CONCISE SECOND EDITION

Worlds Together,
Worlds Apart

CONCISE SECOND EDITION

Worlds Together, Worlds Apart

Elizabeth Pollard, Clifford Rosenberg, Robert Tignor

with Jeremy Adelman, Stephen Aron, Peter Brown,
Benjamin Elman, Stephen Kotkin, Xinru Liu, Suzanne Marchand,
Holly Pittman, Gyan Prakash, Brent Shaw, Michael Tsin

W. W. NORTON & COMPANY • NEW YORK • LONDON

To my parents, John and Catherine, who encouraged me to see the world; and to my husband Brad and children Amelia and Jake, with whom I now share that adventure. —EAP

To my students. —CR

W. W. Norton & Company has been independent since its founding in 1923, when William Warder Norton and Mary D. Herter Norton first published lectures delivered at the People's Institute, the adult education division of New York City's Cooper Union. The firm soon expanded its program beyond the Institute, publishing books by celebrated academics from America and abroad. By midcentury, the two major pillars of Norton's publishing program—trade books and college texts—were firmly established. In the 1950s, the Norton family transferred control of the company to its employees, and today—with a staff of four hundred and a comparable number of trade, college, and professional titles published each year—W. W. Norton & Company stands as the largest and oldest publishing house owned wholly by its employees.

Editor: Jon Durbin
Project Editor: Jennifer Barnhardt
Editorial Assistant: Lily Gellman
Managing Editor, College: Marian Johnson
Managing Editor, College Digital Media: Kim Yi
Production Manager: Ashley Horna
Media Editor: Carson Russell
Associate Media Editor: Sarah Rose Aquilina
Media Project Editor: Rachel Mayer
Media Editorial Assistant: Alexandra Malakhoff
Ebook Production: Michael Hicks
Marketing Manager, History: Sarah England Bartley
Design Director: Rubina Yeh
Designer: Lissi Sigillo
Director of College Permissions: Megan Schindel
Permissions Associate: Elizabeth Trammell
Photo Editor: Agnieszka Czapski
Composition: Cenveo Publishing Services
Illustrations: Mapping Specialists, Ltd.
Manufacturing: LSC Communications–Crawfordsville

Permission to use copyrighted material is included in the credits section of this book, which begins on page C-1.

The Library of Congress has cataloged the Full Edition as follows:

Names: Tignor, Robert L., author.
Title: Worlds together, worlds apart : a history of the world from the beginnings of humankind to the present / Robert Tignor ... [and eleven others].
Description: Fifth edition. | New York : W. W. Norton & Company, [2018] | Includes bibliographical references and index.
Identifiers: LCCN 2017032085 | ISBN 9780393624786 (hardcover)
Subjects: LCSH: World history—Textbooks. | World history—Examinations—Study guides. | Advanced placement programs (Education)—Examinations—Study guides.
Classification: LCC D21 .T53 2018 | DDC 909—dc23 LC record available at https://lccn.loc.gov/2017032085

ISBN this edition: 978-0-393-63980-3 (softcover.)

W. W. Norton & Company, Inc., 500 Fifth Avenue, New York, N.Y. 10110

www.wwnorton.com
W. W. Norton & Company Ltd., 15 Carlisle Street, London W1D 3BS

1 2 3 4 5 6 7 8 9 0

BRIEF CONTENTS

CONTENTS

1

Becoming Human   3

2

Rivers, Cities, and

First States, 3500–2000 BCE   55

3

Nomads, Territorial States, and Microsocieties, 2000–1200 BCE   105

4

First Empires and Common Cultures in Afro-Eurasia, 1250–325 BCE

155

5

Worlds Turned Inside Out,

1000–350 BCE   203

6

Shrinking the Afro-Eurasian World, 350–100 BCE 251

7

Han Dynasty China and Imperial Rome, 300 BCE–300 CE 297

8

The Rise of Universalizing Religions, 300–600 CE   343

9

New Empires and Common Cultures, 600–1000 CE — 393

10

Becoming "The World,"
1000–1300 CE　　443

11

Crisis and Recovery in Afro-Eurasia, 1300–1500   497

12

Contact, Commerce, and Colonization, 1450–1600   545

13

Worlds Entangled, 1600–1750   591

14

Cultures of Splendor and

Power, 1500–1780 645

15

Reordering the World, 1750–1850 693

16

Alternative Visions of the

Nineteenth Century   739

17

Nations and Empires,
1850–1914   787

18

An Unsettled World,

1890–1914   835

19

Of Masses and Visions of the Modern, 1910–1939   883

20

The Three-World Order, 1940–1975   933

21

Globalization, 1970–2000   985

Epilogue: 2001–The Present   1035

CURRENT TRENDS IN WORLD HISTORY

GLOBAL THEMES AND SOURCES

MAPS

Worlds Together, Worlds Apart sets the standard for instructors who want to teach a globally integrated world history survey course. Building on the success of the First Concise Edition, co-authors Elizabeth Pollard (San Diego State University) and Clifford Rosenberg (City University of New York) and general editor Robert Tignor (Princeton University) have created this dynamic and highly accessible new Concise Second Edition of *Worlds Together, Worlds Apart*. A full third shorter than its parent text, written with clear, accessible prose and explanations, and with substantially more pedagogy support than any other text in the marketplace to guide students' reading and develop their historical thinking skills, the Concise Second Edition continues to offer a coherent, cutting-edge survey of the field built around world historical stories of significance. This concise, globally integrated, chronological approach not only makes it easy for students to see connections and comparisons across time and place, but also makes the teaching of the course more manageable for instructors compared with more civilizational and regional approaches. Some of the major stories dealt with in the chapters of the Concise Second Edition are the spread of humans across the planet, the first global agricultural revolution, the creation of empires, the building of the Silk Roads, the spread of the Black Death across Afro-Eurasia, the impact of New World silver on global trade, alternative ways of organizing societies during the rise of nineteenth-century capitalism, and the rise of the nation-state.

The New Concise Second Edition

In response to substantive feedback from highly experienced frontline world history instructors, the new Concise Second Edition has been streamlined and simplified. With its new handy compact format, engaging design, sharpened guided-reading pedagogy, and newly revamped end-of-chapter readings—each highlighting a target historical thinking skill—this edition improves accessibility while strengthening history skills development. Expanded coverage of environmental history, new online **History Skills Tutorials**, a new **Interactive Instructor's Guide**, and **InQuizitive**, Norton's award-winning adaptive learning tool, support a state-of-the-art learning experience.

HIGHLIGHTS of the Concise Second Edition

- **A more accessible global framework** No introductory text does a better job of helping students make comparisons and connections across time and place. Co-authors Beth Pollard and Cliff Rosenberg are experienced teachers who have successfully introduced students to world history in this global way. This edition is more accessible than ever with sharpened guided reading pedagogy and a heavily revised and simplified map program.
  - **Sharpened guided-reading pedagogy** in each chapter helps students make global connections and comparisons as they read:
    - A redesigned chapter-opening spread provides a conceptual road map for the presentation that follows. Revised **Chapter Outlines** and **Core Objectives** identify important global concepts and developments before students start reading. A **(NEW) Global Storylines** feature addresses major chapter themes region by region. And a **(NEW) Big Picture** feature poses a question that highlights the chapter's most important global core objective.
    - Throughout the chapter, **(NEW) Key Term marginal definitions** expand on boldfaced key terms in the text to make the narrative more accessible. And the renamed **Core Objective flags** reference the Core Objectives throughout the chapter so that students know when to focus in on the most relevant material.
    - End-of-chapter features include **Tracing the Global Storylines** summaries that remind students of the overarching global stories introduced at the start of each chapter and show their impact on each region, visual **Chronologies** that compare—region by region—the dates of key events covered in the chapter, and simplified **Thinking about Global Connections** questions.
- **A strengthened focus on global history skills with (NEW) primary sources** In the text and accompanying digital resources, a wealth of features engage students in making connections across time and space. These features promote analysis and interpretation of primary source documents, images, and maps, helping students develop the skills promoted by the American Historical Association, the College Board, and various state guidelines.
  - Chapter-ending **Global Themes and Sources** sections provide an in-text reader:
    - These sections, each containing a handful of primary source documents on a single topic, focus on one of the four major historical thinking skills promoted by the AHA and the College Board (context, causation, comparison, and continuity and change). They replace the shorter "Competing Perspectives" primary sources from the First Concise Edition.

- (**NEW**) pre-reading **Historical Thinking Skills Questions** guide students in the targeted critical thinking skill and in interpretation of the primary sources.
  - (**NEW**) headnotes specific to each source, as well as source-specific questions.
- **Interpreting Visual Evidence** sections engage students in analyzing historical images.
- Updated **Current Trends in World History** features highlight cutting-edge research that is relevant to global issues today.
- A **redesigned visual program** facilitates visual analysis and interpretation while highlighting global comparisons and connections.
  - Enlarged **images** (roughly 10% **NEW** to the Concise Second Edition) are easier to analyze.
  - **A heavily revised and simplified map program**, including (**NEW**) **The Global View**, a two-page map spread that illustrates the overarching story featured in a chapter. Like all of the revised maps, these spreads focus on just one or two developments to simplify interpretation.
- (**NEW**) **scholarship on environmental history** With an author team made up of experts on each global region, *Worlds Together, Worlds Apart* has always reflected exceptionally balanced scholarship. The Concise Second Edition offers new coverage of numerous topics, but it places special emphasis on one overarching issue that is of particular interest to students and instructors: the environment's role in world history.
  Some examples in Volume One:
  - **Chapter 1:** (**NEW**) material on climate change and hominid evolution, and a (**NEW**) section on the environmental impact of the agricultural revolution and herding.
  - **Chapter 4:** (**NEW**) section on environmental crisis, economic decline, and migration, with a fascinating discussion on climate change in India and how it influenced the development of Vedic-Brahmanic culture and the rice economy.
  - **Chapter 10:** (**NEW**) section on environmental challenges and fragmentation discusses the impact of severe climate conditions on eastern Mediterranean and Islamic lands between the eleventh and twelfth centuries, including the fragmentation of Islamic political institutions.
  Some examples in Volume Two:
  - **Chapter 13:** (**NEW**) section on global commerce and climate change that addresses mercantilism and chartered companies, and a fascinating (**NEW**) discussion on the Little Ice Age.
  - **Chapter 14:** (**NEW**) section on formation of American identities that details the environmental impacts of scientific studies that promoted colonization and entrepreneurial activity in the Americas.

- **Chapter 18: (NEW)** section on protecting the environment discusses Teddy Roosevelt's promotion of conservation of nature, as well as parallel movements in Europe. **(NEW)** Current Trends in World History feature, Adapting to the Environment: Russian Peasants Take On the Steppe, reveals growing awareness of the need for sustainable agricultural methods.

- **New support for teaching global history** A team of highly experienced instructors, led by Lead Media Author Alan Karras (University of California, Berkeley), has developed accompanying resources that reflect and complement the Concise Second Edition's distinctive pedagogy while supporting nationally recognized outcomes for the World History survey. Engaging activities and questions move students beyond comprehension to analysis and concept application. These new resources also make it easier than ever for instructors to design and teach a course with a global framework.

  - **(NEW) History Skills Tutorials** combine author videos and interactive assessments in an innovative digital setting to teach students how to analyze the maps, images, and documents in the book and beyond. Instructors can assign these tutorials at the beginning of the semester to prepare students for primary source analysis assignments or incorporate them throughout the semester as a tool for reinforcing skills in working with written and visual sources as well as with maps.

  - **InQuizitive,** W. W. Norton's award-winning adaptive learning tool, features new coverage in every chapter to reflect the new concepts and sources introduced in the book.

  - **(NEW) Interactive Instructor's Guide (IIG)** supports the teaching of global history by providing a searchable, sortable online way to prepare for lectures. The IIG contains resources drawn from the revamped Instructor's Manual. For selected chapters, the authors have created new videos providing best practices for teaching the transregional and comparative connections in the book.

  - **Primary Source Exercises** introduce primary sources from outside the book that build on the key historical developments and global storylines in each chapter. A brief quiz including multiple-choice and short-response questions provides opportunities for assessment.

As you can see, we have worked hard to make the Concise Second Edition of *Worlds Together, Worlds Apart* a powerful learning and teaching tool for students and instructors who want to take a more global approach to world history.

Our Major Themes

The primary organizing framework of *Worlds Together, Worlds Apart*—one that runs through the chapters and connects the different parts of the book—is the theme of **interconnection and divergence**. While describing movements that facilitated global connectedness, this book also shows how different regions developed their own ways of incorporating or resisting connections and change.

Themes that stand out in *Worlds Together, Worlds Apart* highlight the importance of trade and cultural exchange through the recurring efforts of people **crossing borders—religious, political, and cultural—that brought the world together**. Merchants and educated men and women traded goods and ideas. Whole communities, in addition to select groups, moved to safer or more promising environments. This transregional exchange of ideas, goods, and peoples produced **transformations and conflicts**—a second important theme. The movements of ideas, peoples, products, and germs over long distances upset the balance of power across the world and within individual societies. Such movements changed the relationships of population groups with other peoples and areas of the world and led over time to dramatic shifts in the ascendancy of regions. **Changes in power arrangements** within and between regions explain which parts of the world and regional groups benefited from integration and which resisted it. Finally, we highlight **the important roles that gendered roles and identities as well as environmental forces play in shaping the evolution of societies**. These themes (trade and cultural exchange, transformation and conflict, alterations in the balance of power, gender, and the environment) are woven into every chapter of this work. While we highlight these major themes throughout, we tell the stories of the people caught in these currents of exchange, conflict, changing power relations, gendered expectations and environmental developments.

Overview of Volume One

Volume One of *Worlds Together, Worlds Apart* deals with the period from the beginnings of human history through the Mongol invasions of the thirteenth century and the spread of the Black Death across Afro-Eurasia. It is divided into eleven chapters, each of which marks a distinct historical period. Hence, each chapter has an overarching theme or small set of themes that holds otherwise highly diverse material together.

Chapter 1, "Becoming Human," presents cultural and biological perspectives on the way that early hominids became truly human. We believe that this chapter is important in establishing the global context of world history. We believe, too, that our chapter is unique in its focus on a range of creation narratives that explain how humans became humans. We discuss how early humans became bipedal and how they developed complex cognitive processes such as language and artistic abilities. Recent research indicates that *Homo sapiens* originated in Africa, as long as 300,000 years ago. These early men and women migrated out of the African landmass as early as 180,000 years ago, gradually populating all regions of the world. We note, as we update this chapter with some of the newest archaeological discoveries, that the narrative of human evolution and our spread across the planet is a rapidly changing story thanks to new hominid finds and new ways to analyze them. Also in this chapter, we describe the domestication of plants and animals and the founding of the first village settlements around the globe. With our strengthened coverage of environmental history, we include new material on the role of climate in human evolution and in the domestication of plants and animals and ultimately settled village life. Finally, we have updated the **Current Trends in World History** feature in this chapter to discuss "Big History" and how it has affected our thinking and research on the origins of the cosmos and early human development.

Chapter 2, **"Rivers, Cities, and First States, 3500–2000 BCE,"** covers the period during which five of the world's great river basins experienced extraordinary breakthroughs in human activity. On the floodplains of the Tigris and Euphrates in Mesopotamia, the Nile in Egypt, the Indus in modern-day northern India and Pakistan, and the Yellow and Yangzi in China, men and women mastered the annual floods and became expert in seeding and cultivating foodstuffs. In these areas, populations became dense and the world's earliest cities formed. All of these river-basin cultures had much in common. They had highly developed hierarchical political, social, and cultural systems, priestly and bureaucratic classes, and organized religious and cultural systems. The development of these major complex societies is a turning point in world history, ushering in the beginnings of profound distinctions between urban and rural communities as well as between the wealthy and poor. New material in Chapter 2 includes discussions on the role of the Ghaggar-Hakra River in Harappan civilization, the amazing "oldest papyri ever" and the new insights they yielded into Egyptian pyramid construction, and added material on exciting finds at Dhaskalio (off the coast of Keros) in the Aegean Sea.

Extensive climate and technological changes serve as major turning points for **Chapter 3, "Nomads, Territorial States, and Microsocieties, 2000–1200 BCE."** Drought, environmental degradation, and political instability brought the first river-basin societies to an abrupt end around 2000 BCE. When aridity forced tribal and nomadic peoples living on the fringes of the settled populations to move closer to settled areas, they brought with them an insurmountable military advantage. They had become adept at yoking horses to war chariots, and hence they were in a position to subjugate or intermarry with the peoples in the settled societies in the river basins. Around 2000 BCE, these peoples established new territorial kingdoms in Mesopotamia, Egypt, the Indus Valley, and China, which gave way a millennium later (1000 BCE) to even larger, militarily and politically more powerful states. In the Americas, the Mediterranean, sub-Saharan Africa, and the Pacific, microsocieties arose as an alternative form of political organization in which peoples lived in much smaller-scale societies that showcased their own unique and compelling features. New material includes a revised and updated **Current Trends in World History** feature, "Climate Change and the Collapse of River-Basin Societies," updated treatment of Hatshepsut and

Thutmosis III, the Hittites, Lady Fu Hao, and a new discussion on the *Ashvamedha* to give more texture to the Vedic treatment.

Chapter 4, "First Empires and Common Cultures in Afro-Eurasia, 1250–325 BCE," describes the different ways in which larger-scale societies grew and became unified. In the case of the world's first empires, the Neo-Assyrian and Persian, political power was the main unifying element. These two states established different models that future empires would emulate. The Neo-Assyrians used brutal force to intimidate and subjugate different groups within their societies and in neighboring states. The Persians followed a pattern that relied less on coercion and more on tributary relationships while permitting cultural diversity. The Zhou state in China offered a third way of maintaining political unity, basing its rule on the doctrine of the mandate of heaven, which legitimated its rulers' succession as long as they were able to maintain stability and order. Vedic society in South Asia offered a dramatically different model, in which religion and culture were the main unifying forces. Religion moves to the forefront of the narrative in other ways in this chapter. The birth of monotheism occurred in the Zoroastrian and Hebrew faiths. Both religions endure today. A major overhaul of the **Global Themes and Sources** section facilitates a comparison of imperial control in the four major regions, from harshest to least central, making use of two new sources: Sargon II's Lamassu inscription at Dur-Sharrukin, and a text on karma and reincarnation from *The Upanishads*.

The last millennium before the Common Era witnessed some of the most monumental developments in human history. In the six and a half centuries discussed in **Chapter 5, "Worlds Turned Inside Out, 1000–350 BCE,"** teachers and thinkers came to the fore. Confucius, the Buddha, Plato, and Aristotle, to name only the best known of this brilliant group, offered new insights into the natural world and provided new guidelines for governing justly and living ethically. In this era, small-scale societies, benefiting from more intimate relationships, took the place of the first great empires, now in decline. These highly individualistic cultures developed new strategies for political organization, even experimenting with a democratic polity. In Africa, the Bantu peoples spread across sub-Saharan Africa, and the Sudanic peoples of Meroe created a society that blended Egyptian and sub-Saharan influences. These were all dynamic hybrid societies building on existing knowledge. Equally dramatic transformations occurred in the Americas, where the Olmec and Chavín peoples were creating hierarchical societies of a type never before seen in their part of the world. New material includes a substantially revised and updated **Current Trends in World History** feature on Axial Age thinkers and their ideas.

Chapter 6, "Shrinking the Afro-Eurasian World, 350–100 BCE," describes two major forces that simultaneously integrated large segments of the Afro-Eurasian landmass culturally and economically. The first was Hellenism, whose leading figure, Alexander the Great, paved the way in North Africa, Southwest Asia, and central Asia for the first transregional cultural system in world history. Second, a trading network known as the Silk Roads, stretching from Palmyra in the west to central Asia in the east, came into being. Buddhism was the first religion to seize on the Silk Roads' more formal existence as its followers moved quickly, with the support of the Mauryan Empire, to spread their ideas into central Asia. New material includes a substantially revised **Global Themes and Sources** section on the causes and effects of the spread of Hellenism and Buddhism, and new discussions on the Magadha Empire to better lay the groundwork for the Mauryan Empire.

Chapter 7, "Han Dynasty China and Imperial Rome, 300 BCE–300 CE," compares Han China and the Roman Empire, the two political, economic, and cultural systems that dominated much of the Afro-Eurasian landmass from 200 BCE to 200 CE. Both the Han Dynasty and the Roman Empire ruled effectively in their own ways, providing an instructive comparative case study. Both left their imprint on Afro-Eurasia, and rulers for centuries afterward tried to revive these glorious empires and use them as models of greatness. This chapter also discusses the effect of state sponsorship on religion as Christianity came into existence in the context of the late Roman Empire and Buddhism was introduced to China during the decline of the Han. New material has been added on the nature of the connection between the Han Dynasty and the Roman Empire in the **Current Trends in World History** feature.

New political systems and the newly spreading religions that emerged in the aftermath of a crumbling Roman Empire and post-Han Dynasty are the primary emphases of **Chapter 8, "The Rise of Universalizing Religions, 300–600 CE."** In the west, the Byzantine Empire, claiming to be the successor state to the Roman Empire, embraced Christianity as its state religion. In the east, Tang rulers patronized Buddhism to such a degree that Confucian statesmen feared it had become the state religion. Both Buddhism and Christianity enjoyed spectacular success in the politically fragmented post-Han era in China and in the feudal world of western Europe. These dynamic religions represent a decisive transformation in world history. Christianity enjoyed its eventual successes through state sponsorship via the Roman and Byzantine empires and by providing spiritual comfort and hope during the chaotic years of Rome's decline. Buddhism grew through imperial sponsorship and through significant changes to its fundamental beliefs when adherents to the faith deified the Buddha and created notions of an afterlife. In Africa, a wide range of significant developments occurred, and a myriad of cultural practices existed; yet large common cultures also arose. The Bantu peoples that spread throughout the southern half of the landmass spoke closely related languages and developed similar political institutions based on the prestige of individuals of high achievement. In the Americas, the Olmecs established their own form of the city-state, while the Maya owed their success to a decentralized common culture built around a strong religious belief system and a series of spiritual centers. New material comparing the "fall" of the Roman empire and the Han dynasty has been added to the **Current Trends in World History** feature. The Maya coverage has been updated to account for the new LIDAR imaging that challenges the traditional narrative, and the **Global Themes and Sources** section on pilgrimages has been expanded with longer excerpts and new travelers with a focus on continuity and change over time.

In a relatively remote corner of the Arabian Peninsula, another world religion, Islam, exploded with world-changing consequences, as **Chapter 9, "New Empires and Common Cultures, 600–1000 CE,"** describes. The rise of Islam provides a contrast to the ways in which other universalizing religions and political empires interacted. Islam and its empire arose in a fashion quite different from Christianity and the Roman Empire. Christianity took over an already existing empire—the Roman—after suffering persecution at its hands for several centuries. In contrast, Islam created an empire almost at the moment of its emergence. By the time the Abbasid Empire came into being in the middle of the eighth century, Islamic armies, political leaders, and clerics exercised power over much of the Afro-Eurasian landmass, from southern Spain across North Africa all the way to central Asia. The Tang Empire in China, however, served as a counterweight to Islam's power, both politically and intellectually. Confucianism enjoyed a spectacular recovery in this period. With the support of the Tang rulers, Confucianism slowed the spread of Buddhism and further reinforced China's development along different, more secular pathways. Japan and Korea enter our narrative of world history at this time, as tributary states to Tang China and as hybrid cultures that mixed Chinese customs and practices with their own. The Christian world split in this period between western Roman Catholicism and eastern Greek Orthodoxy. Both branches of Christianity played a role in unifying societies, especially in western Europe, which lacked strong political rule. New material includes expanded in-text coverage of the "Green Revolutions" in Islam and Tang China, an updated **Current Trends in World History** feature with the latest research on the origins of Islam, and a completely revised and expanded **Global Themes and Sources** exploration of women and empire.

In the three centuries from 1000 to 1300 CE (**Chapter 10, "Becoming 'The World,' 1000–1300 CE"**), Afro-Eurasia experienced an unprecedented rise in prosperity and population that spread into West Africa and eastern Africa. Just as important, the world in this period divided into regional zones that are recognizable today. At the same time, trade grew rapidly. A view of the major trading cities of this time demonstrates how commerce transformed cultures. Sub-Saharan Africa also underwent intense regional integration via the spread of the Mande-speaking peoples and the Mali Empire. The Americas witnessed their first empire in the form of the Chimú Empire in the Andes. This chapter ends with the Mongol conquests of the twelfth and thirteenth centuries, which brought massive destruction but also significant connectedness to Afro-Eurasia. The Mongol Empire, once in place, promoted long-distance commerce, scholarly exchange, and travel on an unprecedented scale. The Mongol story, highlighted in the new **Current Trends in World History** feature on "A Most Unusual Nomad State," underscores the important role that nomads played throughout the history of the early world. The **Global Themes and Sources** feature picks up on the theme of travelers from Chapter 8 and includes new and expanded sources for analyzing the continuities and changes over time in "world" travel.

The Black Death brought Afro-Eurasia's prosperity and population growth to a catastrophic end, as discussed in **Chapter 11, "Crisis and Recovery in Afro-Eurasia, 1300–1500."** The bubonic plague wiped out as much as two-thirds of the population in many of the densely settled locations of Afro-Eurasia, whose societies had already been brought to their knees by the Mongols' depredations. The destruction and dying of the fourteenth century saw traditional institutions give way and forced peoples to rebuild their cultures. The political systems that came into being at this time and the intense religious experimentation that took place effected a sharp break with the past. In the face of one of humanity's grimmest periods, peoples and societies demonstrated tremendous resilience as they looked for new ways to rebuild their communities, some turning inward and others seeking inspiration, conquests, and riches elsewhere. New material recasts the Renaissance, offers sources for comparing different communities' understandings of the causes and effects of the Black Death, and a new **Current Trends in World History** feature considers Ming fashion. Volume One concludes on the eve of the "Columbian Exchange," the moment when "old" worlds discovered "new" ones and a vast series of global interconnections and divergences commenced

Please note that the primary source readings (Global Themes and Sources) have been heavily revised throughout Volume One—with selections both expanded from the first edition and entirely new selections—to address the four major historical thinking skills as described by the AHA and the College Board. Critical thinking about what sources can reveal of their historical context is emphasized in each chapter.

Overview of Volume Two

The organizational structure for Volume Two reaffirms the authors' commitment to write a decentered, global history of the world. Christopher Columbus is not the starting point, as he is in so many modern world histories. Rather, we begin in the eleventh and twelfth centuries with two major developments in world history: the Mongol conquests and the Black Death. **Chapter 10, "Becoming 'The World,' 1000–1300 CE,"** describes an unprecedented rise in prosperity and population that Afro-Eurasia experienced, which spread into West Africa and eastern Africa. Just as important, the world in this period divided into regional zones that are recognizable today. At the same time, trade grew rapidly. A view of the major trading cities of this time demonstrates how commerce transformed cultures. Sub-Saharan Africa also underwent intense regional integration via the spread of the Mande-speaking peoples and the Mali Empire. The Americas witnessed their first empire in the form of the Chimú Empire in the Andes. This chapter ends with the Mongol conquests of the twelfth and thirteenth centuries, which brought massive destruction but also significant connectedness to Afro-Eurasia. The Mongol Empire, once in place, promoted long-distance commerce, scholarly exchange, and travel on an unprecedented scale. The Mongol story, highlighted in the new **Current Trends in World History** feature on "A Most Unusual Nomad State," underscores the important role that nomads played throughout the history of the early world. The **Global Themes and Sources** feature picks up on the theme of travelers from Chapter 8 and includes new and expanded sources for analyzing the continuities and changes over time in "world" travel.

The Black Death brought Afro-Eurasia's prosperity and population growth to a catastrophic end, as discussed in **Chapter 11, "Crisis and Recovery in Afro-Eurasia, 1300–1500."** The bubonic plague wiped out as much as two-thirds of the population in many of the densely settled locations of Afro-Eurasia, whose societies had already been brought to their knees by the Mongols' depredations. The destruction and dying of the fourteenth century saw traditional institutions give way and forced peoples to rebuild their cultures. The political systems that came into being at this time and the intense religious experimentation that took place effected a sharp break with the past. In the face of one of humanity's grimmest periods, peoples and societies demonstrated tremendous resilience as they looked for new ways to rebuild their communities, some turning inward and others seeking inspiration, conquests, and riches elsewhere. New material recasts the Renaissance, offers sources for comparing different communities' understandings of the causes and effects of the Black Death, and a new **Current Trends in World History** feature considers Ming fashion.

Chapter 12, "Contact, Commerce, and Colonization, 1450–1600," examines commerce and exploration after the collapse of the Mongol Empire. Disease and increasing trade linkages were vital factors. New material includes expanded coverage of the Ottoman Empire—in particular, its centrality to networks of trade and exploration. The chapter provides more specifics about the major sultans; the importance of the conquest of Syria and Egypt (1516–1517), and the resistance of Mamluk rulers; the Ottoman admiral and cartographer Piri Reis and his masterwork *The Book of the Sea*; the Ottomans' earliest military failures against the Safavid Empire; the trade routes that made Ottoman expansion possible and Ottoman expansion's interconnectedness with European expansion overseas; and the multiethnic legacy of centuries of Ottoman rule.

Europeans sailed across the Atlantic Ocean to find a more direct, less encumbered route to Asia and came upon lands, peoples, and products that they had not expected. One item, however, that they had sought in every part of the world, and that they found in abundance in the Americas, was precious metal. **Chapter 13, "Worlds Entangled, 1600–1750,"** discusses how New World silver from Mexico and Peru became the major currency of global commerce, facilitating the long-distance trading networks that had been revived after the Black Death. The effect of New World silver on the world economy was so great that it, even more than the Iberian explorations of the New World, brought the hemispheres together and transformed the terms on which peoples around the world interacted with one another. Sugar also linked the economies and polities of western Europe, Africa, and the Americas and was a powerful force in a triangular trade centered on the Atlantic Ocean. This trade involved the shipment of vast numbers of African captives to the Americas, where they toiled as slaves on sugar, tobacco, cotton, and rice plantations. New material includes new content on leading Ottoman intellectual Mustafa Ali and his magnum opus *The Essence of History* (1591); on the Little Ice Age (the sharp drop in global temperature from 1620 to 1680) and its contribution to a wave of political upheaval across Afro-Eurasia; on the impact of the Thirty Years' War; on the contribution of imported New World silver to the destabilization of the economy; on the Celali Revolt; and on the rising Manchu population's breach of China's Great Wall.

Chapter 14, "Cultures of Splendor and Power, 1500–1780," investigates the Ottoman scientists, Safavid and Mughal artists, and Chinese literati, as well as European thinkers, whose notable achievements were rooted in their own cultures but tempered by awareness of the intellectual activities of others. This chapter looks closely at the creation of culture as a historical process and describes how the massive increase in wealth during this period, growing out of global trade, led to one of the great periods of cultural flourishing in world history. Around 1800, transformations reverberated outward from the Atlantic world and altered economic and political relationships in the rest of the world. New content explores the religion, politics, and consequences of the Enlightenment, including, in particular, a new **Global Themes and Sources** section on commerce, civilization, and the Enlightenment.

Chapter 15, "Reordering the World, 1750–1850," discusses political revolutions in the Americas and Europe, focusing on new ideas about trade and labor. It contends that a powerful rhetoric of freedom and universal rights underlay the beginning of a "great divide" between peoples of European descent and others. The forces of laissez-faire capitalism, industrialization, the nation-state, and republicanism emanating from the Atlantic world not only attracted diverse groups around the world, but also threatened groups that put forth alternative visions. New ideas of freedom, as manifested in trading relations, labor, and political activities, clashed with older notions of inherited rights and statuses and further challenged the way men and women had lived in earlier times. These political, intellectual, and economic reorderings changed the way people around the world saw themselves and thus represent something quite novel in world history.

These new ways of envisioning the world did not go unchallenged, as **Chapter 16, "Alternative Visions of the Nineteenth Century,"** makes clear. Intense resistance to evolving modernity reflected the diversity of peoples around the world and their hopes for the future. Wahhabism in Islam, the "big men" of

Africa, Indian resistance in the United States and Mexico, socialism and communism in Europe, the Taiping Rebellion in China, and the Indian Mutiny in South Asia catapulted to historical prominence prophets and leaders whose visions often drew on earlier traditions and led these individuals to resist rapid change. New material includes a dramatically expanded and refocused **Global Themes and Sources** section on alternatives to nineteenth-century capitalism.

Chapter 17, "Nations and Empires, 1850–1914," deals with the political, economic, military, and ideological power that thrust Europe and North America to the fore of global events and led to an era of nationalism and modern imperialism, new forces in world history. Yet this period of seeming European supremacy was to prove short-lived. New content focuses on the Irish potato famine and its impact, Britain's imperial regime in India and the Caribbean and its application in Africa, and a new **Global Themes and Sources** section on the scramble for empire.

As **Chapter 18, "An Unsettled World, 1890–1914,"** demonstrates, even before World War I shattered Europe's moral certitude, many groups, both at home (feminists, Marxists, and unfulfilled nationalists) and abroad (anticolonial nationalists), had raised a chorus of complaints about European and North American dominance. Like Chapter 14, this chapter looks at the processes by which specific cultural movements arose and how they reflected the concerns of individual societies. Yet here, too, syncretic movements emerged in many cultures that reflected the sway of global imperialism, which by then had become a dominant force. New content includes a new **Current Trends in World History** feature, "Adapting to the Environment: Russian Peasants Take On the Steppe," and a new focus on the 1902 passage of the U.S. National Reclamation Act.

Chapter 19, "Of Masses and Visions of the Modern, 1910–1939," briefly covers World War I, then discusses how, from the end of that war until World War II, different visions of being modern competed around the world. The development of modernism and its effects on multiple cultures is the theme that integrates the diverse developments discussed in this chapter. In the decades between the world wars, proponents of liberal democracy struggled to defend their views and often to impose their will on authoritarian rulers and anticolonial nationalists. New content includes material on the impact of World War I in East Africa; Britain's affiliation with Russia and France in the Triple Entente in 1907; conflict in the Balkans and the chain reaction set off by the assassination of Austrian Archduke Franz-Ferdinand; a new focus on British and French conscription of their colonial subjects; the Ottoman alliance with the Central Powers; hastily drawn postwar borders in the Middle East and their later consequences in the twenty-first century; and an (all-new) **Global Themes and Sources** section, "Comparing and Contextualizing Totalitarianism."

Chapter 20, "The Three-World Order, 1940–1975," presents the effects of World War II as new adversaries arose after the war. A three-world order came into being—the First World, led by the United States and extolling capitalism, the nation-state, and democratic government; the Second World, led by the Soviet Union and favoring authoritarian polities and economies; and the Third World, made up of former colonies seeking an independent status and alternative routes to modernity for themselves in world affairs. The rise of this three-world order, which dominated the second half of the twentieth century, constitutes another major theme of world history. New content includes a revised **Global Themes and Sources** section on independence and nation building.

Chapter 21, **"Globalization, 1970–2000,"** which begins with the end of the Cold War, shows that the modern world, while clearly more unified than before, still had profound cultural differences and political divisions. At the beginning of the twenty-first century, capital, commodities, peoples, and ideas moved rapidly over long distances. But cultural tensions and political impasses continued to exist. The rise of this form of globalism represented a vital new element as humankind headed into a new century and millennium. New content includes a revised **Global Themes and Sources** section with new primary sources on the power of grassroots democracy.

The **Epilogue, 2001–The Present,** tracks developments since the turn of the millennium. These last few years have brought profound changes to the world order, yet we hope that readers of *Worlds Together, Worlds Apart* will see more clearly how this most recent history is, in fact, entwined with the trends of much longer duration that are the chief focus of this book. New material includes a discussion of populist election victories; two new **Current Trends in World History** features, "Global Capitalism and the Great Contraction of 2008" and "Has *Homo sapiens* Entered a New Epoch—the Anthropocene?"; coverage of devastating hurricanes; new coverage of Donald Trump's election as U.S. president in 2016 as well as his policies, particularly regarding the U.S.-Mexico border, and his nativist attacks on immigrants and refugees; new content on ISIS and Syria; the U.S. summit with North Korea; and the U.S. withdrawal from the Joint Comprehensive Plan of Action (Iranian nuclear deal).

Please note that the primary source readings (Global Themes and Sources) have been heavily revised throughout Volume Two—with selections both expanded from the first edition and entirely new selections—to address the four major historical thinking skills as described by the AHA and the College Board. Critical thinking about what sources can reveal of their historical context is emphasized in each chapter.

Media Ancillaries

Lead media author Alan Karras (University of California, Berkeley) helped gather a team of innovative world history instructors, including Shane Carter, Sharon Cohen, Ryba Epstein, Derek O'Leary, Andrew Hardy, and others. Together, this team has ensured that the Concise Second Edition of *Worlds Together, Worlds Apart* is supported by an array of digital media with tools faculty need to meet course goals—in the classroom and online—and activities that will help students to develop core skills in reading comprehension, writing, and analysis and to better understand the geography and contexts in world history survey courses.

For Students

InQUIZITIVE

Quizzing to Learn (Shane Carter, Alan Karras)

InQuizitive, Norton's groundbreaking formative, adaptive quizzing platform, uses interactive questions and guided feedback to motivate students to read and understand the text. Varied question types—featuring images, maps, and primary sources—prompt critical and analytical thinking about each of the chapter's Core Objectives. Robust grading functionality helps instructors track their students' progress on learning outcomes.

(NEW) History Skills Tutorials

Accessible through the digital landing page with the code that is included in each new copy of the book, the History Skills Tutorials featuring author Elizabeth Pollard consist of three online modules that provide a framework for analyzing primary source documents, images, and maps. Each tutorial opens with author videos modeling the analysis process. Subsequent interactive activities challenge students to apply what they have learned.

Student Site

This free site offers students access to additional primary source documents and images, an expansive collection of author videos, and iMaps. It is ideal for instructors interested in granting students access to additional material without creating or administering online assignments.

Norton Ebooks

Norton Ebooks give students and instructors an enhanced reading experience at a fraction of the cost of a printed textbook. Students are able to have an active reading experience and can take notes, bookmark, search, highlight, and even read offline. As an instructor, you can add your own notes for students to see as they read the text. Norton ebooks can be viewed on—and synced between—all computers and mobile devices. The ebook for the Concise Second Edition includes embedded author videos, pop-up key term definitions, and enlargeable images and maps.

For Instructors

Resources for instructors are available at wwnorton.com/instructors.

Norton LMS Resources (Jacob Pomerantz, Alan Karras)

Free Norton Coursepacks (downloadable in learning management systems such as Blackboard, WebCT, D2L, and Moodle; additional formats can be provided upon request) include:

- **Primary Source Exercises:** One exercise per chapter provides 3–5 multiple-choice questions and two short-response questions (with sample answers). Each exercise contains 1–2 primary sources.
- **Online Reader:** Approximately 100 additional primary source documents and images that supplement the ones in the text. Also available grouped as Research Topics.
- **iMaps:** Interactive versions of each map from the text are provided on the Student Site and in the Coursepack, enabling students to explore different layers of information. Each iMap is supported by a Map Worksheet.
- **Chapter Quizzes:** These quizzes include answer references to each chapter's Core Objectives.
- **Office Hours Videos:** Authors Beth Pollard and Cliff Rosenberg as well as media author Alan Karras explain difficult concepts.
- **Flashcards:** Online cards for each chapter align key terms and events with brief descriptions and definitions. The cards can be "flipped," printed, or downloaded.
- **Chapter Outlines**
- **Chronologies**
- **Forum Prompts:** Discussion questions that can be used in face-to-face or online discussion boards to engage students in active discussions about the major themes and concepts in each chapter.
- **Questions from the Text:** The questions from Core Objectives, Global Storylines, Global Themes and Sources, and Thinking about Global Connections from the text are available for online assignments and grading.
- **Analyzing Global Developments:** Previously included in the text of the Concise First Edition, these features have been updated and transferred to the Coursepack for use as assigned activities.
- **StoryMaps:** Available in the Coursepack in PDF format for reference.
- **AHA Student Learning Outcomes:** The student learning outcomes based on the AHA's "Benchmarks for Professional Development" now include suggestions for using *Worlds Together, Worlds Apart*, Second Concise Edition to help students achieve these learning outcomes.

(NEW) Interactive Instructor's Guide (Sharon Cohen, Alan Karras)

The new IIG supports the teaching of global history by providing a searchable, sortable online way to prepare for lectures. For selected chapters, the authors have created videos providing best practices for teaching the trans-regional connections in the book as well as **NEW** suggested image and sylla-bus activities.

Classroom Presentation Tools (Derek O'Leary, Andrew Hardy, Alan Karras)

- **Lecture PowerPoints and Art PowerPoints** feature photographs and maps from the book, retouched for in-class presentation.
- *StoryMaps* break complex maps into a sequence of five annotated screens that focus on the story behind the geography. The ten StoryMaps include such topics as The Silk Roads, The Spread of the Black Death, and Population Growth and the Economy.

Instructor's Manual (Sharon Cohen, Alan Karras)

The Instructor's Manual for the Concise Second Edition of *Worlds Together, Worlds Apart* has everything instructors need to prepare lectures and classroom activities, including lecture outlines, lecture ideas, and suggested classroom activities. Our Popular Fallacy section provides an exercise that helps to dispel common misconceptions students may have about each chapter. The revamped Instructor's Manual features two **NEW** sections, one on the teaching of the primary sources in each chapter, and one on effectively incorporating all of Norton's media resources into a syllabus.

Test Bank (Ryba Epstein, Derek O'Leary, Alan Karras)

The Test Bank features more than 1,050 questions—including multiple-choice, true/false, matching, and essay questions—each aligned to a Global Storyline and Core Objective from the book. Classified according to level of difficulty and Bloom's Taxonomy (remembering, understanding, applying, analyzing, evaluating, and creating), they provide multiple avenues for comprehension and skill assessment. The Test Bank features 25% **NEW** questions. These questions are also available in ExamView Test Generator, where you can more easily create tests and manage test question selection.

Acknowledgments

The quality and range of reviews of this project were truly exceptional. The final version of the manuscript was greatly influenced by the thoughts and ideas of numerous instructors.

First Concise Edition Reviewers

Andreas Agocs, University of the Pacific
Anthony Barbieri-Low, University of California, Santa Barbara
Brett Berliner, Morgan State University

Carolyn Noelle Biltoft, Georgia State University
Gayle Brunelle, California State University, Fullerton
Grace Chee, West Los Angeles College
Stephen Colston, San Diego State University
Paula Devos, San Diego State University
Alan Karras, University of California, Berkeley
Elaine MacKinnon, University of West Georgia
Harold Marcuse, University of California, Santa Barbara
Eva Moe, Modesto Junior College
Alice Pate, Kennesaw State University
Chandrika Paul, Shippensburg University
Jared Poley, Georgia State University
Dana Rabin, University of Illinois
Masako Racel, Kennesaw State University
Charles Reed, Elizabeth City State University
Alice Roberti, Santa Rosa Junior College
Steven Rowe, Chicago State University
Lynn Sargeant, California State University, Fullerton
Robert Saunders, Farmingdale State College
Sharlene Sayegh-Canada, California State University, Long Beach
Jeffrey Shumway, Brigham Young University
Greg Smay, University of California, Berkeley
Lisa Tran, California State University, Fullerton
Michael Vann, California State University, Sacramento
Theodore Weeks, Southern Illinois University
Krzysztof Ziarek, University at Buffalo

Concise Second Edition Reviewers

Christian Davis, James Madison University
Robert Dietle, Western Kentucky University
Holly Hulburt, Southern Illinois University
Senya Lubisich, Citrus College
Anthony Makowski, Delaware County Community College
Anthonette McDaniel, Pellissippi State Community College
Charles Reed, Elizabeth City State University
Jason Sharples, Florida Atlantic University
Kristin Stapleton, University at Buffalo
Pamela Stewart, Arizona State University

For the Concise Second Edition, we have some familiar and new friends at W. W. Norton to thank. Chief among them is Jon Durbin, who once again played a major role in bringing this edition to publication. Sarah England Bartley has put together a creative marketing plan for the book. Lissi Sigillo is responsible for the book's beautiful and effective new design. Lily Gellman has been invaluable with her work on manuscript preparation. Carson Russell, Laura Wilk, Sarah Rose Aquilina, and Alexandra Malakhoff have done a masterful job of strengthening the media support materials to meet the ever more complex classroom and assessment needs of instructors. Agnieszka Czapski and Donna Ranieri have done a great job researching and securing the permissions for the new photos. Mapping Specialists have done a beautiful job transforming and revitalizing the map program. Emily Pace and Leah Gregory have done fantastic work hunting down hard-to-find copies of sources. Jennifer Barnhardt, our project editor, and Ashley Horna, our production manager, have accomplished a genuinely herculean task in getting the book published on time with a very tight schedule, and we are particularly thankful to them. Jennifer Greenstein and Norma Sims Roche each did an assiduous job with the copyediting, turning the chapters around quickly to meet our schedule. A special shout-out goes to Debra Morton-Hoyt and her team of cover designers. *Worlds Together, Worlds Apart* has always had incredibly creative and distinctive covers, and the Concise Second Edition covers are even more eye-catching and memorable than those of the first edition. We also want to thank the authors of the full edition for their participation in this Concise Second Edition while allowing the new authors considerable leeway to have their own input. Bravo!

Elizabeth Pollard (*Ph.D. University of Pennsylvania*) is associate professor of history at San Diego State University. Her research investigates women accused of witchcraft in the Roman world and explores the exchange of goods and ideas between the Mediterranean and the Indian Ocean in the early centuries of the Common Era. Her pedagogical interests include Digital Humanities approaches to Roman history and witchcraft studies as well as the impact of global perspectives on teaching, learning, and writing about the ancient Mediterranean.

Clifford Rosenberg (*Ph.D. Princeton University*) is associate professor of European history at City College and the Graduate Center, CUNY. He specializes in the history of modern France and its empire and is the author of *Policing Paris: The Origins of Modern Immigration Control between the Wars*. He is working now on a book about the spread of tuberculosis between France and Algeria since the mid-nineteenth century.

Robert Tignor (*Ph.D. Yale University*) is professor emeritus and the Rosengarten Professor of Modern and Contemporary History at Princeton University and the three-time chair of the history department. With Gyan Prakash, he introduced Princeton's first course in world history thirty years ago. Professor Tignor has taught graduate and undergraduate courses in African history and world history and has written extensively on the history of twentieth-century Egypt, Nigeria, and Kenya. Besides his many research trips to Africa, Professor Tignor has taught at the University of Ibadan in Nigeria and the University of Nairobi in Kenya.

Alan Karras (*Ph.D. University of Pennsylvania*) is the associate director of International & Area Studies at the University of California, Berkeley, and has previously served as chair of the College Board's test development committee for world history and as co-chair of the College Board's commission on AP history course revisions. The author and editor of several books, he has written about the eighteenth-century Atlantic world and, more broadly, global interactions that focus on illicit activities like smuggling and corruption. An advocate of linking the past to the present, he is now working on a history of corruption in empires, focusing on the East India Company.

Jeremy Adelman (*D.Phil. Oxford University*) has lived and worked in seven countries and on four continents. A graduate of the University of Toronto, he earned a master's degree in economic history at the London School of Economics (1985) and a doctorate in modern history at Oxford University (1989). He is the author or editor of ten books, including *Sovereignty and Revolution in the Iberian Atlantic* (2006) and *Worldly Philosopher: The Odyssey of Albert O. Hirschman* (2013), a chronicle of one of the twentieth century's most original thinkers. He has been awarded fellowships by the British Council, the Social Science and Humanities Research Council of Canada, the Guggenheim Memorial Foundation, and the American Council of Learned Societies (the Frederick Burkhardt Fellowship). He is currently the Henry Charles Lea Professor of History and the director of the Global History Lab at Princeton University. His next book is called *Earth Hunger: Markets, Resources, and the Need for Strangers*.

Stephen Aron (*Ph.D. University of California, Berkeley*) is professor of history at the University of California, Los Angeles, and executive director of the Institute for the Study of the American West, Autry National Center. A specialist in frontier and Western American history, Aron is the author of *How the West Was Lost: The Transformation of Kentucky from Daniel Boone to Henry Clay* and *American Confluence: The Missouri Frontier from Borderland to Border State*. He is currently editing the multivolume *Autry History of the American West* and writing a book with the tentative title *Can We All Just Get Along: An Alternative History of the American West*.

Peter Brown (*Ph.D. Oxford University*) is the Rollins Professor of History emeritus at Princeton University. He previously taught at London University and the University of California, Berkeley. He has written on the rise of Christianity and the end of the Roman Empire. His works include *Augustine of Hippo*; *The World of Late Antiquity*; *The Cult of the Saints*; *Body and Society*; *The Rise of Western Christendom*; and *Poverty and Leadership in the Later Roman Empire*. His most recent book is *Treasure in Heaven*.

Benjamin Elman (*Ph.D. University of Pennsylvania*) is professor of East Asian studies and history at Princeton University. He has served as the chair of the Princeton East Asian Studies Department and as director of the East Asian Studies Program. He taught at the University of California, Los Angeles, for over fifteen years, 1986–2002. His teaching and research fields include Chinese intellectual and cultural history, 1000–1900 CE; the history of science in China, 1600–1930; the history of education in late imperial China; and Sino-Japanese cultural history, 1600–1850. He is the author of seven books, four of them translated into Chinese, Korean, or Japanese: *From Philosophy to Philology: Intellectual and Social Aspects of Change in Late Imperial China*; *Classicism, Politics, and Kinship: The Ch'angchou School of New Text Confucianism in Late Imperial China*; *A Cultural History of Civil Examinations in Late Imperial China*; *On Their Own Terms: Science in China, 1550–1900*; *A Cultural History of Modern Science in China*; *Civil Examinations and Meritocracy in Late Imperial China, 1400–1900*; and *Science in China, 1600–1900: Essays by Benjamin A. Elman*. He is the creator of Classical Historiography for Chinese History at http://libguides.princeton.edu/chinese-historiography, a bibliography and teaching Web site published since 1996.

Stephen Kotkin (*Ph.D. University of California, Berkeley*) is professor of European and Asian history as well as international affairs at Princeton University. He formerly directed Princeton's program in Russian and Eurasian studies (1996–2009). He is the author of *Magnetic Mountain: Stalinism as a Civilization*; *Uncivil Society: 1989 and the Implosion of the Communist Establishment*; and *Armageddon Averted: The Soviet Collapse, 1970–2000*. He is a co-editor of *Mongolia in the Twentieth Century: Landlocked Cosmopolitan*. Professor Kotkin has twice been a visiting professor in Japan.

Xinru Liu (*Ph.D. University of Pennsylvania*) is associate professor of early Indian history and world history at the College of New Jersey. She is associated with the Institute of World History and the Chinese Academy of Social Sciences. She is the author of *Ancient India and Ancient China: Trade and Religious Exchanges, AD 1–600*; *Silk and Religion: An Exploration of Material Life and the Thought of People, AD 600–1200*; *Connections across Eurasia: Transportation, Communication, and Cultural Exchange on the Silk Roads*, coauthored with Lynda Norene Shaffer; and *A Social History of Ancient India* (in Chinese). Professor Liu promotes South Asian studies and world history studies in both the United States and the People's Republic of China.

Suzanne Marchand (*Ph.D. University of Chicago*) is professor of European and intellectual history at Louisiana State University, Baton Rouge. Professor Marchand also spent a number of years teaching at Princeton University. She is the author of *Down from Olympus: Archaeology and Philhellenism in Germany, 1750–1970* and *German Orientalism in the Age of Empire: Religion, Race, and Scholarship*.

Holly Pittman (*Ph.D. Columbia University*) is professor of art history at the University of Pennsylvania, where she teaches art and archaeology of Mesopotamia and the Iranian plateau. She also serves as curator in the Near East Section of the University of Pennsylvania Museum of Archaeology and Anthropology. Previously she served as a curator in the Ancient Near Eastern Art Department of the Metropolitan Museum of Art. She has written extensively on the art and culture of the Bronze Age in Southwest Asia and has participated in excavations in Cyprus, Turkey, Syria, and Iraq as well as in Iran, where she currently works. Her research investigates works of art as media through which patterns of thought, cultural development, and historical interactions of ancient cultures of Southwest Asia can be reconstructed.

Gyan Prakash (*Ph.D. University of Pennsylvania*) is professor of modern Indian history at Princeton University and a member of the Subaltern Studies Editorial Collective. He is the author of *Bonded Histories: Genealogies of Labor Servitude in Colonial India*; *Another Reason: Science and the Imagination of Modern India*; and *Mumbai Fables*. Professor Prakash edited *After Colonialism: Imperial Histories and Postcolonial Displacements* and *Noir Urbanisms*, co-edited *The Space of the Modern City* and *Utopia/Dystopia*, and has written a number of articles on colonialism and history writing. He is currently working on a history of the city of Bombay. With Robert Tignor, he introduced the modern world history course at Princeton University.

Brent Shaw (*Ph.D. Cambridge University*) is the Andrew Fleming West Professor of Classics at Princeton University, where he is director of the Program in the Ancient World. He was previously at the University of Pennsylvania, where he chaired the Graduate Group in Ancient History. His principal areas of specialization as a Roman historian are Roman family history and demography, sectarian violence and conflict in late antiquity, and the regional history of Africa as part of the Roman Empire. He has published *Spartacus and the Slave Wars: A Brief History with Documents*; edited the papers of Sir Moses Finley, *Economy and Society in Ancient Greece*; and published in a variety of books and journals, including the *Journal of Roman Studies*, the *American Historical Review*, the *Journal of Early Christian Studies*, and *Past & Present*.

Michael Tsin (*Ph.D. Princeton*) is associate professor of history and international studies at the University of North Carolina at Chapel Hill. He previously taught at the University of Illinois at Chicago, Princeton University, Columbia University, and the University of Florida. Professor Tsin's primary interests include the histories of modern China and colonialism. He is the author of *Nation, Governance, and Modernity in China: Canton, 1900–1927*. He is currently writing a social history of the reconfiguration of Chinese identity in the twentieth century.

North America, South America, Atlantic Ocean, Pacific Ocean, Mississippi R., Amazon R., Niger R.

0   1000   2000 Miles
0   1000   2000 Kilometers

The Geography of the Ancient and Modern Worlds

Today, geographers usually identify six inhabited continents: Africa, North America, South America, Europe, Asia, and Australia. Inside these continents they locate a vast number of subcontinental units, such as East Asia, South Asia, Southeast Asia, the Middle East, North Africa, and sub-Saharan Africa. Yet this geographic understanding would have been alien to premodern people, who did not think of themselves as inhabiting continents bounded by large bodies of water. Lacking a firm command of the seas, they saw themselves as living on contiguous landmasses. Hence, in this textbook, we have chosen to use a set of geographic terms that more accurately reflect the world of the premoderns.

The most interconnected and populous landmass of premodern times was Afro-Eurasia. The term *Eurasia* is widely used in general histories, but we find it inadequate. The preferred term, from our perspective, must be Afro-Eurasia, for the interconnected land-mass of premodern—and, indeed, much of modern—times included large parts of Europe and Asia and significant regions in Africa—particularly Egypt, North Africa, and even parts of sub-Saharan Africa.

It was only in the period from 1000 to 1300 CE that the divisions of the world that we take for granted today began to take shape. The peoples of the northwestern part of Afro-Eurasia did not see themselves as European Christians, and hence as a distinct cultural entity, until the end of the Middle Ages. Islam did not arise and extend its influence throughout the middle zone of Afro-Eurasia until the eighth and ninth centuries. Nor did the peoples living in what we today term the Indian subcontinent feel a strong sense of their own cultural and political unity until the Delhi Sultanate and the Mughal Empire brought political unity to that vast region. As a result, we use the terms South Asia, Vedic society, and India in place of *Indian subcontinent* for the premodern part of our narrative, and we use Southwest Asia and North Africa to refer to what today is designated as the Middle East.

CONCISE SECOND EDITION

Worlds Together, Worlds Apart

1

Becoming Human

In summer 2017, the story of human origins was rocked by findings that may well push back, and relocate to a different region of Africa, the earliest evidence for *Homo sapiens*. These arguments were grounded in the work of Jean-Jacques Hublin, who in 2004 with his team of paleoanthropologists had returned to Jebel Irhoud in Morocco to establish a better date for remains that had been unearthed by miners in the 1960s. What Hublin's team found were stone tools and fossilized skull fragments (including a jaw) belonging to five individuals. Thermoluminescence dating of objects found with the bones, as well as uranium series dating of a tooth, showed that the possible *Homo sapiens* that Hublin and his team had uncovered had lived as early as 315,000 years ago—more than 100,000 years earlier than the previously accepted date for *Homo sapiens* of 200,000 years ago based on finds in East Africa. While researchers have not been able to extract DNA from the bones found at Jebel Irhoud, other DNA research on a 2,000-year-old skeleton from sub-Saharan Africa has pointed to a split in the branches of *Homo sapiens* lineage more than 250,000 years ago. This genetic split supports the argument, based on the new Jebel Irhoud evidence and other new finds such as *Homo naledi* to be discussed later in this chapter, that the spread of *Homo sapiens* in Africa occurred longer ago and is more complicated than the hypothesis of a 200,000-years-ago origin for *Homo sapiens* that scholars accepted just a decade ago. The modern scientific creation narrative evolves as new evidence unearthed through excavation adds more data to the story that scholars work to piece together.

Most of the common traits of human beings—the abilities to make tools, engage in family life, use language, and refine cognitive abilities—evolved over many millennia and crystallized around the time *Homo sapiens* migrated out of Africa more than 100,000 years ago. Only with the beginning of settled agriculture did significant cultural

Chapter Outline

- Creation Narratives
- Hominids to Modern Humans
- The Life of Early *Homo sapiens*
- Agricultural Revolution: Food Production and Social Change
- Conclusion

Core Objectives

- **DESCRIBE** various creation narratives traced in this chapter, including the narrative of human evolution, and **EXPLAIN** why they differ.

- **TRACE** the major developments in hominid evolution that resulted in the traits that make *Homo sapiens* "human."

- **DESCRIBE** human ways of life and cultural developments from 300,000 to 12,000 years ago.

- **COMPARE** the ways communities around the world shifted to settled agriculture, and **ANALYZE** the significance this shift had for social organization.

differences develop between groups of humans, as artifacts such as tools, cooking devices, and storage containers reveal. Put simply, the differences we think of as separating humankind's cultures today are less than 15,000 or 20,000 years old.

This chapter lays out the origins of humanity from its common source. It shows how many different hominids (represented today by humans, chimpanzees, gorillas, and orangutans) preceded modern humans, and that humans came from one—relatively recent—stock of hominid migrants out of Africa. Fanning out across the world, our ancestors adapted to environmental constraints and opportunities. They created languages, families, and clan systems, often innovating to defend themselves against predators. One of the biggest breakthroughs was the domestication of plants and animals and the creation of settled agriculture. With this development, humans could stop following food and begin producing it where they desired.

Global Storylines

- Communities, from long ago to today, produce creation narratives in order to make sense of how humans came into being.

- Hominid development across millions of years results in modern humans (*Homo sapiens*) and the traits that make us "human."

- During the period from 300,000 to 12,000 years ago, humans live as hunters and gatherers and achieve major breakthroughs in language and art.

- Global revolution in domesticating crops and animals leads to settled agricultural—based communities, while other communities develop pastoral ways of life.

Creation Narratives

For thousands of years, humans have constructed narratives of how the world, and humans, came to be. These **creation narratives** have varied over time and across cultures, depending on a society's values and the evidence available. To understand the origins of modern humans, we must come to terms with scales of time: the billions, millions, and hundreds of thousands of years through which the universe, earth, and life on it developed into what they are today. Though the hominids that eventually evolved into modern humans lived millions of years ago, our tools for telling the modern creation narrative are relatively new.

Only 350 years ago, English clerics claimed on the basis of biblical calculations and Christian tradition that the first day of creation was Sunday, October 23, 4004 BCE. Modern science, however, indicates that the origin of the universe dates back 13.8 billion years, and the hominid separation from African pongids (members of the ape family) began as long as 7 million years ago. These new discoveries have proved as mind-boggling to Hindus and Muslims as to Christians and Jews—all of whom believed, in different ways, that the universe was not so old and that divine beings had a role in creating it and all life, including the first humans. For millennia, human communities across the globe have constructed narratives that extend back differing lengths of time and suggest various roles for humans and gods in the process of universal creation. For instance, the Judeo-Christian narrative portrays a single God creating a universe out of nothingness, populating it with plants, animals, and humans, in a span of six days. The centuries-old creation story of the Yoruba peoples of West Africa depicts a divine being descending from the heavens in human form and becoming the godlike king Oduduwa, who established the Yoruba kingdom and the rules by which his subjects were to live. The foundational texts of Hinduism, which date to the seventh or sixth century BCE, account that the world is millions, not billions, of years old. Chinese Han dynasty (206 BCE–220 CE) astronomers believed that at the world's beginning the planets were conjoined and that they would merge again at the end of time. The Buddhists' cosmos comprised millions of worlds, each consisting of a mountain encircled by four continents, its seas surrounded by a wall of iron.

Yet even the million-year time frames and multiple planetary systems that ancient Asian thinkers endorsed did not prepare their communities for the idea that humans are related to apes. In all traditional cosmologies, humans came into existence fully formed, at a single moment, as did the other beings that populated the world. Modern discoveries about humanity's origins have challenged these traditions, because no tradition conceived that creatures

THE BIG PICTURE

How did we become human? What are the defining characteristics of human beings?

Core Objectives

DESCRIBE the various creation narratives, and **EXPLAIN** why they differ.

creation narratives
Narratives constructed by different cultures that draw on their belief systems and available evidence to explain the origins of the world and humanity.

evolved into new kinds of life, that humans had descended from apes, and that all of humanity originated in Africa.

Hominids to Modern Humans

The modern scientific creation narrative of human evolution would have been unimaginable even just over a century ago, when Charles Darwin was formulating his ideas about human origins. As we will see in this section, scientific discoveries have shown that modern humans evolved from earlier hominids. Through adaptation to their environment, various species of hominids developed new physical characteristics and distinctive skills. Millions of years after the first hominids appeared, the first modern humans—*Homo sapiens*—emerged and spread out across the globe.

EVOLUTIONARY FINDINGS AND RESEARCH METHODS

New insights into the time frame of the universe and human existence have occurred over a long period of time. Geologists made early breakthroughs in the eighteenth century when their research into the layers of the earth's surface revealed a world much older than biblical time implied. Evolutionary biologists, most notably Charles Darwin (1809–1882), concluded that all life had evolved over long periods from simple forms of matter. In the twentieth century astronomers, evolutionary biologists, and archaeologists have developed sophisticated dating techniques to pinpoint the chronology of the universe's creation and the evolution of all forms of life on earth. Their discoveries have radically transformed humanity's understanding of its own history (see Current Trends in World History: Using Big History and Science to Understand Human Origins). A mere century ago, who would have accepted the idea that the universe came into being 13.8 billion years ago, that the earth appeared about 4.5 billion years ago, and that the earliest life forms began to exist about 3.8 billion years ago?

Yet, modern science suggests that human beings are part of a long evolutionary chain stretching from microscopic bacteria to African apes that appeared about 23 million years ago, and that Africa's "Great Ape" population separated into several distinct groups of **hominids**: one becoming present-day gorillas; the second becoming chimpanzees; and the third becoming modern humans only after following a long and complicated evolutionary process. Our focus will be on the third group of hominids, who became modern humans. A combination of traits, evolving over several million years, distinguished humans from other hominids, including (1) lifting the

hominids
The "family," in scientific classification, that includes gorillas, chimpanzees, and humans (that is, *Homo sapiens*, in addition to our now-extinct hominid ancestors such as the various australopithecines as well as *Homo habilis*, *Homo erectus*, and *Homo neanderthalis*).

torso and walking on two legs (bipedalism), thereby freeing hands and arms to carry objects and hurl weapons; (2) controlling and then making fire; (3) fashioning and using tools; (4) developing cognitive skills and an enlarged brain and therefore the capacity for language; and (5) acquiring a consciousness of "self." All these traits were in place at least 150,000 years ago.

Two terms central to understanding any discussion of hominid development are evolution and natural selection. **Evolution** is the process by which species of plants and animals change and develop over generations, as certain traits are favored in reproduction. The process of evolution is driven by a mechanism called *natural selection*, in which members of a species with certain randomly occurring traits that are useful for environmental or other reasons survive and reproduce with greater success than those without the traits. Thus, biological evolution (human or otherwise) does not imply progress to higher forms of life, but instead implies successful adaptation to environmental surroundings.

EARLY HOMINIDS, ADAPTATION, AND CLIMATE CHANGE

The term *modern humans* refers to members of the *Homo sapiens* subspecies that evolved as early as 300,000 years ago. Through evolution, *Homo sapiens* developed the traits that make us distinct from the many other species and subspecies of hominids, such as the australopithecines (both *africanus* and *afarensis*), *Homo habilis*, and *Homo erectus* discussed in this section. "Modern" (and "recent") when applied to humans is relative, especially when compared to the life of the universe (which dates to 13.8 billion years ago) and even to the earliest hominids (7 million years ago). This section's discussion demonstrates that as modern humans evolved from earlier hominids, they passed through successive waves of adaptation, innovation, and migration. (See Table 1.2.)

Australopithecines In 1924, near Johannesburg, South Africa, a scientist named Raymond Dart identified the pint-sized skull and bones of a creature, nicknamed "Taung child," that had both ape-like and humanoid features. Dart officially labeled his bipedal find *Australopithecus africanus*. **Australopithecines** existed not only in southern Africa but in the north as well. In 1974, an archaeological team working at a site in present-day Ethiopia unearthed a relatively intact skeleton of a young adult female australopithecine in the valley of the Awash River. While the technical name for the find became *Australopithecus afarensis*, the researchers who found the skeleton gave it the nickname Lucy, based on the popular Beatles song "Lucy in the Sky with Diamonds."

Using Big History and Science to Understand Human Origins

The historical profession has undergone transformative changes since the end of World War II. One of the most radical changes in historical narratives is what historian David Christian has called "Big History." Just what it is still remains a mystery for many historians, and few departments of history offer courses in Big History. But Big History presents a coherent narrative of the origins of the universe up to the present. Its influence on our sense of who we are and where we came from is impressive.

Big History covers the history of our universe from its creation 13.8 billion years ago to the present. (See Table 1.1.) Because it merges natural history with human history, its study requires knowledge of many fields of science. Big History's use of the sciences enables us to learn of the universe before our solar system (astrophysics), our planet before life (geology), life before humans (biology), and humans before written sources (paleoanthropology). At present, few historians feel comfortable using these findings or integrating these data into their own general history courses. Nevertheless, Big History provides another narrative of how and when our universe, and we as human beings, came into existence.

Most of this chapter deals with how our species, *Homo sapiens*, came into being, and here, too, scholars are dependent on a range of approaches, including the work of linguists, biologists, paleoanthropologists, archaeologists, and many others. The first major advance in the study of the time before written records occurred in the mid-twentieth century, and it involved the use of radiocarbon dating. All living things contain the radiocarbon isotope C^{14}, which plants acquire directly from the atmosphere and animals acquire indirectly when they consume plants or other animals. When these living things die, the C^{14} isotope begins to decay into a stable nonradioactive element, C^{12}. Because the rate of decay is regular and measurable, it is possible to determine the age of fossils that leave organic remains for up to 40,000 years.

The evidence for human evolution, discussed in this chapter, requires dating methods that can extend back much farther than radiocarbon dating. Using the *potassium-argon method*, scientists can calculate the age of nonliving objects by measuring the ratio of potassium to argon in them, since potassium decays into argon. This method allows scientists to calculate the age of objects up to a million years old. Likewise, scientists can use *uranium-thorium dating* to determine the date of objects (like shells, teeth, and bones) more closely linked to living beings. This uranium-series method permits scientists to date objects up to 500,000 years old. A similar date limit can be reached through *thermoluminescence methods* applied to soil deposits and objects with crystalline materials that have been exposed to sunlight or heat (as in the flames of a fire pit or the heat of a kiln). Even if a scientist cannot offer a direct date for an object—teeth, skull, or other bone—such methods offer a date for the sediments in which researchers find fossils, as a gauge of the age of the fossils themselves.

Lucy was remarkable. She stood a little over 3 feet tall, she walked upright, her skull contained a brain within the ape size range (that is, one-third human size), and her jaw and teeth were human-like. Her arms were long, hanging halfway from her hips to her knees—suggesting that she might not have been bipedal at all times and sometimes resorted to arms for locomotion, in the fashion of a modern baboon. Above all, Lucy's skeleton was relatively complete and showed us that hominids were walking around more than 3 million years ago. It is important to emphasize that australopithecines were not humans but they carried the genetic and biological material out of which

As this chapter demonstrates, the environment, especially climate, played a major role in the appearance of hominids and the eventual dominance of *Homo sapiens*. But how do we know so much about the world's climate so far back in time? This brings us to yet another scientific breakthrough, known as *marine isotope stages*. By exploring the marine life, mainly pollen and plankton, deposited in deep seabeds and measuring the levels of oxygen-16 and oxygen-18 isotopes in these life forms, oceanographers and climatologists are able to determine the temperature of the world hundreds of thousands and even millions of years ago and thus to chart the cooling and warming cycles of the earth's climate.

DNA (deoxyribonucleic acid) analysis is another crucial tool for unraveling the beginnings of modern humans. DNA, which determines biological inheritances, exists in two places within the cells of all living organisms—including the human body. *Nuclear DNA* occurs in the nucleus of every cell, where it controls most aspects of physical appearance and makeup. *Mitochondrial DNA* occurs outside the nucleus of cells and is located in mitochondria, structures used in converting the energy from food into a form that cells can use. Nuclear and mitochondrial DNA exists in males and females, but only mitochondrial DNA from females passes to their offspring, as the females' egg cells carry their mitochondria with their DNA to the offspring; sperm cells from males do not donate any DNA to the egg cell at fertilization. By examining mitochondrial DNA, researchers can measure genetic relatedness and variation among living organisms—including human beings. Such analysis has enabled researchers to pinpoint human descent from an original African population and to determine various branches of *Homo sapiens* lineage.

The genetic similarity of modern humans suggests that the population from which all *Homo sapiens* descended originated in Africa more than 250,000 years ago. When these humans began to move out of Africa as long as 180,000 years ago, they spread eastward into Southwest Asia and then throughout the rest of Afro-Eurasia. One group migrated to Australia about 50,000 years ago. Another group moved into the area of Europe about 40,000 years ago. When the scientific journal *Nature* in 1987 published genetic-based findings about humans' spread across the planet, it inspired a groundswell of public interest—and a contentious scientific debate that continues today.

Questions for Analysis

- How has the study of prehistory changed since the mid-twentieth century?
- Why are different dating methods appropriate for different kinds of artifacts?
- How does the study of climate and environment relate to the origins of humans?

Explore Further

Barham, Lawrence, and Mitchell, Peter, *The First Africans: African Archaeology from the Earliest Toolmakers to Most Recent Foragers* (2008).

Barker, Graeme, *Agricultural Revolution in Prehistory: Why Did Foragers Become Farmers* (2006).

Christian, David, *Maps of Time: An Introduction to Big History* (2004).

modern humans would later emerge. These precursors to modern humans had a key trait for evolutionary survival: they were remarkably good adapters. They could deal with dynamic environmental shifts, and they were intelligent.

Adaptation For hominids, like the rest of the plant and animal world, survival required constant adaptation (the ability to alter behavior and to innovate, finding new ways of doing things). During the first millions of years of hominid existence, these slow changes involved primarily physical adaptations to the environment. The places where researchers

Table 1.1 The Age of the Universe and Human Evolution

Development	Time
Big bang moment in the creation of the universe	13.8 BILLION YEARS AGO (BYA)
Formation of the sun, earth, and solar system	4.5 BYA
Earliest life forms appear	3.8 BYA
Multicellular organisms appear	1.5 BYA
First hominids appear	7 MILLION YEARS AGO (MYA)
Australopithecus afarensis appears (including Lucy)	3.4 MYA
Homo habilis appears (including Dear Boy)	2.5 MYA
Homo erectus appears (including Java and Peking Man)	1.8 MYA
Homo erectus leave Africa	1.5 MYA
Neanderthals appear	400,000 YEARS AGO
Homo sapiens appear	300,000 YEARS AGO
Homo sapiens leave Africa	180,000 YEARS AGO
Homo sapiens migrate into Asia	120,000 YEARS AGO
Homo sapiens migrate into Australia	60,000 YEARS AGO
Homo sapiens migrate into Europe	50,000 YEARS AGO
Homo sapiens migrate into the Americas	16,000 YEARS AGO
Homo sapiens sapiens appear (modern humans)	35,000 YEARS AGO

<1% of Earth's Existence

Before the agricultural revolution, dates are usually marked as BP, which counts the number of years before the present. These BP (or "before the present") dates might also be assigned units such as BYA (billions of years ago), MYA (millions of years ago), or KA (thousands of years ago), depending on what scale is most appropriate for the development being described. More recent dates, beginning around 12,000 years ago, are marked with BCE (before [the] Common Era) as the unit of time. To render a BP date into a BCE date, simply subtract 2,000 years to account for the 2,000 years of the Common Era (CE). So 12,000 BP = 10,000 BCE (plus the 2,000 years of the Common Era since the year 1).

have found early hominid remains in southern and eastern Africa had environments that changed from being heavily forested and well watered to being arid and desert-like, and then back again. (See Map 1.1.) Hominids had to keep pace with these changing physical environments or else risk extinction. In fact, many of the early hominid groups did die out.

In adapting, early hominids began to distinguish themselves from other mammals that were physically similar to themselves. It was not their hunting prowess that made the hominids stand out, because plenty of other species chased their prey with skill and dexterity. The single trait that gave early hominids a real advantage for survival was bipedalism: they became "two-footed" creatures that stood upright. At some point, the first hominids were able to remain upright and move about, leaving their arms and hands free for other useful tasks, like carrying food over long distances. Once they ventured into open savannas (grassy plains with a few scattered trees), about 1.7 million years ago, hominids had a tremendous advantage. They were the only primates (an order of mammals consisting of man, apes, and monkeys) to move consistently on two legs. Because they could move continuously and over great distances, they were able to migrate out of hostile environments and into more hospitable locations.

Environmental Changes The climate in eastern and southern Africa, where hominid development began, was conducive to the development of diverse plant and animal species. When the world entered its fourth great ice age approximately 40 million years ago, the earth's temperatures dropped and its continental ice sheets, polar ice sheets, and mountain glaciers increased. This ice age lasted until 12,000 years ago. Like all ice ages, this fourth ice age had alternating warming and cooling phases that lasted between 40,000 and 100,000 years each. Between 15 and 10 million years ago, the climate in Africa went through one such cooling and drying phase. To the east of Africa's Rift Valley, stretching from South Africa north to the Ethiopian highlands, the cooling and drying forced forests to contract and savannas to spread. It was in this region that some apes left the shelter of the trees, stood up, and learned to walk, to run, and to live in savanna lands—thus becoming the precursors to humans, and distinctive as a new species.

Using two feet for locomotion augmented the means for obtaining food and avoiding predators and improved the chances these creatures had to survive in constantly changing environments. In addition to being bipedal, hominids had opposable thumbs. This trait, shared with other primates, gave hominids great physical dexterity, enhancing their ability to explore and to alter materials found in nature. Manual dexterity and standing upright also enabled them to carry young family members if they needed to relocate, or to throw missiles (such as rocks and sticks) with deadly accuracy to protect themselves or to obtain food.

Hominids used their increased powers of observation and memory, what we call cognitive skills, to gather wild berries and grains and to scavenge the meat and marrow of animals that had died of natural causes or as the prey of predators. All primates are good at these activities, but hominids came to excel at them. Cognitive skills, which also included problem

Table 1.2 Human Evolution	
Species	**Time***
Sahelanthropus tchadensis (including Toumai skull)	7 MILLION YEARS AGO (MYA)
Orrorin tugenensis	6 MYA
Ardipithecus ramidus (including Ardi)	4.4 MYA
Australopithecus anamensis	4.2 MYA
Australopithecus afarensis (including Lucy)	3.4 MYA
Australopithecus africanus (including Taung child)	3.0 MYA
Homo habilis (including Dear Boy)	2.5 MYA
Homo erectus and *Homo ergaster* (including Java and Peking Man)	1.8 MYA
Homo heidelbergensis (common ancestor of *Homo neanderthalis* and *Homo sapiens*)	600,000 YEARS AGO
Homo neanderthalis	400,000 YEARS AGO
Homo sapiens	300,000 YEARS AGO
Homo naledi	c. 280,000 YEARS AGO
Homo sapiens sapiens (modern humans)	35,000 YEARS AGO

*Dates are approximate (midpoint on a range), based on multiple finds. Some species are represented with hundreds of examples (more than 300 examples of *Australopithecus afarensis*, of which "Lucy" is the most famous, date across a span of almost 1 million years), while the evidence for other species is more limited (*Sahelanthropus tchadensis* is represented by a single skull).

Source: Smithsonian Institute Human Origins Program

Fossil Bones of Lucy Archaeologist Donald Johanson discovered the fossilized bones of this young female in the Afar region of Ethiopia. Representative of *Australopithecus afarensis*, which lived from 3.9 to 2.9 million years ago, Lucy's bones are believed to date from approximately 3.2 million years ago and provide evidence of some of the first hominids to appear in Africa. This find was of great importance because the bones were so fully and completely preserved.

solving and—eventually—language, were destined to become the basis for further developments. Early hominids were highly social. They lived in bands of about twenty-five individuals, trying to survive by hunting small game and gathering wild plants. Not yet a match for large predators, they had to find safe hiding places. They thrived in places where a diverse supply of wild grains and fruits and abundant wildlife ensured a secure, comfortable existence. In such locations, small hunting bands of twenty-five could swell through alliances with others to as many as 500 individuals. Like other primates, hominids communicated through gestures, but they also may have developed a very basic form of spoken language that led (among other things) to the establishment of rudimentary cultural codes such as common rules, customs, and identities.

Early hominids lived in this manner for up to 3 million years, changing their way of life very little except for moving around the African landmass in their never-ending search for more favorable environments. Even so, their survival is surprising. There were not many of them, and they struggled in hostile environments surrounded by a diversity of large mammals, including predators such as lions.

As the environment changed over the millennia, these early hominids gradually changed as well. Over a period of 3 million years, their brains more than doubled in size; their foreheads became more elongated; their jaws became less massive; and they took on a much more human look. Adaptation to environmental changes also created new skills and aptitudes, which expanded the ability to store and analyze information. With larger brains, hominids could form mental maps of their worlds—they could learn, remember what they learned, and convey these lessons to their neighbors and offspring. In this fashion, larger groups of hominids created communities with shared understandings of their environments.

Diversity Recent discoveries in Kenya, Chad, and Ethiopia suggest that hominids were both older and more diverse than early australopithecine finds (both *afarensis* and *africanus*) had suggested. In southern Kenya in 2000, researchers excavated bone remains, around 6 million years old, of a chimpanzee-sized hominid (named *Orrorin tugenensis*) that walked upright on two feet. In Chad in 2001, another team unearthed the 7 million-year-old

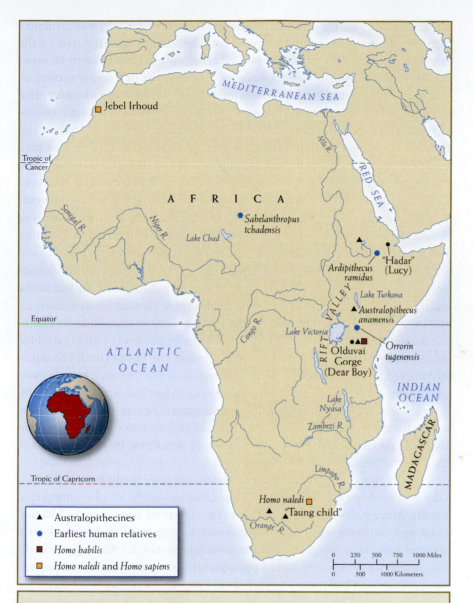

Map legend:

▲ Australopithecines
● Earliest human relatives
■ *Homo habilis*
■ *Homo naledi* and *Homo sapiens*

Map labels:

MEDITERRANEAN SEA
Jebel Irhoud
Tropic of Cancer
Nile R.
RED SEA
AFRICA
Senegal R.
Niger R.
Lake Chad
● *Sahelanthropus tchadensis*
▲
● "Hadar" (Lucy)
Ardipithecus ramidus
RIFT VALLEY
Lake Turkana
▲ *Australopithecus anamensis*
Equator
Congo R.
Lake Victoria
● ▲ ■ *Orrorin tugenensis*
Olduvai Gorge (Dear Boy)
ATLANTIC OCEAN
INDIAN OCEAN
Lake Nyasa
Zambezi R.
MADAGASCAR
Tropic of Capricorn
Limpopo R.
Homo naledi ■
▲ "Taung child"
Orange R.

Scale:
0   250   500   750   1000 Miles
0   500   1000 Kilometers

Map 1.1 Early Hominids

The earliest hominid species evolved in Africa millions of years ago.

- Judging from this map, in which parts of Africa has evidence for hominid species been excavated?

- Use Table 1.2 to assign dates to these hominid finds. What, if any, hypotheses might you suggest to correlate the geographic spread of the finds with the evolution of hominid species over time?

- According to this chapter, how did the changing environment of eastern and southern Africa shape the evolution of these modern human ancestors?

"Toumai skull," with a mix of attributes (small cranial capacity like a chimp's but more human-like teeth and spinal column placement at the base of the skull) that perplexed researchers but led them to place this new find, technically named *Sahelanthropus tchadensis*, in the story of human evolution. These finds indicate that bipedalism must be millions of years older than scientists thought based on discoveries like Lucy (*Australopithecus afarensis*) and "Taung child" (*Australopithecus africanus*). Moreover, *Orrorin* and *Sahelanthropus* teeth indicate that they were closer to modern humans than to australopithecines. In their arms and hands, though, which show characteristics needed for tree climbing, the *Orrorin* hominids seemed more ape-like than the australopithecines. So *Orrorin* hominids were still somewhat tied to an environment in the trees. Only the chimp-sized skull fragments of *Sahelanthropus* have been found, so no conclusions about their bodies, other than that they walked upright, can be drawn.

The story of diversity continues to unfold. Far inside a cave near Johannesburg, South Africa, spelunkers recently made a discovery that led to the excavation of more than 1,550 fossil remains (now named *Homo naledi*, for the cave in which they were found). Researchers have been able to assemble a composite skeleton that revealed that the upper body parts resembled some of the much earlier pre-*Homo* finds, while the hands (both the palms and curved fingers), the wrists, the long legs, and the feet are close to those of modern humans. The males were around 5 feet tall and weighed 100 pounds, while the females were shorter and lighter. Recent publications have suggested a surprisingly late date range of 335,000 to 236,000 years ago, and therefore much research remains to be done to determine how these fossils fit the story of human evolution.

The fact that different kinds of early hominids were living in isolated societies and evolving separately, though in close proximity to one another, in eastern Africa between 4 and 3 million years ago until as recently as 300,000 years ago indicates much greater diversity among their populations than scholars previously imagined. The environment in eastern Africa generated a fair number of different hominid populations, a few of which would provide our genetic base, but most of which would not survive in the long run.

Tool Use by *Homo habilis*

One million years after Lucy, the first beings whom we assign to the genus *Homo*, or "true human," appeared. Like early hominids, *Homo habilis* was bipedal, possessing a smooth walk based on upright posture. *Homo habilis* had an even more important advantage over other hominids: brains that were growing larger. Big brains are the site of innovation: learning and storing lessons so that humans could pass those lessons on to later generations, especially in the making of tools and the efficient use of resources (and, we suspect, in defending themselves). Mary and Louis Leakey, who made astonishing fossil discoveries in the 1950s at Olduvai Gorge in present-day north central Tanzania, identified these important traits. The Leakeys' finds included an intact skull that was 1.8 million years old. They nicknamed the creature whose skull they had unearthed Dear Boy.

Objects discovered with Dear Boy demonstrated that by this time early humans had begun to make tools for butchering animals and, possibly, for hunting and killing smaller animals. The tools were flaked stones with sharpened edges for cutting apart animal flesh and scooping out the marrow from bones. To mimic the slicing teeth of lions, leopards, and other carnivores, these early humans had devised these tools through careful chipping. Dear Boy and his companions had carried usable rocks to distant places where they made their implements with special hammer stones—tools to make tools. Unlike other tool-using animals (for example, chimpanzees), early humans were now intentionally fashioning implements, not simply finding them when needed. More important, they were passing on knowledge of these tools to their offspring and, in the process, gradually improving the tools. The Leakeys, believing that making and using tools represented a new stage in the evolution of human beings, gave Dear Boy and his companions the name **Homo habilis**, or "skillful human." While scholars today may debate whether toolmaking (rather than walking upright or having a large brain) is the key trait that distinguishes the first humans from earlier hominids, *Homo habilis*'s skills made them the forerunners, though very distant ones, of modern men and women.

MIGRATIONS OF *HOMO ERECTUS*

By 1 million years ago, many of the hominid species that flourished together in Africa had died out. One surviving species, which emerged about 1.8 million years ago, had a large brain capacity and walked truly upright; it therefore gained the name **Homo erectus**, or "standing human." Three important features distinguished *Homo erectus* from their competitors and made them more able to cope with environmental changes: their family dynamics, use of fire, and ability to travel long distances. Discoveries in Asia and Europe show that *Homo erectus* migrated out of Africa in some of the earliest waves of hominid migration around the globe.

Family Dynamics One of the traits that contributed to the survival of *Homo erectus* was the development of extended periods of caring for their young.

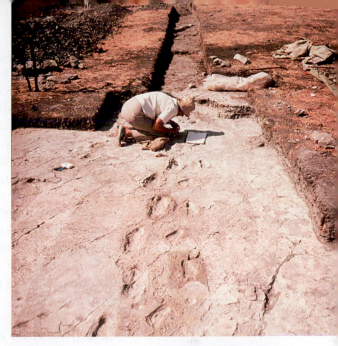

The Leakeys Louis Leakey and his wife, Mary, were dedicated archaeologists whose work in East Africa established the area as one of the starting points of human development. Mary Leakey was among the most successful archaeologists studying hominids in Africa. Her finds, including the one in this photograph from Laetoli, Tanzania, highlight the activities of early men and women in Africa. The footprints, believed to be those of an *Australopithecus afarensis*, date from 3.7 to 3 million years ago.

Homo habilis
Species, confined to Africa, that emerged about 2.5 million years ago and whose toolmaking ability truly made it the forerunner, though a very distant one, of modern humans. *Homo habilis* means "skillful human."

Although their enlarged brain gave these hominids advantages over the rest of the animal world, it also brought one significant problem: their heads were too large to pass through the females' pelvises at birth. Their pelvises were only big enough to deliver an infant with a cranial capacity that was about a third an adult's size. As a result, offspring required a long period of protection by adults as they matured and their brain size tripled.

This difference from other species also affected family dynamics. For example, the long maturing process gave adult members of hunting and gathering bands time to train their children in those activities. In addition, maturation and brain growth required mothers to spend years breast-feeding and then preparing food for children after their weaning. In order to share the responsibilities of child-rearing, mothers relied on other women (their own mothers, sisters, and friends) and girls (often their own daughters) to help in the nurturing and protecting, a process known as *allomothering* (literally, "other mothering").

Use of Fire *Homo erectus* began to make rudimentary attempts to control their environment by means of fire. It is hard to tell from fossils when hominids—*Homo erectus* or *Homo sapiens* (modern humans)—learned to use fire. The most reliable evidence comes from cave sites less than 250,000 years old, where early humans apparently cooked some of their food, but some have suggested that hominid mastery of fire occurred as early as 500,000 years ago, by *Homo erectus*. Fire provided heat, protection, a gathering point for small communities, and a way to cook food. It was also symbolically powerful: here was a source of energy that humans could extinguish and revive at will. The uses of fire had enormous long-term effects on human evolution. Because they were able to boil, steam, and fry wild plants, as well as otherwise undigestible foods (especially raw muscle fiber), hominids who mastered this technology could expand their diets. Because cooked foods yield more energy than raw foods and because the brain, while only 2 percent of human body weight, uses between 20 and 25 percent of all the energy that humans take in, cooking was decisive in the evolution of brain size and functioning.

Early Migrations Being bipedal, *Homo erectus* could move with a smooth and rapid gait, so they could cover large distances quickly. They were the world's first long-distance travelers, forming the first mobile human communities. (See Table 1.3.) Around 1.5 million years ago, *Homo erectus* individuals began migrating out of Africa, first into the lands of Southwest Asia. From there, they traveled along the Indian Ocean shoreline, moving into South Asia and Southeast Asia and later northward into what is now China. Their migration was a response in part to the environmental changes that were transforming the world. The Northern Hemisphere experienced thirty major cold phases during this period, marked by glaciers spreading over vast expanses of the northern parts of Eurasia and the Americas. The glaciers formed as a result of intense cold that froze much of the world's oceans, lowering them some 325 feet below present-day levels. These lower ocean levels made it possible for the migrants to travel across land bridges into Southeast Asia and from East Asia to Japan, as well as from New Guinea to Australia. The last parts of the Afro-Eurasian landmass to be occupied were in Europe.

Discoveries of the bone remains of "Java Man" and "Peking Man" (named according to the places where archaeologists first unearthed their remains) confirmed early settlements of *Homo erectus* in Southeast and East Asia. The remains of Java Man, found in 1891 on the island of Java, turned out to be those of an early *Homo erectus* that had dispersed into Asia between 1.5 and 1 million years ago. Peking Man, found near Beijing in the 1920s, was a cave dweller, toolmaker, and hunter and gatherer who settled in the warmer climate in northern China perhaps 400,000 years ago. Peking Man's brain was larger than that of his Javan cousins, and there is evidence that he controlled fire and cooked meat in addition to hunting large animals. He made tools of vein quartz, quartz crystals, flint, and sandstone. A major innovation was the double-faced axe, a stone instrument whittled down to sharp edges on both sides to serve as a hand axe,

Table 1.3 Migrations of *Homo sapiens*	
Species	**Time**
Homo erectus leave Africa	c. 1.5 MILLION YEARS AGO
Homo sapiens leave Africa	c. 180,000 YEARS AGO
Homo sapiens migrate into Asia	c. 120,000 YEARS AGO
migrate into Australia	c. 60,000 YEARS AGO
migrate into Europe	c. 50,000 YEARS AGO
migrate into the Americas	c. 16,000 YEARS AGO

Skulls of Ancestors of *Homo sapiens* Shown here are seven skulls of ancestors of modern-day men and women, arranged to highlight brain growth over time. The larger the brain, the more developed the regions of the brain that process vision, different kinds of cognition, and communication can be. The skulls represent (left to right): *Adapis*, a lemur-like animal that lived 50 million years ago; *Proconsul*, a primate that lived about 23 million years ago; *Australopithecus africanus*; *Homo habilis*; *Homo erectus*; *Homo sapiens* from the Qafzeh site in Israel, about 90,000 years old; and *Homo sapiens sapiens* from France, about 22,000 years old.

a cleaver, a pick, and probably a weapon to hurl against foes or animals. Even so, these early predecessors still lacked the intelligence, language skills, and ability to create culture that would distinguish the first modern humans from their hominid relatives.

HOMO SAPIENS: THE FIRST MODERN HUMANS

Homo sapiens—a bigger-brained, more dexterous, and more agile species of humans that appeared in the highlands of eastern Africa about 200,000 years ago (and possibly in northwest Africa closer to 300,000 years ago)—differed notably from their precursors, including *Homo habilis* and *Homo erectus*. Their distinctive traits, including greater cognitive skills, made *Homo sapiens* the first modern humans and enabled them to spread out from Africa and flourish in even more diverse regions across the globe than *Homo erectus* did.

Large-scale shifts in Africa's climate and environment several hundred thousand years ago put huge pressures on all types of mammals, including hominids. In these extremely warm and dry environments, the smaller, quicker, and more adaptable mammals survived. What counted now was no longer large size and brute strength, but the ability to respond quickly, with agility, and with great speed. The eclipse of *Homo erectus* by *Homo sapiens* was not inevitable. After all, *Homo erectus* was already scattered around Africa and Eurasia by the time *Homo sapiens* emerged; in contrast, even as late as 100,000 years ago there were only about 10,000 *Homo sapiens* adults living primarily in a small part of the African landmass. When *Homo sapiens* began moving in large numbers out of Africa and the two species encountered each other in the same places across the globe, *Homo sapiens* individuals were better suited to survive—in part because of their greater cognitive and language skills.

The *Homo sapiens* newcomers followed the trails blazed by earlier migrants when they moved out of Africa. (See Map 1.2.) Evidence, including part of a fossilized jaw with teeth, from a cave on Mount Carmel in Israel indicates that *Homo sapiens* were living there as early as 180,000 years ago. Whether that evidence suggests significant migrations or more limited forays by *Homo sapiens* is still unclear. Nevertheless, it is clear that from 120,000 to 50,000 years ago, *Homo sapiens* were moving in ever increasing numbers into the same areas as their genetic cousins, reaching across Southwest Asia and from there into central Asia—but not into the area of Europe.

The Physical Evolution of Hominids These three figures show the femur bones of Lucy, *Orrorin tugenensis* (one of the earliest of the hominids, who may have existed around 6 million years ago), and *Homo sapiens*. *Homo sapiens* have a larger femur bone and were bigger than Lucy—a representative of the hominid species *Australopithecus afarensis*—but have the same bone structure. Particularly useful indicators for determining differences among human ancestors are skull size (which can indicate the size of the brain and thus cognitive ability), the position at the base of the skull where the spine enters the cranium (which can indicate bipedalism), jawbones and teeth (which can indicate the kind of food they could have chewed), femur bones (which can indicate overall size and manner of walking), and foot and hand structure (which can indicate the kind of activities they performed).

They flourished and reproduced. By 30,000 years ago, the population of *Homo sapiens* had grown to about 300,000. Between 60,000 and 12,000 years ago, these modern humans were surging into areas tens of thousands of miles from the Rift Valley and the Ethiopian highlands of Africa.

In the area of present-day China, *Homo sapiens* were thriving and creating distinct regional cultures. Consider Shandingdong Man, a *Homo sapiens* who dates to about 18,000 years ago. His physical characteristics were closer to those of modern humans, and he had a similar brain size. His stone tools, which included choppers and scrapers for preparing food, were similar to those of the *Homo erectus* Peking Man. His bone needles, however, were the first stitching tools of their kind found in China, and they indicated the making of garments. Some of the needles measured a little over an inch in length and had small holes drilled in them. Shandingdong Man also buried his dead. In fact, a tomb of grave goods includes ornaments suggesting the development of aesthetic tastes and religious beliefs.

Homo sapiens were also migrating into the northeastern fringe of East Asia. In the frigid climate there, they learned to follow herds of large Siberian grazing animals. The bones and dung of mastodons made decent fuel and good building material. Pursuing their prey eastward as the large-tusked herds sought pastures in the steppes (treeless grasslands) and marshes, these groups migrated across the ice to Japan. Archaeologists have discovered a mammoth fossil in the colder north of Japan, for example, and an elephant fossil in the warmer south. Elephants in particular roamed the warmer parts of Inner Eurasia. The hunters and gatherers who moved into Japan gathered wild plants for sustenance, and they dried, smoked, or broiled meat by using fire.

About 30,000 years ago, *Homo sapiens* began edging into the weedy landmass that linked Siberia and North America (which hominids had not populated). This thousand-mile-long land bridge, later called Beringia, must have seemed like an extension of familiar steppe-land terrain, and these individuals lived isolated lives there on a broad and (at the time) warm plain for thousands of years before beginning to migrate into North America. The first migrations occurred around 16,000 years ago. Modern humans poured eastward and southward into North America. A final migration occurred about 8,000 years ago by boat, since by then the land bridge had disappeared under the sea. (See Map 1.2 for evidence that demonstrates the complex picture of the peopling of the Americas, both along the western coastline and to the east.)

Using their cognitive abilities to adapt to new environments and to innovate, these migrants, who were the first discoverers of America, began to fill up the landmasses. They found ample prey in the herds of woolly mammoths, caribou, 3-ton giant sloths, and 200-pound beavers. But the explorers could also themselves be prey—for they encountered saber-toothed

Core Objectives

COMPARE the narrative of human evolution to the creation narratives covered earlier.

ARCTIC OCEAN

by 25,000 BP

NORTH SEA

EUROPE

BLACK SEA
50,000–40,000 BP

CASPIAN SEA

MEDITERRANEAN SEA

by 180,000 BP

by 60,000 BP

SOUTHWEST ASIA

EAST ASIA

100,000 BP

SOUTH ASIA

AFRICA

SOUTHEAST ASIA

ATLANTIC OCEAN

100,000 BP

INDIAN OCEAN

120,000 BP

60,000–50,000 BP

AUSTRALIA

Map 1.2 Early Migrations: Out of Africa

Hominid species, like *Homo erectus*, began migrating out of Africa hundreds of thousands of years ago, but only *Homo sapiens* went to all major inhabitable regions.

- According to this map, when and to what regions did *Homo erectus* migrate? *Homo neanderthalis*? *Homo sapiens*? Compare the location, extent, and dates of each species' migration.

- Locate the extent of ice sheets and identify the differences in exposed landmasses, as compared to modern shorelines. How did ice sheets and exposed land shape each species' migration patterns?

- Examine the dates for human settlement of the Americas. What do these dates suggest about human migration in the Americas?

ARCTIC OCEAN

BERINGIA

From Asia 16,000 BP

NORTH
AMERICA

14,000 BP

Clovis
13,000 BP

Buttermilk Creek
15,500 BP

Meadowcroft
16,000 BP

Cactus Hill
15,500 BP

Tropic of Cancer

PACIFIC
OCEAN

12,500 BP

ATLANTIC
OCEAN

Equator

Lapa do Boquete
12,000 BP

SOUTH
AMERICA

Tropic of Capricorn

Monte Verde
14,500 BP

11,000 BP

▲ Pre-Clovis
● Clovis
⟵ Spread of *Homo erectus* before 200,000 years ago
⟵ Colonization of *Homo sapiens*
　Area occupied by *Homo neanderthalensis*
　Area occupied by *Homo erectus*
┈┈ Coastline at time of glacial maximum
　Maximum extent of ice sheets, c.16,000 BP
　Land exposed by lower sea level, c. 16,000 BP

0   1000   2000 Miles

0   1000   2000 Kilometers

tigers, long-legged eagles, and giant bears that moved faster than horses. The melting of the glaciers about 8,000 years ago and the resulting disappearance of the land bridge eventually cut off the first Americans from their Afro-Eurasian origins. Thereafter, the Americas became a world apart from Afro-Eurasia.

Although modern humans evolved from earlier hominids, no straight-line descent tree exists from the first hominids to *Homo sapiens*. Increasingly, scientists view our origins as shaped by a series of progressions and regressions as hominid species adapted or failed to adapt and died out. The remains of now-extinct hominid species, such as *Homo ergaster*, *Homo heidelbergensis*, *Homo neanderthalis*, and now *Homo naledi* (see Table 1.2), offer intriguing glimpses of ultimately unsuccessful branches of the complex human evolutionary tree. Spreading into Europe and parts of Southwest Asia along with other hominids, Neanderthals, for example, had big brains, used tools, wore clothes, buried their dead, hunted, lived in rock shelters, and even interacted with *Homo sapiens*. Yet when faced with environmental challenges, *Homo sapiens* survived, while Neanderthals died out nearly 40,000 years ago.

Indeed, several species could exist simultaneously, but some were more suited to changing environmental conditions—and thus more likely to survive—than others. Although the examples emphasized in this chapter—*Homo habilis* and *Homo erectus*—were among some of the world's first human-like inhabitants, they probably were not direct ancestors of modern men and women. By 25,000 years ago, DNA analysis reveals, nearly all genetic cousins to *Homo sapiens* had become extinct. *Homo sapiens*, with their physical agility and superior cognitive skills, were ready to populate the world.

The Life of Early *Homo sapiens*

Core Objectives

DESCRIBE human ways of life and cultural developments from 300,000 to 12,000 years ago.

In the period from 300,000 to around 12,000 years ago, early *Homo sapiens* were similar to other hominids in that they lived by hunting and gathering, but their use of language and new cultural forms represented an evolutionary breakthrough. Earlier hominids could not form large, lasting communities, as they had limited communication skills. While simple commands and hand signals developed over time, complex linguistic expression escaped them. This achievement was one of the last in the evolutionary process of becoming human; it did not occur until between 100,000 and 50,000 years ago. Many scholars view it as the critical ingredient in distinguishing human beings from other animals. It is this skill that made *Homo sapiens* "sapiens," which is to say "wise" or "intelligent"—humans who could create culture.

LANGUAGE

Few things set *Homo sapiens* off from the rest of the animal world more starkly than their use of language. Although the beginnings and development of language are controversial, scholars agree that the cognitive abilities involved in language development marked an evolutionary milestone. Some earlier hominids could express themselves by grunting, but natural language (the use of sounds to make words that convey meaning to others) is unique to modern humans. The development of language required a large brain and complex cognitive organization to create word groups that would convey symbolic meaning. Verbal communication required an ability to think abstractly and to communicate abstractions. Language was a huge breakthrough, because individuals could teach words and ideas to neighbors and offspring. Language thus enhanced the ability to accumulate knowledge that could be transmitted across both space and time.

Biological research has demonstrated that humans can make and process many more primary and distinctive sounds, called phonemes, than other animals can. Whereas a human being can utter fifty phonemes, an ape can form only twelve. Also, humans can process sounds more quickly than other primates can. With fifty phonemes it is possible to create more than 100,000 words; by arranging those words in different sequences and developing rules in language, individuals can express countless subtle and complex meanings. Recent research suggests that use of complex languages occurred about 100,000 years ago and that the nearest approximation to humanity's earliest language existing today belongs to two African peoples, the !Kung of southern Africa and the Hadza of Tanzania. These peoples make a clicking sound by dropping the tongue down from the roof of the mouth and exhaling. As humans moved out of Africa and spread around the globe, they expanded their original language into nineteen language families, from which all of the world's languages then evolved. (See Map 1.3.) It was the development of language and the cultural forms discussed later in this section that allowed *Homo sapiens* to engage dynamically with their environments.

HUNTING AND GATHERING

Although these early humans were developing language skills that distinguished them from their hominid relatives, like their predecessors they remained hunters and gatherers until around 12,000 years ago (for almost 95 percent of our existence). As late as 1500 CE, as much as 15 percent of the world's population still lived by **hunting and gathering**. Early *Homo sapiens* hunted animals, fished, and foraged for wild berries, nuts, fruit, and grains, rather than planting crops, vines, or trees. Even today hunting and gathering societies endure, although only in the most marginal locations—often at the edge of deserts. Researchers consider the present-day San peoples of

> **hunting and gathering**
> Lifestyle in which food is acquired through hunting animals, fishing, and foraging for wild berries, nuts, fruit, and grains, rather than planting crops, vines, or trees. As late as 1500 CE, as much as 15 percent of the world's population still lived by this method.

Map 1.3 Original Language Family Groups

The use of complex language developed 100,000 years ago among *Homo sapiens* in Africa. As humans dispersed throughout the globe, nineteen language families evolved from which all modern languages originate.

- How many different landmasses did language evolve on? Which landmasses have a greater number of language families, and why might that be?
- On the basis of this map, what geographic features had an impact on the evolution of language groups?
- Why do you think separate languages emerged over time?

southern Africa as an isolated remnant continuing their traditional hunting and gathering modes of life. Modern scholars use the San to reveal how men and women must have lived hundreds of thousands of years ago. The fact that hominid men and women (going back to *Homo erectus* and *habilis* and beyond) survived as hunters and gatherers for millions of years, that early *Homo sapiens* also lived this way, and that a few contemporary communities still forage for food suggests the powerful attractions of this way of life. Hunters and gatherers could find enough food in about three hours of foraging each day, thus affording time for other pursuits such as relaxation, interaction, and friendly competitions with other members of their bands. Scholars believe that these small bands were relatively egalitarian compared with the more male-dominated societies that arose later. They speculate that men

Hadza of Modern Tanzania
Hunting and gathering was the way that most humans lived for hundreds of thousands of years. Although their way of life is dying out, modern hunters and gatherers offer useful ethnographic comparisons for understanding how humans lived in the millennia prior to sedentary agriculture. These Hadza, from modern Tanzania, dig up edible roots that offer a reliable and high-calorie food source for their community.

specialized in hunting and women specialized in gathering and child-rearing. Scholars also believe that women made a larger contribution and had high status because the dietary staples of the community were cereals and fruits, whose harvesting and preparation were likely women's responsibility.

PAINTINGS, SCULPTURE, AND MUSIC

The ability to draw allowed *Homo sapiens* to understand their environment, to bond among their kin groups (groups related by blood ties), and to articulate important mythologies. Accomplished artwork from this era has been found across Afro-Eurasia. For instance, in a deep cave at Altamira in Spain more than two dozen life-size figures of bison, horses, and wild bulls, all painted in vivid red, black, yellow, and brown, are arranged across the ceiling of the huge chamber. More than 50,000 similarly stunning works of art have been found in caves across Europe and elsewhere. The images on cave walls accumulated in some instances over a period of 25,000 years, and they changed little in that time. The subjects are often large game—animals that early humans would have considered powerful symbols. The artists rendered these animals in such a way that the natural contours of the cave wall defined a bulging belly or an eye socket. The remarkably few human images show hunters, naked females, or dancing males. There are also many handprints made by blowing paint around a hand placed on the cave wall, or by dipping hands in paint and then pressing them to the wall. There are even abstract symbols such as circles, wavy lines, and checkerboards; often these appear at places of transition in the caves.

Scholars have rejected an initial theory that these paintings were decorative, for the deep caves were not homes and had no natural light to render the images visible. Perhaps the images helped the early humans define themselves as separate from other parts of nature. Alternatively, they might have been the work of powerful shamans, individuals believed to hold special powers to understand and control the forces of the cosmos. The subjects and the style of the paintings are similar to images engraved or painted on rocks by some hunting and gathering societies living today, especially the San and the !Kung peoples of southern Africa. In those societies, paintings mark important places of ritual: shamans make them during trances while mediating with the spirit world on behalf of their communities.

Paintings were not the only form of artistic expression for early humans. Archaeologists also have unearthed small sculptures of animals shaped out of bone and stone that are even older than the paintings. Most famous are figurines of rotund, and perhaps pregnant, females. Statuettes like the so-called Venus of Willendorf, found in Austria, demonstrate that successful reproduction was a very important theme. Other sculptures represent animals in postures of movement or at rest.

The caves of early men and women also resounded to the strains of music. In 2008 archaeologists working in southwestern Germany discovered a hollowed-out bone flute with five openings that they dated to approximately 35,000 years ago, roughly the same time that humans began to occupy this region. When researchers put the flute to musical tests, they also concluded that the instrument was capable of making harmonic sounds comparable to those of modern-day flutes.

Only *Homo sapiens* had the cognitive abilities to produce the abundant sculptures and drawings of this era, thus leaving a permanent mark on the symbolic landscape of human development. Such visual expressions marked the dawn of human culture and a consciousness of men's and women's place in the world. Symbolic activity of this sort enabled humans to make sense of themselves, nature, and the relationship between humanity and nature. That relationship with nature—which had remained static for hundreds of thousands of years of hunting and gathering—would change with the agricultural revolution.

Agricultural Revolution: Food Production and Social Change

About 12,000 years ago (around 10,000 BCE), a fundamental shift occurred in the way humans produced food for themselves—what some scholars have called an agricultural, or ecological, revolution. Around the same time, a significant warming trend that had begun around 11,000 BCE resulted in a profusion of plants and animals, large numbers of which began to exist closer to humans. In this era of major change, humans established greater control over nature. The transformation consisted of the **domestication** of wild plants and animals. Population pressure was one factor that triggered the move to settled agriculture, as hunting and gathering alone could not sustain the growth in numbers of people. A revolution in agriculture, in turn, led to a vast population expansion because men and women could now produce more calories per unit of land. As various plants and animals were domesticated around the world, people settled in villages and social relationships changed.

THE BEGINNINGS OF SETTLED AGRICULTURE AND PASTORALISM

Learning to control environments through the domestication of plants and animals was a gradual process. Communities shifted from a hunting and gathering lifestyle (which requires moving around in search of food) to one based on agriculture (which requires staying in one place until the soil has been exhausted). **Settled agriculture** refers to the application of human labor and tools to a fixed plot of land for more than one growing cycle. Alternatively, some people adopted a lifestyle based on **pastoralism** (the herding of domesticated animals), which complemented settled farming.

Early Domestication of Plants and Animals The formation of settled communities enabled humans to take advantage of favorable regions and to take risks, spurring agricultural innovation. In areas with abundant wild game and edible plants, people began to observe and experiment with the most adaptable plants. For ages, people gathered grains by collecting seeds that fell freely from their stalks. At some point, observant collectors perceived that they could obtain larger harvests if they pulled grain seeds directly from plants. The process of plant domestication probably began when people noticed that certain edible plants retained their nutritious grains longer than others, so they collected these seeds and scattered them across fertile soils. When ripe, these plants produced bigger and more concentrated crops. Plant domestication occurred when the plant retained its ripe, mature seeds, allowing an easy harvest. People used most seeds for food but saved some for planting in the next growing cycle, to ensure a food supply for the next year.

Dogs were the first animals to be domesticated (although in fact they may have adopted humans, rather than the other way around). At least 15,000 years ago in Central Asia, including Mongolia and Nepal, humans first domesticated gray wolves and made them an essential part of human society. Dogs did more than comfort humans. They provided an example of how to achieve the domestication of other animals and, with their herding instincts, they helped humans control other domesticated animals, such as sheep. In the central Zagros Mountains region, where wild sheep and wild goats

domestication
Bringing a wild animal or plant under human control.

settled agriculture
Humans' use of tools, animals, and their own labor to work the same plot of land for more than one growing cycle. It involves switching from a hunting and gathering lifestyle to one based on farming.

pastoralism
A way of life in which humans herd domesticated animals and exploit their products (hides/fur, meat, and milk). Pastoralists include nomadic groups that range across vast distances, as well as transhumant herders who migrate seasonally in a more limited range.

Domestication This detail from a wall painting in the Tassili-n-Ajjer mountain range in modern Algeria depicts early domestication of cattle and other animals.

were abundant, they became the next animal domesticates. Perhaps hunters returned home with young wild sheep, which then reproduced, and their offspring never returned to the wild. The animals accepted their dependence because the humans fed them. Since controlling animal reproduction was more reliable than hunting, domesticated herds became the primary source of protein in the early humans' diet.

When the number of animals under human control and living close to the settlement outstripped the supply of food needed to feed them, community members could move the animals to grassy steppes for grazing. These pastoralists herded domesticated animals, moving them to new pastures on a seasonal basis. Goats, the other main domesticated animal of Southwest Asia, are smarter than sheep but more difficult to control. The pastoralists may have introduced goats into herds of sheep to better control herd movement. Pigs and cattle also came under human control at this time.

Transhumant Herders and Nomadic Pastoralists Pastoralism appeared as a way of life around 5500 BCE, essentially at the same time that full-time farmers appeared (although the beginnings of plant and animal domestication had begun many millennia earlier). Over time, two different types of pastoralists with different relationships to settled populations developed: transhumant herders and nomadic pastoralists. Transhumant herders were closely affiliated with agricultural villages whose inhabitants grew grains, especially wheat and barley, which required large parcels of land. These herders produced both meat and dairy products, as well as wool for textiles, and exchanged these products with the agriculturalists for grain, pottery, and other staples. Extended families might farm and herd at the same time, growing crops on large estates and grazing their herds in the foothills and mountains nearby. They moved their livestock seasonally, pasturing their flocks in higher lands during summer and in valleys in winter. This movement over short distances is called *transhumance* and did not require herders to vacate their primary living locations, which were generally in the mountain valleys.

In contrast with transhumant pastoralism, *nomadic pastoralism* came to flourish especially in the steppe lands north of the agricultural zone of southern Eurasia. This way of life was characterized by horse-riding herders of cattle and other livestock. Because horses provided decisive advantages in transportation and warfare, they gained more value than other domesticated animals. Thus, horses soon became the measure of household wealth and prestige. Unlike the transhumant herders, the nomadic pastoralists often had no fixed home, though they often returned to their traditional locations. They moved across large distances in response to the size and needs of their herds. The northern areas of the Eurasian landmass stretching from present-day Ukraine across Siberia and Mongolia to the Pacific Ocean became the preserve of these horse-riding pastoral peoples in a region unable to support the extensive agriculture necessary for large settled populations. Historians know much less about these horse-riding pastoral nomads than about the agriculturalists and the transhumant herders, as their numbers were small and they left fewer archaeological traces or historical records. Their role in world history, however, is as important as that of the settled societies. In Afro-Eurasia, they domesticated horses and developed weapons and techniques that at certain points in history enabled them to conquer sedentary societies. As we will see in the next section (and later chapters), they also transmitted ideas, products, and people across long distances, maintaining the linkages that connected east and west.

AGRICULTURAL INNOVATION: AFRO-EURASIA AND THE AMERICAS

The agricultural revolutions that occurred worldwide between 9000 and 2000 BCE had much in common: climatic change; increased knowledge about plants and animals; and the need for more efficient ways to feed, house, and promote the growth of a larger population. These concerns led peoples in Eurasia, the Americas, and Africa to see the advantages of cultivating plants and domesticating wildlife. (See Map 1.4.).

Some communities were independent innovators, developing agricultural techniques based on their specific environments. In Southwest Asia, East Asia, Africa, and the Americas, the distinctive crops and animals that humans first domesticated reflect independent innovation. As we will see in the following section, other communities (such as those in Europe) were borrowers

Core Objectives

COMPARE the ways communities around the world shifted to settled agriculture.

NORTH
AMERICA

Eastern Woodlands
3000 BCE
(Squash)

Mississippi R.

Gulf of Mexico

ATLANTIC
OCEAN

SAHARA

Tehuacan Valley

Sahel
2000 BCE
(Millet,
Sorghum)

Niger R.

Mesoamerica
8000–4000 BCE
(Maize, Squash)

Equator

Amazon R.

SOUTH
AMERICA

ANDES

Mesotropics
8000–5000 BCE
(Manioc, Squash,
Palms, Yams)

Central Andes
8000–5000 BCE
(Llamas, Potatoes,
Guinea Pigs)

PACIFIC
OCEAN

MOUNTAINS

Origin of food domestication

0   1000   2000 Miles

0   1000   2000 Kilometers

Map 1.4 content (labels on map):

Southeastern Europe
6000 BCE
(Pigs, Cattle, Wheat, Barley, Sheep, Goats)

ASIA

GOBI DESERT

BLACK SEA
CAUCASUS MTS.
CASPIAN SEA
TAKLAMAKAN DESERT
MEDITERRANEAN SEA
SYRIAN DESERT
ZAGROS MTS.
Tigris R.
Euphrates R.
Persian Gulf
Indus R.
Yellow R.
Yangzi R.

Yellow River
5500 BCE (Millet)

Yangzi River
6500 BCE (Rice)

PACIFIC OCEAN

EUROPE
Danube R.

DESERT
AFRICA
Nile R.
RED SEA
Congo R.
ETHIOPIAN HIGHLANDS

Fertile Crescent
8000 BCE
(Barley, Cattle, Goats, Pigs, Sheep, Wheat)

KALAHARI DESERT

INDIAN OCEAN

AUSTRALIA

ARCTIC OCEAN

Map 1.4 The Origins of Food Production and Animal Domestication

Agricultural production emerged in many regions at different times. The variety of patterns reflected local resources and conditions.

- In how many different locations, and at what different times, did agricultural production and animal domestication emerge? What is the range of crops and animals domesticated in each region?

- What specific geographic features (for instance, specific mountains, rivers, or latitudes) are common among these early food-producing areas? Do those geographic features appear to guarantee agricultural production?

- Why do you think agriculture emerged in certain areas and not in others?

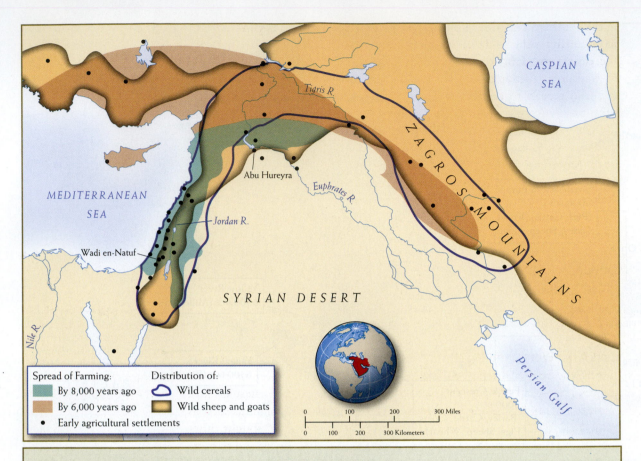

Map 1.5 The Birth of Farming in the Fertile Crescent

....

Agricultural production occurred in the Fertile Crescent starting roughly in 9000 BCE. Though the process was slow, farmers and herders domesticated a variety of plants and animals, which led to the rise of large-scale, permanent settlements.

- Trace the region where the wild cereals were domesticated as well as the density of agricultural settlements. How does the region you traced relate to the reason this area is called the "Fertile Crescent"?
- What topographical features appear to influence the location of agricultural settlements and farming?
- What relationship existed between cereal cultivators and herders of goats and sheep?

of ideas, which spread through migration and contact with other regions. In all of these populations, the shift to settled agriculture was revolutionary.

Southwest Asia: Cereals and Mammals The first agricultural revolution occurred in Southwest Asia in an area bounded by the Mediterranean Sea and the Zagros Mountains, a region known today as the Fertile Crescent because of its rich soils and regular rainfall. (See Map 1.5.) Around 9000 BCE, in the southern corridor of the Jordan River valley, humans began to domesticate the wild ancestors of barley and wheat, which were the easiest to adapt to settled agriculture and the easiest to transport. Although the changeover from gathering wild cereals to regular cultivation took several centuries and saw failures as well as successes, by 8000 BCE cultivators were selecting and storing seeds and then sowing them in prepared seedbeds. Moreover, in the valleys of the Zagros Mountains on the eastern side of the Fertile Crescent, similar experimentation was occurring with animals around the same time. Of the six large mammals—goats, sheep, pigs, cattle, camels, and horses—that have been vital for meat, milk, skins, and transportation, humans in Southwest Asia domesticated all except horses. With the presence of so many valuable plants and animals, Southwest Asia led the agricultural revolution and gave rise to many of the world's first major city-states (see Chapter 2).

East Asia: Water And Rice A revolution in food production also occurred among the coastal dwellers in East Asia, although under different circumstances. (See Map 1.6.) As the rising sea level created the Japanese islands, hunters in that area tracked a diminishing supply of large animals, such as giant deer. When big game became extinct, men and women sought other ways to support themselves, and before long they settled down and became cultivators of the soil. In this postglacial period, divergent human cultures flourished in northern and southern Japan. Hunters in the south created primitive pebble and flake tools, whereas those in the north used sharper blades about a third of an inch wide. Production of earthenware pottery—a breakthrough that enabled people to store food more easily—also may have begun in this period in the south. Throughout the rest of East Asia, the spread of lakes, marshes, and rivers created habitats for population concentrations and agricultural cultivation. Two newly formed river basins, along the Yellow River in northern China and the Yangzi River in central China, became densely populated areas that were focal points for intensive agricultural development.

What barley and wheat were for Southwest Asia, rice along the Yangzi River and millet along the Yellow River were for East Asia—staples adapted to local environments that humans could domesticate to support a large, sedentary population. Archaeologists have found evidence of rice cultivation in the Yangzi River valley in 6500 BCE, and of millet cultivation in the Yellow River valley in 5500 BCE. Innovations in grain production, including the introduction of a faster-ripening rice from Southeast Asia, spread through

Large Two-handled Yangshao Pot In the village of Yangshao in Henan Province, remains were first found in 1921 of a people who lived more than 6,000 years ago. This pot comes from those people, who were named Yangshao after the modern village in which the evidence for their culture was first found. The ancient Yangshao lived in small, rammed-earth fortresses and, without the use of pottery wheels, created fine white, red, and black painted pottery with human faces and animal and geometric designs. This jar was found in Gansu Province and dates to around 2500 BCE.

Map 1.6 The Spread of Farming in East Asia

Agricultural settlements appeared in East Asia between 6500 and 5500 BCE, several thousand years later than they did in the Fertile Crescent.

- According to this map, where did early agricultural settlements appear in East Asia?
- What two main crops were domesticated in East Asia? Where did each crop type originate, and to what regions did each spread?
- How did the physical features of these regions shape agricultural production?

Core Area of Cultivation
- Rice
- Millet
- Initial farming settlement before 3000 BCE
- Spread of rice farming before 3000 BCE

MONGOLIAN STEPPE

GOBI DESERT

Amur R.

Yellow R.

KOREA

JAPAN

CHINA

Yangzi R.

Pearl R.

Irrawaddy R.

Mekong R.

TAIWAN

PACIFIC OCEAN

LUZON

MINDINAO

BORNEO

SUMATRA

CELEBES

NEW GUINEA

INDIAN OCEAN

JAVA

TIMOR

| 0 | 250 | 500 Miles |
| 0 | 250 | 500 Kilometers |

internal migration and wider contacts. Ox plows and water buffalo plow-shares were prerequisites for large-scale millet planting in the drier north and the rice-cultivated areas of the wetter south. By domesticating plants and animals, the East Asians, like the Southwest Asians, laid the foundations for more populous societies.

Africa: The Race with the Sahara The evidence of settled agriculture in the various regions of Africa is less clear. Most scholars think that the Sahel area (spanning the African landmass just south of the Sahara Desert) was most likely where hunters and gatherers became settled farmers and herders without borrowing from other regions. In this area, an apparent move to set-tled agriculture, including the domestication of large herd animals, occurred two millennia before it did along the Mediterranean coast in North Africa. From this innovative heartland, Africans carried their agricultural break-throughs across the landmass.

In the wetter and more temperate locations of the vast Sahel, particu-larly in mountainous areas and their foothills, villages and towns developed. These regions were lush with grassland vegetation and teeming with animals. Before long, the inhabitants had made sorghum, a cereal grass, their principal food crop. Residents constructed stone dwellings, underground wells, and grain storage areas. In one such population center, fourteen circular houses faced each other to form a main thoroughfare, or a street.

The Sahel was colder and moister in 8000 BCE than it is today. As the world became warmer and the Sahara Desert expanded, around 2000 BCE, this region's inhabitants had to disperse and take their agricultural and herd-ing skills into other parts of Africa. (See Map 1.7.) Some went south to the tropical rain forests of West Africa, while others trekked eastward into the Ethiopian highlands. In their new environments, farmers searched for new crops to domesticate. The rain forests of West Africa yielded root crops, particularly the yam and cocoyam, both of which became the principal life-sustaining foodstuffs. The ensete plant, similar to the banana, played the same role in the Ethiopian highlands. Thus, the beginnings of agriculture in Africa involved both innovation and diffusion, as Africans applied the tech-niques that first emerged in the Sahel to new plants and animals.

The Americas: A Slower Transition The shift to settled agriculture occurred more slowly in the Americas. When people crossed Beringia into the Americas around 16,000 years ago (14,000 BCE), the plants and animals were different enough that early settlers devised ways of living that distin-guished them from their ancestors in Afro-Eurasia. When the glaciers melted and water covered the land bridge between East Asia and America, the Americas and their peoples truly became a whole world apart. The traditional narrative has been that early humans in America, called "Clovis people" after

BLACK SEA

CASPIAN SEA

MEDITERRANEAN SEA

Tropic of Cancer

Nile R.

RED SEA

Senegal R.

TROPICAL RAINFORESTS

Niger R.

Lake Chad

S A H E L

A F R I C A

ETHIOPIAN HIGHLANDS

Lake Turkana

Equator

Congo R.

Lake Victoria

ATLANTIC OCEAN

INDIAN OCEAN

Lake Tanganyika

Lake Nyasa

Zambezi R.

Legend

- Sahara Desert, c. 6000 BCE
- Sahara Desert today
- Lakes in the Sahara, c. 6000 BCE
- ○ Early farming site
- ● Early herding site
- Movement of peoples to western tropical rainforests
- Movement of peoples to Ethiopian highlands
- Sahel region

Original Areas of Crop Domestication
- Sorghum
- Yam
- Teff, ensete, and other Ethiopian crops

Map 1.7 The Spread of Farming in Africa

Societies living in the Sahel (the region south of the Sahara Desert) developed their own version of agricultural production after 6000 BCE.

- Why is the Sahel so important in the movement of peoples and ideas about crops? Why did farming spread in the directions that it did?
- What do you note about the location of farming and herding sites?
- How did the expansion of the Sahara Desert affect the diffusion of agriculture in the Sahel?

an archaeological site near Clovis, New Mexico (dating to around 11,000 BCE), used chipped blades and pointed spears to pursue their prey. New excavations, however, are unearthing even earlier evidence for human occupation in the Americas, with "pre-Clovis" sites ranging from Pennsylvania and the southeastern United States to Brazil and Chile (See Map 1.2 for the complicated picture of human migration in the Americas.) Although scientists once thought that early hunting and gathering communities in the Americas had wiped out the large ice-age mammals in the Americas, recent research suggests that climatic change destroyed indigenous plants and trees—the feeding grounds of large prehistoric mammals. This left undernourished mastodons, woolly mammoths, bison, and other mammals vulnerable to human and animal predators. As in Afro-Eurasia, the arrival of a long warming cycle compelled those living in the Americas to adapt to different environments and to create new ways to support themselves. Thus, in the woodland area of the present-day northeastern United States, hunters learned to trap smaller wild animals for food and furs. To supplement the protein from meat and fish, these people also dug for roots and gathered berries. Even as most communities adapted to the settled agricultural economy, they did not abandon basic survival strategies of hunting and gathering.

Food-producing changes in the Americas were different from those in Afro-Eurasia because this area did not undergo the sudden cluster of innovations that revolutionized agriculture in Southwest Asia and elsewhere. Independent innovation occurred more slowly here. Tools ground from stone, rather than chipped implements, appeared in the Tehuacán Valley by 6700 BCE, and evidence of plant domestication there dates back to 5000 BCE. But villages, pottery making, and sustained population growth came later. For many early American inhabitants, the life of hunting, trapping, and fishing went on as it had for millennia. Indeed, researchers have found the remains of ancient shellfishing throughout the coastal Americas from Alaska to Chile on the Pacific Ocean side. On the coast of what is now Peru, people found food by fishing and gathering shellfish from the Pacific. Archaeological remains include the remnants of fishnets, bags, baskets, and textile implements; gourds for carrying water; and stone knives, choppers, scrapers, bone awls, and thorn needles. Some made breakthroughs in the management of fire that enabled them to manufacture pottery; others devised irrigation and water sluices in floodplains. And some even began to send their fish catches inland in return for agricultural produce.

The earliest evidence of plant experimentation in Mesoamerica dates from around 8000 BCE, and the peoples living there continued to domesticate new plants for a long time. Maize, squash, and beans (first found in what is now central Mexico) became dietary staples. The early settlers foraged small seeds of maize, peeled them from ears only a few inches long, and planted them. Maize offered real advantages because it was easy to store over long periods of time, nutritious, and easy to cultivate alongside other plants. Nonetheless, it took 5,000 years for farmers to complete its domestication. Over the years, farmers had to mix and breed different strains of maize for it to evolve from thin spikes of seeds to cobs rich with kernels, with a single plant yielding big, thick ears to feed a growing permanent population. Thus, the agricultural changes afoot in Mesoamerica were slow and late in maturing. The pace was even more gradual in South America, where early settlers clung to their hunting and gathering traditions.

Across the Americas, the settled, agrarian communities found that legumes (beans), grains (maize), and tubers (potatoes) complemented one another in keeping the soil fertile and offering a balanced diet. Unlike the Afro-Eurasians, however, the settlers did not use domesticated animals as an alternative source of protein. In only a few pockets of the Andean highlands is there evidence of the domestication of tiny guinea pigs. Nor did people in the Americas tame animals that could protect villages (as dogs did in Afro-Eurasia) or carry heavy loads over long distances (as cattle and horses did in Afro-Eurasia). Although llamas could haul heavy loads, they were uncooperative and only partially domesticated, and thus mainly useful only for their fur, which was used for clothing.

Nonetheless, the domestication of plants and animals in the Americas, as well as the presence of villages and clans, suggests significant diversification and refinement of agricultural techniques. At the same time, the centers of such activity were numerous, scattered, and more isolated than those in Afro-Eurasia—and thus more narrowly adapted to local geographical climatic conditions, with little exchange among them. This fragmentation was a distinguishing force in the gradual pace of change in the Americas, and it contributed to their taking a path of development separate from Afro-Eurasia's.

BORROWING AGRICULTURAL IDEAS: EUROPE

In some places, agricultural revolution occurred through the borrowing of ideas from neighboring regions, rather than through innovation. Peoples living at the western fringe of Afro-Eurasia, in Europe, learned the techniques of settled agriculture through contact with other regions. By 7000 BCE, people in parts of Europe close to the societies of Southwest Asia, such as Greece and the Balkans, were abandoning their hunting and gathering way of life for an agricultural one. The Franchthi Cave in Greece, for instance, reveals that around 6000 BCE the inhabitants learned how to domesticate animals and plant wheat and barley, having borrowed that innovation from their neighbors in Southwest Asia.

The emergence of agriculture and village life occurred in Europe along two separate paths of borrowing. (See Map 1.8.) The first and most rapid

Map 1.8 **The Spread of Agriculture in Europe**

The spread of agricultural production into Europe after 7000 BCE represents geographic diffusion. Europeans borrowed agricultural techniques and technology from other groups, adapting those innovations to their own situations.

- Trace the two pathways by which agriculture spread across Europe. What shaped the routes by which agriculture diffused?

- How might scholars know that there were two routes of diffusion, and why would the existence of different diffusion routes matter?

- Identify the locations of the early farming communities. What geographical features seem to have influenced where these farming communities sprang up?

trajectory followed the northern rim of the Mediterranean Sea: from what is now Turkey through the islands of the Aegean Sea to mainland Greece, and from there to southern and central Italy and Sicily. Whether the process involved the actual migration of individuals or, rather, the spread of ideas, connections by sea quickened the pace of the transition. Within a relatively short period of time, hunting and gathering gave way to domesticated agriculture and herding.

The second trajectory of borrowing took an overland route: from Anatolia, across northern Greece into the Balkans, then northwestward along the Danube River into the Hungarian plain, and from there farther north and west into the Rhine River valley in modern-day Germany. This route of agricultural development was slower than the Mediterranean route for two reasons. First, domesticated crops, or individuals who knew about them, had to travel by land, as there were few large rivers like the Danube. Second, it was necessary to find new groups of domesticated plants and animals that could flourish in the colder and more forested lands of central Europe, which meant planting crops in the spring and harvesting them in the autumn, rather than the other way around. Cattle rather than sheep became the dominant herd animals.

In Europe, the main cereal crops were wheat and barley (additional plants such as olives came later), and the main herd animals were sheep, goats, and cattle—all of which had been domesticated in Southwest Asia. Hunting, gathering, and fishing still supplemented the new settled agriculture and the herding of domesticated animals.

Thus, across Afro-Eurasia and the Americas, humans changed and were changed by their environments. While herding and gathering remained firmly entrenched as a way of life, certain areas with favorable climates and plants and animals that could be domesticated began to establish settled agricultural communities, which were able to support larger populations than hunting and gathering could sustain.

REVOLUTIONS IN SOCIAL ORGANIZATION

Core Objectives

ANALYZE the significance the shift to settled agriculture had for social organization across global regions.

In addition to creating agricultural villages, the domestication of plants and animals brought changes in social organization, notably changes in gender relationships.

Life in Villages In the many regions across the globe where domestication of plants and animals took hold, agricultural villages were established near fields for accessible sowing and cultivating, and near pastures for herding livestock. Villagers collaborated to clear fields, plant crops, and celebrate rituals in which they sang, danced, and sacrificed to nature and the spirit world for fertility, rain, and successful harvests. They also produced stone tools to work the fields, and clay and stone pots or woven baskets to collect and store the crops. The earliest dwelling places of the first settled communities were simple structures: circular pits with stones piled on top to form walls, with a cover stretched above that rested on poles. Social structures were equally simple, being clan-like and based on kinship networks. With time, however, population growth enabled clans to expand. As the use of natural resources intensified, specialized tasks evolved and divisions of labor arose. Some community members procured and prepared food; others built terraces and defended the settlement. Later, residents built walls with stones or mud bricks and clamped them together with wooden fittings. Some villagers became craftworkers, devoting their time to producing pottery, baskets, textiles, or tools, which they could trade to farmers and pastoralists for food. Craft specialization and the buildup of surpluses contributed to social stratification (the emergence of distinct and hierarchically arranged social classes), as some people accumulated more land and wealth while others led the rituals and sacrifices.

Çatal Hüyük This artist's drawing depicts the settlement at Çatal Hüyük, which offers evidence of a Neolithic community's shift, over a 2,000-year span of time, to settled agriculture and more densely packed living. The one-room houses were entered from the roof (via ladders into the living areas) and included space for daily chores (like food preparation), storage, sleeping, and even the burial of the dead under the floor of the living area.

Archaeological sites in Southwest Asia have provided evidence of what life was like in some of the earliest villages. At Wadi en-Natuf, for example, located about 10 miles from present-day Jerusalem, a group of people known historically as Natufians began to dig sunken pit shelters and to chip stone tools around 12,500 BCE. In the highlands of eastern Anatolia, large settlements clustered around monumental public buildings with impressive stone carvings that reflect a complex social organization. In central Anatolia around 7500 BCE, at the site of Çatal Hüyük, a dense honeycomb settlement featured rooms with artwork of a high quality. The walls were covered with paintings, and sculptures of wild bulls, hunters, and pregnant women enlivened many rooms.

As people moved into the river valley in Mesopotamia (in present-day Iraq) along the Tigris and Euphrates Rivers, small villages began to appear after 5500 BCE. They collaborated to build simple irrigation systems to water their fields. Perhaps because of the increased demands for community work to maintain the irrigation systems, the communities in southern Mesopotamia became stratified, with some people having more power than others. We can see from the burial sites and myriad public buildings uncovered by archaeologists that, for the first time, some people had higher status derived from birth rather than through the merits of their work. A class of people who had access to more luxury goods, and who lived in bigger and better houses, now became part of the social organization.

Men, Women, and Evolving Gender Relations Gender roles became more pronounced during the gradual transition to agriculturally based ways of life. For millions of years, biological differences—the fact that females give birth to offspring and lactate to nourish them and that males do not—determined female and male behaviors and attitudes toward each other. One can speak of the emergence of "gender" relations and roles (as opposed to biological differences) only with the appearance of modern humans (*Homo sapiens*). Only when humans began to think in complex symbolic ways and give voice to these perceptions in a spoken language did true gender categories as *man* and *woman* crystallize. At that point, culture joined biology in governing human interactions.

As human communities became larger, more hierarchical, and more powerful, the rough gender egalitarianism of hunting and gathering societies eroded. Because women had been the primary gatherers, their knowledge of wild plants had contributed to early settled agriculture, but they did not necessarily benefit from that transition. Advances in agrarian tools introduced a harsh working life that undermined women's earlier status as farmers. Men, no longer so involved in hunting and gathering, now took on the heavy work of yoking animals to plows. Women took on the backbreaking and repetitive tasks of planting, weeding, harvesting, and grinding the grain into flour. Thus, although agricultural innovations increased productivity, they also increased the drudgery of work, especially for women. Fossil evidence from Abu Hureyra, Syria, reveals damage to the vertebrae, osteoarthritis in the toes, and curved and arched femurs, all suggesting that the work of bending over and kneeling in the fields took its toll on female agriculturalists. The increasing differentiation of the roles of men and women also affected power relations within households and communities. The senior male figure became dominant in these households, and males became dominant over females in leadership positions.

The agricultural revolution marked a greater division among men, as well as between men and women. Where the agricultural transformation was most widespread, and where population densities began to grow, the social and political differences created inequalities. As these inequalities affected gender relations, patriarchy (the rule of senior males within households) began to spread around the globe.

Conclusion

Over thousands of generations, African hominids evolved from other primates into bipedal, toolmaking, fire-using *Homo erectus*, who migrated far from their native habitats to fill other landmasses. They did so in waves, often in response to worldwide cycles of climatic change. *Homo sapiens*, with bigger brains and consequently greater cognition, emerged in Africa about 300,000 years ago and migrated out of Africa beginning 180,000 years ago. With greater adaptive skills, they were better prepared to face the elements when a cooling cycle returned, and eventually they became the only surviving branch of the tree of human ancestors. *Homo sapiens* used language and art to engage in abstract, representational thought and to convey the lessons of experience to their neighbors and descendants. As modern humans stored and shared knowledge, their adaptive abilities increased.

Although modern men and women shared an African heritage, these individuals adapted over many millennia to the environments they encountered as they began to fill the earth's corners and practice hunting and gathering ways of life. Some settled near lakes and took to fishing, while others roamed the northern steppes hunting large mammals. No matter where they went, their dependence on nature yielded broadly similar social and cultural structures. It took another warming cycle for people ranging from Africa to the Americas to begin putting down their hunting weapons and start domesticating animals and plants.

The changeover to settled agriculture was not uniform worldwide. As communities became more settled, the world's regions began to vary as humans learned to modify nature to fit their needs. The varieties of animals that they could domesticate and the differing climatic conditions and topography that they encountered shaped the ways in which people drifted apart in spite of their common origins. What these settled communities shared, however, was increasing social hierarchy, including the unequal status of men and women.

Focus On
What Makes Us Human

- **Bipedalism:** Hominids come down from the trees in Africa, become upright, and walk on two legs.
- **Big brains:** Ancestors to modern humans make tools and fire and acquire larger brains.

- **Cognitive skills:** Homo sapiens develop the capacity for language and learn to communicate with one another, develop a sense of self, and produce art.
- **Village life:** People domesticate plants and animals and begin to live in more socially complex communities.

Key Terms

australopithecines p. 7	hominids p. 6	*Homo sapiens* p. 18	pastoralism p. 27
creation narratives p. 5	*Homo erectus* p. 15	hunting and	settled agriculture
domestication p. 27	*Homo habilis* p. 15	gathering p. 23	p. 27
evolution p. 7			

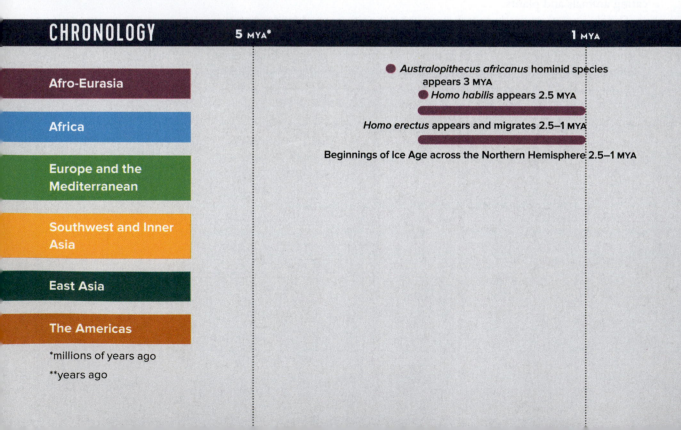

CHRONOLOGY   5 MYA*   1 MYA

Afro-Eurasia

Africa

Europe and the Mediterranean

Southwest and Inner Asia

East Asia

The Americas

- *Australopithecus africanus* hominid species appears 3 MYA
- *Homo habilis* appears 2.5 MYA

Homo erectus appears and migrates 2.5–1 MYA

Beginnings of Ice Age across the Northern Hemisphere 2.5–1 MYA

*millions of years ago
**years ago

- **Thinking about Exchange Networks and Human Evolution** Across several million years, the hominid ancestors of humans, especially *Homo erectus*, and then *Homo sapiens*, migrated out of Africa. What role did evolution play in making it possible for our hominid ancestors and then *Homo sapiens* to migrate across the globe?

- **Thinking about the Environment and Human Evolution** Climate change and environmental conditions have played a recurring role in the narrative recounted in this chapter. In what specific ways did the climate change, and in what specific ways did the environment help shape the evolution of humans and influence the shift from hunting and gathering to settled agriculture?

- **Thinking about Changing Gender Relationships and the Agricultural Revolution** Some scholars have argued that the hunting and gathering ways of life for both *Homo erectus* and *Homo sapiens* allowed women—biologically, through their lactation and child-rearing, and calorically, through their dominant role as gatherers—to make a larger and more significant contribution to their communities than their male counterparts did. In what ways might the development of settled agriculture have ushered in a shift in these gender roles?

Go to **INQUIZITIVE** to see what you've learned—and learn what you've missed—with personalized feedback along the way.

| 200,000 YA** | 150,000 YA | 100,000 YA | 50,000 YA | 10,000 YA | 1 CE |

Human migration from Afro-Eurasia begins 16,000 YA

Ice Age ends 16,000–10,000 BCE

Homo sapiens emerges in Africa 300,000 YA

Homo sapiens migrates out of Africa 180,000–50,000 YA

Cave art develops in Europe 30,000 YA

Beginnings of agricultural revolution in Southwest Asia 9000 BCE

Agricultural settlements emerge in Southwest Asia 6000–5000 BCE

Pastoralism begins in Inner Asia 3000 BCE

Millet cultivation in Yellow River valley develops 6500 BCE

Rice cultivation in Yangzi River valley develops 5500 BCE

Maize cultivation emerges in central Mexico 8000 BCE

Global Themes and Sources

Contextualizing Creation Narratives

Every story told needs a beginning. Where and how the story begins reveals a great deal about who is telling it and the context from which the storyteller comes. Finding a beginning for the narrative of world history is no different. Humans at many times and in many places have attempted to create all-encompassing narratives that explain their place in the world. And, to give those stories a beginning, communities have attempted to explain where they came from in the first place by constructing creation narratives. Creation narratives draw on a particular community's knowledge and beliefs to offer an account of human, and even universal, origins. These narratives reveal a great deal about the historical context from which they come by revealing the context into which they place humans and what makes up the natural world around them. Are humans the first or last thing to come into being? What else is created with them? By what means? What is humanity's relationship to the rest of creation? Analyzing these types of issues within texts that describe creation offers an opportunity to muse on the historical contexts that produced them and the many ways that people through time have attempted to start the story of world history.

The five documents here represent a range of varied creation narratives from many different regions of the world: the sacrifice of Purusha from the Vedic narratives of South Asia (now India); the creation of the universe and all therein from Judeo-Christian sacred text originating in Southwest Asia (the Levant); the creation of the universe in a text from East Asia (China); the creation of humanity by the gods in a text from Mesoamerica (modern Latin America); and the creation of land, palm trees, and humans from a Yoruba narrative (West Africa). Because many communities have credited divine action with their creation, an examination of the context for stories of "beginnings" often has us looking at religious texts. While some of these religious texts no longer have large worship communities that promote them,

many of these narratives—like the account of creation in Genesis or the sacrifice of Purusha in the Rig-Veda—are still important to communities of faith today. When historians examine creation narratives, the goal is not to decide which is "true" or to judge the rationality of the communities that produced or preserved them; rather, the goal is to analyze the narratives to understand what values and beliefs are encoded in these stories of beginnings and to get a sense of the historical context from which they came. In the chapters that follow, you will learn a great deal about the peoples of South Asia, Southwest Asia, East Asia, Mesoamerica, and Africa. The creation narratives excerpted here offer a chance to begin to explore these historical contexts and to think about how the context from which these narratives came shaped communities' understanding of where humans fit.

Analyzing the Context of Creation Narratives

- Compare the stories of creation. What is created, and in what order, in each of these narratives? Who is doing the creating? Out of what? How long does it take? What seem to be the creator's (or creators') motives—if any—for creation?

- What do you think accounts for the differences and similarities in these creation narratives?

- How does each of these narratives reflect the unique context from which the narrative comes? In other words, what does each narrative tell us about what matters to the community that produced and transmitted the narrative?

- Compare these historical creation narratives with the narrative of human origins outlined in this chapter. What does the modern creation narrative of evolution have in common with these creation narratives? How is it different? What do these similarities and differences tell us about what our own modern context values?

"The Sacrifice of Purusha" from the Rig-Veda (1500 BCE)

The Rig-Veda dates to around 1500 BCE, when Vedic peoples migrated into South Asia. These Vedic people sang hymns while making sacrifices to their gods, and the hymns were later collected in the Rig-Veda—the earliest Hindu sacred text. The portion of the hymn excerpted here describes the creation of the universe by the gods' sacrifice of a creature, Purusha, to create the various levels of society.

- How does the text describe Purusha? To what extent can you visualize this being?

- What exactly is produced through the sacrifice of Purusha by the gods?

- How might the product of the sacrifice of Purusha offer a mirror of the Vedic community that produced the text?

Thousand-headed Purusha, thousand eyed, thousand-footed—he, having pervaded the earth on all sides, extends ten fingers beyond it.

Purusha alone is all this—whatever has been and whatever is going to be. Further, he is the lord of immortality and also of what grows on account of food.

Such is his greatness; greater, indeed than this is Purusha. All creatures constitute but one-quarter of him, his three-quarters are the immortal in the heaven.

With his three-quarters did Purusha rise up; one-quarter of him again remains here. With it did he variously spread out on all sides over what eats and what eats not.

From him was Virāj born, from Virāj the evolved Purusha. He, being born, projected himself behind the earth as also before it. When the gods performed the sacrifice with Purusha as the oblation, then the spring was its clarified butter, the summer the sacrificial fuel, and the autumn the oblation.

The sacrificial victim, namely, Purusha born at the very beginning, they sprinkled with sacred water upon the sacrificial grass. With him as oblation, the gods performed the sacrifice, and also the Sādhyas [a class of semidivine beings] and the rishis [ancient seers].

From that wholly offered sacrificial oblation were born the verses and the sacred chants; from it were born the meters [*chandas*]; the sacrificial formula was born from it.

From it horses were born and also those animals who have double rows [i.e., upper and lower] of teeth; cows were born from it, from it were born goats and sheep.

When they divided Purusha, in how many different portions did they arrange him? What became of his mouth, what of his two arms? What were his two thighs and his two feet called?

His mouth became the brāhman; his two arms were made into the rājanya; his two thighs the vaishyas; from his two feet the shūdra was born.

The moon was born from the mind, from the eye the sun was born; from the mouth Indra and Agni, from the breath [*prāna*] the wind [*vāyu*] was born.

From the navel was the atmosphere created, from the head the heaven issued forth; from two feet was born the earth and the quarters (the cardinal directions) from the ear. Thus did they fashion the worlds.

Seven were the enclosing sticks in this sacrifice, thrice seven were the fire-sticks made when the gods, performing the sacrifice, bound down Purusha, the sacrificial victim.

With this sacrificial oblation did the gods offer the sacrifice. These were the first norms [*dharma*] of sacrifice. These greatnesses reached to the sky wherein live the ancient Sādhyas and gods.

Source: *Sources of Indian Tradition*, vol. 1, *From the Beginning to 1800*, 2nd ed., edited and revised by Ainslie T. Embree (New York: Columbia University Press, 1988), pp. 18–19.

Genesis 1:1–31 from the Bible

Genesis opens with an account of a singular God bringing order from chaos over the course of six days. According to the "documentary hypothesis" advanced by biblical scholars, the text of Genesis was collated by Jewish redactors, a specialized, scholarly type of editor, long ago from a range of sources with different emphases (including different Jewish understandings about God and priestly concerns) and likely reached its final form after the sixth century BCE. Genesis, the first book of the Hebrew Bible, was adopted as a part of authoritative scripture by the early Christian community, as well.

....

- What is created in this text, and in what order?
- Who does the creating, and how exactly is creation achieved?
- What is the relationship between God and humans, and between humans and the rest of God's creation?

....

[1]In the beginning God created the heavens and the earth. [2]The earth was without form and void, and darkness was upon the face of the deep; and the Spirit of God was moving over the face of the waters. [3]And God said, "Let there be light"; and there was light. [4]And God saw that the light was good; and God separated the light from the darkness. [5]God called the light Day, and the darkness he called Night. And there was evening and there was morning, one day. [6]And God said, "Let there be a firmament in the midst of the waters, and let it separate the waters from the waters." [7]And God made the firmament and separated the waters which were under the firmament from the waters which were above the firmament. And it was so. [8]And God called the firmament Heaven. And there was evening and there was morning, a second day.

[9]And God said, "Let the waters under the heavens be gathered together into one place, and let the dry land appear." And it was so. [10]God called the dry land Earth, and the waters that were gathered together he called Seas. And God saw that it was good. [11]And God said, "Let the earth put forth vegetation, plants yielding seed, and fruit trees bearing fruit in which is their seed, each according to its kind, upon the earth." And it was so. [12]The earth brought forth vegetation, plants yielding seed according to their own kinds, and trees bearing fruit in which is their seed, each according to its kind. And God saw that it was good. [13]And there was evening and there was morning, a third day. [14]And God said, "Let there be lights in the firmament of the heavens to separate the day from the night; and let them be for signs and for seasons and for days and years, [15]and let them be lights in the firmament of the heavens to give light upon the earth." And it was so. [16]And God made the two great lights, the greater light to rule the day, and the lesser light to rule the night; he made the stars also.

[17]And God set them in the firmament of the heavens to give light upon the earth, [18]to rule over the day and over the night, and to separate the light from the darkness. And God saw that it was good. [19]And there was evening and there was morning, a fourth day.

[20]And God said, "Let the waters bring forth swarms of living creatures, and let birds fly above the earth across the firmament of the heavens." [21]So God created the great sea monsters and every living creature that moves, with which the waters swarm, according to their kinds; and every winged bird according to its kind. And God saw that it was good. [22]And God blessed them, saying, "Be fruitful and multiply and fill the waters in the seas, and let birds multiply on the earth." [23]And there was evening and there was morning, a fifth day.

[24]And God said, "Let the earth bring forth living creatures according to their kinds: cattle and creeping things and beasts of the earth according to their kinds." And it was so. [25]And God made the beasts of the earth according to their kinds and the cattle according to their kinds, and everything that creeps upon the ground according to its kind. And God saw that it was good.

[26]Then God said, "Let us make man in our image, after our likeness; and let them have dominion over the fish of the sea, and over the birds of the air, and over the cattle, and over all the earth, and over every creeping thing that creeps upon the earth." [27]So God created man in his own image, in the image of God he created him; male and female he created them. [28]And God blessed them, and God said to them, "Be fruitful and multiply, and fill the earth and subdue it; and have dominion over the fish of the sea and over the birds of the air and over every living thing that moves upon the earth." [29]And God said, "Behold, I have given you every plant yielding seed which is upon the face of all the earth, and every tree with seed in its fruit; you shall have them for food. [30]And to every beast of the earth, and to every bird of the air, and to everything that creeps on the earth, everything that has the breath of life, I have given every green plant for food." And it was so. [31]And God saw everything that he had made, and behold, it was very good. And there was evening and there was morning, a sixth day.

Source: *The New Oxford Annotated Bible: New Revised Standard Version with the Apocrypha*, 4th ed. (New York: Oxford University Press, 2010), pp. 11–13.

"The Creation of the Universe" from the *Huainanzi* (c. second century BCE)

The *Huainanzi*, from second-century BCE Han China, is a Confucian text that takes the form of dialogues between a prince and court scholars. It also reflects Daoist ideas, such as the role of the complementary forces of *yin* and *yang*. The *Huainanzi*'s creation story does not assign agency on the part of any god or gods and instead focuses on balance.

- **By what means does creation take place in this narrative?**
- **What is created?**
- **What seems to matter to the community that valued this creation narrative?**

Before Heaven and Earth had taken form all was vague and amorphous. Therefore it was called the Great Beginning. The Great Beginning produced emptiness, and emptiness produced the universe. The universe produced material-force, which had limits. That which was clear and light drifted up to become Heaven, while that which was heavy and turbid solidified to become Earth. It was very easy for the pure, fine material to come together but extremely difficult for the heavy, turbid material to solidify. Therefore Heaven was completed first and Earth assumed shape after. The combined essences of Heaven and Earth became the yin and yang; the concentrated essences of the yin and yang became the four seasons; and the scattered essences of the four seasons became the myriad creatures of the world. After a long time the hot Force of the accumulated yang produced fire, and the essence of the fire force became the sun; the cold force of the accumulated yin became water, and the essence of the water force became the moon. The essence of the excess force of the sun and moon became the stars, while Earth received water and soil. [3:1a]

When Heaven and Earth were joined in emptiness and all was unwrought simplicity, then, without having been created, things came into being. This was the Great Oneness. All things issued from this Oneness, but all became different, being divided into various species of fish, birds, and beasts. . . . Therefore while a thing moves it is called living, and when it dies it is said to be exhausted. All are creatures. They are not the uncreated creator of things, for the creator of things is not among things. If we examine the Great Beginning of antiquity we find that man was born out of nothing to assume form as something. Having form, he is governed by things. But he who can return to that from which he was born and become as though formless is called a "true man." The true man is one who has never become separated from the Great Oneness. [14:1a]

Source: *Sources of Chinese Tradition*, vol. 1, *From the Earliest Times to 1600*, 2nd ed., compiled by Wm. Theodore de Bary and Irene Bloom (New York: Columbia University Press, 1999), pp. 346–47.

Popul Vuh (date of origin unknown)

The Mayas of Mesoamerica believed that humans were created by an assembly of divine beings, a story preserved in this excerpt from the *Popul Vuh*. Although many indigenous texts that had been passed down orally for centuries among Mesoamerican peoples were destroyed by Catholic priests when the Spanish entered the region, the copy of the *Popul Vuh* that has been passed down to the present was transcribed and translated by a Dominican friar in the early eighteenth century.

- **Who creates humanity, and what is the process by which that creation takes place?**
- **From what substance are humans made? Why might that be significant in Mesoamerican creation?**
- **What is the relationship of humanity with the gods and with the rest of the world?**

Here, then, is the beginning of when it was decided to make man, and when what must enter into the flesh of man was sought.

And the Forefathers, the Creators and Makers, who were called Tepeu and Gucumatz said: "The time of dawn has come, let the work be finished, and let those who are to nourish and sustain us appear, the noble sons, the civilized vassals: let man appear, humanity, on the face of the earth." Thus they spoke.

They assembled, came together and held council in the darkness and in the night; then they sought and discussed, and here they reflected and thought. In this way their decisions came clearly to light and they found and discovered what must enter into the flesh of man.

It was just before the sun, the moon, and the stars appeared over the Creators and Makers.

From Paxil, from Cayalá, as they were called, came the yellow ears of corn and the white ears of corn. These are the names of the animals which brought the food: *yac* [the mountain cat], *utiú* [the coyote], *quel* [a small parrot], and *hob* [the crow]. These four animals gave tidings of the yellow ears of corn and the white ears of corn, they told them that they should go to Paxil and they showed them the road to Paxil.

And thus they found the food, and this was what went into the flesh of created man, the made man; this was his blood; of this the blood of man was made. So the corn entered [into the formation of man] by the work of the Forefathers.

***

The animals showed them the road. And then grinding the yellow corn and the white corn, Xmucané made nine drinks, and from this food came the strength and the flesh, and with it they created the muscles and the strength of man. This the Forefathers did, Tepeu and Gucumatz, as they were called.

After that they began to talk about the creation and the making of our first mother and father; of yellow corn and of white corn they made their flesh; of corn meal dough they made the arms and the legs of man. Only dough of corn meal went into the flesh of our first fathers, the four men, who were created.

***

These are the names of the first men who were created and formed: the first man was Balam-Quitzé, the second, Balam-Acab, the third, Mahucutah, and the fourth was Iqui-Balam.

These are the names of our first mothers and fathers.

It is said that they only were made and formed, they had no mother, they had no father. They were only called men. They were not born of woman, nor were they begotten by the Creator nor by the Maker, nor by the Forefathers. Only by a miracle, by means of incantation were they created and made by the Creator, the Maker, the Forefathers, Tepeu and Gucumatz. And as they had the appearance of men, they were men; they talked, conversed, saw and heard, walked, grasped things; they were good and handsome men, and their figure was the figure of a man.

They were endowed with intelligence; they saw and instantly they could see far, they succeeded in seeing, they succeeded in knowing all that there is in the world. When they looked, instantly they saw all around them, and they contemplated in turn the arch of heaven and the round face of the earth.

The things hidden [in the distance] they saw all, without first having to move; at once they saw the world, and so, too, from where they were, they saw it.

Great was their wisdom; their sight reached to the forests, the rocks, the lakes, the seas, the mountains, and the valleys. In truth, they were admirable men, Balam-Quitzé, Balam-Acab, Mahucutah, and Iqui-Balam.

Then the Creator and the Maker asked them: "What do you think of your condition? Do you not see? Do you not hear? Are not your speech and manner of walking good? Look, then! Contemplate the world, look [and see] if the mountains and the valleys appear! Try, then, to see!" they said to [the four first men].

And immediately they [the four first men] began to see all that was in the world. Then they gave thanks to the Creator and the Maker: "We really give you thanks, two and three times! We have been created, we have been given a mouth and a face, we speak, we hear, we think, and walk; we feel perfectly, and we know what is far and what is near. We also see the large and the small in the sky and on earth. We give you thanks, then, for having created us, oh, Creator and Maker! for having given us being, oh, our grandmother! oh, our grandfather!" they said, giving thanks for their creation and formation.

Source: *Popol Vuh: The Sacred Book of the Ancient Quiché Maya*, translated into English by Delia Goetz and Sylvanus G. Morley from Spanish translation by Adrián Recinos (Norman: University of Oklahoma Press, 1950), pp. 165–68.

Yoruba Creation Narrative (date of origin unknown)

The Yoruba peoples of West Africa (modern-day Nigeria and Benin) preserve in songs and oral traditions their own creation narrative featuring a range of deities. The portion of the narrative excerpted here recounts how the god Obatala created and populated the land with palm trees and humans.

- How is the world created? Humanity?
- What reason does the story give for the creation of humanity?
- How do the various deities interact with one another? How would you describe the relationship between humans and the gods?

In the beginning was only the sky above, water and marshland below.

The chief god Olorun ruled the sky, and the goddess Olokun ruled what was below.

Obatala, another god, reflected upon this situation, then went to Olorun for permission to create dry land for all kinds of living creatures to inhabit. He was given permission, so he sought advice from Orunmila, oldest son of Olorun and the god of prophecy.

He was told he would need a gold chain long enough to reach below, a snail's shell filled with sand, a white hen, a black cat, and a palm nut, all of which he was to carry in a bag. All the gods contributed what gold they had, and Orunmila supplied the articles for the bag. When all was ready, Obatala hung the chain from a corner of the sky, placed the bag over his shoulder, and started the downward climb. When he reached the end of the chain he saw he still had some distance to go.

From above he heard Orunmila instruct him to pour the sand from the snail's shell, and to immediately release the white hen.

He did as he was told, whereupon the hen landing on the sand began scratching and scattering it about.

Wherever the sand landed it formed dry land, the bigger piles becoming hills and the smaller piles valleys. Obatala jumped to a hill and named the place Ife. The dry land now extended as far as he could see.

He dug a hole, planted the palm nut, and saw it grow to maturity in a flash. The mature palm tree dropped more palm nuts on the ground, each of which grew immediately to maturity and repeated the process. Obatala settled down with the cat for company.

Many months passed, and he grew bored with his routine.

He decided to create beings like himself to keep him company. He dug into the sand and soon found clay with which to mold figures like himself and started on his task, but he soon grew tired and decided to take a break.

He made wine from a nearby palm tree, and drank bowl after bowl. Not realizing he was drunk, Obatala returned to his task of fashioning the new beings; because of his condition he fashioned many imperfect figures.

Without realizing this, he called out to Olorun to breathe life into his creatures.

The next day he realized what he had done and swore never to drink again, and to take care of those who were deformed, thus becoming Protector of the Deformed.

The new people built huts as Obatala had done and soon Ife prospered and became a city.

When Obatala returned to his home in the sky for a visit, Olokun summoned the great waves of her vast oceans and sent them surging across the land. Wave after wave she unleashed, until much of the land was underwater and many of the people were drowned. Those that had fled to the highest land beseeched the god Eshu who had been visiting, to return to the sky and report what was happening to them. Eshu demanded sacrifice be made to Obatala and himself before he would deliver the message.

The people sacrificed some goats, and Eshu returned to the sky.

When Orunmila heard the news he climbed down the golden chain to the earth, and cast many spells which caused the flood waters to retreat and the dry land reappear.

So ended the great flood.

Source: "Yoruba Creation Narrative," translated by P. J. Criss, in Polat Kaya, "'Ak Tengiz': The Disappeared Ice Age Sea-Size Lake of Siberia," *Turk Dunyasi Arastirmalari*, no. 121 (August 1999): 38–39.

Interpreting Visual Evidence

Prehistoric Art

Prehistoric art provides some of the best direct evidence for the thoughts and experiences of humans who lived prior to the invention of writing (which, as we'll see in Chapter 2, has only been around for 5,000 years). Paintings showing the outlines of hands, images of animals, and even hunting scenes adorn the walls of caves across Afro-Eurasia, put there by humans over tens of thousands of years.

The artwork in Chauvet Cave in southwestern France may be the oldest in Europe, dating to about 35,000 years ago. In the first two images below, horses and lions from Chauvet Cave convey both perspective and movement. The overlapping of horses suggests a powerfully galloping herd, and the bison image uses a doubling effect—drawing additional hindquarters and legs—to give the bison the appearance of motion and speed. In central India, cave paintings at Bhimbetka date to as long as 30,000

years ago; the painting reproduced here includes several herds of different types of animals. Other images from this site painted over thousands of years include humans dancing and even having sex. Cave paintings from other areas like Lascaux in southeastern France (20,000 years old), Altamira in Spain (17,000 years old), and Tassili-n-Ajjer in North Africa (8,000 years old) provide similar insights into the artists' lives.

In addition to making paintings, early humans carved figurines. Small female figurines, often with emphasized breasts and genitalia, have been found at Willendorf in Austria, Dolni Vestonice in the Czech Republic, Cernavoda in Romania, and Malta in Siberian Russia. These figurines, carved from limestone, mammoth tusk, and reindeer horn, also range from about 35,000 to 8,000 years old. The figurine known as the Venus of Hohle Fels, found in Germany, dates to more than 35,000 years ago. This 2.4-inch carving

Horses, rhinos, and aurochs from Chauvet Cave

Lions from Chauvet Cave

may have been worn as an amulet. The 6-inch Venus of Willendorf from more than 25,000 years ago wears only a headdress (or braided hairstyle) and rests her arms across her breasts. The apparent continuity in both the cave art and figurines across thousands of years is striking.

Venus of Hohle Fels

Willendorf Venus

Questions for Analysis

1. Based on these cave paintings and figurines, what types of subjects did humans in the prehistoric period depict in their art? Why do you think they chose those subjects?

2. Compare these paintings and figurines. Given that there was not likely any interaction between the communities that produced them, what do you think might account for the similarities and differences?

3. Imagine an artist in a dark cave, painting with plant-made pigments by the light of a flickering torch; or a man or woman spending a hundred hours to carve a figurine from limestone. What might spur the creation of such artworks? How does this art change your understanding of the hunter-gatherer lifestyle?

Cave painting at Bhimbetka

2

Rivers, Cities, and First States

3500–2000 BCE

One of the first urban centers in the world was the ancient city of Uruk. Located in southern Mesopotamia on a branch of the Euphrates River, it was home to more than 10,000 people by the late fourth millennium BCE and boasted many large public structures and temples. One temple had stood there since before 3000 BCE; with plastered mud-brick walls that formed stepped indentations, it perched high above the plain. In another area, administrative buildings and temples adorned with elaborate façades stood in courtyards defined by tall columns. Colored stone cones arranged in elaborate geometric patterns covered parts of these buildings. An epic poem devoted to its later king, Gilgamesh, described Uruk as the "shining city."

Over the years, Uruk became an immense commercial and administrative center. A huge wall with seven massive gates surrounded the metropolis, and down the middle ran a canal carrying water from the Euphrates. On one side of the city were gardens, kilns, and textile workshops. On the other was the temple quarter where priests lived, scribes kept records, and *lu-gal* ("the big man") conferred with the elders. As Uruk grew, many small industries—including pottery crafting, metalworking, stone bowl making, and brickmaking—became centralized in response to the increasing sophistication of construction and manufacturing.

Uruk was the first city of its kind in world history. Earlier humans had settled in small communities

Core Objectives

- **IDENTIFY** the earliest river-basin societies, and **ANALYZE** their shared and distinctive characteristics.
- **EXPLAIN** the religious, social, and political developments that accompany early urbanization from 3500 to 2000 BCE.
- **TRACE** and **EVALUATE** the influence of long-distance connections across Afro-Eurasia during this period.
- **COMPARE** early urbanization with the ways of life in small villages and among pastoral nomads.

scattered over the landscape. As some communities gradually became focal points for trade, a few of these hubs grew into cities with large populations and institutions of economic, religious, and political power. Most inhabitants no longer produced their own food, working instead in specialized professions.

Between 3500 and 2000 BCE, a handful of remarkable societies clustered in a few river basins on the Afro-Eurasian landmass. These regions—in Mesopotamia (between the Tigris and Euphrates Rivers), in northwest India (on the Indus River), in Egypt (along the Nile), and in China (near the Yangzi and Yellow Rivers)—became the heartlands for densely populated settlements with complex cultures. Here the world saw the birth of the first large cities and territorial states. One of these settings (Mesopotamia) brought forth humankind's first writing system, and all laid the foundations for kingdoms radiating out of opulent cities. This chapter describes how each society evolved, and it explores their similarities and differences. It is important to note how exceptional these large cities and territorial states were, and we will see that many smaller societies prevailed elsewhere. The Aegean, Anatolia, western Europe, the Americas, and sub-Saharan Africa offer reminders that most of the world's people dwelt in small communities, far removed culturally from the monumental architecture and accomplishments of the big new states.

Global Storylines

- Complex societies form around five great river basins.
- Early urbanization brings changes, including new technologies, monumental building, new religions, writing, hierarchical social structures, and specialized labor.
- Long-distance trade connects many of the Afro-Eurasian societies.
- Despite impressive developments in urbanization, most people live in villages or in pastoral nomadic communities.

Settlement and Pastoralism

Around 3500 BCE, cultural changes, population growth, and technological innovations gave rise to complex societies. Clustered in cities, these larger communities developed new institutions, and individuals took on a wide range of social roles and occupations, resulting in new hierarchies based on wealth and gender. At the same time, the number of small villages and pastoral nomadic communities grew.

Water was the key to settlement, since predictable flows of water determined where humans settled. Reliable water supplies allowed communities to sow crops adequate to feed large populations. Abundant rainfall allowed the world's first villages to emerge, but the breakthroughs into big cities occurred in drier zones where large rivers formed beds of rich soils deposited by flooding rivers. With irrigation innovations, soils became arable. Equally important, a worldwide warming cycle expanded growing seasons. The **river basins**—with their fertile soil, irrigation, and available domesticated plants and animals—made possible the agricultural surpluses needed to support city dwellers.

EARLY CITIES ALONG RIVER BASINS

The material and social advances of the early cities occurred in a remarkably short period—from 3500 to 2000 BCE—in three locations: the basin of the Tigris and Euphrates Rivers in central Southwest Asia; the northern parts of the Nile River flowing toward the Mediterranean Sea; and the Indus River basin in northwestern South Asia. About a millennium later, a similar process began along the Yellow River and the Yangzi River in China. (See Map 2.1.) In these regions humans farmed and fed themselves by relying on intensive irrigation agriculture. Gathering in cities inhabited by rulers, administrators, priests, and craftworkers, they changed their methods of organizing communities by worshipping new gods in new ways and by obeying divinely inspired monarchs and elaborate bureaucracies. New technologies appeared, ranging from the wheel for pottery production to metalworking and stoneworking for the creation of both luxury objects and utilitarian tools. The technology of writing used the storage of words and meanings to extend human communication and memory.

With cities and new technologies came greater divisions of labor. Dense urban settlement enabled people to specialize in making goods for the consumption of others: weavers made textiles, potters made ceramics, and jewelers made precious ornaments. Soon these goods were traded with outlying areas. As trade expanded over longer distances, raw materials such as wool, metal, timber, and precious stones arrived in the cities and could be fashioned into new, manufactured goods. (See Map 2.2.) One of the most

THE BIG PICTURE

Identify the earliest river-basin societies. What are their shared characteristics?

river basin
Area drained by a river, including all its tributaries. River basins were rich in fertile soil, water for irrigation, and plant and animal life, which made them attractive for human habitation. Cultivators were able to produce surplus agriculture to support the first cities.

The Global View

NORTH AMERICA

Mississippi R.

Colorado R.

Rio Grande

ATLANTIC OCEAN

TEHUACÁN VALLEY

SAHARA

SAHEL

Niger R.

PACIFIC OCEAN

Amazon R.

CHICAMA VALLEY

ANDES MOUNTAINS

SOUTH AMERICA

Desert

Pastoral belt – steppe lands

Tropical rain forest

Agricultural society 3000 BCE

River-basin societies (early cities)

Widespread village culture

0   1000   2000 Miles

0   1000   2000 Kilometers

Map 2.1 The World in the Third Millennium BCE

Human societies became increasingly diversified as agricultural, urban, and pastoral nomadic communities expanded. While urban communities began to develop in several major river basins in the Eastern Hemisphere, not every river basin produced cities in the third millennium BCE. Pastoralism, village life, agricultural communities, and continued hunting and gathering were by far the norm for most of the peoples of the earth.

- In what different regions did pastoralism and river-basin societies emerge? Where did pastoralism and river-basin societies not emerge? What might account for where these ways of life developed and where they did not?

- Considering the geographic features highlighted on this map, why do you think cities appeared in the regions that they did? What might explain why cities did not appear elsewhere?

- How did geographic and environmental factors promote interaction between nomadic pastoral and sedentary agricultural societies?

coveted metals was copper: easily smelted and shaped (not to mention shiny and alluring), it became the metal of choice for charms, sculptures, and valued commodities. When combined with arsenic or tin, copper hardens and becomes **bronze**, which is useful for tools and weapons. Consequently, this period marks the beginning of the so-called Bronze Age, which will extend into the second millennium BCE (see Chapter 3).

The emergence of cities as population centers created one of history's most durable worldwide distinctions: the **urban-rural divide**. Where cities appeared alongside rivers, people adopted lifestyles based on specialized labor and the mass production of goods. In contrast, most people continued to live in the countryside, where they remained on their lands, cultivating the land or tending livestock, though they exchanged their grains and animal products for goods from the urban centers. The two ways of life were interdependent and both worlds remained linked through family ties, trade, politics, and religion.

PASTORAL NOMADIC COMMUNITIES

Around 3500 BCE, Afro-Eurasia also witnessed the growth and spread of pastoral nomadic communities. The transhumant herder communities that had appeared in Southwest Asia around 5500 BCE (see Chapter 1) continued to be small and their settlements impermanent. They lacked substantial public buildings or infrastructure, but their seasonal moves followed a consistent pattern. Across the vast expanse of Afro-Eurasia's great mountains and its desert barriers, and from its steppe lands ranging across inner and central Eurasia to the Pacific Ocean, these transhumant herders lived alongside settled agrarian people, especially when occupying their lowland pastures. They traded meat and animal products for grains, pottery, and tools produced in the agrarian communities.

In the arid environments of Inner Mongolia and central Asia, transhumant herding and agrarian communities initially followed the same combination of herding animals and cultivating crops that had proved so successful in Southwest Asia. However, because the steppe environment could not support large-scale farming, these communities came to focus on animal breeding and herding. As secondary pursuits they continued to fish, hunt, and farm small plots in their winter pastures. Their economy centered on domesticated cattle, sheep, and horses. As their herds increased, these horse-riding nomads had to move often to new pastures, driving their herds across vast expanses of land. By the second millennium BCE, they had become full-scale nomadic pastoral communities, and they dominated the steppes. In these pastoral nomadic economies of the arid zones of central Eurasia, horses became crucial to survival. These nomadic and transhumant groups played a vital role in connecting cities and spreading ideas throughout Afro-Eurasia.

Map 2.2 Trade and Exchange in Southwest Asia and the Eastern Mediterranean, Third Millennium BCE

Extensive commercial networks linked the urban cores of Southwest Asia.

- Of the traded raw materials shown on the map, which ones were used for building materials, and which ones for luxury items?

- Which regions had timber, and which regions did not? How would the needs of river-basin societies have influenced trade with the regions that had timber?

- Using the map, describe the extent and likely routes of trade necessary for the creation of the treasures of Ur in Mesopotamia (with items fashioned from gold, lapis lazuli, and carnelian) and the wealth buried with pharaohs in their pyramids (silver, gold, lapis lazuli, and carnelian)?

Between the Tigris and Euphrates Rivers: Mesopotamia

The world's first complex society arose in Mesopotamia. Here the river and the first cities changed how people lived. Mesopotamia, whose name is a Greek word meaning "[region] between two rivers," is a landmass including all of modern-day Iraq and parts of Syria and southeastern Turkey. From their headwaters in the mountains to the north and east to their destination in the Persian Gulf, the Tigris and Euphrates Rivers are wild and unpredictable. Unpredictable floodwaters could wipe out years of hard work, but when managed properly they could transform the landscape into verdant and productive fields. Both rivers provided water for irrigation and, although hardly navigable, were important routes for transportation and communication by pack animal and by foot. Mesopotamia's natural advantages—its rich agricultural land and water, combined with easy access to neighboring regions—favored the growth of cities and later territorial states (see Chapter 3). These cities and states became the sites of important cultural, political, and social innovations.

Early Mesopotamian Waterworks From the sixth millennium BCE, irrigation was necessary for successful farming in southern Mesopotamia. By the first millennium BCE, sophisticated feats of engineering allowed the Assyrians to redirect water through constructed aqueducts, like the one illustrated here on a relief from the palace of the Assyrian king Sennacherib at Nineveh.

TAPPING THE WATERS

The first rudimentary advances in irrigation occurred in the foothills of the Zagros Mountains along the banks of the smaller rivers that feed the Tigris. Converting the floodplain of the Euphrates River into a breadbasket, however, required mastering the unpredictable waters. (A floodplain is an area where the river overflows and deposits fertile soil.) Both the Euphrates and the Tigris, unless controlled by waterworks, were unfavorable to cultivators because the annual floods occurred at the height of the growing season, when crops were most vulnerable. Low water levels occurred when crops required abundant irrigation. To prevent the river from overflowing during its flood stage, farmers built levees along the banks and dug ditches and canals to drain away the floodwaters. Engineers devised an irrigation system whereby the Euphrates, which has a higher riverbed than the Tigris, essentially served as the supply and the Tigris as the drain. Storing and channeling water year after year required constant maintenance and innovation by a corps of engineers.

The Mesopotamians' technological breakthrough was in irrigation, not in agrarian methods. Because the soils were fine, rich, and constantly replenished by the floodwaters' silt, soil tillage was light work. Farmers sowed a combination of wheat, millet, sesame, and barley (the basis for beer, a staple of their diet).

CROSSROADS OF SOUTHWEST ASIA

Though its soil was rich and water was abundant, southern Mesopotamia had few other natural resources apart from the mud, marsh reeds, spindly trees, and low-quality limestone that served as basic building materials. To obtain high-quality, dense wood; stone; metal; and other materials for constructing and embellishing their cities with their temples and palaces, Mesopotamians interacted with the inhabitants of surrounding regions. In return for their exports of textiles, oils, and other commodities, Mesopotamians imported cedar wood from Lebanon, copper and stones from Oman, more copper from Turkey and Iran, and the precious blue gemstone called lapis lazuli, as well as ever-useful tin, from faraway Afghanistan. Maintaining trading contacts was easy, given Mesopotamia's open boundaries on all sides. The area became a crossroads for the peoples of Southwest Asia, including Sumerians, who concentrated in the south; Hurrians, who lived in the north; and Akkadians, who populated western and central Mesopotamia. Trade and migration contributed to the growth of cities throughout the river basin, beginning with the Sumerian cities of southern Mesopotamia.

THE WORLD'S FIRST CITIES

During the first half of the fourth millennium BCE, a demographic transformation occurred in the Tigris-Euphrates river basin, especially in the southern area called Sumer. The population expanded as a result of the region's agricultural bounty, and many Mesopotamians migrated from country villages to centers that eventually became cities. (A **city** is a large, well-defined urban area with a dense population.) The earliest Sumerian cities—Eridu, Nippur, and Uruk—developed over about 1,000 years, dominating the southern part of the floodplain by 3500 BCE. Buildings of mud brick show successive layers of urban development, as at Eridu, where more than twenty reconstructed temples were piled atop one another across four millennia, resulting in a final temple that rose from a platform like a mountain, visible for miles in all directions.

As the temple grew skyward, the village expanded outward and became a city. From their homes in temples located at the center of cities, the cities' gods broadcast their powers. In return, urbanites provided luxuries, fine clothes, and enhanced lodgings for the gods and their priests. In Sumerian cosmology, created by ruling elites, humans existed solely to serve the gods,

city
Highly populated concentration of economic, religious, and political power. The first cities appeared in river basins, which could produce a surplus of agriculture. The abundance of food freed most city inhabitants from the need to produce their own food, which allowed them to work in specialized professions.

Level XVI   Level IX   Level VII

Layout of Eridu Over several millennia, temples of increasing size and complexity were built atop each other at Eridu in southern Iraq. The culmination came with the elaborate structure of level VII.

so the urban landscape reflected this fact: a temple at the core, with goods and services flowing to the center and with divine protection and justice flowing outward.

Some thirty-five cities with religious sanctuaries dotted the southern plain of Mesopotamia. Sumerian ideology glorified a way of life and a territory based on politically equal city-states, each with a guardian deity and sanctuary supported by its inhabitants. (A **city-state** is a political organization based on the authority of a single, large city that controls outlying territories.) Because early Mesopotamian cities served as meeting places for peoples and their deities, they gained status as religious and economic centers. Whether enormous (like Uruk and Nippur) or modest (like Ur and Abu Salabikh), all cities were spiritual, economic, and cultural homes for Mesopotamian subjects.

Simply making a city was therefore not enough: urban design reflected the city's role as a wondrous place to pay homage to the gods and their human intermediary, the king. Within their walls, early cities contained large houses separated by date palm plantations and extensive sheepfolds. As populations grew, the Mesopotamian cities became denser, houses became smaller, and new suburbs spilled out beyond the old walls. The typical layout of Mesopotamian cities reflected a common pattern: a central canal surrounded by neighborhoods of specialized occupational groups. The temple marked the city center, with the palace and other official buildings on the periphery. In separate quarters for craft production, families passed down their trades across generations. In this sense, the landscape of the city mirrored the growing **social hierarchies** (distinctions between the privileged and the less privileged).

GODS AND TEMPLES

The worldview of the Sumerians and, later, the Akkadians of Mesopotamia included a belief in a group of gods that shaped their political institutions and controlled everything—including the weather, fertility, harvests, and the

city-state
Political organization based on the authority of a single, large city that controls outlying territories.

social hierarchies
Distinctions between the privileged and the less privileged.

underworld. As depicted in the *Epic of Gilgamesh* (a second-millennium BCE composition based on oral tales about Gilgamesh, a historical but mythologized king of Uruk), the gods could give but could also take away—with droughts, floods, and death. Gods, and the natural forces they controlled, had to be revered and feared. Faithful subjects imagined their gods as immortal beings whose habits were capricious and who had contentious relationships and gloriously work-free lives.

Each major god of the Sumerian pantheon (an officially recognized group of gods and goddesses) dwelled in a lavish temple in a particular city that he or she had created; for instance, Enlil, god of air and storms, dwelled in Nippur; Enki (also called Ea), god of water, in Eridu; Nanna, god of the moon, in Ur; and Inanna (also called Ishtar), goddess of love and fertility, in Uruk. These temples, and the patron deity housed within, gave rise to each city's character, institutions, and relationships with its urban neighbors. Inside these temples, benches lined the walls, with statues of humans standing in perpetual worship of the deity's images. By the end of the third millennium BCE, the temple's platform base had changed to a stepped platform called a *ziggurat*, with the main temple on top. Surrounding the ziggurat were buildings that housed priests, officials, laborers, and servants.

Temples functioned as the god's estate, engaging in all sorts of productive and commercial activities. Temple dependents cultivated cereals, fruits, and vegetables by using extensive irrigation and cared for flocks of livestock. Other temples operated workshops for manufacturing textiles and leather goods, employing craftworkers, metalworkers, masons, and stoneworkers. Enormous labor forces were involved in maintaining this high level of production.

ROYAL POWER, FAMILIES, AND SOCIAL HIERARCHY

Like the temples, royal palaces reflected the power of the ruling elites. Royal palaces appeared around 2500 BCE and served as the official residence of a ruler, his family, and his entourage. As access to palaces and temples over time became limited, gods and kings became inaccessible to all but the most elite. Although located at the edge of cities, palaces were the symbols of permanent secular, military, and administrative authority distinct from the temples' spiritual and economic power.

The Royal Cemetery at Ur shows how Mesopotamian rulers used elaborate burial arrangements to reinforce their religious and socioeconomic hierarchies. Housed in a mud-brick structure, the royal burials held not only the primary remains but also the bodies of more than eighty men and women who had been sacrificed. Huge vats for cooked food, bones of animals, drinking vessels, and musical instruments suggest the lifestyle of those who joined their masters in the graves. Honoring the royal dead by including their

DEATH-PIT PG.1237

RAMP

ENTRANCE

Death Pit 1237 from the Royal Tombs of Ur The excavation team at Ur produced careful drawings and notes as they uncovered the Royal Tombs of Ur in 1927–28. Their drawing of Death Pit 1237 illustrates the rich grave offerings of gold, silver, lapis lazuli, and shell (including a lyre, on the left-hand side). It also shows the remains of six men (armed and lined up by the door, along the bottom) and sixty-seven well-dressed women who were likely buried alive as a funerary offering to honor and accompany the most elaborately decked-out female (Body 61, top right corner) in the afterlife.

followers and possessions in their tombs underscored the social hierarchies—including the vertical ties between humans and gods—that were the cornerstone of these early city-states.

Social hierarchies were an important part of the fabric of Sumerian city-states. Ruling groups secured their privileged access to economic and political resources by erecting systems of bureaucracies, priesthoods, and laws. Priests and bureaucrats served their rulers well, championing rules and norms that legitimized the political leadership. Occupations within the cities were highly specialized, and a list of professions circulated across the land so that everyone could know his or her place in the social order. The king and priest in Sumer were at the top of the list, followed by bureaucrats (scribes and household accountants), supervisors, and craftworkers, such as cooks, jewelers, gardeners, potters, metalsmiths, and traders. The biggest group, which was at the bottom of the hierarchy, comprised workers who were not slaves but were dependent on their employers' households. Movement among economic classes was not impossible but, as in many traditional societies, it was rare.

The family and the household provided the bedrock for Sumerian society, and its patriarchal organization, dominated by the senior male, reflected the balance between women and men, children and parents. The family consisted of the husband and wife bound by a contract: she would provide children, preferably male, while he provided support and protection. Monogamy was the norm unless there was no son, in which case a second wife or a slave girl would bear male children to serve as the married couple's offspring. Adoption was another way to gain a male heir. Sons would inherit the family's property in equal shares, while daughters would receive dowries necessary for successful marriage into other families. Some women joined the temple staff as priestesses and gained economic autonomy that included ownership of estates and productive enterprises, although their fathers and brothers remained responsible for their well-being.

FIRST WRITING AND EARLY TEXTS

Mesopotamia was the birthplace of the world's first writing system, inscribed to promote the economic power of the temples and kings. Those who wielded new writing tools were **scribes**; from the very beginning they were near the top of the social ladder, under the big man and the priests. As the writing of texts became more important to the social fabric of cities, and facilitated information sharing across wider spans of distance and time, scribes consolidated their elite status.

Mesopotamians were the world's first record keepers and readers. The precursors to writing appeared in Mesopotamian societies when farming peoples and officials who had been using clay tokens and images carved on stones to seal off storage areas began to use them to convey messages. These images, when combined with numbers drawn on clay tablets, could record the distribution of goods and services.

Around 3200 BCE, someone, probably in Uruk, understood that the marks (most were pictures of objects) could also represent words or sounds. Before long, scribes connected visual symbols with sounds, and sounds with meanings, and they discovered they could record messages by using abstract symbols or signs to denote concepts. Such signs later came to represent syllables, the building blocks of words. By impressing signs into wet clay with the cut end of a reed, scribes pioneered a form of wedge-shaped writing that we call *cuneiform*; it filled tablets with information that was intelligible to anyone who could decipher it, even in faraway locations or in future generations. Developing over 800 years, this Sumerian innovation enhanced the urban elites' ability to trade goods, to control property, and to transmit ideas through literature, historical records, and sacred texts. The result was a profound change in human experience, because representing symbols of spoken language facilitated an extension of communication and memory.

Much of what we know about Mesopotamia rests on our ability to decipher cuneiform script. By around 2400 BCE, texts began to describe the political makeup of southern Mesopotamia, giving details of its history and economy. Adaptable to different languages, cuneiform script was borrowed by other peoples in Mesopotamia to write not only Semitic languages such as Akkadian and, much later, Old Persian, but also the languages of the Hurrians and the Hittites.

City life and literacy gave rise also to written narratives, the stories of a "people" and their origins. "The Temple Hymns," written around 2100 BCE, describe thirty-five divine sanctuaries. The Sumerian King List, known from texts written around 2000 BCE, recounts the reigns of kings by city and dynasty and narrates the long reigns of legendary kings before the so-called Great Flood. A crucial event in Sumerian identity, the Great Flood, a pastoral-focused version of which is also found in biblical narrative, explained Uruk's demise as the gods' doing. Flooding was the most powerful natural force in the lives of those who lived by rivers, and it helped shape the foundations of Mesopotamian societies.

SPREADING CITIES AND FIRST TERRITORIAL STATES

No single state dominated the whole of Mesopotamia in the fourth and third millennia BCE, but the most powerful and influential were the Sumerian

scribes
Those who mastered writing and used it to document economic transactions, keep lists, and record religious and literary texts; from the very beginning, they were at the top of the social ladder, under the major power brokers.

Changes in Cuneiform over Time The world's earliest script, cuneiform, changed over time and was used to write in many different languages. The first image (*top left*) shows the earliest version of cuneiform being used to write in the Sumerian language (here, a c. 2500 BCE accounting text). The next image (*top right*) shows the more formalized cuneiform script used to write in the Akkadian language more than a millennium after its invention by the Sumerians. The third image (*bottom left*) shows the Hittites' use of cuneiform script to render their language (here, in a letter sealed in a clay envelope). The final image (*bottom right*) demonstrates the use of cuneiform more than 2,000 years after its invention, in this case to record in Assyrian the flood story from the *Epic of Gilgamesh.*

city-states (2850–2334 BCE) and their successor, the Akkadian territorial state (2334–2193 BCE). In the north, Hurrians urbanized their rich agricultural zone around 2600 BCE, including cities at Urkesh and Tell Brak. (See Map 2.3.)

Sumerian city-states, with their expanding populations, soon found themselves competing for agrarian lands, scarce water, and lucrative trade routes. And as pastoralists far and wide learned of the region's bounty, they journeyed in greater numbers to the cities, fueling urbanization and competition. The world's first great conqueror—Sargon the Great (r. 2334–2279 BCE), king of Akkad—emerged from one of these cities. By the end of his reign, he had united (by force) the independent Mesopotamian cities south of modern-day Baghdad and brought the era of competitive independent city-states to an end. Sargon's unification of the southern cities by alliance, though relatively

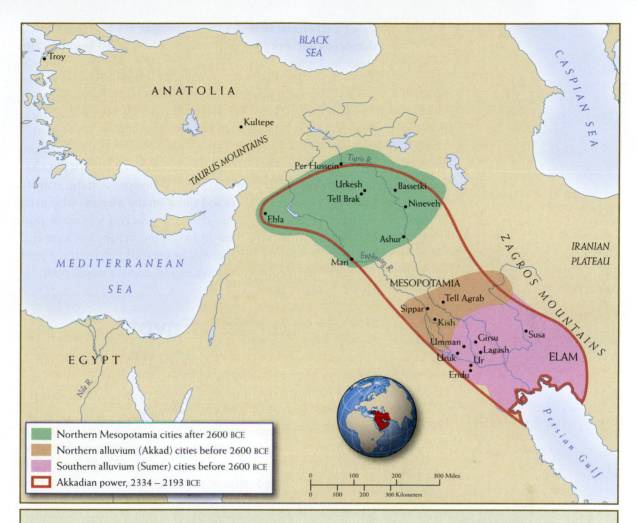

Map 2.3 The Spread of Cities in Mesopotamia and the Akkadian State, 2600–2200 BCE

Urbanization began in the southern river basin of Mesopotamia and spread northward. Eventually, the region achieved unification under Akkadian power.

- According to this map, what natural features influenced the location of Mesopotamian cities?

- Where were cities located before 2600 BCE, as opposed to afterward? What does the area under Akkadian power suggest that the Akkadian territorial state was able to do?

- How did the expansion northward reflect the continued influence of geographic and environmental factors on urbanization?

short-lived, created a territorial state. (A territorial state is a form of political organization that holds authority over a large population and landmass; its power extends over multiple cities.) Sargon's dynasty sponsored monumental architecture, artworks, and literary works, which in turn inspired generations of builders, architects, artists, and scribes. And by encouraging contact with distant neighbors, many of whom adopted aspects of Mesopotamian culture, the Akkadian kings increased the geographic reach of Mesopotamian influence. Just under a century after Sargon's death, foreign tribesmen from the Zagros Mountains conquered the capital city of Akkad around 2190 BCE, setting the beginning of a pattern that would fuel epic history writing, namely the struggles between city-state dwellers and those on the margins who lived a simpler way of life. The impressive state created by Sargon was made possible by Mesopotamia's early innovations in irrigation, urban development, and writing. While Mesopotamia led the way in creating city-states, Egypt went a step further, unifying a 600-mile-long region under a single ruler.

"The Gift of the Nile": Egypt

In Egypt, complex societies grew on the banks of the Nile River, and by the third millennium BCE their peoples created a distinctive culture and a powerful, prosperous state. The earliest inhabitants along the banks of the Nile were a mixed people. Some had migrated from the eastern and western deserts in Sinai and Libya as these areas grew barren from climate change. Others came from the Mediterranean. Equally important were peoples who trekked northward from Nubia and central Africa. Ancient Egypt was a melting pot where immigrants blended cultural practices and technologies.

Like Mesopotamia, Egypt had densely populated areas whose inhabitants depended on irrigation, built monumental architecture, gave their rulers immense authority, and created a complex social order based in commercial and devotional centers. Yet the ancient Egyptian culture was profoundly shaped by its geography. The environment and the natural boundaries of deserts, river rapids, and sea dominated the country and its inhabitants. Only about 3 percent of Egypt's land area was cultivable, and almost all of that cultivable land was in the Nile Delta—the rich alluvial land lying between the river's two main branches as it flows north of modern-day Cairo into the Mediterranean Sea. This environment shaped Egyptian society's unique culture.

THE NILE RIVER AND ITS FLOODWATERS

Knowing Egypt requires appreciating the pulses of the Nile. The world's longest river, it stretches 4,238 miles from its sources in the highlands of central Africa to its destination in the Mediterranean Sea. Egypt was deeply attached to sub-Saharan Africa; not only did its waters and rich silt deposits come from the African highlands, but much of its original population had migrated into the Nile Valley from the west and the south many millennia earlier.

The Upper Nile is a sluggish river that cuts through the Sahara Desert. Rising out of central Africa and Ethiopia, its two main branches—the White and Blue Niles—meet at present-day Khartoum and then scour out a single riverbed 1,500 miles long to the Mediterranean. The annual floods gave the basin regular moisture and enriched the soil. Although the Nile's floodwaters did not fertilize or irrigate fields as broad as those in Mesopotamia, they created green belts flanking the broad waterway. These gave rise to a society whose culture stretched along the navigable river and its carefully preserved banks. Away from the riverbanks, on both sides, lay a desert rich in raw materials but largely uninhabited. (See Map 2.4.) Egypt had no fertile hinterland like the sprawling plains of Mesopotamia. In this way, Egypt was arguably the most river-focused of river-basin cultures.

The Nile's predictability as the source of life and abundance shaped the character of the people and their culture. In contrast to the wild and uncertain Euphrates and Tigris Rivers, the Nile was gentle, bountiful, and reliable. During the summer, as the Nile swelled, local villagers built earthen walls that divided the floodplain into basins. By trapping the floodwaters, these basins captured the rich silt washing down from the Ethiopian highlands. Annual flooding meant that the land received a new layer of topsoil every year. The light, fertile soils made planting simple. Peasants cast seeds into the alluvial soil and then had their livestock trample them to the proper depth. The never-failing sun, which the Egyptians worshipped, ensured an abundant harvest. In the early spring, when the Nile's waters were at their lowest and no crops were under cultivation, the sun dried out the soil.

The peculiarities of the Nile region distinguished it from Mesopotamia. The Greek historian and geographer Herodotus 2,500 years ago noted that Egypt was the gift of the Nile and that the entire length of its basin was one of the world's most self-contained geographical entities. Bounded on the north by the Mediterranean Sea, on the east and west by deserts, and on the south by waterfalls, Egypt was destined to achieve a common culture. Due to these geographical features, the region was far less open to outsiders than was Mesopotamia, which was situated at a crossroads. Egypt created a common culture by balancing a struggle of opposing forces: the north or Lower Egypt versus the south or Upper Egypt; the black, rich soil versus the red sand; life versus death; heaven versus earth; order versus disorder. For Egypt's rulers the primary task was to bring stability or order, known as *ma'at*, out of these opposites. The Egyptians believed that keeping chaos, personified by the desert and its marauders, at bay through attention to *ma'at* would allow all that was good and right to occur.

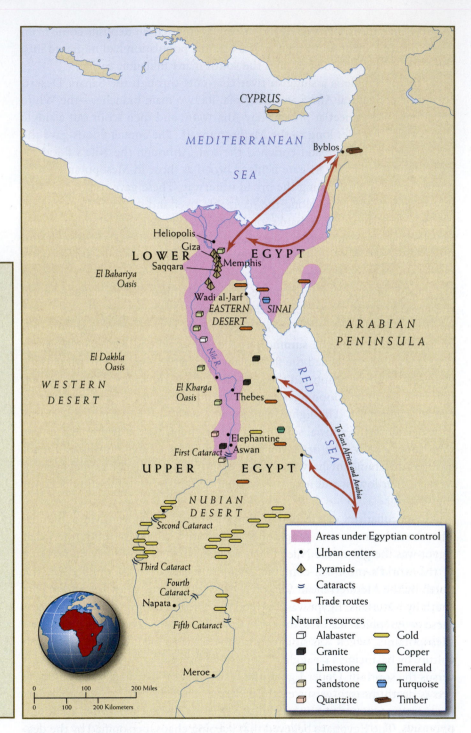

Map 2.4 Old Kingdom Egypt, 2686–2181 BCE

Old Kingdom Egyptian society reflected a strong influence from its geographical location.

- What geographical features contributed to Egypt's isolation from the outside world and the people's sense of their unity?

- What natural resources enabled the Egyptians to build the Great Pyramids? What resources enabled the Egyptians to fill those pyramids with treasures?

- Based on the map, why do you think it was important to the people and their rulers for Upper and Lower Egypt to be united?

Map labels:

CYPRUS

MEDITERRANEAN SEA

Byblos

Heliopolis
Giza
LOWER   EGYPT
Saqqara   Memphis
El Bahariya Oasis
Wadi al-Jarf
EASTERN DESERT   SINAI
ARABIAN PENINSULA

El Dakhla Oasis

Nile R.

WESTERN DESERT

El Kharga Oasis
Thebes

RED SEA

To East Africa and Arabia

Elephantine
First Cataract   Aswan

UPPER   EGYPT

NUBIAN DESERT

Second Cataract

Third Cataract

Fourth Cataract
Napata

Fifth Cataract

Meroe

Legend:

- Areas under Egyptian control
- Urban centers
- Pyramids
- Cataracts
- Trade routes

Natural resources

- Alabaster
- Granite
- Limestone
- Sandstone
- Quartzite
- Gold
- Copper
- Emerald
- Turquoise
- Timber

0   100   200 Miles
0   100   200 Kilometers

THE EGYPTIAN STATE AND DYNASTIES

Once the early Egyptians harnessed the Nile to agriculture, the area changed quickly from being scarcely inhabited to socially complex. A king, called pharaoh and considered semidivine, ensured that the forces of nature, in particular the regular flooding of the Nile, continued without interruption. This task had more to do with appeasing the gods than with running a complex hydraulic system. The king protected his people from chaos-threatening invaders from the eastern desert, as well as from Nubians on the southern borders. In wall carvings, artists portrayed early kings carrying the shepherd's crook and the flail, indicating their responsibility for the welfare of their flocks (the people) and of the land. Under the king an elaborate bureaucracy organized labor and produced public works, sustaining both his vast holdings and general order throughout the realm.

The narrative of ancient Egypt's history follows its thirty-one dynasties, spanning nearly three millennia from 3100 BCE down to its conquest by Alexander the Great in 332 BCE. (See Table 2.1.) Since the nineteenth century, scholars have recast the story around three periods of dynastic achievement: the Old Kingdom, the Middle Kingdom, and the New Kingdom. At the end of each era, cultural flourishing suffered a breakdown in central authority, known respectively as the First, Second, and Third Intermediate Periods.

PHARAOHS, PYRAMIDS, AND COSMIC ORDER

The Third Dynasty (2686–2613 BCE) launched the foundational period known as the Old Kingdom, the golden age of ancient Egypt. By the time it began, the basic institutions of the Egyptian state were in place, as were the ideology and ritual life that legitimized the dynastic rulers.

The pharaoh—king as god—presented himself to the population by means of impressive architectural spaces, and the priestly class performed rituals reinforcing his supreme status within the universe's natural order. One of the most important rituals was the Sed festival, which renewed the king's vitality after he had ruled for thirty years and sought to ensure the perpetual presence of water. King Djoser, of the Third Dynasty, celebrated the Sed festival at his tomb complex at Saqqara. This magnificent complex is the world's oldest stone structure, dating to around 2650 BCE. Djoser's architect, Imhotep, designed a step pyramid that ultimately rose some 200 feet above the plain. The whole complex became a stage for state rituals that emphasized the divinity of kingship and the unity of Egypt.

The step pyramid at Djoser's tomb complex was a precursor to the grand pyramids of the Fourth Dynasty (2613–2494 BCE). These kings erected their monumental structures at Giza, just outside modern-day Cairo and

Table 2.1 Dynasties of Ancient Egypt

Dynasty*	Date
Predynastic Period dynasties I and II	3100–2686 BCE
Old Kingdom dynasties III–VI	2686–2181 BCE
First Intermediate Period dynasties VII–X	2181–2055 BCE
Middle Kingdom dynasties XI–XIII	2055–1650 BCE
Second Intermediate Period dynasties XIV–XVII	1650–1550 BCE
New Kingdom dynasties XVIII–XX	1550–1070 BCE
Third Intermediate Period dynasties XXI–XXV	1070–747 BCE
Late Period dynasties XXVI–XXXI	747–332 BCE

*The term *dynasty* generally refers to a series of rulers who are related to one another. Intermediate periods mark breaks between the kingdoms (Old, Middle, and New). While scholars make attempts to synchronize the dates with modern chronology and other events in the ancient world, the succession of rulers comes from Egyptian texts.

Source: Compiled from Ian Shaw and Paul Nicholson, eds., *The Dictionary of Ancient Egypt* (London: British Museum Press, 1995), pp. 310–11.

not far from the early royal cemetery site of Saqqara, where Djoser's step pyramid stood. The pyramid of the pharaoh Khufu, rising 481 feet above ground, is the largest stone structure in the world, and its corners are almost perfectly aligned to due north, west, south, and east. The oldest papyrus texts ever found—including a set of records kept by an official named Merer around 2550 BCE, which was excavated recently at the ancient port of Wadi al-Jarf—document a meticulous timetable for the gathering of stone for pyramid construction during Khufu's reign and tabulations of food to feed workers.

Surrounding these royal tombs at Giza were those of high officials, almost all members of the royal family. The enormous amount of labor involved in building these monuments came from peasant-workers, slaves brought from Nubia, and captured Mediterranean peoples. Filling these monuments with wealth for the occupants' afterlife similarly required a range of specialized labor (from jewelers, to weavers, to stone carvers, to furniture makers). Long-distance trade was required to bring from far away not only the jewels and precious metals (like lapis lazuli, carnelian, and silver) required for such offerings, but also the materials to construct the ships that helped make that trade possible (like timber from Byblos). Through their majesty and complex construction, the Giza pyramids reflect the degree of centralization and the surpluses in Egyptian society at this time as well as the trade and specialized labor that fueled these undertakings.

Pharaohs used their royal tombs, and the ritual of death leading to everlasting life, to embody the state's ideology and the principles of the Egyptian cosmos. The pharaoh also employed symbols, throne names, and descriptive titles for himself and his advisers to represent his own power and that of his administrators, the priests, and the landed elite. The Egyptian cosmic order was one of inequality and stark hierarchy, not dissimilar to the hierarchies of Mesopotamia. Established at the time of creation, the universe was the king's responsibility to maintain for eternity.

GODS, PRIESTHOOD, AND MAGICAL POWER

Egyptians understood their world as inhabited by three groups: gods, kings, and the rest of humanity. Official records only showed representations of gods and kings. Yet the people did not confuse their kings with gods—at least during the kings' lifetimes. Mortality was the bar between rulers and deities; after death, kings joined the gods whom they had represented while alive.

As in Mesopotamia, every region in Egypt had its resident god. Some gods, such as Amun (believed to be physically present in Thebes, the political center of Upper Egypt), transcended regional status because of the importance of their hometown. Over the centuries the Egyptian gods evolved, combining often-contradictory aspects into single deities, including Horus, the hawk god; Osiris, the god of regeneration and the underworld; Isis, who represented the ideals of sisterhood and motherhood; Hathor, the goddess of childbirth and love; Ra, the sun god; and Amun, a creator considered to be the hidden god.

Official religious practices took place in the main temples. The king and his agents offered respect, adoration, and thanks to the gods in their temples. In return, the gods maintained order and nurtured the king and—through him—all humanity. In this contractual relationship, the gods were passive while the kings were active, a difference that reflected their unequal relationship.

The tasks of regulating religious rituals and mediating among gods, kings, and society fell to one specialist class: the priesthood. Creating this class required elaborate rules for selecting and training the priests. Only priests could enter the temples' inner sanctuaries, and the gods' statues only left the temples for great festivals. Thus, priests monopolized communication between spiritual powers and their subjects.

Unofficial religion was also important. Ordinary Egyptians matched their elite rulers in faithfulness to the gods, but their distance from temple life caused them to find different ways to fulfill their religious needs and duties. They visited local shrines, where they prayed, made requests, and left offerings to the gods. Magic had a special importance for commoners, who believed that amulets held extraordinary powers, such as preventing illness and guaranteeing safe childbirth. To deal with profound questions, commoners looked to omens and divination. Spiritual expression was central to Egyptian culture at all levels, and religion helped shape other cultural achievements, including the development of a written language.

WRITING AND SCRIBES

Egypt, like Mesopotamia, was a scribal culture. By the middle of the third millennium BCE, literacy was well established among small circles of scribes in Egypt and Mesopotamia. The fact that few individuals were literate heightened the scribes' social status. Most high-ranking Egyptians were also trained as scribes for the king's court, the army, or the priesthood. Some kings and members of the royal family learned to write as well. Although in both cultures writing emerged in response to economic needs, people soon grasped its utility for commemorative and religious purposes. As soon as literacy took hold, Mesopotamians and Egyptians were drafting historical records and literary compositions.

Ancient Egyptians used two forms of writing. Elaborate *hieroglyphs* (from the Greek "sacred carving") served in formal temple, royal, or divine contexts. More common, however, was *hieratic* writing, a cursive script written with ink on papyrus or pottery. (*Demotic* writing, from the Greek *demotika*, meaning "popular" or "in common use," developed much later and became the vital transitional key on the Rosetta Stone that ultimately allowed the nineteenth-century decipherment of hieroglyphics. Used for record keeping, hieratic writing also found uses in letters and works of literature—including narrative fiction, manuals of instruction and philosophy, cult and religious hymns, love poems, medical and mathematical texts, collections of rituals, and mortuary books.

Literacy spread first among upper-class families. Most students started training when they were young. After mastering the copying of standard texts in hieratic cursive or hieroglyphs, students moved on to literary works. The upper classes prized literacy as proof of high intellectual achievement. When elites died, they had their student textbooks placed alongside their corpses as evidence of their talents. The literati produced texts mainly in temples, where these works were also preserved. Writing in hieroglyphs and the composition of texts in hieratic, and later demotic, script continued without break in ancient Egypt for almost 3,000 years.

PROSPERITY AND THE DEMISE OF OLD KINGDOM EGYPT

Cultural achievements, agrarian surpluses, and urbanization ultimately led to higher standards of living and rising populations. Under pharaonic rule, Egypt enjoyed spectacular prosperity. Its population swelled from 350,000 in 4000 BCE to 1 million in 2500 BCE and nearly 5 million by 1500 BCE. However, expansion and decentralization eventually exposed the weaknesses of the Old and Middle Kingdom dynasties.

The state's success depended on administering resources skillfully, especially agricultural production and labor. Everyone, from the most powerful elite to the workers in the field, was part of the system. In principle, no one possessed private property; in practice, Egyptians treated land and tools as

Egyptian Hieroglyphs and "Cursive Script" The Egyptians wrote in two distinctive types of script. The more formal is hieroglyphs, which is based on pictorial images that carry values of either ideas (logograms) or sounds (phonemes). All royal and funerary inscriptions, such as this funerary relief from the Old Kingdom (from the tomb of Nefertiabet, c. 2550 BCE), are rendered in hieroglyphic script. Nefertiabet's inscription describes, with a mixture of images and words, the funerary offerings, including food, fabric, and cosmetics. Daily documents, accountings, and literary texts—such as the fragment from the *Book of the Dead* (*top right*)—were most often written in a cursive script called hieratic, which was written with ink on papyrus. The form of the cursive signs is based on the hieroglyphs but is more abstract and can be formed more quickly.

their own—but submitted to the intrusions of the state. The state's control over taxation, prices, and the distribution of goods required a large bureaucracy that maintained records, taxed the population, appeased the gods, organized a strong military, and aided local officials in regulating the Nile's floodwaters.

Royal power, and the Old Kingdom, collapsed in the three years following the death of Pepy II in 2184 BCE. Local magnates assumed hereditary control of the government in the provinces and treated lands previously controlled by the royal family as their personal property. An extended drought strained Egypt's extensive irrigation system, which could no longer water the lands that fed the region's million inhabitants. (See Current Trends in World History: Climate Change at the End of the Third Millennium BCE in Egypt, Mesopotamia, and the Indus Valley.) In this so-called First Intermediate Period (2181 to 2055 BCE), local leaders plunged into bloody regional struggles to keep the irrigation works functioning for their own communities until the century-long drought ended. Although the Old Kingdom declined, it established institutions and beliefs that endured and were revived several centuries later.

Climate Change at the End of the Third Millennium BCE in Egypt, Mesopotamia, and the Indus Valley

During the long third millennium BCE, the first urban centers in Egypt, Mesopotamia, Iran, central Asia, and South Asia flourished and grew in complexity and wealth in a wet and cool climate. This smooth development was sharply if not universally interrupted beginning around 2200 BCE. Both archaeological and written records agree that across Afro-Eurasia, most of the urban, rural, and pastoral societies underwent radical change. Those watered by major rivers were selectively destabilized, while the settled communities on the highland plateaus virtually disappeared. After a brief hiatus, some recovered, completely reorganized, and used new technologies to manage agriculture and water. The causes of this radical change have been the focus of much interest.

After four decades of research by climate specialists working together with archaeologists, a consensus has emerged that climate change toward a warmer and drier environment contributed to this disruption. Whether this disruption was caused solely by human activity, in particular agriculture

on a large scale, or was also related to cosmic causes such as the rotation of the earth's axis away from the sun, is still a hotly debated topic. It was likely a combination of factors.

The urban centers dependent on the three major river systems in Egypt, Mesopotamia, and the Indus Valley, all experienced disruption. In Egypt, the hieroglyphic inscriptions tell us that the Nile no longer flooded over its banks to replenish the fields with fresh soil and with water for crops. Social and political chaos followed for more than a century. In southern Mesopotamia, the deeply downcut rivers changed course, disrupting settlement patterns and taking fields out of cultivation. Other fields were poisoned by salts brought on through overcultivation and irrigation without fallow periods. Fierce competition for water and land put pressure on the central authority. To the east and west, transhumant pastoralists, faced with shrinking pasture for their flocks, pressed in on the river valleys, disrupting the already challenged social and political structure of the densely urban centers.

In northern Mesopotamia, the responses to the challenges of aridity were more varied. Some centers were able to weather the crisis by changing strategies of food production and distribution. Some fell victim to intraregional warfare, while others, on the rainfall margin, were abandoned. When the region was settled again, society was differently organized. The population did not drastically decrease, but rather distributed itself across the landscape more evenly in smaller settlements that required less water and food. It appears that a similar solution was found by communities to the east on the Iranian plateau, where the inhabitants of the huge urban center of Shahr-i Sokhta abruptly left the city and settled in small communities across the oasis landscape.

The solutions found by people living in the cities of the Indus Valley also varied. Some cities, like Harappa, saw their population decrease rapidly. It seems that the bed of the river shifted, threatening the settlement and its hinterland. Mohenjo Daro, on the other hand, continued to be occupied for another several centuries, although the

The Indus River Valley: A Parallel Culture

Cities emerged in the Indus River valley in South Asia in the third millennium BCE. The urban culture of the Indus area is called "Harappan" after the urban site of Harappa that arose on the banks of the Ravi River, a tributary large civic structures fell out of use, replaced by more modest structures. The Ghaggar-Hakra (as a year-round river) had dried up long before Harappan settlements of the third millennium. The urban settlements along the course of its seasonal flow had already formed as an adaptation to an earlier climate change, since their inhabitants had likely clustered along

Millet This hardy grain, cultivated for its resistance to drought, persists in the desert environment of present-day western Pakistan.

the dried-up riverbed as a topographical feature that would focus monsoon flows even in the absence of a year-round river. And to the south, on the Gujarat Peninsula, population and the number of settlements increased. They abandoned wheat as a crop, instead cultivating a kind of drought-enduring millet that originated in West Africa. Apparently conditions there became even more hospitable, allowing farming and fishing communities to flourish well into the second millennium BCE.

The evidence for this widespread phenomenon of climate change at the end of the third millennium BCE is complex and contradictory. This is not surprising, because every culture and each community naturally had an individual response to environmental and other challenges. Those with perennial sources of fresh water were less threatened than those in marginal zones where only a slight decrease in rainfall could mean failed crops and herds. Notably, certain types of social and political institutions were resilient and introduced innovations that allowed them to adapt, while others were too rigid or shortsighted to find local solutions. A feature of human culture is its remarkable ability to adapt rapidly. When people are faced with challenges, the traits of resilience, creativity, and ingenuity lead to cultural innovation and change. This is what we can see, even in our own times, during the period of environmental stress.

Questions for Analysis

- How did the response to drought in the Indus Valley differ from the response in Mesopotamia?
- Imagine that the climate during the third millennium BCE had not changed. How do you think this might have affected the development of ancient Egypt?
- How has our understanding of global climate change affected the way we study prehistory?

Explore Further

Behringer, Wolfgang, *A Cultural History of Climate* (2010).

Bell, Barbara, "The Dark Ages in Ancient History. 1. The First Dark Age in Egypt," *American Journal of Archaeology* 75 (January 1971): 1–26.

Singh, Ajit et al., "Counter-Intuitive Influence of Himalayan River Morphodynamics on Indus Civilisation Urban Settlements," *Nature Communications* 8, article no. 1617 (2017), doi:10.1038/s41467-017-01643-9.

Weiss, Max et al., "The Genesis and Collapse of Third Millennium North Mesopotamian Civilization," *Science (New Series)* 261 (August 20, 1993): 995–1004.

of the Indus. Developments in the Indus basin reflected local tradition combined with strong influences from Iranian plateau peoples, as well as indirect influences from distant Mesopotamian cities. Villages appeared around 5000 BCE on the Iranian plateau along the Baluchistan Mountain foothills, to the west of the Indus. By the early third millennium BCE, frontier villages had spread eastward to the fertile banks of the Indus River and its tributaries. (See Map 2.5.) The river-basin settlements soon yielded agrarian surpluses

Map 2.5 The Indus River Valley in the Third Millennium BCE

Historians know less about the urban society of the Indus Valley in the third millennium BCE than they do about its contemporaries in Mesopotamia and Egypt, in part because of the absence of a written record. Recent scholarship has suggested the importance of a second seasonal flow (as opposed to a year-round river) in the channel of the long dried-up Ghaggar-Hakra to the east of the Indus.

- Where were cities concentrated in the Indus Valley? Why do you think the cities were located where they were?
- How do the trade routes of the fourth and early third millennium BCE differ from those of the later third millennium BCE? What might account for those differences?
- What commodities appear on this map? What is their relationship to urban centers and trade routes?

that supported greater wealth, more trade with neighbors, and public works. Urbanites of the Indus region and the Harappan peoples began to fortify their cities and to undertake public works similar in scale to those in Mesopotamia, but strikingly different in function.

The Indus Valley ecology boasted many advantages—especially compared to the area near the Ganges River, the other great waterway of the South Asian landmass. The melting snows in the Himalayas watered the semitropical Indus Valley, ensuring flourishing vegetation, plus the region did not suffer the yearly monsoon downpours that flooded the Ganges plain. The expansion of agriculture in the Indus basin, as in Mesopotamia, Egypt, and China, depended on the Indus River's annual floods to replenish the soil and avert droughts. From June to September, the river inundated the plain. New evidence has suggested that the monsoons also brought seasonal flows of water into long-dried-up riverbeds (especially the so-called paleochannel of the Ghaggar-Hakra, a river that had dried up almost three thousand years before Harappan society began to thrive). This evidence poses a unique question about river-fueled society in the third millennium: How did the Harappan settlements clustered along this paleochannel to the east of the Indus River harness a seasonal flow of water into an otherwise dried-up riverbed, as compared with a year-round river?

Whether along the year-round-flowing Indus or the seasonal flows of water in the Ghaggar-Hakra paleochannel, farmers planted wheat and barley, harvesting the crops the next spring. Harappan villagers also improved their tools of cultivation. Researchers have found evidence of furrows, probably made by plowing, that date to around 2600 BCE. These developments suggest that, as in Mesopotamia and Egypt, farmers were cultivating harvests that yielded a surplus that allowed many inhabitants to specialize in other activities. In time, rural wealth produced urban splendor. More abundant harvests, now stored in large granaries, brought migrants into the area and supported expanding populations. By 2500 BCE cities began to replace villages throughout the Indus River valley, and within a few generations towering granaries marked the urban skyline. Harappa and Mohenjo Daro, the two largest cities, each covered a little less than half a square mile and may have housed 35,000 residents.

Harappan cities sprawled across a vast floodplain covering 500,000 square miles—two or three times the size of the Mesopotamian cultural zone. At the height of their development, the Harappan peoples reached the edge of the Indus ecological system and encountered the cultures of northern Afghanistan, the inhabitants of the desert frontier, the nomadic hunters and gatherers to the east, and the traders to the west. Although scholars know less about Harappan society than about Mesopotamia or ancient Egypt, what they know about Harappan urban culture and trade routes is impressive.

HARAPPAN CITY LIFE AND WRITING

The well-planned layout of Harappan cities and towns included a fortified citadel housing public facilities alongside a large residential area. The main street running through the city had covered drainage on both sides, with house gates and doors opening onto back alleys. Citadels were likely centers of political and ritual activities. At the center of the citadel of Mohenjo Daro was the famous great bath. The location, size, and quality of the bath's steps, mortar and bitumen sealing, and drainage channel all suggest that the structure was used for public bathing rituals.

The Harappans used brick extensively—in upper-class houses, city walls, and underground water drainage systems. Workers used large ovens to manufacture the durable construction materials, which the Harappans laid so skillfully that basic structures remain intact to this day. A well-built house had private bathrooms, showers, and toilets that drained into municipal sewers, also made of bricks. Houses in small towns and villages were made of less durable and less costly sun-baked bricks.

Many of the remains of Harappan culture lie buried under deep silt deposits accumulated over thousands of years of heavy flooding. Consequently, we know less about it than about other contemporary cultures of Afro-Eurasia. Additionally, scholars are still working to identify the Indus peoples' language and decipher the script of about 400 symbols. Although a ten-glyph-long public inscription has been found at the Harappan site of Dholavira, most of what remains of the Indus Valley script appears on a thousand or more stamp seals and small plaques excavated from the region, which may

Mohenjo Daro Mohenjo Daro, the "mound of dead," is a large urban site of the Harappan culture. The view of the city demonstrates a neat layout of houses and civic facilities such as sewer draining.

represent the names and titles of individuals rather than complete sentences. Moreover, because the Harappans did not produce King Lists (as the Mesopotamians and Egyptians did)—and may not even have had kings—scholars cannot chart a Harappan political history by tracing the rise and fall of dynasties and kingdoms. Relying only on fragmentary archaeological evidence, scholars have been unable to draw the rich portraits of Harappan life that they have supplied for the Mesopotamians and the Egyptians.

TRADE

The Harappans engaged in trade along the Indus River, through the mountain passes to the Iranian plateau, and along the coast of the Arabian Sea as far as the Persian Gulf and Mesopotamia. They traded copper, flint, shells, and ivory, as well as pottery, flint blades, and jewelry created by their craftworkers, in exchange for gold, silver, gemstones, and textiles. Carnelian, a precious red stone, was a local resource, but lapis lazuli had to come from what is now northern Afghanistan. Some of the Harappan trading towns nestled in remote but strategically important places. Consider Lothal, a well-fortified port at the head of the Gulf of Khambhat (Cambay). Although distant from the center of Harappan society, it provided vital access to the sea and to valuable raw materials. Its many workshops processed precious stones, both local and foreign. Because the demand for gemstones and metals was high on the Iranian plateau and in Mesopotamia, control of their extraction and trade was essential to maintaining the Harappans' economic power. So the Harappans built fortifications and settlements near sources of carnelian and copper mines.

Through a complex and vibrant trading system, the Harappans maintained access to mineral and agrarian resources. To facilitate trade, rulers relied not just on Harappan script but also on a system of weights and measures that they devised and standardized. Archaeologists have found Harappan seals, used to stamp commodities with the names of their owners or the nature of the goods, at sites as far away as the Persian Gulf, Mesopotamia, and the Iranian plateau.

The general uniformity in Harappan sites suggests a centralized and structured state. Unlike the Mesopotamians and the Egyptians, however, the Harappans apparently built neither palaces nor grand royal tombs. What the Indus River people show us is how much the urbanized parts of the world were diverging from one another, even as they borrowed from and imitated their neighbors.

> **Core Objectives**
>
> **TRACE** and **EVALUATE** the trade connections stretching from Mesopotamia to the Indus River valley societies.

The Yellow and Yangzi River Basins: East Asia

Like the Mesopotamians, Egyptians, and Harappans, East Asian peoples clustered in river basins. Their settlements along the Yellow River in the north and the Yangzi River to the south became the foundation of the future Chinese state. By 5000 BCE, both millet in the north and rice in the south were under widespread cultivation.

Yet in the following three millennia (when Mesopotamia, Egypt, and the Indus Valley were creating complex, city-based cultures), the Chinese moved slowly toward urbanization. (See Map 2.6.) Like the other regions' waterways, the Yellow and Yangzi Rivers had annual floods and extensive floodplains suitable for producing high agricultural yields and supporting dense populations. In China, however, the evolution of hydraulic works, big cities, priestly and bureaucratic classes, and a new writing system took longer. A lack of easily domesticated animals and plants contributed to the different developmental path in China, as did geographic barriers. The Himalayan Mountains and the Taklamakan and Gobi Deserts prevented large-scale migrations between East Asia and central Asia and hindered the diffusion of cultural breakthroughs occurring elsewhere in Afro-Eurasia.

FROM YANGSHAO TO LONGSHAN CULTURE

China's classical histories have claimed that China's cultural traditions originated in the Central Plains of the Yellow River basin and spread outward to less developed regions inside and even beyond mainland China. These histories place the beginnings of Chinese culture at the Xia dynasty, dating from 2200 BCE. Archaeological studies of river-basin environments in East Asia tell a different story, however. Whether or not the Xia existed as a historical dynasty, archaeological evidence suggests our study of the Yellow River basin and Yangzi delta should begin earlier—in the two millennia from 4000 to 2000 BCE.

China in 4000 BCE was very different geographically and culturally from what it is today. A warmer and moister climate divided its vast landmass into distinctive regions. Recent archaeological research records that at least eight distinct regional cultures appeared between 4000 and 2000 BCE, and only as these communities interacted did their institutions and ways of life come together to create a unified Chinese culture.

Although it was geographically divided, China was never devoid of outside influences. Some travelers did arrive via the ocean, but more came via the Mongolian steppe, through which nomads introduced important technologies such as metalworks. Nomads were drawn to the agricultural settlements (as they were in Mesopotamia), and they brought innovations, such as bronze and other goods, from the west. Through trade and migration, nomadic cultures and technologies filtered from the steppes to settled communities on the rivers.

The major divide in China was between the northern Yellow and more centrally located Yangzi river basins. Not only did inhabitants of these two regions rely on different crops—millet in the north and rice in the

Map 2.6 River-Basin Peoples in East Asia, 5000–2000 BCE

Complex agricultural societies emerged in East Asia during the third millennium BCE.

- Locate the three distinct cultures on the map. Where is each located, and what major crop was grown in each?
- What topographical features may have shaped the extent and spread of the various cultures represented on the map?
- Locate the dots for farming before 3000 BCE and those for farming after 3000 BCE. What hypotheses might you offer based on the location of farming before and after 3000 BCE?

Yangshao Bowl with Dancing Figures, c. 5000–1700 BCE The Yangshao, also referred to as the "painted pottery" culture, produced gray or red pottery painted with black geometric designs and occasionally with pictures of fish or human faces and figures. Because the potter's wheel was unknown at the time, the vessels were probably fashioned with strips of clay.

south—but they built their houses differently, buried their dead in different ways, and produced distinctive pottery styles. The best known of the early cultures developed along the Yellow River and in the Central Plains area and is known as the Yangshao culture.

Yangshao villages typically covered 10 to 14 acres and were composed of houses erected around a central square. Villagers had to move frequently because they practiced slash-and-burn agriculture. Once residents had exhausted the soil, they picked up their belongings, moved to new lands, and constructed new villages. Their lives were hard. Excavated cemeteries reveal that nearly 20 percent of the burials were of children fifteen years and younger; only a little more than half of those buried lived past the age of forty.

Around 3000 BCE, the Yangshao culture gave way to the Longshan culture, which had an even larger geographical scope and would provide some of the cultural foundations for the first strong states that emerged in the Central Plains. Longshan flourished from 3000 BCE to 2000 BCE and had its center in Shandong Province. Although the Longshan way of life first took form in coastal and southern China, outside the Central Plains, it moved quickly into this hub of economic and political activity. Proof of its widespread cultural influence can be seen from the appearance of a unique style of black pottery, stretching all the way from Manchuria in the north through the Central Plains to the coast and beyond to the island of Taiwan.

The Longshan people likely migrated in waves from the peripheries of East Asia to the eastern China seashore. Their achievements, compared to those of the Yangshao, suggest marked development between 5000 and 2000 BCE. Several independent regional cultures in northern and southern China began to produce similar pottery and tools and to plant the same crops, probably reflecting contact. They did not yet produce city-states, but agriculture and small settlements flourished in the increasingly populated Yellow River valley.

Some of the hallmarks of early urban life are evident in the archaeological remains. Longshan communities built defensive walls for protection and dug wells to supply water. They buried their dead in cemeteries outside their villages. Of several thousand graves uncovered in southern Shanxi Province, the largest ones contain ritual pottery vessels, wooden musical instruments, copper bells, and painted murals. Shamans performed rituals using jade axes. Jade quarrying in particular indicated technical sophistication, as skilled craftworkers incised jade tablets with powerful expressions of ritual and military authority. The threat of organized violence among Longshan villages was real. Discoveries at one Longshan site revealed a household whose members were scalped. At this same site, attackers filled the water wells with five layers of human skeletons, some decapitated. Clearly, the villages' defensive walls were essential.

As communities became more centralized, contact between regions increased. Links between northern and southern China arose when Long-shan peoples began to migrate along the East Asian coast to Taiwan and the Pearl River delta in the far south. Similarities in artifacts found along the coast and at Longshan sites in northern China, such as the form and decoration of pottery and jade items, also point to a shared sphere of culture and trade.

Archaeologists also have found evidence of short-lived political organizations. Although they were nothing like the dynastic systems in Egypt, Mesopotamia, and the Indus Valley, they were wealthy—if localized—polities. They constituted what scholars call the era of Ten Thousand States. One of them, the Liangzhu, has drawn particular interest for its remarkable jade objects and its sophisticated farming techniques. The Liangzhu grew rice and fruits and domesticated water buffalo, pigs, dogs, and sheep. Archaeologists have discovered the remains of net sinkers, wooden floats, and wooden paddles, which demonstrate a familiarity with watercraft and fishing. Artisans produced a black pottery from soft paste thrown on a wheel, and like the Longshan, they created ritual objects from several varieties of jade. Animal masks and bird designs adorned many pieces, revealing a shared cosmology that informed the rituals of the Liangzhu elite.

In the late third millennium BCE, a long drought hit China (as it did Egypt, Mesopotamia, and India). Although the climate change limited progress and forced migrations to more dependable habitats, the Chinese recovered early in the second millennium BCE. Now they created elaborate agrarian systems along the Yellow and Yangzi Rivers that were similar to earlier irrigation systems along the Euphrates, Indus, and Nile. Extensive trading networks and a stratified social hierarchy emerged; like the other river-basin complexes of Asia and North Africa, China became a centralized polity. Here, too, a powerful monarchy eventually united the independent communities. But what developed in China was a social and political system that emphasized an idealized past and a tradition represented by sage-kings, which later ages emulated. In this and other ways, China diverged from the rest of Afro-Eurasia.

Longshan Beaker, c. 2500 BCE Longshan has been called the "black pottery" culture, and its exquisite black pottery was not painted but rather decorated with rings, either raised or grooved. Longshan culture was more developed than the Yangshao culture, and its distinctive pottery was likely formed on a potter's wheel.

Life Outside the River Basins

In 3500 BCE, the vast majority of humans lived outside the complex cities that emerged in parts of Afro-Eurasia. At the other end of the spectrum, many peoples continued to live as hunters and gatherers, or in small agricultural villages or nomadic groups. In between were worlds such as those in the Aegean, Anatolia, Europe, and parts of China, where towns emerged and agriculture advanced, but not with the leaps and bounds of the great river-basin societies.

Some cultures outside the river basins—in the Aegean, Anatolia, and Europe—had a distinctive warrior-based ethos, such that the top tiers of the social ladder held chiefs and military men instead of priests and scribes. In Europe and Anatolia especially, weaponry rather than writing, forts rather than palaces, and conquest rather than commerce dominated everyday life. Settlements in the Americas and sub-Saharan Africa were smaller and remained based on agriculture. Here, too, the inhabitants moved beyond stone implements and hunting and gathering, but they remained more egalitarian than river-basin peoples.

AEGEAN WORLDS

Contact with Egypt and Mesopotamia affected the worlds of the Aegean Sea (the part of the Mediterranean Sea between the Greek Peloponnese and Anatolia), but it did not transform them. Geography stood in the way of significant urban development on the mountainous islands of the Aegean, on the Anatolian plateau, and in Europe. Even though people from Anatolia, Greece, and the Levant had populated the Aegean islands in the sixth millennium BCE, their small villages, of 100 inhabitants or fewer, endured for 2,000 years before becoming more complex. On mainland Greece and on the Cycladic islands in the Aegean, fortified settlements housed local rulers who controlled a small area of agriculturally productive countryside.

Metallurgy developed both on the island of Crete and in the Cyclades. There is evidence of more formal administration and organizations in some communities by 2500 BCE, but the norm was scattered settlements separated by natural obstacles. One exciting recent find has been reported by scholars excavating a ritual center at Dhaskalio, a small islet off the coast of the Aegean island of Keros that was likely attached by land to Keros in the early Bronze Age. At this site, excavations have revealed mid-third-millennium BCE workshops for working imported metals like copper, as well as elaborate monumental engineering projects, including staircases and drainage tunnels, constructed with imported stone.

By the early third millennium BCE, Crete had made occasional contact with Egypt and the coastal towns of the Levant, encountering new ideas, technologies, and materials as foreigners arrived on its shores. People coming by ship from the coasts of Anatolia and the Levant, as well as from Egypt, traded stone vessels and other luxury objects for the island's abundant copper. Graves of Aegean elites, such as those at Knossos on Crete, with their gold jewelry and other exotic objects, show that the elites did not reject the niceties of cultured life, but they knew that their power rested as much on their rugged landscape's resources as on self-defense and trade with others.

ANATOLIA

The highland plateau of Anatolia (in the region of modern-day Turkey) shows clear evidence of regional cultures focused on the control of trade routes and mining outposts. True cities did not develop here until the third millennium BCE, and even then they were not the sprawling population centers typical of the Mesopotamian plain. Instead, small communities emerged around fortified citadels housing local rulers who competed with one another. Two impressively fortified centers were Horoz Tepe and Alaça Hüyük, which have yielded more than a dozen graves—apparently royal—full of gold jewelry, ceremonial standards, and elaborate weapons. Similarly, the settlement at Troy—which would be the site of the Trojan War of the late second millennium BCE—was characterized by monumental stone gateways, stone-paved ramps, and high-status graves filled with gold and silver objects, vessels, jewelry, and other artifacts. Parallel grave finds on Crete, the Greek mainland, and as far away as Ur indicate that Troy participated in the trading system linking the Aegean and Southwest Asian worlds. At the same time, Troy faced predatory neighbors and pirates who attacked from the sea—an observation that explains its impressive fortifications.

EUROPE: THE WESTERN FRONTIER

At the western reaches of the Eurasian landmass was a region featuring cooler climates with smaller population densities. Its peoples—forerunners of present-day Europeans—began to make objects out of metal, formed permanent settlements, and started to create complex societies. Here, hierarchies began to undermine egalitarian ways. Yet, as in the Aegean worlds, population density and social complexity had limits.

More than in the Mediterranean or Anatolia, warfare dominated social development in Europe. Two contributing factors were the persistent fragmentation of the region's peoples and the type of agrarian development they pursued. (See Map 2.7.) The introduction of the plow and the clearing of woodlands expanded agriculture. Flint mining at an industrial level slashed the cost and increased the availability of raw materials needed to make tools for clearing forested lands and tilling them into arable fields. Compared to the river-basin societies, Europe was a wild frontier where violent conflicts over resources were common.

By 3500 BCE, the more developed agrarian peoples had combined into large communities, constructing impressive monuments that remain visible today. In western Europe, large ceremonial centers shared the same model: enormous shaped stones, some weighing several tons each, set in common patterns—in alleyways, troughs, or circles—known as *megalithic* ("great stone") constructions. These daunting projects required cooperative planning and work. In the British Isles, where such developments occurred later, the famous megalithic complexes at Avebury and Stonehenge probably reached their highest stages of development just before 2000 BCE.

By 2000 BCE, the whole of the northern European plain shared a common material culture based on agriculture, the herding of cattle for meat and milk, the use of the plough, and the use of wheeled vehicles and metal

Map 2.7 captions and legend:

- Farm settlement
- Urban complexes
- Archaeological site
- Main routes of the spread of agriculture

Traded Commodities
- Copper
- Flint

Labels on map: NORTH SEA, BALTIC SEA, ATLANTIC OCEAN, Grimes Graves, Stonehenge, EUROPE, Rhine R., Dnieper R., CASPIAN SEA, Danube R., Varna, BLACK SEA, Alaça Hüyük, Horoz Tepe, ANATOLIA, SOUTHWEST, MESOPOTAMIA, Euphrates R., Tigris R., ASIA, CORSICA, ADRIATIC SEA, Troy, SARDINIA, BALEARIC ISLANDS, AEGEAN SEA, Mycenae, MEDITERRANEAN, Keros, CYCLADES, RHODES, CYPRUS, MALTA, CRETE, Knossos, SEA, Beginnings of palace-based societies, Nile R., EGYPT, RED SEA

Map 2.7 Settlements outside the River Basins: The Eastern Mediterranean and Europe, 5000–2000 BCE

Urban societies in Southwest Asia, like those in Mesopotamia and the Nile Valley, had profound influences on societies in Anatolia, the Aegean, and western Europe.

- Trace the main routes for the spread of agriculture. Based on those routes, how did agriculture spread in this period?
- Locate the icons for copper and flint. Based on your reading of the chapter, how might these commodities have shaped the culture in the regions in which they were located?

Stonehenge This spectacular site, located in the Salisbury Plain in Wiltshire in southwestern England, is one of several such megalithic structures found in the region. Constructed by many generations of builders, the arrangement of the large stone uprights enabled people to determine precise times in the year through the position of the sun. Events such as the spring and autumn equinoxes were connected with agricultural and religious activities.

tools and weapons, mainly of copper. Increasing communication, exchange, and mobility among the European communities led to increasing wealth but also sparked organized warfare over frontier lands and valuable resources. In an ironic twist, the integration of local communities led to greater friction and produced regional social stratification. The violent men who now protected their communities received ceremonial burials complete with their own drinking cups and weapons. Archaeologists have found these warrior burials in a swath of European lands extending from present-day France and Switzerland to present-day central Russia. Because the agricultural communities now were producing surpluses that they could store, residents had to defend their land and resources from encroaching neighbors.

An aggressive culture was taking shape based on violent confrontations between adult males organized in "tribal" groups. War cultures arose in all western European societies. Armed groups carried bell-shaped drinking cups across Europe, using them to swig beer and mead distilled from grains, honey, herbs, and nuts.

Warfare had the effect of accentuating the borrowing among the region's competing peoples. The violent struggles and emerging kinship groups fueled a massive demand for weapons, alcohol, and horses. Warrior elites borrowed from Anatolia the technique of combining copper with tin to produce harder-edged weapons made of the alloy bronze. Soon smiths were producing them in bulk—as evidenced by hoards of copper and bronze tools and weapons from the period found in central Europe. Traders used the rivers of central and northern Europe to exchange their prized metal products, creating one of the first commercial networks that covered the landmass.

THE AMERICAS

In the Americas, techniques of food production and storage, transportation, and communication restricted the surpluses for feeding those who did not work the land. Thus, these communities did not grow in size and complexity. For example, in the Chicama Valley of Peru, which opens onto the Pacific Ocean, people still nestled in small coastal villages to fish, gather shellfish, hunt, and grow beans, chili peppers, and cotton (to make twined textiles, which they dyed with wild indigo). By around 3500 BCE, these fishermen abandoned their cane and adobe homes for sturdier houses, half underground, on streets lined with cobblestones.

Hundreds if not thousands of such villages dotted the seashores and riverbanks of the Americas. Some made the technological breakthroughs required to produce pottery; others devised irrigation systems and water sluices in areas where floods occurred. Some even began to send their fish catches inland in return for agricultural produce. Ceremonial structures highlighted communal devotion and homage to deities, and rituals to celebrate birth, death, and the memory of ancestors.

In the Americas, the largest population center was in the valley of Tehuacán (near modern-day Mexico City). Here the domestication of corn created a food source that enabled people to migrate from caves to a cluster of pit-house villages that supported a growing population. By 3500 BCE, the valley held nothing resembling a large city. People lived in clusters of interdependent villages, especially on the lakeshores: here was a case of high population density, but not urbanization.

SUB-SAHARAN AFRICA

The same pattern occurred in sub-Saharan Africa, where the population grew but did not concentrate in urban communities. About 12,000 years ago, when rainfall and temperatures increased, small encampments of hunting, gathering, and fishing communities congregated around the large lakes and rivers flowing through the region that would later become the Sahara Desert. Large game animals roamed, posing a threat but also providing a source of food. Over the millennia, in the wetter and more temperate locations of this vast region—particularly the upland mountains and their foothills—permanent villages emerged.

As the Sahara region became drier, people moved to the desert's edges, to areas along the Niger River and the Sudan. Here they grew yams, oil palms, and plantains. In the savannah lands that stretched all the way from the Atlantic Ocean in West Africa to the Nile River basin in present-day Sudan, settlers grew grains such as millet and sorghum, which spread from their places of origin to areas along the lands surrounding the Niger River basin. Residents constructed stone dwellings and dug underground wells and food storage areas. As an increasing population strained resources, groups migrated south toward the Congo River and east toward Lake Nyanza, where they established new farms and villages. Although population centers were often hundreds or thousands of miles apart and were smaller than the urban centers in Egypt and Mesopotamia, the widespread use of the same pottery style, with rounded bottoms and wavy decoration, suggests that they maintained trading and cultural contacts. In these respects, sub-Saharan Africa matched the ways of life in Europe and the Americas.

Conclusion

Over the fourth and third millennia BCE, the world's social landscape changed in significant ways. In a few key locations, where giant rivers irrigated fertile lands, complex human cultures began to emerge. These areas experienced all the advantages and difficulties of expanding populations: occupational specialization; social hierarchy; rising standards of living; sophisticated systems of art and science; and centralized production and distribution of food, clothing, and other goods. Ceremonial sites and trading crossroads became cities that developed centralized religious and political systems. As scribes, priests, and rulers labored to keep complex societies together, social distinctions within the city (including the roles of men and women) and the differences between country folk and city dwellers sharpened.

Although river-basin cultures shared basic features, each one's evolution followed a distinctive path. Where there was a single river—the Nile or the Indus—the agrarian hinterlands that fed cities lay along the banks of the waterway. In these areas cities were small; thus, the Egyptian and Harappan worlds enjoyed more political stability and less rivalry. In contrast, cities in the immense floodplain of the Tigris and Euphrates needed large hinterlands to sustain their populations. Because of their growing power and need for resources, Mesopotamian cities vied for preeminence, and their competition often became violent.

In most areas of the world, however, people still lived in simple, egalitarian societies based on hunting, gathering, and basic agriculture—as in the Americas and sub-Saharan Africa. In Anatolia, Europe, and parts of China, regional cultures emerged as agriculture advanced and populations grew. Some of them, as in the Aegean and Europe, forged warrior societies. Beyond these frontiers, farmers and nomads survived as they had for many centuries. Thriving trading networks connected many, but not all, of these regions to one another.

Changes in climate affected everyone and could slow or even reverse development. How—and whether—cultures adapted depended on local circumstances. As the next chapter will show, the human agents of change often came from the fringes of larger settlements and urban areas.

Focus On
Societies in the Great River Basins

Mesopotamia

- Peoples living along the Tigris River and Euphrates River control floodwaters and refine irrigation techniques.

- Mesopotamians establish the world's first large cities, featuring powerful rulers, social hierarchies, and temples (ziggurats) for worship of their gods.

- Mesopotamia is the birthplace of writing.

Egypt

- Peoples of Egypt use Nile River waters to irrigate their lands and create a bountiful agriculture.

- Egyptian rulers known as pharaohs unify their territory, establish a powerful state, and develop a vibrant economy.

- Egyptians build magnificent burial chambers (pyramids), develop hieroglyphic writing, and worship a pantheon of gods.

Indus Valley

- South Asian peoples harness the Indus River and create cities (like Harappa and Mohenjo Daro), as well as a form of writing called Indus Valley script.

- Harappan cities include residential housing and public structures (like baths) with excellent drainage.

- Indus Valley peoples export copper, shells, and carnelian (as well as lapis lazuli and turquoise, from nearby sources) to peoples of Mesopotamia and Egypt.

East Asia

- Peoples dwelling in the basins of the Yellow River and the Yangzi River control the waters' flow and expand agriculture.

- These people develop elaborate cultures, which scholars later label Yangshao and Longshan.

- While agriculture in East Asia does not produce city-states in this period, Longshan peoples leave behind distinctive pottery and jade artifacts, suggesting evidence of regional trade.

CHRONOLOGY

	4000 BCE	3000 BCE
Southwest Asia and Egypt	Earliest Sumerian cities appear in Mesopotamia 3500 BCE ●	First Dynasty emerges in Egypt 3100 BCE ●
South Asia		
East Asia	Yangshao culture thrives along Yellow River 4000–3000 BCE	
Europe and the Mediterranean		
The Americas	Chicama Valley culture thrives on Pacific coast of South America 3500 BCE ● Tehuacán Valley in Mexico thrives 3500 BCE ●	
Inner and Central Asia	Dense village life along many lakes and rivers 3500 BCE ● Spread of nomadic pastoralism begins 3500 BCE ●	

THINKING ABOUT GLOBAL CONNECTIONS

- **Thinking about River-Basin Societies and the Environment** Human interaction with the environment—including climate, geography, the characteristics of the rivers, and the continued cultivation of crops and herds—played a significant role in shaping each early river-basin community. Describe ways that these environmental factors influenced the unique characteristics of each river-basin society.

- **Thinking about Exchange Networks among Early River-Basin Societies** Carnelian from the Indus region buried in elite tombs of Egypt; lapis lazuli from the region of modern-day Afghanistan on necklaces adorning Harappan necks; shell from the Indus floodplain inlaid on Mesopotamian grave goods—these examples provide evidence of how trade in raw

materials bound river-basin societies together in the third millennium BCE. What routes might such goods have traveled? What does this exchange of commodities suggest about other types of exchange that may have been taking place between these river-basin societies?

- **Thinking about Changing Power Relationships in River-Basin Societies** From 3500 to 2000 BCE, as societies developed in the river basins of Mesopotamia, Egypt, South Asia, and East Asia, more intensive cultivation brought agricultural surpluses that ushered in a wide range of impacts. Explain, with examples from each of the river-basin societies, how food surpluses led to job specialization, wealth accumulation, and the resulting social hierarchies.

Key Terms

bronze p. 60

city p. 63

city-state p. 64

river basin p. 57

scribes p. 66

social hierarchies p. 64

urban-rural divide p. 60

 Go to **INQUIZITIVE** to see what you've learned—and learn what you've missed—with personalized feedback along the way.

2000 BCE	1000 BCE

Old Kingdom Egypt 2686–2181 BCE

Sargon's Akkadian territorial state in Mesopotamia 2334–2200 BCE

Cities appear in Indus Valley 2500 BCE

Longshan culture flourishes in Yellow River valley 3000–2000 BCE

Fortified villages in the Aegean 2500 BCE

Stonehenge constructed 2000 BCE

Global Themes and Sources

Early Writing in Context

Agricultural surplus, and the urbanization and labor specialization that accompanied it, likely prompted the earliest development of writing and the profession of the scribes whose job it was to write. Early forms of writing were employed for a variety of purposes, such as keeping economic and administrative records, recording the reigns of rulers, and preserving religious events and practices (for calendars, rituals, and divinatory purposes). By the third millennium BCE, some early societies—Mesopotamia and Egypt, in particular—used writing to produce literature, religious texts, and historical documents.

Different types of writing developed in early societies at different times. Mesopotamians developed the world's first writing (a script called cuneiform) around 3200 BCE, but Egyptians were not far behind, developing their hieroglyphs within a century. Writing systems were not all the same. In some systems, symbols represented words or concepts. In other systems, symbols represented sounds, usually syllables. Some systems changed over time, beginning with symbols representing concepts, but then those symbols became simplified over time to represent the syllables that make up words. And in alphabetic systems, like the much later Phoenician and Greek, symbols are letters that are assembled to create words. Other record keeping did not use written symbols at all; for example, knotted cords formed a type of record keeping as early as 3000 BCE among the peoples of the Andean highlands of South America.

Unsurprisingly, scholars know more about early cultures whose writing has since been deciphered. This decipherment and the ancient texts that made it possible, however, are perhaps more recent than you might think. Cuneiform was cracked in the early nineteenth century (only two hundred years ago), using a text written more than 2,000 years after cuneiform was invented, namely the multilingual Behistun inscription (written in Akkadian, Elamite, and Old Persian)

dating to 522 BCE. Hieroglyphs were also deciphered in the nineteenth century—almost 5,000 years after their inception—thanks to the trilingual Rosetta Stone (in Greek, demotic script, and hieroglyphs), which recorded a Hellenistic royal decree dating to 196 BCE, almost 3,000 years after hieroglyphs were invented. Some forms of writing, like the glyphs of the Maya of Mesoamerica beginning around 250 BCE, are still in the process of being deciphered. Undeciphered scripts, such as the Indus Valley script or Rongorongo of Pacific Islanders, offer intrigue and promise to those who would attempt their decipherment. Yet, even if the writing has been deciphered and the text can be translated by scholars, students encountering these translated texts must work through unfamiliar words, concepts, forms, and even gaps in the texts as preserved, in order to attempt to understand what that text can reveal about the context from which it comes.

Analyzing Early Writing in the Context of River-Basin Societies

- Looking at the examples, what differences or similarities do you notice in letter/symbol forms as well as the objects on which the writing was etched?

- What sorts of topics does each example of early writing address? What do the topics discussed in these texts suggest about the purpose and context for writing in their respective societies?

- To what extent does the type of society (river basin, seafaring, and so on), namely its context, seem to affect the development of writing in that region (date, type, purpose, and so on)?

- How does the fragmentary nature of the texts affect your ability to interpret them? How has the decipherment, or lack thereof, of these scripts affected scholars' understandings of the societies that produced them?

Items Needed to Build Boats

The text offered here was pressed into a clay tablet in cuneiform script during the late third millennium BCE. Found in southern Mesopotamia (Sumer), it describes the materials required to build "Magan boats." Magan was likely situated on the southern shores of the Arabian Peninsula, either in modern Yemen or Oman, although scholars are not certain of its location.

....

- What sorts of materials are listed in this document, and how do you imagine they would be used for the construction of boats?

- What does the form of the document suggest about its context? What kind of document does this appear to be?

- What do the form and contents of the document suggest about the purpose of at least this example of Sumerian writing in cuneiform script?

....

178 large palm trees
1400 large pine(?) trees
36 large tamarisk trees
32 large acacia(?)-trees
10 tamarisk trees, each 3 cubits
276 talents of palm fibre rope
34 talents of palm leaf rope
418 talents of reeds
207 talents of halfa-grass
753(?) ox hides
44 talents, 48 minas of goat hair
1695 litres of fish oil
. . .
4260 bundles of construction-reeds
12324 bundles of fuel(?)-reeds
3170 GUR-measures of purified bitumen

For making watertight the Magan-boats.
From the governor of Girsu.

10 shekels of oil
2 litres of dates
Magan-offerings

via Urabba, messenger

Expenditure
Month xii

Source: British Museum Collection Database. Reg no. 1895,0329.48; BM no. 18390. www.britishmuseum.org/collection. British Museum, Online. Accessed 12/2/2018.

Egyptian Mouth-Opening Ritual

Although writing appeared in Egypt just 100 years after it did in Mesopotamia, the hieroglyphs preserved in the pyramid of Pharaoh Unis (r. 2375–2345 BCE) offer some of the earliest sustained religious writing from Egypt. These pyramid texts, such as the example included here, contain a range of rituals to facilitate the pharaoh's passage into the afterlife.

....

- What gods are mentioned and for what purpose? What materials are mentioned in the text, and how are they used? What repetition do you see in this text?

- How are the gods, materials, and the repetition suggestive of a ritual, or religious, context for the writing?

- Why would ideas like these be inscribed on the walls inside a pyramid?

....

Libation

Osiris, acquire for yourself all those who hate Unis and anyone who speaks bad of his name.
Thoth, go, acquire him for Osiris: get the one who speaks bad of Unis's name; put him in your hand.
Recitation 4 Times: Don't you let loose of him: beware that you not let loose of him.
Libation.

Censing

Someone has gone with his ka;
Horus has gone with his ka; Seth has gone with his ka;
Thoth has gone with his ka; the god has gone with his ka;
Osiris has gone with his ka; Eyes-Forward has gone with his ka;
you too have gone with your ka.
Ho, Unis! Your ka's arm is before you. Ho, Unis! Your ka's arm is after you.

Ho, Unis! Your ka's foot is before you. Ho, Unis! Your ka's foot is after you.

Osiris Unis, I have given you Horus's eye: provide your face with it. Let the scent of Horus's eye disseminate to you.

Recitation 4 times. Incense, fire.

Cleansing the Mouth with Salt Water

These your cool waters, Osiris—these your cool waters, oh Unis—have come from your son, have come from Horus.

I have come having gotten Horus's eye, that your heart may become cool with it; I have gotten it under your feet.

Accept the outflow that comes from you: your heart will not become weary with it.

Recitation 4 Times: Come, you have been invoked.

Cool Water; 2 pellets of natron.

Condensed milk, condensed milk, that parts your mouth, ho, Unis! may you taste its taste in front of those of the gods' booths: the spittle of Horus, condensed milk; the spittle of Seth, condensed milk; the reconciliation of the two gods' hearts, condensed milk.

Recitation 4 Times: Your natron-salt is among Horus's Followers.

5 pellets of Nile-Valley natron of Nekheb.

Your natron is Horus's natron;
   your natron is Seth's natron;
   your natron is Thoth's natron;
   your natron is the god's natron:
   your own natron is amongst them.

Your mouth is the mouth of a milk-calf on the day he is born.

5 Pellets of Delta natron of Shetpet.

Your natron is Horus's natron, your natron is Seth's natron, your natron is Thoth's natron, your natron is the god's natron; your natron is your ka's natron, your natron is your natron's natron: this your own natron is amongst your brothers, the gods.

Your natron is on your mouth: you should clean all your bones and end what is (bad) against you.

Osiris, I have given you Horus's eye: provide your face with it disseminated.

1 Pellet of natron.

The Mouth-Opening Ritual

Ho, Unis! I have fixed your jaws spread for you.

The flint spreader.

Osiris Unis, Let me part your mouth for you.

An ingot of Nile-Valley god's-metal; an ingot of Delta god's-metal.

Unis, accept Horus's eye, which went away: I have gotten it for you that I might put it in your mouth.

Nile-Valley Zrw-salt; Delta Zrw-salt.

Ho, Unis! Accept Osiris's šjkw-mineral.

Šjkw-mineral.

Here is the tip of the breast of Horus's own body: accept (it) to your mouth.

A jug of milk.

Here is the breast of your lactating sister Isis, which you should take to your mouth.

An empty jar.

Giving cool water; taking around.

Here are Horus's two eyes, black

Pyramid of Unis.

and white: take them to your countenance, that they may brighten your face.

A white jar, a black jar; lifting up.

Source: James P. Allen, *Writings of the Ancient World: The Ancient Pyramid Texts* (Atlanta: Society of Biblical Literature, 2005), pp. 19–20.

PRIMARY SOURCE 2.3

Harappan Seals

As early as 2500 BCE, Indus Valley scribes made notations—usually pictorial emblems and five to six signs—on steatite seal stamps, pots, and even jewelry. The seal stamps shown here offer an example of this still-undeciphered script.

Harappan seal stamps.

- What figures can you make out on the seals? What other notations do you see that are suggestive of writing?

- How do you think scholars go about deciphering these figures and notations?

- The only evidence of writing in the mid-third millennium BCE Indus Valley is these seal stamps and a few other short inscriptions (like the one at Dholavira). What does this fact suggest to you about their Harappan context?

Oracle bone.

PRIMARY SOURCE 2.4

Shang Dynasty Oracle Bone

While marks on pots produced by Yangshao peoples (c. 5000 BCE) may have been used for record keeping, the earliest full writing system did not appear in East Asia until the Shang dynasty (1600–1046 BCE). Shang kings used oracle bone predictions—etched on animal bones (like the one pictured here), which were heated until they cracked—to divine the answers to questions about the will of their ancestors and the weather.

- About what topic is this oracle bone attempting to divine an answer? How do you know?

- What is the ritual process of which this writing seems to be a part?

- What do the process of which this writing is a part and the topic about which it inquires suggest to you about the context for writing when it first appeared in East Asia, more than a millennium after its development in Mesopotamia and Egypt?

A partial translation of the left-hand side of this oracle bone reads:

[PREFACE:] Crack making on gui-si day, Que divined:
[CHARGE:] In the next ten days there will be no disaster.
[PROGNOSTICATION:] The king, reading the cracks, said, "There will be no harm; there will perhaps be the coming of alarming news."
[VERIFICATION:] When it came to the fifth day, ding-you, there really was the coming of alarming news from the west. Zhi Guo, reporting, said, "The Du Fang [a border people] are besieging in our eastern borders and have harmed two settlements." The Gong-fang also raided the fields of our western borders.

Source: This translation follows (with slight modifications by Bryan W. Van Norden) David N. Keightley, *Sources of Shang History* (Berkeley: University of California Press, 1978), p. 44.

PRIMARY SOURCE 2.5

Early Greek Writing (Linear B)

The earliest deciphered Greek writing, known as Linear B, did not appear until around 1450 BCE among the Mycenaeans, although other forms of Greek writing developed several hundred years earlier on Crete among the Minoans. The example here comes from the Mycenaean palace at Pylos, on mainland Greece.

- Who and what are mentioned in this text, and what does this suggest about the text's purpose?

- What evidence for the economic context at Pylos in mainland Mycenaean Greece does the text offer?

- How does the fragmentary nature of the text affect your reading of it?

The plot of Qelequhontas: this much seed: 276 l. of wheat

R. slave of the god, holds a lease: so much seed: 12 l. of wheat

W. the priest holds a lease: so much seed: 12 l. of wheat

Thuriatis, female slave of the god, dependant of P. the old man: so much seed: 108 l. of wheat

The plot of Admaos, so much seed: 216 l. of wheat.
. . .

T. slave of the god, holds a lease: so much seed: 32 l. of wheat

The plot of A . . . eus, so much seed: 144 l. of wheat.
. . .

The plot of T. slave of the god, holds a lease: 18 l. of wheat

The plot of R., so much seed: 138 l. of wheat. . . .

The plot of Aktaios, so much seed: 384 l. of wheat.
. . .

Source: M. Ventris and J. Chadwick, *Documents in Mycenaean Greek*, 2nd ed. (Cambridge, England: Cambridge University Press, 1973), doc. 116.

Linear B from Pylos. From the excavated Mycenaean palace at Pylos, this is a typical Linear B document inscribed on clay with linear marks representing syllables and signs.

Interpreting Visual Evidence

Burials and Long-Distance Trade

One of the most intriguing types of evidence from the river-basin societies discussed in this chapter is the elaborate burials of the elite. These burials often contained tremendous wealth in the form of finely crafted items. A number of these items show not only highly specialized artisanship but also evidence of long-distance trade in raw materials among these third-millennium BCE societies.

Consider the types of objects pictured here and the materials used to make them. Queen Hetepheres I of the Fourth Dynasty of Egypt (c. 2550 BCE) was buried at Giza (near Memphis and Saqqara) with silver bracelets decorated with butterflies made of turquois, lapis lazuli, and carnelian. In southern Mesopotamia, Pu-Abi was interred in the magnificent Royal Tombs of Ur (c. 2600–2400 BCE), which contained artifacts such as the Royal Standard of Ur pictured on the first page of this chapter. Among the many items found in Pu-Abi's tomb was a lyre made with lapis lazuli and shell set in bitumen, shown in the second image below. Excavation reports describe this lyre as being found in the arms of a female lyrist who may have been a sacrificial victim at the death of Pu-Abi. Harappan artisans in the Indus River valley used a bow drill to perforate tiny beads in order to craft the necklace shown here from lapis lazuli, carnelian, and other semiprecious stones. Much earlier, around 4000 BCE, at Varna on the coast of the Black Sea (see Map 2.7), an important person from a farming village was buried with 990 gold objects (mostly decorative pieces sewn onto his clothing), as well as the flint daggers, axes, and spearheads; his burial is shown in the final image.

Bracelets of Queen Hetepheres I.

Harp, or "Queen's Lyre," from the Royal Tombs of Ur.

Male warrior burial at Varna.

Questions for Analysis

1. Looking at Map 2.2, where did the raw materials used to make each of the items here come from? Along what trade routes would these raw materials have traveled? What does that suggest about trade between river-basin societies in the third millennium BCE?

2. What does the presence of these highly crafted items in the graves of elite individuals suggest about river-basin societies, especially in terms of wealth accumulation, labor specialization, and the beginnings of social stratification?

3. What does the ability and willingness to bury so much wealth in the dirt suggest about these third-millennium BCE societies, especially as compared with earlier, more subsistence-based hunting and gathering communities?

Harappan gemstone necklace with lapis lazuli and carnelian.

3

Nomads, Territorial States, and Microsocieties

2000–1200 BCE

Around 2200 BCE, the Old Kingdom of Egypt collapsed. The collapse did not occur because of incompetent rulers, of which there were many, or a decline in the arts and sciences, which is evident in unfinished building projects; the Old Kingdom fell because of radical changes in climate—namely, a powerful warming and drying trend that blanketed Afro-Eurasia between 2200 and 2150 BCE. The Mesopotamians and Harappans were as hard hit as the Egyptians.

In Egypt the environmental disaster yielded a series of low floods of the Nile because the usual monsoon rains did not arrive to feed the river's upper regions. With less water to irrigate crops, farmers could not grow enough food for the river basin's million inhabitants. Documents from this period reveal widespread suffering and despair. Consider the following tomb inscription: "All of Egypt was dying of hunger to such a degree that everyone had come to eating his children." Or another: "The tribes of the desert have become Egyptians everywhere. . . . The plunderer is everywhere, and the servant takes what he finds." Herders and pastoral nomads also felt the pinch. As these outsiders pressed upon permanent settlements in search of food, the governing structures in Egypt—and elsewhere, in Mesopotamia and the Indus Valley—broke down.

Chapter Outline

- Nomadic Movement and the Emergence of Territorial States
- The Territorial State in Egypt
- Territorial States in Southwest Asia
- Nomads and the Indus River Valley
- The Shang Territorial State in East Asia
- Microsocieties in the South Pacific and in the Aegean
- Conclusion

Core Objectives

- **EXPLAIN** the relationship between climate change and human settlement patterns in the second millennium BCE.
- **DESCRIBE** the impact of transhumant herders and pastoral nomads on settled communities.
- **COMPARE** the varied processes by which territorial states formed and interacted with each other across Afro-Eurasia.
- **EXAMINE** the development of microsocieties in the South Pacific and the Aegean, and **EXPLAIN** the role geography played in their development.

The pioneering city-states of the third millennium BCE may have created unprecedented differences between elites and commoners, between urbanites and rural folk, but everyone felt the effects of this disaster.

This chapter focuses on two related developments. The first focus is the impact of climate change on the peoples of Afro-Eurasia: famines occurred, followed by political and economic turmoil. The old order gave way as river-basin states in Egypt, Mesopotamia, and the Indus Valley collapsed. Herders and pastoral nomads, driven from grazing areas that were drying up, forced their way into the heartlands of these great states in pursuit of better-watered lands. Once there, they challenged the traditional ruling elites. The nomads also brought with them a new military weapon—the horse-drawn chariot. Nomads and their chariots form the second focus of this chapter, for chariots introduced a type of warfare that would dominate the plains of Afro-Eurasia for a half a millennium. The nomads' advantage proved only temporary, however. Soon the Egyptians, Mesopotamians, Chinese, and many others learned from their chariot-driving conquerors: they assimilated some of their foes into their own societies and drove others away, adopting the invaders' most useful techniques. This chapter also examines worlds apart from the expanding centers of population and politics, where climate change and chariot-driving nomads were shaping world history. The islanders of the Pacific and the Aegean did not interact with one another with such intensity—and therefore their political systems evolved differently. In these locales, microsocieties (small-scale, loosely interconnected communities) were the norm.

Global Storylines

- Climate change and environmental degradation lead to the collapse of river-basin societies.

- Transhumant migrants (with their animal herds in need of pasturage) and pastoral nomads (with their horse-drawn chariots) interact, in both destructive and constructive ways, with settled agrarian societies.

- A fusion of migratory and settled agricultural peoples produce expanded territorial states—in Egypt, Southwest Asia, the Indus River valley, and Shang China—that supplant earlier river-basin societies.

- Microsocieties emerge in the eastern Mediterranean and South Pacific based on expanding populations and increased trade.

Nomadic Movement and the Emergence of Territorial States

As nomads and herders brought new pressures and new technologies to settled communities, innovations in governance spurred the rise of larger, expansionist territorial states. At the end of the third millennium BCE, drought and food shortages led to the overthrow of ruling elites throughout central and western Afro-Eurasia. Walled cities could not defend their hinterlands. Trade routes lay open to predators, and pillaging became a lucrative enterprise. Clans of horse-riding **pastoral nomads**—from the relatively sparsely populated and isolated Inner Eurasian steppes—swept across vast distances, eventually threatening settled people in cities. **Transhumant herders**—who lived closer to agricultural settlements and migrated seasonally to pasture their livestock—also advanced on populated areas in search of food and resources. These migrations of pastoral nomads and transhumant herders occurred across Eurasia, in the Arabian Desert and Iranian plateau in the west, and in the Indus River valley and the Yellow River valley in the east. (See Map 3.1.) Many transhumant herders and nomadic pastoralists settled in the agrarian heartlands of Mesopotamia, the Indus River valley, the highlands of Anatolia, Iran, China, and Europe. After the first wave of newcomers, more migrants arrived by foot or in wagons pulled by draft animals. Some sought temporary work; others settled permanently. They brought horses and new technologies that were useful in warfare; religious practices and languages; and new pressures to feed, house, and clothe an ever-growing population. This millennia-long process is sometimes referred to as **Indo-European migrations**.

The term Indo-European was created by comparative linguists to trace and explain the similarities within the large language family that includes Sanskrit, Hindi, Persian, Greek, Latin, and what would become German and English. Words and concepts that appear in many languages, such as numbering systems and words like *mother*, *father*, and *god*, suggest these so-called Indo-European languages may have had a common origin. For instance, the number one is *eka* (in Sanskrit), *ek* (in Hindi), *hen* (in Greek), *unus* (in Latin), *un* (in French), and *ein* (in German). The word for mother is *mātr* (in Sanskrit), *mātā* (in Hindi), *meter* (in Greek), *mater* (in Latin), *mère* (in French), and *mutter* (in German). A host of demographic, geographic, and other factors shape the movement and development of languages over time. Nonetheless, migrations of the earliest speakers of the Indo-European language group, who carried not only their language but also their technology and culture, are likely part of the story of the spread of pastoralists from the central Eurasian steppe into Europe, Anatolia, Southwest Asia, and South Asia.

Perhaps the most vital breakthroughs that nomadic pastoralists transmitted to settled societies were the harnessing of horses and the invention of

THE BIG PICTURE

What was the relationship between climate change and human settlement patterns in the second millennium BCE?

pastoral nomads
Pastoral peoples who move with their herds in perpetual motion across large areas, like the steppe lands of Inner Eurasia, and facilitate long-distance trade.

transhumant herders
Pastoral peoples who move seasonally from lowlands to highlands, in proximity to city-states, with which they trade the products of their flocks (milk, fur, hides) for urban products (manufactured goods, such as metals).

Indo-European migrations
The migrations, tracked linguistically and culturally, of the peoples of a distinct language group (including Sanskrit, Persian, Greek, Latin, and German) from central Eurasian steppe lands into Europe, Southwest Asia, and South Asia.

The Global View

BALTIC SEA

EUROPE

URAL MOUNTAINS

Dnieper R.

Dniester R.

HUNGARIAN PLAIN

Danube R.

Volga R.

BLACK SEA

Minoan Mycenaean

Hittites

ANATOLIAN PLATEAU

CASPIAN SEA

ARAL SEA

Oxus R.

CENTRAL ASIA

Lake Balkas

PAMIR MTS.

HINDU KUSH MTS.

Tigris R.

Euphrates R.

ZAGROS MTS.

IRANIAN PLATEAU

MEDITERRANEAN SEA

Amorites Hyksos

SOUTHWEST ASIA

Nile R.

Persian Gulf

Indus R.

HIM...

SOUT...

RED SEA

ARABIAN DESERT

ARABIAN SEA

SOUT...

Legend

← Transhumant migrations
← Spread of wheeled vehicles
← Spread of war chariots
← Dispersal of nomads
■ Pastoral nomads, c. 2000–1500 BCE

Southwest Asian Society
■ Zone of urban civilization

0   500   1000 Miles
0   500   1000 Kilometers

Map 3.1 Nomadic Migrations in Afro-Eurasia, 2000–1000 BCE

Many different groups of nomadic peoples were on the move in the second millennium BCE, migrating into many of the regions that had hosted the river-basin-fueled, city-state-filled cultures of the third millennium BCE.

- According to this map, from what specific parts of the world did pastoral peoples migrate? Into what specific areas did they move? What geographical features may have shaped the migrations in terms of the regions left behind, the routes traveled, and the locations traveled to?
- What regions did these migrations bring into closer connection?
- What technological innovations were spread by these migrations, and across what regions did that technology spread?

Lake
Baikal

ALTAI MOUNTAINS

TIEN SHAN
MTS.

TAKLAMAKAN
DESERT

GOBI DESERT

Yellow R.

EAST ASIA

SEA
OF
JAPAN

JAPAN

Yangzi R.

A MOUNTAINS

Ganges R.

dic Peoples

ASIA

SOUTHEAST

ASIA

Bay of
Bengal

Austronesian

SOUTH
CHINA
SEA

PACIFIC

OCEAN

War Chariots *Upper left:* A large vase typical of Mycenaean art on the mainland areas of Greece. Note the presence of the horse-drawn chariot. The possession of this more elaborate means of transport and warfare characterized the warrior elites of Mycenaean society and linked them to developments over wide expanses of Afro-Eurasia at the time. *Upper right:* This wooden chest covered with stucco and painted on all sides with images of the Egyptian pharaoh in his war chariot was found in the fabulously wealthy tomb of Tutankhamun in the Valley of the Kings in Egypt. The war chariot was introduced into Egypt by the Hyksos. By the reign of Tutankhamun in the New Kingdom, depictions of the pharaoh single-handedly smiting the enemy from a war chariot drawn by two powerful horses were common. *Bottom right:* Spoke-wheeled chariot, with two horse skeletons. Six chariots were excavated at Yin Xu near Anyang (capital of the Shang dynasty), five of them with a male skeleton behind the carriage. The Shang fought with neighboring pastoral nomads from the central Asian steppes. To do this, they imported horses from central Asia and copied the chariots of nomads they had encountered. This gave Shang warriors devastating range and speed for further conquest.

chariot

Horse-drawn vehicle with two spoked and metal-rimmed wheels that revolutionized warfare in the second millennium BCE and was made possible through the interaction of pastoralists and settled communities.

the **chariot**, a two-wheeled horse-drawn vehicle used in warfare and later in processions and races. On the vast steppe lands north of the Caucasus Mountains, during the late fourth millennium BCE, settled people had domesticated horses in their native habitat. Elsewhere, as on the northern steppes of what is now Russia, horses were a food source. Only during the late third millennium BCE did people harness horses with cheek pieces and mouth bits in order to facilitate the control of horses and their use for transportation. Parts of horse harnesses made from wood, bone, bronze, and iron, found in tombs scattered across the steppe, reveal the evolution of headgear from simple mouth bits to full bridles with headpiece, mouthpiece, and reins.

Sometime around 2000 BCE, pastoral nomads in the mountains of the Caucasus joined the bit-harnessed horse to the two-wheeled chariot. Various chariot innovations began to unfold: pastoralists lightened chariots so their warhorses could pull them faster; spoked wheels made of special wood bent into circular shapes replaced solid-wood wheels that were heavier and prone to shatter; wheel covers, axles, and bearings (all produced by settled people) were added to the chariots; and durable metal went into the chariot's moving parts. Hooped bronze and, later, iron rims reinforced the spoked wheels. Initially iron was a decorative and experimental metal, and all tools and weapons were bronze. Iron's hardness and flexibility, however, eventually made it more desirable for reinforcing moving parts and protecting wheels, like those on the chariot. Thus, the horse chariots combined innovations by both nomads and settled agriculturalists.

These innovations—combining new engineering skills, metalworking, and animal domestication—revolutionized the way humans made war. The horse chariot slashed travel time between capitals. Slow-moving infantry now ceded to battalions of chariots. Each vehicle carried a driver and an archer and charged into battle with lethal precision and ravaging speed. The mobility, accuracy, and shooting power of warriors in horse-drawn chariots tilted the political balance. After the nomads perfected this type of warfare (by 1600 BCE), they challenged the political systems of Mesopotamia and Egypt, and chariots soon became central to the armies of Egypt, the Assyrians and Persians of Southwest Asia, the Vedic kings of South Asia, the later Zhou rulers in China, and local nobles as far west as Italy, Gaul, and Spain. Only with the development of cheaper armor made of iron (after 1000 BCE) did foot soldiers recover their military importance. And only after states developed cavalry units of horse-mounted warriors did chariots lose their decisive military advantage. For much of the second millennium BCE, then, charioteer elites prevailed in Afro-Eurasia.

For city dwellers in the river basins, the first sight of horse-drawn chariots must have been terrifying, but they quickly understood that war making had changed, and they scrambled to adapt. The pharaohs in Egypt probably copied chariots from nomads or neighbors, and they came to value them highly. For example, the young pharaoh Tutankhamun (r. c. 1336–1327 BCE) was a chariot archer who made sure his war vehicle and other gear accompanied him in his tomb. A century later, the Shang kings of the Yellow River valley, in the heartland of agricultural China, likewise were entombed with their horse chariots.

While nomads and transhumant herders toppled the river-basin cities in Mesopotamia, Egypt, and China through innovations in warfare such as the chariot, the turmoil that ensued sowed seeds for a new type of regime: the territorial state. While Sargon and the Akkadians set up a short-lived territorial state in earlier Mesopotamia (2334–2200 BCE) (see Chapter 2), the martial innovations and political and environmental crises of the early second millennium BCE helped spur more enduring development of territorial states elsewhere. The **territorial state** was a centralized kingdom organized around a charismatic ruler. The new rulers of these territorial states exerted power not only over localized city-states but also over distant hinterlands. They enhanced their stability through rituals for passing the torch of command from one generation to the next. People no longer identified themselves as residents of cities; instead, they felt allegiance to large territories, rulers, and broad linguistic and ethnic communities. These territories for the first time had identifiable borders, and their residents felt a shared identity. Territorial states differed from the city-states that preceded them in that the new territorial states in Egypt, Mesopotamia, and China based their authority on monarchs, widespread bureaucracies, elaborate legal codes, large territorial expanses, definable borders, and ambitions for continuous expansion.

The Territorial State in Egypt

The first of the great territorial states of this period arose from the ashes of chaos in Egypt. The long era of prosperity associated with Old Kingdom Egypt ended when drought brought catastrophe to the area. For several decades the Nile did not overflow its banks, and Egyptian harvests withered. (See Current Trends: Climate Change and the Collapse of River-Basin Societies.) As the pharaohs lost legitimacy and fell prey to feuding among rivals for the throne, regional elites replaced the authority of the centralized state. Egypt, which had been one of the most stable corners of Afro-Eurasia, endured more than a century of tumult before a new order emerged. The pharaohs of the Middle Kingdom and, later, the New Kingdom reunified the river valley and expanded south and north.

RELIGION AND TRADE IN MIDDLE KINGDOM EGYPT (2055–1650 BCE)

Around 2050 BCE, after a century of drought, the Nile's floodwaters returned to normal and crops grew again. In the centuries that followed, pharaohs at Thebes consolidated power in Upper Egypt and began new state-building activity, ushering in a new phase of stability that historians call the Middle Kingdom. The rulers of this era developed Egypt's religious and political institutions in ways that increased state power, creating the conditions for greater prosperity and trade.

Religion and Rule Spiritual and worldly powers once again reinforced each other in Egypt. Gods and rulers together replaced the chaos that people believed had brought drought and despair. Amenemhet I (1985–1955 BCE), first pharaoh of the long-lasting Twelfth Dynasty (1985–1795 BCE), elevated a formerly less significant god, Amun, to prominence. The king capitalized on the god's name, which means "hidden," to convey a sense of his own invisible omnipresence throughout the realm. Because Amun's attributes of air and breath were largely intangible, believers in other gods were able to embrace his cult. Amun's cosmic power appealed to people in areas that had recently been impoverished.

The pharaoh's elevation of the cult of Amun unified the kingdom and brought even more power to Amun and the pharaoh. Consequently, Amun eclipsed all the other gods of Thebes. Merging with the formerly omnipotent sun god Re, the deity now was called Amun-Re: the king of the gods. Because the power of the gods and kings was intertwined, the pharaoh as Amun's earthly champion enjoyed enhanced legitimacy as the supreme ruler.

The massive temple complex dedicated to Amun-Re offers evidence of the gods' and the pharaoh's joint power. Middle Kingdom rulers tapped into their kingdom's renewed bounty, their subjects' loyalty, and the work of untold slaves and commoners to build Amun-Re's temple complex at Thebes (present-day Luxor). For 2,000 years, Egyptians and slaves toiled to erect monumental gates, enormous courtyards, and other structures in what was arguably the largest, longest-lasting public works project ever undertaken. Blending the pastoral ideals of herders into the institutions of their settled and hierarchical territorial state, Middle Kingdom rulers also nurtured a cult of the pharaoh as the good shepherd whose prime responsibility was to care for his human flock. By instituting charities, offering homage to gods at the palace to ensure regular floodwaters, and performing ceremonies to honor their own generosity, the pharaohs portrayed themselves as these shepherds. As a result, the cult of Amun-Re was both a tool of political power and a source of spiritual meaning for Egyptians.

Expanding Trade Networks Prosperity gave rise to an urban class of merchants and professionals who used their wealth and skills to carve out new opportunities for themselves. They indulged in leisure activities such as formal banquets with professional dancers and singers, and they honed their skills in hunting, fowling, and fishing. In a sign of their upward mobility and autonomy, some members of the middle class constructed tombs filled with representations of the material goods they

Hypostyle Hall The precinct of Amun-Re in the Karnak temple complex (near modern-day Luxor) was made up of a series of gates, courts, and temples that were built over time by many pharaohs from the Middle and New Kingdoms. The lofty, inscribed columns of the Great Hypostyle Hall (pictured here), which was built by Ramses II in the thirteenth century BCE, offer stunning evidence of the construction projects that pharaohs built to underscore their power and their relationship to the divine.

Climate Change and the Collapse of River-Basin Societies

The three great river-basin societies discussed in Chapter 2— Egypt, Mesopotamia, and the Indus Valley—collapsed at around the same time. The collapse in Egypt and Mesopotamia was almost simultaneous (roughly between 2200 BCE and 2100 BCE). In contrast, while the collapse was delayed in the Indus Valley for approximately 200 years, when it came, it virtually wiped out the Harappan state and culture. At first, historians

River-Basin Society	Date of Collapse	Climatological Evidence	Archaeological Evidence	Literary Evidence
Egypt	The Old Kingdom collapsed and ushered in a period of notable political instability, the First Intermediate Period (2181–2055 BCE).	Sedimentation studies reveal markedly lower Nile floods and an invasion of sand dunes into cultivated areas.	Many of the sacred sites of the Old Kingdom and much of their artwork are believed to have been destroyed in this period due to political chaos.	An abundant literary record is full of tales of woe. Poetry and steles call attention to famine, starvation, low Nile floods, and even cannibalism.
Mesopotamia	The last effective ruler of the Kingdom of Akkad (2334–2193 BCE) was Naram Sin (r. 2254–2218 BCE).	Around 2100 BCE, inhabitants abruptly abandoned the Haabur drainage basin, whose soil samples reveal marked aridity as determined by the existence of fewer earthworm holes and wind-blown pellets.	Teil Leilan and other sites indicate that the large cities of this region began to shrink around 2200 BCE and were soon abandoned, and remained unoccupied for 300 years.	Later UR III scribes described the influx of northern "barbarians" and noted the construction of a wall, known as the Repeller of the Amorites, to keep these northerners out.
Indus Valley and the Harappan society	Many of the Harappan peoples migrated eastward, beginning around 1900 BCE, leaving this region largely empty of people.	Hydroclimatic reconstructions show that precipitation began to decrease around 3000 BCE, reaching a low in 2000 BCE, at which point the Himalayan rivers stopped incising. Around 1700 BCE, the Ghaggar-Hakra rivers dried up.	Major Harappan urban sites began to shrink in size and lose their urban character between 1900 and 1700 BCE.	No literary source material because the Harappan script has still to be deciphered.

focused on political, economic, and social causes, stressing bad rulers, nomadic incursions, political infighting, population migrations, and the decline of long-distance trade. In more recent times, however, a group of scientists that included paleobiologists, climatologists, sedimentationists, and archaeologists have studied these societies and found convincing evidence that a truly radical change in the climate—a 200-year-long drought spreading across the Afro-Eurasian landmass—was a powerful factor in the collapse of these cultures. But how can these researchers know so much about the climate 4,000 years ago? The following table assembles the evidence for their assertions, drawing on their scholarly studies on Egypt, Mesopotamia, and the Indus Valley.

Questions for Analysis

- Why did more standard historical explanations for the collapse of the large river-basin societies precede the more recent emphases on climate change?
- Why might some scholars resist climate change as being the overwhelming factor contributing to the collapse of these river-basin societies?
- On the basis of your reading, to what extent do you think the evidence for climate change is convincing for all three societies? For which ones is the evidence more persuasive, and for which ones is it less convincing?

Explore Further

Bell, Barbara, "The Dark Ages in Ancient History," *American Journal of Archaeology* 75 (January 1971): 1–26.

Behringer, Wolfgang, *A Cultural History of Climate* (2010).

Butzer, Karl W., "Collapse, Environment, and Society," *Proceedings of the National Academy of Science* 109 (March 2012): 3632–39.

Cullen, H. M., et al., "Climate Change and the Collapse of the Akkadian Empire," *Geology* 28 (April 2000): 379–82.

Giosan, Liviu, et al., "Fluvial Landscapes of the Harappan Civilization," *Proceedings of the National Academy of Science* 109 (June 2012): E1688–94.

Weiss, Max, et al., "The Genesis and Collapse of Third Millennium North Mesopotamian Civilization," *Science*, New Series, 261 (August 20, 1993): 995–1004.

would use in the afterlife as well as the occupations that would engage them for eternity. This new merchant class did not rely on the king's generosity and took burial privileges formerly reserved for the royal family and a few powerful nobles.

As they centralized power and consolidated their territorial state, Egyptians also expanded their trade networks. (See Map 3.2.) Because the floodplains had long since been deforested, the Egyptians needed to import massive quantities of wood by ship. Most prized were the cedars from Byblos (a city in the land soon known as Phoenicia, roughly present-day Lebanon), which were crafted into furniture and coffins. Commercial networks extended south through the Red Sea to present-day Ethiopia and were used to import precious metals, ivory, livestock, slaves, and exotic animals such as panthers and monkeys. Expeditions to the Sinai Peninsula searched for copper and turquoise. Expansion southward into Nubia for gold and other resources continued in the early New Kingdom. As part of Egyptian colonization southward, a series of forts extended as far south as the second cataract of the Nile River (just south of the modern-day border between Egypt and Sudan).

MIGRATIONS AND EXPANDING FRONTIERS IN NEW KINGDOM EGYPT (1550–1070 BCE)

The success of the new commercial networks lured pastoral nomads who were searching for work. Later, chariot-driving Hyksos invaders from Southwest Asia attacked Egypt, setting in motion the events marking the break between what historians call the Middle and New Kingdoms of Egypt. Although the invaders challenged the Middle Kingdom, they also inspired innovations that enabled the New Kingdom to thrive and expand.

Hyksos Invaders Sometime around 1640 BCE, a western Semitic-speaking people, whom the Egyptians called the **Hyksos** ("Rulers of Foreign Lands"), overthrew the unstable Thirteenth Dynasty (toward the end of Egypt's Middle Kingdom period). The Hyksos had mastered the art of horse chariots. Thundering into battle with their war chariots and their superior bronze axes and composite bows (made of wood, horn, and sinew), they easily defeated the pharaoh's foot soldiers. The victorious Hyksos did not destroy the conquered land, but adopted and reinforced Egyptian ways. Ruling as the Fifteenth Dynasty, the Hyksos asserted control over the northern part of the country and transformed the Egyptian military.

After a century of political conflict, an Egyptian who ruled the southern part of the country, Ahmosis (r. 1550–1525 BCE), successfully used the Hyksos weaponry—horse chariots—against the invaders themselves and became pharaoh. This conquest marked the beginning of what historians call New Kingdom Egypt. Hyksos invasions had taught Egyptian rulers that they must

Hyksos
Chariot-driving, axe- and composite-bow-wielding, Semitic-speaking people (their name means "Rulers of Foreign Lands"), who invaded Egypt, overthrew the Thirteenth Dynasty, set up their own rule over Egypt, and were expelled by Ahmosis to begin the period known as New Kingdom Egypt.

Map 3.2 Territorial States and Trade Routes in Southwest Asia, North Africa, and the Eastern Mediterranean, 1500–1350 BCE

Trade in many commodities brought the societies of the Mediterranean Sea and Southwest Asia into increasingly closer contact.

- What were the major trade routes and the major trading states in Southwest Asia, North Africa, and the eastern Mediterranean during this time?
- What were the major trade goods? Which regions appear to have had more, and more unique, resources than the others?
- What did each region need from the others? What did each region have to offer in exchange for the goods it needed?

vigilantly monitor their frontiers, for they could no longer rely on deserts as buffers. Ahmosis assembled large, mobile armies and drove the Hyksos "foreigners" back. Diplomats followed in the army's path, as the pharaoh initiated a strategy of interference in the affairs of Southwest Asian states. Such policies laid the groundwork for statecraft and an international diplomatic system that future Egyptian kings used to dominate the eastern Mediterranean world.

Migrations and invasions introduced new techniques that the Egyptians adopted to consolidate their power. These included bronze working (which the Egyptians had not perfected), an improved potter's wheel, and a vertical loom. South Asian animals such as humped zebu cattle, as well as vegetable and fruit crops, now appeared on the banks of the Nile for the first time. Other significant innovations pertained to war, such as the horse and chariot, the composite bow, the scimitar (a sword with a curved blade), and other weapons from western Eurasia. These weapons transformed the Egyptian army from a standing infantry to a high-speed, mobile, and deadly fighting force. Egyptian troops extended the military frontier as far south as the fourth cataract of the Nile River (in northern modern-day Sudan), and the kingdom now stretched from the Mediterranean shores to Ethiopia.

Expanding Frontiers By the beginning of the New Kingdom, the territorial state of Egypt was projecting its interests outward: it defined itself as a superior, cosmopolitan society with an efficient bureaucracy run by competent and socially mobile individuals. As mentioned above, Egypt expanded its control southward into Nubia, as a source of gold, exotic raw materials, and manpower.

Historians identify this southward expansion most strongly with the reign of Egypt's most powerful woman ruler, Hatshepsut. She served as regent for her young stepson, Thutmosis III, who came to the throne in 1479 BCE when his father—Hatshepsut's half brother and husband—Thutmosis II died. When her stepson was seven years old, Hatshepsut proclaimed herself "king," ruling as co-regent until she died two decades later. During her reign there was little military activity, but trade contacts into the Levant and Mediterranean and southward into Nubia flourished. When he ultimately came to power, Thutmosis III (r. 1479–1425 BCE) launched another expansionist phase, northeastward into

Hatshepsut The only powerful queen of Egyptian pharaonic history was Hatshepsut, seen here in two portraits created during her reign (1479–1458 BCE). In the earlier statue, a young, feminine Hatshepsut wears a masculine headdress and kilt but is labeled in the accompanying inscription as a "perfect goddess" and "daughter of Re." Because a woman on the throne of Egypt would offend the basic principles of order (*ma'at*), Hatshepsut usually portrayed herself as a man, especially late in her reign, as in the second image here. This masculine portrayal was reinforced by the use of male determinatives in the hieroglyphic renditions of her name.

the Levant. The famed Battle of Megiddo, the first recorded chariot battle in history, took place twenty-three years into his reign. Thutmosis III's army at Megiddo, including nearly 1,000 war chariots, defeated his adversaries and established an Egyptian presence in Palestine. The growth phase launched by Thutmosis III would continue for 200 years. Having evolved into a strong, expanding territorial state, Egypt was now poised to engage in commercial, political, and cultural exchanges with the rest of the region.

Territorial States in Southwest Asia

Climatic change and invasions by migrants also transformed the societies of Southwest Asia, and new territorial kingdoms arose in Mesopotamia and Anatolia. Here, as in Egypt, the drought at the end of the third millennium BCE was devastating. Harvests shrank, the price of basic goods rose, and the social order broke down. In southern Mesopotamia, cities were invaded by transhumant herders (not chariot-driving nomads) who sought grazing lands to replace those swallowed up by expanding deserts. A millennium of intense cultivation, combined with severe drought, brought disastrous consequences: rich soil in the river basin was depleted of nutrients; salt water from the Persian Gulf seeped into the marshy deltas, contaminating the water table; and the main branch of the Euphrates River shifted to the west. Many cities lost access to their fertile agrarian hinterlands and withered away. Mesopotamia's center of political and economic gravity shifted northward, away from the silted, marshy deltas of the southern heartland.

As scarcities mounted, transhumant peoples began to press in upon settled communities more closely. Mesopotamian city dwellers were scornful of the rustic migrants, whom they called **Amorites** ("westerners"), invading their cities. While these transhumant herders may have been western "foreigners" to those living in the urban centers of Mesopotamia, they were not strangers. These rural folk had wintered in villages close to the rivers to water their animals, which grazed on fallow fields. In the scorching summer, they retreated to the cooler highlands. Their flocks provided wools, leather, bones, and tendons to the artisan-based industries of the urban centers of Mesopotamia. In return, the herders purchased crafted products and agricultural goods. They also paid taxes, served as warriors, and labored on public works projects, but had few political rights within city-states.

Around 2000 BCE, Amorites from the western desert joined allies from the Iranian plateau to bring down the Third Dynasty of Ur, which had controlled all of Mesopotamia and southwestern Iran for more than a century. These Amorites and their allies founded the Old Babylonian kingdom, centered on the southern Mesopotamian city of Babylon, near modern-day Baghdad. Other territorial states arose in Mesopotamia in the millennium that

Amorites
Name, which means "westerners," used by Mesopotamian urbanites to describe the transhumant herders who began to migrate into their cities in the late third millennium BCE.

followed, sometimes with one dominating the entire floodplain and sometimes with multiple powerful kingdoms vying for territory. As in Egypt, a century of political instability followed the demise of the old city-state models. Here, too, pastoralists played a role in the restoration of order, increasing the wealth of the regions they conquered and helping the cultural realm to flourish. The Old Babylonian kingdom expanded trade and founded territorial states with dynastic ruling families and well-defined frontiers. As we will see, pastoralists also played a key role in the development of territorial kingdoms in Anatolia.

MESOPOTAMIAN KINGSHIP

The new rulers of Mesopotamia changed the organization of the state and promoted a distinctive culture, as well as expanding trade. Herders-turned-urbanite-rulers mixed their own nomadic social organization with that of the once-dominant city-states to create the structures necessary to support much larger territorial states. The basic social organization of the Amorites, out of which the territorial states in Mesopotamia evolved, was tribal (dominated by a ruling chief) and clan based (claiming descent from a common ancestor). Over time, chieftains drew on personal charisma and battlefield prowess to become kings; kings allied with the merchant class and nobility for bureaucratic and financial support; and kingship became hereditary.

Over the centuries, powerful Mesopotamian kings expanded their territories and subdued weaker neighbors, inducing them to pay tribute in luxury goods, raw materials, and manpower as part of a broad confederation of city-states under the kings' protection. Control over military resources (metals for weaponry and, later, herds of horses for pulling chariots) was necessary for dominance. The ruler's charisma also mattered. Unlike the more institutionalized Egyptian leadership, Mesopotamian kingdoms could vacillate from strong to weak, depending on the leader's personality.

The most famous Mesopotamian ruler of this period was Hammurapi (or Hammurabi) (r. 1792–1750 BCE). Continuously struggling with powerful neighbors, he sought to centralize state authority and to create a new legal order. Using diplomatic and military skills to become the strongest king in Mesopotamia, he made Babylon his capital. He implemented a new system to consolidate power, appointing regional governors to manage outlying provinces and to deal with local elites. Like the Egyptian pharaohs of the Middle Kingdom, Hammurapi was shepherd and patriarch of his people, responsible for proper preparation of the fields and irrigation canals and for his followers' well-being. Balancing elite privileges with the needs of the lower classes, the king secured his power. **Hammurapi's Code**, with its "eye-for-an-eye," if/then, reciprocity of crime and punishment, is an example of this balancing act. Its compilation of 282 edicts outlines crimes and their punishments.

Hammurapi's Code The inscription on the shaft of Hammurapi's Code is carved on a diorite stele in the Akkadian language using a beautiful and orderly rendition of cuneiform script. At the top of the stele, which is more than 7 feet tall, the seated sun-god Shamash bestows authority on Hammurapi, illustrating the point of the code's prologue and epilogue, which describe Hammurapi's god-given authority.

The code places an emphasis on the king's control, as divine agent, over public matters; the vital role of the family in orderly relations; and the rights and responsibilities of each social class (free, dependent, and slave). Such an overarching legal code underscored the authority of the king as well as the hierarchies of power within the territorial state.

Power and Culture Mesopotamian rulers commissioned public art and works projects and promoted institutions of learning. The court supported workshops for skilled artisans and schools for scribes, the transmitters of an expanding literary culture. To dispel their image as rustic foreigners and to demonstrate their familiarity with the region's core values, new Mesopotamian rulers valued the oral tales and written records of the earlier Sumerians and Akkadians. Scribes copied the ancient texts and preserved their tradition. Royal hymns portrayed the king as a legendary hero of quasi-divine status.

Heroic narratives about legendary founders, based on traditional stories about the rulers of ancient Uruk, legitimized the new rulers. The most famous tale was the *Epic of Gilgamesh*, one of the earliest surviving works of literature. Originally composed more than a millennium earlier, in the Sumerian language, this epic narrated the heroism of the legendary king of early Uruk, Gilgamesh. This epic is probably best known for the passage in which Gilgamesh seeks out advice from Utnapishtim, the survivor of a terrible flood, in a story that resonates with that of Noah from Genesis in the Hebrew scriptures. Utnapishtim's flood story, however, is just one part of Gilgamesh's epic, which describes the title character's rivalry and, later, friendship with Enkidu and his quest for immortality after his friend Enkidu's death. Preserved by scribes in royal courts through centuries, the epic offers an example of how the Mesopotamian kings invested in cultural production to explain important political relations, unify their people, and distinguish their subjects from those of other kingdoms.

Trade and the Rise of a Private Economy Another feature of the territorial state in Mesopotamia was its shift away from economic activity dominated by the city-state and toward independent private ventures. Mesopotamian rulers designated private entrepreneurs rather than state bureaucrats to collect taxes. People paid taxes in the form of commodities such as grain, vegetables, and wool, which the entrepreneurs exchanged for silver. They, in turn, passed on the silver to the state after pocketing a percentage for their profit. This process generated more private economic activity and wealth, and more revenues for the state.

Mesopotamia was a crossroads for caravans leading east and west. Peace and good governance allowed trade to flourish. The ability to move exotic foodstuffs, valuable minerals, textiles, and luxury goods across Southwest

Hammurapi's Code
Legal code created by Hammurapi (r. 1792–1750 BCE). The code divided society into three classes—free, dependent, and slave—each with distinct rights and responsibilities.

Gilgamesh in Image and Text (*Left*) This terra-cotta plaque is one of the few visual depictions of Gilgamesh (on the left wielding the knife) and his sidekick, Enkidu. It illustrates one of the episodes in their shared adventures, the killing of Humwawa, the monster of the Cedar Forest. The style of the plaque indicates that it was made during the Old Babylonian period, between 2000 and 1600 BCE. (*Right*) The text of the Gilgamesh epic was preserved on tablets of baked clay, like the now-fragmentary tablets shown here, which were found in the seventh-century BCE library of the Neo-Assyrian king Ashurbanipal. The *Epic of Gilgamesh* had enduring appeal for those in Mesopotamia, who passed the story along for millennia, first orally, then in images like the one here, then in text.

Asia won Mesopotamian merchants and entrepreneurs a privileged position as middlemen. Merchants also used sea routes for trade with the Indus Valley. Before 2000 BCE, mariners had charted the waters of the Red Sea, the Gulf of Aden, the Persian Gulf, and much of the Arabian Sea. And during the second millennium BCE, shipbuilders figured out how to construct larger vessels and rig them with towering masts and woven sails—creating seaworthy craft that could carry bulkier loads. Shipbuilding required wood (particularly cedar from Phoenicia) as well as wool and other fibers (from the pastoral hinterlands) for sails. Such reliance on imported materials reflected a growing regional economic specialization and an expanding sphere of interaction across western Afro-Eurasia. The benefits and risks of trade in Mesopotamia are evident from royal edicts of debt annulment (to help merchants who had overstretched) and formalized commercial rules governing taxes and duties. In trade and other exchanges, Mesopotamia became a crucial link between Egypt, Anatolia, and southwestern Iran. Centralized control of the region facilitated a thriving trade in such precious commodities as horses, chariots, and lapis lazuli, which was exchanged for gold, wood, and ivory.

THE OLD AND NEW HITTITE KINGDOMS (1800–1200 BCE)

Chariot warriors known as the Hittites established territorial kingdoms in Anatolia, to the northwest of Mesopotamia. Anatolia (modern-day Turkey) was an overland crossroads that linked the Black and Mediterranean Seas.

Like other plateaus of Afro-Eurasia, it had high tablelands, was easy to traverse, and was hospitable to large herding communities. During the third millennium BCE, Anatolia had become home to numerous communities run by native elites. These societies combined pastoral ways of life, agriculture, and urban commercial centers. Before 2000 BCE, peoples speaking Indo-European languages began to enter the plateau, probably coming from the steppe lands north and west of the Black Sea. The newcomers lived in fortified settlements and often engaged in regional warfare, and their numbers grew. Splintered into competing clans, they fought for regional supremacy. They also borrowed extensively from the cultural developments of the Southwest Asian urban cultures, especially those of Mesopotamia.

In the early second millennium BCE, the chariot warrior groups of Anatolia grew powerful on the commercial activity that passed through their region. Chief among them were the **Hittites**. Hittite lancers and archers rode chariots across vast expanses to plunder their neighbors and demand taxes and tribute. In the seventeenth century BCE, the Hittite leader Hattusilis I unified these chariot aristocracies, secured his base in Anatolia, defeated the kingdom that controlled northern Syria, and then campaigned along the Euphrates River, even sacking Babylon in 1595 BCE. The Hittites ultimately built their capital at Hattusa, in central Anatolia, complete with massive walls, a monumental gate with lions carved into it, multiple temples and granaries, and a palace. Near Hattusa, the rock-cut sanctuary of Yazilikaya contains reliefs of gods and goddesses marching in procession, as well as images of Hittite kings.

Two centuries after the successes of Hattusilis I, the Hittites enjoyed another period of political and military success. In 1274 BCE, they fought the Egyptians at the Battle of Qadesh (in modern Syria), the largest and best-documented chariot battle of antiquity. Both sides claimed victory. The treaty that records reciprocal promises of nonaggression by the Egyptians and Hittites nearly fifteen years after the battle is the oldest surviving peace treaty, and a replica of it is displayed at the United Nations. Soon after Qadesh, the Egyptian forces withdrew from the region. Hittite control—spanning from Anatolia across the region between the Nile and Mesopotamia—was central to balancing power among the territorial states that grew up in the river valleys.

A COMMUNITY OF MAJOR POWERS (1400–1200 BCE)

Between 1400 and 1200 BCE, the major territorial states of Southwest Asia and Egypt perfected instruments of international diplomacy. A cache of 350 letters, referred to by modern scholars as the Amarna letters after the present-day Egyptian village of Amarna, where they were discovered, offers intimate views of the interactions among the powers of Egypt and Southwest Asia. The letters include communications between Egyptian pharaohs and various leaders of

Hittites

An Anatolian chariot warrior group that spread east to northern Syria, though they eventually faced weaknesses in their own homeland. Rooted in their capital at Hattusa, they interacted with contemporary states both violently (as at the Battle of Qadesh against Egypt) and peacefully (as in the correspondence of the Amarna letters).

Southwest Asia, including Babylonian and Hittite kings. The leaders of these powers settled their differences through treaties and diplomatic negotiations rather than on the battlefield. Each state knew its place in the political pecking order. It was an order that depended on constant diplomacy, based on communication, treaties, marriages, and the exchange of gifts. As nomadic peoples combined with settled urban polities to create new territorial states in Egypt, Mesopotamia, and Anatolia, and as those territorial states came into contact with one another through trade, this diplomacy was vital to maintaining the interactions in this community of major powers in Southwest Asia.

Nomads and the Indus River Valley

Compared with those in Egypt and Mesopotamia, territorial states emerged more slowly in the Indus River valley. Late in the third millennium BCE, drought ravaged the Indus River valley as it did other regions. By 1700 BCE, the population of the old Harappan heartland had plummeted. Here, too, around 1500 BCE, yet another group of nomadic peoples, calling themselves Aryans ("respected ones"), emerged from their homelands in the steppes of Inner Eurasia. In contrast with developments in Egypt, Anatolia, and Mesopotamia, these pastoral nomads did not immediately establish large territorial states. Crossing the northern highlands of central Asia through the Hindu Kush, they descended into the fertile Indus River basin (see Map 3.3) with large flocks of cattle and horses. They sang chants from the Rig-Veda as they sacrificed some of their livestock to their gods. Known collectively as the Vedas ("knowledge"), these hymns served as the most sacred texts for the newcomers, who have been known ever since as the **Vedic peoples**. Sanskrit, the spoken language of the Vedic peoples, is one of the earliest known Indo-European languages and a source for virtually all the European languages, including Greek, Latin, English, French, and German.

Like other nomads from the northern steppe, Vedic peoples brought domesticated animals—especially horses, which pulled their chariots and established their military superiority. Not only were they superb horse charioteers, but they were also masters of copper and bronze metallurgy and wheel making. Their expertise in these areas allowed them to produce the very chariots that transported them into their new lands.

The Vedic peoples were deeply religious. They worshipped a host of deities, the most powerful of which were the sky god and the gods that represented horses. They were confident that their chief god, Indra (the deity of war), was on their side. The Vedic peoples also brought elaborate rituals of worship, which set them apart from the indigenous populations. Perhaps the most striking of these was the year-long Ashvamedha, a ritual that culminated in an elaborate horse sacrifice that reinforced the power and territorial claims of the

Map labels:
BLACK SEA
HITTITES
MEDITERRANEAN SEA
MITANNI
SEMITIC LANGUAGES
CASPIAN SEA
ARAL SEA
Tigris R.
Euphrates R.
Persian Gulf
RED SEA
Nile R.
PROTO-INDO-IRANIANS
HINDU KUSH MTS.
HIMALAYA MOUNTAINS
Indus R.
INDO-ARYAN/VEDIC
Ganges R.
DECCAN PLATEAU
DRAVIDIAN
ARABIAN SEA
Bay of Bengal
INDIAN OCEAN

0   500   1000 Miles
0   500   1000 Kilometers

Suggested Indo-European homeland, 3rd millennium BCE
Spread of Indo-European speakers, 2nd millennium BCE
Indo-European speakers, 2nd millennium BCE

Map 3.3 Indo-European Migrations, Second Millennium BCE

One of the most important developments of the second millennium BCE was the movement of Indo-European peoples.

- Where did the Indo-European migration originate?
- Where did Indo-European migrations spread to during this time?
- How do these migrations relate to the Afro-Eurasian developments that are traced in this chapter?

Indra with Buddha The Vedic peoples worshipped their gods by sacrificing and burning cows and horses and by singing hymns and songs, but they never built temples or sculpted idols. Therefore, we do not know how they envisioned Indra and their other gods. However, when Buddhists started to make images of Buddha in the early centuries CE, they also sculpted Indra and other Vedic deities. This image of Indra riding his elephant, Airavata, dates to the second century BCE and was found in Bhaja Cave 19 on the northwest coast of India.

leader. As with many Afro-Eurasian migrations, the outsiders' arrival led to fusion as well as to conflict. While the native-born peoples eventually adopted the newcomers' language, the newcomers themselves took up the techniques and rhythms of agrarian life. The Vedic peoples used the Indus Valley as a staging area for migrations throughout the northern plain of South Asia. As they mixed agrarian and pastoral ways and borrowed technologies (such as ironworking) from farther west, their population expanded and they began to look for new resources. With horses, chariots, and iron tools and weapons, they marched south and east. By 1000 BCE, they reached the southern foothills of the Himalayas and began to settle in the Ganges River valley. Five hundred years later, they had settlements as far south as the Deccan plateau.

Each wave of occupation involved violence, but the invaders did not simply dominate the indigenous peoples. Instead, the confrontations led them to embrace many of the ways of the vanquished. In particular, the Vedic newcomers were impressed with inhabitants' farming skills and knowledge of seasonal weather. These they adapted even as they continued to expand their territory. They moved into huts constructed from mud, bamboo, and reeds. They refined the already-sophisticated production of beautiful carnelian stone beads, and they further aided commerce by devising standardized weights. In addition to raising domesticated animals, they sowed wheat and rye on the Indus plain, and they learned to plant rice in the marshy lands of the Ganges River valley. Later they mastered the use of plows with iron blades, an innovation that transformed the agrarian base of South Asia. This turn to settled agriculture was a major shift for the nomadic pastoral Vedic peoples. After all, their staple foods had always been dairy products and meat, and they were used to measuring their wealth in livestock (horses were most valuable, and cows were more valuable than sheep). Moreover, because they could not breed their prized horses in South Asia's semitropical climate, they initiated a brisk import trade from central and Southwest Asia.

As the Vedic peoples filled the relative void left by the collapse of the Harappans and adapted to their new environment, their initial political organization took a somewhat different course from that of Southwest Asia. Whereas competitive kingdoms dominated the landscape in Southwest Asia, competitive and balanced regimes were slower to emerge in South Asia. The result was a slower process of political integration.

The Shang Territorial State in East Asia

China's first major territorial state combined features of earlier Longshan culture with new technologies and religious practices. Climatic change affected East Asia much as it had central and Southwest Asia. Stories supposedly written on bamboo strips and later collected into what historians call the "Bamboo Annals" tell of a time at the end of the legendary Xia dynasty when the sun dimmed, frost and ice appeared in summer, and a long drought followed heavy rainfall and flooding. According to Chinese mythology, the first ruler of the Shang dynasty defeated a despotic Xia king and then offered to sacrifice himself so that the drought would end. This leader, Tang, survived to found the territorial state called Shang around 1600 BCE in northeastern China.

The Shang state was built on four elements that the Longshan peoples had already introduced: a metal industry based on copper; pottery making; walled towns; and divination using animal bones. To these Longshan foundations, the Shang dynasty added hereditary rulers whose power derived from their relation to ancestors and gods; written records; large-scale metallurgy (especially in bronze); tribute; and various rituals.

STATE FORMATION

A combination of these preexisting Longshan strengths and Shang innovations produced a strong Shang territorial state and a wealthy and powerful elite, noted for its intellectual achievements and aesthetic sensibilities.

Shang kings used a personalized style of rule, making regular trips around the country to meet, hunt, and conduct military campaigns. With no rival territorial states on its immediate periphery, the Shang state did not create a strongly defended, permanent capital, but rather moved its capital as the frontier expanded and contracted. Bureaucrats used written records to oversee the large and expanding population of the Shang state.

Advanced Shang metalworking—the beginnings of which appeared in northwestern China at pre-Shang sites dating as early as 1800 BCE—was vital to the Shang territorial state. Shang bronze work included weapons, fittings for chariots, and ritual vessels. Because copper and tin were available from the North China plain, only short-distance trade was necessary to obtain the resources that a bronze culture needed. (See Map 3.4.) Shang bronze-working technique involved the use of hollow clay molds to hold the molten metal alloy, which, when removed after the liquid had cooled and solidified, produced firm bronze objects. The casting of modular components that artisans could assemble later promoted increased production and permitted the elite to make

> ### Core Objectives
>
> **COMPARE** state formation in Shang China and in Mesopotamia and Egypt.

Map legend:

- ★ Shang capital
- **WEI** Shang vassal state
- Ren Hostile people
- ● Horse chariot burial
- ▬ Copper source
- ▬ Tin source
- ⚘ Oracle bones
- ⬭ Limit of Shang bronze working

Map labels: Yellow R., Di (Gui), BAIYU SHAN MTS., Yanjing Rong, Dongyi, GUANGXING, WANG, Yuwu Rong, ★ Geng, HUO, Di (Gui), Xiang, Yin, TAI SHAN MTS., YELLOW SEA, Quanrong (Kunyi), Peng, Wei, DANG, Fang, Chaoge, Cao Rong, WEI, Ren, Qiang, ★ Ao?, Bo? ★, Xu-yi, Rong, Bo? ★, Huai-yi, Luhun, ZHOU, QIN LING MTS., DABA SHAN MTS., DABIE SHAN MTS., SHANG CHINA, Yangzi R., EAST CHINA SEA

Scale: 0 100 200 300 Miles / 0 100 200 300 Kilometers

Map 3.4 Shang Dynasty in East Asia

The Shang state was one of the most important and powerful of early Chinese dynasties.

- Based on your analysis of this map, what raw materials were the most important to the Shang state?
- How were the deposits of these raw materials distributed across Shang territory and beyond? How might that distribution have shaped the area marked on the map as the limit of Shang bronze working?
- Locate the various Shang capitals. Why do you think they were located where they were?

extravagant use of bronze vessels for burials. The bronze industry of this period shows the high level not only of material culture (in the practical function of the physical objects) but also of cultural development (in the aesthetic sense of beauty and taste conveyed by the choice of form). Since Shang metalworking required extensive mining, it necessitated a large labor force, efficient casting, and a reproducible artistic style. Although the Shang state highly valued its artisans, it treated its copper miners as lowly tribute laborers. By controlling access to tin and copper and to the production of bronze, Shang kings prevented their rivals from forging bronze weapons and thus increased their own power and legitimacy. With their superior weapons, Shang armies by 1300 BCE could easily destroy armies wielding wooden clubs and stone-tipped spears.

Chariots entered the Central Plains of China with nomads of the north around 1200 BCE, much later than their appearance in Egypt and Southwest Asia. They were quickly adopted by the upper classes. Chinese chariots were larger (fitting three men standing in a box mounted on eighteen- or twenty-six-spoke wheels) and much better built than those of their neighbors. As symbols of power and wealth, they were often buried with their owners. Yet, unlike elsewhere in Afro-Eurasia, they were at first little used in warfare during the Shang era, perhaps because of the effectiveness and shock value of large Shang infantry forces, composed mainly of foot soldiers armed with axes, spears, arrowheads, shields, and helmets, all made of bronze. In Shang China, the chariot was used primarily for hunting and as a mark of high status. Shang metalworking and the incorporation of the chariot gave the Shang state a huge advantage and unprecedented power over its neighbors.

AGRICULTURE AND TRIBUTE

The Shang dynastic rulers also understood the importance of agriculture for winning and maintaining power, so they did much to promote its development. The activities of local governors and the masses revolved around agriculture. Rulers controlled their own farms, which supplied food to the royal family, craftworkers, and the army. Farmers drained low-lying fields and cleared forested areas to expand the cultivation of millet, wheat, barley, and possibly rice. Their tools included stone plows, spades, and sickles. Farmers also cultivated silkworms and raised pigs, dogs, sheep, and oxen. Thanks to the twelve-month, 360-day lunar calendar developed by Shang astrologers, farmers were better able to track the growing season. By including leap months, this calendar maintained the proper relationship between months and seasons, and it relieved fears about solar and lunar eclipses by making them predictable.

The ruler's wealth and power depended on tribute from elites and allies. Elites supplied warriors and laborers, horses and cattle. Allies sent foodstuffs, soldiers, and workers and "assisted in the king's affairs"—perhaps by hunting, burning brush, or clearing land—in return for his help in defending against

Bronze At the height of the Shang state, circa 1200 BCE, its rulers erected massive palaces at the capital of Yin, which required bronze foundries for its wine and food vessels. In these foundries, skilled workers produced bronze weapons and ritual objects and elaborate ceremonial drinking and eating vessels, like the one pictured.

invaders and making predictions about the harvest. Commoners sent their tribute to the elites, who held the land as grants from the king. Farmers transferred their surplus crops to the elite landholders (or to the ruler if they worked on his personal landholdings) on a regular schedule. Tribute could also take the form of turtle shells and cattle scapulas (shoulder blades), which the Shang used for divination by means of oracle bones (see below). Divining the future was a powerful way to legitimate royal power—and then to justify the right to collect more tribute. By placing themselves symbolically and literally at the center of all exchanges, the Shang kings reinforced their power over others.

SOCIETY AND RITUAL PRACTICE

The advances in metalworking and agriculture gave the state the resources to sustain a complex society, in which religion and rituals reinforced the social hierarchy. The core organizing principle of Shang society was familial descent traced back many generations to a common male ancestor. Grandparents, parents, sons, and daughters lived and worked together and held property in common, but male family elders took precedence. Women from other male family lines married into the family and won honor when they became mothers, particularly of sons.

The death ritual, which involved sacrificing humans to join the deceased in the next life, reflected the importance of family, male dominance, and social hierarchy. Members of the royal elite were often buried with their full entourage, including wives, consorts, servants, chariots, horses, and drivers. The inclusion of personal slaves and servants indicates a belief that the familiar social hierarchy would continue in the afterlife. An impressive example of the burial practices of the Shang elite is the tomb of an exceptional prominent woman, Fu Hao (also known as Fu Zi), who was consort to the king, a military leader in her own right, and a ritual specialist. She was buried with a wide range of objects made from bronze and jade (including weapons), ivory, pottery, cowrie shells that were used as currency, and a large cache of oracle bones, as well as six dogs and sixteen humans who appear to have been sacrificed to accompany her at death.

The Shang state was a full-fledged theocracy: it claimed that the ruler at the top of the hierarchy derived his authority through guidance from ancestors and gods. Shang rulers practiced ancestral worship, which was the major form of religious belief in China during this period. Ancestor worship involved performing rituals in which the rulers offered drink and food to their recently dead ancestors with the hope that they would intervene with their more powerful long-dead ancestors on behalf of the living. Divination was the process by which Shang rulers communicated with ancestors and foretold the future by means of **oracle bones**. Diviners applied intense heat to the shoulder bones of cattle or to turtle shells and interpreted the cracks

oracle bones
Animal bones inscribed, heated, and interpreted by Shang ritual specialists to determine the will of the ancestors.

that appeared on these objects as auspicious or inauspicious signs from the ancestors regarding royal plans and actions. On these so-called oracle bones, scribes subsequently inscribed the queries asked of the ancestors to confirm the diviners' interpretations. Thus, Shang writing began as a dramatic ritual performance in which the living responded to their ancestors' oracular signs.

The oracle bones and tortoise shells offer a window into the concerns and beliefs of the elite groups of these very distant cultures. The questions put to diviners most frequently as they inspected bones and shells were about the weather, hardly surprising in communities so dependent on growing seasons and good harvests; about family health and well-being; and especially about the prospects of having male children, who would extend the family line.

In Shang theocracy, because the ruler was the head of a unified clergy and embodied both religious and political power, no independent priesthood emerged. Diviners and scribes were subordinate to the ruler and the royal pantheon of ancestors he represented. Ancestor worship sanctified Shang control and legitimized the rulers' lineage, ensuring that the ruling family kept all political and religious power. Because the Shang gods were ancestral deities, the rulers were deified when they died and ranked in descending chronological order. Becoming gods at death, Shang rulers united the world of the living with the world of the dead.

SHANG WRITING

In the process of scribes' and priests' using their script on oracle bones for the Shang king, the formal character-based writing of East Asia developed over time. So although Shang scholars did not invent writing in East Asia, they perfected it. Evidence for writing in this era comes entirely from oracle bones, which were central to political and religious authority under the Shang. Other written records may have been on materials that did not survive. This accident of preservation may explain the major differences between the ancient texts in China (primarily divinations on bones) and in the Southwest Asian societies that impressed cuneiform on clay tablets (primarily for economic transactions, literary and religious documents, and historical records). In comparison with the development of writing in Mesopotamia and Egypt, the transition of Shang writing from record keeping (for example, questions to ancestors, lineages of rulers, or economic transactions) to literature (for example, myths about the founding of states) was slower. Shang rulers initially monopolized writing through their scribes, who positioned the royal families at the top of the social and political hierarchy. And priests wrote on the oracle bones to address the otherworld and gain information about the future so that the ruling family would remain at the center of the political system.

As Shang China cultivated developments in agriculture, ornate bronze metalworking, and divinatory writing on oracle bones, the state did not face the repeated waves of pastoral nomadic invaders seen in other parts of Afro-Eurasia. It was nonetheless influenced by the chariot culture that eventually filtered into East Asia. Given that so many of the developments in Shang China bolstered the authority of the dynastic rulers and elite, it is perhaps not surprising that the chariot in China was initially more a marker of elite status than an effective tool for warfare.

Microsocieties in the South Pacific and in the Aegean

As environmental circumstances drove pastoral nomads and transhumant herders toward settled agriculturalists, leading ultimately to the development of powerful and somewhat intertwined territorial states in Egypt, Southwest Asia, the Indus River valley, and Shang China, other pressures drove migrations across the South Pacific and Aegean. These maritime migrations led to the development after 2000 BCE, in such places as Austronesia and the Aegean, of **microsocieties**: small-scale, fragmented, and dispersed communities that had limited interaction with others.

THE SOUTH PACIFIC (2500 BCE–400 CE)

Austronesian-speaking peoples with origins in coastal South China migrated into the South Pacific and formed microsocieties there. While the precise date for the beginning of these migrations is debated among scholars, the proliferation of peoples across the South Pacific was well under way by the third millennium BCE. Using their double-outrigger canoes, which were 60 to 100 feet long and bore huge triangular sails, the early Austronesians crossed the Taiwan Straits and colonized key islands in the Pacific. Their vessels were much more advanced than the simple dugout canoes used in inland waterways. In good weather, double-outrigger canoes could cover more than 120 miles in a day. The invention of a stabilization device for deep-sea sailing sometime after 2500 BCE triggered further Austronesian expansion into the Pacific. By 400 CE, these nomads of the sea had reached most of the islands of the South Pacific. Their seafaring skills enabled the Austronesians to monopolize trade wherever they went.

By comparing the vocabularies and grammatical features of languages spoken today by the remaining tribal peoples in Taiwan, the Philippines, and Indonesia, scholars have traced the ancient Austronesian-speaking peoples back to coastal South China in the fourth millennium BCE. Pottery, stone tools, and domesticated crops and pigs also provide markers for tracking Austronesian settlements throughout the coastal islands and in the South Pacific. According

Core Objectives

EXAMINE the development of microsocieties in the South Pacific and the Aegean, and **EXPLAIN** the role geography played in their development.

microsocieties
Small-scale, fragmented communities that had little interaction with others. These communities were the norm for peoples living in the Americas and islanders in the Pacific and Aegean from 2000 to 1200 BCE.

Austronesian Canoe Early Austronesians crossed the Taiwan Straits and colonized key islands in the Pacific using double-outrigger canoes from 60 to 100 feet long equipped with triangular sails. In good weather, such canoes could cover more than 120 miles in a day. This relief, from Borobudur, a later Buddhist temple in Java, shows an eighth-century ce depiction of a double-outrigger canoe.

to archaeologists, the same cultural features had spread from Taiwan to the Philippines (by 2500 BCE), to Java and Sumatra (by 2000 BCE), and to parts of Australia and New Guinea (by 1600 BCE). The Austronesians then ventured farther eastward into the South Pacific, apparently arriving in Samoa and Fiji in 1200 BCE and on mainland Southeast Asia in 1000 BCE. (See Map 3.5.) The Austronesians reached the Marquesas Islands, strategically located for northern and southern exploration, in the central Pacific around 200 CE. Over the next few centuries, some moved on to Easter Island to the south and Hawaii to the north. The immense 30-ton stone structures on Easter Island represent the monumental Polynesian architecture produced after their arrival.

Equatorial lands in the South Pacific have a tropical or subtropical climate and, in many places, fertile soils containing nutrient-rich volcanic ash. In this environment the Austronesians cultivated dry-land crops (yams and sweet potatoes), irrigated crops (more yams, which grew better in paddy fields or in rainy areas), and tree crops (breadfruit, bananas, and coconuts). In addition, colonized areas beyond the landmass, such as the islands of Indonesia, had labyrinthine coastlines rich in maritime resources, including coral reefs and mangrove swamps teeming with wildlife. Island-hopping led the adventurers to encounter new food sources, but the shallow waters and reefs offered sufficient fish and shellfish for their needs.

In the South Pacific, the Polynesian descendants of the early Austronesians shared a common culture, language, technology, and stores of domesticated plants and animals. These later seafarers came from many different island communities (hence the name *Polynesian*, "belonging to many islands"), and after

Map 3.5 Austronesian Migrations

The Pacific Ocean saw many migrations from East Asia.

- Where did the Austronesian migrants come from? What were the boundaries of their migration? Trace the stages of Austronesian migration over time. Why do you think these migrations took place over such a long time period?
- Why, unlike other migratory people during the second millennium BCE, did Austronesian settlers in Polynesia become a world apart?

they settled down, their numbers grew. Their crop surpluses allowed more densely populated communities to support craft specialists and soldiers. Most settlements boasted ceremonial buildings to promote local solidarity and forts to provide defense. On larger islands, communities often cooperated and organized workforces to enclose ponds for fish production and to build and maintain large irrigation works for agriculture. In terms of political structure, Polynesian communities ranged from tribal or village units to multi-island alliances that sometimes invaded other areas.

The expansion of East Asian peoples throughout the South Pacific and their trade back and forth, however, did not integrate the islands into the mainland culture. Expansion could not overcome the tendency of these Austronesian microsocieties, dispersed across a huge ocean, toward fragmentation and isolation.

THE AEGEAN WORLD (2000–1200 BCE)

In the region around the Aegean Sea (the islands and the mainland of present-day Greece), no single power emerged before the second millennium BCE, but island microsocieties (the Minoans and the Mycenaeans) developed an expanding trade network and distinctive cultures. Settled agrarian communities were linked only by trade and culture. Fragmentation was the norm—in part because the landscape had no great river-basin systems or large common plain. In its fragmentation, the island world of the eastern Mediterranean initially resembled that of the South Pacific.

As an unintended benefit of the lack of centralization, there was no single regime to collapse when the droughts arrived. Thus, in the second millennium BCE, peoples of the eastern Mediterranean did not struggle to recover lost grandeur. Rather, they enjoyed a remarkable though gradual development, making advances based on influences they absorbed from Southwest Asia, Egypt, and Europe. Residents of Aegean islands like Crete and Thera enjoyed extensive trade with the Greek mainland, Egypt, Anatolia, Syria, and Palestine. It was also a time of population movements from the Danube region and central Europe into the Mediterranean. Groups of these migrants settled in mainland Greece in the centuries after 1900 BCE; modern archaeologists have named them Mycenaeans after their famous palace at Mycenae. Soon after settling in their new environment, the Mycenaeans turned to the sea to look for resources and interaction with their neighbors.

At the outset, the main influence on the Aegean world came from the east by sea. As the institutions and ideas that had developed in Southwest Asia moved westward, they found a ready reception along the coasts and on the islands of the Mediterranean. Trade was the main source of eastern influences, with vessels carrying cargoes from island to island and up and down the commercial centers along the coast. (See Map 3.6.) Mediterranean trade centered on tin from the east and readily available copper, both essential for making bronze (the primary metal in tools and weapons). Islands such as Cyprus and Crete, located in the midst of the active sea-lanes, flourished. Cyprus had large reserves of copper ore, which started to generate intense activity around 2300 BCE. By 2000 BCE, harbors on the southern and eastern sides of the island were shipping and transshipping goods, along with copper ingots, as far west as Crete, east to the Euphrates River, and south to Egypt.

Minoan Culture Crete, too, was an active trading node in the Mediterranean, and its culture reflected outside influences as well as local traditions. Around 2000 BCE, a large number of independent palace centers began to emerge on Crete, at Knossos (ultimately the most impressive of them) and elsewhere. Scholars have named the people who built these elaborate centers

Map 3.6 Trade in the Eastern Mediterranean World

Greece, Egypt, and Cyprus were trade hubs in the eastern Mediterranean.

- What major commodities were traded in the eastern Mediterranean?
- Why did trade originally move from east to west?
- What role did geographic location play in the Mycenaeans' eventual conquest of the Minoans?

the Minoans, after the legendary King Minos who may have ruled Crete at this time. The Minoans sailed back and forth across the Mediterranean, and by 1600 BCE they were colonizing other Aegean islands as trading and mining centers. The Minoans' wealth soon became a magnet for the Mycenaeans, their mainland competitors, who took over Crete around 1400 BCE.

As the island communities traded with the peoples of Southwest Asia, they borrowed some ideas but also kept their own cultural traditions. In terms of borrowing, the monumental architecture of Southwest Asia found small-scale echoes in the Aegean world—notably in the palace complexes built on Crete between 1900 and 1600 BCE.

In terms of a distinctive cultural element, worship on the islands focused on a female deity, the "Lady," but there are no traces of large temple complexes similar to those in Mesopotamia, Anatolia, and Egypt. Nor, apparently, was there any priestly class of the type that managed the temple complexes of Southwest Asian societies. Moreover, it is unclear whether these societies had full-time scribes.

Perhaps not surprisingly for a fragmented microsociety, there was significant regional diversity within this small Aegean world. On Crete, the large, palace-centered communities controlled centrally organized societies with a high order of refinement. Confident in their wealth and power, the sprawling, airy palaces had no fortifications and no natural defenses. On Thera (modern Santorini), a small island to the north of Crete, a trading city was not centered on a major palace complex but rather featured private houses, with bathrooms including toilets and running water and other rooms decorated with exotic wall paintings. It was this same island of Thera that was the center of a catastrophic volcanic eruption in the mid-second millennium BCE that likely contributed to the decline of the Minoans.

Mycenaean Culture

Mycenaean Culture The Mycenaean culture was more war oriented than that of the peaceful, seafaring Minoans. When the Mycenaeans migrated to Greece from central Europe, they brought their Indo-European language, their horse chariots, and their metalworking skills. Their move was gradual, lasting from about 1850 to 1600 BCE, but ultimately they dominated the indigenous population. They maintained their dominance with their powerful weapon, the chariot, until 1200 BCE. The battle chariots and festivities of chariot racing described in the centuries-later epic poetry of Homer's *Iliad* (recounting the legendary Trojan War in which Mycenaean Greeks attacked the city of Troy, in Anatolia) express memories of glorious chariot feats that echo Vedic legends from South Asia. Homer's "Catalog of Greek Ships" (*Iliad* 2.494–759), detailing the many different Greek communities that sent ships of warriors to fight at Troy, also illustrates the diffuse and fragmented political situation, yet common culture and ideals, that bound together the Greek microsociety.

The Mycenaean material culture emphasized displays of weaponry, portraits of armed soldiers, and illustrations of violent conflicts. The main palace centers at Tiryns and Mycenae were the hulking fortresses of warlords surrounded by rough-hewn stone walls and strategically located atop large rock outcroppings. In these fortified urban hubs, a preeminent ruler (*wanax*)

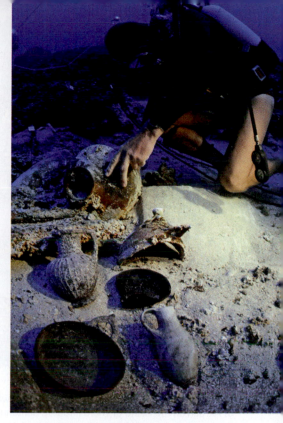

Seaborne trade Shipwrecks recovered by underwater archaeologists, who work methodically to document their cargo, demonstrate the scale of seaborne trade in the late second millennium BCE. The famous Uluburun shipwreck, which sunk off the southern coast of Turkey ca. 1325 BCE, was transporting ten tons of copper and more than one hundred amphorae (large two-handled jars) containing all kinds of high-value commodities.

Aegean Fresco This is one of the more striking wall paintings, or frescoes, discovered by archaeologists in the 1970s and 1980s at Akrotiri on the island of Thera (modern Santorini) in the Aegean Sea. Its brilliant colors, especially the blue of the sea, evoke the lively essence of Minoan life on the island. Note the houses of the wealthy along the port and the flotilla of ships that reflects the seaborne commerce that was beginning to flourish in the Mediterranean in this period.

stood atop a complex bureaucratic hierarchy. At the heart of the palace society were scribes, who recorded in their Linear B script the goods and services allotted to local farmers, shepherds, and metalworkers, among others. Tombs of the Mycenaean elite contain many gold vessels and ostentatious gold masks. Amber beads in the tombs indicate that the warriors had contacts with inhabitants of northern European coniferous forest regions, whose trees secreted that highly valued resin.

Mycenaean expansion eventually overwhelmed the Minoans on Crete. The Mycenaeans created colonies and trading settlements, reaching as far as Sicily and southern Italy. The trade and language of these early Greek-speaking peoples created a veneer of unity linking the dispersed worlds of the Aegean Sea. Yet, at the close of the second millennium BCE, the eastern Mediterranean faced internal and external convulsions that ended the heyday of these microsocieties. Most notable was a series of migrations of peoples from central Europe who moved through southeastern Europe, Anatolia, and the eastern Mediterranean (see Chapter 4 for more on these Sea Peoples). The invasions, although often destructive, did not extinguish but rather reinforced the creative potential of this frontier area. Because theirs was a closed maritime world—in comparison with the wide-open Pacific—the

Greek-speaking peoples around the Aegean quickly reasserted dominance in the eastern Mediterranean that the Austronesians did not match in Southeast Asia or Polynesia.

Conclusion

The second millennium BCE was an era of migrations, warfare, and territorial state building in Afro-Eurasia. Whereas river-basin societies had flourished in the fourth and third millennia BCE in Mesopotamia, Egypt, the Indus Valley, and East Asia, now droughts shook the agrarian foundations of their economies. Old states crumbled; from the steppes and plateaus pastoral nomads and transhumant herders descended in search of food, grazing lands, and other opportunities. As transhumant herders pressed into the river-basin societies, the social and political fabric of these communities changed. Likewise, horse-riding nomads from steppe communities in Inner Eurasia conquered and settled in the agrarian states, bringing key innovations. Foremost were the horse chariots, which became a military catalyst sparking the evolution from smaller states to larger territorial states encompassing crowded cities, vast hinterlands, and broadened trade networks. The nomads and herders also adopted many of the settled peoples' beliefs and customs. On land and sea, migrating peoples created zones of long-distance trade that linked agrarian societies.

Through a range of trade, migrations, and conquest throughout the second millennium BCE, the Nile Delta, the basin of the Tigris and Euphrates rivers, the Indus Valley, and the Yellow River basin were brought into even closer contact than before. In Southwest Asia and the Nile River basin, the interaction led to an elaborate system of diplomatic relations. The first territorial states appeared in this millennium, composed of multiple communities living under common laws and customs. An alliance of farmers and warriors united agrarian production with political power to create and defend territorial boundaries. The new arrangements overshadowed the nomads' historic role as predators and enabled them to become military elites within these new states. Through taxes and drafted labor, villagers repaid their rulers for local security and state-run diplomacy.

The rhythms of state formation differed where regimes were not closely packed together. In East Asia, for example, the absence of strong rivals allowed the emerging Shang dynasty to develop more gradually. Where landscapes had sharper divisions—as in the island archipelagos of the South Pacific and in the Mediterranean—small-scale, decentralized, and fragmented microsocieties emerged. But fragmentation is not the same as isolation. Even peoples in the worlds apart from the developments across Afro-Eurasia were not entirely secluded from the increasing flows of technologies, languages, goods, and migrants.

Focus On
The Emergence of Territorial States

Egypt and Southwest Asia

- Invasions by nomads and transhumant herders lead to the creation of larger territorial states: New Kingdom Egypt, Hittites, Mesopotamian states.

- Creating a centuries-long peaceful era, a community of major powers emerges among the major states as the result of shrewd statecraft and diplomacy.

Indus River Valley

- Migratory Vedic peoples from the steppes of Inner Eurasia use chariots and rely on domesticated animals to spread out and begin integrating the northern half of South Asia.

Shang State (China)

- Shang dynastic rulers promote improvements in metalworking, agriculture, and the development of writing, leading to the growth of China's first major state.

Microsocieties

- Substantial increases in population, migrations, and trade lead to the emergence of microsocieties among peoples in the South Pacific (Austronesians) and the Aegean world (Minoans and Mycenaeans).

Key Terms

Amorites p. 119	Hittites p. 123	microsocieties p. 132	territorial state p. 112
chariot p. 110	Hyksos p. 116	oracle bones p. 130	transhumant herders p. 107
Hammurapi's Code p. 120	Indo-European migrations p. 107	pastoral nomads p. 107	Vedic peoples p. 124

CHRONOLOGY

	2500 BCE	2000 BCE
Egypt and Southwest Asia		Middle Kingdom in Egypt 2055–1650 BCE
		Hammurapi's Babylonia 1792–1750 BCE
South Asia		
East Asia		
The Mediterranean		
South Pacific	Austronesian migrations 2500 BCE–400 CE	

- **Thinking about Environmental Impacts and Territorial States** Around 2000 BCE, a series of environmental disasters helped destroy the societies that had thrived in parts of Afro-Eurasia in the third millennium BCE. What were the short-term and long-term impacts of these environmental troubles? How did they influence the movement of peoples and the formation of territorial states in the second millennium BCE?

- **Thinking about Transformation & Conflict and Territorial States** The second millennium BCE witnessed large-scale migrations of nomadic peoples who brought with them their domesticated horses and their chariot technology. These people are referred to by scholars as Indo-Europeans, largely on the basis of their languages. Contrast the impact of migrations into

Southwest Asia (Anatolia and Mesopotamia), Egypt, South Asia, and East Asia. To what extent did conflict play a role in the impact of Indo-European-language speakers on the formation of territorial states?

- **Thinking about Interconnection & Divergence and Territorial States** While territorial states formed in Egypt, Mesopotamia, South Asia, and East Asia, microsocieties formed in the South Pacific and in the Aegean Sea. What factors influenced whether a region might host a territorial state as opposed to a microsociety? What areas of the planet were still worlds apart? What ways of life continued to predominate in those worlds apart from the territorial states and microsocieties discussed in this chapter?

 Go to INQUIZITIVE to see what you've learned—and learn what you've missed—with personalized feedback along the way.

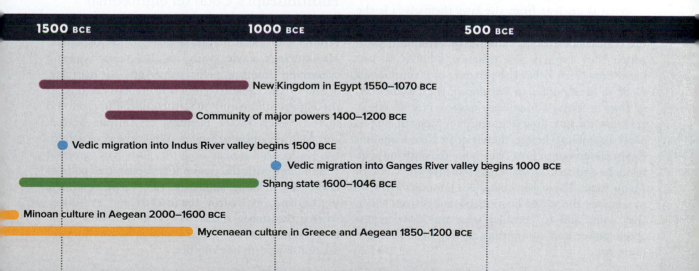

1500 BCE	1000 BCE	500 BCE

New Kingdom in Egypt 1550–1070 BCE

Community of major powers 1400–1200 BCE

Vedic migration into Indus River valley begins 1500 BCE

Vedic migration into Ganges River valley begins 1000 BCE

Shang state 1600–1046 BCE

Minoan culture in Aegean 2000–1600 BCE

Mycenaean culture in Greece and Aegean 1850–1200 BCE

Global Themes and Sources

Law Codes in the Context of Territorial States and Pastoral Nomads

In addition to charismatic monarchs and complex bureaucracies, one of the ways territorial states brought order to the large regions under their control was through clear codes of law. These could range from elaborate legal codes, such as that of Hammurapi, to more general instructions to leaders on how to administer justice. Pastoral nomadic groups, like the Hebrews and Vedic peoples, also developed law codes, especially as they began to settle down.

The logic of the law codes is as varied as their historical context. Some law codes operated on an "if/then" formula (*if* a certain crime is committed, *then* a certain punishment is to be meted out), others laid out clear and forceful rules for proper behavior, and others deliberated on procedure and punishment. Some law codes mention gods specifically, while others appear to focus primarily on human interactions and appeal to earthly authority. Many of the law codes reveal distinctions based on class, occupation, and gender.

What is unclear from the laws themselves is the extent to which they describe ideal behavior or the realities of everyday life in the communities to which they applied. For instance, scholars do not know how often either the penalties of Hammurapi's Code in Mesopotamian Babylon or the *Punishments of Tang* in Shang China were applied. Nor do scholars know for sure how frequently the scene of supplicants assembling before the vizier in New Kingdom Egypt played out or how true to life the husband-wife relations and attitudes toward women in the Code of Manu were. These law codes do, however, allow us to compare the varied historical contexts from which they come and to consider what the laws suggest about power and community in the second millennium BCE.

Analyzing The Context of Early Law Codes

- What issues do territorial states, such as those of Babylon, New Kingdom Egypt, and Shang China, attempt to legislate? What sorts of issues appear to matter to the nomadic Hebrews and Vedic peoples?

- What sorts of social distinctions (class, gender, occupation) are evident in the codes?

- What do the variations in the laws—with respect to issues such as source of authority, punishment, and enforcement—suggest about the source of power at the heart of these societies?

- What can you generalize about the concerns of a settled territorial state as compared with those of a more nomadic group?

PRIMARY SOURCE 3.1

Hammurapi's Code (c. eighteenth century BCE)

From a Babylonian territorial state in Mesopotamia, Hammurapi's Code, with its 282 laws covering everything from property ownership to marriage, is one of the earliest recorded law codes. Dating to the eighteenth century BCE, the code was produced in the context of the blending of Amorite herders and Mesopotamian urbanites. While the prologue to the law code describes how the gods have invested Hammurapi with the power to establish this code of laws and "to bring about the rule of righteousness in the land, to destroy the wicked and evil-doers, so that the strong should not harm the weak," the laws themselves are focused primarily on humans' relationships with one another.

- What are some of the crimes outlined in these laws? What are the punishments for those crimes?
- What evidence do you see in Hammurapi's laws for the relationship between men and women? Between parents and children? Between different levels of society?
- What do these laws suggest about the eighteenth-century BCE Mesopotamian context from which they come? What sorts of issues seem to matter to this community (or its ruler)?

§1. If a man bring an accusation against a man, and charge him with a (capital) crime, but cannot prove it, he, the accuser, shall be put to death.

§2. If a man charge a man with sorcery, and cannot prove it, he who is charged with sorcery shall go to the river, into the river he shall throw himself and if the river overcome him, his accuser shall take to himself his house (estate). If the river show that man to be innocent and he come forth unharmed, he who charged him with sorcery shall be put to death. He who threw himself into the river shall take to himself the house of his accuser.

§3. If a man, in a case (pending judgment), bear false (threatening) witness, or do not establish the testimony that he has given, if that case be a case involving life, that man shall be put to death.

§4. If a man (in a case) bear witness for grain or money (as a bribe), he shall himself bear the penalty imposed in that case.

§5. If a judge pronounce a judgment, render a decision, deliver a verdict duly signed and sealed and afterward alter his judgment, they shall call that judge to account for the alteration of the judgment which he had pronounced, and he shall pay twelve-fold the penalty which was in said judgment; and, in the assembly, they shall expel him from his seat of judgment, and he shall not return, and with the judges in a case he shall not take his seat.

§6. If a man steal the property of a god (temple) or palace, that man shall be put to death; and he who receives from his hand the stolen (property) shall also be put to death.

§7. If a man purchase silver or gold, manservant or maid servant, ox, sheep or ass, or anything else from a man's son, or from a man's servant without witnesses or contracts, or if he receive (the same) in trust, that man shall be put to death as a thief.

§8. If a man steal ox or sheep, ass or pig, or boat—if it be from a god (temple) or a palace, he shall restore thirtyfold; if it be from a freeman, he shall render tenfold. If the thief have nothing wherewith to pay he shall be put to death.

***

§14. If a man steal a man's son, who is a minor, he shall be put to death.

§15. If a man aid a male or female slave of the palace, or a male or female slave of a freeman to escape from the city gate, he shall be put to death.

§16. If a man harbor in his house a male or female slave who has fled from the palace or from a freeman, and do not bring him (the slave) forth at the call of the commandant, the owner of that house shall be put to death.

§17. If a man seize a male or female slave, a fugitive, in the field and bring that (slave) back to his owner, the owner of the slave shall pay him two shekels of silver.

***

§38. An officer, constable or tax-gatherer shall not deed to his wife or daughter the field, garden or house, which is his business (*i. e.*, which is his by virtue of his office), nor shall he assign them for debt.

§39. He may deed to his wife or daughter the field, garden or house which he has purchased and (hence) possesses, or he may assign them for debt.

§40. A woman, merchant or other property-holder may sell field, garden or house. The purchaser shall conduct the business of the field, garden or house which he has purchased.

§41. If a man have bargained for the field, garden or house of an officer, constable or tax-gatherer and given sureties, the officer, constable or tax-gatherer shall return to his field, garden, or house and he shall take to himself the sureties which were given to him.

§42. If a man rent a field for cultivation and do not produce any grain in the field, they shall call him to account, because he has not performed the work required on the field, and he shall give to the owner of the field grain on the basis of the adjacent (fields).

§43. If he do not cultivate the field and neglect it, he shall give to the owner of the field grain on the basis of the adjacent (fields); and the field which he has neglected, he shall break up with hoes, he shall harrow and he shall return to the owner of the field.

**

§45. If a man rent his field to a tenant for crop-rent and receive the crop-rent of his field and later Adad (*i.e.*, the Storm God) inundate the field and carry away the produce, the loss (falls on) the tenant.

§46. If he have not received the rent of his field and he have rented the field for either one-half or one-third (of the crop), the tenant and the owner of the field shall divide the grain which is in the field according to agreement.

**

§128. If a man take a wife and do not arrange with her the (proper) contracts, that woman is not a (legal) wife.

§129. If the wife of a man be taken in lying with another man, they shall bind them and throw them into the water. If the husband of the woman would save his wife, or if the king would save his male servant (he may).

§130. If a man force the (betrothed) wife of another who has not known a male and is living in her father's house, and he lie in her bosom and they take him, that man shall be put to death and that, woman shall go free.

§131. If a man accuse his wife and she has not been taken in lying with another man, she shall take an oath in the name of god and she shall return to her house.

§132. If the finger have been pointed at the wife of a man because of another man, and she have not been taken in lying with another man, for her husband's sake she shall throw herself into the river.

§133. If a man be captured and there be maintenance in his house and his wife go out of her house, she shall protect her body and she shall not enter into another house.

§133A. [If] that woman do not protect her body and enter into another house, they shall call that woman to account and they shall throw her into the water.

§134. If a man be captured and there be no maintenance in his house and his wife enter into another house, that woman has no blame.

§135. If a man be captured and there be no maintenance in his house, and his wife openly enter into another house and bear children; if later her husband return and arrive in his city, that woman shall return to her husband (and) the children shall go to their father.

§136. If a man desert his city and flee and afterwards his wife enter into another house; if that man return and would take his wife, the wife of the fugitive shall not return to her husband because he hated his city and fled.

§137. If a man set his face to put away a concubine who has borne him children or a wife who has presented him with children, he shall return to that woman her dowry and shall give to her the income of field, garden and goods and she shall bring up her children; from the time that her children are grown up, from whatever is given to her children they shall give to her a portion corresponding to that of a son and the man of her choice may marry her.

§138. If a man would put away his wife who has not borne him children, he shall give her money to the amount of her marriage settlement and he shall make good to her the dowry which she brought from her father's house and then he may put her away.

§139. If there were no marriage settlement, he shall give to her one mana of silver for a divorce.

§140. If he be a freeman, he shall give her one-third mana of silver.

§141. If the wife of a man who is living in his house, set her face to go out and play the part of a fool, neglect her house, belittle her husband, they shall call her to account; if her husband say "I have put her away," he shall let her go. On her departure nothing shall be given to her for her divorce. If her husband say: "I have not put her away," her husband may take another woman. The first woman shall dwell in the house of her husband as a maid servant.

§142. If a woman hate her husband, and say: "Thou shalt not have me," they shall inquire into her antecedents for her defects; and if she have been a careful mistress and be without reproach and her husband have been going about and greatly belittling her, that woman has no blame. She shall receive her dowry and shall go to her father's house.

§143. If she have not been a careful mistress, have gadded about, have neglected her house and have belittled her husband, they shall throw that woman into the water.

***

§148. If a man take a wife and she become afflicted with disease, and if he set his face to take another, he may. His wife, who is afflicted with disease, he shall not put away. She shall remain in the house which he has built and he shall maintain her as long as she lives.

§149. If that woman do not elect to remain in her husband's house, he shall make good to her the dowry which she brought from her father's house and she may go.

§150. If a man give to his wife field, garden, house or goods and he deliver to her a sealed deed, after (the death of) her husband, her children cannot make claim against her. The mother after her (death) may will to her child whom she loves, but to a brother she may not.

***

§162. If a man take a wife and she bear him children and that woman die, her father may not lay claim to her dowry. Her dowry belongs to her children.

§163. If a man take a wife and she do not present him with children and that woman die; if his father-in-law return to him the marriage settlement which that man brought to the house of his father-in-law, her husband may not lay claim to the dowry of that woman. Her dowry belongs to the house of her father.

§164. If his father-in-law do not return to him the marriage settlement, he may deduct from her dowry the amount of the marriage settlement and return (the rest) of her dowry to the house of her father.

***

§194. If a man give his son to a nurse and that son die in the hands of the nurse, and the nurse substitute another son without the consent of his father or mother, they shall call her to account, and because she has substituted another son without the consent of his father or mother, they shall cut off her breast.

§195. If a son strike his father, they shall cut off his fingers.

§196. If a man destroy the eye of another man, they shall destroy his eye.

§197. If one break a man's bone, they shall break his bone.

§198. If one destroy the eye of a freeman or break the bone of a freeman, he shall pay one mana of silver.

§199. If one destroy the eye of a man's slave or break a bone of a man's slave he shall pay one-half his price.

§200. If a man knock out a tooth of a man of his own rank, they shall knock out his tooth.

§201. If one knock out a tooth of a freeman, he shall pay one-third mana of silver.

§202. If a man strike the person of a man (*i.e.*, commit an assault) who is his superior, he shall receive sixty strokes with an ox-tail whip in public.

§203. If a man strike another man of his own rank, he shall pay one mana of silver.

§204. If a freeman strike a freeman, he shall pay ten shekels of silver.

§205. If a man's slave strike a man's son, they shall cut off his ear.

Source: *The Code of Hammurabi, King of Babylon, about 2250 B.C.*, 2nd ed., translated by Robert Francis Harper (Union, New Jersey: University of Chicago Lawbook Exchange, 1999): pp. 11, 13, 17, 25, 27, 45, 47, 49, 51, 53, 57, 59, 73, 75.

PRIMARY SOURCE 3.2

Instruction to Vizier Rekhmire (c. fifteenth century BCE)

No comprehensive law codes survive from Middle or New Kingdom Egypt, but a set of instructions from Thutmosis III (stepson of, and co-ruler with, Hatshepsut, before his solo reign) to Rekhmire, a pharaoh's vizier (chief minister), from around 1450 BCE gives a keen sense of how judgments were made at the Egyptian court. These instructions, along with a biography of Rekhmire, were preserved in hieroglyphs on the wall of the mortuary chapel of Rekhmire in Thebes, along with beautifully painted scenes of the collection of taxes and tribute, the labors of workers and other craftspeople, and funerary practices.

- What scene does the opening of these instructions conjure? How does this scene help you imagine the social and political context in which the instructions were meant to be followed?

- Over what issues does the vizier have authority?

- How does this administration of authority and justice by the vizier align with your understanding of the post-Hyksos territorial state context of New Kingdom Egypt?

667. Mayest thou see to it for thyself, to do everything after that which is in accordance with law; to do everything according to the right thereof.

***

669. Be not enraged toward a man unjustly, but be thou enraged concerning that about which one should be enraged; show forth the fear of thee; let one be afraid of thee, (for) a prince is a prince of whom one is afraid. Lo, the true dread of a prince is to do justice. Behold, if a man show forth the fear of him a myriad of times, there is something of violence in him. Be not known to the people; and they shall not say: "He is (only) a man."

670. Lo, one shall say of the chief scribe of the vizier: "A scribe of justice," shall one say of him. Now, as for the hall, wherein thou holdest hearings there shall be a broad-hall therein. ⌈He who dispenses⌉ justice before all the people, he is the vizier. Behold, a man shall be in his office, (as long as) he shall do things according to that which is given to him.

***

675. Arrangement of the sitting of the governor of the (residence) city, and vizier of the Southern City, (and) of the court, in the hall of the vizier. As for every act of this official, the vizier while hearing in the hall of the vizier, he shall sit upon a chair, with a rug upon the floor, and a dais upon it, a cushion under his back, a cushion under his feet, a — upon it, and a baton at his hand; the 40 skins shall be open before him. Then the magnates of the South (shall stand) in the two aisles before him, while the master of the privy chamber is on his right, the ⌈receiver of income⌉ on his left, the scribes of the vizier at his (either) hand; one ⌈corresponding⌉ to another, with each man at his proper place. One shall be heard after another, without allowing one who is behind to be heard before one who is in front. If one in front says: "There is none being heard at my hand," then he shall be taken by the messenger of the vizier.

***

681. Let not any official be empowered to judge ⌈against a superior⌉ in his hall. If there be any assailant against any of these officials in his hall, then he shall cause that he be brought to the judgment-hall. It is the vizier who shall punish him, in order to expiate his fault. . . .

682. As for every messenger whom the vizier sends with a message for an official, from the first official to the last, let him not be ⌈swerved⌉, and let him not be conducted; the official shall repeat his vizierial message while he stands before the official, repeating his message and going forth to wait for him. His messenger shall seize the mayors and village sheiks for the judgment-hall; . . . saying: "I have been sent with a message for the official so and so; he caused that I be conducted, and he caused that something be entrusted to me.

683. He who has not disproved the charge at his hearing, which takes place ⌈—⌉, then it shall be entered in the criminal docket. He who is in the great prison, not able to disprove the charge of his messenger, likewise; when their case comes on another time, then one shall report and determine whether it is in the criminal docket, and there shall be ⌈executed⌉ the things concerning which entry was made, in order to expiate their offense.

***

698. It is he who dispatches the official staff, to attend to the water-supply in the whole land.

699. It is he who dispatches the mayors and village sheiks to plow for harvest time.

700. It is he who ⌈appoints⌉ the overseers of hundreds in the hall of the king's-house.

701. It is he who ⌈arranges⌉ the hearing of the mayors and village sheiks who go forth in his name, of South and North.

702. Every matter is reported to him; there are reported to him the affairs of the southern fortress; and every arrest which is for seizing — — —.

703. It is he who makes the ⌈—⌉ of every nome; it is he who "hears" it. It is he who dispatches the ⌈district⌉ soldiers and scribes to carry out the ⌈administration⌉ of the king. The records of the nome are in his hall. It is he who hears concerning all lands. It is he who makes the boundary of every nome, the field ⌈—⌉, all divine offerings and every contract.

704. It is he who takes every deposition; it is he who hears the rejoinder when a man comes for argument with his opponent.

705. It is he who appoints every appointee to the hall of judgment, when any litigant comes to him from the king's-house. It is he who hears every edict.

Source: *Ancient Records of Egypt: Historical Documents from the Earliest Times to the Persian Conquest*, vol. 2, translated by James Henry Breasted (Chicago: University of Chicago Press, 1906), pp. 269–70, 273, 275–76, 279.

PRIMARY SOURCE 3.3

The Ten Commandments, Exodus 20:1–17 and Leviticus from the Bible

The Ten Commandments are perhaps the clearest, most direct statement of the laws binding the nomadic Hebrew peoples with their god and with one another. Hebrew scriptures describe the scene in which God delivers the Ten Commandments to Moses in the wilderness of Sinai during the Hebrews' sojourn from Egypt. A more elaborate set of laws touching on a wider range of issues, including dietary concerns, sexuality, blasphemy, and religious observances, is contained in the priestly Levitical Code of Hebrew scripture, especially in Leviticus 17–26. Examined together, the Ten Commandments and the Levitical Code give a better context for the laws and penalties by which the Hebrew peoples lived and governed their community.

- What are the range of behaviors addressed by the Ten Commandments? What, if any, rationale is offered in Exodus for why these rules should be followed and the penalty for not doing so?

- How do the Ten Commandments (Exodus 20:1–17) compare with the punishments for disobedience in Leviticus 26?

- What do the concerns addressed in the Ten Commandments and the punishments described in Leviticus suggest about the context of the community living by these rules?

Genesis 20: And God spoke all these words, saying,

2 "I am the Lord your God, who brought you out of the land of Egypt, out of the house of bondage.

3 "You shall have no other gods before[f] me.

4 "You shall not make for yourself a graven image, or any likeness of anything that is in heaven above, or that is in the earth beneath, or that is in the water under the earth; [5]you shall not bow down to them or serve them; for I the Lord your God am a jealous God, visiting the iniquity of the fathers upon the children to the third and the fourth generation of those who hate me, [6]but showing steadfast love to thousands of those who love me and keep my commandments.

7 "You shall not take the name of the Lord your God in vain; for the Lord will not hold him guiltless who takes his name in vain.

8 "Remember the sabbath day, to keep it holy. [9]Six days you shall labor, and do all your work; [10]but the seventh day is a sabbath to the Lord your God; in it you shall not do any work, you, or your son, or your daughter, your manservant, or your maidservant, or your cattle, or the sojourner who is within your gates; [11]for in six days the Lord made heaven and earth, the sea, and all that is in them, and rested the seventh day; therefore the Lord blessed the sabbath day and hallowed it.

12 "Honor your father and your mother, that your days may be long in the land which the Lord your God gives you.

13 "You shall not kill.

14 "You shall not commit adultery.

15 "You shall not steal.

16 "You shall not bear false witness against your neighbor.

17 "You shall not covet your neighbor's house; you shall not covet your neighbor's wife, or his manservant, or his maidservant, or his ox, or his ass, or anything that is your neighbor's."

***

Leviticus 26: [14] "But if you will not hearken to me, and will not do all these commandments, [15]if you spurn my statutes, and if your soul abhors my ordinances, so that you will not do all my commandments, but break my covenant, [16]I will do this to you: I will appoint over you sudden terror, consumption, and fever that waste the eyes and cause life to pine away. And you shall sow your seed in vain, for your enemies shall eat it; [17]I will set my face against you, and you shall be smitten before your enemies; those who hate you shall rule over you, and you shall flee when none pursues you. [18]And if in spite of this you will not hearken to me, then I will chastise you again sevenfold for your sins, [19]and I will break the pride of your power, and I will make your heavens like iron and your earth like brass; [20]and your strength shall be spent in vain, for your land shall not yield its increase, and the trees of the land shall not yield their fruit.

21 "Then if you walk contrary to me, and will not hearken to me, I will bring more plagues upon you, sevenfold as many as your sins. [22]And I will let loose the wild beasts among you, which shall rob you of your children, and destroy your cattle, and make you few in number, so that your ways shall become desolate.

23 "And if by this discipline you are not turned to me, but walk contrary to me, [24]then I also will walk contrary to you, and I myself will smite you sevenfold for your sins. [25]And I will bring a sword upon you, that shall execute vengeance for the covenant; and if you gather within your cities I will send pestilence among you, and you shall be delivered into the hand of the enemy. [26]When I break your staff of bread, ten women shall bake your bread in one oven, and shall deliver your bread again by weight; and you shall eat, and not be satisfied.

Source: *The New Oxford Annotated Bible: New Revised Standard Version with the Apocrypha*, 4th ed. (New York: Oxford University Press, 2010), pp. 92–93, 156–57.

PRIMARY SOURCE 3.4

The Code of Manu (c. 200 BCE)

The Code of Manu is thought to represent some of the earliest legal ideas of the nomadic Vedic peoples of South Asia. The code's nearly 2,700 verses were written down in Sanskrit sometime after 200 BCE, but the laws about social interactions in the excerpt here may well date to a much earlier time. They are presented in the form of a dialogue between the legendary first man, Manu, and wise men who come before him to hear his ideas about social order.

- How does the opening of this code engage the class distinctions you might expect in a Vedic South Asian context?

- What expectations for behavior are outlined in this code?

- What do these "eternal laws for a husband and his wife" suggest about the relationship between men and women in a Vedic context?

Chapter I. 1. The great sages approached Manu, who was seated with a collected mind, and, having duly worshipped him, spoke as follows:

2. 'Deign, divine one, to declare to us precisely and in due order the sacred laws of each of the (four chief) castes (varna) and of the intermediate ones.

3. 'For thou, O Lord, alone knowest the purport, (i.e.) the rites, and the knowledge of the soul, (taught) in this whole ordinance, which is unknowable and unfathomable.

4. He [Manu] whose power is measureless, being thus asked by the high-minded great sages, duly honoured them, and answered, 'Listen!'

***

Chapter IX. 1. [Manu] will now propound the eternal laws for a husband and his wife who keep to the oath of duty, whether they be united or separated.

2. Day and night women must be kept in dependence by the males (of) their (families), and, if they attach themselves to sensual enjoyments, they must be kept under one's control.

3. Her father protects (her) in childhood, her husband protects (her) in youth, and her sons protect (her) in old age; a woman is never fit for independence.

4. Reprehensible is the father who gives not (his daughter in marriage) at the proper time; reprehensible is the husband who approaches not (his wife in due season), and reprehensible is the son who does not protect his mother after her husband has died.

5. Women must particularly be guarded against evil inclinations, however trifling (they may appear); for, if they are not guarded, they will bring sorrow on two families.

6. Considering that the highest duty of all castes, even weak husbands (must) strive to guard their wives.

7. He who carefully guards his wife, preserves (the purity of) his offspring, virtuous conduct, his family, himself, and his (means of acquiring) merit.

***

9. As the male is to whom a wife cleaves, even so is the son whom she brings forth; let him therefore carefully guard his wife, in order to keep his offspring pure.

10. No man can completely guard women by force; but they can be guarded by the employment of the (following) expedients:

11. Let the (husband) employ his (wife) in the collection and expenditure of his wealth, in keeping (everything) clean, in (the fulfilment of) religious duties, in the preparation of his food, and in looking after the household utensils.

12. Women, confined in the house under trustworthy and obedient servants, are not (well) guarded; but those who of their own accord keep guard over themselves, are well guarded.

13. Drinking (spirituous liquor), associating with wicked people, separation from the husband, rambling abroad, sleeping (at unseasonable hours), and dwelling in other men's houses, are the six causes of the ruin of women.

***

46. Neither by sale nor by repudiation is a wife released from her husband; such we know the law to be, which the Lord of creatures (Praĝâpati) made of old.

***

76. If the husband went abroad for some sacred duty, (she) must wait for him eight years, if (he went) to (acquire) learning or fame six (years), if (he went) for pleasure three years.

77. For one year let a husband bear with a wife who hates him; but after (the lapse of) a year let him deprive her of her property and cease to cohabit with her.

81. A barren wife may be superseded in the eighth year, she whose children (all) die in the tenth, she who bears only daughters in the eleventh, but she who is quarrelsome without delay.

82. But a sick wife who is kind (to her husband) and virtuous in her conduct, may be superseded (only) with her own consent and must never be disgraced.

***

95. The husband receives his wife from the gods, (he does not wed her) according to his own will; doing what is agreeable to the gods, he must always support her (while she is) faithful.

96. To be mothers were women created, and to be fathers men; religious rites, therefore, are ordained in the Veda to be performed (by the husband) together with the wife.

***

101. 'Let mutual fidelity continue until death,' this may be considered as the summary of the highest law for husband and wife.

Source: *The Laws of Manu, Translated with Extracts from Seven Commentaries,* translated by Georg Bühler (Oxford: Clarendon Press, 1886), pp. 1–2, 327–29, 335, 341–42, 344–45.

PRIMARY SOURCE 3.5

Adviser Zichan of Zheng's Compilation of Laws (c. sixth century BCE)

The Chinese text included here describes the first set of formal laws in China, dating to the sixth century BCE. The text comes from the Spring and Autumn period (770–476 BCE), whose latter years also produced the thoughtful musings of Confucius. This passage, however, describes a series of earlier contexts for how law worked in early China and offers reflections on rule by king versus rule of law. It suggests that Shang kings did not publicize a penal code, but rather created a clear system of punishments for disorderly conduct brought before the king.

- **What are the problems with law codes, according to this text?**

- **How does this text suggest that Chinese kings established order before there were laws?**

- Based on this text, what do you imagine was the second-millennium BCE legal context of the Shang territorial state? Would people living under Shang authority have known the laws that governed them? Explain.

In the third month, the people of Zheng cast a penal text. Shu Xiang dispatched to Zichan a text. It stated, "Formerly, I had hope for you, but have now given it up. In the past, former kings consulted on affairs to decide them but did not make penal compilations, for they feared that the people would grow litigious. Still unable to control them, they restrained them with rightness, bound them with [good] governance, and raised them with humanness. They institutionalized emoluments and ranks to encourage their obedience and determined strict punishments so as to overawe their perversity. Fearing that that was not enough, they taught them of loyalty, rewarded good conduct, instructed them in their duties, deployed them with harmony, supervised them respectfully, supervised them with might, and adjudged them with firmness. Still they sought sagacious and erudite superiors, intelligent and astute officials, loyal and trustworthy elders, and kind and beneficent masters. It was only under such conditions that the people could be employed without disaster or disorder resulting. When the people are aware of a legal compilation, they will have no wariness of their superiors. All become contentious, appealing to the texts, and achieve their goals through lucky conniving. They cannot be governed. When the Xia had a disorderly government, they composed the *Punishments of Yu*. When the Shang had disorderly administration, they composed the *Punishments of Tang*. When the Zhou had disorderly administration, they composed the *Nine Punishments*. All three of these penal compilations arose in terminal ages. Now as advisor to the kingdom of Zheng you have rectified fields and ditches, established a reviled administration, instituted the tripartite compilation, and cast the penal text [in bronze], in order to calm the populace. Is this not difficult?

Source: *Zuozhuan*, translated by Earnest Caldwell, in "Social Change and Written Law in Early Chinese Legal Thought," *Law and History Review* 32 (February 2014): 15.

Interpreting Visual Evidence

Bronze Working

An important development in many of the territorial states of the second millennium BCE was bronze working, which involved the smelting of copper and tin to make durable objects. Bronze was used for weapons, chariot parts (wheel rims and lynchpins), tools, decorative objects, and ritual vessels.

The methods for casting bronze varied in different parts of Afro-Eurasia. In the east, in Shang China, artisans used an approach called the piece-mold method. In this method, artists would make a model of the item to be cast, cover it in clay to make a mold, cut the clay mold away in pieces (even etching the clay mold to add further detail), cast the bronze into the cut pieces of the clay mold, and then reassemble the bronze pieces to make the finished product. This process allowed the artists to achieve a much greater level of detail than the lost-wax method used in the Mediterranean, in which a model is made in wax, clay is formed around it, the clay form is heated to melt and remove the wax, and then bronze is poured into the cavity where the wax had been.

While bronze working thrived across Afro-Eurasia in the second millennium BCE, scholars agree that Shang bronze metallurgy was far and away the most advanced. Stunning examples of intricate Shang bronze work have been unearthed in tombs in the Yellow River valley. The Shang Chinese developed a range of vessel types, one of which was the jia-type vessel (an example from the fifteenth to fourteenth

century BCE is pictured here), used for heating wine libations for ceremonies venerating ancestors. To the far west, bronze casters in Middle and New Kingdom Egypt crafted a range of items that have been found in burials. One example, dating to the sixteenth to thirteenth century BCE, is this razor handle depicting an African man playing an instrument. From Mycenae in Greece, a gold-inlay dagger from the sixteenth century BCE shows a lion hunt, with five hunters (one of whom has been killed) and three lions.

Shang "jia" vessel.

Egyptian razor handle.

Mycenaean bronze dagger.

Questions for Analysis

1. Compare the bronze work from China, Egypt, and Greece. What does the varied craftsmanship suggest about the spread of this vital skill among territorial states in the second millennium BCE?

2. Compare what each of these items was used for and where they were found. What can you surmise about territorial states—about their hierarchies, their similarity to river-basin societies—based on the findspots for these items (elite graves) and their purpose (ritual, decorative, and so on)?

3. What does the decorative imagery on these bronze items suggest about trade and exchange among territorial states?

4

First Empires and Common Cultures in Afro-Eurasia

1250–325 BCE

Sennacherib—ruler of the Neo-Assyrian Empire early in the seventh century BCE—writes that at the end of one successful campaign he took "200,150 people, great and small, male and female, horses, mules, asses, camels, and sheep without number, I brought away from them and counted them my spoil." The booty about which Sennacherib boasts was unheard of in earlier ages. The immensity of such conquest highlights the arrival of a new era that involved empires with even larger geographical, political, economic, and cultural ambitions and achievements than the territorial states that preceded them (see Chapter 3). Given the nature and process of their formation, these early empires arguably replaced, rather than descended from, the earlier territorial states.

One key factor shaping these developments was warfare spurred by military innovation. Additionally, radical climate change drove many of the warrior/political leaders from the fringes of formerly powerful territorial states to the centers of power. There they established hybrid societies uniting cities and their hinterlands, among the Neo-Assyrians and Persians of Southwest Asia, Vedic parts of South Asia, and Zhou China. Imperial ideologies and religious beliefs supported the

Chapter Outline

- Forces of Upheaval and the Rise of Early Empires
- Empire in Southwest Asia: The Neo-Assyrian and Persian Empires
- Imperial Fringes in Western Afro-Eurasia
- Foundations of Vedic Culture in South Asia
- The Early Zhou Empire in East Asia
- Conclusion

Core Objectives

- **DESCRIBE** the factors that contributed to the rise of early empires in 1250–325 BCE and the characteristics of these empires.
- **COMPARE** empire formation, or the lack thereof, in Southwest Asia, South Asia, and East Asia in this period.
- **EVALUATE** the connection between empires and war, religion, and trade.
- **ANALYZE** the relationships between empires and the peoples on their peripheries.

new empires. Farming yields increased and populations grew. On the fringes of empires, microsocieties arose and made significant contributions to human development: the seafaring Phoenicians developed a simplified alphabet, the Israelites espoused a strict monotheism, and Greek city-states came to the fore and even began to challenge the power of the Persian Empire.

Global Storylines

- Climate change, migrations, technological advances, and administrative innovations contribute to the development of the world's first great empires.

- The Neo-Assyrians and then the Persians employ two different approaches to consolidate and maintain empires in Southwest Asia.

- South Asia becomes more culturally integrated despite the absence of a strong, centralized political authority.

- The Zhou dynasty establishes loose political integration in East Asia.

Forces of Upheaval and the Rise of Early Empires

Four related forces shaped the development of early empires in the first millennium BCE: climate change, migrations, new technologies, and administrative innovations. Migrants driven by climate change mingled with settled peoples. Ambitious leaders used innovations in technology and administration to create new states that went on to conquer other kingdoms. Gradually, a new political organization came into being: the **empire**. An empire is a group of states or different ethnic groups brought together under a single sovereign power. With varying degrees and types of centralization (as we will see in Southwest Asia, South Asia, and East Asia), empires connected distant regions through common languages, unifying political systems, trade, and shared religious beliefs. While most regions of Afro-Eurasia did not experience the rise of empire, those that did, and their neighbors, were profoundly affected by the development.

THE BIG PICTURE

. . . .

What were the factors that contributed to the rise of early empires in 1250–325 BCE, and what were the characteristics of these empires?

CLIMATE CHANGE

Beginning around 1200 BCE, another prolonged period of drought gripped Afro-Eurasia, causing social upheavals and migrations and utterly destroying settled societies and long-established governments. Many regions that had enjoyed rapid population growth in the second millennium BCE now found themselves unable to support such large numbers, forcing peoples to leave their homes in search of food and fertile land. (See Map 4.1.)

From the Mediterranean to East Asia, this wave of drought led to dramatic political shifts. In Egypt, low Nile floods forced pharaohs to spend their time securing food supplies and repelling Libyans from the desert and "Sea People" marauders from the coast. In Anatolia, Hittite kings dispatched envoys to the rulers of all the major agricultural areas, pleading for grain shipments to save their starving people. Even the drastic step of moving their capital to northern Syria, where food was more plentiful, did not prevent Hittite collapse. In mainland Greece, Mycenaean culture disintegrated when diminished rains made it impossible for farmers there to export wine, olives, and timber. Likewise in East Asia, radical climate change was a major factor in political developments. Arid conditions on the plains of central Asia resulted in powerful hot and dry winds that carried immense quantities of dust onto the North China plain. The dust storms reduced the soil's ability to retain moisture and led to a sharp decline in soil fertility. Some groups, like the Zhou peoples, went on the move in search of arable land.

empire
Group of states or ethnic groups governed by a single sovereign power with varying degrees of centralization using a range of methods, including common language, shared religious beliefs, trade, political systems, and military might.

The Global View

NORTH SEA

BALTIC SEA

EUROPE

NORTH SEA

Dniester R.

Dnieper R.

Danube R.

BLACK SEA

URAL MOUNTAINS

ARAL SEA

CASPIAN SEA

Volga R.

CENT

MYCENAEANS Troy

AEGEAN SEA

ANATOLIA

Tiryns

CRETE

CYPRUS

Aleppo

Tigris R.

HITTITES

MITANNI

Nineveh

Ashur

Euphrates R.

ELAMITES

Babylon

IRANIAN PLATEAU

ZAGROS MTS.

MEDITERRANEAN SEA

Tyre

LEVANT

SYRIAN DESERT

Jericho

Jerusalem

SOUTHWEST ASIA

NORTH AFRICA

SAHARA

Amarna

EGYPT Thebes

Nile R.

ARABIAN PENINSULA

Persian Gulf

NUBIA

RED SEA

> **Sub-Saharan periphery:** Increased population and gradual adoption of agriculture

Niger R.

S U B - S A H A R A N   A F R I C A

Congo R.

Lake Victoria

> **Tropical woodlands:** Yams and palm nuts cultivated

ATLANTIC OCEAN

Legend:

- ▮ Urban cores
- ▮ Vedic settlement by 900 BCE
- ← Nomadic incursions (sea peoples)
- ← Nomadic incursions (pastoralists)
- ■ Destroyed site
- • City

Map 4.1 Afro-Eurasia, 1200 BCE—Urban Cores and Nomadic Invaders

Nomadic incursions shattered the social and political status quo in Afro-Eurasia at this time. While destroying old polities, these migrations fostered a new social and political order in a variety of regions.

- Where did nomadic groups originate, and where did they migrate to?
- What is a major difference between the invasions of the Sea Peoples in this period and pastoral invasions?
- Why do you think that so many of the nomadic movements were toward populated areas?

INNER ASIA

ALTAI MOUNTAINS

Lake Balkas

GOBI DESERT

L ASIA

TIEN SHAN

Oxus R.   PAMIR MTS.

HINDU KUSH MTS.

TAKLAMAKAN DESERT

EAST ASIA

Yellow R.

SHANG CHINA

HIMALAYA MOUNTAINS

Indus R.

THAR DESERT

Mithila

Ganges R.

SOUTH ASIA

DECCAN PLATEAU

Dantapura

ARABIAN SEA

Yangzi R.

Ganges Valley: Rice-farming villages

Mainland Southeast Asia: Rice-farming villages, bronze tools and ornaments

SOUTHEAST ASIA

SOUTH CHINA SEA

Bay of Bengal

Maritime Southeast Asia: Slow transition from hunting and gathering to agriculture

INDIAN OCEAN

| 0 | 500 | 1000 Miles |
| 0 | 500 | 1000 Kilometers |

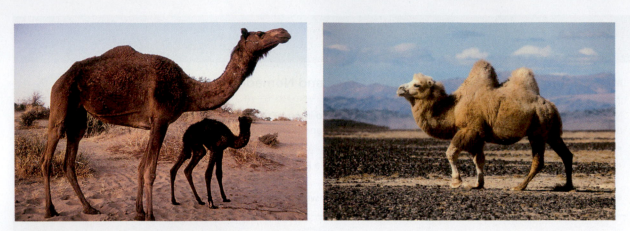

Camels Dromedary camels (*left*) are good draft animals for travel and domestic work in the deserts of Arabia, Afghanistan, and India. Two-hump camels (*right*) are much bigger than dromedary camels. They are more suited to the extreme dry and cold weather in Iran and central Asia. Over time, both types of camel become important for Afro-Eurasian trade.

MIGRATIONS

The violent movement of peoples, driven in part by climate change, disrupted urban societies and destroyed the administrative centers of kings, priests, and dynasties. Invaders, moving out of loosely organized peripheral societies, assaulted the urban centers and territorial kingdoms of mainland Greece, Crete, Anatolia, Mesopotamia, Egypt, and East Asia, causing the collapse of many of these once powerful states. Marauders from the Mediterranean basin and the Syrian desert upset the diplomatic relations and the elaborate system of international trade that had linked Southwest Asia and North Africa. In East Asia, the Zhou peoples, who by the twelfth century BCE were settled in the valley of the Yellow River's most important tributary, the Wei River in northwestern China, tangled with the Shang authorities and eventually overwhelmed the regime. In the Indus Valley, waves of nomads pressed down from the northwest, lured by fertile lands to the south. The upheavals caused by these migrations opened the way for new empires to develop, but only after centuries of turmoil and decline.

NEW TECHNOLOGIES

Technological innovations were crucial in reconstructing communities that had been devastated by drought and violent population movements. Advances in the use of pack camels, seaworthy vessels, iron tools for cultivation, and iron weapons for warfare facilitated the rise of empires.

The camel—first the one-humped Saharan dromedary and later the hardier two-humped Bactrian camel—helped to open up trade routes across

Afro-Eurasia. The fat stored in camels' humps allows them to survive long journeys and harsh desert conditions, and thick pads under their hoofs enable them to walk smoothly over the difficult terrain that had previously hindered such long-distance exchange. Similarly, new shipbuilding technologies made a significant impact. Whereas boats had once been designed for limited transport on rivers and lakes and along shorelines, new ships boasted larger and better-reinforced hulls. Stronger masts and improved rigging allowed billowing sails to harness wind power more effectively. These innovations, along with improvements in ballast and steering, propelled bold mariners to venture out across large bodies of open water like the Mediterranean Sea.

Innovations in metalworking, in which bronze was supplanted by the harder iron, also facilitated the rise of empires. Iron became the most important and widely used metal from this time onward (hence the term Iron Age, sometimes used to describe this period). Although far more abundant than the tin and copper used to make bronze, iron is more difficult to extract from ore and to fabricate into useful shapes. When the technology to smelt and harden iron advanced, iron tools and weapons replaced those made of bronze. This revolution in metallurgy brought shifts in agrarian techniques, such as forged-iron-edged plows that allowed farmers to cultivate crops far beyond the traditional floodplains of riverbanks. Farmers could now till more difficult terrain to remove weeds, break up sod, and unearth fertile subsoil. These technological innovations supported larger, more integrated societies.

ADMINISTRATIVE INNOVATIONS

The expansion of the first empires depended on military might, and control of expanded territories required new administrative techniques. Beginning in the ninth century BCE, fierce Neo-Assyrian soldiers, equipped with iron weaponry and armor, established their king's rule over the countryside. The Neo-Assyrians used mass deportations to break resisters' unity, to provide slave labor in parts of the empire that needed manpower, and to integrate the realm. Over 300 years, they constructed an infrastructure of roads, garrisons, and relay stations throughout the entire territory, making it easier to communicate and to move troops. Moreover, they forced subject peoples to send tribute in the form of grains, animals, raw materials, and people, in addition to precious goods such as gold and lapis lazuli, which they used to build imperial cities and to enrich the royal coffers. In later centuries, such innovations—well-equipped armies, deportation, road systems for transit and communication, and tribute—became common among empires. (See Current Trends in World History: Big Forces in Early Empires.)

Big Forces in Early Empires

Conflict has always been a part of the human condition. But organized warfare and the use of "big force," that is large, well-disciplined armies, appears only with the formation of complex societies. The military units created in these complex societies became crucial vehicles for expanding the lands and peoples under the control of single states and broadcasting the influence of these states well beyond the territories that they controlled militarily.

Evidence for intermittent conflict among the city-states of Sumer in the fourth millennium BCE and in Old Kingdom Egypt (2686–2181 BCE), discussed in Chapter 2, shows that local populations were drafted into a common army when needed. Permanent forces, first recorded in the Old Akkadian period in the third millennium BCE, were used to forge unity, dominate trade routes, and repel threatening "barbarians." Over the next two millennia, across the full extent of Afro-Eurasia, the technologies and structure of war machines developed along similar paths, leading to large standing armies equipped with new and improved weapons, marked by continual innovation and addition of new capabilities.

The earliest armies of Sumer were soldiers on foot arranged in a boxlike formation (generally called a *phalanx*, although that term later becomes associated with military innovations by Alexander of Macedon and his father Philip II). The men were protected by the same types of leather capes and helmets and carried the same large shields to deflect spears and arrows. This mass-formation fighting of infantry that was enabled by uniform training, uniform armaments, and state provisioning became the norm for land forces in Egypt, Neo-Assyria, and, later, the Greek city-states. By the early second millennium, horse-drawn chariots were added to the force, adding mobility and the potential of surprise to an ever-larger infantry force (see Chapter 3). Mounted cavalry was introduced later, toward the middle of the first millennium BCE, by the Neo-Assyrians when fighting in mountainous terrain rendered the chariot impractical. Camels, long used as pack animals, were also used in warfare, primarily by Arab tribesmen conscripted into the Neo-Assyrian army. And elephants were one of the four components of the South Asian Vedic armies, who combined them with cavalry, infantry, and chariots to create a highly effective fighting force.

Even before the rise of complex societies and large military forces, the weapons of warfare had been those of the hunter: bows and arrows,

Assault on -alammu On the reliefs of the palace of Sennacherib (r. c. 700–692 BCE) at Nineveh, slingers launch projectiles while shield-bearing spearmen form up behind them in an assault on a city known from a fragmentary inscription as -alammu.

spears, and slings. Like these weapons, knives, daggers, axes, and maces were also incorporated into armies and were wielded by infantries in hand-to-hand combat. The compound bow, first used in warfare by the Sumerians, was refined by the Neo-Assyrians into a powerful projectile that could achieve an arc of more than 200 yards, raining destruction down on the opposing infantry. Although bronze was the most important metal for weapons, the introduction of iron toward the end of the second millennium BCE expanded the availability of metal for these state war machines. Since war was often conducted to acquire land, cities had to be conquered by force. Battering rams, first documented in Egypt, were added to mobile siege machines; towers supporting archers are pictured on the Neo-Assyrian stone sculptures. Levers and breaking bars as well as tunneling were used to undermine the integrity of the walls. And scaling ladders were thrown against the fortification for the final assault.

In China, the same elements of infantry, chariots, and archers were at the core of the army from as early as the Shang dynasty. While the original goal of the Shang was to capture prisoners needed for sacrifice to the ancestors, soon defensive forces were needed to protect them against their neighbors. The Zhou gradually defeated the Shang through their superior forces and more ingenious and agile tactics. A fundamental advance was made with the invention around 475 BCE of the crossbow, a far more powerful personal killing machine, and the torsion catapult, which threw both heavy projectiles and fiery masses onto the enemy. From the beginning, the techniques and technologies of war were rapidly shared across cultural boundaries as a natural result of adapting and improving on the achievements of the enemy. What mattered most for success was the ability to integrate and coordinate the increasing number of elements that went into a fighting force. The Persians learned at the hands of the Greeks that numbers and sheer firepower could not overcome agility, communication, and integration.

Toward the end of the second millennium BCE, new forms of force were appearing not just on land but also on the sea. The construction of purpose-built ships for the conduct of war on water—the world's first "battleships"—occurred over the course of the eighth century BCE in the eastern Mediterranean. These special ships were built mainly by the Phoenician and the Greek city-states, whose livelihood depended on commerce on the high seas. They were not designed like the slow-sailing bulky ships used for the transport of large cargoes; instead, they were sleek and slim—about 120 feet long and only 15 feet wide—with little room for anything other than the men rowing them. With up to 170 rowers, they were designed and constructed for speed and power. They had no purpose other than the deliberate sinking of other ships. At first, the rowers in ships were arranged with two banks (called *biremes* by the Greeks) and later with three (called *triremes*). The ships were armed with bronze "beaks," or rams, that were used to cave in the sides of enemy ships. These ships were costly to construct, to man, to provision, and to command. As with the maintenance, training, and arming of large land forces, only relatively wealthy states and governments could afford to mount this kind of power on the high seas.

Questions for Analysis

- What were some of the military innovations that were characteristic of "big forces"? In infantry? Cavalry? Naval forces?
- In what specific ways did these military innovations shape the development of empires?
- From your reading of this chapter, in what other ways could you compare empires, in addition to comparing their use of "big forces"?

Explore Further

Briant, Pierre, *From Cyrus to Alexander: A History of the Persian Empire* (2002).

Tanner, Harold M., *China: A History: From Neolithic Cultures through the Great Qing Empire (10,000 BCE–1799 CE)* (2009).

Empire in Southwest Asia: The Neo-Assyrian and Persian Empires

Core Objectives

COMPARE empire formation, or the lack thereof, in Southwest Asia, South Asia, and East Asia between 1250 and 325 BCE.

In Southwest Asia, the Neo-Assyrians and then the Persians offered some of the world's first experiments with true imperial control. The Neo-Assyrians (911–612 BCE) perfected early techniques of imperial rule, many of which became standard in later empires. The Neo-Assyrians also revealed the raw military side of imperial rule: constant, harsh warfare and the brutal exploitation of subjects. On the other hand, the Persians (c. 560–331 BCE), who took control of Southwest Asia after the Neo-Assyrians, balanced their vast multicultural empire through a gentler combination of centralized administration and imperial ideology.

THE NEO-ASSYRIAN EMPIRE (911–612 BCE)

Defining features of the Neo-Assyrian Empire included deportations, forced labor, and a rigid social hierarchy. Neo-Assyrian rulers divided their empire into two parts and ruled them in different ways. The core of empire, which the Neo-Assyrians called the "Land of Ashur," included such ancient cities as Ashur and Nineveh on the upper reaches of the Tigris River, and the lands between the Zagros Mountains and the Euphrates River. (See Map 4.2.) The king's appointees governed these interior lands, whose inhabitants had to supply food for the temple of the national god Ashur, manpower for the god's residence in the city of Ashur, and officials to carry out the state's business. Outside of the "Land of Ashur" proper lay "the Land under the Yoke of Ashur," whose inhabitants were not considered Neo-Assyrians. In these peripheral territories, local rulers held power as subjects of the Neo-Assyrian Empire. These subordinated states were expected to deliver massive amounts of tribute in the form of gold and silver, as opposed to the manpower or agricultural goods supplied by those in the "Land of Ashur." Tribute went directly to the king, who used it to pay for his extravagant court and ever-increasing military costs.

Forced labor—including serving in the military—and deportations helped integrate the empire and undermine local resistance. The Neo-Assyrian armies were hardened and disciplined professional troops led by officers promoted on the basis of merit, not birth. Their military combined infantry, cavalry, iron weapons, horse-drawn chariots armored with iron plates and carrying expert archers, and siege warfare (complete with massive wheeled siege towers and iron-capped battering rams). The Neo-Assyrian army evolved over time from an all-Neo-Assyrian army that conducted annual summer campaigns to a several-hundred-thousand-strong, year-round force composed of Neo-Assyrians and conquered peoples. By the seventh century BCE, different

Map 4.2 The Neo-Assyrian Empire

The Neo-Assyrians built the first strong regional empire in Afro-Eurasia. In the process, they faced the challenge of promoting order and stability throughout their diverse realm.

- Where did the Neo-Assyrian Empire expand? How would you compare the various stages of expansion, in terms of timing and geographic reach?
- Which parts of the empire were "the Land of Ashur," and which were "the Land under the Yoke of Ashur"?
- Why do you think expansion after 720 BCE led to the empire's destruction?

Tiglath Pileser III The walls of the Neo-Assyrian palaces were lined with stone slabs carved with images of the victories of the king. This fragmentary slab from the palace of Tiglath Pileser III (r. 745–728 BCE) originally decorated the wall of his palace at Nimrud. It shows the inhabitants and their herds being forced to leave after the defeat of their town by the Neo-Assyrians. Below is Tiglath Pileser III, shaded by his royal umbrella, in his war chariot.

ethnic groups in the Neo-Assyrian army performed specialized military functions: Phoenicians provided ships and sailors; Medes served as the king's bodyguards; and Israelites supplied charioteers. In addition to a military force, the Neo-Assyrian state needed huge labor forces for agricultural work and for enormous building projects. The Neo-Assyrians recruited most agricultural and construction workers from conquered peoples. Over three centuries, the Neo-Assyrian Empire relocated more than 4 million people—a practice that not only supported its stupendous work projects but also undermined local resistance efforts.

Neo-Assyrian Ideology and Propaganda Neo-Assyrian imperial ideology supported and justified its system of expansion, exploitation, and inequality. Even in the early stages of expansion, Neo-Assyrian inscriptions and art expressed a divinely determined destiny that drove the regime to expand westward toward the Mediterranean Sea. The national god Ashur had commanded all Neo-Assyrians to support the forcible growth of the empire, whose goal was to establish and maintain order and keep an ever-threatening cosmic chaos at bay. Only the god Ashur and his agent, the king, could bring universal order. The king conducted holy war to transform the known world into the well-regulated Land of Ashur, intensifying his campaign of terror and expansion with elaborate propaganda. A three-pronged propaganda program—including elaborate architectural complexes and ceremonies, texts such as inscriptions and year-by-year accounts (annals) of kings' achievements, and vivid images of the army's brutal campaigns—proclaimed that Neo-Assyria's triumph was inevitable.

Neo-Assyrian Social Structure The Neo-Assyrians also exploited a rigid social hierarchy. At the top was the king, who as the sole agent of the god Ashur conducted war to expand the Land of Ashur. Below the king were military elites, rewarded through gifts of land, silver, and exemptions from royal taxes. Over time, these military elites became the noble class and controlled vast estates that included both the land and the local people who worked it. The king and the elites owned the most populous part of the society, the peasantry, in which various categories of workers had differing privileges. Many workers were enslaved because they could not pay their debts, but they were allowed to marry nonslave partners, conduct financial transactions, and even own property with other slaves attached to it. Foreigners enslaved through conquest, however, had no rights and were forced to do hard manual labor on the state's monumental building projects. Those peoples forcibly relocated were not slaves but became attached to the lands that they had to work. Families were small and lived on modest plots of land, where they raised vegetables and planted vineyards.

Women in Neo-Assyria were far more restricted than their counterparts in the earlier periods of Sumerian and Old Babylonian Mesopotamia. Under the Neo-Assyrians' patriarchal social system, women had almost no control over their lives. Because all inheritance passed through the male line, it was crucial that a man be certain of the paternity of the children borne by his wives. As a result, all interactions between men and women outside of the family were highly restricted. The so-called Middle Assyrians of the thirteenth century BCE had introduced the practice of veiling, requiring it of all respectable women. Prostitutes who serviced the men of the army and worked in the taverns were forbidden to wear the veil, so that their revealed faces and hair would signal their disreputable status. Any prostitute found wearing the veil would be dragged to the top of the city wall, stripped of her clothing, flogged, and sometimes even killed.

The queens of Neo-Assyria obeyed the same social norms, but their lives were more comfortable and varied than the commoners'. They lived in a separate part of the palace with servants who were either women slaves or eunuchs (castrated males). Though Neo-Assyrian queens rarely wielded genuine power, they enjoyed respect and recognition, especially in the role of mother of the king. In fact, a queen could serve as regent for her son if the king died while his heir was still a child.

The Instability of the Neo-Assyrian Empire At their peak, the Neo-Assyrians controlled most of the lands stretching from Persia to Egypt. Yet their empire was unstable, as it required occupying armies to be spread across vast territories and a relentless propaganda machine. Discontent among nobles ultimately led to civil war, which made the Neo-Assyrian Empire vulnerable to external threats as well. The conquest of Nineveh by a combined force of Medes, Neo-Babylonians, and other groups contributed to the collapse of the Neo-Assyrian Empire in 612 BCE.

THE PERSIAN EMPIRE (c. 560–331 BCE)

After a brief interlude of Neo-Babylonian rule—including the reign of Nebuchadnezzar II (r. c. 605–562 BCE) and the creation of his legendary Hanging Gardens of Babylon—the Persians asserted power and created a gentler form of imperial rule in Southwest Asia, based more on persuasion and mutual benefit than on raw power. A nomadic group speaking an Indo-Iranian language,

The Annals of Ashurbanipal
This ten-sided baked clay cylinder carries a portion of the annals of the Neo-Assyrian king Ashurbanipal (r. 668–627 BCE). It was found at Nineveh along with thousands of other tablets preserved in his famous library, including many of the earliest fragments of the *Epic of Gilgamesh*. The annals of Ashurbanipal were detailed, almost novelistic accounts of his military and civic achievements. Unlike earlier annals, they include first-person discourse, indirect discourse, flashbacks, and lively descriptions of events and places.

the Persians had arrived on the Iranian plateau from central Asia during the second millennium and gradually spread to the plateau's southwestern part. These expert horsemen shot arrows from horseback with deadly accuracy in the midst of battle. After Cyrus the Great (r. 559–529 BCE) united the Persian tribes, his armies defeated the Lydians in southwestern Anatolia and took over their gold mines, land, and trading routes. He next overpowered the Greek city-states on the Aegean coast of Anatolia. In building their immense empire, the Persians, whose ancestors were pastoralists and had no urban traditions to draw on, adapted the ideologies and institutions of the Neo-Babylonians, the Neo-Assyrians, and indigenous peoples, modifying them to fit their own customs and political aims.

The Integration of a Multicultural Persian Empire From their base on the Iranian plateau, the Persian rulers developed a centralized yet multicultural empire that reached from the Indus Valley to northern Greece and from central Asia to the south of Egypt. (See Map 4.3.) Cyrus, the founder of the Persian Empire, presented himself as a benevolent ruler who had liberated his subjects from the oppression of their own kings. He pointed to his victory in Babylon as a sign that the city's gods had turned against its king as a heretic. Cyrus released the Jews from their captivity in Babylon, to which they had been exiled by the Neo-Babylonian king Nebuchadnezzar II around 587 BCE; they then returned to Jerusalem in 538 BCE to begin rebuilding their temple. Even the Greeks, who later defeated the Persians, saw Cyrus as a model ruler.

In the aftermath of Cyrus's death on the battlefield, Darius I (r. 521–486 BCE) overcame his main rival for power and put the new empire on a solid footing. First he suppressed revolts across the lands, recording this feat on the Behistun inscription, a monumental rock relief overhanging the road to his capital, Persepolis. Then he conquered territories held by dozens of different ethnic groups, stretching from the Indus River in the east to the Aegean and Mediterranean Seas in the west, and from the Black, Caspian, and Aral Seas in the north to the Nile River in the south. To manage this huge domain, Darius introduced dynamic administrative systems that enabled the empire to flourish for another two centuries. Its new bureaucracy combined central and local administration and made effective use of the strengths of local tradition, economy, and rule—rather than forcing Persian customs on subject people via rigid central control.

This empire was both centralized and multicultural. The Persians believed that all subject peoples were equal; the only requirements were to be loyal to the king and to pay tribute—which was considered an honor, not a burden. Although local Persian administrators used local languages, Aramaic (a dialect of a Semitic language long spoken in Southwest Asia) became the empire's official language because many of its literate scribes came from Mesopotamia. Darius brought the wealth of the periphery to the imperial center

Map 4.3 The Persian Empire, 550–479 BCE

Starting in the sixth century BCE, the Persians succeeded the Neo-Assyrians as rulers of the large regional empire of Southwest Asia and North Africa. Compare the Persian Empire's territorial domains to those of the Neo-Assyrian Empire in Map 4.2.

- Geographically, how did the Persian Empire differ from the Neo-Assyrian state?
- Analyzing the map, how many Persian satrapies existed and in what regions? What role do you think they played in the success of the Persian Empire?
- How did *qanats* and road systems help the Persians consolidate their imperial power?

by establishing a system of provinces, or **satrapies**, each ruled by a governor (called a satrap) who was a relative or a close associate of the king. The local bureaucrats and officials who administered the government worked under close monitoring by military officers, central tax collectors, and spies (the so-called eyes of the king) who enforced the satraps' loyalty. Darius established a system of fixed taxation and formal tribute allocations. Moreover, he promoted trade throughout the empire by building roads, establishing a

satrapy
Province in the Persian empire, ruled over by a governor, called a satrap, who was usually a relative or associate of the king.

standardized currency including coinage, and introducing standard weights and measures. These strategies helped integrate and centralize the empire's vast territories.

Zoroastrianism, Ideology, and Social Structure The Persians built their ideology of kingship and their social structure on religious foundations. They drew their religious ideas from their pastoral and tribal roots, and thus their ideology reflected traditions of warrior and priestly classes similar to those preserved in the Vedic texts of the Indus Valley. Zoroaster (also known as Zarathustra), who most likely lived sometime after 1000 BCE in eastern Iran, crystallized the region's traditional beliefs into a formal religious system. The main source for the teachings of Zoroaster is the *Avesta*, a collection of holy works initially transmitted orally by priests and then, according to legend, written down in the third century BCE. **Zoroastrianism** ultimately became the religion of the empire.

Zoroaster promoted belief in the god Ahura Mazda, who had created the world and all that was good. In dualistic contrast, Ahura Mazda's adversary, Ahriman, was deceitful and wicked. The Persians saw these two forces—light and truth versus darkness and lies—as engaged in a cosmic struggle for control of the universe. Zoroastrianism treated humans as capable of choosing between good and evil. Human choices had consequences: rewards or punishments in the afterlife.

Persians believed that their kings were appointed by Ahura Mazda as ruler over all peoples and all lands of the earth and charged by him with maintaining perfect order from which all creation would benefit. As such, kings enjoyed absolute authority. In return, they were expected to follow moral and political guidelines that reflected Zoroastrian notions of ethical behavior. Kings also had to show physical superiority that matched their moral standing. They had to be expert horsemen and peerless in wielding bows and spears. These were qualities valued by all Persian nobles, who revered the virtues of their nomadic ancestors. According to the ancient Greek historian Herodotus, Persian boys were taught three things only: "to ride, to shoot with the bow, and to tell the truth."

The Persian social order included four diverse groups with well-defined roles. A ruling class consisted of priests maintaining the ritual fire in temples, nobles administering the state, and warriors protecting and expanding the empire. An administrative and commercial class included scribes and bureaucrats who kept imperial records and merchants who secured goods from distant lands. The other two groups were made up of artisans and, finally, peasants who grew the crops and tended the flocks that fed the imperial machine.

The powerful Persian hereditary nobility surrounded and supported the king. These nobles had vast landholdings and often served the king as satraps or advisers. Also close to the king were wealthy merchants who directed trade

Persepolis In the highland valley of Fars, the homeland of the Persians, Darius and his successors built a capital city and ceremonial center at the site of Persepolis. On top of a huge platform, there were audience halls, a massive treasury, the harem, and residential spaces. The building was constructed of mud brick. The roof was supported by enormous columns projecting the images of bulls.

across the vast empire. Royal gifts solidified the relations between king and nobles, reinforcing the king's place at the top of the political and social pyramid. In public ceremonies the king presented gold vessels, elaborate textiles, and jewelry to reward each recipient's loyalty and demonstrate dependence on the crown. Any kind of failure would result in the withdrawal of royal favor. Should such failures be serious or treasonous, the offenders faced torture and death. In Persian society, class and royal favor counted for everything.

Public Works and Imperial Identity The Persians undertook significant building projects that helped unify their empire and consolidate imperial identity. For one, the Persians engaged in large-scale road building and constructed a system of rapid and dependable communication. The key element in the system was the Royal Road, which followed age-old trade routes some 1,600 miles from western Anatolia to the heart of the empire in southwestern Iran; trade routes continued eastward across the northern Iranian plateau and into central Asia. Traders used the Royal Road, as did the Persian army; subjects took tribute to the king, and royal couriers carried messages to the satraps and imperial armies over this road.

In addition to the Royal Road, the Persians devised other ways to connect the far reaches of the empire with its center. Darius oversaw the construction of a canal more than 50 miles long linking the Red Sea to the Nile River.

Persian Water-Moving Technique The Persians perfected the channeling of water over long distances through underground channels called *qanats*. This technique, an efficient way to move water without evaporation, is still used today in hot, arid regions. In this example near Yazd, in central Iran, the domed structure leading to the underground tunnel is flanked by two brick towers called *badgir*, an ancient form of air-conditioning that cools the water using wind (*bad* in Persian). See Map 4.3 for the location of these *qanats*.

Additionally, Persians developed a system of *qanats,* underground tunnels through which water flowed over long distances without evaporating or being contaminated. Laborers from local populations toiled on these feats of engineering as part of their obligations as subjects of the empire.

Until Cyrus's time, the Persians had been pastoral nomads who lacked traditions of monumental architecture, visual arts, or written literature or history. Multiple capitals—at Persepolis, Pasargadae, and Susa—expressed a Persian imperial identity. Skilled craftsmen from all over the empire blended their distinct cultural influences into a new Persian architectural style. The Persians used monumental architecture with grand columned halls and huge open spaces to provide reception rooms for thousands of representatives bringing tribute from all over the empire and as a way to help integrate subject peoples by connecting them to one central, imperial authority. In the royal palace, three of the columned halls stood on raised platforms accessed via processional stairways that were lined with elaborate images of subjects bringing gifts and tribute to the king. This highly refined program of visual propaganda showed the Persian Empire as a society of diverse but obedient peoples. The carvings on the great stairway of Persepolis demonstrate the range of peoples each bringing distinctive tribute: the Armenians presenting precious metal vessels, the Lydians carrying gold armlets and bowls, the Egyptians offering exotic animals, and the Sogdians leading proud horses.

While the stream of tribute ebbed and flowed over time, the multicultural Persian Empire was able to hold power in Southwest Asia for more than 200 years. Although the empire was weakened by challenges posed by Greek city-states to its west in the fifth century, it persisted until it fell to the invading army of Alexander the Great in 331 BCE. First the Neo-Assyrians, and then later the Persians, had fashioned their own brands of empire that used a combination of military force, rigid political and social organization, and religious ideology to maintain successive control over Southwest Asia.

Imperial Fringes in Western Afro-Eurasia

A very different world emerged on Afro-Eurasia's western edges. Although their powerful neighbors affected them, western peoples—such as the Sea Peoples, the Greeks, the Phoenicians, and the Israelites—retained their own languages, beliefs, and systems of rule. While their communities were smaller than those in Southwest Asia, each asserted power and had long-lasting influence disproportionate to their size.

Core Objectives

ANALYZE the relationships between empires and the peoples on their peripheries in Southwest Asia, South Asia, and East Asia.

SEA PEOPLES

New migrations brought violent change to long-established kingdoms and states in the Mediterranean and Southwest Asia. Beginning around 1200 BCE, as the full effects of drought struck, new waves of Indo-European-speaking peoples left the Danube River basin in Central Europe. A rapid rise in population and the development of local natural resources, particularly iron, spurred this group, who came to be known as the **Sea Peoples,** to move down the Danube toward the Black Sea. The invaders, armed with iron weaponry, brought turmoil to the peoples living in southeastern Europe, the Aegean, and the eastern Mediterranean.

The Hittites of Anatolia were the first to fall to the migrants' invasion. Once the invaders reached the Mediterranean, they mainly used boats for transportation, hence the label Sea Peoples (not a name they called themselves but rather one from the perspective of those whom they attacked). The Egyptians knew them as the Peleset, and only with great difficulty did the pharaohs repel them. Ramses III's mortuary temple in Thebes displays a massive relief depicting the so-called Battle of the Delta (c. 1175 BCE), in which he and his Egyptian forces fought off their invasion. The Sea Peoples ultimately settled along the southern coast of Southwest Asia, where they became known as the Philistines.

In the Mediterranean, the Sea Peoples' intrusion shook the social order of the Minoans on the island of Crete (see Chapter 3). Agricultural production in the region declined, and as the palace-centered bureaucracies and priesthoods of the second millennium BCE vanished, more violent societies emerged that relied on the newcomers' iron weapons. This was the culture

Sea Peoples
Migrants from north of the Mediterranean who invaded cities of Egypt, Asia Minor, and the Levant in the second millennium BCE.

of warrior-heroes described in the *Iliad*, an epic poem about the Trojan War, based on oral tales passed down for centuries before their compilation by Homer in the eighth century BCE. The Greek descendants of these warrior-heroes of the Mycenaean past developed dynamic communities and, as we will see in the next section, offered one of the most significant challenges to the Persians.

THE GREEKS

Among the small-scale societies that emerged in Persia's shadow, the Greeks were particularly influential. Greek-speaking people in different cities sometimes cooperated with the Persians, even borrowing their ideas, but sometimes strongly resisted them. In 499 BCE, some Greek city-states and others in the eastern Mediterranean revolted against the Persians, who claimed control over the Greek islands and mainland. During the six-year struggle, some Greek communities sided with the Persians and suffered condemnation by other Greeks for doing so. On the mainland, most Greek cities resisted the Persian king's authority. In 490 BCE, Darius and his vast army invaded mainland Greece but suffered a humiliating defeat at the hands of the much smaller force of Athenians at Marathon, near Athens. The Persians retreated and waited another decade before challenging their western foe again. Meanwhile, however, Athens was becoming a major sea power.

Under the leadership of Themistocles in the 480s BCE, Athens became a naval power whose strength was its fleet of triremes (battleships). When Greek and Persian forces clashed again in 480 BCE, Persian land forces led by Darius's successor Xerxes fought through Leonidas's 300 Spartans (and other Greeks) at Thermopylae only to have their navy lose the pivotal sea battle at Salamis. A year later, the Persians suffered a decisive defeat on land and eventually lost the war. Persian military defeats changed the balance of power. For the next 150 years, Persia lost ground to the Greeks, who gradually regained territory in southeastern Europe and western Anatolia. That expanded territory, and its governance, would become in the fifth century BCE the root of Greek civil discord (see Chapter 5).

THE PHOENICIANS

Another important group on the fringes extended their influence across the Mediterranean through their seafaring and trade: these were the Chanani

Mycenaean Arms and Armor
This Mycenaean vase illustrates the central role of arms and war to the societies on mainland Greece through 1200 BCE. The men bear common suits of armor and weapons—helmets, corsets, spears, and shields—most likely supplied to them by the palace-centered organizations to which they belonged. Despite these advantages, they were not able to mount a successful defense against the land incursions that destroyed the Mycenaean palaces toward the end of the thirteenth century BCE.

(called "Canaanites" in Hebrew scriptures) living in the region of modern-day Lebanon. We know these entrepreneurial people by the name that the Greeks gave them—**Phoenicians** ("Purple People")—because of an expensive purple dye that they manufactured and traded. A mixture of the local population and the more recently arrived Sea Peoples, these traders preferred opening up new markets and new ports to subduing frontiers. The Phoenicians maintained their autonomy from Neo-Assyrian kings by supplying them with exotic luxuries. Phoenician coastal cities were ideally situated to develop trade throughout the entire Mediterranean basin. Inland stood an extraordinary forest of massive cedars—perfect timber for making large, seaworthy craft, and a highly desirable export to the treeless heartlands of Egypt and Mesopotamia. (See Map 4.4.)

Innovations in shipbuilding and seafaring enabled Phoenicians to sail as far west as present-day Morocco and Spain, carrying huge cargoes of such goods as timber, dyed cloth, glassware, wines, textiles, copper ingots, and carved ivory. Their trading colonies all around the southern and western rims of the Mediterranean (including Carthage in modern-day Tunisia) became major ports that shipped goods from interior regions throughout the Mediterranean. There they competed with Greek colonies that were similarly settling in the western Mediterranean to pursue commerce and relieve population pressures. While the Phoenicians are noteworthy for their seafaring and trade, they are perhaps best known for their revolutionizing of commerce and communication through their development of the **alphabet** in the mid-second millennium BCE. This new method of writing arrived in the west in 800 BCE, probably through Greek traders working in Phoenician centers. The alphabet allowed educated people to communicate directly with one another, dramatically reducing the need for professional scribes. The Phoenicians' trade and their alphabet allowed this "fringe" group to exert influence far beyond the confines of their political borders.

THE ISRAELITES

To the south of the mountains of Lebanon, the homeland of the Phoenicians, another minor region extended to the borderlands of Egypt. In this narrow strip of land between the Mediterranean Sea to the west and the desert to the east, an important microsociety emerged, that of the Israelites. The Israelites' own later stories emphasized their origins in Mesopotamia to the east, with the patriarch Abraham from Ur on the Euphrates. Later stories stressed connections with the Egypt of the pharaohs to the west and the mass movement of a captive Israelite population out of Egypt under Moses in the late second millennium BCE. Archaeological evidence suggests that a local culture emerged in the area of present-day Israel between 1200 and 1000 BCE. These developments culminated in a kingdom centered at Jerusalem under

Phoenicians

An ethnic group in the Levant known for their ships, trading, and alphabet, and referred to in Hebrew scripture as the Canaanites. The term *Phoenician* (Greek for "Purple People") derives from the major trade good they manufactured, a rare and expensive purple dye.

alphabet

A mid-second-millennium BCE Phoenician system of writing based on relatively few letters (twenty-two) that combined to make sounds and words. Adaptable to many languages, the alphabet was simpler and more flexible than writing based on symbols for syllables and ideas.

Map 4.4 The Mediterranean World, 1000–400 BCE

....

Peoples on the fringes of the great regional empires of Southwest Asia and North Africa had strong influences beyond their borders, despite their political marginalization. Though politically dwarfed by the Neo-Assyrian and Persian Empires, various groups in the Mediterranean basin displayed strong cultural and economic power.

- What were the borderland communities and what did they trade?
- How far did their trading networks and settlement patterns extend?
- According to your reading, why were such small communities able to flourish in terms of trade and settlement?

PHŒNICIAN	ANCIENT GREEK	LATER GREEK	ROMAN
			A
			B
			G
			D
			E
			F
			Z
			H
			Th
			I
			K
			L
			M
			N
			X
			O
			P
			Q
			R
			S
			T

The Phoenician Alphabet (*Left*) The first alphabet was written on clay tablets using the cuneiform script. It was developed by Phoenician traders who needed a script that was easy to learn so that they could record transactions without specially trained scribes. This tablet was found at the port town of Ugarit (Ras Shamra) in Syria and is dated to the fourteenth century BCE. (*Right*) The forms of the letters in the Phoenician alphabet of the first millennium BCE are based on signs used to represent the Aramaic language. These Phoenician letters were then borrowed by the ancient Greeks. Our alphabet is based on the one used by the Romans, who borrowed their letter forms from the later Greek inscriptions.

King David (r. c. 1000–960 BCE). The kingdom that David and his successor Solomon (r. c. 960–930 BCE) established around Jerusalem, centered on the great temple that Solomon built in the city, did not last long. It fragmented immediately after Solomon's reign, forming the small kingdom of Israel in the north and the smaller Judah in the south.

Within the small kingdom founded by David and Solomon, profound religious and cultural changes took place. Solomon's great temple in Jerusalem outranked all other shrines in the land. The educated upper classes especially, who were linked to the temple, focused on one god, YHWH, over other regional deities in a form of reverence modern scholars call *henotheism* (the recognition of the power of one god over other spirits and deities that still exist). Gradually, however, there was a move to **monotheism** (the acceptance of only one god to the exclusion of all others).

monotheism
The belief in only one god; to be distinguished from polytheism (the belief in many gods) and henotheism (the belief that there may be many gods but one is superior to the others).

The long transition to monotheism, completed by the seventh century BCE, did not take place without resistance. Challenging the power of kings and priests, prophets like Isaiah (c. 720s BCE), Ezra (c. 600s BCE), and Jeremiah (c. 590s BCE) helped articulate the Israelites' monotheistic religion. Prophets threatened divine annihilation for groups that opposed the new idea of one temple, one god, and one moral system to the exclusion of all others. The Neo-Assyrians to the east figured large in many of the prophets' warnings. Ultimately, the Torah—a series of five books that encapsulated the laws governing all aspects of life, including family and marriage, food, clothing, sex, and worship—became an exclusive "contract" between all these people and their one and only god. As Jewish people scattered over time across Afro-Eurasia, their monotheism would come to have a far-reaching impact.

Foundations of Vedic Culture in South Asia (1500–600 BCE)

In South Asia, language and belief systems—rather than a unified political system enforced and enlarged by military conquests—brought people together. Indo-European-speaking peoples, also known as Vedic peoples for the religious traditions they brought with them, entered South Asia through the passes in the Hindu Kush Mountains in the middle of the second millennium BCE and eventually occupied the whole of what are today Pakistan, Bangladesh, and northern India (see Chapter 3). Here the migrant population, together with the indigenous inhabitants, fostered a flourishing culture. Unlike in societies in Southwest Asia, the new rulers in this region did not have previous states on which to found their power. Floods and earthquakes had weakened the earlier Harappan urban centers in the Indus River valley (see Chapter 2), and their urban culture had died out several centuries earlier. Vedic newcomers integrated this territory through a shared culture. Even though the Vedic migrants changed the social and cultural landscape of the region, they did not give it greater political coherence by creating a single, unified regional kingdom.

VEDIC CULTURE SETTLES DOWN

The men and women who migrated into the northern lands of South Asia were illiterate, chariot-riding, and cattle-keeping pastoral peoples, who lacked experience of cities and urban life. They brought with them much beloved and elaborate rituals, mainly articulated in hymns, called **Vedas** (Sanskrit for "wisdom" or "knowledge"), which they retained as they entered a radically different environment and which they relied on to provide a foundation for assimilating new ways. Transmitted orally, but eventually written down in

Vedas
Rituals, hymns, and other explanatory texts composed and orally transmitted in Sanskrit by Brahman priests. They shaped the society and religious rituals of Vedic peoples and became central texts in Hinduism.

Sanskrit, Vedic hymns reflected their earlier lives on the plains of central Asia and were infused with images of animals and gods. For example, in some of these Vedic poems storms "gallop" across the heavens, and thunder sounds like the "neigh of horses."

These Indo-European-speaking migrants, equipped with their Vedic traditions, encountered indigenous people who either lived in agricultural settlements or were herders like themselves. They allied themselves with some peoples and made enemies of others. In their interactions with local peoples, the Vedic migrants kept their own language and religious rituals but also absorbed local words and deities. Allies and defeated enemies who became part of their society had to accept Vedic culture. By the middle of the first millennium BCE, the Vedic peoples covered all of what is now northern India, and their language and rituals had become dominant in their new land. (See Map 4.5.)

Vedic elites, with their pastoral nomadic roots, never lost their passion for fine horses, and they created trading routes to the northwest, beyond the Hindu Kush, to maintain a supply of these horses. But as the Vedic people entered the fertile river basins, they gradually settled down and turned to agriculture and herding. Indigenous farmers taught the Vedic newcomers farming techniques. For example, the iron plow was crucial for tilling the Ganges plain and transforming the Deccan plateau into croplands. In the drier north, the Vedic people grew wheat, barley, millet, and cotton; in the wet lowlands, they cultivated rice paddies. Farmers also produced tropical crops such as sugarcane and spices like pepper, ginger, and cinnamon. With farming success came increased populations and urban settlements across the region, fueled by agricultural surplus and trade in goods, both raw (grain) and manufactured (sugarcane into sugar).

SOCIAL DISTINCTIONS: CLANS AND *VARNA*

Over time, Vedic societies became more complex and less egalitarian than those of their pastoral ancestors. In the process of fanning out across the five tributaries of the Indus River and settling in the plain between the Ganges and Yamuna Rivers, the Vedic peoples created small regional governments and chieftainships. Jockeying for land and resources, they fought fiercely with the indigenous peoples and even more fiercely among themselves.

Vedic chieftainships eventually became small kingdoms with inhabitants bound to each other through lines of descent from a common ancestor. They traced their lineage—identified as either solar or lunar—through blood ties, marriage alliances, and invented family relations. The two lineages, solar and lunar, included many *clans* (groups of households claiming descent from a common ancestor) in which seniority determined one's power and importance. The Vedic peoples absorbed many local clans into their own lineages. Clans that adopted the Vedic culture became part of the lineage (through

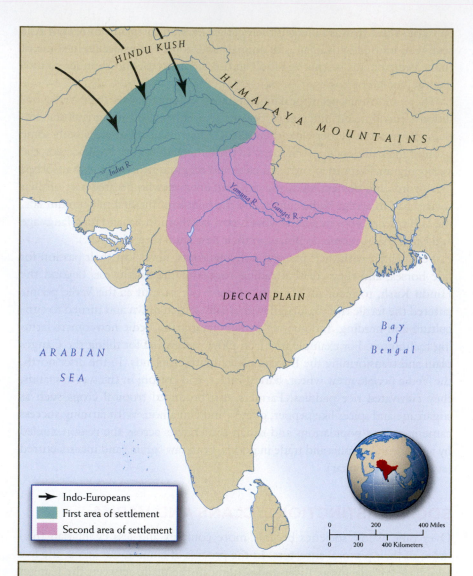

Indo-Europeans
First area of settlement
Second area of settlement

Map 4.5 South Asia, 1500–400 BCE

Indo-European peoples crossed over mountainous areas and entered northern South Asia, bringing with them their nomadic ways. They were, however, quick to learn settled agriculture from the local inhabitants.

- Where did the Indo-Europeans originally come from?
- Where did they settle? What geographical features may have influenced the stages of expansion southward?
- Based on your reading, why did Vedic culture prosper and provide a basis of unity for such large populations?

marriage or made-up ties) and were considered insiders. In contrast, clans that had other languages and rituals were considered to be uncivilized outsiders. These two lineages became less important over time, but were memorialized in the later *Mahabharata*, one of the two major Sanskrit epics of ancient India, which recalls the last phase of the lunar lineage, and the *Ramayana*, the second Sanskrit epic, which celebrates a hero of the solar lineage.

As Vedic peoples settled into agrarian communities after 1000 BCE, their social structure became even more complex and hierarchical. Among other distinctions, divisions developed between those who controlled the land and those who worked it. Vedic peoples used the term **varna** to refer to their rigid status distinction and recognized four ranked social groups into which one was born—Brahmans, Kshatriyas, Vaishyas, and Shudras. Since the Sanskrit word *varna* means "color," its use suggests that the four-class system originated in the encounter between clans and communities of different complexions and cultures. Vedic hymns described the origins of the *varnas* in their creation narrative. When the gods sacrificed Purusha to create the universe, the Brahmans (priests) came from his mouth, his arms produced the Kshatriyas (warriors), the thighs gave birth to the Vaishyas (commoners), and from the feet emerged the Shudras (laborers and servants).

Clan members who had been politically the most powerful and had led their communities into northern India claimed the status of Kshatriyas. It was they who controlled the land. Less powerful clan members, who worked the land and tended livestock, became Vaishyas. Slaves and laborers who served in the households and fields of the Vaishyas came from outside the

varna
Sanskrit for "color"; refers to the four ranked social groups within early Vedic society (priests, warriors, commoners, and laborers). The term *caste*, which derives from the term *casta* ("race/breed" in Spanish and Portuguese) is a later, anachronistic term often used for these divisions.

Scenes from the Mahabharata Reliefs on the walls of the Kailasa Temple in the Ellora Cave complex in northwest India depict scenes from the *Mahabharata* and the *Ramayana*. While these images were carved in the eighth century CE, they illustrate scenes from these epics that recount the distant Vedic past thousands of years earlier when the lunar and solar lineages struggled against one another and among themselves. Archers, war elephants, chariots, hand-to-hand combat, and diplomatic scenes combine on this relief to narrate the main battle from the *Mahabharata* between two rival factions of the lunar lineage.

Gold Coin of Kumaragupta I
Kumaragupta I's coin, dating from the fifth century CE, intentionally drew on much older Vedic concepts (including the ashvamedha, or horse sacrifice from the Yajur-Veda) and imagery (here, a Hindu goddess).

Vedic lineages and became known as Shudras. Brahmans claimed the highest status, for they performed the rituals and understood the religious principles without which life was believed to be unsustainable. Brahmans and Kshatriyas reinforced each other's high status. Brahmans performed the sacrifices that converted warriors into kings, and kings reciprocated by paying fees and gifts to the Brahmans. Vaishyas and Shudras were left with the tasks of ensuring the sustenance of the elite. The Brahmans guided a society in which the proper relationship with the forces of nature as represented by the deities constituted the basis of prosperity. As agriculture became ever more important, Brahmans acted as agents of Agni, the god of fire, to purify the new land for cultivation. This complex hierarchy so inextricably connected with Vedic religion provided the primary unifying structure for society in South Asia.

UNITY THROUGH THE VEDAS AND UPANISHADS

A Vedic culture, transmitted from generation to generation by the Brahmans, unified what political rivalries had divided. A common language (Sanskrit); belief in Agni, Indra, and other gods; and shared cultural symbols linked the dispersed communities and gave Vedic peoples a collective identity. Though Sanskrit was a language imported from central Asia, the people used it to transmit the Vedas orally. By expressing sacred knowledge in the rhythms and rhymes of Sanskrit, the Vedic peoples effectively passed on their culture from one generation to the next.

The Vedas promoted cultural unity and pride through common ritual practices and support for hereditary leaders. As the priests of Vedic society, the Brahmans were responsible for memorizing the Vedic works. These included commentaries on sacred works from early nomadic times as well as new rules and rituals explaining the settled, farming way of life. The main body of Vedic literature includes the four Vedas: Rig-Veda, Sama-Veda, Yajur-Veda, and Atharva-Veda. The Rig-Veda, the earliest text, is a collection of hymns praising the gods, including Indra (god of war), Agni (god of fire), and Varuna (god of water). The Sama-Veda is a textbook of songs for priests to perform when making ritual sacrifices; most of its stanzas also appear in the Rig-Veda. The Yajur-Veda is a prayer book for the priest who conducted rituals for chariot races, horse sacrifices, or the king's coronation. The Atharva-Veda includes charms and remedies; many address problems related to agriculture, a central aspect of life. Although the Vedic period left no impressive buildings and artifacts, the Vedas laid the socioreligious foundations for South Asia.

During the middle of the first millennium BCE, some thinkers (mostly Brahman ascetics dwelling in forests) felt that the Vedic rituals no longer provided satisfactory answers to the many questions of a rapidly changing society.

The result was a collection of works known as the **Upanishads**, or "the supreme knowledge," which expanded the Vedic cultural system. Taking the form of dialogues between disciples and a sage, the Upanishads offered insights into the ideal social order. The Upanishads teach that people are not separate from each other but belong to a cosmic universe called Brahma. While the physical world is always changing and is filled with chaos and illusion, *atman*, the eternal being, exists in all people and all creatures. Atman's presence in each living being makes all creatures part of a universal soul. Although all living beings must die, atman guarantees eternal life, ensuring that souls are reborn and transmigrate into new lives. This cycle continues with humans as they are reborn either as humans or as other living creatures, like cows, insects, or plants.

These unique views of life and the universe, as outlined in the Vedas and Upanishads, were passed along as principles of faith, bringing spiritual unity to the northern half of South Asia because local gods could easily be absorbed into the system. Unlike in Southwest Asia, here in the kingdoms of the Indus Valley and the Ganges plain the common Vedic culture—rather than larger political units—was the unifying bond.

Upanishads
First-millennium BCE Vedic wisdom literature, in the form of a dialogue between students and teacher; together with the Vedas, they brought a cultural and spiritual unity to much of South Asia.

The Early Zhou Empire in East Asia (1045–771 BCE)

In China, the Zhou succeeded the Shang state, and Zhou rulers built a powerful tributary empire, claiming the "mandate of heaven." The Zhou had been only a minor state during the Shang's political preeminence; during that period, the Zhou and the Shang had lived side by side, trading and often allying with one another to fend off raiders from the northwest. The appearance of a dynamic leader among the Zhou peoples, King Wu, and the need to find more resources after drought-related dust storms swept across the North China plain, emboldened the Zhou to challenge the Shang. At a battle in 1045 BCE, the Zhou prevailed. King Wu of the Zhou owed his success to his army of 45,000 troops and their superior weaponry, which included dagger axes, bronze armor, and 300 war chariots (small numbers by Southwest Asian standards, but overwhelming in East Asia). (See Map 4.6.) In the centuries that followed, innovations in politics, agriculture, and social structures helped the Zhou integrate their empire.

Core Objectives

EVALUATE the connection between empires and war, religion, and trade in Southwest Asia and East Asia.

DYNASTIC INSTITUTIONS AND CONTROL OF THE LAND

When the Zhou took over from the Shang, their new state consisted of more than seventy small states, whose rulers accepted the overarching authority of

GOBI DESERT

TAKLAMAKAN
DESERT

Shang
Zhou

Yellow R.

SHANG
DYNASTY

YELLOW
SEA

Hangou Canal

●Xianyang

ZHOU DYNASTY

EAST
CHINA
SEA

PLATEAU
OF
TIBET

HIMALAYA MTS.

Yangzi R.

Irrawaddy R.

Mekong R.

Pearl R.

SOUTHEAST ASIA

Bay
of
Bengal

SOUTH
CHINA
SEA

0   250   500 Miles
0   250   500 Kilometers

Map 4.6 The Shang and Zhou Dynasties, 2200–256 BCE

Toward the end of the second millennium BCE, the Zhou state supplanted the Shang dynasty as the most powerful political force in East Asia. Using the map above, compare and contrast the territorial reach of the Zhou state with that of the Shang.

- In what direction did the Zhou state expand most dramatically?
- As you view the map, why do you think that the Zhou did not expand farther northward and westward?
- Based on your reading, how did the Zhou integrate their geographically large and diverse state?

the Zhou kings. To solidify their power, the Zhou copied the Shang's patrimonial state structure, centered on ancestor worship in which the rulers' power passed down through a lineage of male ancestors reaching back to the gods. Thirty-nine Zhou kings followed one after the other, mostly in an orderly father-to-son succession, over a span of eight centuries.

Even though the Zhou drew heavily on Shang precedents, their own innovations produced some of the most significant contributions to China's distinctive cultural and political development. Regarding all those whom they governed as a single people, the Zhou referred to their subjects using the term *Huaxia*, or "Chinese." Although the various Zhou states were not fully unified, Zhou leaders called their lands *Zhongguo*, a term that came to mean "the middle kingdom" (and is a term still used for the modern state of China). Moreover, the Zhou kings of this middle kingdom, in addition to being required to rule justly, believed that they had a duty to extend their culture to "less civilized" peoples living in outlying regions.

Having defeated the Shang and established Zhou control in northwestern China, King Wu (r. 1049–1043) and his successors expanded north toward what is now Beijing and south toward the Yangzi River valley. Seeking to retain the allegiance of the lords of older states and to gain the support of new lords, whom they appointed in annexed areas, Zhou kings rewarded their political supporters with lands that they could pass on to their descendants. As the Zhou expanded their territory, its new colonies often consisted of garrison towns where the Zhou colonizers lived, surrounded by fields (inhabited by local farmers). As under the Shang, Zhou regional lords supplied military forces as needed, paid tribute, and appeared at the imperial court to pledge their continuing allegiance.

The Zhou leaders promoted the integration of China not only through dynastic institutions but also through agricultural advances (including the iron plow, irrigation, and canals). Wooden and, much later, iron plows enabled farmers to break the hard sod of lands beyond the river basins, and over time cultivators learned the practice of field rotation to prevent soil nutrients from being exhausted. In the middle of the first millennium BCE, regional states organized local efforts to regulate the flow of the main rivers. They built long canals to promote communication and trade, and they dug impressive irrigation networks to convert arid lands into fertile belts. This slow agrarian revolution enabled the Chinese population to soar, reaching perhaps 20 million by the late Zhou era.

Zhou Chariots This seventeenth-century painting (on silk) recalls the memory of a pivotal Zhou king, Emperor Mu Wang (of the tenth century BCE), riding in a chariot driven by a legendary charioteer. The Zhou adapted the use of chariots and archers from their predecessors to defeat the Shang around 1045 BCE. Regional lords who owed allegiance to the Zhou king distinguished themselves in the aristocratic hierarchy by using chariots for battle and travel.

Under the Zhou, landowners and rulers organized the construction of dikes and irrigation systems to control the floodplain of the Yellow River and Wei River valley surrounding the capital at Xianyang (present-day Xi'an). For centuries, peasants labored over this floodplain and its tributaries—building dikes, digging canals, and raising levees as the waters flowed to the sea. When their work was done, the bottom of the floodplain was a latticework of rich, well-watered fields, with carefully manicured terraces rising in gradual steps to higher ground. Eventually, irrigation works grew to such a scale that they required management by the Zhou rulers, centered in the Wei River valley, and their skilled engineers. The engineers also designed canals that connected rivers and supported commerce and other internal exchanges. Tens of thousands of workers spent countless days digging these canals, paying tribute in the form of labor.

The canals linked China's two breadbaskets: wheat and millet fields in the north and rice fields in the south. And as with the Yellow River in the north, engineers controlled the Yangzi River in the south. Nomads in mountainous areas or on the Zhou frontiers, who often fought with the Zhou ruler and his regional lords, began to depend on trade with the fertile heartlands. In these ways, the Zhou promoted greater unity within their territory and among the peoples living in and around it.

"MANDATE OF HEAVEN"

In addition to promoting a Chinese ethnic and political identity and cultivating advances in agriculture, Zhou rulers also introduced the long-enduring concept of the **mandate of heaven**, which provided a justification for their rule. Attributed by later Chinese intellectuals to King Wu's younger brother Zhou Gong (often referred to as the Duke of Zhou), the mandate asserted that Zhou moral superiority justified taking over Shang wealth and territories and that heaven had imposed a moral mandate on them to replace the Shang, whom they characterized as evil men whose policies brought pain to the people through waste and corruption, and return good governance to the people.

At first Zhou leaders presented the mandate of heaven as a religious compact between the Zhou people and their supreme "sky god" in heaven, but over time Zhou kings and the court detached the concept from the sky god and made the mandate into a freestanding Chinese political doctrine. The Zhou argued that since worldly affairs were supposed to align with those of the heavens, heavenly powers conferred legitimate rights to rule only on their chosen representative. In return, the ruler was duty-bound to uphold heaven's principles of harmony and honor. Any ruler who failed in this duty, who let instability creep into earthly affairs, or who let his people suffer, would lose the mandate. Under this system, spiritual authority withdrew support from any wayward dynasts and found other, more worthy, agents. The Zhou rulers had to acknowledge that

mandate of heaven
Religious ideology established by Zhou leaders to communicate legitimate transfer and retention of royal power as the will of their supreme god. The mandate later became Chinese political doctrine.

any group of rulers, even they themselves, could be ousted if they lost the mandate of heaven because of improper practices.

As part of maintaining their mandate and their legitimacy as rulers, Zhou kings created royal calendars, official documents that defined times for undertaking agricultural activities and celebrating rituals. Unexpected events such as solar eclipses or natural calamities could throw into question the ruling house's mandate. Since rulers claimed that their authority came from heaven, the Zhou perfected the astronomical system on which they based their calendar. Zhou astronomers precisely calculated the length of a lunar month (29.53 days) and the solar year. To resolve the discrepancy between a solar year (365.25 days) and a lunar year (354.36 days), the Zhou occasionally inserted a leap month. Scribes dated the reigns of kings by days and years within a repeating sixty-year cycle.

Zhou legitimacy was also grounded in their use of bronze ritual vessels, statues, ornaments, and weapons, the large-scale production of which they borrowed from their Shang predecessors. Like the Shang, the Zhou developed an extensive system of bronze metalworking that required a large force of tribute labor. Many of its members were Shang, who were sometimes forcibly transported to new Zhou towns to produce the bronze ritual objects. These objects, sold and distributed across the lands and used in ceremonial rituals, symbolized Zhou legitimacy.

Zhou Wine Vessel Under the Zhou, bronze metallurgy depended on a large labor force. Many workers initially came from Shang labor groups, who were superior to the Zhou in technology. The use of bronze, such as for this wine vessel, exemplified dynastic continuity between the Shang and the Zhou.

SOCIAL AND ECONOMIC CONTROLS

As the Chinese social order became more integrated, it also became more class based. Directly under the Zhou ruler and his royal ministers were the hereditary nobles, divided into ranks. These regional lords had landholdings of different sizes. They all owed allegiance to the Zhou king, and they supplied warriors to fight in the king's army and laborers to clear land, drain fields, and do other work. The regional lords periodically appeared at court and took part in complex rituals to reaffirm their allegiance to the king. Below the regional lords were high officers at the Zhou court, as well as ministers and administrators who supervised the people's work. Aristocratic warriors stood at the bottom of the noble hierarchy.

Among commoners, an elaborate occupation-based hierarchy developed over time. Early on, most of the population worked as farmers on fields owned by great landholding families, while some commoners were artisans, such as bronze workers or silk weavers. The later occupation-based system, however, divided people more precisely by function—landholders who produced grain, growers of plants and fruit trees, woodsmen, breeders of cattle and chickens, artisans, merchants, weavers, servants, and those with no fixed occupation—and the central government exerted considerable control over how each group did its job. While reports of this control may be overstated, the system does show a unique attempt by the Zhou government to assert power over the empire's diverse peoples.

The Zhou also made political and legal use of family structures. In their patrilineal society, the Zhou established strict hierarchies for both men and women. Both art and literature celebrated the son who honored his parents. Men and women had different roles in family and ceremonial life. On landholdings, men farmed and hunted, while women produced silk and other textiles and fashioned them into clothing. Wealth increasingly trumped other distinctions, however. In particular, rich women high in the Zhou aristocracy enjoyed a greater range of actions than other women did. And wealthy merchants in emerging cities challenged the authority of local lords.

LIMITS AND DECLINE OF ZHOU POWER

The Zhou state relied on culture (its bronzes) and statecraft (the mandate of heaven) to maintain its leadership among competing powers and lesser principalities in its territories. Rather than having absolute control of an empire (like the Neo-Assyrians and Persians had) or a primarily socioreligious unity (like the Vedic peoples of South Asia had), the Zhou state was first among many regional economic and political allies.

The Zhou dynasty was not highly centralized; instead, it expected regional lords to control the provinces. Military campaigns continued to press into new lands or to defend Zhou holdings from enemies. Rulers interacted with neighbors and allies by giving them power, protecting them from aggression, and intermarrying between dynastic family members and local nobles. Consequently, Zhou subordinates had more than autonomy; they had genuine resources that they could turn against the dynasts at opportune moments.

The power of the Zhou royal house over its regional lords declined in the ninth and eighth centuries BCE. In response, the Zhou court at Xianyang introduced ritual reforms with grandiose ceremonies featuring larger, standardized bronze vessels. Even this move could not reverse the regime's growing political weakness in dealing with its steppe neighbors and internal regional lords. In 771 BCE, northern steppe invaders forced the Zhou to flee their western capital, ushering in the beginning of what would come to be known as the Spring and Autumn period of the Eastern Zhou dynasty centered at Luoyi (modern Luoyang).

The Zhou dynastic period, like the Shang, was later idealized by Chinese historians as a golden age of wise kings and officials. In fact, the Zhou model of government, culture, and society became the standard for later generations. Though the Neo-Assyrian and Persian superpowers were capable of greater expansion during this period, China was sowing the seeds of a more durable state.

Conclusion

Around 1000 BCE, dramatic changes in political and social structures took place across Afro-Eurasia. Consolidations of power, with varying degrees and types of centralization, formed in Southwest Asia (Neo-Assyrians and Persians), Vedic South Asia, and East Asia (among the Zhou). Driving these sociopolitical developments were changes in climate, invasions by nomadic peoples, technological innovations, and new administrative strategies.

A spectrum of power consolidation—from the highly centralized to the more culturally unified—occurred across Afro-Eurasia. The tightly consolidated Neo-Assyrian and Persian Empires differed in fundamental ways from the earlier city-states and territorial states of this area. They created ideologies, political institutions, and economic ties that extended their power across vast regions. Their strong imperial institutions enabled them to exploit human and material resources at great distances from the imperial centers. At the other end of Afro-Eurasia, the Zhou in East Asia established loose integration of diverse peoples and territories through a powerful dynastic arrangement buttressed by a mandate from heaven; but they could not overcome the power of local nobles or fully protect the western frontier from nomadic attacks. In the Vedic world of the Indus Valley and Ganges plain, shared values and revered texts did not lead to a single major state. An unparalleled degree of cultural, as opposed to political or economic, integration bound together northern South Asia. Many centuries would pass before a regime would layer a state over this shared cultural world.

Empire building did not occur everywhere. The majority of the world's people still lived in smaller political groupings. Even within Afro-Eurasia, some areas were completely untouched. And even where the Neo-Assyrian and Persian rulers, soldiers, and traders came into contact with certain groups, they did not necessarily crush them. For example, the nomadic peoples of the northern steppes and the southern desert locations throughout Eurasia continued to be autonomous. But fewer and fewer were untouched by the technological, cultural, and political pulses of empires.

The peoples living in Southwest Asia (under the Neo-Assyrians and then Persians), in the Vedic society of South Asia, and in the Zhou kingdom of East Asia made lasting contributions to the cultural and religious history of humanity. Late Vedic South Asia spun out the concept of cyclic universal time in the form of reincarnation. And in late Zhou China, an ideal of statecraft and social order took shape. On the fringes of these empires, other groups made lasting contributions. The Phoenicians traversed the whole of the Mediterranean basin and spread their simplified alphabet. From the land of Israel, a budding monotheism sprouted. All evolved into powerful cultural forms that in time spread their influences far beyond their sites of origin.

Focus On
First Empires and Smaller States

Ancient Near East

- Neo-Assyrians use raw military power and massive population relocations to build and maintain the world's first empire.

- Persians rely on tolerance, their system of satrapies, and Zoroastrianism to build a cosmopolitan empire.

Mediterranean World

- Greeks, Phoenicians, and Israelites show the advantages of small-scale states with innovations in writing, trading, and religious thought.

- Sea Peoples migrate into the region, attacking empires in the eastern Mediterranean, including the Hittites and Egyptians, before settling down in the Levant.

South Asia

- Vedic migrants combine with local populations to build a unified but *varna*-stratified common culture through religious and economic ties.

- Religious texts, like the Vedas and the Upanishads, bring a cultural unity through their rules, rituals, and traditions.

China

- The Zhou dynasty constructs a powerful tributary state through dynastic institutions and agricultural advances.

- Zhou dynasts legitimate their rule through claiming the mandate of heaven (good governance together with upright behavior equates to legitimate rule), a concept that will become a long-lasting political doctrine in China.

CHRONOLOGY	1500 BCE	1200 BCE
Southwest Asia and Northern Africa		
The Mediterranean		
South Asia		
East Asia		

THINKING ABOUT GLOBAL CONNECTIONS

- **Thinking about Power Relationships and the Formation of Empires** From 1250 to 325 BCE, several regional empires with centralized rule developed: in Southwest Asia, the Neo-Assyrians and then Persians established tightly controlled empires; in East Asia, the Zhou achieved loose political unification; and a culturally integrated people thrived in South Asia. Compare the use of military force and its relationship to political centralization in each of these cases. How does religion help to bring unification?

- **Thinking about the Environment and the Formation of Empires** Just as climate change around 2000 BCE contributed to the demise of earlier societies, prolonged drought around 1200 BCE again brought dramatic changes to many areas. Compare the environmental crises in Egypt, Southwest Asia, and East Asia in the late second millennium BCE and their results, especially with respect to empire formation.

- **Thinking about Exchange Networks and the Formation of Empires** While this chapter focuses on the formation of empires, the majority of the world's people lived outside or on the fringes of these empires. The Sea Peoples, after disrupting the Hittites, Greeks, and Egyptians, settled down on the coast of Southwest Asia and became the Philistines; the Phoenicians expanded their trade across the Mediterranean; the Greeks effectively resisted Persian authority; and Jewish Israelites founded a kingdom centered on monotheism. Which had the most significant impact on human history: the centralized empires or the peoples on the fringes and beyond? Why?

Key Terms

alphabet p. 175	monotheism p. 177	Sea Peoples p. 173	Vedas p. 178
empire p. 157	Phoenicians p. 175	Upanishads p. 183	Zoroastrianism p. 170
mandate of heaven p. 186	satrapy p. 169	*varna* p. 181	

Go to **INQUIZITIVE** to see what you've learned—and learn what you've missed—with personalized feedback along the way.

---

900 BCE	600 BCE	300 BCE

Neo-Assyrian Empire 911–612 BCE

Persian Empire 560–331 BCE

Phoenician and Greek colonization 800–500 BCE

Greek/Persian battles 499–480 BCE

Vedic culture develops 1500–600 BCE

Early Zhou dynasty 1045–771 BCE

Global Themes and Sources

Comparing Early Empires

The early empires described in this chapter used a combination of military might, political organization, and religious ideology to control the peoples who lived within their territory. The Neo-Assyrians, for instance, combined brute force and tight political administration to consolidate a highly centralized empire. The Persians used some of the same strategies but allowed greater multicultural variation and self-rule within their domain. Zhou leaders in East Asia justified their rule via the mandate of heaven, but this justification required ongoing demonstration of a mandate in a world of unpredictable events such as sickness and crop devastation. In South Asia, Indo-European Vedic immigrants brought a degree of social, but not political, unification through their religious ideas, most notably the hierarchically arranged *varna* and understandings of reincarnation

The texts presented here facilitate a comparison of the varied methods of control utilized in each of these regions, on a spectrum from the harsh centralized control of the Neo-Assyrians to the looser political, yet strong ideological, ties of South Asia. The Dur-Sharrukin building inscription describes the construction by Sargon II (r. 721–705 BCE) of a new capital for the Neo-Assyrian Empire in Southwest Asia. Over the course of the two decades during which the lavish capital was under construction, Sargon II expanded his empire by force and tribute exaction. Two centuries later, Darius I (r. 522–486 BCE) commissioned the Behistun inscription to commemorate his consolidation of power over the Persian state in roughly the same region of Southwest Asia that the Neo-Assyrians had controlled. This blend of Zoroastrian ideals and military force demonstrates some of the key elements of Persian imperial control. The *Shangshu* (Book of Documents) preserves a narrative of the transition of power around 1043 BCE in East Asia from King Wu to his brother the Duke of Zhou, who was acting as regent for Wu's son, King Ch'eng.

In this account, ancestors were consulted via oracle bones and the mandate of heaven was in doubt. The last excerpt comes from the *Upanishads*, a collection of works sacred to the Vedic peoples of South Asia, dating to the seventh century BCE or earlier. The reassuring message from this text underscores the potentially unifying power of the belief in reincarnation. Each text gives a glimpse of the practical and ideological forces that bound peoples and empires together in the first millennium BCE.

Analyzing Early Empires

- What similarities and differences do you see in the central focus of each text? What does the central focus of each text reveal about political and social control? How is the nature of empire, or social control, within each text a reflection of what you know (from this chapter) about the degree of imperial centralization in each region?

- What is the role of religion in each text? How is the role of religion similar across these texts and the empires they reflect? How is it different?

- Compare the genre and perspective of each text. How do the type of source and the point of view from which it is written add something to your consideration of the nature of empire, or the lack of a consolidated empire, in each region?

PRIMARY SOURCE 4.1

Sargon II's Lamassu Inscription at Dur-Sharrukin (c. 720 BCE)

Sargon II (r. 721–705 BCE) ruled during a time of militaristic expansion for the Neo-Assyrians, undertaking brutal campaigns both within and beyond the borders of his empire. Toward the beginning of his reign, he began the construction of the new capital city of Dur-Sharrukin (modern Khorsabad, near Mosul in Iraq). At the entrance to Sargon II's throne room in the palace at Dur-Sharrukin sat a 40-ton, 16-foot-tall lamassu (human-headed winged bull). The inscriptions included here were carved onto the front and back of this massive creature. Beneath the descriptions of beauty and splendor is a reality of conquest, tribute extraction, and tight-fisted rule.

- What actions and traits does Sargon II highlight throughout the inscription that could justify his imperial power and authority?

- What details does the inscription offer about the construction of Dur-Sharrukin, including its park, the buildings, the city walls, the gates, and other features? Why do you think the text offers such details?

- What does the tone and content of this inscription suggest about the nature of Neo-Assyrian rule?

[Inscription on the back of the lamassu]: Palace of Sargon, ruler appointed by Enlil, priest of Ashur, mighty king, king of the world, king of Assyria, king of the four quarters of the world, favorite of the great gods; who established the exempt status of Sippar, Nippur, and Babylon, and protects them in their weakness; who provides food for the destitute, who makes restitution for their wrongful losses; who reestablished for the city Assur its privileged status which had lapsed; who abolished forced labor for Der and brought rest to its weary people; most powerful of all princes, who stretched his protection over Harran and recorded that city's freedom from taxation in accordance with the will of Anu and Dagan; the king, who since the day he became ruler, has had no equal and has encountered no one superior to him in war or battle; who has smashed all lands like clay pots and has imposed reins on the four quarters of the world, who has set his officials over them as governors, and has imposed tax and tribute upon them comparable to those paid by Assyria.

[Inscription on the front of the lamassu]: [At that time I constructed a city above the water holes at the foot of Mt. Musri north of Nineveh, and I named it Dur-Sharrukin. Around it I laid out a great park

resembling Mt. Amanus, planted with every Syrian aromatic tree and mountain fruit tree. Not one of the 350 ancient princes who reigned over Assyria before me and ruled the subjects of Enlil had thought of this location; not one had known how to settle it or dig its canal or to set out its orchards.] I planned day and night how to settle that city and how to raise its great shrines, the dwellings of the great gods, and my royal residential palaces. I spoke and commanded it to be built. In an auspicious month, on a favorable day, the month Simanu (May/June), on a festival day, I made my workers take up the hoe and mold bricks.

In the month Abu (July/August) . . . , I set out its limestone (masonry) upon (foundation deposits of) gold, silver, precious stones, and aromatic plants of Mt. Amanus; I laid its foundations and firmly set its bricks. There I built awesome shrines, firm as the mass of a mountain, for Ea, Sin, Ningal, Shamash, Nabu, Adad, and Ninurta. At the exalted command of these gods, I constructed palaces of ivory, ebony, boxwood, musukkannu-wood, cedar, cypress, juniper, burashu-juniper, and pistachio-wood for my royal dwelling. I roofed them with large cedar beams. I bound doors made of cypress and musukkannu-wood with bands of shining copper and made them fast in their entrances. In front of the palace gates, I built a portico resembling that of a Hittite palace. . . . Eight lions, in pairs, each weighing 4,610 talents (ca. 14 tons) full measure of shining copper, cast according to the workmanship of Ninagal and of dazzling brightness—on top of these lion figures I placed four equally tall cedar columns, each one ninda (ca. 20 ft.) in diameter, products of Mt. Amanus, and there supported the boards forming the cornice of the palace gates. I skillfully made mountain sheep and great protective deities out of massive mountain stone and set them facing the four directions. I depicted on large limestone slabs the regions which I had personally captured and set these slabs around the walls for display.

I made the length of the wall 16,261½ ninda and 2 cubits (ca. 60 miles) and laid its foundation platform upon a high mountain. In front and in back, on both sides, and facing the four winds I opened eight gates. I called the gates of Shamash and Adad on the east side of the city: "Shamash Gains Victories for Me" and "Adad Establishes My Abundance." I named the gates of Enlil and Ninlil on the north side: "Enlil Makes the Foundation of My City Firm" and "Ninlil Creates Abundance." I named the gates of Anu and Ishtar on the west side: "Anu Makes the Work of My Hands Flourish" and "Ishtar Enriches Its People." I named the gates of Ea and Belet-ili on the south side: "Ea Makes Its Springs Flow Prosperously" and "Belet-ili Increases His Offspring." Its inner wall was called "Ashur Allows the Reign of the King, Its Builder, to Last for Many Years and Guards His Troops"; its outer wall was called "Ninurta Establishes the Foundation Platform of His City So That It Will Last until the Distant Future."

There under a single administration I settled peoples from the four quarters of the world, of alien tongues and different speech, mountain dwellers and lowlanders, as many as the Light of the Gods (Shamash), Lord of All, has shepherded; these peoples I had captured at the command of the god Ashur by the power of my scepter. I commissioned native Assyrians, masters of every craft, as overseers and officials to instruct them (the settlers) in their duties as tenants and in their obligations toward god and king.

When I had finished building the city and my palaces, in the month Tashritu (September/October) I invited the great gods who dwell in Assyria to come here. I held a feast to dedicate the city and palaces. I received rich gifts from the princes of the East and West: gold, silver, and all kinds of costly objects fitting for these palaces. May the gods who dwell in this city deem all my works acceptable. May they decree that they will dwell in their temples here and that my reign may remain firm for ever and ever. Whoever destroys the work of my hands, alters the features of my statue, obliterates the representations which I have had depicted, or erases my insignia—may Sin, Shamash, Adad, and all the great gods who live here pluck out his name and his seed from the land; and may they make him live as a captive under his enemies.

Source: "Featured Object Number 8, May 1990, Human-Headed Winged Bull from Khorsabad (OIM A7369)," translated by John A. Brinkman, Oriental Institute Museum, 1990, pp. 3–4, https://oi.uchicago.edu/sites/oi.uchicago.edu/files/uploads/Lamassu_A7369_1990_factsheet.pdf.

The Behistun Inscription (c. 520 BCE), Darius I

The Behistun inscription was commissioned by Darius I, king of Persia, sometime after 520 BCE. It commemorates a series of nineteen battles over the course of which he defeated nine rebellious kings. The trilingual cuneiform inscription—in Old Persian, Elamite, and Babylonian—was posted high up on a cliff face on a major road connecting Mesopotamia with western Iran. The text was accompanied by a relief that shows the nine kings, ropes around their necks and hands bound, led before the victorious Darius. Zoroastrian themes of truth and righteousness vanquishing lies and wrongdoing are central to the text.

- What role does Ahura Mazda, and Zoroastrianism more generally, play in Darius's claims to have defeated his enemies?

- Apart from religious justification, what other evidence do you see for the way that Darius I asserted power and consolidated his empire?

- Given that this copy at Behistun was high up on the side of a cliff and not likely to have been legible to passersby, why might Darius have posted an inscription like this on a major route through his empire?

4.1–2. Saith Darius the King: This is what was done by me in Babylon.

4.2–31. Saith Darius the King: This is what I did by the favor of Ahuramazda in one and the same year after that I became king. XIX battles I fought; by the favor of Ahuramazda I smote them and took prisoner IX kings. One was Gaumata by name, a Magian; he lied . . . he made Persia rebellious. One, Açina by name, an Elamite; he lied . . . he made Elam rebellious to me. One, Nidintu-Bel by name, a Babylonian; he lied; thus he said: "I am Nebuchadnezzar, the son of Nabonidus; he made Babylon rebellious. One, Martiya by name, a Persian; he lied . . . he made Elam rebellious. One, Phraortes by name, a Mede; he lied . . . he made Media rebellious. One Ciçantakhma by name, a Sagartian; he lied . . . he made Sagartia rebellious. One, Frada by name, a Margian; he lied . . . he made Margiana rebellious. One, Vahyazdata by name, a Persian; he lied . . . he made Persia rebellious. One, Arkha by name, an Armenian; he lied . . . he made Babylon rebellious.

4.31–32. Saith Darius the King: These IX kings I took prisoner within these battles.

4.33–36. Saith Darius the King: These are the provinces which became rebellious. The Lie made them rebellious, so that these [men] deceived the people. Afterwards Ahuramazda put them into my hand; as was my desire, so I did unto them.

4.36–40. Saith Darius the King: Thou who shalt be king hereafter, protect thyself vigorously from the Lie; the man who shall be a Lie-follower, him do thou punish well, if thus thou shalt think, "May my country be secure!"

4.40–43. Saith Darius the King: This is what I did; by the favor of Ahuramazda, in one and the same year I did [it]. Thou who shalt hereafter read this inscription, let that which has been done by me convince thee; do not thou think it a lie.

4.43–45. Saith Darius the King: I turn myself quickly to Ahuramazda, that this [is] true, not false, [which] I did in one and the same year. . . .

4.52–56. Saith Darius the King: Now let that which has been done by me convince thee; thus to the people impart, do not conceal it: if this record thou shalt not conceal, [but] tell it to the people, may Ahuramazda be a friend unto thee, and may family be unto thee in abundance, and may thou live long!

4.57–59. Saith Darius the King: If this record thou shalt conceal, [and] not tell it to the people, may Ahuramazda be a smiter unto thee, and may family not be to thee!

4.59–61. Saith Darius the King: This which I did, in one and the same year by the favor of Ahuramazda I did; Ahuramazda bore me aid, and the other gods who are.

4.61–67. Saith Darius the King: For this reason Ahuramazda bore aid, and the other gods who are, because I was not hostile, I was not a Lie-follower, I was not a doer of wrong—neither I nor my family. According to righteousness I conducted myself. Neither to the weak nor to the powerful did I do wrong. The man who cooperated with my house, him I rewarded well; whoso did injury, him I punished well.

4.67–69. Saith Darius the King: Thou who shalt be king hereafter, the man who shall be a Lie-follower or who shall be a doer of wrong—unto them do thou not be a friend, [but] punish them well.

4.69–72. Saith Darius the King: Thou who shalt hereafter behold this inscription which I have inscribed, or these sculptures, do thou not destroy them, [but] thence onward protect them; as long as thou shalt be in good strength! . . .

4.76–80. Saith Darius the King: If thou shalt behold this inscription or these sculptures, (and) shalt destroy them and shalt not protect them as long as unto thee there is strength, may Ahuramazda be a smiter unto thee, and may family not be unto thee, and what thou shalt do, that for thee may Ahuramazda utterly destroy!

4.80–86. Saith Darius the King: These are the men who were there at the time when I slew Gaumata the Magian who called himself Smerdis; at that time these men cooperated as my followers. . . .

4.86–88. Saith Darius the King: Thou who shalt be king hereafter, protect well the family of these men.

4.88–92. Saith Darius the King: By the favor of Ahuramazda this is the inscription which I made. . . . [O]n clay tablets and on parchment it was composed. Besides, a sculptured figure of myself I made. Besides, I made my lineage. And it was inscribed and was read off before me. Afterwards this inscription I sent off everywhere among the provinces. The people unitedly worked upon it.

Source: Roland G. Kent, *Old Persian: Grammar, Texts, Lexicon*, 2nd rev. ed. (New Haven, CT: American Oriental Society, 1953), pp. 131–32.

PRIMARY SOURCE 4.3

Zhou Succession Crisis (c. 1043 BCE)

This account of the Zhou succession crisis derives from a much larger set of texts known as the *Shangshu*, or Book of Documents. While portions of the collection report on earlier periods of Chinese history (the legendary Xia dynasty, as well as the historical second-millennium BCE Shang dynasty), the majority of the *Shangshu* reports on the history of the Zhou. Despite the complex transmission history of the *Shangshu*, its combination of speeches and narrative are some of the best evidence for developments in the Zhou dynasty. This particular excerpt describes the tricky situation that occurred when the first king of the Zhou dynasty, King Wu, died and his brother the Duke of Zhou (spelled "Chou" in the document) assumed the position of regent for the dead king's young son King Ch'eng (the second king of the Zhou dynasty).

- In what ways does divination by oracle bone and other means factor into this account?
- What role does the mandate of heaven play in establishing Zhou authority?
- What does this account suggest about the nature of imperial rule in Zhou China?

After he had completed the conquest of the Shang people, in the second year, King Wu fell ill and was despondent. The two lords, the duke of Shao and Tai-kung Wang, said, "For the king's sake let us solemnly consult the tortoise oracle." But the duke of Chou [King Wu's younger brother, named Tan] said, "We must not distress the ancestors, the former kings."

The duke of Chou then offered himself to the ancestors, constructing three altars within a single compound. . . . Then he made this announcement to the Great King, to King Chi, and to King Wen, his great grandfather, grandfather, and father, and the scribe copied down the words of his prayer on tablets:

"Your chief descendant So-and-so [King Wu's personal name is tabooed] has met with a fearful disease and is violently ill. If you three kings are obliged to render to Heaven the life of an illustrious son, then substitute me, Tan, for So-and-so's person. I am good and compliant, clever and capable. I have much talent and much skill and can serve the spirits. . . ."

Then he divined with three tortoises, and all were auspicious. He opened the bamboo receptacles and consulted the documents, and they too indicated an auspicious answer. The duke of Chou said to the king, "According to the indications of the oracle, you will suffer no harm."

[The king said,] "I, the little child, have obtained a new life from the three kings. I shall plan for a distant end. I hope that they will think of me, the solitary man."

After the duke of Chou returned, he placed the tablets containing the prayer in a metal-bound casket. The next day the king began to recover.

[Later, King Wu died and was succeeded by his infant son, King Ch'eng. The duke of Chou acted as regent and was slandered by King Wu's younger brothers, whom he was eventually forced to punish.]

In the autumn, when a plentiful crop had ripened but had not yet been harvested, Heaven sent great thunder and lightning accompanied by wind. The grain was completely flattened and even large trees were uprooted. The people of the land were in great fear. The king and his high ministers donned their ceremonial caps and opened the documents of the metal-bound casket and thus discovered the record of how the duke of Chou had offered himself as a substitute for King Wu. The two lords and the king then questioned the scribe and the various other functionaries, and they replied. "Yes it is true. But his lordship forbade us to speak about it."

The king grasped the document and wept. "There is no need for us to make solemn divination about what has happened," he said. "In former times the duke of Chou toiled diligently for the royal house, but I, the youthful one, had no way of knowing it. Now Heaven has displayed its terror in order to make clear the virtue of the duke of Chou. I, the little child, will go in person to greet him, for the rites of our royal house approve such action."

When the king came out to the suburbs to meet the duke of Chou, Heaven sent down rain and reversed the wind, so that the grain all stood up once more. The two lords ordered the people of the land to right all the large trees that had been blown over and to earth them up. Then the year was plentiful. (*Chin t'eng.*)

Source: Burton Watson, *Early Chinese Literature* (New York: Columbia University Press, 1962), pp. 35–36.

PRIMARY SOURCE 4.4

On Karma and Reincarnation (before seventh century BCE), from the Upanishads

The Upanishads began to take their current form in the first millennium BCE. They reflect on the social and cosmic order of which humans and other creatures are a part. While they do not seek to replace Vedic rituals or undermine *varna* structures, they did offer a unifying spiritual message that all living creatures possessed a spark of universal soul (*atman*). The excerpt included here comes from the fourth chapter of the Brihadaranyaka Upanishad and is focused on a somewhat philosophical discussion of the freedom of the soul and its escape from earthly attachments. While Brahmans (the highest of the *varna* levels of Vedic society) are mentioned in this text and the text is divided into Brāhmaṇas (commentaries), neither are to be confused with the larger theme of Brahma (the cosmic universe of everything).

....

- **According to this text, what happens to the self at death?**

- **What evidence in the text offers a view into the realities and political structures of the world that produced it?**

- **How might the ideas expressed in this text offer a sense of unity and belonging to the people who believed its message?**

....

[Third Brāhmaṇa] 35. As a heavily loaded cart goes creaking, just so this bodily self, mounted by the intelligent Self, goes groaning when one is breathing one's last. 36. When he comes to weakness—whether he come to weakness through old age or through disease—this person frees himself from these limbs just as a mango, or a fig, or a berry releases itself from its bond; and he hastens again, according to the entrance and place of origin, back to life. 37. As noblemen, policemen, chariot-drivers, village-heads wait with food, drink, and lodgings for a king who is coming, and cry: "Here he comes! Here he comes!" so indeed do all things wait for him who has this knowledge and cry: "Here is Brahma coming! Here is Brahma coming!" 38. As noblemen, policemen, chariot-drivers, village-heads gather around a king who is about to depart, just so do all the breaths gather around the soul and the end, when one is breathing one's last.

[Fourth Brāhmaṇa] 1. When this self comes to weakness and to confusedness of mind, as it were, then the breaths gather around him. He takes to himself those

particles of energy and descends into the heart. When the person in the eye turns away, back [to the sun], then one becomes non-knowing of forms. 2. "He is becoming one," they say; "he does not see." "He is becoming one," they say; "he does not smell." "He is becoming one," they say; "he does not taste." "He is becoming one," they say; "he does not speak." "He is becoming one," they say; "he does not hear." "He is becoming one," they say; "he does not think." "He is becoming one," they say; "he does not touch." "He is becoming one," they say; "he does not know." The point of his heart becomes lighted up. By that light the self departs, either by the eye, or by the head, or by other bodily parts. After him, as he goes out, the life goes out. After the life, as it goes out, all the breaths go out. He becomes one with intelligence. What has intelligence departs with him. His knowledge and his works and his former intelligence [i.e., instinct] lay hold of him. 3. Now as a caterpillar, when it has come to the end of a blade of grass, in taking the next step draws itself together towards it, just so this soul in taking the next step strikes down this body, dispels its ignorance, and draws itself together [for making the transition]. 4. As a goldsmith, taking a piece of gold, reduces it to another newer and more beautiful form, just so this soul, striking down this body and dispelling its ignorance, makes for itself another newer and more beautiful form like that either of the fathers or of the Gandharvas, or of the gods, or of Prajāpati, or of Brahma, or of other beings. 5. Verily, this soul is Brahma, made of knowledge, of mind, of breath, of seeing, of hearing, of earth, of water, of wind, of space, of energy and non-energy, of desire and non-desire, of anger and of non-anger, of virtuousness and of non-virtuousness. It is made of everything. . . . According as one acts, according as one conducts himself, so does he become. The doer of good becomes good. The doer of evil becomes evil. One becomes virtuous by virtuous action, bad by bad action. . . . As is his desire, such is his resolve; as is his resolve, such the action he performs; what action (*karma*) he performs, that he procures for himself. . . . [6.] Now the man who does not desire.—He who is without desire, who is freed from desire, whose desire is satisfied, whose desire is the Soul—his breaths do not depart. Being very Brahma, he goes to Brahma. 7. On this point there is this verse:—

When are liberated all

The desires that lodge in one's heart,

Then a mortal becomes immortal!

Therein he reaches Brahma!

As the slough of a snake lies on an ant-hill, dead, cast off, even so lies this body. But this incorporeal, immortal Life is Brahma indeed, is light indeed. . . . 22. Verily, he is the great, unborn Soul, who is this [person] consisting of knowledge among the senses. In the space within the heart lies the ruler of all, the lord of all, the king of all. He does not become greater by good action nor inferior by bad action. He is the lord of all, the overlord of beings, the protector of beings. He is the separating dam for keeping these worlds apart.

Such a one the Brahmans desire to know by repetition of the Vedas, by sacrifices, by offering, by penance, by fasting. On knowing him, in truth, one becomes an ascetic. Desiring him only as their home, mendicants wander forth. . . . [23.] Therefore, having this knowledge, having become calm, subdued, quiet, patiently enduring, and collected, one sees the Soul just in the soul. One sees everything as the Soul. Evil does not overcome him; he overcomes all evil. Evil does not burn him; he burns all evil. Free from evil, free from impurity, free from doubt, he becomes a Brahman. . . . 25. Verily, that great, unborn Soul, undecaying, undying, immortal, fearless, is Brahma. Verily, Brahma is fearless. He who knows this becomes the fearless Brahma.

Source: *The Thirteen Principal Upanishads*, translated by Robert Ernest Hume (New York: Oxford University Press, 1934), pp. 139–41, 143–44.

Interpreting Visual Evidence

Tribute

Black obelisk of Shalmaneser III.

One method early empires of the first millennium BCE used to consolidate their power was the collection of tribute from the areas under their control. The examples gathered here depict the payment of various forms of tribute in different empires.

In his palace complex at Nimrud, the Neo-Assyrian king Shalmaneser III (r. 858–824 BCE) erected a black limestone obelisk decorated on four sides with reliefs and inscriptions commemorating his conquests and the peoples who paid tribute to him. This obelisk includes a famous scene thought to show the tribute offered by King Jehu of Israel. Another series of images on the obelisk, shown below, record the exotic

Tribute scene from palace at Persepolis.

gifts from Musri (literally, "Borderlands") including two-humped Bactrian camels, an elephant, and three monkeys. At the Persian capital of Persepolis, grand staircases leading to the main audience hall of the palace were decorated with scenes of the king and his courtiers as well as the delegations bringing tribute to the center of the empire. The second image depicts tribute bearers bringing animals and other items (in bowls) as gifts to the Persian king. Those delivering their tribute would have walked past these scenes on their way to pay obeisance to the Persian king. In Zhou China, tribute was often rendered in human labor, which was needed to build the irrigation system of canals and dikes. But another form of tribute to Zhou dynasts may have been textiles, such as the woven silk with a geometric and dragon motif shown in the final image. The silk was dyed red with cinnabar, a rare and expensive ingredient whose use would have been limited to luxury textiles of the elite. The differing types of tribute and their display indicate the varying levels of centralized control these first-millennium empires exerted over their subject peoples.

Woven textile from Eastern Zhou.

Questions for Analysis

1. Compare the grand display of tribute in the Neo-Assyrian and Persian Empires with the tribute suggested by the Zhou textile. What do these varied tributes (their type and display) suggest about the nature of early empire in each of these regions?

2. Compare the symbolic political value with the actual economic impact of the specific tributes visible here.

3. Imagine yourself as a tribute bearer ascending the steps to the reception hall of the Persian king or visiting the Neo-Assyrian capital of Shalmaneser III. Now imagine yourself as a member of the Persian or Neo-Assyrian elite. How would your experience of viewing these scenes differ depending on your identity?

5

Worlds Turned Inside Out

1000–350 BCE

In the midst of violent struggles for power and territory in China in the sixth century BCE, Master Kong Fuzi instructed his disciples on how to govern, saying: "Guide them by edicts, keep them in line with punishments, and the people will stay out of trouble but will have no sense of shame. Guide them by virtue, keep them in line with the rites, and they will, besides having a sense of shame, reform themselves" (Confucius, *The Analects*, II, 3).

Master Kong, also known as Confucius, represented a new breed of influential leaders who were teachers and thinkers, not kings, priests, or warriors. Nonetheless, it was the convulsions around them—incessant warfare, population growth, migrations, and the emergence of new cities—that motivated their search for insights. By viewing the world in innovative ways, these teachers instructed rulers on how to govern justly and showed ordinary individuals how to live ethically.

The teachers and founders of new ways of thinking from the first millennium BCE, who figure prominently in this chapter, were some of the most influential in history. In China, Confucius elaborated a set of principles for ethical living that has guided the Chinese population up to modern times. In South Asia, Siddhartha Gautama (the Buddha) laid out social and spiritual tenets that challenged the traditional social hierarchy based on birth and, with it, the power of

Chapter Outline

- An "Axial Age"
- Eastern Zhou China
- The New Worlds of South Asia
- The Mediterranean World
- Common Cultures in the Americas and Sub-Saharan Africa
- Conclusion

Core Objectives

- **DESCRIBE** the challenges that Afro-Eurasian empires and states faced in the first millennium bce, and **COMPARE** the range of solutions they devised.

- **IDENTIFY** Axial Age thinkers and **ANALYZE** their distinctive ideas.

- **EXPLAIN** the relationship between Axial Age thinkers across Afro-Eurasia (East Asia, South Asia, and the Mediterranean) and the political and social situations to which they were responding.

- **COMPARE** the political, cultural, and social developments across Afro-Eurasia with those occurring in the Americas and sub-Saharan Africa.

the ruling priests and warriors. In Greece, Socrates, Plato, and Aristotle described a world that conformed to natural laws.

The philosophers, theologians, poets, political leaders, and merchants of this era founded literary traditions, articulated new belief systems, and established new political and economic institutions that spread well beyond the places that inspired them. While wars and havoc raged within their societies and long-distance trade and travel linked societies, these thinkers influenced a world shaped by a search for order and an appetite for new thinking.

Global Storylines

- A range of challenges—warfare, political upheaval, economic pressures, and social developments—transform the empires and states of Afro-Eurasia.

- "Second-generation" societies arise across Afro-Eurasia in a pivotal period sometimes called the "Axial Age."

- Axial Age thinkers in Afro-Eurasia reshape peoples' views of the world and their place in it.

- Complex new societies develop in the Americas and sub-Saharan Africa.

THE BIG PICTURE

Explain why historians refer to the mid-first millennium BCE as an "Axial Age." Was this period an Axial Age in your opinion?

An "Axial Age"

Some modern thinkers call the mid-first millennium BCE the **Axial Age** to emphasize its pivotal and transitional role between the declining old empires of ancient Egypt, Southwest Asia, northern India, and Zhou China, and the later empires of Alexander the Great, Chandragupta's Mauryan Empire, Rome, and the Han Chinese (see Chapters 6 and 7). Instrumental to this dynamic period were the ethical, philosophical, and religious innovations taking place in India, China, and Europe.

In this Axial Age of the first millennium BCE, societies on the edges of regional empires or within declining empires of Afro-Eurasia started to follow innovative paths. (See Map 5.1.) These new communities were not just extensions of old ways of life. In each, dramatic innovations in cultural and religious beliefs were expanding people's social, political, and cultural options. Although each of the resulting cultures—in East Asia, South Asia, and the Mediterranean—was distinct from the others, we might call them all

second-generation societies, given that they built on their predecessors yet represented a departure from ancient legacies. (See Current Trends in World History: What Makes an "Axial Age"?)

While Afro-Eurasia experienced an Axial Age and the emergence of second-generation societies, other parts of the world saw complex, urban-based societies emerge for the first time. The first of these in the Americas was established by the Olmecs in Mesoamerica, with artistic and religious reverberations well beyond their homelands. In Africa, distinct regional identities spread in the Upper Nile (in Nubia) and West Africa (among the Nok). One of the most striking features of the first millennium BCE is the long-lasting impact of both the Axial Age second-generation societies that stretched across Afro-Eurasia and the first complex societies isolated from them by oceans and desert.

Eastern Zhou China

Destruction of the old political order paved the way for radical thinkers and cultural flourishing in Eastern Zhou China. Centered at Luoyang, the turbulent Eastern Zhou dynasty was divided by ancient Chinese chroniclers into the Spring and Autumn period (722–481 BCE) and the Warring States period (403–221 BCE). One writer from the Spring and Autumn period described over 500 battles among states and more than 100 civil wars within states, all taking place within 260 years. Fueling this warfare was the spread of cheaper and more lethal weaponry, made possible by new iron-smelting techniques, which in turn shifted influence from the central government to local authorities and allowed warfare to continue unabated into the Warring States period. Regional states became so powerful that they undertook large-scale projects, including dikes and irrigation systems, which had to this point been feasible only for empires. By the beginning of the Warring States period, seven large territorial states dominated the Zhou world. (See Map 5.2.) Their wars and shifting political alliances involved the mobilization of armies and resources on an unprecedented scale. Qin, the most powerful state, which ultimately replaced the Eastern Zhou dynasty in 221 BCE, fielded armies that combined huge infantries in the tens of thousands with lethal cavalries and skilled archers using state-of-the-art crossbows.

The conception of central power changed dramatically during this era. Royal appointees replaced hereditary officeholders. By the middle of the fourth century BCE, power was so concentrated in the major states' rulers that each began to call himself "king" (*wang*). Despite—or perhaps even as a result of—the constant warfare, scholars, soldiers, merchants, peasants, and artisans thrived in the midst of an expanding agrarian economy and interregional trade.

Axial Age
Pivotal period in the mid-first millennium BCE when radical thinkers, such as Zoroaster in Persia, Confucius and Master Lao in East Asia, Siddhartha Gautama (the Buddha) in South Asia, and Socrates in the Mediterranean, offered dramatically new ideas that challenged their times.

second-generation societies
First-millennium BCE societies that innovated on their older political, religious, and cultural ideas by incorporating new aspects of cultures they encountered to reshape their way of life.

Core Objectives

DESCRIBE the challenges that Afro-Eurasian empires and states faced in the first millennium BCE, and **COMPARE** the range of solutions they devised.

The Global View

NORTH AMERICA

ROCKY MOUNTAINS

NOMADIC HUNTERS AND GATHERERS

Great Lakes

Mississippi R.

St. Lawrence R.

Gulf of Mexico

OLMEC

MESOAMERICA

WEST INDIES

ATLANTIC OCEAN

PACIFIC OCEAN

ANDES

CHAVÍN

NOMADIC HUNTERS AND GATHERERS

Amazon R.

SOUTH AMERICA

MOUNTAINS

CELTIC PEOP

Rhine

IBERIANS

SAHAR

SAHAR PEOPL

SAHEL

Niger

NOK

| NOK | State |
| SLAVS | People |

0 1000 2000 Miles

0 1000 2000 Kilometers

Map 5.1 The World in an Axial Age, c. 500 BCE

By the middle of the first millennium BCE, complex agriculture-based societies beyond the regional empires of Southwest Asia, North Africa, and East Asia contributed to the flowering of new cultural pathways and ideas that reshaped the old empires and territorial states into what we might call second-generation societies.

- According to your reading, where did these second-generation societies appear? What had been located there before?

- Examining the map, how are these second generation societies influenced by peoples on their margins?

- Which states are in regions closely connected to others? Which appear to be geographically isolated? How might proximity to others or relative isolation have shaped these societies' development?

INNOVATIONS IN THOUGHT

Core Objectives

IDENTIFY Axial Age thinkers and **ANALYZE** their distinctive ideas.

Out of this turmoil came new visions that would shape Chinese thinking about the individual's place in society and provide the philosophical underpinnings for the world's most enduring imperial system (lasting from the establishment of the Qin dynasty in 221 BCE until the abdication of China's last monarch in 1912). Often it was the losers among the political elites, seeking to replace their former advantages with new status gained through service, who sparked this intellectual creativity. Many important teachers emerged in China's Axial Age, each with disciples. The philosophies of these "hundred masters," a term mostly used at the time by itinerant scholars, constituted what came to be known as the Hundred Schools of Thought. Among the most influential were Confucianism and Daoism.

Confucius (551–479 BCE) was very much the product of the violent Spring and Autumn period. Serving in minor governmental positions, he believed the founders of the Zhou dynasty had established ideals of good government and principled action. Frustrated, however, by the realities of division and war among rival states all around him, Confucius set out in search of an enlightened ruler. Confucius's teachings stemmed from his belief that human beings behaved ethically not because they wanted to achieve salvation or a heavenly reward but because it was in their human makeup to do so. Humanity's natural tendencies, if left alone, produced harmonious existence. Confucius saw family and filial submission (the duty of children to parents) as the foundation of proper ethical action, including loyalty to the state and rulers. His idea of modeling the state on the patriarchal family—with the ruler respecting heaven as if it were his father and protecting his subjects as if they were his children—became a bedrock principle of Confucian thought. Although he regarded himself as a transmitter of ancient wisdom, Confucius established many of the major guidelines for Chinese thought and action: respect for the pronouncements of scholars, commitment to a broad education, and training for all who were highly intelligent and willing to work, whether noble or humble in birth. This equal access to training for those willing and able offered a dramatic departure from past centuries, when only nobles were believed capable of ruling. Nonetheless, Confucius's distinctions between gentlemen-rulers and commoners continued to support a social hierarchy—although an individual's position in that hierarchy now rested on education rather than on birth.

Confucius's ethical teachings were preserved by his followers in a collection known as *The Analects*. These texts record Confucius's conversations with his students. In his effort to persuade his contemporaries to reclaim what he regarded as the lost ideals of the early Zhou, Confucius proposed a moral framework stressing humaneness (*ren*), correct performance of ritual (*li*),

Confucius

(551–479 BCE) Radical thinker whose ideas—especially about how ethical living that was centered on *ren* (benevolence), *li* (proper ritual), and *xiao* (filial piety toward ancestors living and dead) shaped the politically engaged superior gentleman—transformed society and government in East Asia.

Map 5.2 Zhou China in the Warring States Period, 403–221 BCE

The Warring States period witnessed a fracturing of the Zhou dynasty into a myriad of states.

- Find the Zhou capital of Luoyang on the map. Where was it located relative to the other key states?
- Trace the Zhou state borders. How would you compare the boundaries and sizes of the various Zhou states? What does this suggest about the importance of diplomacy during this period?
- How do you think so many smaller states could survive when they were surrounded first by seven and then by three even larger and more powerful states (Qin, Qi, and Chu)?

loyalty to the family (*xiao*), and perfection of moral character to become a "superior man" (*junzi*)—that is, a man defined by benevolence and goodness rather than by the pursuit of profit. Confucius believed that a society of such superior men would not need coercive laws and punishment to achieve order. Confucius ultimately left court in 484 BCE, discouraged by the continuing state of warfare. His transformational ideology remained, however, and has shaped Chinese society for millennia, both through its followers and through those who adopted traditions that developed as a distinct counterpoint to Confucian engagement.

Another key philosophy was **Daoism**, which diverged sharply from Confucian thought by scorning rigid rituals and social hierarchies. Its ideas originated with a Master Lao (Laozi, "Old Master"), who—if he actually existed—may have been a contemporary of Confucius. His sayings were collected in *The Daodejing*, or *The Book of the Way and Its Power* (c. third century BCE). Master Lao's book was then elaborated by Master Zhuang (Zhuangzi, c. 369–286 BCE). Daoism stressed that the best path (*dao*) for living was to follow the natural order of things. Its main principle was *wuwei*, "doing nothing." Spontaneity, noninterference, and acceptance of the world as it is, rather than attempting to change it through politics and government, were what mattered. In Laozi's vision, the ruler who interfered least in the natural processes of change was the most successful. Zhuangzi focused on the enlightened individual living spontaneously and in harmony with nature, free of society's ethical rules and laws and viewing life and death simply as different stages of existence.

Apart from the philosophical discourse of the "hundred masters," with its far-reaching impact across Chinese society, elites and commoners alike tried to maintain stability in their lives through religion, medicine, and statecraft. The elites' rites of divination to predict the future and medical recipes to heal the body found parallels in the commoners' use of ghost stories and astrological almanacs to understand the meaning of their lives and the significance of their deaths. Elites recorded their political discourses on wood and bamboo slips, tied together to form scrolls. They likewise prepared military treatises, ritual texts, geographic works, and poetry. The growing importance of statecraft and philosophical discourse promoted the use of writing, with 9,000 to 10,000 graphs or signs required to convey these elaborate ideas.

What emerged from all this activity was a foundational alliance between scholars and the state. Scholars became state functionaries who were dependent on rulers' patronage. In return, rulers recognized scholars' expertise in matters of punishment, ritual, astronomy, medicine, and divination. Philosophical deliberations focused on the need to maintain order and stability by preserving the state. These bonds that rulers forged with their scholarly elites were a distinguishing feature of governments in Warring States

China, as compared with other Afro-Eurasian societies at this time.

INNOVATIONS IN STATE ADMINISTRATION

Regional rulers of the Spring and Autumn period enhanced their ability to obtain natural resources, to recruit men for their armies, and to oversee conquered areas. This trend continued in the Warring States period, as the elites in the major states created administrative districts with stewards, sheriffs, and judges and a system of registering peasant households to facilitate tax collection and army conscription. These officials, who had been knights under the Western Zhou, were now bureaucrats in direct service to the ruler. These administrators were the "superior men" (*junzi*) of Confucian thought. They were paid in grain, titles, and gifts of gold and silver from the ruler. The most successful of these ministers was the Qin statesman Shang Yang (fourth century BCE). Lord Shang's reforms—including a head tax, administrative districts for closer bureaucratic control of hinterlands, land distribution for individual households to farm, and reward or punishment for military achievement—positioned the Qin to become the dominant state of its time.

INNOVATIONS IN WARFARE

With administrative reforms came reforms in military recruitment and warfare. In earlier periods, nobles had let fly their arrows from chariots while conscripted peasants fought beside them on the bloodstained ground. The Warring States, however, relied on massed infantries of peasants, whose conscription was made easier by the registration of peasant households. Bearing iron lances and unconstrained by their relationships with nobles, these peasants fought fiercely. In addition to this conscripted peasant infantry, armies boasted elite professional troops equipped with iron armor and weapons, and wielding the recently invented crossbow. The crossbow's tremendous power, range, and accuracy enabled archers to kill lightly armored cavalrymen or charioteers at a distance. With improved siege technology, enemy armies assaulted the new defensive walls of towns and frontiers, either digging under them or using counterweighted siege ladders to scale them. Campaigns were no longer limited to an agricultural season and instead might stretch over a

Qu Yuan In addition to the innovations of Confucian and Daoist thought, the first millennium BCE also saw an outpouring of poetic work. Qu Yuan (339–278 BCE), shown here in a seventeenth-century painting, is known both from his own writing and from the works of later writers who mention him, such as the famous Chinese historian Sima Qian (145–86 BCE). A disgraced politician, diplomat, and poet, Qu Yuan wrote his famous poem *Li Sao* in the context of the decline of his home state, Chu, over the course of the Warring States period.

year or longer. The huge state armies contained as many as 1 million commoners in the infantry, supported by 1,000 chariots and 10,000 bow-wielding cavalrymen. During the Spring and Autumn period one state's entire army would face another state's, but by the Warring States period armies could divide into separate forces and wage several battles simultaneously.

ECONOMIC, SOCIAL, AND CULTURAL CHANGES

While a growing population presented new challenges, the continuous warfare in these periods spurred economic growth in China. An agricultural revolution on the North China plain along the Yellow River led to rapid population growth, and the inhabitants of the Eastern Zhou reached approximately 20 million. Several factors contributed to increased agricultural productivity beginning in the Spring and Autumn period. Some rulers gave peasants the right to own their land in exchange for taxes and military service, which in turn increased productivity because the farmers were working to benefit themselves. Agricultural productivity was also enhanced by innovations such as crop rotation (millet and wheat in the north, rice and millet in the south) and oxen-pulled iron plowshares to prepare fields.

With this increased agricultural yield came the pressures of accompanying population growth. Ever-attentive peasant farmers tilling the fields of North and South China produced more rice and wheat than anyone else on earth, but that agricultural success was often outpaced by their growing families. As more people required more fuel, deforestation led to erosion of the fields. Many animals were hunted to extinction. Many inhabitants migrated south to domesticate the marshes, lakes, and rivers of the Yangzi River delta; here they created new arable frontiers out of former wetlands. When the expansion into arable land invariably hit its limits, Chinese families faced terrible food shortages and famines. The long-term economic result was a declining standard of living for massive numbers of Chinese peasants.

Despite these long-term cycles of population pressures and famine, larger harvests and advances in bronze and iron casting enabled the beginning of a market economy: trade in surplus grain, pottery, and ritual objects. Peasants continued to barter, but elites and rulers used minted coins. Grain and goods traveled along roads, rivers, and canals. Rulers and officials applied their military and organizational skills for public projects enhancing waterworks.

Economic growth had repercussions at all levels of society. Rulers attained a high level of cultural sophistication, as reflected in their magnificent palaces and burial sites. Archaeological evidence also suggests that commoners could purchase bronze metalwork, whereas previously only Zhou rulers and aristocrats could afford to do so. Social relations became more fluid as commoners gained power and aristocrats lost it. In Qin, for example, peasants who served in the ruler's army could be rewarded with land, houses, slaves, and even status change for killing enemy soldiers. While class relations had a revolutionary fluidity, gender relations became more rigid for elites and nonelites alike as male-centered kinship groups grew. The resulting separation of the sexes and male domination within the family affected women's position. An emphasis on monogamy, or at least the primacy of the first wife over additional wives and concubines, emerged. Relations between the sexes became increasingly ritualized and constrained by moral and legal sanctions against any behavior that appeared to threaten the purity of authoritarian male lineages.

Even with the endless cycles of warfare and chaos—or perhaps because of them—many foundational beliefs, values, and philosophies for later dynasties sprang forth during the Spring and Autumn and Warring States periods. By the middle of the first millennium BCE, China's political activities and institutional and intellectual innovations affected larger numbers of people, over a much broader area, than did comparable developments in South Asia and the Mediterranean.

Knife Coin Zhou dynasty coins, like the later Han coin shown here, were made of bronze and produced in a variety of shapes, some resembling spades and knives, depending on the region. Each of the Warring States had its own currency.

The New Worlds of South Asia

While Chinese scholar-officials were theorizing about how to govern and organize their society, the Vedic peoples who settled in the Ganges Valley were assimilating earlier residents and forging their own new political institutions, economic activities, and belief systems. The heartland of South Asian developments in this period was the mid-Ganges plain, a roughly 70,000-square-mile area in the northeast of present-day India and the southern tip of Nepal. (See Map 5.3.) Waves of Vedic peoples migrated into this region around 600 BCE, clearing land, establishing new cities and trade routes, expanding rice cultivation, and experimenting with new political forms. Abundant monsoon rains made the land suitable for rice farming, as opposed to the wheat and barley farming of the Indus Valley. Vedic migrants cleared land by setting fire to the forests and using iron tools—fashioned from ore mined locally—to remove what was left of the jungle. Two major kinds of states appeared in the mid- and lower Ganges plain: those ruled by hereditary monarchs and those ruled by a small elite (oligarchy). South Asian oligarchies were led by the Kshatriya class of warriors and officials. Kshatriya oligarchs controlled the land and other resources, overseeing the work of slaves and foreign workers.

In the kingdoms and oligarchic cities of northern India, a new system of hierarchy emerged alongside the old fourfold *varnas* (Brahman priests, Kshatriya warriors, Vaishya commoners, and Shudra laborers).

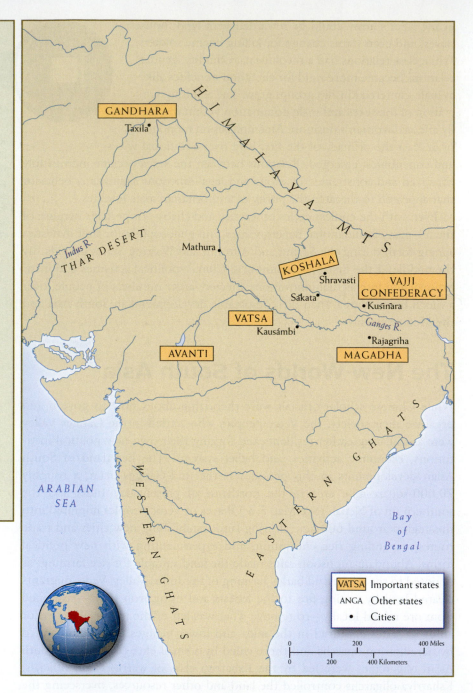

Map 5.3 Major States in the First Millennium BCE in South Asia

South Asia underwent profound transformations in the first millennium BCE that reflected growing urbanization, increased commerce, and the emergence of two types of states: monarchies and oligarchies.

- Where did the new states and cities appear? How do these compare with the location of the earlier cities of the Harappans (Map 2.5)?

- What geographic and environmental features encouraged or hindered social and cultural integration?

- What other regions had influence on South Asia, and where might South Asian culture spread?

Map labels:
GANDHARA
Taxila
HIMALAYA MTS
Indus R.
THAR DESERT
Mathura
KOSHALA
Shravasti
VAJJI CONFEDERACY
Sáketa
Kuśīnāra
VATSA
Kausámbi
Ganges R.
Rajagriha
AVANTI
MAGADHA
ARABIAN SEA
WESTERN GHATS
EASTERN GHATS
Bay of Bengal

Legend:
VATSA Important states
ANGA Other states
• Cities

0 200 400 Miles
0 200 400 Kilometers

Varnas remained the overarching theoretical basis for ranking the social order; however, since booming agriculture allowed for greater variation in professions, occupation and birth received new emphasis. Each occupational group established its own sublevels, called *jatis* (the Sanskrit word for "birth"). *Jatis* were organized not only by kinship and profession but even by product. In the emerging urban centers, for instance, traders were regarded as "purer" than artisans, while those making gold utensils had higher status than those making copper or iron products. Yet members of each group worked together to restrict internal competition, and they closed ranks to preserve their status. Sub-*jatis* banned intermarriage to prevent other groups from accessing their knowledge. Religion buttressed this hierarchical system. Brahmanic texts, some from an earlier period and some from the present, invoked the principle of purity and pollution to rank *varnas* and *jatis* and to hinder movement between them. Occupations were made hereditary, and taboos were placed on intermarriage and interdining. These injunctions ensured that individuals did not move out of their inherited occupation. Thus, the basis of what would later become the caste system, which still plays an important role in Indian society, was laid at this time.

NEW CITIES AND A CHANGING ECONOMY

Supported by rice agriculture, cities began to emerge on the Ganges plain around 500 BCE and became centers of commercial and intellectual exchange. Some, such as Shravasti and Rajagriha, thrived as artisanal centers, while others, like Taxila, prospered through trade. These cities of the Ganges plain were dominated by men and women whose occupations—bankers, merchants, and teachers—did not fit easily into the old *varnas*. Precisely laid out streets were crowded with vendors, and wealthy residents employed elephants and horse-drawn chariots to move them about. Alleys leading from the main streets zigzagged between houses built with pebbles and clay. Although city expansion was often haphazard, civic authorities showed great interest in sanitation. The many squares dotting each city had garbage bins, and dirty water drained away in deep sink wells underground. Streets were graded so that rainfall would wash them clean.

The new cities offered exciting opportunities and innovations. Rural householders who moved into them prospered by importing rice and sugarcane from villages to sell in the markets; they then transported manufactured goods such as sugar, salt, and utensils back to their villages. The less affluent turned to craftwork, fashioning textiles, needles, fine pottery, copper plates, ivory decorations, and gold and silver utensils. Other professions included physicians, launderers, barbers, cooks, tailors, and entertainers. The elaborate

Taxila (*Left*) Taxila became the capital of Gandhara, a kingdom located in what is today northern Pakistan and eastern Afghanistan, when it was occupied by the Persian Empire in the fifth century BCE. Dharmarajika was one of the most important monasteries. The walkway around the stupa, a moundlike structure containing Buddhist relics, was covered with glass tiles, and the stupa itself was decorated with jewels. (*Right*) This corner of a stupa exhibits a variety of the architectural styles that prevailed in Gandharan art. Both square and round columns are covered by Greek-influenced Corinthian capitals. The arch on the right shows the stacked-beam style of Sanchi, the famous stupa in central India.

division of labor suggests high degrees of specialization and commercialization. Those with money became bankers who financed trade and industry. As in Greece and China, coins came into use in these cities at about this time. Traders and bankers established municipal bodies that issued the coins and vouched for their worth. Made of silver, the coins had irregular shapes but specific weights, which determined their value; they also were punch-marked, or stamped with symbols of authority on one side.

Yet the opportunities and innovations of the new cities did not ensure success for everyone. Many came to cities in search of work, and some fared better than others. As a whole, city dwellers had more material wealth, but their lives were far more uncertain. In addition, urban life created a new social class: those who did the dirtiest jobs, such as removing garbage and sewage, and were therefore viewed as physically and ritually impure "untouchables." Even though their work kept the cities clean, they were forced to live in shantytowns outside the city limits. These outcasts became receptive audiences for those who would challenge Vedic rituals and Brahman priests.

BRAHMANS, THEIR CHALLENGERS, AND NEW BELIEFS

To the Brahmans, nothing about the cities seemed good, and their efforts to retain their superior status prompted new challenges to traditional beliefs. The Brahmans thought that *varnas* and *jatis* mixing indiscriminately polluted society. Moreover, lowborn persons grasping at higher status by acquiring wealth or skill skewed established hierarchies. When an alphabetic script appeared around 600 BCE, sacred knowledge became more accessible, and thus the Brahmans' ability to control the definition of right and wrong was undermined. Formerly, all of Vedic literature had been memorized, and only the brightest Brahmans could master the tradition. (See Chapter 4.)

Frightened by these urban threats, Brahmans sought to strengthen their relationships with the kings by establishing the idea of a monarch endowed with divine power. Kingship had been unnecessary in a long-ago golden age, according to Brahmanic scripts; a moral code and priests to uphold it had been enough to keep things in order. Over time, though, the world deteriorated due to rivalry for wealth. According to Brahmanic writings, the gods then decided that people on earth needed a king to maintain order. The gods enticed a reluctant Manu ("Man") with a range of promises, including one-tenth of the grain harvest, one-fiftieth of the cattle, merits for subjects' good behavior, and the most beautiful woman in his domain. The Laws of Manu are associated with this tradition. In the Brahmanic accounts, royal power had a divine origin: the gods chose the king and protected him. Priests and Vedic rituals were essential to royal power, since kingly authority was validated through religious ceremonies carried out by Brahman priests. This emphasis on divine kingship solved some problems but created new ones. The Brahmans' claim to moral authority caused resentment among the Kshatriyas—especially those in the oligarchic republics, whose leaders did not assert divine power. Merchants and artisans also chafed at the Brahmans' claims to superiority. Such resentments provoked challenges to the Brahmans' domination. Some thinkers in South Asia believed that they were in an age of acute crisis because their culture's ancient harmony had been lost. And like many scholars and philosophers elsewhere in this axial era, a new group of South Asian scholars and religious leaders developed their own answers to questions about human existence.

Dissident South Asian thinkers challenged the Brahmans' worldview by refusing to recognize the gods that populated the Vedic world. Some of these rebels sprang from inside the Vedic tradition; though Brahmans, they rejected the idea that sacrificial rituals pleased the gods. To them, God was a universal concept, not a superhuman creature. Also, they felt that the many cows that priests slaughtered for ritual sacrifices could serve more practical uses, such as plowing the land and producing milk. Their discussions and teachings about the universe and life were later collected in the *Upanishads*. Other dissidents, such as Mahavira and the Buddha, came from outside the Vedic tradition.

Mahavira and Jainism Vardhamana Mahavira (c. 540–468 BCE) popularized the doctrines of **Jainism**, which had emerged in the seventh century BCE. Born a Kshatriya in an oligarchic republic, Mahavira left home at age

Jainism
System of thought, originating in the seventh century BCE, that challenged Brahmanism. Spread by Vardhamana Mahavira, Jainism encouraged purifying the soul through self-denial and nonviolence.

thirty to seek the truth about life; he spent twelve years as an ascetic (one who rejects material possessions and physical pleasures) wandering throughout the Ganges Valley before reaching enlightenment. He taught that the universe obeys its own everlasting rules and cannot be affected by any god or other supernatural being. He also believed that the purpose of life is to purify one's soul through asceticism and to attain a state of permanent bliss. The Jains' religious doctrines emphasized the idea that asceticism, rather than knowledge, would enable one to avoid harming other creatures and thereby purify the soul. Since the doctrine of *ahimsa* ("no hurt") held that every living creature has a soul—killing even an ant would result in an unfavorable rebirth—believers had to watch every step to avoid inadvertently becoming murderers. The extreme nonviolence of Jainism was impossible for peasants, who could not work the land without killing insects. Instead, Jainism became a religion of city dwellers and traders. Mahavira's teachings were transmitted orally for nearly a millennium before being compiled into writing by followers in the fifth century CE.

The Buddha and Buddhism The most direct challenge to traditional Brahmanic thinking came from Siddhartha Gautama (c. 563–483 BCE), a contemporary of Mahavira and Confucius. Later known as the **Buddha** (Enlightened One), Gautama objected to Brahmanic beliefs, their rituals and sacrifices, and their preference for kingship that kept the priestly class in power. His Axial Age teachings provided the peoples of South Asia and elsewhere with alternatives to established traditions.

The son of a highly respected Kshatriya warrior, Gautama was born into a comfortable life in a small oligarchic community nestled in the foothills of the Himalayas. Yet, at the age of twenty-nine, he walked away from everything, leaving behind his father, wife, and newborn son. Family and friends wept as he donned a robe and shaved his head and beard, symbols of the ascetic life that he intended to pursue. Gautama struggled with the belief that the life that he and most others were destined to live would consist of little more than endless episodes of suffering, which began with the pain of childbirth, followed by aging, illness, disease, and death, after which reincarnated beings would experience more of the same.

For six years, Gautama lived as an ascetic wanderer before a forty-nine-day meditation led him to the enlightened moment in which he realized that *nirvana* (spiritual contentment) could be achieved by finding a middle ground between self-indulgence and self-denial. He expressed this new credo as the Four Noble Truths: (1) life, from birth to death, is full of suffering; (2) all suffering is caused by desires; (3) the only way to rise above suffering is to renounce desire; and (4) the only way to rid oneself of desire is through adherence to the Eightfold Path, which includes wisdom (right views and right intentions), ethical behavior (right conduct, right speech, and right livelihood), and mental discipline (right effort, right thought, and right meditation). This teaching represented a dramatic shift in thinking about humanity and correct behavior. Like the Jain teachings of Mahavira, the Buddha's doctrines left no space for Brahmanic deities to dictate human lives. The Buddha's logical explanation of human suffering and his guidelines for renouncing desire appealed to many people for their simplicity, accessibility, and challenge to the Vedic hierarchies.

Like other dissident thinkers of this period, the Buddha delivered his message in a vernacular dialect of Sanskrit that all could understand. His many followers soon formed a community of monks called a *sangha* ("gathering"). The Buddha and his followers wandered from one city to another on the Ganges plain, where they found large audiences as well as the alms needed to sustain the expanding *sangha*. It was these followers who would pass on and eventually compile the Buddha's sayings into the Dhammapada. The Buddha's most influential patrons were urban merchants. In struggles between oligarchs and kings, the Buddha sided with the oligarchs, reflecting his upbringing in an oligarchic republic. He inevitably aroused opposition from the Brahmans, who favored monarchical government. While the Buddha himself did not seek to erase the Vedic hierarchies, Buddhism provided an escape from its oppressive aspects and the prestige that it afforded the Brahmans. Together with Jainism, Buddhism's challenge to Brahmanic thinking appealed particularly in the new urban contexts of South Asia and to those who felt disadvantaged by prevailing Vedic hierarchies in the first millennium BCE.

Brahman Recluse When Buddhists started to tell stories in sculptures and paintings, Brahmans were included when appropriate. This character in Gandharan Buddhist art probably represents a Brahman who lived as a recluse, instead of as a priest. He is not shaved or dressed, but his expression is passionate.

The Mediterranean World

Political, economic, and social changes also stimulated new thinking in the Mediterranean world. The violent upheavals that tore through the borderland areas of the northern Levant, the coastal lands of Anatolia, the islands of the Aegean and Mediterranean Seas, and mainland Greece in the few centuries after 1000 BCE freed the people in these regions from the domination of the Neo-Assyrians and Persians (Chapter 4). These borderland communities encircling the Mediterranean basin also created second-generation societies that developed new social and political methods of organization and explored new Axial Age ideas. Phoenicians, Greeks, Cretans, Cypriots, Lydians, Etruscans, and many others exchanged not only trade goods but also ideas about the virtues of self-sufficient cities whose inhabitants shared power more widely than before. (See Map 5.4.)

FORMATION OF NEW CITY-STATES

Core Objectives

EXPLAIN the relationship between Axial Age thinkers across Afro-Eurasia and the political and social situations to which they were responding.

In the ninth and eighth centuries BCE, as order returned to the eastern Mediterranean and the population rebounded, peoples who were clustered in more concentrated settlements formed city-states. Unlike the city-states of earlier Mesopotamia, which were governed by semidivine monarchs, or the great urban centers of Southwest Asian empires, which were run by elite scribes, high priests, and monarchs, the Mediterranean city-states were governed by their citizens. These self-governing city-states were a new political form that profoundly influenced the Mediterranean region. This new urban entity—known first by the Phoenicians as a *qart*, then by the Greeks as a *polis*, and the Romans as a *civitas*—multiplied throughout the Mediterranean by the sixth century BCE.

The new principles of rulership were revolutionary. Ordinary residents, or "citizens," of these cities—such as Carthage and Gadir (modern-day Cádiz in Spain) among the western Phoenicians; Athens, Thebes, Sparta, and Corinth among the Greeks; and Rome and Praeneste among the early Latins— governed themselves and selected their leaders. Their self-government took various forms, including tyranny (rule by a popularly approved individual), oligarchy (rule by the few), and democracy (rule by all free adult males).

The new cities of the Mediterranean basin included adult male citizens, other free persons (including women, who could not vote or hold office), foreign immigrants, and large numbers of unfree persons (including slaves and people tied to the land who could not vote or fight for the polis). The small family unit, or household, was the most important social unit of the city-state, and the city-state was seen as a natural outgrowth of the household. Thus, the free adult male was fully entitled to engage in the city's public affairs. In contrast, adult women of free birth remained enclosed within the private world of the family and had no standing to debate policy in public, vote, or hold office. Those enjoying full citizenship rights—the adult free-born males—in each community decided what tasks, from warfare to public works, the city-state would undertake and what kind of government and laws it would adopt.

City-states were competitive places. Their histories relate rivalries between individuals, social classes, and other groups. Competition for honor and prestige was a value that shaped behavior in the city-states. This extreme competitive ethic found an outlet in organized sporting events. Almost from

Map 5.4 The Mediterranean World, 1000–350 BCE

Phoenician and Greek city-states, as well as the colonies they founded, dotted the coastline of both the Mediterranean and Black Seas.

- What were the main goods traded in the Mediterranean world in this period? Where were they located?
- To what extent might the concentration of goods in certain regions have driven colonization and fostered trade?
- What areas did the Greeks and Phoenicians control with their homeland cities and their colonies? What was their main settlement pattern?

the moment that Greek city-states emerged, athletic contests sprang up. The greatest of these competitions were the Olympic Games, which began in 776 BCE at Olympia in southern Greece. The competitive spirit among communities also took the destructive form of armed conflicts over borderlands, trade, valuable resources, religious shrines, and prestige. The incessant battles among city-states fueled new developments in military equipment, such as the heavy armor that gave its name to the hoplites, or infantrymen, and in tactics, such as the standard blocklike configuration (which the Greeks called a *phalanx*) in which the regular rank and file fought. These wars were so destructive that they threatened to destabilize the city-states' world. The most famous conflicts were the Peloponnesian War (431–404 BCE) between Athens and Sparta, and their respective allies, and the ongoing rivalry between the city-states of Rome and Phoenician Carthage (from c. 500 BCE onward) that led to the Punic Wars. Despite the destabilizing effects of warfare, city-states prospered, and economic innovations facilitated trade and exchange throughout the Mediterranean.

ECONOMIC INNOVATIONS

Without an elaborate top-down bureaucratic and administrative structure, residents of the new cities devised other ways to run their commercial affairs. They developed open trading markets and a system of money that enabled buyers and sellers to know the precise value of commodities so that exchanges were efficient. At their center, the new city-states had a marketplace (*agora* or *forum*), a large open area where individuals bought and sold commodities. These increasingly complex transactions required money, rather than barter or gift exchange. Like the states in Eastern Zhou China and Vedic South Asia,

The Agora The agora, or central open marketplace, was one of the core defining features of Mediterranean city-states. At its center, each city had one of these open-air plazas, the heart of its commercial, religious, social, and political life. When a new city was founded, the agora was one of the first places that the colonists measured out. The large, rectangular, open area in this picture is the agora of the Greek colony of Cyrene (in modern-day Libya).

Mediterranean Coins From the sixth century BCE onward, money in the form of precious metal coins began spreading through the city-states of the Mediterranean, beginning with the Greek city-states in the western parts of what is today Turkey, then spreading to the other Greek poleis and beyond. On the left here is the classic tetradrachm (four-drachma piece) coin of Athens with its owl of the goddess Athena; on the right is a silver coin of shekel weight produced by the city of Carthage in the western Mediterranean.

by the end of the fifth century BCE the Greek city-states were issuing a striking variety of coins, and other peoples such as the Phoenicians, Etruscans, and Persians were using them. Coins bought services, as well, perhaps at first to hire mercenary soldiers. In the absence of large bureaucracies, Mediterranean cities relied on money to connect the producers and buyers of goods and services, especially as city-states became more far-flung.

Indeed, the search for silver, iron, copper, and tin drove traders westward across the Mediterranean. By about 500 BCE, the Phoenicians, Greeks, and others from the eastern Mediterranean had planted new city-states around the shores of the western Mediterranean and the Black Sea. Once established, these colonial communities became completely independent and transformed the coastal world. City-based life was common from southern Spain and western Italy to the Crimea on the Black Sea. With amazing speed, seaborne communications spread a Mediterranean-wide urban culture that bolstered the region's wealthy and powerful elites. Among the local elites of Tartessos in southern Spain, the Gallic chiefs in southern France, and the Etruscan and Roman nobles of central Italy, a new aristocratic culture featured similar public displays of wealth: richly decorated chariots, elaborate armor and weapons, fine dining ware, elaborate houses, and public burials. From the western end of the Mediterranean to the Black Sea, the city-state communities developed a culture founded on market-based economies and private property.

In contrast to the privilege enjoyed by these elites was the traffic in human flesh: slavery. Treating men, women, and children as objects of commerce, to be bought and sold in markets, created a new form of commercial slavery called chattel slavery. Slavery—the forced, unfree labor of war captives or of those who sold themselves to pay debt—had existed since the third millennium, but what was new in this Mediterranean context was the commodification of bodies and the scale of the exchange. When dangerous and exhausting tasks such as mining and farming required extra labor, freeborn citizens purchased slave laborers. The primary source of slaves was still mainly war captives. In some city-states, slaves may have constituted up to a quarter of the population. In every one of the new city-states, slaves provided manual and technical labor of all kinds and produced the agricultural surpluses that supported the urban population.

NEW IDEAS

New ways of thinking about the world emerged from the competitive atmosphere that the Greek city-states fostered. In the absence of monarchical or priestly rule, ideas were free to arise, circulate, and clash. Individuals argued publicly about the nature of the gods, the best state, what is good, and whether to wage war. There was no final authority to give any particular idea a final stamp of approval and force its acceptance. New ideas emerged in science and the arts, and Greek philosophers proposed theories on human society and many other topics.

Naturalistic Science and Realistic Art In this competitive marketplace of ideas, some daring thinkers developed novel ways of perceiving the cosmos and representing the environment. Rather than seeing everything as the handiwork of all-powerful deities, they took a naturalistic view of humans and their place in the universe. This new thinking was evident in their art, which idealized the natural world. Artists increasingly represented humans, objects, and landscapes not in abstract, idealized, or formal ways but in "natural" ways, as they appeared to the human eye. Even their portrayals of gods became more human-like. Later, these objective and natural views of humans and nature became the new ideals, the highest of which was the unadorned human figure: the nude became the centerpiece of Greek art. Individual artists—such as the vase painter Exekias, the sculptor Praxiteles, and the poet Sappho—began to sign their works in a clear manifestation of the new sense of the individual being freed from the restraints of an autocratic state or a controlling religious system.

New Thinking and Greek Philosophers Axial Age thinkers in city-states such as Miletus and Ephesus in western Anatolia did not accept traditional explanations of how and why the universe worked. Each thinker competed to outdo his peers in offering persuasive and comprehensive explanations of the cosmos, and their theories became ever more radical. For instance, Thales (c. 636–546 BCE) believed that water was the primal substance from which all other things were created. Xenophanes (c. 570–480 BCE)

Greek philosophers
"Wisdom lovers" of the ancient Greek city-states, including Socrates, Plato, Aristotle, and others, who pondered such issues as self-knowledge, political engagement and withdrawal, and evidence-based inquiry to understand the order of the cosmos.

doubted the very existence of gods as they had been portrayed, asserting instead that only one general divine aura suffused all creation but that ethnic groups produced images of gods in their own likeness. Pythagoras (c. 570–495 BCE), who devoted himself to the study of numbers, held that a wide range of physical phenomena, like musical sounds, were in fact based in numbers. Democritus (c. 460–370 BCE) claimed that everything was composed of small and ultimately indivisible particles, which he called *atoma* ("uncuttables"). This rich competition among ideas led to a more aggressive mode of public thinking, which the Greeks called *philosophia* ("love of wisdom").

In the fifth century BCE **Greek philosophers** ("wisdom lovers") were focusing on humans and their place in society. Some of these professional thinkers tried to describe an ideal state, characterized by harmonious relationships and free from corruption and political decline. One such thinker was Socrates (469–399 BCE), a philosopher who frequented the agora at Athens and encouraged people to reflect on ethics and morality, even as the Peloponnesian War raged on. He stressed the importance of honor and integrity as opposed to wealth and power (just as Confucius had done in Eastern Zhou China and the Buddha had done in Vedic South Asia). Plato (427–347 BCE), a student of Socrates, presented Socrates's philosophy in a series of dialogues (much as Confucius's students had written down his thoughts). In *The Republic*, Plato envisioned a perfect city that philosopher-kings would rule. He thought that if fallible humans could imitate this model city more closely, their states would be less susceptible to the decline that was affecting the Greek city-states of his own day.

Plato's most famous pupil answered the same questions about nature and the acquisition of knowledge differently. Deeply interested in the natural world, Aristotle (384–322 BCE) believed that by collecting and studying all the facts one could about a given thing, one could achieve a better understanding. His main idea was that the interested inquirer can find out more about the world by collecting as much evidence as possible about a given thing and then making deductions from these data about general patterns.

The Human Form The human body as it appeared naturally, without any adornment, became the ideal set by Greek art. Even gods were portrayed in the same natural nude human form. This statue by Praxiteles is of the god Dionysus and the child Hermes. Such bold nude portraits of humans and gods were sometimes shocking to other peoples.

What Makes an "Axial Age"?

In the mid-twentieth century, the German philosopher Karl Jaspers invented the term "Axial Age" to describe the importance of ideas that originated in the first millennium BCE. These thinkers and their ideas are characterized as "axial" because (1) they were a pivot point, or axis, that seemed to turn the world in a new direction, (2) they occurred along an east-west axis stretching from the Mediterranean to East Asia, and (3) they are central to ethical thought even down to the present day. These Axial Age philosophers were both the product of, and a challenge to, the societies from which they came. Each was responding to a context of economic growth and political infighting. Although the specific socioeconomic and political contexts that spurred them to develop their new ideas were unique—the stratifications of *varna* in South Asia for the Buddha, the warfare of the late Spring and Autumn period in China for Confucius, and the civil war among Greek city-states for Socrates—across the board these new thinkers critiqued and offered alternatives to the status quo.

Ideas about the Axial Age have come a long way since Jaspers. World historians today have a better understanding of how connectedness may have affected the development of these ideas. Where Jaspers saw a relatively disconnected world and marveled at the similarities among the independently proposed ideas, scholars today recognize that exchange between the Mediterranean, Southwest Asia, and South Asia predated these thinkers by almost 2,000 years and may have even had an impact on these developments. Scholars have refined the definition of what makes a tradition axial. For instance, Shmuel Eisenstadt has remarked that the axial philosophers were a sort of intellectual elite who, in a self-examining way, helped negotiate between what he refers to as an "otherworldly" and "worldly" order. David Christian, the historian known for his work with "Big History," has noted the relationship between large, connected empires and these universal philosophical ideas, with their "universal truths and . . . all-powerful gods"; he has even interpreted the spread of these similar ideas as evidence of the connections across Afro-Eurasia. Others have also begun to reflect more critically on the limitations of Axial Age thought as an organizing concept. For instance, although the tenets of Axial Age philosophers were accessible and applicable to urban-living elite men, historians such as Karen Armstrong raise the question of whether they also applied to women, nonelites, and those living in rural contexts. Other scholars, of

This evidence-based inquiry stood in stark contrast to Plato's claim that everything a person observes is in fact only a flawed copy of the "real" thing that exists in a thought-world of abstract patterns accessible only by pure mental meditation—completely the opposite of Aristotle's method. This competition of ideas raged on for centuries, with the new thinking of these Mediterranean Axial Age philosophers at times fueling the aspirations of the city-states and at other times challenging them.

whom Iain Provan is the most recent and vocal, raise concerns about generalizing across very different cultures and not giving enough attention to the unique political situation of each region. Some have challenged outright the concept of the Axial Age, arguing that it is merely a modern, oversimplifying construct that is in no way useful for interpreting the complex philosophical developments of the first millennium BCE.

Even with the modern tweaks and strong critiques of his theory, it is hard to disagree with Jaspers that these mid-first-millennium BCE thinkers, such as Confucius, the Buddha, and Socrates, offered transformational ideas that are still with us today. The axial traditions offer surprisingly similar moral codes that address issues such as the nature of wisdom and divine justice, the need for kindness, and the value of following the "Golden Rule."

Questions for Analysis

- Based on your reading of this chapter, what connections, if any, can be made between the geopolitical situation of a society and the Axial Age philosophy that sprang from that region? In what ways did each philosopher support or challenge the status quo?
- Karl Jaspers was particularly impressed that societies he understood as being disconnected from one another could develop philosophical ideas that were so similar. How might connections with other regions, or the lack thereof, have affected the development of these ideas? What might account for similarities and differences in these Axial Age philosophies?
- How useful, or not, do you find the concept of the Axial Age for thinking about global developments in the first millennium BCE? What are some arguments for and against using such a term/concept?

Explore Further

Armstrong, Karen, *The Great Transformation: The Beginning of Our Religious Traditions* (2006).

Bellah, Robert N., "What Is Axial about the Axial Age?" *European Journal of Sociology 46, no. 1 (2005): 69–89.*

Eisenstadt, S. N., (ed.), *The Origins and Diversity of the Axial Age* (1986).

Jaspers, Karl, *The Origin and Goal of History*, translated by Michael Bullock (1953).

Provan, Iain, *Convenient Myths: The Axial Age, Dark Green Religion, and the World That Never Was* (2013).

Sources: Karen Armstrong, *The Great Transformation: The Beginning of Our Religious Traditions* (New York: Knopf, 2006), pp. xxi–xxii; Robert N. Bellah, "What Is Axial about the Axial Age?" *European Journal of Sociology* 46, no. 1 (2005): 69–89; David Christian, *Maps of Time: An Introduction to Big History* (Berkeley: University of California Press, 2004), p. 319; S. N. Eisenstadt (ed.), *The Origins and Diversity of the Axial Age* (Albany: State University of New York Press, 1986); Karl Jaspers, *The Origin and Goal of History*, translated by Michael Bullock (New Haven, CT: Yale University Press, 1953); Iain Provan, *Convenient Myths: The Axial Age, Dark Green Religion, and the World That Never Was* (Waco, TX: Baylor University Press, 2013).

Common Cultures in the Americas and Sub-Saharan Africa

During what we have termed the Axial Age in Eurasia and North Africa, peoples living in the Americas and most of sub-Saharan Africa built complex, urban-based societies for the first time. These regions did not have the large number of immense cities, the presence of increasingly complex empires, the proliferation of elaborate written texts, the wide variety of load-bearing domesticated animals, and the other ingredients that underlay the radical new ideas of this era in the narrow band above the equator in the Eastern Hemisphere. Nonetheless, among the Chavín of the Andes, the Olmecs of Mesoamerica, the peoples of Nubia, and the West African Nok, exciting new developments were taking place in the first millennium BCE. Since the written record from these communities is limited, however, knowledge of their societies and beliefs is based largely on archaeological remains.

THE CHAVÍN IN THE ANDES

Around 1400 BCE, as the **Chavín** peoples began to share a common belief system, they also began to organize their societies vertically along the steep mountainsides and deep fertile valleys of the Andes. (See Map 5.1.) Valley floors yielded tropical and subtropical produce; the mountains supported maize and other crops; and in the highlands, potatoes became a staple and llamas produced wool and dung (used as fertilizer and fuel) and, eventually, served as beasts of burden. Llamas could not transport humans, however, so the Chavín migratory and political reach remained limited. While most necessities were available nearby thanks to the ecological diversity of the region, the Chavín did undertake some long-distance trade—mainly in dyes and precious stones, such as obsidian. By 900 BCE, the Chavín were erecting elaborate stone carvings, using advanced techniques to weave fine cotton textiles, and making gold, silver, and copper metal goods. Scholars have found evidence that by 400 BCE trade in painted textiles, ceramics, and gold objects spanned the Pacific coast, the Andean highlands, and the watershed eastward to the tropical rain forests of the Amazon basin.

What unified the fragmented Chavín communities was a shared artistic tradition manifested in their devotion to powerful deities. Their spiritual capital was the central temple complex of Chavín de Huántar, in modern Peru's northeastern highlands. The temple boasted a U-shaped platform whose opening to the east surrounded a sunken, circular plaza. From its passageways and underground galleries, priests—whom the Chavín believed were transformed into jaguars through their consumption of hallucinogenic drugs—could make dramatic entrances during ceremonies. Pilgrims brought tribute to Chavín de Huántar, where they worshipped and feasted together. The Chavín drew on influences from as far away as the Amazon and the Pacific coast as they created devotional cults that revered wild animals as representatives of spiritual forces. Carved stone jaguars, serpents, and hawks, baring their large fangs and claws to remind believers of nature's powers, dominated the spiritual landscape. The Chavín cult gave way around 400 BCE

Chavín de Huántar and El Lanzón Chavín de Huántar is nestled in the Peruvian Andes. The temple complex contains several structures; the so-called Northern Platform is pictured here (*above*). Deep within one of the labyrinthine structures stands El Lanzón (*right*), etched with snakes, felines, and humans combined into one hybrid supernatural form.

to local cultural heirs, but some elements of it survived in successor religions adopted by stronger states to the south.

THE OLMECS IN MESOAMERICA

Farther to the north, the first complex society in Mesoamerica emerged around 1500 BCE between the highland plateaus of central Mexico and the Gulf Coast around modern-day Veracruz. (See Map 5.5.) The **Olmecs** are an example of a first-generation community that created new political and economic institutions while contemplating profound questions about the nature of humanity and the world beyond. The culture of the Olmecs—a name meaning "inhabitants in the land of rubber," one of their staples—sprang up from local village roots. The region's peoples formed a loose confederation of villages scattered from the coast to the highlands, mainly nestling in river valleys and along the shores of swampy lakes. Their residents traded with one another, shared a common language, and worshipped the same gods. Around 1500 BCE, the residents of hundreds of hamlets began to develop a single culture and to spread their beliefs, artistic achievements, and social structure far beyond their heartland.

At the core of Olmec culture were its decentralized villages, which housed hundreds—possibly thousands—of households apiece. In these settlements productive subsistence farmers cultivated most of the foodstuffs their

> **Olmecs**
> Mesoamerican people, emerging around 1500 BCE, whose name means "inhabitants of the land of rubber," one of their major trade goods. Living in decentralized agrarian villages, this complex, stratified society shared language and religious ideas that were practiced at sacred ritual centers.

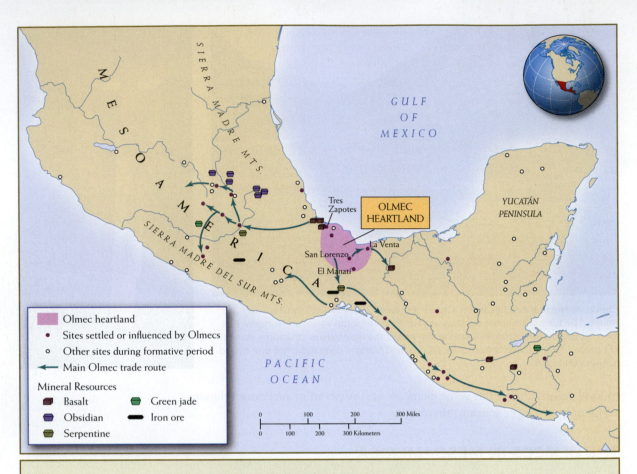

Map Legend:

Olmec heartland
• Sites settled or influenced by Olmecs
○ Other sites during formative period
← Main Olmec trade route

Mineral Resources
Basalt
Obsidian
Serpentine
Green jade
Iron ore

Map labels: SIERRA MADRE MTS., MESOAMERICA, SIERRA MADRE DEL SUR MTS., GULF OF MEXICO, YUCATÁN PENINSULA, PACIFIC OCEAN, Tres Zapotes, OLMEC HEARTLAND, La Venta, San Lorenzo, El Manatí

Scale: 0 100 200 300 Miles / 0 100 200 300 Kilometers

Map 5.5 The Olmec World, 1500–350 BCE

The Olmecs had a strong impact on Mesoamerica's early cultural integration.

- According to this map, how did the Olmecs influence people living beyond the Olmec heartland?
- What geographical factors limited the extent of Olmec influence?
- What is the relationship between resources, trade routes, and Olmec settlements?

communities needed (especially maize, beans, squash, and cacao), while shipping lightweight products including ceramics and precious goods (such as jade, obsidian, or quetzal feathers, used to create masks and ritual figurines) to other villages. Most of the precious objects were for religious purposes rather than everyday consumption. Despite their dispersed social landscape, the Olmec peoples created shared belief systems, a single language, and a priestly class who ensured that villagers and residents of the new urban centers followed highly ritualized practices.

Cities as Sacred Centers The primary Olmec cities, including San Lorenzo, La Venta, and Tres Zapotes, were small compared with the urban centers of Afro-Eurasia, but they served as devotional and secular hubs. The cities featured specialized structures that included massive earthen mounds, platforms, palaces, capacious plazas, and large stone monuments (colossal heads, jaguar sculptures, and basalt thrones). Beneath the mounds of the devotional centers, archaeologists have found axes, knives of sharpened obsidian, other tools, and jade figurines, buried as tokens for those who dwelled in the supernatural world. Olmec devotional art depicted natural and supernatural entities—not just snakes, jaguars, and crocodiles, but also certain humans called shamans, whom the Olmecs believed could commune with the supernatural and transform themselves wholly or partly into beasts. A common figurine is the "were-jaguar," a being that was part man, part animal. Shamans representing jaguars invoked the Olmec rain god, a jaguar-like being, to bring rainfall and secure the land's fertility.

A range of agriculture-linked devotional activity thrived in the Olmecs' major cities. Noble players competed in a complex ball game to honor the rain god, as fans cheered on. Olmec archaeological sites are filled with the remains of game equipment and trophies, some of which were entombed with dead rulers so they could play ball with the gods in the otherworld. It is likely that athletics and human sacrifice were blended in the same rituals. Many monuments depict a victorious and costumed ballplayer (sporting a jaguar headdress or a feathered serpent helmet) atop a defeated, bound human, though scholars are not sure whether the losers were literally executed. Nevertheless, rainmaking rites did include human sacrifice, which involved executing and dismembering captives. The Olmecs believed that the gods defined calendric passages, and thus the seasons and crucial rainfall patterns. Priests, charting celestial movements, devised a complex calendar that marked the passage of seasons and generations. Indeed, the Olmecs' ceremonial life—from ball games to human sacrifice to calendars—was focused on agricultural and rainfall cycles.

A World of Social Distinctions Unlike many decentralized agrarian cultures that were simple and egalitarian, the Olmecs developed an elaborate cultural system marked by many tiers of social rankings. Daily labor kept village-focused Olmecs busy. The vast majority worked the fertile lands as part of household units, with children and parents toiling in the fields with wooden tools, fishing in streams with nets, and hunting turtles and other small animals. Most Olmecs juggled the needs of their immediate families, their village neighbors, and the taxes imposed by rulers.

The priestly class, raised and trained in the palaces at La Venta, San Lorenzo, and Tres Zapotes, directed the exchanges of sacred ritual objects among farming communities. Alongside the priestly elite emerged a secular elite composed of chieftains who supervised agrarian transactions, oversaw artisans, and accepted villagers' tribute. The highest-ranking chieftains commanded villages scattered over a large territory. The chieftains set up workshops, managed by foremen, where craftworkers created pots, painted, sculpted, and wove. Some of their work featured stones and gems imported from surrounding villages.

It is likely that a merchant class also developed to facilitate trade throughout Olmec territories and beyond. As the Olmecs' arts expanded, so did their demand for imported obsidian and jade, seashells, plumes, and other precious goods. The Olmecs exported rubber, cacao, pottery, ceramics, figurines, jaguar pelts, and crocodile skins throughout Mesoamerica. They also conveyed their belief system to neighbors—if not to convert them, at least to influence them and reinforce a sense of superiority.

The Loss of Centers The breakdown of the Olmec culture around the middle of the first millennium is shrouded in mystery. The decline was abrupt in some centers and drawn out in others. At La Venta, the altars and massive basalt heads were defaced and buried, indicating a dramatic shift. Yet there is little evidence of a spasm of war, a peasant uprising, a population shift, or conflict within the ruling classes. Indeed, in many parts of the heartland, the religious centers that had been the hubs of the Olmec world were abandoned but not destroyed. As the bonds between rulers and subjects weakened, so did the exchange of ritual objects that had enlivened the Olmec centers and made them magnets for obedience and piety. Although Olmec hierarchies collapsed, much of the Olmec hinterland remained heavily populated and highly productive. While it lasted, the Olmec combination of an integrated culture, a complex hierarchical social structure, and urban-centered devotional practice offered a degree of cohesion unprecedented in the Americas.

COMMON CULTURES IN SUB-SAHARAN AFRICA

In Africa, too, widespread common cultures emerged in a number of favorable locations. Africa's most significant climate-related historical development in the first millennium BCE was the continued drying up of the northern and central landmass and the sprawl of the great Sahara Desert. (See Map 5.6.) Large areas that had once supported abundant plant and animal life, including human settlements, now became sparsely populated. As a result, the African peoples began to coalesce in a few locations. Most important was the Nile Valley, which may have held more than half of the entire population of Africa at this time.

Climatic change divided Africa from the equator northward to the Sahara Desert into four zones. The first zone was the Sahara itself, which never completely emptied out despite its extreme heat and aridity. Its oases supported

Map legend:

- Meroe
- Kush
- Nok
- Mediterranean settlements
- Persian Empire
- City
- ← Trans-Saharan trade route
- ▲ Spread of iron making from 6th century BCE to the 2nd century BCE
- Sudanic savannah
- Rainforest
- NOK State

Map labels: MEDITERRANEAN COLONIES · BLACK SEA · CASPIAN SEA · PERSIAN EMPIRE · Carthage · MEDITERRANEAN SEA · ATLANTIC OCEAN · MEDITERRANEAN COLONIES · Jerusalem · Memphis · SAHARA DESERT · NORTH AFRICA · SAHARAN PEOPLES · EGYPT · First Cataract · Abu Simbel · KUSH · Fifth Cataract · Kerma · Nile R. · RED SEA · Sixth Cataract · Meroe · SAHEL · Jenne · Gao · Niger R. · Senegal R. · Lake Chad · NOK · Taruga · Congo R. · SUB-SAHARAN AFRICA · Lake Turkana · Lake Victoria · Lake Tanganyika · Equator · INDIAN OCEAN

Scale: 0–400–800 Miles · 0–400–800 Kilometers

Map 5.6 Africa, 500 BCE

The first millennium BCE was a period of cultural, economic, and political integration for North and sub-Saharan Africa.

- According to this map, how might the Mediterranean colonies have had an influence on Africa?
- What main geographic feature integrated Kush and Egypt? What impact might cataracts have on integration?
- Where does the map indicate there was a spread of ironworking? What features on the map may have influenced where ironworking spread?

pastoral peoples, who raised livestock and promoted contacts between the northern and western parts of the landmass. South of the Sahara was the Sahel, literally the "coast" (Arabic *sahil*) of the great ocean of sand, which saw no city of great size in this period. The next zone was the Sudanic savanna, an area of high grasslands stretching from present-day Senegal along the Atlantic Ocean in the west to the Nile River and the Red Sea in the east. Many of West Africa's kingdoms later emerged there because the area was free of the tsetse fly, which was as lethal to animals as to humans, killing off cattle, horses, and goats. The fourth zone comprised the western and central African rain forests, a sparsely populated region characterized by small-scale societies.

Although there was contact across the Sahara by means of trans-Saharan trade routes traversed by camel and via the Nile Valley, Africa below the Sahara differed markedly from North Africa and Eurasia. It did not develop plow agriculture; instead, its farmers depended on hoes. Also, except in densely populated regions, land was held communally and never carried as much value as labor, which was in short supply. African peoples could always move into new locations. They had more difficulty finding workers to turn the soil. In the savanna, millet and sorghum were the primary food crops; in the rain forests, yams and other root crops predominated. Relatively large populations inhabited the Sudanic savanna, the sole area for which substantial historical records exist. Here, in fact, a way of life that historians call Sudanic began to crystallize.

These Sudanic peoples were not completely dependent on their feet to get around (in contrast to their llama-reliant counterparts in the Americas). They had domesticated several animals, including cattle and goats, and even possessed small horses. Although their communities were scattered widely across this region of Africa, they had much in common. For example, they all possessed religious beliefs dominated by a high god, polities led by sacred kings, and burial customs of interring servants alongside dead rulers to serve them in the afterlife. Sudanic peoples were skilled cultivators and weavers of cotton, which they had domesticated. Archaeologists and historians used to believe that the Sudanic peoples borrowed their institutions, notably their sacred kingships, from their Egyptian neighbors, but linguistic evidence and their burial customs indicate that the Sudanic communities developed these practices independently.

Nubia: Kush and Meroe One of the most highly developed locations of common culture in sub-Saharan Africa was Nubia, a region lying between the first Nile cataract (a large waterfall) and the sixth, just north of where the Blue and White Niles come together. From at least the fourth millennium BCE onward, peoples in this region had contact with both the northern and southern parts of the African landmass. It was one of the few parts of sub-Saharan Africa known to the Eurasian world during this period.

Temple of the Lion God at Naqa The small, steep Nubian pyramids of the Meroitic Kingdom, reflecting its Egyptian connections up the Nile, are familiar to many. But the kings and queens of Meroe also built other structures that echoed Egyptian themes and architecture. Pictured here is the façade of the temple of the Lion God, Apedemak, at Naqa in the ancient Meroitic Kingdom. To the right of the entrance, Queen Amanitore (c. 50 CE) strikes down her enemies in a scene reminiscent of images of Thutmosis III (15th century BCE) or Ramses III (12th century BCE) at Luxor.

By the second and first millennia BCE, complex societies formed and developed into states in Nubia. The first of the important Nubian states was Kush. A thriving contemporary of Middle Kingdom Egypt, it flourished between 1700 and 1500 BCE between the first and third cataracts and had its capital at Kerma. Because of its proximity to Egypt, it adopted many Egyptian cultural and political practices, even as it was under constant pressure from the northern powerhouse. Its successor states had to move farther south, up the Nile, to keep free from the powerful Egyptians; the kingdom's capitals were repeatedly uprooted and relocated upriver.

Nubia was Egypt's corridor to sub-Saharan Africa; a source of ivory, gold, and slaves; and an area that Egyptian monarchs wanted to dominate. To the Egyptians, the land of Kush and its people were there to be exploited, not conquered, as Egyptians had no desire to live there. Ramses II left his mark with his magnificent monuments at the Nubian site Abu Simbel around 1250 BCE.

Building on the foundations of earlier kings who had ruled the region of Nubia, the **Meroitic kingdom** arose in the fourth century BCE and flourished until 300 CE. This kingdom was centered in the city of Meroe farther south along the Nile close to its sixth cataract, in the region today known as Sudan. The Meroitic kingdom's rulers were influenced by the pharaonic culture, adapting hieroglyphs, erecting pyramids in which to bury their rulers, viewing their kings as divine, and worshipping the Egyptian god Amun. Meroe became a thriving center of production and commerce. Its residents were especially skilled in iron smelting and the manufacture of textiles, and their products circulated widely throughout Africa. However, Meroe was equally a part of the Sudanic savanna way of life—as evidenced by the distinctiveness of its language and the determination of its inhabitants to retain political autonomy, including, if necessary, moving farther south, out of the orbit of Egypt

Meroitic kingdom

Thriving kingdom from the fourth century BCE to 300 CE. A successor to Kush, it was influenced by both Egyptian and Sudanic cultures.

and more into the orbit of Sudanic polities. Although they called their kings pharaohs, the influential leaders of Meroe selected them from among the many members of the royal family, attempting to ensure that their rulers were men of proven talents. In addition, the Nubian states had close commercial contacts with other merchants and commercial hubs in Sudanic Africa.

West African Kingdoms Complex societies also thrived in West Africa. The most spectacular West African culture of the first millennium BCE was the Nok culture, which arose in the sixth century BCE in an area that is today the geographical center of Nigeria. Though slightly south of the savanna lands of West Africa, the area was (and still is) in regular contact with that region. At Taruga, near the present-day village of Nok, early iron smelting occurred in 600 BCE. Taruga may well have been the first place in western Africa where iron ores were smelted. Ironworking was significant for the Nok peoples, who moved from using stone materials directly to iron, bypassing the bronze working that had been a transitional stage in the technology characteristic of other advanced metallurgists in Afro-Eurasia (as in second-millennium BCE Shang China and the Mediterranean). The Nok made iron axes and hoes, iron knives and spears, and luxury items for trade. They achieved historical fame not for their iron-smelting prowess but for their magnificent terra-cotta figurines, discovered in the 1940s in the tin-mining region of central Nigeria. These naturalistic figures date to at least 500 BCE. They were likely altar-pieces for a cult associated with the land's fertility. Placed next to new lands that were coming into cultivation, they were believed to bless the soil and enhance its productivity.

The Nok were not the only culture developing in this region. Peoples living in the Senegal River basin and Mande peoples around the western branch of the Niger River also began to establish large settlements, in which artisans smelted iron ore and wove textiles and merchants engaged in long-distance trade. West Africa was also home to the Bantu-speaking peoples destined to play a major role in the history of the landmass. Around 300 BCE, small Bantu groups began to migrate southward into the equatorial rain forests, where they cleared land for farming; from there, some moved on to southern Africa. (See Chapter 8 for a discussion of the Bantu peoples.) As impressive as the ironworking, figurines, and trade of West Africa were, these cultures were not yet producing—or at least there is no record of—the type of Axial Age developments that were happening in much of Eurasia.

Conclusion

Afro-Eurasia's great river-basin areas—the Nile, the Tigris-Euphrates, the Indus—were still important in the first millennium BCE, but their time as centers of world cultures was passing. With the development of what we might call second-generation societies, these river-basin areas yielded some of their prominence to regions that had been on their fringes, whether the Mediterranean in the west or the Ganges in the east. Within the territorial states in China, the kingdoms and oligarchies in urbanizing South Asia, and the city-states in the Mediterranean world, great social and intellectual dynamism occurred.

During this Axial Age across much of Eurasia, influential thinkers came to the fore with perspectives quite different from those of the earlier river-basin societies and other contemporary developments elsewhere in worlds apart. In China, the political instability of the Warring States period propelled scholars such as Confucius to engage in political debate, in which they stressed respect for social hierarchy. In South Asia, dissident thinkers challenged the Brahmanic spiritual and political order, and the Buddha articulated a religious belief system that was much less hierarchical than its Vedic predecessor. Mediterranean Greek philosophers offered new views about nature, their political world, and human relations and values—based primarily on secular rather than religious ideas.

Even where contacts with other societies were less intense, innovations occurred as the first complex societies began to arise in the Americas and in sub-Saharan Africa. In the Americas, the Olmecs developed a worldview in which mortals had to appease angry gods through human sacrifice, and built elaborate temples where many peoples could pay homage to the same deities. In West Africa, the Nok peoples promoted interregional trade and cultural contact as they expanded their horizons. In sub-Saharan Africa, settled pockets devised complex cultural foundations for community life. One spectacular example of sub-Saharan and Egyptian synthesis was the Nubian culture of the Meroitic kingdom. As the world was coalescing into culturally distinct regions, many of the ideas newly forged in Eurasia, the Americas, and sub-Saharan Africa had a continuing impact on societies that followed.

Focus On
Innovative Societies

China
- A multistate system emerges from warfare, revolutionizing society and thought.
- Confucius and Master Lao outline new ideals of governing and living.

South Asia
- Small monarchies and urban oligarchies emerge after the Vedic peoples' migrations and rule over societies organized around the *varna* system.
- Dissident thinkers like Mahavira and the Buddha challenge Brahman priests and the caste system.

The Mediterranean World
- Independent city-states emerge from social destruction and facilitate revolutionary principles in rulership, commerce, and thought.

- Thinkers like Socrates, Plato, and Aristotle challenge conventions and encourage public discourse about the role of the individual in society and the way the universe works.

The Americas
- Chavín peoples and the Olmecs produce increasingly hierarchical, agriculture-based societies and connect villages via trade.
- Large-scale common cultures emerge.

Sub-Saharan Africa
- Expansion of the Sahara Desert and population migrations cause people to coalesce in a few locations.
- Early signs of a common culture appear across the Sudanic savanna.

 Go to INQUIZITIVE to see what you've learned—and learn what you've missed—with personalized feedback along the way.

CHRONOLOGY

	1600 BCE	1400 BCE	1200 BCE
East Asia			
South Asia			
The Mediterranean			
The Americas			
Sub-Saharan Africa			

Olmec culture emerges and diffuses through Mesoamerica 1500–400 BCE

Chavín culture flourishes in Central Andes of South America 1400–400 BCE

- **Thinking about Transformation & Conflict and the Axial Age** In the first millennium BCE across Afro-Eurasia, Axial Age thinkers developed radical new ideas in response to their respective political and cultural situations. In what ways did Axial Age thinkers in East Asia (Confucius and Master Lao), South Asia (Mahavira and the Buddha), and the Mediterranean (naturalist philosophers and Socrates) address the unique transformations and conflicts that were taking place where they lived? How do Zoroaster of Persia and the Jewish prophets of Israel, discussed in Chapter 4, fit this model?

- **Thinking about Worlds Together, Worlds Apart and the Axial Age** From the mid-second through the mid-first millennium BCE, "second-generation" societies developed in Eastern Zhou China, the Ganges plain

of South Asia, and the Mediterranean, while parts of South America, Mesoamerica, and sub-Saharan Africa birthed their first complex societies. What are the differences between the second-generation societies of Afro-Eurasia and the first complex societies elsewhere, and what might account for these very different, yet contemporary, developments across the globe?

- **Thinking about Changing Power Relationships and the Axial Age** Axial Age thinkers in East Asia, South Asia, and the Mediterranean offered challenges to both political and social traditions. How did the innovative ideas of thinkers such as Confucius, the Buddha, and Socrates contest and help to reshape power relationships ranging from the political to the familial?

Key Terms

Axial Age p. 204

Buddha p. 218

Chavín p. 228

Confucius p. 208

Daoism p. 210

Greek philosophers p. 224

Jainism p. 217

Meroitic kingdom p. 235

Olmecs p. 229

second-generation societies p. 205

Global Themes and Sources

Comparing Axial Age Thinkers and Their Ideas

Zoroastrianism. Confucianism. Buddhism. Socratic philosophy and questioning. Each of these major developments in the world of ideas is named for a thinker who lived in the first millennium BCE: Zoroaster (after 1000 BCE); Confucius (551–479 BCE); Siddhartha Gautama, later called the Buddha (c. 563–483 BCE); and Socrates (469–399 BCE). But what can we know of these individuals whose ideas were so transformational in their own time and continue to be influential even today? How were their ideas preserved? How can we explore the texts that preserve the ideas attributed to these thinkers in order to get a better sense of the philosophers and the world to which each was responding? Although the "Axial Age" is a contested concept—with scholars ranging from those who find it a useful concept but argue about how best to define it, why it happened, and what impact it may have had, to those who question whether it is a meaningful category for understanding disparate philosophical developments—this chapter has emphasized the challenge that these exceptional thinkers posed to their second-generation societies.

Axial Age thinkers and the ideas they proposed offer an opportunity to compare the radical teachings that surfaced in the first millennium BCE and the distinct contexts within which they were initially put forward. The following excerpts are drawn from Zoroaster's teachings preserved in the Gathas, from Confucius's dialogues with his students in *The Analects*, from the Buddha's reflections in the Dhammapada, and from Socrates's defense of himself in the *Apology*. These texts demonstrate the similarities and differences in how each thinker expressed his ideas—in bold statements and interactive dialogue with others, or rather in poetic phrases and cryptic comments. These selections offer differing ideas about the divine, ranging from the all-powerful Ahura Mazda of the Zoroastrian tradition to the oracular Apollo with whom Socrates had a more transactional relationship,

as well as differing ideas about the role of the individual, ranging from participating in a cosmic battle between good and evil (as in the Gathas of Zoroastrianism) to engaging in a personal struggle to attain inner peace (as in the Dhammapada of Buddhism). These texts show the vibrant nature of political debate involved in axial thought, as students converse with Confucius about the traits of a superior gentleman and as Socrates recounts the charges against himself to the men of Athens assembled to hear his defense. We see each of the thinkers reflect on what it means to be wise and what the meaning of truth is. These texts give us a chance to combine what we know from this chapter about each region with what we see of these philosophical developments in order to investigate why these differences and similarities in thought may have developed in these places at this particular moment in time.

Analyzing Axial Age Thinkers and Their Ideas

- What elements of each Axial Age thinker's ideas, as outlined in this chapter, do you find in these excerpts? What are the similarities and differences among these Axial Age ideas? What do you think accounts for the similarities and differences?

- How do the similarities and differences among these thinkers' ideas help you understand how the so-called Axial Age may have played out in the various regions? Given what you know from this chapter about the political context for each thinker, what is so radical about the ideas in each excerpt?

- The teachings of each of these thinkers were recorded not by the thinker himself but by his students. What evidence in the excerpts suggests transmission of these ideas by disciples? Why do you think these Axial Age thinkers did not write down their own ideas?

- To what extent do these Axial Age ideas apply to nonelite men? To women? Which regions of the world are represented by these Axial Age texts? Which regions are not? Why is this the case, and how might this affect the usefulness of the term "Axial Age" as a global concept for making sense of the first millennium BCE?

PRIMARY SOURCE 5.1

The Gathas from the Hymns of Zoroaster (1000–600 BCE)

In the Gathas, Zoroaster (also called Zarathustra) outlines a philosophy in which opposing forces of light and truth battle those of darkness and lies. These hymns, which are addressed by Zoroaster to the god of light, Ahura Mazda, praise the god and seek his guidance. Initially a challenge to the spirit-focused tradition of the pastoral nomadic culture from which the Persians came, Zoroaster's ideas were eventually adopted by kings to undergird the Persian state and justify their rule.

- How are the ideas in this text about truth and falsehood supposed to influence the actions of the believer?
- What are the rewards for following the ideas and ideals of Ahura Mazda?
- How could a ruler, like Darius in Persia, use these ideas to support his imperial power?

33.1 In accordance with the Primeval Laws of this existence,
The Ratu (Judge) shall deal perfect justice to all;
To the good who chose the Truth,
To the evil who chose Falsehood,
And to those in whom good and evil are mixed.

33.2 He who opposes Evil by his thought or word
Or by the work of his own two hands,
He who instructs people to their good,
Makes a worthy offering of faith to Thy Purpose,
O Ahura Mazda!

33.3 He who is most good to the righteous,
Be he a noble, or a peasant, or a dependent,
He who zealously makes the good living creation flourish,
He shall come to dwell with Truth in the realm of the Good Mind.

33.4 I [Zarathustra] am he who by devotion and prayer shall
Keep disobedience and the Evil Mind far from Thee, O Mazda,
Keep insolent heresy away from the nobles,
The distrust spread by slanderers, from the community,
And the evil of destruction from the pastures of cattle.

33.5 I invoke Thy Sraosha (Inspiration) as the greatest of all aids at the Consummation,
To attain Life Eternal in Thy Kingdom of the Good Mind,
To attain the straight path of Truth wherein Thou dwelleth, O Mazda Ahura!

33.6 I, who as Thy steadfast priest, have learned the straight path of Asha (Truth and Righteousness),
And would learn from the Best Mind how best to do what should be done,
Therefore I ask of Thee, My Lord,
Bless me with Thy Vision and grant me a consultation with Thee!

33.7 Come hither to me, in Thine own self, O Mazda!
Come unmistakably, O Thou Best One, with
The Spirit of Truth and The Good Mind!
Let my message be heard beyond the limits of the community of adherents.
Let the brilliant offerings of reverential prayers be manifest to all.

33.8 Do Thou make known to me, the Ultimate Good, the final end,
That I may bring it about with the help of the Good Mind.
Accept, O Mazda, the homage of Thy faithful worshipper.

Accept, O truth, my hymn of praise for Thee,
Grant to us, O Spirits of Deathless Weal and
Immortality, your own two blessings.

33.9 And with the blessings of these comrade
Spirits of
Perfection and Immortality,
Let all advance to Thee, O Mazda!
Let all promote the cause of Truth!

33.10 All the felicities of life, which have been, which
are, which shall be,
Come to us through Thy Divine Grace, O Mazda:
Through thy Holy Power, let our persons advance to
the wished-for beatitude,
With the help of the Good Mind, with the help of
Truth!

33.11 Hearken unto me, O Most Benevolent Ahura
Mazda!
O ye Spirits of Piety and Truth that bless our
existence!
O ye Good Mind, and the Dominion of Heaven!
Be gracious unto us as we receive our recompense!

33.12 Arise for me, O Ahura!
Through my devotion give me steadfastness of purpose,
Through Thy Most Bounteous Spirit make me pure
in goodness,
Through the Spirit of Righteousness grant me the
courage of spiritual might,
And through the Good Mind give me the trust of
the people.

3.13 With thy divine grace, O Lord.
Make wide the vision of my mind;
Make manifest Thy everlasting attributes;
Make known the blessings of Thy Kingdom of Heaven, and the joyous recompense of the Good Mind,
. . . inspire our consciousness with the Ultimate Truth.

33.14 To the Lord Mazda, as an offering,
Zarathustra dedicates the works of his life, even his
very self.

The noblest essence of his Good Thought.
To Truth, he consecrates obedience to its
principles
In word and deed, and all the might of his spiritual
authority.

Source: Yasna 33, *The Gathas: The Hymns of Zarathushtra*, translated by D. J. Irani, edited by K. D. Irani (Newton, MA: Center for Ancient Iranian Studies, 1998), pp. 47–50.

PRIMARY SOURCE 5.2

The Analects (c. 480 BCE), Confucius

Confucius engaged in philosophical dialogues with his students in the 480s BCE, during the transition from the Spring and Autumn period to the Warring States period. Confucius's teachings about what it meant to be a superior gentleman (*junzi*) became the foundation for Chinese government and society for thousands of years. The passage here shows the lively conversation between Confucius, "the Master" in the text, and his students, including Master You, Master Zeng, Zixia, Ziqin, and Zigong.

- What evidence in the text do you see for the Confucian principles of *ren*, (benevolence), *li* (proper ritual), and *xiao* (filial piety)?

- Based on the exchanges here between Confucius and his pupils, and among his students, what would it have been like to study with Confucius?

- What would be the implications for governing if elite men lived according to the principles laid out in this text?

1.1 The Master said: "To learn something and then to put it into practice at the right time, is this not a joy? To have friends coming from afar: is this not a delight? Not to be upset when one's merits are ignored: is this not the mark of a gentleman?"

1.2. Master You said: "A man who respects his parents and his elders would hardly be inclined to defy his superiors. A man who is not inclined to defy his superiors will never foment a rebellion. A gentleman works at the root. Once the root is secured, the Way unfolds. To respect parents and elders is the root of humanity."

1.3. The Master said: "Clever talk and affected manners are seldom signs of goodness."

1.4. Master Zeng said: "I examine myself three times a day. When dealing on behalf of others, have I been trustworthy? In intercourse with my friends, have I been faithful? Have I practiced what I was taught?"

1.5. The Master said: "To govern a state of middle size, one must dispatch business with dignity and good faith; be thrifty and love all men; mobilize the people only at the right times."

1.6. The Master said: "At home, a young man must respect his parents; abroad, he must respect his elders. He should talk little, but with good faith; love all people, but associate with the virtuous. Having done this, if he still has energy to spare, let him study literature."

1.7. Zixia said: "A man who values virtue more than good looks, who devotes all his energy to serving his father and mother, who is willing to give his life for his sovereign, who in intercourse with friends is true to his word—even though some may call him uneducated, I still maintain he is an educated man."

1.8. The Master said: "A gentleman who lacks gravity has no authority and his learning will remain shallow. A gentleman puts loyalty and faithfulness foremost; he does not befriend his moral inferiors. When he commits a fault, he is not afraid to amend his ways."

1.9. Master Zeng said: "When the dead are honored and the memory of remote ancestors is kept alive, a people's virtue is at its fullest."

1.10. Ziqin asked Zigong: "When the Master arrives in another country, he always becomes informed about its politics. Does he ask for such information, or is it given him?" Zigong replied: "The Master obtains it by being cordial, kind, courteous, temperate, and deferential. The Master has a way of enquiring which is quite different from other people's, is it not?"

1.11. The Master said: "When the father is alive, watch the son's aspirations. When the father is dead, watch the son's actions. If three years later, the son has not veered from the father's way, he may be called a dutiful son indeed."

1.12. Master You said: "When practicing the ritual, what matters most is harmony. That is what made the beauty of the way of the ancient kings; it inspired every move, great or small. Yet they knew where to stop: harmony cannot be sought for its own sake, it must always be subordinated to the ritual; otherwise it would not do."

1.13. Master You said: "If your promises conform to what is right, you will be able to keep your word. If your manners conform to the ritual, you will be able to keep shame and disgrace at bay. The best support is provided by one's own kinsmen."

1.14. The Master said: "A gentleman eats without stuffing his belly; chooses a dwelling without demanding comfort; is diligent in his office and prudent in his speech; seeks the company of the virtuous in order to straighten his own ways. Of such a man, one may truly say that he is fond of learning.

1.15. Zigong said: "'Poor without servility; rich without arrogance.' How is that?" The Master said: "Not bad, but better still: 'Poor, yet cheerful; rich, yet considerate.'" Zigong said: "In the *Poems*, it is said: 'Like carving horn, like sculpting ivory, like cutting jade, like polishing stone.' Is this not the same idea?" The Master said: "Ah, one can really begin to discuss the *Poems* with you! I tell you one thing, and you can figure out the rest."

1.16. The Master said: "Don't worry if people don't recognize your merits; worry that you may not recognize theirs."

Source: Confucius, *The Analects*, translated by Simon Leys, edited by Michael Nylan, A Norton Critical Edition (New York: Norton, 2014), pp. 3–4.

The Dhammapada
(third century BCE), Buddha

The wisdom of Siddhartha Gautama, later called the Buddha, was passed along in a text called the Dhammapada, which was recorded by his followers in the third century BCE. The Buddha's ideas about suffering, desire, and how to escape both, offered a distinct challenge to the prevailing hierarchies of the *varna* system that had thrived in South Asia since the influx of pastoral nomads into the region in the mid-second millennium BCE.

....

- According to this text, what distinguishes the behavior of a fool from that of a wise person? How does one know if one is wise?

- What ways of thinking and acting are encouraged by this text? How do those fit with what you know of Buddhism?

- In what specific ways do the principles laid out in this text challenge the *varna*-stratified community and the religious ideas of South Asia at the time of the Buddha?

....

Long is the night for the sleepless. Long is the road for the weary. Long is samsara (the cycle of continued rebirth) for the foolish, who have not recognized the true teaching. 60

If on one's way one does not come across one's better or an equal, then one should press on resolutely alone. There is no companionship with a fool. 61

"I've got children," "I've got wealth." This is the way a fool brings suffering on himself. He does not even own himself, so how can he have children or wealth? 62

A fool who recognises his own ignorance is thereby in fact a wise man, but a fool who considers himself wise—that is what one really calls a fool. 63

Even if a fool lived with a wise man all his life, he would still not recognise the truth, like a wooden spoon cannot recognise the flavour of the soup. 64

Even if a man of intelligence lives with a wise man only for a moment, he will immediately recognise the truth, like one's tongue recognises the flavour of the soup. 65

Stupid fools go through life as their own enemies, doing evil deeds which have bitter consequences. 66

A deed is not well done if one suffers after doing it, if one bears the consequences sobbing and with tears streaming down one's face. 67

But a deed is well done if one does not suffer after doing it, if one experiences the consequences smiling and contented. 68

A fool thinks it like honey so long as the bad deed does not bear fruit, but when it does bear fruit he experiences suffering. 69 . . .

Like fresh milk a bad deed does not turn at once. It follows a fool scorching him like a smouldering fire. 71

A fool acquires knowledge only to his own disadvantage. It destroys what good he has, and turns his brains. 72 . . .

One way leads to acquisition, the other leads to nirvana. Realising this a monk, as a disciple of the Buddha, should take no pleasure in the respect of others, but should devote himself to solitude. 75

***

Better than a thousand pointless words is one saying to the point on hearing which one finds peace. 100

Better than a thousand pointless verses is one stanza on hearing which one finds peace. 101

Better than reciting a hundred pointless verses is one verse of the teaching (one dhammapada) on hearing which one finds peace. 102

Though one were to defeat thousands upon thousands of men in battle, if another were to overcome just one—himself, he is the supreme victor. 103

Victory over oneself is better than that over others. When a man has conquered himself and always acts with self-control, neither devas, spirits, Mara or Brahma can reverse the victory of a man like that. 104, 105

Though one were to perform sacrifices by the thousand month after month for a hundred years, if another were to pay homage to a single inwardly perfected man for just a moment, that homage is better than the hundred years of sacrifices. 106

Though one were to tend the sacrificial fire for a hundred years in the forest, if another were to pay homage to a single inwardly perfected man for just a moment, that homage is better than the hundred years of sacrifice. 107 . . .

Four principal things increase in the man who is respectful and always honours his elders—length of life, good looks, happiness and health.   109

Though one were to live a hundred years immoral and with a mind unstilled by meditation, the life of a single day is better if one is moral and practises meditation.   110

Though one were to live a hundred years without wisdom and with a mind unstilled by meditation, the life of a single day is better if one is wise and practises meditation.   111

Though one were to live a hundred years without seeing the rise and passing of things, the life of a single day is better if one sees the rise and passing of things.   113 . . .

Though one were to live a hundred years without seeing the supreme truth, the life of a single day is better if one sees the supreme truth.   115

Source: "The Fool," and "The Thousands," *The Dhammapada*, translated by John Richards, Electronic Buddhist Archives, 1993, http://www.cheraglibrary.org/buddhist/dhammapada/.

PRIMARY SOURCE 5.4

The Apology of Socrates (c. 400 BCE), Plato

The ideas of the Greek philosopher Socrates, recorded in dialogues and the speech called the *Apology* (in defense of his influence on youth), called on Athenians to look within, to question, and to reason for themselves. As a citizen of democratic Athens, Socrates was a full participant in the political system and in the Peloponnesian War (431–404 BCE), as well as an influential teacher. The defense speech included here, as reported by his student Plato, preserves Socrates's reflections on wisdom and how his pursuit of understanding led to the charges against him.

- **What are the charges against Socrates? From what you can tell of him from this passage, do you think they are justified?**
- **What does Socrates think of teachers? Of wisdom?**
- **How could the behaviors and ideas promoted by Socrates in this passage have been interpreted by his contemporaries as radical and youth-corrupting?**

19b–e: Let us consider, then, from the beginning, what the accusation is, from which the prejudice against me arose that Meletos believed when he brought this charge against me. Well then. What precisely did the accusers say when they accused me? Just as if they were charging me, it is necessary to read out the indictment: "Socrates is guilty of meddling, of inquiring into things under the earth and in the heavens, of making the weaker speech the stronger and of teaching these very things"—something like this. . . . I call on the majority of you as witnesses, and I expect you to teach and inform one another, those of you who have ever heard me in discussion—and this includes many of you. Inform one another if any of you heard me ever discussing such things, either a lot or a little. And from this you will realize that the same is true of the other things that the many say about me, when really none of this is the case. And if you have heard from anyone that I endeavor to teach people and make money, this is certainly not true. Though again, I think that it is a fine thing if an individual is able to teach people. . . .

20d: Perhaps some of you might respond, "But Socrates, what is your profession? Where have these slanders against you come from? For surely it's not by busying yourself with the usual things that so much hearsay and talk has arisen, but by doing something different from most people. Then tell us what it is, so that we don't judge your case rashly." [Socrates replies:] Listen then. And while I will perhaps appear to some of you to be joking, rest assured that I will tell you the whole truth. For I, men of Athens, have acquired this reputation due to nothing other than a certain wisdom. What sort of wisdom is this? Quite likely a human wisdom. . . .

21a–e: You know Chairephon, I presume. He was a companion of mine from youth and a comrade of yours in the democracy. . . . [W]hen he went to Delphi he was so bold as to ask this—and, as I say, don't interrupt, gentlemen—he asked if there was anyone wiser than me. The Pythia [a priestess of Apollo who was renowned for her advice, which was thought to come from Apollo] then replied that there was no one wiser. And his brother here will bear witness to you about these things, since he [Chairephon] himself has died.

Think about why I am bringing this up: it's because I am going to teach you where the prejudice against me came from. Because when I heard this I pondered in the following way: "Whatever does the god mean? And what riddle is he posing? For I am not aware of being wise in anything great or small. What in the world does he mean, then, when he says that I am wisest? For certainly he does not lie; he is not permitted to." And I for a long time puzzled over his meaning.

Then, very reluctantly, I embarked on a sort of trial of him [Apollo]. I went to one of the people who are thought to be wise, hoping to refute the oracle there if anywhere, and reply to its pronouncement: "This man here is wiser than me, though you said I was. So, scrutinizing this fellow—there's no need to refer to him by name, he was one of the politicians with whom I experienced something of the following sort when examining him, men of Athens—in talking with him it seemed to me that while this man was considered to be wise both by many other people and especially by himself, he was not. And so I tried to show him that he took himself to be wise, but was not. As a result I became hated by this man and by many of those present.

And so, as I was going away, I was thinking to myself, "I am at least wiser than this man. It's likely that neither of us knows anything worthwhile, but whereas he thinks he knows something when he doesn't know it, I, when I don't know something, don't think I know it either. It's likely, then, that by this I am indeed wiser than him in some small way that I don't think myself to know what I don't know." Next, I went to another one of the people thought to be wiser than him and things seemed the same to me, and so I made an enemy of him as well as of many others.

Source: Plato, *Socrates' Defense (The Apology of Socrates)*, translated by Cathal Woods and Ryan Pack, 2016, pp. 2–4, doi:10.2139/ssrn.1023144.

Interpreting Visual Evidence

Elsewhere in the Axial Age

During the time that the Axial Age thinkers such as Confucius, the Buddha, and Socrates were sharing their radical ideas with disciples who recorded them in written texts, other major developments were taking place in preliterate societies. Some of the complex civilizations that formed in this period, like the Nok (in sub-Saharan Africa) and the Olmecs (in Mesoamerica), apparently did not leave written records, so historians rely on artwork—as well as many other sources, such as oral traditions and linguistic analysis—to learn about these peoples.

For example, although the Nok left no written texts that would tell us of their thinking, they did leave behind intriguing figurines. The Nok figurines were shaped from terra-cotta. Their impressive craftsmanship, with finely sculpted poses and carefully shaped hair, clothing, jewelry, and facial features, conveys the artistic tastes of these African peoples dating back to the mid-first millennium BCE. Who these figurines represent, however, is not clear, nor is their purpose.

The second Nok terra-cotta pictured here offers a glimpse of everyday life with its scenes of the harvest and mothers caring for their children.

The Olmecs, who thrived on the other side of the world in first-millennium BCE Mesoamerica, constructed ceremonial centers and also produced a wide range of artifacts, many of which provide evidence of their religious beliefs. So-called Offering 4 from the ritual center at La Venta dates to the mid-first millennium BCE. These seventeen figurines (between 6 and 8 inches tall), including at least one female, were buried together apparently to reenact some political or religious event, perhaps a high-status marriage or an important sacrifice. Wearing a mask that resembles classic Olmec shamanic images—like a jaguar's snarling mouth (see fourth image) and an eagle's beak—these figurines suggests the shape-shifting powers of a shaman. Even without written texts from these first-millennium BCE peoples, artifacts like these help us reconstruct their ideas.

Nok figurine.

Nok terra-cotta.

Offering 4 at La Venta.

Olmec jaguar.

1. Compare the Nok and Olmec figurines with the depictions of the Axial Age thinkers on the first page of this chapter. What do these depictions suggest about what matters to the people who produced them?

2. Looking at Map 5.6, what connection might the Nok have had with the Mediterranean in the first millennium BCE? How might transregional exchange, not just of goods but also of ideas, have affected both the Mediterranean and the sub-Sahara?

3. Looking at Map 5.5, how might trade in Mesoamerica in raw materials such as jade and obsidian have influenced the creation of objects such as Offering 4 from La Venta and the jaguar figurines?

4. Given that the Nok and Olmec cultures were sophisticated and expressed their beliefs through artworks like these, why do you think there is no evidence of singular Axial Age thinkers (like Confucius, the Buddha, or Socrates) among the Nok and the Olmecs?

6

Shrinking the Afro-Eurasian World

350–100 BCE

In the blistering August heat of 324 BCE, at a town on the Euphrates River that the Greeks called Opis (not far from modern Baghdad), Alexander the Great's experienced Macedonian troops declared that they had had enough. They had been fighting far from their homeland for more than a decade. They had marched eastward from the Mediterranean, forded wide rivers, traversed great deserts, trudged over high mountain passes, and slogged through rain-drenched forests. Along the way they had defeated massive armies that not only outnumbered Alexander's own forces but also were armed with fearsome war elephants. Some of his troops had taken wives from the cities and tribes they vanquished, so the army had become a giant swarm of ethnically mixed families. This was an army like no other. It did more than just defeat neighbors and rivals—it forcefully connected entire worlds, bringing together diverse peoples and lands.

Conquering in the name of building a new world, however, was not what the soldiers had bargained for. They loved their leader, but many thought he had gone too far. They had lost companions and grown weary of war. Some had mutinied at a tributary of the Indus River, halting Alexander's advance into South Asia. Now, at Opis, they threatened to desert him altogether. Summoning up their courage, they voiced these resentments to their supreme commander. Alexander's response was immediate and inspired. In order to persuade his troops not to desert him, he evoked

Core Objectives

- **DESCRIBE** Hellenism and **EXPLAIN** its impact across Afro-Eurasia.
- **ANALYZE** the political changes that shaped central and South Asia in the aftermath of Alexander's incursion on the region.
- **EVALUATE** the forces that influenced the spread of Buddhism in this period.
- **TRACE** the early routes of the "Silk Roads" and **ASSESS** their importance in connecting Afro-Eurasia.

the astounding military triumphs and historic achievement they had accomplished: establishing his rule from Macedonia to the Indus Valley. This far-reaching political vision came to a sudden end with Alexander's death a year later, when he was thirty-two years old. Even in his short lifetime, though, he had set in motion cultural and economic forces that would transform Afro-Eurasia.

At the same time that Alexander was expanding eastward, another development was taking form: the Silk Roads. This system of routes constituted the primary commercial network linking East Asia and the Mediterranean world for nearly a thousand years. Many different types of precious commodities were exchanged along its more than 5,000 miles, but the network ultimately took its name from the huge quantities of precious silk that passed along it.

As a result of Alexander's conquests and the political developments that followed, as well as the intensifying of trade along the Silk Roads, two broad cultural movements came to link diverse populations across wide expanses of the Afro-Eurasian landmass: Hellenism and Buddhism. Hellenism, briefly defined, was a shared Greek identity that spread throughout the lands in which Greeks settled and was expressed in their language, art, architecture, politics, and more. Buddhism, as an Axial Age philosophy, was introduced in the previous chapter. A new form of Buddhism, called Mahayana Buddhism, took shape in the period described in this chapter. New empires—namely Alexander's successor states of the Mediterranean and the Mauryan Empire in South Asia—and newly deepening trade routes, both on land and sea, created the circuits through which Hellenism and Buddhism flowed.

Imperial conquests and long-distance trade laid the foundations for widespread cultural systems that were far more enduring than the empires themselves. Merchants, monks, and administrators helped connect widespread parts of Afro-Eurasia, as the busy sea-lanes and Silk Roads flourished. Merely a few centuries after the conquests of Alexander and Mauryan kings, the world looked very different from the realms their armies had traversed.

Global Storylines

- Conquests by Alexander the Great and the influence of his successor states spread Hellenism across Southwest Asia and into South Asia.

- The Mauryan Empire accelerates the integration of South Asia and helps Buddhism spread throughout that region and beyond.

- "Silk Roads," both overland and by sea, facilitate the movement of commodities (spices, metals, and silks) and ideas (especially Buddhism and Hellenism) across Afro-Eurasia.

Alexander and the Emergence of a Hellenistic World

The armed campaigns of the Macedonians led by Alexander the Great (356–323 BCE) began a drive for empire from the west that connected distant regions and spread a Hellenistic culture throughout the conquered lands. (See Map 6.1.) Alexander came from the frontier state of Macedonia to the north of Greece and commanded a highly mobile force armed with advanced military technologies that had developed during the incessant warfare among Greek city-states in the fifth and fourth centuries BCE. Under Alexander's predecessors—especially his father, Philip II—Macedonia had become a large ethnic and territorial state. Philip had unified Macedonia and then gone on to conquer neighboring states. Macedonia boasted gold mines that could finance Philip's new military technology and his disciplined army. Philip's troops included heavily armored infantry that maneuvered in closely arrayed units called phalanxes as well as in large-scale cavalry formations for shock tactics. These infantry and cavalry forces were supported by income not only from Macedonian gold mines but also from the slave trade that passed through Macedonia. By the early 330s BCE, Philip had crushed the Greek city-states to the south, including Athens.

After Philip's assassination, his son Alexander used this new military machine in a series of daring attacks on the Persian Empire. Alexander owed much of his success to a readiness to take risks. In his initial forays into Southwest Asia he outpaced, outflanked, and outthought his adversaries. Through these rapid assaults he brought under the rule of his Greek-speaking elites all the lands of the former Persian Empire, extending from Egypt and the eastern Mediterranean to the Indus River valley.

The result of this expansion was hardly an empire, given that Alexander did not live long enough to establish institutions to hold the distant lands together. But his military campaigns continued a process that the Persians had already set in motion of smashing barriers that had separated peoples on the eastern and western ends of Afro-Eurasia. The conqueror saw himself as a new universal figure, a bridge connecting distant cultures.

Alexander's conquests increased exposure of formerly Persian lands to the commodities of the Mediterranean and to cultural ideas associated with the Greek city-states. Alexander founded dozens of new cities named after himself, not only the famed Alexandria in Egypt but also Iskandariya and Kandahar in modern-day Iraq and Afghanistan. Alexander seized the accumulated wealth that the Persian kings stored in their immense palaces, especially at Persepolis, and dispersed it into the money economies of the Mediterranean city-states. This massive redistribution of wealth fueled a widespread economic expansion in the Mediterranean and beyond.

THE BIG PICTURE

How did Hellenism, Buddhism, and the Silk Road shape Afro-Eurasia?

Legend:

- ✳ Major battles
- ← Campaigns of Alexander the Great
- ▭ Conquests of Alexander the Great
- Qin Empire
- Greek city-state
- Carthage
- Area of Roman control
- Macedonia
- Ptolemaic Empire
- Seleucid Empire
- Graeco-Bactria
- Mauryan Empire
- Empire of Xiongnu

CONQUESTS OF ALEXANDER THE GREAT, 323 BCE

GREEK CITY-STATES

PTOLEMAIC EMPIRE

Granicus (334 BCE)
Issus (333 BCE)
Gaugamela (331 BCE)

0   500   1000 Miles
0   500   1000 Kilometers

Map 6.1 Afro-Eurasia in 250 BCE, after Alexander's Conquests

....

Alexander of Macedonia did not live long enough or establish the institutions necessary to create one large politically unified empire, but his conquests integrated various Afro-Eurasian worlds culturally and economically. Trace the pathways that Alexander followed on his conquests.

- Locate on the map the Hellenistic successor states. What did these states have in common? How were they different from each other?

- Which areas on the map did Greeks *not* rule? How did the spread of Hellenism affect them?

- What features illustrated on the map may have encouraged the spread of Hellenism? What features may have limited the spread of Hellenism?

Battle of Issus Mosaic of the Battle of Issus (333 BCE) between Alexander the Great of Macedon and Darius, the king of Persia (found in a house at Pompeii in southern Italy). Alexander is the bareheaded figure to the far left; Darius is the figure to the right, gesturing with his right hand. The men represent two different types of warfare. On horseback, Alexander leads the cavalry-based shock forces of the Macedonian Greeks, while Darius directs his army from a chariot in the style of the great kings of Southwest Asia.

ALEXANDER'S SUCCESSORS AND THE TERRITORIAL KINGDOMS

Alexander died in Babylon at age thirty-two, struck down by overconsumption of alcohol and other excesses that matched his larger-than-life personality and reflected the war culture of Macedonian warriors. His death in 323 BCE brought on the collapse of the regime he had personally held together. The conquered lands fragmented into large territories over which his generals squabbled for control.

Alexander's successors—his generals Seleucus, Antigonus, Ptolemy, Lysimachus, and others—thought of themselves not as citizens of a Greek city-state but rather as absolute rulers over large blocks of territory, modeling themselves on the regional rulers they had defeated. One effect of powerful families' control of whole kingdoms was that some women could now hold great power, an unthinkable prospect in the democracies of the city-states. Queens in Macedonia, Syria, and Egypt—whether independent or as co-regents with their husbands—established new public roles for women. For example, Berenice I of Egypt (r. c. 320–280 BCE) was the first in a series of powerful women who helped rule the kingdom of the Nile, a line that ended with the famous Cleopatra VII in the 30s BCE.

Three large territorial states stood out in the new Hellenistic world: the Seleucid Empire (established by Seleucus), stretching from Syria to present-day Afghanistan; Macedonia, ruled by the Antigonids (established by Antigonus); and Egypt, ruled by the Ptolemies (established by Ptolemy). In areas between these larger states, middle-sized kingdoms emerged. The old city-states of the Mediterranean, such as Athens and Corinth, still thrived, but now they functioned in a world dominated by these much larger power blocs. On mainland Greece, larger confederations of previously independent city-states formed.

Competition in war remained an unceasing fact of life, but the wars among the kingdoms of Alexander's successors were broader in scope and more complex in organization than ever before. Since the successor kingdoms were nearly equal in strength and employed the same advanced military technology, however, the near-constant state of wars between the new kings never achieved much. After battles that killed tens of thousands, and severely injured and wounded hundreds of thousands more, the three major kingdoms—and even the minor ones—remained largely unchanged.

The great powers therefore settled into a centuries-long game of watching one another and balancing threats with alliances. What emerged was a fierce competition that dominated international relations, in which diplomacy and treaty-making sometimes replaced actual fighting. This equilibrium was reminiscent of the first age of international relations in the second millennium BCE (see Chapter 3). Long periods of peace began to grace the intervals between the new kingdoms' violent and destructive wars.

Berenice Portrait head of Berenice I, wife and consort of Ptolemy I, the first Macedonian king of Egypt after its conquest by Alexander the Great. Berenice was one of the women who, as queens of huge empires, wielded power and commanded wealth in their own right.

HELLENISTIC CULTURE

The unification of large blocks of territory under Alexander's successors helped spread a common Hellenistic culture. Following existing commercial networks, Hellenism was a shared Greek culture that extended across the entire Mediterranean basin and into Southwest Asia. Hellenistic culture included philosophical and political thinking, secular disciplines ranging from history to biology, popular entertainment in theaters, exercising and socializing in gymnasia, competitive public games, and art in many forms. Despite pockets of resistance, Hellenism was remarkably successful at taking root across a large swath of Afro-Eurasia and spreading its influence even farther.

Common Language The core element of Hellenism was a common language known as *Koine*, or "common," Greek. It replaced the city-states' numerous dialects with an everyday form that people anywhere could understand. ***Koine* Greek** quickly became the international language of its day. Peoples in Egypt, Judea, Syria, and Sicily, who all had distinct languages and cultures, could now communicate more easily with one another and enjoy the same dramatic comedies and new forms of art and sculpture.

Koine Greek

Simpler than regional versions of Greek such as Attic or Ionic, this "common Greek" dialect became an international language across the regions influenced by Hellenism and facilitated trade of goods and ideas.

Cosmopolitan Cities Individuals were no longer citizens of a particular city (*polis*); instead they were the first **cosmopolitans**, that is, citizens (*polites*) belonging to the whole world or universe (*kosmos*). Much as Athens had been the model city of the age of the Greek city-state, Alexandria in Egypt became exemplary in the Hellenistic age. Whereas citizens of fifth-century BCE city-states had zealously maintained their exclusive civic identities (as Athenians, Spartans, or Corinthians, for example), Alexandria was a multiethnic city built by immigrants, who rapidly totaled half a million as they streamed in from all over the Mediterranean and Southwest Asia seeking new opportunities. Members of Alexandria's dynamic population, representing dozens of Greek and non-Greek peoples, communicated in the common language that supplanted their original dialects. Soon a new urban culture emerged to meet the needs of so diverse a population.

Hellenistic entertainment in this more connected world had to appeal to broad audiences and a wide variety of people. Plays were now staged in any city touched by Greek influence and had to translate to any environment. Consequently, the distinctive regional humor and local characters of fifth-century Greek city-state drama gave way to dramas populated by the stock characters of standard sitcoms with which any audience could identify: the greedy miser, the old crone, the jilted lover, the golden-hearted whore, the boastful soldier, the befuddled father, the cheated husband, the rebellious son. At performances throughout the Mediterranean basin, laughter would be just as loud in Syracuse on the island of Sicily as in Scythopolis in the Jordan Valley of Judea.

The Theater at Syracuse The great theater in the city-state of Syracuse in Sicily was considerably refurbished and enlarged under the Hellenistic kings. It could seat 15,000 to 20,000 persons. Here the people of Syracuse attended plays written by playwrights who lived on the far side of their world, but whose works they could understand as if the characters were from their own neighborhood. The same plays, performed in similar theaters across the Hellenistic world, deliberately featured typecast characters and situations, thereby broadening their audience while spreading Hellenistic sensibilities.

A new political style of distant, almost godlike kings developed, in part due to the size of the territories over which they ruled. Instead of being accessible, which was not possible when Hellenistic kingdoms and states were so enormous, Hellenistic leaders became larger-than-life figures. Individuals related to political leaders primarily through the personality of the kings and their families. Rulership was personality, and personality could unite large numbers of subjects. For example, Demetrius Poliorcetes, the ruler of Macedonia, stood out in his high-platform shoes and heavy makeup, and he decorated his elaborate, flowing cape with images of the sun, the stars, and the planets. In the presence of a powerful sun-king like Demetrius, ordinary individuals felt small and inconsequential.

Philosophy and Religion Hellenistic religion and philosophy increasingly focused on the individual and his or her place in the larger world. This growing concern with the individual found expression in many new philosophical schools that proposed a range of ideas, including self-sufficiency (Cynicism), detachment (Epicureanism), and involvement (Stoicism). For instance, the Athenian Diogenes (c. 412–323 BCE), an early proponent of the Cynic school of philosophy, sought freedom from society's laws and customs, rejecting cultural norms as human-made inventions not in tune with nature and therefore false. Similarly turning thoughts to the self, Epicurus (341–270 BCE), the founder of a school in Athens that he called The Garden, envisioned an ideal community of adherents regardless of their gender and social status, centered on his school. Seeking out pleasure and avoiding pain, these Epicureans contemplated the answer to the question "What is the good life?" and struggled to develop a sense of "not caring" (*ataraxia*) about their worries. More widespread than Diogenes's Cynicism and Epicurus's philosophy was Zeno's Stoicism. Zeno (c. 334–262 BCE), from the island of Cyprus, initiated it, and other cosmopolitan figures across the Hellenistic world—from Babylon in Mesopotamia to Sinope on the Black Sea—developed its beliefs. Named after the Stoa Poikilē, the roofed colonnade in the Athenian agora in which Zeno first presented his ideas, Stoicism argued that everything was grounded in nature. Stoicism regarded cities and kingdoms as human-made things, important but transient. Being in tune with nature and living a good life required understanding the rules of the natural order and being in control of one's passions, and thus required indifference to pleasure and pain. Stoicism, Epicureanism, and Cynicism offered the individual a range of philosophical responses to the Hellenistic world developing all around.

Long-established religions were also shaped by Hellenism and then re-exported throughout the Mediterranean. For example, Greeks in Egypt drew on the indigenous cult of Osiris and his consort, Isis, to fashion a new narrative about Osiris's death and rebirth that represented personal salvation from death. Isis became a supreme goddess whose "supreme virtues" encompassed the powers of dozens of other Mediterranean gods and goddesses. Believers experienced personal revelations and out-of-body experiences (*exstasis*, "ecstasy"). A ritual of dipping in water (*baptizein*, "to baptize") marked the transition of believers, "born again" into lives devoted to a "personal savior" who delivered an understanding of a new life by direct revelation. These new beliefs, like the worship of Isis, emphasized the spiritual concerns of humans as individuals, rather than the collective worries of towns or cities. Other Hellenistic adaptations from earlier Greek religion, including cults centered on the Eleusinian Mysteries of Demeter and Bacchic worship of Dionysus, similarly focused on the salvation of the individual as they spread throughout the Hellenistic world.

PLANTATION SLAVERY AND MONEY-BASED ECONOMIES

Ironically, philosophical and religious innovations focused on the self were accompanied by the rise of plantation slavery—the ultimate devaluing of an individual—as an engine of the Hellenistic economy. Large numbers of slaves were used in agricultural production—especially in Italy, Sicily, and North African regions close to Carthage. Alexander's conquests and Rome's political rise had produced unprecedented wealth for a small elite. These men and women used their riches to acquire huge tracts of land and to purchase slaves (either kidnapped individuals or conquered peoples) on a scale and with a degree of managerial organization never seen before. The slave plantations, wholly devoted to producing surplus crops for profit, helped to drive a new Mediterranean economy. The estates created vast wealth for their owners—though at a heavy price to others, as reliance on slave labor now left the free peasants who used to work the fields with no option but to move into overcrowded cities, where employment was hard to find.

To pay for the goods that satisfied their newly acquired tastes, Celtic chieftains in the regions encompassing modern-day France began selling their own people in the expanding slave markets of the Mediterranean. Slavery and slave trading also became central to the economies of the Iberian Peninsula—especially in the hinterlands of large river valleys like the Ebro, where local elites founded urban centers imitating Greek styles.

The circulation of money reinforced the effects of forced labor. With more cash in the economy, wealthy landowners, urban elites, and merchants could more easily do business. The increasing use of Greek-style coins to pay for goods and services (in place of barter) promoted the importation of commodities such as wine from elsewhere in the Mediterranean. As coined money became even more available, it led to even more commercial exchanges. The forced transfer of precious metals to the Mediterranean from

Southwest Asia by Alexander's conquests was so large that it actually caused the price of gold to fall.

In the west, Carthage began to mint its own coins—at first mainly in gold, but later in other metals. Rome moved to a money economy at the same time. By the 270s and 260s BCE, the Romans were issuing coins on a large scale under the pressures of their first war with Carthage (264–241 BCE). By the end of the third century, even borderland peoples such as the Gauls had begun to mint coins, imitating the galloping-horse images found on Macedonia's gold coins. So, too, did kingdoms in North Africa, where the coins of Numidian kings bore the same Macedonian royal imagery. By around 100 BCE, inhabitants of the entire Mediterranean basin and surrounding lands were using coins minted by this range of political entities to buy and sell all manner of commodities.

Hellenistic Adaptation and Resistance The new high Greek culture spread far and wide, though it was not fully accepted everywhere in the Mediterranean. It appealed particularly to elites who sought to enhance their position by embracing Hellenistic culture over local values. Syrian, Jewish, and Egyptian elites in the eastern Mediterranean adopted this attitude, as well as Roman, Carthaginian, and African elites in the western Mediterranean.

The Hellenistic influences reached sub-Saharan Africa, where the Meroitic kingdom (see Chapter 5), already influenced by pharaonic forms, now absorbed characteristics of Greek culture as well. It is not surprising that Greek influences were extensive at Meroe, because continuous interaction with the Egyptians also exposed its people to the world of the Mediterranean. Both Meroe and its rival, Axum, located in the Ethiopian highlands, used Greek-style steles (inscribed stone pillars) to boast of their military exploits. Citizens of Meroe worshipped Zeus and Dionysus. The rulers of Meroe, understanding the advantages of the Greek language, employed Greek scribes to record their accomplishments on the walls of Greek-Egyptian temples. In this way, Meroe developed a mix of Greek, Egyptian, and African cultural and political elements.

Not every community succumbed to the allure of Hellenism. The Jews in Judea offer a striking case of resistance and accommodation to its universalizing forces. Having been released from their Babylonian exile by the Persian monarch Cyrus in 538 BCE, the Jews returned to Judea—now a Persian province—and began rebuilding Jerusalem. While the Persians tolerated local customs and beliefs (see Chapter 4), the Hellenism brought by the Seleucid successor state that took Persia's place after Alexander's conquest brought a shock to Judaism. While some among the Jewish ruling elite began to adopt Greek ways—to wear Greek clothing, to participate in the gymnasium with its cult of male nudity, to produce images of gods as art—others rejected the push. Those who spurned assimilation rebelled against the common elements of Hellenism—its language, music, gymnasia, nudity, public art, and secularism—as being deeply immoral and threatening to their beliefs. Ultimately, this resistance to Hellenism led to full-scale armed revolt, headed up by the family of the Maccabees. In 167 BCE, the Seleucids provoked the Maccabees by forbidding the practice of Judaism (by outlawing worship and circumcision) and profaning the Jews' temple (by erecting an altar to Zeus in the sanctuary of the temple and sacrificing pigs on it). Though the Maccabees succeeded in establishing an independent Jewish state centered on the temple in Jerusalem, they did not entirely overcome the impact of the new universal culture on Judaism. A huge Jewish community in the Hellenistic city of Alexandria in Egypt embraced the new culture. Scholars there produced a version of the Hebrew scriptures in *Koine* Greek, and historians (such as Jason of Cyrene) and philosophers (such as Philo of Alexandria) wrote in Greek, imitating Greek models.

Similar resistance and accommodation were taking place elsewhere. In the 330s and 320s BCE, when Alexander was uniting the eastern Mediterranean, the city-state of Rome took the first critical military actions to unify Italy. Rather than beginning as a kingdom like Macedonia, Rome went from being a city-state to flourishing as a large territorial state. During this transformation it adopted significant elements of Hellenistic culture: Greek-style temples, elaborately decorated Greek-style pottery and paintings, and an alphabet based on that of the Greeks. Many Roman elites saw immersion in Hellenistic ideals as a way to appear to the rest of the world as "civilized," while others resisted Greek ways as being overly luxurious and contrary to Roman ideals of manliness. The conservative Roman senator Cato the Elder (234–149 BCE) struggled with the tensions that Hellenism introduced to Roman ways. Although he was devoted to the Roman past, the Latin language, and the ideal of small-scale Roman peasant farmers and their families, Cato embraced many Hellenistic influences. He wrote a standard manual for the new economy of slave plantation agriculture, invested in shipping and trading, learned Greek rhetoric (both speaking and writing the language), and added the genre of history to Latin literature. Cato blended an extreme devotion to Roman tradition with bold Hellenistic innovations in most aspects of daily life.

Rome's long-time rival, the Phoenician colony of Carthage, also adopted Hellenism but with less internal conflict than in Rome. Carthaginian culture took on important elements of Hellenistic culture. For example, some Carthaginians went to Athens to become philosophers. Innovative ideas on political theory and warfare came from the Greek city-states. The design of sanctuaries, temples, and other public buildings in Carthage reveals a mix of Greek-style pediments and columns, Carthaginian designs and measurements, and local North African motifs and structures. Carthaginian women adorned themselves with jewelry that reflected styles from Egypt, such as ornate necklaces of gold and earrings of lapis lazuli.

Already well integrated into the Mediterranean economy, Carthage welcomed the increased communication and exchange that Hellenism facilitated. Carthaginian merchants traded with other Phoenician colonies in the western Mediterranean, with the towns of the Etruscans and the Romans in Italy, with the Greek trading city of Massilia (modern Marseilles) in southern France, and with Athens in the eastern Mediterranean. In addition, the Carthaginians expanded their commercial interests into the Atlantic, moving north along the coast of Iberia and south along the coast of West Africa, even establishing a trading post at the island of Mogador more than 600 miles down the Atlantic coast of Africa. Profoundly shaped by Alexander's conquests, Hellenism spread even farther across Afro-Eurasia with Alexander's successors.

Converging Influences in Central and South Asia

During this period, tighter political organization in South Asia helped spread new influences, like Hellenism and Buddhism, across the region. The high mountains of modern-day Afghanistan were a major geographical barrier to east-west exchange, but they were not impassable. Mountain passes—pinched like the narrow neck of an hourglass between the high plateau of Iran to the west and the towering ranges of Tibet to the east—offered the shortest route through the formidable Hindu Kush range. By crossing these passes, Alexander's armies expanded the routes between the eastern and western portions of Afro-Eurasia and brought about massive political and cultural changes in central and South Asia. Conquerors moved from west to east (like Alexander), from east to west (like the later nomads from central Asia), and from north to south, through the mountains and into the rich plains of the Indus and Ganges River valleys. At the same time, South Asian trade and religious influences, especially Buddhism, moved northward toward routes running west to east along what became known as the Silk Roads.

Core Objectives

ANALYZE the political changes that shaped central and South Asia in the aftermath of Alexander's incursion on the region.

CHANDRAGUPTA AND THE MAURYAN EMPIRE

Alexander's brief occupation of the Indus Valley (327–325 BCE) paved the way for one of the largest empires in South Asian history, the Mauryan Empire. Before the arrival of Alexander's forces, South Asia had been a conglomerate of small warring states. This political instability came to an abrupt halt when, in 321 BCE, an ambitious young man named Chandragupta Mori (or Maurya), inspired by Alexander, seized the throne of the Magadha kingdom and launched a series of successful military expeditions in what is now northern India. These campaigns would lead to the founding of his new Mauryan Empire.

The Magadha kingdom that Chandragupta overthrew had thrived on the lower Ganges plain since the sixth century BCE and had held great strategic advantages over other states. For one thing, it contained rich iron ores and fertile rice paddies. Moreover, on the northeast Deccan plateau ample woods supported herds of elephants, a mainstay of the powerful Magadha mobile military forces, which used elephants to charge down and terrify the enemy. According to Alexander's contemporary Megasthenes, fear of facing those elephants and the large army of Magadha was one of the reasons Alexander's troops refused to cross the Ganges. However, by the time Chandragupta Maurya took over the Magadha kingdom, it was suffering under the heavy taxation and greed of its king.

The Mori family, or Mauryans, did not start out as a distinguished ruling family, but economic strength and military skill elevated them over their rivals. Chandragupta (r. 321–297 BCE), though of lowly origins, probably from the Vaishya *varna*, grew up in the Punjab region of the Indus Valley observing Alexander's onslaught and aspiring to be an equally powerful military and political leader. When Alexander withdrew his forces from northern India, Chandragupta inserted himself into the political vacuum created by the Greek withdrawal.

Chandragupta's **Mauryan Empire** (321–184 BCE) constituted South Asia's first empire and served as a model for later Indian empire builders. After supplanting Magadha's Nanda monarchic dynasty, which had been in place for just over a century, Chandragupta used his military resources to reach westward beyond the Ganges plain into the area where four tributaries join the Indus. Here he pushed up to the border with the Seleucid kingdom, the largest successor kingdom of Alexander's empire, based in Mesopotamia.

Alexander's eastern successor, the Seleucid king Seleucus Nicator (358–281 BCE), responded by invading Mauryan territory—only to face Chandragupta's impregnable defenses. Soon thereafter, a treaty between the two powers gave a large portion of Afghanistan to the Mauryan Empire. One of the daughters of Seleucus went to the Mauryan court, accompanied by a group of Greek women. Seleucus also sent to Chandragupta's court an ambassador named Megasthenes—that same Megasthenes who reported on the elephants of Magadha's army. In return for these gifts and diplomacy, the Mauryans sent Seleucus many South Asian valuables, including hundreds of elephants, which the Greeks soon learned to use in battles.

The Seleucid ambassador Megasthenes lived in South Asia for years and gathered his observations while at the Mauryan court into a book titled *Indica*, after the Greek term for this region. Megasthenes's *Indica* depicted a well-ordered and highly stratified society divided into seven groups: philosophers, farmers, soldiers, herdsmen, artisans, magistrates, and councilors. People respected the boundaries between groups and honored rituals that reinforced their identities: members of different groups did not intermarry

Mauryan Empire
(321–184 BCE) The first large-scale empire in South Asia, stretching from the Indus in the west to the mouth of the Ganges in the east and nearly to the southern tip of the Indian subcontinent; begun by Chandragupta Maurya, in the aftermath of Alexander's time in India, and expanded to its greatest extent by his grandson Aśoka.

or even eat together. Megasthenes also noted the ways in which rulers integrated the region—for example, connecting major cities with extensive tree-lined roads, complete with mile markers. These roads facilitated both trade and the movement of troops. (See Current Trends in World History: Building Roads: Early Highways for Communication, Trade, and Control.) Contrary to Greek expectations of a military closely integrated into civil society, Megasthenes reported that soldiers in India were a profession separate from the rest of the population. Mauryan troops did not pursue any other occupation, but stood ready to obey their commander. This military force was huge, boasting cavalry divisions of mounted horses, war elephants, and scores of infantry.

The Regime of Aśoka The Mauryan Empire reached its height during the reign of its third king, Aśoka (r. 268–231 BCE), Chandragupta's grandson. Aśoka's lands included almost all of South Asia; only the southern tip of the subcontinent remained outside his control. In 261 BCE, Aśoka launched the conquest of Kalinga, a kingdom on the east coast of the South Asian subcontinent. The Mauryan army triumphed, but at a high price: about 100,000 soldiers died in battle, many more perished in its aftermath, and some 150,000 people endured forcible relocation. Aśoka was appalled and shamed by the brutal devastation his army had wrought. He vowed to cease inflicting pain on his people and pledged to follow the peaceful doctrines of Buddhism, issuing a famous edict that renounced brutal ways.

In his Kalinga Edict, Aśoka proclaimed his intention to rule according to the Indian concept of *dhamma*, a vernacular form of the Sanskrit word *dharma*, understood widely in Mauryan lands to mean tolerance of others, obedience to the natural order of things, and respect for all of earth's life forms. *Dhamma* was to apply to everyone, including the priestly Brahmans, Buddhists, members of other religious sects, and even Greeks. *Dhamma* became an all-encompassing moral code that all religious sects in South Asia accepted. With *dhamma* as a unifying symbol, Aśoka required all people, whatever their religious practices and cultural customs, to consider themselves his subjects, to respect him as their father, and to conform to his moral code—starting with the precept that people of different religions or sects should get along with each other. He also praised the benefits of agrarian progress and banned large-scale cattle sacrifice as detrimental to agriculture. Meanwhile, he warned the "forest people," the hunters and gatherers living beyond the reach of government, to avoid making trouble.

To disseminate the ideals of *dhamma*, Aśoka regularly issued decrees, which he had chiseled on stone pillars and boulders in every corner of his domain, selecting locations where people were likely to congregate and where they could hear the words as read to them by the few who were literate. Occasionally he also issued edicts to explain his Buddhist faith. All were

Building Roads: Early Highways for Communication, Trade, and Control

World historians have become fascinated with the history of roads because they provide insight into the way nations and empires functioned, and they allow us to study transnational forces that cross borders, like trade, migration, and the spread of ideas. Indeed, reliable communications and regular trade were among the most important forces that enabled the great regions of the world to be linked. If rivers and seas offered natural waterways to meet this demand, roads were the man-made answer that enabled soldiers, traders, and travelers to cross great stretches of land or go around high mountain ranges more quickly. Road building required huge financial and labor resources. Only empires had the incentives and resources to build large-scale roads and the networks that fed into them; these roads would aid in the empire's rule over their domain and in gathering the revenue that came from transregional trade.

The Persian Empire (560–331 BCE) was the largest state in the Afro-Eurasian world (see Chapter 4) and thus required efficient communications over vast distances and terrain that was varied and forbidding. The problems were overcome by the construction of many "great" or "royal" roads across the empire to connect the royal capitals where the king resided from time to time. One of the best-known great roads connected the far western coast at Sardis in Asia Minor (present-day Turkey) with the heartland of the Persian Empire around Susa (southern Iran) in the east, more than 1,700 miles away. The great roads featured way stations, supply depots, relays of horses and other pack animals, and state personnel, all to enable the local governors, or satraps, of the emperor to dispatch men and missions to the King of Kings.

If the royal Persian road communications system was a marvel of its age, the roads of the Roman Empire (30 BCE–c. 476 CE) are rightly renowned for their extent and quality of construction. At its height, the empire boasted about 250,000 miles of roads; about 55,000 miles were of the formal stone-paved quality that most impresses us today. They were formally called "public roads" and were open to travel by anyone. Provincial, city, and municipal officials were in charge of upkeep. High standards of construction were imposed for the main paved highways—land was leveled and roadbeds were built up of layers of hard-packed sand and gravel, with careful gradients that allowed for drainage. The top layer was paved with heavy flagstones that provided long life.

It is easy to underestimate the amount of hard work and engineering required to construct the roadbeds, drainage, and bridges. The work and materials required to construct one major road in Italy, the Via Appia (the "Appian Way"), would have been several times that required to build the great pyramids in Egypt. The major roads were marked with milestones that informed the traveler about the distance from the point of departure or to the next major town (5,000 or so of these have survived). The English word "mile" comes from the Roman *milia passuum* (slightly less than our mile in

inscribed in local languages, including Sanskrit, as well as Greek and Aramaic in the Hellenistic- and Persian-influenced northwest.

The Mauryan Empire at its height encompassed 3 million square miles, including all of what is today Pakistan, much of what is Afghanistan, the southeastern part of Iran, and the whole of the Indian subcontinent except for the lands at the southern tip. Its extraordinarily diverse geography consisted of jungles, mountains, deserts, and floodplains, and its equally disparate population of 50 to 60 million inhabitants was made up of pastoralists, farmers, forest dwellers, merchants, artisans, and religious leaders. Aśoka's promotion of the Buddhist tenet of *dhamma* and his elaborate administrative

Roman Road System Coursing through Afro-Eurasia, the Roman road system is shown in all its complexity and glory in the only surviving copy of the ancient *Tabula Peutingeriana*. The icon of a seated ruler represents Rome.

length). The system of roads allowed the Roman state to maintain a public relay service called the *cursus publicus* along which imperial officials and units of the army, as well as information, could move efficiently and predictably from one part of the empire to another.

One of the singular achievements of the Qin dynasty (221–207 BCE) was the building of a road system to create sufficient infrastructure to unify its far-flung empire. The Qin network of roads connected the capital at Xianyang to every part of the country. The Qin used peasants, soldiers, and some slaves as forced laborers to build new roads and widen existing ones, so that troops could move quickly and easily to put down revolts anywhere in the empire. These roads were expanded under the succeeding Han dynasty (206 BCE–220 CE) to facilitate travel not only for the military but also for merchants and commoners.

The road system of Qin and Han China paralleled the Persian royal roads and the Roman road network in scale and magnitude. By 100 BCE, many roads were wide, surfaced with stone, and lined with trees; steep mountains were traversed by stone-paved stairways with broad treads and low steps. By the end of the sixth century CE, the internal road network, not counting the Silk Road from the Han and Tang capital of Chang'an to central Asia, had grown to encompass some 25,000 miles. This ingeniously engineered system of roads helped the Chinese—like other empires—to control an empire spanning a vast, geographically diverse area.

Questions for Analysis

- What are three reasons that world historians are particularly interested in roads?
- What political and geographical motives did empires have to build road systems?
- What groups of people benefited most from these road systems?

Explore Further

Liu, Xinru, *The Silk Road in World History* (2010).

Wood, Frances, *The Silk Road: Two Thousand Years in the Heart of Asia* (2004).

structure were not enough to hold together his empire, which did not last long after his death in 231 BCE. The proliferation of Buddhism made possible by Aśoka's adoption and wholehearted sponsorship of the faith, however, was a lasting impact of his reign.

GREEK INFLUENCES IN CENTRAL ASIA

Hellenistic influences shaped politics and culture in the regimes that succeeded direct Greek control in central Asia. Alexander's military had thrust into Asia and reached as far as the Punjab. There he defeated several rulers

Aśoka Buddhist legend claims that Aśoka placed relics of the Buddha in the many stupas he had built. The stupa at Sarnath (*left*) is the best-preserved one from the time of Aśoka. Aśoka had his edicts carved on pillars like the one on the right all over India. The majestic lion at the top of the pillar shows the influence of Persian art, in which the lion was the symbol of royalty.

of Gandhara in 326 BCE. In the course of this campaign he planted many garrison towns—especially in eastern Iran, in northern Afghanistan, and in the Punjab, where he needed to protect his easternmost territorial acquisition. These garrison towns were originally stations for soldiers, but they soon became centers of Hellenistic culture. Many of these outposts displayed the characteristic features of a Greek city-state: a colonnaded main street lined by temples to patron gods or goddesses, a theater, a gymnasium for education, an administrative center, and a marketplace. Following Alexander's death, Seleucus Nicator built more of these Greek garrison towns before he concluded peace with Chandragupta Maurya and withdrew from the region.

The garrison towns founded by Alexander and Nicator remained and grew into Hellenistic centers. Once the Greek soldiers who had been stationed in them realized they would be spending their lives far from their homeland, they married local women and started families. Bringing their Hellenistic customs to the local populations, the soldiers established institutions familiar to them from the Greek city-states. *Koine* Greek was the official language, but because locals used their own languages in daily life, subsequent generations were bilingual. For centuries, traditional Greek institutions—especially Greek language and writing—survived many political changes and much cultural assimilation, providing a common basis of engagement in a long zone stretching from the Mediterranean to South Asia.

Hellenistic influences were even more pronounced in the regimes that succeeded Seleucid control in central Asia in the late third century BCE. The Seleucid state had taken over the entirety of the former Persian Empire, including its central Asian and South Asian territory. The Hellenistic kingdom of **Bactria** broke away from the Seleucids around 200 BCE to establish a strong state that included the Gandhara region in modern Pakistan. As Mauryan power receded from the northwestern part of India, the Bactrian rulers extended their conquests into this area. Because the cities that the Bactrian Greeks founded included many Indian residents, they have been called "Indo-Greek." Those in Gandhara incorporated familiar features of the Greek polis, but inhabitants still revered Indian gods and goddesses.

Hellenistic Bactria served as a bridge between South Asia and the Greek world of the Mediterranean. Among the goods that the Bactrians sent west were elephants, which were vital to the Greek armies there. Not only did the Bactrian Greeks revive the cities in India left by Alexander, but they also founded new Hellenistic cities in the Gandhara region. The Greek king Demetrius, who invaded India around 200 BCE, entrusted the extension of his empire in the northern region of India to his generals, many of whom became independent rulers after his death. Sanskrit literature refers to these Greek rulers as the Yavana kings—a word derived from "Ionia," a region whose name applied to all those who spoke Greek or came from the Mediterranean.

Aï Khanoum, on the Oxus River (now the Amu) in present-day Afghanistan, was the site of an administrative center, possibly the capital of the Bactrian state. Unearthed by archaeologists in the 1960s, Aï Khanoum had avoided the devastations that befell so many other Hellenistic cities in this region. Greek-style architecture and inscriptions indicate that the original residents of Aï Khanoum were soldiers from Greece. Following the typical pattern, they married local women and established the basic institutions of a Greek polis. Aï Khanoum's characteristic Greek structures included a palace complex, a gymnasium, a theater, an arsenal, several temples, and elite residences. Featuring marble columns with Corinthian capitals, the palace contained an administrative section, storage rooms, and a library. A main road divided the city into lower and higher parts, with the main religious buildings located in the lower city. Though far from Greece, the elite Greek residents read poetry and philosophy and staged Greek dramas in the theater. Grape cultivation supported a wine festival associated with the god Dionysus. The remains of various statues indicate that the residents not only revered the Greek deity Athena and the demigod Heracles but also paid homage to the Persian Zoroastrian religion.

Perhaps the ruler most adept at mingling Greek and Indian influences was Menander (also known as Milinda), a Yavana/Hellenistic city-state king of the mid-second century BCE. Using images and legends on coins to promote both traditions among his subjects, Menander claimed legitimacy as an Indian ruler who also cultivated Greek cultural forms. The face of his coins bore his regal image surrounded by the words "King, Savior, Menander," in Greek. The reverse side featured the Greek goddess Athena and the king's title in the local Prakrit language. This mixed Indo-Greek identity was not confined to coins. In his discussions with a Buddhist sage, King Menander debated the nature of the

Buddha (was he human or divine?) and showed a keen interest in South Asian religious influences even as he embraced Hellenism. These Indo-Greek legacies persisted long after the Hellenistic regimes collapsed, because they remained essential to communication and trade around the rim of the Indian Ocean.

The Transformation of Buddhism

Core Objectives

EVALUATE the forces that influenced the spread of Buddhism in this period.

During this time of political and social change, South Asia also experienced upheavals in the religious sphere, as Hellenism and other east-west connections transformed Buddhism. Impressed by Hellenistic thought, South Asian peoples blended it with their own ethical and religious traditions. Beginning among the Yavana city-states in the northwest, where Buddhism's sway was most pronounced, this blended Buddhism rapidly spread to other regions that were experiencing the same changes. In addition to Hellenism, other layers of influence came together in South Asia through increased seafaring and interactions with nomadic peoples. This cultural fusion profoundly transformed and enriched Buddhism.

INDIA AS A SPIRITUAL CROSSROADS

Many land and sea routes now converged in India, rendering the region a melting pot of ideas and institutions. Improved mastery of the monsoon trade winds in this period opened the Indian Ocean to commerce and made India the hub for long-distance ocean traders and travelers. Another major influence on Buddhism was the Kushans, a horse-riding nomadic group who stabilized east-west connectivity through central Eurasia in the first century CE. With Kushan patronage and the thriving commerce their stability brought to the region, Buddhist communities grew so rich that monks began to live in elegant monastic complexes. (We will discuss the Kushans and their role in Silk Road trade later in this chapter.) The center of each monastic community was a stupa, with its Buddhist relics and sculptures depicting the Buddha's life and teachings. Such monasteries provided generously for the monks, furnishing them with halls where they gathered and worshipped and rooms where they meditated and slept. Buddhist monasteries were also open to the public as places for worship.

THE NEW BUDDHISM: THE MAHAYANA SCHOOL

This mixing of new ways—nomadic, Hellenistic, and Persian—with traditional Buddhism produced a spiritual and religious synthesis: **Mahayana** ("Great Vehicle") **Buddhism**. In the first two centuries of the Common Era, Mahayana Buddhists resolved a centuries-long dispute over whether the Buddha was a god or a wise human. They affirmed: the Buddha was indeed a deity. However,

Mahayana Buddhism

"Great Vehicle" Buddhism; an accessible form of Buddhism that spread along the Silk Roads and included in its theology a divine Buddha as well as bodhisattvas.

bodhisattvas

In Mahayana Buddhism, enlightened beings who have earned nirvana but remain in this world to help others reach it.

Mahayana Buddhism was accommodating; it offered a spiritual pluralism that incorporated outside influences and positioned Indian believers as a cosmopolitan people.

Mahayana Buddhism appealed especially to foreigners and immigrants who traded or settled in India because it made the Buddha easier to understand. The Buddha's preaching had stressed life's suffering and the renunciation of desire to end suffering and achieve nirvana. Newcomers to the region and to Buddhism—such as migrants or traders—saw no attraction in a belief that life consisted of painful cycles of birth, growth, death, and rebirth. This sharp dichotomy between a real world of hardship and the Buddha's abstract world of nirvana gave way to the Mahayana Buddhists' vision that **bodhisattvas**—enlightened demigods, ready to reach nirvana—delayed doing so in order to help others attain it. Early Mahayana texts, like "The Practice of Perfect Wisdom," describe in detail the characteristics of bodhisattvas. These bodhisattvas prepared spiritual halfway points to welcome deceased devotees not yet ready to release their desires and enter nirvana. The universe of the afterlife in Mahayana Buddhism presented an array of alternatives to the harsh real existence of worldly living. With its bodhisattvas, Mahayana Buddhism enabled all individuals—the poor and powerless as well as the rich and powerful—to move from a life of suffering into a happy existence.

Stupa Staircase The risers from the staircase of a large stupa in the Gandhara region display scenes from Buddhist stories. The upper one shows men in nomads' clothing playing music, including the Greek-style lyre. On the middle and lower ones, men and women in Greek clothing drink and make merry. The pictures are Buddhist versions of performances in a Greek theater.

NEW IMAGES OF THE BUDDHA IN LITERATURE AND ART

Just as Buddhism absorbed outside influences and became more appealing, it also inspired literature and art that appealed to diverse peoples. A new genre of literature dealing with the Buddha and the bodhisattvas emerged. Buddhist texts written in Sanskrit disseminated the life of the Buddha and his message far and wide, reaching far corners of Asia. Aśvaghosa (c. 80–c. 150 CE), a great Buddhist thinker, wrote a biography of the Buddha, which set the Buddha's life story within the commercial urban environment of the Kushan Empire (instead of in the rural Shakya republic in the Himalaya foothills, where he had actually lived). Aśvaghosa's largely fictive version of the

Buddha's life story spread rapidly throughout India and beyond, introducing Buddha and his teachings to many potential converts.

The colorful images of Sanskrit Buddhist texts of the first centuries CE gave rise to a large repertoire of Buddhist sculptural art and drama. On Buddhist stupas and shrines, artisans carved scenes of the Buddha's life, figures of bodhisattvas, and statues of patrons and donors. Fashioned from gray schist rock, these Buddhist sculptures from the Kushan territory (modern Pakistan and northwest region of India), follow what is called the **Gandharan style**. Those from the central region of India, created mainly from local red sandstone, follow what is called Mathuran style. Gandharan Buddhist art shows strong Greek and Roman influences, whereas the Mathuran style evolved from the carved idols of South Asian folk gods and goddesses.

Despite their stylistic differences, the schools shared themes and cultural elements. Inspired by Hellenistic art and religious tradition, both took the bold step of sculpting the Buddha and bodhisattvas in realistic human form, rather than symbolic form (such as a bodhi tree, which symbolizes Buddha's enlightenment). Though the Buddha wore no decorations because he had cut off all links to the world, bodhisattvas were dressed as princes because they were still in this world, generously helping others. What was important was bringing the symbolic world of Buddhism closer to the people.

Buddhas Greco-Roman influence on the iconography of Buddha was probably responsible for the Gandharan-style attire and facial expression of Buddhas and bodhisattvas. The seated Buddha on the left was crafted from bronze and, with its sun-like crown, looks a lot like Hellenistic images of Helios or Apollo. The Mathuran Buddha of the later Gupta period (*right*), carved from red sandstone, wears a robe so transparent that the artist must have had very fine silk in mind when sculpting it.

Buddhist art reflected a spiritual system that appealed to people of diverse cultural backgrounds. Consider the clothes of the patron figures. For male and female figures alike, the garments were simple and well adapted to tropical climates. Those indigenous to the semitropical land had nude upper bodies and a wrapping like the modern *dhoti*, or loincloth, on their lower bodies. Jewelry adorned their headdresses and bodies. By contrast, the nomadic patron figures wore traditional cone-shaped leather hats, knee-length robes, trousers, and boots. Figures with Greek clothing demonstrate continuing Hellenistic influence. The jumble of clothing styles illustrates that Buddhist devotees could share a faith while retaining their ethnic or regional differences.

The Formation of the Silk Roads

In the first century BCE, trade routes stretching from China to central Asia and westward had merged into one big intertwined series of routes, famously referred to as the **Silk Roads** even though caravans transported many other precious commodities, such as incense, gemstones, and metals. Traders traveled segments of the route, passing their goods on to others who took them farther along the road and, in turn, passed them on again. The Silk Roads owed much to earlier overland routes through which merchants had exchanged frankincense and myrrh from the Arabian Peninsula for copper, tin, gemstones, and textiles. (See Map 6.2.) During this period, seaborne trade also created closer connections between Afro-Eurasian worlds.

The effects of these long-distance exchanges altered the political geography of Afro-Eurasia. Egypt and Mesopotamia faded as sources of innovation and knowledge, becoming instead crossroads for peoples on either side of them. The former borderlands emerged as new imperial centers. What we now call the Middle East literally became a commercial middle ground between the Mediterranean and India. East Asia, principally China, finally connected indirectly with the Mediterranean via central and South Asia. Through China, whose traders reached Bali and other islands now in Indonesia, connections developed with Japan, Korea, and Southeast Asia. China, insulated from the west by the Himalayas and the Pamir Mountains, remained politically and culturally a mysterious land to those from the Mediterranean. Yet products made from silk revealed to the Greeks and Romans that an advanced society lay far to the east.

NOMADS AND TRADE ROUTES

The horse-riding nomads of Inner Eurasia made long-distance trade possible. For centuries, these scattered nomadic peoples had linked entire regions and facilitated trade and interactions between distant communities. Responding to

Core Objectives

TRACE the early routes of the "Silk Roads" and **ASSESS** their importance in connecting Afro-Eurasia.

Silk Roads
More than 5,000 miles of trade routes linking China, central Asia, and the Mediterranean. They were named for the silk famously traded along their land and sea routes, although ideas, people, and many other high-value commodities also moved along their lengths.

NORTH SEA

ROMAN
EMPIRE

SCYTHIANS

BLACK SEA

ANATOLIA

ARAL
SEA

CASPIAN
SEA

URAL

Rome

Athens

from the west to
India and China:
G ○

Antioch
Dura Europos
Palmyra

PARTHIAN
EMPIRE

Carthage

MEDITERRANEAN SEA

Persepolis

Alexandria

Petra
NABATAEAN
KINGDOM

EGYPT

Myos
Hormos

Berenice

NUBIA

Nile R.

RED SEA

ARABIAN

DESERT

Persian Gulf

from Arab
to India:

from Arabia, Ethiopia,
and East Africa
to the west:
I ○ ○

ARABIAN
STATES

from Arabia
and Ethiopia to
India and Chin
I

Meroe

AXUMITE
KINGDOM

Lake
Victoria

from the west
to India and
Southeast Asia:
○ G
○ ○ ○

INDIAN
OCEAN

Bhapta

Legend

- Silk Road
- Incense trade route
- Other trade routes
- **WUSUN** Nomad group
- Boundary of empires, states, and kingdoms
- • Port/trading town
- ○ Buddhist heartland
- ← Spread of Buddhism
- ○ Buddhist centers
- Buddhist rock-carved temples
- ▲ Sacred Buddhist mountains

Traded Goods

Cu	Copper	○	Jewelry and cut gems
	Textiles	▬	Lacquerware
	Fine stone and metal vessels	●	Peacocks
	Furs	○	Pearls
G	Glassware		Silk
	Gems	○○○	Slaves
	Gold	**S**	Spices
Y	Grain	**Sn**	Tin
H	Horses	●	Tortoiseshell
I	Incense		Wine
	Ivory	♣	Wood

0   500   1000 Miles
0   500   1000 Kilometers

Map 6.2 Afro-Eurasian Trade and the Early Spread of Buddhism, c. 150 CE

During the period covered in this chapter, trade along land and sea routes increasingly brought the Afro-Eurasian world together. The early spread of Mahayana Buddhism happened along some of these same routes. This map highlights important commercial routes linking societies and the incredibly wide range of goods traded, as well as the early spread of Buddhism.

- What types of goods were flowing to the east? What goods flowed to the west? What might these flows suggest about the balance of trade in this period?

- Trace the route a trade good might take from Indonesia to Carthage, and from Luoyang to Rome. How do these routes differ? Based on the regions through which each route goes and the various features along the way (ports, Buddhist sites, and so on), what interactions do you imagine might have taken place along either route?

- Based on the location of various Buddhist sites on this map, how were Buddhism and trade interrelated?

the drying out of their homelands in the second millennium BCE, they moved southward (see Chapter 3). Moving from place to place and being in close contact with their animals, the nomads were exposed to—and acquired resistance to—a greater variety of microbes than settled peoples did. Their relative immunity to disease made them ideal agents for linking distant settled communities. Nomads also raced into political vacuums and installed new regimes that linked northwest China and the Iranian plateau. Among the most important of these nomadic peoples were the Xiongnu (also spelled "Hsiung-nu") pastoralists, originally from the eastern part of the Asian steppe in modern Mongolia. By the third century BCE, their mastery of bronze technology made them the most powerful nomadic community in the area.

When Xiongnu power waned, a new empire, that of the Kushans, arose in their place around 50 CE. The Yuezhi, a nomadic group to the west of the Qin, unified the region's tribes, migrated southwestward, and established this Kushan Empire in Afghanistan and the Indus River basin. The Kushans' empire embraced a large and diverse territory and was critical in the formation of the Silk Roads. The Kushans had been an illiterate people, but they adopted Greek as their official language. Kushan coinage, like the Indo-Greek coinage discussed earlier, blended Greek and Indian elements. Mediterranean traders arriving in the Kushan markets to purchase silks from China, as well as Indian gemstones and spices, conducted their transactions in Greek. The coins they used—struck to Roman weight standards (themselves derived from Greek coinage) and inscribed in Greek—served their needs perfectly. Kushan rule stabilized the trading routes through central Asia that stretched from the steppes in the east to the Parthian Empire in the west. This territory became a major segment of the Silk Roads.

Three Kushan Coins The blending of multiple religions into empires that were situated on trade routes is demonstrated on Kushan coinage, which includes a wide variety of deities over time. Kanishka I (r. 127–150 CE), who helped foster the spread of Mahayana Buddhism on the Silk Roads, minted coinage with an image of himself sacrificing at an altar on one side and Buddha on the reverse (*top*). The same king also minted coins with his image encircled with the words "King of Kings" in Greek script on one side and the Greek sun god, Helios, recognizable by the radiate diadem, on the reverse (*middle*). Kanishka II, who ruled over the Kushans in the early third century CE, minted coins featuring the Hindu god Shiva with his bull, Nandi (horned head peeking out from behind Shiva's right leg), on the reverse (*bottom*). The simultaneous commerce of ideas and goods is easy to imagine given that the imagery on coins that facilitated the exchange reflected a range of gods.

CARAVAN CITIES AND THE INCENSE TRADE

As nomads moved southwestward, they produced a new kind of commercial hub: the caravan city. Established at strategic locations (often at the edges of deserts or in oases or at the end points of major trade arteries), these cities became locations where vast trading groups assembled before beginning their arduous journeys. Some caravan cities originating as Greek garrison towns became centers of Hellenistic culture, displaying such staples of the polis as public theaters. **Caravan cities** were among the most spectacular and resplendent urban centers of this era.

One of the most striking of these caravan cities was the Nabatean capital at Petra. The Nabateans were an Arabic-speaking people who eked out a living, primarily as sheepherders, in the Sinai Desert and the northwestern Arabian Peninsula. They also facilitated the movement of frankincense, myrrh, and other spices along the route—sometimes called the Incense or Spice Road—linking the Arabian Peninsula and Indian Ocean with the Mediterranean, where Greeks and Romans used these goods to make perfumes and incense. Because the Greeks and later the Romans needed large quantities of incense to burn in worshipping their gods, the trade passing through this region was extremely lucrative. Although originating in Nabatean herders' practice of carving shelters and cisterns for catching rainwater out of the solid stone of the forbidding landscape, the magnificent "Rock City" of Petra (*petros* in Greek means rock) was made possible by the wealth accumulated from the spice trade. Houses, shrines, tombs, and even the vast theater—carved entirely from the sandstone terrain to seat 6,000 to 10,000 spectators—reflected Hellenistic influences. Petra's power and wealth lasted from the mid-second century BCE to the early second century CE. The caravan traders, the ruling elite of the rock city, controlled the supply of spices and fragrances from Arabia and India to the ever-expanding Roman Empire. Nabatean traders based in Petra traveled throughout the eastern Mediterranean, erecting temples wherever they established trading communities.

With Petra's decline during the Roman period, Palmyra became the most important caravan city at the western end of the Silk Roads. Rich citizens of Rome relied on the Palmyran traders to procure luxury goods for them, importing Chinese silks for women's clothing and incense for religious rituals, as well as gemstones, pearls, and many other precious items. Palmyran traders handled non-silken textiles as well, including cotton from India and cashmere wool from Kashmir or the nearby central Asian highlands. Administered by the chiefs of local tribes, Palmyra maintained considerable autonomy even under formal Roman control. Although the Palmyrans used a Semitic dialect in daily life, for state affairs and business they used Greek, a reminder of the continued influence of Hellenism. Their merchants had learned Greek when the region came under Seleucid rule, and it remained useful when doing business with caravans from afar, long after the political influences of Hellenism had waned.

Palmyrans built a splendid marble city in the desert. A colonnade, theater, senate house, agora, and major temples formed the metropolitan area.

Palmyran Tomb Sculpture This tombstone relief sculpture shows a wealthy young Palmyran, attended by a servant—probably a household slave. Palmyra was at the crossroads of the major cultural influences traversing Southwest Asia at the time. The style of the clothing—the flowing pants and top—and the couch and pillows reflect the trading contacts of the Palmyran elite, in this case with India to the east. The hairstyle and mode of self-presentation signal influences from the Mediterranean to the west.

Complexes of hostels, storage houses, offices, and temples served the needs of traders who passed through. The Palmyrans worshipped many deities, both local and Greek, and seemed concerned about their own afterlife. Like Petra, Palmyra had a cemetery as big as its residential area, with marble sculptures on the tombs depicting city life. Many tombs showed the master or the master and his wife reclining on Greek-style couches, holding drinking goblets. Sculptures of camel caravans and horses tell us that the deceased were caravan traders in this world who anticipated continuing their rewarding occupation in the afterlife.

Caravan cities such as Petra, and later Palmyra, linked the Mediterranean with the silk and incense routes that traversed Afro-Eurasia by land and sea. Goods came into the caravan cities via multiple land routes. One artery stretched from China, then across the Iranian plateau and the Syrian desert to reach the Mediterranean Sea, and another route cut south through modern Afghanistan, into the Indus Valley, then along India's northwest coast and across the Indian Ocean to the Red Sea.

CHINA AND THE SILK ECONOMY

China's flourishing economy owed much to the fact that Chinese silks were the most sought-after commodity in long-distance trade. As thousands of precious silk bales made their way to Indian, central Asian, and Mediterranean markets, silk became the ultimate prestige commodity of the regions' ruling classes. Over time, the exchange between eastern and western portions of the Silk Road was increasingly mediated by Persian, Xiongnu, Kushan, and other middlemen at the great oases and trading centers that grew up in central Asia. Local communities took profitable advantage of the silk trade from China based on their increased knowledge and contacts.

Not only was silk China's most valuable export, but it also served as a tool in diplomacy with the nomadic kingdoms on China's western frontiers and as a source of funds for the Chinese armies. The country's rulers used silk to pay off neighboring nomads and borderlanders, buying both horses and peaceful borders with the fabric. During the Zhou dynasty, it had served as a precious medium of exchange and trade.

People valued silk as a material for clothing; as a filament made by spinning the protein fibers extracted from the cocoons of silkworms, it is smooth yet strong. Whereas cloth spun from hemp, flax, and other fibers tends to be rough, silk looks and feels rich. Moreover, it is cool against the skin in hot summers and warm in the winter. Silk also has immense tensile strength, making it useful for bows, lute strings, and fishing lines. Artisans even wove it into a tight fabric to make light body armor or light bags for transporting liquids (particularly useful for traders crossing arid expanses). Before the Chinese invented paper, silk was a popular writing material that was more durable than bamboo or wood. Texts written on silk often joined other funerary objects in the tombs of aristocratic lords and wealthy individuals.

As the long-distance silk trade grew, commerce within China also expanded. Because of reforms in the Warring States period, economic life in China after 300 BCE centered increasingly on independent farmers producing commercial crops for the marketplaces along land routes as well as rivers, canals, and lakes. As this market economy grew, merchants organized themselves based on family lineages and occupational guilds. Power now shifted away from agrarian elites and into the hands of urban financiers and traders. The traders benefited from the improvement in roads and waterways, which eased the transportation of grain, hides, horses, and silk from the villages to the new towns and cities. Bronze coins of various sizes and shapes, as well as cloth and silk used in barter, spurred long-distance trade. By the second century BCE, wealthy merchants were ennobled as local magnates and wore clothing that marked their official status. As commerce further expanded, regional lords opened local customs offices along land routes and waterways to extract a share of the money and products for themselves.

Though China still had little intellectual interaction with the rest of Afro-Eurasia, its long-distance commercial exchanges skyrocketed due to the Silk Road trade. Southern silk was only the first of many Chinese commodities that reached the world beyond the Taklamakan Desert. China also became an export center for lacquer, hemp, and linen. From Sichuan came iron, steel, flint, hard stone, silver, and animals, while jade came from the

Silk Texts Before the invention of paper, silk was widely used as writing material for correspondence, maps, illustrations, and important texts included as funerary objects in the tombs of aristocrats, because it was more portable and durable than bamboo or wood. The Mawangdui silk texts shown here are from a Hunan tomb that was closed in 168 BCE and opened in 1973.

northwest. At the same time, China was importing Mediterranean, Indian, and central Asian commodities.

Despite its early development of commerce, China still had no major ports that could compare to the caravan cities of Petra and Palmyra. Most cities in the landlocked north were administrative centers where farmers and traders gathered under the regional states' political and military protection. The larger cities had gates that closed between sunset and sunrise; during the night, mounted soldiers patrolled the streets. Newer towns along the southeastern seacoast still looked upriver to trade with inland agrarian communities, which also produced silk for export. Facilitating oceanic trade became more of a concern for the state during this period, and merchant ships now enjoyed the protection of military boats. However, internal, interregional trade predominated, and it fed into the Silk Roads through decentralized networks.

THE SPREAD OF BUDDHISM ALONG THE TRADE ROUTES

In addition to silk traders, monks traveled along Afro-Eurasian trade arteries to spread the word of new religions. While Christians would later take advantage of these trade routes to spread their faith (see Chapter 8), Buddhism was the chief expansionist faith in this period. Under Kushan patronage during the first centuries CE, Buddhism reached out from India to China and central Asia, following the Silk Roads. Monks from the Kushan Empire accompanied traders traveling to China. There they translated Buddhist texts into Chinese and other languages, aided by Chinese converts. Buddhist ideas were slow to gain acceptance everywhere the monks proselytized. It took several centuries, and a new wave of nomadic migrations, for Buddhism to take root in China.

Buddhism fared less well when it followed the commercial arteries westward. The religion never became established on the Iranian plateau and made no further headway toward the Mediterranean. The main barrier was Zoroastrianism, which had been a state religion in the Persian Empire during the fifth and fourth centuries BCE (see Chapter 4); by the time Buddhism began to spread, Zoroastrianism had long been established in Iran. Iranian

Hellenism had done little to weaken the power of Zoroastrianism, whose adherents formed city-based religious communities affiliated primarily with traders. These Zoroastrian traders continued to adhere to their own faith while traveling along the Silk Roads and did nothing to help Buddhism spread westward.

COMMERCE ON THE RED SEA AND INDIAN OCEAN

Using new navigational techniques and larger ships, seafarers eventually expanded the transport of Silk Road commodities via the Red Sea and the Indian Ocean. Although land routes were the tried-and-true avenues for migrants, traders, and wayfarers, they carried only what could be borne on the backs of humans and animals. Travel on them was slow, and they were vulnerable to marauders. With time, some risk takers found ways of traversing waterways—eventually on an unprecedented scale and with an ease unimaginable to earlier merchants. These risk takers were Arabs, from the commercial middle ground of the Afro-Eurasian trading system.

Arab traders had long carried such spices as frankincense and myrrh to the Egyptians, who used them in religious and funerary rites, and later to the Greeks and Romans. Metals such as bronze, tin, and iron passed along overland routes from Anatolia, as did gold, silver, and chlorite from the Iranian plateau. Gold, ivory, and other goods from the northern part of India passed through Taxila (the capital of Gandhara) and the Hindu Kush Mountains into Persia as early as the sixth century BCE. Following the expansion of the Hellenistic world, however, ships increasingly conducted long-distance trade. Mastering the monsoons over time, they sailed down the Red Sea and across the Indian Ocean as they carried goods between the tip of the Arabian Peninsula and the ports of the Indian landmass.

Arab seafarers led the way into the Indian Ocean, forging links that joined East Africa, the eastern Mediterranean, and the Arabian Peninsula with India, Southeast Asia, and East Asia. Such voyages involved longer stays at sea and were far more dangerous than sailing in the Mediterranean. Yet by the first century CE, Arab and Indian sailors were transporting Chinese silks, central Asian furs, and fragrances from Himalayan trees across the Indian Ocean. The city of Alexandria in Egypt soon emerged as a key transit point between the Mediterranean Sea and the Indian Ocean. Boats carried Mediterranean exports of olives and olive oil, wine, drinking vessels, glassware, linen and wool textiles, and red coral up the Nile, stopping at Koptos and other port cities from which camel caravans took the goods to ports on the Red Sea. For centuries, Mediterranean merchants had considered the Arabian Peninsula to be the end of the Spice Road. But after Alexander's expedition and the establishment of colonies between Egypt and Afghanistan, they began to value the wealth and opportunities that lay along the shores of the Indian Ocean.

Arab sailors who ventured into the Indian Ocean benefited from new navigational techniques, especially celestial bearings (using the position of the stars to determine the position of the ship and the direction to sail). They used large ships called dhows, whose sails were rigged to easily capture the wind; these forerunners of modern cargo vessels were capable of long hauls in rough waters. Beginning about 120 BCE, mariners came to understand the seasonal rain-filled monsoon winds, which blow from the southwest between October and April and then from the northeast between April and October—knowledge that propelled the maritime trade connecting the Mediterranean with the Indian Ocean.

Mariners accumulated the new sailing knowledge in books—each called a **periplus** ("sailing around")—in which sea captains recorded the landing spots and ports between their destinations, as well as their precious cargoes. The *Periplus Maris Erythraei*, or *Periplus of the Red Sea*, was one such first-century BCE handbook. It offered advice to merchants traveling and trading along two major, connected routes: one on the Red Sea along the coastline of Egypt and the other on the Arabian Sea heading eastward to India. The author demonstrates keen observation and navigational skill in cataloguing the navigable routes, the marketable goods at each port, and anthropological insights on the inhabitants of the far-flung regions visited. The revolution in sailing techniques, like celestial bearing and the dhows, combined with practical knowledge, like that contained in the *Periplus Maris Erythraei*, dramatically reduced the cost of long-distance shipping and multiplied the ports of call around large bodies of water. Some historians have argued that there were now two Silk Roads: one by land and one by sea.

Conclusion

Alexander's territorial gains were awesome in their scale, but his empire was as transitory as it was huge. Though it crumbled upon his death, Alexander's conquest had effects more profound than those of any military or political regime before. Alexander's armies ushered in an age of thinking and practices that transformed Greek achievements into a common culture—Hellenism—whose influences, both direct and indirect, touched far-flung societies for centuries thereafter.

Hellenism offered a common language, both literally and figuratively, that linked culture, institutions, and trade. However, many Greek-speaking peoples and their descendants in parts of central and Southwest Asia integrated local cultural practices with their own ways, creating diverse and rich cultures. Thus, the influences of culture flowed both ways. The economic story is equally complex. Following pathways forged by previous empires and kingdoms, Alexander's successors strengthened and expanded existing trade routes and centers of commercial activity, which ultimately led to the creation of the Silk Roads.

Although the effects of this Hellenistic age lasted longer than most cultural systems and had a wider appeal than previous philosophical and spiritual ideas, they did not overwrite everything that came before. Some, like the Jewish people of Judea and Alexandria, either fought against Hellenism with all their might or accommodated to it. Others, like the Romans and Carthaginians, took from the new common culture what they liked and discarded the rest.

In South Asia, the immediate successor to Alexander's military was the Mauryan Empire, which established its dominion over much of South Asia and even some of central Asia for close to a century and a half. Once Mauryan control receded, South Asia was opened up even more than before to currents moving swiftly across Afro-Eurasia, including the institutions and cultures of steppe nomads, seafarers, and Hellenists. The most telling South Asian responses occurred in the realm of spiritual and ethical norms, where Buddhist doctrines began to evolve toward a full-fledged world religious system.

Greater political integration helped fashion highways for commerce and enabled the spread of Buddhism. Nomads, like the Kushans, left their steppe lands and exchanged wares across great distances. As they found greater opportunities for business, their trade routes shifted farther south. Eventually merchants, rather than the trading nomads, seized the opportunities provided by new technologies, especially in sailing and navigation, and by thriving caravan cities. These commercial transformations connected distant parts of Afro-Eurasia. The Silk Roads and new sea-lanes connected ports and caravan cities from North Africa to South China, created new social classes, produced new urban settings, supported powerful new polities, and transported Hellenism and Buddhism well beyond their points of origin.

Focus On
Forces That Unify Afro-Eurasia

The Mediterranean World

- The spread of Hellenism around the Mediterranean via Alexander's conquests and his successor kingdoms leads to a common language, cosmopolitan cities, new types of philosophy and religion, plantation slavery, and money-based economies.

Central and South Asia

- The Mauryan Empire, of Chandragupta and his grandson Aśoka, integrates the northern half of India in the aftermath of Alexander's withdrawal from the region.

- The Bactrian kingdom and Kushan Empire further solidify the spread of Hellenism into central Asia.

The Transformation of Buddhism

- The combined influences of Hellenism, Aśoka's adoption of the Buddhist faith, nomadism, and Indian Ocean seafaring transform Buddhism into a world religion.

Formation of Silk Roads

- Nomadic warriors from central Asia complete the final links of the overland Silk Roads, strengthening the ties that join peoples across Afro-Eurasia.

- Overland traders carry spices, transport precious metals, and convey Buddhist thought along the Silk Roads into China.

- Seafaring traders use new navigation techniques and larger ships called dhows to expand the transport of Silk Road commodities to the Mediterranean world via the Indian Ocean.

CHRONOLOGY

	400 BCE	350 BCE	300 BCE	250 BCE
Southwest Asia and Egypt			Conquests of Alexander the Great 334–323 BCE	
	Hellenistic successor states 323–30 BCE			
The Mediterranean				
		Spread of plantation and money-based economies 250–40 BCE		
Central and South Asia				
	Transformation of Buddhism begins third century BCE			
East Asia				
	Growth of market economy third–first centuries BCE			

THINKING ABOUT GLOBAL CONNECTIONS

- **Thinking about Crossing Borders and Shrinking the Afro-Eurasian World** Alexander's conquests and the resulting Hellenistic kingdoms of his successors brought about a never-before-seen cultural unity across huge swaths of Afro-Eurasia. To what extent was this cultural diffusion—comparable in some ways to the globalization or "Americanization" of culture around the world in modern times—a positive development? In what ways might it have been seen by those living through it as a negative development?

- **Thinking about Transformation & Conflict and Shrinking the Afro-Eurasian World** Alexander and his successors brought about unity initially by brutal conquest, then later through diplomatic strategies and the spread of Hellenistic ideas. Likewise, as the conquest of Kalinga demonstrated, Aśoka brutally conquered territories before his change of heart and promotion of *dhamma*. Compare and contrast the role of military conflict and cultural movements (like Hellenism and *dhamma*) in bringing unity to the Hellenistic world and South Asia.

- **Thinking about Worlds Together, Worlds Apart and Shrinking the Afro-Eurasian World** The long-distance trade routes known as the Silk Roads, and sometimes the Incense Roads, brought intensified interactions among societies across Afro-Eurasia in the last centuries BCE. Which societies were closely involved in this exchange? Which appear to have been less involved? What accounts for these regions' involvement, or lack thereof, in Silk Road exchange?

Key Terms

Bactria p. 269	cosmopolitans p. 258	Mahayana Buddhism p. 270	*periplus* p. 282
bodhisattvas p. 271	Gandharan style p. 272	Mauryan Empire p. 264	Silk Roads p. 273
caravan cities p. 277	*Koine* Greek p. 257		

 Go to INQUIZITIVE to see what you've learned—and learn what you've missed—with personalized feedback along the way.

200 BCE	150 BCE	100 BCE	50 BCE

Expansion of Rome and clash with Carthage 330–146 BCE

Mauryan Empire 321–184 BCE

Bactrian kingdom, c. 250–50 BCE

Kushan Empire first–third centuries CE

Warring States period 403–221 BCE

Global Themes and Sources

Exploring Connectivity on the Silk Road

In the aftermath of Alexander's conquests, Hellenistic successor states flourished in western Afro-Eurasia, Indo-Greek states like Bactria reigned in central Eurasia, the Mauryans developed the first "Indian" empire in South Asia, and a web of trade routes through each of these regions joined together to form the Silk Roads. Two powerful movements, Hellenism and Buddhism, thrived as a result of this connectivity and consolidation.

The sources in this section offer a glimpse into this world newly connected through expansive conquest and thickening exchange routes. While Arrian's *Anabasis* emphasizes Alexander's military campaigns as he marched his troops as far as the Ganges River, Arrian also includes in his narrative a number of nonmilitaristic encounters, such as Alexander and his Macedonian forces' contacts with Indian philosophers (which occurred around 325 BCE). The relationship between military conquest and the spread of ideas is also explored in Aśoka's Kalinga Edict (261 BCE). Aśoka, who ruled over an expanding Mauryan Empire in India two generations after Alexander had turned back from the Ganges, describes in detail what he refers to as "conquest through Dharma" when he converts to Buddhism. Just over seventy years later, we see the blending of local Egyptian and Hellenistic ideas in the Third Memphis Decree of Ptolemy V (196 BCE). In this text, local Egyptian priests honor their Hellenistic king with particular Egyptian flair, while that king offers tax relief and other benefits to the Egyptian peoples over whom he rules in the aftermath of a revolt. Farther to the east along the Silk Roads, changes in Buddhism begin to appear in texts like "The Practice of Perfect Wisdom" (c. 100 BCE). This early Mahayana Buddhist text preserves ideas that were transmitted and shaped by Silk Road exchange.

The level of connectivity required to investigate cause-and-effect relationships across far-flung regions can be hard to establish in early world history. What is particularly striking about the closing centuries of the first millennium BCE is that military conquest by Alexander, his successors, and Aśoka; the establishment of realms like the Bactrian kingdom and the Kushan Empire; and Silk Road exchange all bring a new degree of sustained connectivity that allows us to explore causality across regions. With empires and kingdoms from the Mediterranean to East Asia now linked to varying degrees by Silk Road exchange, we can begin to explore the direct effects of that connectivity, namely the spread of ideas like Hellenism and Buddhism.

Analyzing the Causes and Effects of Connectivity on the Silk Roads

- What evidence do you see for conquest and Silk Road connectivity in these texts?

- What evidence do you see for the effects (both short- and long-term) of conquests and Silk Roads, especially with respect to the spread of Hellenism and Buddhism?

- How would you differentiate—in terms of geographic scope, direction, magnitude, effect, and other factors—the role of conquest and the role of Silk Roads in shaping Afro-Eurasia in this period?

PRIMARY SOURCE 6.1

Alexander and the Indian Sages (c. 325 BCE), from *Anabasis of Alexander* (second century CE), Arrian

Although Arrian wrote his account of Alexander's campaigns in the east (which occurred around 325 BCE) more than four hundred years after they took place, he relied on firsthand accounts from Alexander's companions in order to compose his narrative. For this particular vignette of Alexander and the Indian sages, Arrian drew on the writings of Nearchus, who is mentioned at the end of this passage (7.3.6). Nearchus was a naval officer in Alexander's army who was famous for sailing from the Indus River to the Persian Gulf and for his composition of a text in which he recorded his firsthand knowledge of the region. In this particular passage, we can observe the ways that exploration and military expansion led to increased interaction between the peoples and ideas of the Mediterranean and the Indus region.

....

- **What does the text reveal about the ideas of these Indian philosophers?**

- **How do Alexander and his companions respond to the sages, to Dandamis, and to Calanus?**

- **What are the apparent causes for the interaction described here? What are some of the possible effects of this interaction on the Macedonian Greeks and on the Indians?**

....

7.1.5 I have always liked the story of the Indian sages, some of whom Alexander chanced to come upon out of doors in a meadow, where they used to meet to discuss philosophy. On the appearance of Alexander and his army, these venerable men stamped with their feet and gave no other sign of interest. Alexander asked them through interpreters what they meant by this odd behavior, and they replied:

7.1.6 "King Alexander, every man can possess only so much of the earth's surface as this we are standing on. You are but human like the rest of us, save that you are always busy and up to no good, travelling so many miles from your home, a nuisance to yourself and to others. Ah well! You will soon be dead, and then you will own just as much of this earth as will suffice to bury you."

7.2.1 Alexander expressed his approval of these sage words; but in point of fact his conduct was always the exact opposite of what he then professed to admire. . . .

7.2.2 In Taxila, once, he met some members of the Indian sect of Wise Men whose practice it is to go naked, and he so much admired their powers of endurance that the fancy took him to have one of them in his personal train. The oldest man among them, whose name was Dandamis (the others were his

pupils), refused either to join Alexander himself or to permit any of his pupils to do so.

7.2.3 "If you, my lord," he is said to have replied, "are the son of God, why—so am I. I want nothing from you, for what I have suffices. I perceive, moreover, that the men you lead get no good from their world-wide wandering over land and sea, and that of their many journeyings there is no end. I desire nothing that you can give me; I fear no exclusion from any blessings which may perhaps be yours.

7.2.4 "India, with the fruits of her soil in due season, is enough for me while I live; and when I die, I shall be rid of my poor body—my unseemly housemate." These words convinced Alexander that Dandamis was, in a true sense, a free man; so he made no attempt to compel him. . . .

7.3.1 [N]o history of Alexander would be complete without the story of Calanus. In India Calanus had never been ill, but when he was living in Persia all strength ultimately left his body. In spite of his enfeebled state he refused to submit to an invalid regimen, and told Alexander that he was content to die as he was, which would be preferable to enduring the misery of being forced to alter his way of life.

7.3.2 Alexander, at some length, tried to talk him out of his obstinacy, but to no purpose; then, convinced that if he were any further opposed he would find one means or another of making away with himself, he yielded to his request, and gave instructions for the building of a funeral pyre. . . . Some say Calanus was escorted to the pyre by a solemn procession—horses, men, soldiers in armour, and people carrying all kinds of precious oils and spices to throw upon the flames; other accounts mention drinking-cups of silver and gold and kingly robes.

7.3.3 He was too ill to walk, and a horse was provided for him; but he was incapable of mounting it, and had to be carried on a litter, upon which he lay with his head wreathed with garlands in the Indian fashion, and singing Indian songs, which his countrymen declare were hymns of praise to their gods.

7.3.4 The horse he was to have ridden was of the royal breed of Nesaea, and before he mounted the pyre he gave it to Lysimachus, one of his pupils in philosophy. . . .

7.3.5 At last he mounted the pyre and with due ceremony laid himself down. All the troops were watching. Alexander could not but feel that there was a sort of indelicacy in witnessing such a spectacle—the man, after all, had been his friend; everyone else, however, felt nothing but astonishment to see Calanus give not the smallest sign of shrinking from the flames.

7.3.6 We read in Nearchus' account of this incident that at the moment the fire was kindled there was, by Alexander's orders, an impressive salute: the bugles sounded, the troops with one accord roared out their battle-cry, and the elephants joined in with their shrill war-trumpetings.

Source: Arrian, *The Campaigns of Alexander*, translated by Aubrey de Sélincourt (New York: Penguin Books, 1981), pp. 349–52.

PRIMARY SOURCE 6.2

Kalinga Edict (261 BCE), Aśoka

King Aśoka (r. 268–231 BCE) proclaimed his adoption of Buddhism in inscriptions, called rock and pillar edicts, carved in stone throughout his Mauryan Empire in India. Wanting the message to be accessible to as many people as possible, Aśoka posted these inscriptions prominently at multiple sites (many of which, like Kandahar, were situated on the Silk Roads), using several languages (Aramaic, Greek, and Gandhari Prakrit) and different scripts (Aramaic, Greek, and Kharosthi). In the inscription of Edict 13, presented here, Aśoka describes his conversion to Buddhism after his forces brutally slaughtered the people of Kalinga in 261 BCE.

- According to this inscription, why does Aśoka adopt the "duties relating to Dharma" after the war in Kalinga?

- What does Aśoka hope will be the long-term effect of his adoption of Buddhism and his posting of these inscriptions? How exactly does Aśoka envision "conquest through Dharma" working?

- What specific claims does Aśoka make about how far his "conquest through Dharma" has spread?

The country of the Kalingas was conquered by king Piyadasi, Beloved of the Gods, eight years after his coronation. In this war in Kalinga, men and animals numbering one hundred and fifty thousand were carried away captive from that country, as many as one hundred thousand were killed there in action, and many times that number perished. After that, now that the country of the Kalingas has been conquered, the Beloved of the Gods is devoted to an intense practice of the duties relating to Dharma, to a longing for Dharma and to the inculcation of Dharma among the people. This is due to the repentance of the Beloved of the Gods on having conquered the country of the Kalingas.

Verily the slaughter, death and deportation of men which take place in the course of the conquest of an unconquered country are considered extremely painful and deplorable by the Beloved of the Gods. But what is considered even more deplorable by the Beloved of the Gods is the fact that injury to or slaughter or deportation of the beloved ones falls to the lot of the Brahmanas, the Sramanas, the adherents of other sects and the householders, who live in that country and among whom are established such virtues as obedience to superior personages, obedience to mother and father, obedience to elders and proper courtesy and firm devotion to friends, acquaintances, companions and relatives as well as to slaves and servants. And, if misfortune befalls the friends, acquaintances, companions and relatives of persons who are full of affection towards the former, even though they are themselves well provided for, the said misfortune as well becomes an injury to their own selves. In war, this fate is shared by all classes of men and is considered deplorable by the Beloved of the Gods.

Excepting the country of the Yavanas, there is no country where these two classes (the Brahmanas and the Sramanas) do not exist; and there is no place in any country where men are not indeed sincerely devoted to one sect or the other. Therefore, the slaughter, death or deportation of even a hundredth or thousandth part of all those people who were slain or who died or were carried away captive at that time in Kalinga, is now considered very deplorable by the Beloved of the Gods.

Now the Beloved of the Gods thinks that, even if a person should wrong him, the offence would be forgiven if it was possible to forgive it. And the forest-folk who live in the dominions of the Beloved of the Gods, even them he entreats and exhorts in regard to their duty. It is hereby explained to them that, in spite of his repentance, the Beloved of the Gods possesses power enough to punish them for their crimes, so that they should turn from evil ways and would not be killed for their crimes. Verily the Beloved of the Gods desires the following in respect of all creatures: non-injury to them, restraint in dealing with them, and impartiality in the case of crimes committed by them.

So, what is conquest through Dharma is now considered to be the best conquest by the Beloved of the Gods. And such a conquest has been achieved by the Beloved of the Gods not only here in his own dominions but also in the territories bordering on his dominions, as far away as at the distance of six hundred Yojanas, where the Yavana king named Antiyoka [Antiochus II of Syria] is ruling and where, beyond the kingdom of the said Antiyoka, four other kings named Turamaya [Ptolemy II Philadelphus of Egypt], Antikini [Antigonus II Gonatas of Macedon], Maka [Magas of Cyrene], and Alikasundara [Alexander II of Epirus, Greece] are also ruling, and, towards the south, where the Cholas and Pandyas are living as far as Tamraparni. Likewise here in the dominions of His Majesty, the Beloved of the Gods—in the countries of the Yavanas and Kambojas, of the Nabhakas and Nabhapanktis, of the Bhoja-paitryanikas and of the Andhras and Paulindas—everywhere people are conforming to the instructions in Dharma imparted by the Beloved of the Gods.

Even where the envoys of the Beloved of the Gods have not penetrated, there too men have heard of the practices of Dharma and the ordinances issued and the instructions in Dharma imparted by the Beloved of the Gods, and are conforming to Dharma and will continue to conform to it.

So, whatever conquest is achieved in this way, verily that conquest creates an atmosphere of satisfaction everywhere both among the victors and the vanquished. In the conquest through Dharma, satisfaction is derived by both the parties. But that satisfaction is indeed of little consequence. Only happiness of the people in the next world is what is regarded by the Beloved of the Gods as a great thing resulting from such a conquest.

And this record relating to Dharma has been written on stone for the following purpose, that my sons and great-grandsons should not think of a fresh con-

quest by arms as worth achieving, that they should adopt the policy of forbearance and light punishment towards the vanquished even if they conquer a people by arms, and that they should regard the conquest through Dharma as the true conquest. Such a conquest brings happiness to all concerned both in this world and in the next. And let all their intense joys be what is pleasure associated with Dharma. For this brings happiness in this world as well as in the next.

Source: *Inscriptions of Aśoka*, translated by D. C. Sircar (New Delhi: Publications Division, Ministry of Information and Broadcasting, Government of India, 1967), pp. 57–59.

PRIMARY SOURCE 6.3

Third Memphis Decree of Ptolemy V, from the Rosetta Stone (196 BCE)

The Rosetta Stone is widely known as an inscription that was key to the deciphering of hieroglyphs. What is less well known about the Rosetta Stone is what the text of the inscription actually said. The Rosetta Stone recorded a text known as the Third Memphis Decree of Ptolemy V (r. 204–181 BCE), a Hellenistic successor king in Egypt. It was the repeated occurrence of the cartouche containing his title, "Ptolemy, the ever-living, the beloved of Ptah," that helped linguists begin to understand how hieroglyphs worked. The text describes the situation after Ptolemy V quashed a revolt against his control.

- **What evidence do you see in this text for Hellenistic influence on Egypt? For Egyptian influence on its Hellenistic king?**

- **What sorts of gifts and allowances does Ptolemy make, both to his own soldiers and to the Egyptian priests and temples?**

- **What would likely be the long-term effects of the cultural blending and Hellenistic rule in Egypt as a result of the specific developments this decree describes?**

1. On the twenty-fourth day of the month Gorpiaios; which correspondeth to the twenty-fourth day of the fourth month of the season Pert of the inhabitants of Ta-Mert [Egypt], in the twenty-third year of the reign of Horus-Ra the child . . .

2. . . . the King of the South and the North . . . the Son of the Sun, *Ptolemy, the ever-living, the beloved of Ptah* [in cartouche, italicized here to show its recurrence], the god who maketh himself manifest . . .

6. [O]n this day the superintendents of the temples, and the servants of the god, and those who are over the secret things of the god, and the libationers [who] go into the most holy place to array the gods in their apparel,

7. and the scribes of the holy writings, and the sages of the Double House of Life, and the other libationers [who] had come from the sanctuaries of the South and the North to Memphis, on the day of the festival, whereon

8. His Majesty . . . *Ptolemy, the ever-living, the beloved of Ptah* . . . entered into the Sehetch-Chamber, wherein they were wont to assemble, in Makha-Taui [place where Upper and Lower Egypt met], and behold they declared thus:—

9. Inasmuch as the King who is beloved by the gods, *Ptolemy, the ever-living, the beloved of Ptah* . . . hath given things of all kinds in very large quantities unto the lands of Horus and unto all

10. those who dwell in them, and unto each and every one who holdeth any dignity whatsoever in the,—now behold, he is like unto a God . . . and behold, His Majesty

11. possessed a divine heart which was beneficent towards the gods; and he hath given gold in large quantities, and grain in large quantities to the temples and he hath given very many lavish gifts in order to make Ta-Mert [Egypt] prosperous, and to make stable [her] advancement;

12. and he hath given unto the soldiers who are in his august service . . . according to their rank: [and of the taxes] some of them he hath cut off, and some of them [he hath lightened], thus causing the soldiers and those who live in the country to be prosperous

13. under his reign [and as regards the sums which were due to the royal house] from the people of Egypt, and likewise those [which were due] from every one who was in his august service, His Majesty remitted them altogether, howsoever great they were;

14. and he hath forgiven the prisoners who were in prison, and ordered that every one among them should be released from [the punishment] which he had to undergo. And His Majesty made an order saying:—In respect of the things [which are to be given to] the gods, and the money and the

15. grain which are to be given to the temples each year, and all the things [which are to be given to] the gods from the vineyards and from the corn-lands of the nome, all the things which were then due under the Majesty of his holy father

16. shall be allowed to remain [in their amounts] to them as they were then; and he hath ordered:—Behold, the treasury (?) shall not be made more full of contributions by the hands of the priests than it was up to the first year of the reign of His Majesty, his holy father. . . .

22. And His Majesty marched against the town of Shekam, which is in front of (?) the town of Uiset, which was in the possession of the enemy . . .

26. . . . and His Majesty captured the town by assault in a very short time, and he cut to pieces the rebels who were therein, and he made an exceedingly great slaughter among them, even like unto that which Thoth and Horus, the son of Isis and [the son of Osiris], made among those who rebelled against them. . . .

36. . . . And it has entered into the heart(s) of the priests of the temples of the South and of the North, and of each and every temple [that all the honours which are paid] to Ptolemy . . .

38. and to the Saviour-Gods, shall be [greatly increased]; and a statue of . . . *Ptolemy, ever-living, beloved of Ptah* . . . shall be set up [in every temple, in the most prominent place], and it shall be

39. called by his name "Ptolemy, the Saviour of Egypt." . . .

41. . . . [the priests have decreed] that this Decree shall [be inscribed] upon a stele of hard stone in the writing of the words of the gods, and the writing of the books, and in the writing of Haui-Nebui (i.e., Greeks), and it shall be set up in the sanctuaries in the temples which [are called] by his name.

Source: E. A. Wallis Budge, *The Nile, Notes for Travellers in Egypt*, 9th ed. (London: Thos. Cook and Son, 1907), pp. 228–40.

"The Practice of Perfect Wisdom" (c. 100 BCE)

"The Practice of Perfect Wisdom" may date to as early as 100 BCE. The text, which is preserved in the first forty-one verses of a much longer and later Buddhist text called the *Aṣṭasāhasrikā Prajñāpāramitā* (*Perfection of Wisdom in 8,000 Lines*), is one of the earliest texts in Mahayana Buddhism. The transmission history of the "Practice of Perfect Wisdom" offers exciting evidence for the movement of Buddhist ideas on the Silk Roads. Scholars have identified an early Gandharan version of the text that was written on birch-bark scrolls in Kharosthi script (one of the scripts of Aśoka's edict in Primary Source 6.2). The text was also preserved in Chinese by Lokaksema, a monk who traveled from Gandhara (in Pakistan) to Luoyang (the Han capital) in the late second century CE. Its verses offer some of the earliest descriptions of what a bodhisattva is.

....

- What elements of Buddhism do you recognize in this text? How do ideas about suffering and illusion fit in?

- What are the traits of a bodhisattva, as outlined in this text?

- In what ways does the Mahayana (or "Great Vehicle") Buddhism in this text differ from the basics of the Four Noble Truths and the Eightfold Path to achieve nirvana (according to the earliest form of Buddhism outlined in Chapter 5)? How might Silk Road connections and the transmission of these ideas from India to China have influenced the differences?

....

[7.] The Bodhisattva, when he comprehends the dharmas [teachings] as he should

Does not retire into Blessed Rest. In wisdom then he dwells.

8. What is this wisdom, whose and whence, he queries,

And then he finds that all these dharmas are entirely empty.

Uncowed and fearless in the face of that discovery

Not far from Bodhi [enlightenment] is that Bodhi-being then.

9. To course in the skandhas [i.e., the five parts that make up a being: form, feeling, perception, conditioning, and consciousness], in form, in feeling, in perception,

Will and so on, and fail to consider them wisely;

Or to imagine these skandhas as being empty;

Means to course in the sign, the track of non-production ignored.

10. But when he does not course in form, in feeling, or perception,

In will or consciousness, but wanders without home,

Remaining unaware of coursing firm in wisdom,

His thoughts on non-production—then the best of all the calming trances cleaves to him.

11. Through that the Bodhisattva now dwells tranquil in himself,

His future Buddhahood assured by antecedent Buddhas.

Whether absorbed in trance, or whether outside it, he minds not.

For of things as they are he knows the essential original nature.

12. Coursing thus he courses in the wisdom of the Sugatas [Fortunate Ones],

And yet he does not apprehend the dharmas in which he courses.

This coursing he wisely knows as a no-coursing,

That is his practice of wisdom, the highest perfection.

13. What exists not, that non-existent the foolish imagine;

Non-existence as well as existence they fashion.

As dharmic facts existence and non-existence are both not real.

A Bodhisattva goes forth when wisely he knows this.

14. If he knows the five skandhas as like an illusion,

But makes not illusion one thing, and the skandhas another;

If, freed from the notion of multiple things, he courses in peace—

Then that is his practice of wisdom, the highest perfection.

15. Those with good teachers as well as deep insight,

Cannot be frightened on hearing the Mother's deep tenets.

But those with bad teachers, who can be misled by others,

Are ruined thereby, as an unbaked pot when in contact with moisture.

16. What is the reason why we speak of "Bodhisattvas"?

Desirous to extinguish all attachment, and to cut it off,

True non-attachment . . .

"Beings who strive for Bodhi" are they therefore called.

17. What is the reason why "Great Beings" are so called?

They rise to the highest place above a great number of people;

And of a great number of people they cut off mistaken views.

That is why we come to speak of them as "Great Beings." . . .

19. This gnosis shows him all beings as like an illusion,

Resembling a great crowd of people, conjured up at the crossroads,

By a magician, who then cuts off many thousands of heads;

He knows this whole living world as a mock show, and yet remains without fear.

20. Form, perception, feeling, will and awareness

Are ununited, never bound, cannot be freed.

Uncowed in his thought he marches on to his Bodhi,

That for the highest of men is the best of all armours.

21. What then again is "the vessel that leads to the Bodhi"?

Mounted upon it one guides to Nirvana all beings.

Great is that vessel, immense, vast like the vastness of space.

Those who travel upon it are carried to safety, delight and ease.

22. Thus transcending the world, he eludes our apprehensions.

"He goes to Nirvana," but no one can say where he went to.

A fire's extinguished, but where, do we ask, has it gone to?

Likewise, how can we find him who has found the Rest of the Blessed?

23. The Bodhisattva's past, his future and his present must elude us,

Time's three dimensions nowhere touch him.

Quite pure he is, free from conditions, unimpeded.

That is his practice of wisdom, the highest perfection.

24. Wise Bodhisattvas, coursing thus, reflect on non-production,

And yet, while doing so, engender in themselves the great compassion,

Which is, however, free from any notion of a being.

Thereby they practice wisdom, the highest perfection.

25. But when the notion of suffering and beings leads him to think:

"Suffering I shall remove, the weal of the world I shall work!"

Beings are then imagined, a self is imagined,—

The practice of wisdom, the highest perfection, is lacking.

26. He wisely knows that all that lives is unproduced as he himself is;

He knows that all that is no more exists than he or any beings.

The unproduced and the produced are not distinguished,

That is the practice of wisdom, the highest perfection.

27. All words for things in use in this world must be left behind,

All things produced and made must be transcended—

The deathless, the supreme, incomparable gnosis is then won.

That is the sense in which we speak of perfect wisdom.

28. When free from doubts the Bodhisattva carries on his practice,

As skilled in wisdom he is known to dwell.

All dharmas are not really there, their essential original nature is empty.

To comprehend that is the practice of wisdom, perfection supreme.

Source: *The Perfection of Wisdom in Eight Thousand Lines and Its Verse Summary,* translated by Edward Conze (1973; repr., San Francisco: Four Seasons Foundation, 1995), pp. 10–12.

Interpreting Visual Evidence

Coinage

The minting of coins was one of the many ways that rulers asserted their identity and conveyed propaganda about their rule. While minting coins was a statement of political authority, rulers often wanted to suggest not only the new ideals of their rule but also a cultural continuity. They chose for their coins words and images that blended the new with the old and the imported with the local.

The well-preserved gold octadrachm coin pictured below displays the image of Berenice II of Egypt (r. 246–221 BCE), one of the many female Egyptian rulers of this period. The coin's flip side shows a cornucopia brimming with fruit and the words *Berenike Basileia* (Queen Berenice). The next coin shown here was minted by King Menander (r. c. 165–130 BCE), known for his discussions with Indian sages on the nature of the Buddha. Menander stamped his own image on a silver coin, along with his name and his title, *Basileus Soter* (King Savior). On the other side of the coin, the Greek goddess Athena is surrounded by an Indian writing known as Kharosthi script.

Several examples of coins from points farther east look a little different than these Hellenistic examples, but express similarly complex messages of identity and continuity. The knife-shaped coin with Chinese characters on it dates to 250–221 BCE and comes from northeastern China. It shows just how diverse coin types could be; even though the practice of government-issued coins was taking hold in many places, there was no one way to mint them. Even within China, coin types varied. The last coin pictured here is a bronze *ban liang* and was minted under the authority of Qin ruler King Huiwen (r. 338–311 BCE), an ancestor of Shi Huangdi, who later established the short-lived Qin dynasty in 221 BCE.

Questions for Analysis

1. Compare these coins with one another. To what extent do you think the "shrinking Afro-Eurasian world," described in this chapter, may have influenced their similarities and differences?

2. What messages might the images and words on the coins have conveyed to those who used them?

3. Coins of high value (like Berenice's gold octadrachm) are usually far better preserved than lower-value coins (like the bronze coin from the Qin dynasty). Why do you think that is the case?

Gold octadrachm.

Menander coin.

Bronze *ban liang*.

Bronze jimo.

7

Han Dynasty China and Imperial Rome

300 BCE–300 CE

In third-century BCE China, the Eastern Zhou state of Qin absorbed the remaining Warring States (see Chapter 5) and set the stage for the Han dynasty. The chief minister of the Qin state, Li Si, urged his king to seize the opportunity presented by the disarray of his opponents: by combining his fearsome armies and his own personal virtues, the king could sweep away his rivals as if dusting ashes from a kitchen hearth. "This is the one moment in ten thousand ages," Li Si whispered to the man who would become Qin Shi Huangdi. The king listened carefully. He followed the advice and laid the foundations for a mighty empire. Although Shi Huangdi's Qin Empire collapsed in 207 BCE after a mere two decades, his political innovations set the stage for the much more powerful and longer lasting Han Empire (206 BCE–220 CE), which became one of the most successful dynasties in Chinese history. Following the Qin model, the Han defeated other regional groups and established a Chinese empire that would last for four centuries.

Chapter Outline

- Globalizing Empires: The Han Dynasty and Imperial Rome
- The Han Dynasty
- The Roman Empire
- Conclusion

Core Objectives

- **IDENTIFY** the features that made Han China and imperial Rome globalizing empires.
- **DESCRIBE** the development of the Han dynasty from its beginnings through the third century CE.
- **EXPLAIN** the process by which Rome transitioned from a minor city-state to a dominating Mediterranean power.
- **COMPARE** Han China with imperial Rome in terms of political authority, economy, cultural developments, and military expansion.

At the other end of Afro-Eurasia another great state, imperial Rome, also met its rivals in war, emerged victorious, and consolidated its power into a vast empire. The Romans achieved this feat by using violent force on a scale hitherto unseen in their part of the globe. The result was a state of huge size, astonishingly unified and stable. Living in the Roman Empire in the mid-70s CE, Pliny the Elder wrote glowingly about the unity of the imperial Roman state. In his eyes, all the benefits that flowed from Rome's extensive reach derived from the greatness of a peace that joined diverse peoples under one benevolent emperor. In this chapter, we will examine and compare the growth, politics, economies, and societies of the Han and Roman Empires.

Global Storylines

- Flourishing at roughly the same time, Han China and the Roman Empire become powerful and enduring "globalizing empires."

- The Han dynasty, building on Qin foundations, establishes a bureaucratic imperial model and social order in East Asia.

- The Roman Empire becomes a Mediterranean superpower exerting far-reaching political, legal, economic, and cultural influence.

Globalizing Empires: The Han Dynasty and Imperial Rome

The Han and the Roman states became truly **globalizing empires**: they covered immense amounts of territory, included huge, diverse populations, and exerted influence far beyond their own borders. Their major innovation was not that they found new ways to plow resources into big armies and civil bureaucracies or that their rulers gave new justifications for their rule. Rather, what distinguished the Romans and the Han from their predecessors was their commitment to integrating conquered neighbors and rivals into their worlds—by extending laws, offering systems of representation, exporting belief systems, colonizing lands, and promoting trade within and beyond their empires. Subject peoples became members of empires, not just the vanquished. Those who resisted not only waved away the benefits of living under imperial rule but also became the targets for military retribution.

In this period, an estimated one out of every four human beings in Afro-Eurasia fell directly under the authority of China or Rome. Their control shaped the identity of those living within their respective realms. To be "Han Chinese" meant that elites shared a common written language based on the Confucian classics, which qualified them for public office. It also meant that commoners from all walks of life shared the elites' belief system based on ancestor worship, ritual practices stressing appropriate decorum and dress for each social level, and a view that the agrarian-based Han Empire was a small-scale model of the entire cosmos. Those who lived beyond the realm of the Han were considered uncivilized.

What it meant to be "Roman" changed over time as Rome's imperial reach expanded. In the fifth century BCE, being Roman meant being a citizen of the city of Rome, speaking Latin (the regional language of central Italy), and eating and dressing like Latin-speaking people. By the late second century BCE, the concept of citizenship expanded to include not only citizens of the city but also anyone who had formal membership in the larger territorial state that the Romans were building. By the beginning of the third century CE, being Roman meant simply being a subject of the Roman emperors. This Roman identity became so deeply rooted that when the western parts of the empire disintegrated two centuries later, the inhabitants of the surviving eastern parts—who had no connection with Rome, did not speak Latin, and did not dress or eat like the original Romans—still considered themselves "Romans" in this broader sense.

The two empires differed in their patterns of development, types of public servants, and ideals for the best kind of government. For example, the civilian magistrate and the bureaucrat were typical of the Han Empire, whereas the citizen, the soldier, and the military governor were at the heart of the

THE BIG PICTURE

In what ways were Han China and imperial Rome similar? How were they different? What features made Han China and imperial Rome globalizing empires?

globalizing empires
Empires that cover immense territory, exert significant influence beyond their borders, include large, diverse populations, and work to integrate conquered peoples.

Roman Empire. In China, dynastic empires fashioned themselves according to the models of past empires. By contrast, Rome began as a collectively ruled city-state and pursued its road to domination as if creating something new. Nonetheless, like the Chinese, Romans were strongly traditional and also idealized their ancestors. Both new empires united huge landmasses and extraordinarily diverse populations.

While both China and Rome participated in Silk Road exchange, both economies were primarily agrarian. Yet free peasants worked the land in China, whereas a huge enslaved population worked the fields of the Roman Empire. At its height, the Han Empire included around 59 million inhabitants and covered 3 million square miles in China proper and, for a while, another 1 million square miles in central Asia. The Roman Empire governed an area and a population nearly as great as those of Han China.

Both empires left indelible legacies; following their collapses, both survived as models. Successor states in the Mediterranean sought to become the second Rome, and after the Han dynasty fell, the Chinese people identified themselves and their language simply as "Han." Both empires raised life to a new level of bureaucratic and military complexity and offered a common identity on a grander scale than ever before. It was a vision that would never be lost.

The Han Dynasty (206 BCE–220 CE)

Core Objectives

DESCRIBE the development of the Han dynasty from its beginnings through the third century CE.

The Han dynasty (206 BCE–220 CE) oversaw an unprecedented blossoming of peace and prosperity in East Asia. Although supporters of the Han dynasty boasted of the regime's imperial uniqueness, in reality it owed much to its predecessor, the Qin state, which contributed vital elements of political unity and economic growth to its more powerful successor regime. (See Map 7.1.) Together, the Qin and Han created the political, social, economic, and cultural foundations that characterized imperial China thereafter.

THE QIN DYNASTY (221–207 BCE): A CRUCIAL FORERUNNER

Although it lasted only fourteen years, the Qin dynasty integrated much of China and made important administrative and economic innovations. The Qin were but one of many militaristic regimes during the Warring States period (c. 403–221 BCE). What enabled the Qin to prevail over rivals was their expansion into the Sichuan region, which was remarkable for its rich mineral resources and fertile soils. There, a merchant class and the silk trade spurred economic growth, and public works fostered increased food production. These strengths enabled the Qin by 221 BCE to defeat the remaining warring states and unify an empire that covered roughly two-thirds of modern China.

The map legend:

- Qin Empire in 221 BCE
- Han Empire in 206 BCE
- Han Empire by 87 BCE
- Further territory added to the Han Empire by 210 CE
- Xiongnu nomadic tribes
- Western regions under Han Protectorate, 59 BCE–23 CE
- Great Wall
- Xiongnu's invasions

Map 7.1 The Qin and Han Dynasties, 221 BCE–220 CE

The short-lived Qin (221–207 BCE) and the much longer-lasting Han (206 BCE–220 CE) dynasties consolidated much of East Asia into one large regional empire.

- Based on the map, when and where did various phases of expansion take place from the Qin through the Han dynasty? What features shaped that expansion?
- Where was the Great Wall located, and against what was it defending?
- What impact did the pastoral Xiongnu have on the Han dynasty's effort to consolidate a large territorial state?

Supported by able ministers and generals, a large conscripted army, and a system of taxation that financed all-out war, the Qin ruler King Zheng assumed the mandate of heaven from the Zhou. Declaring himself **Shi Huangdi**, or "First August Emperor," in 221 BCE, Zheng harkened back to China's great mythical emperors of antiquity. Forgoing the title of king (*wang*), which had been used by leaders of the Zhou and warring states, Zheng instead took the title of emperor (*di*), a term that had meant "ancestral ruler" for the Shang and Zhou.

Shi Huangdi centralized the administration of the empire. He forced the defeated rulers of the warring states and their families to move to Xianyang, the Qin capital—where they would be unable to gather rebel armies. The First August Emperor then parceled out the territory of his massive state into thirty-six provinces, called **commanderies** (*jun*). Each commandery had a civilian and a military governor, as well as an imperial inspector. Regional and local officials answered directly to the emperor, who could dismiss them at will. Civilian governors did not serve in their home areas, thus preventing them from building up power for themselves. These reforms provided China with a centralized bureaucracy and a hereditary emperor that later dynasties, including the Han, inherited.

The chief minister of the Qin Empire, Li Si, subscribed to the principles of Legalism developed during the Warring States period. This philosophy valued written law codes, administrative regulations, and inflexible punishments more highly than the rituals and ethics that Confucians emphasized or the spontaneity and natural order that the Daoists stressed. Determined to bring order to a turbulent world, Li Si advocated strict laws and harsh punishments that included beheading, mutilation, and loss of rank and office.

Other methods of control further facilitated Qin rule. Registration of the common people at the age of sixteen provided the basis for taxation and conscription both for military service and public works projects. The Qin emperor established standard weights and measures, as well as a standard currency. The Qin also improved communication systems and administrative efficiency by constructing roads radiating out from their capital to all parts of the empire. Just as crucial was the Qin effort to standardize writing. Banning regional variants of written characters, the Qin required scribes and ministers throughout the empire to adopt the "small seal script," which later evolved into the less complicated style of bureaucratic writing known as "clerical script" that became prominent during the Han dynasty. In 213 BCE, a Qin decree ordered officials to confiscate and burn all books in private possession, except for technical works on medicine, divination, and agriculture. Education and learning were now under the exclusive control of state officials.

The agrarian empire of the Qin yielded wealth that the state could tax. Increased tax revenues meant more resources for imposing order. The government issued rules on working the fields, taxed farming households, and conscripted laborers to build irrigation systems and canals so that even more land could come under cultivation. The Qin and, later, the Han dynasties relied on free farmers and conscripted their able-bodied sons into their huge armies. Working their own land and paying a portion of their crops in taxes, peasant families were the economic bedrock of the Chinese empire. Long-distance commerce thrived, as well. In the dynamic regional market centers of the cities, merchants peddled foodstuffs as well as weapons, metals, horses, dogs, hides, furs, silk, and salt—all produced in different regions and transported on the improved road system. Taxed both in transit and in the market at a higher rate than agricultural goods, these trade goods yielded even more revenue for the imperial government.

The Qin grappled with the need to expand and defend their borders, extending those boundaries in the northeast to the Korean Peninsula, in the south to present-day Vietnam, and in the west into central Asia. Relations between the settled Chinese and the nomadic Xiongnu to the north and west (see Chapter 6) teetered in a precarious balance until 215 BCE, when the Qin Empire pushed north into the middle of the Yellow River basin, seizing pasturelands from the Xiongnu and opening the region up for settlement. Qin officials built roads into these areas and employed conscripts and criminals to create a massive defensive wall that covered a distance of 3,000 miles along the northern border (the beginnings of the Great Wall of China—though north of the current wall, which was constructed more than a millennium later). In 211 BCE, the Qin settled 30,000 colonists in the steppe lands of Inner Eurasia.

Despite its military power, the Qin dynasty collapsed quickly, due to constant warfare and the heavy taxation and exhausting conscription that war required. When conscripted workers mutinied in 209 BCE, they found allies in descendants of Warring States nobles, local military leaders, and influential merchants. The rebels swept up thousands of supporters with their call to arms against the "tyrannical" Qin. Shortly before Shi Huangdi died in 210, even the educated elite joined former lords and regional vassals in revolt. The second Qin emperor committed suicide in 207, and his weak successor surrendered to the leader of the Han forces later that year. The resurgent Xiongnu confederacy also reconquered their old pasturelands as the dynasty fell.

Intellectual Censorship This seventeenth-century painting depicts the infamous "Burning of the Books and Burying of the Scholars" edict enacted by Shi Huangdi at the suggestion of his adviser, Li Si. Unfortunately, even the state-approved texts were destroyed a mere six years later, during the fall of the Qin dynasty and sack of the capital.

BEGINNINGS OF THE WESTERN HAN DYNASTY

The civil war that followed the collapse of Qin rule opened the way for the formation of the Western Han dynasty. A commoner and former policeman named Liu Bang (r. 206–195 BCE) declared himself prince of his home area of Han. In 202 BCE, Liu proclaimed himself the first Han emperor. Claiming the mandate of heaven, the Han portrayed the Qin as evil; yet at the same time they adopted the Qin's bureaucratic system. In reality, Qin laws had been no crueler than those of the Han. Under Han leadership, China's armies swelled with some 50,000 crossbowmen who brandished mass-produced weapons made from bronze and iron. Armed with the crossbow, foot soldiers and mounted archers extended Han imperial lands in all directions. Following the Qin practice, the Han also relied on a huge conscripted labor force for special projects such as building canals, roads, and defensive walls.

The first part of the Han dynasty is known as the Western (or Former) Han dynasty (206 BCE–9 CE). The Han brought economic prosperity and the expansion of empire. This was especially the case under **Emperor Wu**, known also as Han Wudi, who presided over one of the longest and most eventful reigns in Chinese history (r. 140–87 BCE). Although called the "Martial Emperor" because of the state's many military campaigns, Emperor Wu rarely inspected his military units and never led them in battle. Wu followed the Daoist principle of *wuwei* (noninterference), striving to remain aloof from day-to-day activities and permitting the empire to function on its own as if it did not require intervention. Still, he used a stringent penal code to eliminate powerful officials who got in his way. In a single year, his court system prosecuted over a thousand such cases.

Qin Archer and Crossbow This kneeling archer was discovered in the tomb of Shi Huangdi, along with the thousands of other bowmen, cavalrymen, and infantry that composed the massive terra-cotta army. Notice his breastplate; its overlapping plates would have enhanced maneuverability. The wooden bow he was holding has disintegrated, but a replica appears above. The bronze arrowhead and trigger mechanism in this reproduction were found with the terra-cotta army.

HAN POWER AND ADMINISTRATION

Undergirding the Han Empire was the tight-knit alliance between the imperial family and the new elite—the scholar-gentry class—who shared a determination to impose order on the Chinese population. Although the first Han emperors had no choice but to compromise with the aristocratic groups who had helped overthrow the Qin, in time the Han created the most highly centralized bureaucracy in the world. No fewer than 130,000 individuals staffed the central and local governments. That structure became the source of its enduring power. As under the Qin, the Han bureaucracy touched everyone because all males had to register, pay taxes, and serve in the military.

The Han court moved quickly to tighten its grip on regional administration. First it removed powerful princes, crushed rebellions, and took over the areas controlled by regional lords. According to arrangements instituted in 106 BCE by Emperor Wu, the empire consisted of thirteen provinces under imperial inspectors. As during the Qin dynasty, commanderies, each administered by a civilian and a military official, covered vast lands inhabited by countless ethnic groups totaling millions of people. These officials maintained political stability and ensured the efficient collection of taxes. However, given the immense numbers under their jurisdiction and the heavy duties they bore, in many respects the local administrative staff was still inadequate to the tasks facing them.

Government schools that promoted the scholar-official ideal became fertile sources for recruiting local officials. In 136 BCE, Emperor Wu founded what became the **Imperial University**, a college for classical scholars that supplied the Han need for well-trained bureaucrats. By the second century CE, the university boasted 30,000 students and faculty. Apart from studying the classics, Han scholars were naturalists and inventors. They made important medical discoveries, dealing with rational explanations of the body's functions and the role of wind and temperature in transmitting diseases. They also invented the magnetic compass and developed high-quality paper. Local elites encouraged their sons to master the classical teachings. This practice could secure future entry into the ruling class and firmly planted the Confucian classics at the heart of the imperial state.

Confucian thought slowly became the ideological buttress of the Han Empire. Under Emperor Wu, the bureaucracy deemed people's welfare to be the essential purpose of legitimate rule. By 50 BCE, *The Analects*, containing Confucius's sayings, was widely disseminated and three Confucian ideals reigned as the official doctrine of the Han Empire: honoring tradition, respecting the lessons of history, and acknowledging the emperor's responsibility to heaven. Scholars used Confucius's words to tutor the princes. By embracing Confucian political ideals, Han rulers established an empire based on the mandate of heaven and crafted a careful balance in which the officials provided a counterweight to the emperor's autocratic strength. When the interests of the court and the bureaucracy clashed, however, the emperor's will was paramount.

Han Coin After the Qin created the first standard imperial currency in China, the copper wuzhu coin was issued by Emperor Xuandi (r. 73–49 BCE) during the Western Han dynasty. *Wuzhu*, which means "five grains," refers to the weight of the coin (1 wuzhu = 5 grains = 4 grams). The wuzhu was in circulation until 621 CE.

Emperor Wu
(r. 140–87 BCE) Also known as Han Wudi, or the "Martial Emperor"; the ruler of the Han dynasty for more than fifty years, during which he expanded the empire through his extensive military campaigns.

Imperial University
founded in 136 BCE by Emperor Wu (Han Wudi) not only to train future bureaucrats in the Confucian classics but also to foster scientific advances in other fields.

ECONOMY AND THE NEW SOCIAL ORDER

Part of the Han leaders' genius was their ability to win the support of diverse social groups that had been squabbling for centuries. The basis of their success was their ability to organize daily life, create a stable social order, promote economic growth, and foster a state-centered religion. One important element in promoting political and social stability was that the Han allowed surviving Qin aristocrats to reacquire some of their former power. The Han also urged enterprising peasants who had worked the nobles' lands to become local leaders in the countryside. Successful merchants won permission to extend their influence in cities, and in local areas scholars found themselves in the role of masters when the state removed their lords.

Out of a massive agrarian base flowed a steady stream of tax revenues and labor for military forces and public works. The Han court drew revenues from many sources: state-owned imperial lands, mining, and mints; tribute from outlying domains; household taxes on the nobility; and taxes on surplus grains from wealthy merchants. Emperor Wu established state monopolies in salt, iron, and wine to fund his expensive military campaigns. His policies encouraged silk and iron production—especially iron weapons and everyday tools—and controlled profiteering through price controls. He also minted standardized copper coins and imposed stiff penalties for counterfeiting.

Han cities were laid out in an orderly grid. Bustling markets served as public areas. Carriages transported rich families up and down wide avenues (and they paid a lot for the privilege: keeping a horse required as much grain as a family of six would consume). Court palaces became forbidden inner cities, off-limits to all but those in the imperial lineage or the government. Monumental architecture in China announced the palaces and tombs of rulers.

Domestic Life Daily life in Han China included new luxuries for the elite and reinforced traditional ideas about gender. Wealthy families lived in several-story homes with richly carved crossbeams and rafters and floors cushioned with embroidered pillows, wool rugs, and mats. Fine embroideries hung as drapes, and screens in the rooms secured privacy. Domestic space reinforced male authority as women and children stayed cloistered in inner quarters, preserving the sense that the patriarch's role was to protect them

Model of a Han Watchtower
Wealthy Han burials contained terra-cotta models of buildings—houses, animal pens, granaries—that would replicate one's life in the afterlife. Shown here is a model of a multistory watchtower standing just over 3 feet tall, the details of which give insight into Han building techniques in the first to third centuries CE. Archers with crossbows stand guard on an upper balcony, while a figure stands in greeting at the front gate.

from a harsh society. Nonetheless, some elite women, often literate, enjoyed respect as teachers and managers within the family while their husbands served as officials away from home. Women who were commoners led less protected lives, working in the fields or even joining entertainment troupes.

Silk was abundant and available to all classes, though in winter only the rich wrapped themselves in furs while everyone else stayed warm in woolens and ferret skins. The rich also wore distinctive slippers lined with leather or silk. Wine and cooked meat came to the dinner tables of the wealthy on vessels fashioned with silver inlay or golden handles. Entertainment for those who could afford it included gambling, performing animals, tiger fights, foreign dancing girls, and even live music in private homes, performed by orchestras in the families' private employ. Although events like these had occurred during the Zhou dynasty, they had marked only public ritual occasions.

Social Hierarchy At the base of Han society was a free peasantry of farmers who owned and tilled their own land. The Han court upheld an agrarian ideal—which Confucians and Daoists supported—honoring the peasants' productive labors, while subjecting merchants to a range of controls (including regulations on luxury consumption) and belittling them for not doing physical labor. Confucians envisioned scholar-officials as working hard for the ruler to enhance a moral economy, which minimized profiteering by greedy merchants.

In reality, however, the first century of Han rule perpetuated the power of elites. At the apex were the imperial clan and nobles, followed, in order, by high-ranking officials and scholars, great merchants and manufacturers, and a regionally based class of local magnates. Below these elites, lesser clerks, medium and small landowners, free farmers, artisans, small merchants, poor tenant farmers, and hired laborers eked out a living. The more destitute became government slaves and relied on the state for food and clothing. At the bottom were convicts and private slaves.

Between 100 BCE and 200 CE, scholar-officials linked the imperial center with local society. At first, their political clout and prestige complemented the power of landlords and large clans, but over time their autonomy grew as they gained wealth by acquiring private property. Following the fall of the Han, they emerged as the dominant aristocratic clans.

In the long run, the imperial court's struggle to limit the power of local lords and magnates failed. Rulers had to rely on local officials to enforce their rule, but those officials could rarely stand up to the powerful men they were supposed to be governing. And when central rule proved too onerous for local elites, they could rebel. Local uprisings against the Han that began in 99 BCE forced the court to relax its measures and left landlords and local magnates as dominant powers in the provinces. Below these privileged groups, powerless agrarian groups turned to Daoist religious organizations that crystallized into potent cells of dissent.

Han Entertainment Han entertainment included dancing girls (*left*), musicians (*middle*), and acrobats (*right*). Music was often played at the homes of rich families, who kept their own orchestras complete with bells and drums.

Religion and Omens Under Emperor Wu, Confucianism took on religious overtones. One treatise portrayed Confucius not as a humble teacher but as an uncrowned monarch, and even as a demigod and a giver of laws, which differed from the portrait in *The Analects* of a more modest, accessible, and very human Confucius.

Although Confucians at court championed classical learning, many local communities practiced forms of a remarkably dynamic popular Chinese religion. Imperial cults, magic, and sorcery reinforced the court's interest in astronomical omens—such as the appearance of a supernova, solar halos, meteors, and lunar and solar eclipses. Unpredictable celestial events, as well as earthquakes and famines, could be taken to mean that the emperor had lost the mandate of heaven. Powerful ministers exploited these occurrences to intimidate their ruler. People of high and low social position alike believed that witchcraft could manipulate natural events and interfere with the will of heaven. Religion in its many forms, from philosophy to witchcraft, was an essential feature of Han society from the elite to the poorer classes.

MILITARY EXPANSION AND THE SILK ROADS

The Han military machine was effective at expanding the empire's borders and enforcing stability around the borderlands. Peace was good for business, specifically for creating stable conditions that allowed the safe transit of goods over the Silk Roads. Emperor Wu did much to transform the military forces. Following the Qin precedent, he made military service compulsory, resulting in a huge force: 100,000 crack troops in the Imperial Guard stationed in the capital and more than a million in the standing army.

Expanding Borders Han forces were particularly active along the borders. During the reign of Emperor Wu, Han control extended from southeastern China to northern Vietnam. When pro-Han Koreans appealed for Han help against rulers in their internal squabbles, Emperor Wu's expeditionary force defeated the Korean king and four Han commanderies sprang up in northern Korea. While incursions into Sichuan and the southwestern border areas were less successful due to mountainous terrain and malaria, a commandery nonetheless took root in southern Sichuan in 135 BCE, and soon it opened trading routes to Southeast Asia.

The Han Empire's most serious military threat, however, came from the Xiongnu and other nomadic peoples in the north. The Han inherited from the Qin a symbiotic relationship with these proud, horse-riding nomads: Han merchants brought silk cloth and thread, bronze mirrors, and lacquerware to exchange for furs, horses, and cattle. After humiliating defeats at the hands of the Xiongnu, the Han under Emperor Wu successfully repelled Xiongnu invasions around 120 BCE and ultimately penetrated deep into Xiongnu territory. The Xiongnu tribes were split in two, with the southern tribes surrendering and the northern tribes moving west, ultimately threatening Roman territory.

The Chinese Peace and the Silk Roads The retreat of the Xiongnu and other nomadic peoples introduced a glorious period of internal peace and prosperity some scholars have referred to as a **Pax Sinica** ("Chinese Peace," 149–87 BCE). During this period, long-distance trade flourished, cities ballooned, standards of living rose, and the population surged. As a result of their military campaigns, Emperor Wu and his successors enjoyed tribute from distant subordinate states, only intervening in their domestic policy if they rebelled. The Han instead relied on trade and markets to incorporate outlying lands as prosperous satellite states within the tribute system. The Xiongnu nomads even became key middlemen in Silk Road trade.

When the Xiongnu were no longer a threat from the north, the Han expanded westward. (See Map 7.2.) By 100 BCE, Emperor Wu had extended the northern defensive wall from the Tianshan Mountains to the Gobi Desert. Along the wall stood signal beacons for sending emergency messages, and its gates opened periodically for trading fairs. The westernmost gate was called the Jade Gate, since jade from the Taklamakan Desert passed through it. Wu also built garrison cities at oases to protect the trade routes. Soldiers at these oasis garrison cities settled with their families on the frontiers. When its military power expanded beyond the Jade Gate, the Han government set up a similar system of oases on the rim of the Taklamakan Desert. With irrigation, oasis agriculture attracted many more settlers. Trade routes passing through deserts and oases now were safer and more reliable—until fierce Tibetan tribes threatened them at the beginning of the Common Era—than the steppe routes, which they gradually replaced.

Pax Sinica
Modern term (paralleling the term *Pax Romana*) for the "Chinese Peace" that lasted from 149 to 87 BCE, a period when agriculture and commerce flourished, fueling the expansion of cities and the growth of the population of Han China.

Map 7.2 *Pax Sinica*: The Han Dynasty in the First Century BCE

Agriculture, commerce, and industry flourished in East Asia under Han rule.

- According to the map, what were the main commodities in the Han dynasty, where were they located, and along what routes might they have moved to pass among the empire's regions?
- Locate the lines marking the commanderies into which Han territory was divided. What do you notice about their comparative size, resources, and other features?
- What do you notice about the location of major trade centers and the areas of intensive agriculture?

SOCIAL UPHEAVAL AND NATURAL DISASTER

The strain of military expenses and the tax pressures those expenditures placed on small landholders and peasants were more than the Han Empire could bear. By the end of the first century BCE, heavy financial expenditures drained the Chinese empire. A devastating chain of events exacerbated the empire's troubles: natural disasters led to crop failures, which led to landowners' being unable to pay taxes that were based not on crop yield but on size of landholding. Wang Mang (r. 9–23 CE), a former Han minister and regent to a child emperor, took advantage of the crisis. Believing that the Han had lost the mandate of heaven, Wang Mang assumed the throne in 9 CE and established a new dynasty. He designed reforms to help the poor and to foster economic activity. He made efforts to stabilize the economy by confiscating gold from wealthy landowners and merchants, introducing a new currency, and attempting to minimize price fluctuations. By redistributing excess land, he hoped to allow all families to work their own parcels and share in cultivating a communal plot whose crops would become tax surplus for the state.

Wang Mang's regime, and his idealistic reforms, failed miserably. Violent resistance from peasants and large landholders, as well as the Yellow River's change in its course in 11 CE, contributed to his demise. When the Yellow River, appropriately called "China's Sorrow," changed course—as it has many times in China's long history—tremendous floods caused mass death, vast migrations, peasant impoverishment, and revolt. The floods of 11 CE likely affected half the Chinese population. Rebellious peasants, led by Daoist clerics, used this far-reaching disaster as a pretext to march on Wang's capital at Chang'an. The peasants painted their foreheads red in imitation of demon warriors and called themselves Red Eyebrows. By 23 CE, they had overthrown Wang Mang. The natural disaster was attributed by Wang's rivals to his unbridled misuse of power, and soon Wang became the model of the evil usurper.

THE EASTERN HAN DYNASTY

After Wang Mang's fall, social, political, and economic inequalities fatally weakened the power of the emperor and the court. As a result, the Eastern (or Later) Han dynasty (25–220 CE), with its capital at Luoyang on the North China plain, followed a hands-off economic policy under which large landowners and merchants amassed more wealth and more property. Decentralizing the regime was also good for local business and long-distance trade, as the Silk Roads continued to flourish. Chinese silk became popular as far away as the Roman Empire. In return, China received from points west on the Silk Roads commodities including glass, jade, horses, precious stones, tortoiseshells, and fabrics. (See Current Trends in World History: Han China, the Early Roman Empire, and the Silk Roads.)

By the second century CE, landed elites enjoyed the fruits of their success in manipulating the Later Han tax system. It granted them so many land and labor exemptions that the government never again firmly controlled its human and agricultural resources as Emperor Wu had. As the court refocused on the new capital in Luoyang, local power fell into the hands of great aristocratic families. These elites acquired even more privately owned land and forced free peasants to become their rent-paying tenants, then raised their rents higher and higher.

Such prosperity bred greater social inequity—among large landholders, tenant farmers, and peasants working their small parcels—and a renewed source of turmoil. Simmering tensions between landholders and peasants boiled over in a full-scale rebellion in 184 CE. Popular religious groups championed new ideas among commoners and elites for whom the many-centuries-earlier Daoist sage Master Laozi, the voice of naturalness and spontaneity, was an exemplary model. Daoist masters challenged Confucian ritual conformity, and they advanced their ideas in the name of a divine order that would redeem all people, not just elites. Officials, along with other political outcasts, headed strong dissident groups and eventually formed local movements. Under their leadership, religious groups such as the Yellow Turbans—so called because they wrapped yellow scarves around their heads—championed Daoist upheaval across the empire. The Yellow Turbans drew on Daoist ideas to call for a just and ideal society. Their message received a warm welcome from a population that was increasingly hostile to Han rule.

Proclaiming the Daoist millenarian belief in a future "Great Peace," the Yellow Turbans demanded fairer treatment by the Han state and equal distribution of all farm lands. As agrarian conditions worsened, a widespread famine ensued. It was a catastrophe that, in the rebels' view, demonstrated the emperor's loss of the mandate of heaven. While Han military forces were successful in quashing the rebellion, significant damage had been dealt to Han rule. The economy disintegrated when people refused to pay taxes and provide forced labor, and internal wars engulfed the dynasty. After the 180s CE, three competing states replaced the Han: the Wei in the northwest, the Shu in the southwest, and the Wu in the south. A long-lasting unified empire did not return for several centuries.

The Roman Empire

At the other end of Afro-Eurasia from Han China, in a centuries-long process, Rome became a great power that ruled over as many as 60 million subjects. The Roman Empire at its height encompassed lands from the highlands of what is now Scotland in Europe to the lower reaches of the Nile River in modern-day Egypt and part of Sudan, and from the borders of the Inner Eurasian steppe in Ukraine and the Caucasus to the Atlantic shores of North Africa. (See Map 7.3.) Whereas the Han Empire dominated an enormous and unbroken landmass, the Roman Empire dominated lands around the Mediterranean Sea. Like the Han Chinese, though, the Romans acquired command over their world through violent military expansion. By the first century CE, almost unceasing wars against their neighbors had enabled the Romans to forge an unparalleled number of ethnic groups and minor states into a single, large political state.

FOUNDATIONS OF THE ROMAN EMPIRE

Three major factors influenced the beginnings of Rome's imperial expansion: migrations of foreign peoples, Rome's military might, and Roman political innovation.

Core Objectives

EXPLAIN the process by which Rome transitioned from a minor city-state to a dominating Mediterranean power.

Population Movements Between 450 and 250 BCE, migrations from northern and central Europe brought large numbers of Celts to settle in lands around the Mediterranean Sea. They convulsed the northern rim of the Mediterranean, staging armed forays into lands from what is now Spain in the west to present-day Turkey in the east. One of these migrations involved Gallic peoples from the region of the Alps and beyond launching a series of violent incursions into northern Italy that ultimately—around 390 BCE—led to the seizure of Rome. The important result for the Romans was not their city's capture, which was temporary yet traumatic, but rather the permanent dislocation that the invaders inflicted on the city-states of the Etruscans. These Etruscans, themselves likely a combination of indigenous people and migrants from Asia Minor centuries before, spoke their own language and were centered in what is now Tuscany. Before the Gallic invasions, the Etruscans had dominated the Italian Peninsula. While the Etruscans with great difficulty drove the invading Gauls back northward, their cities never recovered nor did their ability to dominate other peoples in Italy, including their fledgling rival, the Romans. Thus, the Gallic migrations weakened Etruscan power, one of the most formidable roadblocks to Roman expansion in Italy.

Military Manpower and the War Ethos The Romans achieved unassailable military power by organizing the communities that they conquered in Italy into a system that generated manpower for their army. This development began around 340 BCE, when the Romans faced a concerted attack by their fellow Latin city-states. By then, the other Latins viewed Rome not as an ally in a system of mutual defense but as a growing threat to their own independence. After overcoming these nearby Latins, the Romans charged onward to defeat one community after another in Italy. Demanding from their defeated

MAP LEGEND

Mediterranean Sea current
Roman expansion to 201 BCE
Roman expansion, 201–100 BCE
Roman expansion, 100–44 BCE
Roman expansion, 44 BCE–14 CE
Roman expansion, 14–96 CE
Roman expansion, 96–116 CE
GALLIA Roman province
GAETULI Border peoples
⊙ Important provincial capitals

Map 7.3 Roman Expansion to 120 CE

Roman expansion continued for several centuries before reaching its peak in the second century CE.

- According to the map, what were Rome's earliest provinces? What provinces were incorporated during the last phase of Rome's expansion? What sense, if any, can you make of the stages of Roman expansion, in terms of where and when the Romans expanded their territory?
- What features—geographical or otherwise—limited Roman expansion farther into Europe, Southwest Asia, and Africa?
- How did the sea current influence the movement of peoples and goods in the Mediterranean?

SCYTHI

GOTHI

CASPIAN SEA

ZYGES

DACIA

MOESIA SUPERIOR

MOESIA INFERIOR

THRACIA

BLACK SEA

IBERI

ARMENIA

ACEDONIA

BITHYNIA AND PONTUS

CHAEA

AEGEAN SEA

ASIA

CAPPADOCIA

PARTHIAN EMPIRE

Corinth

GALATIA

MESOPOTAMIA

Tigris R.

LYCIA AND PAMPHYLIA

CILICIA

Antioch

Euphrates R.

RHODES

CYPRUS

SYRIA

CRETE

SEA

Caesarea

ARABI

JUDAEA

Jerusalem

CYRENAICA

Alexandria

AEGYPTUS

ARABIA

Nile R.

RED SEA

Punic Wars

Series of three wars fought between Rome and Carthage from 264 to 146 BCE that resulted in the end of Carthaginian hegemony in the western Mediterranean, the growth of Roman military might (army and navy), and the beginning of Rome's aggressive foreign imperialism.

enemies a supply of men for the Roman army every year, Rome amassed a huge reservoir of military manpower.

In addition to their overwhelming advantage in manpower, the Romans cultivated an unusual war ethos. A heightened sense of honor drove Roman men to push themselves into battle again and again, and never to accept defeat. Guided by the example of great warriors and shaped by a regime of training and discipline, in which minor infractions of duty were punishable by death, the Roman army trooped out to war in annual spring campaigns beginning in the month—still called March today—dedicated to and named for the Roman god of war, Mars.

By 275 BCE, Rome controlled the Italian Peninsula. It next entered into three great **Punic Wars** with Carthage, which had begun as a Phoenician colony and was now the major power centered in the northern parts of present-day Tunisia (see Chapters 4 and 5). The First Punic War (264–241 BCE) was a prolonged naval battle over the island of Sicily. With their victory, the Romans acquired a dominant position in the western Mediterranean. The Second Punic War (218–201 BCE), however, revealed the real strength and might of the Roman army. The Romans drew on their reserve force of nearly 750,000 men to ultimately repulse—with huge casualties and dramatic losses—the Carthaginian general Hannibal's invading force of 20,000 troops and their war elephants. The Romans took the war to enemy soil, winning the decisive battle at Zama near Carthage in late 202 BCE. In a final war of extermination, waged between 149 and 146 BCE, the Romans used their overwhelming advantage in manpower, ships, and other resources to bring the five-centuries-long hegemony of Carthage in the western Mediterranean to an end.

With an unrelenting drive to war, the Romans continued to draft, train, and field extraordinary numbers of men for combat. Soldiers, conscripted at age seventeen or eighteen, served for up to ten years at a time. With so many young men devoted to war for such long spans of time, the war ethos became deeply embedded in the ideals of every generation. After 200 BCE, the Romans unleashed this successful war machine on the kingdoms of the eastern Mediterranean. In 146 BCE, the Romans obliterated the great Greek city-state of Corinth in the same year they annihilated what was left of Carthage, killing all its adult males and selling all its women and children into slavery. Their monopoly of power over the entire Mediterranean basin was now unchallenged.

Roman military forces served under men who knew they could win not just glory and territory for the state, but also enormous rewards for themselves. They were talented men driven by burning ambition, from Scipio Africanus in the late 200s BCE, the conqueror of Carthage, to Julius Caesar, the great general of the 50s BCE. Julius Caesar's eight-year-long cycle of Gallic wars resulted in the deaths of more than 1 million Gauls and the enslavement of another million. Western Afro-Eurasia had never witnessed war on this scale; it had no equal anywhere, except in China.

Political Institutions and Internal Conflict The conquest of the Mediterranean placed unprecedented power and wealth into the hands of a few men in the Roman social elite. The rush of battlefield successes had kept Romans and their Italian allies preoccupied with the demands of army service overseas. Once this process of territorial expansion slowed, social and political problems that had been lying dormant began to resurface.

Following the traditional date of its founding in 509 BCE, the Romans had lived in a state that they called the "public thing" or ***res publica*** (hence the modern word "republic"). In this state, policy issued from the Senate—a body of permanent members, 300 to 600 of Rome's most powerful and wealthy citizens (by definition, male)—and from popular assemblies of the citizens. Every year the citizens elected the officials of state, principally two consuls who held power for a year and commanded the armies. The people also annually elected ten men who, as tribunes of the plebs ("the common people"), had the task of protecting the common people's interests against those of the rich and powerful. In severe political crises, Romans sometimes chose one man, a dictator, whose words, *dicta*, were law and who held absolute power over the state for no longer than six months. These institutions, originally devised for a city-state, were problematic for ruling a Mediterranean-sized empire.

By the second century BCE, Rome's power elite were exploiting the wealth from its Mediterranean conquests to acquire huge tracts of land in Italy and Sicily. They then imported enormous numbers of slaves from all around the Mediterranean to work this land. Free citizen farmers, the backbone of the army, were driven off their lands and into the cities. The result was a severe

> **res publica**
> Term (meaning "the public thing") used by Romans to describe their Republic, which was advised by a Senate and was governed by popular assemblies of free adult males, who were arranged into voting units, based on wealth and social status, to elect officers and legislate.

Roman Farmers and Soldiers In the late Republic, most Roman soldiers came from rural Italy, where small farms were being absorbed into the landholdings of the wealthy and powerful. In the empire, soldiers were recruited from rural provincial regions. They sometimes worked small fields of their own and sometimes worked the lands of the wealthy—like the domain in the Roman province of Africa (in modern-day Tunisia) that is depicted in this mosaic.

agrarian and recruiting crisis. In 133 and 123–121 BCE, two tribunes, the brothers Tiberius and Gaius Gracchus, tried—much as Wang Mang would in China more than a century later—to address these inequalities. The Gracchi brothers attempted to institute land reforms guaranteeing to all of Rome's poor citizens a basic amount of land that would qualify them for army service. But political enemies assassinated the elder brother, Tiberius, and orchestrated violent resistance that drove the younger brother, Gaius, to commit suicide while being chased by an angry mob.

Thereafter, poor Roman citizens looked not to state institutions but to army commanders, to whom they gave their loyalty and support, to provide them with land and income. These generals became increasingly powerful and started to compete with one another, ignoring the Senate and the traditional rules of politics. As generals sought control of the state and their supporters took sides, a long series of civil wars began that lasted from 90 BCE to the late 30s BCE. The Romans now turned inward on themselves the tremendous militaristic resources built up during the conquest of the Mediterranean.

EMPERORS, AUTHORITARIAN RULE, AND ADMINISTRATION

Julius Caesar's adopted son, Octavian (63 BCE–14 CE), ultimately reunited the fractured empire and emerged as undisputed master of the Roman world. Octavian's authoritarian one-man rule marked the beginning of the **Pax Romana** ("Roman Peace," 25 BCE–235 CE). This peace depended on the power of one man with enough authority to enforce an orderly competition among Roman aristocrats.

Octavian concentrated immense wealth and the most important official titles and positions of power in his own hands. Signaling the transition to a new political order in which he alone controlled the army, the provinces, and the political processes in Rome, Octavian assumed a new title, **Augustus** ("the Revered One")—much as the Qin emperor Zheng had assumed the new title of Shi Huangdi ("First August Emperor")—as well as the traditional republican roles of *imperator* ("commander in chief," or emperor), *princeps* ("first man"), and *Caesar* (a name connoting his adoptive heritage, but which over time became a title assumed by imperial successors).

Rome's subjects tended to see these emperors as heroic or even semidivine beings in life and to think of the good ones as becoming gods on their death. Yet emperors were always careful to present themselves as civil rulers whose power ultimately depended on the consent of Roman citizens and the might of the army. They contrasted themselves with the image of "king," a role the Romans had learned to detest from the monarchy they themselves had long ago overthrown to establish their Republic in 509 BCE. Nonetheless, the emperors' powers were immense.

Being a Roman emperor required finesse and talent, and few succeeded at it. Of the twenty-two emperors who held power in the most stable period of Roman history (between the first Roman emperor, Augustus, and the early third century CE), fifteen met their end by murder or suicide. As powerful as he might be, no individual emperor alone could govern an empire of such great size and population, encompassing a multitude of languages and cultures. He needed institutions and competent people to help him. In terms of sheer power, the most important institution was the army. Consequently, the emperors systematically transformed the army into a full-time professional force. Men now entered the imperial army not as citizen volunteers but as paid experts who enlisted for life and swore loyalty to the emperor and his family. It was part of the emperor's image to present himself as a victorious battlefield commander, inflicting defeat on the "barbarians" who threatened the empire's frontiers.

A Roman Town Roman towns featured many of the standard elements of modern towns and cities. Paved streets and avenues crossed at right angles; sidewalks ran between streets and houses. The houses were often several stories high and had wide windows and open balconies. All these elements can be seen in this street from Herculaneum, preserved by the eruption of nearby Mount Vesuvius in August of 79 CE, which buried the town and its inhabitants.

For most emperors, however, governance was largely a daily chore of listening to complaints, answering petitions, deciding court cases, and hearing reports from civil administrators and military commanders. At its largest in the second century CE, the Roman Empire encompassed more than forty administrative units, called provinces. As in Han China, each had a governor appointed or approved by the emperor; but unlike Han China, which had its formal Confucian-trained bureaucracy with ranks of senior and junior officials, the Roman Empire of this period was relatively understaffed in terms of central government officials. The emperor and his provincial governors depended very much on local help, sometimes aided by elite slaves and freedmen (former slaves) serving as government bureaucrats. With a limited staff of full-time assistants and an entourage of friends and acquaintances, each governor was expected to guarantee peace. However, the state relied on private companies for some essential tasks, such as the collection of imperial taxes, in which the profit motives of the publicans (the men in the companies that took up government contracts) were at odds with the expectations of fair government among the empire's subjects.

TOWN AND CITY LIFE

Due to the conditions of peace and the wealth it generated, urban settlements were clustered in core areas of the empire—central Italy, southern

Spain, northern Africa, and the western parts of present-day Turkey. The towns, whose municipal charters echoed Roman forms of government, provided the backbone of local administration for the empire. Towns often were walled, and inside those walls the streets and avenues ran at right angles. A large, open-air, rectangular area called the *forum* dominated the town center. Around it clustered the main public buildings: the markets, the main temples of principal gods and goddesses, and the building that housed city administrators. Residential areas featured regular blocks of houses, close together and fronting on the streets. Larger towns contained large apartment blocks that were not much different from the four- and five-story buildings in any modern city. In the smaller towns, sanitary standards were reasonably good.

The imperial metropolis of Rome was another matter. With well over a million inhabitants, it was larger than any other urban center of its time; Xianyang and Chang'an—the Qin and Han capitals, respectively—each had a population of between 300,000 and 500,000. While Rome's inhabitants were privileged in terms of their access to government doles of wheat and aqueduct-supplied water, their living conditions could be appalling, with people jammed into ramshackle high-rise apartments prone to collapse in a fire. Apart from crime and violence, poor sanitary conditions and the diseases that accompany them were constant threats to the population.

Towns large and small tended to have two major entertainment venues: a theater, adopted from Hellenistic culture and devoted to plays, dances, and other popular events, and an amphitheater, a Roman innovation with a much larger seating capacity that surrounded the oval performance area at its center.

Deadly Roman Entertainment The huge amphitheater (*left*) is in the remains of the Roman city of Thysdrus in North Africa (the town of El Jem in modern-day Tunisia). The wealth of the Africans under the empire enabled them to build colossal entertainment venues that competed with the one at Rome in scale and grandeur. Roman gladiators would fight, sometimes to the death, in such venues. The mosaic from Rome (*right*) shows two gladiators at the end of a full combat in which Astacius has killed Astivus. The Greek letter theta, or "th" (the circle with a crossbar through it), beside the names of Astivus and Rodan indicates that these men are dead—*thanatos* being the Greek word for "death."

In the amphitheaters, Romans could stage exotic beast hunts and gladiatorial matches for the enjoyment of huge crowds of appreciative spectators. These public entertainment facilities of Roman towns stressed the importance of gatherings in which citizens participated in civic life, as compared with the largely private entertainment of the Han elite.

SOCIAL AND GENDER RELATIONS

In Rome's civil society, laws and courts governed formal relationships, including those based on patronage and the family. By the last century BCE, the Roman state's complex legal system featured a rich body of written law, courts, and well-trained lawyers. Deeply entrenched throughout the empire, this legal infrastructure long outlasted the Roman Empire. Also firmly embedded in Roman society was a system of personal relationships that linked the rich and powerful with the mass of average citizens. Men and women of wealth and high social status acted as patrons, protecting and supporting dependents or "clients" from the lower classes. From the emperor at the top to the local municipal man at the bottom, the bonds between these groups in each city found formal expression in legal definitions of patrons' responsibilities to clients; at the same time, this informal social code raised expectations that the wealthy would be civic benefactors, sponsoring the construction of public libraries, bathhouses, and theaters.

While patronage was important, the family was at the very foundation of the Roman social order. Legally speaking, the authoritarian *pater-familias* ("father of the family") had nearly total power over his dependents, including his wife, children, grandchildren, and the slaves whom he owned. Despite this patriarchal system, Roman women, even those of modest wealth and status, had much greater freedom of action and much greater control of their own wealth and property when compared with women in most Greek city-states. As in Han China, some women in the Roman world could be well educated, literate, well connected, and in control of their own lives—despite what the laws and ideas of Roman males might suggest.

Coin Hoard Examining batches of coins buried for safekeeping reveals the range of coins in circulation at any one time. This coin hoard was found near Didcot in Oxfordshire, England. Buried about 165 CE, it contained about 125 gold coins minted between the 50s and 160s CE and represents the equivalent of about eleven years' pay for a Roman soldier. Gold coins were used for expensive transactions or to store wealth. Most ordinary purchases or payments were made with silver or brass coins.

ECONOMY AND NEW SCALES OF PRODUCTION

Rome achieved staggering transformations in agriculture and mining. The area of land surveyed and cultivated rose steadily throughout this period, as Romans spread into arid lands on the periphery of the Sahara Desert to the south and opened up heavily forested regions in present-day France and

Germany to the north. Roman agriculture and mining relied on chattel slaves—human beings purchased as private property (see Chapter 6). The massive concentration of wealth and slaves at the center of the Roman world led to the first large-scale commercial plantation agriculture and the first technical handbooks on how to run such operations for profit; it also led to dramatic slave rebellions, such as the Sicilian Revolt (135–132 BCE) and the Spartacus uprising (73–71 BCE), although the latter began among slaves in a school for gladiators. Slave-worked estates specialized in products destined for the big urban markets: wheat, grapes, and olives, as well as cattle and sheep. An impressive road system connected the far-flung parts of their empire. Milestones marked most of these roads, and complex ancient maps, called itineraries, charted major roads and distances between towns. (See Map 7.4.)

Rome mined copper, tin, silver, and gold—out of which the Roman state produced the most massive coinage system known in western Afro-Eurasia before early modern times. Public and private demand for metals was so great that traces of the air pollution generated by their mining operations remain in ice core samples taken from Greenland today. Rome's standardized currency facilitated taxation and the increased exchange of commodities and services. The economy functioned more efficiently due to this production of coins, which was paralleled only by the coinage output of Han dynasty China and its successors.

THE RISE OF CHRISTIANITY

Over centuries, Roman religion had cultivated a dynamic world of gods, spirits, and demons that was characteristic of earlier periods of Mediterranean history. **Christianity** took shape in this richly pluralistic world. Its foundations lay in a direct confrontation with Roman imperial authority: the trial of Jesus. After preaching the new doctrines of what was originally a sect of Judaism, Jesus was found guilty of sedition and executed by means of crucifixion—a standard Roman penalty—as the result of a typical Roman provincial trial overseen by a Roman governor, Pontius Pilatus.

No historical reference to Jesus survives from his own lifetime. Shortly after the crucifixion, Paul of Tarsus, a Jew and a Roman citizen from southeastern Anatolia, claimed to have seen Jesus in full glory outside the city of Damascus. Paul and the Mediterranean communities to whom he preached and wrote letters between 40 and 60 CE referred to Jesus as the Anointed One (the Messiah, in keeping with Jewish expectations) or the Christ—*ho Christos* in Greek (still the dominant language of the eastern Mediterranean region thanks to Hellenism). Only many decades later did accounts that came to be called the Gospels—such as Matthew, Mark, Luke, and John—describe Jesus's life and record his sayings. Jesus's preaching drew not only on Jewish models but also on the Egyptian and Mesopotamian image of the great king as shepherd of his people (see Chapter 3). With Jesus, this image of the good

Christianity
New religious movement originating in the Eastern Roman Empire in the first century CE, with roots in Judaism and resonance with various Greco-Roman religious traditions. The central figure, Jesus, was tried and executed by Roman authorities, and his followers believed he rose from the dead. The tradition was spread across the Mediterranean by his followers, and Christians were initially persecuted—to varying degrees—by Roman authorities. The religion was eventually legalized in 312 CE, and by the late fourth century CE it became the official state religion of the Roman Empire.

Legend

- ⊙ Important provincial capital
- • Roman trading cities
- ᚁᚁᚁ Defense works
- ᚁᚁᚁ African fortification
- —— Main Roman road
- – – – Sea-lane
- ▪ Legionary base
- ⚓ Naval base
- ▨ Roman territory under *Pax Romana*
- ▨ Territory occupied after 106 CE

Traded items

⬭ Metals		⬭ Slaves	
Y Grain		◗ Marble	
Wine		Ceramics	
Oil		⬭ Amber	
Fish			

Map labels: Antonine Wall, Hadrian's Wall, NORTH SEA, BALTIC SEA, BRITANNIA, Londinium, GERMANIA, Gesoriacum, Colonia Agrippina, ATLANTIC OCEAN, Augusta Treverorum, Limes (fortified line), GALLIA, Rhine, Danube R., Carnuntum, Burdigala, Lugdunum, Aquileia, Sirmium, Istrus, CASPIAN SEA, Narbo, Ravenna, ADRIATIC SEA, BLACK SEA, Trapezus, ARMENIA, Massilia, ITALIA, Rome, Byzantium, Ancyra, PARTHIAN/SASANIAN EMPIRE, Tarraco, Brundisium, Tigris, MESOPOTAMIA, HISPANIA, Corduba, Misenum, AEGEAN SEA, Antioch, ASSYRIA, Gades, Caesarea, Corinth, SYRIA, Euphrates R., Fossatum Africae (ramparts, ditch, and possibly wall), MEDITERRANEAN SEA, Carthage, RHODES, CRETE, CYPRUS, Damascus, Cyrene, Alexandria, AEGYPTUS, RED SEA, Nile R.

Scale: 0 — 250 — 500 Miles; 0 — 250 — 500 Kilometers

Map 7.4 *Pax Romana*: The Roman Empire in the Second Century CE

The Roman Empire enjoyed remarkable peace and prosperity in the second century CE. Economic production increased, and Roman culture expanded throughout the realm.

- According to the map, what commodities cluster in which regions? With what groups did Romans trade beyond their empire, and for what commodity in particular?
- What are some of the major sea-lanes and roads linking the different parts of the empire?
- What do you note about the locations of legionary bases and naval bases? What is the strategic value of their locations? How are the limits of empire delineated?

shepherd took on a new, personal closeness. Not a distant monarch but a preacher, Jesus had set out on God's behalf to gather a new, small flock.

Through the writings of Paul and the Gospels, both written in Greek, this image of Jesus rapidly spread beyond Palestine (where Jesus had preached only to Jews and only in the local language, Aramaic). Core elements of Jesus's message, such as the responsibilities of the well-off for the poor and the promised eventual empowerment of "the meek," appealed to many ordinary people in the wider Mediterranean world. But it was the apostle Paul who was especially responsible for reshaping this message for a wider audience. While Jesus's teachings were directed at villagers and peasants, Paul's message spoke to a world divided by religious identity, wealth, slavery, and gender differences: "There is neither Jew nor Greek, there is neither slave nor free, there is neither male nor female; for you are all one in Christ Jesus" (Galatians 3:28). This new message, universal in its claims and appeal, was immediately accessible to the dwellers of the towns and cities of the Roman Empire.

Just half a century after Jesus's crucifixion, the followers of Jesus saw in his life not merely the wanderings of a Jewish charismatic teacher, but a head-on collision between "God" and "the world." Jesus's teachings came to be understood as the message of a divine being—who for thirty years had moved (largely unrecognized) among human beings. Jesus's followers formed a church: a permanent gathering entrusted to the charge of leaders chosen by God and fellow believers. For these leaders and their followers, death offered a defining testimony for their faith. Early Christians hoped for a Roman trial and the opportunity to offer themselves as witnesses (*martyrs*) for their faith.

Persecutions of Christians were sporadic and responses to local concerns. Not until the emperor Decius, in the mid-third century CE, did the state direct an empire-wide attack on Christians. But Decius died within the year, and Christians interpreted their persecutor's death as evidence of the hand of God in human affairs. By the last decades of the third century, Christian communities of various kinds, reflecting the different strands of their movement through the Mediterranean as well as the local cultures in which they settled, were present in every society in the empire.

THE LIMITS OF EMPIRE

The limitations of Roman force were a pragmatic factor in determining who belonged in, and was subject to, the empire as opposed to who was outside it and therefore excluded. The Romans pushed their authority in the west to the shores of the Atlantic Ocean, and to the south they drove it to the edges of the Sahara Desert. In both cases, there was little additional useful land available to dominate. Roman power was blocked, however, to the east by the Parthians and then the Sasanians and to the north by the Goths and other Germanic peoples.

The Parthians   On Rome's eastern frontiers, powerful Romans, such as Marcus Crassus in the mid-50s BCE, Mark Antony in the early 30s BCE, and the emperor Trajan around 115 CE, wished to imitate the achievements of Alexander the Great and conquer the arid lands lying east of Judea and Syria. Crassus and Antony failed miserably, stopped by the Parthian Empire and its successor, the Sasanian Empire. The Romans, under Trajan, briefly annexed provinces of Armenia and Mesopotamia but abandoned them soon thereafter. The Parthian people had moved south from present-day Turkmenistan and settled in the region comprising the modern states of Iraq and Iran. Parthian social order was founded on nomadic pastoralism and a war capability based on technical advances in mounted horseback warfare. Reliance on horses made the Parthian style of fighting highly mobile and ideal for warfare on arid plains and deserts. They perfected the so-called Parthian shot: the arrow shot from a bow with great accuracy at long distance and from horseback at a gallop. On the flat, open plains of Iran and Iraq, the Parthians had a decisive advantage over slow-moving, cumbersome mass infantry formations that had been developed for war in the Mediterranean. Eventually the expansionist states of Parthia and Rome became archenemies: they confronted each other in Mesopotamia for nearly four centuries.

The Sasanians expanded the technical advances in mounted horseback warfare that the Parthians had used so successfully in open desert warfare against the slow-moving Roman mass infantry formations. King Shapur I (r. 240–270 CE) exploited the weaknesses of the Roman Empire in the mid-third century CE, even capturing the Roman emperor Valerian. One early Christian writer, Lactantius, used Valerian's fate at the hands of the Sasanians—he was forced to serve in captivity as a footstool for the Sasanian king, then flayed and stuffed after death to stand in the Sasanian throne room as a warning to ambassadors—as a lesson for what happens to those who persecute Christians. As successful as the Parthians and the Sasanians were in fighting the Romans, however, they could never challenge Roman sway over Mediterranean lands. Their decentralized political structure limited their coordination and resources, and their horse-mounted style of warfare was ill suited to fighting in the more rocky and hilly environments of the Mediterranean world. (See Chapter 8 for more on the Sasanians.)

German and Gothic "Barbarians"   In the lands across the Rhine and Danube, to the north, environmental conditions largely determined the limits of empire. The long and harsh winters, combined with excellent soil and growing conditions, produced hardy, dense population clusters scattered across vast distances. These illiterate, kin-based agricultural societies had changed little since the first millennium BCE.

As the Roman Empire fixed its northern frontiers along the Rhine and Danube Rivers, two factors determined its relationship with the Germans and Goths

Han China, the Early Roman Empire, and the Silk Roads

This chapter offers detailed information allowing for a comparison of the globalizing empires of imperial Rome and Han China. To what extent, however, were these powerful, contemporary forces in contact with each other? Because the Roman Empire and Han China were separated from one another by 5,000 miles, harsh terrain, and the powerful Parthian Empire, scholars have wondered about their interaction and knowledge of one another. (See Map 7.5.) In the nineteenth century, European archaeologists created the term "Silk Road," stressing the commercial linkages between these two great empires. (See Chapter 6 for more on the early Silk Roads.) Many twentieth-century historians have challenged this view, first, questioning the validity of the term due to its emphasis on silk exchange to the exclusion of other traded commodities, and, second, questioning the extent of direct, or even indirect, commercial exchanges between Han China and the Roman Empire. Some modern historians see the very idea of a Silk Road as part of a de-Europeanizing trend among global historians who are committed to elevating the Chinese as the true entrepreneurs of the age.

David F. Graf's recent exhaustively researched study offers an exciting new look at the Silk Roads and Chinese-Roman relations. He finds clear evidence that already by the reign of Augustus, substantial amounts of Chinese silk were available in the Mediterranean world. Graf observes that the late first-century BCE poets Virgil and Ovid have many references to Chinese silk. Another first-century BCE poet, Horace, was more explicit about the use of Chinese silks, writing that "the sheer and transparent qualities of serica [Chinese] dresses became a symbol of degeneracy of the emperors and aristocratic women, drawing condemnation." In the late first century CE, natural historian Pliny the Elder commented somewhat disdainfully on trade with the Seres (the Silk People): "Though mild in character, the Chinese still resemble wild animals in that they shun the company of the rest of humankind and wait for trade to come to them." While the *Peutinger Table*, a map (or itinerary) thought to reveal early first-century CE geographic knowledge, does not reach as far as China in the east, the Romans had sufficient information by the middle of the second century CE to enable mapmakers drawing on Ptolemy's *Geography*

to locate China and the rest of East Asia on their map of the world.

The Han emperor most responsible for beginning to expand Chinese influence westward, opening up trade routes to China's west and gaining knowledge of western regions, was Emperor Wu (r. 140–87 BCE). In 139 BCE, Wu sent an official, Zhang Qian, accompanied by more than a hundred men, on a mission to the west. The primary goal of this mission was to secure alliances with central Asian states, most importantly the Yuezhi, against the Xiongnu nomads, who threatened the Han at this time. On his way to the Yuezhi, Zhang Qian was detained by a Xiongnu chieftain for ten years, during which he married a Xiongnu woman and had children with her. While in captivity, Zhang Qian gathered information on the commodities from this region and beyond, including Bactria, India, and Persia. He shared this information when he eventually escaped and returned to the Han capital at Chang'an. In short, Wu's diplomatic and military moves expanded China's understanding of the west and knowledge of routes through which silk could be shipped westward.

A second major Chinese initiative regarding the west occurred around

on the rivers' other side. First, these small societies had only one big commodity for which the empire was willing to pay: human bodies. So the slave trade out of the land across the Rhine and Danube became immense: gold, silver, coins, wine, arms, and other luxury items flowed across the rivers in one direction in exchange for slaves flowing into the empire. Second, the wars between the Romans and these societies were unremitting, as every emperor faced the

the end of the first century CE and the beginning of the second. Here, the leading figure was General Ban Ch'ao (brother of Ban Zhao, who wrote the *Lessons for Women* excerpted at the end of this chapter). Ban Ch'ao held the office of Protector of the Western Territories between 91 and 101 CE. He brought the whole of the Tarim Basin under Chinese rule and established a set of forts on routes leading westward. He dispatched one of his adjuncts, Gan Ying, to travel westward and gather information on regions thus far unexplored by the Chinese. Gan Ying did not reach Rome, though his mission was to do so. Nevertheless, journeying only as far as the Black Sea or the Persian Gulf, he did acquire much information about Rome and its dependent states.

The Roman Empire was known to the Chinese as Da Qin. Gan Ying viewed Da Qin accurately in some respects and fantastically in others. In fact, Graf notes that the Chinese sources portrayed the Romans through their own spectacles, seeing Rome as "an idealized China, a Taoist utopia, a fictitious religious world divorced from reality." According to Chinese sources, the first direct contact with the Roman Empire occurred during the ninth year of the reign of Huandi (166 CE), when a private Roman merchant arrived at the Chinese commandery on the central Vietnamese coast with "gifts of elephant tusks, rhinoceros horn, and tortoise shell" during the reign of Marcus Aurelius. The Chinese court was unimpressed by these offerings, even wondering if the reports of Rome's power had been exaggerated.

Most of the Chinese silk that reached the Mediterranean regions came by sea via the route described in the *Periplus Maris Erythraei* (see Chapter 6), often through the Persian Gulf and Red Sea and then overland to ports along the coast of present-day Syria. But the overland route, which most scholars have called the Silk Road, was also in use at this time. The entry point for much Chinese silk was Palmyra. Trade through Palmyra reached its high point in the second century CE. To date, the largest quantity of silk found outside China and dated to ancient times was discovered in Palmyra. The polychrome silk weaving found in Palmyra can be traced back to imperial Chinese workshops. The conclusion of the most recent scholarship on the Silk Roads and Chinese-Roman relations, according to Graf, is that "there was significant movement of peoples and goods along segments of the 'Silk Route' during the Roman imperial era," but the relations between the Chinese and the Romans were remote and "indirect."

Questions for Analysis

- What is the evidence for exchange between the Romans and the Han Chinese? What were the impediments to direct interaction between Rome and China?
- What did the Romans think about trade with China? What did the Chinese think of Rome?
- How does the evidence for interconnectivity between Rome and China influence your understanding of the comparative picture of these two globalizing empires?

Explore Further

Graf, David F., "The Silk Road between Syria and China," in *Trade, Commerce, and the State in the Roman World*, edited by Andrew Wilson and Alan Bowman (2018), pp. 443–529.

Hansen, Valerie, *The Silk Road: A New History* (2012).

Liu, Xinru, *The Silk Road in World History* (2010).

Sources: David F. Graf, "The Silk Road between Syria and China," in *Trade, Commerce, and the State in the Roman World*, edited by Andrew Wilson and Alan Bowman (Oxford: Oxford University Press, 2018), pp. 443–529 (quotations are from pp. 444, 460, 477–78).

expectation of dealing harshly with these so-called barbarians. Ironically, internal conflicts within the Roman Empire ultimately prompted increasing use of "barbarians" as soldiers and even as officers who served the empire.

While the Han Empire had fallen by 220 CE, the Roman Empire in the west continued to exist politically for 250 more years, and its history became intertwined with the rise of Christianity, one of the world's universalizing religions.

Map 7.5 Imperial Rome and Eastern (Later) Han China (C. 200 CE)

Imperial Rome and the Eastern (Later) Han dynasty thrived simultaneously for about 200 years at the start of the first millennium CE. Despite their geographic spread and the Silk Roads running across Afro-Eurasia, the two empires did not have as much direct contact as one might expect.

- What major groups lived on the borders of imperial Rome and Han China?
- What were the geographical limits of the Roman Empire? Of Han China?
- Based on the map and your reading, what drew imperial Rome and Han China together? What kept them apart?

Conclusion

China and Rome both constructed empires of unprecedented scale and duration, yet they differed in fundamental ways. Starting out with a less numerous and less dense population than China, Rome relied on slaves and "barbarian" immigrants to expand and diversify its workforce. While less than 1 percent of the Chinese population were slaves, more than 10 percent of the population in the Roman Empire were slaves. The Chinese rural economy was built on a huge population of free peasant farmers; this enormous labor pool, together with a remarkable bureaucracy, enabled the Han to achieve great political stability. In contrast, the millions of peasant farmers who formed the backbone of rural society in the Roman Empire were much more loosely integrated into the state structure. They never unified to revolt against their government and overthrow it, as did the mass peasant movements of Later Han China. In comparison with their counterparts in China, the peasants in the Roman Empire were not as well connected because they lived farther apart from one another, and they were not as united in purpose. Here, too, the Mediterranean environment accented separation and difference.

In contrast with the elaborate Confucian bureaucracy in Han China, the Roman Empire was relatively fragmented and underadministered. Moreover, no single philosophy or religion ever underpinned the Roman state in the way that Confucianism buttressed the dynasties of China. Both empires, however, benefited from the spread of a uniform language and imperial culture. The process was more comprehensive in China, which possessed a single language that the elites used, than in Rome, where officially a two-language world existed: Latin in the western Mediterranean, Greek in the east. Both states fostered a common imperial culture across all levels of society. Once entrenched, these cultures and languages lasted well after the end of empire.

Differences in human resources, languages, and ideas led the Roman and Han states to evolve in unique ways. In both places, however, faiths that filtered in from the margins—Christianity and Buddhism—eclipsed the classical and secular traditions that grounded the states' foundational ideals. Transmission of these new faiths benefited from expanded communications networks. The new religions added to the cultural mix that outlasted the Roman Empire and the Han dynasty.

At their height, both states surpassed their forebears by translating unprecedented military power into the fullest form of state-based organization. Each state's complex organization involved the systematic control, counting, and taxing of its population. In both cases, the general increase of the population, the growth of huge cities, and the success of long-distance trade contributed to the new scales of magnitude, making these the world's first two long-lasting global empires. The Han were not superseded in East Asia as the model empire until the Tang dynasty in the seventh century CE. In western Afro-Eurasia, the Roman Empire was not surpassed in scale or intensity of development until the rise of powerful European nation-states more than a millennium later.

Soldier versus Barbarian On the frontiers of the Roman Empire, the legionary soldiers faced the non-Roman "barbarians" from the lands beyond. In this piece of a stone-carved picture from Trajan's Forum in Rome, we see a civilized and disciplined Roman soldier, to the left, facing a German "barbarian"—hair uncut and unkempt, without formal armor, his house a thatched hut. Frontier realities were never so clear-cut, of course. Roman soldiers, often recruited from the "barbarian" peoples, were a lot more like them than was convenient to admit, and the "barbarians" were influenced by and closer to Roman cultural models than this picture indicates.

Focus On
Comparing Han China and Imperial Rome

- Han China and imperial Rome assimilate diverse peoples to their ways and regard outsiders as uncivilized.

- Both empires develop professional military elites, codify laws, and value the role of the state (not just the ruler) in supporting their societies.

- Both empires serve as models for successor states in their regions.

- The empires differ in their ideals and the officials they value: Han China values civilian bureaucrats and magistrates; Rome values soldiers and military governors.

Key Terms

Augustus p. 318	Emperor Wu p. 304	*Pax Romana* p. 318	*res publica* p. 317
Christianity p. 322	globalizing empires p. 299	*Pax Sinica* p. 309	Shi Huangdi p. 302
commanderies p. 302	Imperial University p. 305	Punic Wars p. 316	

CHRONOLOGY

300 BCE — 200 BCE — 100 BCE

East Asia

Qin Empire of Shi Huangdi 221–207 BCE

Emperor Wu expands Han Empire 140–87 BCE

The Mediterranean

Roman state expands through Italian Peninsula 340–265 BCE

Rome eliminates Carthage (Punic Wars) 264–146 BCE

Tiberius and Gaius Gracchus attempt agrarian reforms 133–121 BCE

- **Thinking about Worlds Together, Worlds Apart and Globalizing Empires** In the six centuries between 300 BCE and 300 CE, the Han dynasty and imperial Rome united huge populations and immense swaths of territory not only under their direct control but also under their indirect influence. In what ways did this expansive unity at each end of Afro-Eurasia have an impact on the connections between these two empires? In what ways did these two empires remain worlds apart?

- **Thinking about Changing Power Relationships and Globalizing Empires** Both the Han dynasty and the Roman Empire developed new models for heightened

authoritarian control placed in the hands of a single ruler. In what ways did this authoritarian control at the top shape power relationships at all levels of these two societies? What were some potential challenges to this patriarchal, centralized control?

- **Thinking about Transformation & Conflict and Globalizing Empires** Both the Han dynasty and the Roman Empire faced intense threats along their borders. In what ways did Han interactions with nomadic groups like the Xiongnu and Roman interactions with Parthians to the east and Germans and Goths to the north affect these globalizing empires?

Go to INQUIZITIVE to see what you've learned—and learn what you've missed—with personalized feedback along the way.

| 1 CE | 100 CE | 200 CE | 300 CE |

Han Empire 206 BCE–220 CE

Wang Mang seizes the Han throne 9–23 CE

Emperor Augustus reforms the Roman state and creates an empire 30 BCE–14 CE

Roman Empire 30 BCE–476 CE

Christianity expands through the empire 30–300 CE

Global Themes and Sources

Comparing Political and Domestic Order in Han China and Imperial Rome

The four passages included here illustrate views from the Han Chinese and the Romans on how to maintain order within their respective empires. The first two philosophical treatises, on rulership and government, provide a male point of view on legitimate political authority in each empire. The other two philosophical discussions (one written by a woman) describe how to bring harmony to the most basic unit of society in both the Han dynasty and the Roman Empire—the household.

In the first excerpt, the second-century BCE Han Chinese scholar Dong Zhongshu integrates a Confucian rationale into the justification for the legitimacy of Han rule. In the second text, Marcus Tullius Cicero, a leading Roman politician from the 60s through the 40s BCE, presents his view on the responsibilities of political officeholders in the Roman state. In the third selection, Ban Zhao, a female writer from Han China, offers *Lessons for Women* drawing on philosophical ideals. No exact parallel of Ban Zhao's text survives from the Roman Empire. While there are literary fragments, short handwritten notes, and possibly epitaphs (funeral inscriptions) composed by Roman women, we must turn to a male writer, the Stoic philosopher Musonius Rufus, for the fourth text, which gives a Roman perspective on women's education comparable to the *Lessons* of Ban Zhao.

These texts offer an opportunity to compare a range of issues. To begin with, you can compare the models for political order with those for domestic order *within* each empire. For example, examining the model for political harmony between ruler and people in Dong Zhongshu's text together with the model for domestic harmony in Ban Zhao's *Lessons for Women* clarifies the relationship between the public and the private sphere. In addition, you can identify and compare the expectations for political and domestic order in Han China with those of the Roman world. Beyond a mere identification of similarities and differences, you can use what you learned in this chapter to try to explain why those similarities and differences exist and begin to explore why they matter for understanding Han China and imperial Rome on their own terms.

Analyzing Political and Domestic Order in Han China and Imperial Rome

- According to these texts, what are the characteristics of a good ruler? Of good subjects? What are the traits of a good husband? A good wife?

- According to these texts, what brings political and domestic harmony? What brings discord?

- What elements in these texts suggest that they offer an elite, primarily male, perspective? To what extent do the ideas presented in these texts extend beyond elite men to women, children, and nonelites?

- What do these texts suggest about the similarities and differences in ideas about political and domestic harmony in Han China and late republican and imperial Rome? Why do you think those similarities and differences appear in these texts?

On the Responsibilities of Rulership (c. 100 BCE), Dong Zhongshu

Dong Zhongshu was an influential adviser during the reign of Emperor Wu (r. 140–87 BCE). In the late second century BCE, Dong wrote a philosophical treatise called *Chunqiu fanlu*, or *Luxuriant Dew of the Spring and Autumn Annals*. The excerpt provided here discusses the responsibilities of a ruler, the "spontaneous punishment" and "spontaneous reward" that derive from the nature of "he who rules," and the need to attend to the "three foundations." Dong's ideas about the importance of Confucianism were manifested in Emperor Wu's creation of the Imperial University for training bureaucrats.

....

- What are the duties of "he who rules the people," and what is at stake in the fulfillment of these duties?

- What are the "three foundations," and how does a good ruler attend to them?

- What evidence do you see of Confucian values in Dong Zhongshu's model of statecraft?

....

Section 1: He who rules the people is the basis of the state. Issuing edicts and initiating undertakings, he is the pivot of all living things. The pivot of all living things, he is the source of honor and dishonor. If he errs by a millimeter, a team of horses cannot retrieve him. This is why he who acts as the people's ruler is attentive toward the fundamental, careful of the beginning, respectful of the small, and cautious of the subtle. . . . He examines [his people's] past activities to verify their present dispositions. He reckons to what extent their accomplishments are derived from former worthies. He dispels their grievances and observes the causes of their disputes. He separates their factions and clans and observes the men they esteem. He relies upon his position to order his people and employs [correct] words to establish their reputations. . . . This is called "eliminating obstructions."

Section 2: He who rules the people is the foundation of the state. Now in administering the state, nothing is more important for transforming [the people] than reverence for the foundation. If the foundation is revered, the ruler will transform [the people] as if a spirit. If the foundation is not revered, the ruler will lack the means to unite the people. If he lacks the means to unite the people, even if he institutes strict punishments and heavy penalties, the people will not submit. This is called "throwing away the state.". . . Heaven, Earth, and humankind are the foundation of all living things. Heaven engenders all living things, Earth nourishes them, and humankind completes them. . . . These three assist one another just as the hands and feet join to complete the body. None can be dispensed with because without filial and brotherly

love, people lack the means to live; without food and clothing, people lack the means to be nourished; and without rites and music, people lack the means to become complete. If all three are lost, people become like deer, each person following his own desires and each family practicing its own customs. Fathers will not be able to order their sons, and rulers will not be able to order their ministers. Although possessing inner and outer walls, [the ruler's city] will become known as "an empty settlement.". . . Although no one endangers him, he will naturally be endangered; although no one destroys him, he will naturally be destroyed. This is called "spontaneous punishment." When it arrives, even if he is hidden in a stone vault or barricaded in a narrow pass, the ruler will not be able to avoid "spontaneous punishment."

One who is an enlightened master and worthy ruler believes such things. For this reason he respectfully and carefully attends to the three foundations. He reverently enacts the suburban sacrifice, dutifully serves his ancestors, manifests filial and brotherly love, encourages filial conduct, and serves the foundation of Heaven in this way. He takes up the plough handle to till the soil, plucks the mulberry leaves and nourishes the silkworms, reclaims the wilds, plants grain, opens new lands to provide sufficient food and clothing, and serves the foundation of Earth in this way. He establishes academies and schools in towns and villages to teach filial piety, brotherly love, reverence, and humility, enlightens [the people] with education, moves [them] with rites and music, and serves the foundation of humanity in this way.

If these three foundations are all served, the people will resemble sons and brothers who do not dare usurp authority, while the ruler will resemble fathers and mothers. He will not rely on favors to demonstrate his love for his people nor severe measures to prompt them to act. Even if he lives in the wilds without a roof over head, he will consider that this surpasses living in a palace. . . . Although no one assists him, he will naturally be powerful; although no one pacifies his state, peace will naturally come. This is called "spontaneous reward." When "spontaneous reward" befalls him, although he might relinquish the throne and leave the state, the people will take up their children on their backs and follow him as the ruler, so that he too will be unable to leave them. Therefore when the ruler relies on virtue to administer the state, it is sweeter than honey or sugar and firmer than glue or lacquer. This is why sages and worthies exert themselves to revere the foundation and do not dare depart from it.

Source: Dong Zhongshu, "Responsibilities of Han Rulership," in *Sources of Chinese Tradition*, vol. 1, *From the Earliest Times to 1600*, 2nd ed., edited by Wm. Theodore de Bary and Irene Bloom (New York: Columbia University Press, 1999), pp. 298–300.

The Role of the Roman State (mid-first century BCE), Cicero

Cicero was a powerful politician and rhetorician in the mid-first century BCE. He worked his way up through the various offices a Roman nobleman would hold in his political career. Cicero's first low-ranking political office led to a series of powerful speeches against a corrupt politician who had ruled brutally in Sicily. After that, his political and oratorical career thrived: his consulship in 63 BCE forestalled an attempted coup, and his many deliberative speeches shaped legislation for two decades. Cicero is writing from a deep well of experience when he outlines the role of the Roman state in his essay *De Officiis* (*On Offices*), excerpted here.

- **What are the duties of a state to its people?**
- **What are Cicero's views on private property, taxation, and bribery?**
- **To whom do Cicero's ideas on government and office holding apply?**

[73] The man in an administrative office, however, must make it his first care that everyone shall have what belongs to him and that private citizens suffer no invasion of their property rights by act of the state. It was a ruinous policy that Philippus proposed when in his tribuneship he introduced his agrarian bill. However, when his law was rejected, he took his defeat with good grace and displayed extraordinary moderation. But in his public speeches on the measure he often played the demagogue, and that time viciously, when he said that "there were not in the state two thousand people who owned any property." That speech

deserves unqualified condemnation, for it favoured an equal distribution of property; and what more ruinous policy than that could be conceived? For the chief purpose in the establishment of constitutional state and municipal governments was that individual property rights might be secured. For, although it was by Nature's guidance that men were drawn together into communities, it was in the hope of safeguarding their possessions that they sought the protection of cities.

[74] The administration should also put forth every effort to prevent the levying of a property tax, and to this end precautions should be taken long in advance. Such a tax was often levied in the times of our forefathers on account of the depleted state of their treasury and their incessant wars. But, if any state (I say "any," for I would rather speak in general terms than forebode evils to our own; however, I am not discussing our own state but states in general)—if any state ever has to face a crisis requiring the imposition of such a burden, every effort must be made to let all the people realize that they must bow to the inevitable, if they wish to be saved. And it will also be the duty of those who direct the affairs of the state to take measures that there shall be an abundance of the necessities of life. It is needless to discuss the ordinary ways and means; for the duty is self-evident; it is necessary only to mention the matter.

[75] But the chief thing in all public administration and public service is to avoid even the slightest suspicion of self-seeking. "I would," says Gaius Pontius, the Samnite, "that fortune had withheld my appearance until a time when the Romans began to accept bribes, and that I had been born in those days! I should then have suffered them to hold their supremacy no longer." Aye, but he would have had many generations to wait; for this plague has only recently infected our nation. And so I rejoice that Pontius lived then instead of now, seeing that he was so mighty a man! It is not yet a hundred and ten years since the enactment of Lucius Piso's bill to punish extortion; there had been no such law before. But afterward came so many laws, each more stringent than the other, so many men were accused and so many convicted, so horrible a war was stirred up on account of the fear of what our courts would do to still others, so frightful was the pillaging and plundering of the allies when the laws and courts

were suppressed, that now we find ourselves strong not in our own strength but in the weakness of others.

***

[77] There is, then, to bring the discussion back to the point from which it digressed, no vice more offensive than avarice, especially in men who stand foremost and hold the helm of state. For to exploit the state for selfish profit is not only immoral; it is criminal, infamous. And so the oracle, which the Pythian Apollo uttered, that "Sparta should not fall from any other cause than avarice," seems to be a prophecy not to the Lacedaemonians alone, but to all wealthy nations as well. They who direct the affairs of state, then, can win the good-will of the masses by no other means more easily than by self-restraint and self-denial.

[78] But they who pose as friends of the people, and who for that reason either attempt to have agrarian laws passed, in order that the occupants may be driven out of their homes, or propose that money loaned should be remitted to the borrowers, are undermining the foundations of the commonwealth: first of all, they are destroying harmony, which cannot exist when money is taken away from one party and bestowed upon another; and second, they do away with equity, which is utterly subverted, if the rights of property are not respected. For, as I said above, it is the peculiar function of the state and the city to guarantee to every man the free and undisturbed control of his own particular property.

Source: Cicero, *De Officiis*, translated by Walter Miller (Cambridge, MA: Harvard University Press, 1913), pp. 249, 251, 253, 255.

PRIMARY SOURCE 7.3

Lessons for Women (c. 100 CE) Ban Zhao

A well-connected and highly educated woman, Ban Zhao wrote *Nujie*, or *Lessons for Women*, toward the end of the Han dynasty. Widowed at a young age, Ban Zhao was able to devote her attentions to literary and philosophical pursuits. Her father and brother were court historians writing the *Book of Han*, which she finalized herself following their deaths. Another brother was a prominent general who was Protector of the Western Territories (91–101 CE). Not only were Ban Zhao's life and literary career truly exceptional, but her articulation of a proper code for female behavior shaped expectations for mothers, wives, and daughters living during the Han dynasty and for hundreds of years later.

- **According to Ban Zhao, what are the characteristics of a proper woman, and how are these reflected in a woman's behavior? How does Ban Zhao compare a woman's behavior with her husband's?**

- **What Chinese philosophical concepts inform Ban Zhao's *Lessons for Women*?**

- **How, if at all, does the fact that Ban Zhao was a woman influence your reading of this text?**

Chapter I: Humility—Let a woman modestly yield to others; let her respect others; let her put others first, herself last. Should she do something good, let her not mention it; should she do something bad, let her not deny it. Let her bear disgrace; let her even endure when others speak or do evil to her. Always let her seem to tremble and to fear. (When a woman follows such maxims as these,) then she may be said to humble herself before others.

Let a woman retire late to bed, but rise early to duties; let her not dread tasks by day or by night. Let her not refuse to perform domestic duties whether easy or difficult. That which must be done, let her finish completely, tidily, and systematically. (When a woman follows such rules as these,) then she may be said to be industrious.

Let a woman be correct in manner and upright in character in order to serve her husband. Let her live in purity and quietness (of spirit), and attend to her own affairs. Let her love not gossip and silly laughter. Let her cleanse and purify and arrange in order the wine and the food for the offerings to the ancestors. (When a woman observes such principles as these,) then she may be said to continue ancestral worship.

No woman who observes these three (fundamentals of life) has ever had a bad reputation or has fallen into disgrace. If a woman fail to observe them, how can her name be honored; how can she but bring disgrace upon herself?

Chapter II: Husband and Wife—The Way of husband and wife is intimately connected with *Yin* and *Yang*, and relates the individual to gods and ancestors.

Truly it is the great principle of Heaven and Earth, and the great basis of human relationships. . . .

If a husband be unworthy then he possesses nothing by which to control his wife. If a wife be unworthy, then she possesses nothing with which to serve her husband. If a husband does not control his wife, then the rules of conduct manifesting his authority are abandoned and broken. If a wife does not serve her husband, then the proper relationship (between men and women) and the natural order of things are neglected and destroyed. . . .

Now examine the gentlemen of the present age. They only know that wives must be controlled, and that the husband's rules of conduct manifesting his authority must be established. They therefore teach their boys to read books and (study) histories. But they do not in the least understand that husbands and masters must (also) be served, and that the proper relationship and the rites should be maintained.

Yet only to teach men and not to teach women,—is that not ignoring the essential relation between them? According to the "Rites," it is the rule to begin to teach children to read at the age of eight years, and by the age of fifteen years they ought then to be ready for cultural training. Only why should it not be (that girls' education as well as boys' be) according to this principle?

Chapter III: Respect and Caution—As *Yin* and *Yang* are not of the same nature, so man and woman have different characteristics. The distinctive quality of the *Yang* is rigidity; the function of the *Yin* is yielding. Man is honored for strength; a woman is beautiful on account of her gentleness. . . .

Now for self-culture nothing equals respect for others. To counteract firmness nothing equals compliance. Consequently it can be said that the Way of respect and acquiescence is woman's most important principle of conduct. So respect may be defined as nothing other than holding on to that which is permanent; and acquiescence nothing other than being liberal and generous. Those who are steadfast in devotion know that they should stay in their proper places; those who are liberal and generous esteem others, and honor and serve (them). . . .

Chapter IV: Womanly Qualifications—A woman (ought to) have four qualifications: (1) womanly virtue; (2) womanly words; (3) womanly bearing; and

(4) womanly work. Now what is called womanly virtue need not be brilliant ability, exceptionally different from others. Womanly words need be neither clever in debate nor keen in conversation. Womanly appearance requires neither a pretty nor a perfect face and form. Womanly work need not be work done more skillfully than that of others.

To guard carefully her chastity; to control circumspectly her behavior; in every motion to exhibit modesty; and to model each act on the best usage, this is womanly virtue.

To choose her words with care; to avoid vulgar language; to speak at appropriate times; and not to weary others (with much conversation), may be called the characteristics of womanly words.

To wash and scrub filth away; to keep clothes and ornaments fresh and clean; to wash the head and bathe the body regularly, and to keep the person free from disgraceful filth, may be called the characteristics of womanly bearing.

With whole-hearted devotion to sew and to weave; to love not gossip and silly laughter; in cleanliness and order (to prepare) the wine and food for serving guests, may be called the characteristics of womanly work.

Source: Pan Chao, *Lessons for Women*, in *Pan Chao: Foremost Woman Scholar of China*, translated by Nancy Lee Swann (New York: Century, 1932), pp. 83–86.

PRIMARY SOURCE 7.4

On Women's Education in Rome (first century CE), Musonius Rufus

Musonius Rufus was a Stoic philosopher who lived during the first century CE. As a proponent of Stoicism, he valued virtue, knowledge, and civic engagement. His discourses touch on everything from the food one should consume and the proper length of one's hair and beard to women's education and marriage. His optimism about the value of training women in philosophy can be offset against the views of the satirist Juvenal, his rough contemporary, who wrote, "Don't let the woman who shares your marriage bed adhere to a set style of speaking or hurl well rounded sentences. . . . [L]et there be things in books she does not understand."

- What are the qualities a woman must possess, according to Musonius Rufus? How do those expectations compare with those placed on men in this same text?
- Why does Musonius Rufus suggest it is a good idea for a woman to be educated and to study philosophy?
- How does the fact that this text represents the views of a male philosopher influence your reading of it? Do you think these views were widely held when he wrote this text? Why or why not?

(3) When he [Musonius Rufus] was asked whether women ought to study philosophy, he began to answer the question approximately as follows. Women have received from the gods the same ability to reason that men have. We men employ reasoning in our relations with others and so far as possible in everything we do, whether it is good or bad, or noble or shameful. Likewise women have the same senses as men, sight, hearing, smell, and all the rest. . . . In addition, it is not men alone who possess eagerness and a natural inclination towards virtue, but women also. Women are pleased no less than men by noble and just deeds, and reject the opposite of such actions. Since that is so, why is it appropriate for men to seek out and examine how they might live well, that is, to practice philosophy, but not women? Is it fitting for men to be good, but not women?

Let us consider in detail the qualities that a woman who seeks to be good must possess, for it will be apparent that she could acquire each of these qualities from the practice of philosophy.

In the first place a woman must run her household and pick out what is beneficial for her home and take charge of the household slaves.

In these activities I claim that philosophy is particularly helpful, since each of these activities is an aspect of life, and philosophy is nothing other than the science of living. . . . Next, a woman must be chaste, and capable of keeping herself free from illegal love affairs, and pure in respect to the other pleasures of indulgence, and not enjoy quarrels, not be extravagant, or preoccupied with her appearance. . . . There are still other requirements: she must control anger, and not be overcome by grief, and be stronger than every kind of emotion.

That is what the philosopher's rationale entails, and the person who knows it and practices it seems to me to be perfectly controlled, whether it is a man or a woman. So much for the subject of self-control.

Now, wouldn't the woman who practices philosophy be just, and a blameless partner in life, and a good worker in common causes, and devoted in her responsibilities towards her husband and her children, and free in every way from greed or ambition? Who could be like this more than the woman who practices philosophy, so long as she truly is a philosopher, since she must inevitably think that doing wrong is worse than being wronged, because it is more disgraceful to do wrong, and to think that being inferior is preferable to being ambitious, and in addition, to love her children more than her own life? What woman would be more just than someone who behaves like that? Surely it follows that an educated woman would be more courageous than an uneducated woman. . . . Wouldn't such a woman be a great help to her husband, and an ornament to her family, and a good example to all who know her? . . .

(4) . . . But it is easy to apprehend that there are not different sets of virtues for men and women. First, men and women both need to be sensible; what need could there be for a foolish man or woman? Second, both need to live just lives. An unjust man could not be a good citizen, and a woman could not run her household well, if she did not run it justly, since if she were unjust she would do wrong to her husband, as they say Eriphyle did to hers. Third, a wife ought to be chaste, and so should a husband, for the laws punish both parties in cases of adultery. Over-indulgence in food and drink and similar problems, excesses that bring disgrace to those who indulge in them, prove that moderation is essential for every human being, whether male or female, for it is only through moderation that we can avoid excess. . . .

It is reasonable, then, for me to think that women ought to be educated similarly to men in respect of virtue, and they must be taught starting when they are children, that this is good, and that bad, and that they are the same for both, and that this is beneficial and that harmful, and that one must do this, and not that. From these lessons reasoning is developed in both girls and boys, and there is no distinction between them. Then they must be told to avoid all base action. When these qualities have been developed both men and women will inevitably be sensible, and the well-educated person, whether male or female, must be able to endure hardship, accustomed not to fear death, and accustomed not to be humbled by any disaster, for this is how one can become manly.

* * *

(13a) He said that a husband and wife come together in order to lead their lives in common and to produce children, and that they should consider all their property to be common, and nothing private, not even their bodies. . . . In marriage there must be complete companionship and concern for each other on the part of both husband and wife, in health and in sickness and at all times. . . . When such caring for another is perfect, and the married couple provide it for one another, and each strives to outdo the other, then this is marriage as it ought to be and deserving of emulation, since it is a noble union.

Sources: Musonius Rufus, in *Women's Life in Greece and Rome*, 2nd ed., edited by Mary Lefkowitz and Maureen Fant (Baltimore: Johns Hopkins Press, 1992), pp. 50–54.

Interpreting Visual Evidence

Images of Power

While their empires were gained and maintained largely through military force, Shi Huangdi and Octavian Augustus also expressed their power through elaborate construction projects. Both men commissioned elaborate mausoleums in which they were buried. Shi Huangdi's massive mausoleum, located in Chang'an (modern-day Xi'an), contained not only the emperor's tomb but also as many as 8,000 life-sized terra-cotta warriors, their horses, and chariots. One ancient Chinese historian reported that the emperor's concubines and the craftsmen who designed the tomb were buried alive with the emperor, though the tomb itself has not been excavated. Augustus's mausoleum was constructed on the Field of Mars just outside the city walls of Rome and was meant to entomb him and his close relatives upon their deaths. While his mausoleum is much more modest than Shi Huangdi's, Augustus's burial site was just one component of his elaborate building program in Rome, which included a forum with its temple to Mars the Avenger, as well as an Altar of Peace and a massive sundial.

Power and authority could also be conveyed through portraiture. The so-called Prima Porta statue of Augustus, pictured here, depicts him as a triumphant general. The statue's iconography suggests

Shi Huangdi's terra-cotta army in Xi'an.

Emperor Augustus's mausoleum in Rome (*top*, aerial view; *bottom*, entrance).

several messages: for example, the breastplate shows his adopted son and heir, Tiberius, receiving back the military standards lost to the Parthians, and the Cupid on a dolphin calls to mind Augustus's divine ancestry reaching back to Venus. While there is no statue or other image from the Qin or Han period showing what Shi Huangdi looked like, the standard picture, dating to a much later period, shows him with an elaborate headpiece, draped in a robe with a dragon on it, and with a sword at his waist.

Questions for Analysis

1. Compare the mausoleums of Shi Huangdi and Augustus. What do you think each ruler was attempting to convey through his burial monument?

2. Looking at the images of these two rulers, what in the representations gives a visual cue of their authority? Why do you think there are no contemporary images of Shi Huangdi, but so many of Augustus?

3. What do these images of Shi Huangdi and Augustus and their burial monuments suggest about the nature of power in the Roman and Chinese worlds?

Augustus of Prima Porta.

Portrait of Shi Huangdi.

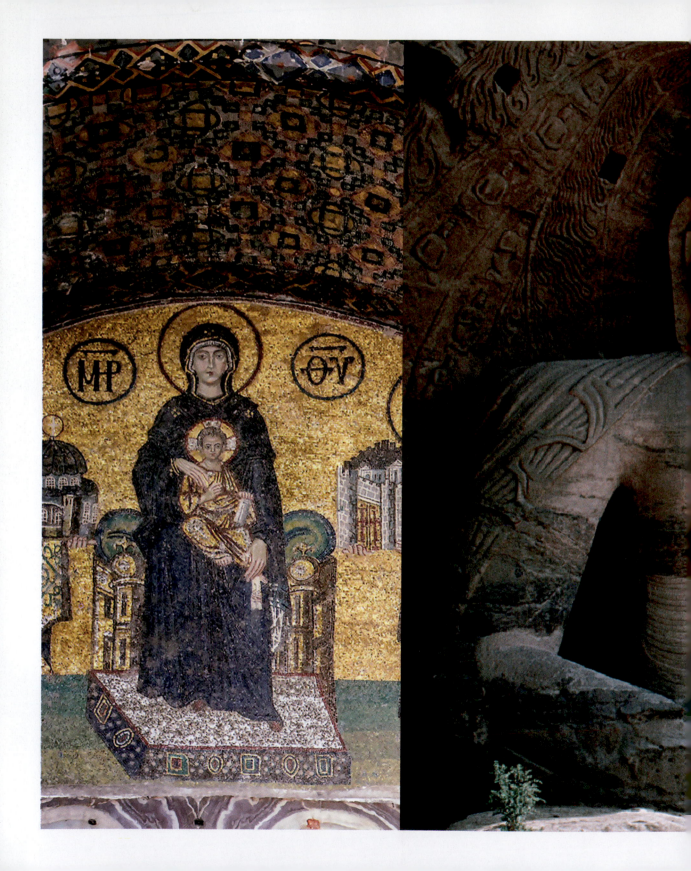

8

The Rise of Universalizing Religions

300–600 CE

Around 180 CE, twelve Christians, seven men and five women, stood trial before the provincial governor at Carthage. Their crime was refusal to worship the gods of the Roman Empire. While the governor argued for the simplicity of his religion with its devotion to "the protecting spirit of our lord the emperor," one Christian retorted that his own lord was "the king of kings and emperor of all nations." This distinction was an unbridgeable gap between the governor and the Christians. The governor condemned them all. "Thanks be to God!" cried the Christians, and straightaway they were beheaded. As the centuries unfolded, the governor's old Roman ideas of the supremacy of an emperor-lord would give way to the martyrs' devotion to their Lord God as emperor over all. As with Christianity's claim of an "emperor of all nations," a religion's capacity for universalizing—particularly its broad appeal across diverse peoples and cultures—became ever more important to its success.

From 300 to 600 CE, the entire Afro-Eurasian landmass experienced a surge of religious activity. In the west, Christianity became the state faith of the Roman Empire. In India, Vedic religion (Brahmanism) evolved into a more formal spiritual system called Hinduism. Buddhism spread across northern India, central Asia, and China. Around the same time, the peoples living in sub-Saharan Africa reached

Chapter Outline

- Religious Change and Empire in Western Afro-Eurasia
- The Silk Roads
- Political and Religious Change in South Asia
- Political and Religious Change in East Asia
- Faith and Cultures in the Worlds Apart
- Conclusion

Core Objectives

- **DESCRIBE** the characteristics of universalizing religions, and **EXPLAIN** why universalizing religions developed to varying degrees in Afro-Eurasia but did not develop elsewhere in the world.

- **ANALYZE** the relationship between empires and universalizing religions across Afro-Eurasia in this period.

- **ASSESS** the connections between political unity and religious developments in sub-Saharan Africa and Mesoamerica in the fourth to sixth centuries CE.

- **COMPARE** the unifying political and cultural developments in sub-Saharan Africa and Mesoamerica with those that took place across Eurasia in this period.

beyond their local communities, creating common cultures across wider geographical areas. The Bantu-speaking peoples, residing in the southeastern corner of present-day Nigeria, began to spread their way of life throughout the entire southern half of the landmass. Similarly, across the Atlantic Ocean, the Maya established political and cultural institutions over a large portion of Mesoamerica. Across much of the world, spiritual concerns integrated scattered communities through shared faiths. (See Map 8.1.)

This integration was facilitated in Afro-Eurasia in part by the spread of what we might call universalizing religions. Two faiths in this era—Christianity and Buddhism—fit the model for this type of religion particularly well. Six main features characterize **universalizing religions**: their appeal to diverse populations (men and women, free-born and slaves, rich and poor); their adaptability as they moved from one cultural and geographical area to another; their promotion of universal rules and principles to guide behavior that transcended place, time, and specific cultural practices; their proselytizing of new believers by energetic and charismatic missionaries; the deep sense of community felt by their converts despite, and perhaps because of, their many demands on followers; and—in the case of Christianity, and to a lesser extent Buddhism—the support given to them by powerful empires. Even as the Roman Empire and the Han dynasty began to crumble, these universalizing traditions continued to flourish.

Across Afro-Eurasia, universalizing religions were on the move. (See Map 8.2.) Religious leaders carrying written texts (books, scrolls, or tablets of wood or palm leaf) traveled widely. Christians from Persia went to China. Buddhists journeyed from South Asia to Afghanistan and used the caravan routes of central Asia to reach China. Voyages, translations, long-distance pilgrimages, and sweeping conversion campaigns remapped the spiritual landscape of the world. New religious leaders were the brokers of more universal but also more intolerant worldviews, premised on a distinct relationship between gods and their subjects. Religions and their brokers profoundly integrated societies. But they also created new ways to drive them apart.

Global Storylines

- Universalizing religions—notably Christianity and Buddhism—appeal to diverse, widespread populations and challenge the power of secular rulers and thinkers.

- Across Afro-Eurasia, these universalizing religions offer continuity even as powerful empires, specifically the Roman Empire in the west and the Han dynasty in China, are transformed.

- Along the Silk Roads, the merchants and rulers of Sasanian Persia, Sogdiana, and South Asia profoundly influence the exchange of goods, people, and ideas between east and west.

- In the "worlds apart," common cultural beliefs help unify newly organized polities in Mesoamerica and new communities of Bantu speakers in sub-Saharan Africa.

Religious Change and Empire in Western Afro-Eurasia

By the fourth century CE in western Afro-Eurasia, the Roman Empire was hardly the political and military juggernaut it had been 300 years earlier. Surrounded by peoples who coveted its wealth while resisting its power, Rome was fragmenting. So-called barbarians eventually overran the western part of the empire, but in many ways those areas still felt "Roman." Rome's endurance was a boon to the new religious activity that thrived in the turmoil of the immigrations and contracting political authority of the empire. Romans and so-called barbarians alike looked to the new faith of Christianity to maintain continuity with the past, eventually founding a central church in Rome to rule the remnants of empire.

THE APPEAL OF CHRISTIANITY

The spread of new religious ideas, including Christianity, in the Roman Empire changed the way people viewed their existence. Believing implied that an important otherworld loomed beyond the world of physical matter. Feeling contact with that other world gave worshippers a sense of worth; it guided them in this life, and they anticipated someday meeting their guides and spiritual friends there. No longer were the gods understood by believers as local powers to be placated by archaic rituals in sacred places. Many gods became omnipresent figures whom mortals could touch through loving attachment. As ordinary mortals now could hope to meet these divine beings in another, happier world, the sense of an afterlife glowed more brightly.

Christians' emphasis on obedience to their Lord God, rather than to a human ruler, sparked a Mediterranean-wide debate on the nature of religion as well as texts that explored these issues. Christians, like the Jews from whose tradition their sect had sprung, read and followed divinely inspired scriptures that told them what to believe and do, even when those actions went against the empire's laws. Christians spoke of their scriptures as "a divine codex." Bound in a compact volume or set of volumes, this was the definitive code of God's law that outlined proper belief and behavior. By the late fourth century CE, Christians had largely settled on a combination of Jewish scriptures and newly authoritative Christian texts—including history, laws, prophecy, biography, poetry, letters, and ideas about the end of days—that would come to be known as the Bible.

Another central feature of early Christianity was the figure of the **martyr**. Martyrs were women and men whom the Roman authorities executed for persisting in their Christian beliefs instead of submitting to emperor worship,

THE BIG PICTURE

What are the characteristics of universalizing religions? What was the relationship between empire and universalizing religion in the Roman Empire, Sasanian Persia, China, and elsewhere along the Silk Roads?

martyr
Literally meaning "witness," a person executed by Roman authorities for maintaining his or her Christian beliefs rather than worshipping the emperor.

The Global View

FOREST NOMADIC HUNTERS AND GATHERERS

NORTH AMERICA

R O C K Y   M O U N T A I N S

Great Lakes

Mississippi R.

St. Lawrence R.

PLAINS NOMADIC HUNTERS AND GATHERERS

Gulf of Mexico

Teotihuacán

MAYA CITY STATES

ATLANTIC OCEAN

PACIFIC OCEAN

CHAVIN

Amazon R.

SOUTH AMERICA

A N D E S   M O U N T A I N S

CELTIC PEOPLES

GERMAN

GOTHS
Carthage

KINGDOM OF THE VANDALS

SAHARA

SAHARAN PEOPLES

Niger R.

Qi	
Northern Wei Dynasty	
Sogdians	
Sasanian	
Gupta	
Eastern Roman	
Goths	
Maya	

VANDALS Kingdom

BANTU People

• City

0   1000   2000 Miles

0   1000   2000 Kilometers

Map 8.1 Empires and Universalizing Religions, 300–600 CE

....

The period from 300 to 600 CE was a time of tumultuous political change accompanied by the spread of adaptable and accessible universalizing faiths.

- Comparing this map with those in Chapters 6 and 7, which polities are new? Which polities have disappeared? Which ones have expanded or contracted?

- Where on the map are the world's empires located? Why might that be the case?

- Looking at Map 8.2, what seems to be the relationship between these empires and religions or philosophies such as Christianity, Buddhism, Judaism, Hinduism, and Confucianism?

Map 8.2 The Spread of Universalizing Religions in Afro-Eurasia, 300–600 CE

The spread of universalizing religions and the shifting political landscape were intimately connected.

- Where did Hinduism, Buddhism, and Christianity emerge? Where did Zoroastrianism and Confucianism thrive? Which traditions coexisted, and where did they coexist?

- Along what routes did each religion expand? What comparisons can you draw about the directional spread and extent of these religions' expansion?

- What features appear to foster the diffusion of these traditions? What features appear to limit their expansion?

as we saw in this chapter's opening story of the twelve Scillitan martyrs—so-called for the town in North Africa from which they came. While other religions, including Judaism and later Islam, honored martyrs who died for their faith, Christianity claimed to be based directly on "the blood of martyrs," in the words of the North African Christian theologian Tertullian (writing around 200 CE).

The story of Vibia Perpetua, a well-to-do mother in her early twenties, offers a striking example of martyrdom. Refusing to sacrifice to the Roman gods, Perpetua and her maid-servant Felicitas, along with their companions, were condemned in 203 CE to face wild beasts in the amphitheater of Carthage, a venue small enough that the condemned and the spectators would have had eye contact with one another throughout the fatal encounter. The prison diary that Perpetua dictated before her death offered to Christians and potential converts a powerful religious message that balanced heavenly visions and rewards with her concerns over responsibility to her father, brother, and infant son. The remembered heroism of women martyrs like Perpetua and Felicitas offset the increasingly male leadership—bishops and clergy—of the institutionalized Christian church.

Christian Martyrs This detail from a mosaic found in a Roman circus in North Africa shows a criminal tied to a stake and being pushed on a little cart toward a lunging leopard. Christian martyrs were treated much the same as criminals: they were executed, sometimes thrown to wild animals. How might the treatment of martyrs like criminals have influenced those watching such "entertainment"?

Constantine: From Conversion to Creed Crucial in spurring Christianity's spread was the transformative experience of Constantine (c. 280–337 CE). Born near the Danubian frontier, he belonged to a class of professional soldiers whose careers took them far from the Mediterranean. Constantine's troops proclaimed him emperor after the death of his father, the emperor Constantius. In the civil war that followed, Constantine looked for signs from the gods. Before the decisive battle for Rome, which took place at a strategic bridge in 312 CE, he supposedly had a dream in which he saw an emblem bearing the words "In this sign conquer." The "sign," which he then placed on his soldiers' shields, was the first two letters of the Greek *christos*, a title for Jesus meaning "anointed one." Constantine's troops won the ensuing battle and, thereafter, Constantine's visionary sign became known all over the Roman world. Constantine showered imperial favor on this once-persecuted faith, not only legalizing Christianity (in 313 CE) but also praising the work of Christian bishops and granting them significant tax exemptions.

creed

From the Latin *credo* meaning "I believe," an authoritative statement of belief. The Nicene Creed, formulated by Christian bishops at the Council of Nicaea in 325 CE, is an example of one such formal belief statement.

By the time that Constantine embraced Christianity, it had already made considerable progress within the Roman Empire. It had prevailed in the face of stiff competition and periodically intense persecution from the imperial authorities. Apart from the new imperial endorsement, Christianity's success could be attributed to the sacred aura surrounding its authoritative texts, the charisma of its holy men and women, the fit that existed between its doctrines and popular preexisting religious beliefs and practices, and its broad, universalizing appeal to rich and poor, city dwellers and peasants, slaves and free people, young and old, and men and women.

In 325 CE, hoping to bring unity to the diversity of belief within Christian communities, Constantine summoned all bishops to Nicaea (modern Iznik in western Turkey) for a council to develop a statement of belief, or **creed** (from the Latin *credo*, "I believe"). The resulting Nicene Creed balanced three separate divine entities—God "the father," "the son," and "the holy spirit"—as facets of one supreme being. Also at Nicaea the bishops agreed to hold Easter, the day on which Christians celebrate Christ's resurrection, on the same day in every church of the Christian world. Writing near the end of Constantine's reign, an elderly bishop in Palestine named Eusebius noted that the Roman Empire of his day would have surprised the martyrs of Carthage, who had willingly died rather than recognize any "empire of this world."

Christianity in the Cities and Beyond After 312 CE, the large churches built in every major city, many with imperial funding, signaled Christianity's growing strength. These gigantic meeting halls were called basilicas, from the Greek word *basileus*, meaning "king." They were modeled on Roman law-court buildings and could accommodate over a thousand worshippers. Inside a basilica's vast space, oil lamps shimmered on marble and brought mosaics to life. Rich silk hangings, swaying between rows of columns, increased the sense of mystery and directed the eye to the far end of the building—a splendidly furnished semicircular apse. Under the dome of the apse, which represented the dome of heaven, and surrounded by priests, the bishop sat and preached from his special throne, or *cathedra*.

These basilicas became the new urban public forums, ringed with spacious courtyards where the city's poor would gather. In return for the tax exemptions that Constantine had granted them, bishops cared for the metropolitan poor. Bishops also became judges, as Constantine turned their arbitration process for disputes between Christians into a kind of small claims court. Offering the poor shelter, quick justice, and moments of unearthly splendor in grand basilicas, Christian bishops perpetuated "Rome" for centuries after the empire had disappeared.

The spread of Christianity outside the cities and into the hinterlands of Africa and Southwest Asia required the breaking of language barriers.

In Egypt, Christian clergy replaced hieroglyphics with Coptic, a more accessible script based on Greek letters, in an effort to bridge the linguistic and cultural gap between town and countryside. In the crucial corridor that joined Antioch to Mesopotamia, Syriac, an offshoot of the Semitic language Aramaic, became a major Christian language. As Christianity spread farther north, to Georgia in the Caucasus and to Armenia, Christian clergy created written languages that are still used in those regions.

THE "FALL" OF ROME IN THE WEST

By the third and fourth centuries CE, the political and economic fabric of the old Roman world was unraveling. (See Map 8.3.) The so-called barbarian invasions of the late fourth and fifth centuries CE further contributed to that demise. These "invasions" were not so much an assault as a violent and chaotic immigration of young fighting men from the frontiers of the empire. Today the term *barbarian* implies uncultivated or savage, but its meaning in antiquity was "foreigner" (with overtones of inferiority). Inhabitants of the empire's western provinces had become accustomed to non-Roman soldiers from across the frontiers, and for them *barbarian* was synonymous with "soldier." The popular image of bloodthirsty barbarian hordes streaming into the empire bears little resemblance to reality. (See Current Trends in World History: Fall of the Roman and Han Empires: A Comparative Perspective.)

Basilica Interior The interior of a basilica, illustrated here with Old Saint Peter's Basilica in Rome, was dominated by rows of ancient marble columns and was filled with light from upper windows, so that the eye was led directly to the apse of the church, where the bishop and clergy would sit under a dome, close to the altar.

The Goths It was the Romans' need for soldiers that drew the barbarians in. The process reached a crisis point when tribes of Goths petitioned the emperor Valens (r. 365–378 CE) to let them immigrate into the empire. These Goths were no strangers to Roman influence: in fact, many had been evangelized into an anti-Nicene version of Christianity by the Gothic bishop Ulfilas, who had even translated the Bible into the Gothic language using an alphabet he developed for that purpose.

Valens, desperate for manpower, encouraged the Goths' entrance into Roman territory but mistreated these new immigrants. A lethal combination of famine and anger at the breakdown of supplies—not innate bloodlust—turned the Goths against Valens. When he marched against them at Adrianople in the hot August of 378 CE, Valens was not seeking to halt a barbarian invasion but rather intending to teach a lesson in obedience to

Map 8.3 Western Afro-Eurasia: War, Immigration, and Settlement in the Roman World, 375–450 CE

Invasions and migrations brought about the reconstitution of the Roman Empire at this time.

- Using the map, identify the people who migrated to or invaded the Roman Empire. Where were they from, and where did they go?
- How did these migrations and invasions reshape the political landscape of western Afro-Eurasia?
- Considering these effects, to what extent was the Roman depiction of these groups as "barbarians" a fair assessment?

his new recruits. The Gothic cavalry, however, proved too much for Valens's imperial army, and the Romans were trampled to death by the men and horses they had hoped to hire. As the pattern of disgruntled "barbarian" immigrants, civil war, and overextension continued, the Roman Empire in western Europe crumbled.

Rome's maintenance of its northern borders required constant efforts and high taxes. But after 400 CE the western emperors could no longer raise enough taxes to maintain control of the provinces. In 418 CE, the Goths settled in southwest Gaul as a kind of local militia to fill the absence left by the contracting Roman authority. Ruled by their own king, who kept his military in order, the Goths suppressed alarmingly frequent peasant revolts. Roman landowners of Gaul and elsewhere anxiously allied themselves with the new military leaders rather than face social revolution and the raids of even more dangerous armies. Although they practiced a different, "heretical" version of Christianity, the Goths came as Christian allies of the aristocracy, not as godless enemies of Rome.

The Huns Romans and non-Romans also drew together to face a common enemy: the Huns. Led by their king Attila (406–453 CE) for twenty years, the Huns threatened both Romans and Germanic peoples (like the Goths). While the Romans could hide behind their walls, the Hunnish cavalry regularly plundered the scattered villages and open fields in the plains north of the Danube.

Attila intended to be a "real" emperor of a warrior aristocracy. Having seized (perhaps from the Chinese empire) the notion of a "mandate of heaven"—in his case, a divine right to rule the tribes of the north—he fashioned the first opposing empire that Rome ever had to face in northern Europe. Rather than selling his people's services to Rome, Attila extracted thousands of pounds of gold coins in tribute from the Roman emperors who hoped to stave off assaults by his brutal forces. Drained both militarily and economically by this Hunnish threat, the Roman Empire in the west disintegrated only twenty years after Attila's death. In 476 CE, the last Roman emperor of the west, a young boy named Romulus Augustulus (namesake of both Rome's legendary founder and its first emperor), resigned to make way for a so-called barbarian king in Italy.

The political unity of the Roman Empire in the west now gave way to a sense of unity through the church. The Catholic Church (*Catholic* meaning "universal," centered in the bishops' authority) became the one institution to which all Christians in western Europe, Romans and non-Romans alike, felt that they belonged. The bishop of Rome became the symbolic head of the western churches. Rome became a spiritual capital instead of an imperial one. By 700 CE, the great Roman landowning families of the Republic and early empire had vanished, replaced by religious leaders with vast moral authority.

Byzantium

Modern term for the Eastern Roman Empire (which would last until 1453), centered at its "New Rome," Constantinople, which was founded in 324 CE by Constantine on the site of the Greek city Byzantium.

CONTINUITY OF ROME IN THE EAST: BYZANTIUM

Elsewhere the Roman Empire was alive and well. From the borders of Greece to the borders of modern Iraq, and from the Danube River to Egypt and the borders of Saudi Arabia, the empire survived undamaged. The new Roman Empire of the east—to which historians gave the name **Byzantium**—had its own "New Rome," Constantinople. Founded in 324 CE by its namesake, Constantine, on the Bosporus straits separating Europe from Asia, this strategically located city was well situated to receive taxes in gold and to control the sea-lanes of the eastern Mediterranean.

Constantinople was one of the most spectacularly successful cities in Afro-Eurasia, soon boasting a population of over half a million and 4,000 new palaces. Every year, more than 20,000 tons of grain arrived from Egypt, unloaded on a dockside over a mile long. A gigantic hippodrome echoing Rome's Circus Maximus straddled the city's central ridge, flanking an imperial palace whose opulent enclosed spaces stretched down to the busy shore. As they had for centuries before in Rome, emperors would sit in the imperial box, witnessing chariot races as rival teams careened around the stadium. The hippodrome also featured displays of eastern imperial might, as ambassadors came from as far away as central Asia, northern India, and Nubia.

Similarly, the future emperor Justinian came to Constantinople as a young man from an obscure Balkan village, to seek his fortune. When he became emperor in 527 CE, he considered himself the successor of a long line of forceful Roman emperors—and he was determined to outdo them. Most important, Justinian reformed Roman laws. Within six years a commission of lawyers had created the *Digest*, a massive condensation and organization of the preexisting body of Roman law. Its companion volume was the *Institutes*, a teacher's manual for schools of Roman law. These works were the foundation of what later ages came to know as "Roman law," followed in both eastern and western Europe for more than a millennium.

Reflecting the marriage of Christianity with empire was Hagia Sophia, a church grandly rebuilt by Justinian on the site of two earlier basilicas. The basilica of Saint Peter in Rome, the largest church built by Constantine two centuries earlier, would have reached only as high as the lower galleries of Hagia Sophia. Walls of multicolored marble, gigantic columns of green and purple granite, audaciously curved semicircular niches placed at every corner, and a spectacular dome lined with gleaming gold mosaics inspired awe in those who entered its doors. Hagia Sophia represented the flowing together of Christianity and imperial culture that for another 1,000 years would mark the Eastern Roman Empire centered in Constantinople.

Internal discord, as well as contacts between east and west, intensified during Justinian's reign. Justinian quelled riots at the heart of Byzantium, like the weeklong Nika riots in 532 CE in which thousands died when a group of senators used the unrest and high emotions of the chariot races as a cover for revolt. He also undertook wars to reclaim parts of the western Mediterranean and to hold off the threat from Sasanian Persia in the east (see next section). Perhaps the most grisly reminder of this increased connectivity was a sudden onslaught in 541–542 CE of the bubonic plague from the east. One-third of the population of Constantinople died within weeks. Justinian himself survived, but thereafter he ruled an empire whose heartland was decimated. Nonetheless, Justinian's contributions—to the law, to Christianity, to the maintenance of imperial order—helped Byzantium last almost a millennium after Rome in the west had fallen away.

Hagia Sophia The domed ceiling of Justinian's Hagia Sophia in Constantinople soared high above worshippers. Intricate mosaics decorated many of the walls and ceilings. The mosaic adorning the southwestern entryway, shown here, depicts Jesus sitting in the lap of the Virgin Mary. On the right, Constantine presents to Jesus and Mary his new city of Constantinople; on the left, Justinian offers his Hagia Sophia.

The Silk Roads

Although exchange along the Silk Roads had been taking place for centuries (see Chapter 6), the sharing of knowledge between the Mediterranean world and China began in earnest during this period. Wending their way across the difficult terrains of central Asia, a steady parade of merchants, scholars, ambassadors, missionaries, and other travelers transmitted commodities, technologies, and ideas between the Mediterranean worlds and China, and across the Himalayas into northern India, exploiting the commercial routes of the Silk Roads. Ideas, including the beliefs of the universalizing religions described in this chapter, traveled along with goods on these exchange routes. Christianity spread through the Mediterranean and beyond, and as we shall see later in this chapter, Buddhism and the Vedic religion (Brahmanism) also continued to spread.

The great oasis cities of central Asia played a crucial role in the effective functioning of the Silk Roads. While the Sasanians controlled the city of Merv in the west, nomadic rulers became the overlords of Sogdiana and Tukharistan and extracted tribute from the cities of Samarkand and Panjikent in the east. The tribal confederacies in this region maintained the links between west and east by patrolling the Silk Road between Iran and China. They also joined north to south as they passed through the mountains of Afghanistan into the plains of northern India. As a result, central Asia between 300 and 600 CE was the hub of a vibrant system of religious and cultural contacts covering the whole of Afro-Eurasia. (See Map 8.4.)

Map 8.4 Exchanges across Afro-Eurasia, 300–600 CE

....

Southwest Asia remained the crossroads of Afro-Eurasia in a variety of ways. Trade goods flowing between west and east passed through this region, as did universalizing religions.

- Trace the principal trade routes and maritime routes. Locate the cities of Merv, Samarkand, and Panjikent. How do the locations of these cities compare with the locations of some of the major cities of the west in the Mediterranean and the east in India and China?
- Based on your reading of the chapter and their location on the map, what role did the kingdom of Sogdiana and the Sasanian Empire play in trade in this era?
- What was the relationship between trade routes and the spread of the bubonic plague?

SASANIAN PERSIA

Beginning at the Euphrates River and stretching for eighty days of slow travel across the modern territories of Iraq, Iran, Afghanistan, and much of central Asia, the Sasanian Empire of Persia encompassed all the land routes of western Asia that connected the Mediterranean world with East Asia. In the early third century CE, the Sasanians had replaced the Parthians as rulers of the Iranian plateau and Mesopotamia. The Sasanian ruler called himself the "King of Kings of Iranian and non-Iranian lands," a title suggestive of the Sasanians' aspirations to universalism. The ancient, irrigated fields of what is modern Iraq became the economic heart of this empire. Its capital, Ctesiphon, arose where the Tigris and the Euphrates rivers come close to one another, only twenty miles south of modern Baghdad.

Symbolizing the king's presence at Ctesiphon was the 110-foot-high vaulted Great Arch of Khusro, named after Justinian's rival, Khusro I

Anoshirwan (Khusro of the Righteous Soul). As his name implied, Khusro Anoshirwan (r. 531–579 CE) exemplified the model ruler: strong and just. His image in the east as an ideal monarch was as glorious as that of Justinian in the west as an ideal Christian Roman emperor. For both Persians and Arab Muslims of later ages, the Arch of Khusro was as awe-inspiring as Justinian's Hagia Sophia was to Christians.

The Sasanian Empire controlled the trade crossroads of Afro-Eurasia and posed a military threat to Byzantium. Its Iranian armored cavalry was a fighting machine adapted from years of competition with the nomads of central Asia. These fearless horsemen fought covered from head to foot in flexible armor (small plates of iron sewn onto leather) and chain mail, riding "blood-sweating horses" draped in thickly padded cloth. Their lethal swords were light and flexible owing to steel-making techniques imported from northern India. With such cavalry, Khusro in 540 CE sacked Antioch, a city of great significance to early Christianity. The campaign was a warning, at the height of Justinian's glory, that Mesopotamia could reach out once again to conquer the eastern Mediterranean shoreline. Under Khusro II the confrontation between Persia and Rome escalated into the greatest war that had been seen for centuries. Between 604 and 628 CE, Persian forces under Khusro II conquered Egypt and Syria and even reached Constantinople before being defeated in northern Mesopotamia.

Politically united by Sasanian control, Southwest Asia also possessed a cultural unity. Syriac was the dominant language. While the Sasanians themselves were devout Zoroastrians (see Chapter 4), Christianity and Judaism enjoyed tolerance in Mesopotamia. Nestorian Christians—so named by their opponents for their acceptance of a hotly contested understanding of Jesus's divine and human nature, promoted by a former bishop of Constantinople named Nestorius—exploited Sasanian trade and diplomacy to spread their faith as far as Chang'an in China and the western coast of southern India. Protected by the Sasanian King of Kings, the Jewish rabbis of Mesopotamia compiled the monumental Babylonian Talmud at a time when their western peers, in Roman Palestine, were feeling cramped under the Christian state. The Sasanian court also embraced offerings from northern India, including the *Panchatantra* stories (moral tales played out in a legendary kingdom of the animals), polo, and the game of chess. In this regard Khusro's was truly an empire of crossroads, where the cultures of central Asia and India met those of the eastern Mediterranean.

THE SOGDIANS AS LORDS OF THE SILK ROADS

The Sogdians, who controlled the oasis cities of Samarkand and Panjikent, served as human links between the two ends of Afro-Eurasia. Their religion was a blend of Zoroastrian and Mesopotamian beliefs, touched with

Brahmanic influences. Their language was the common tongue of the early Silk Roads, and their shaggy camels bore the commodities that passed through their entrepôts (transshipment centers). Moreover, their splendid mansions such as those excavated at Panjikent show strong influences from the warrior aristocracy culture of Iran. The palace walls display gripping frescoes of armored riders, reflecting the revolutionary change to cavalry warfare from Rome to China. The Sogdians were known as merchants as far away as China.

Through the Sogdians, products from Southwest Asia and North Africa found their way to the eastern end of the landmass. Carefully packed for the long trek on jostling camel caravans, Persian and Roman goods rode side by side. Along with Sasanian silver coins and gold pieces minted in Constantinople, these exotic products found eager buyers as far east as China and Japan.

BUDDHISM ON THE SILK ROADS

South of the Hindu Kush Mountains, in northern India, nomadic groups made the roads into central Asia safe to travel, enabling Buddhism to spread northward and eastward via the mountainous corridor of Afghanistan into China. Buddhist monks were the primary missionary agents, the bearers of a universal message who traveled across the roads of central Asia, carrying holy books, offering salvation to commoners, and establishing themselves more securely in host communities than did armies, diplomats, or merchants.

At Bamiyan, a valley of the Hindu Kush—two gigantic statues of the Buddha, 121 and 180 feet in height, were carved from a cliffside during the fourth and fifth centuries CE (and stood there for 1,500 years until dynamited by the Taliban in 2001). Travelers found welcoming cave monasteries here and at oases all along the way from the Taklamakan Desert to northern China, where—2,500 miles from Bamiyan—travelers also encountered five huge Buddhas carved from cliffs in Yungang, China. While those at Bamiyan stood tall with royal majesty, the Buddhas of Yungang sat in postures of meditation. In the cliff face and clustered around the feet of the Bamiyan Buddhas various elaborately carved cave chapels housed intricate paintings with Buddhist imagery. Surrounding the Yungang Buddhas, over fifty caves sheltered more than 50,000 statues representing Buddhist deities and patrons. The Yungang Buddhas, seated just inside the Great Wall, welcomed travelers to the market in China and marked the eastern end of the central Asian Silk Road. (See Map 8.5.) The Bamiyan and Yungang Buddhas are a reminder that by the fourth century CE religious ideas were creating world empires of the mind, transcending kingdoms of this world and bringing a universal message contained in their holy scriptures.

Map 8.5 Buddhist Landscapes, 300–600 CE

Buddhism spread from its heartland in northern India to central and East Asia at this time. Trade routes, along with the merchants and pilgrims who traveled along them, fostered that spread.

- Trace the trade routes and the routes showing the spread of Buddhism. According to the map, what role did increasingly extensive trade routes play in spreading Buddhism?
- Locate the Buddhist centers and rock-carved temples, especially at Bamiyan, Dunhuang, and Yungang. How might their location on trade routes have influenced the spread of this universalizing faith?
- Trace the travels of Faxian and Xuanzang. How are their routes similar and different, and what do they suggest about growing connections between East Asia and South Asia?

Bamiyan and Yungang Buddhas Compare the Buddhas at Bamiyan (*left*) and Yungang (*right*). Note the Gandharan dress and standing pose of the Bamiyan Buddha, whose majesty and ornamentation the pilgrim Xuanzang described in the mid-seventh century CE. The Buddha in Yungang, one of five created under the emperors of the Northern Wei, sits at the foothills of the Great Wall, marking the eastern destination of the central Asian Silk Roads.

Political and Religious Change in South Asia

Core Objectives

ANALYZE the relationship between empires and universalizing religions in South Asia and China.

South Asia, especially the area of modern India, enjoyed a surge of religious enthusiasm during the Gupta dynasty, the largest political entity in South Asia from the early fourth to the mid-sixth century CE. Its kings facilitated commercial and cultural exchange, much as the Roman Empire had done in the west. Chandragupta (r. c. 320–335 CE, not to be confused with Chandragupta Maurya from Chapter 6), calling himself "King of Kings, Great King," together with his son, expanded Gupta territory to the entire northern Indian plain and made a long expedition to southern India. The development of Hinduism out of the *varna*-bound Vedic Brahmanic religion and the continued spread of Buddhism helped unify a diverse region and the diverse peoples who lived there.

THE HINDU TRANSFORMATION

During this period, the ancient Brahmanic Vedic religion spread widely in South Asia. Because Buddhism and Jainism had many devotees in cities and commercial communities (see Chapter 5), conservative Brahmans turned their attention to rural India and brought their religion into accord with rural life and agrarian values. This refashioned Brahmanic religion emerged as the dominant faith in Indian society in the form of what we today call **Hinduism**.

In the religion's new, more accessible form, believers became vegetarians, abandoning the animal sacrifices that had been important to their earlier rituals. Their new rituals were linked to self-sacrifice—denying themselves meat rather than offering up slaughtered animals to the gods, as they had done previously. Three major deities—Brahma, Vishnu, and Shiva—formed a trinity representing the three phases of the universe—birth, existence, and destruction, respectively—and the three expressions of the eternal self, or *atma*. Vishnu was the most popular of the three and was thought by believers to reveal himself through various avatars (or incarnations).

Poets during the reign of Chandragupta, a generous patron of the arts, expressed the religious sentiments of the age. Working with the motifs and episodes from two early epics, the *Mahabharata* and the *Ramayana* (see Chapter 4), these poets addressed new problems and praised new virtues. What had once been lyric dramas and narrative poems written to provide entertainment now served as collective memories of the past and underscored Brahmanic religious beliefs about ideal behavior. The heroes and deeds that the poets praised in classical Sanskrit served as models for kings and their subjects.

A central part of the *Mahabharata* revolves around the final battle between two warring confederations of Vedic tribes. The hero Arjuna, the best warrior of one of these confederations, is unwilling to fight against his enemies because many of them are his cousins. At a crucial moment on the battlefield, Krishna—an avatar of Vishnu, who was Arjuna's charioteer and religious teacher—intervenes, commanding Arjuna to slay his foes, even those related to him. Krishna reminds Arjuna that he belongs to the Kshatriya *varna*, the warriors put on earth to govern and to fight against the community's enemies. The *Bhagavad Gita*, which preserves this tale of Krishna and Arjuna, became part of the authoritative literature of Hindu spirituality. It prescribed religious and ethical teachings and behaviors, called *dharma* in Hinduism, for people at every level of society.

Hindus also adopted the deities of other religions, even regarding the Buddha as an avatar of Vishnu. Thus, the Hindu world of gods became larger and more accessible than the earlier Vedic one, enabling more believers to share a single faith. Hindus did not wish to approach the gods only through the sacrificial rituals at which Brahmans alone could officiate. Individuals, therefore, also developed an active relationship with particular gods through personal devotion, in a practice called *bhakti*. This individualized, personal *bhakti* devotion attracted Hindus of all social strata, while the mythological literature wove the deities into a heavenly order presided over by the trinity

Hinduism
Ancient Brahmanic Vedic religion that emerged as the dominant faith in India in the third century CE. It reflected rural and agrarian values and focused on the trinity of Brahma (birth), Vishnu (existence), and Shiva (destruction).

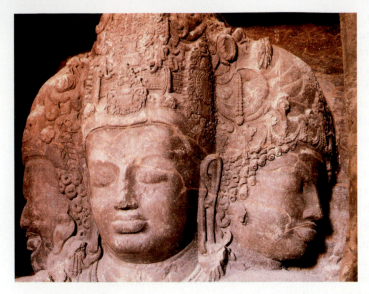

Hindu Statue This huge statue of a three-headed god in a cave on a small island near Mumbai represents the theology of Hinduism. Brahma, the creator; Vishnu, the keeper; and Shiva, the destroyer are all from one atma, or the single soul of the universe.

of Brahma, Vishnu, and Shiva as universal gods. During this period Hinduism lived side by side with Buddhism, competing for followers by building ornate temples and sculptures of gods and by holding elaborate rituals and festivals.

While the stories of human-divine interaction, the larger number of gods, and the development of *bhakti* devotion made Hinduism more personal than the old Vedic Brahmanism had been, Hinduism was still very much rooted in the hierarchical *varna* system. While Hinduism was more accessible to a wider audience than Brahmanism had been, there were limits to how universalizing this tradition could be since the *varna* system, with which it was closely intertwined, did not extend outside South Asia.

THE TRANSFORMATION OF THE BUDDHA

During the Gupta period, the two main schools of Buddhism—the Mahayana (Greater Vehicle) school and the Hinayana (Lesser Vehicle) school—acquired universalizing features that were different from what the Buddha had preached centuries earlier. The historical Buddha was a sage who was believed to enter *nirvana*, ending the pain of consciousness. In the earliest Buddhist doctrine, god and supernatural powers were not a factor (see Chapter 5). But by 200 CE a crucial transformation had occurred: his followers started to view the Buddha as a god. Mahayana Buddhism not only recognized the Buddha as a god but extended worship to the many bodhisattvas who bridged the gulf between the Buddha's perfection and the world's sadly imperfect peoples (see Chapter 6). It was especially in the Mahayana school that Buddhism became a universalizing religion, whose adherents worshipped divinities, namely the Buddha and the bodhisattvas, rather than recognizing them merely as great men.

Some Buddhists fully accepted the Buddha as god but could not accept the divinity of bodhisattvas; these adherents belonged to the more monkish school of old-fashioned **Hinayana Buddhism**, later called Theraveda in Sri Lanka and Southeast Asia. Rejecting Sanskrit authoritative scripture on the supernatural power of bodhisattvas, they remained loyal to the early Buddhist texts, which were probably based on the words of the Buddha himself. Hinayana temples barred all colorful idols of the bodhisattvas and other

Hinayana Buddhism
(termed "Lesser Vehicle" Buddhism by the Mahayana/ "Greater Vehicle" school; also called Theraveda Buddhism) A more traditional, conservative branch of Buddhism that accepted the divinity of the Buddha but not of bodhisattvas.

heavenly beings; they contained images of only the Buddha. Buddhism, with its vibrant competing Mahayana and Hinayana schools, spread along the Silk Roads far beyond its South Asian point of origin.

CULTURE AND IDEOLOGY INSTEAD OF AN EMPIRE

Unlike China and Rome, India did not have a centralized empire that could establish a code of laws and an overarching administration. Instead, what emerged to unify South Asia was a distinctive form of cultural synthesis—called by scholars the **Sanskrit cosmopolis**—based on Hindu spiritual beliefs and articulated in the Sanskrit language.

Spearheading this development from 300 to 1300 CE were priests and intellectuals well versed in the Sanskrit language and literary and religious texts. As Sanskrit spread, it stepped beyond religious scriptures and became the public language of politics, although local languages retained their prominence in day-to-day administration and everyday life. Kings and emperors used Sanskrit to express the ideals of royal power and responsibility. Rulers issued inscriptions in it, recording their genealogies and their prestigious acts. Poets celebrated ruling dynasties and recorded important moments in the language.

The emergence of Sanskrit as the common language of the elites in South and Southeast Asian societies also facilitated the spread of Brahmanism. Possessing an unparalleled knowledge of the language, Brahmans circulated their ideals on morality and society in Sanskrit texts, the most influential of which was the **Code of Manu**. This document records a discourse given by the sage, Manu, to a gathering of wise men seeking answers on how to organize their communities after the destruction wrought by a series of floods. The text lays out a set of laws designed to address the problems of assimilating strangers into expanding towns and refining the hierarchical Brahmanic order as the agricultural frontier expanded. Above all, the Code of Manu offered guidance for living within the *varna* and *jati* system, including whom to marry, which profession to follow, and even what to eat. The Code of Manu provided mechanisms for absorbing new groups into the system of *varnas* and *jatis*, thus propelling Hinduism into every aspect of life, far beyond the boundaries of imperial control.

During this period, settlers from northern India pushed southward into lands formerly outside the domain of the Brahmans. In these territories Brahmans encountered Buddhists and competed with them to win followers. The mixing of these two groups and the intertwining of their ideas and institutions ultimately created a common "Indic" culture organized around a shared vocabulary addressing concepts such as the nature of the universe and the cyclical pattern of life and death. Much of this mixing of ideas took place in schools, universities, and monasteries. The Buddhists already possessed large

Sanskrit cosmopolis
Cultural synthesis based on Hindu spiritual beliefs expressed in the Sanskrit language that unified South Asia in place of a centralized empire.

Code of Manu
Brahmanic code of law that took shape in the third to fifth centuries CE and expressed ideas going back to Vedic times. Framed as a conversation between Manu (the first human and an ancient lawgiver) and a group of wise men, it articulated the rules of the hierarchical *varna* system.

monasteries, such as Nalanda in northeast India, where 10,000 residential faculty and students assembled, and more than 100 smaller establishments in southeast India housing at least 10,000 monks. In these settings Buddhist teachers debated theology, cosmology, mathematics, logic, and botany. Brahmans also established schools where similar intellectual topics were discussed and where Buddhist and Brahmanic Hindu ideas were fused.

The resulting Indic cultural unity covered around 1 million square miles (an area as great as the extent of the Roman Empire) and a highly diverse population. Although India did not have a single governing entity like China and did not adhere to one religious system as in the Christian Roman Empire, it was developing a distinctive culture based on the intertwining of two shared, accessible, and—to varying degrees—universalizing religious traditions.

Political and Religious Change in East Asia

With the fall of the Han dynasty, China experienced a period of political disunity and a surge of new religious and cultural influences. In the first century CE, Han China was the largest state in the world, with as great a population as the Roman Empire had at its height. Its emperor extracted an annual income of millions of pounds of rice and bolts of cloth and conscripted millions of workers whose families paid tribute through their labor. Later Chinese regarded the end of the Han Empire as a disaster just as great as western Europeans regarded the end of the Roman Empire. In post-Han China, new influences arrived via the Silk Roads through contact with nomadic "barbarians" and the proselytizing of Buddhist monks, and new forms of Daoism responded to a changing society.

THE WEI DYNASTY IN NORTHERN CHINA

After the fall of the Han in 220 CE, several small kingdoms—at times as many as sixteen of them—competed for control. Civil wars raged for roughly three centuries, a time called the Six Dynasties period (220–589 CE), when no single state was able to conquer more than half of China's territory. The most successful regime was that of the Tuoba, a people originally from Inner Mongolia. In 386 CE, the Tuoba founded the Northern Wei dynasty, which lasted 150 years and administered part of the Han territory. Although technically Mongolian "barbarians," the Northern Wei had lived for generations within the Chinese orbit as tributary states.

The Northern Wei maintained many Chinese traditions of statecraft and court life: they taxed land and labor on the basis of a census, conferred official ranks and titles, practiced court rituals, preserved historical archives, and promoted classical learning and the use of classical Chinese for record keeping and political discourse. Though they were nomadic warriors, they adapted their large standing armies to city-based military technology, which required drafting huge numbers of workers to construct dikes, fortifications, canals, and walls.

Among the challenges facing the Northern Wei rulers was the need to consolidate authority over their own highly competitive nomadic people. One strategy was to make their own government more "Chinese." Under Emperor Xiaowen (r. 471–499 CE), for example, the Tuoba royal family adopted the Chinese family name of Yuan and required all court officials to speak Chinese and wear Chinese clothing. However, the Tuoba warrior families resisted these policies. Xiaowen also rebuilt the old Han imperial capital of Luoyang based on classical architectural models dating from the Han dynasty and made it the seat of his government.

Wei rulers sought stronger relationships with the Han Chinese families of Luoyang that had not fled south. The Wei offered them political power as officials in the Wei bureaucracy and more land. For example, the Dowager Empress Fang (regent for Xiaowen 476–490 CE) attempted progressive land reforms that offered land to all young men—whether Han or Wei—who agreed to cultivate it. But even this plan failed to bridge the cultural divides between the "civilized" Han Chinese of Luoyang and the "barbarian" Tuoba Wei, because the latter showed no interest in farming.

Members of the Wei court supported Buddhist temples and monumental cave sites in an appeal to their Tuoba roots while also honoring Confucian traditions dating to the ancient Zhou period. Emperor Xiaowen's death cut short his efforts to unify the north. Several decades of intense fighting among military rulers followed, leading ultimately to the downfall of the Northern Wei dynasty.

CHANGING DAOIST TRADITIONS

Daoism, a popular Chinese religion under the Han and a challenge to the Confucian state and its scholar-officials, lost its political edge and adapted to the new realities in this period of disunity. Two new traditions of Daoist thought flourished in this era of self-doubt. The first was organized and community oriented, and involved heavenly masters who as mortals guided local religious groups or parishes. Followers sought salvation through virtue, confession, and ceremonies, including a mystical initiation rite. A second Daoist tradition was more individualistic, attempting to reconcile Confucian classical learning with Daoist religious beliefs in the occult and magic. It used trance and meditation to control human physiology. Through such mental and physical efforts, a skilled practitioner could accumulate enough religious merit to prolong his life. The concept of religious merit and demerit in Daoist circles echoed the Buddhist notion of karmic retribution (the cosmic assessment of

Fall of the Roman and Han Empires: A Comparative Perspective

Both the Roman Empire and the Han Empire had an extraordinary number of similarities. Initially, they knew little about each other. With 5,000 miles of steppes, mountains, and deserts separating the empires, their knowledge of each other was based on traded commodities. Although they arose at slightly different times (the Han Empire at the end of the third century BCE and the Roman Empire at the end of the first century BCE), they both lasted approximately 400 years and had the same population (around 60 million, together half of the entire world population). The rulers of both empires resided in capital cities that were the largest in the world (Rome and Chang'an, each at 1 million). Both rulers were thought to have godlike powers, aspired to domination of their known world, and commanded huge militaries. Moreover, both empires were so powerful and long-lasting that subsequent Chinese and western European rulers sought to revive them. In China the imperial system, in spite of periods of considerable turmoil and fragmentation (especially from 300 to 600 CE), lasted more than 2,000 years, from the establishment of the Qin dynasty in 221 BCE to the abdication of the last Qing emperor on February 12, 1912, when the Chinese republic came into existence. In contrast, in western Europe, while political leaders sought to revive the

fallen Roman Empire and claimed to have done so first under Charlemagne and later under the Habsburgs as the Holy Roman Empire, these states were never true empires.

A variety of reasons exist for the endurance of China's imperial system and the failure of western European leaders to revive anything that resembled the Roman Empire. Three reasons stand out. First, China and Rome emerged as empires in markedly different ways. Second, during their four centuries of existence, their ruling elites created different political institutions and were guided by different ideologies. Third, their collapses were notably different.

The Road to Empire

The short-lived Qin Empire (221–207 BCE) cleared the way for the Han Empire and created the institutional foundations and solidified the ideological bases for the Han and subsequent dynasties. The Qin arose after the Shang and Zhou dynasties, which were important states but far from being true empires. Although the rulers of the Zhou dynasty, founded in 1045 BCE, remained on the throne until the third century BCE, the Zhou ceased to be a dynamic and powerful state in the eighth century BCE, giving way to the Spring and Autumn period (722–481 BCE) and the Warring States period (403–221 BCE). The Warring

States period was crucial in establishing the ideological foundations for China's imperial history. During this long period China experienced constant warfare, in which the size of armies and the number of casualties skyrocketed. According to China scholar Yuri Pines, the carnage of warfare led all the major Chinese intellectuals and scholar-officials, including Confucius, Mencius, Laozi, Mo Di, and the Legalists, to "endorse the idea that a single savior-like person would bring about unity and peace." These Axial Age philosophers in China created the ideological foundations for empire—foundations that compelled China's ruling elites to return over and over again to imperial rule through an emperor.

In contrast, the Roman state emerged as the dominant city-state in the Italian Peninsula beginning in the fifth century BCE. Rome warred continuously with other city-states on the peninsula right down to the first century CE (against Etruscans, Samnites, Greeks in southern Italy, and Italian allies). Additionally, Rome warred against other groups in the Mediterranean, from the Carthaginians in North Africa and Spain to the Hellenistic successor kingdoms to the east. Nonetheless, Rome's experience with warfare did not produce foundational philosophies. Moreover, its political ideology, drawn to some extent from the Greek city-states of the Axial Age, was based on republicanism.

The empire emerged only at the end of the first century BCE.

Different Imperial Political Institutions and Ideologies

Geography was an important difference between Rome and Han China. The Roman Empire was not easy to govern territorially. Its ruler had to govern both sides of the Mediterranean Sea. In addition, Italy was a peninsula, Iberia was separated from northern Europe by the Pyrenees, and the British Isles were divided from mainland Europe by the English Channel. China had geographical barriers also. It was crisscrossed by rivers, mountains, and deserts that created diverse regional cultures. Thus, like the rulers of the Roman Empire, China's ruling elites had to impose their will on disparate ethnic and linguistic groups. Ideology, handed down from the Warring States period, proved immensely crucial in solidifying this unity. Equally important, however, was the role of the scholar-gentry class, who insisted that a detailed knowledge of the classics was the only way to enter the ruling class. Moreover, China was more closely governed than its Roman counterpart. The central and local governments were staffed by around 130,000 individuals, of whom 20,500 worked for the central administration. The far-flung Chinese bureaucracy made the Roman Empire seem undergoverned.

Rome was much more of a patchwork empire, governed in cooperation with local elites and nowhere as dependent on direct administration or a complex bureaucracy. Rome maintained its authority through its immense army and military coercion rather than ideological preeminence. Even considering Rome's late third-century CE system of more than 100 provinces managed as twelve dioceses, Rome never developed the kinds of administrative institutions that existed in the Han Empire.

The Decline and Fall of the Roman and Han Empires

While both the Roman and Han Empires lasted four centuries, their overthrows were decidedly different. Both succumbed to nomadic pastoral peoples—the Goths overwhelming the Roman state and the northern steppe peoples bringing the Han to their knees. European nomads entered the Roman Empire and destroyed Rome's power to rule in the west, while Christianity offered a degree of continuity. In the east, steppe peoples who invaded China did not destroy the Han imperial system but instead emulated it, even while maintaining their traditional political, social, and ideological practices in their homelands. Ultimately, western Europe and China diverged dramatically after the fall of the Roman and Han Empires. Europe ended up with many fledgling states and vernacular languages, but one God, one papacy, and one dominant religion. In contrast, China had many minor gods, but one emperor, one dominant language, and a long-lasting Confucian bureaucracy.

Questions for Analysis

- What are some of the similarities and differences in the processes through which the Roman and Han Empires formed, were maintained, and fell?
- What might account for the differing outcomes in the aftermaths of the fall of the Han Empire and the fall of the Roman Empire in the west?

Explore Further

Pines, Yuri, *Envisioning Eternal Empire: Chinese Political Thought of the Warring States Era* (2009).

Pines, Yuri, *The Everlasting Empire: The Political Culture of Ancient China and Its Imperial Legacy* (2012).

Rosenthal, Jean-Laurent, and R. Bin Wong, *Before and Beyond Divergence: The Politics of Economic Change in China and Europe* (2011).

Scheidel, Walter (ed.), *Rome and China: Comparative Perspectives on Ancient World Empires* (2009).

Source: Yuri Pines, *Envisioning Eternal Empire: Chinese Political Thought of the Warring States Era* (Honolulu: University of Hawaii Press, 2009), p. 26.

Mogao Caves at Dunhuang
This scene comes from Mogao Cave 285 (c. 540 CE, during the Northern Wei dynasty) at Dunhuang on the Silk Roads. Winged apsaras (heavenly spirits) float above a landscape of brilliant blue-hued mountains and deer-filled forests. On the left, five robbers, who have been blinded by troops in a previous scene, wander aimlessly, but in the central scene, their sight having been restored after adopting Buddhism, they sit peacefully at the foot of the Buddha. Hundreds of beautifully painted caves were created at Mogao over several centuries through the painstaking devotion of monks and with the sponsorship of wealthy donors, whose names are often inscribed on the walls.

one's acts in this life that determines one's rebirth into a better or worse next life). For the Daoists, however, eternal life was the ultimate goal, and not the Buddhists' ideal of release from the cycle of life, death, and rebirth.

BUDDHISM IN CHINA

Buddhism's universalizing message appealed to many people living in the fragmented Chinese empire. By the third and fourth centuries CE, travelers from central Asia who had converted to Buddhism had become frequent visitors in the streets and temples of the competing capitals: Chang'an, Luoyang, and Nanjing. Spreading the faith required intermediaries, endowed with texts and explanations, to convey its message. Kumarajiva (344–413 CE), a renowned Buddhist scholar and missionary, was the right man, in the right place, at the right time to spread Buddhism in China—where it already coexisted with other faiths.

Kumarajiva's influence on Chinese Buddhist thought was critical. Not only did he translate previously unknown Buddhist texts into Chinese, but he also clarified Buddhist terms and philosophical concepts. He and his disciples established a Mahayana branch known as Madhyamika (Middle Way) Buddhism, which used irony and paradox to show that reason was limited. For example, they contended that all reality was transient because nothing remained unchanged over time. They sought enlightenment by means of transcendental visions and spurned experiences in the material world of sights and sounds.

Kumarajiva represented the beginning of a profound cultural shift. After 300 CE, Buddhism began to expand in northwestern China, taking advantage of imperial disintegration and the decline of Daoism and state-sponsored Confucian classical learning. The Buddhists stressed devotional acts, such as daily prayers and mantras, which included seated meditations in solitude requiring mind and breath control, as well as the saving power of the Buddha and the saintly bodhisattvas who postponed their own salvation for the sake of others. They even encouraged the Chinese to join a new class—the clergy. The idea that persons could be defined by faith rather than kinship was not new in Chinese society, but it had special appeal in a time of serious crisis like that of the turbulent Six Dynasties period. In the south, the immigrants from the north found that membership in the Buddhist clergy and monastic orders offered a way to restore their lost prestige.

Even more important, in the northern states—now part Chinese, part "barbarian"—Buddhism provided legitimacy. With Buddhists holding prominent positions in government, medicine, and astronomy, the Wei ruling houses could espouse a philosophy that was just as legitimate as that of the Han Chinese. As a Tuoba who ruled at the height of the Northern Wei in the early sixth century CE, Emperor Xuanwu was an avid Buddhist who made Mahayana Buddhism the state religion during his reign.

In 643 CE, the Chinese Buddhist Xuanzang brought back to Chang'an (then the world's largest city) an entire library of Buddhist scriptures—527 boxes of writings and 192 birch-bark tablets—that he had collected on a pilgrimage to Buddhist holy sites in South Asia. He lodged them in the Great Wild Goose Pagoda and immediately began to translate every line into Chinese. Although the importation of these texts from India was profoundly important, Buddhism did not seek to be the same in all places and at all times. On the contrary, as the expression of a cosmic truth as timeless and varied as the world itself, Buddhism showed a high level of adaptability, easily absorbing the gods and the wisdom of every country it touched.

By 400 CE, China had more than 1,700 Buddhist monasteries and about 80,000 monks and nuns. By contrast, in 600 CE (after two centuries of monastic growth), Gaul and Italy—the two richest regions of western Europe—had,

Xuanzang This painting portrays the Chinese pilgrim Xuanzang accompanied by a tiger on his epic travels in South Asia to collect important Buddhist scriptures.

altogether, only 320 monasteries, many with fewer than 30 monks. Yet, in the two ends of Afro-Eurasia the principal bearers of the new religions were monks. Set apart from "worldly" affairs in their refuges, they enjoyed the pious support of royal courts and warriors whose lifestyles differed sharply from their own. Through their devoted faith in the divine and the support of secular rulers, these two universalizing religions—Buddhism and Christianity—would continue to grow, flourish, and revitalize themselves.

Faith and Cultures in the Worlds Apart

Core Objectives

ASSESS the connections between political unity and religious developments in sub-Saharan Africa and Mesoamerica in the fourth to sixth centuries CE.

In most areas of sub-Saharan Africa and Mesoamerica, it was not easy for ideas, institutions, peoples, and commodities to circulate broadly. Thus, we do not see the development of universalizing faiths like those in Eurasia. Rather, belief systems and their associated deities remained local. Nonetheless, sub-Saharan Africans and peoples living in Mesoamerica revered prophetic figures who, they believed, communicated with deities and brought to humankind divinely prescribed rules of behavior. Peoples in both regions honored beliefs and rules that were passed down orally across generations. These unifying spiritual traditions guided behavior and established social customs.

BANTUS OF SUB-SAHARAN AFRICA

Today, most of Africa south of the equator is home to peoples who speak some variant of more than 400 Bantu languages. Although scholars using oral traditions and linguistic evidence can trace a clear narrative of the Bantu people no farther back than 1000 CE, it appears that the first Bantu speakers lived in the southeastern part of modern Nigeria, where about 4,000 or 5,000 years ago they likely shifted from hunting, gathering, and fishing to practicing settled agriculture. Preparing just one acre of tropical rain forest for farming required removing 600 tons of moist vegetation. To accomplish this arduous task, Bantus used mainly machetes, billhooks, and controlled burning. Bantus cultivated woodland plants such as yams and mushrooms, as well as palm oils and kernels. Yet the difficulties in preparing the land for settled agriculture did not keep the Bantus from being the most expansionist of African peoples. (See Map 8.6.)

Bantu Migrations Following riverbeds and elephant trails, Bantu migrants traveled out of West Africa in two great waves. One wave moved across the Congo forest region to East Africa. Their knowledge of iron smelting enabled them to deploy iron tools for agriculture. Because their new habitats supported a mixed economy of animal husbandry and sedentary agriculture, this group became relatively prosperous. A second wave of migrants moved

Map 8.6 Bantu Migrations in Africa

The migration of Bantu speakers throughout much of sub-Saharan Africa in the first millennium CE dramatically altered the cultural landscape.

- According to the map, where did the Bantu speakers originate? Into which areas did the Bantu speakers migrate? Why might they have migrated in that direction?
- Trace the spread of ironworking with the Bantu speakers. How might ironworking have enabled Bantu speakers to dominate the peoples already living there?
- What range of topography and ecological zones did the Bantu speakers encounter as they moved southward and eastward? How might that have influenced their spread into new regions?

southward through the rain forests in present-day Congo, eventually reaching the Kalahari Desert. The tsetse fly–infested environment did not permit them to rear livestock, so they were limited to subsistence farming. These Bantus learned to use iron later than those who had moved to the Congo region in the east.

Precisely when these **Bantu migrations** began is unclear, but once under way, the travelers moved rapidly. Genetic and linguistic evidence reveals that they absorbed most of the hunting and gathering populations who originally inhabited these areas. What enabled the Bantus to prevail and prosper was their skill as settled agriculturalists. They adapted their farming techniques and crops to widely different environments, including the tropical rain forests of the Congo River basin, the savanna lands of central Africa, the high grasslands around Lake Nyanza, and the highlands of Kenya.

For the Bantu of the rain forests of Central Africa (the western Bantu), the introduction of the banana plant from tropical South and Southeast Asia was decisive. Linguistic evidence suggests that it first arrived in the Upper Nile region and then traveled into the rest of Africa with small groups migrating from one favorable location to another; the earliest proof of its presence is a record from the East African coast dating to 525 CE. The banana adapted well to the equatorial rain forests, withstanding the heavy rainfalls, requiring less clearing of rain forests, reducing the presence of the malaria-carrying *Anopheles* mosquito, and providing more nutrients than the indigenous yam crop. Exploiting banana cultivation, the western Bantu filled the equatorial rain forests of central Africa between 500 and 1000 CE.

Bantu Cultures, East and West The widely different ecological zones into which the Bantu-speaking peoples spread made it difficult to establish the same political, social, and cultural institutions. In the Great Lakes area of the East African savanna lands and the savanna lands of Central Africa, where communication was relatively easy, the eastern Bantu speakers developed centralized polities whose kings ruled by divine right. They moved into heavily forested areas similar to those they had left in southeastern Nigeria. These locations supported a way of life that remained fundamentally unaltered until European colonialism in the twentieth century.

The western Bantu-speaking communities of the lower Congo River rain forests formed small-scale societies based on family and clan connections. They organized themselves socially and politically into age groups, the most important of which were the ruling elders. Within these age-based networks, individuals who demonstrated talent in warfare, commerce, and politics provided leadership. Certain rights and duties were imposed on different social groups based mainly on their age. Males moved from child to warrior to ruling elder, and females transitioned from child to married child-bearer. Bonds among age groups were powerful, and movement from one to the next was marked by meaningful and well-remembered rituals. So-called big men, supported by followers attracted by their valor and wisdom as opposed to inheritance, promoted territorial expansion. Individuals who could attract a large community of followers, marry many women, and sire many children could lead their bands into new locations and establish dominant communities.

These rain forest communities held a common belief that the natural world was inhabited by spirits, many of whom were their own heroic ancestors. These spiritual beings intervened in mortals' lives and required constant appeasement. Diviners helped men and women understand the spirits' ways, and charms warded off the misfortune that aggrieved spirits might wish to inflict. Diviners and charms also protected against the injuries that living beings—witches and sorcerers—could inflict. In fact, much of the misfortune that occurred in the Bantu world was attributed to these malevolent forces. The Bantu migrations ultimately filled up more than half the African landmass. The Bantus spread a political and social order based on family and clan structures that rewarded individual achievement—and maintained an intense relationship to the world of nature that they believed was imbued with supernatural forces.

MESOAMERICANS

As in sub-Saharan Africa, the process of settlement and expansion in Mesoamerica differed from that in the large empires of Afro-Eurasia. Mesoamerica had no integrating artery of a giant river and its floodplain, and so it lacked the extensive resources that a state could harness for monumental ambitions. Nonetheless, some remarkable polities developed in the region, ranging from the city-state of Teotihuacán to the more widespread influence of the Maya. (See Map 8.7.)

Teotihuacán Around 300 BCE, people in the central plateau and the southeastern districts of Mesoamerica where the dispersed villages of Olmec culture had risen and fallen (see Chapter 5) began to gather in larger settlements. Soon, political and social integration led to city-states. Teotihuacán, in the heart of the fertile valley of central Mexico, became the largest center of the Americas before the Aztecs almost 1,500 years later.

Core Objectives

COMPARE the unifying political and cultural developments in sub-Saharan Africa and Mesoamerica with those that took place across Eurasia in this period.

Teotihuacán The ruins of Teotihuacán convey the importance of monumental architecture to its culture. Looking down from the Pyramid of the Moon, in the foreground is the Plaza of the Moon leading to the Street of the Dead. The Pyramid of the Sun stands in the distance and beyond it, out of sight, are the remains of the Pyramid of the Feathered Serpent. These massive structures were meant to confirm the importance of spiritual affairs in urban life.

Faith and Cultures in the Worlds Apart | **373**

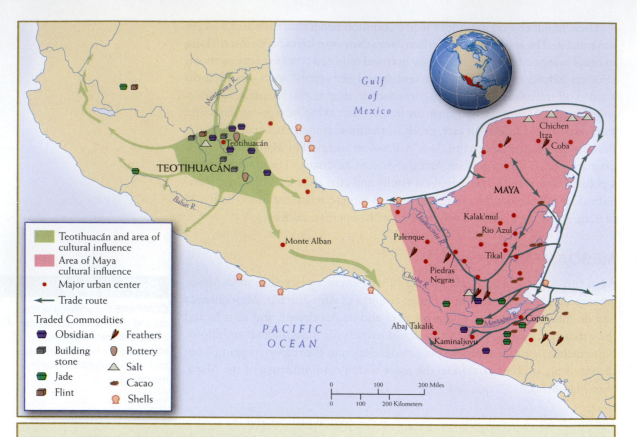

Map 8.7 Mesoamerican Worlds, 200–700 CE

At this time, two groups dominated Mesoamerica: one was located at the city of Teotihuacán in the center, and the other—the Maya—was in the south.

- Locate the traded commodities on the map. What do you note about the distribution of these commodities?
- Where are the trade routes located? What might have fostered interaction between Teotihuacán and the Maya?

Fertile land and ample water from the valley's marshes and lakes fostered high agricultural productivity despite the inhabitants' technologically rustic methods of cultivation. The local food supply sustained a metropolis of between 100,000 and 200,000 residents, living in more than 2,000 apartment compounds lining the city's streets. At one corner rose the massive pyramids of the sun and the moon—the focus of spiritual life for the city dwellers. Marking the city's center was the huge royal compound; the grandeur and refinement of its stepped stone pyramid, the Temple of the Feathered Serpent, were famous throughout Mesoamerica.

The feathered serpent was the anchor for the people's spiritual lives. It was a symbol of fertility that governed reproduction and life. The feathered serpent's temple was the core of a much larger structure. From it radiated the awesome promenade known as the Street of the Dead, which culminated in the hulking Pyramid of the Moon, where foreign warriors and dignitaries were mutilated, sacrificed, and often buried alive to consecrate the holy structure.

Teotihuacán was a powerful city-state that flexed its military muscle to overtake its rivals. By 300 CE, Teotihuacán controlled the entire basin of the Valley of Mexico. It dominated its neighbors and demanded gifts, tribute, and humans for ritual sacrifice. Its massive public architecture displayed art that commemorated decisive battles, defeated neighbors, and captured fighters. While the city's political influence beyond the basin was limited, its cultural and economic diffusion were significant. Making use of porters, Teotihuacán's merchants traded their ceramics, ornaments of marine shells, and all sorts of decorative and valued objects (especially of green obsidian) far and wide. At the same time, Teotihuacán imported pottery, feathers, and other goods from distant lowlands.

This kind of expansion left much of the political and cultural independence of neighbors intact, with only the threat of force keeping them in check. In the fifth century CE, however, invaders burned Teotihuacán and smashed the carved figurines of the central temples and palaces, targeting Teotihuacán's institutional and spiritual core.

The Maya In the Caribbean region of the Yucatán and its interior, the Maya people flourished from about 250 CE to their zenith in the eighth century. The Maya lived in an inhospitable region—hot, infertile, lacking navigable river systems, and vulnerable to hurricanes. Yet the Maya established hundreds, possibly thousands, of agrarian villages scattered across the diverse ecological zones of present-day southern Mexico to western El Salvador. Villages were linked by a shared Mayan language and through tribute payments, chiefly from lesser settlements to sacred towns. At their peak the Maya may have numbered as many as 10 million.

Maya Political and Social Structure The Maya established a variety of kingdoms around major ritual centers—such as Palenque, Copán, and Piedras Negras—and their hinterlands. Such hubs were politically independent but culturally and economically interconnected through commerce. Some larger settlements, such as Tikal and Kalak'mul, became sprawling centers with dependent provinces. In 2018, scientists using jungle-penetrating laser scanning determined that many of the Maya centers were much larger and more densely settled than had been previously thought and that they had defensive walls, had extensive irrigation systems, and were connected by roads.

Maya culture encompassed about a dozen kingdoms that shared many features. Ambitious rulers in these larger states frequently engaged in hostilities with one another. Highly stratified, with an elaborate class structure,

Palenque Deep in the Lacandon jungle of present-day Mexico lies the ruin of the Maya city of Palenque. Its pyramid, on the left, overlooks the site; on the right, the Tower of the Palace shadows a magnificent courtyard where religious figures and nobles gathered. There is no mistaking how a city like Palenque could command its hinterland with religious authority.

each kingdom was topped by a shamanistic king who legitimated his position via his lineage, reaching back to a founding father and, ultimately, the gods. The vast pantheon of gods included patrons of each subregion, as well as a creator god and deities for rain, maize, war, and the sun. Gods were neither especially cruel nor benevolent; rather, they focused on the dance that sustained the axis connecting the underworld and the skies. What humans had to worry about was making sure that the gods got the attention and reverence they needed.

This was the job of Maya rulers. Kings sponsored elaborate public rituals to reinforce their divine heritages, including ornate processions down their cities' main boulevards to honor gods and their descendants, the rulers. Lords and their wives performed ritual blood sacrifice to feed their ancestors. A powerful priestly elite, scribes, legal experts, military advisers, and skilled artisans were vital to the hierarchy.

Most of the Maya people remained tied to the land, which could sustain a high population only through dispersed settlements. Poor soil quality and limited water supply prevented large-scale agriculture. Through terraces, the draining of fields, and slash-and-burn agriculture, Maya managed a subsistence economy of diversified agrarian production. Villagers cultivated maize, beans, and squash, rotating them to prevent the depletion of soil nutrients. Farmers supplemented these staples with root crops such as sweet potato and cassava. Cotton—the basic fiber used for clothing—frequently grew amid rows of other crops as part of a diversified mix.

Maya Writing, Mathematics, and Architecture A common set of beliefs, codes, and values connected the dispersed Maya villages. Sharing a similar language, the Maya developed writing and an important class of scribes, who were vital to the society's integration. Rulers rewarded scribes for writing grand epics about dynasties and their founders, major battles, marriages, deaths, and sacrifices. Such writings offered to Maya shared common histories, beliefs, and gods—always associated with the narratives of ruling families.

The best-known surviving text is the *Popol Vuh*, a "Book of Community." It narrates one community's creation myth, extolling its founders (twin heroes) and the experiences—wars, natural disasters, human ingenuity—that enabled a royal line to rule the Quiché kingdom. The text begins with the gods' creation of the earth and ends with the rituals the kingdom's tribes must follow to avoid a descent into social and political anarchy, which had occurred several times throughout their history.

The Maya also had skilled mathematicians, who devised a calendar and studied astronomy. They accurately charted regular celestial movements and marked the passage of time by precise lunar and solar cycles. The Maya kept sacred calendars, by which they rigorously observed their rituals at the proper times. Each change in the cycle had particular rituals, dances, performances, and offerings to honor the gods with life's sustenance.

Cities reflected a ruler's ability to summon his subjects to contribute to the kingdom's greatness. Plazas, ball courts, terraces, and palaces sprawled out from neighborhoods. Activity revolved around grand royal palaces and massive ball courts, where competing teams treated enthusiastic audiences to contests that were more religious ritual than game. The Maya also excelled at building monumental structures. In Tikal, for instance, surviving buildings include six massive, steep funerary pyramids featuring elaborately carved and painted masonry walls, vaulted ceilings, and royal burial chambers; the tallest temple soars more than 220 feet high (40 feet higher than Justinian's Hagia Sophia).

Maya Bloodletting and Warfare
Maya elites were obsessed with spilling blood as a way to honor rulers and ancestors as well as gods. This gory rite led to frequent warfare, especially among rival dynasties, the goal of which was to capture victims for the bloody rituals. Rulers also would shed their own blood at intervals set by the calendar. Royal wives drew blood from their

Wood Tablet This detail of a carved-wood tablet from a temple in the city of Tikal (c. 741 CE) is a fine example of the ornate form of scribal activity, which combined images and portraits with glyphs that tell a narrative.

tongues and men had their penises perforated. Such bloodletting by means of elaborately adorned and sanctified instruments was reserved for those of noble descent. Carvings and paintings portray blood cascading from rulers' mutilated bodies.

Internal warfare eventually doomed the Maya, especially after devastating confrontations between Tikal and Kalak'mul during the fourth through seventh centuries CE. With each outbreak, rulers drafted larger armies and sacrificed greater numbers of captives. Crops perished. People fled. After centuries of misery, it must have seemed as if the gods themselves were abandoning the Maya people. The cycle of violence destroyed the cultural underpinnings of elite rule that had held the Maya world together. There was no single catastrophic event, no great defeat by a rival power. The Maya people simply abandoned their spiritual centers, and cities became ghost towns. As populations declined, jungles overtook temples. Eventually, the hallmark of Maya unity—the ability to read a shared script—vanished. While vibrant religious traditions thrived in sub-Saharan Africa and in Mesoamerica, they served more to reinforce the political and social situations from which they came rather than to spread a universalizing message far beyond their original context.

Conclusion

The breakdown of two imperial systems—Rome around the Mediterranean, and Han China in East Asia—introduced an era in which religion and shared culture rather than military conquest and political institutions linked large areas of Afro-Eurasia.

The Roman Empire gave way to a new religious unity, first represented by Christian dissenters and then co-opted by the emperor Constantine. In western Europe, the sense of unity unlimited by imperial frontiers gave rise to a universal, or "Catholic," church—the "true" Christian religion that believers felt all peoples should share. In the eastern Mediterranean, where the Roman Empire survived, Christianity and empire coalesced to reinforce one another. Christians here held that beliefs about God and Jesus found their most correct expression within the Eastern Roman Empire and in its capital, Constantinople.

Similarly, in East Asia, the weakening of the Han dynasty enabled Buddhism to dominate Chinese culture. Without a unified state in China, Confucian officials lost their influence, while Buddhist priests and monks enjoyed patronage from regional rulers, local warriors, and commoners. In India, Brahman elites exploited population movements beyond the reach of traditional rulers as they established ritual forms for daily life on every level of society, while melding aspects of their own Vedic faith with those of Buddhism to create a new Hindu synthesis.

Not all regions felt the spread of universalizing religions, however. In most of sub-Saharan Africa belief systems were much more localized. Similarly in Mesoamerica, where long-distance transportation was harder and political authority more diffuse, religion was a unifying force but nothing like the widespread universalizing religions of Afro-Eurasia. Nevertheless, spiritual life was no less profound. Here, a strong sense of a shared worldview, a shared sense of purpose, and a shared sense of faith enabled common cultures to develop. Indeed, the Bantus and Maya became large-scale common cultures—but ruled at the local level.

Thus, the period 300–600 CE saw the emergence of three great cultural units in Afro-Eurasia, each defined in religious terms: Christianity in the Mediterranean and parts of Southwest Asia, Hinduism in South Asia, and Buddhism in East Asia. They illustrate the ways in which peoples were converging under larger religious tents, while also becoming more distinct. Universalizing religions, whether Christian or Buddhist, and codes of behavior, such as the Brahmanic Code of Manu, gave people a new way to define themselves and their loyalties.

Focus On
Religions and Regions

Europe and Southwest Asia

- Christianity moves from a minority, persecuted faith to a state religion in the Roman Empire.

- The Sasanian state in Iran provides fertile ground for a tolerant mixture of Zoroastrianism, Nestorian Christianity, Judaism, Buddhism, and Brahmanic religion.

Sub-Saharan Africa and Mesoamerica

- Large parts of sub-Saharan Africa are influenced by the spread of Bantu-speaking, ironworking migrants who adapt to a range of ecological zones.

- In Mesoamerica, urban kingdoms thrive in Teotihuacán (central Mexico) and among the Maya (of the Yucatán).

South Asia and East Asia

- Brahmanism, or Hinduism, becomes the dominant religion among the Vedic peoples of South Asia.

- Buddhism spreads out of South Asia along the Silk Roads through central Asia and into East Asia (now fractured politically, but with the Buddhist-leaning Northern Wei having a dominant influence).

Key Terms

Bantu migrations p. 372	creed p. 350	martyr p. 345	universalizing religions p. 344
Byzantium p. 354	Hinayana Buddhism p. 362	Sanskrit cosmopolis p. 363	
Code of Manu p. 363	Hinduism p. 361		

CHRONOLOGY

	1 CE	100 CE	200 CE	300 CE	400 CE

The Mediterranean and Southwest Asia
Emperor Constantine legalizes Christianity in Roman Empire 313 CE

Central Asia

South Asia
Transformation of Brahmanism into Hinduism begins fir or second century CE

East Asia
Six Dynasties period 220–589 CE

Sub-Saharan Africa
Bantu migrations from western Africa to south, central, and east first millennium CE

Mesoamerica
Maya culture dominates Yucatán Peninsula and surrounding area third–ninth centuries CE

- **Thinking about Crossing Borders and Universalizing Religions** Why did borders seem to infuse vitality into Christianity and Buddhism from the fourth through the sixth centuries CE? Which religions in this period did not seem to cross borders and why? What effect did this have on those religions?

- **Thinking about Changing Power Relationships and Universalizing Religions** Universalizing religions, like Christianity and Buddhism, were successful in part because of their diverse personalized appeal to men and women, rich and poor, and the upper and lower classes. How might this diverse appeal enable a universalizing religion like Christianity to undermine and alter traditional power relationships? In what ways did Buddhism do the same?

- **Thinking about Worlds Together, Worlds Apart and Universalizing Religions** Why did universalizing religions like Christianity and Buddhism develop in some parts of the world but not in others in the period 300 to 600 CE? How did these universalizing religions allow for continuity in Eurasia, even as empires fell away? In the "worlds apart," how might the lack of universalizing religion have influenced continuity, as political entities rose and fell over time?

Go to **INQUIZITIVE** to see what you've learned—and learn what you've missed—with personalized feedback along the way.

500 CE	600 CE	700 CE	800 CE	900 CE	1000 CE

Sasanian Empire flourishes in Iran and Mesopotamia third–sixth centuries CE

"Barbarian" invasions of Roman Empire fourth–fifth centuries CE

Byzantine Empire flourishes in eastern Mediterranean fifth–seventh centuries CE

Byzantine and Sasanian wars sixth–seventh centuries CE

Buddhism spreads through central Asia fourth–sixth centuries CE

Sogdian merchant communities dominate Silk Road trade through central Asia fourth–sixth centuries CE

Gupta Empire 320–550 CE

Buddhism gains in popularity fourth–sixth centuries CE

City of Teotihuacán dominates Valley of Mexico fourth–fifth centuries CE

Global Themes and Sources

Continuity and Change in Pilgrimage

Pilgrimage went hand in hand with the spread of universalizing religions along the trade routes that stretched across Eurasia. Christians and Buddhists traveled the religious geography of their faith, visiting sacred sites and relics and hearing stories of holy women and men. The pilgrimages described here are arranged chronologically by journey (not date of composition) and grouped by tradition (Christianity, then Buddhism), in order to track changes within a tradition over time in this all-important practice, as well as to see the similarities and differences in how pilgrimage worked for each. The account from Hinduism was written in the mid-first millennium CE, roughly at the same time the Christian and Buddhist pilgrims were traveling, but describes a legendary character's travel to holy sites and people almost 1,500 years earlier. It thus offers a Hindu perspective on pilgrimage that can be contrasted with the pilgrimages within the universalizing traditions of Christianity and Buddhism.

The church historian Socrates (not to be confused with the ancient Greek philosopher of the same name) recounts the faith-inspired travels of Helena, the mother of the emperor Constantine, as well as those of individuals who traveled into Africa and India to spread the Gospel. That historical account (reported almost 200 years after the fact) can be compared with the first-person travel diary kept by a woman named Egeria who journeyed to holy sites across the eastern Mediterranean in the late fourth century CE, recording the places she visited and her experiences at each location. At roughly the same time Egeria was traveling, an elderly Chinese Buddhist monk named Faxian was making his way from Chang'an in China to South Asia to look for Buddhist scriptures and to visit sites sacred to Buddhism. More than 200 years later, another Buddhist monk, named Xuanzang, traveled west along the Silk Roads to Samarkand, where he turned south into India, visiting Buddhist sites along the way before returning to China. The passage from the *Bhagavata Purana* describes the travels of Vidura, a major character in the *Mahabharata* whose legendary storyline extends back to 1000 BCE.

Taken together, these sources offer an excellent opportunity to track how certain aspects of pilgrimage endure while others change over time. Religiously motivated travel and monasticism were central to the spread of universalizing religious traditions in the mid-first millennium CE. Consequently, the similarities and differences in pilgrimage, over time and across traditions, make it possible to track the relative importance of this religious tourism within the larger context of the ever-expanding influence of Christianity and Buddhism.

Analyzing Continuity and Change in Pilgrimage

- What do these pilgrims—Helena, Egeria, Faxian, Xuanzang, and Vidura—see and do when they visit a holy site? To what extent does pilgrimage within Christianity and Buddhism seem to change over time? In what ways is there continuity in the practice of pilgrimage?

- What appears to be the role of storytelling in pilgrimage? What do these excerpts suggest about the relationship between monasteries and holy sites? Between pilgrims and written text?

- How do the similarities and differences over time and across traditions—in terms of where religious travelers go, what they do, how and to whom they report their experiences—indicate the extent to which a tradition was a universalizing faith?

Recovery of the Cross of Christ by Helena (c. 325 CE), from *Ecclesiastical History* (fifth century CE), Socrates

Socrates wrote his *Ecclesiastical History* in the early fifth century CE to describe the important years from 305 CE (when Constantine, the emperor who legalized Christianity, began to consolidate his imperial power) through 439 CE (when Theodosius II, who oversaw a major codification of Roman law, was emperor in the east and the Vandals and Huns were threatening the western empire). In the passages here, Socrates offers the story of how Helena, the mother of Constantine, reputedly found the cross on which Jesus was crucified, as well as how Christianity spread into Africa and India during Constantine's reign. Helena's travels to Jerusalem and the voyage of Meropius and Frumentius to India illustrate early attempts by Christians to mark sacred space and to spread their tradition beyond the boundaries of the Roman empire.

- **What does Helena find when she travels to Jerusalem, and how does she verify its legitimacy to her satisfaction? What are the impediments to her success?**

- **How are Helena's finds marked? What might be the significance of this building activity in the short and long term?**

- **What does the text reveal about how Christianity spread into new territories?**

Chapter 18: Helena, the emperor's mother . . . being divinely directed by dreams went to Jerusalem. Finding that which was once Jerusalem, desolate . . . she sought carefully the sepulcher of Christ, from which he arose after his burial; and after much difficulty, by God's help she discovered it. What the cause of the difficulty was I will explain in a few words. Those who embraced the Christian faith, after the period of his passion, greatly venerated this tomb; but those who hated Christianity, having covered the spot with a mound of earth, erected on it a temple to Venus, and set up her image there, not caring for the memory of the place. This succeeded for a long time; and it became known to the emperor's mother. Accordingly she having caused the statue to be thrown down, the earth to be removed, and the ground entirely cleared, found three crosses in the sepulcher: one of these was that blessed cross on which Christ had hung, the other two were those on which the two thieves that were crucified with him had died. With these was also found the tablet of Pilate, on which he had inscribed in various characters, that the Christ who was crucified was king of the Jews. Since, however, it was doubtful which was the cross they were in search of, the emperor's mother was not a little distressed; but from this trouble the bishop of Jerusalem, Macarius, shortly relieved her. And he solved the doubt by faith, for he sought a sign from God and obtained it. The sign was this: a certain woman of the neighborhood, who had been long afflicted with disease, was now just at the point of death; the bishop therefore arranged it so that each of the crosses should be brought to the dying woman, believing that she would be healed on touching the precious cross. Nor was he disappointed in his expectation: for the two crosses having been applied which were not the Lord's, the woman still continued in a dying state; but when the third, which was the true cross, touched her, she was immediately healed, and recovered her former strength. In this manner then was the genuine cross discovered. The emperor's mother erected over the place of the sepulcher a magnificent church, and named it *New Jerusalem*, having built it facing that old and deserted city. There she left a portion of the cross, enclosed in a silver case, as a memorial to those who might wish to see it: the other part she sent to the emperor, who being persuaded that the city would be perfectly secure where that relic should be preserved, privately enclosed it in his own statue, which stands on a large column of porphyry in the forum called Constantine's at Constantinople. I have written this from report indeed; but almost all the inhabitants of Constantinople affirm that it is true. Moreover the nails with which Christ's hands were fastened to the cross (for his mother having found these also in the sepulcher had sent them) Constantine took and had made into bridle-bits and a helmet, which he used in his military expeditions. The emperor supplied all materials for the construction of the churches, and wrote to Macarius the bishop to expedite these edifices. When the emperor's mother had completed the

New Jerusalem, she reared another church not at all inferior, over the cave at Bethlehem where Christ was born according to the flesh: nor did she stop here, but built a third on the mount of his Ascension. . . . She was also very munificent to the churches and to the poor; and having lived a life of piety, she died when about eighty years old. Her remains were conveyed to New Rome, the capital, and deposited in the imperial sepulchers. . . .

Chapter 19: We must now mention in what manner Christianity was spread in this emperor's reign: for it was in his time that the nations both of the Indians in the interior, and of the Iberians first embraced the Christian faith. . . . When the apostles went forth by lot among the nations, Thomas received the apostleship of the Parthians; Matthew was allotted Ethiopia; and Bartholomew the part of India contiguous to that country: but the interior of India, in which many barbarous nations using different languages lived, was not enlightened by Christian doctrine before the times of Constantine. I now come to speak of the cause which led them to become converts to Christianity. A certain philosopher, Meropius, a Tyrian by race, determined to acquaint himself with the country of the Indians, being stimulated to this by the example of the philosopher Metrodorus, who had previously traveled through the region of India. Having taken with him therefore two youths to whom he was related, who were by no means ignorant of the Greek language, Meropius reached the country by ship. . . . It so happened that a little before that time the treaty between the Romans and Indians had been violated. The Indians, therefore, having seized the philosopher and those who sailed with him, killed them all except his two youthful kinsmen; but sparing them from compassion for their tender age, they sent them as a gift to the king of the Indians. He being pleased with the personal appearance of the youths, constituted one of them, whose name was Edesius, cupbearer at his table; the other, named Frumentius, he entrusted with the care of the royal records. . . . Thus Frumentius controlled all things and made it a task to enquire whether among the Roman merchants trafficking with that country, there were any Christians to be found: and having discovered some, he informed them who he was, and exhorted them to select and occupy some appropriate places for the celebration of Christian worship. In the course of a little while he built a house of prayer; and having instructed some of the Indians in the principles of Christianity, they fitted them for participation in the worship.

Source: Socrates Scholasticus, *Ecclesiastical History*, in *Nicene and Post-Nicene Fathers of the Christian Church*, vol. 2, translated by A. C. Zenos (Grand Rapids, MI: Wm. B. Eerdmans, 1957), pp. 21–23.

PRIMARY SOURCE 8.2

Diary of a Pilgrimage (late fourth century CE), Egeria

Egeria was a nun who traveled from Spain to the eastern Mediterranean (modern Turkey, Syria, Israel, and Egypt) to visit sites important to early Christianity. Her writing is striking not only because it was composed by a far-traveling woman but also because it is the earliest recorded Christian pilgrimage account. Egeria's rich descriptions of the places she visits, the people she meets, and the religious rituals performed at each site demonstrate how pilgrimage could enliven the faith of the adherents of universalizing traditions.

- What details does Egeria offer that give you a sense of what her travel was like?

- What does Egeria do at the places she visits? How are people, place, and story a significant part of that experience?

- How has pilgrimage changed from Helena's time to Egeria's time, just two generations later? How has it remained the same? What do you think accounts for these similarities and differences?

Chapter 22: After I had returned to Antioch, I remained there for a whole week, until whatever was necessary for our journey had been prepared. I then set out from Antioch and, after journeying for several days, arrived in the province called Cilicia, the capital city of which is Tarsus, the same Tarsus in which I had already been on my trip down to Jerusalem. Since the shrine of Saint Thecla is located a three-day journey from Tarsus, in Isauria, it was a great pleasure for me to go there, particularly since it was so near at hand.

Chapter 23: I set out from Tarsus and I came to a certain city by the sea, still in Cilicia, called

Pompeiopolis. From there I crossed over in the regions of Isauria, and I stayed at a city called Corycus. On the third day I arrived at a city called Seleucia of Isauria. On arriving there, I went to the bishop, a very holy man and a former monk. I also saw there in the same city a very beautiful church. Since it is around fifteen hundred feet from the city to the shrine of Saint Thecla, which lies beyond the city on a rather flat hill, I thought it best to go out there to make the overnight stop which I had to make.

At the holy church there is nothing but countless monastic cells for men and women. I met there a very dear friend of mine, and a person to whose way of life everyone in the East bears witness, the holy deaconess Marthana, whom I had met in Jerusalem, where she had come to pray. She governs these monastic cells of *aputactitae*, or virgins. Would I ever be able to describe how great was her joy and how great mine when she saw me? But to return to the subject: There are many cells all over the hill, and in the middle there is a large wall which encloses the church where the shrine is. It is a very beautiful shrine. The wall is set there to guard the church against the Isaurians, who are evil men, who frequently rob and who might try to do something against the monastery which is established there. Having arrived there in the name of God, a prayer was said at the shrine and the complete Acts of Saint Thecla was read. I then gave unceasing thanks to Christ our God, who granted to me, an unworthy woman and in no way deserving, the fulfillment of my desires in all things. And so, after spending two days there seeing the holy monks and the *aputactitae*, both men and women, who live there, and after praying and receiving Communion, I returned to Tarsus and to my journey.

I made a three-day stop before setting out on my journey from there, in the name of God. On the same day I arrived at the resting station called Mansocrenae, located at the base of Mount Tarsus, and I stopped there. The next day I climbed Mount Tarsus and travelled by a route, already known to me, through several provinces that I had already crossed on my journey down, that is, Cappadocia, Galatia, and Bithynia. Then I arrived at Chalcedon, where I stopped because of the very famous shrine of Saint Euphemia, already known to me from before. On the following day, after crossing the sea, I arrived in Constantinople, giving thanks to Christ our God who deigned to bestow such favor on me, an unworthy and undeserving person. Not only did He deign to fulfill my desire to go there, but He granted also the means of visiting what I desired to see, and of returning again to Constantinople.

After arriving there, I did not cease giving thanks to Jesus our God, who had deigned to bestow His grace upon me, in the various churches, that of the apostles and the numerous shrines that are here. As I send this letter to Your Charity and to you, reverend ladies, it is already my intention to go, in the name of Christ our God, to Asia, that is, to Ephesus, to pray at the shrine of the holy and blessed apostle John. If, after this, I am still living, I will either tell Your Charity in person—if God will deign to grant that—about whatever other places I shall have come to know, or certainly I will write you of it in letters, if there is anything else I have in mind.

You, my sisters, my light, kindly remember me, whether I live or die.

Source: Egeria, *Ancient Christian Writers: Diary of a Pilgrimage*, translated by George E. Gringras (Mahwah, NJ: Newman Press, 1970), pp. 86–89.

PRIMARY SOURCE 8.3

A Record of Buddhistic Kingdoms (early fifth century CE), Faxian

Faxian's journeys blended two elements of universalizing tradition: pilgrimage and texts. He was motivated to travel to the homeland of Buddhism to gather or copy as many Buddhist texts as possible so he could bring them back to China. His description of his travels—from China to India to Sri Lanka and back again—offers a view of the varied worship practices within different schools of Buddhism, as well as the many different regions where Buddhism flourished.

- What specific details does Faxian offer about the sites he visits? What do you think is the purpose of that level of detail?
- How are the holy sites visited by Faxian marked out?
- What role do other monks and monasteries play in Faxian's travel?

Chapter 31: From this place, after travelling to the west for four yojanas [Vedic unit of measure, approximately

8 miles], (the pilgrims) came to the city of Gayâ; but inside the city all was emptiness and desolation. Going on again to the south for twenty le [Chinese unit of measure, roughly one-third of a mile], they arrived at the place where the Bodhisattva for six years practised with himself painful austerities. All around was forest.

Three le west from here they came to the place where, when Buddha had gone into the water to bathe, a deva [divine being] bent down the branch of a tree, by means of which he succeeded in getting out of the pool.

Two le north from this was the place where the Grâmika girls presented to Buddha the rice gruel made with milk; and two le north from this (again) was the place where, seated on a rock under a great tree, and facing the east, he ate (the gruel). The tree and the rock are there at the present day. The rock may be six cubits in breadth and length, and rather more than two cubits in height. In Central India the cold and heat are so equally tempered that trees will live in it for several thousand and even for ten thousand years.

Half a yojana from this place to the north-east there was a cavern in the rocks, into which the Bodhisattva entered, and sat cross-legged with his face to the west. (As he did so), he said to himself, "If I am to attain to perfect wisdom (and become Buddha), let there be a supernatural attestation of it." On the wall of the rock there appeared immediately the shadow of a Buddha, rather more than three feet in length, which is still bright at the present day. At this moment heaven and earth were greatly moved, and devas in the air spoke plainly, "This is not the place where any Buddha of the past, or he that is to come, has attained, or will attain, to perfect Wisdom. Less than half a yojana from this to the south-west will bring you to the patra tree, where all past Buddhas have attained, and all to come must attain, to perfect Wisdom." When they had spoken these words, they immediately led the way forwards to the place, singing as they did so. . . .

At the place mentioned above . . . men subsequently reared topes [or stupas, Buddhist shrines with relics] and set up images, which all exist at the present day.

Where Buddha, after attaining to perfect wisdom, for seven days contemplated the tree, and experienced the joy of vimukti; where, under the patra tree, he walked backwards and forwards from west to east for seven days; where the devas made a hall appear, composed of the seven precious substances, and presented offerings to him for seven days; where the blind dragon Muchilinda encircled him for seven days; where he sat under the nyagrodha tree, on a square rock, with his face to the east, and Brahma-deva came and made his request to him; where the four deva kings brought to him their alms-bowls; where the 500 merchants presented to him the roasted flour and honey; and where he converted the brothers Kaśyapa and their thousand disciples;—at all these places topes were reared.

At the place where Buddha attained to perfect Wisdom, there are three monasteries, in all of which there are monks residing. The families of their people around supply the societies of these monks with an abundant sufficiency of what they require, so that there is no lack or stint. The disciplinary rules are strictly observed by them. The laws regulating their demeanour in sitting, rising, and entering when the others are assembled, are those which have been practised by all the saints since Buddha was in the world down to the present day. The places of the four great topes have been fixed, and handed down without break, since Buddha attained to nirvâna. Those four great topes are those at the places where Buddha was born; where he attained to Wisdom; where he (began to) move the wheel of his Law; and where he attained to pari-nirvâna.

***

Chapter 36: From Vârânasî (the travellers) went back east to Pâtaliputtra. Faxian's original object had been to search for (copies of) the Vinaya [texts governing monastic communities in Buddhism]. In the various kingdoms of North India, however, he had found one master transmitting orally (the rules) to another, but no written copies which he could transcribe. He had therefore travelled far and come on to Central India. Here in the mahâyâna monastery, he found a copy of the Vinaya, containing the Mahâsânghika rules,—those which were observed in the first Great Council, while Buddha was still in the world. . . . [The account then describes a range of texts collected by Faxian.]

In consequence (of this success in his quest) Faxian stayed here for three years, learning Sanskrit books and the Sanskrit speech, and writing out the Vinaya rules.

Source: Faxian, *A Record of Buddhistic Kingdoms, Being an Account by the Chinese Monk Fâ-Hien of His Travels in India and Ceylon* (A.D. 399–414) *in Search of the Buddhist Books of Discipline*, translated by James Legge (Oxford: Clarendon Press, 1886), pp. 87–90, 98–99.

Travels of Xuanzang (seventh century CE)

Like Faxian, the Chinese monk Xuanzang traveled along the Silk Roads encountering many varieties of Buddhism as it was practiced in different regions and many texts produced within those different Buddhist communities. And like Faxian's writings, Xuanzang's vivid descriptions of the places he visits offer wide-eyed wonder and storytelling leavened with practical analyses of distances between cities, the sizes of structures and communities, and the local cultures he encounters. Read closely, however, for the subtle differences in the ways that Xuanzang describes the world through which he moves more than 200 years after Faxian.

- What does Xuanzang note about the sites that he visits? Why do you think he offers these details?

- How do monasteries and convents fit into Xuanzang's travel? What does this text reveal about the development of stupas and the placement of relics within them?

- How does Xuanzang's travel compare with that of his fellow Buddhist Faxian, more than 200 years earlier? What are the similarities and differences over time in how pilgrimage is described and what a pilgrim does?

Po-Ho [Balkh, in northern Afghanistan]. This country is about 800 *li* from east to west, and 400 *li* from north to south; on the north it borders on the Oxus. The capital is about 20 *li* in circuit. It is called generally the little Râjagriha [site in northeastern India, important in Buddhism and Jainism, first capital of Magadha kingdom]. This city, though well (*strongly*) fortified, is thinly populated. The products of the soil are extremely varied, and the flowers, both on the land and water, would be difficult to enumerate. There are about 100 convents and 3000 monks, who all study the religious teaching of the Little Vehicle [i.e., Hinayana Buddhism].

Outside the city, towards the south-west, there is a convent called Navasaṅghârâma, which was built by a former king of this country. The Masters (of Buddhism), who dwell to the north of the great Snowy Mountains, and are authors of Śâstras, occupy this convent only, and continue their estimable labours in it. There is a figure of Buddha here, which is lustrous with (reflects the glory of) noted gems, and the hall in which it stands is also adorned with precious substances of rare value. This is the reason why it has often been robbed by chieftains of neighbouring countries, covetous of gain.

This convent also contains (possesses) a statue of Pisha-men (Vaiśravaṇa) Dêva, by whose spiritual influence, in unexpected ways, there is protection afforded to the precincts of the convent. . . .

Within the convent, in the southern hall of Buddha, there is the washing-basin which Buddha used. It contains about a peck, and is of various colours, which dazzle the eyes. It is difficult to name the gold and stone of which it is made. Again, there is a tooth of Buddha about an inch long, and about eight or nine tenths of an inch in breadth. Its colour is yellowish white; it is pure and shining. Again, there is the sweeping brush of Buddha, made of the plant "Ka-she" (kâśâ). It is about two feet long and about seven inches round. Its handle is ornamented with various gems. These three relics are presented with offerings on each of the six fast-days by the assembly of lay and cleric believers. Those who have the greatest faith in worship see the objects emitting a radiance of glory.

To the north of the convent is a stûpa, in height about 200 feet, which is covered with a plaster hard as the diamond, and ornamented with a variety of precious substances. It encloses a sacred relic (she-li), and at times this also reflects a divine splendour.

To the south-west of the convent there is a Vihâra [monastery]. Many years have elapsed since its foundation was laid. It is the resort (of people) from distant quarters. There are also a large number of men of conspicuous talent. As it would be difficult for the several possessors of the four different degrees (fruits) of holiness to explain accurately their condition of saintship, therefore the Arhats [people who have reached nirvana] . . . , when about to die, exhibit their spiritual capabilities (miraculous powers), and those who witness such an exhibition found stûpas in honour of the deceased saints. These are closely crowded together here, to the number of several hundreds. Besides these there are some thousand others, who, although they had reached the fruit of holiness (i.e., Arhatship), yet having exhibited no spiritual changes at the end of life, have no memorial erected to them.

At present the number of priests is about 100; so irregular are they morning and night in their duties, that it is hard to tell saints from sinners.

To the north-west of the capital about 50 *li* or so we arrive at the town of Ti-wei; 40 *li* to the north of this town is the town of Po-li. In each of these towns there is a stûpa about three chang (30 feet) in height. In old days, when Buddha first attained enlightenment after advancing to the tree of knowledge, he went to the garden of deer; at this time two householders meeting him, and beholding the brilliant appearance of his person, offered him from their store of provisions for their journey some cakes and honey. The lord of the world, for their sakes, preached concerning the happiness of men and Dêvas, and delivered to them, his very first disciples, the five rules of moral conduct and the ten good qualities (shen, virtuous rules). When they had heard the sermon, they humbly asked for some object to worship (offer gifts). On this Tathâgata delivered to them some of his hair and nail-cuttings. Taking these, the merchants were about to return to their own country, when they asked of Buddha the right way of venerating these relics. Tathâgata forthwith spreading out his Sanghâti on the ground as a square napkin, next laid down his Uttarâsanga and then his Sankakshikâ; again over these he placed as a cover his begging-pot, on which he erected his mendicant's staff. Thus he placed them in order, making thereby (the figure of) a stûpa. The two men taking the order, each went to his own town, and then, according to the model which the holy one had prescribed, they prepared to build a monument, and thus was the very first Stûpa of the Buddhist religion erected.

Source: *Buddhist Records of the Western World, Translated from the Chinese of Hiuen Tsiang (A.D. 629)*, vol. 1, translated by Samuel Beal (London: Trübner, 1884), pp. 43–48.

Travels of Vidura in Distant Vedic Past (c. 1000 BCE[?]), from the *Bhagavata Purana* (recorded c. 500 CE)

The excerpt of the *Bhagavata Purana* offered here tells the story of Vidura, the brother of the king Dhṛtarāṣṭra, and the sacred journey Vidura takes through India. The increasing popularity of accessible *bhakti* devotion at the time this text reached its written form can be traced in the personal relationship that several of the characters, including Vidura, have with Krishna, who is the human incarnation of the Hindu god Vishnu. Even with those hints of personal connection, Vidura's pilgrimage stands in striking contrast to those in the other texts offered here.

- Why does Vidura go on pilgrimage? What does Vidura do when he visits holy sites?

- What in the text suggests Vidura's personalized relationship with Krishna?

- How is Vidura's pilgrimage similar to travels by the Christians Helena and Egeria and the Buddhists Faxian and Xuanzang? How is it different? What do you think accounts for these similarities and differences?

SB 3.1. (10) When Vidura was invited by his elder brother [Dhṛtarāṣṭra] for consultation, he entered the house and gave instructions which were exactly to the point. His advice is well-known, and instructions by Vidura are approved by expert ministers of state. (11) [Vidura said:] You must now return the legitimate share to Yudhiṣṭhira who has no enemies and who has been forebearing through untold sufferings due to your offenses. He is waiting with his younger brothers, among whom is the revengeful Bhīma, breathing heavily like a snake. Surely you are afraid of him. (13) You are maintaining offense personified, Duryodhana, as your infallible son, but he is envious of Lord Kṛṣṇa. And because you are thus maintaining a nondevotee of Kṛṣṇa, you are devoid of all auspicious qualities. Relieve yourself of this ill fortune as soon as possible and do good to the whole family! (14) While speaking thus, Vidura, whose personal character was esteemed by respectable persons, was insulted by Duryodhana, who was swollen with anger and whose lips were trembling. Duryodhana was in company with Karna, his younger brothers and his maternal uncle Śakuni. (15) "Who asked him to come here, this son of a kept mistress? He is so crooked that he spies in the interest of the enemy against those on whose support he has grown up. Toss him out of the palace immediately and leave him with his only breath." (16) Thus being pierced by arrows through his ears and afflicted to the core of his heart, Vidura placed his bow on the door and quit his brother's palace. He was not sorry, for he considered the acts of the external energy to be supreme. (17) By his piety, Vidura achieved the advantages of the pious Kauravas [i.e., children of Dhṛtarāṣṭra]. After leaving Hastināpura, he took shelter of many places of pilgrimages, which are the Lord's lotus feet. With a desire to gain a high order of pious life, he traveled to holy places where thousands of transcendental forms of the Lord are situated. (18) He began to travel along, thinking only of Kṛṣṇa [i.e., Krishna], through various holy places like Ayodhyā, Dvārakā and Mathurā [all cities in India]. He traveled where the grove, hill, orchard, river and lake are all pure and sinless and where the forms of the Unlimited decorate the temples. Thus he performed the pilgrim's progress. (19) While so traversing the earth, he simply performed duties to please the Supreme Lord Hari. His occupation was pure and independent. He was constantly sanctified by taking his bath in holy places, although he was in the dress of a mendicant and had no hair dressing nor a bed on which to lie. Thus he was always unseen by his various relatives. (20) Thus, when he was in the land of Bhāratavarṣa [i.e., India] traveling to all the places of pilgrimage, he visited Prabhāsakṣetra. At that time Mahārāja Yudhiṣṭhira was the emperor and held the world under one military strength and one flag. (21) At the place of pilgrimage at Prabhāsa, it came to his knowledge that all his relatives had died due to violent passion, just as an entire forest burns due to fire produced by the friction of bamboos. After this he proceeded west, where the river Sarasvatī flows. (22) On the bank of the river Sar-

asvatī there were eleven places of pilgrimage, namely (1) Trita, (2) Uśanā, (3) Manu, (4) Pṛthu, (5) Agni, (6) Asita, (7) Vāyu, (8) Sudāsa, (9) Go, (10) Guha and (11) Śrāddhadeva. Vidura visited all of them and duly performed rituals. (23) There were also many other temples of various forms of the Supreme Personality of Godhead Viṣṇu, established by great sages and demigods. These temples were marked with the chief emblems of the Lord, and they reminded one always of the original Personality of Godhead, Lord Kṛṣṇa. (24) Thereafter he passed through very wealthy provinces like Surat, Sauvīra and Matsya and through western India, known as Kurujāṅgala. At last he reached the bank of the Yamunā, where he happened to meet Uddhava, the great devotee of Lord Kṛṣṇa. (25) Then, due to his great love and feeling, Vidura embraced him [Uddhava] who was a constant companion of Lord Kṛṣṇa and formerly a great student of Bṛhaspati. Vidura then asked him for news of the family of Lord Kṛṣṇa, the Personality of Godhead. (26) [Please tell me] whether the original Personalities of Godhead, who incarnated Themselves at the request of Brahmā [who is born out of the lotus flower from the Lord] and who have increased the prosperity of the world by elevating everyone, are doing well in the house of Śurasena. (27) [Please tell me] whether the best friend of the Kurus, our brother-in-law Vasudeva, is doing well. He is very munificent. He is like a father to his sister, and he is always pleasing to his wives. (33) As the Vedas are the reservoir of sacrificial purposes, so the daughter of King Devaka-bhoja conceived the Supreme Personality of Godhead in her womb, as did the mother of the demigods. Is she [Devakī] doing well? (45) O my friend, please, therefore, chant the glories of the Lord, who is meant to be glorified in the places of pilgrimage. He is unborn, and yet He appears by His causeless mercy upon the surrendered rulers of all parts of the universe. Only for their interest did He appear in the family of His unalloyed devotees the Yadus.

Source: *Śrīmad Bhāgavatam*, Third Canto, "The Status Quo" (Part 1, Chapters 1–8), translated by His Divine Grace A. C. Bhaktivedanta Sawmi Prabhupāda (Los Angeles: The Bhaktivedanta Book Trust, 1972), pp. 9–11, 13–16, 19–23, 25–28, 34, 47.

Interpreting Visual Evidence

Representations of Holiness

One of the features of universalizing religions discussed in this chapter is that they offered individuals a more personal connection with the divine. This accessibility is visible in the religious art from the period.

As the images here show, artists expressed what it means to be holy in various ways. The Yungang Caves in northeastern China were situated at the eastern end of the Silk Roads. The large statues and interior painting and carvings pictured here were created between 450 and 525 CE, during the Northern Wei dynasty. Many different Buddhas reside in individual niches on the walls surrounding the large central Buddha statue. Thousands of miles away, in the crumbling Western Roman Empire, the Archbishop's Chapel from Ravenna (c. 500 CE) in northern Italy preserved depictions of martyrs and other religious figures, notably Perpetua and Felicitas. These women appear here not as violently bloodied witnesses to their faith but rather as a serenely modest matron and her humble servant.

The two relief sculptures pictured here provide additional perspectives on sacred subjects. The Hindu relief depicts the Kalyanasundara, or "beautiful marriage," of Parvati and Shiva (the Hindu god of destruction and rejuvenation). This particular relief was carved in the mid-sixth century CE in Cave 1 at Elephanta on an island in the harbor of modern-day Mumbai. Its imagery recurs in numerous versions throughout the ancient Hindu temples of India and beyond. In this carving, Parvati, a reincarnation of Shiva's first wife, Sati, is married to Shiva as a reward for her patient devotion. The final image is a limestone relief from Yaxchilán, Mexico, and shows a royal Maya bloodletting ritual. In the image (dated by the glyphs to October 26, 709 CE), the queen pierces her tongue with a thorny rope in a reenactment of the bloodletting by the gods in the Maya creation narrative.

Perpetua and Felicitas.

Yungang Caves.

Kalyanasundara of Parvati and Shiva.

Questions for Analysis

1. Compare these visual representations of what it means to be holy. To what extent do they convey a message that is particular to their tradition?

2. What might account for the similarities in these depictions of what it means to be holy?

3. Given what you know about the features of these universalizing traditions, what in these images might suggest human access to holiness or the possibility of a personal connection to the divine?

4. How does the location of these images (where they were created and displayed) contribute to an understanding of how universalizing these traditions were?

Royal bloodletting ritual.

9

New Empires and Common Cultures

600–1000 CE

In 754 CE al-Mansur, ruler of the new Muslim Abbasid dynasty, decided to relocate his capital city from Damascus (the capital of Islam's first dynasty) closer to the Abbasids' home region on the Iranian plateau. Islam was barely a century old, yet it flourished under this second dynasty. The caliph al-Mansur chose, for both practical and symbolic reasons, to build his capital near an unimposing village called Baghdad. Not only did the site lie between Mesopotamia's two great rivers, at the juncture of the canals that linked them, but it was also close to the ancient capital of the earlier Sasanian Empire and the site of ancient Sumerian and Babylonian power. By building at Baghdad, al-Mansur could reaffirm Mesopotamia's centrality in the world and promote the universalizing ambitions of Islam.

Al-Mansur's choice had enduring effects. Baghdad became a vital crossroads for commerce. Overnight, the city exploded into a bustling world entrepôt. Chinese goods arrived by land and sea; commodities from Inner Eurasia flowed in over the Silk Roads; and cargo-laden camel caravans wound across Baghdad's western desert, linking the capital with Syria, Egypt, North Africa, and southern Spain. The unity that the Abbasids imposed from Baghdad intensified the movement of peoples, ideas, innovations, and commodities.

While Islam was gaining ground in central Afro-Eurasia, Chinese might was surging in East Asia under the Tang dynasty. Yet Islam and Tang China were clearly different worlds. The Islamic state had a universalizing religious mission: to bring humankind under the

Chapter Outline

- The Origins and Spread of Islam
- The Tang State
- The Emergence of European Christendom
- Conclusion

Core Objectives

- **DESCRIBE** and **EXPLAIN** the spread of Islam, Buddhism, and Christianity from 600 to 1000 CE.
- **COMPARE** the organizational structures of the Abbasids, Tang China, and Christendom.
- **COMPARE** the internal divisions within the Islamic, Tang, and Christian worlds.
- **EVALUATE** the relationships between religion, empire, and commercial exchange across Afro-Eurasia during this period.

authority of the religion espoused by the Prophet Muhammad. In contrast, the Tang state had no such grandiose religious goals; the ruling elite supported religious variety within China, and they did not use Buddhism to expand their control into areas outside China. Instead, the Tang rulers expected that their neighbors would copy Chinese institutions and pay tribute as symbols of respect to the greatness of the Tang Empire. Though not as expansive as Islam and the Tang Empire, Christianity also strived in this period to extend its domain and add to its converts. With Islam's warriors, traders, and scholars crossing into Europe, Chinese influences taking deeper root in East Asia, and Christendom extending itself across Europe, religion and empire once again intertwined to serve as the social foundation across much of Afro-Eurasia.

Global Storylines

- The universalizing religion of Islam, based on the message of the prophet Muhammad, originates on the Arabian Peninsula and spreads rapidly across Afro-Eurasia.

- The expanding Tang dynasty in East Asia consolidates its bureaucracy, struggles with religious pluralism, and extends its influence into Korea and Japan.

- Christianity splits over religious and political differences, leading to a divide between Roman Catholicism in the west and Greek Orthodoxy in the east.

The Origins and Spread of Islam

Islam began inside Arabia. Despite its remoteness and sparse population, by the sixth century CE Arabia was brushing up against exciting outside currents: long-distance trade, religious debate, and imperial politics. The Hijaz—the western region of Arabia bordering the Red Sea—knew the outside world through trading routes reaching up the coast to the Mediterranean. Mecca, located in the Hijaz, was an unimposing village of simple mud huts. Mecca's inhabitants included both merchants and the caretakers of a revered sanctuary called the Kaaba, a dwelling place of deities. In this remote region, one of the world's major prophets emerged, and the universalizing faith he founded soon spread from Arabia through the trade routes stretching across Southwest Asia and North Africa.

A VISION, A TEXT, A NEW COMMUNITY

Born in Mecca around 570 CE into a well-respected tribal family, Muhammad enjoyed only moderate success as a trader. Then came a revelation that would convert him into a proselytizer of a new faith. In 610 CE, while Muhammad was on a monthlong spiritual retreat in the hills near Mecca, he believed that God came to him in a vision and commanded him to recite a series of revelations.

The early revelations were short and powerful, emphasizing a single, all-powerful God (Allah) and providing instructions for Muhammad's fellow Meccans to carry this message to nonbelievers. Muhammad's early preaching had a clear message. He urged his small band of followers to act righteously, to set aside false deities, to submit themselves to the one and only true God, and to care for the less fortunate—for the Day of Judgment was imminent. Muhammad's most insistent message was the oneness of God, a belief that has remained central to the Islamic faith ever since.

These teachings, compiled into an authoritative version after the Prophet's death, constituted the foundational text of Islam: the Quran. Accepted as the word of God, the Quran's verses were understood to have flowed flawlessly through God's perfect instrument, the Prophet Muhammad. Muhammad believed that he was a prophet in the tradition of Moses, other Hebrew prophets, and Jesus and that he communicated with the same God that they did. The Quran and Muhammad proclaimed the tenets of a new faith to unite a people and expand the faith's spiritual frontiers. Islam's message already had universalizing elements, though how far it was to be extended, whether to the tribesmen living in the Arabian Peninsula or well beyond, was not at all clear at first.

In 622 CE, Muhammad and a small group of followers, opposed by Mecca's leaders because of their radical religious beliefs and their challenge to the

THE BIG PICTURE

What cultural, political, and economic factors influenced the expansion of Islam, Buddhism, and Christianity from 600 to 1000 CE?

Mecca At the great mosque at Mecca, which many consider the most sacred site in Islam, hundreds of thousands of worshippers gather for Friday prayers. Many are performing their religious duty to go on a pilgrimage to the holy places in the Arabian Peninsula.

ruling elite's authority, escaped to Yathrib (later named Medina). The perilous 200-mile journey, known as *the hijra* ("breaking off of relations" or "departure"), yielded a new form of communal unity: the *umma* ("band of the faithful"). So significant was this moment that Muslims date the beginning of the Muslim era from this year.

Medina became the birthplace of a new faith called Islam ("submission"— in this case, to the will of God) and a new community called Muslims ("those who submit"). The city of Medina had been facing tribal and religious tensions, and by inviting Muhammad and his followers to take up residence there, its elders hoped that his leadership and charisma would bring peace and unity to their city. Early in his stay Muhammad put forth the Constitution of Medina, which required the community's people to refer all disputes to God and him. Now the residents were expected to replace traditional family, clan, and tribal affiliations with loyalty to Muhammad as the last and the truest Prophet of God.

Over time, the core practices and beliefs of every Muslim would crystallize as the **five pillars of Islam**. Muslims were expected to (1) *proclaim* the phrase "there is no God but God and Muhammad is His Prophet"; (2) *pray* five times daily facing Mecca; (3) *fast* from sunup until sundown during the month of Ramadan; (4) *travel* on a pilgrimage to Mecca at least once in a lifetime if their personal resources permitted; and (5) *pay* alms in the form of taxation that would alleviate the hardships of the poor. These clear-cut expectations gave the imperial system that soon developed a doctrinal and legal structure and a broad appeal to diverse populations.

five pillars of Islam
Five practices that unite all Muslims: (1) proclaiming that "there is no God but God and Muhammad is His Prophet"; (2) praying five times a day; (3) fasting during the daylight hours of the holy month of Ramadan; (4) traveling on pilgrimage to Mecca; and (5) paying alms to support the poor.

MUHAMMAD'S SUCCESSORS AND THE EXPANDING *DAR AL-ISLAM*

In 632 CE, in his early sixties, the Prophet passed away; but Islam remained vibrant thanks to the energy of its early followers—especially Muhammad's first four successors, the "rightly guided caliphs" (the Arabic word *khalīfa* means "successor"). These caliphs ruled over Muslim peoples and the expanding state. They institutionalized the new faith. They set the new religion on the pathway to imperial greatness by linking religious uprightness with territorial expansion, empire building, and an appeal to all peoples. (See Current Trends in World History: The Origins of Islam in the Late Antique Period: A Historiographical Breakthrough.)

Driven by religious fervor and a desire to acquire the wealth of conquered territories, Muslim soldiers embarked on military conquests and sought to found a far-reaching territorial empire. This expansion of the Islamic state was one aspect of the struggle that they called *jihad*, between the *dar al-Islam* ("the world of Islam") and the *dar al-harb* ("the world of warfare"). Within fifteen years, their skill in desert warfare and their inspired military leadership enabled Muslim soldiers to expand the *dar al-Islam* into Syria, Egypt, and Iraq—centerpieces of the former Byzantine and Sasanian Empires. The Byzantines saved the core of their empire by pulling back to the highlands of Anatolia, where they could defend their frontiers. In contrast, the Sasanians hurled their remaining military resources against the Muslim armies, only to be annihilated.

A political vacuum opened in the new and growing Islamic empire with the assassination of Ali, the last of the "rightly guided caliphs." Ali was arguably the first male convert to Islam and had proved a fierce leader in the early battles for expansion. The Umayyads, a branch of one of the Meccan clans, laid claim to Ali's legacy. Having been governors of the province of Syria under Ali, the Umayyads relocated the capital to the Syrian city of Damascus and introduced a hereditary monarchy, the Umayyad caliphate, in 661 CE to resolve leadership disputes. Although tolerant of conquered populations, Umayyad dynasts did not permit non-Arabic-speaking converts to hold high political offices, an exclusive policy that contributed to their ultimate demise.

DIFFICULTIES IN DOCUMENTATION

Little can be gleaned about Muhammad himself and the evolution of Islam from Arabic-Muslim sources known to have been written in the seventh century CE. Non-Muslim sources, especially Christian and Jewish texts, which are often unsympathetic to Muhammad and early Islam, are more abundant and contain useful data on the Prophet and the early messages of Islam. These non-Muslim sources raise questions about Muhammad's birthplace, his relationship to the most powerful of the clans during his stay in Mecca, and

The Origins of Islam in the Late Antique Period: A Historiographical Breakthrough

The recent explosion of historical writing on the origins of Islam owes an enormous debt to the creation of the field of Late Antiquity, in particular the 1971 publication of Peter R. Brown's pioneering work *The World of Late Antiquity, AD 150 to 750*. Although the study itself predated the surge in globally oriented studies, it was part of a powerful globalist impulse to create new chronologies and new geographies. Its impact compelled scholars of classical and Islamic history to expand their research boundaries as well as their linguistic abilities.

Late Antiquity, according to Brown, was characterized by cultural Hellenism, centered in the Mediterranean basin. While Christianity was a decidedly new religion, Christian theologians and philosophers like Origen, Athanasius, and Augustine employed Hellenic thought to assimilate Christianity to the Hellenism of the Greco-Roman world. Brown similarly recognized Islam's incorporation of Mediterranean ideas. The Arabs, spilling out of the Arabian Peninsula, created an empire like that of the Roman-Byzantine and Sasanian Empires, even assimilating many Byzantine and Sasanian practices and preserving and adding to Greek learning, a heritage that they passed on to Europe at the time of the Renaissance. According to Brown, "[T]he religion of Islam . . . [was] the most rapid crisis in the religious history of the Late Antique period." In another work, he added that "early Islam trembled on the brink of becoming (like its ancestors—Judaism and Christianity) a Mediterranean civilization." For Brown, the true end of the Late Antique period came only in 750 CE with the foundation of the Abbasid dynasty. Islam's new capital at Baghdad (rather than the more Mediterranean-oriented Umayyad capital in Damascus), along with its thrust eastward into Iran and farther east into Khurasan, turned Islam away from the Mediterranean basin and its Greco-Roman culture and institutions.

Brown's challenge to Islamicists was to determine whether Islam in the first century of its existence was in fact an extension of Late Antiquity. In truth, historians of Islam were slow to accept the challenge, noting that other than the Quran itself, what we know about Islam's first two centuries comes from Muslim sources written in the eighth, ninth, and even tenth centuries CE. But in reality, there was a substantial non-Muslim literature on the origins of Islam that in spite of biases against Islam contained vital information on its origins.

Nearly four decades after Brown issued his challenge, classicists and Islamicists started exploring the beginnings of Islam using non-Muslim sources, including Greek, Armenian, Aramaic, Latin, Hebrew, Samaritan, Pahlavi, Syriac, and Arabic texts. Now scholars have revised our understanding of Muhammad's career, the emergence of a monotheistic creed in the Arabian Peninsula, and the Arabs' aspiration to create a universal empire. One of these scholars, Aziz al-Azmeh, has asserted that the birth of Islam was not a rupture with earlier traditions but "an even the date of his death. Many of these sources, as well as the Quran itself, stress the end-times content of Muhammad's preachings and the actions of his followers. The conclusion that scholars derive from these sources is that it was only during the eighth century CE, in the middle of the Umayyad period, that Islam lost its end-of-the-world emphasis and settled into a long-term religious and political system.

The only Muslim source that we have on Muhammad and early Islam is the Quran itself, which, according to Muslim tradition, was compiled during the caliphate of Uthman (r. 644–655 CE). Recent scholarship has questioned this claim, suggesting a later date, sometime in the early eighth century CE, for the standardization of the Quran. Some scholars even contend that the integral part of late antiquity." An important finding from these new sources is that when Islam originated, Jews and Christians were welcomed and some became Muhammad's early followers. Moreover, as the Arabs poured out of the Arabian Peninsula into Syria, Iraq, and Egypt, they did not see themselves as carrying a new religion. As monotheists, they welcomed alliances with Christians, Jews, and Zoroastrians. Islam did not emerge as a separate confessional religion, with many of the features that exist today, until the reign of the Umayyad ruler Abd al-Malik ibn Marwan (r. 685–705). Much of the evidence comes from non-Muslim sources, but evidence also appears on coins minted in the name of Abd al-Malik and, especially, on the Dome of the Rock, a building constructed in 692 in Jerusalem by Abd al-Malik. The coins and the building bear numerous inscriptions, many of them from the Quran, that proclaim the distinctiveness of Islam from Christianity and Judaism.

Questions for Analysis

- How did Brown's *World of Late Antiquity* pose a challenge to scholars of early Islam?
- Why do you think scholars of Islam were slow to respond to Brown's challenge?
- How has the understanding of Islam's beginnings changed with the contributions of recent scholarship?

Explore Further

al-Azmeh, Aziz, *The Emergence of Islam in Late Antiquity: Allah and His People* (2014).

Bowersock, G. W., *The Crucible of Islam* (2017).

Donner, Fred M., *Muhammad and the Believers at the Origins of Islam* (2010).

Grabar, Oleg, *The Shape of the Holy: Early Islamic Jerusalem* (1996).

Hoyland, Robert G., *In God's Path: The Arab Conquests and the Creation of an Islamic Empire* (2015).

Robinson, Chase F., 'Abd al-Malik (2005).

Shoemaker, Stephen J., *The Death of a Prophet: The End of Muhammad's Life and the Beginnings of Islam* (2012).

Sources: Peter R. Brown, *The World of Late Antiquity, AD 150 to 750* (London: Thames & Hudson, 1971; reprint as Norton Paperback, 1989), p. 189; Peter R. Brown, *Society and the Holy in Late Antiquity* (Berkeley: University of California Press, 1982), p. 68; Aziz al-Azmeh, *The Emergence of Islam in Late Antiquity: Allah and His People* (Cambridge, England: Cambridge University Press, 2014), pp. 2–3.

text by then had additions to, and redactions of, Muhammad's message. The Quran, in fact, is quiet on some of the most important events of Muhammad's life. It mentions the name of Muhammad only four times. For more information, scholars have depended on biographies of Muhammad, one of the first of which was compiled by Ibn Ishaq (704–767 CE); this work is not available to present scholars, but it was used by later Muslim authorities, notably Ibn Hisham (d. 833 CE), who wrote *The Life of Muhammad*, and Islam's most illustrious historian, Muhammad Ibn al-Jarir al-Tabari (838–925 CE). Although the works of these later writers come from the ninth and tenth centuries CE, Muslim tradition ever since has held these sources to be reliable on Muhammad's life and the evolution of Islam after the death of the Prophet.

THE ABBASID REVOLUTION

As the Umayyads spread Islam beyond Arabia, some peoples resisted what they experienced as Arab Umayyad religious impurity and repression. In particular, these peoples believed that the continuing discrimination against them despite their conversion to Islam was humiliating and unfair. The Arab Umayyad conquerors enslaved large numbers of non-Arabs. These slaves could leave their servile status only through manumission. Even so, these formerly enslaved or non-Arab peoples who converted found that they, too, were still regarded as lesser persons although they lived in Arab households and had become Muslims. This situation existed even though the Arabs totaled about 250,000 to 300,000 during the Umayyad era, while non-Arab populations were 100 times as populous, totaling between 25 and 30 million. The area where protest against Arab domination reached a crescendo was in the east, notably in Khurasan, where most of the Arab conquerors did not live separately from the local populations but instead lived in close contact with them and intermarried local, ethnically different women. Ultimately, a new coalition emerged under the Abbasi family, which claimed descent from the Prophet. Disgruntled provincial authorities and their military allies, as well as non-Arab converts, joined the movement.

After amassing a sizable military force, the Abbasid coalition trounced the Umayyad ruler in 750 CE and began its caliphate, which would last 500 years. The center of the Muslim state then shifted to Baghdad in Iraq (as we saw at the start of this chapter), signifying the eastward sprawl of the faith and its empire. This shift represented a success for non-Arab groups within Islam without eliminating Arab influence at the dynasty's center—the capital, Baghdad, in Arabic-speaking Iraq.

Islam's appeal to converts during the Abbasid period was diverse. Some turned to it for practical reasons, seeking reduced taxes or enhanced power. Others, particularly those living in ethnically and religiously diverse regions, welcomed the message of a single all-powerful God and a single community united by a clear code of laws. Islam, drawing its original impetus from the teachings and actions of a prophetic figure, followed the trajectory of Christianity and Buddhism and became a faith with a universalizing message and appeal. It owed much of its success to its ability to merge the contributions of vastly different geographic, economic, and intellectual territories into a rich yet unified culture. (See Map 9.1.)

caliphate
Islamic state, headed by a caliph—chosen either by election from the community (Sunni) or from the lineage of Muhammad (Shia)—with political authority over the Muslim community.

The Caliphate An early challenge for the Abbasid rulers was to determine how traditional, or "Arab," they could be and still rule so vast an empire. They chose to keep the bedrock political institution of the early Islamic state—the **caliphate** (the line of political rulers reaching back to Muhammad). Although the caliphs exercised political authority over the Muslim community, they were not understood to have inherited Muhammad's prophetic powers or any authority in religious doctrine. That power was reserved for religious scholars, called *ulama*.

Abbasid rule borrowed practices from successful predecessors in its mixture of Persian absolute authority and the royal seclusion of the Byzantine emperors who lived in palaces far removed from their subjects. This blend of absolute authority and decentralized power involved a delicate and ultimately unsustainable balancing act. As the empire expanded, it became increasingly decentralized politically, enabling wily regional governors and competing caliphates in Spain and Egypt to grab power. Even as Islam's political center diffused, though, its spiritual center remained fixed in Mecca, where many of the faithful gathered to fulfill their pilgrimage obligation.

The Army The Abbasids, like all rulers, relied on force to integrate their empire. Yet they struggled with what the nature of that military force should be: a citizen-conscript, all-Arab force or a professional, even non-Arab, army. In the early stages, leaders conscripted military forces from local Arab populations, creating citizen armies. Ultimately, however, the Abbasids recruited professional soldiers from Turkish-speaking communities in central Asia and from the non-Arab, Berber-speaking peoples of North and West Africa. Their reliance on foreign—that is, non-Arab—military personnel represented a major shift in the Islamic world. Not only did the change infuse the empire with dynamic new populations, but soon these groups gained political authority. Having begun as an Arab state and then incorporated strong Persian influence, the Islamic empire now embraced Turkish elements from the pastoral belts of central Asia.

Islamic Law (the *Sharia*) and Theology Islamic law, or the **sharia**, began to take shape in the Abbasid period. The work of generations of religious scholars, the *sharia* covers all aspects of practical and spiritual life, providing legal principles for marriage contracts, trade regulations, and religious prescriptions such as prayer, pilgrimage rites, and ritual fasting. The most influential early scholar of the *sharia* was an eighth-century Palestinian-born Arab, al-Shafi'i, who insisted that Muhammad's laws as laid out in the Quran, in addition to his sayings and actions as written in later reports (*hadith*), provided all the legal guidance that Islamic judges needed. This shift gave *ulama* (Muslim scholars) a central place in Islam since only their spiritual authority, and not the political authority of the caliphs, was qualified to define religious law. The *ulama*'s ascendance opened a sharp division within Islam: between the secular realm of the caliphs and the religious sphere of religious judges, experts on Islamic law, teachers, and holy men.

Gender in Early Islam Pre-Islamic Arabia was one of the last regions in Southwest Asia where patriarchy had not triumphed. Instead, men still

sharia
Body of Islamic law that has developed over centuries, based on the Quran, the sayings of Muhammad (*hadith*), and the legal opinions of Muslim scholars (*ulama*).

The Global View

NORTH SEA

EUROPE

ATLANTIC
OCEAN

FRANKISH
EMPIRE

Aachen

Tours
732 ✗

Danube R.

KINGDOM
OF THE
VISIGOTHS

Toledo
712

Lisbon
711

Cordoba
711

711 ✗

PYRENEES
714   721 ✗ 720
720

BYZANTINE

EMPIRE

Constantinople
717

BLACK

ANATOLIA

Rhodes
654

TAURUS MTS.

670, 674, 717   654

654

64

Carthage
697

702
720

720

MEDITERRANEAN   SEA

Tripoli
647

Barca
643

Jerusalem
638

Alexandria
642 ✗

Al-Fustat
(Cairo)

ATLAS MOUNTAINS

NORTH

AFRICA

SAHARA DESERT

EGYPT

Nile R.

Niger R.

Legend

🟫	Muslim lands by 634 CE
🟩	Muslim lands by 656 CE
🟨	Muslim lands by 756 CE
→	Muslim raid
✗	Muslim victory, with date
✗	Muslim defeat, with date
656	Date of Muslim conquest
◀	Further expansion of Islam
——	Byzantine Empire, 610 CE
——	Sasanian Empire, 610 CE
——	Frankish Empire, 610 CE
•	City

Map 9.1 The Spread of Islam during the First Millennium

Islam emerged in the Arabian Peninsula in the seventh century CE. Within 150 years, leaders of this religious community had conquered a vast amount of territory.

- What regions did the Muslims take over by 634 CE? By 756 CE?
- What were the limits to Muslim expansion during the first 150 years, according to the map? How would you explain these limits?
- Beyond the initial areas of Islamic conquest, where did Islam continue to expand? What do you think drew Islam into these regions?

CENTRAL ASIA

Lake Balkas

ARAL SEA

Talas River 751 ✕

CASPIAN SEA

SOGDIANA

Bukhara •   • Samarkand

Euphrates R.

✕ Nineveh 627
Mosul

• Nishapur

• Balkh

ZAGROS MTS.

IRANIAN PLATEAU

Samarra

• Herat

Indus R.

THAR DESERT

Damascus

• Baghdad

• Isfahan

SASANIAN

Tigris R.

✕✕ Qadisiya 636

EMPIRE

• Kandahar

ASIA

Persian Gulf

Hormuz

Ganges R.

SOUTHWEST

SOUTH ASIA

ARABIAN DESERT

• Medina

✕ Badr 624

RED SEA

• Mecca

ARABIAN

PENINSULA

ARABIAN SEA

| 0 | | 500 | | 1000 Miles |
| 0 | 500 | | 1000 Kilometers | |

married into women's families and moved to those families' locations, as was common in tribal communities. Some women engaged in a variety of occupations and, if they became wealthy, even married more than one husband. But contact with the rest of Southwest Asia, where men's power over women prevailed, was already altering women's status in the Arabian Peninsula before the birth of Muhammad.

Muhammad's relations with women reflected these changes. As a young man, he married a woman fifteen years his senior—Khadija, an independent trader—and took no other wives before she died. It was Khadija to whom he went in fear following his first revelations. She wrapped him in a blanket and assured him of his sanity. She was also his first convert. Later in life, however, he took younger wives, some of whom were widows of his companions, and insisted on their veiling (partly as a sign of their modesty and privacy). He married his favorite wife, Aisha, when she was only nine or ten years old. As a major source for collecting Muhammad's sayings, Aisha became an important figure in early Islam.

By the time Islam reached Southwest Asia and North Africa, where strict gender rules and women's subordinate status were entrenched, the new faith was adopting a patriarchal outlook. Muslim men could divorce freely; women could not. A man could take four wives and numerous concubines; a woman could have only one husband. Well-to-do women, always veiled, lived secluded from male society. Still, the Quran did offer women some protections. Men had to treat each wife with respect if they took more than one. Women could inherit property (although only half of what a man inherited). Marriage dowries went directly to the bride rather than to her guardian, indicating women's independent legal standing; and while a woman's adultery drew harsh punishment, its proof required eyewitness testimony. The result was a legal system that reinforced men's dominance over women but empowered magistrates to oversee the definition of male honor and proper behavior.

THE BLOSSOMING OF ABBASID CULTURE

Core Objectives

EVALUATE the relationships between religion, empire, and commercial exchange across Afro-Eurasia during this period.

The arts flourished during the Abbasid period, a blossoming that left its imprint throughout society. Within a century of Abbasid rule, Arabic had superseded Greek as the Muslim world's preferred language for poetry, literature, medicine, science, and philosophy. Arabic spread beyond native speakers to become the language of the educated classes. Arabic scholars preserved and extended Greek and Roman thought, in part through the transmission of treatises by Aristotle, Hippocrates, Galen, Ptolemy, and Archimedes, among others. To house such manuscripts, patrons of the arts and sciences—including the caliphs—opened magnificent libraries.

The Muslim world absorbed scientific breakthroughs from China and other areas: Muslims incorporated the use of paper from China, adopted siege warfare from China and Byzantium, and assimilated knowledge of plants from the ancient Greeks. From Indian sources, scholars borrowed a numbering system based on the concept of zero and units of ten—what we today call Arabic numerals. Arab mathematicians were pioneers in arithmetic, geometry, algebra, and trigonometry. Since much of Greek science had been lost in the west and later was reintroduced via the Muslim world, the Islamic contribution to the west was of immense significance. Thus, this intense borrowing, translating, storing, and diffusing of ideas brought worlds together.

ISLAM IN A WIDER WORLD

As Islam spread and decentralized, it generated dazzling and often competitive dynasties in Spain, North Africa, and points farther east. Each dynastic state revealed the Muslim talent for achieving high levels of artistry far from its heartland. But growing diversity led to a problem: Islam fragmented politically. No single political regime could hold its widely dispersed believers together. (See Map 9.2.)

Cities in Spain One extraordinary Muslim state arose in Spain under Abd al-Rahman III (r. 912–961 CE), the successor ruler of a Muslim kingdom founded there over a century earlier. Abd al-Rahman brought peace and stability to a violent frontier region where civil conflict had disrupted commerce and intellectual exchange. His evenhanded governance promoted amicable relations among Muslims, Christians, and Jews, and his diplomatic relations with Christian potentates as far away as France, Germany, and Scandinavia generated impressive commercial exchanges between western Europe and North Africa. He expanded and beautified the capital city of Cordoba, and his successor made the Great Mosque of Cordoba one of Spain's most stunning sites. In the nearby city Madinat al-Zahra, Abd al-Rahman III surrounded the city's administrative offices and mosque with verdant gardens of lush tropical and semitropical plants, tranquil pools, fountains that spouted cooling waters, and sturdy aqueducts that carried potable water to the city's inhabitants.

Talent in Central Asia In the eastern regions of the Islamic empire, Abbasid rulers in Baghdad surrounded themselves with learned men from Sogdiana, the central Asian territory where Greek learning had flourished. The Barmaki family, who for several generations held high administrative offices under the Abbasids, came from the central Asian city of Balkh. Loyal servants of the caliph, the Barmakis made sure that wealth and talent from the crossroads of Asia were funneled into Baghdad. Devoted patrons of the arts, the Barmakis promoted and collected Arabic translations of Persian, Greek, and Sanskrit manuscripts. They also encouraged central Asian scholars to enhance their

Map 9.2 Political Fragmentation in the Islamic World, 750–1000 CE

By 1000 CE, the Islamic world was politically fractured and decentralized. The Abbasid caliphs still reigned in Baghdad, but they wielded very limited political authority.

- What are the regions where major Islamic powers emerged?
- What areas were Sunni? Which were Shiite?
- Looking back to empires in the Mediterranean and Southwest Asia in earlier periods, how would you compare the area controlled by Islam with the extent of the Roman Empire (Chapter 7), Hellenistic kingdoms (Chapter 6), and the Persian Empire (Chapter 4)? What do you think accounts for the differences?

learning by moving to Baghdad. These scholars included the Islamic cleric al-Bukhari (d. 870 CE), who was a renowned collector of *hadith*; the mathematician al-Khwarizmi (c. 780–850 CE), who modified Indian digits into Arabic numerals and wrote the first book on algebra; and the philosopher al-Farabi (d. 950 CE), from a Turkish military family, who also made his way to Baghdad, where he studied eastern Christian teachings and promoted the Platonic ideal of a philosopher-king. Even when the Abbasid caliphate began to decline, intellectual vitality continued under the patronage of local rulers. The best example of this is, perhaps, the polymath Ibn Sina (known in the

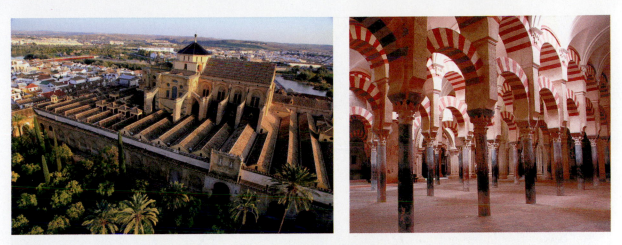

The Great Mosque of Cordoba The Great Mosque of Cordoba was built in the eighth century CE by the Umayyad ruler Abd al-Rahman I and added to by other Muslim rulers. Built on the site of a Gothic church, which had been placed on the site of an earlier Roman temple, the mosque's most striking features were alternating red and white arches, made of jasper, onyx, marble, and granite and fashioned from materials from the Roman temple and other buildings in the vicinity. Around the doors and across the walls Arabic calligraphy proclaimed Muhammad's message and asserted the superiority of Arabic as God's chosen language.

west as Avicenna; 980–1037), whose *Canon of Medicine* stood as the standard medical text in both Southwest Asia and Europe for centuries.

Trade in Sub-Saharan Africa Carried by traders and scholars, Islam also crossed the Sahara Desert and penetrated well into Africa, where merchants exchanged weapons and textiles for gold, salt, and slaves. (See Map 9.3.) Trade did more than join West Africa to North Africa. It generated prodigious wealth, which allowed centralized political kingdoms to develop. The most celebrated was Ghana, which lay at the terminus of North Africa's major trading routes and was often hailed in Arab sources for its gold, as well as its pomp and power. Seafaring Muslim traders carried Islam into East Africa via the Indian Ocean. As early as the eighth century CE, coastal trading communities in East Africa were exporting ivory and possibly slaves. By the tenth century, the East African coast featured a mixed African-Arab culture. The region's evolving Bantu language absorbed Arabic words and before long gained a new name, Swahili (derived from the Arabic plural of the word meaning "coast").

Green Revolution in the Islamic World New crops, especially food crops, leaped across political and cultural borders during this period, offering expanding populations more diverse and nutritious diets and the ability to feed increased numbers. Most of them originated in Southeast Asia, made their way to India, and dispersed throughout the Muslim world and into China. These crops included new strains of rice, taro, sour oranges, lemons,

Map 9.3 Islam and Trade in Sub-Saharan Africa, 700–1000 CE

Islamic merchants and scholars, not Islamic armies, carried Islam into sub-Saharan Africa. Trace the trade routes in Africa, being sure to follow the correct direction of trade.

- According to the map key and icons, what commodities were Islamic merchants seeking below the Sahara?
- What were the major trade routes and the direction of trade in Africa?
- How did trade and commerce shape the geographic expansion of the Islamic faith?

limes, and most likely coconut palm trees, sugarcane, bananas, plantains, and mangoes. Sorghum and possibly cotton and watermelons arrived from Africa.

Once Muslims conquered the Sindh in northern India in 711 CE, the crop innovations pioneered in Southeast Asia made their way to the west. Soon a "green revolution" in crops and diet swept through the Muslim world. Sorghum supplanted millet and the other grains of antiquity because it was hardier, had higher yields, and required a shorter growing season. Citrus trees added flavor to the diet and provided refreshing drinks during the summer heat. Increased cotton cultivation led to a greater demand for textiles.

For over 300 years, farmers from northwest India to Spain, Morocco, and West Africa made impressive use of the new crops. They increased agricultural output, slashed fallow periods, and grew as many as three crops on lands that formerly had yielded one. (See Map 9.4.) As a result, farmers could feed larger communities; even as cities grew, the countryside became more densely populated and even more productive.

OPPOSITION WITHIN ISLAM: SHIISM AND THE FATIMIDS

Islam's whirlwind rise generated internal tensions from the start. It is hardly surprising that a religion that extolled territorial conquests and created a large empire in its first decades would also spawn dissident religious movements that challenged the existing imperial structures. Muslims shared a reverence for a basic text and a single God but often had little else in common. Religious and political divisions only grew deeper as Islam spread into new corners of Afro-Eurasia.

Sunnis and Shiites Early division within Islam was fueled by disagreements about who should succeed the Prophet, how the succession should take place, and who should lead Islam's expansion into the wider world. **Sunnis** (from the Arabic word meaning "tradition") accepted that the political succession from the Prophet to the four "rightly guided caliphs" and then to the Umayyad and Abbasid dynasties was the correct one. The vast majority of Muslims today are Sunni. Dissidents, like the Shiites, contested the Sunni understanding of political and spiritual authority. **Shiites** ("members of the party of Ali") felt that the proper successors should have been Ali, who had married the Prophet's daughter Fatima, and then his descendants. Ali was one of the early converts to Islam and one of the band of Meccans who had migrated with the Prophet to Medina. The fourth of the "rightly guided caliphs," he ruled over the Muslim community from 656 to 661 CE, dying at the hands of an assassin who struck him down as he was praying in a mosque in Kufa, Iraq. Shiites believed that Ali's descendants, whom they called *imams*, had

Sunnis
Majority sect within modern Islam that follows a line of political succession from Muhammad, through the first four caliphs (Abu Bakr, Umar, Uthman, and Ali), to the Umayyads and beyond, with caliphs chosen by election from the *umma* (not from Muhammad's direct lineage).

Shiites
Minority tradition within modern Islam that traces political succession through the lineage of Muhammad and breaks with Sunni understandings of succession at the death of Ali (cousin and son-in-law of Muhammad and fourth caliph) in 661 CE.

Map 9.4 Agricultural Diffusion in the First Millennium

The second half of the first millennium saw a revolution in agriculture throughout Afro-Eurasia. Agriculturalists across the landmass increasingly cultivated similar crops.

- Where did the staple crops originate? In what direction and where did most of them flow?
- What role did the spread of Islam and the growth of Islamic empires (see Map 9.1) play in the process?
- What role did Southeast Asia and the Tang dynasty play in the spread of these crops?

religious and prophetic power as well as political authority—and thus should be spiritual leaders.

Shiism appealed to regional and ethnic groups whom the Umayyads and Abbasids had excluded from power; it became Islam's most potent dissident force and created a permanent divide within Islam. Shiism was well established in the first century of Islam's existence, and over time the Sunnis and Shiites diverged even more than these early political disputes over succession might have indicated. Both groups had their own versions of the *sharia*, their own collections of *hadith*, and their own theological tenets.

The Jenne Mosque and al-Azhar Mosque The Jenne Mosque (*left*) arose in the kingdom of Mali when that kingdom was at the height of its power. The mosque speaks to the depth and importance of Islam's roots in the Malian kingdom. The mosque of al-Azhar (*right*) is Cairo's most important ancient mosque. Built in the tenth century CE by the Fatimid conquerors and rulers of Egypt, it quickly became a leading center for worship and learning, frequented by Muslim clerics and admired in Europe.

The Fatimids Repressed in what is present-day Iraq and Iran, Shiite activists made their way to North Africa, where they joined with dissident Berber groups to topple several rulers. In 909 CE, a Shiite religious and military leader, Abu Abdallah, overthrew the Sunni ruler there. Thus began the Fatimid regime.

After conquering Egypt in 969 CE, the Fatimids set themselves against the Abbasid caliphs of Baghdad, refusing to acknowledge their legitimacy and claiming to speak for the whole Islamic world. The Fatimid rulers established their capital at al-Qahira (or Cairo). Early on they founded al-Azhar Mosque, which attracted scholars from all over Afro-Eurasia and spread Islamic learning outward. They also built other elegant mosques and centers of learning. The Fatimid regime lasted until the late twelfth century, though its rulers made little headway in persuading the Egyptian population, most of whom remained Sunnis, to embrace their Shiite beliefs.

By 1000 CE Islam, which had originated as a radical religious revolt in a small corner of the Arabian Peninsula, had grown into a vast political and religious empire. It had become the dominant force in the middle regions of Afro-Eurasia. Like its rival in this part of the world, Christianity, it aspired to universality. But unlike Christianity, it was linked from its outset to political power. Muhammad and his early followers created an empire to facilitate the expansion of their faith, while their Christian counterparts inherited an empire when Constantine embraced the new faith. A vision of a world under the jurisdiction of Muslim caliphs, adhering to the dictates of the *sharia*, drove Muslim armies, merchants, and scholars to territories thousands of miles away from Mecca and Medina. Yet as Islam's reach stretched thin, political fragmentation within the Muslim world meant that Islam's reach could not extend to much of western Europe and China.

The Tang State

Core Objectives

COMPARE the organizational structures of the Abbasids, Tang China, and Christendom.

The rise of the powerful Tang Empire (618–907 CE) in China paralleled Islam's explosion out of Arabia and its impact throughout Afro-Eurasia. Once again the landmass had two centers of power, as Islam replaced the Roman Empire in counterbalancing the power and wealth of China. Like the Umayyads and the Abbasids, the Tang dynasty promoted a cosmopolitan culture. Under Tang rule Buddhism, medicine, and mathematics from India gave China's chief cities an international flavor. China became a hub for East Asian integration and spread its influence to Korea and Japan.

TERRITORIAL EXPANSION UNDER THE TANG DYNASTY

The Tang dynasty expanded the boundaries of the Chinese state and reestablished its dominance in East and central Asia. After the fall of the Han, China had faced a long period of political fragmentation (see Chapter 8). As had happened several times before, yet another sudden change in the course of the Yellow River caused extensive flooding on the North China plain and set the stage for the emergence of the Tang dynasty. Revolts ensued as the population faced starvation. Li Yuan, the governor of a province under the short-lived Sui dynasty (589–618 CE) marched on Chang'an and took the throne in 618. He promptly established the Tang dynasty and began building a strong central government by increasing the number of provinces and doubling the number of government offices. By 624 CE, the initial steps of establishing the Tang dynasty were complete; but Li Yuan's ambitious son, Li Shimin, forced his father to abdicate and took the throne in 627 CE.

An expanding Tang state required a large and professionally trained army, capable of defending far-flung frontiers and squelching rebellious populations. Toward these efforts the Tang built a military organization of aristocratic cavalry and peasant soldiers. The cavalry regularly clashed on the northern steppes with encroaching nomadic peoples, who also fought on horseback; at its height the Tang military had 700,000 horses. At the same time, between 1 and 2 million peasant soldiers garrisoned the south and toiled on public works projects.

Much like the Islamic forces, the Tang's frontier armies increasingly relied on pastoral nomadic soldiers from the Inner Eurasian steppe. Notable were the Uighurs, Turkish-speaking peoples who had moved into western China and by 750 CE constituted the empire's most potent military force. These warriors mobilized fearsome cavalries, fired longbows at distant range, and wielded steel swords and knives in hand-to-hand combat. The Tang military also pushed the state into Tibet, the Red River valley in northern Vietnam, Manchuria, and Bohai (near Korea).

Legend:
- Tang Empire, 618–907 CE
- Chinese cultural region outside empire
- Area under Tang control, 645–763 CE
- City
- TURKS People
- Canal
- Area of high population density
- Abbasid Empire, c. 750 CE

Map 9.5 The Tang State in East Asia, 750 CE

The Tang dynasty, at its territorial peak in 750 CE, controlled a state that extended from central Asia to the East China Sea.

- Which parts of the Tang dynasty benefited from the canal system that had been enhanced by its short-lived predecessor, the Sui?
- How did the area under Tang control change over time? Based on your reading of the chapter and the information on the map, what factors shaped the area controlled by the Tang?
- What foreign areas were under Tang control? What areas were heavily influenced by Tang government and culture?

At the empire's height, Tang armies controlled more than 4 million square miles of territory (see Map 9.5)—an area as large as the entire Islamic world in the ninth and tenth centuries CE. Once the Tang administrators brought South China's rich farmlands under cultivation (by draining swamps, building an intricate network of canals and channels, and connecting lakes and rivers to the rice lands), the state was able to collect taxes from roughly

10 million families, representing 57 million individuals. Most of these taxes took the form of agricultural labor, which propelled the expansion of cultivated frontiers throughout the south.

ORGANIZING THE TANG EMPIRE

The Tang Empire emulated the Han in many ways, but its rulers also introduced new institutions. The heart of the agrarian-based Tang state was the magnificent capital city of Chang'an, the population of which reached 1 million, half of whom lived within its impressive city walls. The outer walls enclosed a 30-square-mile area. Internal security arrangements made it one of the safest urban locales for its age. Its more than 100 quarters were separated from each other by interior walls with gates that were closed at night, after which no one was permitted on the streets. Horsemen patrolled the streets until the gates reopened in the morning. Chang'an had a large foreign population, estimated at one-third of its total, and a diverse religious life. Zoroastrian fires burned as worshippers sacrificed animals and chanted temple hymns. Nestorian Christians from Syria found a welcoming community, and Buddhists could boast ninety-one of their own temples in Chang'an in 722 CE.

Confucian Administrators Despite the Tang's reliance on the fruits of agriculture and a military force, the day-to-day control of the empire required an efficient and loyal civil service. Entry into the Tang ruling group required knowledge of Confucian ideas and all the commentaries on the Confucian classics. It also required skill in the intricate classical Chinese language, in which this literature was written.

The Tang state introduced the world's first fully written **civil service examinations**, which tested sophisticated literary skills and knowledge of the Confucian classics. The Tang also allowed the use of Daoist classics as texts for the exams, believing that the early Daoists represented another important stream of ancient wisdom. Candidates for office, whom local elites recommended, gathered in the capital triennially to take qualifying exams. They had been trained since the age of three in the classics and histories, either by their families or in Buddhist temple schools. Most failed, but those who were successful underwent further trials to evaluate their character and determine the level of their appointments. New officials were selected from the pool of graduates on the basis of social conduct, eloquence, skill in calligraphy and mathematics, and legal knowledge.

Although official careers were in theory open to anyone of proven talent, in practice they were closed to certain groups. Women were not permitted to serve, nor were sons of merchants or those who could not afford a classical education. Over time, though, Tang civil examinations forced aristocrats to compete with commoner southern families, whose growing wealth gave them

civil service examinations
Set of challenging exams instituted by the Tang to help assess potential bureaucrats' literary skill and knowledge of the Confucian classics.

access to educational resources that made them the equals of the old elites. Through examinations, this new elite eventually outdistanced the sons of the northern aristocracy in the Tang government in effect by out-studying them.

The system underscored education as the primary avenue for success. Even impoverished families sought the best classical education they could afford for their sons. Although few succeeded in the civil examinations, many boys and even some girls learned the fundamentals of reading and writing. The Buddhists played a crucial role in extending education across society: as part of their charitable mission, their temple schools introduced many children to primers based on classical texts. Many Buddhist monks, in fact, entered the clergy only after not qualifying for or failing the civil examinations.

China's Female Emperor Not all Tang power brokers were men. The wives and mothers of emperors wielded influence in the court—usually behind the scenes, but sometimes publicly. The most striking example is Empress Wu.

Born into a noble family, Wu Zhao played music and mastered the Chinese classics as a young girl. Because she was witty, intelligent, and beautiful, Wu was recruited before age thirteen to Li Shimin's court and became his favorite concubine. When Li Shimin died, his son assumed power and became Emperor Gaozong. Wu became the new emperor's favorite concubine and gave birth to the sons he required to succeed him. As the mother of the future emperor, Wu enjoyed heightened political power. Subsequently, she took the place of Gaozong's empress, Wang, by accusing her of killing Wu's newborn daughter.

After Gaozong suffered a stroke, Wu became administrator of the court, a position equal to the emperor's. She created a secret police force to spy on her opposition, and she jailed or killed those who challenged her. Following her husband's death, she made herself Empress Wu (r. 684–705 CE). She expanded the military and recruited her administrators from the civil examination candidates to oppose her enemies at court.

Wu ordered scholars to write biographies of famous women, and she empowered her mother's clan by assigning high political posts to her relatives. Later, she moved her court from Chang'an to Luoyang, where she tried to establish a new "Zhou dynasty," seeking to imitate the widely admired era of Confucius. Empress Wu elevated Buddhism over Daoism as the favored state religion, invited the most gifted Buddhist scholars to her capital at Luoyang, built Buddhist temples, and subsidized spectacular cave sculptures. In fact, Chinese Buddhism achieved its highest officially sponsored development in this period.

Eunuchs Tang rulers protected themselves, their possessions, and especially their women with loyal and well-compensated **eunuchs** (men surgically castrated as youths and thus sexually impotent). By the late eighth century CE,

eunuchs
Surgically castrated men who rose to high levels of military, political, and personal power in several empires (for instance, the Tang and the Ming Empires in China; the Abbasid and Ottoman Empires; and the Byzantine Empire).

The Tang Court This tenth-century CE painting of elegant ladies of the Tang imperial court enjoying a feast and music (*left*) tells us a great deal about the aesthetic tastes of elite women in this era. It also shows the secluded "inner quarters," where court ladies passed their daily lives far from the hurly-burly of imperial politics. Castrated males, known as eunuchs (*right*), guarded the women and protected the royal family of Tang emperors. By the late eighth century CE, eunuchs were fully integrated into the government and wielded a great deal of military and political power.

more than 4,500 eunuchs were fully entrenched in the Tang Empire's institutions, wielding significant power not only within the imperial household but at the court and beyond. For instance, the Chief Eunuch controlled the military. Through him, the military power of court eunuchs extended to every province and garrison station in the empire, forming an all-encompassing network. This eunuch bureaucracy mediated between the emperor and the provincial governments.

Under Emperor Xianzong (r. 806–820 CE), eunuchs acted as a third pillar of the government, working alongside the official bureaucracy and the imperial court. Yet by 838 CE, the delicate balance of power among throne, eunuchs, and civil officials had evaporated. Eunuchs became an unruly political force in late Tang politics, and their competition for influence produced political instability.

AN ECONOMIC REVOLUTION

At its height, Tang China's economic achievements included agricultural production based on an egalitarian land allotment system, an increasingly fine handicrafts industry, a diverse commodity market, and a dynamic urban life. The earlier short-lived Sui dynasty had started this economic progress by reunifying China and building canals, especially the Grand Canal linking the north and south. The Tang continued by centering their efforts on the Grand Canal and the Yangzi River, which flows from west to east. These waterways aided communication and transport throughout the empire. The south grew richer, largely through the backbreaking labor of immigrants from the north. Fertile land along the Yangzi became China's new granary, and areas south of the Yangzi became its demographic center.

Green Revolution in Tang China The same agricultural revolution that was sweeping through South Asia and the Muslim world also took East Asia by storm. China received the same crops that Muslim cultivators were carrying westward. Rice was critical. New varieties entered from the south, and groups migrating from the north (after the collapse of the Han Empire) eagerly took them up. Soon Chinese farmers became the world's most intensive wet-field rice cultivators. Early- and late-ripening seeds supported two or three plantings a year. Champa rice, introduced from central Vietnam, was especially popular for its drought resistance and rapid ripening.

Because rice needs ample water, Chinese hydraulic engineers went into the fields to design water-lifting devices, which peasant farmers used to construct hillside rice paddies. This new rice cultivation was also the partial impetus for the canal building already mentioned. Engineers dug canals linking rivers and lakes, and they even drained swamps, alleviating the malaria that had long troubled the region. Their efforts yielded a booming and constantly moving rice frontier.

Trade in Luxuries Chinese merchants took full advantage of the Silk Roads to trade with India and the Islamic world; when rebellions in northwest China and the rise of Islam in central Asia jeopardized the land route, the "silk road by the sea" became the avenue of choice. From all over Asia and Africa, merchant ships arrived in South China ports bearing spices, medicines, and jewelry in exchange for Chinese silks and porcelain. In the large cities of the Yangzi delta, workshops produced rich brocades (silk fabrics), fine paper, intricate woodblock prints, unique iron casts, and exquisite porcelains. Art collectors all across Afro-Eurasia especially valued Tang "tricolor pottery," decorated with brilliant hues. Chinese artisans transformed locally grown cotton into highest-quality clothing. Painting and dyeing technology improved, and the resulting superb silk products generated significant tax revenue. These Chinese luxuries dominated the trading networks that reached Southwest Asia, Europe, and Africa via the Silk Roads and the Indian Ocean.

ACCOMMODATING WORLD RELIGIONS

The early Tang emperors tolerated remarkable religious diversity. Nestorian Christianity, Zoroastrianism, and Manichaeanism (a radical Christian sect) had entered China from Persia during the time of the Sasanian Empire. Islam came later. These spiritual impulses—together with Buddhism and the indigenous teachings of Daoism and Confucianism—spread throughout the Tang Empire and at first were widely used to enhance state power.

The Growth of Buddhism Buddhism, in particular, thrived under Tang rule. Initially, Emperor Li Shimin distrusted Buddhist monks because they avoided serving the government and paying taxes. Yet after Buddhism gained acceptance as one of the "three ways" of learning—joining Daoism and Confucianism—Li endowed huge monasteries, sent emissaries to India to collect texts and relics, and commissioned Buddhist paintings and statuary. Caves along the Silk Roads, such as those at Dunhuang, provided ideal venues for monks to paint the inside walls where religious rites and meditation took place.

Anti-Buddhist Campaigns By the mid-ninth century CE, however, the growing influence of China's hundreds of thousands of Buddhist monks and nuns threatened Confucian and Daoist leaders, who responded by arguing that Buddhism's values conflicted with native traditions. One Confucian-trained scholar-official, Han Yu, even attacked Buddhism as a foreign doctrine of barbarian peoples who were different in language, culture, and knowledge. Although Han Yu was exiled for his objections, two decades later the state began suppressing Buddhist monasteries and confiscating their wealth, fearing that religious loyalties would undermine political ones. Increasingly

One of the Four Sacred Mountains This monastery on Mount Song is famous because in 527 CE an Indian priest, Bodhidharma, arrived there to initiate the Zen school of Buddhism in China.

intolerant Confucian scholar-administrators argued that the Buddhist monastic establishment threatened the imperial order.

By the mid-ninth century CE, the Tang state openly persecuted Buddhism. Emperor Wuzong (814–846 CE), for instance, closed more than 4,600 monasteries and destroyed 40,000 temples and shrines. More than 260,000 Buddhist monks and nuns endured a forced return to secular life, after which the state parceled out monastery lands to taxpaying landlords and peasant farmers. To expunge the cultural impact of Buddhism, classically trained literati revived ancient prose styles and the teachings of Confucius and his followers. Their efforts reversed some of the early Buddhist successes in China.

Although Buddhism remained important, the Tang era represented the triumph of homegrown ideologies (Confucianism and Daoism) over a foreign universalizing religion (Buddhism). In addition, by permanently dismantling huge monastic land holdings, the Tang ensured that no religion would rival its power. Successor dynasties continued to keep religious establishments weak and fragmented, although Confucianism maintained a more prominent role within society as the basis of the ruling classes' ideology and as a quasi-religious belief system for a wider portion of the population. The result was persistent religious diversity within China.

TANG INTERACTIONS WITH KOREA AND JAPAN

While China was opening up to the cultures of its western regions, its own culture was reaching out to the east—to Korea and, eventually, to Japan. (See Map 9.6.) Chinese influence, both indirect and direct, had reached into Korea for more than a millennium, and later into Japan, but not without local resistance and the flourishing of entirely indigenous and independent political and religious developments.

Early Korea Interactions with China played a fundamental role in the history of the Korean Peninsula. Unification in 668 CE under the Silla—one of three rival states in Korea—enabled Koreans to establish an autonomous government, but their opposition to the Chinese did not deter them from modeling their government on the Tang imperial state. The Silla rulers dispatched annual emissaries bearing tribute payments to the Chinese capital and regularly sent students and monks. As a result, literary Chinese—not their own dialect—became the written language of Korean elites. Chinese influence extended to the way in which the Silla state organized its court and bureaucracy and to the construction of the Silla capital city of Kumsong, which imitated the Tang capital of Chang'an. Silla's fortunes became entwined with the Tang's to such an extent, however, that once the Tang declined, Silla also began to fragment and ultimately surrendered to the Goryeo kingdom in 935 CE.

Map legend:

- Extent of Silla power, 670–935 CE
- Extent of Nara state by 600 CE
- Capital
- City
- Buddhist temple
- Shinto shrine
- Holy mountain
- Bohai
- Tang Empire

Amur R.

BOHAI

HOKKAIDO AINU

SEA OF JAPAN

HONSHŪ

Wonsan
Lelang
KOREA
SILLA
Kumsong (Kyongju)

JAPAN

Heian-kyo
Ise
Osaka
Heijo-kyo
Nara

Yellow R.

YELLOW SEA

SHIKOKU

KYŪSHŪ

PACIFIC OCEAN

EAST CHINA SEA

Yangzi R.

0   50   100 Miles
0 50 100 Kilometers

Map 9.6 Tang Borderlands: Korea and Japan, 600–1000 CE

The Tang dynasty held great power over emerging Korean and Japanese states, although it never directly ruled either region.

- Based on the map, what connections do you see between Korea and Japan and the Tang Empire?
- What, if any, relationship do you see between the proliferation of Buddhist temples and Shinto shrines?

Early Japan Like Korea, Japan also felt influences emanating from China, and it responded by thwarting and accommodating them at the same time. But Japan enjoyed added autonomy: it was an archipelago of islands, separated from the mainland although internally fragmented. In the mid-third century CE, a warlike group had arrived by sea from Korea and imposed military and social control over southern Japan. These conquerors—known as the "Tomb Culture" because of their elevated burial sites—unified Japan by extolling their imperial ancestors and maintaining their social hierarchy. In time, the complex aristocratic society that had developed within the Tomb Culture gave rise to a Japanese state on the Yamato plain in the region now known as Nara. In becoming the ruling faction in this area, the Yamato clan incorporated native Japanese as well as Korean migrants.

After 587 CE, the Soga kinship group—originally from Korea but by 500 CE a minor branch of the Yamato imperial family—became Japan's leading family and controlled the Japanese court through intermarriage. Soon they were attributing their cultural innovations to their own Prince Shotoku (574–622 CE), of Soga and Yamato descent. Contemporary Japanese scribes claimed that Prince Shotoku, rather than Korean immigrants, introduced Buddhism to Japan and that his illustrious reign sparked Japan's rise as an exceptional island kingdom. Shotoku promoted both Buddhism and Confucianism, thus enabling Japan, like its neighbor China, to accommodate numerous religions.

Indeed, religious influences flowed into Japan, contributing to spiritual diversity while bolstering the Yamato rulers. Although Prince Shotoku and later Japanese emperors turned to Confucian models for government, they also dabbled in occult arts and Daoist purification rituals. In addition, governmental edicts promoted Buddhism as the state religion of Japan. Association with Buddhism gave the Japanese state extra status by lending it the prestige of a universal religion whose appeal stretched to Korea, China, and India. State-sponsored spiritual diversity led native Shinto cults—which believed that after death a person's soul (or spirit) became a Shinto *kami*, or local deity, provided that it was nourished and purified through proper rituals and festivals—to formalize a creed of their own. The introduction of Confucianism and Buddhism motivated Shinto adherents to assemble their diverse religious practices into a well-organized belief system. Shinto priests now collected ancient liturgies, and Shinto rituals (such as purification rites to ward off demons and impurities) gained recognition in the state's official Department of Religion.

Political integration under Prince Shotoku did not mean political stability, however. In 645 CE, the Nakatomi kinship group seized the throne and eliminated the Soga and their allies. Via intermarriage with the imperial clan, the Nakatomi became the new spokesmen for the Yamato tradition. Thereafter, Nakatomi no Kamatari (614–669 CE) enacted a series of reforms that

Horyuji Temple The main hall of the Horyuji Temple in Nara, Japan (*left*), was built in the seventh century CE. Several murals from the seventh and eighth centuries CE cover the walls inside the temple. In this fresco (*right*), the Yakushi (or medicine/healing) Buddha of Pure Land Buddhism sits with bodhisattvas and other attendants, while winged celestial beings, called *apsaras* (or *tennin*, in Japanese Buddhism), fly above. Some scholars have argued that the artists who created the frescoes in the Horyuji Temple based the images on drawings made of the Buddha in Tang China.

reflected Confucian principles of government allegedly enunciated by Sho-toku. These reforms enhanced the power of the ruler, no longer portrayed simply as an ancestral kinship group leader but now depicted as an exalted "emperor" (*tenno*) who ruled by the mandate of heaven, as in China, and exercised absolute authority.

THE FALL OF TANG CHINA

Hence, at the eastern end of Afro-Eurasia, the Tang, as well as the Silla of Korea and the Yamato state of Japan, interacted with one another and blended both religious and political authority to maintain stability. The peak of Chinese power in East Asia occurred just as the Abbasids were expanding into Tang portions of central Asia. Yet, despite the Abbasid Empire's spread, China in 750 CE was still the most powerful and best-administered empire in the world. When Muslim forces drove the Tang from Turkistan in 751 CE at the Battle of Talas River, however, their success emboldened groups such as the Sogdians and Tibetans to challenge the Tang and even take their cap-ital. As a result, the Tang gradually retreated into the old heartlands along the Yellow and Yangzi Rivers. Thereafter, misrule, court intrigues, economic exploitation, and popular rebellions weakened the empire, but the dynasty held on for over a century more until northern invaders toppled it in 907 CE.

The Emergence of European Christendom

European historians debate whether or not to label this period in Europe "the Dark Ages." Scholars who have spurned the term "Dark Ages," in favor of the term "Late Antiquity," emphasize the political and cultural continuities between Rome and its successor states, especially in the eastern Mediterranean, and the new dynamic institutions that arose in Rome's wake. Scholars who favor the term "Dark Ages" stress what they see as a sharp cultural, political, and economic decline accompanying the Roman Empire's fall, especially in the western Mediterranean. "The Dark Ages," as a label for this period, has been resurrected by environmental historians, who argue that the period was indeed dark, as a result of a colder and drier climate. Agricultural production declined, famines occurred year after year, and infectious diseases spread across Afro-Eurasia (for example, the plague during the reign of Justinian; see Chapter 8). This harsher climate and the diseases that accompanied it between 400 and 900 CE caused dying and mortality on a large scale. The drought that was wreaking havoc in Europe is the same one that helped spur Arab tribal peoples, carrying the banner of Islam, to pour out of their severely affected lands in the Arabian Peninsula in search of better lands and a better life, as other nomadic groups had done.

Although western Europe lacked a highly developed political empire like that of the Abbasids or the Tang dynasty, Christianity increasingly unified the peoples of Europe. In fifth-century CE western Europe, the mighty Roman military machine gave way to a multitude of warrior leaders whose principal allegiances were local. The political ideal of the Roman Empire certainly influenced western Europeans, but the true inheritor of Rome in the west was the Roman Catholic Church, with its priests, missionaries, and monks. In northern Europe, a frontier mentality and the Viking threat shaped Christianity. In eastern Europe and Byzantium, a form of Christianity known as Greek Orthodoxy had become dominant by 1000 CE. Together, these two major strands of the faith—the western Roman Catholic Church and eastern Greek Orthodoxy—constituted the realm of Christendom, the entire portion of the world in which Christianity prevailed as a unifying institution. (See Map 9.7.)

CHARLEMAGNE'S FLEDGLING EMPIRE

Far removed from the old centers of high culture, Charlemagne (r. 768–814 CE), ruler of the Franks, expanded his western European kingdom through constant warfare and plunder. In 802 CE, Harun al-Rashid, the Abbasid ruler of Baghdad, sent the gift of an elephant to Charlemagne, already the king

Core Objectives

COMPARE the internal divisions within the Islamic, Tang, and Christian worlds.

Map 9.7 Christendom, 600–1000 CE

The end of the first millennium saw much of Europe divided between two versions of Christianity, each with different traditions. On the map, locate Rome and Constantinople, the two seats of power in Christianity.

- According to the map, what were the two major regions where Christianity held sway? In what directions did Roman Catholic Christianity and Greek Orthodox Christianity spread?

- Where were important churches and monasteries heavily concentrated? Why do you think they were focused in those regions?

- The map suggests that missionaries played important roles in spreading Roman Catholicism and Greek Orthodoxy. Why do you think this was the case?

of the Franks for three decades and recently crowned by the pope in Rome as "Holy Roman Emperor" (on Christmas Day in 800 CE). While the Franks interpreted the caliph's gift as an acknowledgment of Charlemagne's power, al-Rashid more likely sent the rare beast as a gracious reminder of his own formidable sway. In al-Rashid's eyes, Charlemagne's "empire" was a minor principality. Although Charlemagne claimed the lofty title of emperor and ultimately controlled much of western Europe, compared with the Islamic world's rulers and vast domain, he was a political lightweight.

Charlemagne's empire had a population of less than 15 million; he rarely commanded armies larger than 5,000; and his tax system was rudimentary. At a time when the caliph's palace at Baghdad covered nearly 250 acres, Charlemagne's palace at Aachen was merely 330 by 655 feet. Baghdad itself was almost 40 square miles in area, whereas there was no "town" outside the palace at Aachen. The palace was essentially a large country house set in open countryside, where Charlemagne and his Franks hunted wild boar from horseback.

Charlemagne and his men were representatives of the warrior class that dominated post-Roman western Europe. After Roman control faded away, war became once again the duty and joy of the aristocrats. Although the Franks vigorously engaged in trade, even that trade was based on war. Europe's principal export at this time was Europeans, and the massive sale of prisoners of war, in markets at Alexandria, Tunis, and southern Spain, financed the Frankish Empire. The main victims of this trade were Slavic-speaking peoples, tribal hunters and cultivators from eastern Europe. This trade in Slavs gives us the modern term *slave*.

Yet Charlemagne's seemingly uncivilized and inhospitable empire offered fertile ground for Christianity to sink down roots. As Christianity grew in western and northern Europe, the rough frontier mentality fueled its expansionist ambitions.

Charlemagne's Palace and Chapel Though not large by Byzantine or Islamic standards, Charlemagne's palace and chapel were heavy with symbolic meaning. A royal hall for banqueting in Frankish, "barbarian" style was linked by a covered walkway to the imperial domed chapel, which was meant to look like a miniature version of Hagia Sophia in Constantinople. Outside the chapel was a courtyard, like that outside the shrine of Saint Peter at Rome.

CHRISTIANITY IN WESTERN EUROPE

Christians of the west, including those in northern Europe, felt that theirs was the one truly universal religion. Their goal was to bring rival groups into a single **Roman Catholic Church** that was replacing a political unity lost in western Europe when the Roman Empire fell. Drawing on the ideas of Augustine of Hippo (c. 410 CE), the western Christians believed that the

Roman Catholic Church
Western European Christianity, centered on the papacy at Rome, that emphasizes the atoning power of Jesus's death and aims to expand as far as possible.

monasticism

From the Greek word *monos* (meaning "alone"), the practice of living without the ties of marriage or family, forsaking earthly luxuries for a life of prayer and study. While Christian monasticism originated in Egypt, a variant of ascetic life had long been practiced in Buddhism.

"city of God" would take earthly shape in the form of the Catholic Church, and that the Catholic Church was not just for Romans—it was for all times and for all peoples.

The arrival of Christianity in northern Europe provoked a cultural revolution. Preliterate societies now encountered a sacred text—the Bible—in a language that seemed utterly strange. Latin had become a sacred language, and books themselves were vehicles of the holy. The bound codex, which had replaced the clumsy scroll, was still messy: it had no divisions between words, no punctuation, no paragraphs, no chapter headings. Readers who knew Latin as a spoken language could understand the script. But Irishmen, Saxons, and Franks could not, for they had never spoken Latin. Consequently, great care was lavished on the few parchment texts—like the Gospels in the Book of Kells (c. 800 CE)—that were prepared with words separated, sentences correctly punctuated and introduced by uppercase letters, and chapter headings.

Those producing these stunning Bibles were starkly different from ordinary men and women. They were monks and nuns. Christian **monasticism** had originated in Egypt, but it suited well the missionary tendencies of Christianity in northern Europe. The root of "monastic" and "monk" is the Greek *monos*, "alone": a monastic was a man or a woman who chose to live alone, without the support of marriage or family. In Muslim (and Jewish) communities, religious leaders emphasized what they had in common with those around them. Many Islamic scholars, theologians, and mystics were married men, even merchants and courtiers. In the Christian west, the opposite was true: warrior societies honored small groups of monks and nuns who were utterly unlike themselves: unmarried, unfit for warfare, and intensely literate in an incomprehensible tongue.

Monasticism appealed to a deep sense that the very men and women who had little in common with ordinary people were best suited to mediate between believers and God. Laypersons (common believers, not clergy) gave gifts to the monasteries and offered them protection. In return, they gained the prayers of monks and nuns and the reassurance that although they themselves were warriors and men of blood, the monks' and nuns' interventions on their behalf would keep them from going to hell. Payment for human sin, the atoning power of Jesus's crucifixion, and the efficacy of monastic prayers were significant theological emphases for western Roman Catholics.

The Catholic Church of northern Europe was a religion of monks, whose communities represented an otherworldly alternative to the warrior societies of the time. By 800 CE, most regions of northern Europe held great monasteries, many of which were far larger than the local villages. Supported by thousands of serfs donated by kings and local warlords, the monasteries became powerhouses of prayer that kept the regions safe.

Northern Christianity also gained new ties to an old center: the city of Rome. The Christian bishop of Rome had always enjoyed much prestige but

Monasticism The great monasteries of the age of Charlemagne, such as the St. Gallen Monastery (*left*), were like Roman legionary settlements. Placed on the frontiers of Germany, they were vast stone buildings, around which entire towns would gather. Their libraries, the largest in Europe, were filled with parchment volumes, carefully written out and often lavishly decorated in a "northern," Celtic style. Monasticism was also about the lonely search for God at the very end of the world, which took place in these Irish monasteries (*right*) on the Atlantic coast. The cells, made of loose stones piled in round domes, are called "beehives."

often took second place to other bishops in Carthage, Alexandria, Antioch, and Constantinople. Though people spoke of him with respect as *papa* ("the grand old man"), many others shared that title.

By the ninth century CE, this picture had changed. Believers from the distant north saw only one *papa* left in western Europe: Rome's pope. New Christians in northern borderlands wanted to find a religious leader for their hopes, and the Catholic Church of western Europe united behind the symbolic center of Rome and its popes. Charlemagne fed this desire when, in 800 CE, he went out of his way to celebrate Christmas Day by visiting the shrine of Saint Peter at Rome. There, Pope Leo III acclaimed him as the new "emperor" of the west. A "modern" Rome—inhabited by popes, famous for shrines of the martyrs, and protected by a "modern" Christian monarch from the north—was what Charlemagne's subjects wanted.

VIKINGS AND CHRISTENDOM

Vikings from Scandinavia exposed the weakness of Charlemagne's Christian empire. When al-Rashid's elephant died in 813 CE, the Franks viewed it as an omen of coming disasters. The great beast keeled over when his handlers marched him out to confront a Viking army from Denmark. Charlemagne died the next year. In the next half century, Charlemagne's empire of borderland peoples met its match on the wide border between the European landmass and the Atlantic. (See Map 9.8.)

Map 9.8 The Age of Vikings and the Slave Trade, 800–1000 CE

Vikings from Scandinavia dramatically altered the history of Christendom.

- In what directions did the Vikings carry out their voyages, trade routes, and raids?
- What were the geographic limits of the Viking explorations in each direction?
- In what direction did the slave trade move, and what role did the Vikings and the Holy Roman Emperors play in expanding the slave trade?

Vikings

Warrior group from Scandinavia that used its fighting skills and sophisticated ships to raid and trade deep into eastern Europe, southward into the Mediterranean, and westward to Iceland, Greenland, and North America.

The **Vikings**' motives were announced in their name, which derives from the Old Norse *vik*, "to be on the warpath." The Vikings sought to loot the now-wealthy Franks and replace them as the dominant warrior class of northern Europe. They succeeded in their plundering and enslaving because of a deadly technological advantage: ships of unparalleled sophistication. Light and agile, Viking ships traveled far up the rivers of northern Europe and could even be carried overland from one river system to another. Under sail, the same boats could tackle open water and cross the North Atlantic. In the ninth century CE, the Vikings set their ships on both courses.

They sacked the great monasteries along the coasts of Ireland and Britain and overlooking the Rhine and Seine Rivers. At the same time, Norwegian adventurers colonized the uninhabited island of Iceland, and then Greenland. By 982 CE, they had even reached continental North America and established a settlement at L'Anse aux Meadows on the Labrador coast.

More long-lasting than their settlements in North America was the Viking incursion into eastern Europe. The Vikings sailed east along the Baltic and then turned south, edging up the rivers that crossed the watershed of central Russia. Here the Dnieper, the Don, and the Volga Rivers flow south into the Black Sea and the Caspian. Consequently, the Vikings created an avenue of commerce that linked Scandinavia and the Baltic directly to Constantinople and Baghdad. Muslim geographers bluntly called this route "The Highway of the Slaves" because so much of the trade was in human cargo.

Oseberg Ship The Viking ship was a triumph of design. It could be rowed up the great rivers of Europe, or its sails could take it across the Atlantic. The Oseberg ship pictured here contained the early ninth-century CE burial of a high-status Viking woman.

In 860 CE, more than 200 Viking longships gathered ominously beneath the walls of Constantinople in the straits of the Bosporus. What they found was not poorly defended monasteries or Charlemagne's rustic Aachen, but a city with a population exceeding 100,000 protected by well-engineered late-Roman walls. For nearly two centuries, Constantinople had resisted almost yearly campaigns launched by the successive Islamic empires of Damascus and later Baghdad. These campaigns were deflected by Constantinople's highly professional generals, a line of skillfully constructed fortresses that controlled the roads across Anatolia, and a deadly technological advantage in naval warfare: Greek fire. This combination of petroleum and potassium, when sprayed from siphons, would explode in a great sheet of flame on the water. The experience and weaponry of Byzantium were too much for the Vikings, and their raid of the most significant city in eastern Christendom was a spectacular failure. Despite their inability to take Byzantium, the Vikings asserted an enduring influence through their forays across the North Atlantic, their brutal interactions with Christian communities in northern Europe, and their expansion into eastern Europe, especially the slave trade they facilitated there.

GREEK ORTHODOX CHRISTIANITY

Outlasting so many military emergencies bolstered the morale of the eastern Christians and led to a flowering of Christianity in this region.

Greek Orthodoxy
Branch of eastern Christianity, originally centered in Constantinople, that emphasizes the role of Jesus in helping humans achieve union with God.

Jelling Stone Carved on the side of this great stone, Christ appears to be almost swallowed up in an intricate pattern of lines. For the Vikings, complicated interweaving like serpents or twisted gold jewelry was a sign of majesty: hence, in this, the first Christian monument in Denmark, Christ is part of an ancient pattern of carving, which brought good luck and victory to the king.

Not just Constantinople but Justinian's Hagia Sophia—its heart—had survived significant threats. That great building and the solemn Greek divine liturgy that reverberated within its domed spaces symbolized the branch of Christian belief that dominated in the east: **Greek Orthodoxy**. Greek Orthodox theology held that Jesus became human less to atone for humanity's sins (as emphasized in Roman Catholicism) and more to facilitate *theosis* (a transformation of humans into divine beings). This was a truly distinct message from that which prevailed in the Roman Catholicism of the west.

In the tenth century CE, as Charlemagne's empire collapsed in western Europe, large areas of eastern Europe became Greek Orthodox, not Roman Catholic. In addition, Greek Christianity gained a spiritual empire in Southwest Asia. The conversion of Russian peoples, Balkan Slavs, and Arab peoples to Greek Orthodox Christianity was a complex process. It reflected a deep admiration for Constantinople on the part of Russians, Bulgarians, Arabs, and Slav princes. It was an admiration as intense as that of any western Catholic for the Roman popes.

By the year 1000 CE, then, there were two Christianities: the new and confident "borderland" Roman Catholicism of western Europe and an ancient Greek Orthodoxy. Western Roman Catholics believed that their church was destined to expand everywhere. Greek Orthodox Christians were less euphoric but believed that their church would forever survive the regular ravages of invasion. This was a significant difference in attitude; Greek Orthodox Christians considered the Franks barbarous and grasping, and western Roman Catholics contemptuously called the eastern Christians "Greeks" and condemned them for "Byzantine" cunning.

Thus, like Islam, the Christian world was divided, with differences in heritage, theology, customs, and levels of urbanization. At that time, the Orthodox world was considerably more ancient and more cultured than the world of the Catholic west. And each dealt with Islam differently. At Constantinople, eastern Christianity held off Muslim forces that constantly threatened the great city and its Christian hinterlands. In the west, by contrast, Muslim expansionism reached all the way to the Iberian Peninsula. Western Christendom, led by the Roman papacy, set about spreading Christianity to pagan tribes in the north, and it began to contemplate retaking lands from the Muslims. Yet in spite of their deep political, ethnic, and theological differences, the two regions of Christianity conducted a brisk trade in commodities and ideas.

Conclusion

Despite the intermixing of peoples, ideas, and goods across Afro-Eurasia, new political and cultural boundaries were developing that would split this landmass in ways previously unimaginable. The most important dividing force was religion, as Islam challenged and slowed the spread of Christianity and as Buddhism challenged the ruling elite of Tang China. As a consequence, Afro-Eurasia's major cultural zones began to compete in terms of religious and cultural doctrines. The Islamic Abbasid Empire pushed back the borders of the Tang Empire. But the conflict grew particularly intense between the Islamic and Christian worlds, where the clash involved faith as well as frontiers.

The Tang Empire revived Confucianism, insisting on its political and moral primacy as the foundation of a new imperial order, and it embraced the classical written language as another unifying element. By doing so, the Tang counteracted universalizing foreign religions—notably Buddhism but also Islam—spreading into the Chinese state. The same adaptive strategies influenced new systems on the Korean Peninsula and in Japan.

In some circumstances, faith followed empire and relied on rulers' support or tolerance to spread the word. This was the case especially in East Asia. At the opposite extreme, empire followed faith—as in the case of Islam, whose believers endeavored to spread their empire in every direction. The Islamic empire and its successors represented a new force: expanding political power backed by one God whose instructions were to spread his message. In the worlds of Christianity, a common faith absorbed elements of a common culture (shared books, a language for the learned classes). But in the west, political rulers never overcame inhabitants' intense allegiance to local authority.

While universalizing religions expanded and common cultures grew, debate raged within each religion over foundational principles. In spite of the diffusion of basic texts in "official" languages, regional variations of Christianity, Islam, and Buddhism proliferated as each belief system spread. The period from 600 to 1000 CE demonstrated that religion, reinforced by prosperity and imperial resources, could bring peoples together in unprecedented ways. But it could also, as the next chapter will illustrate, drive them apart in bloody confrontations.

Focus On
Faith and Empire

The Islamic Empire

- Warriors from the Arabian Peninsula defeat Byzantine and Sasanian armies and establish an Islamic empire stretching from Morocco to South Asia.

- The Abbasid state takes over from the Umayyads, crystallizes the main Islamic institutions of the caliphate and Islamic law, and promotes cultural achievements in religion, philosophy, and science.

- Disputes over Muhammad's succession lead to a deep and enduring split between Sunnis and Shiites.

Tang China

- The Tang dynasty dominates East Asia and exerts a strong influence on Korea and Japan.

- Tang rulers balance Confucian and Daoist ideals with Buddhist thought and practice.

- A common written language and shared philosophy, rather than a single universalizing religion, integrate the Chinese state.

Christian Europe

- Charlemagne establishes an empire in part of western Europe, while the Vikings raid and trade from their homeland in Scandinavia westward to North America, southward to the Mediterranean, and eastward to the Caspian Sea.

- Monks, nuns, and Rome-based popes spread Christianity throughout western Europe.

- Constantinople-based Greek Orthodoxy survives the spread of Islam.

CHRONOLOGY

	600 CE	700 CE
The Islamic World	Life of Muhammad 570–632 CE	
	Umayyad caliphate 661–750 CE	
East Asia	Prince Shotoku initiates reforms in Japan 574–622 CE	
Europe	Arab armies conquer much of Byzantine Empire, but the empire survives 632–661 CE	

THINKING ABOUT GLOBAL CONNECTIONS

- **Thinking about Crossing Borders and Faith & Empire** As Islam spread outside its initial Arabian context, the faith underwent a range of developments. As Christianity and Buddhism continued to spread, these traditions underwent changes as well. Compare the shifts that took place within Islam as it expanded (600–1000 CE) with those within Buddhism and Christianity, not only in their earlier periods (see Chapter 8) but also during the period from 600 to 1000 CE.

- **Thinking about Changing Power Relationships and Faith & Empire** As each of the empires discussed in this chapter matured, divisions developed within the faiths that initially had helped to bring unity to their respective regions. In the Abbasid world, a split developed between Sunni and Shiite Muslims. In Tang China, Buddhism and Confucianism vied for political influence.

Christendom divided into the Roman Catholic west and the Greek Orthodox east. What was the exact nature of each religious disagreement? How do these divisions compare in terms of the root of the internal rifts and their impact in the political realm?

- **Thinking about Worlds Together, Worlds Apart** The empires described in this chapter reached across wide swaths of territory and interacted with vibrant societies on their margins. The peoples of Europe struggled with the onslaught of the fierce Vikings. The peoples of Tang China interacted with neighboring Korea and Japan. How does the interaction of Europe and the Vikings compare with the relations of the Tang and the external influences that they experienced? To what extent did the Abbasids contend with similar exchanges?

Key Terms

caliphate p. 400

civil service
    examinations p. 414

eunuchs p. 415

five pillars of Islam p. 396

Greek Orthodoxy p. 430

monasticism p. 426

Roman Catholic
    Church p. 425

sharia p. 401

Shiites p. 409

Sunnis p. 409

Vikings p. 428

 Go to **INQUIZITIVE** to see what you've learned—and learn what you've missed—with personalized feedback along the way.

800 CE	900 CE	1000 CE

Abbasid caliphate 750–1258 CE

Fatimid Shiite regime founded in Egypt 969 CE ●

Tang dynasty in China 618–907 CE

Silla rulers unify Korean state 668–935 CE

Catholic Church based in Rome begins converting much of northern Europe into Christian communities eighth century CE

Charlemagne unites much of western Europe into a short-lived Christian kingdom 768–814 CE

Vikings raid much of Europe and establish strong commercial links across eastern Europe ninth–tenth centuries CE

Global Themes and Sources

Women and Community in the Context of New Empires

Within each of the new empires discussed in this chapter, belief systems addressed the diverse and influential roles—as daughters, wives, mothers, caregivers, and more—that women played in family and community. In historical contexts ranging from the early Islamic states and western Christendom to Tang China and Viking Scandinavia, practical concerns as well as religious and philosophical ideals influenced the realities that governed women's lives.

Muslim ideas about women and family originated in the Arabian Peninsula and spread as the Umayyad and Abbasid Empires extended their reach from Southwest Asia into central Asia and across North Africa and into Spain. As Christendom expanded across western Europe, so too did the influence of both the monastics at the heart of Christianity and Christian ideas about women's roles. Although Tang authorities vacillated in their official support of Buddhism, there was no doubt about the enduring importance of Confucian thought in political and social matters, including its ideas about family and filial piety. And, as Vikings set out from Scandinavia into the British Isles, Iceland, and beyond, as well as into the interior of central Europe, Viking expectations for women went with them and were shaped by the new ideas, including Christianity, that they encountered.

The four sources included here offer an opportunity to explore the factors shaping women's lives, as well as the ways that women shaped the expanding empires described in this chapter. Working with sources about women in this, and every, historical context presents challenges. We must account for the (sometimes hostile) male authorship and audience of the sources, balance ideal expectations for women against the realities of lived experience, and work around the sources' frequent focus on elite and exceptional women, for instance, Empress Wu of the Tang or Khadija, the wife of Muhammad, rather than on unnamed nonelite women. By examining primary sources to identify societal expectations regarding women, we can better understand the broader historical context of each empire. Conversely, each of these empires provides a context for exploring the role of women within the diverse communities that spanned Eurasia from 600 to 1000 CE.

Analyzing Women in the Context of New Empires

- What do these texts (and the empires they represent) reveal about societal expectations for women's behavior and for men's behavior toward women? What might account for any similarities and differences?

- Which women and men are included, explicitly and implicitly, in the expectations laid out in these texts? Who is excluded? What do these inclusions and exclusions suggest about the historical contexts of these texts?

- Based on the historical sources, how did the belief systems of Islam, Christianity, and Confucianism offer contexts for gender expectations and family structures?

- In what ways do the expectations about women's behavior and their role in the community challenge your impression of women's roles in the historical contexts of Abbasid Islam, western Christendom, Tang China, and the Viking world?

- How might an increasingly connected world have modified gender roles as the belief systems that created those roles came into contact with one another?

PRIMARY SOURCE 9.1

Surah 4, An-Nisa, from the Quran (seventh century CE)

Surah 4 ("On Women") of the Quran outlines rules about marriage, inheritance, and the treatment of orphans, among other family-oriented topics. Recorded in the seventh century CE, the Quran, along with *hadith* (sayings of Muhammad), formed the basis for later *sharia* (law) that regulated community matters. As you read the source, imagine the community shaped by the expectations laid out in this excerpt from the Quran.

....

- Who is the presumed audience of these rules? How do you know?

- What are the rules with respect to women? The rules with respect to orphans? The rules about inheritance?

- What are the benefits of abiding by the rules? The penalties for breaking them?

- What conclusions might you draw about the wider context of the early Islamic world, given the ideals laid out in this text for how to treat women and children?

....

4.1 O people! be careful of (your duty to) your Lord, Who created you from a single being and created its mate of the same (kind) and spread from these two, many men and women; and be careful of (your duty to) Allah, by Whom you demand one of another (your rights), and (to) the ties of relationship; surely Allah ever watches over you.

4.2 And give to the orphans their property, and do not substitute worthless (things) for (their) good (ones), and do not devour their property (as an addition) to your own property; this is surely a great crime.

4.3 And if you fear that you cannot act equitably towards orphans, then marry such women as seem good to you, two and three and four; but if you fear that you will not do justice (between them), then (marry) only one or what your right hands possess; this is more proper, that you may not deviate from the right course.

4.4 And give women their dowries as a free gift, but if they of themselves be pleased to give up to you a portion of it, then eat it with enjoyment and with wholesome result.

4.5 And do not give away your property which Allah has made for you a (means of) support to the weak of understanding, and maintain them out of (the profits of) it, and clothe them and speak to them words of honest advice.

4.6 And test the orphans until they attain puberty; then if you find in them maturity of intellect, make over to them their property, and do not consume it extravagantly and hastily, lest they attain to full age; and whoever is rich, let him abstain altogether, and whoever is poor, let him eat reasonably; then when you make over to them their property, call witnesses in their presence; and Allah is enough as a Reckoner.

4.7 Men shall have a portion of what the parents and the near relatives leave, and women shall have a portion of what the parents and the near relatives leave, whether there is little or much of it; a stated portion.

4.8 And when there are present at the division the relatives and the orphans and the needy, give them (something) out of it and speak to them kind words.

4.9 And let those fear who, should they leave behind them weakly offspring, would fear on their account, so let them be careful of (their duty to) Allah, and let them speak right words.

4.10 (As for) those who swallow the property of the orphans unjustly, surely they only swallow fire into their bellies and they shall enter burning fire.

4.11 Allah enjoins you concerning your children: The male shall have the equal of the portion of two females; then if they are more than two females, they shall have two-thirds of what the deceased has left, and if there is one, she shall have the half; and as for his parents, each of them shall have the sixth of what he has left if he has a child, but if he has no child and (only) his two parents inherit him, then his mother shall have the third; but if he has brothers, then his mother shall have the sixth after (the payment of) a bequest he may have bequeathed or a debt; your parents and your children, you know not which of them is the nearer to you in usefulness; this is an ordinance from Allah: Surely Allah is Knowing, Wise.

4.12 And you shall have half of what your wives leave if they have no child, but if they have a child, then you shall have a fourth of what they leave after (payment of) any bequest they may have bequeathed or a debt; and they shall have the fourth of what you leave if you have no child, but if you have a child then they shall have the eighth of what you leave after (payment of) a bequest you may have bequeathed or a debt; and if a man or a woman leaves property to be inherited by neither parents nor offspring, and he (or she) has a brother or a sister, then each of them two shall have the sixth, but if they are more than that, they shall be sharers in the third after (payment of) any bequest that may have been bequeathed or a debt that does not harm (others); this is an ordinance from Allah: and Allah is Knowing, Forbearing.

4.13 These are Allah's limits, and whoever obeys Allah and His Apostle, He will cause him to enter gardens beneath which rivers flow, to abide in them; and this is the great achievement.

4.14 And whoever disobeys Allah and His Apostle and goes beyond His limits, He will cause him to enter fire to abide in it, and he shall have an abasing chastisement.

Source: Sura 4, translated by Marmaduke Pickthall, revised by Jane Dammen McAuliffe, in *The Norton Anthology of World Religions*, vol. 2, *Islam*, edited by Jack Miles et al. (New York: W. W. Norton, 2015), pp. 87–89.

PRIMARY SOURCE 9.2

Law of Adamnan (700 CE)

The *Law of Adamnan* demonstrates both the brutal realities of tribal warfare as Christianity spread into Ireland and the efforts of Christian clergy and lay leaders to do something about it. This text describes how a monk named Adamnan of Iona was inspired by his mother and an angel to develop a law protecting noncombatants that was then signed by kings, nobles, and religious authorities. As you read the *Law of Adamnan*, consider how the source describes the impact of the Christian context on the treatment of women.

- According to the text, what were the lives of women and children like before Adamnan's Law?

- What protections for women, children, and clergy does Adamnan's Law create? What are the penalties for not treating women and children the way the law demands?

- What rationale, explicit and implicit, does the source offer to explain the reasoning for these new protections?

1. Five ages before the birth of Christ, to wit, from Adam to the Flood, from the Flood to Abraham, from Abraham to David, from David to the Captivity in Babylon, from the Babylonian Captivity to the birth of Christ. During that time women were in bondage and in slavery, until Adamnan, son of Ronan, son of Tinne, son of Aed, son of Colum, son of Lugaid, son of Setne, son of Fergus, son of Conall, son of Niall, came.

2. *Cumalach* [slave] was a name for women till Adamnan come to free them. . . .

3. The work which the best women had to do, was to go to battle and battlefield, encounter and camping, fighting and hosting, wounding and slaying. On one side of her she would carry her bag of provisions, on the other her babe. Her wooden pole upon her back. Thirty feet long it was, and had on one end an iron hook, which she would thrust into the tress of some woman in the opposite battalion. Her husband behind her, carrying a fence-stake in his hand, and flogging her on to battle. For at that time it was the head of a woman, or her two breasts, which were taken as trophies.

4. Now after the coming of Adamnan no woman is deprived of her testimony, if it be bound in righteous deeds. For a mother is a venerable treasure, a mother is a goodly treasure, the mother of saints and bishops and righteous men, an increase in the Kingdom of Heaven, a propagation on earth.

5. Adamnan suffered much hardship for your sake, O women, so that ever since Adamnan's time one half of your house is yours, and there is a place for your chair in the other half; so that your contract and your safeguard are free; and the first law made in Heaven and on earth for women is Adamnan's Law. . . .

***

33. Here begins the speech of the angel to Adamnan: . . . On Pentecost eve a holy angel of the Lord came to him, and again at Pentecost after a year, and seized a staff, and struck his side and said to him; "Go forth into Ireland, and make a law in it that women be not in any manner killed by men, through slaughter or any other death, either by poison, or in water, or in fire, or by any other beast, or in a pit, or by dogs, but that they shall die in their lawful bed. Thou shalt establish a law in Ireland and Britain for the sake of the mother of each one, because a mother has borne each one, and for the sake of Mary mother of Jesus Christ, through whom all are. Mary besought her Son on behalf of

Adamnan about this Law. For whoever slays a woman shall be condemned to a twofold punishment, that is, his right hand and his left foot shall be cut off before death, and then he shall die, and his kindred shall pay seven full *cumals* [1 *cumal* (unit of measure) = 3 cows], and one-seventh part of the penance. If, instead of life and amputation, a fine has been imposed, the penance is fourteen years, and fourteen *cumals* shall be paid. But if a host has done it, every fifth man up to three hundred shall be condemned to that punishment; if few, they shall be divided into three parts. The first part of them shall be put to death by lot, hand and foot having been first cut off; the second part shall pay fourteen full *cumals*; the third shall be cast into exile beyond the sea, under the rule of a hard regimen; for the sin is great when any slays the mother and sister of Christ's mother and the mother of Christ, and her who carries a spindle and who clothes every one. But he who from this day forward shall put a woman to death and does not do penance according to the Law, shall not only perish in eternity, and be cursed for God and Adamnan, but all shall be cursed that have heard it and do not curse him, and do not chastise him according to the judgement of this Law" . . .

34. This is the enactment of Adamnan's Law in Ireland and Britain. . . . The enactment of this Law of Adamnan is a perpetual law on behalf of clerics and women and innocent children until they are capable of slaying a man, and until they take their place in the tribe, and their (first) expedition is known.

Source: Adamnan, *Anecdota Oxoniensia: Cáin Adamnáin: An Old-Irish Treatise on the Law of Adamnan*, edited and translated by Kuno Meyer (Oxford: Clarendon Press, 1905), pp. 3, 5, 23, 25.

PRIMARY SOURCE 9.3

Analects for Women (800 CE), Song Ruoxin and Song Ruozhao

In the late eighth century CE, two young women, Song Ruoxin and Song Ruozhao, composed their *Analects for Women* while in attendance at the court of the Tang emperor. This text, which expands on Ban Zhao's ideas from almost 700 years earlier, adapted Confucian thought to create a set of advice for women living around 800 CE in Tang China. As you read the text, watch for clues that suggest a Confucian context.

- Who is the presumed audience of this text? How do you know?
- What are the responsibilities of a Tang woman, according to this text? What would her life be like?
- In what ways does the text adapt Confucian values such as *ren* (benevolence), *li* (proper conduct/ritual), and *xiao* (filial piety) to women's experience?

[Ban Zhou] said: I am the wife of a virtuous man, the daughter of an eminent family. I observe all the four proprieties and am well-read in history. As I pause from women's work and read, (I find that) there have been many heroines praiseworthy and some virtuous women admirable. I feel sorry that posterity has not followed their model. I thus write this work entitled The Analects for Women in the hope of teaching women to inherit the good and guard against the evil. Those who follow these teachings will be regarded as virtuous women, whose names will rank among those of their predecessors and be passed down to future generations.

Book One: On Deportment

The first thing for any woman to learn is the principle of deportment: that of purity and chastity. If you are pure, then chastity will follow; if you are chaste, then you will be honored. Don't turn your head and look while walking. Don't show your teeth while speaking. Don't move your knees while sitting. Don't sway your dress while standing. Don't laugh out loud when happy. Don't shout when angry. Indoors or out, men and women should be in separate groups. . . . Don't give your name to a man who is not your relative. Don't become friendly with a woman who is not from a good family. Only by being decorous and proper will you be a [proper] person.

Book Five: On Serving the Parents

While still at home, every woman should revere her parents. Every morning get up early and ask after their health. When it's cold, start a fire. Use a fan to cool them when it is hot. Serve food when they are hungry, and bring tea when they are thirsty. If your parents rebuke you, don't become flustered; listen attentively and think about what they have said day and night. If there is anything that is not done accordingly, correct it as you were told. Don't take what they have said as commonplace, but obey their instructions, and never argue with them. If there is something you don't understand, don't hesitate to ask them.

When parents get old, be concerned for them morning and evening, making shoes, darning socks, and sewing clothes for them. . . . When parents suffer from any illness, don't leave their bedside. . . . Steep the medicine and try it yourself. Pray for the help of the spirits and Buddha, and hope for recovery. In case misfortune should occur or death take them, let pain penetrate to the marrow of your bones, wail and lament, never forgetting the three years of suckling. Clothe the dead and don mourning clothes. Prepare for burial and arrange the sacrifices. Do obeisance and burn joss sticks. Continue to cultivate dignity so that your parents can rise to Heaven. . . .

Book Seven: On Serving One's Husband

When a woman is married, her husband will be her master among relatives. The affinity to the former life becomes the marriage of the present life. To compare one's husband to Heaven is not meaningless. The husband [should be] firm and the wife yielding. An affectionate couple rely on each other. At home, treat your husband as respectfully as you would a guest. When he speaks to you, listen attentively. If your husband has some evil ways, remonstrate repeatedly. Don't learn from those ignorant women who bring evil on themselves. . . .

Book Eleven: On Conciliation and Yielding

The rules for managing a household for a wife are to prize harmony and filial piety above all else. When your mother-in-law rebukes you, don't feel hurt. When your father-in-law has any criticism, listen to it quietly. In the upper rooms and in the lower chambers, with nephews and nieces, you should behave harmoniously. Whether [disagreements are] right or wrong, don't get involved. [Whether an issue involves] good or bad, don't argue. Shameful family matters should never be exposed to the public. . . .

Book Twelve: On Preserving Chastity

Women of old, both chaste and virtuous, have had their names recorded in the annals of history and passed down to the present day. Women nowadays who have not learned from them should not consider it too difficult to begin. The first [principle] is that of preserving chastity; the second, that of purity and virtuousness. If there is a daughter in a family, don't [let her] leave the inner chambers. When there are guests, don't go beyond the main hall. Don't spread gossip, or speak in vile language. . . . If there occurs the misfortune of the husband dying at a young age, wear mourning clothes for three years, and remain firm in your will to preserve your chastity. Protect your family and manage your property. Clean and sweep your husband's tomb. In life or in death, it is one life shared.

Source: Song Ruoxin and Song Ruozhao, "Book of Analects for Women: Consort Song (Tang)," translated by Heying Jenny Zhan and Roger Bradshaw, *Journal of Historical Sociology* 9, no. 3 (1996): 261, 263–65, 267–68.

Unn the Deep-Minded, from the *Laxdale Saga* (c. 900 CE)

Viking sagas—such as the *Gísla saga*, the *Njáls saga*, and the *Grettis saga*—record the travels and interactions of Vikings. Women often feature as major characters in these tales. While the *Laxdale Saga* focuses on the four marriages of Guðrún and ends with her death as a Christian nun in Iceland, the saga opens in northern Scotland with the unusual life of another woman, Unn (also called Aud, in other sagas), who lived around 900 CE. Unn is certainly an exceptional character, but her matchmaking and wealth accumulation offer a glimpse into the power that a Viking woman could wield within her community.

- What are some of Unn's accomplishments, and what makes her exceptional, according to the *Laxdale Saga*?

- How is Unn able to achieve all that she does?

- What can you learn about the context of Viking family and community, and women's roles within each, by examining Unn's life in the *Laxdale Saga*?

Unn the Deep-minded was in Caithness [northern Scotland] when her son Thorstein fell. When she heard that Thorstein was dead, and her father had breathed his last, she deemed she would have no prospering in store there. So she had a ship built secretly in a wood, and when it was ready built she arrayed it, and had great wealth withal; and she took with her all her kinsfolk who were left alive; and men deem that scarce may an example be found that any one, a woman only, has ever got out of such a state of war with so much wealth and so great a following. From this it may be seen how peerless among women she was. Unn had with her many men of great worth and high birth. . . . When she was ready, Unn took her ship to the Orkneys; there she stayed a little while, and there she married off Gro, the daughter of Thorstein the Red. . . . After that Unn steered her ship to the Faroe Isles, and stayed there for some time. There she married off another daughter of Thorstein, named Olof, and from her sprung the noblest race of that land, who are called the Gate-Beards.

. . . Unn now got ready to go away from the Faroe Isles, and made it known to her shipmates that she was going to Iceland. She had with her Olaf "Feilan," the son of Thorstein, and those of his sisters who were unmarried. After that she put to sea, and, the weather being favourable, she came with her ship to the south of Iceland to Pumice-Course (Vikrarskeid). There they had their ship broken into splinters, but all the men and goods were saved.

. . . Then she went about all the Broadfirth-Dales, and took to her lands as wide as she wanted. After that Unn steered her ship to the head of the bay, and there her high-seat pillars were washed ashore, and then she deemed it was easy to know where she was to take up her abode. She had a house built there: it was afterwards called Hvamm, and she lived there. . . .

After that Unn gave to more men parts of her land-take. . . . [The text then recounts the men to whom Unn doles out parcels of land, describing their female relatives in great detail.]

Olaf "Feilan" was the youngest of Thorstein's children. He was a tall man and strong, goodly to look at, and a man of the greatest mettle. Unn loved him above all men, and made it known to people that she was minded to settle on Olaf all her belongings at Hvamm after her day. Unn now became very weary with old age, and she called Olaf "Feilan" to her and said: "It is on my mind, kinsman, that you should settle down and marry." . . . That same summer Olaf "Feilan" married Alfdis. Their wedding was at Hvamm. Unn spent much money on this feast. . . . The wedding feast was very crowded; yet there did not come nearly so many as Unn had asked, because the Islefirth people had such a long way to come. Old age fell now fast upon Unn, so that she did not get up till mid-day, and went early to bed. No one did she allow to come to her for advice between the time she went to sleep at night and the time she was aroused, and she was very angry if any one asked how it fared with her strength. . . . Unn went into the hall and a great company with her, and when all seats were taken in the hall, everyone was much struck by the lordliness of the feast. Then Unn said: "Bjorn and Helgi, my brothers, and all my other kindred and friends, I call witnesses to this, that this dwelling with all its belongings that you now see before you, I give into the hands of my kinsman, Olaf, to own and to manage." After that Unn stood up and said she would go to the bower where she was wont to sleep, but bade everyone have for pastime whatever was most to his mind, and that ale should be the cheer of the common folk. . . . But the day after Olaf went to the sleeping bower of Unn, his grandmother, and when he came into the chamber there was Unn sitting up against her pillow, and she was dead. Olaf went into the hall after that and told these tidings. Everyone thought it a wonderful thing, how Unn had upheld her dignity to the day of her death. So they now drank together Olaf's wedding and Unn's funeral honours, and the last day of the feast Unn was carried to the [burial mound] that was made for her. She was laid in a ship in the cairn, and much treasure with her, and after that the cairn was closed up.

Source: *Laxdaela Saga*, translated by Muriel A. C. Press (London: J. M. Dent, 1899; Project Gutenberg, 2006), pp. 6–12, http://www.gutenberg.org/files/17803/17803-h/17803-h.htm.

Interpreting Visual Evidence

Transmission of Religious Knowledge

A major development in the period from 600 to 1000 CE was the production of authoritative versions of religious texts. The images gathered here show the variety of forms these texts took—ranging from scroll to codex, handwritten manuscript to printed text—and the diverse materials used in making them.

The Lindisfarne Gospel was created around 700 CE by a Christian monk named Eadfrith on a remote island off England. A beautifully "illuminated" (decorated) page opens each Gospel, followed by Latin text, to which a monk named Aldred in the tenth century CE added an Old English translation between the lines. Pictured here are two pages: one showing the

beginning of the Gospel of Matthew and the other showing the last page of the codex, on which Aldred added some information about the gospels.

The "Diamond Sutra," shown in the next image, was printed in 868 CE, during the Tang dynasty, in Dunhuang, China. Using carved wooden blocks, this text with illustrations was printed on separate sheets of paper, then glued onto a scroll nearly 16 feet long. It is the oldest surviving printed text that has a date on it. In this text, written in Chinese, the Buddha instructs an elderly student that one must cut through, as with a diamond, the illusion that masks all perception.

Early manuscripts of the Quran show a variety of geometric embellishments and beautifully flowing

The Lindisfarne Gospel (700 CE, with tenth-century CE interlinear comments).

Arabic calligraphy. Pictured here are a ninth-century CE manuscript page from Tunis and a tenth-century CE Persian folio of the Quran in the Kufic lettering style. The image of the Persian Quran shows not only how the pages were laid out but also the construction of the codex.

From a world apart, the Maya Dresden Codex dates to around 1100 CE but records a text originally written perhaps 300 years before. It includes astronomical tables and ritual instructions on both sides of the bark paper, which is nearly 12 feet long. As many as six different scribes used around 350 glyphs and numerical symbols in composing this text.

Finally, the palm-leaf manuscript pictured here dates to around 1300 CE and preserves a copy of a Jain text, the *Kalpa Sutra*, the content of which dates to as early as the fourth century BCE. In the scene here, Vimal-aprava, a Jain monk, offers instruction to a prince. Like many of the Hindu and Buddhist texts that circulated in Southeast Asia, this later copy of the *Kalpa Sutra* was written in Sanskrit in ink on palm leaves that were then stacked between wooden slats and strung together.

The "Diamond Sutra" (868 CE).

Quran from Tunis (ninth century CE).

Quran from Persia (tenth century CE).

The *Kalpa Sutra* (c. 1300 CE).

The Dresden Codex (c. 1100 CE).

Questions for Analysis

1. Compare the various texts. What are the similarities and differences in terms of content, form, and decoration, and what do you think accounts for them?

2. Consider the languages in which these texts are written. What role does translation seem to play in the transmission of these texts and the preservation of the ideas they contain?

3. Given what you know from this chapter about the Abbasid caliphate, Tang China, Charlemagne's Europe, and the Vikings, what role do you think empires played in the preservation, or destruction, of religious texts?

10

Becoming "The World"

1000–1300 CE

In the late 1270s two Christian monks, Bar Sāwmā and Markōs, voyaged from what is now Beijing into the heart of the Islamic world. They were not Europeans. They were Uighurs, a Turkish people of central Asia, many of whom had converted to Christianity centuries earlier. The monks hoped to make a pilgrimage to Jerusalem in order to visit the tombs of the martyrs.

On their journey westward, Bar Sāwmā and Markōs traveled a world bound together by economic and cultural exchange. The two monks lingered at the magnificent trading hub of Kashgar in what is now western China, where caravan routes converged in a market for jade, exotic spices, and precious silks. Unable to continue on to Jerusalem due to the route's dangers (including murderous robbers), the monks parted ways at Baghdad. Bar Sāwmā was appointed an ambassador by the Buddhist Mongol il-Khan of Persia to drum up support among European leaders for an attack on Jerusalem to wrest it from Muslim control. He visited Constantinople (where the Byzantine emperor gave him gold and silver), Rome (where he met with the pope at the shrine of Saint Peter), and Paris (where he saw that city's vibrant university). In the end, neither monk ever reached Jerusalem or returned to China. Bar Sāwmā ended his days in Baghdad, and Markōs became patriarch of the Nestorian branch of Christianity, centered in modern-day Iran. Yet their voyages exemplified

Core Objectives

- **IDENTIFY** technological advances of this period, especially in ship design and navigation, and **EXPLAIN** how they facilitated the expansion of Afro-Eurasian trade.

- **DESCRIBE** the varied social and political forces that shaped the Islamic world, India, China, and Europe, and **EVALUATE** the degree to which these forces integrated cultures and geographic areas.

- **COMPARE** the internal integration and external interactions of sub-Saharan Africa with those of the Americas.

- **ASSESS** the impacts that the Mongol Empire had on Afro-Eurasian peoples and places.

the crisscrossing of people, money, goods, and ideas along the trade routes and sea-lanes that connected the world's regions.

Three related themes dominate the period from 1000 to 1300 CE. First, trade along sea-based routes increased and coastal trading cities began to expand dramatically. Second, greater trade and religious integration generated the world's four major cultural "spheres," whose inhabitants were linked by shared institutions and beliefs: the Islamic world, India, China, and Europe. Sub-Saharan Africa and the Americas also thrived during this period; however, they remained more fragmented, experiencing more limited political and economic integration. Third, the Mongol Empire, stretching from China to Persia and as far as eastern Europe, ruled over huge swaths of land in many of the world's major cultural spheres. Each of these three themes contributes to an understanding of how Afro-Eurasia became a "world" unified through trade, migration, and even religious conflict.

Global Storylines

- Advances in maritime technology lead to increased sea trade, transforming coastal cities into global trading hubs and elevating Afro-Eurasian trade to unprecedented levels.

- Intensified trade and religious integration shape four major cultural "spheres": the Islamic world, India, China, and Europe.

- Sub-Saharan Africa is drawn into Eurasian exchange, resulting in a true Afro-Eurasia—wide network, while the Americas experience more limited political, economic, and cultural integration.

- The Mongol Empire integrates many of the world's major cultural spheres.

Development of Maritime Trade

By the tenth century CE, sea routes were becoming more important than land networks for long-distance trade. Improved navigational aids, better map-making, refinements in shipbuilding, and new political support for shipping made seaborne trade easier and slashed its cost. These developments also fostered the growth of maritime commercial hubs (called anchorages), which further facilitated the expansion of maritime trade.

A new navigational instrument spurred this boom: the magnetic needle compass. This Chinese invention initially identified promising locations for houses and tombs, but eleventh-century sailors from Guangzhou (Canton) used it to find their way on the high seas. The use of this device eventually spread among navigators. The compass not only allowed sailing under cloudy skies, but it also improved mapmaking.

An array of new ship types—dhows, junks, and cogs—allowed for more impressive mastery of the seas. Dhows, ships with triangular sails called lateens, maximized the power of the monsoon trade winds on the Arabian Sea and the wider Indian Ocean. Sailing the South China seas were junks, large, flat-bottomed ships with internal sealed bulkheads, stern-mounted rudders, as many as four decks, six masts with a dozen sails, and the space to carry as many as 500 men. And, in the Atlantic, cogs, with their single mast and square sail, linked Genoa to locations as distant as the Azores and Iceland. The numbers testify to the power of the maritime revolution: while a porter could carry about 10 pounds over long distances, and animal-drawn wagons could move 100 pounds of goods over small distances, the Arab dhows could transport up to 5 tons of cargo, Atlantic cogs as much as 200 tons, and Chinese junks more than 500 tons.

Maritime traders enjoyed the protection of political authorities such as the Song rulers in China, who maintained a standing navy that protected traders and lighthouses that guided trading fleets in and out of harbors. The Fatimid caliphate in Egypt profited from maritime trade and defended merchant fleets from pirates, using armed convoys of ships to escort commercial fleets and regulate the ocean traffic. This system of protection soon spread to North Africa and southern Spain.

Long-distance trade spawned the growth of commercial cities. These cosmopolitan **entrepôts** served as transshipment centers, located on land between borders or in ports where ships could drop anchor. In these cities, traders exchanged commodities and replenished supplies. Beginning in the late tenth century CE, several regional centers became major anchorages of the maritime trade: in the west, the Egyptian port city of Alexandria on the Mediterranean (and Cairo, just up the Nile); near the tip of the Indian sub-continent, the port of Quilon (now Kollam); in the Malaysian Archipelago,

Core Objectives

IDENTIFY technological advances of this period, especially in ship design and navigation, and **EXPLAIN** how they facilitated the expansion of Afro-Eurasian trade.

the city of Melaka; and in the east, the Chinese city of Quanzhou. (See Map 10.1.) These hubs thrived under the political stability of powerful rulers who recognized that trade would generate wealth for their regimes.

Cairo and Alexandria were the Mediterranean's main maritime commercial centers. Cairo was home to numerous Muslim and Jewish trading firms, and Alexandria was their lookout post on the Mediterranean. The Islamic legal system prevalent in Egypt promoted a favorable business environment. Through Alexandria, Europeans acquired silks from China, especially the coveted *zaytuni* (satin) fabric from Quanzhou. But many more goods passed through the Egyptian anchorage: from the Mediterranean, olive oil, glassware, flax, corals, and metals; from India, gemstones and aromatic perfumes; and from elsewhere, minerals and chemicals for dyeing or tanning, and raw materials such as timber and bamboo. Paper and books (including hand-copied Bibles, Talmuds, and Qurans) traveled along this network as well.

In South India during the tenth century CE, the Chola dynasty supported the port of Quilon, which was the nerve center of maritime trade between China and the Red Sea and the Mediterranean. Trade through Quilon continued to flourish long after the Chola golden age passed away. Personal relationships were key to trade at this anchorage, as elsewhere; for instance, when striking a deal with a local merchant, a Chinese trader might mention his Indian neighbor in Quanzhou and that family's residence in Quilon. Dhows arrived in Quilon laden not only with goods from the Red Sea and Africa, but also with traders, sojourners, and fugitives. Chinese junks unloaded silks and porcelain, and picked up passengers and commodities for East Asian markets. Muslims, the largest foreign community in Quilon, lived in their own neighborhoods and shipped horses from Arab countries to India and the southeast islands, where kings viewed them as symbols of royalty. There was even trade through Quilon in elephants and cattle from tropical countries, though the most common goods were spices, perfumes, and textiles.

East of Quilon, across the Bay of Bengal, Melaka became a key cosmopolitan entrepôt because of its strategic location and proximity to Malayan tropical produce. Indian, Javanese, and Chinese merchants and sailors spent months in such ports selling their goods, purchasing return cargo, and waiting for the winds to change direction so they could reach their next destination.

Antique Chinese Compass
Chinese sailors from Guangzhou (Canton) started to use magnetic needle compasses in the eleventh century. By the thirteenth century, magnetic needle compasses were widely used on ships in the Indian Ocean and were starting to appear in the Mediterranean.

entrepôts
Multiethnic trading stations, often supported and protected by regional leaders, where traders exchanged commodities and replenished supplies in order to facilitate long-distance trade.

During peak season, Southeast Asian ports were crowded with colorfully dressed foreign sailors, local Javanese artisans who produced finely textured batik handicrafts, and traders eager for profit. The traders converged from all over Asia to flood the markets with their merchandise and to search for pungent herbs, aromatic spices, and agrarian staples such as quick-ripening strains of rice to ship out.

In China, the Song government set up offices of seafaring affairs in its three major ports: Quanzhou, Guangzhou (Canton), and a third near present-day Shanghai. In return for a portion of the taxes on the goods passing through these entrepôts, these offices registered cargoes, sailors, and traders, while guards kept a keen eye on the traffic. All foreign traders in Song China were guests of the governor, who doubled as the chief of seafaring affairs. Every year, the governor conducted a wind-calling ritual. Traders of every origin—Arabs, Persians, Jews, Indians, and Chinese—witnessed the ceremony, then joined together for a sumptuous banquet. Although most foreign merchants did not reside apart from the rest of the city, they did maintain buildings for religious worship according to their faiths. A mosque from this period still stands on a busy street in Quanzhou. Hindu traders living in Quanzhou worshipped in a Buddhist shrine where statues of Hindu deities stood alongside those of Buddhist gods. Each of these bustling ports teemed with a cosmopolitan mix of peoples, goods, and ideas that flowed through growing maritime networks thanks to improved ships and better navigational tools.

Dhow This modern dhow in the harbor of Zanzibar displays the characteristic triangular sail. The sail can make good use of the monsoon winds and thus has guided dhows on the Arabian Sea since ancient times.

Map 10.1 Afro-Eurasian Trade, 1000–1300 CE

During the early second millennium, Afro-Eurasian merchants increasingly turned to the Indian Ocean to transport their goods. Locate the global hubs of Quilon, Alexandria, Cairo, Melaka, and Quanzhou on this map.

- What regions do each of these global hubs represent?
- Based on the map, why would sea travel have been preferable to overland travel?
- According to the text, what revolutions in maritime travel facilitated this development?

The Islamic World in a Time of Political Fragmentation

While the number of Muslim traders began to increase in commercial hubs from the Mediterranean to the South China Sea, it was not until the ninth and tenth centuries CE that Muslims became a majority within their own

Abbasid Empire (see Chapter 9), and even then rulers struggled to unite the diverse Islamic world. From the outset, Muslim rulers and clerics dealt with large non-Muslim populations, even as these groups were converting to Islam. Rulers accorded non-Muslims religious toleration as long as the non-Muslims accepted Islam's political dominion. Jewish, Christian, and Zoroastrian communities within Muslim lands were free to choose their own religious leaders and to settle internal disputes in their own religious courts. They did, however, have to pay a special tax, the *jizya*, and defer to their Muslim rulers. While tolerant, Islam was an expansionist, universalizing faith. Intense proselytizing—especially by Sufi missionaries (whose ideas are discussed later in this chapter)—carried the sacred word to new frontiers and, in the process, reinforced the spread of Islamic institutions that supported commercial exchange.

Slave Market Slaves were a common commodity in the marketplaces of the Islamic world. Turkish conquests during the years from 1000 to 1300 CE put many prisoners on the slave market.

ENVIRONMENTAL CHALLENGES AND POLITICAL DIVISIONS

Severe climate conditions—freezing temperatures and lack of rainfall—afflicted the Eastern Mediterranean and the Islamic lands of Mesopotamia, the Iranian plateau, and the steppe region of central Asia in the late eleventh and early twelfth centuries. The Nile's low water levels devastated Egypt, the breadbasket for much of the area. At least one-quarter of the summer floods that normally brought sediment-enriching deposits to Egypt's soils and guaranteed abundant harvests failed in this period. Driven in part by drought, Turkish nomadic pastoralists poured out of the steppe lands of central Asia in search of better lands, wreaking political and economic havoc everywhere they invaded.

At the same time these climate-driven Turkish pastoralists were migrating and the Islamic faith was increasing its reach across Afro-Eurasia, the political institutions of Islam were fragmenting. (See Map 10.2.) From 950 to 1050 CE, it appeared that Shiism would be the vehicle for uniting the Islamic world. The Fatimid Shiites had established their authority over Egypt and much of North Africa (see Chapter 9), and the Abbasid state in Baghdad was controlled by a Shiite family, the Buyids. Each group created universities, in Cairo and Baghdad respectively, ensuring that leading centers of higher

jizya
Special tax that non-Muslims were forced to pay to their Islamic rulers in return for which they were given security and property and granted cultural autonomy.

learning were Shiite. But divisions also sapped Shiism, and Sunni Muslims began to challenge Shiite power and establish their own strongholds. In Baghdad, the Shiite Buyid family surrendered to the invading Seljuk Turks, a Sunni group, in 1055. A century later, the last of the Shiite Fatimid rulers gave way to a new Sunni regime in Egypt.

The Seljuk Turks who took Baghdad had been migrating into the Islamic heartland from the Asian steppes as early as the eighth century CE, bringing superior military skills and an intense devotion to Sunni Islam. When they flooded into the Iranian plateau in 1029, they contributed to the end of the magnificent cultural flourishing of the early eleventh century. When Seljuk warriors ultimately took Baghdad in 1055, they established a nomadic state in Mesopotamia over a once powerful Abbasid state that now lacked the resources to defend its lands and its peoples, weakened by famines and pestilence. The Seljuk invaders destroyed institutions of learning and public libraries and looted the region's antiquities. Once established in Baghdad, they founded outposts in Syria and Palestine, then moved into Anatolia after defeating Byzantine forces in 1071.

By the thirteenth century the Islamic heartland had fractured into three regions. In the east (central Asia, Iran, and eastern Iraq), the remnants of the old Abbasid state persevered, with a succession of caliphs claiming to speak for all of Islam yet deferring to their Turkish military commanders. In the core of the Islamic world—Egypt, Syria, and the Arabian Peninsula— where Arabic was the primary language, military men of non-Arab origin held the reins of power. Farther west in North Africa, Arab rulers prevailed, but the influence of Berbers, some from the northern Sahara, was extensive. Islam was a vibrant faith, but its polities were splintered.

THE SPREAD OF SUFISM

Even in the face of this political splintering, Islam's spread was facilitated by a popular, highly mystical and communal form of the religion, called **Sufism**. The term *Sufi* comes from the Arabic word for wool (*suf*), which many of the early mystics wrapped themselves in to mark their penitence. Seeking closer union with God, Sufis performed ecstatic rituals such as repeating over and over again the name of God. In time, groups of devotees gathered to read aloud the Quran and other religious tracts. Sufi mystics' desire to experience God's love found ready expression in poetry. Most admired of Islam's mystical love poets was Jalal al-Din Rumi (1207–1273), spiritual founder of the Mevlevi Sufi order, which became famous for the ceremonial dancing of its whirling devotees, known as dervishes.

Although many *ulama* (scholars) despised the Sufis and loathed their seeming lack of theological rigor, the movement spread with astonishing speed and offered a unifying force within Islam. Sufism's emotional content

Sufism
Emotional and mystical form of Islam that appealed to the common people.

Map 10.2 The Islamic World, 900–1200 CE

....

The Islamic world experienced political disintegration in the first centuries of the second millennium.

- According to the map key, what were the two major types of Islamic states in this period? What were some of the major political entities?
- What were the sources of instability in this period according to the map?
- What do you note about the locations of Jewish and Christian communities, as well as Sufi shrines, across the Islamic world?

and strong social bonds, sustained in Sufi religious orders, or brotherhoods, added to its appeal for many. Sufi missionaries from these brotherhoods carried the universalizing faith to India, to Southeast Asia, across the Sahara Desert, and to many other distant locations. It was through these brotherhoods that Islam became truly a religion for the people. As trade increased and more converts appeared in the Islamic lands, urban and peasant populations came to understand the faith practiced by the political, commercial, and scholarly upper classes even while they remained attached to their Sufi brotherhood ways. Over time, Islam became even more accommodating, embracing Persian literature, Turkish ruling skills, and Arabic-language contributions in law, religion, literature, and science.

WHAT WAS ISLAM?

Buoyed by Arab dhows on the high seas and carried on the backs of camels following commercial routes, Islam had been transformed from Muhammad's original vision of a religion for Arab peoples. By 1300, its influence spanned Afro-Eurasia and reached multitudes of non-Arab converts. While Arabic remained the primary language of religious devotion, Persian became the language of Islamic philosophy and art and Turkish the language of Islamic law and administration. Islam attracted city dwellers and rural peasants alike, as well as its original audience of desert nomads. Muslim scholars formed universities, such as al-Qarawiyyin in Fez, Morocco (859 CE) and al-Azhar in Cairo, Egypt (970 CE). Islam's extraordinary universal appeal generated an intense cultural flowering around 1000 CE.

That cultural blossoming in all fields of high learning was marked by diversity in both language and ideas. Representing the new Persian ethnic pride was Abu al-Qasim Firdawsi (920–1020 CE), a devout Muslim who believed in the importance of pre-Islamic Sasanian traditions. In the epic poem *Shah Namah* (Book of Kings), he celebrated the origins of Persian culture and narrated the history of the Iranian highland peoples from the dawn of time to the Muslim conquest. Indicative of the enduring prominence of the Islamic faith and the Arabic language in thought was the legendary Ibn Rushd (1126–1198), known as Averroës in the western world. Steeped in the writings of Aristotle, Ibn Rushd's belief that faith and reason were compatible even influenced the thinking of the Christian world's leading philosopher and theologian, Thomas Aquinas (1225–1274).

During this period, the Islamic world became one of the four cultural spheres that would play a major role in world history, laying the foundation for what would become known as the Middle East up through the middle of the twentieth century. Islam became the majority religion of most of the inhabitants of Southwest Asia and North Africa, Arabic language use became widespread, and the Turks began to establish themselves as a dominant force, ultimately creating the Ottoman Empire, which would last into the twentieth century. The Islamic world became integral in transregional trade and in the creation and transmission of knowledge.

India as a Cultural Mosaic

With its pivotal location along land- and sea-based trade routes, India became an intersection for the trade, migration, and culture of Afro-Eurasian peoples. With 80 million inhabitants in 1000 CE, it had the second-largest population

Map 10.3 South Asia in 1300

As the fourteenth century began, India was a blend of many cultures. Politically, the Turkish Muslim regime of the Delhi Sultanate dominated the region.

- What region was controlled by the Delhi Sultanate in 1236? How did the area controlled by the Delhi Sultanate change in just 100 years?
- How does the map suggest that trade routes helped to spread the Muslims' influence in India?
- Where on the map do Hindu areas resist Muslim political control? Based on your reading, what factors may have accounted for Hinduism's continued appeal despite the Muslims' political power?

in the region, not far behind China's 120 million. Turks ultimately spilled into India as they had into the Islamic heartlands, bringing their newfound Islamic beliefs. But the Turkish newcomers encountered an ethnic and religious mix of which they were just one part. (See Map 10.3.)

SHIFTING POLITICAL STRUCTURES

Before the Turks arrived, India was splintered among rival chiefs called *rajas*. These leaders gained support from Brahmans by doling out land grants to them. Since much of the land was uncultivated, the Brahmans first built temples, then converted the indigenous hunter-gatherer peoples to the Hindu traditions, and finally taught the converts how to cultivate the land. In this way, Brahmans simultaneously spread their faith and expanded the agrarian tax base for themselves and the rajas. They also repaid the rajas' support by compiling elaborate genealogies for them, endowing them with lengthy and legitimizing ancestries. In return, the rajas demonstrated that they, too, were well versed in Sanskrit culture, including equestrian skills and courtly etiquette, and were prepared to patronize artists and poets.

When Turkish warlords began entering India, the rajas had neither the will nor resources to resist them after centuries of fighting off invaders. For example, Mahmud of Ghazna (r. 998–1030 CE) launched many expeditions from the Afghan heartland into northern India and, eager to win status within Islam, made his capital, Ghazni, a center of Islamic learning. Mahmud's expansion in the early eleventh century marked the height of what came to be known as the Ghaznavid Empire (977–1186 CE). Later, in the 1180s, Muhammad Ghuri led another wave of Islamic Turkish invasions from Afghanistan across the Delhi region in northern India. Wars raged between the Indus and Ganges Rivers until, one by one, all the way to the lower Ganges Valley, the fractured kingdoms of the rajas toppled. The Turks introduced their own customs while accepting local social structures, such as the hierarchical *varna* system. The Turks constructed grand mosques and built impressive libraries where scholars could toil and share their wisdom with the court.

While the Ghaznavids were impressive, the most powerful and enduring of the Turkish Muslim regimes of northern India was the **Delhi Sultanate** (1206–1526), whose rulers brought political integration but also strengthened the cultural diversity and tolerance that were already a hallmark of the Indian social order. Sultans recruited local artisans for numerous building projects, and palaces and mosques became displays of Indian architectural tastes adopted by Turkish newcomers. But Islam never fully dominated South Asia because the sultans did not force their subjects to convert. Nor did they display much interest in the flourishing commercial life along the Indian coast. The sultans permitted these areas to develop on their own: Persian Zoroastrian traders settled on the coast around modern-day Mumbai while farther south, Arab traders controlled the Malabar coast. The Delhi Sultanate was a rich and powerful regime that brought political integration but did not enforce cultural homogeneity.

WHAT WAS INDIA?

During the eleventh, twelfth, and thirteenth centuries India became the most diverse and, in some respects, the most tolerant region in Afro-Eurasia. India

Delhi Sultanate (1206–1526)
A Turkish Muslim regime in northern India that, through its tolerance for cultural diversity, brought political integration without enforcing cultural homogeneity.

Hindu Temple When Buddhism started to decline in India, Hinduism was on the rise. Numerous Hindu temples were built, many of them adorned with ornate carvings like this small tenth-century temple in Bhubaneshwar, east India.

in this era arose as an impressive but fragile mosaic of cultures, religions, and ethnicities. When the Turks arrived, the local Hindu population, having had much experience with foreign invaders and immigrants, assimilated these intruders as they had done earlier peoples. Before long, the newcomers thought of themselves as Indians who, however, retained their Islamic beliefs and steppe ways. They continued to wear their distinctive trousers and robes and flaunted their horse-riding skills. At the same time, the local population embraced some of their conquerors' ways, donning the tunics and trousers that characterized central Asian peoples.

Diversity and cultural mixing became most visible in the multiple languages that flourished in India. Although the sultans spoke Turkish languages, they regarded Persian literature as a high cultural achievement and made Persian their courtly and administrative language. Meanwhile, most of their Hindu subjects spoke local languages, adhered to the regulations of the *varna* system of hierarchies, and practiced diverse forms of Hindu worship. The rulers in India did what Muslim rulers in Southwest Asia and the Mediterranean did with Christian and Jewish communities living in their midst: they collected the *jizya* tax and permitted communities to worship as they saw fit and to administer their own communal law. Ultimately, Islam proved in India that it did not have to be an intolerant conquering religion to prosper.

Although Buddhism had been in decline in India for centuries, it, too, became part of the cultural intermixing of this period. As Vedic Brahmanism evolved into Hinduism (see Chapter 8), it had absorbed many Buddhist doctrines and practices, such as nonviolence (*ahimsa*) and vegetarianism. The two religions became so similar in India that Hindus simply considered the Buddha to be one of their deities—an incarnation of the great god Vishnu. Many Buddhist moral teachings mixed with and became Hindu stories. Artistic motifs reflected a similar process of adoption and adaptation. Goddesses, some beautiful and others fierce, appeared alongside Buddhas, Vishnus, and Shivas as their consorts. The Turkish invaders' destruction of major monasteries in the thirteenth century deprived Buddhism of local spiritual leaders. Lacking dynastic support, Buddhists in India were more easily assimilated into the Hindu population or converted to Islam.

Once the initial disruptive effects of the Turkish invasions were absorbed, India remained a highly diverse and tolerant region during this period. Most important, India also emerged as one of the four major cultural spheres, enjoying a tremendous level of integration as Turkish-Muslim rulers and their traditions and practices were successfully intermixed with the native Hindu society, leading to a more integrated and peaceful India.

Song China: Insiders versus Outsiders

The preeminent world power in 1000 CE was still China, despite its recent turmoil. In 907 CE the Tang dynasty splintered into regional kingdoms, mostly led by military generals. In 960 CE one of these generals, Zhao Kuangyin, ended the fragmentation, reunified China, and assumed the mandate of heaven for the Song dynasty (960–1279 CE). The following three centuries witnessed many economic and political successes, but northern nomadic tribes kept the Song dynasty from completely securing its reign. (See Map 10.4 and Map 10.5.) Ultimately, one of those nomadic groups, the Mongols, would bring the Song dynasty to an end, but not before Song influence had fanned out into Southeast Asia, helping to create new identities in the polities that developed there.

ECONOMIC AND POLITICAL DEVELOPMENTS

Chinese merchants, like those from India and the Islamic world, participated in Afro-Eurasia's powerful long-distance trade. Yet China's commercial successes could not have occurred without the country's strong agrarian base—especially its vast wheat, millet, and rice fields, which fed a population that reached 120 million. Crop cultivation benefited from breakthroughs in metalworking that produced stronger iron plows, which Song farmers harnessed to sturdy water buffalo to extend the agricultural frontier.

Map 10.4 East Asia in 1000 CE

....

Several states emerged in East Asia between 1000 and 1300 CE, but none were as strong as the Song dynasty in China. Using the key to the map, try to identify the factors that contributed to the Song state's economic dynamism.

- What do you note about the location of the major trading centers?
- What do you note about the distribution of the other trading centers?
- According to the map, what external factors kept the Song dynasty from completely securing its reign?

Manufacturing also flourished. With the use of piston-driven bellows to force air into furnaces, Song iron production in the eleventh century equaled that of Europe in the early eighteenth century. In the early tenth century, Chinese alchemists mixed saltpeter with sulfur and charcoal to produce a product that would burn and could be deployed on the battlefield: gunpowder. Song entrepreneurs were soon inventing a remarkable array of incendiary

MONGOLS

Karakorum

GOBI DESERT

WESTERN LIAO
KHITAI

JIN

Datong Beijing Liaoyang

SEA
OF
JAPAN

KAMAKURA
SHOGUNATE

JAPAN

Heian

Nara

XIA
TANGUT

Yellow R.

KORYO

Yellow R.

YELLOW
SEA

TIBET

Lhasa

HIMALAYA
MTS.

Kaifeng
(Song capital)

Yangzhou

Suzhou

Hangzhou

EAST
CHINA
SEA

Yangzi R.

SOUTHERN
SONG

PACIFIC

OCEAN

Dali

DALI
KINGDOM

Quanzhou Fuzhou

BURMESE
STATES

Guangzhou

*Bay of
Bengal*

ANNAM

KHMER

CHAMPA

SOUTH
CHINA
SEA

	Original Song Empire
	Area lost in 1126
KHITAI	Peoples

0 250 500 Miles
0 250 500 Kilometers

Map 10.5 East Asia in 1200

The Song dynasty regularly dealt with "barbarian" neighbors with a balance of military response and outright bribery.

- What were the major "barbarian" tribes on the borders of Song China during this period?
- Approximately what percentage of Song China was lost to the Jin in 1126?
- Apart from so-called barbarians, what other polities existed on the borders of Song China?

devices that flowed from their mastery of techniques for controlling explosions and high heat. At the same time, artisans were producing increasingly light, durable, and exquisitely beautiful porcelains. Before long, their porcelain was the envy of all Afro-Eurasia (hence the modern term "china" for fine dishes). Also flowing from the artisans' skillful hands were vast amounts of clothing and handicrafts, made from the fibers grown by Song farmers. In effect, the Song Chinese oversaw the world's first manufacturing revolution, producing finished goods on a large scale for consumption far and wide.

Expanding commerce transformed the role of money and its wide circulation. By now the Song government was annually minting nearly 2 million strings of currency, each containing 1,000 copper coins. As the economy grew, the supply of metal currency could not match the demand, which fueled East Asia's desire for gold from East Africa. At the same time, merchant guilds in northwestern Shanxi developed the first letters of exchange, or paper money, which they called **flying cash**. These letters linked northern traders with their colleagues in the south. Before long, printed money became more common than minted coins for trading purposes. Eventually, the Song dynasty began to issue more notes to pay its bills—a practice that ultimately contributed to runaway inflation.

Song emperors built on Tang political institutions by expanding a central bureaucracy of scholar-officials chosen even more extensively through competitive civil service examinations. Zhao Kuangyin, or Emperor Taizu (r. 960–976 CE), himself administered the final test for all who had passed the highest-level palace examination. In subsequent dynasties, the emperor was the nation's premier examiner, symbolically demanding oaths of allegiance from successful candidates. By 1100 these ranks of learned men had accumulated sufficient power to become China's new ruling elite. This expansion of the civil service examination system was crucial to a shift in power from the still significant hereditary aristocracy to a less wealthy but more highly schooled class of scholar-officials.

CHINA'S NEIGHBORS: NOMADS, JAPAN, AND SOUTHEAST ASIA

China's prosperity influenced its neighbors and its interactions with them. As Song China flourished, nomads on the outskirts eyed the Chinese successes closely. To the north, nomadic societies formed their own dynasties and adopted Chinese institutions. These non-Chinese nomads sought both to conquer and to copy China proper. Despite its sophisticated weapons, the Song army could not match its enemies on the steppe when the nomads united against them. Steel tips improved the arrows that Song soldiers shot from their crossbows, and flamethrowers and "crouching tiger" catapults sent incendiary bombs streaking into their enemies' ranks. But none of these

flying cash
Letters of exchange—early predecessors of paper money—first developed by guilds in the northern Song province Shanxi that eclipsed coins by the thirteenth century.

Core Objectives

DESCRIBE the social and political forces that shaped Song China, and **EVALUATE** the degree to which they integrated the cultures of East Asia.

Chinese and Barbarian After losing the north, the Chinese grew resentful of outsiders. They drew a dividing line between their own agrarian society and the nomadic warriors, calling them "barbarians." Such identities were not fixed, however. Chinese and so-called barbarians were mutually dependent.

breakthroughs was secret. Warrior neighbors on the steppe mastered the new arts of war more fully than did the Song military. Consequently, China drew on its economic success (and the innovation of paper money) to "buy off" the borderlanders. This short-term solution, however, led to economic instability (particularly inflation) and military weakness, especially as the Song forces were cut off, via the steppe nomads, from their supply of horses for warfare purposes.

Feeling the pull of China's economic and political gravity, cultures around China consolidated their own internal political authority and defined their own identities in order to keep from being swallowed up by China. At the same time, they increased their commercial transactions with China. In Japan, for instance, leaders distanced themselves from Chinese influences, but they also developed a strong sense of their islands' distinctive identity. Even so, the long-standing dominance of Chinese ways remained apparent at virtually every level of Japanese society, and was most pronounced at the imperial court in the capital city of Heian (present-day Kyoto), which was modeled after the Chinese capital city of Chang'an. Outside Kyoto, however, a less China-centered way of life existed and began to impose itself on the center. Here, local notables, mainly military leaders and large landowners, began to challenge the imperial court for dominance. This challenge was accompanied by the arrival of an important new social group in Japanese society—samurai warriors. By the beginning of the fourteenth century, Japan had multiple sources of political and cultural power: an imperial family with prestige but little authority; an endangered and declining aristocracy; powerful landowning notables based in the provinces; and a rising and increasingly ambitious class of samurai.

During the Song period, Southeast Asia became a crossroads of Afro-Eurasian influences. The Malay Peninsula became home to many entrepôts for traders shuttling between India and China, because it connected the Bay of Bengal and the Indian Ocean with the South China Sea. (See Map 10.6.) Consequently, Southeast Asia was characterized by a fusion of religions and cultural influences: Vedic Brahmanism in Bali and other islands, Islam in Java and Sumatra, and Mahayana Buddhism in Vietnam and other parts of mainland Southeast Asia. Important Vedic and Buddhist kingdoms emerged in Southeast Asia. The most powerful and wealthy of these kingdoms was the Khmer Empire (889–1431 CE), with its capital at Angkor, in present-day Cambodia. Public works and magnificent temples dedicated to the revived

Angkor Wat Mistaken by later European explorers for a remnant of Alexander the Great's conquests, the enormous temple complexes built by the Khmer people in Angkor borrowed their intricate layout and stupa (a moundlike structure containing religious relics) architecture from the Brahmanic Indian temples of the time. As their capital, Angkor was a microcosm of the world for the Khmer, who aspired to represent the macrocosm of the universe in the magnificence of Angkor's buildings and their geometric layout.

Vedic gods from India went hand in hand with the earlier influence of Indian Buddhism. One of the greatest temple complexes in Angkor—Angkor Wat—exemplified the Khmers' heavy borrowing from Vedic Indian architecture and the revival of the Hindu pantheon within the Khmer royal state. Kingdoms like the Khmer Empire functioned as political buffers between the strong states of China and India and brought stability and further commercial prosperity to the region.

WHAT WAS CHINA?

Paradoxically, the increasing exchange between outsiders and insiders within China hardened the lines that divided them and gave residents of China's interior a highly developed sense of themselves as a distinct people possessing a superior culture. Exchanges with outsiders nurtured a "Chinese" identity among those who considered themselves true insiders and referred to themselves as "Han." Song Chinese grew increasingly suspicious and resentful toward the outsiders living in their midst. They called these outsiders "barbarians" and treated them accordingly.

Print culture crystallized the distinct Chinese identity. Of all Afro-Eurasian societies in 1300, the Chinese were the most advanced in their use of printing, book publishing, and circulation, in part due to the invention of a movable type printing press by the artisan Bi Sheng around 1040. Song dynasty printed books established classical Chinese as the common language of educated classes in East Asia. The Song government used its plentiful

Map 10.6 Southeast Asia, 1000–1300 CE

Cross-cultural influences affected Southeast Asian societies during this period.

- What geographic features (rivers, mountains, islands, straits, etc.) shape Southeast Asia?
- What makes Southeast Asia unique geographically compared to other regions of the world?
- Based on the map, why were the kingdoms of Southeast Asia exposed to so many cross-cultural influences?

supply of paper to print books, especially medical texts, and to distribute calendars. The private publishing industry expanded, and printing houses throughout the country produced Confucian classics, works on history, philosophical treatises, and literature—all of which figured in the civil service examinations. Buddhist publications, too, were available everywhere.

China's huge population base, coupled with a strong agrarian base and manufacturing innovations, made it the wealthiest of the four major cultural spheres, and its common language and Confucian civil service system, which enabled a transfer of power from hereditary aristocrats to Confucian scholars, made it the most unified. China's influence on the surrounding region was tremendous.

Christian Europe

Europe, from 1000 to 1300 CE, was a region of strong contrasts. Intensely localized power was balanced by a shared sense of Europe's place in the world, especially with respect to Christian identity. Some inhabitants even began to believe in the existence of something called "Europe" and increasingly referred to themselves as "Europeans," especially in contrast to the world of Islam to the east and south. (See Map 10.7.)

Core Objectives

COMPARE the role that religions and migration played in forging unified identities in Europe, India, and the Islamic worlds.

LOCALIZATION OF POWER

From the agriculture-based manors of western Europe to the cities of Russia, power structures in Europe were localized. For example, in western Europe of the eleventh and twelfth centuries, the Franks became the unchallenged rulers after the collapse of Charlemagne's empire, yet they oversaw a somewhat fragmented manor-based economy and social structure. The peasantry's subjugation to this knightly class was at the heart of a system scholars have called feudalism (emphasizing the power of the local lords over the peasantry); but a more accurate term for the system is **manorialism**, which emphasizes instead the manor's role as the basic unit of economic power. The manor comprised the lord's fortified home (or castle), the surrounding fields controlled by the lord but worked by peasants (as free tenants or as serfs tied to the land), and the village in which those peasants lived. Although manorialism was driven by agriculture, limited manufacturing and trade augmented the manor economy. This system harnessed agrarian energy and helped western Europe shed its identity as a somewhat "barbarian" appendage of the Mediterranean.

Between 1100 and 1200, as many as 200,000 pioneering peasants emigrated from present-day Belgium, Holland, and northern Germany to the frontiers of Europe (now Poland, the Czech Republic, Hungary, and the

manorialism
System in which the manor (a lord's home, its associated industry, and surrounding fields) served as the basic unit of economic power; an alternative to the concept of feudalism (the hierarchical relationships of king, lords, and peasantry) for thinking about the nature of power in western Europe from 1000 to 1300 CE.

Map 10.7 legend annotations:

1. Spread of western Christianity into eastern Europe and Baltic regions through conquest and migration

2. Spread of western Christianity through Spanish Reconquista

3. Spread of western Christianity through Norman conquest of Sicily

4. Spread of western Christianity through Crusades

Map labels: NORWAY, SWEDEN, SCOTLAND, IRELAND, NORTH SEA, DENMARK, BALTIC SEA, LITHUANIA, RUSSIAN PRINCIPALITIES, Novgorod, TEUTONIC ORDER, POLISH STATES, Kiev, *Dnieper R.*, FRONTIER OF ISLAMIC WORLD, 1300, To New Sarai, ENGLAND, Cambridge c. 1209, Oxford early 12th C., London, Bruges, Ghent, Rouen, Paris c. 1200, c. 1250, Orléans c. 1236, FRANCE, ATLANTIC OCEAN, Prague 1348, HUNGARY, *Danube R.*, BLACK SEA, To Tabriz, *Tigris R.*, To Baghdad 1065, *Euphrates R.*, Toulouse 1229, c.12th C., 1332, 1339, Milan 1248, 1204, Venice, Avignon 1303, Genoa, Bologna 1088, Florence, 1215, 1246, 1308, SERBIA, BULGARIA, Constantinople, BYZANTINE EMPIRE, SELJUK STATES, PORTUGAL, 1308, 1250, c. 1218, CASTILE, ARAGON, c. 1300, Marseille, Barcelona, Rome 1245, 1224 since 9th century, Lisbon c. 1290, Seville c. 1254, Granada, GRANADA, *MEDITERRANEAN SEA*, Palermo, Fez 859, CRUSADER STATES, Jerusalem, Alexandria, MAMLUKS, Cairo 970, *Rhine R.*, ALPS, PYRENEES

Legend:
- Areas and direction of expansion of western Christendom with annotations
- ● Cities over 50,000 population
- • Important cities with less than 50,000
- ■ University

Scale: 0 — 250 — 500 Miles; 0 — 250 — 500 Kilometers

Map 10.7 Western Christendom in 1300

Catholic Europe expanded geographically and integrated culturally during this era.

- According to this map, into what areas did western Christendom successfully expand?
- What were the different means by which western Christianity expanded?
- Which are the earliest universities on the map? What might account for the flourishing of universities where they were located?

Baltic states). Despite its harsh climate and landscape, the area offered the promise of freedom from feudal lords' arbitrary justice and the imposition of forced labor that the peasants had experienced in western Europe. In a fragile balance between the native elites and liberty-seeking newcomers, castles and villages echoing the landscape of manorial France now replaced local economies that had been based on gathering honey, hunting, and the slave trade. For a thousand miles along the Baltic Sea, forest clearings dotted with new farmsteads and small towns edged inward from the coast up the river valleys.

Russian lands modeled themselves after Byzantium, not Rome or western Europe. Set in a giant borderland between the steppes of Inner Eurasia and the booming centers of Europe, Russia's cities lay at the crossroads of overland trade and migration. These cities were not agrarian centers, but hubs of expanding long-distance trade. Kiev became one of the region's greatest urban centers, a small-scale Constantinople with its own miniature Hagia Sophia. Russian Christians looked not to the Roman Catholic faith associated with the popes in Rome, but rather to Byzantium's Hagia Sophia and the Orthodoxy of the east as the source of religious authority. Russian Christianity remained that of a borderland—vivid oases of high culture set against the backdrop of vast forests and widely scattered settlements. Like the agricultural manors of western Europe, these Russian cities demonstrate the highly localized nature of power in Europe in this period.

WHAT WAS CHRISTIAN EUROPE?

Christianity in this era—primarily the Roman Catholicism of the west, but also the Orthodoxy of the east—became a universalizing faith that transformed the region becoming known as "Europe." The Christianity of post-Roman Europe had been a religion of monks, and its most dynamic centers were great monasteries. Members of the laity were expected to revere and support their monks, nuns, and clergy, but not to imitate them. By 1200, all this had changed. The internal colonization of western Europe—the clearing of woods and founding of villages—ensured that parish churches arose in all but the wildest landscapes. Now the clergy reached more deeply into the private lives of the laity. Marriage and divorce, previously considered family matters, became the domain of the church.

New understandings of religious devotion and innovative institutions for learning developed in the west. For instance, the followers of Francis of Assisi (1182–1226) emerged as an order of preachers who brought a message of repentance. Franciscans encouraged the laity—from the poorest to the elite—to feel remorse for their wrongdoings, to confess their sins to local priests, and to strive to be better Christians. At nearly the same time, intellectuals were beginning to gather in Paris to form one of the first European universities, a sort of trade guild of scholars. These professional thinkers endeavored to prove that Christianity was the only religion that fully addressed the concerns of all rational human beings. Such was the message of Thomas Aquinas, who wrote *Summa contra Gentiles* (Summary of Christian Belief against Non-Christians) in 1264. The growing number of churches, new religious orders, and universities began to change what it meant to live in a "Christian Europe."

RELATIONS WITH THE ISLAMIC WORLD

In the late eleventh century, western Europeans launched the Crusades, a wave of attacks against the Muslim world. The First Crusade began in 1095, when Pope Urban II appealed to the warrior nobility of France to put their violence to good use: they should combine their role as pilgrims to Jerusalem with that of soldiers in order to free the Christian "holy land" from Muslim rule. Such a just war, the clergy proposed, was a means for absolution, not a source of sin.

Starting in 1097, an armed host of around 60,000 men set out from northwestern Europe to seize Jerusalem. The crusading forces included knights in heavy armor as well as people drawn from Europe's impoverished masses, who joined the movement to help besiege cities and construct a network of castles as the Christian knights drove their frontier forward. The fleets of Venice, Genoa, and Pisa helped transport later Crusaders and supplied the kingdoms they created as they moved eastward. Later Crusaders, especially those from the upper class, brought their wives, who found a degree of autonomy away from their homeland. There are even accounts of a children's crusade (1212), inspired by the visions of a boy. Over time, the Crusades drew together a range of peoples from varied walks of life in common purpose.

No fewer than nine Crusades were fought over the two centuries that followed Urban II's call; but none of the coalitions, in the end, created lasting Christian kingdoms in the lands they "reconquered." Most knights returned home, their epic pilgrimages completed. The remaining fragile network of Crusader lordships barely threatened the Islamic heartland. The real prosperity and the capital cities of Muslim kingdoms lay inland, away from the coast—at Cairo, Damascus, and Baghdad. The assaults' long-term effect was

Crusader Kneeling, this Crusader promises to serve God (as he would serve a feudal lord) by going to fight on a Crusade (as he would fight for any lord to whom he had sworn loyalty). The two kinds of loyalty—to God and to one's lord—were deliberately confused in Crusader ideas. Both were about war, but fighting for God was unambiguously good, while fighting for a lord was not always so clear-cut.

to harden Muslim feelings against the Franks and the millions of nonwestern Christians who had previously lived peacefully in Egypt and Syria.

Even so, a range of sources offer Muslim and Christian perspectives that show tolerance of, and curiosity about, each other. For example, Usāmah ibn Munqidh (1095–1188), a learned Syrian leader, describes his shock at the Frankish Crusaders' backward medical practices and the freedom they offered their wives, in addition to well-meaning exchanges such as a particular Frank's confusion about the direction in which Muslims pray. Similarly, Jean de Joinville (1224/1225–1317), a French chronicler of Louis X of France who led the Seventh Crusade, marveled at the order within the sultan's camp and the role of musicians in calling the Muslim forces to hear the sultan's orders.

Other campaigns of Christian expansion, like the Iberian efforts to drive out the Muslims, were more successful. Beginning with the capture of Toledo in 1061, the Christian kings of northern Spain slowly pushed back the Muslims. Eventually they reached the heart of Andalusia in southern Iberia and conquered Seville, adding more than 100,000 square miles of territory to Christian Europe. Another force, from northern France, crossed Italy to conquer Muslim-held Sicily, ensuring Christian rule in that strategically located mid-Mediterranean island. Unlike the Crusaders' fragile foothold at the edge of the Middle East, these two conquests were a turning point in relations between Christian and Muslim power in the Mediterranean. Christianity—and in particular the rise of the Roman Catholic Church, the spread of universities, and the fight against the Muslims in their native and spiritual homelands—was a force that helped create a cultural sphere known as Europe, whose peoples would become known as European, at the western end of the Afro-Eurasian landmass during this period.

Worlds Coming Together: Sub-Saharan Africa and the Americas

From 1000 to 1300 CE, sub-Saharan Africa and the Americas became far more internally integrated—culturally, economically, and politically—than before. Islam's spread and the growing trade in gold, slaves, and other commodities brought sub-Saharan Africa more fully into the exchange networks of the Eastern Hemisphere, but the Americas remained isolated from Afro-Eurasian networks for several more centuries.

Core Objectives

COMPARE the internal integration and external interactions of sub-Saharan Africa with those of the Americas.

SUB-SAHARAN AFRICA COMES TOGETHER

During this period, sub-Saharan Africa's relationship to the rest of the world changed dramatically. While sub-Saharan Africa had never been a world entirely apart before 1000 CE, its integration with Eurasia now became much stronger. Increasingly, its hinterlands found themselves touched by the commercial and migratory impulses emanating from the Indian Ocean and Arabian Sea transformations. (See Map 10.8.)

West Africa and the Mande-Speaking Peoples Once trade routes bridged the Sahara Desert (see Chapter 9), the flow of commodities and ideas linked sub-Saharan Africa to North Africa and Southwest Asia. As the savanna region became increasingly connected to developments in Eurasia, Mande-speaking peoples became the primary agents for integration within and beyond West Africa. Exploiting their expertise in commerce and political organization, the Mande edged out rivals. The Mande homeland was a vast area, 1,000 miles wide between the bend in the Senegal River to the west and the bend of the Niger River to the east, and stretching more than 2,000 miles from the Senegal River in the north to the Bandama River in the south.

By the eleventh century, Mande-speaking peoples were spreading their cultural, commercial, and political hegemony from the savanna grasslands southward into the woodlands and tropical rain forests stretching to the Atlantic Ocean. Those dwelling in the rain forests organized small-scale societies led by local councils, while those in the savanna lands developed centralized forms of government under sacred kingships. Mande speakers believed that their kings had descended from the gods and that they enjoyed the gods' blessing.

As the Mande extended their territory to the Atlantic coast, they gained access to tradable items that residents of Africa's interior were eager to have—notably kola nuts and malaguetta peppers, for which the Mande exchanged iron products and manufactured textiles. Mande-speaking peoples, with their far-flung commercial networks and highly dispersed populations, dominated trans-Saharan trade in salt from the northern Sahel, gold from the Mande homeland, and slaves. By 1300, Mande-speaking merchants had followed the Senegal River to its outlet on the Atlantic coast and then pushed their commercial frontiers farther inland and down the coast. Thus, even before European explorers and traders arrived in the mid-fifteenth century, West African peoples had created dynamic networks linking the hinterlands with coastal trading hubs.

Mali Empire

West African empire, founded by the legendary king Sundiata in the early thirteenth century. It facilitated thriving commerce along routes linking the Atlantic Ocean, the Sahara, and beyond.

The Mali Empire In the early thirteenth century, the **Mali Empire** became the Mande successor state to the kingdom of Ghana (see Chapter 9). The origins of the Mali Empire and its legendary founder are enshrined in *The Epic of Sundiata*. Sundiata's triumph, which occurred in the first half of the thirteenth century, marked the victory of new cavalry forces over traditional foot soldiers. Horses now became prestige objects for the savanna peoples, symbols of state power.

Map 10.8 Sub-Saharan Africa, 1300

Increased commercial contacts influenced the religious and political dimensions of sub-Saharan Africa at this time. Compare this map with Map 9.3.

- Where had strong Islamic communities emerged by 1300? By what routes might Islam have spread to those areas?

- According to this map, what types of activity were taking place in sub-Saharan West Africa?

- What goods were traded in sub-Saharan Africa, and along what routes did those exchanges take place?

Map legend:
- Pilgrimage route of Mansa Musa
- Trans-Saharan trade routes
- Maritime trade routes
- State nucleus and sphere of influence
- Islamic areas
- Spread of Islam
- Gold deposits
- Copper deposits
- Salt
- Ivory
- Slaves

Under the Mali Empire, commerce was in full swing. With Mande trade routes extending to the Atlantic Ocean and spanning the Sahara Desert, West Africa was no longer an isolated periphery of the central Muslim lands. The Mali king Mansa Musa (r. 1312–1332) made a celebrated hajj, or pilgrimage to Mecca, in 1324–1325, traveling through Cairo and impressing crowds with the size of his retinue—including soldiers, wives, consorts, and as many as 12,000 slaves—and his displays of wealth, especially many dazzling items made of gold. Mansa Musa's stopover in Cairo, one of Islam's primary cities,

West African Asante Gold This picture from the 1375 Catalan Atlas shows Mansa Musa, the king of Mali, on his throne, surrounded by images of gold. When Mansa Musa traveled on pilgrimage to Mecca (1324–1325), his entourage included soldiers, wives, consorts, and as many as 12,000 slaves, many wearing rich brocades woven of Persian silk. His caravan brought immense quantities of gold—nearly 100 camels each bearing 300-pound sacks of gold—and Mansa Musa distributed it lavishly. Preceding his retinue as it crossed the desert were 500 slaves, each carrying a golden staff.

astonished the Egyptian elite and awakened much of the world to the fact that Islam had spread far below the Sahara and that a sub-Saharan state could mount such an impressive display of power and wealth.

The Mali Empire boasted two of West Africa's largest cities. Jenne, an entrepôt dating back to 200 BCE, was a vital assembly point for caravans laden with salt, gold, and slaves preparing for journeys west to the Atlantic coast and north over the Sahara. More spectacular was the city of Timbuktu; founded around 1100 as a seasonal camp for nomads, it grew in size and importance under the patronage of various Mali kings. By the fourteenth century it was a thriving commercial, intellectual, and religious center famed for its three large mosques, which are still standing.

Trade between East Africa and the Indian Ocean Africa's eastern and southern regions were also integrated into long-distance trading systems. Because of the monsoon winds, East Africa was a logical end point for much of the Indian Ocean trade. Swahili peoples living along that coast became brokers for trade from the Arabian Peninsula, the Persian Gulf territories, and the western coast of India. Merchants in the city of Kilwa on the coast of present-day Tanzania brought ivory, gold, slaves, and other items from the interior and shipped them to destinations around the Indian Ocean.

Shona-speaking peoples grew rich by mining the gold ore in the highlands between the Limpopo and Zambezi Rivers. By 1000 CE, the Shona had founded up to fifty small religious and political centers, each one erected from stone to display its power over the peasant villages surrounding it. Around 1100, one of these centers, Great Zimbabwe, stood supreme among the Shona. Built on the fortunes made from gold, its most impressive landmark was a massive elliptical building made of stones fitted so expertly that they needed no grouting.

African slaves were as valuable as African gold in shipments to Indian Ocean as well as Mediterranean markets. Although the Quran mitigated the severity of slavery, requiring Muslim slave owners to treat their slaves kindly and praising those who freed their slaves, the African slave trade flourished under Islam. Africans became slaves either taken as prisoners of war or as criminals sold into slavery as punishment. Slaves might work as soldiers, seafarers on dhows, domestic servants, or plantation workers. Conditions for plantation laborers on the agricultural estates of lower Iraq were so oppressive that they led, in the ninth century CE, to one of the largest slave wars documented in world history (the Zanj rebellion). Yet in this era, plantation slave labor, like that which later became prominent in the Americas in the nineteenth century, was the exception, not the rule.

THE AMERICAS

During this period, the Americas were untouched by the connections reverberating across Afro-Eurasia. Apart from limited Viking contacts in North America (see Chapter 9), navigators still did not cross the large oceans that separated the Americas from other lands. Yet, here, too, commercial and expansionist impulses fostered closer contact among peoples who lived there.

Andean States of South America Growth and prosperity in the Andean region gave rise to South America's first empire. The **Chimú Empire** developed early in the second millennium in the fertile Moche Valley bordering the Pacific Ocean. (See Map 10.9.) Ultimately the Moche people expanded their influence across numerous valleys and ecological zones, from pastoral highlands to rich valley floodplains to the fecund fishing grounds of the Pacific coast. As their geographic reach grew, so did their wealth.

The Chimú economy was successful because it was highly commercialized. Agriculture was its base, and complex irrigation systems turned the arid coast into a string of fertile oases capable of feeding an increasingly dispersed population. Cotton became a lucrative export to distant markets along the Andes. Parades of llamas and porters lugged these commodities up and down the steep mountain chains that form the spine of South America. A well-trained bureaucracy oversaw the construction and maintenance of canals, and a hierarchy of provincial administrators watched over commercial hinterlands.

The Chimú Empire's biggest city, Chan Chan, held a core population of 30,000 inhabitants. A sprawling walled metropolis covering nearly 10 square miles, with extensive roads circulating through its neighborhoods, Chan Chan boasted ten huge palaces at its center. Protected by thick walls 30 feet high, these opulent residence halls symbolized the rulers' power. Within the compound, emperors erected burial complexes for storing their accumulated riches: fine cloth, gold and silver objects, splendid *Spondylus* shells, and other luxury goods. Around the compound spread neighborhoods for nobles and artisans; farther out stood rows of commoners' houses. The Chimú regime, centered at Chan Chan, lasted until Incan armies invaded in the 1460s and incorporated the Pacific state into their own immense empire.

Toltecs in Mesoamerica Additional hubs of regional trade developed farther north. By 1000 CE, Mesoamerica had seen the rise and fall of several complex societies, including Teotihuacán and the Maya (see Chapter 8). Caravans of porters bound the region together, working the intricate roads that connected the coast of the Gulf of Mexico to the Pacific and the southern lowlands of

Chimú Empire
South America's first empire, centered at Chan Chan, in the Moche Valley on the Pacific coast from 1000 through 1470 CE, whose development was fueled by agriculture and commercial exchange.

Map 10.9 Andean
States, c. 700–1400
CE

Although the Andes
region of South America
was isolated from Afro-
Eurasian developments
before 1500, it was not
stagnant. Indeed, political
and cultural integration
brought the peoples
of this region closer
together.

- Where are the areas
  of Chimú Empire and
  Tiahuanaco influence
  on the map?
- What was the ecology
  and geography of each
  region, and how might
  that have shaped each
  region's development?
- What crops and animals
  did the Chimú and
  Tiahuanaco benefit
  from?

CARIBBEAN SEA

PACIFIC OCEAN

SOUTH AMERICA

AMAZON BASIN

Amazon R.

ANDES MOUNTAINS

ANDEAN COAST

CHIMÚ EMPIRE

Chan Chan
Moche

Huari

Pucara

Nazca

Chuquibamba

Lake Titicaca

Tiahuanaco

ATACAMA DESERT

Lake Poopó

0   250   500 Miles

0   250   500 Kilometers

- Chimú Empire, c. 1200
- Tiahuanaco, c. 700
- Area of Tiahuanaco influence, c. 700
- Irrigated river valley
- Underground aqueduct
- Guinea pigs
- Maize
- Peanuts
- Peppers
- Potatoes
- Squash
- Turkeys

Toltecs

Mesoamerican peoples who
filled the political vacuum
left by Teotihuacán's decline;
established a temple-filled
capital and commercial hub
at Tula.

Central America to the arid regions of modern Texas. (See Map 10.10.) The
Toltecs filled the political vacuum left by the decline of Teotihuacán and tapped
into the commercial network radiating from the rich valley of central Mexico.

The Toltecs were a combination of migrant groups, farmers from the north
and refugees from the south fleeing the strife that followed Teotihuacán's

Chan Chan The image shows some of the remains of Chan Chan. The city covered 15 square miles and was divided into neighborhoods for nobles, artisans, and commoners, with the elites living closest to the hub of governmental and spiritual power.

demise. These migrants settled northwest of Teotihuacán as the city waned, making their capital at Tula. They relied on a maize-based economy supplemented by beans, squash, and dog, deer, and rabbit meat. Their rulers made sure that enterprising merchants provided them with status goods such as ornamental pottery, rare shells and stones, and precious skins and feathers.

Tula was a commercial hub, a political capital, and a ceremonial center. While its layout differed from Teotihuacán's, many features revealed borrowings from other Mesoamerican peoples. Temples consisted of giant pyramids topped by colossal stone soldiers, and ball courts where subjects and conquered peoples alike played their ritual sport were found everywhere. The architecture and monumental art reflected the mixed and migratory origins of the Toltecs in a combination of Maya and Teotihuacáno influences. At its height, the Toltec capital teemed with 60,000 people, a huge metropolis by contemporary European standards (if small by Song Chinese and Abbasid standards).

Cahokians in North America As in South America and Mesoamerica, cities took shape at the hubs of trading networks across North America. The largest was **Cahokia**, along the Mississippi River near modern-day East St. Louis. A city of about 15,000, it approximated the size of London at the time. Farmers and hunters had settled in the region around 600 CE, attracted by its rich soil, its woodlands that provided fuel and game, and its access to trade via the Mississippi. Eventually, fields of maize and other crops fanned out toward the horizon. The hoe replaced the trusty digging stick, and satellite towns erected granaries to hold the growing harvests.

Cahokia
Commercial city on the Mississippi for regional and long-distance trade of commodities such as salt, shells, and skins and of manufactured goods such as pottery, textiles, and jewelry; marked by massive artificial hills, akin to earthen pyramids, used to honor spiritual forces.

Map 10.10 Commercial Hubs in Mesoamerica and North America, 1000 CE

Both Cahokia and Tula were commercial hubs of vibrant regional trade networks.

- What routes linked Tula and the Toltecs with other regions?
- What goods circulated in the regions of Pueblo and Cahokia?
- Based on the map, what appear to be some of the differences between Canyon culture, Mississippian culture, and the Toltecs?

Cahokia became a commercial center for regional and long-distance trade. The hinterlands produced staples for Cahokia's urban consumers, and in return its crafts rode inland on the backs of porters and to distant markets in canoes. Woven fabrics and ceramics from Cahokia were exchanged for mica from the Appalachian Mountains, seashells and sharks' teeth from the Gulf of Mexico, and copper from the upper Great Lakes. Cahokia became more than an importer and exporter: it was the exchange hub for an entire regional network trading in salt, tools, pottery, woven stuffs, jewelry, and ceremonial goods.

Dominating Cahokia's urban landscape were enormous earthen mounds of sand and clay (thus the Cahokians' nickname of "mound people"). It was from these artificial hills that the people honored spiritual forces. Building these types of structures without draft animals, hydraulic tools, or even wheels was labor-intensive, so the Cahokians recruited neighboring people to help. A palisade around the city protected the metropolis from marauders.

Toltec Temple Tula, the capital of the Toltec Empire, carried on the Mesoamerican tradition of locating ceremonial architecture at the center of the city. The Pyramid of the Morning Star cast its shadow over all other buildings. And above them stood columns of the Atlantes, carved Toltec god-warriors, the figurative pillars of the empire itself. The walls of this pyramid were likely embellished with images of snakes and skulls. The north face of the pyramid has the image of a snake devouring a human.

Ultimately Cahokia's success bred its downfall. As woodlands fell to the axe and the soil lost its nutrients, timber and food became scarce. In contrast to the sturdy dhows of the Arabian Sea and the bulky junks of the China Sea, Cahokia's river canoes could carry only limited cargoes. Cahokia's commercial networks met their limits. When the creeks that fed its water system could not keep up with demand, engineers changed their course, but to no avail. By 1350 the city was practically empty. But Cahokia represented the growing networks of trade and migration in North America and the ability of North Americans to organize vibrant commercial societies.

Two forces contributed to greater integration in sub-Saharan Africa and the Americas from 1000 to 1300 CE: commercial exchange (of salt, gold, ivory, and slaves in sub-Saharan Africa and shells, pottery, textiles, and metals in the Americas) and urbanization (at Jenne, Timbuktu, and Great Zimbabwe in sub-Saharan Africa and at Chan Chan, Tula, and Cahokia in the Americas). By 1300, trans-Saharan and Indian Ocean exchange had brought Africa into full-fledged Afro-Eurasian networks of exchange and, as we will see in Chapter 12, transatlantic exchange would soon bring the Americas into a global network.

The Mongol Transformation of Afro-Eurasia

Commercial networks were clearly one way to integrate the world. But just as long-distance trade could connect people, so could conquerors. The Inner Eurasian steppes had already unleashed horse-riding warriors such as the Kushans and Xiongnu (see Chapters 6 and 7). Now, the Mongols created an empire that straddled east and west, expanding their reach not only through brutal conquest but also through intensified trade and cultural exchange. (See Map 10.11.)

Core Objectives

ASSESS the impacts that the Mongol Empire had on Afro-Eurasian peoples and places.

Map 10.11 Mongol Conquests and Campaigns, 1200–1300

Mongol campaigns and conquests brought Afro-Eurasian worlds together as never before. Trace the outline of the entire area of Mongol influence shaded on this map.

- What regions and cultural groups did the Mongol armies conquer, partially conquer, or invade? Which did the Mongols not invade?
- How many different khanates did the Mongols establish across Eurasia, and what were they? In what ways do these khanates essentially rewrite the political map of Eurasia?
- What role did geography play in shaping the spread of their influence?

SIBERIA

MONGOL ANCESTRAL
HOMELAND

Karakorum

Lake
Baikal

GOBI DESERT

AGATAI

TIBET

OUNTAINS

BURMA

Shangdu
(Xanadu)

Khan-balik/Dadu
(modern Beijing)

KHANATE OF THE
GREAT KHAN
(YUAN EMPIRE)

Kaifeng

Yangzi R.

Yangzhou

Hangzhou

KORYO

SEA
OF
JAPAN

KAMAKURA
SHOGUNATE

JAPAN

Kyoto

1279

YUNNAN

Pagan

Guangzhou

ANNAM

CHAMPA

KHMER
EMPIRE

SOUTH
CHINA
SEA

SUMATRA

BORNEO

JAVA

PACIFIC

OCEAN

500   1000 Miles
500   1000 Kilometers

→ Mongol campaigns beyond controlled lands
■ Mongol ancestral homeland
■ Mongol controlled
▨ Area of loose or temporary Mongol control
✕ Battle

WHO WERE THE MONGOLS?

The Mongols were a combination of forest and steppe peoples. Residing in circular, felt-covered tents, which they shared with some of their animals, they lived by hunting and livestock herding. They changed campgrounds with the seasons. Life on the steppes was such a constant struggle that only the strong survived. Their food, primarily animal products, provided high levels of protein, which built up their muscle mass and their strength. Always on the march, their society resembled a perpetual standing army with bands of well-disciplined military units led by commanders chosen for their skill.

Wielding heavy compound bows made of sinew, wood, and horn, Mongol archers were deadly accurate at over 200 yards—even at full gallop. Their small but sturdy horses, capable of withstanding extreme cold, bore saddles with high supports in front and back, enabling the warriors to maneuver at high speeds. With their feet secure in iron stirrups, the archers could rise in their saddles to aim their arrows without stopping. These expert horsemen often remained in the saddle all day and night, even sleeping while their horses continued on. Each warrior kept many horses, replacing tired mounts with fresh ones so that the armies could cover up to 70 miles per day.

Mongol tribes solidified their conquests by extending kinship networks, building an empire out of an expanding confederation of familial tribes. Women were a vital link in those networks. Households sealed alliances by the exchange of daughters in marriage. In addition to their role in linking kinship networks, women in Mongol society were responsible for child-rearing, shearing and milking livestock, and processing pelts for clothing. But they also took part in battles. Although women could be bought and sold, Mongol wives had the right to own property and to divorce. Elite women, such as the mother and wife of the Mongol ruler Kublai Khan, even played important political roles.

CONQUEST AND EMPIRE

The Mongols' need for grazing lands contributed to their desire to conquer distant fertile belts and rich cities. The Mongols depended on settled peoples for grain and manufactured goods, including iron for tools, wagons, weapons, bridles, and stirrups. Their first expansionist forays followed caravan routes.

The Mongol expansion began in 1206 under a united cluster of tribes. These tribes were unified by a gathering of clan heads who chose one of those present, Temüjin (c. 1162–1227), as Khan, or Supreme Ruler. Taking the name Chinggis (Genghis) Khan, he launched a series of conquests southward across the Great Wall of China and westward to Afghanistan and Persia. The Mongols even invaded Korea in 1231. The armies of Chinggis's sons reached both the Pacific Ocean and the Adriatic Sea. Chinggis's grandsons founded dynasties in Persia, in China, and on the southern Eurasian steppes. Thus, a realm took shape that touched all four of Afro-Eurasia's cultural spheres.

Mongols in Abbasid Baghdad In the thirteenth century, Mongol tribes were streaming out of the steppes, crossing the whole of Asia and entering the eastern parts of Europe. Mongke Khan, a grandson of Chinggis, made clear the Mongol aspiration to world domination: he commanded his brother, Hulagu, to conquer Iran, Syria, Egypt, Byzantium, and Armenia, and he appointed another brother, Kublai, to rule over China, Tibet, and the northern parts of India.

When Hulagu reached Abbasid Baghdad in 1258, he encountered a feeble foe and a city that was a shadow of its former glorious self. Merely 10,000 horsemen faced his army of 200,000 soldiers, who were eager to acquire the booty of a wealthy city. Even before the battle had taken place, Baghdadi poets were composing elegies for their dead and mourning the defeat of Islam. The slaughter was vast. Hulagu himself boasted of taking the lives of at least 200,000 people. The Mongols hunted their adversaries in wells, latrines, and sewers and followed them into the upper floors of buildings, killing them on rooftops until, as an Iraqi Arab historian observed, "blood poured from the gutters into the streets. . . . The same happened in the mosques." In a few weeks of sheer terror, the Abbasid caliphate was demolished. Hulagu's forces showed no mercy to the caliph himself, who was rolled up in a carpet and trampled to death by horses. With Baghdad crushed, the Mongol armies pushed on to Syria, slaughtering Muslims along the way.

Mongols in China In the east, Mongol forces under Chinggis Khan had entered northern China at the beginning of the thirteenth century, defeating the Khitai army, which was no match for the Mongols' superior cavalry on the North China plain. Despite some serious setbacks due to the climate (including malaria for the men and the deaths of horses from the heat), Chinggis's grandson Kublai Khan (1215–1294) seized southern China from the Song dynasty beginning in the 1260s. The Song army fell before Mongol warriors brandishing the latest gunpowder-based weapons, technology the Mongols had borrowed from Chinese inventors and now used against them.

Hangzhou, the last Song capital, fell in 1276. Kublai Khan's most able commander, Bayan, led his crack Mongol forces in seizing town after town, moving ever closer to the capital, while the Dowager Empress tried to buy them off, proposing substantial tribute payments, but Bayan was uncompromising. Once conquered, the Dowager Empress and Hangzhou were treated well by the Mongols. In fact, Hangzhou was still one of the greatest cities in the world when it was visited by the Venetian traveler Marco Polo in the 1280s and by the Muslim traveler Ibn Battuta in the 1340s. Both men agreed that neither Europe nor the Islamic world had anything like it.

Kublai Khan founded his Yuan dynasty with a capital at Khan-balik (also called Dadu, which became present-day Beijing). The Mongol conquest of both north and south changed China's political and social landscape. But Mongol rule did

A Most Unusual Nomad State

Although nomadic pastoralists and sedentary agriculturalists depended on each other to flourish, their deep commitments to their institutions and ways of life made cooperation difficult. Pastoralists endeavored to be as self-sufficient as possible. They scorned peoples who dug in the soil. On the other hand, as we noted in Chapter 3, sedentary peoples, most notably their literate members, regarded herders as uncivilized barbarians. The Chinese, for instance, saw the steppe peoples who lived to the north of them, and who often invaded their state, as occupying the "inhospitable land of the barbarian" and its people as "avaricious and violent marauders."

The Mongols were the quintessential pastoral nomads. Very little is known of their early history, largely because they were a small, fragmented, and powerless people living along the borderlands of southern Siberia, eastern Mongolia, and northwestern Manchuria. To their east lived the Tatars, and to their west the Uighurs and Khitai, far more powerful pastoral peoples from whom the Mongols learned many of their political and military skills. The Mongols first surface

in Chinese sources during the Tang dynasty (618–907 CE). The Chinese, who feared the military capabilities of steppe peoples and were regularly invaded and even conquered by those peoples, had little fear of the Mongols at this time, regarding them as an insignificant community far from the empire's northern frontier. The Mongols were well known, however, for raiding, looting, and violence toward outsiders and among themselves.

Few individuals have had a greater impact on world history than the founder of the Mongol state, Temüjin (c. 1162–1227). His youthful travails hardened him as a warrior and made him a leader. Having lost his father at a young age and being the eldest of his siblings, he, along with his mother, endured a harsh existence. But as an adult, he unified warring Mongol clans and defeated the Mongols' enemies, either assimilating them to the Mongol way of life or exterminating them if they refused his leadership. In 1206, as a result of his spectacular military successes, he took the name Chinggis Khan, meaning Supreme Ruler. Not only did he bring most of Inner Asia under his rule, but his armies pushed southward into Manchuria and

northern China and west toward central Asia and the Islamic states. At his death in 1227, he divided his vast territorial conquests among the four sons of his first wife, Borte. These men and their successors created four Mongol states, called khanates, loosely linked as an empire: Yuan China; the Khanate of the Golden Horde; the northern steppe (Khanate of the Chagatai); and Persia, known as the Il-Khanate.

The Mongols established their rule over settled societies in China, Iran, central Asia, and Russia, but then had to decide how to rule over sedentary populations. Specifically, the issue facing Mongol rulers was whether to foster close relations with the ruling classes of the conquered societies or stay apart, relying on military force. In truth, the Mongol empire fragmented and each state was ruled in manifestly different ways. Yet one quality underlay all of the Mongol states—the dominant presence of the Mongol military and the high prestige that attached to being a Mongol. Commonly, pastoral nomads who conquered sedentary peoples kept their distance from those settled societies with their cities, bureaucracies, artisans, and priests, instead extracting tribute

not impose rough steppe-land ways on the "civilized" urbanite Chinese. While non-Chinese outsiders took political control, they were a conquering elite that ruled over a vast Han majority. The result was a divided ruling system in which incumbent Chinese elites governed locally, while the newcomers managed the unifying central dynasty and collected taxes for the Mongols.

Southeast Asia also felt the whiplash of Kublai Khan's conquest. Circling Song defenses in southern China, the Mongols galloped southwest and conquered from them while maintaining their own distinctive way of life. For example, Chinggis forbade his followers to live in towns, and the Golden Horde Mongols lived separate from the peoples they conquered, maintaining their pastoral norms, content to receive tribute payments.

Early on, some of Chinggis's followers wanted to annihilate the northern Chinese population and turn the region into pure pastureland. Ogodei, Chinggis's third son and successor as the Great Khan, was opposed to Chinggis's merciless and destructive practices and ordered that "no peaceable inhabitants of the country be killed and forbade arbitrary pillage." One of Ogodei's successors, Kublai, became the founder of the Yuan dynasty in China, claiming for himself the Chinese mandate of heaven. Even so, Kublai cherished his Mongol identity, never learned Chinese, never consulted a book in Chinese, and "never identified with the values of the Chinese cultural legacy other than to recognize

the utility of systemic and reasoned explanation in the Chinese pattern." Moreover, the Yuan rulers divided the populations under their rule into four ranked tiers: the first of which were the Mongols themselves; the second, the non-Han Chinese of the western parts of Inner Asia, mainly nomads like themselves; the third, the northern Chinese, conquered early in the Mongol expansion; and the fourth, the southern Chinese, once the domain of the Song dynasty and the center of Confucian culture. In such a fashion, the Yuan dynasty, although centered in China proper—the heartland of urbanization and high culture—did not allow itself to be swallowed up by the Han population or its culture.

Thus, the Mongol empire, which lasted for more than two centuries, made an uneasy accommodation with sedentary populations, with its rulers partially embracing the institutions of the sedentary peoples, but never fully renouncing their pastoral, nomadic ways.

Questions for Analysis

- How did nomads and sedentary peoples view one another?
- Why might one consider the Mongols in general, and Temüjin in particular, to be unlikely conquerors?
- In what ways did different Mongol leaders negotiate the difference between pastoral and sedentary ways?

Explore Further

Di Cosmo, Nicola, Allen J. Frank, and Peter Golden (eds.), *The Cambridge History of Inner Asia: The Chinggisid Age* (2009).

Khazanov, Anatoly M., *Nomads and the Outside World*, 2nd ed., trans. Julia Crookurden, with a foreword by Ernest Gellner (1994).

Mote, Frederick W., *Imperial China, 900–1800* (1999).

Rossabi, Morris, *A History of China* (2014).

Tanner, Harold M., *China: A History* (2009).

Sources: Nicola Di Cosmo, Allen J. Frank, and Peter Golden (eds.), *The Cambridge History of Inner Asia: The Chinggisid Age* (New York: Cambridge University Press, 2009), p. 9; Anatoly M. Khazanov, *Nomads and the Outside World*, 2nd ed., trans. Julia Crookurden, with a foreword by Ernest Gellner (Madison: University of Wisconsin Press, 1994), p. 245; Frederick W. Mote, *Imperial China, 900–1800* (Cambridge, MA: Harvard University Press, 1999), p. 451.

states in Yunnan and in Burma. From there, in the 1270s, the armies headed directly back east into the soft underbelly of the Song state. In this sweep, portions of mainland Southeast Asia became annexed to China for the first time. Kublai Khan used the conquered Chinese fleets to push his expansionism onto the high seas—meeting with failure during his unsuccessful 1274 and 1281 invasions of Japan from Korea. An ill-fated Javanese expedition to extend Mongol reach beyond the South China Sea in 1293 was Kublai Khan's last.

Mongol Warriors This miniature painting is one of the illustrations for *History* by Rashid al Din, the most outstanding scholar under the Mongol regimes. Note the relatively small horses and strong bows used by the Mongol soldiers.

In the end, the Mongol Empire reached its outer limits. In the west, the Egyptian Mamluks stemmed the advancing Mongol armies and prevented Egypt from falling into their hands. In the east, the waters of the South China Sea and the Sea of Japan foiled Mongol expansion into Java and Japan. Better at conquering than governing, the Mongols struggled to rule their vast possessions in makeshift states. Bit by bit, they yielded control to local administrators and rulers who governed as their surrogates. There was also frequent feuding among the Mongol rulers themselves. In China and in Persia, Mongol rule collapsed in the fourteenth century. Ultimately, the Mongols would meet a deadly adversary even more brutal than they were: the plague of the fourteenth century (see Chapter 11).

Mongol conquest reshaped Afro-Eurasia's social landscape. Islam would never again have a unifying authority like the caliphate or a powerful center like Baghdad. China, too, was divided and changed by the Mongols' introduction of Persian, Islamic, and Byzantine influences into China's architecture, art, science, and medicine. The Yuan policy of benign tolerance brought elements from Christianity, Judaism, Zoroastrianism, and Islam into the Chinese mix. The Mongol thrust also facilitated the flow of fine goods, traders, and technology from China to the rest of the world. Finally, the Mongol conquests encouraged an unprecedented Afro-Eurasian interconnectedness, surpassing even the Hellenistic connections that Alexander's conquests had brought in the late fourth century BCE (see Chapter 6). Out of Mongol conquest and warfare would come centuries of trade, migration, and increasing contacts among Africa, Europe, and Asia.

Conclusion

Between 1000 and 1300 CE, Afro-Eurasia was forming large cultural spheres. As trade and migration spanned longer distances, these spheres prospered and became more integrated. In central Afro-Eurasia, Islam was firmly established, and its merchants, scholars, and travelers acted as commercial and cultural intermediaries joining the landmass together as they spread their universalizing faith. As seaborne trade expanded, India, too, became a commercial crossroads. Merchants in its port cities welcomed traders arriving from Arab lands to the west, from China, and from Southeast Asia. China also boomed, pouring its manufactures into trading networks that reached throughout Eurasia and even into Africa. Christian Europe had two centers—at Rome and at Constantinople—both of which were at war with Islam.

Neither sub-Saharan Africa nor the Americas saw the same degree of integration, but trade and migration in these areas had profound effects. Certain African cultures flourished as they encountered the commercial energy of trade on the Indian Ocean. Africans' trade with one another linked coastal and interior regions in an ever more integrated world. American peoples also built cities that dominated cultural areas and thrived through trade. American cultures shared significant features: reliance on trade, maize, and the exchange of goods such as shells and precious feathers. And larger areas honored the same spiritual centers.

By 1300, trade, migration, and conflict were connecting Afro-Eurasian worlds in unprecedented ways. When Mongol armies swept into China, into Southeast Asia, and into the heart of Islam, they applied a thin coating of political integration to these widespread regions and built on existing trade links. At the same time, most people's lives remained quite localized, driven by the need for subsistence and governed by spiritual and governmental representatives acting at the behest of distant authorities.

Still, locals noticed the evidence of cross-cultural exchanges everywhere—in the clothing styles of provincial elites, such as Chinese silks in Paris or quetzal plumes in northern Mexico; in enticements to move (and forced removals) to new frontiers; in the news of faraway conquests or advancing armies. Worlds were coming together within themselves and across territorial boundaries, while remaining apart as they sought to maintain their own identities and traditions. In Afro-Eurasia especially, as the movement of goods and peoples shifted from ancient land routes to sea-lanes, these contacts were more frequent and far-reaching. Never before had the world seen so much activity connecting its parts, nor had there ever been so much cultural similarity within those parts. By the time the Mongol Empire arose, the regions composing the globe were those that we now recognize as the cultural spheres of today's world.

Focus On
Foundational Cultural Spheres

The Islamic World

- The Islamic world undergoes a burst of expansion, prosperity, and cultural diversification but remains politically fractured.

- Arab merchants and Sufi mystics spread Islam over great distances and make it more appealing to other cultures, helping to transform Islam into a distinct cultural sphere.

- Islam travels across the Sahara Desert; the powerful gold- and slave-supplying empire of Mali arises in West Africa.

China

- The Song dynasty reunites China after three centuries of fragmented rulership, reaching into the past to re-establish a sense of a "true" Chinese identity as the Han through a widespread print culture and denigration of outsiders.

- Agrarian success and advances in manufacturing—including the production of both iron and porcelain— fuel an expanding economy, complete with paper money.

India

- India remains a mosaic under the canopy of Hinduism despite cultural interconnections and increasing prosperity.

- The invasion of Turkish Muslims leads to the Delhi Sultanate, which rules over India for three centuries, strengthening cultural diversity and tolerance.

Christian Europe

- Roman Catholicism becomes a "mass" faith and helps to create a common European cultural identity.

- Feudalism organizes the elite-peasant relationship, while manorialism forms the basis of the economy.

- Europe's growing confidence is manifest in its efforts, including the Crusades and the reconquering of Iberia, to drive Islam out of "Christian" lands.

CHRONOLOGY

	900	1000	1100
Sub-Saharan Africa			Great Zimbabwe flourishes 1100
The Americas	Moche people found city of Chan Chan in South America 900 CE — Cahokia flourishes as a commercial hub in North America 1000 CE — Toltecs dominate central Mexico 900–1100 CE		
The Islamic World	Turkish migrants and armies spread into Islamic world's heartland 1000 CE		Sufism spreads through Islamic world c. 1100
South Asia		Central Asian invasions begin 1000 CE	
East Asia	Song dynasty in China 906–1279 CE		
Southeast Asia			
Europe		Reconquering of the Iberian Peninsula 1061–1492 — Crusades 1095–1272	

- **Thinking about *Worlds Together, Worlds Apart***
From 1000 to 1300 CE, a range of social and political developments contributed to the consolidation of four cultural spheres that still exist today: Europe, the Islamic world, India, and China. In what ways did these spheres interact with one another? In what ways was each sphere genuinely distinct from the others? To what extent were sub-Saharan Africa and the Americas folded into these spheres and with what result?

- **Thinking about Transformation & Conflict and Becoming the World** As the four cultural spheres of Afro-Eurasia consolidated, shocking examples of conflict between them began to take place. Whether Pope Urban II's call in 1095 to reclaim the "holy land" from Muslims or the Mongol Hulagu's brutal sack of Baghdad in 1258, this period was marked by large-scale warfare between rival cultural spheres. To what extent was such conflict inevitable? In what ways did conflict transform the groups involved?

- **Thinking about Crossing Borders and Becoming the World** Major innovations facilitated economic exchange in the Indian Ocean and in Song China. The magnetic needle compass, better ships, and improved maps shrank the Indian Ocean to the benefit of traders. Similarly, paper money in Song China changed the nature of commerce. How did these developments shift the axis of Afro-Eurasian exchange? What evidence suggests that bodies of water and the routes across them became more significant than overland exchange routes in binding together Afro-Eurasia? What might be the longer-term implications of these developments?

Key Terms

Cahokia p. 473	entrepôts p. 446	Mali Empire p. 468	Sufism p. 450
Chimú Empire p. 471	flying cash p. 459	manorialism p. 463	Toltecs p. 472
Delhi Sultanate p. 454	*jizya* p. 449		

Go to INQUIZITIVE to see what you've learned—and learn what you've missed—with personalized feedback along the way.

1200   1300   1400

Mali Empire emerges

King Mansa Musa 1312–1332

Chimú Empire in South America 1000–1460 CE

Mongol forces sack Baghdad and end Abbasid caliphate 1258

Delhi Sultanate 1206–1526

Mongol Yuan dynasty 1279–1368

Khmer Empire 899–1431 CE

Global Themes and Sources

Comparing "World" Travelers Over Time

The maritime revolution described in this chapter, along with the Silk Roads across Inner Eurasia, facilitated travel for trade, diplomacy, and religious pilgrimage on a scale previously unseen. While earlier travelers, like the Spanish nun Egeria or the Buddhist monks Faxian and Xuanzang, had covered great distances and for reasons similar to those of some of the travelers whose accounts you'll read here, the sheer distances traveled by Bar Sāwmā or Ibn Battuta eclipse the journeys of their centuries-earlier counterparts. Like the earlier pilgrims, however, several travelers who moved between the worlds of Afro-Eurasia in this period left records of their stunning journeys or were written about by others.

As we saw at the start of this chapter, Bar Sāwmā traveled primarily along land routes from Yuan dynasty China all the way to modern-day France in the late thirteenth century. A Nestorian Christian monk, Bar Sāwmā appears to have made his journeys, which were recorded in a Syriac text shortly after his death in 1294, with both diplomacy and religious pilgrimage in mind. The Venetian merchant Marco Polo was traveling at nearly the same time as Bar Sāwmā, but in the opposite direction. Long after his travels were completed, Marco Polo recounted his twenty-four year voyage (1271–1295), including his time in the Mongol court of China. About a generation after Bar Sāwmā and Marco Polo completed their journeys, the North African Muslim scholar Ibn Battuta set out to traverse a combination of land and sea routes through much of Africa, Southwest Asia, Southeast Asia, and East Asia between 1325 and 1354. Writing after his travels were completed, Ibn Battuta offered details about the places he visited and their customs, as well as the hardships of travel. A rough contemporary of Ibn Battuta, a Syrian Islamic historian by the name of al-Umari who lived in the first half of the fourteenth century, provides the fourth passage here, a description of the pilgrimage of yet another famous traveler, Mansa Musa, King of Mali, in 1324–1325. The final "world" traveler represented here is the Chinese naval commander Zheng He, whose voyages came later (1405–1433; see Chapter 11) but can be usefully compared with those of Bar Sāwmā, Marco Polo, Ibn Battuta, and Mansa Musa. In a series of expeditions, Zheng He's fleet sailed from China through Southeast Asia, to Sri Lanka, into the northern Indian Ocean, and even to the Persian Gulf and the Red Sea, leaving stone inscriptions at many of the sites he visited.

The records of these travelers—Bar Sāwmā, Marco Polo, Ibn Battuta, Mansa Musa, and Zheng He—allow us to study the realities of pilgrimage and exploration in this period, but also to analyze how they are similar and how they change over time. Together with what you've learned in this chapter about the political situations across Afro-Eurasia, you can begin to explain the similarities and differences in patterns of "world" travel over hundreds of years and to think about the historical significance of those journeys.

Analyzing Comparisons of World Travelers

- Based on these excerpts, what sorts of details seem to interest each traveler? How does the form of each text (life of revered holy figure, post-trip travelogue, inscription) influence the reliability of the account?

- What sorts of dangers are explicitly mentioned, or implied, in these texts?

- What in the texts suggests the exchange of goods and ideas?

- Compare these travel accounts with those from the Global Themes and Sources feature of Chapter 8. What are some of the similarities and differences in the "world" travels of these two groups of individuals? What accounts for those changes and continuities over time?

Pilgrimage to Jerusalem (c. 1300), Bar Sāwmā

This passage illustrates the realities of travel for Bar Sāwmā and his travel companion Markōs in the late thirteenth century. Setting out from the Mongol capital Khan-balik, they enter the territory of Mar Denha (or Mar Catholicus), the Patriarch of the Nestorian Church, who, after greeting them warmly, sends them on their way to visit holy sites. Just in this one passage, we can see the territory these pilgrims covered, starting in Khan-balik, arriving at Maraghah (in the territory of modern Azerbaijan), continuing on to Baghdad, and then into Armenia and Georgia. Many of the interactions and travel issues they describe resonate with those of the Spanish nun Egeria. (Titles of sites have been capitalized, as in the original translation.)

• **What are some of the practical travel issues Bar Sāwmā and his travel companion face?**

• **How do Bar Sāwmā and his companion interact with people and places on their travels?**

• **How do those travel issues and interactions compare with those of the Spanish nun Egeria, 900 years earlier?**

And having enjoyed the conversation of those brethren they set out to go to ADHÔRBÎJÂN . . . so that they might travel from there to BAGHDÂD, to MÂR DENHÂ, the Catholicus. . . . Now it happened that Mâr Catholicus had come to MÂRÂGHÂH [a town of ADHÔRBÎJÂN, the capital of HÛLÂGÛ KHÂN], and they met him there. And at the sight of him their joy grew great, and their gladness was increased. . . . And when [Mar Catholicus] asked them, "Whence [come] ye?" they replied, "From the countries of the East, from KHÂN BÂLÎK, the city of the King of Kings [KÛBLÂI] KHÂN. We have come to be blessed by you, and by the Fathers (i.e. Bishops), and the monks, and the holy men of this quarter of the world. And if a road [openeth] to us, and God hath mercy upon us, we shall go to JERUSALEM."

. . . [Catholicus] comforted them and said unto them, "Assuredly, O my sons, the Angel of Provi-dence shall protect you on this difficult journey, and he shall be a guide unto you until the completion of your quest." . . .

[After a few days, Bar Sāwmā and his companion] request [of Mar Catholicus]: "If we have found mercy (i.e. favour) in the eyes of Mâr our Father, let him permit us to go to BAGHDÂD, in order that we may receive a blessing from the holy sepulchers (or relics?) of MÂR MÂRÊ, . . . the Apostle, the teacher of the East, and those of the Fathers that are there. And from there we would go to the monasteries that are in the country of BÊTH GARMAI and in NISIBIS that we may be blessed there also, and demand assistance."

And when the Catholicus saw the beauty of their object, and the innocence of their minds, and the hon-esty of their thoughts, he said unto them, "Go ye, my sons, and may Christ, the Lord of the Universe, grant unto you your petition." . . . And he wrote for them a *pêthîkhâ* (i.e. a letter of introduction) to these countries so that they might be honourably entreated whitherso-ever they went; and he sent with them a man to show them the way, and to act as a guide along the roads.

And they arrived in Baghdad, and thence they went to the Great Church of KÔKÊ [at Ctesiphon]. . . . And they went to the monastery of MÂR MÂRÎ, the Apostle, and received a blessing from the sepul-chers (or relics?) of that country. And from there they turned back and came to the country of BÊTH GAR-MAI, and they received blessings from the shrine (or tomb) of MÂR EZEKIEL [the prophet, near Dâkôk], which was full of helps and healings. And from there they went to ARBÎL, and thence to MÂWSIL (i.e. Môsul on the Tigris). And they went [to] SHÎGAR (SINJÂR), and NISIBIS, and MERDÂ (MARDÎN); and were blessed by the shrine [containing] the bones of MÂR AWGÎN, the second CHRIST. And thence they went to GÂZARTÂ of BÊTH ZABHDAI, and they were blessed by all the shrines and monasteries, and the religious houses, and monks, and the Fathers (i.e. Bishops) in their dioceses. . . .

And when they arrived at the city of Animto [i.e. ANÎ, the ancient capital of Christian ARMENIA, situated on an affluent of the river Araxes], and saw the monasteries and the churches therein, they mar-velled at the great extent of the buildings and at their magnificence. And thence they went towards BÊTH

GÛRGÂYÊ (i.e. the country of Georgia), so that they might travel by a clear (or safe?) road, but when they arrived there they heard from the inhabitants of the country that the road was cut because of the murders and robberies which had taken place along it.

Chapter 4. And the two monks turned back and came to Mâr Catholicus, who rejoiced [at the sight of] them, and said unto them, "This is not the time for a journey to JERUSALEM. The roads are a disturbed state, and the ways are cut. Now behold, ye have received blessings from all the Houses of God, and the shrines (or relics?) which are in them, and it is my opinion that when a man visits them with a pure heart, the service thus paid to them is in no way less than that of a pilgrimage to Jerusalem."

Source: Rabban Bar Sāwmā. *The Monks of Kublai Khan, Emperor of China, or The History of the Life and Travels of Rabban Sāwmā*, trans. E. A. Wallis Budge (London: Religious Tract Society, 1928), pp. 140–43, 145–46.

PRIMARY SOURCE 10.2

The Mongol Capital at Kanbalu (Khan-Balik) (c. 1300), Marco Polo

In the last quarter of the thirteenth century, the Venetian merchant Marco Polo, together with his father and uncle, undertook a magnificent trek eastward on the Silk Roads. They ultimately arrived at Khan-balik, capital of the Mongol Yuan dynasty (and the place from which Bar Sāwmā set out, in the previous passage). There, they encountered Kublai Khan. Long after his journey was completed, Marco Polo offered this thorough description of the city, which would ultimately become Beijing. While some scholars have questioned the veracity of Polo's travels, arguing that he may never have made it all the way to China, the detail offered in this passage suggests firsthand experience.

- What does Marco Polo emphasize in his description of Kanbalu (Khan-balik)?

- What different groups of people live in greater Khan-balik? How are they organized and distributed?

- Why do you think Marco Polo focuses on the issues that he describes?

The city of Kanbalu is situated near a large river in the province of Cathay, and was in ancient times eminently magnificent and royal. The name itself implies "the city of the sovereign;" but his majesty having imbibed an opinion from the astrologers, that it was destined to become rebellious to his authority, resolved upon the measure of building another capital, upon the opposite side of the river, where stand the palaces just described: so that the new and the old cities are separated from each other only by the stream that runs between them. The new-built city received the name of Tai-du, and all the Cathaians, that is, all those of the inhabitants who were natives of the province of Cathay, were compelled to evacuate the ancient city, and to take up their abode in the new. Some of the inhabitants, however, of whose loyalty he did not entertain suspicion, were suffered to remain, especially because the latter, although of the dimensions that shall presently be described, was not capable of containing the same number as the former, which was of vast extent.

This new city is of a form perfectly square, and twenty-four miles in extent, each of its sides being neither more nor less than six miles. It is enclosed with walls of earth, that at the base are about ten paces thick, but gradually diminish to the top, where the thickness is not more than three paces. In all parts the battlements are white. The whole plan of the city was regularly laid out by line, and the streets in general are consequently so straight, that when a person ascends the wall over one of the gates, and looks right forward, he can see the gate opposite to him on the other side of the city. In the public streets there are, on each side, booths and shops of every description. All the allotments of ground upon which the habitations throughout the city were constructed are square, and exactly on a line with each other; each allotment being sufficiently spacious for handsome buildings, with corresponding courts and gardens. One of these was assigned to each head of a family; that is to say, such a person of such a tribe had one square allotted to him, and so of the rest. Afterwards the property passed from hand to hand. In this manner the whole interior of the city is disposed in squares, so as to resemble a chessboard, and planned out with a degree of precision and beauty impossible to describe. The wall of the city has twelve gates, three on each side of the square, and over each gate and compartment of the wall there is a handsome building; so that on each side of the square there are five such buildings, containing large rooms, in which are disposed the arms of those who form the garrison of the city, every gate being guarded by a thousand men. It is not to be understood that such a force is stationed there in consequence of the apprehension of danger from any hostile power whatever, but as a guard suitable to the honour and dignity of the sovereign. Yet it must be allowed that the declaration of the astrologers has excited in his mind a degree of suspicion with regard to the Cathaians. . . .

Outside of each of the gates is a suburb so wide that it reaches to and unites with those of the other nearest gates on both sides, and in length extends to the distance of three or four miles, so that the number of inhabitants in these suburbs exceeds that of the city itself. Within each suburb there are, at intervals, as far perhaps as a mile from the city, many hotels, or caravanserais, in which the merchants arriving from various parts take up their abode; and to each description of people a separate building is assigned, as we should say, one to the Lombards, another to the Germans, and a third to the French. . . .

Guards, in parties of thirty or forty, continually patrol the streets during the course of the night, and make diligent search for persons who may be from their homes at an unseasonable hour, that is, after the third stroke of the great bell. When any are met with under such circumstances, they immediately apprehend and confine them, and take them in the morning for examination before officers appointed for that purpose, who, upon the proof of any delinquency, sentence them, according to the nature of the offence, to a severer or lighter infliction of the bastinade beating with a cudgel, usually on the soles of the feet, which sometimes, however, occasions their death. It is in this manner that crimes are usually punished amongst these people, from a disinclination to the shedding of blood, which their *baksis* or learned astrologers instruct them to avoid.

Source: Marco Polo, *The Travels of Marco Polo, The Venetian*, ed. Thomas Wright (London: George Bell and Sons, 1904), pp. 181–86. Notes in brackets added by the author.

The Holy Sites of Jerusalem (c. 1360), Ibn Battuta

Ibn Battuta's travels dwarf those of any other world traveler in this period. What began as a *hajj* became a journey of tens of thousands of miles. Traveling for more than a quarter century, Ibn Battuta was particularly interested in the role and practice of Islam in each place he visited. While he was sometimes called into action to serve as a learned Muslim *qadi* (judge) in the places he visited, his travels often took the form of engaged and devoted religious tourism, as when he visited Jerusalem, as described in the passage here.

- What can you make out of Ibn Battuta's itinerary? What sites does he visit? What, and how, does he learn about the history of each site?

- How does Ibn Battuta describe mosques? Churches? What do you think accounts for the differences in his descriptions?

- How do Ibn Battuta's descriptions of holy sites compare with those in Bar Sāwmā's account?

From Gaza I travelled to the city of Abraham [Hebron], the mosque of which is of elegant, but substantial, construction, imposing and lofty, and built of squared stones. At one angle of it there is a stone, one of whose faces measures twenty-seven spans. It is said that Solomon commanded the *jinn* to build it. Inside it is the sacred cave containing the graves of Abraham, Isaac, and Jacob, opposite which are three graves, which are those of their wives. I questioned the imám, a man of great piety and learning, on the authenticity of these graves, and he replied: "All the scholars whom I have met hold these graves to be the very graves of Abraham, Isaac, Jacob and their wives. No one questions this except introducers of false doctrines; it is a tradition which has passed from father to son for generations and admits of no doubt.". . .

On the way from Hebron to Jerusalem, I visited Bethlehem, the birthplace of Jesus. The site is covered by a large building; the Christians regard it with intense veneration and hospitably entertain all who alight at it.

We then reached Jerusalem (may God ennoble her!), third in excellence after the two holy shrines of Mecca and Medína, and the place whence the Prophet was caught up into heaven. Its walls were destroyed by the illustrious King Saladin and his successors, for fear lest the Christians should seize it and fortify themselves in it. The sacred mosque is a most beautiful building, and is said to be the largest mosque in the world. Its length from east to west is put at 752 "royal" cubits and its breadth at 435. On three sides it has many entrances, but on the south side I know of one only, which is that by which the imám enters. The entire mosque is an open court and unroofed, except the mosque al-Aqsá, which has a roof of most excellent workmanship, embellished with gold and brilliant colours. Some other parts of the mosque are roofed as well. The Dome of the Rock is a building of extraordinary beauty, solidity, elegance, and singularity of shape. It stands on an elevation in the centre of the mosque and is reached by a flight of marble steps. It has four doors. The space round it is also paved with marble, excellently done, and the interior likewise. Both outside and inside the decoration is so magnificent and the workmanship so surpassing as to defy description. The greater part is covered with gold so that the eyes of one who gazes on its beauties are dazzled by its brilliance, now glowing like a mass of light, now flashing like lightning. In the centre of the Dome is the blessed rock from which the Prophet ascended to heaven, a great rock projecting about a man's height, and underneath it there is a cave the size of a small room, also of a man's height, with steps leading down to it. Encircling the rock are two railings of excellent workmanship, the one nearer the rock being artistically constructed in iron, and the other of wood.

Among the grace-bestowing sanctuaries of Jerusalem is a building, situated on the farther side of the valley called the valley of Jahannam [Gehenna] to the east of the town, on a high hill. This building is said to mark the place whence Jesus ascended to heaven. In the bottom of the same valley is a church venerated by the Christians, who say that it contains the grave of Mary. In the same place there is another church which the Christians venerate and to which they come on pilgrimage. This is the church of which they are falsely persuaded to believe that it contains the grave of Jesus. All who come on pilgrimage to visit it pay a stipulated tax to the Muslims, and suffer very unwillingly various humiliations. Thereabouts also is the place of the cradle of Jesus, which is visited in order to obtain blessing.

Source: Ibn Battúta, *Ibn Battúta: Travels in Asia and Africa, 1325–1354*, trans. and ed. H. A. R. Gibb (London: George Routledge & Sons, Ltd., 1929), pp. 55–57.

PRIMARY SOURCE 10.4

The Hajj of Mansa Musa (1324–1325), al-Umari

Al-Umari was a historian who lived in the first half of the fourteenth century. While his personal life reflected the vicissitudes of court politics in Mamluk-controlled Syria (complete with a period of imprisonment when he fell out of favor), his well-researched history was much appreciated by his contemporaries. The passage included here, in which al-Umari describes the famed *hajj* of Mansa Musa, shows that al-Umari himself traveled to Cairo to gather information from local informants about Mansa Musa's sojourn in the city.

- **What are the layers of reporting in this passage? How does the traveling historian al-Umari come by his information on Mansa Musa?**

- **How does Mansa Musa's *hajj* influence the peoples with whom he and his retinue come into contact?**

- **How typical was Mansa Musa's *hajj*? Even if it is atypical, what can you generalize about the role of *hajj* in the Mediterranean and Indian Ocean worlds based on Mansa Musa's and Ibn Battuta's experiences?**

The emir Abū 'l-Ḥasan 'Alī b. Amīr Ḥajib told me that he was often in the company of sultan Mūsā the king of this country when he came to Egypt on the Pilgrimage. He was staying in [the] Qarāfa [district of Cairo] and Ibn Amīr Ḥājib was governor of Old Cairo and Qarāfa at that time. A friendship grew up between them and this sultan Mūsā told him a great deal about himself and his country and the people of the Sūdān who were his neighbours. One of the things which he told him was that his country was very extensive and contiguous with the Ocean. By his sword and his armies he had conquered 24 cities each with its surrounding district with villages and estates. It is a country rich in livestock—cattle, sheep, goats, horses, mules—and different kinds of poultry—geese, doves, chickens. The inhabitants of his country are numerous, a vast concourse, but compared with the peoples of the Sūdān who are their neighbours and penetrate far to the south they are like a white birth-mark on a black cow. He has a truce with the gold-plant people, who pay him tribute.

Ibn Amīr Ḥājib said that he asked him about the gold-plant, and he said: "It is found in two forms. One is found in the spring and blossoms after the rains in open country (ṣaḥrā'). It has leaves like the najīl grass and its roots are gold (tibr). The other kind is found all the year round at known sites on the banks of the Nīl and is dug up. . . .

Sultan Mūsā told Ibn Amīr Ḥājib that gold was his prerogative and he collected the crop as a tribute except for what the people of that country took by theft. . . .

"This sultan Mūsā, during his stay in Egypt both before and after his journey to the Noble Ḥājib, maintained a uniform attitude of worship and turning towards God. It was as though he were standing before Him because of His continual presence in his mind. He and all those with him behaved in the same manner and were well-dressed, grave, and dignified. He was noble and generous and performed many acts of charity and kindness. He had left his country with 100 loads of gold which he spent during his Pilgrimage on the tribes who lay along his route from his country to Egypt, while he was in Egypt, and again from Egypt to the Noble Hijāz and back. . . .

From the beginning of my coming to stay in Egypt I heard talk of the arrival of this sultan Mūsā on his Pilgrimage and found the Cairenes eager to recount what they had seen of the Africans' prodigal spending. . . .

This man flooded Cairo with his benefactions. He left no court emir (amīr muqarrab) nor holder of a royal office without the gift of a load of gold. The Cairenes made incalculable profits out of him and his suite in buying and selling and giving and taking. They exchanged gold until they depressed its value in Egypt and caused its price to fall. . . .

Merchants of Miṣr and Cairo have told me of the profits which they made from the Africans, saying that one of them might buy a shirt or cloak (thawb) or robe (izār) or other garment for five dinars when it was not worth one. Such was their simplicity and trustfulness that it was possible to practice any deception on them. They greeted anything that was said to them with credulous acceptance. But later they formed the very poorest opinion of the Egyptians because of the obvious falseness of everything they said to them and their outrageous behaviour in fixing the prices of the provisions and other goods which were sold to them. . . .

Muhanna' b. 'Abd al-Bāqī al-'Ujrumī the guide informed me that he accompanied sultan Mūsā when he made the Pilgrimage and that the sultan was very open-handed towards the pilgrims and the inhabitants of the Holy Places. He and his companions maintained great pomp and dressed magnificently during the journey. He gave away much wealth in alms. "About 200 mithqals of gold fell to me" said Muhanna' "and he gave other sums to my companions." Muhanna' waxed eloquent in describing the sultan's generosity, magnanimity, and opulence.

Gold was at a high price in Egypt until they came in that year. The mithqal did not go below 25 dirhams and was generally above, but from that time its value fell and it cheapened in price and has remained cheap till now. The mithqal does not exceed 22 dirhams or less. This has been the state of affairs for about twelve years until this day by reason of the large amount of gold which they brought into Egypt and spent there.

Source: al-Umari, *Corpus of Early Arabic Sources for West African History*, trans. J. F. P Hopkins (Cambridge: Cambridge University Press, 1981), pp. 267, 269–71.

PRIMARY SOURCE 10.5

The Galle Trilingual Stone Inscription (1411), Zheng He

No discussion of world travelers in this increasingly connected Afro-Eurasian world would be complete without evidence from Zheng He's travels, although he lived in a slightly later period than the other travelers discussed here (namely, during the Ming dynasty, which took the mandate of heaven from the

Mongol Yuan dynasty of China in the aftermath of the Black Death; see Chapter 11). The seven far-reaching naval expeditions undertaken by Zheng He from 1405 to 1433 illustrate Ming patronage of voyages of exploration that demonstrated their might. This trilingual inscription (in Chinese, Persian, and Tamil), set up in 1411 by Zheng He and his companions at Sri Lanka [called Ceylon in the source], demonstrates the pragmatic religious devotion of those voyaging for nonreligious aims.

....

- **What range of goods does Zheng He's embassy offer? Why these specific commodities?**

- **Why do Zheng He, who was born and raised a Muslim, and his companions make offerings to Buddha?**

- **How do Zheng He's reasons for travel and what he does at this holy site compare with the other travelers in this section?**

....

His Majesty, the Emperor of the Great Ming dynasty has despatched the eunuchs Ching-Ho [Zheng He], Wang Ch'ing-Lien, and others to set forth his utterance before Buddha, the World Honoured one, as follows:

"Deeply do we reverence you, Merciful and Honoured One, whose bright perfection is wide-embracing, and whose way of virtue passes all understanding, whose law enters into all human relations, and the years of whose great Kalpa (period) are like the sand of the river in number, you whose controlling influence ennobles and converts, whose kindness quickens, and whose strength discerns, whose mysterious efficacy is beyond compare! Whereas Ceylon's mountainous isle lies in the south of the ocean, and its Buddhist temples are sanctuaries of your gospel, where your miraculous responsive power imbues and enlightens. Of late, we have dispatched missions to announce our mandate

to foreign nations, and during their journey over the ocean they have been favoured with the blessing of your beneficent protection. They escaped disaster or misfortune and journeyed in safety to and fro. In everlasting recognition of your supreme virtue, we, therefore, bestow offerings in recompense, and do now reverently present before Buddha, the Honoured One, oblations of gold and silver, gold embroidered jewelled banners of variegated silk, incense burners, and flower vases, silks of many colours in lining and exterior, lamps and candles with other gifts, in order to manifest the high honour of our worship. Do you, Lord Buddha, bestow on them, your regard!"

List of Alms bestowed at the shrine of the Buddhist temple in the Mountain of Ceylon as offerings:

1000 pieces of gold; 5000 pieces of silver; fifty rolls of embroidered silk in many colours; fifty rolls of silk taffeta in many colours; four pairs of jewelled banners, gold embroidered, and of variegated silk; two pairs of the same picked in red; one pair of the same in yellow; one pair in black; five antique brass incense burners; five pairs of antique brass flower vases picked in gold on lacquer, with gold stands; five pairs of yellow brass candle-sticks, picked in gold on lacquer, with gold stand; five yellow brass lamps picked in gold on lacquer, with gold stands; five incense vessels in vermilion red, lacquered gold picked on lacquer, with gold stands; six pairs of golden lotus flowers; 2500 catties of scented oil; ten pairs of wax candles; ten sticks of fragrant incense.

The date being the seventh year of Yung-Lo (1410 a.d.) marked Chi ch'ou in the sixty years' cycle, on the Chia Hsu day of the sixty days cycle in the second moon, being the first day of the month. A reverent oblation.

Source: "Appendix I. Translation of the Chinese Inscription," trans. Edmund Backhouse, in "The Galle Trilingual Stone," *Spolia Zeylanica* 8 (Issued from the Colombo Museum; Ceylon: H. M. Richards, Acting Government Printer, 1913), pp. 125–26. Bracketed notes added by the author.

Interpreting Visual Evidence

Imagining the World

During this period when Afro-Eurasia was "becoming the world," cartographers began producing "world" maps. In 1154 al-Idrisi, a Muslim cartographer sponsored by King Roger II of Sicily, produced his *Tabula Rogeriana*. Al-Idrisi's map was accompanied by a commentary that contained information about the ten regions (numbered west to east; but note that the map was drawn so that the south is at the top) and seven climate zones (numbered south to north and following the scheme set forth by the second-century CE Greco-Roman geographer Ptolemy). In 1375, a Jewish mapmaker named Abraham Cresques, from the island of Majorca off the east coast of Spain, produced the second map included here, which is known as the *Catalan Atlas*. Cresques's map is a mixture of practical information

and storytelling. The crisscrossed lines that mark compass bearings, suggestive of a nautical chart, reflect the influence of the compass on European mapmaking beginning around 1300. The ornate depictions of the Mali king Mansa Musa and the caravan of Marco Polo offer historical information. In 1459, a monk named Fra Mauro, from Venice, created his *Mappa Mundi* (Map of the World), the third map pictured here. Fra Mauro's map is striking in its detail and information. Not only does it carefully mark out shorelines, rivers, cities, and other geographic features, it also includes banners with detailed information and even drawings of the different types of ships (such as the North Atlantic cogs, Chinese junks, and Arabian dhows, discussed in this chapter) that sailed the different seas.

Al-Idrisi's *Tabula Rogeriana*.

Cresques's *Catalan Atlas*.

Fra Mauro's *Mappa Mundi*.

11

Crisis and Recovery in Afro-Eurasia

1300–1500

When Mongol armies besieged the Genoese trading outpost of Caffa on the Black Sea in 1346, they not only damaged trading links between East Asia and the Mediterranean but also unleashed a devastating disease: the bubonic plague. Defeated Genoese merchants and soldiers withdrew, unknowingly taking the germs with them aboard their ships. By the time they arrived in Messina, Sicily, half the passengers were dead. The rest were dying. People waiting on shore for the ships' trade goods were horrified at the sight and turned the ships away. Desperately, the captains went to the next port, only to face the same fate. Despite these efforts at isolation, Europeans could not keep the plague (later called the Black Death) from reaching their shores. As it spread from port to port, it eventually contaminated all of Europe, killing more than half of the population.

This story illustrates the disruptive effects of both the Mongol invasions and the long-distance trade routes that the Mongols foisted on Afro-Eurasian societies. In the thirteenth and early fourteenth centuries, Mongol armies swept into and took control of vast regions of Afro-Eurasia. Although the invasions ushered in an age of intensified cultural and political contact, the channels of exchange—the land routes and sea-lanes of human voyagers—became accidental conduits for deadly microbes. These germs devastated societies far more decisively than did Mongol warfare. They were the real "murderous hordes" of world

Chapter Outline

- Collapse and Consolidation
- The Islamic Heartland
- Western Christendom
- Ming China
- Conclusion

Core Objectives

- **DESCRIBE** the nature and origins of the crises spanning Afro-Eurasia during the fourteenth century.

- **ASSESS** the impact of the Black Death on China, the Islamic world, and Europe.

- **COMPARE** the ways in which regional rulers in postplague Afro-Eurasia attempted to construct unified states and **ANALYZE** the extent and nature of their successes.

- **EXPLAIN** the role that religious belief systems played in rebuilding the Islamic world, Europe, and Ming China in the fourteenth and fifteenth centuries.

- **EXAMINE** the way art and architecture reflected the political realities of the Islamic world, Europe, and Ming China after the Black Death.

- **COMPARE** how Ottoman, Iberian, and Ming rulers extended their territories and regional influence.

history, infecting people from every community, class, and culture they encountered. So staggering was the Black Death's toll that population densities did not recover for 200 years. The most severely affected regions were those that the Mongols had brought together: settlements and commercial hubs along the old Silk Roads and around the Mediterranean Sea and the South China Sea. While segments of the Indian Ocean trading world experienced death and disruption, South Asian societies, which had escaped the Mongol conquest, also escaped the dying and political disruptions associated with the Black Death.

This chapter explores the ways in which Afro-Eurasian peoples restored what they thought was valuable from old traditions after these crises, while discarding what they thought had failed them in favor of radically new institutions and ideas. Much of the recovery had striking similarities across Afro-Eurasia, as societies reaffirmed their most deeply held and long-standing beliefs. Chinese rulers looked to Confucian thought and well-known dynastic institutions to provide guidance going forward. In the Muslim heartland, a small band of Turkish-speaking warriors—the Ottomans—channeled the energies of a revived Islam to expand their own territory and the Muslim world. Europeans also invoked their traditions. In the Iberian Peninsula, political elites used a resurgent Catholicism to spread their political power and drive Muslim communities out of Europe. Europeans also created new dynastic monarchies and looked to their distant past in Greek and Roman culture for inspiration.

Radically new institutions and ideas appeared across Afro-Eurasia in the aftermath of the Black Death. Notable among these was the outburst of cultural activity

Global Storylines

- The spread of the Black Death and the collapse of the Mongol Empire sets off crises across Afro-Eurasia, with major demographic, political, economic, and cultural consequences.

- Across Afro-Eurasia, continuity in religious beliefs and cultural institutions accompanies changes in political structures in Europe, the Muslim world, and China.

- In central Eurasia, new rulers—most notably the Ottomans—rebuild dynasties in place of the Mongols, using a blend of religion, military expansion, administrative control, and cultural tolerance.

- In western Christendom, new monarchies establish political order, and the Renaissance brings a cultural rebirth to societies devastated by plague.

- In East Asia, the Ming dynasty replaces the Mongol Yuan dynasty, using an elaborate Confucian bureaucracy to oversee infrastructure and long-distance exchange.

that took place in western Europe. Historians have called this flourishing the Renaissance (rebirth), for during this era Europeans rediscovered their Greek and Roman pasts and used inspiration drawn from classical antiquity to bring about far-reaching innovations in art, architecture, thought, and political and financial institutions. While significant changes reshaped institutions and ideas in this period, there were also many continuities. Considering how grievously people suffered and how many died, it is perhaps surprising how much of the old—particularly religious beliefs and institutions—survived the aftermath of Mongol rule and the Black Death.

Collapse and Consolidation

Although the Mongol invasions overturned political systems, the plague devastated society itself. The pandemic killed millions, disrupted economies, and threw communities into chaos. Rulers could explain to their people the assaults of "barbarians," but it was much harder to make sense of an invisible enemy. Nonetheless, in response to the upheaval, new ruling groups moved to reorganize their states. By making strategic marriages and building powerful armies, these rulers enlarged their territories, formed alliances, and built dynasties.

THE BLACK DEATH

The spread of the Black Death was the fourteenth century's most significant historical development. (See Map 11.1.) Originating in Inner Asia, the disease afflicted peoples from China to Europe and killed 25 to 65 percent of infected populations.

How did the **Black Death** move so far and so fast? One explanation may lie in climate changes. The cooler climate of this period—scholars refer to a "Little Ice Age"—may have weakened populations and left them vulnerable to disease. In Europe, for instance, beginning around 1310, harsh winters and rainy summers shortened growing seasons and ruined harvests. Exhausted soils no longer supplied the resources required by growing urban and rural populations, while nobles squeezed the peasantry in an effort to maintain their luxurious lifestyle. The ensuing famine lasted from 1315 to 1322, during which time millions of Europeans died of starvation or of diseases against which the malnourished population had little resistance. This climate change and famine laid the groundwork for the Black Death that soon followed. Another climate-related factor in the spread of the plague lay in the drying up of the central Asian steppe borderlands, where bubonic plague had existed for centuries. This drought may have forced rodents out of their usual dwelling places and pressed pastoral peoples, who carried the infectious strains, closer to settled agricultural communities. Fleas transmitted plague from rodent to rodent, and to humans. The resulting epidemic was terrifying, for its causes

THE BIG PICTURE

What crises affected fourteenth-century Afro-Eurasia and what was the range of responses to those crises?

Black Death
Great epidemic of the bubonic plague that ravaged Europe, East Asia, and North Africa in the fourteenth century, killing large numbers of people, including perhaps as much as one-third of the European population.

Plague Victim The plague was highly contagious and quickly led to death. Here a physician and his helper cover their noses to avoid the unbearable stench emanating from the patient.

were unknown at the time. Infected victims died quickly—sometimes overnight—and in agony, coughing up blood and oozing pus and blood from black sores the size of eggs.

But it was the trading network that spread the germs across Afro-Eurasia into famine-struck western Europe. This wider Afro-Eurasian population was vulnerable because its members had no immunity to the disease. The first outbreak in a heavily populated region occurred in the 1320s in southwestern China. From there, the disease spread through China and then continued its death march along the major trade routes. Many of these routes terminated at the Italian port cities, where ships with dead and dying people aboard arrived in 1347. From there, what Europeans called the Pestilence or the Great Mortality engulfed the western end of the landmass. Societies in China, the Muslim world, and Europe suffered the disastrous effects of the Black Death.

Plague in China China was ripe for the plague pandemic. Its population had increased under the Song dynasty (960–1279) and subsequent Mongol rule. But by 1300, hunger and scarcity spread as resources were stretched thin. The weakened population was especially vulnerable. For seventy years, the Black Death ravaged China, reduced the size of the already small Mongol population, and shattered the Mongols' claim to a mandate from heaven. In 1331, plague may have killed 90 percent of the population in Bei Zhili (modern Hebei) Province. From there it spread throughout other provinces, reaching Fujian and the coast at Shandong. By the 1350s, most of China's large cities had suffered severe outbreaks.

Even as the Black Death was engulfing China, bandit groups and dissident religious sects were undercutting the power of the last Mongol Yuan rulers. Popular religious movements warned of impending doom. Most prominent was the Red Turban movement, which blended China's diverse cultural and religious traditions, including Buddhism, Daoism, and other faiths. Its leaders emphasized strict dietary restrictions, penance, and ceremonial rituals, and made proclamations that the world was drawing to an end.

Plague in the Islamic World The plague devastated parts of the Muslim world as well. The Black Death reached Baghdad by 1347. By the next year, the plague overtook Egypt, Syria, and Cyprus, causing as many as 1,000 deaths a day according to a Tunisian report. Animals, too, were afflicted. One Egyptian writer commented: "The country was not far from being ruined. . . . One found in the desert the bodies of savage animals with the bubos under their arms. It was the same with horses, camels, asses, and all the beasts in general, including birds, even the ostriches." In the eastern Mediterranean, plague left much of the Islamic world in a state of near political and economic collapse. The great Arab historian Ibn Khaldûn (1332–1406), who lost his mother and father and a number of his teachers to the Black Death in Tunis, underscored the desolation: "Cities and buildings were laid waste, roads and way signs were obliterated, settlements and mansions became empty, dynasties and tribes grew weak," he wrote. "The entire world changed."

Plague in Europe In Europe, the Black Death first ravaged the Italian Peninsula; then it seized France, the Netherlands, Belgium, Luxembourg, Germany, and England in its deathly grip. Overcrowded and unsanitary cities were particularly vulnerable. All levels of society—the poor, craftspeople, aristocrats—were at risk, although flight to the countryside offered some protection from infection. Nearly 50 million of Europe's 80 million people perished between 1347 and 1351. After 1353, the epidemic waned, but the plague returned every seven years or so for the rest of the century and sporadically through the fifteenth century. Consequently, the European population continued to decline, until by 1450 many areas had only one-quarter the number of a century earlier.

In the face of the Black Death, some Europeans turned to debauchery, determined to enjoy themselves before they died. Others, especially in urban settings in Flanders, the Netherlands, and parts of Germany, claimed to find God's grace outside what they saw as a corrupt Catholic Church. Semimonastic orders like the Beghards and Beguines, which had begun in the century or so before the plague, expanded in its wake. These laypeople (unordained men and women) argued that people should trust their own "interior instinct" more than the Gospel as then preached. By contrast, the Flagellants were so convinced that man had incurred God's wrath that they whipped themselves to atone for human sin.

For many who survived the plague, disappointment with the clergy smoldered. Famished peasants resented priests and monks for living lives of luxury. In addition, they despaired at the absence of clergy when they were so greatly needed. While many clerics had perished attending to their parishioners during the Black Death, others had fled to rural retreats far from the ravages of the plague, leaving their followers to fend for themselves.

Core Objectives

ASSESS the impact of the Black Death on China, the Islamic world, and Europe.

Map 11.1 The Spread of the Black Death

The Black Death was an Afro-Eurasian pandemic of the fourteenth century.

- What was the origin point of the Black Death? How far did it travel?
- Which trade routes did the Black Death follow? Which trade routes did the Black Death appear not to have followed? What do you think accounts for the difference?
- Where was the earliest instance of the Black Death? Where did it occur latest? What hypotheses can you assert about the Black Death based on the dates on the map?

Map labels:

SCANDINAVIA 1349
NORTH SEA
BALTIC SEA
Novgorod
Moscow
MUSCOVY 1351
KHANATE OF THE GOLDEN HORDE
Edinburgh 1350
Dublin 1349
BRITAIN
London 1348
Bremen 1349
Lübeck 1349
Danzig
Kiev
Rostov
New Sarai
ARAL SEA
Oxford 1348
Amiens 1348
Cologne 1349
EUROPE
Cracow
Caffa 1346
CASPIAN SEA
Paris 1348
Buda 1349
Venice 1347
Florence 1347
BLACK SEA
Bukhara
Avignon 1347
Genoa 1347
Siena 1347
Constantinople 1347
Trebizond
Tabriz
Samark
Bordeaux 1348
Marseille
Pisa 1347
Naples
Athens 1347
ANATOLIA
Maraghah
IL-KHANATE
Barcelona 1348
Palermo 1347
Messina 1347
Aleppo 1347
PERSIA
Lisbon 1349
Madrid
SPAIN 1348
Algiers
Tunis
Damascus 1347
Baghdad 1347
Isfahan
Ceuta
Fez
MEDITERRANEAN SEA
Tripoli 1348
Alexandria 1347
Jerusalem 1347
Basra
Shiraz
Hormuz
Marrakesh 1349
Cairo 1347
ARABIA
Persian Gulf
AFRICA
Medina
Mecca 1348
ARABIAN SEA
RED SEA
Aden 1351
Mogadishu
INDIAN

Legend:

➤ Progress of bubonic plague
— Trade routes
• Known areas of major outbreaks
* Modern Chinese provincial names for regions affected by outbreak of plague

MONGOL
ANCESTRAL
HOMELAND

Lake Baikal

Karakorum

Shangdu

Tashkent

Kashgar

kh

Kabul

Beijing
1354

HEBEI*
1331

SHANDONG*
1353

SEA
OF
JAPAN

1351

1352

1353 1351 1354

1345

1346

TIBET

KHANATE OF THE

GREAT KHAN

1335 Kaifeng

1332

Lhasa

Delhi

HUBEI*
1320

1321

1323

Hangzhou

1351 Nanchang
1352

Nagasāki

JAPAN

DELHI

SULTANATE

YUNNAN*
1320

1353 Fuzhou

1356

BURMA

1354

Guangzhou
1354

FUJIAN*
1345

PACIFIC

OCEAN

Pagan
before 1320

Calicut

Angkor

SOUTH

CHINA

SEA

OCEAN

Melaka

Brunei

SUMATRA

BORNEO

JAVA

0   500   1000 Miles

0   500   1000 Kilometers

Bubonic Plague and the Destruction of Society Bubonic plague devastated the countries of western Christendom. Here, in Pieter Bruegel the Elder's *The Triumph of Death* (1562), skeletons murder indiscriminately, rich and poor alike, and dogs devour unburied corpses.

The Black Death wrought devastation throughout Afro-Eurasia. The Chinese population plunged from around 115 million in 1200 to 75 million or less in 1400, as the result of the Mongol invasions of the thirteenth century and the disease and disorder of the fourteenth century. Over the course of the fourteenth century, Europe's population shrank by more than 50 percent. In the most densely settled Islamic territory—Egypt—a population that had totaled around 6 million in 1400 was cut in half. When farmers fell ill with the plague, food production collapsed. Famine followed and killed off the survivors. Worst afflicted were the crowded cities, especially coastal ports. Some cities lost up to two-thirds of their population. Refugees from urban areas fled their homes, seeking security and food in the countryside. The shortage of food and other necessities led to rapidly rising prices, work stoppages, and unrest. Political leaders added to their unpopularity by repressing the unrest. Everywhere, regimes trembled and collapsed. The Mongol empire, which had held so much of Eurasia together commercially and politically, disintegrated. Thus, the way was prepared for experiments in state building, religious beliefs, and cultural understandings.

REBUILDING STATES

Starting in the late fourteenth century, Afro-Eurasians began the task of reconstructing both their political order and their trading networks. By then the plague had died down, though it continued to afflict peoples for centuries. However, the rebuilding of military and civil administrations—no easy task—also required political legitimacy. With their people deeply shaken by the extraordinary loss of life, rulers needed to revive confidence in themselves and their regimes, which they did by fostering beliefs and rituals that confirmed their legitimacy and by increasing their control over subjects.

The basis for power was a political institution well known to Afro-Eurasians for centuries, the dynasty—the hereditary ruling family that passed control from one generation to the next. Like those of the past, the new dynasties sought to establish their legitimacy in three ways. First, ruling families insisted that their power derived from a divine calling: Ming emperors in China claimed for themselves what previous dynastic rulers had asserted—the "mandate of heaven"—while European monarchs claimed to rule by "divine right." From their base in Anatolia, Ottoman warrior-princes asserted that they now carried the banner of Islam. In these ways, ruling households affirmed that God or the heavens intended for them to hold power. Second, leaders attempted to prevent squabbling among potential heirs by establishing clear rules about succession to the throne. Many European states tried to standardize succession by passing titles to the eldest male heir, thus ensuring political stability at a potential time of crisis, but in practice there were countless complications and quarrels. In the Islamic world, successors could be designated by the current ruler or elected by the community; here, too, struggles over succession were frequent. Third, ruling families elevated their power through conquest or alliance—by ordering armies to extend their domains forcibly, or by marrying their royal offspring to rulers of other states or members of other elite households, a technique widely practiced in Europe. Once it established legitimacy, the typical royal family would consolidate power by enacting coercive laws and punishments and sending emissaries to govern distant territories. A ruling family would also establish standing armies and new administrative structures to collect taxes and to oversee building projects that proclaimed royal power.

As we will see in the next three sections of this chapter, the innovative state building that occurred in the wake of the plague's devastation would not have been as successful had it not drawn on older traditions. In Europe, a cultural flourishing based largely on ancient Greek and Roman models gave rise to thinkers who proposed new views of governance. The peoples of the Islamic world held fiercely to their religion as successor states, notably the Ottoman Empire, absorbed numerous Turkish-speaking groups. The Ming renounced the Mongol expansionist legacy and emphasized a return to Han rulership, consolidating control of Chinese lands and concentrating on internal markets rather than overseas trade. Many of these regimes lasted for centuries, promoting political institutions and cultural values that became deeply embedded in the fabric of their societies.

The Islamic Heartland

The devastation of the Black Death followed hard on the heels of the Mongol destruction of Islam's most important city, Baghdad, and Islam's old political order. Nonetheless, these two catastrophes prepared the way for new Islamic states to emerge. The old, Arabic-speaking Islamic world remained vital, still at the heart of Islam geographically, but it now had to yield authority to new rulers and religious men. This new Islamic world included large Turkish- and Persian-speaking populations as well. It occupied a vast geographic triangle that stretched from Anatolia in the west to the Khurasan region of Persia and Afghanistan in the east and to Baghdad in the south.

The Ottomans, the Safavids, and the Mughals emerged as the dominant states in the Islamic world in the early sixteenth century. They exploited the rich agrarian resources of the Indian Ocean regions and the Mediterranean basin, and they benefited from a brisk seaborne and overland trade. By the mid-sixteenth century the Mughals controlled the northern Indus River valley; the Safavids occupied Persia; and the Ottomans ruled Anatolia, the Arab world, and much of southern and eastern Europe. Here we will explore in depth the Ottoman Empire, which emerged first and endured the longest of the three. (See Chapter 12 for a fuller discussion of the Mughals and Chapter 14 for more on the Safavids.)

THE OTTOMAN EMPIRE

The rise of the **Ottoman Empire** owed as much to innovative administrative techniques and religious tolerance as to military strength. Although the Mongols considered Anatolia to be a borderland region of little economic importance, their military forays in the late thirteenth century opened up the region to new political forces. The ultimate victors here were the Ottoman Turks. They transformed themselves from warrior bands roaming the borderlands between the Islamic and Christian worlds into rulers of a settled state and, finally, into sovereigns of a far-flung, highly bureaucratic empire. (See Map 11.2.)

Under their chief, Osman (r. 1299–1326), the Turkish Ottomans formalized a stern and disciplined warrior ethos. In addition to deploying their

Ottoman Empire
A Turkish warrior band that transformed itself into a vast, multicultural, bureaucratic empire that lasted from the early fourteenth century through the early twentieth century and encompassed Anatolia, the Arab world, and large swaths of southern and eastern Europe.

Map 11.2 The Ottoman Empire, 1300–1566

This map charts the expansion of the Ottoman state from the time of its founder, Osman, through the reign of Suleiman, the empire's most illustrious ruler.

- Where did the Ottoman Empire originate under Osman? Into what regions did the Ottomans expand between the years 1326 and 1566?
- What were the geographic limits of the Ottoman Empire?
- What governments were able to resist Ottoman expansion?

fierce warriors, knowns as *ghazis*, Osman and his son Orhan (r. 1326–1362), both Sunni Muslims, proved skilled at working with those who held different religious beliefs, including Byzantine Christians, Sufi dervishes, and Shiites. Osman and Orhan offered genuine opportunities for others to exercise power and gain wealth. While other Turkish warrior bands fought for booty under charismatic military leaders, they failed because, unlike the Ottomans, they did not integrate these religious groups and the range of artisans, merchants, bureaucrats, and clerics whose support was essential in the Ottoman rise to power. The Ottomans triumphed over their rivals by adapting techniques of administration from neighboring groups and by attracting those groups to their rule. In time, not only did the Ottoman state win the favor of Islamic clerics, but it also became the champion of Sunni Islam throughout the Islamic world.

By the mid-fourteenth century, the Ottomans had expanded into the Balkans, becoming the most powerful force in the eastern Mediterranean and western Asia. By the early sixteenth century, the Ottoman state controlled a vast territory, stretching in the west to the Moroccan border, in the north to Hungary and Moldavia, in the south through the Arabian Peninsula, and in the east to the Persian border. What was impressive and new within the Islamic world was the Ottomans' elaborate administrative hierarchy, atop which stood the sultan. Below him was a military and civilian bureaucracy whose task was to demand obedience and revenue from subjects. The bureaucracy's discipline enabled the sultan to expand his realm, which in turn forced him to invest in an even larger bureaucracy.

The empire's spectacular expansion was primarily a military affair. To recruit followers, the Ottomans promised wealth and glory to new subjects. This was an expensive undertaking, but territorial expansion generated vast financial and administrative rewards. Moreover, by spreading the spoils of conquest and lucrative administrative positions, rulers bought off potentially unhappy subordinates. Still, without military might, the Ottomans would not have enjoyed the successes associated with the brilliant reigns of Murad II (r. 1421–1451) and his appropriately named successor, Mehmed the Conqueror (r. 1451–1481).

Mehmed's most spectacular triumph was the conquest of Constantinople, an ambition for Muslim rulers ever since the birth of Islam. Mehmed left no doubt that this was his primary goal: shortly after his coronation, he vowed to capture Constantinople, the ancient Roman and Christian capital of the Byzantine Empire, and a city of immense strategic and commercial importance, which had withstood Muslim efforts at conquest for centuries. First, Mehmed built a fortress of his own to prevent European vessels from reaching the capital. Then, by promising his soldiers free access to booty and portraying the city's conquest as a holy cause, he amassed a

The Fall of Constantinople The use of heavy artillery in the forty-day siege of Constantinople was instrumental to the Ottoman victory. At the center of this Turkish miniature is one such cannon, possibly of Hungarian origin, which required hundreds of men and oxen to transport and secure outside the city walls.

huge army that outnumbered the defending force of 7,000 by more than ten times. For forty days his troops bombarded Constantinople's massive walls with artillery that included enormous cannons built by Hungarian and Italian engineers. On May 29, 1453, Ottoman troops overwhelmed the surviving defenders and took Constantinople—which Mehmed promptly renamed Istanbul.

The Tools of Empire Building The Ottomans adopted Byzantine administrative practices to unify their enlarged state and incorporated many of Byzantium's powerful families into it. Their dynastic power, however, was not only military; it also rested on a firm religious foundation. At the center of this empire was the sultan, who combined a warrior ethos with an unwavering devotion to Islam. Describing himself as the "shadow of God" on earth, the sultan claimed the role of caretaker for the Islamic faith. Throughout the empire, he devoted substantial resources to the construction of elaborate mosques and to the support of Islamic schools. As self-appointed defender of the faith, the sultan assumed the role of protector of the holy cities on

The Suleymaniye Mosque Built by Sultan Suleiman in the mid-sixteenth century to crown his achievements, the Suleymaniye Mosque was designed by the architect Sinan to dominate the city. Location mattered to Suleiman. The Bosporus Strait, the vital route connecting the Mediterranean with the Black Sea, is visible beyond the mosque, and Justinian's Hagia Sophia (not visible above) is located just across a park from the mosque.

the Arabian Peninsula and of Jerusalem, while working to unite the realm's diverse lands and peoples and constantly striving to extend the borders of Islam. During the reign of Suleiman (r. 1520–1566), the Ottomans reached the height of their territorial expansion. Under his administration, the Ottoman state ruled 20 to 30 million people. By the time Suleiman died, the Ottoman Empire bridged Europe and the Arab world. Istanbul by then was a dynamic imperial hub, dispatching bureaucrats and military men to oversee a vast domain.

Istanbul's **Topkapi Palace** exhibited the Ottomans' view of governance, the sultans' emphasis on religion, and the continuing influence of Ottoman familial traditions. Laid out by Mehmed II, the palace complex projected a vision of Istanbul as the center of the world. As a way to promote the sultan's magnificent power, architects designed the complex so that the buildings containing the imperial household were nestled behind layers of outer courtyards, in a mosaic of mosques, courts, and special dwellings for the sultan's harem. The harem had its own hierarchy of thousands of women, from the sultan's mother and consorts to the slave women who waited on them, and it became a formidable political force at the heart of Ottoman power.

The growing importance of Topkapi Palace as the command post of empire represented a crucial transition in the history of Ottoman rulers. Not only was the palace the place where future bureaucrats received their training; it was also the place where the chief bureaucrat, the grand vizier, carried out the day-to-day running of the empire. Whereas the early sultans had led their soldiers into battle personally and had met face-to-face with their kinsmen, the later rulers withdrew into the sacredness of the palace, venturing out only occasionally for grand ceremonies. Still, every Friday, subjects lined up outside the palace to introduce their petitions, ask for favors, and seek justice. If they were lucky, the sultans would be there to greet them—but they did so behind grated glass, issuing their decisions by tapping on the window. The palace thus projected a sense of majestic, distant wonder, a home fit for semidivine rulers.

Diversity and Control The fact that the Ottoman Empire endured into the twentieth century owed much to the ruling elite's ability to gain the support and employ the talents of exceedingly diverse populations. After all, neither conquest nor conversion eliminated cultural differences among the empire's distant provinces. Thus, for example, the Ottomans' language policy was one of flexibility and tolerance. Although Ottoman Turkish was the official language of administration, Arabic was the primary language of the Arab provinces, the common tongue of street life. Within the empire's European lands, many people spoke their own languages. From the fifteenth century onward, the Ottoman Empire was perhaps more multilingual than any of its rivals.

In politics, as in language, the Ottomans showed flexibility and tolerance. The imperial bureaucracy permitted extensive regional autonomy. In fact,

Ottoman military cadres perfected a technique for absorbing newly conquered territories into the empire by parceling them out as revenue-producing units among loyal followers and kin. Regional appointees could collect local taxes, part of which they earmarked for Istanbul and part of which they pocketed for themselves. This approach was a common administrative device for many world dynastic empires ruling extensive domains.

Like other empires, the Ottoman state was always in danger of losing control over its provincial rulers. Local potentates—the group that the imperial center allowed to rule in their distant regions—found that great distances enabled them to operate independently from central authority. These rulers kept larger amounts of tax revenues than Istanbul deemed proper. So, to limit their autonomy, the Ottomans established the janissaries, a corps of infantry soldiers and bureaucrats who owed direct allegiance to the sultan. The system at its high point involved conscription of Christian youths from the empire's European lands. This conscription, called the **devshirme**, required each village to hand over a certain number of males between the ages of eight and eighteen. Uprooted from their families and villages, selected for their fine physiques and good looks, these young men were converted to Islam and sent to farms to build up their bodies and learn Turkish. A select few were moved on to Topkapi Palace to learn Ottoman military, religious, and administrative techniques. Some of these men later enjoyed exceptional careers in the arts and sciences—such as the architect Sinan, who designed the Suleymaniye Mosque. Recipients of the best education available in the Islamic world, trained in Ottoman ways, instructed in the use of modern weaponry, and deprived of family connections, the *devshirme* recruits were prepared to serve the sultan (and the empire as a whole) rather than the interests of any particular locality or ethnic group.

Thus, the Ottomans established their legitimacy via military skill, religious backing, and a loyal bureaucracy. They artfully balanced the decentralizing tendencies of the outlying regions with the centralizing forces of the imperial capital. Relying on a careful mixture of religious faith, imperial patronage,

devshirme
The Ottoman system of taking non-Muslim children in place of taxes in order to educate them in Muslim ways and prepare them for service in the sultan's bureaucracy.

and cultural tolerance, the sultans curried loyalty and secured political stability. Indeed, the Ottoman Empire was so strong and stable that it dominated the coveted and highly contested trading crossroads between Europe and Asia for many centuries. Thus, its consolidation had powerful consequences for Europeans' efforts to rebuild their societies after the plague; above all, it closed off their traditional overland trade routes to India and China.

Western Christendom

No region suffered more from the Black Death than western Christendom, and arguably no region made a more spectacular comeback. From 1100 to 1300, Europe had enjoyed a surge in population, rapid economic growth, and significant technological and intellectual innovations, only to see these achievements halted in the fourteenth century by famine and the Black Death. Europeans responded by creating new political and cultural forms. New dynastic states arose, competing with one another, and a movement called the Renaissance revived Europe's connections with its Greek and Roman past and produced masterpieces of art, architecture, and other forms of thought.

THE CATHOLIC CHURCH, STATE BUILDING, AND ECONOMIC RECOVERY

Core Objectives

EXPLAIN the role that religious belief systems played in rebuilding the Islamic world, Europe, and Ming China in the fourteenth and fifteenth centuries.

In the aftermath of famine and plague, the peoples of western Christendom, like those in the Muslim world, looked to their religious beliefs and institutions as foundations for recovery. The faith of many had been severely tested, and religious authorities had to struggle to reclaim their power. To begin with, the late medieval western church found itself divided at the top (at one point during this period there were three popes) and challenged from below, both by individuals pursuing alternative kinds of spirituality and by increasing demands on the clergy and church administration. Disappointment with the clergy smoldered. The peasantry despaired at the absence of clergy when they were so greatly needed during the famines and Black Death. With groups like the Beghards and Beguines challenging the clergy's right to define religious doctrine and practices, the church fought back, identifying all that was suspect and demanding strict obedience to the true faith. This response included the persecution of heretics, Jews, Muslims in the Iberian Peninsula, homosexuals, prostitutes, and "witches." During this period the church also expanded its charitable and bureaucratic functions, providing alms to the urban poor and registering births, deaths, and economic transactions. Crucially, when faced with challenges to its authority, the church associated itself with secular rulers, lending moral authority to kings who claimed to rule "by divine right."

Europe's political rulers aligned themselves with church leaders to rebuild their states and consolidate their power. One royal family, the Habsburgs, drew on their Catholic religious traditions and established a powerful, long-lasting dynasty that would rule large parts of central Europe for centuries to follow. Habsburg leaders were elected to head the federation of states known as the Holy Roman Empire almost continuously from 1438 to 1806, and for a time they ruled Spain and its New World colonies. Yet even at the height of its power in the early sixteenth century, the Habsburg monarchy never succeeded in restoring an integrated empire to western Europe.

In 1450, western Christendom had no central government, no official tongue, and only a few successful commercial centers, mostly in the Mediterranean basin. (See Map 11.3.) The feudal system of a lord's control over the peasantry (see Chapter 10), which was now in decline, left a legacy of political fragmentation and enduring elite privileges, which made the consolidation of a unified Christian Europe even more difficult to achieve. Europe's linguistic diversity reflected its political fragmentation. No single ruler or language united peoples, even when they shared a religion. Latin lost ground as rulers chose various regional dialects (e.g., French, Spanish, English) to be their official state languages, in contrast with China, whose written literary Chinese script remained a key administrative tool for the new dynasts, and the Islamic world, where Arabic was the common language of faith and Turkish the language of administration.

Those who sought to rule the emerging states faced numerous obstacles. For example, rival claimants to the throne financed threatening private armies. Also, the clergy demanded and received privileges in the form of access to land and relief from taxation; they often meddled in politics themselves, and the church became a formidable economic powerhouse. And once the printing press became more widely available in Europe in the 1460s, printers circulated anonymous pamphlets criticizing the court and the clergy. Some states had consultative political bodies—such as the Estates General in France, the Cortes in Spain, and Parliament in England—in which princes formally asked representatives of their people for advice and, in the case of the English Parliament, for consent to new forms of taxation. Such political bodies gave no voice to common men and no representation to women. But they did allow the collective expression of grievances against overbearing policies.

Out of the chaos of famine, disease, and warfare, the diverse peoples of Europe found a political way forward. This path involved the formation of centralized dynastic monarchies. While not new to this period, the political institution of **monarchy** was particularly instrumental to western Christendom in the fifteenth century. Often in competition with the new monarchies, a handful of European city-states, in which a narrow group of wealthy and influential voters selected their leaders, survived right up to the nineteenth

monarchy
Political system in which one individual holds supreme power and passes that power on to his or her next of kin.

Legend:
- English territories, 1420–1428
- Possessions of House of Burgundy, 1429–1453
- Holy Roman Empire
- ✳ Popular uprising
- ✗ Battle
- ← Campaigns of Henry V, 1415, 1421–1422
- ← Campaign of Joan of Arc, 1429
- Ottoman advance, 1453

Map labels include: NORWAY, 1434, SWEDEN, RUSSIAN PRINCIPALITIES, NORTH SEA, BALTIC SEA, TEUTONIC ORDER, Moscow, DENMARK, Hamburg, Lübeck 1408, Brunswick 1374, PRUSSIA, Danzig 1378, POLAND–LITHUANIA, ENGLAND, London 1381, 1450, Bruges 1438, Amsterdam, ARTOIS, HOLY ROMAN EMPIRE, Kiev, Calais, Agincourt 1415, Ghent 1379, 1450, BOHEMIA, Prague 1419, Cracow, NORMANDY, Verneuil 1424, Reims, Metz 1405, Paris 1413, BRITTANY, Patay 1429, Orleans, Tours, Cravant 1423, AUSTRIA, Vienna, Buda, HUNGARY, MOLDAVIA, ATLANTIC OCEAN, Poitiers 1356, FRANCE, SWISS CONFED., Geneva, GUYENNE, Castillon 1453, Lyons, DAUPHINÉ, Milan, Venice, VENETIAN REPUBLIC, Belgrade 1456, WALLACHIA, BLACK SEA, GASCONY, Genoa, ADRIATIC SEA, Jajce 1463, SERBIA, BULGARIA, NAVARRE, Avignon, PROVENCE, REPUBLIC OF GENOA, PAPAL STATES, Kosovo 1449, Istanbul, PORTUGAL, LEON, 1391, ARAGON, 1409, CORSICA, Florence 1378, Rome, Naples, ALBANIA, Istanbul (Constantinople) 1453, CASTILE, CROWN OF ARAGON, SARDINIA, KINGDOM OF NAPLES, OTTOMAN EMPIRE, GRANADA, BALEARIC ISLANDS (ARAGON), Strait of Gibraltar, Cueta, SICILY, MEDITERRANEAN SEA

Scale: 0 – 250 – 500 Miles; 0 – 250 – 500 Kilometers

Map 11.3 Western Christendom, 1400–1500

Europe was a region divided by dynastic rivalries during the fifteenth century. Locate the most powerful regional dynasties on the map: Portugal, Castile, Aragon, France, Burgundy, England, and the Holy Roman Empire.

- Using the scale, contrast the sizes of political units in this map with those in Maps 11.2 (Ottoman Empire) and 11.4 (Ming China). Explain the significance of the differences.
- Where did popular uprisings take place? Based on your reading, why did those regions experience popular unrest?
- Based on the map, why might the Venetian Republic have been particularly engaged, both in trade and intermittent warfare, with the Ottomans?

century and in some cases into the twentieth. Consolidation of these states occurred sometimes through strategic marriages but more often through warfare, both between princely families and with local aristocratic allies and foreign mercenaries.

One striking example of this political turmoil was the Hundred Years' War (1337–1453), in which the French sought to throw off English domination. The Black Death raged in the early years of this intermittent conflict. A central figure toward the end of the war was the peasant girl Joan of Arc, whose visions of various saints inspired her to support the French monarch Charles VII and see him crowned at Reims Cathedral. While Joan was a charismatic leader of troops, commanding as many as 8,000 at the decisive battle at Orleans, eventually the French nobility turned on her, and she was captured by the English. Joan was tried for heresy and burned at the stake in Rouen in 1431. Joan's brief, but remarkable, part in the Hundred Years' War illustrates the role an exceptional woman, even a peasant girl, could play on the predominantly male, elite political stage.

Elsewhere, in southern Europe, where economies rebounded through seaborne trade with Southwest Asia, political stabilization was swifter. The stabilization of Italian city-states such as Venice and Florence, and of monarchical rule in Portugal and Spain, led to an economic and cultural flowering known as the Renaissance. In northern and western Europe, the process took longer. In England and France, in particular, internal feuding, regional warfare, and religious fragmentation delayed recovery for decades (see Chapter 12).

POLITICAL CONSOLIDATION AND TRADE IN THE IBERIAN PENINSULA

War and overseas trade played a central role in the emergence of new dynasties in Portugal and Spain. Through the fourteenth century, Portuguese Christians devoted themselves to fighting the Moors, who were Muslim occupants of North Africa, the western Sahara, and the Iberian Peninsula. After the Portuguese crossed the Strait of Gibraltar and seized the Moorish fortresses at Ceuta, in Morocco, their ships could sail between the Mediterranean and the Atlantic without Muslim interference. With that threat diminished, the Portuguese perceived their neighbor, Castile (a region in what is now Spain), as their chief foe. Under João I (r. 1385–1433), Portugal defeated the Castilians, becoming the dominant power on the Iberian peninsula. No longer preoccupied with Castilian competition, the Portuguese sought new territories and trading opportunities in the North Atlantic and along the West African coast. João's son, Prince Henrique, known later as Henry the Navigator, further expanded the royal family's domain by supporting expeditions down the coast of Africa and offshore to the Atlantic islands of Madeira and the Azores. The west and central coasts of Africa and the islands of the North and

South Atlantic, including the Cape Verde Islands, São Tomé, Principe, and Fernando Po, soon became Portuguese ports of call.

Portuguese monarchs granted the Atlantic islands to nobles as hereditary possessions on condition that the grantees colonize them, and soon the colonizers were establishing lucrative sugar plantations. In gratitude, noble families and merchants threw their political weight behind the king. Subsequent monarchs continued to cultivate local aristocrats' support for monarchical authority, thus ensuring smooth succession to the crown for members of the royal family.

In Spain, a new dynasty also emerged, though the road was difficult. Medieval Spain comprised rival kingdoms that quarreled ceaselessly. Within those kingdoms, several religions coexisted: Muslims, Jews, and Christians lived side by side in relative harmony, and Muslim armies still occupied strategic posts in the south. Over time, marriages and the formation of kinship ties among nobles and between royal lineages yielded a new political order. One by one, the major houses of the Spanish kingdoms intermarried, culminating in the wedding of Isabella of Castile and Ferdinand of Aragon (1469). This marriage linked Castile, wealthy and populous, to Aragon, which enjoyed an extended trading network in the Mediterranean. Together, the monarchs brought unruly nobles and distant towns under their control. They topped off their achievements by marrying their children into other European royal families—especially the Habsburgs, central Europe's most powerful dynasty. Thus, Spain's two most important provinces were joined, and Spain later became a state to be reckoned with.

The new Spanish rulers sent Christian armies south to push Muslim forces out of the Iberian Peninsula. By the mid-fifteenth century only Granada, a strategic linchpin overlooking the straits between the Mediterranean and the Atlantic, remained in Muslim hands. After a long and costly siege, Christian forces captured the fortress there in 1492. This was a victory of enormous symbolic importance, as joyous as the fall of Constantinople to Mehmed and the Ottomans in 1453 was depressing (for Christians).

The Inquisition and Westward Exploration Isabella and Ferdinand sought to drive all non-Catholics out of Spain. Terrified by Ottoman incursions into Europe, they launched an **Inquisition** in 1481, taking aim especially against *conversos*—converted Jews and Muslims, whom they suspected were Christians only in name. When Granada fell, the crown ordered the expulsion of all Jews from Spain. After 1499, a more tolerant attempt to convert the Moors (Muslims) by persuasion gave way to forced conversion—or emigration. All told, almost half a million people were forced to flee the Spanish kingdoms. This lack of tolerance meant that Spain, like other European states in this era, became increasingly homogeneous. With fewer groups vying for influence within their territories, rulers' attention turned outward, fueling rivalries between the various European states.

Inquisition
General term for a tribunal of the Roman Catholic Church that enforced religious orthodoxy. Several inquisitions took place over centuries, seeking to punish heretics, witches, Jews, and those whose conversion to Christianity was called into doubt.

So strong was the tide of Spanish fervor by late 1491 that the monarchs listened now to a Genoese navigator whose pleas for patronage they had previously rejected. Christopher Columbus promised them unimaginable riches that could finance their military campaigns and bankroll a crusade to liberate Jerusalem from Muslim hands. Off he sailed with a royal patent that guaranteed the monarchs a share of all he discovered. Soon the Spanish economy was reorienting itself toward the Atlantic, and Spain's merchants, missionaries, and soldiers were preparing for conquest and profiteering in what had been, just a few years before, a blank space on the map.

THE RENAISSANCE

Just as the Ming invoked Han Chinese traditions and the Ottomans looked to Sunni Islam to point the way forward, European elites drew on their own traditions for guidance as they rebuilt after the devastation of the plague. They found inspiration in ancient Greek and Roman institutions and ideas. Europe's extraordinary political and economic revival also involved a powerful outpouring of cultural achievements, led by Italian scholars and artists and financed by bankers, churchmen, and nobles. Much later, scholars coined the word **Renaissance** to characterize the cultural flourishing of the Italian city-states, France, the Netherlands, England, and the Holy Roman Empire in the period 1430–1550. What was being "reborn" was ancient Greek and Roman art and learning—knowledge that could help people understand an expanding world and support the rights of secular individuals to exert power in it.

Although the Renaissance was largely funded by popes, Christian kings, and powerful wealthy merchants, it challenged the authority of traditional religious elites, breaking the medieval church's monopoly on answers to the big questions. Religious topics and themes, such as David and Goliath, Judith and Holophernes, and various scenes from Jesus's story (annunciation of his birth to Mary, Jesus's adoration by the magi, and his baptism and crucifixion) dominated much of Renaissance art, but these themes took on new meaning as warnings to overbearing rulers and reminders to the obscenely

Ferdinand and Isabella Entering Granada This altar relief, sculpted by Felipe Vigarny in the early sixteenth century, depicts the triumphant entrance of King Ferdinand and Queen Isabella into the city of Granada after their conquest of this last Muslim stronghold in Spain.

Renaissance
Term meaning "rebirth" used by historians to characterize the cultural flourishing of European nations between 1430 and 1550, which emphasized a break from the church-centered medieval world and a new concept of humankind as the center of the world.

wealthy, who sponsored many of these works, of their place in the cosmos and the civic responsibility that stemmed from their wealth. These religious themes were also joined by classical topics, such as scenes from mythology and the ancient past. The movement valued secular forms of learning, rather than just Christian doctrine, and a more human-centered understanding of the cosmos.

The Renaissance was all about new exposure to the old—to classical texts and ancient art and architectural forms. Although some Greek and Roman texts were known in Europe and the Islamic world, the use of the printing press made others accessible to western scholars for the first time. Scholars now realized that the pre-Christian Greeks and Romans had developed powerful means of representing and caring for the human body. Having studied the world directly, without the need to square their observations with biblical information, the ancients had much to teach about geography, astronomy, and architecture and about how to govern states and armies. For Renaissance scholars it was no longer enough to understand Christian doctrine and to concern themselves with the next world. One had to go back to the original, classical sources in order to understand the human condition. This in turn required the learning of languages and history. Scholarship that attempted to return to Greek and Roman sources became known as **humanism**.

Because political and religious powers were not united in Europe (as they were in China and the Islamic world), scholars and artists seeking sponsors for their work could play one side against the other or, alternatively, could suffer both clerical and political persecution. Michelangelo (1475–1564), a leading painter, sculptor, architect, and engineer of the age, completed commissions for the famous Florentine bankers and political leaders of the Medici family, for the Florentine Wool Guild, and for Pope Julius II. Peter Paul Rubens painted for the courts of France, Spain, England, and the Netherlands, as well as selling paintings on the open market. These two painters, renowned for showing a great deal of flesh, frequently offended conservative church officials. Even so, most support for the arts came either from the church or from individual clergymen, and virtually all secular donors were devout believers who commissioned works with religious themes. The Dutch scholar Desiderius Erasmus ridiculed corrupt popes and the clergy under the patronage of English, Dutch, and French supporters while remaining a Catholic, an ordained cleric, and an opponent of Reformation doctrines. Conflicts within the Catholic Church, between the church and secular leaders, and among secular leaders and wealthy private citizens enabled artists to present challenging images and ideas with an unusual independence.

Gradually, a network of educated men and women took shape that was not wholly dependent on the church, the state, or a single princely patron. Classical knowledge gave individuals the means to challenge political, clerical, and aesthetic authority. Moreover, rivalries between Europe's relatively small

Core Objectives

EXAMINE the way art and architecture reflected the political realities of the Islamic world, Europe, and Ming China after the Black Death.

humanism

The Renaissance aspiration to develop a greater understanding of the human experience than the Christian scriptures offered by reaching back into ancient Greek and Roman texts.

Renaissance Masterpieces Leonardo da Vinci's *The Last Supper* (*left*) depicts Christ's disciples reacting to his announcement that one of them will betray him. Michelangelo's *David* (*right*) stands over seventeen feet high and was conceived as an expression of Florentine civic ideals.

states and city-states allowed many of these scholars to dodge the authorities by fleeing to neighboring communities. Of course, they could also use their learning to defend the older elites: for example, numerous lawyers and scholars continued to work for the popes in defending the papacy. At the same time, men like Erasmus and later Martin Luther (the leading figure of the Reformation in the sixteenth century) looked to secular princes to support their critical scholarship. In Florence, Niccolò Machiavelli wrote the most famous treatise on authoritarian power, *The Prince* (1513). Machiavelli argued that political leadership required mastering the rules of modern statecraft, even if in some cases this meant disregarding moral imperatives. Holding and exercising power were vital ends in themselves, he claimed; traditional ideas of civic virtue should not deter rulers, like those of the Medici family, from maintaining control over society.

With Renaissance ideas challenging traditional authority and rulers facing a range of internal and external obstacles, the new monarchies of Europe were not all immediately successful in consolidating power and unifying peoples. In France and England, for example, the great age of monarchy had yet to dawn. Even when stable states did arise in Europe, they were fairly small compared with the Ottoman and Ming empires. In the mid-sixteenth century, Portugal and Spain, Europe's two most expansionist states, had populations of 1 million and 9 million, respectively. England, excluding Wales, had a mere 3 million in 1550. Only France, with 17 million, had a population close to the Ottoman Empire's 25 million. And these numbers paled in comparison with Ming China's population of nearly 200 million in 1550. But in Europe, small could be advantageous. Portugal's relatively small population meant that the crown had fewer groups to control. In the world of finance, the most successful merchants were those inhabiting the smaller Italian city-states and, a bit later, the cities of the northern Netherlands. The Florentines developed sophisticated banking techniques, created extensive networks of agents throughout Europe and the Mediterranean, and served as bankers to the popes. At the same time, the Renaissance—which flourished in the city-states and newly stabilized monarchies—made elite European culture more cosmopolitan and independent from government authority, even if it could not unify the states and peoples who cultivated it.

Ming China

Like the Europeans, the Chinese saw their stable worldview and political order crumble under the catastrophes of human and microbial invasions. Moreover, like the Europeans, people in China had long regarded outsiders as "barbarians" and balked at being ruled by them. Together, the Mongols and the Black Death upended the political and intellectual foundations of what had appeared to be the world's most integrated society. The Mongols brought the Yuan dynasty to power; then the plague devastated China and prepared the way for the emergence of a new dynasty. The **Ming dynasty**, ruled by ethnically Han Chinese, defined itself against its foreign predecessors. Ming emperors sought to reinforce everything Chinese. In particular, they supported China's vast internal agricultural markets in an attempt to minimize dependence on merchants and foreign trade.

RESTORING ORDER

Ming dynasty
Successor to the Mongol Yuan dynasty that reinstituted and reinforced Han Chinese ceremonies and ideals, including rule by an ethnically Han bureaucracy.

Red Turban movement
Diverse religious movement in China during the fourteenth century that spread the belief that the world was drawing to an end as Mongol rule was collapsing.

In the chaotic fourteenth century, as plague and famine ravaged China and the Mongol Yuan dynasty collapsed, only a strong military movement capable of overpowering other groups could restore order. That intervention began at the hands of a poor young man who had trained in the **Red Turban movement**: Zhu Yuanzhang, a successful warlord who had led a rebellion against the waning power of the Mongols and any others who would assert control in their wake.

It soon became clear that Zhu had a much grander design for China than the ambitions of most warlords. When he took Nanjing in 1356, he renamed it Yingtian (in response to heaven). Lifted by subsequent successful military campaigns, Zhu (r. 1368–1398) took the imperial title of Hongwu (expansive and martial) Emperor and proclaimed the founding of the Ming (brilliant) dynasty in 1368. Soon thereafter, his troops met little resistance when they seized the Yuan capital of Khan-balik (soon renamed Beijing), causing the Mongol emperor to flee to his homeland in the steppe. It would, however, take Hongwu almost another twenty years to reunify the entire country.

CENTRALIZATION UNDER THE MING

Hongwu and successive Ming emperors had to rebuild a devastated society from the ground up. Although in the past China had experienced natural catastrophes, wars, and social dislocation, the plague's legacy was devastation on an unprecedented scale. It left the new rulers with the formidable challenge of rebuilding the great cities, restoring respect for ruling elites, and reconstructing the bureaucracy.

Imperial Grandeur and Kinship The rebuilding began with the Hongwu Emperor, whose capital at Nanjing reflected imperial grandeur. When the dynasty's third emperor, the Yongle (perpetual happiness) Emperor, relocated the capital to Beijing, he flaunted an even more grandiose style, employing around 100,000 artisans and 1 million laborers to build this new capital. The city had three separate walled enclosures. Inside the outer city walls sprawled the imperial city; within its walls lay the palace compound, the Forbidden City. Traffic within the walled sections navigated through broad boulevards leading to the different gates, above which imposing towers soared. The palace compound, where the imperial family resided, had more than 9,000 rooms. Anyone standing in the front courts, which measured more than 400 yards on a side and boasted marble terraces and carved railings, would gasp at the awe-inspiring projection of power. That was precisely the effect the Ming emperors wanted, just as the Ottoman sultans did in building Topkapi Palace.

Marriage and kinship buttressed the power of the Ming imperial household, much as dynastic strategies did in Europe. The Ming dynasty's founder married the adopted daughter of a leading Red Turban rebel (her father, according to legend, was a convicted murderer), thereby consolidating his power and eliminating a threat. Empress Ma, as she was known, became Hongwu's principal wife and was praised for her compassion. Emerging as the kinder face of the regime, she tempered the harsh and sometimes cruel disposition of her spouse. He had numerous other consorts as well, including Korean and Mongol women, who bore him twenty-six sons and sixteen daughters (similar to, although on a smaller scale than, the Ottoman sultan's harem at Topkapi Palace).

Building a Bureaucracy Faced with the challenge of reestablishing order out of turmoil, Hongwu initially sought to rule through his kinsmen—by giving imperial princes generous stipends, command of large garrisons, and

Ming Fashion

Ming rulers liked to represent themselves as custodians of "civilized" Han traditions, in contrast to the "barbarian" ways of the previous Mongol Yuan dynasty. However, from governmental practices to clothing fashions, there were visible signs everywhere that the Ming, despite their rhetoric, followed in the footsteps of the Yuan and became more and more linked to an ever-growing, interconnected world. As trade with neighboring and faraway lands continued unabated and merchants and travelers kept moving, it proved to be impossible for the Ming to keep outside influences at arm's length. At the same time, the rhetoric of a return to Han traditions did generate moves to invoke antiquity in the realm of fashion. Status-conscious elites with newfound wealth eagerly purchased clothes in what they believed to be the ancient Han style, hoping to set themselves apart from the common people. Their flirtation with antiquity, however, often ended up being more of a reinvention to satisfy the surging demands of the market than a genuine return to earlier conventions.

Founder Zhu Yuanzhang set the tone of the Ming by trying to rid the

An example of headwear used by Ming officials, reputedly following the style of earlier dynasties. The beams attached to the crown of the cap indicate the official's rank, so the cap is known as a "beamed cap."

country of the close-fitting tunics worn by the Mongols. He advocated instead the wearing of the reputedly Tang-style garment of earlier times. While this measure did meet with some success, the vibrant clothing industry was hardly free of its fascination with the "exotic," such as horsehair skirts from

Korea for men. These skirts were a rare commodity when they first arrived, probably via trade missions, but by the late fifteenth century, local weavers had become so skilled in making them, and consumers so eager to obtain them, that craftspeople were caught stealing the tails of horses to satisfy the soaring demand for the raw materials. Indeed, undoubtedly to the chagrin of the first Ming emperor and his descendants, much of the Yuan style and even terminology in both male and female clothing persisted during the Ming era.

Hats for men—a convenient yet highly visible way to make a statement of social standing—were another striking example of Ming retro taste in fashion. Invoking the names of earlier dynasties were the Han cap, the Jin cap, the Tang cap, and so on. The most interesting, however, was the Chunyang hat, which allegedly drew upon both Han and Tang styles in its design but had actually become a symbol of the so-called new and strange fashion that so often attracted commentary in Ming writings. In fact, it was favored by the young, who had nothing but disdain for ancient styles!

significant autonomy in running their domains. However, when the princes' power began to threaten the court, Hongwu slashed their stipends, reduced their privileges, and took control of their garrisons. No longer dependent on these men, he established an imperial bureaucracy beholden only to him and to his successors. Its officials won appointments through their outstanding performance on a reinstated civil service examination.

In addition, Hongwu took other steps to install a centralized system of rule. He assigned bureaucrats to oversee the manufacture of porcelain, cotton, and silk products as well as tax collection. He reestablished the Confucian

The "paddy-field gown" for women might have had its origins in Buddhist robes.

Nor was the rage for fashion reserved for men only, or even for just the privileged. As one Ming writer lamented, perhaps with a hint of exaggeration: "Nowadays the very servant girls dress in silk gauze, and the singsong girls look down on brocaded silks and embroidered gowns." Respectable women, we are told, looked to the clothing and style of the courtesans of the prosperous southern region of the country for ideas and inspiration for fashion. Indeed, much of our visual knowledge of Ming women's clothing comes from paintings that probably show highly trained courtesans or the female "entertainers" that were ubiquitous in Ming urban centers. These paintings reveal the different and consistently evolving styles of clothing for Ming women—including the "paddy-field gown," which might have owed its origins to Buddhist robes—that were the focus of much criticism from those who frowned on the growing penchant for the exotic, the strange, the outrageous, and the irreverent in the realm of fashion. If nothing else, this debate about clothing certainly tells us that despite the often conservative stance and policies of the Ming regime, the everyday life of many Ming subjects was a constant exercise in negotiating the multiple impacts of both the old and the new, as well as the familiar and the foreign, in different arenas of their rapidly changing society.

Questions for Analysis

- What are some examples of Ming "retro" fashion? Why did the Ming elite cultivate an "ancient" Han style?
- How do we know about changes in women's fashion in the Ming era? Are there any dangers in using these sources to understand the dress of all Ming women?
- Flipping back through the illustrations in this chapter, what do you see of the clothing from other regions? What questions does the analysis of Ming clothing presented here raise for you as you reexamine the images of Ottomans and western Europeans?

Explore Further

Clunas, Craig and Harrison-Hall, eds., *Ming: 50 Years that Changed China* (2014).

Finnane, Antonia, *Changing Clothes in China: Fashion, History, Nation* (2008).

school system as a means of selecting a cadre of loyal officials (not unlike the Ottoman janissaries and administrators). He also set up local networks of villages to rebuild irrigation systems and to supervise reforestation projects to prevent flooding—with the astonishing result that the amount of land reclaimed nearly tripled within eight years. For water supply and flood control, over 40,000 reservoirs underwent repairs or new construction. Historians estimate that Hongwu's reign oversaw the planting around Nanjing of about 1 billion trees, which were later used in building a maritime expedition fleet in the early fifteenth century.

The Forbidden City The Yongle Emperor relocated the capital to Beijing, where he began the construction of the Forbidden City, or imperial palace compound, in the early fifteenth century. The palace was designed to inspire awe in all who saw it.

The imperial palace not only projected the image of a power center, it *was* the center of power. Every official received his appointment by the emperor through the Ministry of Personnel. Hongwu eliminated the post of prime minister (he executed the man who held the post) and ruled directly. Ming bureaucrats had to kneel before the emperor. The drawback of this centralized control, of course, was that the Ming emperor had to keep tabs on this immense system. Hongwu constantly moved his bureaucrats around, sometimes fortifying the administration, sometimes undermining it lest it become too autonomous. Over time, Hongwu nurtured a bureaucracy far more extensive than that of the Ottomans. The Ming thus established the most highly centralized system of government of all the monarchies of this period.

Religion under the Ming Just as the Ottoman sultans projected themselves as Muslim rulers, calling themselves the shadow of God, and European monarchs claimed to rule by divine right, the Ming emperors enhanced their legitimacy by drawing on ancient Chinese religious traditions. Citing the mandate of heaven, the emperor revised and strengthened the elaborate rites and ceremonies that had supported dynastic power for centuries. Official rituals, such as those related to the gods of soil and grain, reinforced political and social classes, portraying the rulers as the moral and spiritual benefactors of their subjects. In lavish ceremonies, the emperor engaged in sacrificial rites, cultivating his image as mediator between the human and the spiritual worlds. The message was clear: the gods were on the side of the Ming household.

MING RULERSHIP

Conquest and defense helped establish the Ming empire, and bureaucracy kept it functioning. The empire's scale required complex administration. (See Map 11.4.) To many outsiders (especially Europeans, whose region was in a state of constant war), Ming stability and centralization appeared to be political wizardry.

Ming rulers worried in particular about maintaining the support of ordinary people in the countryside. The emperor wished to be seen as the special guardian of his subjects. He wanted their allegiance as well as their taxes and labor. But during hard times, poor farmers were reluctant to provide resources—taxes or services—to distant officials. A popular Chinese proverb was "The mountain is high and the emperor is far away." For these reasons, and because he distrusted state bureaucrats, Hongwu preferred to entrust the management of rural communities to local leaders, whom he appointed as village chiefs, village elders, or tax captains. Within these communities, the dynasty created a social hierarchy based on age, sex, and kinship. While women's labor remained critical for the village economy, the government reinforced a gender hierarchy by promoting women's chastity and constructing commemorative arches for widows who honored their husbands by refraining from remarrying.

Like the European and Islamic states, the Ming Empire faced periodic unrest and rebellion. Rebels often proclaimed their own brand of religious beliefs and local elites resented central control. Outright terror helped stymie these threats to central authority. In a massive wave of carnage, Hongwu slaughtered anyone who posed a threat to his authority, from the highest of ministers to the lowliest of scribes. From 1376 to 1393, four of his purges condemned close to 100,000 subjects to execution. Yet, despite the emperor's immense power, the Ming Empire remained undergoverned. Indeed, as the population multiplied, there were too few loyal officials to handle local

Ming Deities The pantheon of deities worshipped during the Ming dynasty demonstrates the rich religious culture of the period.

Map 11.4 Ming China, 1500s

The Ming state was one of the largest empires at this time—and the most populous. Using the scale, determine the length of its coastline and its internal borders.

- What were the two Ming capitals and the three main seaport trading cities? How far are they from one another?
- According to the map, where did the Ming rulers expect the greatest threat to their security?
- How many provinces are outlined on the map? How far is Beijing from some of the more distant provinces? What sorts of challenges might that create for the centralized style of Ming rule, and how does the chapter suggest those challenges were resolved?

affairs. By the sixteenth and early seventeenth centuries, for example, some 10,000 to 15,000 officials shouldered the responsibility of managing a population exceeding 200 million people. Nonetheless, Hongwu bequeathed to his descendants a set of tools for ruling that drew on subjects' direct loyalty to the emperor and on the intricate workings of an extensive bureaucracy. His legacy enabled his successors to balance local sources of power with the needs of dynastic rulership.

TRADE AND EXPLORATION UNDER THE MING

Gradually, the political stability brought by the Ming dynasty allowed trade to revive. Now the new dynasty's merchants reestablished China's preeminence in long-distance commercial exchange. Chinese silk and cotton textiles, as well as fine porcelains, ranked among the world's most coveted luxuries. When a Chinese merchant ship sailed into a port, trading partners and onlookers crowded the docks to watch the unloading of precious cargoes. Although Ming rulers' support for overseas ventures wavered and eventually declined, this period saw important developments in Chinese trade and exploration.

Core Objectives

COMPARE how Ottoman, Iberian, and Ming rulers extended their territories and regional influence.

Overseas Trade: Success and Suspicion During the Ming period, Chinese traders based in the three main ports—Hangzhou, Quanzhou, and Guangzhou (Canton)—were as energetic as their Muslim counterparts in the Indian Ocean. These and other ports were home to prosperous merchants and the point of convergence for vast sea-lanes. Leaving the mainland ports, Chinese vessels carried precious wares to offshore islands, the Pescadores, and Taiwan. From there, they sailed on to the ports of Southeast Asia. As entrepôts for global goods, East Asian ports flourished. Former fishing villages developed into major urban centers.

The Ming dynasty viewed overseas expansion with suspicion, however. Hongwu feared that too much contact with the outside world would cause instability and undermine his rule. In fact, he banned private maritime commerce in 1371. But enforcement was lax, and by the late fifteenth century maritime trade had once again surged. Because much of the thriving business took place in defiance of official edicts, it led to constant friction between government officials and maritime traders. Although the Ming government ultimately agreed to issue licenses for overseas trade in the mid-sixteenth century, its policies continued to vacillate. To Ming officials, unlike their counterparts in Portugal and Spain, the sea represented problems of order and control rather than opportunities.

The Expeditions of Zheng He One spectacular exception to the early Ming attitude toward maritime trade was a series of officially sponsored expeditions in the early fifteenth century. It was the ambitious third Ming emperor, the Yongle Emperor, who took this initiative. One of his loyal followers was a Muslim whom the Ming army had captured as a boy. The youth was castrated and sent to serve at the court (as a eunuch, he could not continue his family line and so theoretically owed allegiance solely to the emperor). Given the name **Zheng He** (1371–1433), he grew up to be an important military leader. The emperor entrusted him with venturing out to trade, collect tribute, and display China's power to the world.

From 1405 to 1433, Zheng He commanded the world's greatest armada and led seven naval expeditions. His larger ships stretched 400 feet in length (Columbus's *Santa Maria* was 85 feet), carried hundreds of sailors on four tiers of decks, and maneuvered with sophisticated rudders, nine masts, and watertight compartments. The first expedition set sail with 28,000 men aboard a flotilla of sixty-two large ships and over 200 lesser ones. Zheng He and his entourage aimed to establish tributary relations with far-flung territories—from Southeast Asia to the Indian Ocean ports, to the Persian Gulf, and to the east coast of Africa. (See Map 11.5.) These expeditions did not seek territorial expansion, but rather control of trade and tribute. When

Zheng He's Ships and Exotic Cargo The largest ship in Zheng He's armada had nine staggered masts and twelve silk sails. This graphic demonstrates just how large and complex Zheng He's ships were, compared with Christopher Columbus's *Santa Maria*. With ships so large, Zheng He's fleet could return to China with magnificent and exotic cargo, like the giraffes brought as tribute from Bengal in 1414 and Malindi in 1415. These tribute giraffes were recorded in several paintings, some inscribed with a poem attributed to contemporary Shen Du that described the giraffes as *qilin*, mythical creatures that appear during the rule of a great leader.

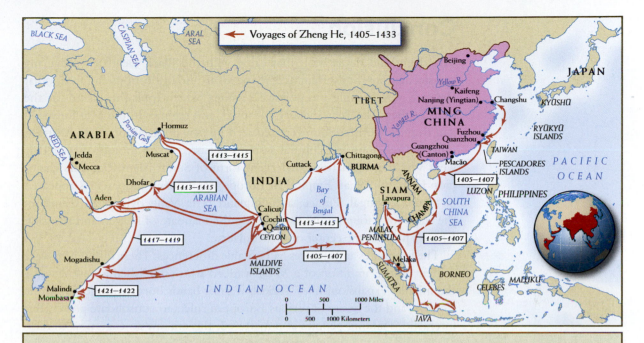

Map 11.5 Voyages of Zheng He, 1405–1433

Zheng He's voyages are some of the most famous in world history. Many have speculated about how history might be different if the Chinese emperors had allowed the voyages to continue.

- What routes did Zheng He's armada follow?
- Referring to other maps in this chapter and earlier chapters, with what peoples did Zheng He's armada come into contact?
- Using the scale on the map, estimate how far Zheng He's armada sailed. How does that distance compare with those covered by other world travelers you've encountered in this text?

the Yongle Emperor died in 1424, the expeditions lost their most enthusiastic patron. Moreover, by the mid-fifteenth century, there was a revival of military threats from the north, recalling how the maritime-oriented Song dynasty had been overrun by invaders from the north (see Chapter 10). Consequently, Ming officials withdrew imperial support for seagoing ventures and instead devoted their energies to overland ventures and defense.

Even though maritime commerce continued without official patronage, the Ming decision to forgo overseas ventures was momentous. Although China remained the wealthiest, most densely settled region of the world, with fully developed state structures and thriving markets, the empire's wariness of overseas projects deprived merchants and would-be explorers of vital support in an age when others were beginning to look outward and overseas.

Conclusion

The dying and devastation that came with the Black Death caused many transformations, but certain underlying ideals and institutions endured. What changed were mainly the political regimes, which took the blame for the catastrophes. The Yuan dynasty collapsed, and regimes in the Muslim world and western Christendom were replaced by new political forms. In contrast, universal religions and cultural systems persisted, even though they underwent vast transformations. A fervent form of Sunni Islam found its champion in the Ottoman Empire. In Europe, centralizing monarchies appeared in Spain, Portugal, France, and England. The Ming dynasts in China set the stage for a long tenure by claiming the mandate of heaven and stressing China's place at the center of their universe.

The new states and empires had notable differences. These differences were evident in the ambition of a Ming warlord who established a new dynasty, the military expansionism of Turkish warrior bands bordering the Byzantine Empire, and the desire of various European rulers to consolidate power. But interactions among peoples also mattered; this era saw an eagerness to reestablish and expand trade networks and a desire to convert unbelievers to "the true faith"—be it a form of Islam or an exclusive Christianity.

All of the dynasties surveyed in this chapter faced similar problems. They had to establish legitimacy, ensure smooth succession, deal with religious movements, and forge working relationships with nobles, townspeople, merchants, and peasants. Yet each state developed a distinctive identity. They all combined political innovation, traditional ways of ruling, and ideas borrowed from neighbors. European monarchies achieved significant internal unity, often through warfare with competing states. Ottoman rulers perfected techniques for ruling an ethnically and religiously diverse empire: they moved military forces swiftly, allowed local communities a degree of autonomy, and trained a bureaucracy dedicated to the Ottoman and Sunni Islamic way of life. The Ming fashioned an imperial system based on a Confucian bureaucracy and intense subordination to the emperor so that it could manage a mammoth population. The rising monarchies of Europe and the Ottoman state all blazed with religious fervor and sought to eradicate or subordinate the beliefs of other groups.

The new states displayed unprecedented political and economic powers. All demonstrated military prowess, a desire for stable political and social hierarchies and secure borders, and a drive to expand. Each legitimized its rule via dynastic marriage and succession, state-sanctioned religion, and administrative bureaucracies. Each supported vigorous commercial activity. The Islamic regimes, especially, engaged in long-distance commerce and, by conquest and conversion, extended their holdings.

For western Christendom, the Ottoman conquests were decisive. They provoked Europeans to establish commercial connections to the east, south, and west. The consequences of their new toeholds would be momentous—just as the Chinese decision to turn away from overseas exploration and commerce meant that China's contact with the outside world would be overland and more limited. As we shall see in Chapter 12, both decisions were instrumental in determining which worlds would come together and which would remain apart.

TRACING THE GLOBAL STORYLINES

Focus On
Crisis and Recovery in Afro-Eurasia

Collapse and Consolidation

- Bubonic plague originates in Inner Asia and afflicts people from China to Europe.
- Climate change and famine leave people vulnerable to infection, while commerce facilitates the spread of disease.
- The plague kills 25 to 65 percent of infected populations and leaves societies in turmoil.

The Islamic Heartland

- Ottomans overrun Constantinople and become the primary Sunni regime in the Islamic world.
- The Ottomans establish their legitimacy with military prowess, religious backing, and a loyal bureaucracy.
- Sultans manage the decentralizing tendencies of outlying provinces with flexibility and tolerance, relying on religious faith, patronage, and bureaucracy.

Western Christendom

- New dynastic monarchies that claim to rule by divine right appear in Portugal, Spain, France, and England.
- The Inquisition takes aim against conversos—converted Jews and Muslims.
- A rebirth of classical learning, known as the Renaissance, originates in Italian city-states and spreads throughout western Europe.

Ming China

- The Ming dynasty replaces the Mongol Yuan dynasty and rebuilds a strong state from the ground up, claiming a mandate from heaven.
- An elaborate, centralized bureaucracy oversees the revival of infrastructure and long-distance trade.
- The emperor and bureaucracy concentrate on developing internal markets and overland trade at the expense of overseas commerce.

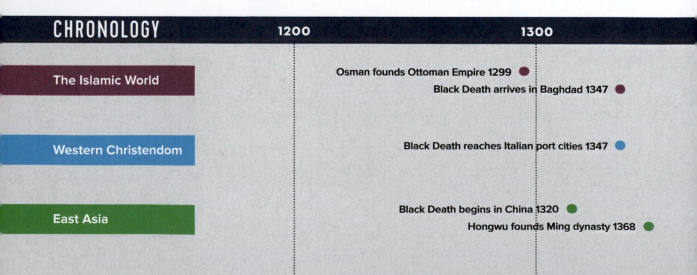

CHRONOLOGY

	1200	1300
The Islamic World		Osman founds Ottoman Empire 1299 ● Black Death arrives in Baghdad 1347 ●
Western Christendom		Black Death reaches Italian port cities 1347 ●
East Asia		Black Death begins in China 1320 ● Hongwu founds Ming dynasty 1368 ●

THINKING ABOUT GLOBAL CONNECTIONS

- **Thinking about Exchange Networks** By the fourteenth century, most of the Afro-Eurasian landmass was bound together by multiple exchange networks that functioned on many levels—political, cultural, and commercial. How did these exchange networks facilitate the spread of the plague? In what ways did the spread of the Black Death correspond with and diverge from existing political, cultural, and commercial networks?

- **Thinking about Changing Power Relationships** Fourteenth-century famine and plague, and the accompanying political, economic, and natural crises, together triggered powerful, often differing, responses in western Europe, the Ottoman lands, and Ming China. How did men and women at different levels of society respond to the fourteenth-century crises? How did their responses reshape their societies? Pay special attention to the relationships among ordinary men and women, elites, and imperial bureaucracies in all three regions.

- **Thinking about Environmental Impacts** Climate change laid the groundwork for the devastation of the Black Death. What environmental developments in Europe, central Asia, and China set the stage for the Black Death?

Key Terms

Black Death p. 499
devshirme p. 511
humanism p. 518
Inquisition p. 516

Ming dynasty p. 520
monarchy p. 513
Ottoman Empire p. 506

Red Turban movement p. 520
Renaissance p. 517

Topkapi Palace p. 510
Zheng He p. 528

Go to **INQUIZITIVE** to see what you've learned—and learn what you've missed—with personalized feedback along the way.

1400   1500   1600

Ottoman armies conquer Constantinople 1453

Suleiman expands and consolidates Ottoman Empire 1520–1566

Castile and Aragon unite to form Spain 1469

Spain conquers Granada 1492

Zheng He's voyages 1405–1433

Global Themes and Sources

Causes and Effects of the Black Death

The devastation wrought by the plague in Afro-Eurasia and the upheaval that followed were unprecedented and far-reaching in their impact. Families were broken as parents, spouses, and children deserted one another for fear of contagion. Religious responses varied from hopelessness to ecstatic devotion. The plague affected the economy as well, causing skyrocketing prices, diminished availability of goods and labor, and unmet demand for certain products and services. Dramatic population losses demonstrate its demographic impact: beginning in southwestern China in the 1320s, the Pestilence or Great Mortality, as it came to be known in Europe, wiped out between 25 and 65 percent of the populations it afflicted.

The plague traveled along the trade routes of Inner Eurasia, taking advantage of the connectivity that had bound the Afro-Eurasian world together and facilitated the movement of people, goods, and ideas. The plague also took advantage of an already weakened population that had experienced a "Little Ice Age" and a resulting famine in the early years of the fourteenth century. Modern scholars have scrutinized sources to determine answers to such questions as what the precise death tolls were, why the plague's effects were so much more devastating in some regions than in others, and what kind of disease it was—septicemic (blood borne and spread by fleas on rats and other animals), pneumonic (airborne, spread by the coughing that accompanied the spewing of blood that so many of the sources report), or a combination of the two. No less fascinating, however, are the attempts by writers of the fourteenth and early fifteenth centuries to understand the plague's causes and immediate effects.

The sources here offer a mix of perspectives. Some come from authors who experienced plague firsthand and others from authors who lived in the plague's aftermath and considered its causes and its effects.

There are regional accounts from two different cultural spheres: the Islamic world, particularly Syria and Egypt, and Europe. Ibn al-Wardi, from Aleppo in Syria, recorded his thoughts on what was causing the plague and described immediate responses to, and effects of, the disease. His understanding offers only the most short-term perspective because he died from the plague in 1349 and thus did not live to see the long-term aftermath. The Florentine Baldasarre de Buonaiuti experienced the plague in one of the European cities hit the hardest, and perhaps the most memorably, by the disease, given the description, with echoes of Baldasarre, in the introduction to Boccaccio's famed *Decameron*, in which elite youth withdraw from the city and entertain one another with stories having locked themselves away in a country villa to escape the sickness in the city. In his later years, Baldasarre recollected the events of 1348 in his *Florentine Chronicle*. The plague offered Ibn Khaldûn (c. 1375) an opportunity to ruminate on the patterns of civilization in his *Muqadimmah*. Written in Cairo, his historiographical masterpiece gives a North African perspective on the effects of the plague a full generation after its impact. Finally, a student of Ibn Khaldûn, al-Maqrizi, gives yet another Cairene, Islamic perspective, yet another generation later.

These sources, with their different perspectives—Christian and Islamic, contemporary and from the plague's aftermath, by chronicler and philosophical historian, European as well as Southwest Asian and North African—encourage us to think about the complexity of cause and effect. We can see how those who lived in proximity to this catastrophic event described the causes of what they, or their recent relatives, had lived through. The sources allow us to consider the short- and long-term effects of the disease as experienced in the fourteenth and fifteenth centuries. And, together with the material in the chapter, the sources give us an opportunity to reflect both on the complexity of causation, teasing out the primary and secondary causes for how the plague played out, and on the larger historical significance of the plague and its aftermath.

Analyzing the Causes and Effects of the Black Death

- How do the responses to, and the effects of, plague in the Muslim world (as reported by Ibn Khaldûn, al-Wardi, and al-Maqrizi) compare with those in Florence (as reported in the *Florentine Chronicle*)?

- What patterns in explaining causation and effects of plague do you detect in these sources? How do the various causes, and effects, explicitly or implicitly discussed in each text build on one another?

- Based on your reading of these sources, what do you think is the short- and long-term historical significance of the effects of the plague?

PRIMARY SOURCE 11.1

Plague in Southwest Asia, Ibn al-Wardi (1349)

Al-Wardi wrote two major works, one a natural history of the Islamic world and the other a history, from which this excerpt on the plague's devastation is taken. His is the most thorough extant contemporary Muslim description of the Black Death. Al-Wardi's discussion of the plague is rendered all the more poignant by the fact that he became one of its victims as the plague swept through Aleppo in 1349.

- **What role does religion, and/or God, play in al-Wardi's account of the plague? How do the Sunni-Shia division and other rifts factor into al-Wardi's account?**

- **How does al-Wardi describe the plague's progress across Afro-Eurasia, and what does that description suggest about al-Wardi's understanding of causation?**

- **What are some of the attempted remedies described by al-Wardi, and what do those remedies suggest about the understanding of the plague's causes?**

God is my security in every adversity. My sufficiency is in God alone. Is not God sufficient protection for His servant? Oh God, pray for our master, Muḥammad, and give him peace. Save us for his sake from the attacks of the plague and give us shelter.

The plague frightened and killed. It began in the land of darkness. Oh, what a visitor! It has been current for fifteen years. China was not preserved from it nor could the strongest fortress hinder it. The plague afflicted the Indians in India. It weighed upon the Sind. It seized with its hand and ensnared even the lands of the Uzbeks. How many backs did it break in what is Transoxiana! The plague increased and spread further. It attacked the Persians, extended its steps toward the land of Khiṭai, and gnawed away at the Crimea. It pelted Rūm with live coals and led the outrage to Cyprus and the islands. The plague destroyed mankind in Cairo. Its eye was cast upon Egypt, and behold, the people were wide-awake. It stilled all movement in Alexandria. . . .

Then, the plague turned to Upper Egypt. It, also, sent forth its storm to Barqah. The plague attacked Gaza, and it shook Asqalān severely. The plague oppressed Acre. The scourge came to Jerusalem and paid the *zakāt* [with the souls of men]. It overtook those people who fled to the al-'Aqsā Mosque, which stands beside the Dome of the Rock. If the door of mercy had not been opened, the end of the world would have occurred in a moment. It, then, hastened its pace and attacked the entire maritime plain. The plague trapped Sidon and descended unexpectedly upon Beirut, cunningly. Next, it directed the shooting of its arrows to Damascus. There the plague sat like a king on a throne and swayed with power, killing daily one thousand or more and decimating the population. It destroyed mankind with its pustules. May God the Most High spare Damascus to pursue its own path and extinguish the plague's fires so that they do not come close to her fragrant orchards.

Oh God, restore Damascus and protect her from insult.

Its morale has been so lowered that people in the city sell themselves for a grain. . . .

The plague and its poison spread to Sarmīn. It reviled the Sunni and the Shī'ī. It sharpened its spearheads for the Sunni and advanced like an army. The plague was spread in the land of the Shīʿī with a ruinous effect. To Antioch the plague gave its share. Then, it left there quickly with a shyness like a man who has forgotten the memory of his beloved. . . . The plague subjected Dhulūl and went straight through the lowlands and the mountains. It uprooted many people from their homes. Then, the plague sought Aleppo, but it did not succeed. By God's mercy the plague was the lightest oppression. . . . How amazingly does it pursue the people of each house! One of them spits blood, and everyone in the household is certain of death. It brings the entire family to their graves after two or three nights. . . .

Oh God, it is acting by Your command. Lift this from us. It happens where You wish; keep the plague from us. Who will defend us against this horror other than You the Almighty? . . .

Oh, if you could see the nobles of Aleppo studying their inscrutable books of medicine. They multiply its remedies by eating dried and sour foods. The buboes which disturb men's healthy lives are smeared with Armenian clay. Each man treated his humours and made life more comfortable. They perfumed their homes with ambergris and camphor, cyperus and sandal. They wore ruby rings and put onions, vinegar, and sardines together with the daily meal. They ate less broth and fruit but ate the citron and similar things.

If you see many biers and their carriers and hear in every quarter of Aleppo the announcements of death and cries, you run from them and refuse to stay with them. In Aleppo the profits of the undertakers have greatly increased. . . .

We ask God's forgiveness for our souls' bad inclination; the plague is surely part of His punishment. We take refuge from His wrath in His pleasure and from His chastisement in His restoring. . . .

Among the things which exasperated the Muslims and brought suffering is that our enemy, the damned people of Sis, are pleased by our trial. They act as if they are safe from the plague—that there is a treaty so that it will not approach them or that they have triumphed over it. Our Lord does not create us as an enticement for those who disbelieve. . . .

This plague is for the Muslims a martyrdom and a reward, and for the disbelievers a punishment and a rebuke. When the Muslim endures misfortune, then patience is his worship. It has been established by our Prophet, God bless him and give him peace, that the plague-stricken are martyrs. This noble tradition is true and assures martyrdom. And this secret should be pleasing to the true believer. If someone says it causes infection and destruction, say: God creates and recreates.

Source: Michael Dols, "Ibn al-Wardi's Risalah al-Naba an al-Waba, A translation of a major source for the history of the Black Death in the Middle East," in *Near Eastern Numismatics, Iconography, Epigraphy, and History: Studies in Honor of George C. Miles*, edited by Dickran K. Kouymjian (American University of Beirut, 1974), pp. 447–54.

PRIMARY SOURCE 11.2

The Florentine Chronicle: Rubric 643 (late fourteenth Century)

Marchione di Coppo Stefani (the pseudonym for Baldasarre de Buonaiuti) wrote his chronicle in the late fourteenth century after he retired from Florentine business and politics. When he was about 12 years old, in 1348, the Black Death swept through Florence. Buonaiuti's later recollection of the plague balances the practical effects of the pestilence, such as inflation, with the pathos of the plague—namely, family members deserting one another and abandoned sick people calling out for help.

- **How does Buonaiuti describe the plague and its ferocity? What details does he report to support that description?**

- **While Buonaiuti may not directly assert an explanation for the causes of the plague, what are some indirect indicators for what those experiencing the plague thought were its causes?**

- **What are the effects of the plague on family? On religion? On the economy? On the population?**

Concerning a Mortality in the City of Florence in Which Many People Died

In the year of the Lord 1348 there was a very great pestilence in the city and district of Florence. It was of such a fury and so tempestuous that in houses in which it took hold previously healthy servants who took care of the ill died of the same illness. Almost none of the ill survived past the fourth day. Neither physicians nor medicines were effective. Whether because these illnesses were previously unknown or because physicians had not previously studied them, there seemed to be no cure. There was such a fear that no one seemed to know what to do. When it took hold in a house it often happened that no one remained who had not died. And it was not just that men and women died, but even sentient animals died. Dogs, cats, chickens, oxen, donkeys, sheep showed the same symptoms and died of the same disease. And almost none, or very few, who showed these symptoms, were cured. The symptoms were the following: a bubo in the groin, where the thigh meets the trunk; or a small swelling under the armpit; sudden fever; spitting blood and saliva (and no one who spit blood survived it). It was such a frightful thing that when it got into a house, as was said, no one remained. Frightened people abandoned the house and fled to another. Those in town fled to villages. Physicians could not be found because they had died like the others. And those who could be found wanted vast sums in hand before they entered the house. And when they did enter, they checked the pulse with face turned away. They inspected the urine from a distance and with something odoriferous under their nose. Child abandoned the father, husband the wife, wife the husband, one brother the other, one sister the other. In all the city there was nothing to do but to carry the dead to a burial. And those who died had neither confessor nor other sacraments. And many died with no one looking after them. And many died of hunger because when someone took to bed sick, another in the house, terrified, said to him: "I'm going for the doctor." Calmly walking out the door, the other left and did not return again. Abandoned by people, without food, but accompanied by fever, they weakened. There were many who pleaded with their relatives not to abandon them when night fell. But [the relatives] said to the sick person, "So that during the night you did not have to awaken those who serve you and who work hard day and night, take some sweetmeats, wine or water. They are here on the bedstead by your head; here are some blankets." And when the sick person had fallen asleep, they left and did not return. . . .

No one, or few, wished to enter a house where anyone was sick, nor did they even want to deal with those healthy people who came out of a sick person's house. And they said to them: "He is stupefied, do not speak to him!" saying further: "He has it because there is a bubo in his house." They call the swelling a bubo. Many died unseen. So they remained in their beds until they stank. And the neighbors, if there were any, having smelled the stench, placed them in a shroud and sent them for burial. . . .

At every church, or at most of them, they dug deep trenches. . . . And those who were responsible for the dead carried them on their backs in the night in which they died and threw them into the ditch, or else they paid a high price to those who would do it for them. The next morning, if there were many [bodies] in the trench, they covered them over with dirt. And then more bodies were put on top of them, with a little more dirt over those; they put layer on layer just like one puts layers of cheese in a lasagna.

The *beccamorti* [literally, vultures] who provided their service, were paid such a high price that many were enriched by it. Many died from [carrying away the dead], some rich, some after earning just a little, but high prices continued. Servants, or those who took care of the ill, charged from one to three florins per day and the cost of things grew. . . .

Some fled to villas, others to villages in order to get a change of air. Where there had been no [pestilence], there they carried it; if it was already there, they caused it to increase. None of the guilds in Florence was working. All the shops were shut, taverns closed; only the apothecaries and the churches remained open. If you went outside, you found almost no one. And many good and rich men were carried from home to church on a pall by four *beccamorti* and one tonsured clerk who carried the cross. Each of them wanted a florin. This mortality enriched apothecaries, doctors, poultry vendors, *beccamorti*, and greengrocers who sold poultices of mallow, nettles, mercury and other herbs necessary to draw off the infirmity. And it was those who made these poultices who made a lot of money. . . .

This pestilence began in March, as was said, and ended in September 1348. And people began to return to look after their houses and possessions. And there were so many houses full of goods without a master that it was stupefying. . . .

Now it was ordered by the bishop and the Lords [of the city government] that they should formally inquire as to how many died in Florence. When it was seen at the beginning of October that no more persons were dying of the pestilence, they found that among males, females, children and adults, 96,000 died between March and October.

Source: Marchione di Coppo Stefani, Cronaca Fiorentina, edited by Niccolo Rodolico, Vol. 30 of *Rerum Italicarum Scriptores* (Citta di Castello: S. Lapi, 1903–1913). As translated by Duane Osheim.

Berbers, Arabs, and Plague in the Maghrib, from the *Muqadimmah*, Ibn Khaldûn (c. 1375)

Born in Tunis, Ibn Khaldûn came from a family that had been active in the political development of Spain and the Maghrib (North Africa) in the century before his birth. Ibn Khaldûn followed in his family's tradition of public service. In his forties, however, he stepped back from public life and composed a grand multivolume history, in the introduction to which, the *Muqadimmah*, he outlines a far-reaching analytical philosophy of history. Essential to his analysis is a theory of causation and considerations about the rise and fall of civilizations. (Ibn Khaldun offers dates according to the Muslim calendar, which marks time from Mohammad's migration from Mecca to Medina in 632. CE equivalents are provided in brackets.)

- What are the causes of population shifts of Berbers and Arabs in the Maghrib, according to Ibn Khaldûn?

- What does Ibn Khaldûn say were the effects of the plague on civilization?

- How does Ibn Khaldûn use earlier writers of history, al-Masûdî and al-Bakrî, to explore the purpose of history? How does the plague fit into Ibn Khaldûn's ideas about history writing?

History refers to events that are peculiar to a particular age or race. Discussion of the general conditions of regions, races, and periods constitutes the historian's

foundation. Most of his problems rest upon that foundation, and his historical information derives clarity from it. It forms the topic of special works, such as the *Murúj adh-dhahab* of al-Mas'ūdī. In this work, al-Mas'ūdī commented upon the conditions of nations and regions in the West and in the East during his period (which was) the three hundred and thirties [the nine hundred and forties]. He mentioned their sects and customs. He described the various countries, mountains, oceans, provinces, and dynasties. He distinguished between Arabic and non-Arabic groups. His book, thus, became the basic reference work for historians, their principal source for verifying historical information.

Al-Mas'ūdī was succeeded by al-Bakri who did something similar for routes and provinces, to the exclusion of everything else, because, in his time, not many transformations or great changes had occurred among the nations and races. However, at the present time—that is, at the end of the eighth [fourteenth] century—the situation in the Maghrib, as we can observe, has taken a turn and changed entirely. The Berbers, the original population of the Maghrib, have been replaced by an influx of Arabs, (that began in) the fifth [eleventh] century. The Arabs outnumbered and overpowered the Berbers, stripped them of most of their lands, and (also) obtained a share of those that remained in their possession. This was the situation until, in the middle of the eighth [fourteenth] century, civilization both in the East and the West was visited by a destructive plague which devastated nations and caused populations to vanish. It swallowed up many of the good things of civilization and wiped them out. It overtook the dynasties at the time of their senility, when they had reached the limit of their duration. It lessened their power and curtailed their influence. It weakened their authority. Their situation approached the point of annihilation and dissolution. Civilization decreased with the decrease of mankind. Cities and buildings were laid waste, roads and way signs were obliterated, settlements and mansions became empty, dynasties and tribes grew weak. The entire inhabited world changed. The East, it seems, was similarly visited, though in accordance with and in proportion to (the East's more affluent) civilization. It was as if the voice of existence in the world had called out for oblivion and restriction, and the world had responded to its call. God inherits the earth and whomever is upon it.

When there is a general change of conditions, it is as if the entire creation had changed and the whole world been altered, as if it were a new and repeated creation, a world brought into existence anew. Therefore, there is need at this time that someone should systematically set down the situation of the world among all regions and races, as well as the customs and sectarian beliefs that have changed for their adherents, doing for this age what al-Mas'ūdī did for his. This should be a model for future historians to follow. In this book of mine, I shall discuss as much of that as will be possible for me here in the Maghrib. I shall do so either explicitly or implicitly in connection with the history of the Maghrib, in conformity with my intention to restrict myself in this work to the Maghrib, the circumstances of its races and nations, and its subjects and dynasties, to the exclusion of any other region. (This restriction is necessitated) by my lack of knowledge of conditions in the East and among its nations, and by the fact that secondhand information would not give the essential facts I am after.

Source: Ibn Khaldûn, *The Muqaddimah, An Introduction to History*, Vol. 1, translated by Franz Rosenthal (New York: Pantheon Books, 1958), pp. 63–65.

PRIMARY SOURCE 11.4

Plague in Syria and Egypt (1348–1350), by al-Maqrizi (early fifteenth century)

Al-Maqrizi wrote his extensive historical works in Cairo in the early fifteenth century. His roots in Cairo were deep, but his family also had connections in Damascus, and he lived there for about ten years in his forties. Given that al-Maqrizi was so prolific a historian, it is surprising that much of what is known about him is based on writing about him by contemporaries and later biographers. Interestingly for our purposes, he was a student of Ibn Khaldûn in Cairo.

- **What part of the population seems to have been hardest hit by the plague? Why might the death toll from plague have been higher during Ramadan?**

- **What was the effect of the plague on religious practice?**

- **What impact did the plague have on the workforce in terms of wages, available workers, and employment opportunities?**

News reached [Cairo from Syria] that the plague in Damascus had been less deadly than in Tripoli, Hama, and Aleppo. From . . . [October 1348] death raged with intensity. 1200 people died daily and, as a result, people stopped requesting permits from the administration to bury the dead and many cadavers were abandoned in gardens and on the roads.

In New and Old Cairo, the plague struck women and children at first, then market people, and the numbers of the dead augmented. . . . The [ravages of the] plague intensified in . . . [November] in [New] Cairo and became extremely grave during *Ramadan* [December], which coincided with the arrival of winter. . . . The plague continued to spread so considerably that it became impossible to count how many died. . . .

In [January 1349], new symptoms developed and people began spitting up blood. One sick person came down with internal fever, followed by an unrestrained need to vomit, then spat blood and died. Those around him in his house fell ill, one after the other and in one or two nights they all perished. Everyone lived with the overwhelming preoccupation that death was near. People prepared themselves for death by distributing alms to the poor, reconciled with one another, and multiplied their acts of devotion.

None had time to consult doctors or drink medicinal syrups or take other medications, so rapidly did they die. By [January 7th,] bodies had piled up in the streets and markets; [town leaders] appointed burial brigades, and some pious people remained permanently at places of prayer in New and Old Cairo to recite funeral orations over the dead. The situation worsened beyond limits, and no solution appeared possible. Almost the entire royal guard disappeared and the barracks in the sultan's citadel contained no more soldiers.

Statistics of the dead from funerals in Cairo during . . . [November and December] attained 900,000. . . . There were 1,400 litters on which they carried the dead and soon even they did not suffice. So they began carrying dead bodies in boxes, on doors taken from stores and on plain boards, on each of which they placed two to three bodies.

People began searching for *Quran* readers for funerals, and many individuals quit their trades to recite prayers at the head of burial procession[s]. A group of people devoted themselves to applying a coat of clay to the inner sides of the graves. Others volunteered to wash corpses, and still others to carry them. Such volunteers received substantial wages. For example, a *Quran* reader earned 10 *dirhams:* the moment he finished with one funeral, he ran off to another. A body carrier demanded six *dirhams* in advance, and still it was hard to find any. A grave digger wanted 50 *dirhams* per grave. But most of them died before they had a chance to spend their earnings.

Family celebrations and marriages no longer took place. . . . No one had held any festivities during the entire duration of the epidemic, and no voice was heard singing. In an attempt to revive these activities, the *wazir* [prime minister] reduced by a third the taxes paid by the woman responsible for collecting dues on singers. The call to prayer was suspended at many locations, and even at the most important ones, there remained only a single *muezzin* [caller to prayer].

The drum batteries before most of the officers' quarters no longer functioned, and the entourage of a commander [who controlled a thousand men] was reduced now from about fifteen to three soldiers.

Most of the mosques and *zawiyas* [Sufi lodges] were closed. It was also a known fact that during this epidemic no infant survived more than one or two days after his birth, and his mother usually quickly followed him to the grave.

At [the end of February], all of Upper Egypt was afflicted with the plague. . . . According to information that arrived . . . from . . . other regions, lions, wolves, rabbits, camels, wild asses and boars, and other savage beasts, dropped dead, and were found with scabs on their bodies.

The same thing happened throughout Egypt. When harvest time arrived, many farmers had already perished [and no field hands remained to gather crops]. Soldiers and their young slaves or pages headed for the fields. They tried to recruit workers by promising them half of the proceeds, but they could not find anyone to help them gather the harvest. They threshed the grain with their horses [hoofs], and winnowed the grain themselves, but, unable to carry all the grain back, they had to abandon much of it.

Most craft workshops closed, since artisans devoted themselves to disposing of the dead, while others, not less numerous, auctioned off property and textiles [which the dead left behind]. Even though the prices of fabric and other such commodities sold for a fifth of their original value . . . they remained unsold. . . . Religious texts sold by their weight, and at very low prices.

Workers disappeared. You could not find either water carriers, or launderers or servants. The monthly salary of a horse groom rose from 30 to 80 *dirhams.* . . . This epidemic, they say, continued in several countries for 15 years.

Source: al-Maqrizi, *The Guide to the Knowledge of Dynasties and Kings*, excerpted in *The Middle East and Islamic World Reader*, edited by Marvin Gettleman and Stuart Schaar (New York: Grove Press, 2012), pp. 52–53.

Interpreting Visual Evidence

Marking Boundaries, Inspiring Loyalty

The fourteenth century witnessed the emergence of dynastic states across Afro-Eurasia that endured for centuries. The size of these new states and the ethnic and religious diversity of their populations posed formidable challenges to those in power. Rulers had to distinguish those who belonged to the community—and owed taxes or military service—from those who did not. They used a careful mixture of privilege and punishment to create a sense of unity among their subjects while at the same time justifying their own right to rule and reinforcing traditional social hierarchies. The three images below show different ways rulers approached this problem.

The first painting, from around 1500, is by the Spanish artist Pedro Berruguete. It portrays a scene

Spanish painting by Berruguete.

The *devshirme* system.

from two centuries earlier in which Spanish authorities burned people at the stake for their alleged heretical beliefs. Notice in the foreground members of the Dominican Order, who were instrumental in the administration of the Inquisition, and soldiers loyal to the crown. The second image, a miniature painting from 1558, depicts the *devshirme* system in the Ottoman Empire. Authorities took non-Muslim children from their families in Europe as a human tribute in place of cash taxes, which the poor region could not pay. The children would then be educated in Ottoman Muslim ways and prepared for service in the sultan's civil and military bureaucracy. The final image, a painting on silk by Ch'iu Ying, represents a group of Confucian scholars waiting for the results of their civil service examination. Candidates spent three days and two nights taking examinations as they sought to enter the Ming bureaucracy.

Chinese painting by Ch'iu Ying.

Questions for Analysis

1. Assess the combinations of privilege and punishment conveyed by these images. What kinds of assistance or special privileges did leaders grant, to whom did they offer this assistance, and what kinds of punishments did they impose?

2. Describe the original context for these images. Who might have created these images, for whom, and who might have seen them?

3. Interpret the role religion plays in these images. How does the artist present the relationship between religion and social order?

4. Explain how Berruguete's use of the past alters the relationship between royal authorities and traditional elites presented in the first painting, compared to the relationship between rulers and elites shown or implied by the other two images.

12

Contact, Commerce, and Colonization

1450–1600

At the time of Christopher Columbus's birth in 1451, the great world power on the rise was neither Spain nor Portugal, but the Ottoman Empire. For the Ottomans, unlike the other major Asian empires, the fifteenth and sixteenth centuries marked a period of frenzied territorial expansion in the Mediterranean as well as the Indian Ocean. The Ottomans were eager to fulfill what they considered to be Islam's primary mission: world dominion. Sultans Bayezid II (r. 1481–1512), Selim I (r. 1512–1520), and Suleiman the Magnificent (r. 1520–1566) continued the conquests of Mehmed the Conqueror and led the thrust into Arab lands and the Indian Ocean even while pressing ahead in Europe. Indeed, Selim I boasted that "he was the ruler of the east and the west."

As the Ottomans turned their attention to conquest of the Red Sea, the Arabian Peninsula, and North Africa, reestablishing under their own control trade routes disrupted by the Mongols and the Black Death, they forced others seeking shares in South and East Asian luxuries to seek new sea passages. European states gave the Ottomans no cause for alarm when they began to make inroads in South Asia in the mid-sixteenth century. After all, it was not Ottoman territory they were contesting, and the Ottomans, looking westward, had bigger fish to fry.

No one could have predicted that European conquests of a few South Asian trading cities were particularly significant, compared with the

Core Objectives

- **DESCRIBE** the broad patterns of world trade after 1450, and **COMPARE** major features of world trade in Asia, the Americas, Africa, and Europe.

- **ANALYZE** the factors that enabled Europeans to increase their trade relationships with Asian empires in the fifteenth and sixteenth centuries, and **ASSESS** their significance.

- **COMPARE** the practices and the impact of European explorers in Asia and the Americas.

- **ANALYZE** the social and political relationships, and **EXPLAIN** the sources of conflict within the Afro-Eurasian polities.

- **ASSESS** how European colonization of the Americas affected African and Amerindian peoples, and **DESCRIBE** their responses.

Ottomans' relentless annexations of large territories, including great stretches of southeastern Europe. Even more unpredictable, though hugely consequential, was the accidental discovery made by Christopher Columbus.

Seeking to circumvent Ottoman power in the eastern Mediterranean, Columbus opened up a "New World" about which Afro-Eurasians had no previous knowledge. Although Christopher Columbus did not intend to "discover" America when he went looking for Asia, his voyages convinced Europeans that there were still new territories to exploit and peoples to convert to Christianity. For the first time since the Ice Age migrations, large numbers of people moved from Afro-Eurasian land-masses to the Americas. So did animals, plants, commercial products, and—most momentous—deadly germs. Europeans now began building empires—but of a different nature than the land empires of Africa and Asia. Their empires were overseas. While the new colonies generated vast riches, they also brought unsettling changes to the rulers and the ruled.

Despite the significance of Europeans' activity in the Americas, most Africans and Asians were barely aware of the Americas. Asian empires continued to flourish after recovering from the Black Death. Nor was Europe's attention exclusively on the Americas, for its royal houses competed with one another for power and territory at home. Religious revolt in the form of the Protestant Reformation intensified these rivalries. In the wake of Columbus, the drive to build and protect empires across oceans began to change the terms on which people around the globe interacted with one another.

Global Storylines

- The European "discovery" of the Americas begins a complex process that changes the ways peoples around the world interact with one another.

- For the first time, major world empires are oceanic, overseas empires rather than continental empires.

- Despite the long-term significance of European activity in the Americas, most Africans and Asians are barely aware of the Americas or the expansion of long-distance trade.

- Within Europe, dynastic states concentrate attention and resources on their own internal rivalries. Religious revolts, especially the Protestant Reformation, intensify those rivalries.

- Asian empires thrive in the sixteenth century, thanks to commercial expansion and political consolidation.

Ottoman Expansion and World Trade

Ottoman expansion overland continued as European expansion overseas began. Both caused important global shifts in the organization of polities as well as in patterns of trade. The two were interconnected, as increasing Ottoman control in the eastern Mediterranean motivated Portuguese and Spanish explorers to turn toward the Atlantic in hopes of reaching the rich trading posts of China and the Indian Ocean by another route. Ottoman expansion was made possible by the Ottomans' domination of Afro-Eurasian trade routes as they recovered in the wake of the Black Death, and it was marked by the sultanate's co-optation of local elites and a relatively tolerant attitude toward other peoples and religions.

For the Europeans, in contrast, expansion overseas was quite new and experimental. Mariners and traders, searching for new routes to South and East Asia, began exploring the Atlantic coast of Africa. Lured by spices, silks, and slaves, and aided by new maritime technology, Portuguese expeditions made their way around Africa and onward to India. Although Europeans still had little to offer would-be trading partners in Asia, their developing capability in overseas trade laid the foundations for a new kind of global commerce.

Both the new and the old expansionism knitted worlds together that had previously been apart or only loosely interconnected. Together they laid the foundations for a new chapter in world history. But we must not forget that even in the midst of this global transformation, the peoples of each continent continued to focus on local, and often religious, struggles closer to their everyday lives.

THE REVIVAL OF ASIAN ECONOMIES

Trade all across Afro-Eurasia benefited enormously from China's economic dynamism, which was driven primarily by China's vast internal economy. Chinese demand for silver fueled a revival of trade across the Indian Ocean and traditional overland routes. After the Ming dynasty relocated its capital from Nanjing in the prosperous south to the northern city of Beijing, Chinese merchants, artisans, and farmers exploited the surging domestic market. Reconstruction of the Grand Canal now opened a major artery that allowed food and riches from the economically vibrant lower Yangzi area to reach the capital region of Beijing. Urban centers, such as Nanjing with a population approaching a million and Beijing at half a million, became massive and lucrative markets. Despite official restrictions on trade, merchants thrived and coastal cities remained active harbors. (See Map 12.5.)

What did foreign buyers have to trade with the Chinese? The answer was silver, which became essential to the Ming monetary system. Whereas their

THE BIG PICTURE

How would you describe the broad patterns of world trade after 1450?

Chinese Porcelain Box There were two distinct markets for Chinese porcelains in this period, one external and one internal, for consumption within China itself. Although it ultimately ended up in a French museum, this box was produced for the vibrant internal Chinese market, for Persian eunuchs serving the Ming court. The inscription on top, in Arabic script, says, "Strive for excellence in penmanship, for it is one of the keys of livelihood"; the inscription on the sides, in Persian, says, "Ignorance is an irremediable evil, [but] knowledge is a priceless elixir." Neither comes from the Quran, but they both express Islamic sentiments in favor of calligraphy and intellectualism glorying God and testify to extensive commercial activity in China.

predecessors had used paper money, Ming consumers and traders mistrusted anything other than silver or gold for commercial dealings. Once the rulers adopted silver as a means of tax payment in the 1430s, it became the predominant medium for larger transactions. China, however, did not produce sufficient silver for its booming economy. Indeed, silver and other precious metals were about the only commodities for which the Chinese would trade their precious manufactures. Through most of the sixteenth century, China's main source of silver was Japan, which one Florentine merchant called the "silver islands." After the 1570s, however, the Philippines, now under the control of the Spanish, became a gateway for silver coming from the New World. One-third of all silver mined in the Americas during the sixteenth and seventeenth centuries wound up in Chinese hands.

China's economic expansion contributed to the revival of Indian Ocean trade. Long-distance merchants developed a brisk commerce that tied the whole of the Indian Ocean together. Ports as far off as East Africa and the Red Sea enjoyed links with coastal cities of India, South Asia, and the Malay Peninsula. Muslims dominated this trade. India was the geographic and economic center of numerous trade routes. With a population expanding as rapidly as China's, its large cities (such as Agra, Delhi, and Lahore) each boasted nearly half a million residents. India's manufacturing center, Bengal, exported silk and cotton textiles and rice throughout South and Southeast Asia. Like China, India exported more than it imported, selling textiles and pepper in exchange for silver.

Overland commerce also thrived anew. One well-trafficked route linked the Baltic Sea, Muscovy, the Caspian Sea, the central Asian oases, and China. Other land routes carried goods to the ports of China and the Indian Ocean; from there, they crossed to the Ottoman Empire's heartland and went by land farther into Europe. Ottoman authorities took a keen interest in the caravan trade, since the state gained considerable tax revenue from it. To facilitate the caravans' movement, the government maintained refreshment and military stations along the route. The largest had individual rooms to accommodate the chief merchants and could provide lodging for up to 800 travelers, as well as care for all their animals. But gathering so many traders, animals, and cargoes could also attract marauders, especially desert tribesmen. To stop the raids, authorities and merchants offered cash payments to tribal chieftains as "protection money." This was a small price to pay in order to protect the caravan trade, whose revenues ultimately supported imperial expansion.

Overland Caravans and Caravanserais Muslim governments and merchants' associations constructed inns, or caravanserais, along the major trading routes. These areas were capable of accommodating a large number of traders and their animals in great comfort.

OTTOMAN EXPANSION

Having built the period's most powerful military forces and armed themselves with the latest maps and scientific instruments, the Ottomans began the sixteenth century in possession of Constantinople and great swaths of southeastern Europe and Anatolia. During the sultanate of Suleiman the Magnificent (r. 1520–1566), Ottoman forces carried the empire southward into Egypt, eastward to the Iranian borderlands, and westward into Europe. By 1550, the Ottoman Empire stretched from Hungary and the Crimea in the north to the Arabian Peninsula in the south, from Morocco in the west to the contested border with Safavid Iran in the east (see Map 12.1 and Chapter 13).

The Ottomans had become a world power, and their armada dwarfed that of all others at the time. It consisted of seventy-four ships, including twenty-seven large and small galleys and munitions ships, mounted with cannons. Piri Reis—an Ottoman admiral and cartographer—conducted research in the Indian Ocean, an area previously unknown to the Ottomans. Not only did he produce a map of the world, but in 1526 he presented to Sultan Suleiman a masterpiece of geography and cartography known as *The Book of the Sea*. The book drew on Arab sources as well as Indian maps obtained from the Portuguese and offered full information on the geography of the world. In no small part thanks to Piri, the Ottomans made important gains in the Red Sea and ventured into the Indian Ocean as rivals to the Portuguese. But their main energies were devoted to the lands around the eastern Mediterranean, the Black Sea, and the Arabian Peninsula.

The conquest of Syria and Egypt in 1516–1517 was decisive in allowing Ottoman leaders to regard their Sunni state as the preeminent Muslim empire from that moment forward, even enabling some sultans to call themselves caliphs. Egypt became the Ottomans' most lucrative and important acquisition, the breadbasket of the empire and the province that provided Istanbul with the largest revenue stream. But the conquest was no easy matter. The Mamluk rulers resisted mightily, losing a bloody battle in 1516 at Marj Dabiq, north of Aleppo, after which, according to Ibn Iyas, the Arab chronicler of the age, "the battlefield was strewn with corpses and headless bodies and faces covered with dust and grown hideous." Nor did the conquest of Egypt prove any easier, for the Mamluks were determined to hold on to their most precious possession. The conquest of Constantinople and the Arab lands transformed the Ottoman Empire, creating a Muslim majority in an empire once mainly populated by conquered Christians and enabling Ottoman sultans to see themselves as heirs of a long line of empires that had ruled over these regions.

Yet on the eastern front, in conflicts with the Safavid Empire, the Ottomans encountered their earliest military failures and their most determined foe, an enemy state that plagued the Ottoman Empire until its collapse early in the eighteenth century (see Chapters 11 and 13). Blocked from eastward expansion, the Ottomans moved westward into Europe, which terrified Europeans. Having taken Constantinople in 1453, Sultan Mehmed II took Athens in 1458. The Ottomans also took large swaths of Balkan territory before turning to North Africa and Egypt and exerted more control than ever over commerce in the Mediterranean.

Ottoman conquests in southeastern and central Europe resulted in the subordination of Christians and Jews to Muslim rule. Centuries of Ottoman rule left a multiethnic legacy in places like Bosnia, including large populations of Muslims in areas later taken by the Habsburg Empire. Thus, the Ottomans, too, from the eastern end of the Mediterranean, became key players in the transformation of Europe in the age of da Gama and Columbus.

EUROPEAN EXPLORATION AND EXPANSION

The emergence of the Ottoman Empire prompted Europeans to probe unexplored links to the east in the sixteenth century. When the Ottomans took control of traditional overland trade routes from Europe to Asia, Europeans

Core Objectives

ANALYZE the factors that enabled Europeans to increase their trade relationships with Asian empires, and **ASSESS** their significance.

began to look south and west—and ventured across the seas. (See Map 12.1.) Taking the lead were the Portuguese, whose search for new routes to Asia led them first to Africa. Europeans had long believed that Africa was a storehouse of precious metals. In fact, a fourteenth-century map, the Catalan Atlas, had depicted a single black ruler controlling a vast quantity of gold in the interior of Africa. As the price of gold skyrocketed during and after the Black Death, ambitious men decided to venture southward in search of this commodity and its twin, silver. Having found sea routes around Africa, European merchants sought to reap the riches abounding in Asian ports, especially once Asian states were firmly established across the Indian Ocean in the seventeenth century.

Innovations in maritime technology and information from other mariners helped Portuguese sailors navigate the treacherous waters along the African coast. New vessels included the carrack, a three- or four-masted ship, developed by the Portuguese to deal with rough waters like the Atlantic Ocean and the Mediterranean. Equally important was the caravel, with specially designed triangular sails, which enabled European sailors to nose in and out of estuaries and navigate unpredictable currents and winds. By using highly maneuverable caravels and perfecting the technique of tacking (sailing into the wind rather than before it), the Portuguese advanced far along the West African coast. In addition, newfound expertise with the compass and the astrolabe helped navigators determine latitude.

Portuguese seafarers ventured from the coasts of Africa into the Indian Ocean and inserted themselves into its thriving commerce. In Asia, Portugal did not attempt to rule directly or to establish colonies. Rather, it aimed to exploit Asian commercial networks and trading systems. To do so, the Portuguese took advantage of a technology developed centuries earlier in China: gunpowder. Mounting small cannons on their warships, they bombarded ports and rival navies or merchant vessels.

The first Portuguese mariner to reach the Indian Ocean was Vasco da Gama (1469–1524). Like Columbus, da Gama was relatively unknown before his extraordinary voyage commanding four ships around the Cape of Good Hope. He found a network of commercial ties spanning the Indian Ocean, as well as skilled Muslim mariners who knew the currents, winds, and ports of call. Once established in the key ports, the Portuguese attempted to take over the trade or, failing this, to tax local merchants. From Sofala, Kilwa, and other important ports on the East African coast, from Goa and Calicut in India, and from Macao in southern China, the Portuguese soon dominated the most active sea-lanes of the Indian Ocean. The Portuguese did not interrupt the flow of luxuries among Asian and African elites; rather, their naval captains simply kept a portion of the profits for themselves, content to benefit from Asian prosperity without imposing Portuguese rule. Only with the discovery of the Americas and the conquest of Brazil did Portugal become an empire with large overseas colonies. For this to transpire, mariners would have to traverse the Atlantic Ocean itself.

The Global View

GREENLAND

NORTH AMERICA

CARTIER 1534–1541

NEWFOUNDLAND (1497)

CABOT 1497–1498

ENGLAND

FRANCE

PORTUGAL

SPAIN

Lisbon

ATLANTIC OCEAN

AZORES

MADEIRA

St. Augustine

SAN SALVADOR

COLUMBUS 1492

CANARY ISLANDS

DRAKE 1577–1580

CORTÉS 1519

Havana

Tenochtitlán

YUCATAN

CUBA

COLUMBUS 1493–1494

CAPE VERDE ISLANDS

AZTEC EMPIRE

HISPANIOLA (1482)

VESPUCCI 1501–1502

MAGELLAN 1519

CABRAL 1500

VASCO DA GAMA 1497–1498

FERNANDO PO

GOLD COAST

SÃO TOMÉ

DEL CANO (after Magellan's death) 1521–1522

PACIFIC OCEAN

SOUTH AMERICA

INCA EMPIRE

Cuzco

Potosí

PIZARRO 1531

MAGELLAN AND DEL CANO 1520

DRAKE 1577–1580

CABRAL 1500

Line of Tordesillas 1494

Straits of Magellan

Cape Horn

Legend

- → Portuguese exploration
- → Spanish exploration
- → English exploration
- → French exploration
- Portuguese controlled islands
- Spanish controlled islands
- • Portuguese controlled cities
- • Spanish controlled cities

Map 12.1 European Exploration, 1420–1580

In the fifteenth and sixteenth centuries, sailors from Portugal, Spain, England, and France explored and mapped the coastline of most of the world. Their activities took place in the shadow of the leading empires of the day, with the Ottomans, Safavids, Mughals, and Ming largely unconcerned and unthreatened by them. They established contacts and made connections that, over time, became increasingly important.

- Explain why Europeans would have chosen sea routes to reach Asia rather than land routes.
- Trace the voyages that started from Portugal, and then the voyages that started from Spain. Explain why Portuguese explorers concentrated on Africa and the Indian Ocean, whereas their Spanish counterparts focused on the Americas.
- Contrast the different patterns of exploration in the New World with those in the Indian Ocean and the South China Sea.

The Catalan Atlas This 1375 map shows the world as it was then known. Not only does it depict the location of continents and islands, but it also includes information on ancient and medieval tales, regional politics, astronomy, and astrology.

The Atlantic World

By opening new sea-lanes in the Atlantic, European explorers set the stage for a major transformation in world history: the establishment of overseas colonies. After the discovery of the Americas, Europeans conquered the native peoples and created colonies for the purpose of enriching themselves and their monarchs.

Crossing the Atlantic was a feat of monumental importance. It did not occur, however, with an aim to discover new lands. Columbus set out to open a more direct—and more lucrative—route to Japan and China. As we saw in Chapter 11, Ferdinand and Isabella hoped Columbus would bring them riches that would finance a crusade to liberate Jerusalem. Neither they nor Columbus expected he would find a "New World."

Europeans arrived in what they soon called the New World with cannons, steel weapons and body armor, horses, and, above all, deadly diseases that caused a catastrophic decline of Amerindian populations. Europeans arrived at a time of political upheaval and took advantage of divisions among the indigenous peoples. The combination of material advantages and local allies enabled Europeans to conquer and colonize the Americas, as they could not do in Asia or Africa, where long-standing patterns of trade had resulted in the development of shared immunities and stable states resisted outside incursions.

Core Objectives

COMPARE the practices and the impact of European explorers in Asia and the Americas.

The devastation of the Amerindian population also resulted in severe labor shortages. Thus began the large-scale introduction of slave laborers imported from Africa, which led to the "Atlantic system" that connected Europe, the Americas, and Africa. The precious metals of the New World now gave Europeans something to offer their trading partners in Asia and enabled them to grow rich. In the process, they brought together peoples and ecosystems that had developed separately for thousands of years.

FIRST ENCOUNTERS

Christopher Columbus set sail from Spain in early 1492, stopped in the Canary Islands for supplies and repairs, and cast off into the unknown. When he stepped onto the beach of San Salvador (in the Bahamas) on October 12, 1492, the explorer ushered in a new era in world history. Once established in the Americas, Columbus and the other mariners, like other expansion-minded Europeans, aimed to Christianize the world while enriching themselves and their backers. These goals—to save souls and to make money—drove the European colonization of the Americas and the formation of an Atlantic system. They also shaped Europeans' early interactions with Amerindians and Africans captured in the slave trade.

When Columbus made landfall in the Caribbean Sea, he unfurled the royal standard of Ferdinand and Isabella and claimed the "many islands filled with people innumerable" for Spain. It is fitting that the first encounter with Caribbean inhabitants, in this case the Tainos, drew blood. Columbus noted, "I showed them swords and they took them by the edge and through

Columbus As Columbus made landfall and encountered Indians, he planted a cross to indicate the spiritual purpose of the voyage and read aloud a document proclaiming the sovereign authority of the king and queen of Spain. Quickly, he learned there was barter for precious stones and metals.

ignorance cut themselves." The Tainos had their own weapons but did not forge steel—and thus had no knowledge of such sharp edges.

For Columbus, the Tainos' naïveté in grabbing his sword symbolized the child-like primitivism of these people, whom he would mislabel "Indians" because he thought he had arrived off the coast of Asia. In Columbus's view the Tainos had no religion, but they did have at least some gold (found initially hanging as pendants from their noses). Likewise, Pedro álvares Cabral, a Portuguese mariner whose trip down the coast of Africa in 1500 was blown off course across the Atlantic, wrote that the people of Brazil had all "the innocence of Adam." He also noted that they were ripe for conversion and that the soils "if rightly cultivated would yield everything." But, as with Africans and Asians, Europeans also developed a contradictory view of the peoples of the Americas. From the Tainos, Columbus learned of another people, the Caribs, who (according to his informants) were savage, warlike cannibals. For centuries, these contrasting images—innocents and savages—structured European (mis)understandings of the native peoples of the Americas.

We know less about what the Indians thought of Columbus or other Europeans on their first encounters. Certainly they were impressed with the Europeans' appearance and their military prowess. The Tainos fled into the forest at the approach of European ships, which they thought were giant monsters; others thought they were floating islands. European metal goods, in particular weaponry, struck them as otherworldly. The Amerindians found the newcomers different not for their skin color (only Europeans drew the distinction based on skin pigmentation), but for their hairiness. Indeed, the Europeans' beards, breath, and bad manners repulsed their Indian hosts. The newcomers' inability to live off the land also stood out. In due course, the Indians realized not just that the strange, hairy people bearing metal weapons were odd trading partners, but that they meant to stay and to force the local population to labor for them. The explorers had become **conquistadors** (conquerors).

FIRST CONQUESTS

First contacts between peoples gave way to dramatic conquests in the Americas; then conquests paved the way to mass exploitation of native peoples. After the first voyage, Columbus claimed that on Hispaniola (present-day Haiti and the Dominican Republic) "he had found what he was looking for"—gold. That was sufficient to persuade the Spanish crown to invest in larger expeditions. Whereas Columbus first sailed with three small ships and 87 men, ten years later the Spanish outfitted an expedition with 2,500 men.

Between 1492 and 1519, the Spanish experimented with institutions of colonial rule over local populations on the Caribbean island that they renamed Hispaniola. Ultimately they created a model that the rest of the New World colonies would adapt. But the Spaniards faced problems that would recur. The first was Indian resistance. As early as 1494, starving Spaniards raided and pillaged Indian villages. When the Indians revolted, Spanish soldiers replied with punitive expeditions and began enslaving them to work in mines extracting gold. As the crown rewarded conquistadors with grants (*encomiendas*) giving them control over Indian labor, a rich class of **encomenderos** arose who enjoyed the fruits of the system. Although the surface gold mines soon ran dry, the model of granting favored settlers the right to coerce Indian labor endured. In return, those who received the labor rights paid special taxes on the precious metals that were extracted. Thus, both the crown and the *encomenderos* benefited. The same cannot be said of the Amerindians, who perished in great numbers from disease, malnutrition, and overwork.

As Spanish colonists saw the bounty of Hispaniola dry up, they set out to discover and conquer new territories. Finding their way to the mainlands of the American landmasses, they encountered larger, more complex, and more militarized societies than those they had overrun in the Caribbean. Great civilizations had arisen there centuries before, boasting large cities, monumental buildings, and riches based on wealthy agrarian societies. In both Mesoamerica, starting with the Olmecs (see Chapter 5), and the Andes, with the Chimú (see Chapter 10), large states had laid the foundations for the subsequent Aztec Empire and **Inca Empire**. These empires were powerful. But they had evolved untouched by Afro-Eurasian developments; as worlds apart, they were unprepared for the kind of assaults that European invaders had honed. In pre-Columbian Mesoamerica and then the Andes, warfare was more ceremonial, less inclined to wipe out enemies than to make them pay tribute. As a result, the wealth and vulnerability of these empires made them irresistible to outside conquerors.

Aztec Society In Mesoamerica, the Mexica had created an empire known to us as "Aztec." Around Lake Texcoco, Mexica cities grew and in 1430 formed a three-city league, which then expanded through the Central Valley of Mexico to incorporate neighboring peoples. Gradually the **Aztec Empire** united numerous small, independent states under a single monarch who ruled with the help of counselors, military leaders, and priests. By the late fifteenth century, the Aztec realm may have embraced 25 million people. Tenochtitlán, situated on an immense island in Lake Texcoco, ranked among the world's largest cities.

Tenochtitlán spread in concentric circles, with the main religious and political buildings in the center and residences radiating outward. The city's outskirts connected a mosaic of floating gardens producing food for urban markets. Canals irrigated the land, waste served as fertilizer, and high-yielding produce found easy transport to markets. Entire households worked: men, women, and children all had roles in Aztec agriculture.

encomenderos
Commanders of the labor services of the colonized peoples in Spanish America.

Inca Empire
Empire of Quechua-speaking rulers in the Andean valley of Cuzco that encompassed a population of 4 to 6 million. The Incas lacked a clear inheritance system, causing an internal split that Pizarro's forces exploited in 1533.

Aztec Empire
Mesoamerican empire that originated with a league of three Mexica cities in 1430 and gradually expanded through the Central Valley of Mexico, uniting numerous small, independent states under a single monarch who ruled with the help of counselors, military leaders, and priests. By the late fifteenth century, the Aztec realm may have embraced 25 million people. In 1521, the Aztecs were defeated by the conquistador Hernán Cortés.

Extended kinship provided the scaffolding for Aztec statehood. Marriage of men and women from different villages solidified alliances and created clan-like networks. In Tenochtitlán, powerful families married their children to each other or found nuptial partners among the prominent families of other important cities. Soon a lineage emerged to create a corps of "natural" rulers. Priests legitimized new emperors in rituals to convey the image of a ruler close to the gods and to distinguish the elite from the lower orders.

Ultimately Aztec power spread though much of Mesoamerica, but the empire's constant wars and conquests deprived it of stability. In military campaigns, the Aztecs defeated their neighbors, forcing the conquered peoples to pay tribute of crops, gold, silver, textiles, and other goods that financed Aztec grandeur. Such conquests also provided a constant supply of humans for sacrifice, because the Aztecs believed that the great god of the sun required human hearts to keep on burning and blood to replace that given by the gods to moisten the earth through rain. Priests escorted captured warriors the temple steps and tore out their hearts, offering their lives and blood as a sacrifice to the sun god.

Those whom the Aztecs sought to dominate did not submit peacefully. From 1440, the empire faced constant turmoil as subject populations rebelled. Tlaxcalans and Tarascans waged a relentless war for freedom, holding at bay entire divisions of Aztec armies. To pacify the realm, the empire diverted more and more men and money into a mushrooming military. By the time the electoral committee chose Moctezuma II as emperor in 1502, divisions among elites and pressures from the periphery had placed the Aztec Empire under extreme stress.

Cortés and Conquest Not long after Moctezuma became emperor, news arrived from the coast of ships bearing pale, bearded men and monsters (horses and dogs). Here distinguishing fact from fiction is difficult. Some accounts left after the conquest by indigenous witnesses reported that Moctezuma consulted with his ministers and priests, and the observers wondered if these men were the god Quetzalcoatl and his entourage. Most historians dismiss the importance of these omens, describing them as the efforts of rival elites to blame Moctezuma for their own inaction. In any case, Moctezuma sent emissaries bearing gifts, but he did not prepare for a military engagement.

Tenochtitlán At its height, the Aztec capital, Tenochtitlán, was as populous as Europe's largest city. As can be seen from this map, it spread in concentric circles, with the main religious and political buildings in the center and residences radiating outward.

Cortés Meets Mesoamerican Rulers (*Left*) This colonial image depicts the meeting of Cortés (second from right) and Moctezuma (seated on the left), with Doña Marina serving as an interpreter and informer for the Spanish conquistador. Notice at the bottom what are likely Aztec offerings for the newcomer. As Mexicans began to celebrate their mixed-blood heritage, Doña Marina became the symbolic mother of the first mestizos. But she remains controversial and has also been viewed in Mexico as a traitor for the help she provided to the Spanish. (*Right*) This detail from a twentieth-century Mexican mural depicts the meeting of Cortés and the king of Tlaxcala, enemy of the Aztecs.

Aboard one of the ships was Hernán Cortés (1485–1547), a former law student from one of the Spanish provinces. He would become the model conquistador, just as Columbus was the model explorer. For a brief time, Cortés was an *encomendero* in Cuba; but when news arrived of a potentially wealthier land to the west, he set sail with over 500 men, eleven ships, sixteen horses, and artillery. When the expedition arrived near present-day Veracruz, Cortés acquired two translators, including the daughter of a local Indian noble family, who became known as Doña Marina, also known as La Malinche. With the assistance of Doña Marina and other native allies, Cortés marched his troops to Tenochtitlán. Upon entering, he gasped in wonder, "This city is so big and so remarkable [that it is] almost unbelievable." One of his soldiers wrote, "It was all so wonderful that I do not know how to describe this first glimpse of things never heard of, seen or dreamed of before."

How was this tiny force to overcome an empire of many millions with an elaborate warring tradition? Crucial to Spanish conquest was their alliance, negotiated through translators, with Moctezuma's enemies—especially the

Tlaxcalans. After decades of yearning for release from the Aztec yoke, the Tlaxcalans and other Mesoamerican peoples embraced Cortés's promise of help. The Spaniards' second advantage was their method of warfare. The Aztecs were seasoned fighters, but they fought to capture, not to kill. Nor were they familiar with gunpowder or sharp steel swords. Although outnumbered, the Spaniards killed their foes with abandon, using superior weaponry, horses, and war dogs. When Cortés arrived at Tenochtitlán, the Aztecs were still unsure who these strange men were and allowed Cortés to enter their city. With the aid of the Tlaxcalans and a handful of his own men, in 1519 Cortés captured Moctezuma, who became a puppet of the Spanish conqueror.

The Aztecs quickly changed their approach to fighting. When Spanish troops massacred an unarmed crowd in Tenochtitlán's central square while Cortés was away, they provoked a massive uprising. The Spaniards led Moctezuma to one of the palace walls to plead with his people for a truce, but the Aztecs kept up their barrage of stones, spears, and arrows—striking and killing Moctezuma. Cortés returned to reassert control; but realizing this was impossible, he gathered his loot and escaped. He left behind hundreds of Spaniards, many of whom were dragged up the temple steps and sacrificed by Aztec priests.

With the Tlaxcalans' help, Cortés regrouped. This time he bombarded Tenochtitlán with artillery, determined to defeat the Aztecs completely. Even more devastating was the spread of smallpox, brought by the Spanish, which ran through the Aztec soldiers and commoners like wildfire. In the end, starvation, disease, lack of artillery, and Cortés's ability to rally Amerindian allies to his side vanquished the Aztec forces. More died from disease than from fighting—the total number of Aztec casualties may have reached 240,000. As Spanish troops retook the capital, now in ruins, the Spaniards and their allies had to engage in house-to-house combat to secure control over Tenochtitlán. The Aztecs lamented their defeat in verse: "We have pounded our hands in despair against the adobe walls, for our inheritance, our city, is lost and dead." Cortés became governor of the new Spanish colony, renamed "New Spain." He promptly allocated *encomiendas* to his loyal followers and dispatched expeditions to conquer the more distant Mesoamerican provinces.

The Mexica experience taught the Spanish an important lesson: an effective conquest had to be swift—and it had to remove completely the symbols of legitimate authority. Their winning advantage, however, was disease. The Spaniards unintentionally introduced germs that made their subsequent efforts at military conquest much easier.

The Incas The other great Spanish conquest occurred in the Andes, where Quechua-speaking rulers, called Incas, had established an impressive state. Sometime around 1200, a band of Andean villagers settled into the valleys near what is now Cuzco, in Peru, which soon became the hub of South America's greatest empire. A combination of raiding neighbors and intermarrying into elite families raised the Incas to regional supremacy. Their power radiated along the valley routes that carved up the chain of great mountains until they finally ran up against the mighty warrior confederacy of the Chanca. After defeating the Chanca rivals around 1438, the Inca warrior Yupanqui renamed himself Pachacuti and began the royal line of Inca emperors. They eventually ruled a vast domain from what is now Chile to southern Colombia. At its center was the capital, Cuzco, with the magnificent fortress of Sacsayhuamán as its head. Built of huge boulders, the citadel was the nerve center of a complex network of strongholds that held the empire together.

As in most empires of the day, political power depended on a combination of tribute and commercial exchange to finance an extensive communication and military network. The empire developed an elaborate system of sending messages by runners who relayed up and down a system of stone highways carrying instructions to allies and roving armed divisions. None of this would have been possible without a wealthy agrarian base. Peasants paid tribute to village elders in the form of labor services to maintain public works, complex terraces, granaries, and food storage systems in case of drought or famine. In return, Inca rulers were obliged to shelter their people and allies in case of hardship. They oversaw rituals, festivals, and ceremonies to give spiritual legitimacy to their power. At their peak, the Incas may have governed a population of up to 6 million people. But as the empire stretched into distant provinces, especially into northern frontiers, ruling Incas lost touch with their base in Cuzco. Fissures began to open in the Andean empire as European germs and conquistadors appeared on South American shores.

When the Spaniards arrived in 1532, they found a divided empire, a situation they quickly learned to exploit. Francisco Pizarro, who led the Spanish campaign, had been inspired by Cortés's victory and yearned for his own glory. Commanding a force of about 600 men, he invited Atahualpa, the Inca ruler, to meet at the town of Cajamarca. There he laid a trap, intending to overpower the Incas and capture their ruler. As columns of Inca warriors and servants covered with colorful plumage and plates of silver and gold entered the main square, the Spanish soldiers were awed. One recalled, "many of us urinated without noticing it, out of sheer terror." But Pizarro's plan worked. His guns and horses shocked the Inca forces. Atahualpa himself fell into Spanish hands, later to be decapitated. Pizarro's conquistadors overran Cuzco in 1533 and then vanquished the rest of the Inca forces, a process that took decades in some areas.

The defeat of the New World's two great empires had enormous repercussions for world history. First, it set the Europeans on the road to controlling the human and material wealth of the Americas and opened a new frontier that the Europeans could colonize. Second, it gave Europeans a market for their own products—goods that found little favor in Afro-Eurasia. Now, following the Portuguese push into Africa and Asia (as well as a Russian push into northern Asia; see Chapter 13), the New World conquests introduced Europeans to a new scale of imperial expansion.

Core Objectives

ASSESS how European colonization of the Americas affected African and Amerindian peoples, and **DESCRIBE** their responses.

The Columbian Exchange The Spanish came to the Americas for gold and silver, but in the course of conquest and settlement they also learned about crops such as potatoes and corn. They brought with them horses, wheat, grapevines, and sugarcane, as well as devastating diseases. Historians call this transfer of previously unknown plants, animals, people, diseases, and products in the wake of Columbus's voyages the **Columbian exchange**. Over time, this exchange transformed environments, economies, and diets in both the new and the old worlds.

The first and most profound effect of the Columbian exchange was a destructive one: the decimation of the Amerindian population by European diseases. For millennia, the isolated populations of the Americas had been cut off from Afro-Eurasian microbe migrations. Africans, Europeans, and Asians had long interacted, sharing disease pools and gaining immunities; in this sense, in contrast, the Amerindians were indeed worlds apart. Sickness spread from almost the moment the Spaniards arrived. One Spanish soldier noted, upon entering the conquered Aztec capital, "The streets were so filled with dead and sick people that our men walked over nothing but bodies." As each wave of disease retreated, it left a population weaker than before, even less prepared for the next wave. The scale of death was unprecedented: imported pathogens wiped out up to 90 percent of the Indian population. A century after smallpox arrived on Hispaniola in 1519, no more than 5 to 10 percent of the island's population was alive. Diminished and weakened by disease, Amerindians could not resist European settlement and colonization of the Americas. Thus were Europeans the unintended beneficiaries of a horrifying catastrophe.

As time passed, all sides adopted new forms of agriculture from one another. After Amerindians taught Europeans how to grow potatoes and corn, the crops became staples all across Afro-Eurasia. The Chinese found that they could grow corn in areas too dry for rice and too wet for wheat, and in Africa corn gradually replaced sorghum, millet, and rice to become the continent's principal food crop by the twentieth century. (See Current Trends in World History: Corn and the Rise of Slave-Supplying Kingdoms in West Africa.) Europeans also took away tomatoes, beans, cacao, peanuts, tobacco, and squash, while importing livestock such as cattle, swine, and horses to the New World. The environmental effects of the introduction of livestock to the Americas were significant. For example, in regions of central Mexico where Native Americans had once cultivated maize and squash, Spanish settlers introduced large herds of sheep and cattle. Without natural

Columbian exchange Movements between Afro-Eurasia and the Americas of previously unknown plants, animals, people, diseases, and products that followed in the wake of Columbus's voyages.

predators, these animals reproduced with lightning speed, destroying entire landscapes with their hooves and their foraging.

As Europeans cleared trees and other vegetation for ranches, mines, or plantations, they undermined the habitats of many indigenous mammals and birds. On the islands of the West Indies, described by Columbus as "roses of the sea," the Spanish chopped down lush tropical and semitropical forests to make way for sugar plantations. Before long, nearly all of the islands' tall trees as well as many shrubs and ground plants were gone, and residents lamented the absence of birdsong. Over ensuing centuries, the plants and animals of the Americas took on an increasingly European appearance. At the same time, the interactions between Europeans and Native Americans would continue to shape societies on both sides of the Atlantic.

THE IBERIAN EMPIRES IN THE AMERICAS

The European presence in the New World went beyond the control of commercial outposts. Unlike in the Indian Ocean—where they had to contend with stable, powerful states—European colonizers in the Americas controlled large amounts of territory, and ultimately the entire landmass (see Map 12.2). Those Native Americans who survived the original encounters were harnessed as a means to siphon tribute payments to the new masters.

By fusing traditional tribute taking with their own innovations, Spanish masters made villagers across their new American empire deliver goods and services. But because the Spanish authorities also bestowed *encomiendas*, those favored individuals could demand labor from their lands' Indian inhabitants—for mines, estates, and public works. Whereas Aztec and Inca rulers had used conscripted labor to build up their public wealth, the Spaniards did so for private gain.

Spanish migrants and their descendants preferred towns to the countryside. With the exception of ports, the major cities of Spanish America were the former centers of Indian empires. Mexico City took shape on the ruins of Tenochtitlán; Cuzco arose from the razed Inca capital. In their architecture, economy, and family life, the Spanish colonies adopted as much as they transformed the worlds they encountered.

The next European power to seize land in the Americas, the Portuguese, were no less interested in immediate riches than the Spanish were. Disappointed by the absence of tributary systems and precious metals in the area they controlled, Brazil, they found instead abundant, fertile land, which they doled out with massive royal grants. These estate owners governed their plantations like feudal lords (see Chapter 10). Failing to find established cities, the Portuguese created enclaves along the coast and lived in more dispersed settlements than the Spanish settlers did.

Corn and the Rise of Slave-Supplying Kingdoms in West Africa

New World varieties of corn spread rapidly throughout the Afro-Eurasian landmass soon after the arrival of Columbus in the Americas. Its hardiness and fast-ripening qualities made it more desirable than many of the Old World grain products. In communities that consumed large quantities of meat, it became the main product fed to livestock.

Corn's impact on Africa was as substantial as it was on the rest of Afro-Eurasia. Seeds made their way to western regions more quickly than to the south of the Sahara along two routes. One was via European merchants calling into ports along the coast; the second was via West African Muslims returning across the Sahara after participating in the pilgrimage to Mecca. The first evidence of corn cultivation in sub-Saharan Africa comes from a Portuguese navigator who identified the crop being grown on the island of Cape Verde in 1540. By the early seventeenth century, corn was replacing millet and sorghum as the main grain

being grown in many West African regions and was destined to transform the work routines and diets of the peoples living in the region's tropical rain forests all the way from present-day Sierra Leone in the east to Nigeria in the west. In many ways this area, which saw the rise of a group of powerful slave-supplying kingdoms in the eighteenth century, notably Asante, Dahomey, Oyo, and Benin, owed its prosperity to the cultivation of this New World crop. (See Chapter 14 for a fuller discussion of these states.)

The tropical rain forests of West and central Africa were thick with trees and ground cover in 1500. Clearing them so that they could support intensive agriculture was exhausting work, requiring enormous outlays of human energy and man-hours. Corn, a crop first domesticated in central Mexico 7,000 years ago, made this task possible. It added much-needed carbohydrates to the carbon-deficient diets of rain-forest dwellers. In addition, as a crop that matured more quickly than those that

were indigenous to the region (millet, sorghum, and rice) and required less labor, it yielded two harvests in a single year. Farmers also cultivated cassava, another New World native, which in turn provided households with more carbohydrate calories. Yet corn did more than produce more food per unit of land and labor. Households put every part of the plant to use—grain, leaves, stalks, tassels, and roots were made to serve useful purposes.

Thus, at the very time that West African groups were moving southward into the rain forests, European navigators were arriving along the coast with new crops. Corn gave communities of cultivators the caloric energy to change their forest landscapes, expanding the arable areas. In a select few of these regions, enterprising clans emerged to dominate the political scene, creating centralized kingdoms like Asante in present-day Ghana, Dahomey in present-day Benin, and Oyo and Benin in present-day Nigeria. These

The problem was where to find labor to work the rich lands of Brazil. Because there was no centralized government to deal with the labor shortage, Portuguese settlers initially tried to enlist the dispersed native population; but when recruitment became increasingly coercive, Indians turned on the settlers. Some Indians fought; others fled to the vast interior. Reluctant to pursue the Indians inland, the Portuguese hugged their beachheads, extracting brazilwood (the source of a beautiful red dye) and sugar from their coastal enclaves.

Silver, Sugar, and Slaves The Iberian empires in the Americas concentrated on three commodities that would transform Europe's relationship

Corn Plantation This nineteenth-century engraving by famed Italian explorer Savorgnan de Brazza shows women of the West African tribe Bateke working in corn plantations. Brazza would later serve as the governor general of the French colony in the Congo.

elites transformed what had once been thinly settled environments into densely populated states, with elaborate bureaucracies, big cities, and large and powerful standing armies.

There was much irony in the rise of these states, which owed so much of their strength to the linking of the Americas with Afro-Eurasia. The armies that they created and the increased populations that the new crops allowed were part and parcel of the Atlantic slave trade. That which the Americas gave with one hand (new crops), it took back with the other in warfare, captives, and New World slavery.

Questions for Analysis

- What were the major effects of growing corn in West Africa?
- How did the growing of corn reshape the history of the Atlantic world during this period?

Explore Further

McCann, James, *Maize and Grace: Africa's Encounter with a New World Crop, 1500–2000* (2005).

to the rest of the world: silver, sugar, and slaves. Silver enabled Spain and Portugal to enter established trade networks in Asia. The slave trade was a big business in itself: it subsidized shipbuilding and new insurance schemes. Above all, the use of slave labor made sugar cultivation fantastically profitable, fueling economic growth and political instability around the world.

The first Europeans in the Americas hoarded vast quantities of gold and silver for themselves and their monarchs. But they also introduced precious metals into the world's commercial systems, which electrified them. In the twenty years after the fall of Tenochtitlán, conquistadors took more gold and

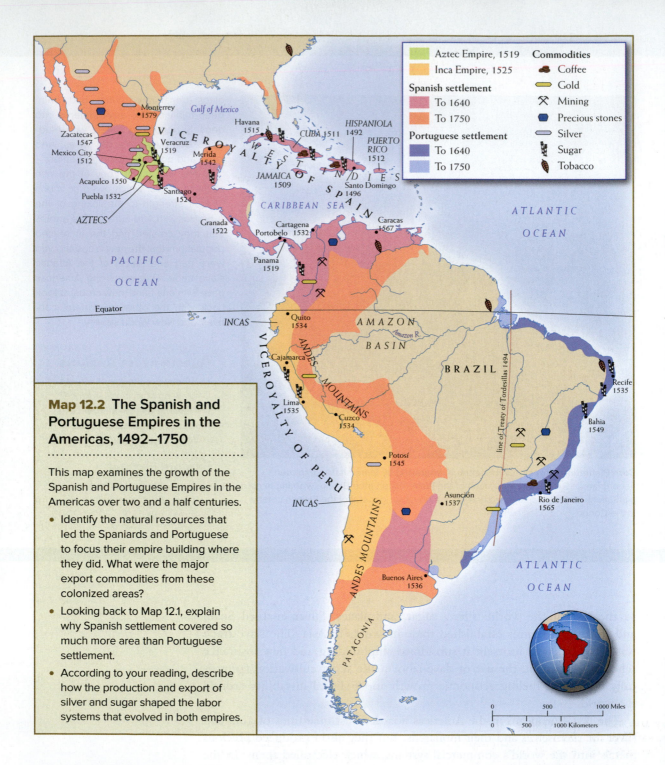

Map 12.2 The Spanish and Portuguese Empires in the Americas, 1492–1750

This map examines the growth of the Spanish and Portuguese Empires in the Americas over two and a half centuries.

- Identify the natural resources that led the Spaniards and Portuguese to focus their empire building where they did. What were the major export commodities from these colonized areas?

- Looking back to Map 12.1, explain why Spanish settlement covered so much more area than Portuguese settlement.

- According to your reading, describe how the production and export of silver and sugar shaped the labor systems that evolved in both empires.

Map legend:

Aztec Empire, 1519	
Inca Empire, 1525	
Spanish settlement	
To 1640	
To 1750	
Portuguese settlement	
To 1640	
To 1750	

Commodities
- Coffee
- Gold
- Mining
- Precious stones
- Silver
- Sugar
- Tobacco

Silver Silver was an important discovery for Spanish conquerors in Mesoamerica and the Andes. Conquerors expanded the customs of Inca and Aztec labor drafts to force Amerindians to work in mines, often in brutal conditions.

silver from Mexico and the Andes than all the gold accumulated by Europeans over the previous centuries.

Having looted Indian coffers, the Spanish entered the business of mining directly, opening the Andean Potosí mines in 1545. Between 1560 and 1685, Spanish America sent 25,000 to 35,000 tons of silver annually to Spain. From 1685 to 1810, this sum doubled. The two mother lodes were Potosí in present-day Bolivia and Zacatecas in northern Mexico. Silver brought bounty not only to the crown but also to a privileged group of families based in Spain's colonial capitals; thus, private wealth funded the formation of local aristocracies.

Colonial mines epitomized the Atlantic world's new economy. They relied on an extensive network of Amerindian labor, at first enslaved, subsequently drafted. Here again, the Spanish adopted Inca and Aztec practices of requiring labor from subjugated villages. Each year, under the *mita*, the local system for recruiting labor, village elders selected a stipulated number of men to toil in the shafts, refineries, and smelters. Under the Spanish, the digging, hauling, and smelting taxed human limits to their capacity—and beyond. Mortality rates were appalling. The system pumped so much silver into European commercial networks that it transformed Europe's relationship to all its trading partners, especially those in China and India. It also shook up trade and politics within Europe itself.

Along with silver, sugar emerged as the most valuable export from the Americas. It also was decisive in rearranging relations between peoples around the Atlantic. Cultivation of sugarcane had originated in India, spread to the Mediterranean region, and then reached the coastal islands of West Africa. The Portuguese, the Spanish, and other European settlers transported the

West African model to the Americas, first in the sixteenth century in Brazil, and then in the Caribbean. By the early seventeenth century, sugar had become a major export from the New World. Because Amerindians resisted recruitment and their numbers were greatly reduced by disease, European plantation owners began importing African slaves. By the eighteenth century, sugar production required continuous and enormous transfers of labor from Africa, and its value surpassed that of silver as an export from the Americas to Europe.

At first, most sugar plantations were fairly small, employing between 60 and 100 slaves. But they were efficient enough to create an alternative model of empire, one that resulted in more complete and dislocating control of the existing population. The slaves lived in wretched conditions: their barracks were miserable, and their diets were insufficient to keep them alive under backbreaking work routines. Moreover, these slaves were disproportionately men. As they rapidly died off, the only way to ensure replenishment was to import more Africans. This model of settlement relied on the transatlantic flow of slaves.

As European demand for sugar increased, the slave trade expanded. Although African slaves were imported into the Americas starting in the fifteenth century, the first direct voyage carrying them from Africa to the Americas occurred in 1525. From the time of Columbus until 1820, five times as many Africans as Europeans moved to the Americas: approximately 2 million Europeans (voluntarily) and 10 million Africans (involuntarily) crossed the Atlantic.

Well before European merchants arrived off its western coast, Africa had known long-distance slave trading. In fact, the overall number of Africans sold into captivity in the Muslim world exceeded that of the Atlantic slave trade. Moreover, Africans maintained slaves themselves. African slavery, like its American counterpart, was a response to labor scarcities. In many parts of Africa, however, slaves did not face permanent servitude. Instead, they were assimilated into families, gradually losing their servile status.

With the additional European demand for slaves to work New World plantations alongside the ongoing Muslim slave trade, pressure on the supply of African slaves intensified. Only a narrow band stretching down the spine of the African landmass, from present-day Uganda and the highlands of Kenya to Zambia and Zimbabwe, escaped the impact of African rulers engaged in the slave trade and Asian and European slave traders.

By the late sixteenth century, important pieces had fallen into place to create a new Atlantic world, one that could not have been imagined a century earlier. This was the three-cornered **Atlantic system**, with Africa supplying labor, the Americas land and minerals, and Europeans the technology and military power to hold the system together. In time, the wealth flows to Europe and the slave-based development of the Americas would alter the world balance of power.

The Transformation of Europe

Despite the flow of American silver into Spanish coffers, most European rulers and their subjects were focused on Europe, not the New World, in the sixteenth century. The period's frequent warfare centered on purely European concerns, above all on a religious split within the Roman Catholic Church, known as the Reformation. This conflict led to profound religious rifts among states and brought additional political rivalries to the continent.

Core Objectives

ANALYZE the social and political relationships, and **EXPLAIN** the sources of conflict within the Afro-Eurasian polities.

THE REFORMATION

Like the Renaissance, the **Protestant Reformation** in Europe began as a movement devoted to returning to ancient sources—in this case, to biblical scriptures. Yet returning to the sources and interpreting Christian doctrine for oneself was dangerous in the fourteenth and fifteenth centuries, for the church feared that challenges to its authority would arise if laypersons were allowed to read the scriptures as they pleased. The church was right: when Luther and his followers seized the right to read and interpret the Bible in a new way, they paved the way for a "Protestant" Reformation that split Christendom for good.

The opening challenge to the authority of the Catholic Church originated in Germany. Here a monk and a professor of theology, **Martin Luther** (1483–1546), used his knowledge of the Bible to criticize the church's ideas and practices. For Luther, God's gift of forgiveness did not depend on taking sacraments or performing good deeds. This faith was something Christians could obtain from reading the Bible—rather than by having a priest tell them what to believe. Finally, Luther concluded that Christians did not need specially appointed mediators to speak to God for them; all believers were equally bound by God's laws and obliged to minister to one another's spiritual needs.

These became the three main principles that launched Luther's reforming efforts: (1) belief that faith alone saves, (2) belief that the scriptures alone hold the key to Christian truth, and (3) belief in the priesthood of all believers. Luther also reacted against corrupt practices in the church, such as the keeping of mistresses by monks, priests, and even popes; and the selling of indulgences, certificates that would supposedly shorten the buyer's time in purgatory. In the 1510s, clerics were hawking indulgences across Europe in an effort to raise money for the sumptuous new Saint Peter's Basilica in Rome. In 1517, Luther formulated ninety-five statements, or theses, and posted them on the doors to the Wittenberg cathedral, hoping to stir up his colleagues in debate.

In response, Pope Leo X and the Habsburg emperor, Charles V, demanded that Luther take back his criticisms and theological claims. When he refused, he was declared a heretic and narrowly avoided being burned

Protestant Reformation
Religious movement initiated by sixteenth-century monk Martin Luther, who openly criticized the corruption in the Catholic Church and voiced his belief that Christians could speak directly to God. His doctrines gained wide support, and those who followed this new view of Christianity rejected the authority of the papacy and the Catholic clergy, broke away from the Catholic Church, and called themselves "Protestants."

Martin Luther
(1483–1546) A German monk and theologian who sought to reform the Catholic Church; he believed in salvation through faith alone, the importance of reading scripture, and the priesthood of all believers. His Ninety-Five Theses, which enumerated the abuses by the Catholic Church as well as his reforms, started the Protestant Reformation.

at the stake. Luther wrote many more pamphlets attacking the church and the pope, whom he now described as the anti-Christ. Luther also translated the New Testament from Latin into German so that laypersons could have direct access, without the clergy, to the word of God. This act spurred many other reformers across Europe to undertake translations of their own, and it encouraged the Protestant clergy to teach children (and adults) to read their local languages.

Spread by printed books and ardent preachers in all the common languages of Europe, Luther's doctrines and those put forward by other reformers won widespread support in some regions, particularly among urban populations. In France and Switzerland, the reformer **Jean Calvin** (1509–1564) emphasized moral regeneration through church teachings and laid out a doctrine of predestination—the notion that each person is "predestined for damnation or salvation even before birth." Those who followed the new faith of Luther and Calvin identified themselves as "Protestants." They promised that their reformed version of Christianity provided both an answer to individual spiritual needs and a new moral foundation for community life. The renewed Christian creed appealed to commoners as well as elites, especially in communities that resented rule by Catholic "outsiders." For example, Protestantism was popular among the Dutch, who resented being ruled by Philip II, an Austrian Catholic who lived in Spain. Although Protestants were rarely a majority before the seventeenth century, the new ideas gained a wide following in the German states, France, Switzerland, the Low Countries, England, and Scotland (see Map 12.3). Later, following the sociologist Max Weber (1864–1920), many European historians and economists, in their efforts to explain the origins of capitalism, would look back to these ideas—especially the emphasis on discipline, industriousness, and the individual's relation to God—as distinguishing Europeans from other peoples.

Counter-Reformation The Catholic Church responded to Luther and Calvin by embarking on its own renovation, which became known as the **Counter-Reformation**. At the Council of Trent, whose twenty-five sessions stretched from 1545 to 1563, Catholic leaders reaffirmed the church's doctrines. But the council also enacted reforms to answer the Protestants' assaults on clerical corruption. Like the Protestants, the reformed Catholics carried their message overseas—especially through an order established by a Spaniard, Ignatius Loyola (1491–1556). Loyola founded a brotherhood of priests, the Society of Jesus, or **Jesuits**, dedicated to the revival of the Catholic Church. From bases in Lisbon, Rome, Paris, and elsewhere in Europe, the Jesuits opened missions as far as South and North America, India, Japan, and China. The Reformation split European society deeply as both Catholics and Protestants vigorously promoted their faiths.

Map 12.3 Religious Divisions in Europe after the Reformation, 1590

The Protestant Reformation divided Europe religiously and politically.

- Within the formerly all-Catholic Holy Roman Empire, list the Protestant groups that took hold.
- Looking at the map, what geographic patterns can you identify in the distribution of Protestant communities?
- List the regions in which you would expect Protestant-Catholic tensions to be the most intense, and explain why.

RELIGIOUS WARFARE IN EUROPE

The religious revival led Europe into another round of ferocious wars. Their ultimate effect was to weaken the **Holy Roman Empire**—a loose confederation of principalities that were clustered mainly in central Europe and presided over in this period by the Habsburgs (see Chapter 11)—and strengthen the English, French, and Dutch. Already in the 1520s, the circulation of books presenting Luther's ideas sparked peasant revolts across central Europe. Some peasants, hoping that Luther's assault on the church's authority would help liberate them, rose up against repressive feudal landlords. In contrast to earlier wars in which one noble's retinue fought a rival's, the defense of the Catholic mass and the Protestant Bible brought crowds of simple folk to arms. Now wars between and within central European states raged for nearly forty years.

Religious conflicts weakened European dynasties. Spain, with its massive empire and its silver mines in the New World, spent much of its new fortune waging war in Europe. Most debilitating was its costly effort to subdue recently acquired Dutch territories. After a series of wars spanning nearly a hundred years, Catholic Spain finally conceded the Protestant Netherlands its independence. Wars took their toll on the Spanish Empire, which was soon wallowing in debts; not even the riches of its American silver mines could bail out the court. In the late 1550s, Philip II could not meet his obligations to creditors, and, within two decades, Spain was declared bankrupt three times. Its decline opened the way for the Dutch and the English to extend their trading networks into Asia and the New World, and the center of power within Europe shifted to the north.

Religious conflicts also sparked civil wars. In France, the divide between Catholics and Protestants exploded in the St. Bartholomew's Day Massacre of 1572. Catholic crowds rampaged through the streets of Paris murdering Huguenot (Protestant) men, women, and children and dumping their bodies into the Seine River. The number of dead reached 3,000 in Paris and 10,000 in provincial towns. Slaughter on this scale did not break the Huguenots' spirit, but it did bring more disrepute to the monarchy for failing to ensure peace. Another round of warfare exhausted the French and brought Henry of Navarre, a Protestant prince, to the throne. To become king, Henry IV converted to Catholicism. Shortly thereafter, he issued the Edict of Nantes, a proclamation that declared France a Catholic country but also tolerated some Protestant worship.

As princes sought to resolve religious questions within their domains, states increasingly became identified with one or another form of Christian faith—and, for Protestants, with a local language. (Protestants translated the Bible from Latin so that more people could read it.) In this way, religious strife propelled forward the process of state building and the forming of national identities. At the same time, religious conflict fueled rivalries for wealth and territory overseas. Thus, Europe entered its age of overseas exploration as a collection of increasingly powerful yet irreconcilably competitive rival states, whose differences stemmed not just from language but from the ways they worshipped the Christian God.

Prosperity in Asia

While Europe was experiencing religious warfare, Asian empires were expanding and consolidating their power, and trade was flourishing. If anything, the arrival of European sailors and traders in the Indian Ocean strengthened trading ties across the region and enhanced the political power and expansionist interests of Asia's imperial regimes. The Mughal ruler of India, Akbar, and the Ottoman sultan, Suleiman the Magnificent (see Chapter 11), were effective and esteemed rulers. The Ming dynasty's elegant manufactures enjoyed worldwide renown, and its ability to govern vast numbers of highly diverse peoples led outsiders to consider China the model imperial state.

Core Objectives

COMPARE the major features of world trade in Asia, the Americas, Africa, and Europe.

MUGHAL INDIA AND COMMERCE

The **Mughal Empire** became one of the world's wealthiest empires just when Europeans were establishing sustained connections with India. These connections, however, only touched the outer layer of Mughal India, one of Islam's greatest regimes. Established in 1526, it was a vigorous, centralized state whose political authority encompassed most of modern-day India. During the sixteenth century, it had a population of between 100 and 150 million.

The Mughals' strength rested on their military power. The dynasty's founder, Babur, had introduced horsemanship, artillery, and field cannons from central Asia, and gunpowder had secured his swift military victories over northern India. Under his grandson, Akbar (r. 1556–1605), the empire enjoyed expansion and consolidation that continued (under his own grandson, Aurangzeb) until it covered almost all of India (see Map 12.4). Known as the "Great Mughal," Akbar was skilled not only in military tactics but also in the art of alliance making. Deals with Hindu chieftains through favors and intermarriage also undergirded his empire.

Mughal rulers were flexible toward their realm's diverse peoples, especially in spiritual affairs. Though its primary commitment to Islam stood firm, the imperial court also patronized other beliefs, displaying a tolerance that earned it widespread legitimacy. The contrast with Europe, where religious differences drove deep fractures within and between states, was stark. Unlike European monarchs, who tried to enforce religious uniformity, Akbar studied comparative religion and hosted regular debates among Hindu, Muslim,

Mughal Empire
One of Islam's greatest regimes. Established in 1526, it was a vigorous, centralized state whose political authority encompassed most of modern-day India. During the sixteenth century, it had a population of between 100 and 150 million.

Map 12.4 Expansion of the Mughal Empire, 1556–1707

Under Akbar and Aurangzeb, the Mughal Empire expanded and dominated much of South Asia. Yet, by looking at the trading ports along the Indian coast, one can see the growing influence of Portuguese, Dutch, French, and English interests.

- Look at the dates for each port, and identify which traders came first and which came last.

- Compare this map with Map 12.2 (showing a period that begins earlier, 1492–1750). To what extent do the trading posts shown here reflect increased European influence in the region?

- According to your reading, explain how these European outposts affected Mughal policies.

Legend:
- Akbar's domain, 1556–1605
- Areas added by Aurangzeb, to 1707
- ■ Trading port

Commodities
- Cinnamon
- Coffee
- Cotton
- Diamonds
- Dyestuffs
- Gold
- Pepper
- Saltpetre
- Sugar

UZBEKS
AFGHANISTAN
SAFAVIDS
Kabul · Khyber Pass
KABUL
Lahore ·
THAR DESERT
Delhi ·
Agra ·
HIMALAYAS
BENGAL
Plassey
Dacca
Chandernagore 1673 (French)
Calcutta 1690 (British)
Hooghly 1537 (Portuguese) 1640 (Dutch) 1651 (British)
Ahmadabad 1612 (British)
Surat 1618–83 (British)
Diu 1535 (Portuguese)
Daman 1558 (Portuguese)
Bombay 1661 (British)
MARATHAS
BIDAR
Godavari R.
Masulipatam 1570 (Portuguese) 1605 (Dutch) 1611 (British)
ARABIAN SEA
Bay of Bengal
Goa 1510 (Portuguese)
Pulicat 1609 (Dutch)
Bhatkal 1637 (Dutch) 1638 (British)
Madras (Ft. St. George) 1639 (British)
São Thomé c. 1520 (Portuguese)
Tellicherry 1683 (British)
Pondicherry 1699 (French)
Nagappattinam 1658 (Dutch)
Calicut (Portuguese)
MALABAR COAST
Cochin 1503 (Portuguese) 1661 (Dutch)
Jaffna 1560 (Portuguese) 1658 (Dutch)
Quilan 1512 (Portuguese) 1661 (Dutch)
Negmobo 1640 (Dutch)
Trincomali 1639 (Dutch)
Colombo 1518 (Portuguese) 1640 (Dutch)
Galle 1518 (Portuguese) 1640 (Dutch)
CEYLON
INDIAN OCEAN

0   200   400 Miles
0   200   400 Kilometers

Jain, Parsi, and Christian theologians. His tolerance kept a multifaceted spiritual kingdom under one political roof.

During the sixteenth century, expanded trade with Europe brought more wealth to the Mughal polity, while the empire's strength limited European incursions. Although the Portuguese occupied Goa and Bombay on the Indian coast, they had little presence elsewhere and dared not antagonize the Mughal emperor. In 1578, Akbar recognized the credentials of a Portuguese ambassador and allowed a Jesuit missionary to enter his court. Thereafter, commercial ties between Mughals and Portuguese intensified, but the merchants were still restricted to a handful of ports. In the 1580s and 1590s, the Mughals ended the Portuguese monopoly on trade with Europe by allowing Dutch and English merchantmen to dock in Indian ports.

Centered in northern India, the Mughal Empire used surrounding regions' wealth and resources—military, architectural, and artistic—to glorify the court. Over time, the enhanced wealth caused friction between wealthy and poorer Indian regions, and even between merchants and rulers. Yet as long as merchants relied on rulers for their commercial gains, and as long as rulers balanced local and imperial interests, the realm maintained a formal unity and kept Europeans on its margins.

PROSPERITY IN MING CHINA

China also prospered from increased commerce in the late sixteenth century. Like the Mughals, the Ming seemed unconcerned with the increasing appearance of foreigners, including Europeans bearing silver. As in India, the Ming confined European traders to port cities. Silver from the Americas did, however, circulate widely in China. It allowed employers to pay their workers with money rather than with produce or goods, which in turn motivated those workers to produce more. China also experienced soaring production in agriculture and handicrafts. A cotton boom, for example, made spinning and weaving China's largest industry.

One measure of greater prosperity under the Ming was its population surge. By the mid-seventeenth century, China's population probably accounted for more than one-third of the total world population. Although 90 percent of Chinese people lived in the countryside, large numbers filled the cities. Beijing, the Ming capital, grew to over 1 million; Nanjing, the secondary capital, nearly matched that number. Cities offered diversions ranging from literary and theatrical societies to schools of learning, religious societies, urban associations, and manufactures from all over the empire. The elegance and material prosperity of Chinese cities dazzled European visitors. One Jesuit missionary described Nanjing as surpassing all other cities "in beauty and grandeur. . . . It is literally filled with palaces and temples and towers and bridges. . . . There is a gaiety of spirit among the people who are well mannered and nicely spoken."

Urban prosperity fostered entertainment districts where people could indulge themselves anonymously and in relative freedom. Some Ming women found a place here as refined entertainers and courtesans, others as midwives, poets, sorcerers, and matchmakers. Female painters, mostly from scholar-official families, emulated males who used the home and garden for creative pursuits. The expanding book trade also accommodated women, who were writers as well as readers, not to mention literary characters and archetypes (especially of Confucian virtues). But Chinese women made their greatest fortunes inside the emperor's Forbidden City as healers, consorts, and power brokers. The vitality that commerce brought to Ming society continued even after the dynasty's fall in 1644, laying the foundation for further population growth and territorial expansion.

ASIAN RELATIONS WITH EUROPE

Europeans' overseas expansion had originally looked toward Asia, and now the products from their New World colonies enabled them to realize some of those dreams. The Portuguese led the way, with Vasco da Gama's rounding of the Cape of Good Hope in 1497–1498. In 1557, their arrival at Macao, a port along the southern coast of China, enabled them to participate in China's expanding import-export trade. Within five years the number of Portuguese in Macao neared 1,000 (see Map 12.5).

Seeing how much the Portuguese were earning on Asian trade, the Spanish, English, and Dutch also ventured into Asian waters. With its monopoly on American silver, Spain enjoyed a competitive advantage. In 1565, the first Spanish trading galleon reached the Philippines; in 1571, after capturing Manila and making it a colonial capital, the Spanish established a brisk trade with China. Each year, ships from Spain's colonies in the Americas crossed the Pacific to Manila, bearing cargoes of silver. They returned carrying porcelain and silks for well-to-do European consumers. Merchants in Manila also procured silks, tapestries, and feathers from the China seas for shipment to the Americas, where the mining elite eagerly awaited these imports.

The year 1571 was altogether decisive in the history of the modern world. For the first time, Spanish ships were able to circle the globe from the New World to China and from China back to Europe. Silver was the commodity that linked the world commercially, the only foreign commodity for which the Chinese had an insatiable demand. From the mother lodes of the Andes and Mesoamerica, silver made the commerce of the world go round.

Other Europeans, too, wanted their share of Asia's wealth. The English and the Dutch reached the South China Sea by 1594. Five years later, 101 English investors pooled their funds and formed a joint-stock company (an association in which each member owned shares of capital) called the English East India Company. Soon this company won a royal charter

MONGOLS

Horses

Horses
Hide

Beijing

Tea

Tea

Horses

Yellow R.

MING CHINA

Cotton
Tea

Soya
Beans

KOREA

Swords
Copper
Gold
Silver
Hide

JAPAN

Sugar
Silk
Cannons
Coins
Ceramics
Paper

PACIFIC
OCEAN

Horses

Tea

Yangzi R.

Guangzhou

Macao

ANNAM

Spices
Gems
Ivory

Ceramics

Silver
Rice
Spices
Cotton (raw)
Swords
Timber
Medicinal herbs

TAIWAN

Sugar
Silk (raw)
Silk (cloth)
Cotton (cloth)
Cannons
Coins
Ceramics
Paper

PHILIPPINES

SOUTH
CHINA
SEA

MALAY

	Ming boundary, 1600
	Main area of ceramic production
	Main area of agricultural production
←	Main trade route
	Export
	Import
MONGOLS	People

0   250   500 Miles
0   250   500 Kilometers

Map 12.5 Trade and Production in Ming China

The Ming Empire in the early seventeenth century was the world's most populous state and arguably its wealthiest.

- According to this map, list the main items involved in China's export-import trade, and identify some of the regions that purchased its exports.
- Evaluate the relative importance of China's internal and overland trade, and contrast it with overseas commerce.
- Evaluate the balance between raw materials, agricultural products, and manufactured goods.

Macao This Chinese painting depicts the Portuguese enclave of Macao on the southern border of China around 1800. The Portuguese first arrived in the Indian Ocean in the early sixteenth century and took control of Macao in 1557. Chinese and Portuguese merchants settled there, and it soon became a vital hub of overseas trading. Macau's golden age coincided with the union of the Spanish and Portuguese crowns between 1580 and 1640.

granting it exclusive rights to import East Indian goods. The company displaced the Portuguese in the Arabian Sea and the Persian Gulf. Doing a brisk trade in indigo, saltpeter, pepper, and cotton textiles, the English East India Company eventually acquired control of ports on both coasts of India—Fort St. George at the coastal city of Madras (1639), Bombay (1661), and Calcutta (1690).

The Europeans' arrival in the South China Sea and the Indian Ocean hardly spelled the beginning of the end of Asian autonomy. Confined to the coasts and a limited number of trading posts, the Europeans forged very weak connections to the ruling elites of Asian societies. For the moment, the Europeans' increased presence enhanced the wealth and might of Asian dynasties.

Conclusion

In the multicentered world of the fifteenth century, Europe was a poor cousin. However, a new spirit of adventure and achievement animated its peoples, stirred up by the rediscovery of antiquity (the Renaissance), the ambitions of merchants and other elites, and the spiritual fervor of the Reformation and Counter-Reformation. Desiring Asian luxury goods, European merchants and mariners were eager to exploit trade routes leading eastward, and new navigational techniques enabled them to sail into dangerous waters. More important, Europe's location promoted expansion across the largely unknown Atlantic Ocean. With the Ottomans controlling Constantinople and the eastern Mediterranean, Atlantic sea-lanes offered an alternative route to Asia. As Europeans searched for routes around Islamic territory, they first sailed down the coast of Africa and then across the Atlantic.

Encountering the "New World" was an accident of monumental significance. In the Americas, Europeans found riches. Mountains of silver and rivers of gold gave them the currency they needed for dealing with Asian traders. Europeans also found opportunities for exchange, conquest, and colonization. Yet, establishing these transatlantic empires heightened tensions within Europe, as rivals fought over the spoils and a religious schism turned into a divisive political and spiritual struggle.

Thus, two conquests characterize this age of increasing world interconnections. The Islamic conquest of Constantinople drove Europeans to find new links to Asia. In turn, the Spanish conquest of the Aztecs and the Incas gave Europeans access to silver, which bought them an increased presence in Asian trading networks.

Amerindians also played an important role, as Europeans sought to conquer their lands, exploit their labor, and confiscate their gold and silver. Sometimes Amerindians worked with Europeans, sometimes under Europeans, sometimes against Europeans—and sometimes none were left to work at all. Then Europeans brought in African laborers, compounding the calamity of the encounter with the tragedy of slavery. Out of the catastrophe of contact, a new oceanic system arose to link Africa, America, and Europe. This was the Atlantic system. Unlike the Indian Ocean and China seas, which supported a system of tributary and trading orders, the Atlantic Ocean supported a system of formal imperial control and settlement of distant colonies. These would become more important to how worlds connected and collided in the following centuries.

Focus On
Regional Developments in the Age of Exploration

Europe

- Portugal creates a trading empire in the Indian Ocean and the South China Sea.
- Spain and Portugal establish colonies in the Americas, discover silver, and establish export-oriented plantation economies.
- The Protestant Reformation breaks out in northern and western Europe, splitting the Catholic Church.

The Americas

- Millions of Amerindians, lacking immunity to European diseases, perish in every region of the New World.

- Spanish conquest and disease destroy the two great Native American empires in Mexico (the Aztecs) and Peru (the Incas).

Africa

- Trade in African captives fuels the Atlantic slave trade, which furnishes labor for European plantations in the Americas.

Asia

- Asian empires—the Mughals in India, the Ming in China, and the Ottomans in western Asia and the eastern Mediterranean—barely notice the Americas but profit economically from enhanced global trade.

Key Terms

Atlantic system p. 568

Aztec Empire p. 557

Jean Calvin p. 570

Columbian exchange p. 562

conquistadors p. 556

Counter-Reformation p. 570

encomenderos p. 557

Holy Roman Empire p. 572

Inca Empire p. 557

Jesuits p. 570

Martin Luther p. 569

Mughal Empire p. 573

Protestant Reformation p. 569

CHRONOLOGY

1500

Europe	Luther begins Protestant Reformation 1517
The Americas	Columbus discovers the "New World" 1492
	Cortés conquers Aztec Empire 1521
	Pizarro conquers Inca Empire 1533
South Asia	Da Gama sails to India 1498
	Portuguese establish bases around Indian Ocean 1508–1511
East Asia	

- **Thinking about Exchange Networks and the Age of Exploration** In the fifteenth and sixteenth centuries, the densest trade networks and most powerful states remained centered in Asia. How did Columbus's "discovery" of the New World alter the terms on which peoples across Afro-Eurasia interacted with one another? What commodities and trade networks brought peoples together, and on what terms? What new inequalities did those contacts create around the world?

- **Thinking about Changing Power Relationships and the Age of Exploration** The effort to expand empires and trading networks differed substantially across Afro-Eurasia and the Americas in the fifteenth and

sixteenth centuries. How did men and women at all levels of society contribute to this expansion? How did that participation shape or reshape their societies? Pay particular attention to the relationship between lower classes and elites.

- **Thinking about Environmental Impacts and the Age of Exploration** The Columbian exchange led to demographic catastrophe and environmental transformation in the New World. Why did the indigenous populations of the Americas get sick so much more often than Europeans did? Why did the plants and animals of the New World increasingly come to resemble those of Afro-Eurasia?

Go to **INQUIZITIVE** to see what you've learned—and learn what you've missed—with personalized feedback along the way.

1600

Religious and dynastic wars 1520s–1570s

Expansion and consolidation of Mughal Empire 1556–1605

Portuguese establish trading port in Macao 1557

Spanish make Manila their major port in the Pacific Ocean 1571

Global Themes and Sources

Cultural Contexts in the Age of Exploration

Overseas exploration and commerce brought new contacts between Amerindians, Europeans, Africans, and Asians in the fifteenth and sixteenth centuries. The primary sources brought together here document important examples of cultural contact in this era and allow us to see how people from radically different cultures perceived one another. They also provide clues about conflict within each of the communities.

The first two documents present opposing views of the initial confrontation between the Spaniards, led by Hernán Cortés (1485–1547), and the Mexica. The third document, a selection from *The History and Description of Africa* by Leo Africanus (al-Ḥasan ibn Muḥammad al-Wazzān al-Zayyātī or al-Fāsī, born c. 1485, died c. 1554), recounts the author's travels in Egypt, Morocco, and Mali, especially Timbuktu (Tombuto), a great center of Islamic learning. The final document, from a Ming official named He Ao, complains that Europeans were untrustworthy. Such sentiments were also common among officials in subsequent centuries, even as China thrived in the commercial exchanges of an increasingly connected world.

Making sense of these sources requires careful attention to context. It's important to note how the prior experiences of the different communities shaped their responses to alien cultures, and how prior exposure to outsiders influenced the ways communities marked the boundaries between "us" and "them." You should pay just as much attention to divisions within each cultural group as to those between the groups.

Analyzing Contexts: The Age of Exploration

- How did prior experiences of different cultures shape the encounters in these sources?

- All of these documents were produced by elite men. How do you think the authors' gender and status influenced their portrayal of events?

How did the authors' gender and status shape their attribution of responsibility for the problems they identified within their societies?

- Compare Cortés's description of Tenochtitlán in his letter to Charles V with Leo Africanus's description of Timbuktu.

PRIMARY SOURCE 12.1

Mexica Views of the Spaniards (c. sixteenth century), Florentine Codex

The Florentine Codex compiled accounts of the Spanish conquest from Mexica elites a generation after the fall of Tenochtitlán. The passages about Moctezuma's response to the Spaniards are drawn largely from interviews with elites from Tenochtitlán's junior partner, the city-state of Tlatelolco, in the aftermath of the Mexica defeat.

- **What about the Spaniards most struck the authors of the Florentine Codex? Identify the factors— appearance, animals, behavior, beliefs—they used to mark the Spaniards as different.**

- **Explain why the Mexica elite (of the 1550s–1560s) might have portrayed Moctezuma as afraid. Pay special attention to local politics before the Spaniards arrived.**

- **Evaluate the claim that Moctezuma believed the Spaniards to be gods. Is it plausible?**

During this time Montezuma neither slept nor touched food. Whatever he did, he was abstracted; it seemed as though he was ill at ease, frequently sighing. He tired and felt weak. He no longer found anything tasteful, enjoyable, or amusing.

Therefore he said, "What is to come of us? Who in the world must endure it? Will it not be me [as ruler]?

My heart is tormented, as though chile water were poured on it; it greatly burns and smarts. Where in the world [are we to turn], o our lord?"

Then [the messengers] notified those who guarded [Montezuma], who kept watch at the head of his bed, saying to them, "Even if he is asleep, tell him. 'Those whom you sent out on the sea have come back.'"

But when they went to tell him, he replied, "I will not hear it here. I will hear it at the Coacalco; let them go there." And he gave orders, saying, "Let some captives be covered with chalk [for sacrifice]."

Then the messengers went to the Coacalco, and so did Montezuma. Thereupon the captives died in their presence; they cut open their chests and sprinkled blood on the messengers. (The reason they did it was that they had gone to very dangerous places and had seen, gazed on the countenances of, and spoken to the gods.)

Seventh chapter, where is told the account that the messengers who went to see the boat gave to Montezuma.

When this was done, they talked to Montezuma, telling him what they had beheld, and they showed him what [the Spaniards'] food was like.

And when he heard what the messengers reported he was greatly afraid and taken aback, and he was amazed at their food. It especially made him faint when he heard how the guns went off at [the Spaniards'] command, sounding like thunder, causing people actually to swoon, blocking the ears. And when it went off, something like a ball came out from inside, and fire went showering and spitting out. And the smoke that came from it had a very foul stench, striking one in the face. And if they shot at a hill, it seemed to crumble and come apart. And it turned a tree to dust; it seemed to make it vanish, as though someone had conjured it away. Their war gear was all iron. They clothed their bodies in iron, they put iron on their heads, their swords were iron, their bows were iron, and their shields and lances were iron.

And their deer that carried them were as tall as the roof. And they wrapped their bodies all over; only their faces could be seen, very white. Their faces were the color of limestone and their hair yellow-reddish, though some had black hair. They had long beards, also yellow-reddish. [The hair of some] was tightly curled. And their food was like fasting food, very large, white, not heavy, like chaff, like dried maize stalks, as tasty as maize stalk flour, a bit sweet or honeyed, honeyed and sweet to eat.

And their dogs were huge creatures, with their ears folded over and their jowls dragging. They had burning eyes, eyes like coals, yellow and fiery. They had thin, gaunt flanks with the rib lines showing; they were very tall. They did not keep quiet, they went about panting, with their tongues hanging down. They had spots like a jaguar's, they were vari-colored.

When Montezuma heard it, he was greatly afraid; he seemed to faint away, he grew concerned and disturbed.

Eighth chapter, where it is said how Montezuma sent witches, wizards, and sorcerers to do something to the Spaniards.

Then at that time Montezuma sent out emissaries. Those whom he sent were all bad people, soothsayers and witches. He also sent elders, strong warriors, to see to all [the Spaniards] needed as to food: turkey hens, eggs, white tortillas, and whatever they might request, and to look after them well so that they would be satisfied in every way. He sent captives in case [the Spaniards] should drink their blood. And the emissaries did as indicated.

Montezuma did this because he took them for gods, considered them gods, worshiped them as gods. They were called and given the name of gods who have come from heaven, and the blacks were called soiled gods.

They say that Montezuma sent the witches, the rainmakers, to see what [the Spaniards] were like and perhaps be able to enchant them, cast spells on them, to use conjury or the evil eye on them or hurl something else at them, perhaps addressing some words of wizardry to them so that they would take sick, die, or turn back. But when they performed the assignment they had been given concerning the Spaniards, they could do nothing; they had no power at all. Then they quickly returned to tell Montezuma what they were like, how strong they were, [saying,] "We are not their match; we are as nothing."

Source: The Florentine Codex, translated by James Lockhart, in *Victors and Vanquished: Spanish and Nahua Views of the Conquest of Mexico*, edited by Stuart B. Schwartz (Boston: Bedford/St. Martin's, 2000), pp. 96–98.

Approaching Tenochtitlán (1520), Hernán Cortés

Written in the midst of the Spanish invasion of Mexico, Cortés's Second Letter was addressed to Emperor Charles V of Spain. In it, Cortés provides an account of his meeting with Moctezuma. He also describes the capital city of Tenochtitlán and its houses of worship.

- Explain how Tenochtitlán compares to Spanish cities, in Cortés's view.

- Why does Cortés mention mosques in Tenochtitlán when there were no Muslims there?

- Analyze the relationship between respect and contempt in this source. What does Cortés admire about the Mexica, and what does he dismiss?

This great city of Tenochtitlan is built on the salt lake, and from the mainland to the city is a distance of two leagues, from any side from which you enter. It has four approaches by means of artificial causeways, two cavalry lances in width. The city is as large as Seville or Cordoba. Its streets (I speak of the principal ones) are very broad and straight, some of these, and all the others, are one half land, and the other half water on which they go about in canoes. All the streets have openings at regular intervals, to let the water flow from one to the other, and at all of these openings, some of which are very broad, there are bridges, very large, strong, and well constructed, so that, over many, ten horsemen can ride abreast. Perceiving that, if the inhabitants wished to practise any treachery against us, they had plenty of opportunity, because the said city being built as I have described, they might, by raising the bridges at the exits and entrances, starve us without our being able to reach land, as soon as I entered the city, I made great haste to build four brigantines, which I had completed in a short time, capable whenever we might wish, of taking three hundred men and the horses to land.

The city has many squares where markets are held and trading is carried on. There is one square, twice as large as that of Salamanca, all surrounded by arcades, where there are daily more than sixty thousand souls, buying and selling, and where are found all the kinds of merchandise produced in these countries, including food products, jewels of gold and silver, lead, brass, copper, zinc, stone, bones, shells, and feathers. Stones are sold, hewn and unhewn, adobe bricks, wood, both in the rough and manufactured in various ways. There is a street for game, where they sell every sort of bird, such as chickens, partridges, quails, wild ducks, fly-catchers, widgeons, turtle-doves, pigeons, reed-birds, parrots, owls, eaglets, owlets, falcons, sparrow-hawks and kestrels, and they sell the skins of some of these birds of prey with their feathers, heads, beaks, and claws. They sell rabbits, hares, and small dogs which they castrate, and raise for the purpose of eating.

***

This great city contains many mosques, or houses for idols, very beautiful edifices situated in the different precincts of it; in the principal ones of The Aztec which are the religious orders of their sect. Priests for whom, besides the houses in which they keep their idols, there are very good habitations provided. All these priests dress in black, and never cut or comb their hair from the time they enter the religious order until they leave it; and the sons of all the principal families, both of chiefs as well as noble citizens, are in these religious orders and habits from the age of seven or eight years till they are taken away for the purpose of marriage. This happens more frequently with the first-born, who inherit the property, than with the others. They have no access to women, nor are any allowed to enter the religious houses; they abstain from eating certain dishes, and more so at certain times of the year than at others.

Amongst these mosques, there is one principal one, and no human tongue is able to describe its greatness and details, because it is so large that within its circuit, which is surrounded by a high wall, a village of five hundred houses could easily be built. Within, and all around it, are very handsome buildings, in which there are large rooms and galleries, where the religious who live there are lodged. There are as many as forty very high and well-built towers, the largest having fifty steps to reach the top; the principal one is higher than the tower of the chief church in Seville. They are so well built, both in their masonry, and their wood work, that they could not be better made nor constructed anywhere; for all the masonry inside the chapels, where they keep their idols, is carved with figures, and the wood work is all wrought with designs of monsters, and other shapes. All these towers are places of burial for the chiefs, and each one of their chapels is dedicated to the idol to which they have a particular devotion. Within this great mosque, there are three halls wherein stand the principal idols of marvelous grandeur in size, and much decorated with carved figures, both of stone and wood; and within these halls there are other chapels, entered by very small doors, and which have no light, and nobody but the religious are admitted to them. Within these are the images and figures of the idols, although, as I have said, there are many outside.

The principal idols in which they have the most faith and belief I overturned from their seats, and rolled down the stairs, and I had those chapels, where they kept them, cleansed, for they were full of blood from the sacrifices; and I set up images of Our Lady, and other Saints in them, which grieved Montezuma, and the natives not a little. At first they told me not to do it, for, if it became known throughout the town, the people would rise against me, as they believed that these idols gave them all their temporal goods, and, in allowing them to be ill-treated, they would be angered, and give nothing, and would take away all the fruits of the soil, and cause the people to die of want. I made them understand by the interpreters how deceived they were in putting their hope in idols, made of unclean things by their own hands, and I told them that they should know there was but one God, the Universal Lord of all, who had created the heavens, and earth, and all things else, and them, and us, who was without beginning, and immortal; that they should adore, and believe in Him, and not in any creature, or thing.

Source: *Letters of Cortes*, translated and edited by Francis Augustus MacNutt (New York: G. P. Putnam's Sons, 1908), vol. 1, pp. 256–57, 259–61.

Leo Africanus's Travels in Africa (1550)

Published in Italian in 1550, *The History and Description of Africa* was the first European account of the geography of Africa. The author, Leo Africanus,
was a Berber, born in Spanish Grenada. His family moved to Morocco when he was a young child, and he later served as a diplomat. (Archaic spelling from the original translation has been preserved.)

- Leo describes the people of Egypt as savages. Explain how he uses the term.
- Explain how Leo divides up the peoples of Africa he encounters. What groups does he describe? How does he distinguish them?
- Does this document reveal more about Europe or Africa?

Wherein he intreateth of the land of Negros, and of the confines of Egypt.

Our ancient Chroniclers of Africa, to wit, *Bichri* and *Meshudi* knew nothing of the land of Negros but onely the regions of Guechet and Cano: for in their time all other places of the land of Negros were vndiscouered. But in the yeere of the Hegeira 380, by the meanes of a certaine Mahumetan which came into Barbarie, the residue of the said land was found out, being as then inhabited by great numbers of people, which liued a brutish and sauage life, without any king, gouernour, common wealth, or knowledge of husbandrie. Clad they were in skins of beasts, neither had they any peculiar wiues: in the day time they kept their cattell; and when night came they resorted ten or twelue both men and women into one cottage together, using hairie skins instead of beds, and each man choosing his leman which he had most fancy vnto. Warre they wage against no other nation, ne yet are desirous to trauell out of their owne countrie. Some of them performe great adoration vnto the sunne rising: others, namely the people of Gualata, worship the fire: and some others, to wit, the inhabitants of Gaoga, approch (after the Egyptians manner) neerervnto the Christian faith. These Negros were first subject vnto king *Ioseph* the founder of Maroco, and afterward vnto the fiue nations of Libya; of whom they learned the Mahumetan lawe, and diuers needfull handycrafts: a while after when the merchants of Barbarie began to resort vnto them with merchandize, they learned the Barbarian language also. But the foresaid fiue people or nations of Libya diuided this land so among themselues, that euery third part of each nation possessed one region. Howbeit the king of Tombuto that now raigneth, called *Abuacre Izchia*, is a Negro by birth: this *Abuacre* after the decease of the former king, who was a Libyan borne, slue all his sonnes, and so vsurped the kingdome. And hauing by warres for the space of fifteen yeeres conquered many large dominions, he then concluded a league with all nations, and went on pilgrimage to Mecca, in which iournie he so consumed his treasure, that he was constrained to borrow great summes of money of other princes. Moreouer the fifteene kingdomes of Negros knowen to vs, are all situate vpon the riuer of Niger, and vpon other riuers which fall thereinto. And all the land of Negros standeth betweene two vast deserts, for on the one side lieth the maine desert betweene Numidia and it, which extendeth it selfe vnto this very land: and the south side thereof adioineth vpon another desert, which stretcheth from thence to the maine Ocean: in which desert are infinite nations vnknowen to vs, both by reason of the huge distance of place, and also in regarde of the diuersitie of languages and religions. They haue no traffique at all with our people, but we haue heard oftentimes of their traffique with the inhabitants of the Ocean sea shore.

A description of the kingdome of Gualata.

This region in regarde of others is very small: for it containeth onely three great villages, with certaine granges and fields of dates. From Nun it is distant southward about three hundred, from Tombuto northward fiue hundred, and from the Ocean sea about two hundred miles. In this region the people of Libya, while they were lords of the land of Negros, ordained their chiefe princely seate: and then great store of Barbarie-merchants frequented Gualata: but afterward in the raigne of the mighty and rich prince *Heli*, the said merchants leauing Gualata, began to resort vnto Tombuto and Gago, which was the occasion that the region of Gualata grew extreme beggerly. The language of this region is called Sungai, and the inhabitants are blacke people, and most friendly vnto strangers. In my time this region was conquered by the king of Tombuto, and the prince thereof fled into the deserts, whereof the king of Tombuto hauing intelligence, and fearing least the prince would returne with all the people of the deserts, graunted

him peace, conditionally that he should pay a great yeerely tribute vnto him, and so the said prince hath remained tributarie to the king of Tombuto vntill this present. The people agree in manners and fashions with the inhabitants of the next desert. Here groweth some quantitie of Mil-seed, and great store of a round & white kind of pulse, the like whereof I neuer saw in Europe; but flesh is extreme scarce among them. Both the men & the women do so couer their heads, that al their countenance is almost hidden. Here is no forme of a common wealth, nor yet any gouernours or iudges, but the people lead a most miserable life.

Source: Leo Africanus, *The History and Description of Africa and of the Notable Things Therein Contained*, edited by Robert Brown (London: Printed for the Hakluyt Society, Lincoln's Inn Fields W.C., 1896), pp. 819–21.

Commentary on Foreigners (c. 1420), Ming Official He Ao

He Ao was a censor, a high official in the provincial bureaucracy of the Ming Empire. The censorate was part of the central state. Responsible directly to the emperor, it was tasked with rooting out corruption at the local level. This document, in which He describes the threats posed by Europeans (called Feringis), is an official government report to his superiors.

- Identify the factors He used to mark foreigners as different, and evaluate their relative significance. Pay special attention to his language and the terms he used.

- What specific threats resulting from European influence does He identify, and what remedies does he propose?

- Explain the distinction this document draws between the way trade was conducted in the past, in the "time of our ancestors," and in the present. What is He's view of commerce?

The Feringis are most cruel and crafty. Their arms are superior to those of other foreigners. Some years ago they came suddenly to the city of Canton, and the noise of their cannon shook the earth [these were cannon-shots fired as a salute by the fleet of Fernão Peres]. Those who remained at the post-station [places where foreigners were lodged] disobeyed the law and had intercourse with others. Those who came to the Capital were proud and struggled [among themselves?] to become head. Now if we allow them to come and go and to carry on their trade, it will inevitably lead to fighting and bloodshed, and the misfortune of our South may be boundless.

In the time of our ancestors, foreigners came to bring tribute only at fixed periods, and the law provided for precautionary measures, therefore the foreigners who could come were not many. But some time ago the Provincial Treasurer, Wu T'ing-chü, saying that he needed spice to be sent to the Court, took some of their goods no matter when they came.

It was due to what he did that foreigner ships have never ceased visiting our shores and that barbarians have lived scattered in our departmental cities. Prohibition and precaution having been neglected, the Feringis became more and more familiar with our fair ways. And thus availing themselves of the situation the Feringis came into our port. I pray that all the foreign junks in our bay and the foreigners who secretly live (in our territory) be driven away, that private intercourse be prohibited and that our strategical defence be close, so that that part of our country will have peace.

Source: T'ien-Tse Chang, *Sino-Portuguese Trade from 1514 to 1644: A Synthesis of Portuguese and Chinese Sources* (Leyden: E. J. Brill, 1934), pp. 51–52.

Interpreting Visual Evidence

Conflict and Consent

In the fifteen and sixteenth centuries, new contacts led to conflict and, in some cases, consent. The consolidation of existing land empires, especially in Asia, required rulers to manage vast, diverse populations. They often used policies of tolerance to win the consent of their new subjects. European overseas empires, by contrast, almost immediately came into conflict with indigenous societies, decimating the Amerindian population and drafting African slaves to perform labor the remaining Amerindians refused. This resulted in societies in the Americas that initially had extremely pronounced cultural differences.

Depictions of these encounters show the dynamics between the groups involved, as well as the artist's point of view. The first image below, an anonymous Mexican painting (c. 1520), portrays Spanish soldiers in gleaming body armor with muskets firing on Amerindians, who are barely visible at the painting's edges and armed only with bows and arrows. The second, *The Conquest of the Aztecs*, was drawn by a converted Amerindian later in the sixteenth century and relied on indigenous oral histories and familiar artistic forms. It shows the Aztec (Mexica) warriors in full battle dress and also portrays their battles with other Amerindians who had sided with the Spanish. In the final image, *Akbar Hears a Petition*, the individuals gathered before Akbar represent the diversity of people who sought the assistance of the Mughal emperor. This miniature reflects the multiethnic and multireligious character of Akbar's empire and the tolerance required to maintain social cohesion.

Anonymous Mexican painting of the Spanish conquest.

The Conquest of the Aztecs, drawn by a converted Amerindian.

Akbar Hears a Petition.

Questions for Analysis

1. In the first two images, note the divisions within each camp, Spanish and Aztec. Explain how each portrays the Aztec defeat. What do the images present to explain the defeat, and what factors, emphasized in this chapter, do they both omit?

2. Interpret the artist's portrayal of Akbar's authority in the third image. Describe the audience presented in the painting. What can you tell about the different groups present?

3. Contrast the first two images with the third. Pay special attention to the center of each image. Describe which elements the artists emphasize, in visual terms. What does that say about the social order?

4. Explain who you think was the audience for each image. Were all three produced for rulers, their court, the elite in general, a particular ethno-religious or social group, or the general public?

13

Worlds Entangled

1600–1750

The leading Ottoman intellectual of the sixteenth century, Mustafa Ali, was a gloomy man, convinced that the Ottoman Empire had slipped into an irreversible decline. When he published his magnum opus, *The Essence of History* (1591), the empire's fortunes looked grim. The first half of the century had witnessed the conquest of Egypt and the reign of Suleiman the Magnificent and the Lawgiver, arguably the most successful of sultans. But by century's end, the Ottomans had lost territory to their main European adversaries; military rioting had occurred in protest against payments in debased silver coinage; and uprisings against the empire were widespread in eastern Anatolia.

Historians now know that many of these problems stemmed from a cold spell that descended on the entire world, which has come to be called the Little Ice Age. Historians have seen the seventeenth century as the most intense phase of a decline in global temperatures that spanned the adjoining centuries. Declining temperatures laid waste to agricultural and pastoral lands, spreading hunger and famines worldwide. As global empires ramped up their competition, they squeezed their peasants for resources to pay for warfare when they could least afford to contribute. A wave of suffering, peasant unrest, and political upheaval swept across Afro-Eurasia.

In spite of the turmoil, the period 1600–1750 saw the world's oceans give way to booming sea-lanes for global trading networks. Europeans conquered and colonized more of the Americas, the demand for African slaves to work New World

Core Objectives

- **DESCRIBE** and **EXPLAIN** the impact of climate change on societies are economies across the globe.

- **IDENTIFY** and **EXPLAIN** the major steps in the integration of global trade networks in the seventeenth and eighteenth centuries, and **ANALYZE** examples of resistance to this integration.

- **ANALYZE** the consequences of the Atlantic slave trade across the Atlantic world.

- **EXPLAIN** the effects of New World silver and increased trade on the Asian empires, and their response to them.

- **COMPARE** the impact of trade and religion on state power in various regions.

- **EXPLAIN** the significance of European consumption of goods (like tobacco, textiles, and sugar) for the global economy.

plantations leaped upward, and global trade intensified, fueled by New World silver. In the Americas, Spain and Portugal faced new competitors—primarily England and France. With religious tensions added to the mix, the stage was set for decades of bloody warfare in Europe and the Americas. At the same time, in the East, rulers in India, China, and Japan enlarged their empires, while Russia's tsars incorporated Siberian territories into their domain. Meanwhile, the Ottoman, Safavid, and Mughal dynasties, though resisting most European intrusions, found their stability profoundly shaken by climate change and global commerce.

Global Storylines

- Transoceanic trade networks (on an unprecedented scale) create vast wealth and new kinds of inequality.

- Silver gives Europeans a commodity to exchange with Asians and begins to tilt the balance of wealth and power from Asia toward Europe.

- New World sugar also accelerates the shift of power in the Atlantic world from the Spanish and Portuguese to the British and French.

- European merchants and African leaders radically increase the volume and violence of the slave trade, destabilizing African societies.

- Asian rulers in India, China, and Japan and Russian tsars enlarge their empires.

- The Ottoman, Safavid, and Mughal dynasties all struggle to resist European assaults.

Global Commerce and Climate Change

In spite of the worldwide trauma brought on by the plunge in temperatures, global trade flourished during this period. Increasing economic ties brought new places and products into world markets. (See Current Trends in World History: Stimulants, Sociability, and Coffeehouses.) Closer economic contact enhanced the power of certain states and destabilized others. It bolstered the legitimacy of England and France, and it prompted strong local support of new rulers in Japan and parts of sub-Saharan Africa. But also in England, France, Japan, Russia, and Africa, linkages led to civil wars and social unrest. In the Ottoman state, outlying provinces slipped from central control; the Safavid regime foundered and then collapsed; the Ming dynasty gave way to the Qing. In India, rivalries among princes and merchants eroded the Mughals' authority, compounding the instability caused by peasant uprisings.

EXTRACTING WEALTH: MERCANTILISM

Transformations in global relations began in the Atlantic, where the extraction and shipment of gold and silver siphoned wealth from the New World (the Americas) to the Old World (Afro-Eurasia). (See Map 13.1.) American exports were so lucrative for Spain and Portugal that other European powers wanted a share in the bounty, so they too launched colonizing ventures in the New World. Although these latecomers found few precious minerals, they devised other ways to extract wealth, for the Americas had fertile lands on which to cultivate sugarcane, cotton, tobacco, indigo, and rice.

If silver quickened the pace of global trade, sugar transformed the European diet. First domesticated in Polynesia, sugar rarely appeared in European diets before the New World plantations started exporting it. Previously, Europeans had used honey as a sweetener, but they soon became insatiable consumers of sugar. Between 1690 and 1790, Europe imported 12 million tons of sugar—approximately 1 ton for every African enslaved in the Americas.

No matter what products they supplied, colonies were supposed to provide wealth for their "mother countries"—according to the economic theory of mercantilism, which drove European empire builders. The term **mercantilism** describes a system that saw the world's wealth as fixed, meaning that any one country's wealth came at the expense of other countries. Mercantilism further assumed that overseas possessions existed solely to enrich European motherlands. Thus, colonies should ship more "value" to the mother country than they received in return. Colonies were supposed

THE BIG PICTURE

What were the major steps in the integration of global trade networks in the seventeenth and eighteenth centuries?

Core Objectives

EXPLAIN the significance of European consumption of goods (like tobacco, textiles, and sugar) for the global economy.

mercantilism
Economic theory that drove European empire builders. In this economic system, the world had a fixed amount of wealth, which meant one country's wealth came at the expense of another's. Mercantilism assumed that colonies existed for the sole purpose of enriching the country that controlled the colony.

Stimulants, Sociability, and Coffeehouses

While armies, travelers, missionaries, and diseases have breached the world's main political and cultural barriers, commodities have been the least respectful of the lines that separate communities. It has been difficult for ruling elites to curtail the desire of their populations to dress themselves in fine garments, to possess jewelry, and to consume satisfying food and drink no matter where these products may originate. The history of commodities, thus, is a core area for world historical research, for products span cultural barriers and connect peoples over long distances. As the world's trading networks expanded in the seventeenth and eighteenth centuries, merchants in Europe, Asia, Africa, and the Americas distributed many new commodities. By far the most popular were a group of stimulants—coffee, cocoa, sugar, tobacco, and tea—all of which (except for sugar) were addictive and also produced a sense of well-being.

Previously, many of these products had been grown in isolated parts of the world: the coffee bean in Yemen, tobacco and cocoa in the New World, and sugar in Bengal. Yet, by the seventeenth century, in nearly every corner of the world, the well-to-do began to congregate in coffeehouses, consuming these new products and engaging in sociable activities.

Coffeehouses everywhere served as locations for social exchange, political discussions, and business activities. Yet they also varied from cultural area to cultural area, reflecting the values of the societies in which they arose.

The coffeehouse first appeared in Islamic lands late in the fifteenth century. As coffee consumption caught on among the wealthy and leisured classes in the Arabian Peninsula and the Ottoman Empire, local growers protected their advantage by monopolizing its cultivation and sale and refusing to allow any seeds or cuttings from the coffee tree to be taken abroad.

Despite some religious opposition, coffee spread into Egypt and throughout the Ottoman Empire in the sixteenth century. Ottoman bureaucrats, merchants, and artists assembled in coffeehouses to trade stories, read, listen to poetry, and play chess and backgammon. Indeed, so deeply connected were coffeehouses with literary and artistic pursuits that people referred to them as schools of knowledge.

From the Ottoman territories, the culture of coffee drinking spread to western Europe. The first coffeehouse in London opened in 1652, and within sixty years the city claimed no fewer than 500 such establishments. In fact, the Fleet Street area of London had so many that the English essayist Charles Lamb commented, "[T]he man must have a rare recipe for melancholy who can be dull in Fleet Street." Although coffeehouses attracted people from all levels of society, they especially appealed to the new mercantile and professional classes as locations where stimulating

to be closed to competitors, so that foreign traders would not drain precious resources from an empire's exclusive domain. As the mother country's monopoly over its colonies' trade generated precious metals for royal treasuries, European states grew rich enough to wage almost unceasing wars against one another. Ultimately, mercantilists believed, as did the English philosopher Thomas Hobbes (1588–1679), that "wealth is power and power is wealth."

The mercantilist system required an alliance between the state and its merchants. Mercantilists understood economics and politics as interdependent, with the merchant needing the monarch to protect his interests and the monarch relying on the merchant's trade to enrich the state's treasury. **Chartered companies**, such as the (English) Virginia Company and the Dutch East India Company were the most visible examples of the collaboration between

chartered companies
Private firms that were awarded monopoly trading rights over vast areas by European monarchs (for example, the Virginia Company and the Dutch East India Company).

beverages like coffee, cocoa, and tea promoted lively conversations. Here, too, opponents claimed that excessive coffee drinking destabilized the thinking processes and even caused conversions to Islam. But against such opposition, the pleasures of coffee, tea, and cocoa prevailed. These bitter beverages in turn required liberal doses of the sweetener sugar. A smoke of tobacco topped off the experience. In this environment of pleasure, patrons of the coffeehouses indulged their addictions, engaged in gossip, conducted business, and talked politics.

Coffee Coffee drinkers at an Ottoman banquet (*left*) and in an English coffeehouse (*right*).

Questions for Analysis
- What factors drove the consumption of stimulants like coffee on a global scale?
- What other commodities from earlier in world history played a similar role? Were there differences in the underlying factors such as scale of consumption between the different periods?

Explore Further
Hattox, Ralph S., *Coffee and Coffeehouses: The Origins of a Social Beverage in the Medieval Near East* (1985).

the state and the merchant classes. European monarchs awarded these firms monopoly trading rights over vast areas.

THE LITTLE ICE AGE

Global cooling occurred unevenly around the world. In some places, the effect of falling temperatures, shorter growing seasons, and irregular precipitation patterns was felt as early as the fourteenth century. But the impact of the **Little Ice Age** reached farther and deeper in the seventeenth century. What caused this climate change is a matter of debate. But a combination of low sunspot activity, changing ocean currents, and volcanic eruptions that filled the atmosphere with dust shocked an increasingly integrated world. While the seventeenth century was especially severe, the cold lasted well into

Little Ice Age
A period of global cooling—not a true ice age—that extended roughly from the sixteenth to the nineteenth century. The dates, especially for the start of the period, remain the subject of scientific controversy.

The Global View

GREENLAND

ICELAND

ALASKA

DENMARK
NETHERLANDS

ENGLAND
Amsterdam
London

Far
FRANCE

PORTUGAL

SPAIN
Lisbon
Seville
Cadiz

RUPERT'S
LAND

NEWFOUND-
LAND

Québec

NEW
FRANCE

Boston
Philadelphia
New York
THIRTEEN
COLONIES

NOVA
SCOTIA

LOUISIANA

From North
America
Tobacco
Rice
Furs
Indigo
Meat
Timber
Grain
Taxes

Manufactures

Silk
Spices

VICEROYALTY
OF
NEW SPAIN

New Orleans

Zacatecas

MEXICO
Mexico City
Acapulco
Veracruz

CURAÇAO

From South
America
Sugar
Gold
Hides
Coffee
Diamonds
Calico
Taxes

Iron
Copper
Textiles
Cutlery
Firearms

Timbuktu

HAUS

ATLANTIC
OCEAN

Slaves

ASANTE
Accra

OYO
Lagos

FERNANDO PO

Cartagena
Panama
VICEROYALTY
OF
GRANADA
Quito

SURINAM

Lima

DUTCH
BRAZIL
Recife
Bahia

PACIFIC
OCEAN

VICEROYALTY
OF BRAZIL

Slaves

VICEROYALTY
OF PERU

Potosí

Tobacco
Sugar

Rio de Janeiro

Buenos Aires

Line of
Tordesillas
1494

Map 13.1 Trade in Silver and Other Commodities, 1650–1750

The seventeenth and eighteenth centuries were the first centuries of true global commerce. Silver was the one item that was traded all over the world.

- Trace the flows of silver from the Americas around the globe (by following the thick orange arrows), and identify the commodities that silver was exchanged for in different parts of the world.
- Explain the relationship between the trade of manufactures and natural resources.
- According to this map, how did increased trade shape European states' territorial ambitions?

ARCTIC OCEAN

St. Petersburg

Danzig

POLAND

TRIA

SWEDEN

OTTOMAN EMPIRE
Aleppo
Baghdad   SAFAVID
Isfahan   EMPIRE
Alexandria   Suez   Basra   Hormuz
ARABIA
Muscat

ETHIOPIA

Mogadishu

Malindi
Mombasa
ZANZIBAR
Kilwa

Mozambique
Sofala   MADAGASCAR
MAURITIUS
RÉUNION
Delagoa
Bay

Cape
Town

of
pe

Delhi
MUGHAL
EMPIRE   BIHAR
Diu   Calcutta
Bombay   Goa   Madras
Tellicherry   Pondicherry
Cochin
CEYLON
Plassey   BENGAL

QING CHINA
Guangzhou
Rangoon   Da Nang
ANNAM   Manila
(VIETNAM)
PHILIPPINES

JAPAN

PACIFIC
OCEAN

Silk
Spices

Melaka
SUMATRA   BORNEO   MALUKU
Banten   Batavia   NEW GUINEA
JAVA   TIMOR   BANDA

INDIAN
OCEAN

**From China and
Southeast Asia**
Silk
Calico
Coffee
Pepper
Spices
Drugs

From India
Silk   Pepper
Calico   Indigo
Coffee   Drugs

| 0 | 1000 | 2000 Miles |
| 0 | 1000 | 2000 Kilometers |

Spanish territory
Portuguese territory
English territory
French territory
Dutch territory
Anglo-French contested area

Silver flow
Trade route
Battle
Silk   Commodity

Winter Landscape Hendrick Avercamp was one of the most prolific Dutch painters of the seventeenth century. He often painted skaters on frozen ponds, lakes, and canals. This painting is from around 1608, when the Little Ice Age was at its most intense, and shows skaters on one of the large frozen-over canals in Amsterdam.

the next century and in parts of North America into the nineteenth. Climate change brought mass suffering because harvests failed. Famine spread across Afro-Eurasia. In West Africa, colder and drier conditions saw an advance of the Sahara Desert, leading to repeated famines in the Senegambia region. Timbuktu and the region around the Niger bend suffered their greatest famines in the seventeenth century. It was still so cold in the early nineteenth century that the English novelist Mary Shelley and her husband spent their summer vacation indoors in Switzerland telling each other horror stories, which inspired Shelley to write *Frankenstein*.

There were also political consequences. As droughts, freezing, and famine spread across Afro-Eurasia, herding societies invaded settled societies. Starving peasants rose up against their lords and rulers. Political divides opened up. In Europe, the Thirty Years' War raged out of control, stoked by farmers' anger (see later in this chapter). Although the war was deeply influenced by religious and dynastic conflicts, it owed much to the decline of food production. In the Americas, indigenous populations were already suffering grievously from the previous centuries' plagues. But the long cold snap brought more mayhem. Tensions between Iroquois and Huron rose in the Great Lakes region of North America. Civil war between Portugal and Spain in Europe wreaked havoc in Iberian colonies and led to invasion and panic.

The Ottomans faced a crippling revolt, while in China the powerful Ming regime could not deal with the climate shock. It was invaded, as was so often the case when pastures turned to dust, by Manchurian peoples from beyond the Great Wall. They installed a new regime, the Qing dynasty. The English philosopher Thomas Hobbes famously wrote in *Leviathan* (1651) that "[m]an's natural state . . . was war; and not simply war, but the war of every man against every other man." "The life of man," he continued, is "solitary, poor, nasty, brutish, and short."

The Little Ice Age had a devastating impact on populations. It is hard, however, to separate the victims of starvation from the victims of war, since warfare aggravated starvation and famine contributed to war. But in continental Europe, the Thirty Years' War carried off an estimated two-thirds of the total population, on a par with the impact of the Black Death (see Chapter 11). Elsewhere, estimates were closer to one-third. Not until the twentieth century did the world again witness such extensive warfare. For some Afro-Eurasian regimes, the global crisis led to collapse and decline; for others, it became an opportunity for renewal and reinvention.

Exchanges and Expansions in North America

As rulers in England, France, and Holland granted monopolies to merchant companies, those countries began to dominate the settlement and trade of new colonies in the Americas and compete with the established colonies of Spain and Portugal. (See Map 13.2.) Although the search for precious metals or water routes to Asia had initially spurred British, French, and Dutch efforts to establish New World colonies, colonizers soon learned that only by exploiting other resources could they generate profits.

EXPANDING MAINLAND COLONIES

While the Dutch relied primarily on commerce, the British and the French exploited natural resources in their North American colonies: the British established farms in a number of ecological zones, while the French relied primarily on the fur trade, especially in the interior.

In their colonies along the Atlantic seaboard, the English established one model for new colonies in the Americas. Although these territories failed to yield precious metals or a waterway across the continent, they did boast land suitable for growing a variety of crops. Different climates and soils made for very different agricultural possibilities: wheat, rye, barley, and oats in the Middle Colonies; tobacco in Virginia and North Carolina; and rice and indigo farther south. In all of England's North American colonies,

Map 13.2 Colonies in North America, 1607–1763

France, England, and Spain laid claim to much of North America at this time.

- Where was each of these colonial powers strongest before the outbreak of the Seven Years' War in 1756? (See p. 631 for a discussion of the Seven Years' War.)

- Which empire gained the most North American territory, and which lost the most at the end of the war in 1763?

- How do you think Native American peoples reacted to the territorial arrangements agreed to by Spain, France, and England at the Peace of Paris, which ended the war?

English claims, 1756
French claims, 1756
Spanish claims, 1756
Dutch claims until 1664
Anglo-French contested area
Seven Years' War battle area

English possessions, 1763
Spanish possessions, 1763

population growth fed greater hunger for farmlands, which put pressure on Indian holdings. The result: a souring of relations between Native Americans and colonists, often ferocious wars between natives and newcomers, and, over the course of the seventeenth and eighteenth centuries, the dispossession of Indians from lands between the Atlantic Ocean and the Appalachian Mountains.

By contrast, Dutch and French colonies rested not on the expulsion of natives, but on dependence on them. Holland's North American venture, however, proved short-lived, as the English took over New Netherland and renamed it New York in 1664. French claims were more enduring and extended across a vast swath of the continent, encompassing eastern Canada, the Great Lakes, and the Mississippi Valley. Crucial to the trade between Europeans and Native Americans in the northern parts of North America was the beaver, an animal for which Native Americans previously had little use.

The distinctive aspect of the fur trade was the Europeans' utter dependence on Native American know-how. After all, trapping required familiarity with the beavers' habits and habitats, which Europeans lacked. This reliance forced the French to adapt to Native American ways, which is evident in their pattern of exchange. Responding to Native American desires to use trade as an instrument to cement familial bonds, the French gave gifts, participated in Native American diplomatic rituals, and even married into Native American families. As a result, *métis* (French–Native American offspring) played an important role in New France as interpreters, traders, and guides. Thus, the French colonization of the Americas—owing to their reliance on Native Americans as trading partners, military allies, and mates—rested more on cooperation than conquest, especially compared to the empires built by their Spanish and English rivals.

As French (and English) traders introduced guns into the exchange networks, however, they initiated an arms race among Native Americans. To get more guns, Native Americans had to collect more skins, which resulted in the depletion of the beaver population in heavily trapped areas. That, in turn, pushed Native Americans to expand their hunting/trapping zones, which heightened conflicts between groups now increasingly competing for hunting territories. Alcohol, too, became a potent weapon for Europeans. It gave them a commodity that Native Americans wanted badly enough to undermine long-standing understandings of the relationship between humans and animals and to overwhelm strictures against overhunting.

The initial agricultural endeavors in the New World were modest. They relied on crops like tobacco that required relatively modest capital investments and could be profitably farmed on a small scale, with few workers. Sugar, by contrast, required major investments. It had to be processed near

The Fur Trade For Europeans in northern North America, no commodity was as important as beaver skins. For the French especially, the fur trade determined the character of their colonial regime in North America. For Native Americans, it offered access to European goods, but overhunting depleted resources and provoked intertribal conflicts.

the cane fields, which meant mills had to be built, and it required massive amounts of labor. Produced on a large scale with slave labor, sugar was enormously profitable. From the middle of the seventeenth century, the British and French devoted their energies to replicating the Portuguese sugar plantations of Brazil on the islands they controlled in the Caribbean. All was not sweet there, however.

The Plantation Complex in the Caribbean

Large European plantations in the Caribbean relied on slave labor to produce sugar for export. Sugar was a killing crop. So deadly was the hot, humid environment in which sugarcane flourished (as fertile for disease as for sugarcane) that many sugar barons spent little time on their plantations. Management fell to overseers, who worked their slaves to death. Despite having immunities to yellow fever and malaria from their homelands' similar environment, the African slaves who worked on the plantations could not withstand the regimen. Inadequate food, atrocious living conditions, and a lack of sanitation added to their miseries. Moreover, plantation managers on large sugar plantations treated their slaves as nonhumans: one English gentleman commented that slaves were like cows, "as near as beasts may be, setting their souls aside."

More than disease and inadequate rations, the work itself decimated the enslaved. Average life expectancy was three years. Six days a week slaves rose before dawn, labored until noon, ate a short lunch, and then worked until dusk. At harvest time, sixteen-hour days saw hundreds of men, women, and children doubled over to cut the sugarcane and transport it to refineries, sometimes seven days per week. Under this brutal schedule, slaves occasionally dropped dead from exhaustion.

Amid disease and toil, the enslaved resisted as they could. The most dramatic expression of resistance was violent revolt. A more common form of resistance was flight. Seeking refuge from overseers, thousands of slaves took to the hills—for example, to the remote mountains of Caribbean islands or to Brazil's vast interior. Those who remained on the plantations resisted via foot dragging, pilfering, and sabotage.

Caribbean settlements and slaveholdings were not restricted to any single European power. But it was the latecomers—especially the English and the French—who concentrated on the islands of the Caribbean. (See Map 13.3.) The English took Jamaica from the Spanish and made it the premier site of Caribbean sugar by the 1740s. When the French seized half of Santo Domingo in the 1660s (renaming it Saint-Domingue, which is present-day Haiti), they created one of the wealthiest societies based on slavery of all time. This French colony's exports eclipsed those of all the Spanish and English islands combined. By 1789, French Saint-Domingue produced nearly half of the world's supply of sugar and coffee. Its principal port city, Cap-Français, was among the richest in the Atlantic world. The colony's merchants and planters built immense mansions worthy of the highest European nobles. Thus, the Atlantic system benefited elite Europeans, who amassed new fortunes by exploiting the colonies' rich soil (which they eroded) and tropical climate and the African slaves' labor.

The Slave Trade and Africa

Although the slave trade began in the mid-fifteenth century, only in the seventeenth and eighteenth centuries did the numbers of human exports from Africa begin to soar. (See Map 13.4.) By 1820, four slaves had crossed the Atlantic for every European. Those numbers were essential to the prosperity of Europe's American colonies. At the same time, the departure of so many inhabitants depopulated and destabilized many parts of Africa.

Core Objectives

DESCRIBE the consequences of the Atlantic slave trade across the Atlantic world.

Map 13.3 Caribbean Colonies, 1625–1763

The Caribbean was a region of expanding trade in the seventeenth and eighteenth centuries.

- What were its major exports and imports?
- Who were its main colonizers and trading partners?
- According to your reading, how did the transformation of this region shape other societies in the Atlantic world?

Tobacco The cultivation of tobacco saved the Virginia colony from ruin and brought prosperity to increasing numbers of planters. The spread of tobacco plantations also pushed Native Americans off their lands and led planters to turn to Africa for a labor force.

CAPTURING AND SHIPPING SLAVES

Merchants in Europe and the New World prospered as the slave trade grew, but their fortunes depended on trading and political networks in Africa. In fact, before the nineteenth-century discovery of quinine, European slavers could not survive in the African interior. Instead they took advantage of Africans' rivalries. Using firearms supplied by Europeans, African elites controlled the capturing of slaves; their networks linked moneylenders and traders on the coast with allies in the interior.

Before the Europeans' arrival, Africa had an already existing system of slave commerce, mainly flowing across the Sahara to North Africa and Egypt and eastward to the Red Sea and the Swahili coast of East Africa. From the Red Sea and Swahili coast destinations, Muslim and Hindu merchants shipped slaves to ports around the Indian Ocean. However, the number of these slaves could not match the volume destined for the Americas once plantation agriculture began to spread. Indeed, 12.5 million Africans survived forcible enslavement and shipment to Atlantic ports from 1525 (the date of the first direct voyage from Africa to the Americas) until 1867 (when the last voyage took place).

Now the slave ports along the African coast became gruesome holding pens. Many slaves who perished did so before losing sight of Africa. Stuck in vast camps where disease and hunger were rampant, the slaves were then

Hudson
Bay

NORTH
AMERICA

ATLANTIC
OCEAN

NORTH
AMERICAN
MAINLAND

50,000

Gulf of
Mexico

367,000

CUBA

779,000

ST.-DOMINGUE

792,000

VERACRUZ

JAMAICA

1,000,000

BARBADOS

4.75 million

CARTAGENA

BRITISH
GUIANA

73,000

294,000

DUTCH
GUIANAS

FRENCH
GUIANA

31,000

PACIFIC
OCEAN

AMAZONIA

192,000

SOUTH
AMERICA

BRAZIL

4.72 million

RÍO DE LA
PLATA

98,000

Map 13.4 The African Slave Trade, 1440–1867

The Atlantic slave trade flourished in the seventeenth, eighteenth, and nineteenth centuries, linking many parts of Africa with the Americas.

- What were the main areas in Africa from which the slaves were taken?
- What were the main areas that they were taken to in the Americas?
- Based on your reading, how and where did the slave trade reshape African societies?

NORTH
SEA

EUROPE

BLACK SEA

CASPIAN
SEA

ARAL
SEA

ASIA

MEDITERRANEAN SEA

ALGERIA TUNISIA

MOROCCO

LIBYA

EGYPT

PERSIA

Persian Gulf

2 million (1700-1900)

S A H A R A

RED SEA

ARABIA

ARABIAN
SEA

1.32 million

YEMEN

SENEGAMBIA

WINDWARD
COAST

SIERRA
LEONE

ASANTE
OF
GOLD
COAST

STATE

BIGHT
OF
BENIN

BIGHT
OF
BIAFRA

A F R I C A

ETHIOPIA

892,000

280,000

533,000

756,000

389,000

337,000

1.2 million

1.99 million

1.6 million

AMERICAS
12.57 million
(1501-1867)

KONGO
KINGDOM

WEST
CENTRAL
AFRICA

SWAHILI
COAST

INDIAN

OCEAN

5.7 million

SOUTHEAST
AFRICA

200,000

MADAGASCAR

MASCARENE
ISLANDS
359,000

0   500   1000   1500 Miles

0   500   1000   1500 Kilometers

The Slave Trade (*Left*) Africans were captured in the interior and then bound and marched to the coast. (*Right*) After reaching the coast, the captured Africans would be crammed into the holds of slave vessels, where they suffered grievously from overcrowding and unsanitary conditions. Long voyages were especially deadly. If the winds failed or ships had to travel longer distances than usual, many of the captives would die en route to the slave markets across the ocean.

forced aboard vessels in cramped and wretched conditions. These ships waited for weeks to fill their holds while their human cargoes wasted away below deck. Crew members tossed dead Africans overboard as they loaded on other Africans from the shore. When the cargo was complete, the ships set sail. In their wake, crews continued to dump bodies. Most died of dehydration brought on by gastrointestinal diseases and a lack of fresh water. Smallpox and dysentery were also scourges. Either way, death was slow and agonizing.

SLAVERY'S GENDER IMBALANCE

In moving so many Africans to the Americas, the slave trade played havoc with the ratios of men to women in both places because most of the slaves shipped to the Americas were adult men. Although the numbers indicated Europeans' preferences for male laborers, they also reflected African slavers' desire to keep female slaves, primarily for household work. The gender imbalance made it difficult for slaves to reproduce in the Americas. So planters and slavers had to return to Africa to procure more captives—especially for the Caribbean islands, where slaves' death rates were so high.

Male slaves outnumbered females in the New World, but in the slave-supplying regions of Africa women outnumbered men. Female captives were especially prized in Africa because of their traditional role in the production of grains, leathers, and cotton. Moreover, the slave trade reinforced the traditional practice of polygamy—allowing relatively scarce men to take several wives, which helped minimize the loss of population.

AFRICA'S NEW SLAVE-SUPPLYING STATES

Africans did not passively let captives fall into the arms of European slave buyers; instead, local political leaders and merchants were active suppliers. This activity promoted the growth of centralized political structures, particularly in West African rain forest areas. The trade also shifted control of wealth away from households owning large herds or lands to those who profited from the capture and exchange of slaves—urban merchants and warrior elites.

In some parts of Africa, the booming slave trade created chaos as local leaders feuded over control of the traffic. In the Kongo kingdom, for example, civil wars raged for over a century after 1665, and captured warriors were sold as slaves. As members of the royal family clashed, entire provinces saw their populations vanish. Europeans fueled these conflicts and provided weapons to their African allies. Moreover, kidnapping became so prevalent that farmers worked their fields bearing weapons, leaving their children behind in guarded stockades.

As some African merchants and warlords sold other Africans, their commercial success enabled them to consolidate political power and grow wealthy. Their wealth financed additional weapons, with which they subdued

The Port of Loango Partly as a result of the profits of the slave trade, African rulers and merchants were able to create large and prosperous port cities such as Loango (pictured), which was on the west coast of south-central Africa.

neighbors and extended political control. Among the most durable new polities was the Asante state, which arose in the West African tropical rain forest in 1701 and expanded through 1750. This state benefited from its access to gold, which it used to acquire firearms (from European traders) to raid nearby communities for captives to be sold into slavery in the Americas. From its capital city at Kumasi, the state eventually encompassed almost all of present-day Ghana. Main roads spread out from the capital like spokes of a wheel, each approximately twenty days' travel from the center. Through the Asante trading networks African traders bought, bartered, and sold captives, who wound up in the hands of European merchants waiting in ports with vessels carrying manufactures and weaponry.

Slavery and the emergence of new states enriched and empowered some Africans, but they cost Africa dearly. For the princes, warriors, and merchants who organized the slave trade, their business enabled them to obtain European goods—especially alcohol, tobacco, textiles, and guns. The Atlantic system also tilted wealth away from rural dwellers and village elders and increasingly toward port cities. Across the landmass, the slave trade thinned the population. True, Africa was spared a demographic catastrophe equal to the devastation of American Indians. The introduction of American food crops—notably maize and cassava, producing many more calories per acre than the old staples of millet and sorghum—blunted the trade's depopulating aspects. Yet some areas suffered grievously from three centuries of heavy involvement in the slave trade. The Atlantic trade enhanced the warrior class, who carried out raids for captives; the dislocations, internal power struggles, and economic hardships that followed precipitated the rise and fall of West African kingdoms.

Asia in the Seventeenth and Eighteenth Centuries

Core Objectives

EXPLAIN the effects of New World silver and increased trade on the Asian empires, and their responses to them.

Global trading networks grew as vigorously in Asia as they did in the Americas. In Asia, however, the Europeans were less dominant. Although they could gain access to Asian markets with American silver, they could not conquer Asian empires or colonize vast portions of the region. Nor were they able to enslave Asian peoples as they had Africans. The Mughal Empire continued to grow, and the Qing dynasty, which had wrested control from the Ming, significantly expanded China's borders. China remained the richest state in the world, but in some places the balance of power was tilting in Europe's direction. Not only did the Ottomans' borders contract, but by the late eighteenth century Europeans had established economic and military dominance in parts of India and much of Southeast Asia.

THE DUTCH IN SOUTHEAST ASIA

In Southeast Asia the Dutch already enjoyed considerable influence by the seventeenth century. Although the Portuguese had seized the vibrant port city of Melaka in 1511 and the Spaniards had taken Manila in 1571, neither was able to monopolize the lucrative spice trade. To challenge them, the Dutch government persuaded its merchants to charter the Dutch East India Company (abbreviated as VOC) in 1602. Benefiting from Amsterdam's position as the most efficient money market with the lowest interest rates in the world, the VOC raised ten times the capital of its English counterpart—the royal chartered English East India Company. The advantages of chartered companies were evident in the VOC's scale of operation: at its peak the company had 257 ships and employed 12,000 persons. Throughout two centuries it sent ships manned by a total of 1 million men to Asia.

The VOC's main impact was in Southeast Asia, where spices, coffee, tea, and teak wood were key exports (see again Map 13.1). The company's objective was to secure a trade monopoly wherever it could, fix prices, and replace the local population with Dutch planters. Under the leadership of Jan Pieterszoon Coen (who once said that trade could not be conducted without war and war could not be conducted without trade), the Dutch swept into the Javanese port of Jakarta in 1619 and took over the nearby Banda Islands two years later. In Banda, the traditional chiefs and almost the entire population were killed outright, left to starve, or taken into slavery. Dutch planters and their slaves replaced the decimated local population and sent their produce to the VOC. The motive for such rapacious action was the huge profit to be made by buying nutmeg at a low price in the Banda Islands and selling it at many times that price in Europe. Although this aggressive expansion met widespread resistance from the local population and other merchants involved in the region's trade, by 1670 the Dutch had also taken Melaka from the Portuguese and controlled all of the lucrative spice trade from the Maluku islands. Next, the VOC set its sights on pepper. However, the Dutch had to share this commerce with Chinese and English competitors. Moreover, since there was no demand for European products in Asia, the Dutch had to participate more in inter-Asian trade as a way to reduce their need to make payments in precious metals.

TRANSFORMATIONS IN THE ISLAMIC HEARTLAND

Compared with Southeast Asia, the major Islamic empires did not feel such direct effects of European intrusion. They did, however, face internal difficulties, which were exacerbated by trade networks that eluded state control and, in some important instances, by climate change. From its inception, the Safavid Empire had always required a powerful, religiously inspired ruler to enforce Shiite religious orthodoxy and to hold together the realm's tribal, pastoral, mercantile, and agricultural factions. With a succession of weak rulers and declining tax revenues—aggravated by a series of droughts and epidemics—the state foundered, and ultimately collapsed in 1722 (see Chapter 14). The Ottoman and Mughal Empires, in contrast, remained more resilient.

The Ottoman Empire Climate change hit the eastern Mediterranean earlier than other regions. Fierce cold and endless drought brought famine and high mortality. In 1620, the Bosporus froze over, enabling people to walk from the European side of Istanbul into the Asian side. In lands dependent on floodwaters for their well-being, such as Egypt and Iraq, food was in short supply and death rates skyrocketed. In addition, the import of New World silver led to high levels of inflation and a destabilized economy.

Having attained a high point under Suleiman (see Chapter 11), the Ottoman Empire ceased expanding. After Suleiman's reign, Ottoman armies and navies tried unsuccessfully to expand the empire's borders—losing, for example, on the western flank to the European Habsburgs. As military campaigns and a growing population strained the realm's limited resources, Ottoman intellectuals worried that the empire's glory was ebbing. A series of administrative reforms in the seventeenth century reinvigorated the state, but it never recaptured the vast power it enjoyed at its height.

Even as the empire's strength waned, by the seventeenth century its sultans faced a commercially more connected world. The introduction of New World silver into Ottoman networks of commerce and moneylending eventually destabilized the empire. Although early Ottoman rulers had avoided trade with the outside world, the lure of silver broke through state regulations. Now Ottoman merchants established black markets for commodities that eager European buyers paid for in silver—especially wheat, copper, and wool. Because these exports were illegal, their sale did not generate tax revenues to support the state's civilian and military administration. So Ottoman rulers had to rely on loans of silver from the merchants. Some European royal houses, notably the Dutch and English, would grant those who bankrolled them a say in government, which vastly increased the crown's credit and ultimately its power. Ottoman sultans, by contrast, feuded with their financiers, which undermined the sultans' authority.

More silver and budget deficits were a recipe for inflation. Prices tripled between 1550 and 1650. Runaway inflation caused hard-hit peasants in Anatolia, suffering from bad harvests and increasing taxes (used to pay off dynastic debts), to join together in uprisings that threatened the state's stability. A revolt, begun in central Anatolia in the early sixteenth century, continued in fits and starts throughout the century, reaching a crescendo in the early seventeenth century. Known as the Celali Revolt, after Shaykh Celali, who had led one of the initial uprisings, the rebellion challenged the sultan's authority with an army of 30,000 and turned much of Anatolia into a danger zone. Disorder at the center of the empire was accompanied by difficulties in the provinces, where breakaway regimes appeared.

The most threatening of the breakaway pressures occurred in Egypt beginning in the seventeenth century. In 1517, Egypt had become the Ottoman Empire's greatest conquest. As the wealthiest Ottoman territory, it was an important source of revenue, and its people shouldered heavy tax burdens. The group that asserted Egypt's political and commercial autonomy consisted of military men, known as **Mamluks** (Arabic for "owned" or "possessed"), who had ruled Egypt as an independent regime until the Ottoman

Mamluks
(Arabic for "owned" or "possessed") Military men who ruled Egypt as an independent regime from 1250 until the Ottoman conquest in 1517.

Siege of Vienna This seventeenth-century painting depicts the Ottoman siege of Vienna, which began on July 14, 1683, and ended on September 12. The city might have fallen if the Polish king, John III, had not answered the pope's plea to defend Christendom and sent an army to assist German and Austrian troops in defeating the Ottomans.

conquest. Although the Ottoman army had routed Mamluk forces on the battlefield, Ottoman governors in Egypt allowed the Mamluks to reform themselves. By the seventeenth century, these military men were nearly as powerful as their ancestors had been in the fifteenth century when they ruled Egypt independently. Mamluk leaders enhanced their power by aligning with Egyptian merchants and catering to the religious elites of Egypt, the *ulama*. Turning the Ottoman administrator of Egypt into a mere figurehead, this new provincial elite kept much of the area's fiscal resources for themselves at the expense not only of the imperial coffers but also of the local peasantry.

Amid new economic pressures and challenges from outlying territories, the Ottoman system also had elements of resilience—especially at the center, where decaying leadership provoked demands for reform from administrative elites. Known as the Köprülü reforms, a combination of financial reform and anticorruption measures gave the state a new burst of energy and enabled the military to reacquire some of its lost possessions. Revenues again increased, and inflation decreased. Fired by revived expansionist ambitions, Istanbul decided to renew its assault on Christianity—beginning with rekindled plans to seize Vienna. Although the Ottomans gathered an enormous force outside the Habsburg capital in 1683, both sides suffered heavy losses and the Ottoman forces ultimately retreated. Under the treaty that ended the Austro-Ottoman war, the Ottomans lost major European territorial possessions, including Hungary.

Thus, the Ottoman Empire began the eighteenth century dealing with serious economic and environmental challenges. Whereas in the sixteenth century rulers of the Ottoman Empire had wanted to create a self-contained and self-sufficient imperial economy, silver undermined this vision as it had elsewhere in the global economy. Indeed, the influx of silver opened Ottoman-controlled lands to trade with the rest of the world, producing breakaway regimes, widespread inflation, social discontent, and conflict between the state and its financiers. The crop shortages and population crises of the Little Ice Age made all of those problems more difficult to manage.

The Mughal Empire In contrast to the Ottomans' military reversals, the Mughal Empire reached its height in the seventeenth century. The period saw Mughal rulers extend their domain over almost all of India and enjoy increased domestic and international trade. But they, too, eventually had problems governing dispersed and resistant provinces, where many villages retained traditional religions and cultures and suffered from the effects of the Little Ice Age on their land's productivity.

Before the Mughals, India had never had a single political authority. Akbar and his successors had conquered territory in the north (see Chapter 12, Map 12.4), so now the Mughals turned to the south and gained control over most of that region by 1689. As the new provinces provided an additional source of resources, local lords, and warriors, the Mughal bureaucracy grew better at extracting services and taxes.

Imperial stability and prosperity did not depend entirely on the Indian Ocean trading system. Indeed, although the Mughals profited from seaborne trade, they never undertook overseas expansion. The main source of their wealth was land rents, which increased via incentives to bring new land into cultivation. But the imperial economy also benefited from Europeans' increased demand for Indian goods, including a sixfold rise in the English East India Company's textile purchases.

Eventually, the Mughals were victims of their own success. More than a century of imperial expansion, commercial prosperity, and agricultural development placed substantial resources in the hands of local and regional authorities. As a result, local warrior elites became more autonomous. By the late seventeenth century, many regional leaders were well positioned to resist Mughal authority. As in the Ottoman Empire, distant provinces began to challenge central rulers. Now the Indian peasants (like their counterparts in Ming China, Safavid Persia, and the Ottoman Empire) capitalized on weakening central authority. Many rose in rebellions, especially when drought and famine hit; others took up banditry.

At this point, the Mughal emperors had to accept diminished power over a loose unity of provincial states. Most of these areas accepted Mughal control in name only, administering their own affairs with local resources. Yet India still flourished, and landed elites brought new territories into agrarian production. Cotton, for instance, supported a thriving textile industry as peasant households focused on weaving and cloth production. Much of their production was destined for export as the region deepened its integration into world trading systems.

The Mughals themselves paid scant attention to commercial matters, but local rulers welcomed Europeans into Indian ports. As more European ships arrived, these authorities struck deals with merchants from Portugal and, increasingly, from England and Holland. Some Indian merchants formed trading companies of their own to control the sale of regional produce to competing Europeans; others established intricate trading networks that reached as far north as Russia. Mercantile houses grew richer and gained greater political influence over financially strapped emperors. Thus, even as global commercial entanglements enriched some in India, the effects undercut the Mughal dynasty.

FROM MING TO QING IN CHINA

Like India, China prospered in the seventeenth and eighteenth centuries; but here, too, growing wealth and climate change undermined central control and, in this case, contributed to the fall of a long-lasting dynasty.

Core Objectives

ANALYZE examples of resistance in Southeast Asia and China to the growth of global trade networks.

As in Mughal India, local power holders in China increasingly defied the Ming government. Moreover, because Ming sovereigns discouraged overseas commerce and forbade travel abroad, they did not reap the rewards of long-distance exchange. Rather, such profits went to traders and adventurers who evaded imperial edicts. Together, the persistence of local autonomy and the accelerating economic and social changes brought unprecedented challenges until finally, in 1644, the Ming dynasty collapsed.

Administrative and Economic Problems How did a dynasty that in the early seventeenth century governed the world's most economically advanced society (and perhaps a third of the world's population) fall from power? As in the Ottoman Empire, responsibility often lay with the rulers and their inadequate response to economic and environmental change. Zhu Yijun, the Wanli Emperor (r. 1573–1620), was secluded despite being surrounded by a staff of 20,000 eunuchs and 3,000 women. The "Son of Heaven" rarely ventured outside the palace compound, and when he moved within it a large retinue accompanied him, led by eunuchs clearing his path with whips. Ming emperors like Wanli quickly discovered that despite the elaborate arrangements and ritual performances affirming their position as the Son of Heaven, they had little control over the vast bureaucracy. An emperor frustrated with his officials could do little more than punish them or refuse to cooperate.

The timing of administrative breakdown in the Ming government was unfortunate, because expanding opportunities for trade led many individuals to circumvent official rules. From the mid-sixteenth century, bands of supposedly Japanese pirates ravaged the Chinese coast. Indeed, the Ming government had difficulties regulating trade with Japan and labeled all pirates as Japanese, but many of the marauders were in fact Chinese who flouted imperial authority. In tough times, the roving gangs terrorized sea-lanes and harbors. In better times, some functioned like mercantile groups: their leaders mingled with elites, foreign trade representatives, and imperial officials. What made these predators so resilient—and their business so lucrative—was their ability to move among the mosaic of East Asian cultures.

Just like in the Islamic empires, the influx of silver from the New World and Japan, while at first stimulating the Chinese economy, led to severe economic and, eventually, political problems. As we saw in Chapter 12, Europeans used New World silver to pay for their purchases of Chinese goods. As a result, by the early seventeenth century China imported more than twenty times more silver bullion (uncoined gold or silver) than it produced. Increasing monetization of the economy—which meant that silver currency became the primary medium of exchange—bolstered market activity and state revenues at the same time.

Yet the use of silver pressured peasants, who now needed that metal to pay their taxes and purchase goods. When silver supplies were abundant, the peasants faced inflationary prices. When supplies were low, the peasants could not meet their obligations to state officials and merchants, and they took up arms in rebellion.

The Collapse of Ming Authority By the seventeenth century, the Ming's administrative and economic difficulties were affecting their subjects' daily lives. This was particularly evident when the regime failed to cope with devastation caused by natural disasters, as in the northwestern province of Shanxi after a drop in average temperatures shortened growing seasons and reduced harvests.

While the Little Ice Age was not wholly responsible for the fall of the Ming, it played a major role. As the price of grain soared there in 1627–1628, the poor and the hungry fanned out to find food by whatever means they could muster. To deal with the crisis, the government imposed heavier taxes and cut the military budget. Bands of dispossessed Chinese peasants and mutinous soldiers then vented their anger at local tax collectors and officials.

Now the cycle of rebellion and weakened central authority that played out in so many other places took its predictable toll. Outlaw armies grew large under charismatic leaders. The most famous rebel leader, the "dashing prince" Li Zicheng, arrived at the outskirts of Beijing in 1644. Only a few companies of soldiers and a few thousand eunuchs were there to defend the capital's 21 miles of walls, so Li Zicheng seized Beijing easily. Two days later, the emperor hanged himself. On the following day, the triumphant "dashing prince" rode into the capital and claimed the throne.

News of the fall of the Ming capital sent shock waves around the empire. One hundred and seventy miles to the northeast, where China meets Manchuria, the army's commander received the news within a matter of days. His task in the area was to defend the Ming against their menacing neighbor, a group that had begun to identify itself as Manchu. Immediately the commander's position became precarious. Caught between an advancing rebel army on the one side and the Manchus on the other, he made a fateful decision: he appealed for the Manchus' cooperation to fight the "dashing prince," promising his new allies that "gold and treasure" awaited them in the capital. Thus, without shedding a drop of blood, the Manchus joined the Ming forces. After years of coveting the Ming Empire, the Manchus were finally on their way to Beijing. (See Map 13.5.)

The Qing Dynasty Asserts Control Despite their small numbers, the Manchus overcame early resistance to their rule and oversaw an impressive expansion of their realm. The **Manchus**—the name was first used in 1635— were descendants of a Turkic-speaking group known as the Jurchens. They emerged as a force early in the seventeenth century, when their leader claimed the title of khan after securing the allegiance of various Mongol groups in

Manchus
Descendants of the Jurchens who helped the Ming army recapture Beijing in 1644 after its seizure by the outlaw Li Zicheng. The Manchus numbered around 1 million but controlled a domain that included perhaps 250 million people. Their rule lasted more than 250 years and became known as the Qing dynasty.

Map 13.5 From Ming to Qing China, 1644–1760

Qing China under the Manchus expanded its territory significantly during this period. Find the Manchu homeland and then the area of Manchu expansion after 1644, when the Manchus established the Qing dynasty.

- Where did the Qing dynasty expand? Explain what this tells us about the priorities of the ruling elite, in particular with respect to global commerce.
- Explain the significance of the chronology of Chinese expansion. Does this qualify your answer to the first question?
- What does the chronology of Chinese expansion tell us about the evolution of the ruling elite's priorities?
- Consider the scope of Chinese territorial expansion in this period, and, based on your reading, explain the challenges this posed for central authorities.

northeastern Asia, paving the way for their eventual conquest of China. By that time, a rising Manchu population, based in Inner China and unable to feed their people in Manchuria, was posed to breach the Great Wall in search of better lands. The Manchus found a Chinese government in disarray from warfare and fiscal crisis, with central authorities overwhelmed by roving bands of peasant rebels.

When the Manchus defeated Li Zicheng and seized power in Beijing, they numbered around 1 million. Assuming control of a domain that included perhaps 250 million people, they were keenly aware of their minority status. Taking power was one thing; keeping it was another. But keep it they did. In fact, during the eighteenth century the Manchu **Qing** ("pure") **dynasty** (1644–1911) incorporated new territories, experienced substantial population growth, and sustained significant economic growth.

The key to China's relatively stable economic and geographic expansion lay in its rulers' shrewd and flexible policies. The early Manchu emperors were able and diligent administrators. They also knew that to govern a diverse population, they had to adapt to local ways. At the same time, Qing rulers were determined to convey a clear sense of their own majesty and legitimacy. Rulers relentlessly promoted patriarchal values. Widows who remained "chaste" enjoyed public praise, and women in general were urged to lead a "virtuous" life serving male kin and family. To the majority Han population, the Manchu emperor represented himself as the worthy upholder of familial values and classical Chinese civilization. However, insinuating themselves into an existing order and appeasing subject peoples did not satisfy the yearning of the Manchus to leave their imprint. They also introduced measures that emphasized their authority, their distinctiveness, and the submission of their mostly Han Chinese subjects. For example, Qing officials composed or translated important documents into Manchu and banned intermarriage between Manchu and Han, although this proved difficult to enforce.

Manchu impositions fell mostly on the peasantry, for the Qing financed their administrative structure through taxes on peasant households. In response, the peasants sought new lands to cultivate in border areas, often planting New World crops that grew well in difficult soils. This move introduced an important change in Chinese diets: while rice remained the staple of the wealthy, peasants increasingly subsisted on corn and sweet potatoes.

While officials redoubled their reliance on an agrarian base, trade and commerce flourished. Chinese merchants continued to ply the waters stretching from Southeast Asia to Japan, exchanging textiles, ceramics, and medicine for spices and rice. Although the Qing state vacillated about permitting maritime trade with foreigners in its early years, it sought to regulate external commerce more formally as it consolidated its rule. In 1720, in Canton, a group of merchants formed a monopolistic guild to trade with Europeans seeking coveted Chinese goods and peddling their own wares. Although the

Qing dynasty
(1644–1911) Minority Manchu rule over China that incorporated new territories, experienced substantial population growth, and sustained significant economic growth.

Canton system

System officially established by imperial decree in 1759 that required European traders to have Chinese guild merchants act as guarantors for their good behavior and payment of fees.

Tokugawa shogunate

Hereditary military administration founded in 1603 that ruled Japan while keeping the emperor as a figurehead; it was toppled in 1868 by reformers who felt that Japan should adopt, not reject, Western influences.

guild disbanded in the face of opposition from other merchants, it revived after the Qing restricted European trade to Canton. The **Canton system**, officially established by imperial decree in 1759, required European traders to have guild merchants act as guarantors for their good behavior and payment of fees.

Despite public disregard for certain imperial edicts, the Qing dynasty enjoyed a heyday during the eighteenth century. It forced Korea, Vietnam, Burma, and Nepal to pay tribute, and its territorial expansion reached far into central Asia, Tibet, and Mongolia. China, in sum, negotiated a century of political upheaval and climate change without dismantling established ways in politics and economics. The peasantry continued to practice popular faiths, cultivate crops, and stay close to fields and villages. Trade with the outside world was marginal to overall commercial life; like the Ming, the Qing cared more about the agrarian than the commercial health of the empire, believing the former to be the foundation of prosperity and tranquility. As long as China's peasantry could keep the dynasty's coffers full, the government was content to squeeze the merchants when it needed funds. Some historians view this practice as a failure to adapt to a changing world order, as it ultimately left China vulnerable to outsiders—especially Europeans. But this view projects later developments onto the past. By the mid-eighteenth century, Europe still needed China more than the other way around. For the majority of Chinese, no superior model of belief, politics, or economics was conceivable. Indeed, although the Qing had taken over a crumbling empire in 1644, a century later China was enjoying a new level of prosperity.

TOKUGAWA JAPAN

Integration with the Asian trading system exposed Japan to new external pressures, even as the islands grappled with internal turmoil. But the Japanese dealt with these pressures more successfully than the mainland Asian empires (Ottoman, Safavid, Mughal, and Ming), which saw political fragmentation and even the overthrow of ruling dynasties. In Japan, a single ruling family emerged. This dynastic state, the **Tokugawa shogunate**, accomplished something that most of the world's other regimes did not: it regulated foreign intrusion. While Japan played a modest role in the expanding global trade, it remained free of outside exploitation.

Unification of Japan During the sixteenth century, Japan had suffered from political instability as banditry and civil strife disrupted the countryside. Regional ruling families, called *daimyos*, had commanded private armies of warriors known as samurai. The daimyos sometimes brought order to their domains, but no one family could establish preeminence over others. Although Japan had an emperor, his authority did not extend beyond the court in Kyoto.

Outer daimyos
Hereditary daimyos
Tokugawa domains

0   50   100 Miles
0   50   100 Kilometers

RUSSIAN EMPIRE

CHINA

KOREA

EZO
(HOKKAIDO)

SEA OF
JAPAN

JAPAN

HONSHŪ

Edo
(Tokyo)

Kyoto

Osaka

Shimabara
1638
Uprising of
Christian
converts
put down

Hirado
1609
Dutch
trading post

Nagasaki
1570
opened to
European trade

DESHIMA ISLAND
1641
Dutch traders
confined there

SHIKOKU

KYŪSHŪ

TANEGASHIMA
1542
Portuguese
trading post

PACIFIC
OCEAN

YELLOW
SEA

EAST
CHINA
SEA

RYŪKYŪ ISLANDS

Map 13.6 Tokugawa Japan, 1603–1867

· ·

The Tokugawa shoguns created a strong central
state in Japan at this time.

- According to this map, how extensive was their
  control?

- Based on your reading, what foreign states were
  interested in trade with Japan?

- How, according to the chapter, did Tokugawa
  leaders attempt to control relations with foreign
  states and other entities?

Following an effort by military leaders to unify Japan, one of the daimyos, Tokugawa Ieyasu, seized power. This was a decisive moment. In 1603, Ieyasu assumed the title of shogun (military ruler), retaining the emperor in name only while taking the reins of power himself. He also solved the problem of succession, declaring that rulership would be hereditary and that his family would be the ruling household. Administrative authority shifted from Kyoto to the site of Ieyasu's domain headquarters: the castle town called Edo (later renamed Tokyo; see Map 13.6). By the time Ieyasu died, Edo had become a major urban center with a population of 150,000. This hereditary Tokugawa shogunate lasted until 1867.

The Tokugawa shoguns ensured a flow of resources from the working population to the rulers and from the provinces to the capital. Villages paid taxes to the daimyos, who transferred resources to the seat of shogunate authority. No longer engaged in constant warfare, the samurai became administrators. Peace brought prosperity. Agriculture thrived. Improved farming techniques and land reclamation projects enabled the country's population to grow from 10 million in 1550 to 16 million in 1600 and 30 million in 1700.

Foreign Affairs and Foreigners Internal peace and prosperity did not insulate Japan from external challenges. When Japanese rulers tackled foreign affairs, their most pressing concern was the intrusion of Christian missionaries and European traders. Initially, Japanese officials welcomed these foreigners out of an eagerness to acquire muskets, gunpowder, and other new technology. But once the ranks of Christian converts swelled, Japanese authorities realized

Edo in the Rain This facsimile of an *ukiyo-e* ("floating world") print by Hiroshige (1797–1858) depicts one of several bridges in the bustling city of Edo (later Tokyo), with Mount Fuji in the background.

that Christians were intolerant of other faiths, believed Christ to be superior to any authority, and fought among themselves. The government suppressed Christianity and drove European missionaries from the country.

Even more troublesome was the lure of trade with Europeans. The Tokugawa knew that trading at various Japanese ports would pull the commercial regions in various directions, away from the capital. When it became clear that European traders preferred the ports of Kyūshū (the southernmost island), the shogunate restricted Europeans to trade only in ports under Edo's direct rule in Honshū. Then, Japanese authorities expelled all European competitors. Only the Protestant (and nonproselytizing) Dutch won permission to remain in Japan, confined to an island near Nagasaki. The Dutch were allowed to unload just one ship each year, under strict supervision by Japanese authorities.

These measures did not close Tokugawa Japan to the outside world, however. Trade with China and Korea flourished, and the shogun received missions from Korea and the Ryūkyū islands. Edo also gathered information about the outside world from the resident Dutch and Chinese (who included monks, physicians, and painters). A few Japanese were permitted to learn Dutch and to study European technology, shipbuilding, and medicine (see Chapter 14). By limiting such encounters, the authorities ensured that foreigners would not threaten Japan's security.

The arrival of New World silver provided at least an initial boost to the major Asian economies. The Mughal Empire achieved its greatest influence in the seventeenth century. Despite a change in the ruling dynasty, China remained the world's center of wealth and power, although there, as elsewhere in Asia, silver caused inflation and altered relations between center and periphery. Ottoman domains shrank, and Europeans achieved important commercial footholds in parts of India and Southeast Asia.

Transformations in Europe

Between 1600 and 1750, religious conflict and the consolidation of dynastic power, spurred on by long-distance trade and climate change, transformed Europe. Commercial centers shifted northward, and Spain and Portugal lost ground to England and France. To the east, the state of Muscovy expanded dramatically to become the sprawling Russian Empire.

Core Objectives

COMPARE the impact of trade and religion on state power in Europe and the Mughal Empire.

EXPANSION AND DYNASTIC CHANGE IN RUSSIA

During this period the Russian Empire expanded to become one of the world's largest-ever states. It gained positions on the Baltic Sea and the Pacific

Ocean, and it established political borders with both the Qing Empire and Japan. These momentous shifts involved the elimination of steppe nomads as an independent force. Culturally, Europeans as well as Russians debated whether Russia belonged more to Europe or to Asia. The answer was both.

Muscovy Becomes the Russian Empire The principality of Moscow, or Muscovy, like Japan and China, used territorial expansion and commercial networks to consolidate a powerful state. This was the Russian Empire, the name given to Muscovy by Tsar Peter the Great around 1700. (*Tsar* was a Russian word derived from the Latin *Caesar* to refer to the Russian ruler.) Originally a mixture of Slavs, Finnish tribes, Turkic speakers, and many others, **Muscovy** spanned parts of Europe, much of northern Asia, numerous North Pacific islands, and even—for a time—a corner of North America (Alaska).

Like Japan, Russia emerged out of turmoil. Security concerns inspired the Muscovite regime to seize territory in the fifteenth and sixteenth centuries. Because the steppe, which stretches deep into Asia, remained a highway for nomadic peoples (especially descendants of the powerful Mongols), Muscovy sought to dominate the areas south and east of Moscow. Beginning in the 1590s, Russian authorities built forts and trading posts along Siberian rivers, and by 1639 the state's borders reached the Pacific. Thus, in just over a century Muscovy had claimed an empire straddling Eurasia and incorporating peoples of many languages and religions. (See Map 13.7.)

Much of this expansion occurred despite the dynastic chaos that followed the death of Tsar Ivan IV in 1584. Ultimately, a group of prominent families reestablished central authority and threw their weight behind a new family of rulers. These were the Romanovs, court barons who set about reviving the Kremlin's fortunes. (The Kremlin was a medieval walled fortress where the Muscovite grand princes—later, tsars—resided.) Like the Ottoman and Qing dynasts, Romanov tsars and their aristocratic supporters would retain power into the twentieth century.

Absolutist Government and Serfdom In the seventeenth and eighteenth centuries, the Romanovs created an absolutist system of government. Only the tsar had the right to make war, tax, judge, and coin money. The Romanovs also made the nobles serve as state officials. Now Russia became a despotic state that had no political assemblies for nobles or other groups, other than mere consultative bodies like the imperial senate. Indeed, away from Moscow, local aristocrats enjoyed nearly unlimited authority in exchange for loyalty and tribute to the tsar.

During this period, Russia's peasantry bore the burden of maintaining the wealth of the nobility and the monarchy. Most peasant families gathered into communes, isolated rural worlds where people helped one another deal

Legend:

- Muscovy, 1462
- Expansion, 1462–1598
- Expansion, 1598–1689
- Expansion, 1689–1795
- Occupied by Russia, 1644–1689
- Qing Empire, 1760

Map 13.7 Russian Expansion, 1462–1795

The state of Muscovy incorporated vast territories through overland expansion as it grew and became the Russian Empire.

- Using the map key, identify the different expansions the Russian Empire underwent between 1462 and 1795 and the directions it generally expanded in.
- With what countries and cultures did the Russian Empire come into contact?
- According to the text, what drove such dramatic expansion?

with the harsh climate, severe landlords, and occasional poor harvests. Communes functioned like extended kin networks in which members supported one another. In 1649, peasants were legally bound as serfs to the nobles and the tsar, meaning that, in principle, they had to perform obligatory services and deliver part of their produce to their lords.

Imperial Expansion and Migration A series of military victories in the eighteenth century made it possible to consolidate the empire and sparked significant population movements. The conquest of Siberia brought vast territory and riches in furs. Victory in a prolonged war with Sweden and then the incorporation of the fertile southern steppes, known as Ukraine, proved decisive. Peter the Great (r. 1682–1725) accomplished the victory in Sweden, after which he founded a new capital at St. Petersburg. Under Peter's successors, including the brilliant and ruthless Catherine the Great, Russia, already a harsh and colossal space, added even more territory. By the late eighteenth century, Russia's grasp extended from the Baltic Sea, Ukraine, and the Crimea on the Black Sea, and stretched eastward all the way to Siberia.

Many people migrated eastward to Siberia. Some were fleeing serfdom; others were being deported for rejecting religious reforms. Battling astoundingly harsh temperatures (falling to –40 degrees Celsius/Fahrenheit) and frigid Arctic winds, these individuals traveled on horseback and trudged on foot to resettle in the east. But the difficulties of clearing forested lands or planting crops in boggy Siberian soils, combined with extraordinarily harsh winters, meant that many settlers died or tried to return. Isolation was a problem, too. There was no established land route back to Moscow until the 1770s, when exiles completed the Great Siberian Post Road through the swamps and peat bogs of western Siberia. The writer Anton Chekhov later called it "the longest and ugliest road in the whole world."

ECONOMIC AND POLITICAL FLUCTUATIONS IN CENTRAL AND WESTERN EUROPE

During this period European economies became more commercialized, especially after the Thirty Years' War. As in Asia, developments in distant parts of the world shaped the region's economic upturns and downturns. Underlying the economic and political fluctuations taking place in Europe, especially the brutal warfare of the Thirty Years' War, was the powerful impact of the Little Ice Age. Freezing temperatures shortened agricultural growing seasons by one to two months. The result was escalating prices for essential grain products, now in short supply. Famines and death from diseases because of malnourishment followed. The cooling had a few benefits, however, including

The Thirty Years' War The mercenary armies of the Thirty Years' War were renowned for pillaging and tormenting civilians. Here the artist Jacques Collot, from Nancy in eastern France, depicts the officially sanctioned punishment of renegade soldiers before an orderly group of townspeople. The caption that appeared with the image indicted the soldiers as "damned and infamous thieves, [hanging] like bad fruit, from this tree."

the magnificent violins, still prized today, crafted by Antonio Stradivari (1644–1737) from the denser wood that freezing temperatures produced.

The Thirty Years' War For a century after Martin Luther broke with the Catholic Church (see Chapter 12), religious warfare raged in Europe. So did contests over territory, power, and trade. The **Thirty Years' War** (1618–1648) was all three of these—a war between Protestant princes and the Catholic emperor for religious predominance in central Europe; a struggle for regional control among Catholic powers (the Spanish and Austrian Habsburgs and the French); and a bid for independence (from Spain) by the Dutch, who wanted to trade and worship as they liked.

The brutal conflict began as a struggle between Protestants and Catholics within the Habsburg Empire, but it soon became a war for preeminence in Europe. It took the lives of civilians as well as soldiers. In total, fighting, disease, and famine wiped out a third of the German states' urban population and two-fifths of their rural population. Ultimately the Treaty of Westphalia (1648) stated that as there was a rough balance of power between

> **Thirty Years' War**
> (1618–1648) Conflict begun between Protestants and Catholics in Germany that escalated into a general European war fought against the unity and power of the Holy Roman Empire.

Protestant and Catholic states, they would simply have to put up with each other. The Dutch won their independence, but the war's enormous costs provoked severe discontent in Spain, France, and England. Central Europe was so devastated that it did not recover in economic or demographic terms for more than a century.

The Thirty Years' War transformed war making. Whereas most medieval struggles had been sieges between nobles leading small armies, centralized states fielding standing armies now waged decisive, grand-scale campaigns. The war also changed the ranks of soldiers: local enlisted men defending their king, country, and faith gave way to hired mercenaries or criminals doing forced service. Even officers, who previously obtained their stripes by purchase or royal decree, now had to earn them. Gunpowder, cannons, and muskets became standardized. By the eighteenth century, Europe's wars featured huge standing armies boasting a professional officer corps, deadly artillery, and long supply lines bringing food and ammunition to the front. The costs—material and human—of war began to soar.

Western European Economies In spite of the toll that warfare took on economic activity, the European states enjoyed significant commercial expansion in the seventeenth century. Northern Europe gained more than did the south, however. Spain, for example, started losing ground to its rivals as the costs of defending its empire soared and merchants from Northern Europe cut in on its trading networks. The weighty costs of its involvement in the Thirty Years' War dealt the Spanish economy a final, disastrous blow.

As European commercial dynamism shifted northward, the Dutch led the way with innovative commercial practices and a new mercantile elite. They specialized in shipping and in financing regional and long-distance trade. Their famous *fluitschips* carried heavy, bulky cargoes (like Baltic wood) with relatively small crews. Now shipping costs throughout the Atlantic world dropped as Dutch ships transported their own and other countries' goods. Amsterdam's merchants founded an exchange bank, established a rudimentary stock exchange, and pioneered systems of underwriting and insuring cargoes.

England and France also became commercial powerhouses, establishing aggressive policies to promote national business and drive out competitors. By stipulating that only English ships could carry goods between the mother country and its colonies, the English Navigation Act of 1651 protected English shippers and merchants—especially from the Dutch.

Economic development was not limited to port towns: the countryside, too, enjoyed breakthroughs in production. Most important was expansion in the production of food. In northwestern Europe, investments in water drainage, larger livestock herds, and improved cultivation practices generated much greater yields. Also, a four-field crop rotation involving wheat, clover, barley, and turnips kept nutrients in the soil and provided year-round fodder for livestock. As a result (and as we have seen many times before), increased agricultural output supported a growing urban population.

Production rose most where the organization of rural property changed. In England, in a movement known as **enclosure**, landowners took control of lands that traditionally had been common property serving local needs. Claiming exclusive rights to these lands, the landowners planted new crops or pastured sheep with the aim of selling the products in distant markets—especially cities. The largest landowners put their farms in the hands of tenants, who hired wage laborers to till, plant, and harvest. Thus, in England, peasant agriculture gave way to farms run by wealthy families who exploited the marketplace to buy what they needed (including labor) and to sell what they produced. In this regard, England led the way in a Europe-wide process of commercializing the countryside.

Dynastic Monarchies: France and England European monarchs had varying success with centralizing state power. In France, Louis XIII (r. 1610–1643) and especially his chief minister, Cardinal Richelieu, concentrated power in the hands of the king. Instead of sharing power with the aristocracy, much less commoners, the king and his counselors wanted him to rule free of external checks, to create an **absolute monarchy**. The ruler was not to be a tyrant, but his authority was to be complete and thorough, and his state free of bloody disorders. The king's rule would be lawful; but he, not his jurists, would dictate the last legal word. If the king made a mistake, only God could call him to account. Thus, the Europeans believed in the "divine right of kings," a political belief not greatly different from that of imperial China, where the emperor was thought to rule with the mandate of heaven.

In absolutist France, privileges and state offices flowed from the king's grace. All patronage networks ultimately linked to the king: these included financial supports the crown provided directly, as well as tax exemptions and a wide array of permissions—such as consent for a writer to publish a book or for people ranging from lawyers and professors to apothecaries, bookbinders, and butchers to work in a regulated trade. The great palace Louis XIV built at Versailles teemed with nobles from all over France seeking favor, dressing according to the king's expensive fashion code, and attending the latest tragedies, comedies, and concerts.

The French dynastic monarchy provided a model of absolute rule for other European dynasts, like the Habsburgs of the Holy Roman Empire, the Hohenzollerns of Prussia, and the Romanovs of Muscovy. The king and his ministers controlled all public power, while other social groups, from the nobility to the peasantry, had no formal body to represent their interests. Nonetheless, French absolutist government was not as absolute as the king would have wished. Pockets of stalwart Protestants practiced their religion secretly in the plateau villages of central France, despite Louis XIV's

enclosure
A movement in which landowners took control of lands that traditionally had been common property serving local needs.

absolute monarchy
Form of government in which one body, usually the monarch, controls the right to tax, judge, make war, and coin money. The term *enlightened absolutist* was often used to refer to state monarchies in seventeenth- and eighteenth-century Europe.

Versailles Louis XIV's Versailles, just southwest of Paris, was a hunting lodge that was converted at colossal cost in the 1670s–1680s into a grand royal chateau with expansive grounds. Much envied and imitated across Europe, the palace became the epicenter of a luxurious court life that included entertainments such as plays and musical offerings, state receptions, royal hunts, boating, and gambling. Thousands of nobles at Versailles vied with each other for closer proximity to the king in the performance of court rituals.

discriminatory measures against them. Peasant disturbances continued. Criticism of court life, wars, and religious policies filled anonymous pamphlets, jurists' notebooks, and courtiers' private journals. Members of the nobility also grumbled about their political misfortunes, but since the king had suppressed the traditional advisory bodies they had dominated, they had no formal way to express their concerns.

England might also have evolved into an absolutist regime, but there were important differences between England and France. Queen Elizabeth (r. 1558–1603) and her successors used many policies similar to those of the French monarchy, such as control of patronage and elaborate court festivities. Above all, the English Parliament remained an important force. Whereas the French kings did not consult the Estates-General to enact taxes, the English monarchs had to convene Parliament to raise money.

Under Elizabeth's successors, fierce quarrels broke out over taxation, religion, and royal efforts to rule without parliamentary consent. Tensions ran high between Puritans (who preferred a simpler form of worship and more egalitarian church government) and Anglicans (who supported the state-sponsored, hierarchically organized Church of England headed by the king). Those tensions erupted in the 1640s into civil war that saw the victory of the largely Puritan parliamentary army and the beheading of the king, Charles I. Although the monarchy was restored a dozen years later, in 1660, the king's relation to Parliament and the relationship between the crown and religion remained undecided (in particular the right of Protestants to assume the throne).

Subsequent monarchs who aspired to absolute rule came into conflict with Parliament, whose members insisted on shared sovereignty and the right of Protestant succession. This dispute culminated in the Glorious Revolution of 1688–1689. In a bloodless upheaval, King James II fled to France and Parliament offered the crown to William of Orange and his wife, Mary (both Protestants). The outcome of the conflict established the principle that English monarchs must rule in conjunction with Parliament. Although the Church of England was reaffirmed as the official state church, Presbyterians and Jews were allowed to practice their religions. Catholic worship, still officially forbidden, was tolerated as long as the Catholics kept quiet. By 1700, then, England's nobility and merchant classes had a guaranteed say in public affairs and assurance that state activity would privilege the propertied classes as well as the ruler. As a result, English rulers could borrow money much more effectively than their rivals could.

Mercantilist Wars The rise of new powers in Europe, especially France and England, intensified rivalries for control of Atlantic trade. As conflicts over colonies and sea-lanes replaced earlier religious and territorial struggles, commercial struggles became worldwide wars. Across the globe, European empires constantly skirmished over control of trade and territory. English and Dutch trading companies took aim at Portuguese outposts in Asia and the Americas, and then at each other. Ports in India suffered repeated assaults and counterassaults. In response, European powers built huge navies to protect their colonies and trade routes and to attack their rivals.

After 1715, a series of wars occurred mainly outside Europe, as empires feuded over colonial possessions. These conflicts were especially bitter in border areas, particularly in the Caribbean and North America. Each round of warfare ratcheted up the scale and cost of fighting.

The **Seven Years' War** (known as the French and Indian War in North America) marked the culmination of this rivalry among European empires around the globe. Fought from 1756 to 1763, it saw Native Americans, African slaves, Bengali princes, Filipino militiamen, and European foot

Seven Years' War (1756–1763) Also known as the French and Indian War; worldwide war that ended when Prussia defeated Austria, establishing itself as a European power, and when Britain gained control of India and many of France's colonies through the Treaty of Paris.

soldiers dragged into a contest over imperial possessions and control of the seas. The battles in Europe were relatively indecisive (despite being large), except in the hinterlands. After all, what sparked the war was a skirmish of British colonial troops (featuring a lieutenant colonel named George Washington) allied with Seneca warriors against French soldiers in the Ohio Valley (see Map 13.2 for North American references). In India, the war had a decisive outcome, for here the East India Company trader Robert Clive rallied 850 European officers and 2,100 Indian recruits to defeat the French (there were but 40 French artillerymen) and their 50,000 Maratha allies—men from an independent Indian empire in northern India—at Plassey. The British seized the upper hand, over everyone. Not only did the British drive off the French from the rich Bengali interior, but they also crippled Indian rulers' resistance against European intruders (see Map 12.4 for India references).

The Seven Years' War changed the balance of power around the world. Britain emerged as the foremost colonial empire. Its rivals, especially France and Spain, took a pounding; France lost its North American colonies, and Spain lost Florida (though it gained the Louisiana Territory west of the Mississippi in a secret deal with France). In India, as well, the French were losers and had to acknowledge British supremacy in the wealthy provinces of Bihar and Bengal. But overwhelmingly, the biggest losers were indigenous peoples everywhere. With the rise of one empire over all others, it was harder for Native Americans to play the Europeans off against each other. Maratha princes faced the same problem. Clearly, as worlds became more entangled, the gaps between winners and losers grew more pronounced.

Conclusion

A radical decline in temperatures worldwide made the seventeenth century a time of famine, dying, epidemic disease, and political turmoil that contributed to regime change in China, Persia, and England and threatened the rulers of the Ottoman and Mughal Empires. But by the 1750s, the world's regions were more economically connected than they had been a century and a half earlier. The process of integrating the resources of previous worlds apart that had begun with Christopher Columbus's voyages intensified during this period. Traders shipped a wider variety of commodities—from Baltic wood to Indian cotton, from New World silver and sugar to Chinese silks and porcelain—over longer distances. People increasingly wore clothes manufactured elsewhere, consumed beverages made from products cultivated in far-off locations, and used imported guns to settle local conflicts.

Everywhere, this integration and the consumer opportunities that it made possible came at a heavy price. Nowhere was it more costly than in the

Americas, where colonization and exploitation led to the expulsion of Native Americans from their lands and the decimation of their numbers. The cost was also very high for the millions of Africans forced across the Atlantic to work New World plantations and for the millions more who did not survive the journey.

Silver was the product from the Americas that most transformed global trading networks and that showed how greater entanglements could both enrich and destabilize. Although Spanish colonizers mined New World silver and shipped it to western Europe and Asia, it was Spain's main competitors in Europe that gained the upper hand in the seventeenth and eighteenth centuries. Nearly one-third of the silver from the New World ended up in China as payment for products like porcelains and silks that consumers still regarded as the world's finest manufactures. But if China's economy remained vibrant, silver did play a part in the fall of one dynasty and the rise of another. For the Ottoman and Mughal Empires, the influx of silver created rampant inflation and undermined their previous economic autonomy.

Certain societies coped with increased commercial exchange, environmental change, and internal challenges more successfully than others did. The Safavid and Ming dynasties could not withstand the pressures; both collapsed. The Spanish, Ottoman, and Mughal dynasties managed to survive but faced increasing pressure from aggressive rivals. For newcomers to the integrating world, the opportunity to trade helped support new dynasties. Japan, Russia, and England emerged on the world stage. But even in these newer regimes, commerce and competition did not erase conflict. To the contrary, while the world was more fully integrated in economic terms than ever before, greater prosperity for some hardly translated into peace for most.

Focus On
Regional Impact of World Trade

The Americas
- England, France, and Holland join Spain and Portugal as colonial powers in the Americas.
- The English and French colonies in the Caribbean become the world's major exporters of sugar.

Africa
- The Atlantic slave trade increases to record proportions, creating gender imbalances, impoverishing some regions, and elevating the power of slave-supplying states.

Southeast Asia
- The Dutch East India Company takes over the major islands of Southeast Asia.

The Islamic World
- World trade destabilizes the Safavid, Ottoman, and Mughal Empires.

East Asia
- The Ming dynasty in China loses the mandate of heaven and is replaced by the Qing.
- The Tokugawa shogunate unifies Japan and limits the influence of Europeans in the country.

Europe
- Tsarist Russia expands toward the Baltic Sea and the Pacific Ocean and becomes the largest state in the world.
- Europe recovers from the Thirty Years' War (1618–1648), with Holland, England, and France emerging as economic powerhouses.

CHRONOLOGY

1600

Region	
The Americas	Sugar complex emerges in the Caribbean region seventeenth century French and Dutch merchants establish fur trade in North America seventeenth century
Africa	Massive expansion of Atlantic slave trade 1650–1800
South Asia	
East Asia	Tokugawa shogunate formed in Japan 1603 Ming dynasty falls, Qing dynasty founded 1644
Europe	Thirty Years' War 1618–1648 England, France, Netherlands pursue mercantilist expansion abroad 1600–1800
The Islamic World	Köprülü reforms stabilize Ottoman Empire mid-seventeenth century
Russia	Expansion into Siberia seventeenth century Romanov dynasty founded 1613

THINKING ABOUT GLOBAL CONNECTIONS

- **Thinking about Exchange Networks and World Trade** How did silver, and then sugar, transform world trade? What political and cultural forces benefited from the development of long-distance trading networks? Which groups suffered and how? Contrast the effects of long distance trade in major world regions.

- **Thinking about Changing Power Relationships and World Trade** The seventeenth and eighteenth centuries witnessed the rise of new powers in England, Japan, and Russia, as well as regional powers on the west coast of Africa. Several established empires continued to expand but confronted powerful new challenges to their authority. How did leaders of the Ottoman, Mughal, and Qing Empires respond to challenges to their authority? What major challenges did they face? How would you characterize the new powers that emerged around the world in this period?

- **Thinking about the Impact of World Trade on Gender Relations** The Atlantic slave trade wreaked havoc on sex ratios both in Africa and in the slave societies of the New World because most slaves taken from Africa were men. How did this affect social life on New World plantations? What strategies did African communities utilize to mitigate the loss of so many men? Elsewhere around the world, increased trade challenged established social hierarchies. How did ruling elites mobilize gender to reinforce their authority?

Key Terms

absolute monarchy p. 629
Canton system p. 620
chartered companies p. 594
enclosure p. 629

Little Ice Age p. 595
Mamluks p. 613
Manchus p. 617
mercantilism p. 593

Muscovy p. 624
Qing dynasty p. 619
Seven Years' War p. 631

Thirty Years' War p. 627
Tokugawa shogunate p. 620

Go to **INQUIZITIVE** to see what you've learned—and learn what you've missed—with personalized feedback along the way.

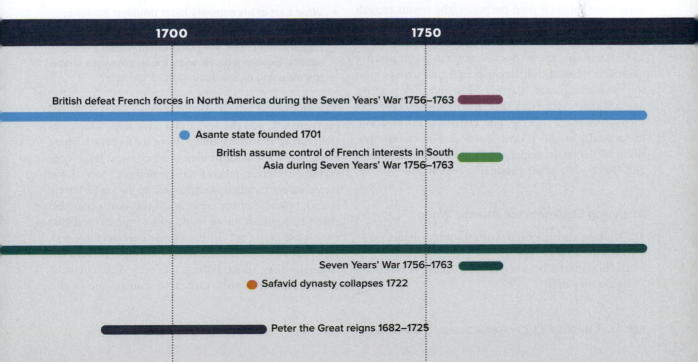

1700 — 1750

British defeat French forces in North America during the Seven Years' War 1756–1763

Asante state founded 1701

British assume control of French interests in South Asia during Seven Years' War 1756–1763

Seven Years' War 1756–1763

Safavid dynasty collapses 1722

Peter the Great reigns 1682–1725

Global Themes and Sources

Comparing Perceptions on Slavery in the Atlantic World

The documents gathered here present different aspects of slavery in the Atlantic world. For African slaves, the Atlantic system was an abomination. For slave owners, merchants, and political leaders—in Africa and Europe—the slave trade was a business. Each document highlights a different aspect and presents a different perspective on Atlantic slavery.

In the first document, Olaudah Equiano describes the horrifying conditions captives endured on the African coast as they awaited the arrival of slaving ships from the point of view of a captive. In the second, Richard Ligon explains the absence of slave revolts from the planters' perspective, while in the third, the Baron de Wimpffen, a Swiss aristocrat and explorer, describes the centrality of race, as opposed to family lineage or nobility, in the colonial society of Saint-Domingue. The final three documents show data from the 1835 household census for Santiago do Iguape, Bahia, a parish in the heart of a sugar plantation region in Brazil. Created by Portuguese colonial authorities for their own purposes, the census records provide basic demographic statistics about the region's population, over half of which was enslaved.

Collectively, these documents raise comparative questions: How did different people and groups view the same institution, slavery? How did they perceive one another? How did they distinguish people like themselves from others? The statistical information, in particular, makes it possible to see how the composition of plantation society changed—to identify cause and effect—in a sugar-producing region.

Analyzing Slavery in the Atlantic World

- Compare the way each written source divides people into racial groups. How do the sources mark the boundaries between communities? What criteria do they use?

- Contrast de Wimpffen's account of Saint-Domingue with Ligon's history of Barbados. What are their biggest fears?

- Does the evidence from the graphs support or undermine the claims of the written sources?

PRIMARY SOURCE 13.1

The Interesting Narrative of the Life of Olaudah Equiano (1789), Olaudah Equiano

Taught to read and write by his masters, Olaudah Equiano (c. 1745–1797) published *The Interesting Narrative of the Life of Olaudah Equiano, or Gustavus Vassa, the African* (1789) after purchasing his freedom in 1766. Known as Gustavus Vassa during his lifetime, he was active in the British abolitionist movement.

- **Explain the significance of nation (or community) in this document.**

- **What part of his captivity most troubled Equiano, and how did he cope?**

- **Equiano describes the punishment meted out to whites. Explain why. How do those passages shape the meaning of the document as a whole?**

The first object which saluted my eyes when I arrived on the coast, was the sea, and a slave ship, which was then riding at anchor, and waiting for its cargo. These filled me with astonishment, which was soon converted into terror, when I was carried on board. I was immediately handled, and tossed up to see if I were sound, by some of the crew; and I was now persuaded that I had gotten into a world of bad spirits, and that they were going to kill me. Their complexions, too, differing so much from ours, their long hair, and the language they spoke (which was very different from any I had ever heard), united to confirm me in this belief. Indeed, such were the horrors of my views and fears at the moment, that, if ten thousand worlds had been my own, I would have freely parted with them all to have exchanged my condition with that of the meanest slave in my own country. When I looked round the ship too, and saw a large furnace of copper boiling, and a multitude of black people of every description chained together, every one of their countenances expressing dejection and sorrow, I no longer doubted of my fate; and, quite overpowered with horror and anguish, I fell motionless on the deck and fainted. When I recovered a little, I found some black people about me, who I believed were some of those who had brought me on board, and had been receiving their pay; they talked to me in order to cheer me, but all in vain. . . .

I now saw myself deprived of all chance of returning to my native country, or even the least glimpse of hope of gaining the shore, which I now considered as friendly; and I even wished for my former slavery in preference to my present situation, which was filled with horrors of every kind, still heightened by my ignorance of what I was to undergo. I was not long suffered to indulge my grief; I was soon put down under the decks, and there I received such a salutation in my nostrils as I had never experienced in my life; so that, with the loathsomeness of the stench, and crying together, I became so sick and low that I was not able to eat, nor I had the least desire to taste anything. . . .

In a little time after, amongst the poor chained men, I found some of my own nation, which in a small degree gave ease to my mind. I inquired of these what was to be done with us? They gave me to understand, we were to be carried to these white people's country to work for them. I then was a little revived, and thought, if it were no worse than working, my situation was not so desperate; but still I feared I should be put to death, the white people looked and acted, as I thought, in so savage a manner; for I had never seen among any people such instances of brutal cruelty; and this not only shown towards us blacks, but also to some of the whites themselves. One white man in particular I saw, when we were permitted to be on deck, flogged so unmercifully with a large rope near the foremast, that he died in consequence of it; and

they tossed him over the side as they would have done a brute. This made me fear these people the more; and I expected nothing less than to be treated in the same manner. . . .

At last, when the ship we were in, had got in all her cargo, they made ready with many fearful noises, and we were all put under deck, so that we could not see how they managed the vessel. But this disappointment was the least of my sorrow. The stench of the hold while we were on the coast was so intolerably loathsome, that it was dangerous to remain there for any time, and some of us had been permitted to stay on the deck for the fresh air; but now that the whole ship's cargo were confined together, it became absolutely pestilential. The closeness of the place, and the heat of the climate, added to the number in the ship, which was so crowded that each had scarcely room to turn himself, almost suffocated us. This produced copious perspirations, so that the air soon became unfit for respiration, from a variety of loathsome smells, and brought on a sickness among the slaves, of which many died. . . . The shrieks of the women, and the groans of the dying, rendered the whole a scene of horror almost inconceivable. Happily perhaps, for myself, I was soon reduced so low here that it was thought necessary to keep me almost always on deck; and from my extreme youth I was not put in fetters. In this situation I expected every hour to share the fate of my companions, some of whom were almost daily brought upon deck at the point of death, which I began to hope would soon put an end to my miseries.

Source: Olaudah Equiano, *The Interesting Narrative of the Life of Olaudah Equiano, or Gustavus Vassa, the African, Written by Himself* (New York: Norton, 2001), pp. 38–41.

A True and Exact History of the Island of Barbadoes (1673), Richard Ligon

Richard Ligon (c. 1585–1662) lost most of his fortune in the English Civil War (1642–1651). He bought half a sugar plantation on the English island of Barbados to recover from his losses and rebuild his fortune.

- **How does Ligon distinguish slaves from slave owners?**

- How does Ligon explain the absence of slave revolts?
- Analyze the role of religion in this document.

....

It has been accounted a strange thing that the Negroes, being more than double the numbers of the Christians that are there, and they accounted a bloody people where they think they have power or advantages; and the more bloody by how much they are more fearful than others: that these should not commit some horrid massacre upon the Christians, thereby to enfranchise [empower] themselves and become Masters of the Island. But there are three reasons that take away this wonder; the one is, They are not suffered [allowed] to touch or handle any weapons: The other, That they are held in such awe and slavery as they are fearful to appear in any daring act; and seeing the mustering of our men and hearing their Gun-shot (that which nothing is more terrible to them), their spirits are subjugated to so low a condition as they dare not look up to any bold attempt. Besides these, there is a third reason, which stops all designs [plans] of that kind, and that is, They are fetch'd from several parts of Africa, who speak several languages, and by that means one of them understands not another: For, some of them are fetch'd from Guinny and Binny, some from Cutchew, some from Angola, and some from the River of Gambia. And in some of these places where petty Kingdoms are, they sell their Subjects and such as they take in Battle, whom they make slaves; and some mean men sell their Servants, their Children, and sometimes their Wives; and think all good traffic [acceptable trade] for such commodities as our Merchants send them. When they are brought to us, the Planters buy them out of the Ship where they find them stark naked and therefore cannot be deceived in any outward infirmity. They choose them as they do Horses in a Market; the strongest, youthfulest, and most beautiful, yield the greatest prices. Thirty pound sterling is a price for the best man Negro; and twenty five, twenty six, or twenty seven pound for a Woman; the Children are at easier rates. . . .

When any of them die, they dig a grave, and at evening they bury him, clapping and wringing their hands and making a doleful sound with their voices.

They are a people of a timorous and fearful disposition, and consequently bloody when they find advantages [opportunities]. If any of them commit a fault, give him present [immediate] punishment, but do not threaten him; for if you do, it is an even lay, he will go and hang himself to avoid the punishment. What their other opinions are in matter of Religion, I know not; but certainly they are not altogether of the sect of the Sadduces [Hebrew sect (second century BCE–first century CE) that rejected belief in the resurrection of the soul]: For, they believe a Resurrection and that they shall go into their own Country again and have their youth renewed. And lodging this opinion in their hearts, they make it an ordinary practice, upon any great fright or threatening of their Master, to hang themselves. But Colonel Walrond, having lost three or four of his best Negroes this way, and in a very little time, caused one of their heads to be cut off and set upon a pole a dozen foot high; and having done that, caused all his Negroes to come forth and march round about this head and bid them look on it, whether this were not the head of such an one that hang'd himself. Which they acknowledging, he then told them, That they were in a main error in thinking they went into their own Countries after they were dead; for, this man's head was here, as they all were witnesses of; and how was it possible the body could go without a head. Being convinc'd by this sad yet lively spectacle, they changed their opinions; and after that, no more hanged themselves.

Source: Richard Ligon, *A True and Exact History of the Island of Barbadoes* (London: Peter Parker, 1673), excerpts available online at http://nationalhumanitiescenter.org/pds/amerbegin/power/text8/LigonBarbadosSlavery.pdf.

<hr>

PRIMARY SOURCE 13.3

A Voyage to Saint Domingue (1797), Alexandre-Stanislas, Baron de Wimpffen

Alexandre-Stanislas, Baron de Wimpffen, served as a captain under the French general Count Rochambeau in 1781–1782 and was an aristocratic military figure and explorer. He served in the West Indies and resigned in 1788.

- Analyze the significance of "intimacy" in this document.
- What does de Wimpffen mean by the "compulsatory precautions arising from the prejudice of colour"?
- Explain the relationship between "whites from Europe" and "white Creoles."

Although the distance between the slave and the free man is immense, yet, to avoid subdivisions, and minute distinctions, I have adopted the division of color, as the most simple. For I must further observe to you, that the male and female negroes, as well as the male and female mulattos, in spite of the acquisition of liberty, remain in a state of abjectness, which not only disqualifies them from any public employ, but forbids them to contract with the whites a sufficient degree of intimacy, I will not say to sleep with them, but even to eat. If I visit a rich mulatto, he will call me Sir, and not master, like the rest. I call him friend, dear friend, &c. he will ask me to dinner; but if he be correct, he will not presume to sit at table with me.

Such, Sir, is the total division. Each of the three classes has besides its shades—such as those which, in despite of complexion, separate the governor from the other whites, the mulatto from the free negro, &c. &c.

The compulsatory precautions arising from the prejudice of colour, have procured for the inhabitants two advantages, which in some degree compensate for the ridiculousness of it. They render the government more circumspect in its arbitrary proceedings; and they imprint on the colonists a character of haughty independence, from which despotic administrators have more than once experienced a resistance so inflexible, that the court has been finally obliged to recall a governor, whom the habit of playing the nabob [a European who returned from India having made a fortune] in the East, has daily tempted to transgress the bounds of his authority.

The natural consequence of the order of things which prevails here, is, that all those titles of honour which are elsewhere the *pabula* [source] of emulation, of rivalry and of discord; which inspire so much pride, and create so many claims in some; so much ambition and envy in others; shrink to nothing, and entirely disappear before the sole title of WHITE. It is by your skin, however branded it may be, and not by your parchment [titles of nobility], however worm-eaten, that your pretensions to gentility are assessed. Thus you see that vanity, which on your side of the water torments and turns herself a thousand ways, to impose on the public, and usurp the tribute of respect which it accords to the claims of birth, would here lose both her time and her labor.

Each of the different classes of the inhabitants of St. Domingo has, as you will readily imagine, a turn of thinking, a style of living, more or less approximate or distinct; which, after all, has little resemblance to what you will find elsewhere; because the climate, the regimen, the manners, the wants, the occupations, the degree of reciprocal dependency, establish here connections of the slightest nature; very different from those which, with you, Sir, bind together the members of the same society. . . .

The first thing that strikes every traveller who arrives here with the faculty of observation, is, that in spite of the conformity of origin, colour and interests, the whites from Europe, and the white Creoles, form two classes, which, by their reciprocal pretentions, are so widely foundered, that necessity alone can bring them together. The former, with more breeding, more politeness, and more knowledge of the world, affect over the latter a superiority which is far from contributing to unite them. Yet, if the Creoles were a little more cautious than they are at present in their too early connections with women; if they cultivated with more care their extraordinary propensities to excel in all bodily exercises; if they seconded by a better method of education the natural facility of their genius; I am persuaded, that not having to struggle against the influence of the climate under which they were born, nor against the habitudes of a kind of life, differing essentially from that to which a European is obliged to submit himself on his arrival here, I am persuaded, I say, that all the advantages would be on their side. Nothing is wanting to the Creole, but a sufficient degree of good sense, to enable him to use, without abusing, the faculties with which nature has endued [sic] him.

Source: Francis Alexander Stanislaus, Baron de Wimpffen, *A Voyage to Saint Domingue, in the Years 1788, 1789, and 1790,* translated by J. Wright (London: T. Cadell, Junior, and W. Davies, 1797), pp. 62–65.

Population Statistics of the Bahia Sugar Plantations, Brazil (1835)

These documents show data from the 1835 household census for Santiago do Iguape, Bahia, a parish in the heart of a sugar plantation region in Brazil. They provide basic demographic statistics about the region's population, over half of which was enslaved. Created by colonial authorities for their own purposes, the census records make it possible to reconstruct the experience of people who left no written records themselves.

Population pyramids are graphs that present a population's composition by age and sex, and, here, by racial classification as well. A pyramid equally divided between men and women with a wide base represents an expanding population with a large proportion of children and young adults. Iguape's free and freed populations follow this pattern, but the enslaved population does not.

- Compare the data for each racial group in the first graph, and consider why the Brazilian state organized its records according to racial categories. How do you think the demands of sugar production shaped the racial categories Brazilian officials used to sort the local population?

- Considering the second two graphs, on the free and enslaved populations, how was plantation society changing? Which groups managed to achieve a level of stability, and which did not?

- Describe the challenges slaves would have faced in establishing families on the sugar plantations of Santiago do Iguape, and contrast their experience with the experiences of freed people of different racial classifications.

Source: Katherine Holt, "Population by Racial Classification, Santiago do Iguape 1835," "Free and Freed Population by Racial Classification, Iguape 1835," and "Enslaved Population by Place of Birth, Santiago do Iguape, 1835," The Bahian History Project: The 1835 Santiago do Iguape Household Census Database, http://www.mappingbahia.org/project/.

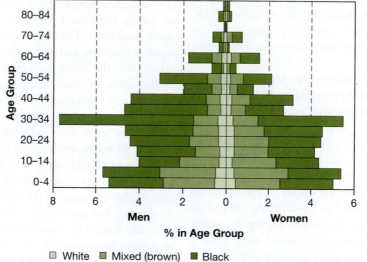

Population by Racial Classification in 1835, Santiago do Iguape

☐ White   ☐ Mixed (brown)   ■ Black

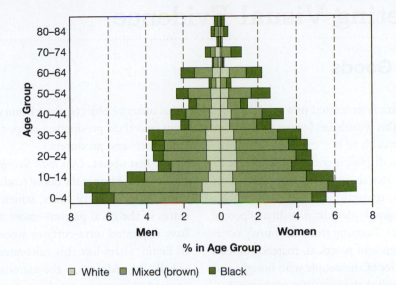

Free and Freed Population by Racial Classification in 1835, Santiago do Iguape

□ White   ■ Mixed (brown)   ■ Black

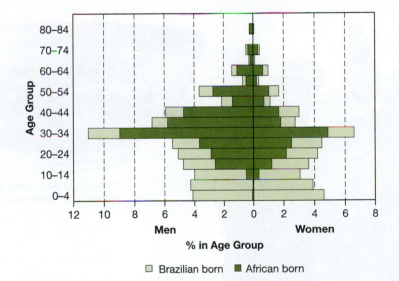

□ Brazilian born   ■ African born

Enslaved Population by Place of Birth in 1835, Santiago do Iguape

Interpreting Visual Evidence

A World of Goods

As overseas trade generated new wealth, elites displayed this wealth in diverse ways. Some used new wealth to buy expensive local materials, while others displayed their power by incorporating foreign materials into local designs. Near commercial centers, opportunities for consumption and display of new goods also drew ordinary people into market activities. Ranging from the purely ornamental to the modest and practical, material objects reflected the identities of the people who bought and displayed them, as well as the identities of the producers who made them. They reinforced and sometimes altered status hierarchies as people's appreciation of these material objects, their beauty, and the skill that went into their production shaped the status of both consumers and producers.

The first object, *Oba with Sacrificial Animals from the Ezomo's Altar of the Hand* (eighteenth–nineteenth century), is made of brass, which signified the elite status of the royal patron—more modest men would have requested terra-cotta or wood. In the kingdom of Benin, altars like this celebrated exceptional individuals. In addition to the materials chosen, the artist used costume and scale to show the status of the figures depicted. The king, Ehenua, dressed in full military regalia, appears in the center of a group of

Chinese porcelain bowl, with painting by Francis Hayman.

Oba with Sacrificial Animals from the Ezomo's Altar of the Hand.

smaller soldiers, aids, and priests. Two rows of musketeers above the frieze include Portuguese soldiers, showing the support Europeans provided Benin's leaders. The second object is a porcelain bowl produced in China for the British market, with a painting of a cricket match by the English painter Francis Hayman (1708–1776). The third object, a Chinese lacquer tray from the Qing dynasty, likely crafted for the internal Chinese market, portrays a pastoral scene. The final object, a British-manufactured teapot, was made for middle-class consumers who could not afford imported porcelain from China. This example, with a handle, was intended to match European decorative style; the factory left off the handle for "Oriental" designs.

Tray (lacquer and mother of pearl), Chinese School, Qing dynasty.

British-manufactured teapot.

Questions for Analysis

1. Describe how these objects were used. What functions did they serve?

2. Analyze the relationship between display and function in these objects. What impression do you think these objects made on people who saw them?

3. Explain the significance of these works for the people who produced them. What roles do you think artistry, craft skill, and financial gain played for the artists and artisans who produced them?

4. How did the conditions in which these objects were produced relate to the identities consumers sought to project? Consider also the relationship between the production of commodities—such as the tea and sugar associated with the final object—and consumer identity.

14

Cultures of Splendor and Power

1500–1780

In 1664, a sixteen-year-old girl from the provinces of New Spain asked her parents for permission to attend the university in the capital. Although she had mastered Greek logic, taught Latin, and become a proficient mathematician, she had two strikes against her: she was a woman, and her thinking ran against the grain of the Catholic Church. So keen was she to pursue her studies that she proposed to disguise herself as a man. But her parents denied her requests, and instead of attending the university she entered a convent in Mexico City, where she would spend the rest of her life. The convent turned out to be a sanctuary for her. There she studied science and mathematics and composed remarkable poetry. Sor (Sister) Juana Inés de la Cruz was her name, and she spoke for a new world where people mixed in far-away places, where new wealth created new customs, and where new ideas began to take hold.

Sor Juana's story attests to the conflicts between new ideas and old orders that occurred as commerce and the consolidation of empires intensified contact between diverse cultures. On the one hand, global commerce created riches that supported arts, architecture, and scientific ventures. On the other, experiments with new ways caused discomfort among defenders of the old order and provoked backlashes against innovation.

Chapter Outline

- Trade and Culture
- Culture in the Islamic World
- Culture and Politics in East Asia
- African Cultural Flourishing
- The Enlightenment in Europe
- Creating Hybrid Cultures in the Americas
- The Influence of European Culture in Oceania
- Conclusion

Core Objectives

- **EXPLAIN** the connections between cultural growth and the creation of a global market.
- **DESCRIBE** and **COMPARE** how each culture in this period reflected the ideas of the state in which it was produced.
- **ANALYZE** the different responses to foreign cultures across Afro-Eurasia in the period from 1500 to 1780.
- **DESCRIBE** how hybrid cultures emerged in the Americas, and **EXPLAIN** the connection between these cultures and Enlightenment ideology.
- **ANALYZE** the role that race and cultural difference played in the process of global integration.

This chapter explores how global commerce enriched and reshaped cultures in the centuries after the Americas ceased to be worlds apart from Afro-Eurasia. As New World commodities invigorated global trade and states consolidated power, rulers and merchants on both sides of the Atlantic displayed their power by commissioning fabulous works of art and majestic palaces and sprawling plazas. These cultural splendors were meant to impress, which they surely did. They also demonstrated the growing connections between distant societies, reflecting how foreign influences could blend with domestic traditions. Book production and consumption soared, with some publications finding their way around the world. The spread of books and ideas and increasing cultural contact led to experiments in religious toleration and helped foster cultural diversity. Yet even as Europeans, who were the greatest beneficiaries of New World riches, claimed to advance new universal truths, cultures around the globe still showed the resilience of inherited traditions.

Global Storylines

- Growing global commerce enriches rulers and merchants, who express their power through patronage for the arts.

- Distinctive cultures flourish in the major regions of the world, blending new influences with local traditions to varying degrees.

- While the Islamic and Asian worlds confidently retain their own belief systems, the Americas and Oceania increasingly face European cultural pressures.

Trade and Culture

New wealth amassed by global commerce in the aftermath of Columbus's "discovery" created the conditions for cultural dynamism in the centuries after 1500. With newfound wealth, rulers promoted learning and the arts in order to legitimize their power and show their sophistication. In Europe, monarchs known as enlightened absolutists restricted the clergy and nobility and hired loyal bureaucrats who championed the knowledge of the new age. Mughal emperors, Safavid shahs, and Ottoman sultans glorified their regimes by bringing artists and artisans from all over the world to give an Islamic flavor to their major cities and buildings. Rulers in China and Japan also looked to artists to extol their achievements. In Africa, the wealth garnered from slave trading underwrote cultural productions of extraordinary merit.

Some rulers were more eager for change than others. Moreover, certain societies—in the Americas and the South Pacific, for example—found that contact, conquest, and commerce undermined indigenous cultural life. Although Europeans and native peoples often exchanged ideas and practices, these transfers were not equal. Native Americans, for example, adapted to European missionizing by creating mixed forms of religious worship—but only because they were under pressure to do so. And as the Europeans swallowed up new territories, it was *their* culture that spread and diversified. Indeed, the Europeans absorbed much from Native Americans and African slaves but offered them little share of sovereignty or wealth in return.

Despite the unifying aspects of world trade, each society retained core aspects of its individuality. Ruling classes disseminated values based on cherished classical texts and long-established moral and religious principles. They used space in new ways to establish and project their power. They mapped their geographies and wrote their histories according to their traditional visions of the universe.

It is not surprising that in 1500 the world's most dynamic cultures remained in Asia, in areas profiting from the Indian Ocean and China Sea trades. It was in China and the Islamic world that the spice and luxury trades first flourished; here, too, rulers had successfully established political stability and centralized control of taxation, law making, and military force. Although older ways did not die out, both trade and empire building contributed to the spread of knowledge about distant people and foreign cultures.

Culture in the Islamic World

As the Ottoman, Safavid, and Mughal Empires gained greater expanses of territory in the sixteenth and seventeenth centuries, they acquired new resources to fund cultural development. Rulers supported new schools and

THE BIG PICTURE

What are the connections between cultural growth and the creation of a global market?

building projects, and the elite produced books, artworks, and luxury goods. Cultural life was connected to the politics of empire building, as emperors and elites sought greater prestige by patronizing intellectuals and artists.

Forged under different empires, Islamic cultural and intellectual life now reflected three distinct worlds. In place of an earlier Islamic cosmopolitanism, unique cultural patterns prevailed within each empire. Although the Ottomans, the Safavids, and the Mughals shared a common faith, each developed a relatively autonomous form of Muslim culture.

THE OTTOMAN CULTURAL SYNTHESIS

By the sixteenth century, the Ottoman Empire enjoyed a remarkably rich culture that reflected a variety of mixing influences. As the Ottoman Empire absorbed more cultures and territories, its blend of ethnic, religious, and linguistic elements exceeded the diversity of previous Islamic empires. It also balanced the interests of military men and administrators with those of clerics. Finally, it allowed autonomy to the minority faiths of Christianity and Judaism. That ability to balance a wide array of local traditions and interests and yet maintain authority in the center, supported by new revenues drawn from global trade, constituted the Ottoman synthesis.

Religion and Education A sophisticated educational system was crucial for the empire's religious and intellectual integration and for its cultural achievements. Here, as in religious affairs, the Ottomans tolerated difference. They encouraged three educational systems that produced three streams of talent—civil and military bureaucrats, *ulama*, and Sufi religious masters. The administrative elite attended hierarchically organized schools that culminated in the palace schools at Topkapi (see Chapter 11). In the religious sphere, an equally elaborate system took students from elementary schools (where they learned reading, writing, and numbers) on to higher schools, or *madrasas* (where they learned law, religion, the Quran, and the natural sciences). These graduates became *ulama* who served as judges, experts in religious law, or teachers. Yet another set of schools, *tekkes*, taught the devotional strategies and religious knowledge for students to enter Sufi orders.

Science and the Arts During this period, the Ottomans integrated some foreign elements into their culture, especially in science and philosophy, while furthering their own traditions in architecture, literature, and music. Most of the foreign influences came from Europe, with which the Ottomans were in constant contact. The Ottomans' most impressive effort to spread European knowledge occurred when a Hungarian convert to Islam, Ibrahim Muteferrika, set up a printing press in Istanbul in 1729. Muteferrika published works on science, history, and geography. One included sections on

Core Objectives

DESCRIBE and COMPARE how each Islamic culture in this period reflected the ideas of the state in which it was produced.

The Ottomans and the Tulip The Ottomans used tulip motifs to decorate tiles in homes and mosques and pottery wares, as on the plate shown here.

geometry; others included the works of Copernicus, Galileo, and Descartes and a plea to the Ottoman elite to learn from Europe. When his patron was killed, however, the *ulama* promptly closed off this avenue of contact with western learning.

The Ottomans combined inherited traditions with new elements in art as well. For example, portraiture became popular after the Italian painter Gentile Bellini visited Istanbul and painted a portrait of Mehmed II. In other areas, though, the Ottomans kept their own styles. The magnificent architectural monuments built in the sixteenth through eighteenth centuries, including mosques, gardens, tombs, forts, and palaces, showed scant western influence. Nor were the Ottomans interested in western literature or music. For the most part, they believed that God had given the Islamic world a monopoly on truth and enlightenment and that their military successes proved his favor.

The Ottomans' capacity to celebrate their well-being and prosperity spread from elites to the broader public during the so-called Tulip Period, which occurred in the 1720s. The elite had long admired the tulip's bold colors and graceful blooms, and for centuries the flower served as the sultans' symbol.

In fact, both Mehmed the Conqueror and Suleiman the Magnificent grew tulips in the most secluded and prestigious courtyards at Topkapi Palace in Istanbul. And many Ottoman warriors heading into battle wore undergarments embroidered with tulips to ensure victory. By the early eighteenth century, tulip designs appeared on tiles, fabrics, and public buildings, and authorities sponsored elaborate tulip festivals. Indeed, Ottoman enjoyment of luxury goods (including lemons, soap, pepper, metal tools, coffee, and wine) grew so extensive that a well-traveled diplomat looked askance at the supposed wealth of Europe. He wrote, "In most of the provinces [of Europe], poverty is widespread, as a punishment for being infidels. Anyone who travels in these areas must confess that goodness and abundance are reserved for the Ottoman realms." Thus, despite challenges from western Europe and fears that their best days were behind them, the Ottomans' cultural traditions flourished into the eighteenth century and beyond.

SAFAVID CULTURE, SHIITE STATE

If global trade ultimately strengthened Safavid rivals both within the empire and without (see Chapter 13), it also provided the wherewithal for a period of spectacular artistic and architectural creativity, especially at the height of Safavid power in the seventeenth century. The Safavid Empire in Persia (1501–1722) was not as long-lived as the Ottoman Empire, but it was significant for giving the Shiite branch of Islam a home base and a location for displaying Shiite culture. The brilliant culture that emerged during the Safavid period provided a unique blend of Shiism and Persia's distinctive historical identity.

The Safavids created a mixed political and religious system based on Shiism and loyalty to the royal family. The most effective architect of a cultural life based on Shiite religious principles and Persian royal absolutism was Shah Abbas I (r. 1587–1629). The location that he chose to display the wealth and royal power of his state, its Persian and Shiite heritages, and its artistic sensibility was Isfahan, the capital city from its creation in 1598 until the empire's end in 1722.

Architecture and the Arts The Safavid shahs were unique among Afro-Eurasian rulers of this era, for they sought to project both absolute authority and accessibility. Their dwellings were unlike those of other rulers—such as Topkapi Palace in Istanbul, the Citadel in Cairo, and the Red Forts of the Mughals. Those were enclosed and fortified buildings, designed to enhance rulers' power by concealing them from their subjects. In contrast, the buildings of Isfahan were open to the outside, demonstrating the Safavid rulers' desire to connect with their people. Isfahan's centerpiece was the great plaza next to the royal palace and the royal mosque at the heart of the capital.

Other aspects of intellectual life reflected the elites' aspirations, wealth, and commitment to Shiite principles. Safavid artists perfected the illustrated book, the outstanding example being *The King's Book of Kings*, which contained 250 miniature illustrations. Here, artists demonstrated their mastery of three-dimensional representation and their ability to harmonize different colors. Weavers produced ornate silks and carpets for trade throughout the world; artisans painted tiles in vibrant colors and created mosaics that adorned mosques and other buildings. Moreover, the Safavids developed an elaborate calligraphy that was the envy of artists throughout the Islamic world. All of these works celebrated Shiite visions of the sacred while at the same time reinforcing the authority and prestige of the empire's ruling elite.

POWER AND CULTURE UNDER THE MUGHALS

Like the Safavids and the Ottomans, the Mughals fostered a lavish high culture, supported primarily by taxes on agriculture but reliant on silver for its currency and, at its high point, open to global trade. Because the Mughals ruled over a large non-Muslim population, the culture they developed in South Asia was initially broad and open, welcoming non-Muslims into its circle. Thus, while Islamic traditions dominated the empire's political and judicial systems, Hindus shared with Muslims the flourishing of learning, music, painting, and architecture, especially from the middle of the sixteenth century to the middle of the seventeenth.

Akbar Leading Religious Discussion This miniature painting from 1604 shows Akbar receiving Muslim theologians and Jesuits. The Jesuits (in the black robes on the left) hold a page relating, in Persian, the birth of Christ. A lively debate will follow the Jesuits' claims on behalf of Christianity.

Religion, Architecture, and the Arts In the sixteenth and early seventeenth centuries, Mughal culture mixed diverse elements from within South Asia and the broader Islamic world. The promise of an open Islamic high culture found its greatest fulfillment under the Mughal emperor Akbar (r. 1556–1605). This skillful military leader was also a popular ruler who allowed common people as well as nobles from all ethnic groups to converse with him at court. His quest for universal truths outside the strict *sharia* led him to develop a religion of his own, which incorporated many aspects of Hindu belief and ritual practice (see Chapter 12).

In architecture, too, the Mughals produced masterpieces that blended styles. This was already evident as builders combined Persian, Indian, and Ottoman elements in tombs and mosques built by Akbar's predecessors. But

Akbar enhanced this mixture in the elaborate city he built at Fatehpur Sikri, beginning in 1571. The buildings included residences for nobles (whose loyalty Akbar wanted), gardens, a drinking and gambling zone, and even an experimental school devoted to studying language acquisition in children.

Akbar's descendant Shah Jahan was also a lavish patron of architecture and the arts. In 1630, Shah Jahan ordered the building in Agra of a magnificent white marble tomb for his beloved wife, Mumtaz Mahal. Like many other women in the Mughal court, she had been an important political counselor. Designed by an Indian architect of Persian origin, this structure, the **Taj Mahal**, took twenty years and 20,000 workers to build. The 42-acre complex included a main gateway, a garden, minarets, and a mosque. The translucent marble mausoleum lay squarely in the middle of the structure, enclosed by four identical façades and crowned by a majestic central dome rising to 240 feet. The stone inlays of different types and hues, organized in geometrical and floral patterns and featuring Quranic verses inscribed in Arabic calligraphy, gave the surface an appearance of delicacy and lightness. Blending Persian and Islamic design with Indian materials and motifs, this poetry in stone represented the most splendid example of Mughal high culture and the combining of cultural traditions.

Foreign Influences versus Islamic Culture Although later emperors were less tolerant than Akbar, Mughal culture remained vibrant. Well into the eighteenth century, the Mughal nobility lived in unrivaled luxury. The presence of foreign scholars and artists enhanced the courtly culture, and the elite eagerly consumed exotic goods from China and Europe. Foreign trade also brought in more silver, advancing the money economy and supporting the nobles' sumptuous lifestyles. In addition, the Mughals assimilated European military technology: they hired Europeans as gunners and military engineers in their armies, employed them to forge guns, and bought guns and cannons from them.

For all their openness to outside influences, the Mughals, like the Ottomans, remained supremely confident of their own traditions. The centers of the Islamic world were still Istanbul, Cairo, and Delhi. Even while incorporating a few new European elements into their cultural mix, most Muslims regarded Europeans as rude barbarians. Elites in Persia, India, and the Ottoman Empire looked to China and the east, not to Europe and the west, for inspiration.

Culture and Politics in East Asia

In East Asia, prosperity, facilitated by China's vast importation of silver from Japan and the Americas, promoted cultural dynamism in the sixteenth through eighteenth centuries. Still, it was China's booming internal market, more than global trade, that fueled a Chinese culture inspired mainly by its own traditions. China had long been a renowned center of learning, with its emperors and elites supporting artists, poets, musicians, scientists, and teachers. But in late Ming and early Qing China, a growing population and extensive commercial networks propelled the circulation of ideas as well as goods.

In Japan, too, economic growth supported elite and popular culture. Because of its giant neighbor across the sea, the Japanese people had always been aware of outside influences. Like the Chinese government, the Tokugawa shogunate tried to promote Confucian notions of a social hierarchy organized on the basis of social position, age, gender, and kin. It also tried to shield the country from egalitarian ideas that would threaten the strict social hierarchy. But the forces that undermined governmental control of knowledge in China proved even stronger in Japan.

CHINA: THE CHALLENGE OF EXPANSION AND DIVERSITY

While China had become increasingly connected with the outside world in the sixteenth and seventeenth centuries, the sources for its cultural flourishing during the period came primarily from within. The circulation of books spread ideas among the literate, and religious rituals instilled cultural values among the broader population. Advances in cartography reflected the distinctive worldview of Chinese elites.

Publishing and the Transmission of Ideas The decentralization of book production and the domestic market helped circulate ideas within China. Woodblock and movable type printing had been present in China for centuries. Although initially the state had spurred book production by printing Confucian texts, before long the economy's increasing commercialization weakened government controls over what got printed. Even as officials clamped down on unorthodox texts, there was no centralized system of censorship, and unauthorized opinions circulated freely.

By the late Ming era, a burgeoning publishing sector catered to the diverse social, cultural, and religious needs of educated elites and urban populations. European visitors admired the vast collections of printed materials housed in Chinese libraries, describing them as "magnificently built" and "finely adorn'd." Perhaps more important, books and other luxury goods were now more affordable. Increasingly, publishers offered a mix of wares: guidebooks for patrons of the arts, travelers, or merchants; handbooks for performing rituals, choosing dates for ceremonies, or writing proper letters; almanacs and encyclopedias; morality books; medical manuals; and, above all, study guides.

Study aids for the civil service examination dominated the literary marketplace. In 1595, Beijing reeled with scandal over news that the second-place graduate had reproduced verbatim several model essays published by commercial printers. Ironically, then, the increased circulation of knowledge led critics to bemoan a decline in real learning; instead of mastering the classics, they charged, examination candidates were simply memorizing the work of others.

Elite women also joined China's literary culture. Women's poetry was especially popular, not only in anthologies published for the general market but in volumes produced for limited circulation to celebrate the refinement of the writer's family. Men of letters soon recognized the market potential of women's writings; some also saw women's less regularized style (usually acquired through family channels rather than state-sponsored schools) as a means to challenge stifling stylistic conformity. On rare occasions, women even served as publishers themselves.

Although elite women enjoyed success in the world of culture, the period brought increasing restrictions on their lives. The practice of footbinding (which elite women first adopted at least as far back as the twelfth century) continued to spread among common people, as small, delicate feet came to signify femininity and respectability. The thriving publishing sector indirectly promoted stricter morality by printing plays and novels that echoed the government's conservative attitudes.

Popular Culture and Religion Important as the book trade was, it had only an indirect impact on most men and women in late Ming China. Those who could not read well or at all absorbed cultural values through oral communication, ritual performance, and daily practices.

Villagers participated in various religious and cultural practices, such as honoring local guardian spirits, patronizing Buddhist and Daoist temples, or watching performances by touring theater groups. At the grassroots level, there was little distinction among Buddhist, Daoist, and local cults. The Chinese believed in cosmic unity, and although they celebrated spiritual forces, they did not consider any of them to be a Supreme Being who favored one sect over another. They believed it was the emperor, rather than any religious group, who held the mandate of heaven. (See Current Trends in World History: The Political Uses of Space.) Unless sects posed an obvious threat, the emperor had no reason to regulate their spiritual practices. This situation promoted religious tolerance and avoided the sectarian warfare that plagued post-Reformation Europe.

Technology and Cartography Belief in cosmic unity did not prevent the Chinese from devising technologies to master nature's operations in this world. For example, the magnetic compass, gunpowder, and the printing press were all Chinese inventions. Chinese astronomers also compiled accurate records of eclipses, comets, novae, and meteors. In part, the emperor's

Footbinding Two images of bound feet: (*left*) as an emblem of feminine respectability when wrapped and concealed, as on this well-to-do Chinese woman; (*right*) as an object of curiosity and condemnation when exposed for the world to see.

needs drove their interest in astronomy and calendrical science. It was the emperor's job as the Son of Heaven, and thus mediator between heaven and earth, to determine the best dates for planting, holding festivities, scheduling mourning periods, and convening judicial court sessions.

Convinced that their sciences were superior, Christian missionaries in China tried to promote their own knowledge in areas such as astronomy and cartography (mapmaking). In 1583, the Jesuit missionary Matteo Ricci brought European maps to China, hoping to impress the elite with European learning. Challenging their belief that the world was flat, his maps demonstrated that the earth was spherical—and that China was just one country among many others. Chinese critics complained that Ricci treated the Ming Empire as "a small unimportant country." As a concession, he placed China closer to the center of the maps and provided additional textual information. Still, his maps had a negligible impact, as neither the earth's shape nor precise scale was particularly important to most Chinese geographers.

Before the nineteenth century, the Chinese had fairly incomplete knowledge about foreign lands despite a long history of contact. Chinese writers, for example, often identified groups of other people through distinctive and,

The Political Uses of Space

The use of space for political purposes is a theme we can trace across world history. In the early modern period, many kings and emperors opted to build grand palaces to create lavish power centers, from which they could project their influence over their kingdoms; petitioners and potential rivals would have to come to *them* to ask for favors or to complete their business. Monarchs sculpted these environments, creating a series of spaces, each of them open to a smaller and smaller number of the king's favorites. Both palaces and their surrounding grounds were ornate and splendid, were expensive to construct, and involved the best craftsmen and artists available, which often meant borrowing ideas and designs from neighboring cultures. Palace complexes of this type, built in Beijing, in Istanbul, in Isfahan, and just outside of Paris, used space to project the rulers' power and to show who was boss.

The **Forbidden City of Beijing** was the earliest of these impressive sites of royal power (see illustration on p. 524). Its construction took about four years—from 1416 to 1420—although the actual name "Forbidden City" did not appear until 1576. The entrance of the city was straddled by the Meridian Gate, the tallest structure of the entire complex, which towered over all other buildings at more than 115 feet above the ground. It was from this lofty position that the emperor extended his gaze toward his empire, as he oversaw various court ceremonies, including the important annual proclamation of the calendar that governed the entire country's agricultural and ritual activities. Foreign emissaries received by the court were also often allowed to use one of the passageways through the gate, where they were expected to be duly awed. As for the officials' daily audience with the emperor, they had to line up outside the Meridian Gate around 3 a.m. before proceeding to the Hall of Supreme Harmony. It was typical of the entire construction project that this impressive hall with vermilion walls and golden tiles was built at considerable cost. For the columns of the hall, fragrant hardwood had to be found in the tiger-ridden forests of the remote southwest, while the mountain forests of the south and southwest were searched for other timbers that eventually made their way to the capital through the Grand Canal.

The Topkapi Palace in Istanbul, capital of the Ottoman Empire, began to take shape in 1458 under Mehmed II and underwent steady expansion over the years (see illustration on p. 511). Topkapi projected royal authority in much the same way as the Forbidden City emphasized Chinese emperors' power: governing officials worked enclosed within massive walls, and monarchs rarely went outside their inner domain.

More than two centuries later, in the 1670s and 1680s, the French monarch Louis XIV built the **Palace of Versailles** on the site of a royal hunting lodge 11 miles from Paris, the French capital (see illustration on p. 630). This enormously costly complex was built to house Louis's leading clergymen and nobles, who were obliged to visit at least twice a year. Louis hoped that by taking wealthy and powerful men and women away from their local power bases, and by diverting them with entertainments, he could keep them from plotting new forms of religious schism or challenging his right to rule. Going to Versailles also allowed him to escape the pressures and demands of the population of Paris. Many European monarchs—including Russia's Peter the Great—would build palace complexes modeled on Versailles.

If in China, the Ottoman Empire, and France, emperors built what were essentially private spaces in which to conduct and dominate state business, Shah Abbas (r. 1587–1629) of the Safavid Empire chose to create a great new public space instead. In the early seventeenth century, Shah Abbas oversaw

Forbidden City of Beijing
Palace city of the Ming and Qing dynasties.

to them, odd physical features. A Ming geographical publication portrayed the Portuguese as "seven feet tall, having eyes like a cat, a mouth like an oriole, an ash-white face, thick and curly beards like black gauze, and almost red hair." Chinese elites glorified their "white" complexions against the peasants' dark skin; against the black, wavy-haired "devils" of Southeast Asia; and

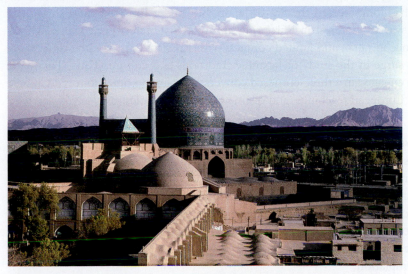

Isfahan On the great plaza at Isfahan, markets and government offices operated in close proximity to the public Shah Abbas Mosque, shown here, and the shah's private mosque. This structure represented Shah Abbas's desire to unite control of trade, government, and religion under one leader.

exchange of ideas. World history is full of palaces and plazas (the Piazza San Marco in Venice might be compared to the royal plaza at Isfahan); we can still visit and admire them. But when we do, we should also remember that space, and the architecture that either opens up to the public or sets aside privileged spaces, has always had political as well as cultural functions.

the construction of the **great plaza at Isfahan**, a structure that reflected his desire to bring trade, government, and religion together under the authority of the supreme political leader. An enormous public mosque, the Shah Abbas Mosque, dominated one end of the plaza, which measured 1,667 feet by 517 feet. At the other end were trading stalls and markets. Along one side sat government offices; the other side offered the exquisite Mosque of Shaykh Lutfollah. If the other rulers of

this era devoted their (considerable) income to creating rich private spaces, Shah Abbas used the vast open space of the plaza to open up his city to all comers, keeping only the Mosque of Shaykh Lutfollah for his personal use.

The royal use of space says a great deal about how monarchs in this era wished to be seen and remembered and about how they wanted to rule. While some wanted to retreat from the rest of society, Shah Abbas wanted to create an open space for trade and the

Questions for Analysis

- Choose one of the places discussed in this feature. Explain how the architectural layout shaped the political power exercised by that space.
- Contrast private spaces, like the palace at Versailles, with public spaces, like the great plaza at Isfahan. What political goals could be accomplished by each?

Explore Further

Babaie, Sussan, *Isfahan and Its Palaces: Statecraft, Shi'ism and the Architecture of Conviviality in Early Modern Iran* (2008).

Necipoğlu, Gülru, *Architecture, Ceremonial, and Power: The Topkapi Palace in the Fifteenth and Sixteenth Centuries* (1991).

against the Europeans' "ash-white" pallor. Qing authors in the eighteenth century confused France with the Portugal known during Ming times, and they characterized England and Sweden as dependencies of Holland. During this period of cultural flourishing, in short, most Chinese did not feel compelled to revise their view of the world.

CULTURAL IDENTITY AND TOKUGAWA JAPAN

The culture that developed in Japan in this period drew on local traditions and, increasingly, foreign influences from China and Europe. Chinese cultural influence had long crossed the Sea of Japan, but under the Tokugawa shogunate there was also interest in European culture. This interest grew via the Dutch presence in Japan and limited contacts with Russians. At the same time, there was a surge in the study of Japanese traditions and culture. Thus, Tokugawa Japan engaged in a three-cornered conversation among time-honored Chinese ways, European teachings, and distinctly Japanese traditions.

Native Arts and Popular Culture Elite and popular culture featured elements that were distinctly Japanese. Until the seventeenth century, the main patrons of Japanese culture were the imperial court in Kyoto, the hereditary shogunate, religious institutions, and a small upper class. These groups developed an elite culture of theater and stylized painting. Samurai (former warriors turned bureaucrats) and daimyos (regional lords) favored a masked theater, called Noh and an elegant ritual for making tea and engaging in contemplation.

Alongside the elite culture arose a rougher urban one that artisans and merchants patronized. Urban dwellers could purchase works of fiction and colorful prints made from carved wood blocks, and they could enjoy the company of female entertainers known as geisha. These women were skilled (*gei*) in playing the three-stringed instrument (*shamisen*), storytelling, and performing; some were also prostitutes. Geisha worked in the cities' pleasure quarters, which were famous for their geisha houses, public baths, brothels, and theaters. Kabuki—a type of theater that combined song, dance, and skillful staging to dramatize conflicts between duty and passion—became wildly popular. This art form featured dazzling acting, brilliant makeup, and sumptuous costumes.

Much popular entertainment chronicled the world of the common people rather than politics or high society. The urbanites' pleasure-oriented culture was known as "the floating world" (*ukiyo*), and the woodblock prints depicting it as *ukiyo-e* (*e* meaning "picture"). Here, the social order was temporarily turned upside down. Those who were usually considered inferior—actors, musicians, courtesans, and others seen as possessing low morals—became idols.

Literacy in Japan now surged, especially among men. The most popular novels sold 10,000 to 12,000 copies. In the late eighteenth century, Edo had some sixty booksellers and hundreds of book lenders. In fact, the presence of so many lenders allowed books to spread to a wider public that previously could not afford to buy them. By the late eighteenth century, as more books circulated and some of them criticized the government, officials tried to censor certain publications. The government's response testified to the uncommon power wielded by people of modest means and the relative significance of popular culture in Japan.

Religion and Chinese Influence In the realm of higher culture and religion, China loomed large in the Tokugawa world. Japanese scholars wrote imperial histories of Japan in the Chinese style, and Chinese law codes and other books attracted a significant readership. Some Japanese traveled south to Nagasaki to meet Zen Buddhist masters and Chinese residents there. Buddhism originally came to Japan from China and remained associated with Chinese monks. A few of those monks even won permission to found monasteries outside Nagasaki and to give lectures and construct temples in Kyoto and Edo.

Although Buddhist temples grew in number, they did not displace the native Japanese practice of venerating ancestors and worshipping gods in nature. Later called Shintō ("the way of the gods"), this practice boasted a network of shrines throughout the country. Shintō developed from time-honored beliefs in spirits, or *kami*, who were associated with places (mountains, rivers, waterfalls, rocks, the moon) and activities (harvest, fertility). Seeking healing or other assistance, adherents appealed to these spirits in nature and daily life through incantations and offerings. Some women under Shintō served as *mikos*, a kind of shaman with special divinatory powers.

Reacting to the influence of Chinese Buddhism and desiring to honor their own country's greatness, some thinkers promoted intellectual traditions from Japan's past. These efforts stressed "native learning," Japanese texts, and Japanese uniqueness. In so doing, they formalized a Japanese religious and cultural tradition, and they denounced Buddhism as a foreign contaminant.

European Influences Not only did Chinese intellectual influences compete with revived native learning, but by the late seventeenth century Japan was also tapping other sources of knowledge. By 1670, a guild of Japanese interpreters in Nagasaki who could speak and read Dutch accompanied Dutch merchants on trips to Edo. As European knowledge spread to high circles in Edo, in 1720 the shogunate lifted its ban on foreign books. Thereafter European ideas, called "Dutch learning," circulated more openly. Scientific, geographical, and medical texts appeared in Japanese translations and in

Artist and Geisha at Tea The erotic, luxuriant atmosphere of Japan's urban pleasure quarters was captured in a new art form, the *ukiyo*-e, or "pictures from a floating world." In this image set in Tokyo's celebrated Yoshiwara district, several geisha flutter about a male artist.

some cases displaced Chinese texts. A Japanese-Dutch dictionary appeared in 1745, and the first official school of Dutch learning followed. Students of Dutch and other European teachings remained a limited segment of Japanese society, but the demand for translations intensified.

Japan's internal debates about what to borrow from the Europeans and the Chinese illustrate the changes that the world had undergone in recent centuries. A few hundred years earlier, products and ideas generally did not travel beyond coastal regions and had only a limited effect (especially inland) on local cultural practices. By the eighteenth century, though, expanded networks of exchange and new prosperity made the integration of foreign ideas feasible and, sometimes, desirable. The Japanese did not consider the embrace of outside influences as a mark of inferiority or subordination, particularly when they could put those influences to good use. This was not the case for the cultures that thrived within the great Asian land-based empires, which were eager lenders but hesitant borrowers.

African Cultural Flourishing

The wealth that spurred artistic achievement and displays of power in Asia and the Islamic world did not bypass African states. Proceeds from the slave trade enabled African upper classes to fund cultural activities and invigorate strong artisanal and artistic traditions that dated back many centuries. African artisans, like those in East Asia, maintained local forms of cultural production, such as wood carving, weaving, and metalworking.

Cultural traditions in Africa varied from kingdom to kingdom, but there were patterns among them. For example, all West African elites encouraged craftsmen to produce carvings, statues, masks, and other objects that would glorify the power and achievements of rulers. (Royal patrons in Europe, Asia, and the Islamic world did the same with architecture and painting.) There was also a widespread belief that rulers and their families had the blessing of the gods. Arts and crafts not only celebrated royal power but also captured the energy of a universe that people believed was suffused with spiritual beings. Starting in the sixteenth century and continuing through the eighteenth century when the slave trade reached its peak, African rulers who benefited from that trade had even more reason—and means—to support cultural pursuits.

THE ASANTE, OYO, AND BENIN CULTURAL TRADITIONS

The kingdom of Asante led the way in cultural attainments, and the Oyo Empire and Benin also promoted rich artistic traditions.

The Asante kingdom's access to gold and the revenues that it derived from selling captives made it the richest state in West Africa, perhaps even in the whole of sub-Saharan Africa. The citizens of Asante accorded the highest respect to entrepreneurs who made money and were able to surround themselves with retainers and slaves. The adages of the age were inevitably about becoming rich: "money is king" or "nothing is as important as money" or "money is what it is all about."

Asante's artisans celebrated these traditions through the crafting of magnificent seats or stools coated with gold as symbols of authority; the most ornate were reserved for the head of the Asante federation, the Asantehene, who ruled this far-flung empire from the capital city of Kumasi. By the eighteenth century, these monarchs ventured out from the secluded royal palace only on ceremonial and feast days, when they wore sumptuous silk garments featuring many dazzling colors and geometric patterns all joined together in interwoven strips. Known as Kente cloth, this fabric could be worn only by the rulers. Kings also had a golden elephant tail, which was carried in front of them. It symbolized the highest level of wealth and power. Also held aloft on these celebratory occasions were maces, spears, staffs, and other symbols of power fashioned from the kingdom's abundant gold supplies. These reminded the common people of the Asantehene's connection to the gods.

Equally resplendent were rulers of the Oyo Empire and Benin, located in the territory that now constitutes Nigeria. Elegant, refined metalwork in the form of West African bronzes reflects these rulers' power and their peoples' high esteem. In the Oyo Empire, the Yoruba people drew on craft and artistic traditions dating back to the first millennium CE. The bronze heads of Ife, capital city of the Yoruba Oyo Empire, are among the world's most sophisticated pieces of art. According to one commentator, "[L]ittle that Italy or Greece or Egypt ever produced could be finer, and the appeal of their beauty is immediate and universal." Artisans fashioned the best known of these works in the thirteenth century (before the slave trade era), but the tradition continued and became more elaborate in the seventeenth and eighteenth centuries.

Stunning bronzes were produced in Benin as well. Although historical records have portrayed Benin as one of Africa's most brutal slave-trading regimes, it produced art of the highest order. Whether Benin's reputation for brutality was deserved or simply part of Europeans' desire to label African rulers as "savage" in order to justify their intervention in African affairs, it cannot detract from the splendor of its artisans' creations.

Brass Oba Head The brass head of an Oba, or king, of Benin. The kingdom's brass and bronze work was among the finest in all of Africa.

Although supported by funds from the Atlantic slave trade, the cultural traditions of western Africa remained little influenced by intellectual and artistic influences from the wider world. African culture during this period was relatively autonomous, even as Africa became increasingly entangled in the global webs of economic exchange and political domination.

The Enlightenment in Europe

An extraordinary cultural flowering also blossomed in Europe during the seventeenth and eighteenth centuries, driven by trade and internal commerce. Often the **Enlightenment** is defined purely in intellectual terms as the spreading of faith in reason and in universal rights and laws, but this era encompassed broader developments, such as the expansion of literacy, the spread of critical thinking, and the decline of religious persecution. Contact between Europe and the wider world after the fifteenth century played a formative role in Europeans' view of the world and their place in it. They quickly became eager consumers of other people's goods and practices. From Amerindian trapping methods to African slaves' cultivation techniques, from Chinese porcelain to New World tobacco and chocolate, contact with others influenced Europe in the seventeenth and eighteenth centuries. The more they learned, the more European intellectuals became convinced not only that their culture was superior—for that was hardly rare—but that they had discovered a set of universal laws that applied to everyone, everywhere around the world.

Abandoning the Christian belief in divine intervention, Enlightenment thinkers sought universal, objective knowledge that did not reflect any particular religion, political view, class, gender, or culture. These scholars struggled to formulate universal, natural laws, although most of these thinkers were unaware of how culture-bound their vision was. They ignored the extent to which European, upper-class male perspectives colored their "objective" knowledge.

THE NEW SCIENCE

Interest in scientific discoveries increased gradually over the seventeenth and eighteenth centuries. While the sixteenth century had brought new prosperity, the seventeenth century produced civil and religious wars, dynastic conflicts, and famines that devastated central Europe. These events bankrupted the Spanish, caused chaos in France, led to the execution of the English king, and saw the Dutch break free from Spanish control. They also contributed to the spread of Protestantism in Europe. At the same time, the crises made some intellectuals wish to turn their backs on religious strife and develop useful ways for understanding and improving *this* world—by imposing order on the chaos and instability they saw around them. By 1750, in some western countries, a significant minority of the population was eager to join in these discussions, which concentrated on the natural sciences, especially physics and astronomy.

The search for new, testable knowledge began centuries before the Enlightenment, in the efforts of Nicolaus Copernicus (1473–1543) and Galileo Galilei (1564–1642) to understand the behavior of the heavens. These men were both astronomers and mathematicians. Making their own mathematical calculations and observations of the stars and planets, they came to conclusions that contradicted age-old assumptions. This entailed considerable risk: when Galileo confirmed Copernicus's claims that the earth revolved around the sun, he was tried for heresy.

In the seventeenth century, a small but influential group of scholars committed themselves, similarly, to experimentation, calculation, and observation. They adopted a method for "scientific" inquiry laid out by the philosopher Sir Francis Bacon (1561–1626), who claimed that real science entailed the formulation of hypotheses that could be tested in carefully controlled experiments. Bacon was chiefly wary of classical and medieval authorities, but his principle also applied to traditional knowledge that European scientists were encountering in the rest of the world. Confident of their calculations performed according to the new **scientific method**, scientists like Isaac Newton (1642–1727) sought universal laws that applied to all matter and motion; they criticized older conceptions of nature (from Aristotelian ideas to folkloric and foreign ones) as absurd and obsolete. Thus, in his *Principia Mathematica* (1687) Newton set forth the laws of motion—including the famous law of gravitation, which simultaneously explained falling bodies on earth and planetary motion.

Most historians no longer call these changes a scientific revolution, for European thinking did not change overnight. Only gradually did thinkers come to see the natural world as operating according to inviolable laws that experimenters could figure out, like gravity and inertia. But by the late seventeenth century, many rulers had developed a new interest in science, and they established royal academies to encourage research. This patronage, of course, had a political function. By incorporating the British Royal Society in 1662, for example, Charles II hoped to show not only that the crown backed scientific progress but also that England's great minds backed the crown. Similar reasoning lay behind Louis XIV's founding of the French Royal Academy of Sciences.

Gradually, the new science expanded beyond the court to gain popularity among elite circles. Marquise de Châtelet-Lomont built a scientific laboratory in her home and translated Newton's *Principia* into French, which her lover, Voltaire, one of the most influential of the Enlightenment figures, popularized. By about 1750, even artisans and journalists were applying Newtonian mechanics to their practical problems and inventions. In Italy, numerous female natural philosophers emerged, and the genre of scientific literature

scientific method
Method of inquiry based on experimentation in nature. Many of its principles were first laid out by the philosopher Sir Francis Bacon (1561–1626), who claimed that real science entailed the formulation of hypotheses that could be tested in carefully controlled experiments.

for "ladies" took hold. A consensus emerged among proponents of the new science that useful knowledge came from collecting data and organizing them into universally valid systems, rather than from studying revered classical texts.

By no means, however, did the scientific worldview dominate European thinking. Most people still understood their relationships with God, nature, and fellow humans via Christian doctrines and local customs. Although literacy was increasing, it was far from universal; schools remained church-governed or elite, male institutions. All governments employed censors and punished radical thinkers, peasants still suffered under arbitrary systems of taxation, and judicial regimes were as harsh as during medieval times. Nonetheless, the promise of universal scientific truths inspired Enlightenment thinkers, who in turn held them out as an ideal.

ENLIGHTENMENT THINKERS

Enlightenment thinkers, called **philosophes** in France, applied scientific reasoning to human interaction and society as opposed to nature. Such thinkers included the French writers Voltaire (1694–1778) and Denis Diderot (1713–1784) and the Scottish moral philosopher and political economist Adam Smith (1723–1790). These writers also called attention to the evils and flaws of human society: Voltaire criticized the torture of criminals, Diderot denounced the despotic tendencies of the French kings Louis XIV and Louis XV, and Smith exposed the inefficiencies of mercantilism. Other Enlightenment thinkers, similarly, criticized contemporary European conditions, and they often suffered imprisonment or exile for writing about what they considered to be superstitious beliefs and corrupt political structures.

The Enlightenment touched all of Europe, but the extent of its reach varied. In France and Britain, enlightened learning spread widely; in Spain, Poland, and Scandinavia, enlightened circles were small and had little influence on rulers or the general population. Enlightened thought flourished in commercial centers like Amsterdam and Edinburgh and in colonial ports like Philadelphia and Boston.

Popular Culture In the emerging marketplace for new books and new ideas, some of the most popular works were not from high intellectuals. Pamphlets charging widespread corruption, fraudulent stock speculation, and insider trading circulated widely. Sex, too, sold well. Works like *Venus in the Cloister, or the Nun in a Nightgown* racked up as many sales as the now-classic works of the Enlightenment. Bawdy and irreligious, these vulgar best-sellers exploited consumer demand—but they also seized the opportunity to mock authority figures, such as nuns and priests. Some even dared to go after the royal family, portraying Marie Antoinette as having sex with her court confessor. Such works displayed the seamier side of the Enlightenment, but they also revealed a willingness on the part of high- and low-brow intellectuals alike to challenge established beliefs and institutions and to undermine royal authority.

The reading public itself helped generate new cultural institutions and practices. In Britain and Germany, book clubs and coffeehouses sprang up to cater to sober men of business and learning; here, aristocrats and well-to-do commoners could read news sheets or discuss stock prices, political affairs, and technological novelties. The same sort of noncourtly socializing occurred in Parisian salons, where aristocratic women presided. The number of female readers, and writers, soared, and the relatively new genre of the novel, as well as specialized women's journals, appealed especially to them. A public sphere emerged that was radically democratic and beyond the control of kings or any corporate body: all it took to participate was the ability to read and the willingness to debate the issues of the day.

Challenges to Authority and Tradition Even though they took the aristocracy's money, many Enlightenment thinkers tried to overturn the status distinctions that characterized European society. They emphasized merit rather than birth as the basis for status. In his *Treatise on Human Understanding* (1690), John Locke claimed that man was born with a mind that was a clean slate (*tabula rasa*) and acquired all his ideas through experience. Locke stressed that cultural differences were the result not of unequal natural abilities but of unequal opportunities to develop one's abilities. Similarly, in *The Wealth of Nations* (1776), Adam Smith remarked that there was little difference (other than education) between a philosopher and a street porter: both were born, he claimed, with the ability to reason, and both should be free to rise in society according to their talents. Yet Locke and Smith still believed that a mixed set of social and political institutions was necessary to regulate relationships among ever-imperfect humans. Moreover, they did not believe that women could act as independent, rational individuals in the same way that all men, presumably, could. Although educated women like Mary Wollstonecraft and Olympe de Gouges took up the pen to protest these inequities (see Chapter 15 for further discussion), the Enlightenment did little to change the subordinate status of women in European society.

Universal Laws and Religious Tolerance Efforts to discover the "laws" of human behavior linked up with criticism of existing governments. Explaining the laws of economic relations was chiefly the work of Adam Smith, whose book *The Wealth of Nations* described universal economic principles. According to Smith, all people have what he called the propensity to truck, barter, and exchange—an innate desire to trade with one another. He complained that mercantilist controls and guild restrictions stifled economic growth and argued instead that a division of labor, spurred on by free and fair competition, provided the best conditions for producing wealth (though he did not advocate completely free, unregulated markets). Assuming that all people, everywhere, shared Protestant notions of thrift and discipline, Smith claimed that by pursuing their own rational self-interest, virtuous individuals would advance the common good without meaning to do so—as if, as he put it, by an "invisible hand." Smith was conscious of growing economic gaps between "civilized and thriving" nations and "savage" ones. Yet he believed that until the poorer nations learned to abide by nature's laws and behaved virtuously, they could not expect a happy fate.

One of the most controversial areas for applying universal laws was religion. Although few Enlightenment thinkers were atheists (people who do not believe in any god), most of them called for religious toleration. They insisted that the use of reason, not force, was the best way to create a community of believers and morally good people. Governments often reacted by censoring books or exiling writers who criticized the authority of the church, but the arguments managed to persuade some rulers. Thus, in the late eighteenth century, governments from Denmark to Austria passed acts offering religious minorities some freedom of worship. However, toleration did not mean full civil rights—especially for Catholics in England or Jews anywhere in Europe. Religious minorities enjoyed much greater freedom in this period in the Ottoman Empire than they did in any European country.

The Enlightenment produced numerous works that attempted to encompass universal knowledge. Most important was the French *Encyclopédie*, which ultimately comprised twenty-eight volumes containing essays by nearly 200 intellectuals. It was popular among the elite despite its political, religious, and intellectual radicalism. Its purpose was "to collect all the knowledge scattered over the face of the earth" and to make it useful to men and women in the present and future. Indeed, the *Encyclopédie* offered a wealth of information about the rest of the world, including more than 2,300 articles on Islam. Here, the authors typically praised Arab culture for preserving and extending Greek and Roman science—and in doing so, preparing the way for scientific advances in Europe. But at the same time, the authors portrayed Islam with the same ill will that they applied to other organized religions, condemning Muhammad for promoting a bloodthirsty religion and Muslim culture in general for not rejecting superstition.

CONSEQUENCES OF THE ENLIGHTENMENT

The Enlightenment—or, more properly, Enlightenments, as there was much variation across Europe—was a movement with numerous ambivalent consequences, both for religious and political institutions and for Europe's relationship with the rest of the world.

Religion and the Enlightenment Although few Enlightenment thinkers were atheists, most criticized what they perceived to be the irrational rituals,

The _Encyclopédie_ Originally published in 1751, the _Encyclopédie_ was the most comprehensive work of learning of the French Enlightenment. (_Top_) The title page features an image of light and reason being dispersed throughout the land. The title itself identifies the work as a dictionary, based on reason, that deals not just with the sciences but also with the arts and occupations. It identifies two of the leading men of letters (_gens de lettres_), Denis Diderot and Jean le Rond d'Alembert, as the primary authors of the work. Contributors to the _Encyclopédie_ included craftsmen as well as intellectuals. (_Bottom_) The detailed illustrations of a pin factory and the processes and machinery employed in pin making are from a plate in the fourth volume of the _Encyclopédie_ and demonstrate its emphasis on practical information.

superstitions, persecutions, and expenditures defended by clergy. The Scottish philosopher and historian David Hume attacked biblical miracles, and Voltaire underscored the bloodiness of the Crusades. They insisted that the use of reason, rather than force or rote repetition of formulas, was the best way to create a community of believers and morally good people. Some governments bowed to clerical pressure and censored the most radical books or exiled writers, but many absolutist monarchs saw an advantage in reducing the church's power and introducing at least some measure of tolerance of religious minorities into their realms.

Tolerance did not mean full civil rights—for Catholics in England, for example, or for Jews anywhere in Europe. Tolerance simply meant a loosening of religious uniformity, and the population as a whole often resented even this. Few Europeans entirely lost their faith as a result of the spread of enlightened ideas and critiques. But it is unquestionably the case that the Enlightenment succeeded in spreading the suspicion of religious authorities and the distaste for religious persecution, and it did create new forms of religious belief and practice.

The application of enlightened ideas to non-European religions had conflicting effects. On the one hand, enlightened thinkers sought information about other religions and wrote books discussing similarities between Christian and non-Christian practices and beliefs. But their imposition of enlightened categories and principles often resulted in severe misunderstandings, as differences were increasingly explained as others' "backward" refusal to evolve along European lines.

The Enlightenment and Politics Absolutist governments did not entirely reject enlightened ideas, which included ideas that were in most cases reformist or critical of religious authorities rather than directly political. Rulers, like astronomers, recognized the virtues of universality (as in a universally applicable system of taxation) and precision (as in a well-drilled army). Also, social mobility allowed more skilled bureaucrats to rise through the ranks, while commerce provided the state with new riches. The idea of collecting knowledge, too, appealed to states that wanted to have greater control over their subjects and to extend their reach overseas. Consider Louis XIV, who was persuaded to establish a census (though he never carried it out) so that he could "know with certitude in what consists his grandeur, his wealth, and his strength." Many enlightened princes supported innovations in the arts and agriculture or sent scientific missions out to explore the world and plant their flags. Like the philosophes, they were convinced that the improvement of trade, agriculture, and national productivity was the right way forward, even though some also were beholden to the older values of the nobility and clergy. Merit and religious tolerance could also be useful in attempts to make states more profitable and armies more efficient. In this way, cultural efflorescence and secular state building in Europe went hand in hand.

The Enlightenment and the Origins of Racial Thought The Enlightenment introduced new ways of thinking about human difference. Scientists sought objective, rational ways to classify peoples and cultures in the same way that botanists classified plants—indeed, many leaders in this field were botanists. To do so, they relied on new concepts of race.

Before the eighteenth century, the word *race* referred to a swift current in a stream or a test of speed; sometimes it meant a family lineage (mainly that of a royal or noble family). The Frenchman François Bernier, who had traveled in Asia, may have been the first European to attempt to classify the peoples of the world. He used a variety of criteria, including those that were to become standard from the late eighteenth century down to the present, such as skin color, facial features, and hair texture. Bernier published these views in his *New Division of the Earth by the Different Groups or Races Who Inhabit It* (1684). In addition, the Swedish naturalist Carolus Linnaeus (1707–1778), the French scholar Georges Louis Leclerc, the comte de Buffon (1707–1788), and the German anatomist Johann Friedrich Blumenbach (1752–1840) also were among the first to use racial principles to classify humankind.

In his *Systema Naturae* (first published in 1735), Europe's most accomplished naturalist, Carolus Linnaeus, identified five subspecies of *Homo sapiens*, or "wise man." He gave each of the continents a subspecies: there was *Homo europaeus*, *Homo americanus*, *Homo afar*, and *Homo asiaticus*, to which he added a fifth category, *Homo monstrosus*, for "wild" men and "monstrous" types. He believed that each of these groups was marked by distinctive social and intellectual characteristics, contrasting light-skinned Europeans, who he believed were governed by laws, to "sooty" Asians, who were governed by opinion. Custom governed copper-skinned Americans, while only personal whim ruled Africans, whom he consigned to the lowest rung of the human ladder.

Linnaeus thought these categories were malleable, both under environmental pressure and through mixing to create new species. Skin color, facial features, and hair type did not directly and permanently correlate to intelligence or morality—this was far removed from the racial thought that emerged a century later. But the idea that human beings could be classified in a few large groups proved enormously influential both in scientific discourse and popular opinion, and the categories he devised were profoundly marked by the biases of his European upbringing.

THE EUROPEAN ENLIGHTENMENT IN GLOBAL PERSPECTIVE

Europe's new science and enlightened thought arose in reaction both to Europe's expanding interaction with the rest of the world and to the period's environmental, religious, and political chaos. But why Europe? Why not China or the Islamic world? As we have seen, Chinese and Muslim scholars could boast rich traditions of scientific and technological development and literary production. Why, then, did Chinese literati and, perhaps more important, Muslim scholars, who still had the most advanced knowledge of the natural sciences even as late as the fourteenth century, let the Europeans assume the lead in understanding the natural world? Answers are difficult to provide, but some suggestions are now coming to light.

For Islam, the rise of Sufi orders and Sufi mysticism posed a challenge to the dominance that the *ulama* believed that they should have over all fields of thought and principles of belief. The *ulama* responded to this threat

Matteo Ricci Adapts to Chinese Culture This image depicts Jesuit father Matteo Ricci. Behind him stands a painting of the Madonna and baby Jesus with a text in literary Chinese, demonstrating Ricci's commitment to adapting Christianity and European culture to the text-oriented Chinese cultural world.

in conservative, even fundamentalist ways, reiterating the importance of the religious sciences, which included studies of the Quran, the sayings of the Prophet (*hadith*), the *sharia* (religious law), theology, poetry, and the Arabic language, and questioning the value of the foreign sciences and the study of the natural world. Occasionally scholars were able to challenge the *ulama*'s monopoly on learning and to look outward for inspiration, but such efforts relied on reformist patrons, who were not in great abundance. While in Europe a diverse set of quarreling and competing churches and patrons made possible the articulation of new and more secular sciences, in Ottoman lands the established authorities and ideas could not so easily be dislodged.

Chinese elites welcomed European learning, but they did so on their own terms. The two first Jesuit missionaries to reach China, Michele Ruggieri (1543–1607) and Matteo Ricci (1552–1610), arrived in China in 1582 and 1583, respectively. As was the case with many Jesuits at this time, both were brilliantly educated not just in religious and theological matters but in Europe's evolving new science. At the time of their arrival, China was in the midst of debates over its solar calendar, which now was out of sync with the seasons and causing difficulties coordinating ceremonial rites and rituals. Thus, Chinese officials were eager to employ Jesuit knowledge of mathematics and astronomy—based on Copernican and Galilean heliocentrism—to assist them in bringing ceremonial dates and political and economic activities into a better relationship with the seasons.

For their part, the Jesuits participated in Confucian ceremonies, hoping to win favor with the emperor and arguing that the rites were compatible with Catholicism. But, to the Jesuits' great disappointment, the Chinese did not accept their religious and theological tenets, and the men made only a very small number of converts. When Pope Clement XI issued a papal bull in 1715 condemning the missionaries' participation in the rites, the project of cultural exchange broke down. Offended, the Kangxi emperor, who had once been sympathetic to the Jesuits, banned Christian missionaries from practicing in China. His successor went even further, ordering the closing of all churches and the expulsion of Jesuits from China. Thus, starting in the mid-eighteenth century, the European window on China and the Chinese window on Europe were closed. China turned away from European contact, most notably Europe's new science that had once intrigued Chinese ruling classes.

Creating Hybrid Cultures in the Americas

As European empires expanded in the Americas, mingling between colonizers and native peoples, as well as African slaves, produced hybrid cultures. But the mixing of cultures grew increasingly unbalanced as Europeans imposed authority over more of the Americas. In addition to guns and germs, many European colonizers brought Bibles, prayer books, and crucifixes. With these, they set out to Christianize and "civilize" Amerindian and African populations in the Americas. Yet missionary efforts produced uneven and often unpredictable outcomes. Even as Amerindians and African slaves adopted Christian beliefs and practices, they often retained older religious practices too.

European colonists likewise borrowed from the peoples they subjugated and enslaved. This was especially true in the sixteenth and seventeenth centuries, when the colonists' survival in the New World often depended on adapting. New sorts of hierarchies emerged, and elites in Latin America and North America increasingly followed the tastes and fashions of European aristocrats. Yet, even as they imitated Old World ways, these colonials forged identities that separated them from Europe.

SPIRITUAL ENCOUNTERS

Although the Jesuits had little impact in China and the Islamic world, Christian missionaries in the Americas had armies and officials to back up their insistence that Native Americans and African slaves abandon their own deities and spirits for Christ. Nonetheless, their attempts to force conversions were rarely a complete success, and some European settlers became interested in Amerindian culture.

Core Objectives

DESCRIBE how hybrid cultures emerged in the Americas, and EXPLAIN the connection between these cultures and Enlightenment ideology.

European missionaries, especially Catholics, used numerous techniques to bring Amerindians within the Christian fold. They smashed idols, razed temples, and whipped backsliders. Catholic orders (principally Dominicans, Jesuits, and Franciscans) also learned what they could about Indian beliefs and rituals—and then exploited that knowledge to make converts to Christianity. For example, many missionaries found it useful to demonize local gods, subvert indigenous spiritual leaders, and transform Indian iconography into Christian symbols.

Neither gentle persuasion nor violent coercion produced the results that missionaries desired. When conversions did occur, the Christian practices that resulted were usually syncretic: mixed forms in which indigenous deities and rituals merged with Christian ones. Those who did convert saw Christian spiritual power as an addition to, not a replacement for, their own religions.

Europeans also attempted to Christianize slaves from Africa, though many slave owners doubted the wisdom of converting persons they regarded as mere property. Sent forth with the pope's blessing, Catholic priests targeted slave populations in the American colonies of Portugal, Spain, and France. Applying many of the same techniques that missionaries used with Indian "heathens," these priests produced similarly mixed results.

More distressing to missionaries than the blending of beliefs or outright defiance were the Amerindians' successes in assimilating captured colonists. It deeply troubled the missionaries that quite a few captured colonists adjusted to their situation, accepted adoptions into local societies, and refused to return to colonial society when given the chance. Moreover, some Europeans voluntarily chose to live among the Amerindians. Comparing the records of cultural conversion, one eighteenth-century colonist suggested that "thousands of Europeans are Indians," yet "we have no examples of even one of those Aborigines having from choice become European." (Aborigines are original, native inhabitants of a region, as opposed to invaders, colonizers, or later peoples of mixed ancestry.) While this calculation was no doubt exaggerated, it shows that despite the missionaries' intentions, cultural exchange went in more than one direction.

INTERMARRIAGE AND CULTURAL MIXING

In the early stages of colonization, Europeans mixed with Amerindians in part because there were many more men than women among the colonists. Almost all the early European traders, missionaries, and settlers were men (although the British North American settlements saw more women arrive relatively early on). In response to the scarcity of women and as a way to help Amerindians accept the newcomers' culture, the Portuguese crown authorized intermarriage between Portuguese men and local women. These

Racial Mixing (*Left*) This *casta* painting shows racial mixing in colonial Mexico—the father is a Spaniard, the mother an Amerindian, and the child a mestizo. (Like the word *caste*, *casta* refers to a group within a social hierarchy, in this case defined by race and racial mixing.) The image indicates that Indians who married whites achieved elevated status. (*Right*) Here, too, we see a racially mixed family. The father is a Spaniard, the mother is an African, and the child is what was then called a mulatto (a term for a person of mixed white and black ancestry that is considered offensive today). Observe, however, the less aristocratic and markedly less peaceful nature of this family.

relations often amounted to little more than rape, but longer-lasting relationships developed in places where Amerindians kept their independence—as among French fur traders and Amerindian women in Canada, the Great Lakes region, and the Mississippi Valley. Whether by coercion or consent, sexual relations between European men and Amerindian women resulted in offspring of mixed ancestry. In fact, the mestizos of Spanish colonies and the *métis* of French outposts soon outnumbered settlers of wholly European descent.

The increasing numbers of African slaves in the Americas complicated the mix of New World cultures even further. Unlike marriages between fur traders and Indian women, in which the women held considerable power because of their connections to Indian trading partners, sexual intercourse between European men and enslaved African women was almost always forced. Children born from such unions swelled the ranks of mixed-ancestry people in the colonial population, contributing to the new cultural mix that was emerging.

FORMING AMERICAN IDENTITIES

Over time, as European colonies in the Americas became more securely established, the colonists developed a sense of their own distinctive "American" identities. The colonization of the Americas brought Europeans, Africans, and Indians into sustained contact, though the nature of the colonies and the character of the contact varied considerably. Where European dominance was most secure, colonists imposed their ways on subjugated populations and

creoles
Persons of mixed European and African (or other) descent who were born in the Americas.

peninsulares
Spaniards who, although born in Spain, resided in the Spanish colonial territories. They regarded themselves as superior to Spaniards born in the colonies (creoles).

imported what they took to be the chief cultural and institutional attributes of the countries they had left behind. Yet Europeans were not immune to cultural influences from the groups they dispossessed and enslaved.

The Creole Identity In Spanish America, ethnic and cultural mixing produced a powerful new class, the **creoles**—people born in the Americas. By the late eighteenth century, creoles increasingly resented the control that **peninsulares**—men and women born in Spain or Portugal but living in the Americas—had over colonial society. Creoles especially resented the exclusive privileges given to peninsular rulers, like those that forbade creoles from trading with other colonial ports. Also, they disliked the fact that royal ministers gave most official posts to peninsulares.

In many cities of the Spanish and Portuguese empires, reading clubs and salons hosted energetic discussions of fresh Enlightenment ideas and contributed to the growing creole identity. The Spanish crown, recognizing the role of printing presses in spreading troublesome ideas, strictly controlled the number and location of printers in the colonies. In Brazil, royal authorities banned them altogether. Nonetheless, books, pamphlets, and simple gossip allowed new notions of science, history, and politics to circulate among literate creoles.

Anglicization In one important sense, wealthy colonists in British America were similar to the creole elites in Spanish and Portuguese America: they, too, copied European ways. For example, they constructed "big houses" (in Virginia and elsewhere—especially the Caribbean) modeled on the country estates of English gentlemen and imported opulent furnishings and fashions from the finest British stores. Imitating the British also involved tightening patriarchal authority. In seventeenth-century Virginia, men had vastly outnumbered women, which gave women some power (widows in particular gained greater control over property and more choices when they remarried). During the eighteenth century, however, sex ratios became more equal, and women's property rights diminished as British customs took precedence.

Intellectually, too, British Americans were linked to Europe. Importing enormous numbers of books and journals, these Americans played a significant role in the Enlightenment as producers and consumers of political pamphlets, scientific treatises, and social critiques. Indeed, drawing on the words of numerous Enlightenment thinkers, American intellectuals created the most famous of enlightened documents: the Declaration of Independence. It announced that all men were endowed with equal rights and were created to pursue worldly happiness. In this way, Anglicized Americans showed themselves, like the creole elites of Latin America, to be products of both European and New World cultures.

The Influence of European Culture in Oceania

In the South Pacific, as in the Americas, European influence had powerful consequences in the eighteenth century. Although in centuries past Hindu, Buddhist, and Islamic missionaries and Chinese traders had traveled to Malaysia and nearby islands, they had not ventured beyond Timor. (See Map 14.1.) Europeans began to do so in the years after 1770, turning their sights on **Oceania** (Australia, New Zealand, and the islands of the southwest Pacific). Using their new wealth to fund voyages with scientific and political objectives, Europeans invaded these remaining unexplored areas. The results were mixed: while some islands maintained their autonomy, the biggest prize, Australia, underwent thorough Anglicization.

Until Europeans colonized it in the late eighteenth century, Australia was, like the Americas before Columbus, truly a world apart. Separated by water and sheer distance from other regions, Australia's main features were harsh natural conditions and a sparse population. At the time of the European colonization, the island was home to around 300,000 people, mostly hunters and gatherers. Now the intrusion into Oceania presented Europeans with a previously unknown region that could serve as a laboratory for studying other peoples and geographical settings.

THE SCIENTIFIC VOYAGES OF CAPTAIN COOK

In Oceania and across the South Pacific, Europeans experimented with a scientific form of imperialism. The story of the region's most famous explorer, Captain James Cook (1728–1779), shows how closely related science and imperialist ventures could be. Cook's voyages and his encounter with the South Sea Islanders opened up the Pacific, particularly Australia, to European colonizers.

Captain Cook has become a legendary figure in European cultural history, portrayed as one of the saintly scientists of enlightened progress. His first voyage had two objectives. The Royal Society charged him with the scholarly task of observing the movement of the planet Venus from the Southern Hemisphere, and the British government assigned him the secret mission of finding and claiming "the southern continent" for Britain. Cook set sail in 1768, and his voyage was so fruitful that he subsequently undertook two more scientific-imperial adventures.

Cook was chosen to head the first expedition because of his scientific interests and skills. Besides Cook, the Royal Society sent along one of its members who was a botanist; a doctor and student of the renowned Swedish naturalist Carolus Linnaeus; and numerous artists and other scientists. The crew

The Global View

Pacific Ocean

Map 14.1 Cook's Global Voyages

Captain Cook's voyages throughout the Pacific Ocean symbolized a new era in European exploration of other societies.

- Where did Cook explore, and what peoples did he encounter?
- Contrast the routes Cook selected for his three voyages. How do they differ? What does that tell us about his project?

Route of James Cook, 1768–71
Route of James Cook, 1772–75
Route of James Cook, 1776–80

The Voyages of Captain James Cook (*Left*) During his celebrated voyages to the South Pacific, Cook kept meticulous maps and diaries. Although he had little formal education, he became one of the great exemplars of enlightened learning through experience and experiment. (*Right*) Kangaroos were unknown in the west until Cook and his colleagues encountered (and ate) them on their first visit to Australia. This engraving of the animal (which unlike most animals, plants, and geographical features, actually kept the name the Aborigines had given it) from Cook's 1773 travelogue, *A Voyage Round the World in the Years 1768–1771*, lovingly depicts the kangaroo's environs and even emotions.

also carried sophisticated instruments and had instructions to keep detailed diaries. This was to be a grand data-collecting journey. Cook's voyages surpassed even the Royal Society's hopes. The scientists made approximately 3,000 drawings of Pacific plants, birds, landscapes, and peoples never seen in Europe.

ECOLOGICAL AND CULTURAL EFFECTS

More than science was at stake, however, for Australia was intended to supply Britain with raw materials. As in the Americas, extracting those materials required a labor force, and the Aborigines of Australia, like the Indians of the Americas, perished in great numbers from imported diseases. Those who survived generally fled to escape control by British masters. Thus, to secure a labor force, plans arose for grand-scale conquest and resettlement by British colonists. On his third voyage, Cook took along a wide array of animals and plants with which to turn the South Pacific into a European-style garden, with massive ecological consequences. His lieutenant later brought apples, quinces, strawberries, and rosemary to Australia; the seventy sheep imported in 1788 laid the foundations for the region's wool-growing economy. In fact, the domestication of Australia arose from the Europeans' certainty about their superior know-how and a desire to make the entire landmass serve British interests.

In 1788, a British military expedition took official possession of the eastern half of Australia. The intent was, in part, to establish a prison colony far from home. This plan belonged as well to the realm of "enlightened" dreams: removing people from an environment that did not suit them and sending them to new climes where they could be reformed, or, if they couldn't be, at least limiting problems back home. The intent was also to exploit Australia for its timber and flax and to use it as a strategic base against Dutch and French expansion. In the next decades, immigration—free and forced—increased the Anglo-Australian population from an original 1,000 to about 1.2 million by 1860. Importing their customs and their capital, British settlers turned Australia into a frontier version of home, just as they had done in British America. Yet, such large-scale immigration had disastrous consequences for the surviving Aborigines. Like the Native Americans, the original inhabitants of Australia were decimated by diseases and increasingly forced westward by European settlement. As in the Americas, European ideas and institutions proved to be far more influential and disruptive in Oceania than they were in the major land empires of Afro-Eurasia.

Conclusion

New wealth produced by commerce and state building created the conditions for a global cultural renaissance in the sixteenth, seventeenth, and eighteenth centuries. It began in the Chinese and Islamic empires and then stretched into Europe, Africa, and previous worlds apart in the Americas and Oceania. Experiments in religious toleration encouraged cultural exchange; book production and consumption soared; grand new monuments took shape; luxury goods became available for wider enjoyment.

Although the Islamic and Chinese worlds confidently retained their own systems of knowing, believing, and representing, the Americas and Oceania increasingly faced European cultural pressures. Here, while hybrid practices became widespread by the late eighteenth century, European beliefs and habits took over as the standards for judging degrees of "civilization." African cultures largely escaped this influence, though their homelands felt the impact of European expansionism because of the slave trade.

From a commercial standpoint, the world was more integrated than ever before. But the exposure and cultural borrowing that global trade promoted did not obliterate established cultural traditions. The Chinese, for instance, still believed in the superiority of their traditional knowledge and customs. Muslim rulers, confident of the primacy of Islam, allowed others to form subordinate cultural communities within their realm and adopted the Europeans' knowledge only when it served their own imperial purposes.

Only the Europeans were constructing knowledge that they believed was both universal and objective, enabling mortals to master the world of nature and all its inhabitants. This view would prove consequential, as well as controversial, in the centuries to come.

◤◥◣◢ Focus On
The Flourishing of Regional Cultures

The Islamic World

- The Ottomans' unique cultural synthesis accommodates not only mystical Sufis and ultraorthodox *ulama* but also military men, administrators, and clerics.

- The Safavid state proclaims the triumph of Shiism and Persian influences in the sumptuous new capital, Isfahan.

- Mughal courtly culture values art and learning and, at its high point, welcomes non-Muslim contributions.

East Asia

- China's cultural flourishing, coming from within, is evident in the broad circulation of traditional ideas, publishing, and mapmaking.

- Japan's imperial court at Kyoto develops an elite culture of theater, stylized painting, tea ceremonies, and flower arranging.

Europe

- Cultural flourishing known as the Enlightenment yields a faith in reason and a belief in humans' ability to fathom the laws of nature and human behavior.

- European thinkers articulate a belief in unending human progress.

- Europeans expand into Australia and the South Pacific.

Africa

- Slave-trading states such as Asante, Oyo, and Benin celebrate royal power and wealth through art.

The Americas

- Even as Euro-Americans participate in the Enlightenment, their culture reflects Native American and African influences.

CHRONOLOGY

	1500	1550	1600
The Islamic World		Shah Abbas I builds Isfahan 1598–1629	
Africa			
Europe			
East Asia			
The Americas			

THINKING ABOUT GLOBAL CONNECTIONS

- **Thinking about Exchange Networks and Cultural Change** How did increased exchanges of goods and ideas change established traditions? What institutions and ideas proved most hospitable to foreign influence, even in established cultures, and why? Which fields proved more resistant to outside ideas? Why were some regions more receptive to foreign influences than others were? Consider religion, natural science, and art.

- **Thinking about Changing Power Relationships and Cultural Change** How did established cultures respond to the inclusion of the Americas in an increasingly integrated world? Which cultures flourished, and why? What relationship(s) can you see between new wealth and cultural change?

- **Thinking about Environmental Impacts and Cultural Change** The isolation of the Americas and Oceania paved the way for ecological catastrophe when Europeans arrived. How, in turn, did ecological catastrophes leave indigenous cultures vulnerable? Consider the nature of religious change in the Americas and the Afro-Eurasian core regions and population movements in Australia.

Key Terms

creoles p. 674

Enlightenment p. 662

Forbidden City of Beijing p. 656

great plaza at Isfahan p. 657

Oceania p. 675

Palace of Versailles p. 656

peninsulares p. 674

philosophes p. 664

scientific method p. 663

Taj Mahal p. 652

 Go to **INQUIZITIVE** to see what you've learned—and learn what you've missed—with personalized feedback along the way.

1650 — 1700 — 1750 — 1800

Taj Mahal built in Mughal dynasty 1630–1650

Tulip Period in Ottoman Empire 1720s

Oyo and Asante kingdoms produce vibrant artistic works seventeenth century

Isaac Newton publishes *Principia Mathematica* 1687

Enlightenment philosophy spreads among educated elites eighteenth century

Carolus Linnaeus publishes *Systema Naturae* 1735

Adam Smith publishes *The Wealth of Nations* 1776

Voyages of Captain Cook 1768–1779

Growing circulation of books and ideas in China seventeenth century

"Floating worlds" appear in Japanese cities seventeenth century

Hybrid cultures appear seventeenth century

Enlightenment philosophy spreads among colonial elites eighteenth century

Global Themes and Sources

Comparing Changes to Global Commerce and Society

Commerce spread around the globe as never before in the centuries after 1500. Although business practices differed in different settings, the same questions confronted merchants, men of letters, and political leaders everywhere trade flourished: Was trade natural—consistent with the right order of things—or unnatural? Did it bring out the best or worst in people? Did the arrival of new wealth and goods support or undermine established cultures and social elites?

Commerce was a central issue in the European Enlightenment; the first three documents all present trade as central to modern European culture. The fourth, by a Japanese merchant named Shimai Soshitsu, instructed future generations on how to keep business interests from compromising their values. The final selection, drawn from edicts issued by the Chinese Qianlong Emperor, shows both fear about the dangers business interests posed and a recognition that they were too important to abolish altogether.

To make sense of these documents, you will need to think comparatively and evaluate how a range of authors responded to the same set of issues. Given the centrality of commerce, they offer the opportunity to think about cause and effect. What change or changes can you identify?

Analyzing Changes to Global Commerce and Societies

- Place the following documents on a continuum from those that supported commerce to those that rejected it.

- Analyze the relationship between commerce and the social order in each document. Does the document present commerce as upholding the social order or as subverting it?

- Analyze the tension between progress and backwardness in each source, from the author's point of view.

"Doux Commerce" (1748), Charles de Secondat, Baron de Montesquieu

Charles de Secondat, Baron de Montesquieu (1689–1755) was a magistrate in the *parlement* (law court) of Bordeaux and a man of letters, one of the most influential figures in the French Enlightenment. The French term *doux commerce* refers to the gentle, taming, civilizing force of commerce.

- Explain the relationship between commerce and "barbarous behavior."

- Which values does trade promote, in Montesquieu's view, and which does it stifle?

- Identify the central assumption at work in this text. What does Montesquieu take for granted, and what does he defend with argument?

Commerce is a cure for the most destructive prejudices; for it is almost a general rule, that wherever we find agreeable manners, there commerce flourishes; and that wherever there is commerce, there we meet with agreeable manners.

Let us not be astonished, then, if our manners are now less savage than formerly. Commerce has everywhere diffused a knowledge of the manners of all nations: these are compared one with another, and from this comparison arise the greatest advantages.

Commercial laws, it may be said, improve manners for the same reason that they destroy them. They corrupt the purest morals. This was the subject of Plato's complaints; and we every day see that they polish and refine the most barbarous.

Peace is the natural effect of trade. Two nations who traffic with each other become reciprocally dependent; for if one has an interest in buying, the other has an interest in selling; and thus their union is founded on their mutual necessities.

But if the spirit of commerce unites nations, it does not in the same manner unite individuals. We see that in countries [Holland] where the people move only by the spirit of commerce, they make a traffic of all the humane, all the moral virtues; the most trifling things, those which humanity would demand, are there done, or there given, only for money.

The spirit of trade produces in the mind of a man a certain sense of exact justice, opposite, on the one hand, to robbery, and on the other to those moral virtues which forbid our always adhering rigidly to the rules of private interest, and suffer us to neglect this for the advantage of others.

The total privation of trade, on the contrary, produces robbery, which Aristotle ranks in the number of means of acquiring; yet it is not at all inconsistent with certain moral virtues. Hospitality, for instance, is most rare in trading countries, while it is found in the most admirable perfection among nations of vagabonds.

Source: Charles de Secondat, Baron de Montesquieu, *The Spirit of the Laws* (Cambridge, England: Cambridge University Press, 1989), pp. 338–39.

PRIMARY SOURCE 14.2

"The Propensity to Truck, Barter, and Exchange" (1776), Adam Smith

Adam Smith (1723–1790) was a Scottish moral philosopher and leading figure of the Scottish Enlightenment whose 1776 book, *The Wealth of Nations*, was a pioneering work of political economy.

- According to Smith, where does the division of labor come from?
- What challenges stand in the way of economic growth, in Smith's view?
- What do you think Smith would say about economic inequality?

The division of labour, from which so many advantages are derived, is not originally the effect of any human wisdom, which foresees and intends that general opulence to which it gives occasion. It is the necessary, though very slow and gradual consequence of a certain propensity in human nature which has in view no such extensive utility; the propensity to truck, barter, and exchange one thing for another.

Whether this propensity be one of those original principles in human nature of which no further account can be given; or whether, as seems more probable, it be the necessary consequence of the faculties of reason and speech, it belongs not to our present subject to inquire. It is common to all men, and to be found in no other race of animals, which seem to know neither this nor any other species of contracts. Two greyhounds, in running down the same hare, have sometimes the appearance of acting in some sort of concert. Each turns her [the hare being hunted] towards his companion, or endeavours to intercept her when his companion turns her towards himself. This, however, is not the effect of any contract, but of the accidental concurrence of their passions in the same object at that particular time.

***

As it is by treaty, by barter, and by purchase that we obtain from one another the greater part of those mutual good offices which we stand in need of, so it is this same trucking disposition which originally gives occasion to the division of labour. In a tribe of hunters or shepherds a particular person makes bows and arrows, for example, with more readiness and dexterity than any other. He frequently exchanges them for cattle or for venison with his companions; and he finds at last that he can in this manner get more cattle and venison than if he himself went to the field to catch them. From a regard to his own interest, therefore, the making of bows and arrows grows to be his chief business, and he becomes a sort of armourer. Another excels in making the frames and covers of their little huts or movable houses. He is accustomed to be of use in this way to his neighbours, who reward him in the same manner with cattle and with venison, till at last he finds it his interest to dedicate himself entirely to this employment, and to become a sort of house-carpenter. In the same manner a third becomes a smith or a brazier, a fourth a tanner or dresser of hides or skins, the principal part of the clothing of savages. And thus the certainty of being able to exchange all that surplus part of the produce of his own labour, which is over and above his own consumption, for such parts of the produce of other men's labour as he may have occasion for, encourages every man to apply himself to a particular occupation, and to cultivate and bring to perfection whatever talent or genius he may possess for that particular species of business.

The difference of natural talents in different men is, in reality, much less than we are aware of; and the very different genius which appears to distinguish men of different professions, when grown up to maturity, is not upon many occasions so much the cause as the effect of the division of labour. The difference between the most dissimilar characters, between a philosopher and a common street porter, for example, seems to arise not so much from nature as from habit, custom, and education. When they came into the world, and for the first six or eight years of their existence, they were, perhaps, very much alike, and neither their parents nor playfellows could perceive any remarkable difference. About that age, or soon after, they come to be employed in very different occupations. The difference of talents comes then to be taken notice of, and widens by degrees, till at last the vanity of the philosopher is willing to acknowledge scarce any resemblance. But without the disposition to truck, barter, and exchange, every man must have procured to himself every necessary and conveniency of life which he wanted. All must have had the same duties to perform, and the same work to do, and there could have been no such difference of employment as could alone give occasion to any great difference of talents.

As it is this disposition which forms that difference of talents, so remarkable among men of different professions, so it is this same disposition which renders that difference useful. Many tribes of animals acknowledged to be all of the same species derive from nature a much more remarkable distinction of genius, than what, antecedent to custom and education, appears to take place among men. By nature a philosopher is not in genius and disposition half so different from a street porter, as a mastiff is from a greyhound, or a greyhound from a spaniel, or this last from a shepherd's dog. Those different tribes of animals, however, though all of the same species, are of scarce any use to one another. The strength of the mastiff is not, in the least, supported either by the swiftness of the greyhound, or by the sagacity of the spaniel, or by the docility of the shepherd's dog. The effects of those different geniuses and talents, for want of the power or disposition to barter and exchange, cannot be brought into a common stock, and do not in the least contribute to the better accommodation and conveniency of the species. Each animal is still obliged to support and defend itself, separately and independently, and derives no sort of advantage from that variety of talents with which nature has distinguished its fellows. Among men, on the contrary, the most dissimilar geniuses are of use to one another; the different produces of their respective talents, by the general disposition to truck, barter, and exchange, being brought, as it were, into a common stock, where every man may purchase whatever part of the produce of other men's talents he has occasion for.

Source: Adam Smith, *An Inquiry into the Nature and Causes of the Wealth of Nations* (London: Methuen, 1904), pp. 15, 17–18.

On Inequality (1755), Jean-Jacques Rousseau

Jean-Jacques Rousseau (1712–1778) was a political philosopher from Geneva with deep connections to the Enlightenment in France and across Europe. In the nineteenth century, his work particularly influenced Karl Marx and Sigmund Freud, among many others.

- Analyze the role of private property in this text.
- What role does competition play? Does Rousseau see competition as essential for innovation or as a problem?
- What does Rousseau mean when he says, "To be and to appear became two entirely different things"?

The first man who, having enclosed a piece of ground, thought to say *this is mine*, and found people sufficiently simple to believe him, was the true founder of civil society. How many crimes, wars, murders, how many miseries and horrors Mankind would have been spared by him who, pulling up the stakes or filling in the ditch, had cried out to his kind: Beware of listening to this impostor; You are lost if you forget that the fruits are everyone's and the Earth no one's: But in all likelihood things had by then reached a point where they could not continue as they were; for this idea of property, depending as it does on many prior ideas which could only arise successively, did not take shape all at once in man's mind: Much progress had to have been made, industry and enlightenment acquired, transmitted, and increased from one age to the next, before this last stage of the state of Nature was reached. Let us therefore take up the thread earlier, and try to fit this slow succession of events and of knowledge together from a single point of view, and in their most natural order.

***

Things having reached this point, it is easy to imagine the rest. I shall not pause to describe the successive invention of the other arts, the progress of languages, the testing and exercise of talents, the inequalities of fortune, the abuse of Wealth, nor all the details that attend them and which everyone can easily add. I shall limit myself to a brief glance at Mankind placed in this new order of things.

Here, then are all our faculties developed, memory and imagination brought into play, amour propre interested, reason become active, and the mind almost at the limit of the perfection of which it is capable. Here are all natural qualities set in action, every man's rank and fate set, not only as to the amount of their goods and the power to help or to hurt, but also as to mind, beauty, strength or skill, as to merit or talents, and, since these are the only qualities that could attract consideration, one soon had to have or to affect them; for one's own advantage one had to seem other than one in fact was. To be and to appear became two entirely different things, and from this distinction arose ostentatious display, deceitful cunning, and all the vices that follow in their wake. Looked at in another way, man, who had previously been free and independent, is now so to speak subjugated by a multitude of new needs to the whole of Nature, and especially to those of his kind, whose slave he in a sense becomes even by becoming their master; rich, he needs their services; poor, he needs their help, and moderate means do not enable him to do without them. He must therefore constantly try to interest them in his fate and to make them really or apparently find their own profit in working for his: which makes him knavish and artful with some, imperious and harsh with the rest, and places him under the necessity of deceiving all those he needs if he cannot get them to fear him and does not find it in his interest to make himself useful to them. Finally, consuming ambition, the ardent desire to raise one's relative fortune less out of genuine need than in order to place oneself above others, instills in all men a black inclination to harm one another, a secret jealousy that is all the more dangerous as it often assumes the mask of benevolence in order to strike its blow in greater safety: in a word, competition and rivalry on the one hand, conflict of interests on the other, and always the hidden desire to profit at another's expense; all these evils are the first effect of property, and the inseparable train of nascent inequality.

Before its representative signs were invented, wealth could scarcely consist in anything but land and livestock, the only real goods that men can possess. Now, once inheritances had increased in number and size to the point where they covered all the land and all adjoined one another, men could no longer aggrandize themselves except at one another's expense, and the supernumeraries whom weakness or indolence had kept from acquiring an inheritance of their own, grown poor without having lost anything because they alone had not changed while everything was changing around them, were obliged to receive or to seize their subsistence from the hands of the rich; and from this began to arise, according to the different characters of the poor and the rich, domination and servitude, or violence and plunder. The rich, for their part, had scarcely become acquainted with the pleasure of dominating than they disdained all other pleasures, and using their old Slaves to subject new ones, they thought only of subjugating and enslaving their neighbors; like those ravenous wolves which once they have tasted human flesh, scorn all other food, and from then on want to devour only men.

Source: Jean-Jacques Rousseau, Second Discourse, Part 2, in *Rousseau's Political Writings: Discourse on Inequality, Discourse on Political Economy, on Social Contract* (New York: Norton, 1988), pp. 34, 42–43.

Merchant Codes in Tokugawa Japan (1610)

Shimai Soshitsu (1539–1615) was a sake merchant in Hakata, Japan. In his testament, Shimai sets out a list of instructions, echoing military codes, to help subsequent generations remain virtuous while pursuing commerce.

- Identify the values expressed in this document.
- Analyze the merchant's relationship to money. What purpose do profits serve?
- Does commerce threaten the social order or support it, in Shimai's view?

1. Live an honest and sincere life. Respect your parents, your brothers, and your relatives, and try to live harmoniously with them all. Honor and treat with respect everyone you meet, even those you see only occasionally. Never behave discourteously or selfishly. Never lie. In fact, never say anything that even resembles a lie, even something you heard from someone else.

2. Although those who are elderly may reasonably pray about the life to come, you should ignore all such issues until you are fifty. You may follow only the Pure Land or Zen Buddhist faiths, and you must have absolutely nothing to do with the Christian religion. . . . Such a faith is an intolerable obstacle to anyone devoted to his house. Not one person in ten understands the things of this life or of the next. Birds and beasts worry only about what is immediately before them, and humans are no different. In this life they first should make certain that they do not sully their reputations. If even Buddha himself is said to have known nothing of the world to come, how can any ordinary mortal know such things? Until you reach fifty, therefore, do not worry about the future life. . . .

3. Dice, backgammon, and all other forms of gambling are strictly forbidden in this life. Even *go*, chess, the martial arts, the nō chants, and the nō dances are forbidden for people under forty. . . .

4. Until you are forty, avoid every luxury, and never act or think like one above your station in life. In matters of business and moneymaking, however, work harder than anyone else. . . . Always behave as one whose station in life is half that of yours. Although some people may suggest that you [should] be more visible and assertive, ignore all such advice and maintain a low profile. Until you turn fifty, be temperate in all things, and avoid all ostentation and finery, anything, in fact, that might call attention to yourself. Do not cultivate expensive tastes, for you should ignore such things as the tea ceremony, swords, daggers, and fine clothes. . . . Do not build a new house unless you are over fifty. Those who are that old may build what they like and can afford. Yet most people are poor by the time they die, for fewer than one in ten or twenty who build a fortune by their own talent carry it to their graves, and those who inherit their wealth are even more likely to lose it and die impoverished. Remember this.

5. Until you are forty, do not invite out others or let others invite you out. Once or twice a year you may invite out your parents, brothers, or relatives, or go out at their invitation, but—do not forget—even this you may do only occasionally. . . .

***

8. Never wander outside the shop or visit places where you have no business being. . . . Since you will generally be in the house, you yourself should tend the morning and evening cooking fires and handle the firewood and embers. You should pick up all trash inside and behind the house, chop up the pieces of rope and short bits of trash to use in plaster, and use the long pieces to make rope. Collect and clean pieces of wood and bamboo longer than five *bu* and use them as firewood. Save all paper scraps, even pieces only three or five *bu* long, to use in making fresh paper. Do as I have done, and waste absolutely nothing.

9. When you need something, go and buy it yourself, regardless of whether it is firewood, two or three *bu* of small fish or sardines, other purchases from the seaside or the town, or even timber. Bargain for the items and pay as little as you can. . . .

10. In general, use few servants, especially few female ones. . . .

11. Keep a steady supply of coarse *miso* on hand for your servants, and when you make the *miso* soup in

the mornings and evenings, carefully filter the *miso*. You should add to the residue salt and cucumbers, eggplants, gourd melons, and onions, and serve this as a side dish to the servants. You can give them the stalks as well, and when rice is expensive, you may feed them some sort of hodgepodge. But if you do give your servants such a dish, you and your wife should eat it as well. Even if you intend to eat rice, first sip at least a bit of the hodgepodge, for your servants will resent it if you do not. . . .

***

13. Those with even a small fortune must remember that their duty in life is to devote themselves to their house and its business. They must not become careless, for if they buy what they want, do as they please, and, in general, live sumptuously, they will soon spend that fortune. . . . Although a samurai can draw on the produce of his tenured lands to earn his livelihood, a merchant must rely on the profit from his business, for without that profit, the money in his bags would soon disappear. No matter how much profit he makes and packs into his bags, however, if he continually wastes that money, he may as well pack it into bags full of holes. Remember this.

14. Rise early in the morning, and go to bed as soon as the sun sets, for you will waste oil if you burn lamps during evenings when you have nothing important to do. . . .

***

17. Live in harmony with your wife, for the two of you must work together diligently. Both of you should live modestly and carefully and consider always the good of the house and its business. A contentious, unhappy marriage destroys a house, for it distracts the husband and wife from their work. . . .

These seventeen articles were written not for Sōshitsu's sake but for yours. They are his testament, and you should follow them closely. They should be as important to you as the Great Constitution of Prince Shōtoku. Read them every day, or even twice a day, and be careful to forget nothing. Write a vow on the back of a votive tablet promising never to violate any of the articles and put it in my coffin when I die.

Source: Wm. Theodore de Bary, Carol Gluck, and Arthur E. Tiedemann (eds.), *Sources of Japanese Tradition*, vol. 2, *1600 to 2000*, 2nd ed. (New York: Columbia University Press, 2001), pp. 268–71.

An Edict on Trade (1793), the Qianlong Emperor

The Qianlong Emperor (1711–1799) was the sixth emperor of the Manchu-led Qing dynasty in China. In the late eighteenth century, the English East India Company sought to expand its trade with China. Here the Chinese governments seeks to regulate the activity of English merchants.

- What was the Qianlong Emperor trying to accomplish?
- How does the Qianlong Emperor justify trading with foreign powers?
- From the emperor's point of view, what effect does trade have on the social order?

You, O King, live beyond the confines of many seas, nevertheless, impelled by your humble desire to partake of the benefits of our civilization, you have dispatched a mission respectfully bearing your memorial. Your Envoy has crossed the seas and paid his respects at my Court on the anniversary of my birthday. To show your devotion, you have also sent offerings of your country's produce.

***

As to your entreaty to send one of your nationals to be accredited to my Celestial Court and to be in control of your country's trade with China, this request is contrary to all usage of my dynasty and cannot possibly be entertained.

***

You, O King from far, have yearned after the blessings of our civilization, and in your eagerness to come into touch with our converting influence have sent an Embassy across the sea bearing a memorial. I have already taken note of your respectful spirit of submission, have treated your mission with extreme favour and loaded it with gifts, besides issuing a mandate to you, O King, and honouring you with the bestowal of valuable presents. Thus has my indulgence been manifested.

. . . Hitherto, all European nations, including your own country's barbarian merchants, have carried on their trade with Our Celestial Empire at Canton. Such has been the procedure for many years, although Our Celestial Empire possesses all things in prolific abundance and lacks no product within its borders. There was therefore no need to import the manufactures of outside barbarians in exchange for our own produce. But as the tea, silk, and porcelain which the Celestial Empire produces are absolute necessities to European nations and to yourselves, we have permitted, as a signal mark of favour, that foreign hongs [trading firms licensed by the Chinese government] should be established at Canton, so that your wants might be supplied and your country thus participate in our beneficence. But your Ambassador has now put forward new requests which completely fail to recognize the Throne's principle to "treat strangers from afar with indulgence," and to exercise a pacifying control over barbarian tribes, the world over. . . .

Your Ambassador requests facilities for ships of your nation to call at Ningpo, Chusan, Tientsin and other places for purposes of trade. Until now trade with European nations has always been conducted at Macao, where the foreign hongs are established to store and sell foreign merchandise. Your nation has obediently complied with this regulation for years past without raising any objection. In none of the other ports named have hongs been established, so that even if your vessels were to proceed thither, they would have no means of disposing of their cargoes. Furthermore, no interpreters are available, so you would have no means of explaining your wants, and nothing but general inconvenience would result. For the future, as in the past, I decree that your request is refused and that the trade shall be limited to Macao.

Source: Gentzler J. Mason, *Changing China: Readings in the History of China from the Opium War to the Present* (New York: Praeger, 1977), pp. 23–28.

Interpreting Visual Evidence

Envisioning the World

Although maps give the impression of objectivity and geographic precision, the arrangement of names and locations, as well as the areas placed at the center and the margins, reveal the mapmakers' views of the world. In most cultures, official maps located their own major administrative and religious sites at the center of the universe and reflected local elites' ideas about how the world was organized.

There were, however, important differences. For example, Chinese maps, like the first two below, typically devoted more attention to textual explanations with moral and political messages than to locating places accurately. The Codex Xolotl presents a cartographic history, showing mountains and waterways and using hieroglyphic place-names for sites in the Valley of Mexico, marking historic conquests of an Aztec group, the Acolhuas of Texcoco. The Iranian

The *Huayi tu* map, 1136.

Chinese wheel map, 1760s.

Codex Xolotl, early sixteenth century.

Iranian map, seventeenth century.

Japanese map of the world, 1761.

Waldseemüller map, 1507.

Mercator projection, 1569.

map presents an unabashedly Islamic vision, with a grid that measures the distances from any location in the Islamic world to Mecca. The Japanese map shows Dutch influence, with much information about distant lands both in the map and in the two-person images to the left. Finally, the European maps (the Waldseemüller map and the Mercator projection) appear objective at first glance, but they, too, group the rest of the world around their own territory, which they distort to make appear disproportionately large.

Questions for Analysis

1. Describe the organizing principles, and therefore priorities, of each map.

2. Compare the maps. How are they different from one another?

3. Evaluate the relative awareness each map shows of distant cultures and territories.

15

Reordering the World

1750–1850

In 1798, the French commander Napoleon Bonaparte invaded Egypt. At the time, Europeans regarded this territory as the cradle of a once-great culture, a land bridge to the Red Sea and trade with Asia, and an outpost of the Ottoman Empire. Occupying the country would allow Napoleon to introduce some of the principles of the French Revolution and to seize control of trade routes to Asia. Napoleon also hoped that by defeating the Ottomans, who controlled Egypt, he would augment his and France's historic greatness. But events did not go as Napoleon planned, for his troops faced a resentful Egyptian population. Although Napoleon soon returned to France and his dream of a French Egypt was short-lived, his invasion challenged Ottoman rule and threatened the balance of power in Europe. Indeed, Napoleon's actions in Africa, the Americas, and Europe, combined with the principles of the American and French Revolutions, laid the foundations for a new era—one based on a radically new understanding of freedom as the absence of constraint, the opposite of privileges handed down by a lord or master.

That new idea of freedom first rang out across western Europe and the Americas and reverberated around the world. It destroyed the American colonial domains of Spain, Portugal, Britain, and France; brought new nations to the stage; and challenged established elites everywhere, leading in some cases to the expansion of colonial

Core Objectives

- **DESCRIBE** the new ideas of freedom, and **EXPLAIN** how they differed from earlier understandings of this term.

- **COMPARE** political and economic developments in the Atlantic world with those of regions elsewhere around the globe during the period 1750–1850.

- **IDENTIFY** and **EXPLAIN** the key developments that constituted the industrial revolution.

- **EXPLAIN** patterns of global trade and economic growth, and **CONNECT** them to political changes during the period 1750–1850.

- **COMPARE** the groups of people who held power in each of the regions in 1750 and then in 1850, and **EXPLAIN** the changes that took place during this period in these societies.

rule. The impulse for change was a belief that governments should enact laws that apply to all people, though in practice there were significant exceptions (slaves, women, and colonized subjects). Free speech, free markets, free labor, and governments freely chosen by freeborn men, it was thought, would benefit everyone. In Europe and the Americas, though not elsewhere, the era also witnessed the emergence of the nation-state. This new form of political organization derived legitimacy from its inhabitants, often referred to as citizens, who, in theory, if not always in practice, shared a common culture, ethnicity, and language.

Yet freedom in some corners of the globe set the stage for depriving people of freedom elsewhere and led inexorably to changes in the worldwide balance of power. Even as western European countries lost their New World colonies, they gained economic and military strength, which further challenged Asian and African governments.

Global Storylines

- A new era based on radically new ideas of freedom and the nation-state emerges in the Atlantic world.

- The industrious and industrial revolutions transform communities and the global economy.

- The worldwide balance of power shifts decisively toward northwestern Europe.

Revolutionary Transformations and New Languages of Freedom

In the eighteenth century, the circulation of goods, people, and ideas created pressures for reform around the Atlantic world. As economies expanded, many people felt that the restrictive mercantilist system prevented them from sharing in the new wealth and power. Similarly, an increasingly literate public called for their states to adopt just practices, including the abolition of torture and the accountability of rulers. In several places, power holders could not stamp out these demands before they became full-scale revolutions.

Reformers wanted to expand the franchise, to enable property holders to vote. Claims of **popular sovereignty**, the idea that political power depends on "the people," became rooted in the idea of the nation: people who shared a common language, common culture, and common history. This in turn gave rise to the nation-state as a form of political organization. Over the course of the nineteenth century, political movements began to emphasize nationalism, the idea that a fully fledged nation should have a state of its own, and democracy, the idea that the people, the *demos*, should choose their own representatives and be governed by them (see Chapter 16). In this chapter, we concentrate on the first expressions of this new thinking, in thirteen of Britain's North American colonies and in France. In both places, the "nation" and the "people" toppled their former rulers.

This chapter also concentrates on far-reaching economic developments that came in tandem with revolutionary political change. Economic reformers argued that unregulated economies would produce faster economic growth. Going well beyond the work of Adam Smith, they called for **free trade** (or **laissez-faire**), unencumbered by tariffs, quotas, and fees; free markets, which would be unregulated; and free labor, which meant using paid rather than slave labor. They insisted that these economic freedoms would yield more just and more efficient societies, ultimately benefiting everyone, everywhere in the world.

Yet the same European and Euro-American elites who wanted a freer world often exploited slaves, denied women equal treatment, restricted colonial economies, and tried forcibly to open Asia's and Africa's markets to European trade and investment. In Africa, idealistic upheavals led not to free and sovereign peoples but to greater enslavement.

Political Reorderings

Late in the eighteenth century, revolutionary ideas spread across the Atlantic world (see Map 15.1) following the trail of Enlightenment ideas about

THE BIG PICTURE

Why did the worldwide balance of power shift during this period?

popular sovereignty
The idea that the power of the state resides in the people.

free trade (laissez-faire)
Domestic and international trade unencumbered by tariff barriers, quotas, and fees.

Core Objectives

DESCRIBE the new ideas of freedom, and **EXPLAIN** how they differed from earlier understandings of this term.

The Global View

RUSSIA

BRITISH NORTH AMERICA

Hudson Bay

OREGON
(Claimed by Spain, Russia, and Britain)

LOUISIANA

Quebec

Boston
New York
Philadelphia
Washington, D.C.

UNITED STATES
✴1776
(independence recognized by Great Britain 1783)

Santa Fe

Charleston

MEXICO
✴1821

FLORIDA

Gulf of Mexico

A T L A N T I C

O C E A N

Mexico City

CUBA

PUERTO RICO

GUADELOUPE (Fr.)

BELIZE
JAMAICA
REPUBLIC OF HAITI
✴1804

MARTINIQUE (Fr.)

UNITED PROVINCES OF CENTRAL AMERICA
✴1823

Cartagena

TRINIDAD (Br.)

Caracas

REPUBLIC OF COLOMBIA
✴1819

GUIANA

P A C I F I C

Quito

O C E A N

PERU
✴1821

B R A Z I L
✴1822

Lima

BOLIVIA
✴1825

Rio de Janeiro

PARAGUAY
✴1811

CHILE
✴1818

PROVINCES OF LA PLATA
✴1816

URUGUAY
✴1828

Buenos Aires
Montevideo

■	British possessions
■	Spanish possessions
■	French possessions
■	Portuguese possessions
■	Dutch possessions
■	Ottoman possessions
■	Russian Empire
✴1776	Date of political independence from European (or Ottoman) colonial rule

0   1000   2000 Miles
0   1000   2000 Kilometers

Map 15.1 Revolutions and Empires in the Atlantic World, 1776–1829

....

Influenced by Enlightenment thinkers and the French Revolution, colonies gained independence from European powers (and in the case of Greece, from the Ottoman Empire) in the late eighteenth and early nineteenth centuries.

- Which European powers granted independence to their colonial possessions in the Americas during this period?
- What were the first two colonial territories to become independent in the Americas?
- Based on the chronology presented in this map and on your reading, consider the relative importance of European influence and local developments in the Americas in accounting for the timing of independence in different countries. Why, in particular, did colonies in Spanish and Portuguese America obtain political independence decades after the United States won its independence?

freedom and reason. As more newspapers, pamphlets, and books circulated in European countries and American colonies, readers began to discuss their societies' problems and to believe they had the right to participate in governance.

The slogans of independence, freedom, liberty, and equality seemed to promise an end to oppression, hardship, and inequities. In the North American colonies and in France, revolutions ultimately brought down monarchies and blossomed into republics. The examples of the United States and France soon encouraged other people in the Caribbean and Central and South America to reject the rule of monarchs. In these revolutionary environments, new institutions—such as written constitutions and permanent parliaments—claimed to represent the people.

THE NORTH AMERICAN WAR OF INDEPENDENCE, 1776–1783

Core Objectives

COMPARE political and economic developments in the Atlantic world with those of regions elsewhere around the globe during the period 1750–1850.

The American Revolution ended British rule in North America. It was the first of a series of revolutions to shake the Atlantic world, inspired by new ideas of freedom.

By the mid-eighteenth century, Britain's colonies in North America swelled with people and prosperity. Bustling port cities like Charleston, Philadelphia, New York, and Boston saw inflows of African slaves, European migrants, and manufactured goods, while agricultural staples flowed out. A "genteel" class of merchants and landowning planters dominated colonial affairs.

Land was a constant source of dispute. Planters struggled with independent farmers (yeomen). Sons and daughters of farmers, often unable to inherit or acquire land near their parents, moved westward, where they came into conflict with Amerindian peoples. To defend their lands, many Amerindians allied with Britain's rival, France. After losing the Seven Years' War (see Chapter 13), however, France ceded its Canadian colony to Britain to secure the return of its much more lucrative Caribbean colonies, especially Saint-Domingue. This left many Indians no choice but to turn to the British government to help them resist the aggressive advances of land-hungry colonists. British officials did make some concessions to Indian interests, but they did not have the troops or financial strength to enforce them.

Asserting Independence from Britain Despite these tensions, Britain stood supreme in the Atlantic world in the mid-1760s, with its greatest foes defeated and its empire expanding. Political revolution in North America seemed unimaginable. And yet, a decade later, that is what occurred.

The spark came from the government of King George III, which insisted that colonists contribute to the crown that protected them, notably in the Seven Years' War (known in North America as the French and Indian War).

The king's officials imposed taxes on a variety of commodities and tried to put an end to smuggling by colonists who sought to evade mercantilist restrictions on trade. To the king's surprise and dismay, colonists objected to the new measures and protested having to pay taxes when they lacked political representation in the British Parliament.

In 1775, resistance in the form of petitions and boycotts turned into open warfare between a colonial militia and British troops in Massachusetts. Once blood was spilled, more radical voices came to the fore. Previously, leaders of the protest had claimed to revere the British Empire. Now calls for severing the ties to Britain became more prominent. Thomas Paine, a recent immigrant from England, captured the new mood in a pamphlet he published in 1776, arguing that it was "common sense" for people to govern themselves. Later that year, the Continental Congress (in which representatives from thirteen colonies gathered) adapted part of Paine's popular pamphlet for the Declaration of Independence.

Drawing on Enlightenment themes (see Chapter 14), the declaration written by Thomas Jefferson stated the people's "natural right" to govern themselves. It also drew inspiration from the writings of the British philosopher John Locke, notably the idea that governments should be based on a **social contract** in which the law binds both ruler and people. Locke had written nearly a century earlier that the people had the right to rebel against their government if it broke the contract and infringed on their rights. With the Declaration of Independence, the rebels announced their right to rid themselves of the English king and form their own government.

The Declaration's assertion that "all men are created equal" overturned former social hierarchies in the thirteen colonies (now calling themselves states). Thus, common men no longer automatically deferred to gentlemen of higher rank. Many women claimed that their contributions to the revolution's cause (by managing farms and shops in their husbands' absence) earned them greater equality in marriage, including property rights. However, the political arrangements Americans designed during their War of Independence gave voting rights only to white, male property owners—not women, not slaves, not Amerindians, not poor white men without property. Indeed, many slaves sided against the revolution, for it was the British who

The Boston Massacre Paul Revere's idealized view of the Boston Massacre of March 5, 1770. In the years after the Seven Years' War, Bostonians grew increasingly disenchanted with British efforts to enforce imperial regulations. When British troops fired on and killed several members of an angry mob in what came to be called the "Boston Massacre," the resulting frenzy stirred revolutionary sentiments among the populace.

social contract
The idea, drawn from the writings of British philosopher John Locke, that the law should bind both ruler and people.

offered them freedom most directly, in exchange for military service. Their hopes for freedom were thwarted when Britain conceded the loss of its rebellious American colonies. With the Treaty of Paris (1783), the United States gained its independence.

Building a Republican Government With independence, the former colonists had to build a new government. They generally agreed that theirs was not to be a monarchy. But what it *was* to be remained through the 1780s a source of much debate, involving heated words and sometimes heated action. As a loose confederation of relatively autonomous states, the new national state struggled to deal with local rebellions, foreign relations, and crushing levels of debt. To save the young nation from falling into "anarchy," propertied men convened the Constitutional Convention in Philadelphia in 1787.

This gathering aimed to forge a document that would create a more powerful national government and a more unified nation. After fierce debate, the convention drafted a charter for a republican government in which power would rest with representatives of the people—not with a king. When it went before the states for approval, the Constitution was controversial. Its critics, known as Anti-Federalists, feared the growth of a potentially tyrannical national government and insisted on including a Bill of Rights to protect individual liberties from abusive government intrusions. Ultimately the Constitution was ratified by the states and then amended by the Bill of Rights.

Ratification of the Constitution and the addition of the Bill of Rights did not end arguments about the scope and power of the national government of the United States. Some Americans called for the national government to abolish slavery. However, many others—especially leaders in the south, where slavery was a mainstay of the economy—argued that the national government did not have the power to do so. In an uneasy truce, political leaders agreed not to let the debate over whether to abolish slavery escalate into a cause for disunion. As the frontier pushed westward, however, the question of which new states would or would not allow slavery again posed a vexing challenge. Initially the existence of ample land postponed a confrontation. In 1800, Thomas Jefferson's election as the third president of the United States marked the triumph of a model of sending pioneers out to new lands in order to reduce conflict on old lands. In the same year, however, a Virginia slave named Gabriel Prosser raised an army of slaves to seize the state capital at Richmond and won support from white artisans and laborers for a more inclusive republic. His dream of an egalitarian revolution fell victim to white terror and black betrayal, though: twenty-seven slaves, including Prosser, went to the gallows. With them, for the moment, died the dream of a multiracial republic in which all men were truly created equal.

In the larger context of the Atlantic world, the successful defiance of Europe's most powerful empire and the establishment of a nonmonarchical, republican form of government sent shock waves through the Americas and Europe and even into distant corners of Asia and Africa. It also helped pave the way for other revolts over the next several decades.

THE FRENCH REVOLUTION, 1789–1799

Partly inspired by the American Revolution, French men and women soon began to call for liberty too—and the result profoundly shook Europe's dynasties and social hierarchies. Its impact, though, reached well beyond Europe, for the French Revolution, even more than the American, inspired rebels and terrified rulers around the globe.

Origins and Outbreak The French king himself opened the door to revolution. Eager to weaken his rival, England, Louis XVI spent huge sums in support of the American rebels—and thereby overloaded the state with debt. To restore his credit, Louis needed to raise taxes on the privileged classes; to do so, he was forced to convene the Estates-General, a medieval advisory body that had not met for over a century. Like the American colonists, French nobles argued that taxation gave them the right of representation.

When the delegates assembled in 1789, however, a procedural dispute spun out of control. The delegates of the clergy (the First Estate) and the aristocracy (the Second Estate) hoped to vote by estate and overrule the delegates representing everyone else (the Third Estate). But the Third Estate, which had more representatives than the first two estates combined, refused to be outvoted. It demanded that all delegates sit together in one chamber and vote as individuals. Soon delegates of the Third Estate declared themselves to be the "National Assembly," the body that should determine France's future.

Afraid that the king would crush the reform movement, a Parisian crowd attacked a medieval armory in search of weapons on July 14, 1789. Not only did this armory—the Bastille—hold gunpowder, but it was also an infamous prison for political prisoners. The crowd stormed the prison and murdered the commanding officer, then cut off his head and paraded it through the streets of Paris. On this day (Bastille Day), the king made the fateful decision not to call out the army, and the capital city belonged to the crowd. As news spread to the countryside, peasants torched manor houses and destroyed municipal archives containing records of feudal dues, payments they owed to landlords of specially designated properties. Barely three weeks later, the French National Assembly abolished the privileges of the nobility and the clergy. It declared a new era of liberty, equality, and fraternity. Liberty, like freedom, now meant the absence of constraint rather than a special privilege granted by the king.

The "Tennis Court Oath"
Locked out of the chambers of the Estates-General, the deputies of the Third Estate reconvened at a nearby indoor tennis court in June 1789; there they swore an oath not to disband until the king recognized the sovereignty of a national assembly.

Revolutionary Transformations The French Revolution connected the concept of a people more closely with a nation. The Declaration of the Rights of Man and of the Citizen (1789) echoed the Americans' Declaration of Independence, but in more radical terms. It guaranteed all citizens of the French nation inviolable liberties and gave all men equality under the law. It also proclaimed that "the principle of all sovereignty rests essentially in the nation." Both the rhetorical and the real war against old-regime privileges threatened to end dynastic and aristocratic rule in Europe.

Social relations changed too, as women felt that the new principles of citizenship should include women's rights. In 1791, a group of women demanded the right to bear arms to defend the revolution, but they stopped short of claiming equal rights for both sexes. In their view, women would become citizens by being good revolutionary wives and mothers, not because of any natural rights. In the same year, Olympe de Gouges composed the Declaration of the Rights of Woman and the Female Citizen, proposing rights to divorce, hold property in marriage, be educated, and have public careers. The all-male assembly did not take up these issues, believing that a "fraternity" of free *men* composed the nation.

As the revolution gained momentum, deep divisions emerged. In 1790, all clergy had to take an oath of loyalty to the new state—an action that bitterly divided the country. The most divisive, destructive turn in the revolution came in 1792, when the French declared a preemptive war against Austria, and then Prussia, Britain, and Russia. They soon had foreign armies on their soil and a civil war to contend with, when peasants outraged by the loyalty oath and city dwellers in major provincial cities rose up against the revolutionary government and its wartime demands.

The Terror In response to this self-induced crisis, elite reformers made common cause with urban radicals in Paris, who demanded price controls, direct democracy, and the violent suppression of dissent. Together, they launched the Reign of Terror. The Committee of Public Safety, including the lawyer Maximilien Robespierre, oversaw the execution of as many as 40,000 so-called enemies of the people—mostly peasants and laborers who had taken up arms against them—justified in terms of defending the Republic. If most victims were of modest means, the term *aristocrat* was often equated with treason. Even before terror was declared as government policy, Louis XVI and his wife, Marie Antoinette, had lost their heads to the guillotine (itself a novel and supposedly rational, enlightened way to execute prisoners painlessly).

By 1794 France's army numbered some 800,000 soldiers, making it the world's largest. Most French officers now came from the middle classes, some even from the lower class. Foot soldiers identified with the French fatherland. Having vowed to wage a defensive war, they now pushed foreign armies off French soil and waged a war to "liberate" the disenfranchised from their rulers across Europe.

When the military emergency ended, enthusiasm for Robespierre's measures lost popular support, and Robespierre himself went to the guillotine on 9 Thermidor (according to the new, revolutionary calendar, or July 28, 1794). His execution marked the end of the Terror but did not restore order. Several years later, following yet more political turmoil, a coup d'état brought to power a thirty-year-old general from the recently annexed Mediterranean island of Corsica.

The general, **Napoleon Bonaparte** (1769–1821), put security and order ahead of social reform. His regime retained significant revolutionary changes, especially those associated with more efficient state government. He eased religious tensions by working out an accord with the Vatican. However, Napoleon was determined not only to reform France but also to prevail over its enemies, and he retreated from republican principles. Taking the title Emperor of the French, he centralized government administration and established a system of rational tax collection. Most important, he created a civil legal code—the Napoleonic Code—that applied throughout all of France (and the French colonies).

THE NAPOLEONIC ERA, 1799–1815

Determined to extend the reach of French influence, Napoleon launched a series of military campaigns in an effort to build a vast empire. He had his armies trumpet the principles of liberty, equality, and fraternity wherever they went. Many local populations initially embraced the French, regarding them as liberators from the old order. Although Napoleon thought the entire world would take up his cause, this was not always the case.

Napoleon Bonaparte (1769–1821) General who rose to power in a postrevolutionary coup d'état, eventually proclaiming himself emperor of France. He placed security and order ahead of social reform and created a civil legal code. Napoleon expanded his empire through military action, but after his disastrous Russian campaign, the united European powers defeated Napoleon and forced him into exile. He escaped and reassumed command of his army but was later defeated at the Battle of Waterloo.

In Portugal, Spain, and Russia, French troops faced fierce popular resistance. Portuguese and Spanish soldiers and peasants formed bands of resisters called guerrillas, and British troops joined them to fight the French in the Peninsular War (1808–1813). In Germany and Italy, as local inhabitants grew tired of paying tribute, many looked to their past for inspiration to oppose the French. Now they discovered something they had barely recognized before: *national* traditions and borders. One of the ironies of Napoleon's attempt to bring all of Europe under French rule was that it laid the foundations for nationalist strife.

In Europe, Napoleon extended his empire from the Iberian Peninsula to the Austrian and Prussian borders. (See Map 15.2.) By 1812, when he invaded Russia, however, his forces were too overstretched and undersupplied to survive the harsh winter. After his failed attack on Russia, all the major European powers united against him. At the Battle of Waterloo in Belgium in 1815, armies from Prussia, Austria, Russia, and Britain crushed his troops as they made their last stand. The stage was now set for a century-long struggle on the continent between those who wanted to restore society as it had been before the French Revolution and those who wanted to guarantee a more liberal order based on individual rights, limited government, and free trade.

REVOLUTION IN SAINT-DOMINGUE (HAITI)

France also saw colonies break away in this age of new freedoms, notably Saint-Domingue. Unlike most of British North America, revolution here came from the bottom rungs of the social ladder: slaves. In this Caribbean colony, freedom therefore meant not just liberation from Europe but emancipation from white planters. It posed a powerful question: How universal were these new rights?

At the outset of the French Revolution the island's black slave population numbered 500,000, compared with 40,000 white French settlers and about 30,000 free "people of color" (individuals of mixed black and white ancestry, as well as freed black slaves). Almost two-thirds of the slaves were relatively recent arrivals, brought to the colony to toil on its renowned sugar plantations, which were exceptional in their brutality. The slave population was an angry majority without local ties, producing wealth for rich absentee landlords of a different race.

The breakdown of authority in France unleashed conflict in Saint-Domingue, where local tensions were already high. White settlers sought self-government; they wanted to break free of the exclusive trade arrangement with France and to control the island themselves. Free blacks wanted to end racial discrimination among property holders without, initially, calling slavery into question. Slaves, by contrast, invoked revolutionary language

French Empire
Under French control
Allied to France
← Napoleon's route, 1812

Map 15.2 Napoleon's Empire, 1812

Early in the first decade of the nineteenth century, Napoleon controlled almost all of Europe.

- What major states were under French control? What countries were allied to France?

- Compare this map with the European part of Map 15.1, and explain how Napoleon redrew the map of Europe. What major country was not under French control?

- According to your reading, how was Napoleon able to control and build alliances with so many states and kingdoms?

Revolution in Saint-Domingue
In 1791, slaves took up arms against white planters. This engraving was based on a German report on the uprising and reflects white fears of slave rebellion as much as the actual events themselves.

to denounce their masters and air long-standing grievances. As civil war erupted, slaves fought French forces that had arrived to restore order. In 1793, the National Convention in France abolished slavery. In part, the motive was to declare the universality of liberty, equality, and fraternity within the French nation, which included colonies. In part, it was to restore order to the colony. Once liberated, the former slaves took control of the island. (See Current Trends in World History: Two Case Studies in Political Change and Environmental Degradation.)

The specter of a free country ruled by former slaves sent shudders across the Western Hemisphere, and above all in Britain and Spain, which had neighboring colonies. A version of martial law was declared in Venezuela. Thomas Jefferson, author of the Declaration of Independence and U.S. president at the time, refused to recognize Haiti. Like other American slave owners, he worried that the example of a successful slave uprising might inspire similar revolts in the United States and elsewhere in the Americas.

REVOLUTIONS IN SPANISH AND PORTUGUESE AMERICA

Revolutionary enthusiasm also spread through Spanish and Portuguese America. As in Haiti, subordinated people of color took advantage of the period's political instability; they mobilized European ideas against European colonizers and challenged the established order. (See Map 15.3.)

Even before the French Revolution, Andean Indians rebelled against Spanish colonial authority. In a major uprising in the 1780s, they demanded freedom from forced labor and compulsory consumption of Spanish wares. After an army of 40,000 to 60,000 Andean Indians besieged the ancient capital of Cuzco and nearly vanquished Spanish armies, it took Spanish forces many years to eliminate the insurgents.

After this uprising, Iberian American elites who feared their Indian or slave majorities renewed their loyalty to the Spanish or Portuguese crown. Ultimately, however, the French Revolution and Napoleonic wars shattered the ties between Spain and Portugal and their American colonies.

Brazil and Constitutional Monarchy Brazil was a prized Portuguese colony whose path to independence saw little political turmoil and no social revolution. In 1807, French troops stormed Lisbon, the capital of Portugal, but not before the royals and their associates fled to Rio de Janeiro, then the capital of Brazil. There they settled down, enacting reforms in administration, agriculture, and manufacturing and establishing schools, hospitals, and a library. Brazil now became the center of the Portuguese Empire. Furthermore, the royal family willingly shared power with the local planter aristocracy, so the economy prospered and slavery expanded.

When the king returned to Portugal in 1821, his son Pedro remained. Fearing an uprising among local elites, Pedro declared Brazil an independent state and established a constitutional monarchy. Local elites soon embraced Pedro's rule and cooperated to minimize conflict, lest a slave revolt erupt. By the 1840s, Brazil had achieved a political stability unmatched in the Americas.

Mexico's Independence When Napoleon occupied Spain, he sparked a crisis in the Spanish Empire that eventually led Mexico to secede. Because the ruling Spanish monarchy fell captive to Napoleon in 1807, colonial elites in Buenos Aires (Argentina), Caracas (Venezuela), and Mexico City (Mexico) found themselves without an emperor. After Napoleon's defeat, locally born creoles resented the fact that Spain reinstated *peninsulares* (people born in Spain) as colonial officials with the help of the royal army. Inspired by Enlightenment thinkers and chafing at the efforts to restore Iberian authority, the creoles wanted to keep their privileges and get rid of the peninsulares.

Mexico's creoles identified themselves more as Mexicans than as Spanish Americans, and as the Spanish king appeared less and less able to govern effectively, Mexican generals (with support of the creoles) proclaimed Mexican independence in 1821. Unlike the situation in Brazil, Mexican secession did not lead to stability.

Other South American Revolutions The loosening of Spain's grip on its colonies was more prolonged and militarized than Britain's separation from its American colonies. Venezuela's Simón Bolívar (1783–1830), the son of a merchant-planter family, who was educated on Enlightenment texts, dreamed of a land governed by reason. He revered Napoleonic France as a model state built on military heroism and constitutional proclamations. So did the Argentine leader General José de San Martín (1778–1850). Men like Bolívar, San Martín, and their many generals waged extended wars of independence against Spanish armies and their allies between 1810 and 1824.

What started in South America as a political revolution against Spanish colonial authority escalated into a social struggle among Indians, mestizos, slaves, and whites. The armed populace threatened the planters and

Two Case Studies in Political Change and Environmental Degradation

Overthrowing slavery and colonial domination did not necessarily halt environmental degradation. In fact, in two important New World countries, the new nations of Haiti and Brazil, the transition to independence aggravated environmental problems created by former colonial regimes.

Two hundred and fifty years ago, Haiti, which was under French colonial rule at that time and known as Saint-Domingue, was the richest colony in the Americas, perhaps even the richest colony in the world, accounting for two-thirds of France's worldwide investment. Saint-Domingue's extraordinary wealth came from large, white-owned sugar plantations that used a massive and highly coerced slave population. The slaves' lives were short and brutal, lasting on average only fifteen years; hence the wealthy planter class had to replenish their labor supplies from Africa at frequent intervals.

White planters on the island were eager to amass quick fortunes so that they could sell out and return to France. Vastly outnumbered by enslaved Africans at a time when abolitionist sentiments were gaining ground in Europe and even circulating among slaves in the Americas, the planters' families knew that their prosperity was unlikely to last. They gave little thought to sustainable growth and were not troubled that they were destroying their environment.

The planters greeted the onset of the French Revolution in 1789 with enthusiasm. They saw an opportunity to assert their independence from France, to engage in wider trading contacts with North America and the rest of the world, and thus to become even richer. They ignored the possibility that the ideals of the French Revolution—especially its slogan of liberty, equality, and fraternity—could inspire the island's free blacks and slaves. Indeed, no sooner had the white planters thrown in their lot with the Third Estate in France than a slave rebellion broke out in Saint-Domingue. From its beginnings in 1791, it led, after great loss of life to African slaves and French soldiers, to the proclamation of an independent state in Haiti in 1804, ruled by African Americans. Haiti became the Americas' second independent republican government. Although the revolt brought political independence to its black population, it only intensified the land's environmental deterioration. Not only did sugarcane fields become scorched battlefields, but freed slaves rushed to stake out independent plots on the old plantations and in wooded areas. In both places, the new peasant class energetically cleared the land. The small country became even more deforested, and intensive cultivation increased erosion and soil depletion. Haiti fell into a more vicious cycle of environmental degradation and poverty.

The second case study of political change leading to the destruction of the environment comes from the independent Brazilian state, where the ruling elite, having achieved autonomy from Portugal, expanded the agrarian frontier. Landowners oversaw the clearing of ancient hardwood forests so that slaves and squatters could plant coffee trees. The clearing process had begun with sugarcane in the coastal regions, but it accelerated with coffee plantings in the hilly regions of São Paulo.

In fact, coffee was a worse threat to Brazil's forests than any other invader in the previous 300 years. Coffee trees thrive on soils that are neither soggy nor overly dry. Therefore, planters razed the virgin forest, which contained a balanced variety of trees and

merchants; rural folk battled against aristocratic creoles; Andean Indians fled the mines and occupied great estates. Popular armies, having defeated Spanish forces by the 1820s, fought civil wars over the new postcolonial order.

New states and collective identities of nationhood now emerged. A narrow elite led these political communities, and their guiding principles were often contradictory. Bolívar, for instance, encouraged his followers to

Slaves Cutting Cane Sugar was the preeminent agricultural export from the New World for centuries. Owners of sugarcane plantations relied almost exclusively on African slaves to produce the sweetener. Labor in the fields was especially harsh, as slaves worked in the blistering sun from dawn until dusk.

undergrowth, and Brazil's once-fertile soil suffered rapid depletion by a single-crop industry. Within one generation the clear-cutting led to infertile soils and extensive erosion, which drove planters farther into the frontier to destroy even more forest and plant more coffee groves. The environmental impact was monumental: between 1788 and 1888, when slavery was abolished, Brazil produced about 10 million tons of coffee and lost 300 million tons of ancient forest biomass (the accumulated biological material from living organisms).

Questions for Analysis

- Who intensified the deforestation and degradation in each case, and why did they do it?
- Why do you think deforestation increased in intensity after Haitians and Brazilians gained their autonomy/independence?

Explore Further

Diamond, Jared, and James A. Robinson (eds.), *Natural Experiments of History* (2010).

Geggus, David (ed.), *The Impact of the Haitian Revolution in the Atlantic World* (2001).

become "American," to overcome their local identities. He wanted the liberated countries to form a Latin American confederation, urging Peru and Bolivia to join Venezuela, Ecuador, and Colombia in the "Gran Colombia." But local identities prevailed, giving way to unstable national republics. Bolívar died surrounded by opponents; San Martín died in exile. The real heirs to independence were local military chieftains, who often forged alliances

Map 15.3 Latin American Nation Building

Creating strong, unified nation-states proved difficult in Latin America. The map shows where boundaries were drawn in Mexico, the United Provinces of Central America, and the Republic of Colombia. In each case, the governments' territorial and nation-building ambitions failed to some degree.

- During what period did a majority of the colonies in Latin America gain independence?

- Which European countries lost the most in Latin America during this period?

- Why did all these colonies gain their independence during this time?

with landowners. Thus, the legacy of the Spanish American revolutions was contradictory and echoed developments elsewhere around the world: the triumph of wealthy elites under a banner of liberty, yet often at the expense of poorer, nonwhite, and mixed populations.

Change and Trade in Africa

Africa also was swept up in revolutionary tides, as increased domestic and world trade—including the selling of African slaves—shifted the terms of state building across the continent. The main catalyst for Africa's political shake-up was the rapid growth and then the demise of the Atlantic slave trade.

ABOLITION OF THE SLAVE TRADE

Even as it enriched and empowered some Africans and many Europeans, the slave trade became a subject of fierce debate in the late eighteenth century. Some European and American revolutionaries argued that slave labor was inherently less productive than free wage labor and ought to be abolished. At the same time, another group favoring abolition of the slave trade insisted that traffic in slaves was immoral. In London they created committees, often led by Quakers, to lobby Parliament for an end to the slave trade. Quakers in Philadelphia did likewise. Pamphlets, reports, and personal narratives denounced the traffic in people.

In response to abolitionist efforts, North Atlantic powers moved to prohibit the slave trade. Denmark acted first in its Caribbean colonies in 1803, Great Britain followed in 1807, and the United States joined the campaign in 1808. Over time, the British persuaded the French and other European governments to do likewise. To enforce the ban, Britain posted a naval squadron off the coast of West Africa to prevent any slave trade above the equator and compelled Brazil's emperor to end slave imports. After 1850, Atlantic slave shipping dropped sharply, though slavery did not end for several decades due to the continued profitability of cotton in the southern United States, sugar in the Caribbean, and coffee in Brazil. The last known Atlantic slave ship discharged its cargo in Cuba in 1867.

NEW TRADE WITH AFRICA

Even as the Atlantic slave trade died down, Europeans promoted commerce with Africa. Now they wanted Africans to export raw materials and to purchase European manufactured goods. What Europeans liked to call "legitimate" trade aimed to raise the Africans' standards of living by substituting trade in produce for trade in slaves. West Africans responded by exporting palm kernels and peanuts. The real bonanza was in vegetable oils to lubricate machinery and make candles and in palm oil to produce soap. European merchants argued that by becoming vibrant export societies, Africans would earn the wealth to profitably import European wares.

The new trade gave rise to a generation of successful West African merchants. There were many rags-to-riches stories, like that of King Jaja of Opobo (1821–1891). Kidnapped and sold into slavery as a youngster, he started out paddling canoes carrying palm oil to coastal ports. Ultimately becoming the head of a coastal canoe house, he founded the port of Opobo and could summon a flotilla of war canoes on command. Another freed slave, a Yoruba, William Lewis, made his way back to Africa and in 1828 settled in Sierra Leone (a British colony for freed slaves, notably blacks from the United States who were loyal to Great Britain). Starting with a few utensils and a small plot of land, he became a successful merchant and sent his son Samuel to England for his education. Samuel eventually became an important political leader in Sierra Leone.

However, the rise of free labor in the Atlantic world and the dwindling foreign slave trade had an unanticipated effect. It strengthened slavery within Africa. In some areas, by the mid-nineteenth century slaves accounted for more than half the population. No longer did they comfortably serve in domestic employment; instead, they toiled on palm oil plantations or, in East Africa, on clove plantations. They also served in the military forces, bore palm oil and ivory to markets as porters, or paddled cargo-carrying canoes along rivers leading to the coast. In 1850, northern Nigeria's ruling class had more slaves than independent Brazil and almost as many as the United States. As Africa ceased to be the world's supplier of slaves, it became in time the world's largest slaveholding region.

Economic Reordering

Core Objectives

IDENTIFY and **EXPLAIN** the key developments that constituted the industrial revolution.

Behind the political and social upheavals, profound changes were occurring in the world economy. Until the middle of the eighteenth century, global trade touched only the edges of most societies, which produced for their own subsistence. Surpluses of special goods, from porcelains to silks, entered trade arteries but did not change the cultures that produced them. A century later, by the middle of the nineteenth century, global trade networks had expanded their reach. The desire for cash, for silver or gold, drove market relations much farther than they had ever reached before. People increasingly worked to produce goods they could sell, which transformed social relations in agricultural hinterlands as well as bustling urban centers.

New Farming Technologies
Although major technological changes in agriculture emerged only late in this period, the spread of more intensive cultivation led to increased yields, especially with the introduction of synthetic fertilizers.

AN INDUSTRIOUS REVOLUTION

Many of these developments took place first in northwestern Europe and British North America. Here, as elsewhere in the world, households had always produced mainly for themselves and made available for marketplaces only meager surpluses of goods and services. But dramatic changes occurred when family members, including wives and children, decided to work harder and longer in order to produce more for the market and purchase more in the market. In these locations, households devoted less time to leisure activities and more time to working, using the additional income from hard work to purchase products produced elsewhere. Scholars recently have come to call this change an **industrious revolution**. Beginning in the second half of the seventeenth century, it gained speed in the eighteenth century and laid the foundations for the industrial revolution of the late eighteenth and early nineteenth centuries.

The willingness on the part of families to work more and an eagerness to eat more diverse foods, to wear better clothes, and to consume products that had once been available as luxuries only to the wealthy classes led in turn to a large expansion in trade. Sugar and silver were the pioneering products. But by the eighteenth century, other staples joined the long-distance trading business, including tea: its leaves came from China, the sugar to cut its bitterness from the Caribbean, the slaves to harvest the sweetener from Africa, and the ceramics to serve a proper cup from the English Midlands. Even ordinary

industrious revolution
Dramatic economic change in which households that had traditionally produced for themselves decided to work harder and longer hours in order to produce more for the market, which enabled them to increase their income and standard of living. Areas that underwent the industrious revolution shifted from peasant farming to specialized production for the market.

people could purchase imported goods with their earnings. Thus, the poor began to enjoy coffee, tea, and sugar. European artisans and farmers purchased tools, furnishings, and home decorations. Slaves and colonial laborers also used their meager earnings to buy imported cotton cloth made in Europe from the raw cotton they themselves had picked several seasons earlier.

The expansion of global trade had important social and political consequences. As new goods flowed from ever more distant corners of the globe, immense fortunes grew. To support their enterprise, traders needed new services in insurance, bookkeeping, and the recording of legal documents. Trade supported the growth of the liberal professions—accountants and lawyers. The new cities of the commercial revolution, hubs like Bristol, Bombay, and Buenos Aires, provided the homes and flourishing neighborhoods for the growing class of men and women known as the **bourgeoisie**: urban businessmen, financiers, and other property owners without aristocratic origins.

THE INDUSTRIAL REVOLUTION

Trade and finance repositioned western Europe's relationship with the rest of the world. So did the emergence of manufacturing. Like agricultural production, output of industrial commodities surged. The heart of this process was a gradual accumulation and diffusion of technical knowledge. Lots of little inventions, their applications, and their spread across the Atlantic world gradually built up a stock of technical knowledge and practice. Historians have traditionally called these changes the **industrial revolution**.

Nowhere was this industrial revolution more evident than in Britain. Britain had access to waterways, constructed a network of canals, and had large supplies of coal and iron—key materials used in manufactured products. It also had a political and social environment that allowed merchants and industrialists to invest heavily while also expanding their internal and international markets. Among their investments was the application of steam power to textile production, which enabled Britain's manufacturers to produce cheaper goods in larger quantities. Finally, Britain had access to New World lands as sources of financial investment, raw materials, and markets for manufactured goods. These factors' convergence promoted self-sustaining economic growth.

Consider the relationship between inventor and investor in the advent of the steam engine. Such engines burned coal to boil water, and the resulting steam drove mechanized devices. There were several tinkerers working on such an engine. But the most famous was James Watt (1736–1819) of Scotland, who managed to separate steam condensers from piston cylinders so that pistons could stay hot and run constantly; he joined forces with the industrialist Matthew Boulton, who marketed the steam engine and set up a laboratory where Watt could refine his device. Invented in 1769, the steam engine catalyzed a revolution in transportation. Steam-powered engines also improved sugar refining, pottery making, and other industrial processes, generating more products at lower cost than when workers had made them by hand.

Textile production was critical. Most raw cotton for the British cloth industry had come from colonial India until 1793, when the American inventor Eli Whitney (1765–1825) patented a "cotton gin" that separated cotton seeds from fiber. After that, cotton farming spread so quickly in the southern United States that by the 1850s it was producing more than 80 percent of the world's cotton supply. In turn, every black slave in the Americas and many Indians in British India were consumers of cheap, British-produced cotton shirts. The price of cotton cloth declined by nearly 50 percent between 1780 and 1850, as textiles became the world's most dynamic industry. England became the world's largest cloth producer, driving most of the other centers of textile production, notably those in the Indian subcontinent, out of business.

Wherever the industrial revolution took hold, it allowed societies to outdistance rivals in manufacturing and elevated them to a new place in the emerging global economic order. (See Map 15.4.) But why did this revolution cluster mainly in the Atlantic world? This is an important question because the unequal distribution of global wealth, the gap between the haves and have-nots, really took off in this era of revolutions. In much of Asia and Africa, technical change altered modes of production and business practices, but it was not followed by a continuous cascade of changes. The great mystery was China, the home of astronomical water clocks and gunpowder. Why did China not become the epicenter of the industrial revolution?

There are two reasons. First, China did not foster experimental science of the kind that allowed Watt to stumble onto the possibility of steam,

A Cotton Textile Mill in the 1830s The region of Lancashire became one of the major industrial hubs for textile production in the world. By the 1830s, mills had made the shift from artisanal work to highly mechanical mass production. Among the great breakthroughs was the shift from wool to cotton textiles, which were printed with designs such as paisley or calico (as in this image) and marketed to middle-class consumers.

Legend:
- Railroads in 1850
- ▲ Center of industry
- ● Iron ore deposit
- ○ Coal and lignite deposits

Percent of Population Living in Cities of 100,000 or More
- 5 percent or less
- 6 to 10 percent
- 20 percent or more

Map 15.4 Industrial Europe around 1850

By 1850 much of western Europe was industrial and urban, with major cities linked to one another through a network of railroads.

- According to this map, what natural resources contributed to the growth of the industrial revolution? What effects did it have on urban population densities?

- Compare the course of major rivers with those of the railways.

- Why did the United Kingdom have such a large concentration of cities with more than 100,000 inhabitants? How was the United Kingdom able to support such large population centers?

or Whitney the cotton gin. Experimentation, testing, and the links between thinkers and investors were a distinctly Atlantic phenomenon. The Qing, like the Mughal and Ottoman dynasties, swept the great minds into the bureaucracy and reinforced the old agrarian system based on peasant exploitation and tribute. Second, Chinese, Mughal, and Ottoman rulers did not support the overseas expansion and trade that helped create the commercial revolution in the Atlantic world. The agrarian dynasties of China and India neither showered favors on local merchants nor effectively shut out interlopers. This made them vulnerable to cheap manufactured imports from European traders backed by their governments extolling the virtues of free trade.

The effects were profound. Historically, Europe had a trade imbalance with partners to the east—furs from Russia and spices and silks from Asia. It made up for this with silver from the Americas. But the new economic order meant that by the nineteenth century, western Europe not only had manufactures like cotton textiles to export to Asia but also had capital. One of Europe's biggest debtors was none other than the sultan of the Ottoman Empire, whose tax system could not keep up with the spending necessary to keep the realm together. More and more, Asian, African, and American governments found themselves borrowing from Europe's financiers just as their people were buying industrial products from Europe and selling their primary products to European consumers and producers.

WORKING AND LIVING

The industrial revolution brought more demanding work routines—not only in the manufacturing economies of western Europe and North America but also on the farms and plantations of Asia and Africa.

Urban Life and Work Routines Increasingly, Europe's workers made their livings in cities. London, Europe's largest city in 1700, saw its population nearly double over the next century to almost 1 million. By the 1820s, population growth was even greater in the industrial hubs of Leeds, Glasgow, Birmingham, Liverpool, and Manchester.

For most urban dwellers, cities were not healthy places. Water that powered the mills, along with chemicals used in dyeing, went directly back into waterways that provided drinking water. Overcrowded tenements shared just a few outhouses. Most European cities as late as 1850 had no running water, no garbage pickup, and no underground sewer system. The result was widespread disease. (In fact, no European city at this time had as clean a water supply as the largest towns of the ancient Roman Empire once had.)

Changes in work affected the understanding of time. Whereas most farmers' workloads had followed seasonal rhythms, after 1800 industrial settings imposed a rigid concept of work discipline. To keep the machinery operating, factory and mill owners installed huge clocks and used bells or horns to signify the workday's beginning and end. Employers also measured output per hour and compared workers' performance.

Industrialization imposed numbing work routines and paltry wages. Worse, however, was having no work at all. As families abandoned their farmland and depended on wages, being idle meant having no income. Periodic downturns in the economy put wage workers at risk, and many responded by organizing protests.

Social Protest and Emigration While entrepreneurs accumulated private wealth, the effects of the industrial revolution on working-class families raised widespread concern, sometimes leading to protests or emigration. In the 1810s in England, groups of jobless craftsmen, called Luddites, smashed the machines that had left them unemployed. Social advocates sought protective legislation for workers, including curbing child labor, limiting the workday, and, in some countries, legalizing prostitution for the sake of monitoring the prostitutes' health.

Some people, however, could not wait for legislative reform. The period saw unprecedented emigration, as unemployed workers or peasants abandoned their homes to seek their fortunes in America, Canada, and Australia. During the Irish Potato Famine of 1845–1849, at least 1 million Irish citizens left their country (and a further million or so died) when fungi attacked their subsistence crop. Desperate to escape starvation, they booked cheap passage to North America on ships so notorious for disease and malnutrition that they earned the name "coffin ships."

The industrial revolution produced wealth on an unprecedented scale, but that wealth was distributed unevenly. Enormous inequalities resulted, both within societies and between them. Free trade resulted, in the long run, not in the proliferation of ever-more-productive small workshops but in massive industrial concentration, a concentration that would prove dynamic, creative, and unstable.

Persistence and Change in Afro-Eurasia

Western Europe's military might, its technological achievements, and its economic strength represented a threat to the remaining Afro-Eurasian empires. Western European merchants and industrialists sought closer economic and (in some cases) political ties. They did so in the name of gaining "free" access to Asian markets and products. Rulers in Russia, the Ottoman Empire, India, and China all sought to borrow from the ideas and institutions emerging from western Europe, but they did so on their own terms, intent on defending the core of their social and political traditions.

REVAMPING THE RUSSIAN MONARCHY

Russian rulers responded to the pressures by strengthening their traditional authority through modest reforms and the suppression of domestic opposition. Tsar Alexander I (r. 1801–1825) was fortunate that Napoleon committed several blunders and lost his formidable army in the Russian snows. Yet the French Revolution and its massive armies struck at the heart of Russian political institutions, which rested upon a huge peasant population laboring as serfs. The tsars could no longer justify their absolutism by claiming that enlightened despotism was the most advanced form of government, since a new model, rooted in popular sovereignty and the concept of the nation, had arisen.

In December 1825, when Alexander died unexpectedly and childless, there was a question over succession. Some Russian officers launched a patriotic revolt. The Decembrists, as they were called, came primarily from elite families and were familiar with western European life and institutions. Some called for a constitutional monarchy to replace Russia's despotism; others favored a tsar-less republic and the abolition of serfdom. Their conspiracy failed to win over conservatives or the peasantry, who still believed in the tsar's divine right to rule. Nicholas (r. 1825–1855) became tsar and brutally suppressed the insurrectionists.

Still, Alexander's successors faced a world in which powerful European states had constitutions and national armies of citizens, not subjects. In trying to maintain absolutist rule, Russian tsars portrayed the monarch's family as the ideal historical embodiment of the nation with direct ties to the people. Nicholas himself prevented rebellion by expanding the secret police, enforcing censorship, conducting impressive military exercises, and maintaining serfdom. And in the 1830s he introduced a conservative ideology that stressed religious faith, hierarchy, and obedience. For the time being, the influence of the French Revolution was quashed in Russia.

REFORMING EGYPT AND THE OTTOMAN EMPIRE

Unlike Russia, where Napoleon's army had reached Moscow, the Ottoman capital in Istanbul never faced a threat by French troops. Still, Napoleon's invasion of Egypt shook the Ottoman Empire. Even before this trauma, Ottoman authorities faced the challenge posed by increased trade with Europe—and the greater presence of European merchants and missionaries. In addition, many non-Muslim religious communities in the sultan's empire wanted the European powers to advance their interests. In the wake of Napoleon, who had promised to remake Egyptian society, reformist energies swept from Egypt to the center of the Ottoman domain.

Reforms in Egypt In Egypt, far-reaching changes came with the rule of **Muhammad Ali**. After the French withdrawal in 1801, Muhammad Ali (r. 1805–1848) won a chaotic struggle for supreme power in Egypt and

Muhammad Ali
(r. 1805–1848) Ruler of Egypt who initiated a set of modernizing reforms that sought to make it competitive with the great powers.

Core Objectives

EXPLAIN patterns of global trade and economic growth, and CONNECT them to political changes during the period 1750–1850.

aligned himself with influential Egyptian families. Yet he looked to revolutionary France for a model of modern state building. As with Napoleon (and with Simón Bolívar in Latin America), the key to his hold on power was the army.

Muhammad Ali also made reforms in education and agriculture. He established a school of engineering and opened the first modern medical school in Cairo under the supervision of a French military doctor. And his efforts in the countryside made Egypt one of the world's leading cotton exporters. A summer crop, cotton required steady watering when the Nile's irrigation waters were in short supply. So Muhammad Ali's Public Works Department, advised by European engineers, deepened the irrigation canals and constructed a series of dams across the Nile. These efforts transformed Egypt, making it the most powerful state in the eastern Mediterranean and alarming the Ottoman state (which still controlled Egypt) and the great powers in Europe. At the same time, European merchants pressed for free access to Egyptian markets, just as they did in Latin America and Africa.

Ottoman Reforms Under political and economic pressures like those facing Muhammad Ali in Egypt, Ottoman rulers also made reforms. Indeed, military defeats and humiliating treaties with Europe were painful reminders of the sultans' vulnerability. In 1805, Sultan Selim III tried to create a new infantry, trained by western European officers. But before he could bring this force up to fighting strength, the janissaries stormed the palace, killed its officers, and deposed Selim in 1807. Over the next few decades, janissary military men and clerical scholars (*ulama*) cobbled together an alliance that thwarted reformers.

Why did reform falter in the Ottoman state before it could be implemented? Reform was possible only if the forces opposed to reform—especially in the military—were weak and the reformers strong. In the Ottoman Empire, the janissary class had grown powerful, providing the main resistance to change. Ottoman authority depended on clerical support, and the Muslim clergy also resisted change. Blocked at the top, Ottoman rulers hesitated to appeal for popular support. Such an appeal, in the new age of popular sovereignty and national feeling, would be dangerous for an unelected dynast in a multiethnic and multireligious realm.

Mahmud II (r. 1808–1839) broke the political deadlock, shrewdly manipulating his conservative opponents. Like Muhammad Ali in Egypt, Mahmud brought in European officers to advise his forces. Here, too, military reform spilled over into nonmilitary areas. The Ottoman modernizers created a medical college, then a school of military sciences. To understand Europe better and to create a first-rate diplomatic corps, the Ottomans schooled their officials in European languages and had European classics translated into Turkish. As Mahmud's successors extended reforms into civilian life, this era—known as the Tanzimat, or Reorganization period (1826–1839)—saw legislation that guaranteed equality for all Ottoman subjects, regardless of religion.

The reforms, however, stopped well short of revolutionary change. Reform relied too much on the personal whim of rulers, and the bureaucratic and religious infrastructure remained committed to old ways. Any effort to reform the rural sector met resistance by the landed interests. Finally, the merchant classes profited from business with a debt-ridden sultan. By preventing the empire's fiscal collapse through financial support to the state, bankers lessened the pressure for reform and removed the spark that had fired revolutions in Europe.

COLONIAL REORDERING IN INDIA

Europe's most important colonial possession in Asia between 1750 and 1850 was British India. Unlike in North America, the changes that the British fostered in Asia did not lead to political independence. Instead, India was increasingly dominated by the **East India Company**, which the crown had chartered in 1600. The company's control over India's imports and exports in the eighteenth and nineteenth centuries, however, contradicted British claims about their allegiance to a world economic system based on "free trade."

The East India Company's Monopoly In enforcing the East India Company's monopoly on trade, the British soon took control of much of the region. Initially, the British tried to control India's commerce by establishing trading posts along the coast without taking complete political control. After conquering the state of Bengal in 1757, the company began to fill its coffers and its officials began to amass personal fortunes. In spite of violent opposition, the British secured the right for the East India Company to collect tax revenues in Bengal, Bihar, and Orissa and to trade free of duties throughout Mughal territory. In return, the Mughal emperor would receive a hefty annual pension. The company went on to annex other territories, bringing much of South Asia under its rule by the early nineteenth century. (See Map 15.5.)

To rule with minimal interference required knowing the conquered society. This led to Orientalist scholarship: British scholar-officials wrote the first modern histories of South Asia, translated Sanskrit and Persian texts, identified philosophical writings, and compiled Hindu and Muslim law books. Through their efforts, the company-state presented itself as a force for revitalizing authentic Hinduism and recovering India's literary and cultural treasures. However, although the Orientalist scholars admired Sanskrit language and literature, they still supported British colonial rule and did not necessarily agree with local beliefs.

Effects in India Company rule and booming trade altered India's urban geography. By the early nineteenth century, colonial cities like Calcutta, Madras, and Bombay became the new centers at the expense of older Mughal

Map 15.5 The British in India, 1767–1857

Starting from locations in eastern and northeastern India, the British East India Company extended its authority over much of South Asia prior to the outbreak of the Indian Rebellion of 1857.

- What type of locations did the British first acquire in India?
- According to your reading, how did the company expand into the interior of India and administer these possessions?
- Why did it choose a strategy of direct rule over some areas and indirect rule over other areas in India?

cities like Agra, Delhi, Murshidabad, and Hyderabad. As the colonial cities attracted British merchants and Indian clerks, artisans, and laborers, their populations surged. Calcutta's reached 350,000 in 1820; Bombay's jumped to 200,000 by 1825. In these cities, Europeans lived close to the company's fort and trading stations, while migrants from the countryside clustered in crowded quarters called "black towns."

India now became an importer of British textiles and an exporter of raw cotton—a reversal of its traditional pattern of trade. In the past, India had been an important textile manufacturer, exporting fine cotton goods throughout the Indian Ocean and to Europe. But its elites could not resist the appeal of cheap British textiles. As a result, India's industrial sector declined. In addition, the import of British manufactures caused unfavorable trade balances that changed India from a net importer of gold and silver to an exporter of these precious metals.

Led by evangelical Christians and liberal reformers, the British did more than alter the Indian economy; they also advocated far-reaching changes in

Indian Resistance to Company Rule Tipu Sultan, the Mysore ruler, put up a determined resistance against the British. This painting by Robert Home shows Cornwallis, the East India Company's governor, receiving Tipu's two sons as hostages after defeating him in the 1792 war. The boys remained in British custody for two years. Tipu returned to fighting the British and was killed in the war of 1799.

Indian culture. For example, they sought to stop the practice of *sati*, by which women burned to death on the funeral pyres of their dead husbands. Now the mood swung away from the Orientalists' respect for India's classical languages, philosophies, cultures, and texts. In 1835, when the British poet, historian, and Liberal politician Lord Macaulay was making recommendations on educational policies, he urged that English replace Persian as the language of administration and that European education replace Oriental learning. The result, reformers hoped, would be a class that was Indian in blood and color but English in tastes and culture.

This was a new colonial order, but it was not stable. Most wealthy landowners resented the loss of their land and authority. Peasants, thrown to the mercy of the market, moneylenders, and landlords and subject to high taxation, were in turmoil. The non-Hindu forest dwellers and roaming cultivators, faced with the hated combination of a colonial state and moneylenders, revolted. Dispossessed artisans stirred up towns and cities. And merchants and industrialists chafed under the British-dominated economy. As freedom expanded in Europe, exploitation expanded in India.

PERSISTENCE OF THE QING EMPIRE

The Chinese empire was largely unaffected by the upheavals in Europe and America until the Opium Wars (1839–1842, 1856–1860) forced the Chinese to acknowledge their military weaknesses. The Qing dynasty, which had taken power in 1644, was still enjoying prosperity and territorial expansion as the nineteenth century dawned. Their sense of imperial splendor continued to rest on the political structure and social order inherited from the Ming (see Chapter 11). However, they could not resist European demands for access to their resources and markets.

The Qing had a talent for extending the empire's boundaries and settling frontier lands. Before 1750, they conquered Taiwan (the stronghold of remaining Ming forces), pushed westward into central Asia, and annexed Tibet. To secure these territorial gains, the Qing encouraged settlement of frontier lands like Xinjiang. New crops from the Americas aided this process—especially corn and sweet potatoes, which grow well in less fertile soils.

Like their European counterparts, Chinese peasants were on the move. But migration occurred in Qing China for different reasons. The state-sponsored westward movement into Xinjiang, for example, aimed to secure a recently pacified frontier region through military colonization, after which civilians would follow. So peasants received promises of land, tools, seed, and the loan of silver and a horse—all with the dual objectives of producing enough food to supply the troops and relieving pressure on the poor and arid northwestern part of the country. These efforts brought so much land under cultivation by 1840 that the region's ecological and social landscape completely changed.

Despite their success in expanding the empire, the Qing faced nagging problems. As a ruling minority, they looked warily at innovation, and only late in the eighteenth century did they deal with their rapidly expanding population. On the one hand, the tripling of China's population since 1300 demonstrated the realm's prosperity; on the other, a population of over 300 million severely strained resources—especially soil for growing crops and wood for fuel. In the late eighteenth and early nineteenth centuries, uprisings inspired by mystical beliefs in folk Buddhism, and at times by the idea of restoring the Ming, engulfed northern China.

By the mid-nineteenth century, extraordinary changes had made western European powers stronger than ever before, and the Qing could no longer dismiss their demands. The first clear evidence of an altered global balance of power was not the rise of Napoleon but a British-Chinese war over a narcotic. Indeed, the **Opium Wars** exposed China's vulnerability in a new era of European ascendancy.

Opium Wars
(1839–1842, 1856–1860) Wars fought between the British and Qing China over British trade in opium; the result was that China granted to the British the right to trade in five different ports and ceded Hong Kong to the British.

The Opium Wars and the "Opening" of China Europeans had been selling staples and intoxicants in China for a long time, and by the late eighteenth century opium, which had previously been used as a medicine or an aphrodisiac, was being smoked in long-stemmed pipes at every level of Chinese society. Sensing opium's economic potential, the East India Company established a monopoly over the export of opium from India in 1773 to help pay for a rapid growth in the company's purchase of tea from China. Because the Chinese showed little taste for British goods, the British had been financing their tea imports with exports of silver to China. But by the late eighteenth century, the company's tea purchases had become too large to finance with silver. Fortunately for the company, the Chinese were eager for Indian cotton and opium, and then mostly just opium.

Opium's impact on China's balance of trade was devastating. In a reversal from earlier trends, silver began to flow out of instead of into China. Once silver shortages occurred, the peasants' tax burden grew heavier. Consequently, long-simmering unrest in the countryside gained momentum. At the Qing court, some officials wanted to legalize the opium trade so as to eliminate corruption and boost revenues. (After all, as long as opium was an illegal substance, the government could not tax its traffic.) In 1838, the emperor sent a special commissioner to Canton, the main center of the trade, to eradicate the influx of opium.

When British merchants in Canton resisted, war broke out. In June 1840, British warships bombarded coastal regions near Canton and sailed upriver for a short way. On land, Qing soldiers used spears, clubs, and a few imported matchlock muskets against the modern artillery of British troops, many of whom were Indians supplied with percussion cap rifles. Along the Yangzi River, outgunned Qing forces fought fiercely, as soldiers killed their own wives and children before committing suicide themselves. But they were no match for British military technology.

The Qing ruling elite capitulated, and through the 1842 Treaty of Nanjing, the British acquired the island of Hong Kong and the right to trade directly with the Chinese in five treaty ports and to reside there.

Opium (*Left*) A common sight in late Qing China was establishments catering specifically to opium smoking. Taken from a volume condemning the practice, this picture shows opium smokers idling their day away. (*Right*) Having established a monopoly in the 1770s over opium cultivation in India, the British greatly expanded their manufacture and export of opium to China to balance their rapidly growing import of Chinese tea and silk. This picture from the 1880s shows an opium warehouse in India where the commodity was stored before being transported to China.

Map 15.6 The Qing Empire and the Opium Wars

The Opium Wars demonstrated the superiority of British military technology. Their victory granted the British control of Hong Kong and established a series of treaty ports, which gave Europeans access to Chinese trade and were subject to the laws of designated European countries.

- How many treaty ports were there after the Opium Wars? What was their significance?
- How were the treaty ports distributed along China's coastline?
- According to the text, how did the Opium Wars change relations between China and the western powers?

Legend:
- Qing Empire
- Treaty ports
- Opium War battles
- British naval forces
- Great Wall
- Grand Canal

(See Map 15.6.) They also forced the Chinese to repay the costs that the British had incurred in the war.

Subsequent treaties guaranteed that the British and other foreign nationals would be tried in their own courts for crimes, rather than in Chinese courts, and would be exempt from Chinese law. Moreover, the British insisted that any privileges granted through treaties with other parties would also apply to them. Other western nations followed the British example in demanding the same right, and the arrangement thus guaranteed all Europeans and North Americans a privileged position in China.

Still, China did not become a formal colony. To the contrary, in the mid-nineteenth century Europeans and North Americans were trading only on its outskirts. Most Chinese did not encounter Europeans. Daily life for most people went on as it had before the Opium Wars. Only the political leaders and urban dwellers were beginning to feel the foreign presence and wondering what steps China might take to acquire European technologies, goods, and learning.

Conclusion

During the period 1750–1850, changes in politics, commerce, industry, and technology reverberated throughout the Atlantic world and, to varying degrees, elsewhere around the globe. By 1850, the world was more integrated economically, with Europe increasingly at the center.

In the Americas, colonial ties broke apart. In France, the people toppled the monarchy. Dissidents threatened the same in Russia. Such upheavals introduced a new public vocabulary—the language of the nation—and made the idea of revolution empowering. In the Americas and parts of Europe, nation-states took shape around redefined hierarchies of class, gender, and color. Britain and France emerged from the political crises of the late eighteenth century determined to expand their borders. Their drive forced older empires such as Russia and the Ottoman state to make reforms.

As commerce and industrialization transformed economic and political power, European governments compelled others (including Egypt, India, and China) to expand their trade with European merchants. Ultimately, such countries had to participate in a European-centered economy as exporters of raw materials and importers of European manufactures. By the 1850s, many of the world's peoples became more industrious, producing less for themselves and more for distant markets. Through changes in manufacturing, some areas of the world also made more goods than ever before. With its emphasis on free trade, Europe began to force open new markets—even to the point of colonizing them. Gold and silver now flowed out of China and India to pay for European products like opium and textiles.

However, global reordering did not mean that Europe's rulers had uncontested control over other people or that the institutions and cultures of Asia and Africa ceased to be dynamic. Some countries became dependent on Europe commercially; others became colonies. China escaped colonial rule but was forced into unfavorable trade relations with the Europeans. In sum, dramatic changes combined to unsettle systems of rulership and to alter the economic and military balance between western Europe and the rest of the world.

Focus On
The Global Effects of the "New Ideas"

The Atlantic World

- North American colonists revolt against British rule and establish a nonmonarchical, republican form of government.

- In the wake of the American Revolution, the French citizenry proclaims a new era of liberty, equality, and fraternity and executes opponents of the revolution, notably the king and queen of France.

- Napoleon's French Empire extends many principles of the French Revolution throughout Europe.

- In the midst of the French Revolution, Haitian slaves throw off French rule, abolish slavery, and create an independent state.

- Napoleon's invasion of Iberia frees Portuguese and Spanish America from colonial rule.

- The British lead a successful campaign to abolish the Atlantic slave trade and promote new sources of trade with Africa.

- An industrial revolution spreads outward from Britain to a few other parts of the Atlantic world.

Africa, India, and Asia

- In Egypt, a military leader, Muhammad Ali, modernizes the country and threatens the political integrity of the Ottoman Empire.

- The British East India Company increasingly dominates the Indian subcontinent.

- The Qing Empire persists despite major European encroachments on its sovereignty.

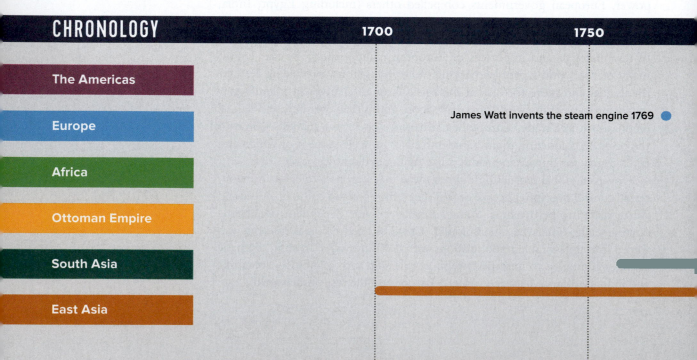

CHRONOLOGY	1700	1750
The Americas		
Europe		James Watt invents the steam engine 1769 ●
Africa		
Ottoman Empire		
South Asia		
East Asia		

THINKING ABOUT GLOBAL CONNECTIONS

- **Thinking about Exchange Networks and Sociopolitical Change** How did established dynasties respond to pressures created by increased exchanges of goods, ideas, and peoples? To what degree did established elites respond by forging a partnership with "the people"? Who defined "the people," and on what terms?

- **Thinking about Changing Power Relationships and Sociopolitical Change** What new kinds of political organizations emerged in this period? Where did new political systems take root, and where did established elites resist most successfully?

- **Thinking about Environmental Impacts and Sociopolitical Change** Although new technologies only gradually transformed agriculture—by far the most common economic activity in the world—the spread of more intensive cultivation demanded considerable capital investment. How did the relationship between town and countryside change as a result? How did living conditions change in cities as their populations swelled?

Key Terms

Muhammad Ali p. 719

Napoleon Bonaparte p. 703

bourgeoisie p. 714

East India Company p. 721

free trade (laissez-faire) p. 695

industrial revolution p. 714

industrious revolution p. 713

Opium Wars p. 724

popular sovereignty p. 695

social contract p. 699

 Go to **INQUIZITIVE** to see what you've learned—and learn what you've missed—with personalized feedback along the way.

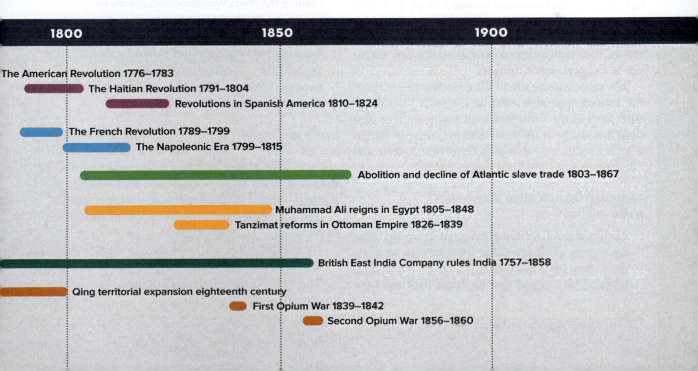

1800 · 1850 · 1900

The American Revolution 1776–1783
The Haitian Revolution 1791–1804
Revolutions in Spanish America 1810–1824
The French Revolution 1789–1799
The Napoleonic Era 1799–1815
Abolition and decline of Atlantic slave trade 1803–1867
Muhammad Ali reigns in Egypt 1805–1848
Tanzimat reforms in Ottoman Empire 1826–1839
British East India Company rules India 1757–1858
Qing territorial expansion eighteenth century
First Opium War 1839–1842
Second Opium War 1856–1860

Global Themes and Sources

Revolution for Whom?

Although Enlightenment *philosophes* argued that the laws of reason applied to everyone and the American Declaration of Independence declared that all men are created equal, their ideas immediately provoked a wide range of opposition during the political reordering of the Age of Revolution. In Europe and the United States, women and the enslaved protested their exclusion, while elite men in territories occupied by western colonizers pointed to the hypocrisy of the occupiers' egalitarian rhetoric. In different ways, they all probed the central, often hidden, assumptions of European elites about hierarchy and difference.

Two of the documents were written in wealthy corners of western Europe and the United States; one was written in Egypt, then occupied by the French army; and one was written in newly independent Haiti, recently liberated from French control. One of the texts was written by a woman; the remaining three were written by men. All four were written by elites upset at their exclusion. Collectively, they highlight tensions and divisions within Europe as well as between Europeans and others. Making sense of them requires grappling with the degree to which people around the world accepted or rejected the basic premises of Enlightenment thinkers.

The sources invite you to think comparatively about the various ways that men and women viewed the same parts of the Enlightenment tradition. They also challenge you to think about whether critiques written outside Europe were similar to those from within, and which ideas resonated most deeply and why.

Analyzing Comparative Viewpoints on Revolutions

- Analyze the role of Enlightenment ideas. Do these documents challenge those ideas or seek to apply them more fully? Do they reject the Enlightenment tradition or contend that its values have not been fully realized? Which document is the most critical? Which is the least critical?

- Compare the documents written in Europe and the United States to those written in Egypt and Haiti.

- Evaluate the degree to which these documents make universal arguments and the degree to which their claims are rooted in local traditions, communities, and beliefs.

PRIMARY SOURCE 15.1

On the Rights of Women (1792), Mary Wollstonecraft

One of the founding figures of modern feminism, Mary Wollstonecraft was born in London in 1759. Her *Vindication of the Rights of Woman* (1792), written in the midst of the French Revolution, took aim at notions of women as helpless, emotional adornments, dependent by their nature on men.

- Identify the limits Wollstonecraft places on women's participation in politics. What role does reason play in setting those limits?

- Explain what Wollstonecraft means by virtue.

- Explain the comparison Wollstonecraft draws between male superiority and the divine right of kings.

Surely there can be but one rule of right, if morality has an eternal foundation, and whoever sacrifices virtue, strictly so called, to present convenience, or whose duty it is to act in such a manner, lives only for the passing day, and cannot be an accountable creature.

The poet then should have dropped his sneer when he says,

If weak women go astray,
The stars are more in fault than they.

For that they are bound by the adamantine chain of destiny is most certain, if it be proved that they are never to exercise their own reason, never to be independent, never to rise above opinion, or to feel the dignity of a rational will that only bows to God, and often forgets that the universe contains any being but itself and the model of perfection to which its ardent gaze is turned, to adore attributes that, softened into virtues, may be imitated in kind, though the degree overwhelms the enraptured mind.

If, I say, for I would not impress by declamation when Reason offers her sober light, if they be really capable of acting like rational creatures, let them not be treated like slaves; or, like the brutes who are dependent on the reason of man, when they associate with him; but cultivate their minds, give them the salutary, sublime curb of principle, and let them attain conscious dignity by feeling themselves only dependent on God. Teach them, in common with man, to submit to necessity, instead of giving, to render them more pleasing, a sex to morals.

Further, should experience prove that they cannot attain the same degree of strength of mind, perseverance, and fortitude, let their virtues be the same in kind, though they may vainly struggle for the same degree; and the superiority of man will be equally clear, if not clearer; and truth, as it is a simple principle, which admits of no modification, would be common to both. Nay, the order of society as it is at present regulated, would not be inverted, for woman would then only have the rank that reason assigned her, and arts could not be practiced to bring the balance even, much less to turn it.

These may be termed Utopian dreams. Thanks to that Being who impressed them on my soul, and gave me sufficient strength of mind to dare to exert my own reason, till, becoming dependent only on him for the support of my virtue, I view, with indignation, the mistaken notions that enslave my sex.

I love man as my fellow; but his sceptre, real or usurped, extends not to me, unless the reason of an individual demands my homage; and even then the submission is to reason, and not to man. In fact, the conduct of an accountable being must be regulated by the operations of its own reason; or on what foundation rests the throne of God?

It appears to me necessary to dwell on these obvious truths, because females have been insulated, as it were; and while they have been stripped of the virtues that should clothe humanity, they have been decked with artificial graces that enable them to exercise a short-lived tyranny. Love, in their bosoms, taking the place of every nobler passion, their sole ambition is to be fair, to raise emotion instead of inspiring respect; and this ignoble desire, like the servility in absolute monarchies, destroys all strength of character. Liberty is the mother of virtue, and if women be, by their very constitution, slaves, and not allowed to breathe the sharp invigorating air of freedom, they must ever languish like exotics, and be reckoned beautiful flaws in nature. Let it also be remembered, that they are the only flaw.

As to the argument respecting the subjection in which the sex has ever been held, it retorts on man. The many have always been enthralled by the few; and monsters, who scarcely have shown any discernment of human excellence, have tyrannized over thousands of their fellow-creatures. Why have men of superior endowments submitted to such degradation? For, is it not universally acknowledged that kings, viewed collectively, have ever been inferior, in abilities and virtue, to the same number of men taken from the common mass of mankind—yet have they not, and are they not still treated with a degree of reverence that is an insult to reason? China is not the only country where a living man has been made a God. *Men* have submitted to superior strength to enjoy with impunity the pleasure of the moment; *women* have only done the same, and therefore till it is proved that the courtier, who servilely resigns the birthright of a man, is not a moral agent, it cannot be demonstrated that woman is essentially inferior to man because she has always been subjugated.

Brutal force has hitherto governed the world, and that the science of politics is in its infancy, is evident from philosophers scrupling to give the knowledge most useful to man that determinate distinction.

I shall not pursue this argument any further than to establish an obvious inference, that as sound politics diffuse liberty, mankind, including woman, will become more wise and virtuous.

Source: Mary Wollstonecraft, *A Vindication of the Rights of Woman*, A Norton Critical Edition, edited by Deidre Shauna Lynch (New York: Norton, 2009), pp. 39–41.

An Egyptian Reaction to French Occupation (1798), Abd al-Rahman al-Jabarti

In 1798, revolutionary France authorized a military campaign in "the Orient," present-day Syria and Egypt, to protect French trade interests and disrupt British access to India. Napoleon Bonaparte sought to win support for the French invasion by presenting himself as a liberator and invoking the ideals of the French Revolution. Here the Cairo scholar Abd al-Rahman al-Jabarti responds.

- Describe the significance of equality in this document.
- Identify the criteria al-Jabarti uses to criticize Napoleon and the French.
- Analyze the role of religion in this document.

On Monday news arrived that the French had reached Damanhur and Rosetta [in the Nile Delta]. . . . They printed a large proclamation in Arabic, calling on the people to obey them. . . . In this proclamation were inducements, warnings, all manner of wiliness and stipulations. Some copies were sent from the provinces to Cairo and its text is:

In the name of God, the Merciful, the Compassionate. There is no god but God. He has no son nor has He an associate in His Dominion.

On behalf of the French Republic which is based upon the foundation of liberty and equality, General Bonaparte, Commander-in-Chief of the French armies makes known to all the Egyptian people that for a long time the Sanjaqs [its Mamluk rulers] who lorded it over Egypt have treated the French community basely and contemptuously and have persecuted its merchants with all manner of extortion and violence. Therefore the hour of punishment has now come.

Unfortunately, this group of Mamluks . . . have acted corruptly for ages in the fairest land that is to be found upon the face of the globe. However, the Lord of the Universe, the Almighty, has decreed the end of their power.

O ye Egyptians . . . I have not come to you except for the purpose of restoring your rights from the hands of the oppressors and that I more than the Mamluks serve God. . . .

And tell them also that all people are equal in the eyes of God and the only circumstances which distinguish one from the other are reason, virtue, and knowledge. . . . Formerly, in the lands of Egypt there were great cities, and wide canals and extensive commerce and nothing ruined all this but the avarice and the tyranny of the Mamluks.

[Al-Jabarti then challenged the arguments in the French proclamation and portrayed the French as godless invaders, inspired by false ideals.]

Here is an explanation of the incoherent words and vulgar constructions which he put into this miserable letter.

His statement "In the name of God, the Merciful, the Compassionate. There is no god but God. He has no son, nor has He an associate in His Dominion." In mentioning these three sentences there is an indication that the French agree with the three religions [Islam, Judaism, and Christianity], but at the same time they do not agree with them, nor with any religion. They are consistent with the Muslims in stating the formula "In the name of God," in denying that He has a son or an associate. They disagree with the Muslims in not mentioning the two Articles of Faith, in rejecting the mission of Muhammad, and the legal words and deeds, which are necessarily recognized by religion. They agree with the Christians in most of their words and deeds, but disagree with them by not mentioning the Trinity, and denying the mission and furthermore in rejecting their beliefs, killing the priests, and destroying the churches. Then, their statement "On behalf of the French Republic, etc.," that is, this proclamation is sent from their Republic, that means their body politic, because they have no chief or sultan with whom they all agree, like others, whose function is to speak on their behalf. For when they rebelled against their sultan six years ago and killed him, the people agreed unanimously that there was not to be a single ruler but that their state, territories, laws, and administration of their affairs, should be in the hands of the intelligent and wise men among them. They appointed persons chosen by them and made them heads of the army, and below them generals and commanders of thousands, two hundreds, and tens, administrators and advisers, on condition that they were all to be equal and none superior to any other in view of the equality of creation and nature. They made this the foundation and basis of their system. This is the meaning of their statement "based upon the foundation of liberty and equality." Their term "liberty" means that they are not slaves like the Mamluks; "equality" has the aforesaid meaning. Their officials are distinguished by the cleanliness of their garments. They wear emblems on their uniforms and upon their heads. . . .

They follow this rule: great and small, high and low, male and female are all equal. Sometimes they break this rule according to their whims and inclinations or reasoning. Their women do not veil themselves and have no modesty. . . . Whenever a Frenchman has to perform an act of nature he does so where he happens to be, even in full view of people, and he goes away as he is, without washing his private parts after defecation. . . .

His saying "[all people] are equal in the eyes of God" the Almighty is a lie and stupidity. How can this be when God has made some superior to others as is testified by the dwellers in the Heavens and on Earth? . . .

So those people are opposed to both Christians and Muslims, and do not hold fast to any religion. You see that they are materialists, who deny all God's attributes. . . . May God hurry misfortune and punishment upon them, may He strike their tongues with dumbness, may He scatter their hosts, and disperse them.

Source: Abd al-Rahman al-Jabarti, *Al-Jabarti's Chronicle of the First Seven Months of the French Occupation of Egypt,* translated by Shmuel Moreh (Leiden: E. J. Brill, 1975), pp. 39–40, 42–43, 46–47.

PRIMARY SOURCE 15.3

The Haitian Declaration of Independence (1804)

Drafted by Jean-Jacques Dessalines, a former slave who went on to become the first ruler of an independent Haiti, the Haitian Declaration of Independence was issued on January 1, 1804, in the port city of Gonaïves. The Declaration marked the end of the thirteen-year-long Haitian Revolution—the only successful slave revolution in history—and established Haiti's independence from France. Haiti was the first independent nation of Latin America and only the second in the Americas, after the United States.

- Identify the terms the Declaration uses to describe the French.

- How does the Declaration distinguish Haitians from the French? Do you think race is a factor?

- How does the Declaration explain Haiti's (temporary) defeat by the French army?

Citizens:

It is not enough to have expelled the barbarians who have bloodied our land for two centuries; it is not enough to have restrained those ever-evolving factions that one after another mocked the specter of liberty that France dangled before you. We must, with one last act of national authority, forever assure the empire of liberty in the country of our birth; we must take any hope of re-enslaving us away from the inhuman government that for so long kept us in the most humiliating torpor. In the end we must live independent or die.

Independence or death . . . let these sacred words unite us and be the signal of battle and of our reunion.

Citizens, my countrymen, on this solemn day I have brought together those courageous soldiers who, as liberty lay dying, spilled their blood to save it; these generals who have guided your efforts against tyranny have not yet done enough for your happiness; the French name still haunts our land.

Everything revives the memories of the cruelties of this barbarous people: our laws, our habits, our towns, everything still carries the stamp of the French. Indeed! There are still French in our island, and you believe yourself free and independent of that Republic, which, it is true, has fought all the nations, but which has never defeated those who wanted to be free.

What! Victims of our [own] credulity and indulgence for 14 years; defeated not by French armies, but by the pathetic eloquence of their agents' proclamations; when will we tire of breathing the air that they breathe? What do we have in common with this nation of executioners? The difference between its cruelty and our patient moderation, its color and ours the great seas that separate us, our avenging climate, all tell us plainly that they are not our brothers, that they never will be, and that if they find refuge among us, they will plot again to trouble and divide us.

Native citizens, men, women, girls, and children, let your gaze extend on all parts of this island: look there for your spouses, your husbands, your brothers, your sisters. Indeed! Look there for your children, your suckling infants, what have they become? . . . I shudder to say it . . . the prey of these vultures.

Instead of these dear victims, your alarmed gaze will see only their assassins, these tigers still dripping with their blood, whose terrible presence indicts your lack of feeling and your guilty slowness in avenging them. What are you waiting for before appeasing their spirits? Remember that you had wanted your remains to rest next to those of your fathers, after you defeated tyranny; will you descend into their tombs without having avenged them? No! Their bones would reject yours.

And you, precious men, intrepid generals, who, without concern for your own pain, have revived liberty by shedding all your blood, know that you have done nothing if you do not give the nations a terrible, but just example of the vengeance that must be wrought by a people proud to have recovered its liberty and jealous to maintain it let us frighten all those who would dare try to take it from us again; let us begin with the French. Let them tremble when they approach our coast, if not from the memory of those cruelties they perpetrated here, then from the terrible resolution that we will have made to put to death anyone born French whose profane foot soils the land of liberty.

We have dared to be free, let us be thus by ourselves and for ourselves. Let us imitate the grown child: his own weight breaks the boundary that has become an obstacle to him. What people fought for us? What people wanted to gather the fruits of our labor? And what dishonorable absurdity to conquer in order to be enslaved. Enslaved? . . . Let us leave this description for the French; they have conquered but are no longer free.

Let us walk down another path; let us imitate those people who, extending their concern into the future, and dreading to leave an example of cowardice for posterity, preferred to be exterminated rather than lose their place as one of the world's free peoples.

Let us ensure, however, that a missionary spirit does not destroy our work; let us allow our neighbors to breathe in peace; may they live quietly under the laws that they have made for themselves, and let us not, as revolutionary firebrands, declare ourselves the lawgivers of the Caribbean, nor let our glory consist in troubling the peace of the neighboring islands. Unlike that

which we inhabit, theirs has not been drenched in the innocent blood of its inhabitants; they have no vengeance to claim from the authority that protects them.

Fortunate to have never known the ideals that have destroyed us, they can only have good wishes for our prosperity.

Peace to our neighbors; but let this be our cry: "Anathema to the French name! Eternal hatred of France!"

Natives of Haiti! My happy fate was to be one day the sentinel who would watch over the idol to which you sacrifice; I have watched, sometimes fighting alone, and if I have been so fortunate as to return to your hands the sacred trust you confided to me, know that it is now your task to preserve it. In fighting for your liberty, I was working for my own happiness. Before consolidating it with laws that will guarantee your free individuality, your leaders, who I have assembled here, and I, owe you the final proof of our devotion. . . .

Swear, finally, to pursue forever the traitors and enemies of your independence.

Source: Laurent Dubois and John D. Garrigus, *Slave Revolution in the Caribbean, 1789–1804: A Brief History with Documents* (Boston: Bedford/St. Martins, 2006), pp. 188–91.

"What to the Slave Is the Fourth of July?" (1852), Frederick Douglass

Frederick Douglass spent the first twenty years of his life as a slave, before becoming a leading abolitionist. In this public lecture, delivered on July 5, 1852 to the Ladies' Anti-Slavery Society in Rochester, New York, Douglass contrasts the freedoms and natural rights championed in the Declaration of Independence and celebrated on the Fourth of July with the substantial lack of freedom endured by African American slaves.

- **Analyze Douglass's use of the term *citizens*. What is the significance of citizenship?**

- **Analyze the role of patriotism in this document. Is this a patriotic speech?**

- **Explain the significance of capital punishment in this document.**

Fellow-Citizens—pardon me, and allow me to ask, why am I called upon to speak here today? What have I, or those I represent, to do with your national independence? Are the great principles of political freedom and of natural justice, embodied in that Declaration of Independence, extended to us? and am I, therefore, called upon to bring our humble offering to the national altar, and to confess the benefits, and express devout gratitude for the blessings, resulting from your independence to us? . . .

But, such is not the state of the case. I say it with a sad sense of the disparity between us. I am not included within the pale of this glorious anniversary! Your high independence only reveals the immeasurable distance between us. The blessings in which you this day rejoice, are not enjoyed in common. The rich inheritance of justice, liberty, prosperity, and independence, bequeathed by your fathers, is shared by you, not by me. The sunlight that brought life and healing to you, has brought stripes and death to me. This Fourth of July is *yours,* not *mine. You* may rejoice, *I* must mourn. To drag a man in fetters into the grand illuminated temple of liberty, and call upon him to join you in joyous anthems, were inhuman mockery and sacrilegious irony. Do you mean, citizens, to mock me, by asking me to speak today? If so, there is a parallel to your conduct. And let me warn you that it is dangerous to copy the example of a nation whose crimes, lowering up to heaven, were thrown down by the breath of the Almighty, burying that nation in irrecoverable ruin! I can to-day take up the plaintive lament of a peeled and woe-smitten people! . . .

Fellow-citizens; above your national, tumultuous joy, I hear the mournful wail of millions! whose chains, heavy and grievous yesterday, are, to-day, rendered more intolerable by the jubilee shouts that reach them. If I do forget, if I do not faithfully remember those bleeding children of sorrow this day, "may my right hand forget her cunning, and may my tongue cleave to the roof of my mouth!" To forget them, to pass lightly over their wrongs, and to chime in with the popular theme, would be treason most scandalous and shocking, and would make me a reproach before God and the world. My subject, then fellow-citizens, is AMERICAN SLAVERY. I shall see, this day, and its popular characteristics, from the slave's point of view. Standing, there, identified with the American bondman, making his wrongs mine, I do not hesitate

to declare, with all my soul, that the character and conduct of this nation never looked blacker to me than on this 4th of July! Whether we turn to the declarations of the past, or to the professions of the present, the conduct of the nation seems equally hideous and revolting. America is false to the past, false to the present, and solemnly binds herself to be false to the future. Standing with God and the crushed and bleeding slave on this occasion, I will, in the name of humanity which is outraged, in the name of liberty which is fettered, in the name of the constitution and the Bible, which are disregarded and trampled upon, dare to call in question and to denounce, with all the emphasis I can command, everything that serves to perpetuate slavery—the great sin and shame of America! "I will not equivocate; I will not excuse"; I will use the severest language I can command; and yet not one word shall escape me that any man, whose judgment is not blinded by prejudice, or who is not at heart a slaveholder, shall not confess to be right and just. . . .

Must I undertake to prove that the slave is a man? That point is conceded already. Nobody doubts it. The slaveholders themselves acknowledge it in the enactment of laws for their government. They acknowledge it when they punish disobedience on the part of the slave. There are seventy-two crimes in the state of Virginia, which, if committed by a black man (no matter how ignorant he be) subject him to the punishment of death; while only two of these same crimes will subject a white man to the like punishment. What is this but the acknowledgment that the slave is a moral, intellectual, and responsible being. The manhood of the slave is conceded. It is admitted in the fact that southern statute books are covered with enactments forbidding, under severe fines and penalties, the teaching of the slave to read or write. When you can point to any such laws, in reference to the beasts of the field, then I may consent to argue the manhood of the slave. When the dogs in your streets, when the fowls of the air, when the cattle on your hills, when the fish of the sea, and the reptiles that crawl, shall be unable to distinguish the slave from a brute, then will I argue with you that the slave is a man!

Source: Frederick Douglass, *Narrative of the Life of Frederick Douglass, an American Slave, Written by Himself,* A Norton Critical Edition, edited by William L. Andrews and William S. McFeely (New York: Norton, 1997), pp. 123–25.

Interpreting Visual Evidence

Framing the Subject

Important currents of Enlightenment thought (which fed into classical liberalism in the nineteenth century—see Chapter 16) stressed the autonomy of the individual. All men were thought to be created equal, endowed with reason and the ability to master nature and the world around them. European liberals celebrated individual initiative, self-control, and material success through hard work as signs of virtue. They also drew from the Enlightenment a faith that the natural world follows observable laws. This faith gave rise, as we have seen, to advances in the natural sciences and then the social sciences. In the arts, that faith corresponded to a renewed interest in representing the external world in precise, objective terms, called realism. Painters sought to capture and reflect an independent, external, stable reality—this in a period before photography.

It was a confident but also a self-centered view of the world.

Here we consider efforts to represent the individual in portraiture. Jean-Auguste-Dominique Ingres painted the French newspaper baron and businessman Louis-François Bertin, in a portrait from 1832. Bertin's *Journal des Débats* served as the recognized organ of the opposition to the Bourbon Restoration in early nineteenth-century France and helped put the constitutional July Monarchy in power. The painter Édouard Manet described Bertin as "the Buddha of the self-satisfied, well-to-to, triumphant bourgeoisie." Unlike Ingres, who painted a real historical figure, Jean-Léon Gérôme, in *Bashi-Bazouk* (1868–69), painted a model dressed in garments made of textiles he had acquired on a trip to the Near East, to represent the unpaid, irregular mercenary soldiers who lived from

Ingres, *Louis-François Bertin*.

Gérôme, *Bashi-Bazouk*.

plunder and fought in Ottoman armies. Gérôme conceived and executed this painting of an Ottoman soldier in a European studio. In the *Portrait of an Indian*, French artist Anne-Louis Girodet-Trioson painted a man in Ottoman clothing. Finally, the *Portrait of the Imperial Bodyguard Zhanyinbao* was probably sketched by a (European) Jesuit artist in the Chinese court and then transferred to a silk scroll by a Chinese master.

Portrait of the Imperial Bodyguard Zhanyinbao.

Girodet-Trioson, *Portrait of an Indian*.

Questions for Analysis

1. Create a psychological profile for each portrait. What clues does the artist give you about the men, their values, and their standing in the world?

2. What is the effect of the sparse backgrounds and the intricate detail in the foregrounds? What do you think the artists left out of these portraits that might influence your profiles?

3. Do the painters create coherent images of their subjects? What contradictions can you see—for

example, between violent aggression and delicate refinement, or between order and disorder—with respect to discipline and control?

4. Compare the two "Orientalist" paintings—the *Portrait of an Indian* and *Bashi-Bazouk*—with the other two. What does Orientalist mean in this context? How, in particular, do they differ from the *Portrait of the Imperial Bodyguard Zhanyinbao*?

16

Alternative Visions of the Nineteenth Century

By the late nineteenth century, territorial expansion in the United States confined almost all Native Americans to reservations. The buffalo that once supported many tribes disappeared: white settlers built towns, farms, and railroads throughout the buffalo's natural habitat, and Native Americans overhunted the shrinking herds. Across the American West, many Native Americans fell into despair. One was a Paiute named Wovoka. But in 1889, he had a vision of a much brighter future. In his dream, the "Supreme Being" told Wovoka that if Native Americans lived harmoniously, shunned white ways (especially alcohol), and performed the cleansing Ghost Dance, then the buffalo would return, and Native Americans, including the dead, would be reborn to live in eternal happiness.

As word spread of Wovoka's vision, Native Americans from hundreds of miles around made pilgrimages to the lodge of this new prophet. Many proclaimed him the Native Americans' messiah or the "Red Man's Christ," an impression fostered by scars on his hands. Soon, increasing numbers joined in the ritual Ghost Dance, hoping it would restore the good life that European colonialism in the Americas had extinguished. Among the hopefuls was Sitting Bull, a revered Sioux chief who was himself famous for his visions. Yet, less than two years after Wovoka's vision, Sitting Bull died at the hands of police forces on a Sioux reservation.

Chapter Outline

- Reactions to Social and Political Change
- Prophecy and Revitalization in the Islamic World and Africa
- Prophecy and Rebellion in China
- Socialists and Radicals in Europe
- Insurgencies against Colonizing and Centralizing States
- Conclusion

Core Objectives

- **DESCRIBE** the challenges to the ideals of industrial capitalism, colonialism, and nation-states in this period.
- **COMPARE** the utopian goals, immediate outcomes, and long-term influence of rebel movements around the world.
- **ANALYZE** the connections between nineteenth-century protest movements and organized religion.
- **ASSESS** the role religion played in these alternative social visions.

A few days later, on December 29, 1890, the U.S. Seventh Cavalry Regiment massacred Sioux Ghost Dancers at a South Dakota creek called Wounded Knee.

Though it failed, this movement was one of many prophetic crusades that challenged an emerging nineteenth-century order. The ideals of the French and American Revolutions in politics—equality before the law, and government for and by property-holding citizens in a world of nation-states—now provided the dominant answers to age-old questions of who should govern and how. Emerging from the industrial revolution, the ideas of free market (laissez-faire) capitalism, in which private owners competed against one another to maximize profits using new technologies and industrial organizations, provided the dominant answers to questions about how productive activity should be organized. But these political and economic answers were not powerful enough entirely to stamp out other views. A diverse assortment of political radicals, charismatic prophets, peasant rebels, and anticolonial insurgents put forward striking counterproposals to those that capitalists, colonial modernizers, and nation-state builders had developed. The people making these counterproposals were motivated by the impending loss of their existing worlds and were energized by visions of ideal, utopian futures.

This chapter presents the voices and visions of those who opposed a nineteenth-century world in which capitalism, colonialism, and nation-states held sway. It puts the spotlight on challengers who shared a dislike of global capitalism and European (and North American) colonialism. Beyond that similarity, these challengers differed in significant ways, for the alternatives they proposed reflected the local circumstances in which each of them developed. Although many of these challengers suffered devastating defeats, like the Ghost Dancers at Wounded Knee, the dreams that aroused their fervor did not always die with them. Some of these alternative visions of the nineteenth century endured to propel the great transformations of the twentieth.

Global Storylines

- Protest movements challenge the nineteenth-century order based on industrial capitalism, the nation-state, and colonization.

- Led by prophets, political radicals, and common people, the movements arise among marginal groups and regions and express visions of ideal, utopian futures.

- The movements differ markedly depending on distance from the centers of change (Europe and the Americas) and reflect local circumstances.

- Although most movements are defeated, they give voice to the views of peasants and workers and have a lasting effect on the policies of ruling elites.

Reactions to Social and Political Change

The alternatives to the emerging order of the nineteenth century varied considerably. Some rebels and dissidents called for the revitalization of traditional religions; others wanted to strengthen village and communal bonds; still others imagined a society where there was no private property and where people shared goods equally. The actions of these dissenters depended on their local traditions and the degree of contact they had with the effects of industrial capitalism, European colonialism, and centralizing nation-states.

This era of rapid social change, when differing visions of power and justice vied with one another, offers unique opportunities to hear the voices of the lower orders—the peasants and workers, whose perspectives the elites often ignored or suppressed. While there are few written records that capture the views of the illiterate and the marginalized, we do have traditions of folklore, dreams, rumors, and prophecies. Handed down orally from generation to generation, these resources illuminate the visions of common people.

THE BIG PICTURE

What were the similarities and differences between the challenges to global industrialization, colonialism, and the rise of the nation-state during the nineteenth century?

Prophecy and Revitalization in the Islamic World and Africa

In regions that experienced European and North American influence but not direct colonial rule, alternative perspectives were strongest far from the main trade and cultural routes. People outside the emerging capitalist world order led these movements. In the Islamic world and Africa, leaders on the margins were especially important in articulating alternative views.

Even though much of the Islamic world and non-Islamic Africa had not been colonized and was only partially involved with European-dominated trading networks, these regions had reached turning points. By the late eighteenth century, the era of Islamic expansion and cultural flowering under the Ottomans, Safavids, and Mughals was over. Their empires had extended Muslim trading orbits, facilitated cross-cultural communication, and promoted common knowledge over vast territories. Their political and military decline, however, brought new challenges to the faithful. The sense of alarm intensified as Christian Europe's power spread from the edges of the Islamic world to its centers. While this perception of danger motivated military men in Egypt and the Ottoman sultans to modernize their states (see Chapter 15), it also bred religious revitalization movements that sought to recapture the glories of past traditions. Led by prophets who feared that the Islamic faith was in trouble, these movements spoke the language of revival and restoration

Core Objectives

ANALYZE the connections between nineteenth-century protest movements and organized religion in Islam, China, and the Americas.

as they sought to establish new religiously based governments across lands in which Muslims ruled and Islamic law prevailed.

Prophecy also exerted a strong influence in non-Islamic Africa, where long-distance trade and population growth were upending the social order. Just as Muslim clerics and political leaders sought solutions to unsettling changes by rereading Islamic classics, African communities looked to charismatic leaders who drew strength from their peoples' spiritual and magical traditions. Often uniting disparate groups behind their dynamic visions, prophetic leaders and other "big men" gained power because they were able to resolve local crises—mostly caused by drought, a shortage of arable land, or some other issue related to the harsh environment.

ISLAMIC REVITALIZATION

Movements to revitalize Islam took place on the peripheries—at a certain remove from trade networks and the changes wrought by global capitalism. (See Map 16.1.) Here, religious leaders rejected the westernizing influences they felt encroaching on their authority and way of life. Revitalization movements looked back to Islamic traditions and modeled their revolts on the life of Muhammad. But even as they looked to the past, they attempted to establish something new: full-scale theocracies. These reformers conceived of the state as the primary instrument of God's will and as the vehicle for purifying Islamic culture. (See Current Trends in World History: Islam: An Enduring Alternative in Algeria.)

Wahhabism   One of the most powerful reformist movements arose on the Arabian Peninsula, the birthplace of the Muslim faith. In the Najd region, an area surrounded by mountains and deserts, a religious cleric named Muhammad Ibn Abd al-Wahhab (1703–1792) galvanized the population by attacking what he regarded as lax religious practices. His message found a ready response among local inhabitants, who felt threatened by the new commercial activities and fresh intellectual currents swirling around them. Abd al-Wahhab demanded a return to the pure Islam of Muhammad and the early caliphs.

Although Najd was far removed from the centers of the expanding world economy, Abd al-Wahhab himself was not. Having been educated in Iraq, Iran, and the Hijaz (a region on the western end of modern Saudi Arabia, on the Red Sea), he believed that Islam had fallen into a degraded state, particularly in its birthplace. He railed against the polytheistic beliefs that had taken hold of the people, complaining that in defiance of Muhammad's tenets men and women were worshipping trees, stones, and tombs and making sacrifices to false images. Abd al-Wahhab's movement stressed the absolute oneness of Allah and severely criticized Sufi sects for extolling the lives of saints over the worship of God.

Map 16.1 Muslim Revitalization Movements in the Middle East and Africa and the *Mfecane* Movement in Southern Africa

During the nineteenth century, a series of Muslim revitalization movements took place throughout the Middle East and North Africa.

- According to this map, in how many different areas did the revitalization movements occur?
- Based on their geographic location within their larger regions, did these movements occur in central or peripheral areas?
- According to your reading, were any of the same factors that led to Islamic revitalization involved in the *Mfecane* developments in southern Africa?

Islam: An Enduring Alternative in Algeria

Many of the alternative movements featured in this chapter derived their impetus from deeply held religious beliefs. Religion played a role in the Indian mutiny and in the visions that spurred the Taiping rebels. In Muslim locations far from the main currents of western influence, like the Arabian Peninsula and northern Nigeria, it generated revivalist movements. But elsewhere it became a political force, and one that developed a palpably anti-European nature as well as the power to endure long beyond the victory of European invaders. World historians like to study political and social movements because they bring into relief the relationship between the colonizer and the colonized and, in the case of these alternative movements, the relationship between peoples living on the peripheries of empires and those living in the center who are part of the ruling elite, including indigenous elites.

This was the case in particular along the old Ottoman periphery, one of the major targets for European colonization. Strikingly, in the first decades of the nineteenth century, in the Ottomans' Balkan domains of Serbia and Greece, Christianity had linked together opponents against the empire. In the

decades to follow, as Ottoman power receded, it left behind it Islamic groups who also used religion as the glue that bound together otherwise diverse peoples. The following example highlights the importance of Islam in galvanizing resistance to French imperialism in Algeria. But there are examples: in the 1840s and 1850s in the Caucasus Mountains, another Ottoman periphery, Islam linked together Chechen and other groups in opposition to Russian colonization; and in the early twentieth century, Libyans attempted to oppose Italian colonization by rallying behind the green flag of the Prophet. Unquestionably, the more Europeans sought to dominate lands inhabited by Muslims, the more they called forth in reaction Islamic alternatives and a politicized form of Islamic resistance.

In 1830, through a series of mishaps and miscalculations, the French found themselves in possession of the Regency of Algiers, a territory of 60,000 square miles where previously 10,000 Ottoman Turks had ruled over 3 million Arab and Berber tribesmen. The French invasion had been an ill-considered adventure, designed to divert attention from the fact that the backward-looking French king, Charles X, had lost his legitimacy at

home. In 1830, Charles was toppled by the so-called July Revolution, but his successor, King Louis Philippe (r. 1830–1848), decided to pursue France's adventure abroad. This was a risky and ultimately costly plan, however, as the French controlled only a few coastal enclaves and the capital city of Algiers; in 1831, the European civilian population was a mere 3,228. Moreover, although the French had driven out the Turks, they had emboldened Arab tribes in the western part of the land to found their own independent state.

In seeking a leader to unite them, the Arab tribes turned to Abd al-Qadir (1807–1883), a charismatic and domineering personality even though only twenty-five years of age. His father, head of the most important Sufi Brotherhood in Algeria, had groomed his son to be a leader and had taught him to despise the Ottoman overlords. Abd al-Qadir and his followers had already committed themselves to overthrowing the Ottomans, but once the French arrived, they were even more determined to rid their area of invaders they regarded as infidels who were intent on seizing their lands and imposing their way of life on them. In organizing resistance to the French, Abd al-Qadir relied on his reputation as a holy man

Wahhabism
Early eighteenth-century reform movement organized by Muhammad Ibn Abd al-Wahhab, who preached the absolute oneness of Allah and a return to the pure Islam of Muhammad.

As **Wahhabism** swept across the Arabian Peninsula, the movement threatened the Ottomans' hold on the region. Wahhabism gained a powerful political ally in the Najdian House of Saud, a leading family whose followers, inspired by the Wahhabis' religious zeal, undertook a militant religious campaign in the final years of the eighteenth century. Frightened by the Wahhabi challenge, the Ottoman sultan persuaded the provincial ruler of Egypt to send troops to the Arabian Peninsula to suppress the movement.

Abd al-Qadir in Exile, Damascus, Syria (1862) Having surrendered to a massive French army in December 1847, Abd al-Qadir was imprisoned in France. After the Revolution of 1848, the new French president, Louis-Napoleon Bonaparte (Napoleon's nephew) released Abd al-Qadir and gave him a government pension in return for the latter's promise not to disturb Algeria.

and a scholar, rather than as merely the head of one of the tribes. In preparation for battle, he called on his soldiers to follow him in a holy war (*jihad*) against Christian invaders, promising those who joined him in battle that "anyone of you who dies, will die a martyr; those of you who survive will gain glory and live happily." Tribes that might not have fought together, or fought together

so long, did so because they were united by their loyalty to a religious as well as a political leader. Abd al-Qadir succeeded in part because he was a forceful personality, but in part because he stood for Islam, which the native Algerians shared, whatever their kinship ties or loyalties to local leaders.

For fifteen years, Abd al-Qadir's forces held out, only surrendering to a massive French force of 108,000 men in 1847. Although often defeated in pitched battles, Abd al-Qadir used his superior knowledge of the terrain and his ability to wait in ambush for French columns to frustrate the French. The French government was finally compelled to send its most accomplished military man, Marshal Thomas-Robert Bugeaud, and to provide him with one-third of its entire military force to finish the job of "pacifying" Algeria.

The French conquest of Algeria marks one of the bloodiest episodes in the history of those two lands. No fewer than 300,000 Algerians perished during these years. Although the French portrayed Abd al-Qadir as a Muslim fanatic, determined to take his people back to a dark age, their message fell on deaf ears. The Algerians extolled him for resisting the French and later made him an iconic figure

of the nationalist movement. One of the first acts carried out by the independent Algerian government in 1962 was to tear down the statue of Marshal Bugeaud and to replace it with one of Abd al-Qadir. The religiously motivated resistance leader had prevailed over the secular political conquerors after all.

Questions for Analysis

- What impact did Algeria's geographic location have on its role in these revolutionary events?
- How did native Algerians view their former Ottoman rulers compared to French Europeans? What was their ultimate goal?

Explore Further

Brower, Benjamin Claude, *A Desert Named Peace: The Violence of France's Empire in the Algerian Sahara, 1844–1902* (2009).

Clancy-Smith, Julia, *Rebel and Saint: Muslim Notables, Populist Protest, Colonial Encounter (Algeria and Tunisia, 1800–1904)* (1994).

Danziger, Raphael, *Abd al-Qadir: Resistance to the French and Internal Consolidation* (1977).

The Egyptians defeated the Saudis in 1818, but Wahhabism and the House of Saud continued to represent a pure Islamic faith that attracted clerics and ordinary people throughout the Muslim world.

Usman dan Fodio and the Fulani In West Africa, Muslim revolts erupted from Senegal to Nigeria in the early nineteenth century, partly in response to increased trade with the outside world and the circulation of religious ideas from across the Sahara Desert. In this region, the Fulani people were decisive in religious uprisings that sought, like the Wahhabi movement, to re-create a supposedly purer Islamic past. The majority were cattle keepers, practicing a pastoral and nomadic way of life. But some were sedentary, living in settled communities, and people in this group converted to Islam, read the Islamic classics, and communicated with holy men of North Africa, Egypt, and the Arabian Peninsula. They concluded that West African peoples were violating Islamic beliefs and engaging in irreligious practices.

The most powerful of these reform movements flourished in what is today northern Nigeria. Its leader was a Fulani Muslim cleric, **Usman dan Fodio** (1754–1817), who ultimately created a vast Islamic empire. Dan Fodio's movement had all the trappings of the Islamic revolts of this period. It sought inspiration in the life of Muhammad and demanded a return to early Islamic practices. It attacked false belief and urged followers to wage holy war (*jihad*) against unbelievers.

Dan Fodio blamed local leaders for what he saw as their failure to respect Islamic law. He won the support of devout Muslims in the area, who agreed that the people were not properly practicing Islam. He also gained the backing of his Fulani tribes and many Hausa-speaking peasants, who had suffered under the rule of the Hausa landlord class. The revolt, initiated in 1804, resulted in the overthrow of the Hausa rulers and the creation of a confederation of Islamic emirates, almost all of which were in the hands of the Fulani allies of dan Fodio.

Fulani women of northern Nigeria made critical contributions to the success of the religious revolt. Although dan Fodio and other male leaders of the purification movement expected women to obey the *sharia* (Islamic law), being modest in their dress and their association with men outside the family, they also expected women to support the community's military and religious endeavors. In this effort, they cited women's important role in the first days of Islam. The best known of the Muslim women leaders was Nana Asma'u (1793–1864), daughter of dan Fodio. Fulani women of the upper ranks acquired an Islamic education, and Asma'u was as astute a reader of Islamic texts as any of the learned men in her society. Like other Muslim Fulani devotees, she accompanied the warriors on their campaigns, encamped with them, prepared food for them, bound up their wounds, and provided daily encouragement. According to many accounts, Asma'u inspired the warriors at their most crucial battle, hurling a burning spear into the midst of the enemy army. Her poem "Song of the Circular Journey" celebrates the triumphs of military forces that trekked thousands of miles to bring a reformed Islam to the area.

Usman dan Fodio considered himself a cleric first and a political and military man second. Although his political leadership was decisive in the revolt's success, thereafter he retired to a life of scholarship and writing. He delegated the political and administrative functions of the new empire to his brother and his son. An enduring decentralized state structure, which became known as the Sokoto caliphate in 1809, developed into a stable empire that helped spread Islam through the region. In 1800, on the eve of dan Fodio's revolt, Islam was the faith of a small minority of people living in northern Nigeria; a century later, it had become the religion of the vast majority, thanks to dan Fodio's military prowess and success in creating a stable political structure, and the increasing Fulani contacts with the broader Islamic world.

CHARISMATIC MILITARY MEN IN NON-ISLAMIC AFRICA

Non-Islamic Africa saw revolts, new states, and prophetic movements arise from the same combination of factors that influenced the rest of the world—particularly long-distance trade and population increase. Local communities here also looked to religious traditions and, as was so often the case in African history, expected charismatic clan leaders, known as "big men," to provide political leadership.

In southern Africa, early in the nineteenth century, a group of political revolts reordered the political map. Collectively known as the *Mfecane* ("the crushing" in Zulu) **movement**, its epicenter was a large tract of land lying east of the Drakensberg Mountains, an area where growing populations and land resources existed in a precarious balance (see again Map 16.1). Many branches of Bantu-speaking peoples had inhabited the southern part of the African landmass for centuries. At the end of the eighteenth century, however, their political organizations still operated on a small scale. These tiny polities could not cope with the competition for land that now dominated southern Africa. That competition intensified with the arrival of British colonizers, who fought both with Dutch settlers and indigenous African communities over natural resources. The import of European goods that flowed into southern Africa from Delagoa Bay also was a destabilizing factor. A branch of the Nguni, the Zulus, produced a fierce war leader, Shaka (1787–1828), who created a ruthless warrior state. It drove other populations out of the region and forced a shift from small clan communities to large, centralized monarchies throughout southern and central Africa.

The son of a minor chief, Shaka emerged victorious in a struggle for cattle-grazing and farming lands that arose during a severe drought. A physically imposing figure, Shaka used terror to intimidate his subjects and to overawe his adversaries. His enemies knew that the price of opposition would be a massacre, even of women and children. Nor was he kinder to his own people. Following the death of his beloved mother, he executed those who were not properly contrite and did not weep profusely. Reportedly, it took 7,000 lives to assuage his grief.

Mfecane movement
African political revolts in the first half of the nineteenth century that were caused by the expansionist methods of King Shaka of the Zulu people.

Shaka and His Zulu Regiments
(*Left*) This illustration, the only one from the time, may be an exaggeration, but it does not exaggerate the view that many had of the awesome strength and power of Shaka, the leader who united the Zulu peoples into an invincible warrior state. (*Right*) The Battle of Isandl-wana (1879) was the first major encounter in the war between the British and Shaka's Zulu state. The larger Zulu army over-whelmed the British, despite the latter's superior firepower.

CHAKA KING OF THE ZOOLUS.

London, Published by E.Churton, 26 Holles St.

Shaka built a new Zulu state around his military and organizational skills and the fear that his personal ferocity produced. He drilled his men relentlessly in the use of short stabbing spears and in discipline under pressure. Like the Mongols, he had a remarkable ability to incorporate defeated communities into the state and to absorb young men into his military. His army of 40,000 men comprised regiments that lived, studied, and fought together. Forbidden from marrying until they were discharged from the army, Shaka's warriors developed an intense esprit de corps and regarded no sacrifice as too great in the service of the state. So overpowering were these forces that other peoples of the region fled from their home areas, and Shaka claimed their estates for himself and his followers. Peoples in nearby areas who weren't absorbed into the Zulu state adopted many of Shaka's military and political innovations, at first to defend themselves and then to take over new land as they fled their old areas. The new states of the Ndebele in what later became Zimbabwe and the Sotho of South Africa came into existence in this way in the mid-nineteenth century.

In turning southern Africa from a region of smaller polities into an area with larger and more powerful states, Shaka seemed very much a man of the modern, nineteenth-century world. Yet he was, in his own unique way, a familiar kind of African leader. He shared a charismatic and prophetic style with others who emerged during periods of acute social change. His new state built an enduring Zulu community and established its traditions against encroachments by outside, European forces.

Prophecy and Rebellion in China

In the mid-nineteenth century, China experienced an explosive popular rebellion that incorporated Christian beliefs into its long tradition of peasant revolts. Whereas movements promoting alternative visions in the Islamic world and Africa appeared in areas distant from western influences and drew substantially on their own traditions, China was no longer isolated. In fact, it had been conducting a brisk trade in opium with Europe. Until 1842, the Chinese had confined trade with Europeans to the port city of Canton. After the Opium War, however, westerners forced Qing rulers to open up a number of other ports to trade.

As in the Islamic world and other parts of sub-Saharan Africa, population increases in China—from 250 million in 1644 to around 450 million by the 1850s—were putting considerable pressure on land and other resources. Moreover, the rising consumption of opium, grown in India and brought to China by British traders, produced further social instability and financial crisis. As banditry and rebellions spread, the Qing rulers turned to the landed elites, the gentry, to maintain order in the countryside. But as the gentry raised its militia to suppress these troublemakers, it whittled away at the authority of the Qing Manchu rulers. Faced with these changes, the Qing dynasty struggled to maintain control.

Searching for an alternative present and future, hundreds of thousands of disillusioned peasants joined what became known as the Taiping Rebellion. Beginning in 1850, the uprising drew on China's long history of peasant revolts. Traditionally, these rebellions ignited within popular religious sects whose visions were egalitarian or **millenarian** (convinced of the imminent coming of a just and ideal society). Moreover, in contrast to orthodox institutions, here women played important roles. Inspired by Daoists, who revered a past golden age before the world was corrupted by human conventions, or by Buddhist sources, these sects threatened the established order.

THE DREAM OF HONG XIUQUAN

The story of the rebellion begins with a complex dream that inspired its founding prophet, Hong Xiuquan (1813–1864). A native of Guangdong Province in the southernmost part of the country (see Map 16.2), Hong first encountered Christian missionaries in the 1830s. He was then trying, unsuccessfully, to pass the civil service examination. After failing the exam for the third time, Hong suffered a strange "illness" in which he had visions of combating demons; these dreams included a mysterious "Old Father" and an "Elder Brother." He also began proclaiming himself the Heavenly King. Relatives and neighbors thought he might have gone mad, but Hong gradually returned to his normal state.

millenarian
Believer (usually religious) in the cataclysmic destruction of a corrupt, fallen society and its replacement by an ideal, utopian future.

Map 16.2 The Taiping Rebellion in China, 1850–1864

....

The Taiping Rebellion started in the southwestern part of the country. The rebels, however, went on to control much of the lower Yangzi region and part of the coastal area.

- What cities did the rebels' march start and end in?

- Why do you think the Taiping rebels were so successful in southern China and not in northern regions?

- How did western powers react to the Taiping Rebellion? Would they have been as concerned if the rebellion took place farther to the north or west?

Map legend:

- Area controlled by rebels, c. 1861
- Hong's march to establish Heavenly Capital in Nanjing, 1850–1853
- Unsuccessful northern campaign, 1853–1854
- Advance of Western troops, 1864
- Advance of Qing troops, 1864

0   100   200   300 Miles
0 100 200 300 Kilometers

Taiping Rebellion

(1850–1864) Rebellion by followers of Hong Xiuquan and the Taiping Heavenly Kingdom against the Qing government over the economic and social turmoil caused by the Opium War. Despite raising an army of 100,000 rebels, the rebellion was crushed.

In 1843, after failing the exam for the fourth time, Hong immersed himself in a Christian tract titled *Good Words for Exhorting the Age*. Reportedly, reading this tract enabled Hong to realize the full significance of his earlier visions. All the pieces suddenly fell into place, and he began to grasp their meaning. The "Old Father," he concluded, was the Lord Ye-huo-hua (a Chinese rendering of "Jehovah"), the creator of heaven and earth. His visions of cleansing rituals in heaven foretold Hong's baptism. The "Elder Brother" was Jesus the Savior, the son of God. He, Hong Xiuquan, was the younger brother of Jesus—God's other son. Just as God had previously sent Jesus to save mankind, Hong thought, God was now sending *him* to rid the world of evil. What was once a series of dreams now became a prophetic vision.

THE REBELLION

Hong's prophecy tapped into a millenarian tradition, inspiring a movement that spread rapidly from southern China. Unlike earlier sectarian leaders whose plots for rebellion were secret before exploding onto the public arena, Hong chose a more audacious path. Once convinced of his vision, he began to preach his doctrines openly, baptizing converts and destroying Confucian idols and ancestral shrines. Such assaults on the establishment testified to his conviction that he was carrying out God's will. Hong's message of revitalization of a troubled land and restoration of the "heavenly kingdom," imagined as a just and egalitarian order, appealed to the subordinate classes caught in the flux of social change. Drawing on a largely rural social base and asserting allegiance to Christianity, the **Taiping** ("Great Peace") **Rebellion** (1850–1864) claimed to herald a new era of economic and social justice.

Many early followers came from the margins of local society—those whose anger at social and economic dislocations caused by the Opium War was directed not at the Europeans but at the Qing government. The Taiping identified the ruling Manchus as the "demons" and as the chief obstacle to realizing God's kingdom on earth. Taiping policies were strict: they prohibited the consumption of alcohol, the smoking of opium, and any indulgence in sensual pleasure. Men and women were segregated for administrative and residential purposes. At the same time, in a drastic departure from dynastic practice, women joined the army in segregated units.

By 1850, Hong's movement had amassed a following of over 20,000, giving Qing rulers cause for concern. When they sent troops to arrest Hong and other rebel leaders, Taiping forces repelled them and then took their turmoil beyond the southwestern part of the country. In January 1851, Hong declared himself Heavenly King of the "Taiping Heavenly Kingdom" (or "Heavenly Kingdom of Great Peace"). By 1853, the rebels had captured major cities. Upon capturing Nanjing, the Taiping cleansed the city of "demons" by systematically killing all the Manchus they

Taiping Rebellion A painting depicting the Taiping rebels attacking a town. Had the Taiping succeeded in overthrowing the Qing, it would have changed the course of Chinese history and profoundly affected the rest of the world.

could find—men, women, and children. Then they established their own "heavenly" capital in the city.

But the rebels could not sustain their vision. Several factors contributed to the fall of the Heavenly Kingdom: struggles within the leadership, an excessively rigid code of conduct, and the rallying of Manchu and Han elites around the embattled dynasty. Disturbed by the Taiping's rejection of Confucianism and wanting to protect their property, landowning gentry led militias against the Taiping. Moreover, western governments also opposed the rebellion, claiming that its doctrines represented a perversion of Christianity. Thus, a mercenary army led by foreign officers took part in suppressing the rebellion. Hong himself perished as his heavenly capital fell in 1864. All told, at least 20 million people died in the Taiping Rebellion.

Like their counterparts in the Islamic world and Africa, the Taiping rebels promised to restore lost harmony. Despite all the differences of cultural and historical background, what Abd al-Wahhab, dan Fodio, Shaka, and Hong had in common was the perception that the present world was unjust. Thus, they sought to reorganize their communities—an endeavor that involved confronting established authorities. In this regard, the language of revitalization used by prophets in Islamic areas and China was crucial, for it provided an alternative vocabulary of political and spiritual legitimacy. By mobilizing masses eager to return to an imagined golden age, these prophets and charismatic leaders gave voice to those dispossessed by global change, while producing new, alternative ways of organizing society and politics.

Socialists and Radicals in Europe

Core Objectives

DESCRIBE the challenges to the ideals of industrial capitalism and nation-states in this period in Europe and the Americas.

Europe and North America were the core areas of economic growth, based on the industrial revolution and free trade, nation-state building, and colonial expansion. But there, too, the main currents of thought and activity encountered challenges. Prophets of all stripes—political, social, cultural, and religious—voiced antiestablishment values and dreamed of alternative arrangements. Radicals, liberals, utopian socialists, nationalists, abolitionists, and religious mavericks made plans for better worlds to come.

RESTORATION AND RESISTANCE

The social and political ferment of the efforts to restore the old order, known as the Restoration period (1815–1848), owed a great deal to the ambiguous legacies of the French Revolution and the Napoleonic wars. (See Map 16.3.) Kings had been toppled and replaced by republics, and then by Napoleon and his relatives; these experiments gave Restoration-era states and radicals many political options from which to choose in the years between Napoleon's downfall in 1815 and the revolutions of 1848.

Map legend:

— German Confederation
★ Revolutionary activity

Foreign intervention to put down revolutions
— Austrian
— French
— British
— Russian
— Egyptian

Map labels:

NORWAY
SWEDEN
NORTH SEA
DENMARK
BALTIC SEA
RUSSIAN EMPIRE
St. Petersburg 1825
GREAT BRITAIN
IRELAND 1822–1829
Manchester 1819
Chartist agitation 1840s
NETHERLANDS
BELGIUM
Brussels 1830
ATLANTIC OCEAN
Hanover 1817–1831
PRUSSIA
Berlin 1848
Cologne 1848
Warsaw 1830–1831, 1848
1830–1831
Kiev 1825
Trier
Frankfurt 1848
Paris 1830, 1848
Stuttgart 1848
Munich 1848
Prague 1848
Krakow (to Austria 1847) 1848
Vendean uprising 1846
FRANCE
SWITZ. 1847–1848
Milan 1820, 1831, 1848
AUSTRIAN EMPIRE
Buda Pest 1848
La Coruña 1820
Oviedo 1820
First Carlist War 1833–1839
Pamplona 1820
Turin 1820
PIEDMONT
Brescia 1820
Venice 1831, 1848
Oporto 1820
Zaragoza 1820
Genoa 1820
Bologna 1831, 1848
PORTUGAL
SPAIN
Madrid 1820
Barcelona 1820
Florence 1820, 1848
CORSICA
Macerata 1820
Belgrade 1807–1833
Bucharest 1821, 1848
BLACK SEA
Lisbon 1820
Second Carlist War 1846–1848
Valencia 1820
KINGDOM OF PIEDMONT-SARDINIA
PAPAL STATES
Rome 1831, 1848
Cádiz 1820
SARDINIA
Naples 1820, 1848
Salerno 1820
Bari 1820
OTTOMAN EMPIRE
MEDITERRANEAN
KINGDOM OF THE TWO SICILIES
Palermo 1820, 1848
SICILY
Reggio 1820
IONIAN IS.
GREECE 1821–1829
Navarino 1827
1827–1829
CRETE
MALTA
SEA
1825–1829

Scale: 0   250   500 Miles
0   250   500 Kilometers

Map 16.3 Civil Unrest and Revolutions in Europe, 1819–1848

Civil unrest and revolutions swept Europe after the Congress of Vienna established a peace settlement at the end of the French Revolution and Napoleon's conquests. Conservative governments had to fight off liberal rebellions and demands for change.

- How many sites of revolutionary activity can you locate on this map?
- What parts of Europe appear to have been politically stable, and what parts rebellious? Based on your reading and the map, can you explain the stability of some parts of Europe and the instability of others?

This period has often been called the Age of Ideology because revolutionary upheavals forced everyone, even those in power, to justify their vision of the social order. Appeals to tradition no longer sufficed. Those called reactionaries or conservatives wanted a return to the world that existed before the French Revolution; they rejected change. Liberals, by contrast, accepted the French Revolution's overthrow of aristocratic privilege. They wanted to hold on to the principles of 1789—above all free trade and equality before the law—without accepting the price controls and political violence of the Terror. Free markets rather than government controls, they believed, would make the most sensible decisions. These proponents of **liberalism** insisted on the individual's right to think, speak, act, and vote as he or she pleased without government interference, so long as no harm came to people or property. Both reactionaries and liberals could find elements to their taste in all the states of the post-Napoleonic world. Much more threatening to the ruling elite were the radicals who believed that the French Revolution had not gone far enough. They longed for a grander revolution that would sweep away the Restoration's political *and* economic order.

RADICAL VISIONS

Reactionaries and liberals did not form the only alternative groups of importance at this time. Most discontented of all—and most determined to effect grand-scale change—were the radicals.

The term *radicals* refers to those who favored the total reconfiguration of the old regime's state system: going to the root of the problem and continuing the revolution, not reversing it or stopping reform. In general, radicals shared a bitter hatred for the status quo and an insistence on popular sovereignty, but beyond this consensus much disagreement remained. If some radicals demanded the equalization or abolition of private property, others—like Serbian, Greek, Polish, and Italian nationalists—were primarily interested in throwing off the oppressive overlordship of the Ottoman and Austrian Empires and creating their own nation-states. It was the radicals' threat of a return to revolutions that ultimately reconciled both liberals and reactionaries to preserving the status quo.

Nationalists In the period before the revolutions of 1848, nationalism was a cause dear to both liberals and radicals, and it threatened conservative rulers who claimed to rule by divine right. The idea of popular sovereignty spread, especially during and after Napoleon's occupation of the continent, but who exactly were "the people"? The "people," or the nation, were generally considered to be those who shared a common language, culture, and history, but nationalists fought bitterly over which people counted and who decided.

All nationalists believed that governments should represent the "people" and that each people—or, at least, their people—should have a state of their own.

Each fledgling nationalist movement—whether Polish, Czech, Greek, Italian, or German—had different contours, but they all drew backers from the liberal aristocracy and the well-educated, commercially active middle classes. Most nationalist movements were, at first, weak and easily crushed, such as attempted Polish uprisings inside tsarist Russia in 1830–1831 and 1863–1864. Unable to win political power, the movements' leaders instead pursued educational and cultural programs to arouse and unite their nation for eventual statehood. By contrast, the Greeks, inspired by religious revivalism and enlightened ideas, managed to wrest independence from the Ottoman Turks after a years-long series of skirmishes, in 1832.

Other nationalist movements were suppressed or at least slowed down with little bloodshed. In places like the German principalities, the Italian states, and the Hungarian parts of the Habsburg Empire, secret societies of young men—students and intellectuals—gathered to plan bright, republican futures. Regrettably for these patriots, however, organizations like Young Italy, founded in 1832 to promote national unification and renewal, had little popular or foreign support. Censorship and a few strategic executions suppressed them. Yet many of these movements ultimately succeeded in the century's second half, when conservatives and liberals alike in western Europe employed nationalist fervor to advance their own ambitions. Kings, aristocrats, and bourgeois businessmen realized that they could mobilize popular support in their capacity as Germans, Frenchmen, or Italians, even as they limited poor people's political rights. However, in central Europe, nationalism pitted many claimants for the same territories against one another, like the Czechs, Serbs, Slovaks, Poles, and Ruthenians (Ukrainians). They did not understand why they could not have a nation-state too. Indeed, the idea of a "nation," like that of a "people," was so abstract and vague that it unleashed a series of competing claims that were incompatible with one another and would prove enormously destructive in the twentieth century.

Socialists and Communists Early socialists and communists (the terms were more or less interchangeable in the nineteenth century) insisted that political reforms offered no effective answer to the more pressing "social question": What was to be done about the inequalities so powerfully magnified by industrial capitalism? The socialists worried in particular about two things. One was the growing gap between impoverished workers and newly wealthy employers. The other concern was that the division of labor—that is, the dividing up and simplifying of tasks so that each worker performs most efficiently—might make people into soulless, brainless machines. Socialists believed that the whole free market economy, not just the state, had to be transformed to save the human race from self-destruction. Liberty and equality, they insisted, could not be separated; liberal capitalism and free markets belonged on history's ash heap, in their view, along with aristocratic privilege.

No more than a handful of radical prophets hatched revolutionary plans in the years after 1815, but they were not the only participants in strikes, riots, peasant uprisings, and protest meetings. Indeed, ordinary workers, artisans, domestic servants, and women employed in textile manufacturing all joined in attempts to answer the "social question" to their satisfaction. A few socialists and feminists—like the English thinker John Stuart Mill and his wife, Harriet—campaigned for social and political equality of the sexes. In Britain in 1819, Manchester workers at St. Peter's Field demonstrated peacefully for increased representation in Parliament, but panicking guardsmen fired on the crowd, leaving 11 dead and 460 injured in an incident later dubbed the Peterloo Massacre. In 1839 and 1842, nearly half the adult population of Britain signed the People's Charter, which called for universal suffrage for all adult males, the secret ballot, equal electoral districts, and annual parliamentary elections. Like most such endeavors, this mass movement, known as Chartism, ended in defeat. Parliament rejected the charter in 1839, 1842, and 1848.

Fourier and Utopian Socialism Despite their many defeats, the radicals kept trying. Charles Fourier's **utopian socialism** was perhaps the most visionary and influential of all Restoration-era alternative movements.

Fired by the egalitarian hopes and the cataclysmic failings of the French Revolution, Fourier (1772–1837) believed himself to be the scientific prophet of the new world to come. He was an imaginative, self-taught man who earned his keep in the cloth trade, an occupation that gave him an intense hatred for merchants and middlemen. Convinced that the division of labor and repressive moral conventions were destroying mankind's natural talents and passions, Fourier concluded that a revolution grander than that of 1789 was needed. But this utopian transformation of economic, social, and political conditions, he thought, could occur through organization, not through bloodshed. Indeed, by 1808 Fourier believed that the thoroughly corrupt world was on the brink of giving way to a new and harmonious age, of which he was the oracle.

First formulated in 1808, his "system" envisioned the reorganization of human communities into what he called phalanxes. In these harmonious collectives of 1,500 to 1,600 people, diversity would be preserved but efficiency maintained; best of all, work would become enjoyable. All members of the phalanx, rich and poor, would work, though not necessarily at the same tasks. All would work in short spurts of no more than two hours, so as to make labor more interesting and sleep, idleness, and overindulgence less attractive. Truly undesirable jobs, like sweeping out stables or cleaning

The Phalanx The phalanx, as one of Fourier's German followers envisioned it. In this rendering, the idealized home for the residents of the cooperative social system is represented as a building architecturally similar to the home of the French kings, the Louvre.

latrines, would fall to young adolescents, who, Fourier argued, actually liked mucking about in filth.

Fourier's writings gained popularity in the 1830s, appealing to radicals who supported a variety of causes. In France, women were particularly active in spreading his ideas, notably founders of the feminist press in France, including Désirée Gay and Jeanne Deroin. Longing for social and moral reforms that would address problems such as prostitution, poverty, illegitimacy, and the exploitation of workers (including women and children), some women saw in Fourier's ideas a higher form of Christian communalism. By reshaping the phalanx to accommodate monogamous families and Christian values, women helped make his work more respectable to middle-class readers. In Russia, Fourier's works inspired the imaginations of the young writer Fyodor Dostoyevsky. He and fourteen others in the radical circle to which he belonged were sentenced to death for their views (though their executions were called off at the last minute). The German thinker Karl Marx read Fourier with great care, and there are many remnants of utopian thought in his work. In *The German Ideology*, Marx describes life in an ideal communist society; in a postrevolutionary world, he predicts, people would no longer have to commit to a single profession or sphere of activity. Everyone could develop their talents in a range of areas. A well-ordered society would make it possible, as he put it in a famous phrase, "for me to do one thing today and another tomorrow, to hunt in the morning, fish in the afternoon, rear cattle in the evening, [and] criticize after dinner."

Marxism University-educated and philosophically radical, Karl Marx (1818–1883) elaborated what he called a scientific socialism. After being expelled from the university for his radical views, Marx took up a career in journalism. In that capacity, he covered legislative debates over property rights and taxation and developed an interest in economics. His understanding of capitalism, a term he was instrumental in popularizing, deepened through his collaboration with Friedrich Engels (1820–1895). Engels was a German-born radical who, after observing conditions in the factories owned by his wealthy father in Manchester, England, published a devastating indictment of industrial wage labor titled *The Condition of the Working Class in England*.

Together, Marx and Engels developed what they called "scientific socialism," which they contrasted with the "utopian socialism" of others like Fourier. Scientific socialism was rooted, they argued, in a materialist theory of history: what mattered in history were the production of material goods and the ways in which society was organized into classes of producers and exploiters. History, they claimed, consisted of successive forms of exploitative production and rebellions against them. Capitalist exploitation of the wage worker was only the latest, and worst, version of class conflict, Marx and Engels contended. In industrialized societies, capitalists owned the means of production (the factories and machinery) and exploited wage workers. Marx and Engels were confident that the clashes between industrial wage workers with nothing to sell but their labor—or **proletarians**—and capitalists would end in a colossal transformation of human society and would usher in a new world of true liberty, equality, and fraternity. These beliefs constituted the fundamentals of **Marxism**. For Marx and Engels, history moved through stages: from feudalism to capitalism, and then, finally, to socialism (or communism).

From these fundamentals, Marx and Engels issued a comprehensive critique of post-1815 Europe. They identified a whole class of the exploited—the working class. They believed that more and more people would fall into this class as industrialization proceeded and that the masses would not share in the rising prosperity that capitalists monopolized. Marx and Engels predicted that there would be overproduction, and underconsumption of goods would lead to lower profits for capitalists and, consequently, to lower wages or unemployment for workers—which would ultimately spark a proletarian revolution. This revolution would result in a "dictatorship of the proletariat" and the end of private property. With the destruction of capitalism, the men claimed, exploitation would cease and the state would wither away.

After a decade of hardship across Europe known as the hungry forties, revolutions erupted in 1848 in France, Austria, Russia, Italy, Hungary, and the German states. After hearing that revolution had broken out in France, Marx and Engels published *The Communist Manifesto*, calling on the workers of all nations to unite in overthrowing capitalism. These were not proletarian

proletarians
Industrial wage workers.

Marxism
A current of socialism created by Karl Marx and Friedrich Engels. It stressed the primacy of economics and technology—and, above all, class conflict—in shaping human history. Economic production provided the foundation, the "base" for society, which shaped politics, values, art, and culture (the superstructure). In the modern, industrial era, they believed class conflict boiled down to a two-way struggle between the bourgeoisie (who controlled the means of industrial production) and the proletariat (workers who had only their labor power to sell).

revolutions. By midcentury, modern industry had not developed beyond a few key locations, mostly in northern and western Europe. Instead the revolutions were cross-class affairs, lead by an uneasy coalition of liberal doctors, lawyers, and university professors; often-radical students and urban artisans; and a mass of poor peasants. As a group, they shared little more than a frustration with old elites and a desire for independent nations. Marx and Engels were sorely disappointed (not to mention exiled) by the reactionary crackdowns that quickly crushed the 1848 revolutions. The failure of those revolutions, however, did not doom their prophecy itself or diminish commitment to alternative social landscapes.

Insurgencies against Colonizing and Centralizing States

Outside Europe, for Native Americans and for Britain's colonial subjects in India, the greatest threat to traditional worlds was colonialism. While European radicals looked back to revolutionary legacies in imagining a transformed society, Native American insurgents and rebels in British India drew on their traditional cultural and political resources to imagine local alternatives to foreign impositions. Like the peoples of China, Africa, and the Middle East, native groups in the Americas and India met the period's challenges with prophecy, charismatic leadership, and rebellion. The insurgents all sought to defend their cultures and looked to an idealized past free from outside influences, but the new worlds they envisioned bore unmistakable marks of the present as well.

NATIVE AMERICAN PROPHETS

Like other native peoples threatened by imperial expansion, the Native Americans of North America dreamed of a world in which intrusive colonizers disappeared. Taking such dreams as prophecies, many Native Americans in the Ohio Valley flocked in 1805 to hear the revelations of a Shawnee named Tenskwatawa. Facing a dark present and a darker future, they enthusiastically embraced the Shawnee Prophet's visions, which (like those of the Paiute prophet Wovoka nearly a century later) foretold how invaders would vanish if Native Americans returned to their customary ways and traditional rites.

Early Calls for Resistance and a Return to Tradition Tenskwatawa's visions—and the anticolonial uprising they inspired—drew on a long tradition of visionary leaders. Often these prophets inspired their followers not only to engage in cleansing ceremonies but also to cooperate in violent, anticolonial uprisings. In the 1760s, for example, the preachings of the Delaware shaman Neolin encouraged Native Americans of the Ohio Valley and Great Lakes to take up arms against the British, leading to the capture of several British military posts. Although the British put down the uprising, imperial officials learned a lesson from the conflict: they assumed a less arrogant posture toward Ohio Valley and Great Lakes Native Americans, and they forbade colonists from trespassing on lands west of the Appalachian Mountains. The British, however, were incapable of restraining the flow of settlers across the mountains, and the problem became much worse for the Native Americans once the American Revolution ended. With the Ohio Valley transferred to the new United States, American settlers crossed the Appalachians and flooded into Kentucky and Tennessee.

Despite the settlers' considerable migration, much of the territory between the Appalachian Mountains and the Mississippi River, which Americans referred to as the "western country," remained a Native American country. North and south of Kentucky and Tennessee, Native American warriors more than held their own against American forces. But in 1794 Native American warriors failed to repel invading American armies, and their leaders had to surrender lands in what is now the state of Ohio to the United States. (See Map 16.4.)

Tenskwatawa: The Shawnee Prophet The Shawnees, who lost most of their land, were among the most bitter—and bitterly divided—of Native American peoples living in the Ohio Valley. Some Shawnee leaders concluded that their people's survival now required that they cooperate with American officials and Christian missionaries. This strategy, they realized, entailed wrenching changes in Shawnee culture. European reformers, after all, insisted that Native American men give up hunting and take up farming, an occupation that the Shawnees and their neighbors had always considered "women's work." Moreover, the Shawnees were pushed to abandon communal traditions in favor of private property rights.

Among the demoralized Shawnees was **Tenskwatawa** (1775–1836), whose story of overcoming personal failures through religious visions and embracing a strict moral code has parallels with that of Hong Xiuquan, the Taiping leader. In his first thirty years, Tenskwatawa could claim few accomplishments. He had failed as a hunter and as a medicine man, had blinded himself in one eye, and had earned a reputation as an obnoxious braggart. All this changed in the spring of 1805, however, after he fell into a trance and experienced a vision. In this dream, Tenskwatawa encountered a heaven where the virtuous enjoyed the traditional Shawnee way of life and a hell where evildoers suffered punishments. Additional revelations followed, and Tenskwatawa soon stitched these together into a new social gospel that urged disciples to abstain from alcohol and return to traditional customs.

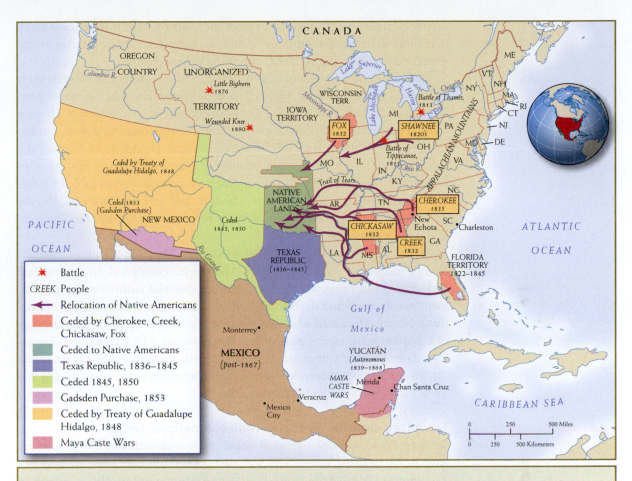

Map 16.4 Native American Revolts in the United States and Mexico

The new world order of expanding nation-states and industrial markets strongly affected indigenous peoples in North America.

- According to this map, where did the fiercest resistance to centralizing states and global market pressures occur?

- What regions of the United States were Native Americans forced to leave?

- According to your reading, to what extent, if any, did the natives' alternative visions create or preserve an alternative to the new emerging order?

Like other prophets, Tenskwatawa exhorted Native Americans to avoid contact with outside influences, to reduce their dependence on European trade goods and to sever their connections to Christian missionaries. If Native Americans obeyed these dictates, Tenskwatawa promised, the deer, which "were half a tree's length under the ground," would come back in abundant numbers to the earth's surface. Likewise, he claimed, Native Americans killed in conflict with colonial intruders would be resurrected, while evil Americans would depart from the country west of the Appalachians.

Like the Qing who responded to Hong's visions, American officials grew concerned as the Shawnee Prophet gathered followers. The spread of Tenskwatawa's message raised fears of a pan–Native American confederacy. Hoping to undermine the Shawnee Prophet's claims to supernatural power, territorial governor William Henry Harrison challenged Tenskwatawa to make the sun stand still. But Tenskwatawa one-upped Harrison. Having learned of an impending eclipse from white astronomers, Tenskwatawa assembled his followers on June 16, 1806. Right on schedule, and as if on command, the sky darkened. Claiming credit for the eclipse, Tenskwatawa saw his standing soar, as did the ranks of his disciples.

At the same time, however, Tenskwatawa had made plenty of enemies among his fellow Native Americans. His visions consigned drinkers to hell and singled out those who cooperated with colonial authorities for punishment in this world and the next. Indeed, Tenskwatawa condemned as witches those Native Americans who rejected his preaching in favor of the teachings of Christian missionaries and American authorities. (To be sure, Tenskwatawa's damnation of Christianized Native Americans was somewhat paradoxical, for missionary doctrines obviously influenced his vision of a burning hell for sinners and his crusade against alcohol.)

Tecumseh and the Wish for Native American Unity Although Tenskwatawa's accusations alienated some Native Americans, his prophecies gave heart to many more. This was particularly the case once his brother, Tecumseh (1768–1813), helped circulate the message of Native American renaissance among Native American villages from the Great Lakes to the Gulf Coast. On his journeys after 1805, Tecumseh did more than spread his brother's visions; he also wedded them to the idea of an enlarged Native American confederation. Moving around the Great Lakes and traveling across the southern half of the western country, Tecumseh preached the need for Native American unity. Always, he insisted that Native Americans resist any American attempts to get them to sell more land. In response, thousands of followers renounced their ties to colonial ways and prepared to combat the expansion of the United States.

By 1810, Tecumseh had emerged, at least in the eyes of American officials, as even more dangerous than his brother. Impressed by Tecumseh's charismatic organizational talents, William Harrison warned that this new "Indian menace" was forming "an Empire that would rival in glory" that of the Aztecs and the Incas. In 1811, while Tecumseh was traveling among southern tribes, Harrison had his troops attack Tenskwatawa's village, Prophet's Town, on the Tippecanoe River in what is now the state of Indiana.

The resulting battle was evenly fought, but the Native Americans eventually gave ground and American forces burned Prophet's Town. That defeat discredited Tenskwatawa, who had promised his followers protection from destruction at American hands. Spurned by his former disciples, including his brother, Tenskwatawa fled to Canada. Tecumseh soldiered on, supporting the British in the War of 1812 in the hope that a British victory would check American expansionism. But in 1813, with the war's outcome still in doubt and the pan–Native American confederacy still fragile, he perished at the Battle of the Thames, north of Lake Erie.

Native American Removals The discrediting of Tenskwatawa and the death of Tecumseh damaged the cause of Native American unity; then British betrayal dealt it a fatal blow. Following the war's end in 1814, the British withdrew their support and left the Native Americans south of the Great Lakes to fend for themselves against land-hungry American settlers and the armies of the United States. By 1815, American citizens outnumbered Native Americans in the western country by a seven-to-one margin, and this

Visions of Native American Unification (*Left*) A portrait of Tenskwatawa, the "Shawnee Prophet," whose visions stirred thousands of Native Americans in the Ohio Valley and Great Lakes to renounce dependence on colonial imports and resist the expansion of the United States. (*Right*) A portrait of his brother, Tecumseh, who succeeded in building a significant pan–Native American confederation, although it unraveled following his death at the Battle of the Thames in 1813 and the end of warfare between the United States and Britain the following year.

gap dramatically widened in the next few years. Recognizing the hopelessness of military resistance, Native Americans south of the Great Lakes resigned themselves to relocation. During the 1820s, most of the peoples north of the Ohio River were removed to lands west of the Mississippi River. During the 1830s, the southern tribes were cleared out, completing what amounted to an ethnic cleansing of Native American peoples from the region between the Appalachians and the Mississippi.

In the midst of these final removals, Tenskwatawa died, though his dream of an alternative to American expansion had faded for his people years earlier. Through the rest of the nineteenth century, however, other Native American prophets emerged, and their visions continued to inspire followers with the hope of an alternative to life under the colonial rule of the United States. But like Wovoka and the Ghost Dancers in 1890, these dreams failed to halt the expansion of the United States and the contraction of Native American lands.

THE CASTE WAR OF THE YUCATÁN

As in North America, the Spanish establishment of an expansionist nation-state in Mexico sparked widespread revolts by indigenous peoples. The most protracted was the Maya revolt in the Yucatán Peninsula. The revolt started in 1847, and its flames were not finally doused until the full occupation of the Yucatán by Mexican national troops in 1901.

The strength and endurance of the Maya revolt stemmed in large measure from the unusual features of the Spanish conquest in southern Mesoamerica. Because this area lacked precious metals and fertile lands, Spain and its rivals focused elsewhere—on central and northern Mexico and the Caribbean islands. As a result, the Maya Indians escaped forced recruitment for silver mines or sugar plantations. This does not mean that global processes side-stepped the Maya Indians. In fact, the production of dyes and foodstuffs for shipment to other regions drew the Yucatán into long-distance trading networks. Nonetheless, cultivation and commerce were much less disruptive to indigenous lives in the Yucatán than elsewhere in the New World.

Growing Pressures from the Sugar Trade Local developments, however, encroached on the Maya world in the nineteenth century. First, regional elites—mainly white, but often with the support of mixed-race (mestizo) populations—bickered for supremacy so long as the central authority of Mexico City remained weak. Weaponry flowed freely through the peninsula, and some combatants even appealed for Maya support. At the same time, regional and international trade spurred the spread of sugar estates, which threatened traditional corn cultivation in the Yucatán. Over the decades, plantations encroached on Maya properties. Planters used several devices to lure independent Maya to work, especially in the harvest. The most important device, debt peonage, involved giving small cash advances to Indian families, which obligated fathers and sons to work for meager wages to pay off the debts. In addition, Mexico's costly wars, culminating in a showdown with the United States in 1846, drove tax collectors and army recruiters into villages in search of revenues and soldiers.

The combination of material and physical threats was explosive. When a small band of Maya, fed up with rising taxes and ebbing autonomy, used firearms to drive back white intruders in 1847, they sparked a war that took a half century to complete. The rebels were primarily free Maya who had not yet been absorbed into the sugar economy. They wanted to dismantle old definitions of Indians as a caste—a status that deprived the Indians of legal and political equality with whites and that also subjected the Indians to special taxes. Thus, local Maya leaders, like Jacinto Pat and Cecilio Chi, upheld a republican model in the name of formal equality of all political subjects and devotion to a spiritual order that did not distinguish between Christians and non-Christians. "If the Indians revolt," one Maya rebel explained, "it is because the whites gave them reason; because the whites say they do not believe in Jesus Christ, because they have burned the cornfield."

The Caste War Horrified, the local white elites reacted to the uprising with vicious repression and dubbed the ensuing bloody conflict a caste war. In their view, the **Caste War of the Yucatán** was a struggle between forward-looking liberals and backward-looking Indians. At first, whites and mestizos were no match for the determined Maya, whose forces seized town after town. They especially targeted symbols of white power. With relish they demolished the whipping posts where Indians had endured public humiliation and punishment.

In the end, fortune, not political savvy, saved the Yucatán's whites. Settlement of the war with the United States in 1848 enabled Mexico City to rescue local elites in the Yucatán. With the help of a $15 million payment from Washington for giving up its northern provinces, Mexico could spend freely to build up its southern armies. The Mexican government soon fielded a force of 17,000 soldiers and waged a scorched-earth campaign to drive back the depleted Maya forces.

By 1849, the confrontation had entered a new phase in which Mexican troops engaged in mass repression of the Maya. Mexican armies set Indian fields and villages ablaze. Between 30 and 40 percent of the Maya population perished in the war and its repressive aftermath. The inhabitants of entire Maya cities pulled up stakes and withdrew to isolated districts protected by fortified villages. War between armies degenerated into guerrilla warfare between an occupying Mexican army and mobile bands of Maya squadrons, inflicting a gruesome toll on the invaders. As years passed, the war ground to a stalemate, especially once the U.S. funds ran out and Mexican soldiers began deserting in droves.

Caste War of the Yucatán
(1847–1901) Conflict between Maya Indians and the Mexican state over Indian autonomy and legal equality, which resulted in the Mexican takeover of the Yucatán Peninsula.

Caste War of the Yucatán
Fernando Castro Pacheco captured the violence of the Caste War in this 1974 painting.

Reclaiming a Maya Identity Warfare prompted a spiritual transformation that reinforced a purely Maya identity against the Mexican invaders' efforts to create a strong, centralized state. Thus, a struggle that began with demands for legal equality and relative cultural autonomy became a crusade for spiritual salvation and the complete cultural separation of the Maya Indians. A particularly influential group under José María Barrera retreated to a hamlet called Chan Santa Cruz. There, at the site where he found a cross shape carved into a mahogany tree, Barrera had a vision of a divine encounter. Thereafter, people in a swath of Yucatán villages around Chan Santa Cruz refashioned themselves as moral communities. Leaders created a polity, with soldiers, priests, and tax collectors pledging loyalty to the Speaking Cross. Like the followers of Hong in China's Taiping Rebellion, Indian rebels forged an alternative religion: it blended Christian rituals, faiths, and icons with Maya legends and beliefs. At the center was a stone temple, Balam Na ("House of God"), 100 feet long and 60 feet wide. Through pilgrimages to Balam Na and the secular justice of Indian judges, the Maya soon governed their domain in the Yucatán autonomously, almost completely cut off from the rest of Mexico.

The Mexican government threw its weight behind the strong-arm ruler General Porfirio Díaz (r. 1876–1911). The general sent one of his veteran commanders, Ignacio Bravo, to do what no other Mexican could accomplish: vanquish Chan Santa Cruz. When General Bravo finally entered the town, he found the once-imposing temple Balam Na covered in vegetation. Nature was reclaiming the territories of the Speaking Cross. Hunger and

Bravo's soldiers finally drove the Maya to work on white Mexican plantations; the alternative vision was vanquished. A combination of declining economic conditions and the soldiers under Ignacio Bravo brought an end to the Maya revolt.

THE REBELLION OF 1857 IN INDIA

Like Native Americans, the peoples of nineteenth-century India had a long history of opposition to colonial domination. Armed revolts had occurred since the onset of rule by the British East India Company (see Chapter 15). Nonetheless, the uprising of 1857 was unprecedented in its scale, and it posed a greater threat than had any previous rebellion.

India under Company Rule During the first half of the nineteenth century, the British rulers of India had dismantled most of the traditional powers of the nobility and the rights of peasants. Believing that the princely powers and landed aristocracies were out of date, the East India Company instituted far-reaching changes in administration. Lord Dalhousie, upon his appointment as governor-general in 1848, immediately began annexing what had been independent princely domains and stripping native aristocrats of their privileges. Swallowing one princely state after another, the British removed their former allies.

The government also decided to collect taxes directly from peasants, displacing the landed nobles as intermediaries. In disarming the landed nobility, the British threw the retainers and militia of the notables into unemployment, and by demanding high taxes from peasants, the British forced them to rely on moneylenders, who could take ownership of land when peasant proprietors failed to pay. Meanwhile, the company transferred judicial authority to an administration that was insulated from the Indian social hierarchy.

The most prized object for annexation was the kingdom of Awadh in northern India. (See Map 16.5.) Founded in 1722 by an Iranian adventurer, it was one of the first successor states to have gained a measure of independence from the Mughal ruler in Delhi. With access to the fertile resources of the Ganges plain, its opulent court in Lucknow was one place where Mughal splendor still survived. In 1765, the company imposed a treaty on Awadh under which the ruler paid an annual tribute for British troops stationed in his territory to "protect" his kingdom from internal and external enemies.

Treaty Violations and Annexation In 1856, citing misgovernment and deterioration in law and order, the East India Company violated its treaty obligations and sent its troops to Lucknow to take control of the province. Nawab Wajid Ali Shah, the poet-king of Awadh, whom the British saw as weak and immoral, refused to sign the treaty ceding control to the British.

DISTINGUISH the long-term influence of protest movements from their immediate political accomplishments in Asia, Islam, and Africa.

Map 16.5 Indian Rebellion of 1857

The Indian Rebellion of 1857 broke out first among the Indian soldiers of the British army. Other groups soon joined the struggle.

- According to this map, how many centers of rebellion were located in British territory and how many in dependent states?

- Why do you think the rebellion occurred in the interior of the subcontinent rather than along the coasts?

- In what way was the company's expansion into formerly autonomous areas during the first half of the nineteenth century a factor in the rebellion?

British empire
Dependent states
✳ Center of rebellion

The annexation of princely domains and the abolition of feudal privileges formed part of the developing practices of European imperialism. To the policy of annexation, Dalhousie added an ambitious program of building railroads, telegraph lines, and a postal network to unify the disjointed territory into a single "network of iron sinew" under British control. Dalhousie saw these infrastructures as key to developing India into a productive colony—a supplier of raw materials for British industry, and a market for its manufactures.

A year after Dalhousie's departure in 1856, India went up in flames. The spark that ignited the simmering discontent into a furious rebellion—the Rebellion of 1857—was the "greased cartridge" controversy. At the end of 1856, the British army, which consisted of many Hindu and Muslim recruits (sepoys) commanded by British officers, introduced the new Enfield rifle to replace the old-style musket. To load the rifle, soldiers had to bite the cartridge open. Although manufacturing instructions stated that linseed oil and beeswax be used to grease the cartridge, a rumor circulated that cow and pig fat had been used. Biting into cartridges greased with animal fat meant violating the Hindu and Muslim sepoys' religious traditions. The sepoys became convinced that there was a plot afoot to defile them and to compel their conversion to Christianity. So a wave of rebellion spread among the 270,000 Indian soldiers, who greatly outnumbered the 40,000 British soldiers employed to rule over 200 million Indians.

Rebellion Breaks Out The mutiny broke out on May 10, 1857, at the military barracks in Meerut. The revolt soon turned from a limited military mutiny into a widespread civil rebellion that involved peasants, artisans, day laborers, and religious leaders. While the insurgents did not eliminate the power of the East India Company, which managed to retain the loyalty of princes and landed aristocrats in some places, they did throw the company into a crisis. Before long, the mutineers in Delhi issued a proclamation declaring that because the British were determined to destroy the religion of both Hindus and Muslims, it was the duty of the wealthy and the privileged to support the rebellion. To promote Hindu-Muslim unity, rebel leaders asked Muslims to refrain from killing cows in deference to Hindu sentiments.

Although the dispossessed aristocracy and petty landholders led the rebellion, leaders also appeared from the lower classes. Bakht Khan, who had been a junior noncommissioned officer in the British army, became commander in chief of the rebel forces in Delhi, replacing one of the Mughal emperor's sons. And Devi Singh, a wealthy peasant, set himself up as a peasant king. Dressed in yellow, the insignia of Hindu royalty, he constituted a government of his own, modeling it on the British administration. While his imitation of company rule showed his respect for the British bureaucracy, he defied British authority by leading an armed peasantry against the hated local moneylenders. The call

The Indian Sepoys The sepoys were drawn from indigenous groups that the British considered to be "martial races." This photograph shows two rebels hanging from a gallows following the British suppression of the rebellion, in 1858, in Lucknow, Uttar Pradesh, India.

to popular forces also marked the rebel career of Maulavi Ahmadullah Shah, a Muslim theologian. He stood at the head of the rebel forces in Lucknow, leading an army composed primarily of ordinary soldiers and people from the lower orders. Claiming to be an "Incarnation of the Deity" and thus inspired by divine will, he emerged as a prophetic leader of the common people. He voiced his undying hatred of the British in religious terms, calling on Hindus and Muslims to destroy British rule and warning his followers against betrayal by landed authorities.

Participation by the Peasantry The presence of popular leadership points to the important role of the lower classes. Although feudal chieftains often brought them into the rebellion, the peasantry made it their own. The organizing principle of their uprising was the common experience of oppression. Thus, they destroyed anything that represented the authority of the company: prisons, factories, police posts, railway stations, European bungalows, and law courts. Equally significant, the peasantry attacked native moneylenders and local power holders who were seen as benefiting from company rule.

Vigorous and militant as the popular rebellion was, it was limited in its territorial and ideological horizons. To begin with, the uprisings were local in scale and vision. Peasant rebels attacked the closest seats of administration and sought to settle scores with their most immediate and visible oppressors. They generally did not carry their action beyond the village or collection of villages. Their loyalties remained intensely local, based on village attachments and religious, caste, and clan ties. Nor did popular militants seek to undo traditional hierarchies of caste and religion.

British Response Convinced that the rebellion was the result of plotting by a few troublemakers, the British reacted with brutal vengeance. Villages were torched, and rebels were tied to cannons and blown to bits to teach Indians a lesson in power.

By July 1858, the vicious campaign to restore British control had achieved its goal. Yet, in August, the British Parliament abolished company rule and the company itself and transferred responsibility for the governing of India to the crown. In November, Queen Victoria issued a proclamation guaranteeing religious toleration, promising improvements, and allowing Indians to serve in the government. She promised to honor the treaties and agreements with princes and chiefs and to refrain from interfering in religious matters. The insurgents had risen up not as a nation but as a multitude of communities acting independently; their determination to find a new order shocked the British and threw them into a panic. Having crushed the uprising, the British resumed the work of transforming India into a modern colonial state and economy. But the desire for radical alternatives and traditions of popular insurgency, though vanquished, did not vanish.

Conclusion

The nineteenth century was a time of turmoil and transformation. Powerful forces reconfigured the world as a place for capitalism, colonialism, and nation-states, while prophets, charismatic leaders, radicals, peasant rebels, and anticolonial insurgents arose to offer alternatives. Reflecting local circumstances and traditions, the struggles of these men and women for a different future opened up spaces for the ideas and activities of the lower classes.

Conventional historical accounts either neglect these struggles or fail to view them as a whole. These individuals were not just romantic, last-ditch resisters, as some scholars have argued. Even after defeat, their messages remained alive within their communities. Nor were their actions isolated and atypical events, for when viewed on a global scale they bring to light a world that looks very different from the one that became dominant. To see the Wahhabi movement in the Arabian Peninsula together with the Shawnee Prophet in North America, the utopians and radicals in Europe with the peasant insurgents in British India, and the Taiping rebels with the Maya in the Yucatán is to glimpse a world of marginalized regions and groups. It was a world that more powerful groups endeavored to suppress but could not erase.

In this world, prophets and rebel leaders usually cultivated power and prestige locally; the emergence of an alternative political or social movement in one region did not impinge on communities and political organizations in others. As much as these individuals had in common, they envisioned widely different kinds of futures. Even Karl Marx, who called the workers of the world to unite, was acutely aware that the call for a proletarian revolution applied only to the industrialized countries of Europe. Other dissenters had even more localized horizons. A world fashioned by movements for alternatives meant a world with multiple centers and different historical timelines.

What gave force to a different mapping of the world was the fact that common people were at the center of these alternative visions, and their voices, however muted, gained a place on the historical stage. The quest for various forms of equality defined efforts to reconstitute alternative worlds. In Islamic regions, the emphasis on equality in revitalization movements was evident in their mobilization of all Muslims, not just the elites. Likewise, charismatic military leaders in Africa, for all their use of raw power, used the framework of community to build new polities. The Taiping Rebellion distinguished itself by seeking to establish an equal society of men and women in service of the Heavenly Kingdom. Operating under very different conditions, European radicals imagined a society free from aristocratic privileges and bourgeois property. Anticolonial rebels and insurgents depended on local solidarities and proposed alternative moral communities. In so doing, these movements compelled ruling elites to adjust the way they governed. The next chapter explores this challenge.

TRACING THE GLOBAL STORYLINES

Focus On
Regional Variations in Alternative Visions

Europe
- European socialists and radicals envision a world free of exploitation and inequalities, while nationalists work to create new independent nation-states.

The Americas
- Native American prophets in the United States imagine a world restored to its customary ways and traditional rites.
- The Maya defy the central Mexican government in a rebellion known as the Caste War of the Yucatán.

The Islamic World and Africa
- Revivalist movements in the Arabian Peninsula and West Africa demand a return to traditional Islam.
- A charismatic warrior, Shaka, creates a powerful state in southern Africa.

Semi-colonial China
- An inspired prophetic figure, Hong Xiuquan, leads the Taiping Rebellion against the Qing dynasty and European encroachment on China.

Colonial India
- Indian troops mutiny against the British and attempt to restore Mughal rule.

CHRONOLOGY

	1750	1800	1850

The Islamic World and Africa
- Dan Fodio's movement in West Africa 1804–1809
- Wahhabis wage militant religious campaigns in Arabian Peninsula late eighteenth century–181
- Shaka creates Zulu state in South Africa 1818–1828

China
- Taiping Rebellion 1850–1864

Europe
- Free markets spread 1830s
- Fourier's utopian socialism gains popularity 1830s
- Revolutions across Europe; Marx and Engels publish *The Communist Manifesto* 1848

The Americas
- Tecumseh's rebellion in North America 1810–1813

India
- Indian Rebellion 1857–1858

THINKING ABOUT GLOBAL CONNECTIONS

- **Thinking about Exchange Networks and Alternative Visions** How did people around the world respond to the major changes of the French, American, and Industrial Revolutions? What difference did proximity to the European and American "core" make?

- **Thinking about Changing Power Relationships and Alternative Visions** What kind of challenges did the new order provoke? What kinds of traditions did those challenges draw on, and what kind of success did they have?

- **Thinking about Gender and Alternative Visions** Describe the role women played in millenarian protest movements during the nineteenth century, and explain the significance of gender to those movements.

Key Terms

Caste War of the Yucatán p. 765

Usman dan Fodio p. 746

liberalism p. 754

Marxism p. 758

Mfecane movement p. 747

millenarian p. 749

proletarians p. 758

Taiping Rebellion p. 750

Tenskwatawa p. 760

utopian socialism p. 756

Wahhabism p. 744

Go to **INQUIZITIVE** to see what you've learned—and learn what you've missed—with personalized feedback along the way.

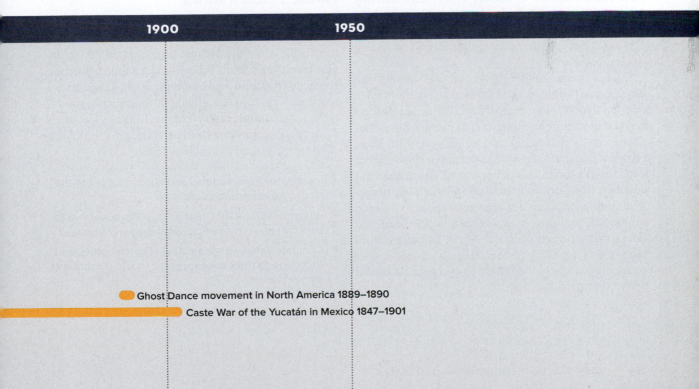

1900

1950

Ghost Dance movement in North America 1889–1890

Caste War of the Yucatán in Mexico 1847–1901

Global Themes and Sources

Comparing Alternatives to Nineteenth-Century Capitalism

While European capitalism and colonialism drove transformative changes in the nineteenth century, protest movements around the world envisioned a future based on other values. These selections provide radically different visions for the future—different from European capitalism and colonialism, and different from one another.

Tenskwatawa, Nana Asma'u, and Bahadur Shah all sought to revive local traditions, reject outside influences, and return to what they viewed as a pure, authentic past that had existed before market forces and new ideas began to unsettle the social order. The Taiping leaders, inspired by a millenarian Christianity, challenged central values of conventional Chinese society; they confronted the central role of the family and ancestral worship and urged their followers to see themselves as belonging to a single family. *The Communist Manifesto* sought nothing less than the complete transformation of society everywhere, starting from the industrial heartland of Europe and taking advantage of the technical advances of the machine age to satisfy everyone's basic needs and put an end to class conflict.

These sources highlight the causes behind the development of these alternative visions and provide an opportunity for comparison. It is particularly important to note the impact that market forces and new ideas of citizenship and equality had on these protests. Some of the protesters came in close contact with market forces and new ideas of citizenship and equality, while others flourished beyond their immediate influence. Consider how each society or group responded, and how it was shaped by the ideas and forces that emerged from the North Atlantic core in the period from 1750 to 1850. Finally, consider what common elements all of these documents share and where they part company.

Analyzing Alternatives to Nineteenth-Century Capitalism

- Analyze the influence of market forces and new ideas of equality in each document.

- Analyze the role of religion—whether explicit or implicit—in each document. Pay special attention to ideas of virtue, sin, and redemption.

- The creators of these sources all opposed capitalism and colonialism, but they reacted differently to what they viewed as outside influences. Place the authors of these sources on a continuum in terms of their rejection of those influences and their efforts to recapture an unsullied past.

PRIMARY SOURCE 16.1

Visions of the Great Good Spirit (1810), Tenskwatawa

In the first decade of the nineteenth century, the Shawnee leader Tenskwatawa recalled an earlier, happier time for the Native American peoples of the Great Lakes and Ohio Valley—it was a time before the coming of the Europeans. In this speech, Tenskwatawa recounts how contact with the "white men's goods" contaminated and corrupted the Indians. He urges them to reject the ways of white Americans and return to the pure ways of a precolonial past.

- Identify the commodities and habits that led to the Native Americans' decline.

- What rules did "Our Creator" give Tenskwatawa to help him make his people what they were before?

- Compare Tenskwatawa's view of commodities and exchange to the view expressed in *The Communist Manifesto*.

I died and went to the World Above, and saw it.

The punishments I saw terrify you! But listen, those punishments will be upon you unless you follow me through the door that I am opening for you!

Our Creator put us on this wide, rich land, and told us we were free to go where the game was, where the soil was good for planting. That was our state of true happiness. We did not have to beg for anything. Our Creator had taught us how to find and make everything we needed, from trees and plants and animals and stone. We lived in bark, and we wore only the skins of animals.

Thus were we created. Thus we lived for a long time, proud and happy. We had never eaten pig meat, nor tasted the poison called whiskey, nor worn wool from sheep, nor struck fire or dug earth with steel, nor cooked in iron, nor hunted and fought with loud guns, nor ever had diseases which soured our blood or rotted our organs. We were pure, so we were strong and happy.

For many years we traded furs to the English or the French, for wool blankets and guns and iron things, for steel awls and needles and axes, for mirrors, for pretty things made of beads and silver. And for liquor. This was foolish, but we did not know it. We shut our ears to the Great Good Spirit. We did not want to hear that we were being foolish.

But now those things of the white men have corrupted us, and made us weak and needful. Our men forgot how to hunt without noisy guns. Our women don't want to make fire without steel, or cook without iron, or sew without metal awls and needles, or fish without steel hooks. Some look in those mirrors all the time, and no longer teach their daughters to make leather or render bear oil. We learned to need the white men's goods, and so now a People who never had to beg for anything must beg for everything!

Some of our women married white men, and made half-breeds. Many of us now crave liquor. He whose filthy name I will not speak, he who was I before, was one of the worst of those drunkards. There are drunkards in almost every family. You know how bad this is.

And so you see what has happened to us. We were fools to take all these things that weakened us. We did not need them then, but we believe we need them

now. We turned our backs on the old ways. Instead of thanking the Great Spirit for all we used to have, we turned to the white man and asked them for more. So now we depend upon the very people who destroy us! This is our weakness! Our corruption! Our Creator scolded me, "If you had lived the way I taught you, the white men could never have got you under their foot!"

And that is why Our Creator purified me and sent me down to you full of the shining power, to make you what you were before!

No red man must ever drink liquor, or he will go and have the hot lead poured in his mouth!

No red man shall take more than one wife in the future. No red man shall run after women. If he is single, let him take a wife, and lie only with her.

Any red woman who is living with a white man must return to her people, and must leave her children with the husband, so that all nations will be pure in their blood.

Now hear what I was told about dealing with white men! These things we must do, to cleanse ourselves of their corruption!

Do not eat any food that is raised or cooked by a white person. It is not good for us. Eat not their bread made of wheat, for Our Creator gave us corn for our bread. Eat not the meat of their filthy swine, nor of their chicken fowls, nor the beef of their cattle, which are tame and thus have no spirit in them. Their foods will seem to fill your empty belly, but this deceives you for food without spirit does not nourish you.

There are two kinds of white men. There are the Americans, and there are the others. You may give your hand in friendship to the French, or the Spaniards, or the British. But the Americans are not like those. The Americans come from the slime of the sea, with mud and weeds in their claws, and they are a kind of crayfish serpent whose claws grab in our earth and take it from us. . . .

. . . Remember it is the wish of the Great Good Spirit that we have no more commerce with white men!

We may keep our guns, and if we need to defend ourselves against American white men, the guns will kill them because they are a white man's weapon. But arrows will kill American intruders, too! You must go to the grandfathers and have them teach you to make good bows and shape arrowheads, and you must recover the old hunting skills. . . .

We will no longer do the frolic dances that excite lust. The Great Good Spirit will teach me the old dances we did before the corruption, and from these dances we will receive strength and happiness!

Source: Elizabeth Cobbs Hoffman, Edward J. Blum, and Jon Gjerde (eds.), *Major Problems in American History*, vol. 1, *To 1877*, 3rd ed. (Boston: Wadsworth Cengage Learning, 2012), pp. 207–9.

PRIMARY SOURCE 16.2

A Female Muslim Voice in Africa (1838–1839), Nana Asma'u

The Islamic scholar, writer, and poet Nana Asma'u was the daughter of Usman dan Fodio, the leader of the Fulani Revolt in northern Nigeria at the turn of the nineteenth century. She was also deeply attached to her brother, Muhammad Bello, who succeeded their father as head of the Sokoto caliphate. Nana Asma'u composed this poem in praise of her brother, underlining his commitment to an Islamic way of life.

- Identify the values that the poet celebrates. What does she praise?

- What threats to the community does the poem identify? What is their nature, and where do they come from? Do they come from the outside world or the community's inner failings, or from some combination of these?

- What role does gender play in the poem? Why does Nana Asma'u write about her brother?

I give thanks to the King of Heaven, the One God. I invoke blessings on the Prophet and set down my poem.

The Lord made Heaven and earth and created all things, sent prophets to enlighten mankind.

Believe in them for your own sake, learn from them and be saved, believe in and act upon their sayings.

I invoke blessings on the Prophet who brought the Book, the Qur'an: he brought the *hadith* to complete the enlightenment.

Muslim scholars have explained knowledge and used it, following in the footsteps of the Prophet.

It is my intention to set down Bello's characteristics and explain his ways.

For I wish to assuage my loneliness, requite my love, find peace of mind through my religion.

These are his characteristics: he was learned in all branches of knowledge and feared God in public and in private.

He obeyed religious injunctions and distanced himself from forbidden things: this is what is known about him.

He concentrated on understanding what is right to know about the Oneness of God.

He preached to people and instructed them about God: he caused them to long for Paradise.

He set an example in his focus on eternal values: he strove to end oppression and sin.

He upheld the *shari'a*, honored it, implemented it aright, that was his way, everyone knows.

And he made his views known to those who visited him: he said to them "Follow the *shari'a*, which is sacred."

He eschewed worldly things and discriminated against anything of ill repute; he was modest and a repository of useful knowledge.

He was exceedingly level-headed and generous, he enjoyed periods of quietude: but was energetic when he put his hand to things.

He was thoughtful, calm, a confident statesman, and quick-witted.

He honored people's status: he could sort out difficulties and advise those who sought his help.

He had nothing to do with worldly concerns, but tried to restore to a healthy state things which he could. These were his characteristics.

He never broke promises, but faithfully kept them: he sought out righteous things. Ask and you will hear.

He divorced himself entirely from bribery and was totally scrupulous: He flung back at the givers money offered for titles.

One day Garange [chief of Mafora] sent him a splendid gift, but Bello told the messenger Zitaro to take it back.

He said to the envoy who had brought the bribe, "Have nothing to do with forbidden things."

And furthermore he said, "Tell him that the gift was sent for unlawful purposes; it is wrong to respond to evil intent."

He was able to expedite matters: he facilitated learning, commerce, and defense, and encouraged everything good.

He propagated good relationships between different tribes and between kinsmen. He afforded protection; everyone knows this.

When strangers came he met them, and taught about religious matters, explaining things: he tried to enlighten them.

He lived in a state of preparedness, he had his affairs in order and had an excellent intelligence service.

He had nothing to do with double agents and said it was better to ignore them, for they pervert Islamic principles.

He was a very pleasant companion to friends and acquaintances: he was intelligent, with a lively mind.

He fulfilled promises and took care of affairs, but he did not act hastily.

He shouldered responsibilities and patiently endured adversities.

He was watchful and capable of restoring to good order matters which had gone wrong.

He was resourceful and could undo mischief, no matter how serious, because he was a man of ideas.

He was gracious to important people and was hospitable to all visitors, including non-Muslims.

He drew good people close to him and distanced himself from people of ill repute.

Those are his characteristics. I have recounted a few examples that are sufficient to provide a model for emulation and benefit.

May God forgive him and have mercy on him: May we be united with him in Paradise, the place we aspire to.

For the sake of the Prophet, the Compassionate, who was sent with mercy to mankind.

May God pour blessings on the Prophet and his kinsmen and all other followers.

May God accept this poem. I have concluded it in the year 1254 AH [after *hijra*, the Muslim dating system].

Source: "Gikku Bello," in *One Woman's Jihad: Nana Asma'u, Scholar and Scribe*, by Beverly B. Mack and Jean Boyd (Bloomington: Indiana University Press, 2000), pp. 97–99.

PRIMARY SOURCE 16.3

The Azamgarh Proclamation (1857), Bahadur Shah

The Indian leaders of the Rebellion of 1857 issued numerous proclamations. The Azamgarh Proclamation, excerpted below, is one of many. The emperor, Bahadur Shah, issued it in August 1857 on behalf of the mutineers who had seized the garrison town of Azamgarh. It attacks the British for subverting Indian traditions and calls on the rebellion's followers to restore the precolonial order.

- Identify the rebels' main grievances against the English.
- Analyze the role of religion in the rebellion.
- Explain the significance of commerce and property for the rebels.

25th. August, 1857.

It is well known to all, that in this age the people of Hindoostan, both Hindoos and Mohammedans, are being ruined under the tyranny and oppression of the infidel and treacherous English. It is therefore the bounden duty of all the wealthy people of India, especially of those who have any sort of connection with any of the Mohammedan royal families, and are considered the pastors and masters of their people, to stake their lives and property for the well being of the public. With the view of effecting this general good, several princes belonging to the royal family of Delhi, have dispersed themselves in the different parts of India, Iran, Turan, and Afghanistan, and have been long since taking measures to compass their favourite end; and it is to accomplish this charitable object that one of the aforesaid princes has, at the head of an army of Afghanistan, &c., made his appearance in

India; and I, who am the grandson of Abul Muzuffer Serajuddin Bahadur Shah Ghazee, King of India, having in the course of circuit come here to extirpate the infidels residing in the eastern part of the country, and to liberate and protect the poor helpless people now groaning under their iron rule, have, by the aid of the *Majahdeens* [religious warriors], erected the standard of Mohammed, and persuaded the orthodox Hindoos who had been subject to my ancestors, and have been and are still accessories in the destruction of the English, to raise the standard of Mahavir.

Several of the Hindoo and Mussalman chiefs, who have long since quitted their homes for the preservation of their religion, and have been trying their best to root out the English in India, have presented themselves to me, and taken part in the reigning Indian crusade, and it is more than probable that I shall very shortly receive succours from the West. Therefore, for the information of the public, the present *Ishtahar*, consisting of several sections, is put in circulation, and it is the imperative duty of all to take it into their careful consideration, and abide by it. Parties anxious to participate in the common cause, but having no means to provide for themselves, shall receive their daily subsistence from me; and be it known to all, that the ancient works, both of the Hindoos and the Mohammedans, the writings of the miracle-workers, and the calculations of the astrologers, pundits, and rammals, all agree in asserting that the English will no longer have any footing in India or elsewhere. Therefore it is incumbent on all to give up the hope of the continuation of the British sway, side with me, and deserve the consideration of the Badshahi, or imperial Government, by their individual exertion in promoting the common good, and thus attain their respective ends; otherwise if this golden opportunity slips away, they will have to repent of their folly, as it is very aptly said by a poet in two fine couplets, the drift whereof is "Never let a favourable opportunity slip, for in the field of opportunity you are to meet with the ball of fortune; but if you do not avail yourself of the opportunity that offers itself, you will have to bite your finger through grief."

No person, at the misrepresentation of the well-wishers of the British Government, ought to conclude from the present slight inconveniences usually attendant on revolutions, that similar inconveniences and troubles should continue when the Badshahi Government is established on a firm basis; and parties badly dealt with by any sepoy or plunderer, should come up and represent their grievances to me, and receive redress at my hands; and for whatever property they may lose in the reigning disorder, they will be recompensed from the public treasury when the Badshahi Government is well fixed. . . .

Section II—Regarding Merchants. It is plain that the infidel and treacherous British Government have monopolized the trade of all the fine and valuable merchandise, such as indigo, cloth, and other articles of shipping, leaving only the trade of trifles to the people, and even in this they are not without their share of the profits, which they secure by means of customs and stamp fees, &c. in money suits, so that the people have merely a trade in name. Besides this, the profits of the traders are taxed, with postages, tolls, and subscriptions for schools, &c. Notwithstanding all these concessions, the merchants are liable to imprisonment and disgrace at the instance or complaint of a worthless man. When the Badshahi Government is established, all these aforesaid fraudulent practices shall be dispensed with, and the trade of every article, without exception, both by land and water, shall be open to the native merchants of India, who will have the benefit of the Government steam-vessels and steam-carriages for the conveyance of their merchandise gratis; and merchants having no capital of their own shall be assisted from the public treasury. It is therefore the duty of every merchant to take part in the war, and aid the Badshahi Government with his men and money, either secretly or openly, as may be consistent with his position or interest, and forswear his allegiance to the British Government.

Section III—Regarding Public Servants. It is not a secret thing, that under the British Government, natives employed in the civil and military services, have little respect, low pay, and no manner of influence; and all the posts of dignity and emolument in both the departments, are exclusively bestowed on Englishmen for natives in the military service, after having devoted the greater part of their lives, attain to the post of soobadar (the very height of their hopes) with a salary of 60r. or 70r. per mensem; and those in the civil service obtain the post of Sudder Ala, with a salary of 500 r. a month, but no influence, jagheer, or present. . . .

Therefore, all the natives in the British service ought to be alive to their religion and interest, and, abjuring their loyalty to the English, side with the Badshahi Government, and obtain salaries of 200 or 300 rupees per month for the present, and be entitled to high posts in future. If they, for any reason, cannot at present declare openly against the English, they can heartily wish ill to their cause, and remain passive spectators of passing events, without taking any active share therein. But at the same time they should indirectly assist the Badshahi Government, and try their best to drive the English out of the country. . . .

Section IV—Regarding Artisans. It is evident that the Europeans, by the introduction of English articles into India, have thrown the weavers, the cotton dressers, the carpenters, the blacksmiths, and the shoemakers, &c., out of employ, and have engrossed their occupations, so that every description of native artisan has been reduced to beggary. But under the Badshahi Government the native artisans will exclusively be employed in the services of the kings, the rajahs, and the rich; and this will no doubt ensure their prosperity. Therefore these artisans ought to renounce the English services, and assist the *Majahdeens,* engaged in the war, and thus be entitled both to secular and eternal happiness.

Section V—Regarding Pundits, Fakirs and other learned persons. The pundits and fakirs being the guardians of the Hindoo and Mohammedan religions respectively, and the Europeans being the enemies of both the religions, and as at present a war is raging against the English on account of religion, the pundits and fakirs are bound to present themselves to me, and take their share in the holy war. . . .

Lastly, be it known to all, that whoever, out of the above named classes, shall after the circulation of this Ishtahar, still cling to the British Government, all his estates shall be confiscated, and his property plundered, and he himself, with his whole family, shall be imprisoned, and ultimately put to death.

Source: Ainslie T. Embree (ed.), *1857 in India: Mutiny or War of Independence?* (Boston: D. C. Heath, 1963), pp. 1–3.

The Principles of the Heavenly Nature (1854), Taiping Heavenly Kingdom

In this excerpt from 1854, written after the Taiping had established a capital in Nanjing and after initial victories had given way to a decline in morale and cohesion, the Taiping leaders envision a radically new community based on the values of a messianic Christianity.

- Explain the significance of the family. Why do the authors speak of their members as brothers and sisters?

- What do the authors mean by "degeneration"? What "degenerated" and why?

- Analyze the relationship between external challenges and internal weakness in this text.

We marquises and chancellors hold that our brothers and sisters have been blessed by the Heavenly Father and the Heavenly Elder Brother, who saved the ensnared and drowning and awakened the deluded; they have cast off worldly sentiments and now follow the true Way. They cross mountains and wade rivers, not even ten thousand *li* being too far for them to come, to uphold together the true Sovereign. Armed and bearing shield and spear, they carry righteous banners that rise colorfully. Husband and wife, men and women, express common indignation and lead the advance. It can be said that they are determined to uphold Heaven and to requite the nation with loyalty.

In the ten thousand nations of the world everyone is given life, nourished, protected, and blessed by the Heavenly Father, the Supreme Ruler and Lord God-on-High. Thus the Heavenly Father, the Supreme Ruler and Lord God-on-High, is the universal father of man in all the ten thousand nations of the world. There is no man who should not be grateful, there is no man who should not reverently worship Him. . . .

However, worldly customs daily degenerated. There were even those who likened themselves to rulers, and, being deluded in heart and nature, arrogant yet at fault, and falsely self-exalted, forbade the prime minister and those below to sacrifice to Heaven. Then [these men] competed in establishing false gods and worshiping them, thus opening up the ways of the devilish demons. The people of the world all followed in like fashion, and this became firmly fixed in their minds. Thereupon, after a considerable time, they did not know their own errors. Hence the Heavenly Father, the Lord God, in view of mortal man's serious crime of disobedience, at his first anger, sent down forty days and forty nights of heavy rain, the vast waters spreading in all directions and drowning mortal man. Only Noah and his family had unceasingly worshiped the Heavenly Father, the Supreme Ruler and Lord God-on-High; therefore, relying on the Heavenly grace, they were fortunate and they alone were preserved. In this, the first instance of the Heavenly Father's great anger, was the great proof of his great powers displayed.

After the Flood, the devilish king of Egypt, whose ambition was mediocrity and who was possessed by the demons, envied the Israelites in their worship of God and bitterly persecuted them. Therefore, the Heavenly Father in his great anger led the Israelites out of Egypt. In this, the second instance of the Heavenly Father's great anger, was the great proof of his great powers displayed.

However, the rulers and people of that time still had not completely forgotten the Heavenly grace. But since the emergence of Daoism in the [Chinese] Qin [dynasty] and the welcoming of Buddhism in the Han [dynasty], the delusion of man by the demons has day by day increased, and all men have forgotten the grace and virtue of the Heavenly Father. . . . The Heavenly Father once again became greatly angered; yet if he were to annihilate them completely, he could not bear it in his heart; if he were to tolerate them, it would not be consonant with righteousness. At that time, the elder son of the Heavenly Father, the Heavenly Elder Brother Jesus, shouldered the great burden and willingly offered to sacrifice his life to redeem the sins of the men of the world. . . .

Let us ask your elder and younger brothers: formerly the people sacrificed only to the demons; they worshiped the demons and appealed to the demons only because they desired the demons to protect them. Yet how could they think that the demons could really protect them? . . . To worship them is of no avail. However, the men of the world sank even

deeper, not knowing how to awaken themselves. Therefore, the Heavenly Father again became angry.

In the *dingyou* year [1837], our Heavenly Father displayed the heavenly grace and dispatched angels to summon the Heavenly King up to Heaven. There He clearly pointed out the demons' perversities and their deluding of the world. He also invested the Heavenly King with a seal and a sword; He ordered the Savior, the Heavenly Elder Brother, Jesus, to take command of the Heavenly soldiers and Heavenly generals and to aid the Heavenly King, and to attack and conquer from Heaven earthward, layer by layer, the innumerable demons. After their victory they returned to Heaven and the Heavenly Father, greatly pleased, sent the Heavenly King down upon the earth to become the true Taiping Sovereign of the ten thousand nations of the world and to save the people of the world. He also bade him not to be fearful and to effect these matters courageously, for whenever difficulties appeared, the Heavenly Father would assume direction and the Heavenly Elder Brother would shoulder the burden.

***

We brothers and sisters, enjoying today the greatest mercy of our Heavenly Father, have become as one family and are able to enjoy true blessings; each of us must always be thankful. Speaking in terms of our ordinary human feelings, it is true that each has his own parents and there must be a distinction in family names; it is also true that as each has his own household, there must be a distinction between this boundary and that boundary. Yet we must know that the ten thousand names derive from the one name, and the one name from one ancestor. Thus our origins are not different. Since our Heavenly Father gave us birth and nourishment, we are of one form though of separate bodies, and we breathe the same air though in different places. This is why we say, "All are brothers within the four seas." Now, basking in the profound mercy of Heaven, we are of one family. . . .

We brothers, our minds having been awakened by our Heavenly Father, joined the camp in the earlier days to support our Sovereign, many bringing parents, wives, uncles, brothers, and whole families. It is a matter of course that we should attend to our parents and look after our wives and children, but when one first creates a new rule, the state must come first and the family last, public interests first and private interests last. Moreover, as it is advisable to avoid suspicion [of improper conduct] between the inner [female] and the outer [male] and to distinguish between male and female, so men must have male quarters and women must have female quarters; only thus can we be dignified and avoid confusion. There must be no common mixing of the male and female groups, which would cause debauchery and violation of Heaven's commandments. Although to pay respects to parents and to visit wives and children occasionally are in keeping with human nature and not prohibited, yet it is only proper to converse before the door, stand a few steps apart and speak in a loud voice; one must not enter the sisters' camp or permit the mixing of men and women. Only thus, by complying with rules and commands, can we become sons and daughters of Heaven.

At the present time, the remaining demons have not yet been completely exterminated and the time for the reunion of families has not yet arrived. We younger brothers and sisters must be firm and patient to the end, and with united strength and a single heart we must uphold God's principles and wipe out the demons immediately. With peace and unity achieved, then our Heavenly Father, displaying his mercy, will reward us according to our merits. Wealth, nobility, and renown will then enable us brothers to celebrate the reunion of our families and enjoy the harmonious relations of husband and wife. Oh, how wonderful that will be! The task of a thousand times ten thousand years also lies in this; the happiness and emoluments of a thousand times ten thousand years also lie in this; we certainly must not abandon it in one day.

Source: Wm. Theodore de Bary and Richard Lufrano (eds.), *Sources of Chinese Tradition*, vol. 2, *From 1600 through the Twentieth Century*, 2nd ed. (New York: Columbia University Press, 2000), pp. 226–30.

Bourgeoisie and Proletariat (1848), Karl Marx and Friedrich Engels

At the behest of an international revolutionary organization, the Communist League, in 1847 Karl Marx and Friedrich Engels set out to draft a confession of faith. While Engels's initial draft was set in the form of a catechism, the final document, rewritten by Marx, took the following, combative, critical form. Published in January 1848, just before revolution in Paris set off rebellion across Europe, *The Communist Manifesto* foretold the inevitable overthrow of bourgeois-dominated capitalism by the working classes.

....

- According to Marx and Engels, how does class conflict change over time? Pay special attention to the range of groups opposed to one another.

- Define the term *bourgeois*. How are the bourgeoisie different from all the prior dominant classes in history?

- This document was initially conceived as a declaration of faith. What role, if any, does religion play in this final version?

....

A spectre is haunting Europe—the spectre of communism. . . .

The history of all hitherto existing society is the history of class struggles.

Freeman and slave, patrician and plebeian, lord and serf, guild-master and journeyman, in a word, oppressor and oppressed, stood in constant opposition to one another, carried on an uninterrupted, now hidden, now open fight, a fight that each time ended, either in a revolutionary reconstitution of society at large, or in the common ruin of the contending classes.

In the earlier epochs of history, we find almost everywhere a complicated arrangement of society into various orders, a manifold gradation of social rank. In ancient Rome we have patricians, knights, plebeians, slaves; in the Middle Ages, feudal lords, vassals, guild-masters, journeymen, apprentices, serfs; in almost all of these classes, again, subordinate gradations.

The modern bourgeois society that has sprouted from the ruins of feudal society has not done away with class antagonisms. It has but established new classes, new conditions of oppression, new forms of struggle in place of the old ones.

Our epoch, the epoch of the bourgeoisie, possesses, however, this distinct feature: it has simplified class antagonisms. Society as a whole is more and more splitting up into two great hostile camps, into two great classes directly facing each other—Bourgeoisie and Proletariat.

From the serfs of the Middle Ages sprang the chartered burghers of the earliest towns. From these burgesses the first elements of the bourgeoisie were developed. . . .

The bourgeoisie, wherever it has got the upper hand, has put an end to all feudal, patriarchal, idyllic relations. It has pitilessly torn asunder the motley feudal ties that bound man to his "natural superiors," and has left remaining no other nexus between man and man than naked self-interest, than callous "cash payment.". . .

We see then: the means of production and of exchange, on whose foundation the bourgeoisie built itself up, were generated in feudal society. At a certain stage in the development of these means of production and of exchange, the conditions under which feudal society produced and exchanged, the feudal organisation of agriculture and manufacturing industry, in one word, the feudal relations of property became no longer compatible with the already developed productive forces; they became so many fetters. They had to be burst asunder; they were burst asunder. . . .

It is enough to mention the commercial crises that by their periodical return put the existence of the entire bourgeois society on its trial, each time more threateningly. In these crises, a great part not only of the existing products, but also of the previously created productive forces, are periodically destroyed. In these crises, there breaks out an epidemic that, in all earlier epochs, would have seemed an absurdity—the epidemic of over-production. . . .

Because there is too much civilisation, too much means of subsistence, too much industry, too much commerce. The productive forces at the disposal of society no longer tend to further the development of the conditions of bourgeois property; on the contrary, they have become too powerful for these conditions, by which they are fettered, and so soon as they overcome these fetters, they bring disorder into the whole of bourgeois society, endanger the existence of bourgeois property. The conditions of bourgeois society are too narrow to comprise the wealth created by them. . . .

The weapons with which the bourgeoisie felled feudalism to the ground are now turned against the bourgeoisie itself.

But not only has the bourgeoisie forged the weapons that bring death to itself; it has also called into existence the men who are to wield those weapons—the modern working class—the proletarians. . . .

Owing to the extensive use of machinery, and to the division of labour, the work of the proletarians has lost all individual character, and, consequently, all charm for the workman. He becomes an appendage of the machine, and it is only the most simple, most monotonous, and most easily acquired knack, that is required of him. Hence, the cost of production of a workman is restricted, almost entirely, to the means of subsistence that he requires for maintenance, and for the propagation of his race. But the price of a commodity, and therefore also of labour, is equal to its cost of production. . . .

Modern Industry has converted the little workshop of the patriarchal master into the great factory of the industrial capitalist. Masses of labourers, crowded into the factory, are organised like soldiers. As privates of the industrial army they are placed under the command of a perfect hierarchy of officers and sergeants. Not only are they slaves of the bourgeois class, and of the bourgeois State; they are daily and hourly enslaved by the machine, by the overlooker, and, above all, by the individual bourgeois manufacturer himself. The more openly this despotism proclaims gain to be its end and aim, the more petty, the more hateful and the more embittering it is. . . .

But with the development of industry, the proletariat not only increases in number; it becomes concentrated in greater masses, its strength grows, and it feels that strength more. The various interests and conditions of life within the ranks of the proletariat are more and more equalised, in proportion as machinery obliterates all distinctions of labour, and nearly everywhere reduces wages to the same low level. The growing competition among the bourgeois, and the resulting commercial crises, make the wages of the workers ever more fluctuating. The increasing improvement of machinery, ever more rapidly developing, makes their livelihood more and more precarious; the collisions between individual workmen and individual bourgeois take more and more the character of collisions between two classes. Thereupon, the workers begin to form combinations (Trades' Unions) against the bourgeois; they club together in order to keep up the rate of wages; they found permanent associations in order to make provision beforehand for these occasional revolts. Here and there, the contest breaks out into riots.

Now and then the workers are victorious, but only for a time. The real fruit of their battles lies, not in the immediate result, but in the ever expanding union of the workers. This union is helped on by the improved means of communication that are created by modern industry, and that place the workers of different localities in contact with one another. It was just this contact that was needed to centralise the numerous local struggles, all of the same character, into one national struggle between classes. But every class struggle is a political struggle. And that union, to attain which the burghers of the Middle Ages, with their miserable highways, required centuries, the modern proletarian, thanks to railways, achieve in a few years. . . .

Of all the classes that stand face to face with the bourgeoisie today, the proletariat alone is a really revolutionary class. The other classes decay and finally disappear in the face of Modern Industry; the proletariat is its special and essential product. . . .

The advance of industry, whose involuntary promoter is the bourgeoisie, replaces the isolation of the labourers, due to competition, by the revolutionary combination, due to association. The development of Modern Industry, therefore, cuts from under its feet the very foundation on which the bourgeoisie produces and appropriates products. What the bourgeoisie therefore produces, above all, are its own grave-diggers. Its fall and the victory of the proletariat are equally inevitable.

Source: *The Marx-Engels Reader*, edited by Robert C. Tucker (New York: Norton, 1972), pp. 335–45.

Interpreting Visual Evidence

The Gender of Nations

Nations are abstractions. They have no material form. The scholar Benedict Anderson famously referred to them as "imagined communities," groups of people who have never met, who may not even speak the same language or worship the same god(s), and yet who come to think of themselves as sharing something profound in common, such as being an American, or an Egyptian, or Chinese. In order to create this sort of community, nationalists have had to represent their nations visually, often in human form and more often as women than as men. For every John Bull (England) or Uncle Sam (the United States), there were several Mariannes (France) or Ranis of Jhansi (India). Especially in areas where few people could read, images and iconography played a vital role in spreading the idea of nationalism to the masses.

The attributes of the chosen figures provide insight into different nationalist movements. The figures' ties to real or invented historical traditions often reflect how these movements defined themselves in opposition to established authorities. In the first image, *Liberty Leading the People* (1830), the French Romantic painter Eugène Delacroix represents a barefoot, bare-chested woman, Marianne, leading a cross-class group of rebels against King Charles X. She wears a Phrygian bonnet, which had become popular during the Revolution of 1789–1799. In the 1890s, an Egyptian Jew named Ya'qub Sanu'a published a nationalist journal in Paris called *Abu Naddara*, which helped introduce Egypt to cartoons. In one issue he presents a veiled Egypt, with France and Russia by her side, confronting Great Britain. Finally, the Rani of Jhansi was the queen of the Maratha-ruled state of Jhansi in the north-central part of India and a leading figure in the Rebellion of 1857. She later became a nationalist icon, as the twentieth-century watercolor here illustrates, and a symbol of heroic resistance against the British.

Questions for Analysis

1. Why do you think nationalists in all of these countries, unlike those in Great Britain and the United States, used female symbols for the nation? What kind of established political authority did they challenge, and how did that challenge differ from the British and American cases?

2. Why do you think Sanu'a, a cosmopolitan liberal who had criticized the subordination of women,

presented Egypt as a fully covered, veiled woman? To whom do you think he was appealing?

3. To what extent does the image of the Rani of Jhansi look backward and invoke history, at least implicitly? To what extent does it look forward and make claims about the nature of contemporary India?

Delacroix, *Liberty Leading the People*.

ILLUSION DÉTRUITE

Sanu'a, cartoon in *Abu Naddara*.

The Rani of Jhansi.

17

Nations and Empires

1850–1914

In 1895, the Cuban patriot José Martí launched a rebellion against the last Spanish holdings in the Americas. The anti-Spanish struggle continued until 1898, when Spain withdrew from Cuba and Puerto Rico. Martí hoped to bring freedom to a new Cuban nation and equality to all Cubans. But even as he helped secure freedom from the declining Spanish Empire, he could not prevent military occupation and political domination of Cuba by the world's newest imperial power, the United States. Martí's hopes and frustrations found parallels around the world.

After 1850, the building of nation-states in Europe, the Americas, and Oceania and the expansion of their empires changed the map of the world, exhilarating some peoples and frustrating others. Those who benefited most were Europeans and peoples of European descent. During these decades the nation-states of Europe, now locked in intense political and economic rivalry, projected their power across the entire world. Much of the rivalry among European states intensified through disruptions in the European balance of power, caused by the unification of two new states (Italy and Germany). Across the Atlantic, the United States abandoned its anticolonial origins and annexed overseas possessions. Yet imperial expansion did not go unchallenged. It encountered resistance from communities being incorporated into the new empires. In Asia and Africa resisters struggled to repel their invaders, often demanding the right to govern themselves.

The second half of the nineteenth century witnessed the simultaneous—and entwined—advance

Core Objectives

- **IDENTIFY** the institutions that enabled elites in western Europe, the Americas, and Japan to consolidate nation-states, and **ANALYZE** the degree to which they succeeded during this period.

- **EXPLAIN** the roles that industrialization, science, and technology played in the expansion of powerful states into the rest of the world.

- **COMPARE** the reactions to imperialism in Africa and Asia, and **EVALUATE** how effective these responses were.

- **ANALYZE** the extent to which colonies contributed to the wealth and political strength of the nation-states that controlled them.

of nationalism and imperialism. These decades also saw the further expansion of industrialization. Taken together, the era's political and economic developments allowed western Europe and the United States to attain primacy in world affairs. But tensions inside these states and their empires, as well as within other states, made the new world order anything but stable.

Global Storylines

- Nation-state building and imperial expansion change the map of the world.

- Industrialization, science, and technology enable states in North America and western Europe—and, to a lesser extent, Japan—to overpower other regions politically, militarily, and economically.

- European, American, and Japanese imperialists encounter significant opposition in Africa and Asia.

Consolidating Nations and Constructing Empires

During the second half of the nineteenth century, the idea of building nation-states engulfed the globe, and nationalism became closely linked to imperialism. Enlightenment thinkers had emphasized the importance of nations, defined as peoples who shared a common past, territory, and culture. To many people it seemed natural that once absolutist rulers had fallen, governments should draw their power and legitimacy from those who lived within their borders and that the body of institutions governing each territory should be uniquely concerned with promoting the welfare of that particular people. This seemed such a natural process that little thought was given to the relationship between "nation" and "state," between the people and their government; national states were simply supposed to well up from the people's longing for liberty and togetherness.

BUILDING NATIONALISM

More often than not, however, local elites created nations. They did so by compelling diverse groups of people and regions to accept a unified network of laws, a central administration, time zones, national markets, and a single regional dialect as the "national" language. To overcome strong regional identities, state administrators broadened public education in the national language and imposed universal military service to build a national army. In this way, dominant elites spread their values and institutions outward to regions throughout each nation and beyond their borders. While a handful of nation-states were already well established in the mid-nineteenth century, two of the most important—Italy and Germany—were newly created in this period, forged through strategic military contests.

EXPANDING THE EMPIRES

The processes of nation building also required the acquisition of new territories, often overseas, a development that was called **imperialism**. Rulers measured national strength not only by their people's unity but also by their economic power and the conquest of new territories. Thus, Germany, France, the United States, Russia, and Japan challenged Britain's leadership in overseas trade by developing their industries and seizing new territories.

Imperial rule facilitated a widespread movement of labor, capital, commodities, and information. As scholars studied previously unknown tribes and races, new schools taught colonized peoples the languages, religions, scientific practices, and cultural traditions of their colonizers. Publications and

THE BIG PICTURE

What institutions enabled elites in western Europe, the Americas, and Japan to consolidate nation-states?

imperialism
Acquisition of new territories by a state and the incorporation of these territories into a political system as subordinate colonies.

products from the "mother country" circulated widely among indigenous elites. Yet colonies were seen as subordinate to the mother country and were given little or no representation in home governments. In this sense, nation and empire were in tension with one another.

Expansion and Nation Building in the Americas

Core Objectives

ANALYZE the degree to which elites in the Americas succeeded in consolidating nation-states.

Once freed from European control, the elites of the Americas set about creating political communities of their own. By the 1850s, they shared a desire both to create widespread loyalty to their political institutions and to expand territorial domains. This also meant finding ways to settle hinterlands that previously belonged to indigenous populations.

Although nation-states took shape throughout the world, the Americas saw the most complete assimilation of new possessions. Instead of treating outlying areas as colonial outposts, American nation-state builders turned them into new provinces. With the help of rifles, railroads, schools, and land surveys, frontiers became staging areas for the expanding populations of North and South American societies. For indigenous peoples, however, such national expansion meant the loss of traditional lands on a vast scale, and many lost lives.

THE UNITED STATES

Military might, diplomacy, and the power of numbers enabled the United States to claim territory that spanned the North American continent. (See Map 17.1.) At its independence, the new country established a barely united confederation of states. Native American resistance and Spanish and British rivalry hemmed in the Americans of European descent. At the same time, the disunited states threatened to break apart, as questions of states' rights and of slavery versus free labor intruded into national politics. Yet, rallying to the rhetoric of **Manifest Destiny**, which maintained that it was God's will for the United States to "overspread" North America, American whites pushed their territorial claims and boundaries westward. They acquired territories via purchase agreements and treaties with France, Spain, and Britain, and via warfare and treaties with diverse Native American nations and Mexico.

Manifest Destiny
Belief that it was God's will for the American people to expand their territory and political processes across the North American continent.

Civil War and States' Rights Westward expansion proved the undoing of the American nation. The question was whether newly acquired lands would be open to slavery or restricted to free labor. Following the 1860 election of Abraham Lincoln, who pledged to halt the expansion of slavery, the United States divided between North and South and plunged into a gruesome Civil War (1861–1865).

Canadian Westward Expansion
- Settled before 1825
- Settled between 1825 and 1871
- Settled between 1871 and 1891
- Settled between 1891 and 1911
- Boundary of original Confederation, 1867
- Rupert's Land territories added to provinces, 1912

United States Westward Expansion
- United States, 1783
- Louisiana Purchase, 1803
- West Florida annexation, 1810, 1813
- East Florida ceded by Spain, 1819
- Acquired from Britain, 1818, 1842
- Texas annexation, 1845
- Oregon Country, 1846
- Ceded by Mexico, 1848
- Gadsden Purchase, 1853
- Acquired from Russia, 1867
- Annexed, 1894
- Railroad

Map 17.1 U.S. and Canadian Westward Expansion, 1803–1912

Americans and Canadians expanded westward in the second half of the nineteenth century, aided greatly by railways.

- How do you account for the differences between the transcontinental railroads in the United States and Canada?
- When did Canada and the United States complete their respective territorial expansions? Why were these expansions not continuous, moving from east to west?
- How did territorial expansion strengthen Canadian and American nationalism?

The bloody conflict led to the abolition of slavery, and the struggle to extend voting and citizenship rights to male freed slaves qualified the Civil War as a second American Revolution. Abraham Lincoln had promised a new model of freedom for a state reborn out of bloodshed. Its cornerstone would be the incorporation of freed slaves as citizens of the United States. Yet experiments in biracial democracy during the Reconstruction period (1867–1877) were short-lived. In the decades after the Civil War, counterrevolutionary pressure led to the denial of voting rights to African Americans and the restoration of (white, patriarchal) planter rule in the Southern states. This pressure was spearheaded by the terrorism of some former Confederates who sought to reverse African Americans' legal and political gains and to restore white planters to power in the South.

Nonetheless, the war brought enduring changes across the United States. The defeat of the South established the preeminence of the national government. After the Civil War, Americans learned to speak of their nation in the singular ("the United States is" in contrast to "the United States are"). With an invigorated nationalism came a stronger national government.

Economic and Industrial Development Even more dizzying were social and economic changes that followed the Civil War. Within ten years of the war's end, the industrial output of the United States had climbed by 75 percent. Americans made such impressive industrial gains that the United States soon joined Britain and Germany atop the list of economic giants.

A potent instrument of capital accumulation appeared at this time—the **limited-liability joint-stock company**. Firms such as Standard Oil and U.S. Steel attracted money from well-to-do investors via a stock market. These investors, called shareholders, in theory owned the company; nonetheless, they left the running of these enterprises to paid managers. Intermediaries, like J. Pierpont Morgan, the New York financial giant who became the world's wealthiest man, loaned money and brokered big deals on the New York Stock Exchange. So great were the fortunes amassed by leading financiers and industrialists that by 1890 the richest 1 percent of Americans owned nearly 90 percent of the nation's wealth.

The expansion of railroad lines symbolized American economic and territorial growth. In 1865, the United States boasted 35,000 miles of track. By 1900, nearly 200,000 miles of track connected the Atlantic to the Pacific and crisscrossed the American territory in between. Americans continued their migrations west. Joined by throngs of immigrants from Europe, they were attracted by homestead acts promising nearly free acreage to settlers and by promoters from the railroads.

By now the United States had become a major world power. It boasted an economy that, despite troubles in the 1890s, had expanded rapidly over the last decades of the nineteenth century. It also was a more integrated nation after the Civil War, with an amended constitution that claimed to uphold the equality of all members of the American nation, even those men who were not white. But there was disagreement on what that equality should involve (for example, should it include women as voters?) and how the country would adjust to a new century in which the nation's "destiny" had already been fulfilled.

limited-liability joint-stock company
Company that mobilized capital from a large number of investors, called shareholders, who were not to be held personally liable for financial losses incurred by the company.

CANADA

Canadians also built a new nation, enjoyed economic success, and followed an expansionist course. Like the United States, Canada had access to a vast frontier prairie for growing agricultural exports. And as in the United States, these lands became the homes and farms of more European immigrants. However, whereas the United States had waged a war to gain independence, Canada's separation from Britain was peaceful. From the 1830s to the 1860s, Britain gradually passed authority to the colony, leaving Canadians to grapple with the task of creating a shared national community.

Building a Nation Sharp internal divisions made that task especially difficult. For one thing, there was a well-established French population. Wanting to keep their villages, their culture, their religion, and their language intact, these French Canadians did not feel integrated into the emerging Canadian national community. Nor were they eager to join the English-speaking population in settling new areas, lest such migration dilute their French-Canadian presence.

The English speakers were equally unenthusiastic about creating an independent Canadian state. Fear of being absorbed into the American republic reinforced these Canadians' loyalty to the British crown and made them content with colonial status. Indeed, when Canada finally gained its independence in 1867, it was by an Act of Parliament in London and not by revolution.

Territorial Expansion Lacking cultural and linguistic unity, Canadians used territorial expansion to build an integrated state. In response to the U.S. purchase of Alaska from Russia in 1867 and the movement of settlers onto the American plains, Canadian leaders realized that they had to incorporate their own western territories, lest these, too, fall into American hands.

The Canadian state also faced friction with indigenous peoples. Frontier warfare threatened to drive away investors and settlers, who could always find property south of the border instead. To prevent the kind of bloodletting that characterized the United States' westward expansion, the Canadian government signed treaties with indigenous peoples to ensure strict separation between natives and newcomers.

The Canadian government acquired significant powers to intervene in, regulate, and mediate social conflict between Anglo and French residents, and among both groups and the Native American population. These powers, in fact, were fuller than those of the U.S. government. But even though the state was relatively strong, the sense of a national identity was comparatively weak. Expansionism helped Canada remain an autonomous state, but it did not solve the question of what it meant to belong to a Canadian nation.

LATIN AMERICA

Latin American elites also engaged in nation-state building and expanded their territorial borders. But unlike in the United States and Canada, expansion did not always create homesteader frontiers that could help expand democracy and forge national identities. Instead, civil conflict fractured certain countries in the region (see Chapters 15 and 16), although a few, most notably Brazil and Mexico, remained united.

Much of Latin America shared a common social history. Far more than in North America, the richest lands in Latin America went to large estate holders producing exports such as sugar, coffee, or beef. As a result, privileged elites monopolized power more than in North America's young democracies.

Amerindian and peasant uprisings were a major worry in new Latin American republics. Fearing insurrections, elites devised governing systems that protected private property while limiting the political rights of the poor. Likewise, the specter of slave revolts, driven home not just by earlier, brutal events in Haiti (see Chapter 15) but also by daily rumors of rebellions, kept elites in a state of alarm. Creating strong states, it seemed to many Latin American elites, required excluding large groups of people from power.

Brazil's "Exclusive" Nation-State Brazil illustrates the process by which Latin American rulers built nation-states that excluded much of the population from both the "nation" and the "state." Through the nineteenth century, rulers in Rio de Janeiro defused political conflict by allowing planters to retain the reins of power.

The official prohibition of the importation of slaves in 1830, coupled with slave resistance, began to choke the planters' system by driving up the price of slaves within the region. Thereafter, Brazilian elites retained some former slaves as gang-workers or sharecroppers (who received tools and seeds in return for a share of the crop), and they also imported new workers—especially from Italy, Spain, and Portugal—as seasonal migrant workers or indentured tenant farmers. Indeed, European and even Japanese migration to Brazil helped planters preserve their holdings in the post-slavery era. In all, 2 million Europeans and some 70,000 Japanese moved to Brazil.

The Brazilian state was deliberately exclusive. As in the United States, elites imposed severe restrictions on suffrage and set rules that reduced political competition. However, given the greater share of the black population in Brazil, restrictions there excluded a larger share of the potential electorate than in the United States.

Brazilian Expansion and Economic Development Like Canada and the United States, the Brazilian state extended its reach to distant areas and incorporated them as provinces. The largest land grab occurred in the Amazon River basin, the world's largest drainage watershed and tropical forest. Here, the Brazilian state gave giant concessions to local capitalists to extract rubber latex. When combined with sulfur, rubber was a key raw material for tire manufacturing in European and North American bicycle and automobile industries.

For a time, Brazil became the world's exclusive exporter of rubber; as a result, its planters, merchants, and workers prospered. Rich merchants became lenders and financiers, not only to workers but also to landowners. The mercantile elite of Manaus, the capital of the Amazon region, designed and decorated their city to reflect their new fortunes. Although the streets were still paved with mud, the town's elite built a replica of the Paris Opera House, and Manaus became a regular stopover for European opera singers on the circuit between Buenos Aires and New York. Rubber workers also benefited from the boom. Mostly either Amerindians or mixed-blood people, they sent their wages home to families elsewhere in the Amazon jungle or on the northeastern coast of Brazil.

One problem was the ecosystem. Such a diversified biomass could not tolerate a regimented form of production. Cultivating rubber trees at the expense of other vegetation made the forest vulnerable to nonhuman predators. Leaf blights and ferocious ants destroyed all experiments at creating more sustainable rubber plantations.

The Brazilian rubber boom, moreover, soon went bust. As competition led to increased supplies and reduced prices, Brazilian producers went bankrupt. Merchants called in their loans, landowners forfeited their titles, and rubber workers returned to their small subsistence farms. Tropical vines crept over the Manaus Opera House, and it gradually fell into disrepair.

Throughout the Americas, nineteenth-century elites, working with outdated ideas of who should wield power, nonetheless attempted to satisfy popular demands for inclusion. While the ideal was to construct nation-states that could reconcile differences among their citizens and pave the way for economic prosperity, political autonomy did not bring prosperity, or even the right to vote, to all. As each nation-state expanded its territorial boundaries, many inhabitants were left out of the political realm.

Opera House in Manaus The turn-of-the-century rubber boom brought immense wealth to the Amazon jungle. As in many boom-and-bust cycles in Latin America, the proceeds flowed to a small elite and diminished when the rubber supply outstripped the demand. But the wealth produced was sufficient to prompt the local elite to build temples of modernity in the midst of the jungle. Pictured here is the Opera House in the rubber capital of Manaus. Like other works built by Latin American elites of the period, this one emulated the original in Paris.

Consolidation of Nation-States in Europe

Core Objectives

COMPARE the challenges elites in Europe and in the Americas faced in consolidating their nation-states, and the degrees to which they succeeded.

In Europe, no "frontier" existed into which new states could expand. Instead, nation-states took shape out of older monarchies and empires, and their borders were determined by diplomats or by battles. In the wake of the French Revolution, the idea caught on that "the people" should form the basis for the nation and that nations should share a common culture—but no one could agree on who "the people" should be. Yet, over the course of the nineteenth century, as literacy, cities, industrial production, and the number and prosperity of property owners expanded, ruling elites had no choice but to share power with a wider group of citizens. These citizens, in turn, increasingly defined themselves as, say, French or German, rather than as residents of Marseilles or subjects of the king of Bavaria.

DEFINING "THE NATION"

For a very long time, in most places, "the nation" was understood to comprise kings, clergymen, nobles—and occasionally rich merchants or lawyers—and no one else. Although some peoples, such as the English and the Spanish, were already self-conscious about their unique histories, only in the late eighteenth century were the crucial building blocks of European nationalism put in place.

Cultural changes laid the foundations of the nation. Increasingly literate urban populations met in coffeehouses and other public places to discuss the issues of the day. Their collective debates—public opinion—weighed for the first time on the decisions of kings and statesmen. During the nineteenth century, a huge expansion of the periodical press made it possible for people all across Europe to read books and newspapers in their own languages. The emerging industrial economy made merchants anxious to standardize laws, taxation policies, and weights and measures. States invested huge sums in building roads and then railroads—and these linked provincial towns and bigger cities, laying the foundations for a closer political integration.

But who were the people, and what constituted a viable nation-state? For some, the nation was a collection of all those who spoke one language; for others, it was all those who lived in a certain territory and who shared a common religious heritage. This was a particularly acute problem in multiethnic central and southeastern Europe, where many people were multilingual, rich and poor alike. But some who shared the same language objected to being lumped into one nation-state. The Irish, for example, spoke English but were predominantly Catholics and wanted to be free from Anglican rule.

UNIFICATION IN GERMANY AND ITALY

Two of Europe's fledgling nation-states came into being when the dynastic states of Prussia and Piedmont-Sardinia incorporated their smaller, linguistically related neighbors, creating the German and Italian nation-states. (See Map 17.2.) In both regions, conservative prime ministers—Count Otto von Bismarck of Prussia and Count Camillo di Cavour of Piedmont—exploited liberal, nationalist sentiment to rearrange the map of Europe.

Building Unified States The unifications of Germany and Italy, both completed in 1871, posed all the familiar problems of who should be included in the new nation-states. To begin with, German speakers were spread all across central and eastern Europe; for centuries they had lived in many different states. Similarly, Italians had lived separately in city-states and small kingdoms on the Italian Peninsula and spoke a range of dialects. The historical experiences and economic developments had made Bavarian Germans (Catholic) quite different from Prussian Germans (Protestant); likewise, the Milanese (who lived in a wealthy urban industrial center) shared little, language included, with the typical Sardinian peasant. But liberal nationalists had made the case that their high culture—especially their literary, musical, and theatrical traditions—overrode these differences, and emotional appeals by poets, composers, and orators convinced many people that this was indeed the case. Bismarck and Cavour merged this nationalist rhetoric with clever diplomacy—and the use of military force in a series of small conflicts—to forge united German and Italian nation-states.

These "unified" states rejected democracy. In the new Italy, which was a constitutional monarchy, less than 5 percent of the 25 million people could vote. The new German Empire (the Second Reich) had an assembly elected by all adult males (the Reichstag), but it had little power. The country was ruled by a combination of aristocrats and bureaucrats under a monarch. Liberals dominated in many localities, but only the emperor (the kaiser) could depose the prime minister. In fact, Bismarck continued to dominate Prussian politics for twenty-eight years, until fired in 1890 by Kaiser Wilhelm II. By that time, unification had yielded brisk economic growth both in Italy and, especially, Germany, but conflict between regions and political groups continued.

NATION BUILDING AND ETHNIC CONFLICT IN THE AUSTRO-HUNGARIAN EMPIRE

Bismarck's unification of Germany came at the expense of Habsburg supremacy in central Europe and (as we will see in the next section) of French territory and influence in the west. After Germany won a victory over the Austrian army in 1866, the Hungarian nobles who controlled the eastern Habsburg Empire forced the weakened dynasts to grant them home rule.

Map 17.2 Italian Unification and German Unification, 1815–1871

Italian unification and German unification altered the political map of Europe.

- What were the names of the two original states that grew to become Italy and Germany?
- Who were the big losers in these territorial transfers?
- According to your reading, what problems did the new Italian and German states face in creating strong national communities?

In the Compromise of 1867, the Habsburgs agreed that their state would officially be known as the Austro-Hungarian Empire. But this move did not solve Austria-Hungary's nationality problems. In both the Hungarian and the Austrian halves of the dual state, Czechs, Poles, and other Slavs now began to clamor for their own power-sharing "compromise" or autonomous national homelands. They would, however, have to wait until the end of World War I.

DOMESTIC DISCONTENTS IN FRANCE AND BRITAIN

Although already unified as nation-states, Britain and France faced major difficulties. For the French, dealing with defeat at the hands of the Germans was the primary national concern in the decades leading up to World War I. For the British, issues of Irish separatism, the rise of the working class, and feminists' demands troubled the political arena.

Destabilization in France The Franco-Prussian War of 1870–1871 completed the unification of Germany. Germany took the French provinces of Alsace and Lorraine, and its victory destabilized France. The German siege of Paris, which lasted for more than three months, devastated the capital. Unprepared, Parisians had no food stocks and were compelled to eat all sorts of things, including two zoo elephants. Under terrible conditions and without effective leadership, the French capital resisted until January 1871, when the government signed a humiliating peace treaty. The Germans left in place a weak provisional French government. Refusing the negotiated peace, furious Parisians vented their rage and established their own government, proclaiming the city a utopia for workers. The leftist commune they established lasted until the provisional national government's army stormed Paris a few months later. At least 25,000 Parisians died in the bloody mop-up that followed. A "Third Republic" took the place of Napoleon III's empire, but it struggled to achieve stability. In the years following the Franco-Prussian War, France saw increasing conflict between classes and the rise of anti-German nationalism.

Irish Nationalism in Great Britain Although the English had long thought of themselves as a nation, the idea that all British people belonged in the same state was much more problematic. The kingdom of England—which was originally composed of England, clearly the dominant state, and Wales—became the kingdom of Great Britain when it united with Scotland in 1707 and Ireland in 1801. It was home to peoples whose historical experiences, religious backgrounds, and economic opportunities were very different. In the nineteenth century, British leaders wrestled in particular with demands for independence from Irish nationalists and lower-class agitation, especially in England. Beginning in 1832, England responded to class conflict at home by extending political rights to most men but not women. England finally

The Irish Potato Famine Many families in Ireland were left desperate and starving in the aftermath of the potato crop failure and were forced to find sustenance wherever they could. In this engraving from the late nineteenth century, a group of people by the coast collects limpets and seaweed to eat.

established universal suffrage for all adult males after World War I, in 1918; roughly one-quarter of British women gained the right to vote at that time and the rest a decade later.

Yet Ireland remained Britain's Achilles' heel. The British government was widely condemned for its failure to relieve Irish suffering during the potato famine of 1845–1849. Over the course of the early nineteenth century, Irish peasants had planted energy-rich and easy-to-cultivate potatoes on their remaining rocky and sandy land. A relatively healthy diet of potatoes and milk had fueled population growth and put more pressure on the land. When a continent-wide potato blight ravaged the island's crops in 1845, this monoculture turned into a recipe for widespread famine. Although the blight continued to decimate harvests for the next four years, the English stuck to their laissez-faire principles and were slow to send grain to relieve Irish suffering, resulting in the death of as many as a million and the emigration of about the same number. Many of these Irish emigrants made their way to England, seeking either passage to North America or work in the English mill towns. Like their Scottish brethren, they did not assimilate easily and often got the lowliest jobs. All of this, on top of 300 years of repressive English domination, spawned a mass movement for Irish home rule that continued into the twentieth century.

Born in opposition to the old monarchical regimes, European nationalism by the end of the nineteenth century had become a means used by liberal and conservative leaders alike to unite the people behind them. But just what they meant by "the people" remained bitterly contested. Continental powers increasingly resorted to an aggressive foreign policy and imperial expansion to maintain popular support without granting political power to ordinary people. France alone, of the European great powers, had a parliamentary democracy elected by universal manhood suffrage.

Industry, Science, and Technology

A powerful combination of industry, science, and technology shaped the emerging nation-states in North America and western Europe. It also reordered the relationships among different parts of the world. One critical factor was that after 1850 western Europe and North America experienced a new phase of industrial development—essentially a second industrial revolution. Japan, too, joined the ranks of industrializing nations as its state-led program of industrial development started to pay dividends. These changes transformed the global economy and intensified rivalries among industrial societies.

Core Objectives

EXPLAIN the roles that industrialization, science, and technology played in expansion of powerful states into the rest of the world.

NEW TECHNOLOGIES, MATERIALS, AND BUSINESS PRACTICES

New technologies and materials drove economic development in the late nineteenth century and led to new business practices. This period witnessed major technological changes with the arrival of new organic sources of power (like oil) and new ways to get old organic sources (like coal) to processing plants. These changes freed manufacturers from having to locate their plants close to their fuel sources. Not only did the most important new source of energy—electricity—permit factories to arise in areas with plenty of skilled workers, but it also slashed production costs. **Steel**, now cheaply produced because of technical innovations, became essential for shipbuilding and railways. Electricity and steel were part of a bundle of innovations that included chemicals and pharmaceuticals, which together transformed northwestern Europe, the United States, and Japan.

The breakthroughs of the second industrial revolution ushered in new business practices, especially mass production and the giant integrated firm. No longer would modest investments suffice, as they had in Britain a century earlier. Now large banks were the major providers of funds. In Europe, limited-liability joint-stock companies were as wildly successful in raising capital on stock markets as they were in the United States. Companies like Standard Oil, U.S. Steel, and Siemens mobilized investments from large numbers of shareholders. The scale of these firms was awesome. U.S. Steel alone produced over half of the world's steel ingots, castings, rails, and heavy structural shapes—and nearly half of all its steel plates and sheets, which were vital in the construction of buildings, railroads, ships, and the like.

steel
A metal more malleable and stronger than iron that became essential for industries like shipbuilding and railways.

INTEGRATION OF THE WORLD ECONOMY

Not only did industrial change concentrate power in North Atlantic societies, but it also reinforced their power on the world economic stage and created a more integrated global economy. Europe and the United States increased their exports in new products; they also grew eager to control the importation of tropical commodities such as cocoa and coffee. While the North Atlantic societies were still largely self-sufficient in coal, iron, cotton, wool, and wheat (the major commodities of the first industrial revolution), the second industrial revolution bred a need for rubber, copper, oil, and bauxite (an ore used to make aluminum), which were not available domestically. Equally important, large pools of money became available for investing overseas.

Movements of Labor and Technology Vast movements of workers took place to satisfy the labor demands of an increasingly integrated world economy. Indians moved thousands of miles from Asia to work on sugar plantations in the Caribbean, Mauritius, and Fiji; to labor in South African mines; and to build railroads in East Africa. Chinese workers constructed railroads in the western United States and toiled on sugar plantations in Cuba. The Irish, Poles, Jews, Italians, and Greeks flocked to North America to fill its burgeoning factories. Italians also moved to Argentina to harvest wheat and corn.

With steam-powered gunboats and breech-loading rifles, Europeans opened new territories for trade and conquest. At home and in their colonial possessions, imperial powers constructed networks of railroads that carried people and goods from hinterlands to the coasts. From there, steamships bore them across the seas. Completion of the Suez Canal in 1869 shortened ship voyages between Europe and Asia and lowered the costs of interregional trade. Information moved even faster than cargoes, thanks to the laying of telegraph cables under the oceans, supplemented by overland telegraph lines.

Charles Darwin and Natural Selection Although machines were the most visible evidence that humans could master the universe, perhaps the most momentous shift in the conception of nature derived from the travels of one British scientist: **Charles Darwin** (1809–1882).

Darwin's theory, articulated in his *On the Origin of Species* (1859), laid out the principles of **natural selection**. Inevitably, he claimed, populations grew faster than the food supply; this condition created a "struggle for existence" among species. In later work he showed how the passing on of individual traits was also determined by what he called sexual selection—according to which the "best" mates are chosen for their strength, beauty, or talents and the less fit fail to reproduce at comparable rates. Although Darwin's book dealt exclusively with animals (and mostly with birds), his readers immediately wondered what his theory implied for humans.

Charles Darwin
(1809–1882) British scientist who became convinced that the species of organic life had evolved under the uniform pressure of natural laws, not by means of a special, one-time creation as described in the Bible.

natural selection
Charles Darwin's theory that populations grew faster than the food supply, creating a "struggle for existence" among species. In later work he showed how the passing on of individual traits was also determined by what he called sexual selection—according to which the "best" mates are chosen for their strength, beauty, or talents. The outcome: the "fittest" survived to reproduce, while the less adaptable did not.

A passionate debate began among scientists and laymen, clerics and anthropologists. Some read Darwin's doctrine of natural selection to mean that it was natural for the strong nations to dominate the weak, or justifiable to allow disabled persons to die—something Darwin explicitly rejected. As more groups (mis)interpreted Darwin's theory to suit their own objectives, a set of beliefs known as social Darwinism legitimated the suffering of the underclasses in industrial society. In subsequent years Europeans would repeatedly suggest that they had evolved more than Africans and Asians. Extending Darwinian ideas far beyond the scientist's intent, some Europeans came to believe that nature itself gave them the right to rule others.

Imperialism and the Origins of Anticolonial Nationalism

Increasing rivalries among nations and social tensions within them produced an expansionist wave late in the nineteenth century. Although Africa became the primary focus of interest, a frenzy of territorial conquest overtook Asia as well. In China's territories, competition by foreign powers to establish spheres of influence heated up in the 1890s. And in India, imperial ambitions provoked the British to conquer Burma (present-day Myanmar). Moreover, Britain and Russia competed for preeminence from their respective outposts in Afghanistan and central Asia. In the Americas, new territories were usually incorporated as provinces of the expansionist state, making them integral parts of the nation.

In Asia and Africa, however, European and American imperialism turned far-flung territories into colonial possessions. The inhabitants of these colonial possessions were generally designated as subjects of the empire without the rights and privileges of citizens. Britain's imperial regime in India provided lessons to a generation of European colonial officials in Africa and other parts of Asia. Yet, even as Europe's colonial administrators looked to earlier imperial practices in India and the Caribbean for use in Africa, they also regarded African communities as less economically and culturally developed than Asian communities. Hence, they believed that Africans would require an extended period of colonial tutelage.

The proponents of European and North American colonization argued that colonial rule produced benefits for both the colonial peoples and the colonizers. Economically, colonies would be drawn into and profit from an emerging world economy. They would export primary products in high demand in the industrialized parts of the global economy—most notably cocoa, tea, coffee, diamonds, gold, and copper from Africa; rubber from the Dutch East Indies; huge quantities of cotton from India and Egypt; and beginning mainly after World War I, oil from the Middle East to fuel industrial economies. In return, colonial peoples would import much-needed

Core Objectives

COMPARE the different western colonial models used in various regions of the world and the responses of those regions.

manufactured commodities—clothing made from their raw cotton; processed foods made from coffee, cocoa, and tea; railway engines; and ocean-going vessels. But were the benefits evenly distributed, as some imperialist proponents claimed? A balance sheet of imperialism is difficult to construct, but the biggest beneficiaries were clearly not African and Asian peasant cultivators, as apologists asserted, or even the workers in western factories, whose wages, while rising, still remained low. Profits flowed mainly to European-run export-import firms, large global banks, and wealthy industrialists.

Not surprisingly, colonized peoples resisted the imposition of economic systems that destroyed older trading and agricultural systems and benefited only the colonial extractors. Resistance took different forms, including the demand for national self-determination. In many parts of colonial Asia, early forms of resistance, usually put down with savage reprisals, were followed by organized political protest and the formation of nationalist political parties. The African continent, the last to be colonized, at first went through an early phase of armed resistance to colonial rule, which was repressed with considerable bloodshed. After World War I, colonial critics followed in the footsteps of the Asian anticolonial nationalists. They, too, created anticolonial, mainly nonviolent, political organizations, seeking at first the redress of colonial grievances, such as lost lands. Many of these nations would have to wait until the post–World War II period to achieve full independence.

INDIA AND THE IMPERIAL MODEL

Britain's rule in India provided a model for other imperialist governments by developing the colony's infrastructure in order to maximize

The Raj Strengthens Control (*Left*) In the aftermath of the Indian Rebellion of 1857, the British government, called the Raj (meaning "rule" in Hindi), intervened much more actively in India. It built an extensive system of railroads to develop India as a profitable colony and to maintain military security. This engraving shows the East India Railway around 1863. (*Right*) Skeletal human remains can be seen scattered among the ruins of the Palace of Secundra Bagh on the outskirts of Lucknow, after the Siege of Lucknow. The Secundra Bagh was attacked by the troops of Sir Colin Campbell in November 1857. This photograph is thought to be among the first to show casualties of war.

British profits from trade. Having suppressed the Indian Rebellion of 1857 (see Chapter 16), authorities revamped the colonial administration. From the British point of view, Indians were not to be appeased—and certainly not brought into British public life. But they did have to be governed, and the economy had to be revived. So, after replacing the East India Company's rule by crown government in 1858, the British set out to make India into a more secure and productive colony. This period of British sovereignty was known as the **Raj** ("rule").

raj
British crown's administration of India following the end of the East India Company's rule after the Rebellion of 1857.

The most urgent tasks facing the British in India were modernizing its transportation and communication systems and transforming the country into an integrated colonial state. These changes had begun under the governor-general of the East India Company, Lord Dalhousie, who oversaw the development of India's modern infrastructure. After the British suppressed the revolt, they took up the construction of public works with renewed vigor. Railways were a key element both in the pacification (they shuttled troops to danger zones) and in the later reform project. The first railway line opened in 1853, and by 1910 India had 30,627 miles of track in operation—making it the fourth-largest railway system in the world.

Construction of other public works followed. Engineers built dams across rivers to tame their force and to irrigate lands; workers installed a grid of telegraph lines that opened communication between distant parts of the region. These public works served imperial and economic purposes: India was to become a consumer of British manufactures and a supplier of primary staples such as cotton, tea, and wheat. On the hillsides of the island of Ceylon (now Sri Lanka) and the northeastern plains of India, the British established vast plantations to grow tea—which was then marketed in England as a healthier alternative to Chinese green tea. India also became an important consumer of British manufactures, especially textiles, in an ironic turnabout of its centuries-old tradition of exporting its own cotton and silk textiles.

The reform efforts of the Raj made India into a unified territory and enabled its inhabitants to begin to regard themselves as "Indians." These were the first steps to becoming a "nation" like Italy and the United States, but there were profound differences. Above all, as colonial subjects Indians did not enjoy basic civic and human rights, and even elites lacked the vote. Other European powers followed the British example in trying to modernize and integrate their colonies economically without welcoming colonial peoples into the life of the nation.

COLONIZING AFRICA

No region felt the impact of European colonialism more powerfully than Africa. In 1880, the only two large European colonial possessions there were French Algeria and two British-ruled South African states, the Cape Colony and Natal. But within a mere thirty years, seven European states had carved almost all of Africa into colonial possessions.

Partitioning the African Landmass In the context of heightened international rivalries, Portugal called for an international conference to discuss claims to Africa. Meeting in Berlin between 1884 and 1885, delegates from Europe, the United States, and the Ottoman Empire agreed to carve up Africa and to recognize the claims of the first European power that claimed control of a given territory. Colonizers rushed to plant their flags as widely as possible, lest they be outmaneuvered by their rivals.

The consequences for Africa were devastating. Nearly 70 percent of the newly drawn borders failed to correspond to older demarcations of ethnicity, language, culture, and commerce—for Europeans knew little of the landmass beyond its coast and rivers. They based their new colonial boundaries on European trading centers rather than on the location of African population groups. (See Map 17.3.)

Several motives led the European powers into their frenzied partition of Africa. Although European businesses were primarily interested in Egypt and South Africa, where their investments were lucrative, small-scale traders and investors harbored fantasies of great treasures locked in the vast uncharted interior. Politicians, publicists, and the reading public also took an interest. The writings of explorers like David Livingstone (1813–1873), a Scottish doctor and missionary, and Henry Morton Stanley (1841–1904), an adventurer in the pay of the *New York Herald*, excited readers with accounts of Africa as a continent of unlimited economic potential.

The most determined of the African empire builders was Leopold II (r. 1865–1909), king of the Belgians. (See Current Trends in World History: Africa's Newest Hunters and Gatherers: Greed, Environmental Degradation, and Resistance for Leopold's activities in central Africa and their effects on Africans and the environment.) In southern Africa, the British champion of imperialism Cecil Rhodes (1853–1902) brought the Rhodesias, Nyasaland, Bechuanaland, the Transvaal, and the Orange Free State into the British Empire as part of a design to have British territories stretching all the way from the Cape of Good Hope in South Africa to Cairo in Egypt.

Other Europeans saw Africa as a grand opportunity for converting souls to Christianity. In fact, Europe's civilizing mission was an important motive in the scramble for African territory. In Uganda, northern Nigeria, and central and western Africa, missionaries went ahead of European armies, begging the European statesmen to follow their lead.

African Resistance Africans faced two unappealing options: they could capitulate to the Europeans and negotiate to limit the loss of their autonomy, or they could fight to preserve their sovereignty. Only a few chose to negotiate.

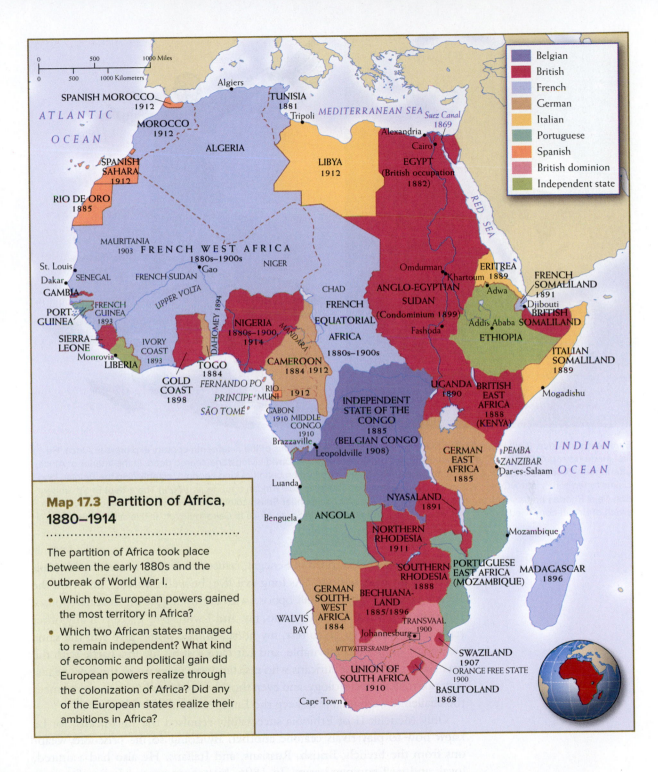

Legend	
Belgian	
British	
French	
German	
Italian	
Portuguese	
Spanish	
British dominion	
Independent state	

SPANISH MOROCCO
1912

ATLANTIC
OCEAN

Algiers

TUNISIA
1881
Tripoli

MEDITERRANEAN SEA

Suez Canal
1869

MOROCCO
1912

ALGERIA

LIBYA
1912

Alexandria

Cairo

EGYPT
(British occupation
1882)

SPANISH
SAHARA
1912

RED SEA

RIO DE ORO
1885

MAURITANIA
1903

FRENCH WEST AFRICA
1880s–1900s

NIGER

Omdurman
Khartoum

ERITREA
1889

FRENCH
SOMALILAND
1891

St. Louis
Dakar
SENEGAL
GAMBIA

FRENCH SUDAN

Gao

UPPER VOLTA

CHAD

ANGLO-EGYPTIAN
SUDAN
(Condominium 1899)

Adwa

Djibouti
BRITISH
SOMALILAND

PORT.
GUINEA

FRENCH
GUINEA
1893

DAHOMEY 1894

NIGERIA
1880s–1900,
1914

FRENCH
EQUATORIAL
AFRICA
1880s–1900s

Addis Ababa
Fashoda

ETHIOPIA

ITALIAN
SOMALILAND
1889

SIERRA
LEONE
Monrovia
LIBERIA

IVORY
COAST
1893

MANDARA

CAMEROON
1884 1912

TOGO
1884
FERNANDO PO
PRINCIPE
SÃO TOMÉ

RIO
MUNI
1912

UGANDA
1890

BRITISH
EAST
AFRICA
1888
(KENYA)

Mogadishu

GOLD
COAST
1898

GABON
1910

MIDDLE
CONGO
1910

Brazzaville
Leopoldville 1908

INDEPENDENT
STATE OF THE
CONGO
1885
(BELGIAN CONGO)

GERMAN
EAST
AFRICA
1885

PEMBA
ZANZIBAR
Dar-es-Salaam

INDIAN
OCEAN

Luanda

NYASALAND
1891

Benguela

ANGOLA

NORTHERN
RHODESIA
1911

Mozambique

PORTUGUESE
EAST AFRICA
(MOZAMBIQUE)

MADAGASCAR
1896

SOUTHERN
RHODESIA
1888

GERMAN
SOUTH-
WEST
AFRICA
1884

BECHUANA-
LAND
1885/1896

WALVIS
BAY

TRANSVAAL
1900

Johannesburg

WITWATERSRAND

UNION OF
SOUTH AFRICA
1910

Cape Town

SWAZILAND
1907
ORANGE FREE STATE
1900
BASUTOLAND
1868

Map 17.3 Partition of Africa, 1880–1914

The partition of Africa took place between the early 1880s and the outbreak of World War I.

- Which two European powers gained the most territory in Africa?
- Which two African states managed to remain independent? What kind of economic and political gain did European powers realize through the colonization of Africa? Did any of the European states realize their ambitions in Africa?

Europeans in Africa (*Left*) Henry Morton Stanley was one of the most famous of the nineteenth-century explorers in Africa. He first made his reputation when he located the British missionary-explorer David Livingstone, feared dead, in the interior of Africa, uttering the famous words, "Dr. Livingstone, I presume." Stanley worked on behalf of King Leopold, establishing the Belgian king's claims to territories in the Congo and often using superior weaponry to cow African opponents. (*Right*) The ardent British imperialist Cecil Rhodes endeavored to bring as much of Africa as he could under British colonial rule. He had an ambition to create a swath of British-controlled territory that would stretch from the Cape in South Africa to Cairo in Egypt, as this cartoon shows.

Lat Dior, a Muslim warlord in Senegal, refused to let the French build a railway through his kingdom. "As long as I live, be well assured," he wrote the French commandant, "I shall oppose with all my might the construction of this railway. I will always answer no, no, and I will never make you any other reply. Even were I to go to rest, my horse, *Malay*, would give you the same answer." Conflict was inevitable, and Lat Dior lost his life in a battle with the French in 1886. Most Africans who resisted were unaware of the Europeans' superior military technology, and even those who adapted their tactics to meet the challenge were unable to keep the Europeans out indefinitely.

Only Menelik II of Ethiopia successfully repulsed the Europeans, for he knew how to play rivals off one another. By doing so, he procured weapons from the French, British, Russians, and Italians. He also had a united, loyal, and well-equipped army. In 1896, his troops routed Italian forces at the Battle of Adwa, after which Adwa became a celebrated moment in African history. Its memory inspired many of Africa's later nationalist leaders.

Colonial Administrations in Africa Once the Europeans' euphoria over the gains of the partition and conquest had worn off, the power to rule the colonies fell to "men on the spot"—military adventurers, settlers, and entrepreneurs whose main goal was to get rich quick. As these individuals established little kingdoms in some areas, Africans (like Amerindians on the other side of the Atlantic) found themselves confined to territories where they could barely provide for themselves.

Eventually, these rough-and-ready systems led to violent revolts from aggrieved Africans, and in their aftermath the colonial rulers had to create more efficient administrations, dedicated to providing health care and education for the colonized. As in India, colonial powers in Africa laid the foundations for future nation-state organizations. Once information trickling out of Africa revealed that the imperial governments were not realizing their goal of bringing "civilization" to the "uncivilized" and creating easy profits, each European power implemented a new form of colonial rule, stripping the strongman conquerors of their absolute powers, monitoring them more closely, and assuming greater responsibility for the colonized peoples.

Eventually, stabilized colonies began to deliver on their economic promise. Whereas early imperialism in Africa had relied on the export of ivory and wild rubber, after these resources became depleted, the colonies pursued other exports. From the rain forests came cocoa, coffee, palm oil, and palm kernels. From the highlands of East Africa came tea, coffee, sisal (used in cord and twine), and pyrethrum (a flower used to make insecticide). Another important commodity was long-staple, high-quality cotton, grown in Egypt and the Anglo-Egyptian Sudan. Indeed, tropical commodities from all across Africa (as from India and Latin America) flowed to industrializing societies.

Thus, European colonial administrators saw Africa as fitting into the world economy in the same way that British administrators viewed India—as an exporter of raw materials and an importer of manufactures. They expected Africa to profit from this role. But, in truth, African workers gained little from participating in colonial commerce, while the price they paid in disruption to traditional social and economic patterns was substantial.

To observers, the European empires in Africa seemed solid and durable, but in fact European colonial rule there was fragile. For all of British Africa, the only all-British force was 5,000 men garrisoned in Egypt. Elsewhere, European officers depended on African military and police forces. And prior to 1914, the number of British administrative officers available for the whole of northern Nigeria was less than 500. These were hardly strong foundations for colonial rule. It would not take much to destabilize the European order in Africa.

Core Objectives

ANALYZE the extent to which colonies contributed to the wealth and political strength of the nation-states that controlled them.

Africa's Newest Hunters and Gatherers: Greed, Environmental Degradation, and Resistance

Africa was the birthplace of hunting and gathering (see Chapter 1). Ironically, although the European colonizers justified their partition of Africa on the grounds of bringing civilization to a benighted people, in fact, in their quest to enrich themselves, the first generation of colonizers exploited the most available resources of the continent, enslaved and killed huge numbers of people, and returned parts of the continent to a hunting and gathering mode of production. The most driven and greediest of these figures was Leopold II, king of the Belgians, who was determined, in spite of sweet-sounding rhetoric, to do whatever it took to line his pockets and make himself a formidable figure in European politics. King Leopold's story and others like it fascinate world historians because it conveys in stark detail the nature of the relationship between the rulers and the Africans they ruled. It also provides a point of comparison for the different models of

ruling that each European power instituted in its colonies.

Even before ascending the throne in 1865, Leopold cast about for ways to become more than the constitutional monarch of a small, recently established, and neutral state. A voracious reader on colonialism, he was struck forcefully by one book: *How the Dutch Ruled Java*, published in 1861. By demonstrating how the Dutch colonial state had expropriated money from the East Indies (today called Indonesia) to spend on projects at home, the book fired his imagination. Could he not do the same? Could he not stake out a colony, take money from it to swell his own exchequer, and use some of it on public works at home—to beautify the cities of Belgium the way Paris had been beautified in the 1850s and 1860s?

Fixing his gaze on central Africa, in the 1880s Leopold manipulated the other European states into recognizing him as the sovereign head of a "Congo Free State," in which he led a European

effort to "civilize" (and especially to exploit) the Congo River basin. Leopold hired the world-famous explorer Henry Stanley to "pacify" the country and ready it for economic development.

But how to make these lands pay off? They were almost entirely unexplored and unsurveyed, and though in time they would yield some of the richest mineral deposits in the world, these prospects were unknown to Leopold and his administrators at first. What the rain forests of Africa had was wild products, especially rubber and ivory. But how to get Africans, who at that point hardly participated in world trade, to tap wild rubber vines and hunt elephants? The solution here and elsewhere in similar African environments was to create large armies (known in Leopold's state as the Force Publique), fix quotas for districts to procure, and compel villagers to bring in baskets of rubber and elephant tusks.

For Leopold the results were little short of astonishing. He extracted vast

THE AMERICAN EMPIRE

The United States, like Europe, was drawn into the mania of overseas expansion and empire building. Echoing the earlier rhetoric of Manifest Destiny, the expansionists of the 1890s claimed that Americans still had a divine mission to spread their superior civilization and their Christian faith around the globe. However, America's new imperialists followed the European model of colonialism from Asia and Africa: colonies were to provide harbors for American vessels, supply raw materials to American industries, and purchase the surplus production of American farms and factories. These new territorial acquisitions were not intended for American settlement or statehood. Nor were their inhabitants to become American citizens, for nonwhite foreigners were considered unfit for incorporation into the American nation.

King Leopold Despite the inhumane way in which he funded his vast array of public buildings, Leopold is sometimes called, not unaffectionately, the "Builder King" by Belgians today.

sums from the Congo, spending lavishly on himself and on Belgium. He sank millions of francs into making the seaside city of Ostend one of the finest resorts in the world. At Tervuren, while a choir sang the new Congo anthem, Leopold laid the foundation stone of a world college for overseas colonial administration. In Brussels he spent over $5 million renovating royal palaces and constructing parks, avenues, casinos, and racecourses.

For the Congolese, Leopold's state was nothing more than a reign of terror. Forced to roam farther and farther from their home villages in search of rubber and elephants to keep pace with ever-escalating quotas, villagers suffered an immense loss of life through famine and conflicts with the Force Publique. Perhaps as many as 10 million Africans perished in a population that had been roughly 20 million before Leopold's agents arrived.

Leopold's brutality did not go unobserved, however. In 1899, the writer Joseph Conrad took the Congo as his model of rapacious European imperialism in his novella *Heart of Darkness*. African villagers rebelled, though unsuccessfully, and by the first decade of the twentieth century, rumors and then detailed reports painted a stark picture of terror and environmental degradation as the villagers rooted out almost all wild rubber and began the hunt for elephants that would ultimately render them an endangered species. In 1908, a year before his death, Leopold was compelled, against his wishes, to turn the administration of the Congo over to the Belgian parliament.

Questions for Analysis

- Why was King Leopold such an important figure in the European partition of Africa?
- While the Congo story is one of the most brutal stories of colonial exploitation and environmental degradation, which other episodes in world history does it remind you of and why?

Explore Further

Herbst, Jeffrey, *States and Power in Africa: Comparative Lessons in Authority and Control* (2000).
Hochschild, Adam, *King Leopold's Ghost* (1998).

The pressure to expand came to a head in the late 1890s, when the United States declared war on Spain and invaded the Philippines, Puerto Rico, and Cuba. The United States annexed Puerto Rico after minimal protest, but Cubans and Filipinos resisted becoming colonial subjects. Bitterness ran particularly high among Filipinos, to whom American leaders had promised independence if they joined in the war against Spain. Betrayed, Filipino rebels launched a war for independence in the name of a Filipino nation. In two years of fighting, over 5,000 Americans and perhaps 200,000 Filipinos perished. The outcome: the Philippines became a colony of the United States.

Colonies in the Philippines and Puerto Rico laid the foundations for a revised model of U.S. expansionism. The earlier pattern had been to turn Native American lands into privately owned farmsteads and to extend the Atlantic

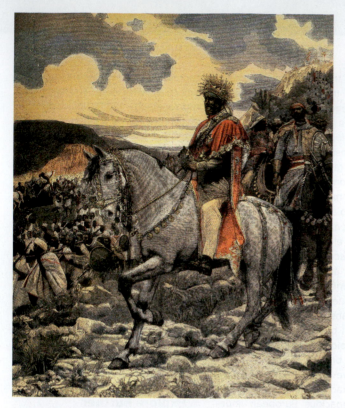

Battle of Adwa Portrait of King Menelik, who defeated the Italian forces at the battle of Adwa in 1896, thus saving his country from European colonization.

market across the continent. But now, in this new era, the nation's largest corporations (with government support) aggressively intervened in the affairs of neighbors near and far. Following the Spanish-American War, the United States repeatedly sent troops to many Caribbean and Central American countries. The Americans preferred to turn these regimes into dependent states, rather than making them part of the United States itself (as with Alaska and Hawaii) or converting them into formal colonies (as the Europeans had done in Africa and Asia).

IMPERIALISM AND CULTURE

Europeans and Americans set out to bring "civilization" to the peoples of their colonies. At least since the Crusades, Europeans had regularly written and thought about others. These images and ideas had grown more numerous and varied as commerce and colonialism in Asia and the Atlantic world increased; they served various purposes, including those of informing, entertaining, flattering, and criticizing European culture. As Europeans and Americans grew more and more confident in their achievements, they became convinced that their arts and sciences were superior—and curiosity often turned to disdain. In time Europeans presumed that the only true modern civilization was their own; other peoples might have reigned over great empires in antiquity but had since fallen into decadence and decline. Artists and writers portrayed nonwestern peoples as exotic, sensuous, and economically backward in a genre scholars have come to call "Orientalism."

If Darwin remained ambivalent about the nature of race, his followers embraced the idea of stable racial differences that evolved only on the longest of time horizons, at a glacial pace, over thousands of years rather than decades or centuries. They ratified a view of "lower" and "higher" races, the former stuck in the past and the latter anointed by God (or in the case of social Darwinists, by nature itself) to define and dictate civilization's future. Europeans' relationship to others might now be one of condescending sympathy or of ruthless exploitation, but the result was that it was up to white Europeans and Americans to create modern culture. The darker people, social Darwinists argued, were not nearly as fully "evolved" as the Europeans and could not hope to catch up. At best they could be taught European languages, sciences, and religions, and perhaps be made to evolve more quickly.

It is telling that French colonial subjects who did well at French schools were known as *evolués*, "the evolved ones."

Celebrating Imperialism Especially in middle- and upper-class circles, Europeans celebrated their imperial triumphs. After the invention of photographic film and the Eastman Kodak camera in 1888, imperial images surfaced in popular forms such as postcards and advertisements. Imperial themes also decorated packaging materials; tins of coffee, tea, tobacco, and chocolates featured pictures highlighting the commodities' colonial origins. Cigarettes often had names like "Admiral," "Royal Navy," "Fighter," and "Grand Fleet." Some of this served as propaganda, produced by investors in imperial commodities or by colonial pressure groups.

Propaganda promoted imperialism abroad but also inspired changes at home. For example, champions of empire argued that if the British population did not grow fast enough to fill the world's sparsely settled regions, then the population of other nations would. Population was power, and the number of healthy children provided an accurate measure of global influence. "Empire cannot be built on rickety and flat-chested citizens," warned a British member of Parliament in 1905. Empire and imperialism carried European, American, and, to a lesser extent, Japanese power and culture throughout the world. In terms of the size of the populations they ruled, this era was the high point of European and Euro-American predominance.

The Women of Algiers in Their Apartment An oil painting by Eugène Delacroix (1798–1863) of Algerian women being attended by a black servant. European painters in the nineteenth century often used images of women to portray Arab Muslim society.

Pressures of Expansion in Japan, Russia, and China

Core Objectives

COMPARE the challenges elites faced in Japan, China, and Russia in consolidating nation-states to those faced by western elites.

The challenge of integrating political communities and extending territorial borders was a problem not just for western Europe and the United States. Other societies also aimed to overcome domestic dissent and establish larger domains. Japan, Russia, and China provide three contrasting models; their differing forms of expansion eventually led them to fight over possessions in East Asia.

JAPAN'S TRANSFORMATION AND EXPANSION

Starting in the 1860s, Japanese rulers tried to recast their country less as an old dynasty and more as a modern nation-state. Since the early seventeenth century, the Tokugawa shogunate had kept outsiders within strict limits and thwarted internal unrest. But after an American naval officer, Commodore Matthew Perry, entered Edo Bay in 1853 with a fleet of steam-powered ships, other Americans, Russians, Dutch, and British followed in his wake. These outsiders forced the Tokugawa rulers to sign humiliating treaties that opened Japanese ports, slapped limits on Japanese tariffs, and exempted foreigners from Japanese laws. Younger Japanese, especially among the military (samurai) elites, felt that Japan should respond by adopting, not rejecting, western practices.

In 1868, a group of reformers toppled the Tokugawa shogunate and promised to return Japan to its mythic greatness. Then Emperor Mutsuhito—the Meiji ("Enlightened Rule") Emperor—became the symbol of a new Japan.

Perry Arrives in Japan A Japanese wood-block print portraying the uninvited arrival into Edo (Tokyo) Bay on August 7, 1853, of a tall American ship, which was commanded by Matthew Perry. This arrival marked the end of Japan's ability to fully control the terms of its interactions with foreigners.

His reign (1868–1912) was called the **Meiji Restoration**. By founding schools, initiating a propaganda campaign, and revamping the army to create a single "national" fighting force, the Meiji government promoted a political community that stressed linguistic and ethnic homogeneity, as well as superiority compared to others. In this way the Meiji leaders overcame age-old regional divisions, subdued local political authorities, and mobilized the country to face the threat from powerful Europeans.

Economic Development One of the Meiji period's remarkable achievements was the nation's economic transformation. After 1871, when the government banned the feudal system and allowed peasants to become small landowners, farmers improved their agrarian techniques and saw their standard of living rise. The energetic new government unified the currency around the yen, created a postal system, introduced tax reforms, and established an advanced civil service system. In 1889, the Meiji government introduced a constitution (based largely on the German model). The following year, 450,000 people—about 1 percent of the population—elected Japan's first parliament, the Imperial Diet.

As the government sold valuable enterprises to the people who had provided strong support, it created private economic dynasties. The new large companies (such as Sumitomo, Yasuda, Mitsubishi, and Mitsui) were trusted family organizations. Fathers, sons, cousins, and uncles ran different parts of large integrated corporations—some in charge of banks, some running the trade wing, some overseeing factories. Women played a crucial role, not just as custodians of the home but also as cultivators of important family alliances, especially among potential marriage partners. In contrast to American limited-liability firms, which issued shares on stock markets to anonymous buyers, Japan's version of large-scale managerial capitalism was a personal affair.

Expansionism and Conflict with Neighbors As in many other emerging nation-states, expansion was a tempting prospect to the Japanese. It offered the promise of more markets for selling goods and obtaining staples, and it was a way to burnish the image of national superiority and greatness. The Meiji moved first to take over the kingdom of the Ry–uky–us southwest of Japan. (See Map 17.4.) A small show of force, only 160 Japanese soldiers, was enough to establish the new Okinawa Prefecture there in 1879. The Japanese regarded the people of the Ry–uky–us as an ethnic minority and refused to incorporate them into the nation-state on equal terms. In contrast with the British in India or the Americans in Puerto Rico, the Japanese conquerors refused to train a native Ry–uky–uan governing class. Meiji intellectuals insisted that the "backward" Okinawans were unfit for local self-rule and representation.

The Japanese fixed upon Korea, which put their plans on a collision course with China's. In a formal treaty, the Japanese recognized Korea as an

Map 17.4 Japanese Expansion, 1870–1910

Under the Meiji Restoration, the Japanese state built a strong national identity and competed with foreign powers for imperial advantage in East Asia.

- According to the map, what were the first areas that the Japanese Empire acquired as it started to expand?
- What two empires' spheres of influence were affected by Japan's aggressive attempts at expansion?
- According to your reading, what were the new Japanese state's objectives? How were they similar to or different from those of expansionist European states in the same period?

Map labels:
RUSSIA
AMUR PROVINCE
NORTH SAKHALIN ISLAND
SEA OF OKHOTSK
SOUTH SAKHALIN ISLAND 1905
KURILE ISLANDS 1875
MONGOLIA
MANCHURIA (Japanese sphere of influence from 1905)
EZO (HOKKAIDŌ)
Mukden
Vladivostok
Shenyang
Haicheng
SEA OF JAPAN
Yingkou
KWANTUNG (leased 1905)
Beijing
Dalian
Pyongyang
JAPAN
Lüshun
Weihaiwei
Seoul
KOREA (Protectorate 1905, Colony 1910)
Tokyo
HONSHU
Kyoto
CHINA
Qingdao
Osaka
Hiroshima
YELLOW SEA
SHIKOKU
PACIFIC OCEAN
Nagasaki
KYŪSHŪ
Nanjing
BONIN ISLANDS 1876
Shanghai
EAST CHINA SEA
VOLCANO ISLANDS 1890
RYUKYU ISLANDS 1874 (Japanese establish Okinawa Prefecture 1879)
OKINAWA
TAIWAN 1895
PESCADORE ISLANDS 1895

Legend:
Japanese Empire, 1870
Japanese acquisition, 1874–1895
Japanese attacks in Sino-Japanese War, 1894–1895
Japanese attacks in Russo-Japanese War, 1904–1905
Japanese acquisition, 1905–1910

independent state (expected to be no longer dominated by China), opened Korea to trade, and won the right to apply Japanese law in Korea. As a result, the Chinese worried that soon the Japanese would try to take over Korea. These fears were well founded, for Japanese designs on Korea eventually sparked the Sino-Japanese War of 1894–1895, in which the Chinese suffered a humiliating defeat.

The Sino-Japanese War accelerated Japan's rapid transformation into a nation-state and a colonial power with no peer in Asia. Having lost the war, China ceded the province of Taiwan to the Japanese. Japan also annexed Korea in 1910 and converted Taiwan and Korea into the twin jewels of its young empire. Like the British in India, the Japanese regarded their colonial subjects as racially inferior and unworthy of the privileges of citizenship. And like other imperial powers, the Japanese expected their possessions to serve the metropolitan center.

RUSSIAN TRANSFORMATION AND EXPANSION

Russia expanded out of a sense of a civilizing mission and a need to defend against other countries expanding along its immense borders. Facing an emerging Germany, a British presence in the Middle East and Persia, a consolidating China, and an increasingly powerful Japan, Russia knew it would have to extend its already large territorial domain. So it established a number of expansionist fronts simultaneously: southwest to the Black Sea, south into the Caucasus and Turkestan, and east into Manchuria. (See Map 17.5.) Success depended on annexing territories and establishing protectorates over conquered peoples.

Modernization and Internal Reform In the 1860s, Tsar Alexander II launched a wave of "Great Reforms" to make Russia more modern and to preserve its status as a great power. In 1861, for example, a decree emancipated peasants from serfdom. Other changes included a sharp reduction in the duration of military service, a program of education for the conscripts, and the beginnings of a mass school system to teach children reading, writing, and Russian culture. Starting in the 1890s, state-sponsored industrialization led to the building of railroads and factories and stimulated the expansion of the steel, coal, and petroleum industries. But while the reforms strengthened the state, they did not enhance the lives of common people. Workers in Russia were brutally exploited, even by the standards of the industrial revolution. Also, large landowners had kept most of the empire's fertile land, and the peasants had to pay substantial redemption fees for the poorer-quality plots they received.

Before long, in the press, courtrooms, and streets, men and women denounced the regime. Revolutionaries engaged in terror and assassination. In 1881, a terrorist bomb killed the tsar. In the 1890s, following a period of famine, the radical doctrines of Marxism (see Chapter 16) gained popularity in Russia. Even aristocratic intellectuals, such as the author of *War and Peace*, Count Leo Tolstoy, lamented their despotic government.

Territorial Expansion Yet the critics of internal reform did not hold back the Russian expansionists, who believed they had to take over certain lands to keep them out of rivals' hands. So they conquered the highland people of the Caucasus Mountains to prevent Ottomans and Persians from encroaching on Russia's southern flank. And they battled the British over areas between Turkestan and British India, such as Persia (Iran) and Afghanistan. Although

Map 17.5 Russian Expansion, 1801–1914

The Russian state continued to expand in the nineteenth century.

- According to this map, what lands did Russia acquire during the period 1796–1855? What lands did it acquire next?
- Compare this map of Russian expansion with Map 13.7. How did the direction of Russia's expansion change in the nineteenth century?
- Which states did the expanding Russian Empire more resemble in this era, western European states (such as Great Britain) or American states (such as the United States)?

some Russians moved to these lands, they never became a majority there. The new provinces were multiethnic, multireligious communities that were only partially integrated into the Russian nation.

Perhaps the most impressive Russian expansion occurred in East Asia, where the Amur River basin offered rich lands, mineral deposits, and access to the Pacific Ocean. The Chinese also wanted to colonize this area, which lay just north of Manchuria. After twenty years of struggle, Russia claimed the land north and south of the Amur River and in 1860 founded Vladivostok, a port on the Pacific Ocean whose name signified "Rule the East." Deciding to focus on these areas in Asia, the Russian government sold its one territory in North America (Alaska) to the United States. Then, to link central Russia and the western part of the country to its East Asian spoils, the government began construction of the Trans-Siberian Railroad in the 1890s. When it was completed in 1916, the new railroad bridged the east and the west.

Governing a Diverse Empire Russia was a huge empire whose rulers were only partially effective at integrating its diverse parts into a political community. Unlike the United States, which displaced or slaughtered native populations during its expansion across an entire continent, Russia tolerated and taxed many of the new peoples. The state's approach ranged from outright repression (of Poles and Jews) to favoritism (toward Baltic Germans and Finns), although the beneficiaries of favoritism often later lost favor if they became too strong. Further, unlike the United States, which managed to pacify borders with its weaker neighbors, Russia faced the constant suspicions of Persians and Ottomans and the menace of British troops in Afghanistan. In East Asia, a clash with expansionist Japan loomed on the horizon.

CHINA UNDER PRESSURE

While the Russians and Japanese scrambled to copy European models of industrialism and imperialism, the Qing were slower to mobilize against threats from the west. Even as the European powers were dividing up China into spheres of influence, Qing officials were much more worried about internal revolts and threats from their northern borders than European incursions.

Adopting Western Learning and Skills A growing number of Chinese officials recognized the superior armaments and technology of rival powers and were deeply troubled by the threat posed by European military might. Starting in the 1860s, reformist bureaucrats sought to adopt elements of western learning and technological skills—but with the intention of keeping the core Chinese culture intact.

This so-called **Self-Strengthening movement** included a variety of new ventures: arsenals, shipyards, coal mines, a steamship company to contest the foreign domination of coastal shipping, and schools for learning foreign ways and languages. Most interesting was the dispatch abroad of about 120 schoolboys under the charge of Yung Wing. The first Chinese graduate of an American college (Yale University, 1854), Yung believed that western education would greatly benefit Chinese students, so he took his charges to Connecticut in the 1870s to attend school and live with American families. Conservatives at the Qing court were soon dismayed by reports of the

Self-Strengthening movement
A movement of reformist Chinese bureaucrats in the latter half of the nineteenth century that attempted to adopt western elements of learning and technological skill while retaining their core Chinese culture.

students' interest in Christianity and aptitude for baseball. In 1881, after the U.S. government refused to admit the boys into military academies, they summoned the students home.

Yung Wing's abortive educational mission was not the only setback for the Self-Strengthening movement, for skepticism about western technology was rife among conservative officials. Some insisted that the introduction of machinery would lead to unemployment; others worried that railways would facilitate western military maneuvers and lead to an invasion; still others complained that the crisscrossing tracks disturbed the harmony between humans and nature. The first short railway track ever laid in China was torn up in 1877 shortly after being built, and the country had only 179 miles of track prior to 1895.

Although they did not acknowledge the railroad's usefulness, the Chinese did adopt other new technologies to access a wider range of information. For example, by the early 1890s there were about a dozen Chinese-language newspapers (as distinct from the foreign-language press) published in major cities, with the largest ones having a circulation of 10,000 to 15,000. To avoid government intervention, these papers sidestepped political controversy; instead, they featured commercial news and literary contributions. In 1882, the newspaper *Shenbao* made use of a new telegraph line to publish dispatches within China.

Internal Reform Efforts China's defeat by Japan in the Sino-Japanese War (1894–1895), sparked by quarrels over Korea, prompted a more serious attempt at reform by the Qing. Known as the Hundred Days' Reform, the episode lasted only from June to September 1898. The force behind it was a thirty-seven-year-old scholar named Kang Youwei and his twenty-two-year-old student Liang Qichao. Citing rulers such as Peter the Great of Russia and the Meiji Emperor of Japan as their inspiration, the reformers urged Chinese leaders to develop a railway network, a state banking system, a modern postal service, and institutions to foster the development of agriculture, industry, and commerce. The reform failed when a group of conservative leaders placed the Dowager Cixi on the throne, rescinded the reformist laws, and executed six of the reform movement's major leaders. They did not, however, capture Kang Youwei, who fled to Japan.

But, in truth, the reforms of the Self-Strengthening movement were ineffectual: they were too modest and poorly implemented. Very few Chinese acquired new skills. Despite talk of modernizing, the civil service examination remained based on Confucian classics and still opened the only doors to government service. Governing elites were not yet ready to reinvent the principles of their political community, and they adhered instead to the traditional dynastic structure.

By the late nineteenth century, the success of the Qing regime in expanding its territories a century earlier seemed like a distant memory, as various powers repeatedly forced it to make economic and territorial concessions. Unlike Japan or Russia, however, the Qing government resisted comprehensive social reforms (until after the turn of the twentieth century), and its policies left the country vulnerable to both external aggression and internal instability.

Conclusion

Between 1850 and 1914, most of the world's people lived not in nation-states but in land empires or in the overseas colonies of nation-states. But leaders in colonial territories, often responding to popular upheavals and destabilizing economic changes, began to see independent nation-states as the most desirable form of governance for their regions.

Although the ideal of "a people" united by territory, history, and culture grew increasingly popular worldwide, it was not easy to make it a reality. Official histories, national heroes, novels, poetry, and music helped, but central to the process of nation formation were the actions of bureaucrats. Asserting sovereignty over what it claimed as national territory, the state "nationalized" diverse populations by creating a unified system of law, education, military service, and government.

Colonization beyond borders was another part of nation building in many societies. In these efforts, territorial conquests took place under the banner of nationalist endeavors. In Europe, the Americas, Japan, and to some extent Russia, the intertwined processes of nation building and territorial expansion were most effective. Expansion abroad consolidated national identities at home.

However, the integrating impulses of imperialist nation-states did not wipe out local differences, mute class antagonisms, or eliminate gender inequalities. Even as Europeans and Americans came to see themselves as chosen—by God or by natural selection—to rule the rest, they suffered deep divisions. Not everyone identified with the nation-state or the empire, or agreed on what it meant to belong or to conquer. But by the century's end, racist advocates and colonial lobbyists seem to have convinced many that their interests and destinies were bound up with their countries' unity, prosperity, and global clout.

Ironically, imperial expansion had an unintended consequence, for self-determination could also apply to racial or ethnic minorities at home and in the colonies. Armed with the rhetoric of progress and uplift, colonial authorities tried to subjugate distant people, but colonial subjects themselves often asserted the language of "nation" and accused imperial overlords of betraying their own lofty principles. As the twentieth century opened, Filipino and Cuban rebels used Thomas Jefferson's Declaration of Independence to oppose American invaders, Koreans defined themselves as a nation crushed under Japanese heels, and Indian nationalists made colonial governors feel shame for violating British standards of "fair play."

TRACING THE GLOBAL STORYLINES

Focus On
Nationalism, Imperialism, and Technological Innovations

The Americas and Europe: Consolidating Nations

- Residents of the United States claim territory across the North American continent after fighting a bloody civil war to preserve the union and abolish slavery.

- Canadians also build a new nation and expand across the continent.

- Brazilians create a prosperous nation-state that excludes much of the population from the privileges of belonging to the "nation" and the "state."

- The dynastic states of Prussia and Piedmont-Sardinia create German and Italian nation-states at the expense of France and the Austrian Empire.

Industry, Science, and Technology on a Global Scale

- Continued industrialization transforms the global economy.

- New technologies of warfare, transportation, and communication lead to greater global economic integration.

- Charles Darwin's *On the Origin of Species* overturns previous conceptions of nature, arguing that present-day life forms evolved from simpler ones over long periods.

Empires

- After suppressing the Indian Rebellion of 1857, the British reorganize their rule in India, providing a model for other imperialist powers.

- European powers partition the entire African continent (except for Ethiopia and Liberia) despite intense African resistance.

- Americans win the Spanish-American War, annex Puerto Rico, and establish colonial rule over the Philippines.

- The expansionist aims of Japan, Russia, and China lead to clashes over possessions in East Asia, with Russia gaining much territory and Japan defeating the Chinese.

- Colonial rule spurs nationalist sentiments among the colonized.

CHRONOLOGY

1800 **1850**

The Americas
- Brazil abolishes the importation of slaves 1830
- U.S. Civil War 1861–1865
- Canada gains self-rule 1867

Europe
- *On the Origin of Species* published 1859
- Unifications of Germany and Italy 1870–1871

East Asia and Southeast Asia
- Commodore Perry "opens" Japan 1853

Africa and the Middle East

South Asia

Russia
- Great Reforms to modernize Russia 1860s

- **Thinking about Worlds Together, Worlds Apart and Nations & Empires** Compare the eighteenth-century empires of Spain, Portugal, and Britain with the new empires arising in Africa at the end of the nineteenth century. What were the sources of their wealth and power? How and to what degree were colonial territories and economies integrated with their imperialist states?

- **Thinking about Changing Power Relationships and Nations & Empires** How did the growth of western influence and Japanese power lay the basis for

opposition movements in Africa and Asia? How did people respond to imperialism? Where was resistance most effective?

- **Thinking about Environmental Impacts and Nations & Empires** Describe the second industrial revolution and explain how it differed from the first industrial revolution. Pay special attention to the new technologies used in the late nineteenth century, especially the sources of power and new materials that were used.

Key Terms

Charles Darwin p. 802

imperialism p. 789

limited-liability joint-stock company p. 792

Manifest Destiny p. 790

Meiji Restoration p. 815

natural selection p. 802

Raj p. 805

Self-Strengthening movement p. 819

steel p. 801

 Go to INQUIZITIVE to see what you've learned—and learn what you've missed—with personalized feedback along the way.

1900	1950

Spanish-American War 1898

Meiji era in Japan 1868–1912

Sino-Japanese War 1894–1895

European expansion in sub-Saharan Africa 1870s–1890s

British occupation of Egypt 1882

British Raj 1858–1947

Construction of Trans-Siberian Railroad 1890s

Global Themes and Sources

Contextualizing the Scramble for Empire

In the second half of the nineteenth century, a handful of nation-states, most but not all of them in Europe, renewed their competition for colonial territory. Class conflict at home and resistance to their efforts abroad bred a new, conflictual vision that stressed competition and struggle in nature as well as human affairs. Doubts arose about the progressive nature of the changes ushered in by the era of the French and industrial revolutions, in particular the idea that granting more people the vote and spreading free markets would lead to peace and prosperity for everyone. Colonizers increasingly believed that they must control ever-greater expanses of territory or risk defeat by rival powers.

The documents presented here show imperialist powers' efforts to explain their actions, to defend their right to rule others, and to mark boundaries of inclusion and exclusion. The sources start in the Americas: John L. O'Sullivan asserts divine support for "Anglo-Saxon" expansion westwards. Next, Count Shigenobu Okuma celebrates Japanese dynamism over the course of the prior generation. In Russia, writing in the context of the empire's expansion eastward, Prince Esper Ukhtomskii considers his country's role as a colonial power in Asia by comparing the Romanov regime to its rivals. In the final document, the General Act of the Conference of Berlin concerning the Congo, the great powers of Europe set ground rules for their competition for territory in Africa.

All written at roughly the same time, these documents demand attention to historical context. Each, in different ways, asserts its country's right to dominate others. Pay special attention to the justifications each mobilizes and the authors' efforts to distinguish colonizer from colonized, those with the right to rule from everyone else.

Analyzing the Context of the Scramble for Empire

- How do the authors justify their country's right to rule others? What kind of reasons do they present (ethnic, moral, technological)?

- Compare the efforts to divide insiders from outsiders in these documents.

- Evaluate the balance between confidence and insecurity in each source.

PRIMARY SOURCE 17.1

"Manifest Destiny" (1845), John L. O'Sullivan

John L. O'Sullivan (1813–1895) was an American newspaper columnist and editor who urged the annexation of Texas to the United States in this 1845 article. He justified it on the basis of what he called "manifest destiny."

- Why does O'Sullivan dismiss slavery as a cause for U.S. expansion?

- Explain the relationship between the United States and Mexico in this document.

- What role does technology play in O'Sullivan's justification for U.S. expansion?

No—Mr. Clay was right when he declared that Annexation was a question with which slavery had nothing to do. The country which was the subject of Annexation in this case, from its geographical position and relations, happens to be—or rather the portion of it now actually settled, happens to be—a slave country. But a similar process might have taken place in proximity to a different section of our Union; and indeed there is a great deal of Annexation yet to take place, within the life of the present generation, along the whole line of our northern border. Texas has been absorbed into the Union in the inevitable fulfilment of the general law which is rolling our population westward; the connexion of which with that ratio of growth in population which is destined within a hundred years to swell our numbers to the enormous population of *two hundred and fifty millions* (if not more), is too evident to leave us in doubt of the manifest design of Providence in regard to the occupation of this continent. It was disintegrated from Mexico in the natural course of events, by a process perfectly legitimate on its own part, blameless on ours; and in which all the censures due to wrong, perfidy and folly, rest on Mexico alone. And possessed as it was by a population which was in truth but a colonial detachment from our own, and which was still bound by myriad ties of the very heartstrings to its old relations, domestic and political, their incorporation into the Union was not only inevitable, but the most natural, right and proper thing in the world—and it is only astonishing that there should be any among ourselves to say it nay. . . .

California will, probably, next fall away from the loose adhesion which, in such a country as Mexico, holds a remote province in a slight equivocal kind of dependence on the metropolis. Imbecile and distracted, Mexico never can exert any real governmental authority over such a country. The impotence of the one and the distance of the other, must make the relation one of virtual independence; unless, by stunting the province of all natural growth, and forbidding that immigration which can alone develope its capabilities and fulfil the purposes of its creation, tyranny may retain a military dominion which is no government in the legitimate sense of the term. In the case of California this is now impossible. The Anglo-Saxon foot is already on its borders. Already the advance guard of the irresistible army of Anglo-Saxon emigration has begun to pour down upon it, armed with the plough and the rifle, and marking its trail with schools and colleges, courts and representative halls, mills and meeting-houses. A population will soon be in actual occupation of California, over which it will be idle for Mexico to dream of dominion. They will necessarily become independent. All this without agency of our government, without responsibility of our people—in the natural flow of events, the spontaneous working of principles, and the adaptation of the tendencies and wants of the human race to the elemental circumstances in the midst of which they find themselves placed. And they will have a right to independence—to self-government—to the possession of the homes conquered from the wilderness by their own labors and dangers, sufferings and sacrifices—a better and a truer right than the artificial title of sovereignty in Mexico a thousand miles distant, inheriting from Spain a title good only against those who have none better. Their right to independence will be the natural right of self-government belonging to any community strong enough to maintain it—distinct in position, origin and character, and free from any mutual obligations of membership of a common political body, binding it to others by the duty of loyalty and compact of public faith. This will be their title to independence; and by this title, there can be no doubt that the population now fast streaming down upon California will both assert and maintain that independence.

Whether they will then attach themselves to our Union or not, is not to be predicted with any certainty. Unless the projected rail-road across the continent to the Pacific be carried into effect, perhaps they may not; though even in that case, the day is not distant when the Empires of the Atlantic and Pacific would again flow together into one, as soon as their inland border should approach each other. But that great work, colossal as appears the plan on its first suggestion, cannot remain long unbuilt. Its necessity for this very purpose of binding and holding together in its iron clasp our fast settling Pacific region with that of the Mississippi valley—the natural facility of the route—the ease with which any amount of labor for the construction can be drawn in from the overcrowded populations of Europe, to be paid in the lands made valuable by the progress of the work itself—and its immense utility to the commerce of the world with the whole eastern coast of Asia, alone almost sufficient for the support of such a road— these considerations give assurance that the day cannot be distant which shall witness the conveyance of the representatives from Oregon and California to Washington within less time than a few years ago was devoted to a similar journey by those from Ohio; while the magnetic telegraph will enable the editors of the "San Francisco Union," the "Astoria Evening Post," or the "Nootka Morning News" to set up in type the first half of the President's Inaugural, before the echoes of the latter half shall have died away beneath the lofty porch of the Capitol, as spoken from his lips.

Away, then, with all idle French talk of *balances of power* on the American Continent. There is no growth in Spanish America! Whatever progress of population there may be in the British Canadas, is only for their own early severance of their present colonial relation to the little island three thousand miles across the Atlantic; soon to be followed by Annexation, and destined to swell the still accumulating momentum of our progress. And whosoever may hold the balance, though they should cast into the opposite scale all the bayonets and cannon, not only of France and England, but of Europe entire, how would it kick the beam against the simple solid weight of the two hundred and fifty, or three hundred millions—and American millions—destined to gather beneath the flutter of the stripes and stars, in the fast hastening year of the Lord 1945!

Source: John L. O'Sullivan, "Manifest Destiny," in *The American West: A Source Book*, edited by Clark C. Spence (New York: Crowell, 1966), pp. 108–11.

Fifty Years of New Japan (1909), Count Shigenobu Okuma

Count Shigenobu Okuma (1838–1922) held high-ranking positions in the Meiji government and served as prime minister of Japan during World War I (1914–1916). The founder of Waseda University, he was an early advocate of western science and culture in Japan. In this document, he celebrates Japan's ability to draw on foreign influences.

- Identify the sources of Japan's strength, according to Okuma.

- Compare the justification for expansion in this document to the justifications in the documents by O'Sullivan and Ukhtomskii.

- Evaluate the balance in this document between internal sources of Japanese strength and borrowed foreign influences.

By comparing the Japan of fifty years ago with the Japan of today, it will be seen that she has gained considerably in the extent of her territory, as well as in her population, which now numbers nearly fifty million. Her government has become constitutional not only in name, but in fact, and her national education has attained to a high degree of excellence. In commerce and industry, the emblems of peace, she has also made rapid strides, until her import and export trades together amounted in 1907 to the enormous sum of 926,000,000 yen. Her general progress, during the short space of half a century, has been so sudden and swift that it presents a rare spectacle in the history of the world. This leap forward is the result of the stimulus which the country received on coming into contact with the civilization of Europe and America, and may well, in its broad sense, be regarded as a boon conferred by foreign intercourse. Foreign intercourse it was that animated the national consciousness of our people, who under the feudal system lived localized and disunited, and foreign intercourse it is that has enabled Japan to stand up as a world power. We possess today a powerful army and navy, but it was after Western models that we laid their foundations by establishing a system of conscription in pursuance of the principle "all our sons are soldiers," by promoting military education, and by encouraging the manufacture of arms and the art of shipbuilding. We have reorganized the systems of central and local administration, and effected reforms in the educational system of the empire. All this is nothing but the result of adopting the superior features of Western institutions. That Japan has been enabled to do so is a boon conferred on her by foreign intercourse, and it may be said that the nation has succeeded in this grand metamorphosis through the promptings and the influence of foreign civilization. For twenty centuries the nation has drunk freely of the civilizations of Korea, China, and India, being always open to the different influences impressed on her in succession. Yet we remain politically unaltered under one Imperial House and sovereign, that has descended in an unbroken line for a length of time absolutely unexampled in the world. We have welcomed Occidental civilization while preserving their old Oriental civilization. They have attached great importance to Bushido, and at the same time held in the highest respect the spirit of charity and humanity. They have ever made a point of choosing the middle course in everything, and have aimed at being always well-balanced. We are conservative simultaneously with being progressive; we are aristocratic and at the same time democratic; we are individualistic while also being socialist. In these respects we may be said to somewhat resemble the Anglo-Saxon race.

Source: Count Shigenobu Okuma, *Fifty Years of New Japan* (*Kaikoku Gojunen Shi*), 2nd ed., edited by Marcus B. Huish, vol. 2 (London: Smith, Elder, 1910), pp. 554–55, 571–72.

Russia's Imperial Destiny (1896), Prince Esper Ukhtomskii

Prince Esper Ukhtomskii (1861–1921), a poet, publisher, and ardent advocate of eastern expansion, was a close confidant of Tsar Nicholas II of Russia. He accompanied Nicholas on an Asian tour in 1890–1891, before the latter assumed the throne. Nicholas approved each chapter of Ukhtomskii's three-volume account of the journey before publication, which was part of his preparation to assume the throne.

- **How does Ukhtomskii justify Russian influence in Asia?**
- **What role does technology play in Russian expansion, according to Ukhtomskii?**
- **Which rival powers does Ukhtomskii discuss? What role do those rivalries play in Russian expansion?**

Our stay at Saigon, the base of French operations in the advance against important borderlands of China, will in its turn be marked by enthusiasm in the greeting of a friendly nation. For us Russians, who scarcely ever visit the distant lands of Asia to study the powers and the means of European colonists, a visit to the central point of the "Indo-Chinese" empire governed from Paris, will be doubly instructive, doubly useful after seeing the British domains and patriarchally protected Java. This will be the more appropriate in that every figure, every vivid detail, every living fact, must and will lead us to reflect, in what a marked degree we Russians, as regards our prestige in Asia, voluntarily resign to every comer from Europe our historical part and our inherited mission as leaders of the East.

In such an abnormal state of affairs all the gain, as regards material prosperity, falls to the share of the representatives of Western principles—representatives foreign in spirit, and in reality hateful to thsoe peoples of an ancient type on whom they have forced themselves by means of their cannon. Burmah, Cambodia, and Annam are no more; Siam is on the eve of dangerous external catastrophes; Japan is on the threshold of terrible internal dissensions; China alone, standing guard over its own, and unconsciously over Russian interests, holds its ground with the wisdom of the serpent, gathers its forces against the foe from beyond the seas, and anxiously glances towards the silent North, where is situated the only State from which the Celestial Empire, educated in autocratic principles, can expect moral support, disinterested assistance, and a practical alliance based on community of interests.

This northern land of mist, forest, and ice, the extreme east of Siberia, opened up by Khabaroff, and other bold pioneers like him, the land re-united to Russia by the genius of Mooravioff-Amoorsky—is still a realm of primitive quiet, of deepest stillness and stagnation. It is only with the end of the century, with the opening up of new ways of communication with our eastern coast, that a new era with all its unforeseen consequences may begin. Meanwhile the land bears the stamp of something unformed and sad, like the life of its original settlers. All the more attention and unprejudiced judgment, then, is required of any one who would draw a parallel between the lands of the Pacific south now opening out before us, with the emerald island of Java, the inexhaustible natural riches of the Indo-Chinese soil, the self-confident vitality of the Celestial Empire, and the marshes and retired nooks, the boundless desert borders, of the country whose mission, in spite of all this, is to be a source of light for the neighbouring expanse, with its countless population.

The tiny kingdom of Holland holds sway in Asia over more than thirty million human beings (and that, too, at the equator, in an earthly paradise), while in the third part of the same continent the most important Power in it cannot reckon up one-half the number.

European colonisers, though not without envy and enmity, have shared among them the best coast-districts of these lands. Towns of such universal commercial importance as Hong-Kong and Singapore are the most eloquent witnesses to the indefatigable enterprise of Europeans amidst the prevailing Asiatic torpor. But while drawing the juices out of this gigantic continent, and, wherever possible, holding hundreds of millions in a state of economic slavery, do the pioneers of civilisation hope for final success? Holding on to the brink and ledges of a precipice, are they not in a state of constant alarm, lest the stones should give way and hurl them into the abyss? When the whole East awakes, as it will sooner or later: when it realises its mighty power and determines to speak its mind, then threats, violence, and superficial victories will not remedy the internal discord. This is why it is Russia's part to grow in power unobserved amidst the wastes and deserts of the North in expectation of the conflict between two worlds, in which the decision will depend on neither of them.

The idea of invading a complex foreign life, of using Asia as a tool for the advancement of the selfish interests of modern, so-called civilised, mankind, was repugnant to us. For more than two hundred years we have remained at home; for our natural union with Turkestan and the region of the Amur cannot be regarded as political annexations. We have remained at home with our traditional carelessness and indolence, while the Pacific has become the arena of Western European advance against a native world with an ancient political constitution and an undoubted civilisation of its own.

The results are patent. The strangers have dethroned and oppressed the East. Coming here to live and make money, they do not find a home. (But any Asiatic borderland soon becomes a home for a Russian.) The natives are not brothers in humanity to them; for them the land is one of voluntary exile, and the people are considered as miserable and inferior beings. The latter gradually realise the meaning of these outrageous views, and repay their "masters" with intense hatred. But where and how are they to find protection and a bulwark against the foreign foe?

But the mythologising spirit is still alive amongst them. The more actively Europe presses on Asia, the brighter becomes the name of the White Tsar in popular report and tradition.

***

From that remote period when our great golden-domed Moscow, which but a little earlier was no more than a small town in an insignificant subordinate principality, received the blessing of the saints and was irradiated by the creative glow of the autocratic idea, the East, advancing on us with fire and sword, has masterfully drawn toward it the eyes of the Russians: has wakened in them sleeping powers and heroic daring: and now calls them onward to deeds of glory, to advancement beyond the bounds of a dull reality, to a bright, glorious, and ineffable future! There neither is nor ever has been a nation whose past is so closely bound up with its future, as may be seen in the growth of the Russian Empire. The man of the West (the German, the Frenchman, the Englishman, the Italian) must cross the seas to find relief from the pressure which overwhelms him at home. Far from his native land, he must build his temporal prosperity on a foundation of sand, and the more firmly he takes root there under conditions of the most favourable nature, the more evident does it become that his old home, and he the voluntary exile, belong to two perfectly alien worlds. Beyond the seas, away from the life of his native land, he may gain money and position, but cannot (except artificially and but for a short time) retain completely untouched the spirit of his people, their ideals and traditions.

Source: Prince E. Ukhtomskii, *Travels in the East of Nicholas II Emperor of Russia, When Cesarewitch 1890–1891*, vol. 2 (London: Archibald Constable and Company, 1890), pp. 142–43, 444–46.

General Act of the Conference of Berlin concerning the Congo (1885)

The Berlin Conference of 1884–1885 (also known as the Congo Conference) regulated European trade and colonization in sub-Saharan Africa in the late nineteenth century. The following selection is an excerpt from the General Act of the Conference.

- The document opens by expressing a desire for mutual understanding and a desire for economic growth. What challenges to progress and economic prosperity does the document suggest?
- Identify the priorities expressed in this document.
- What limits, if any, does this document impose on the colonizers?

In the name of Almighty God:

. . . Wishing to regulate in a spirit of good mutual understanding the conditions most favorable to the development of commerce and of civilization in certain regions of Africa, and to assure to all peoples the advantages of free navigation upon the two principal African rivers which empty into the Atlantic ocean; desirous on the other hand to prevent misunderstandings and contentions to which the taking of new possessions on the coast of Africa may in the future give rise, and at the same time preoccupied with the means of increasing the moral and material well being of the indigenous populations, have resolved, upon the invitation which has been addressed to them by the Imperial Government of Germany in accord with the Government of the French Republic, to assemble for this object a Conference at Berlin. . . .

Chapter I.

Declaration relative to the liberty of commerce in the basin of the Congo, its embouchures and neighboring country, and dispositions connected therewith.

Article 1.

The commerce of all nations shall enjoy complete liberty. . . .

Article 2.

All flags, without distinction of nationality, shall have free access to all the littoral of the territories above enumerated, to the rivers which there empty into the sea, to all the waters of the Congo and its affluents including the lakes, to all the ports situated upon the borders of these waters, as well as to all the canals which may in the future be excavated with the object of connecting together the water courses or lakes comprised in the whole extent of the territories described in Article 1. They may undertake every kind of transport and exercise the coastwise navigation by sea and river as also small boat transportation upon the same footing as the allegiants.

Article 3.

Merchandise of every origin imported into these territories, under whatever flag it may be, by route of sea or river or land, shall have to discharge no other taxes than those which may be collected as an equitable compensation for expenses useful to commerce and which, under this head, must be equally borne by the allegiants and by strangers of every nationality.

All differential treatment is prohibited in respect to ships as well as merchandise.

Article 4.

Merchandise imported into these territories shall remain free from entrance and transit dues.

The Powers reserve to themselves to decide, at the end of a period of twenty years, whether freedom of entry shall or shall not be maintained.

Article 5.

Every Power which exercises or shall exercise rights of sovereignty in the territories under consideration shall not concede there either monopoly or privilege of any kind in commercial matters.

Strangers shall enjoy there without distinction, for the protection of their persons and their goods, the acquisition and transmission of their movable and immovable property and for the exercise of the professions, the same treatment and the same rights as the allegiants.

Article 6.

Depositions relative to the protection of the natives, of missionaries and of travelers, and also to religious liberty.

All Powers exercising rights of sovereignty or an influence in the Said territories engage themselves to watch over the conservation of the indigenous populations and the amelioration of their moral and material conditions of existence and to strive for the suppression of slavery and especially of the negro slave trade; they shall protect and favor without distinction of nationality or of worship, all the institutions and enterprises religious, scientific or charitable, created and organized for these objects or tending to instruct the natives and to make them understand and appreciate the advantages of civilization.

The christian missionaries, the savants, the explorers, their escorts, properties and collections shall be equally the object of special protection.

Liberty of conscience and religious toleration are expressly guaranteed to the natives as well as to allegiants and to strangers.

The free and public exercise of all forms of worship, the right to erect religious edifices and to organize missions belonging to all forms of worship shall not be subjected to any restriction or hindrance.

***

Chapter II.

Declaration concerning the slave trade.

Article 9.

Conformably to the principles of the law of nations, as they are recognized by the signatory Powers, the slave trade being interdicted, and as the operations which, by land or sea, furnish slaves to the trade ought to be equally considered as interdicted, the Powers who exercise or shall exercise rights of sovereignty or an influence in the territories forming the conventional basin of the Congo declare that these territories shall not serve either for a market or way of transit for the trade in slaves of any race whatever. Each of these Powers engages itself to employ all the means in its power to put an end to this commerce and to punish those who are occupied in it.

Chapter III.

Declaration relative to the neutrality of the territories comprised in the conventional basin of the Congo.

Article 10.

In order to give a new guarantee of security to commerce and to industry and to favor, by the maintenance of peace, the development of civilization in the countries mentioned in Article 1 and placed under the regime of commercial liberty, the high signatory parties of the present Act and those who shall subsequently adhere to it engage themselves to respect the neutrality of the territories or parts of territories depending on said countries, including therein the territorial waters, so long as the Powers who exercise or shall exercise rights of sovereignty or protectorate over these territories, making use of the option to proclaim themselves neutrals, shall fulfill the duties which belong to neutrality.

***

Article 17.

There is instituted an International Commission charged to assure the execution of the dispositions of the present navigation Act.

The signatory Powers of this Act, as well as those who shall adhere to it hereafter, can, at all times, have themselves represented in the said Commission, each by one delegate. No delegate can dispose of more than one vote even in the case where he may represent several governments.

***

Article 19.

. . . In case of an abuse of power or of an injustice on the part of an agent or employé of the International Commission, the individual who shall regard himself as injured in his person or in his rights may address himself to the consular agent of his nation. The latter shall examine the complaint; if he finds it prima facie reasonable, he shall have the right to present it to the Commission. Upon his initiative, the Commission represented by at least three of its members, shall join itself to him to make an investigation touching the conduct of its agent or employé. If the consular agent considers the decision of the

Commission as giving rise to objections of right, he shall make a report of it to his government which may have recourse to the Powers represented in the Commission and invite them to come to agreement upon the instructions to be given to the Commission.

***

Chapter VI.

Declaration relative to the conditions essential to be fulfilled in order that new occupations upon the coasts of the African continent may be considered as effective.

Article 34.

The Power which henceforth shall take possession of a territory upon the coast of the African continent situated outside of its present possessions, or which, not having had such possessions hitherto, shall come to acquire them, and likewise, the Power which shall assume a protectorate there, shall accompany the respective act with a notification addressed to the other signatory Powers of the present Act, in order to put them in a condition to make available, if there be occasion for it, their reclamations.

Source: "The Treaty of Berlin," *American Journal of International Law* 3, no. 1, supplement: Official Documents (January 1909): 7–24

Interpreting Visual Evidence

Occidentalism: Representing Western Influence

Ever since the publication of Edward Said's landmark work *Orientalism* (1978), scholars have carefully examined European and American efforts to represent nonwestern peoples in disciplines ranging from art, languages, and literature to law, biology, and philosophy. The field of postcolonial studies that emerged in Said's wake has emphasized the degree to which western descriptions of "Orientals" were really efforts to describe themselves—as the rational, disciplined opposite of the supposedly sensual Orient—and to affirm their own values. More recently, scholarly attention has turned to different peoples' efforts to make sense of European and American influences on their societies—representations that we might call "Occidentalism" (the "Occident" meaning the west).

Here we consider a range of visual materials that both reflected and shaped ordinary people's views of western influence. These depictions circulated widely; notice the combination of text and images, for those who could not read. While Japan was not colonized, the Meiji Restoration relied heavily on European models for its constitution and economic plans. In *Bake-Bake Gakkō* (School of Demons) from the series *Kyosai Rakuga* (1874), Kawanabe Kyosai satirizes the European-inspired Japanese school reforms of the Meiji Restoration. The second image, *The Beating of the (Foreign) Devils and the Burning of the (Christian) Books* (c. 1890), shows Chinese Boxer rebels attacking foreign influence. In the final image, the Mexican

Kawanabe Kyosai's *Bake-Bake Gakkō*, number 3 of the *Kyosai Rakuga* series (Kawanabe Kyosai Memorial Museum).

The Beating of the (Foreign) Devils and the Burning of the (Christian) Books.

caricaturist José Guadalupe Posada mocks American influence in *The American Mosquito* (1910–1913). Whether the mosquitoes in question represent American tourists, the Americans brought in by Mexico's President Díaz to manage railroads and mines, or the American dollar remains unclear.

The American Mosquito.

Questions for Analysis

1. Compare the representation of foreign influence in all three works. Are those influences purely oppressive? Do any local actors appear to find outside influence appealing? What is the greater threat, according to these images, internal weakness or a coercive foreign intervention?

2. Analyze the relationship between local traditions and progress in each work. Do the images present a vision of progress? From the perspective of the artists, what is the relationship, if any, between foreign influence and progress?

3. Do the artists present a homegrown vision of progress, or is progress something that comes from abroad? Is it possible, from the artists' point of view, to be Japanese, Chinese, or Mexican and modern at the same time?

4. What messages do these works convey about their own societies? Do the artists present their own people as powerless victims, as vulnerable and divided, as caught between their own autocratic rulers and outside invaders, or perhaps as unified and defiant?

18

An Unsettled World

1890–1914

In 1905 a young African man, Kinjikitile Ngwale, began to move among various ethnic groups in German East Africa, spreading a message of opposition to German colonial authorities. In the tradition of visionary prophets (see Chapter 16), Kinjikitile claimed that by anointing his followers with blessed water (*maji* in Swahili), he could protect them from European bullets and drive the Germans from East Africa. Kinjikitile's reputation spread rapidly, drawing followers from across 100,000 square miles of territory. Although German officials soon executed Kinjikitile, they could not prevent a broad uprising, called the Maji Maji Revolt (1905–1907). The Germans brutally suppressed the revolt, killing between 200,000 and 300,000 Africans.

The Maji Maji Revolt and its aftermath revealed the intensity of opposition to the world of nations and their empires. In Europe and North America, critics who felt deprived of the full benefits of industrializing nation-states—especially women, workers, and frustrated nationalists—demanded far-reaching reforms. In Asia, Africa, and Latin America, anticolonial critics and exploited classes protested European domination. In the face of so much unrest from within their nations and from their colonies, Europeans' faith in the idea of progress and the superiority of their "civilization" was shaken. Ironically, this occurred at the very moment when Europeans and people of European descent seemed to have established preeminence in world affairs.

This chapter tackles the anxieties and insecurities that unsettled the world around the turn of the

Chapter Outline

- Progress, Upheaval, and Movement
- Discontent with Imperialism
- Worldwide Insecurities
- Cultural Modernism
- Rethinking Race and Reimagining Nations
- Conclusion

Core Objectives

- **EXPLAIN** the connections between migration and the development of nationalism in this period.
- **COMPARE** Chinese responses to imperialism with responses to imperialism in Africa.
- **IDENTIFY** and **DESCRIBE** political, economic, and social crises that swept through the world in this period, and **ANALYZE** the impact they had on different regions of the world.
- **EXPLAIN** the ways in which new cultural forms at the turn of the century reflected challenges to the world order as it then existed.
- **EVALUATE** the ways in which race, nation, and religion unified populations but also made societies more difficult to govern and economies more difficult to manage.

twentieth century. It ties them in particular to several key factors: (1) the uprooting of millions of people from countryside to city and from one continent to another, (2) discontent with the poverty that many suffered even as economic production increased, and (3) resentment of and resistance to European domination. Around the globe, this tumult caused a questioning of established ideas that led to a flowering of new thinking and fresh artistic expression under the label of "modernism." This unsettling movement was a defining feature of the era.

Global Storylines

- Numerous factors lead to global instability: vast population movements, worldwide financial crises, class conflict, the rise of women's consciousness, and hatred of colonial domination.

- Class conflict, economic instability, and great power rivalry within Europe combine with growing protest from overseas to undermine Europe's dominant position in world affairs.

- New scientific thinking and artistic expression, known as cultural modernism, challenge the dominant western view of progress and open Europe and North America to the cultural achievements of nonwestern societies.

Progress, Upheaval, and Movement

Rapid economic progress in the decades leading up to 1914 brought challenges to the established order and the people in power. In Europe and the United States, radicals and middle-class reformers agitated for political and social change. In areas colonized by European countries and the United States, resentment focused on either colonial rulers or indigenous elites. Even in nations such as China, which had not been formally colonized but which faced repeated intrusions, popular discontent targeted domination by Europeans. At the same time, millions of people migrated to cities and different countries in search of a better life.

In the late nineteenth century, whole new industries fueled economic growth, especially in the industrial countries and in territories that exported vital raw materials to Europe and the United States. But industrial capitalism also spurred inequalities within industrial countries and, especially, between the world's industrial and nonindustrial regions. Periodic economic downturns left thousands out of work. This led, in some cases, to organized opposition to authoritarian regimes or to the free market system; it also provoked new critiques of the new industrial order and the values that supported it.

In Europe and North America, a generation of young artists, writers, and scientists broke with older conventions and sought new ways of seeing and describing the world. In Asia, Africa, and South America as well, many of these innovators were energized by the idea of moving beyond traditional forms of art, literature, music, and science. But this generation's exuberance worried those who were not ready to give up their cultural traditions and institutions.

THE BIG PICTURE

What are the connections between migration and the development of nationalism in this period?

PEOPLES IN MOTION

If the world was being *unsettled* by political, economic, and cultural changes, it was also being *resettled* by mass emigration. (See Map 18.1.) The emigration of throngs of Europeans to temperate zones in the Americas and Oceania began after the Napoleonic wars and gathered momentum in the 1840s, when the Irish fled their starving communities to seek better lives in North America. After 1870, the flow of Europeans became a torrent. The United States was the favored destination, with six times as many European immigrants arriving there as in Argentina (the second-place receiving country) between 1871 and 1920. The high point occurred between 1901 and 1910, when over 6 million Europeans entered the United States. This was nothing less than a demographic revolution.

Emigration, Immigration, Internal Migration Europeans were not the only peoples on the move. Between the 1840s and the 1940s, 29 million

The Global View

Inset map labels (Europe):

NORTH SEA
Glasgow
BRITAIN
Bradford
Manchester and Leeds
Liverpool Sheffield
Birmingham
Bristol London
DENMARK Copenhagen
NETHERLANDS
Amsterdam Hamburg Berlin
Rotterdam GERMANY
Antwerp Wuppertal Dresden
BELGIUM Cologne Leipzig
Brussels Frankfurt
LUX. Nuremberg
Paris Munich
FRANCE SWITZ. AUSTRIA-HUNGARY
Lyons Milan
Bordeaux Turin ITALY
Marseilles

Main map labels:

CANADA

BRITISH COLUMBIA

UNITED STATES

Cleveland Pittsburgh
Montréal
Detroit Buffalo
Chicago Boston
San Francisco New York
St. Louis Philadelphia
Baltimore
Washington, D.C.
Cincinnati

CALIFORNIA

New Orleans

MEXICO
Mexico City

CUBA

CENTRAL AMERICA

TRINIDAD

VENEZUELA
COLOMBIA
GUYANA
ECUADOR
BRAZIL
PERU
BOLIVIA
PARAGUAY
CHILE
Rio de Janeiro
ARGENTINA
Santiago URUGUAY
Buenos Aires Montevideo

PACIFIC OCEAN

ATLANTIC OCEAN

NORWAY
Inset area
IRELAND Belfast
Dublin
PORTUGAL Barcelona
Lisbon Madrid
SPAIN TUNISIA
SPANISH MOROCCO
MOROCCO ALGERIA
SPANISH SAHARA
FRENCH WEST AFRICA
GAMBIA
PORT. GUINEA
SIERRA LEONE NIGERIA
LIBERIA TOGO
GOLD COAST SP. GUINEA

Migration figures:

32 million (1620–1914)
7.4 million (1530–1914)
12 million (1530–1860)
1.5 million (1850–1914)

Legend:

Boundary in 1914

Percentage Population Increase, 1700–1900
- 0–49%
- 50–99%
- 100–249%
- 250–1000%
- Over 1000%

City Population in 1900
- • 250,000–500,000
- • 500,000–1,000,000
- • Over 1,000,000

Major Population Movements, 1500–1914
Migration originating from:
- Europe, Scandinavia, and western Russia
- Asia
- Africa

Scale: 1000 2000 Miles
1000 2000 Kilometers

ARCTIC OCEAN

SWEDEN
Stockholm • St. Petersburg
Riga • Moscow

10 million
(1880–1914)

RUSSIAN

EMPIRE

SIBERIA

Breslau
Warsaw
Lodz
Vienna
Budapest
Bucharest
Istanbul
ITALY
Naples

AUSTRO-
HUNGARIAN
EMPIRE
Odessa

2.2 million
(1880–1914)

OTTOMAN
EMPIRE

Rome

Alexandria
Cairo
RIPOLI
EGYPT

PERSIA   AFGHANISTAN

OMAN

NEPAL BHUTAN

Lucknow

INDIA
Calcutta
Bombay
Hyderabad
Madras

MONGOLIA

MANCHURIA

Beijing
Tianjin

KOREA

CHINA

Wuhan
Chongqing

Shanghai

Guangzhou

BURMA

SIAM FRENCH
INDOCHINA
Bangkok

2 million

Nagoya **JAPAN**
Kyoto
Kobe Tokyo
Osaka Yokohama

1 million
(1880–1914)

22 million
(1820–1914)

8 million
(1900–1914)

**PACIFIC
OCEAN**

PHILIPPINES

FRENCH
SOMALILAND
BRITISH
SOMALILAND
ITALIAN
SOMALILAND

ANGLO-
EGYPTIAN
SUDAN
RENCH
EQUA-
TORIAL
AFRICA
ETHIOPIA

ERITREA

CAMEROON
BELGIAN
CONGO
CABINDA
GERMAN
EAST
AFRICA
NGOLA
RHODESIA

RM
UTH
EST
RICA
CAPE
COLONY

UGANDA
BRITISH
EAST
AFRICA

MADAGASCAR

BECHUANALAND

MOZAMBIQUE

4.3 million
(1500–1900)

3 million
(1850–1914)

BRUNEI
MALAYA N. BORNEO
SARAWAK
Singapore

DUTCH EAST INDIES

EAST
TIMOR

KAISER
WILHELMSLAND
PAPUA

**INDIAN
OCEAN**

3 million
(1790–1914)

AUSTRALIA

Sydney
Melbourne

**NEW
ZEALAND**

Map 18.1 Nineteenth-Century Migration

The nineteenth century witnessed a demographic revolution in terms of migration, urbanization patterns, and population growth. The world's population also rose from roughly 625 million in 1700 to 1.65 billion in 1900 (a two-and-a-half-fold increase).

- To what areas did most of the migrants from Europe go? What about the migrants from China, India, and Africa?
- What four areas saw the greatest population increase by 1900?
- How were migration flows and urbanization connected? What factors most accounted for these global population changes? Was internal growth more important than external migration in the case of the world's population growth? In what countries was population growth most affected by external or internal migration?

South Asians migrated into the Malay Peninsula and Burma (British colonies), the Dutch Indies (Indonesia), East Africa, and the Caribbean. Most were recruited to labor on plantations, railways, and mines in British-controlled territories. Meanwhile, the Chinese, too, emigrated in massive numbers. Between 1845 and 1900, population pressure, a shortage of cultivable land, and social turmoil drove 800,000 Chinese to seek new homes in North and South America, New Zealand, Hawaii, and the West Indies. Nearly four times as many settled in Southeast Asia. Moreover, industrial changes caused millions to migrate *within* their own countries or to neighboring ones, seeking employment in the burgeoning cities or other opportunities in frontier regions.

From the 1860s until 1914, governments imposed almost no controls on immigration or emigration. In China, the Qing government failed in its effort to restrict emigration into the dominant Manchus' northeastern homelands. The United States allowed entry to anyone who was not a prostitute, a convict, or a "lunatic"; but in 1882, racist reactions spurred legislation that barred entry to almost all Chinese. Travel within Europe required no passports or work permits; foreign-born criminals were subject to deportation, but that was the extent of immigration policy.

Urban Life Cities boomed, with both positive and negative effects. Tokyo's population climbed from 500,000 in 1863 to 1,750,000 in 1908, and London's passed 6.5 million. Major cities faced housing shortages, despite governments' massive rebuilding and beautification projects. This was the era when city planning came into its own—to widen and regularize thoroughfares for train and streetcar traffic, and to make crowded city life attractive to new inhabitants. City governments in New York, Cairo, Buenos Aires, Bombay, and Brussels spent lavishly on opera houses, libraries, sewers, and parks, hoping to ward off disease and crime and to impress others with their modernity. And yet, for all those efforts, cholera and tuberculosis remained major killers, and suicide and alcoholism became growing problems. Population movement and the growth of cities were distinct features of the later nineteenth century all over the world, opening up new opportunities to become rich or to sink into poverty.

Urban Transportation Streetcars in Tokyo, Japan's capital, are watched over by sword-bearing patrolmen in 1905, during the Russo-Japanese War. The first electric streetcar began running in Japan in 1895. Note the elevated electricity lines, which dated from the 1880s.

Discontent with Imperialism

In the decades before the Great War, opposition to European domination in Asia and Africa gathered strength. During the nineteenth century, as Europeans touted imperialism as a "civilizing mission," local prophets had voiced alternative visions contesting European supremacy (see Chapter 16). While imperialists consolidated their hold, suppression of unrest in the colonies required ever more force and bloodshed. As the cycle of resistance and repression escalated, many Europeans back home, mainly on the left and out of power, questioned the harsh means of controlling their colonies. By 1914, these questions were intensifying as colonial subjects across Asia and Africa challenged imperial domination.

UNREST IN AFRICA

Africa witnessed many anticolonial uprisings in the first decades of colonial rule. (See Map 18.2.) Violent conflicts embroiled not only the Belgians and the Germans, who paid little attention to African political traditions, but also the British, whose colonial system left traditional African rulers in place. These uprisings made Europeans uneasy. Why, they wondered, were Africans resisting regimes that had huge advantages in firepower and transport and that were bringing medical skills, literacy, and other fruits of European civilization? Some Europeans concluded that Africans were too stubborn or unsophisticated to appreciate Europe's generosity. Others, shocked by colonial cruelty, called for reform. A few radicals even demanded an end to imperialism.

The Anglo-Boer War The continent's most devastating anticolonial uprising occurred in South Africa. This unique struggle pitted two white communities against each other: the British in the Cape Colony and Natal against the Afrikaners, descendants of original Dutch settlers who lived in the Transvaal and the Orange Free State. (See Map 18.2 inset). Although two white regimes were the main adversaries, the Anglo-Boer War (1899–1902) involved the area's 4 million black inhabitants as fully as its 1 million whites.

The war's origins lay in the discovery of gold in the Transvaal in the mid-1880s. As the area rapidly became Africa's richest state, the prospect that Afrikaner republics might become the powerhouse in southern Africa was more than British imperialists could accept. Fearing that war was inevitable, the president of the Transvaal launched a preemptive strike against the British. In late 1899, Afrikaner forces crossed into South Africa. Fighting a relentless guerrilla campaign, Afrikaners waged a war that would last three years and cost Britain 20,000 soldiers and £200 million.

Core Objectives

COMPARE Chinese responses to imperialism with responses to imperialism in Africa.

Map 18.2 Uprisings and Wars in Africa

The European partition and conquest of Africa were violent affairs.

- How many separate African resistance movements can you count on this map?

- Where was resistance the most prolonged?

- According to your reading, why were Ethiopians, who sustained their autonomy, able to do what other African opponents of European armies were not?

Legend:
- Belgian
- British
- French
- German
- Italian
- Portuguese
- Spanish
- British dominion
- Independent state
- African resistance movement

- Area of Afrikaner settlements, c. 1800
- Great trek
- Afrikaner states at outbreak of war
- Afrikaners, 1899–1900
- ✕ Afrikaner victory, 1899–1900
- ✕ British victory, 1900
- ⚐ Diamond mining
- ● Gold mining

In a frustrated effort to respond to Afrikaner hit-and-run tactics, the British instituted a terrifying innovation: the concentration camp. At one moment in the war, at least 155,000 captured men, women, and children were held in camps surrounded by barbed wire. The British rounded up Afrikaners and Africans, whom they feared would side with the "anticolonial" Dutch descendants. Ultimately, the British won the war, bringing the Transvaal and the Orange Free State—with their vast gold reserves—into their empire. But the horrors of the war traumatized the British, who regarded themselves as Europe's most enlightened and efficient colonial rulers.

Other Struggles in Colonized Africa The disgust that some Europeans felt toward imperial violence deepened after Germany's activities in Africa also went brutally wrong. Germany had established colonies in South West Africa (present-day Namibia), Cameroon, and Togo in 1884 and in East Africa in 1885. In German South West Africa, the Herero and San people resisted the Germans in the Herero Revolt, and in German East Africa (modern-day Tanzania), the Muslim Arab peoples rebelled. Between 1904 and 1906, fighting in German South West Africa escalated to such an extent that the German commander issued an extermination order against the Herero population.

According to those who favored European imperialism, however, the atrocities of the Boer War and German South West Africa, like the horrors of Leopold's Belgian Congo (see Chapter 17), were exceptions to what they considered Europeans' enlightened rule. Europeans saw Africans either as accepting subjects or childlike primitives when they resisted—as in the Maji Maji Revolt in German East Africa, described at the beginning of this chapter—and redoubled their efforts to impose colonial order. The problem, in their view, was that they had not tried hard enough to bring civilization. In many cases, the number of officials stationed in the colonies increased.

Extermination of the Herero
This 1906 photograph shows a soldier guarding Herero women and children in a prison camp on the coast of German South West Africa (present-day Namibia). The Germans carried out a campaign of near-extermination against the Herero population in German South West Africa in 1904–1906. Nearly 90 percent of the Herero were killed.

THE BOXER UPRISING IN CHINA

Although not formally colonized, China too struggled against European intrusions. As the population swelled to over half a billion and outstripped the country's resources, problems of landlessness, poverty, and peasant discontent (long-standing concerns in China's modern history) left the established order vulnerable to internal revolts and foreign intervention.

The breakdown of dynastic authority originated largely with foreign pressure. For one thing, China's defeat in the Sino-Japanese War of 1894–1895 (see Chapter 17) was deeply humiliating. Japan acquired Taiwan as its first major colony, and European powers demanded that the weakened Qing government grant them specific areas within China as their respective "spheres of influence." (See Map 18.3.) The United States argued instead for maintaining an "open door" policy in China that would keep access available to all traders, while supporting missionary efforts to spread Christianity.

Unrest and Revolt The most explosive reaction to these pressures, the **Boxer Uprising,** started within the peasantry in 1899. Like colonized peoples in Africa, the Boxers violently resisted European meddling. And like the Taiping Rebellion decades earlier (see Chapter 16), the story of the Boxers was tied to missionary activities. Whereas in earlier centuries Jesuit missionaries had sought to convert the court and the elites, by the mid-nineteenth century the missionary goal was to convert commoners. After the Taiping Rebellion, Christian missionaries had streamed into China, impatient to make new converts in the hinterlands and confident of their governments' backing.

The Boxers rejected claims of western superiority. Especially in regions suffering from natural disasters and economic hardship, activists provided assistance to the dispossessed. Women played a prominent role. The so-called Red Lanterns were mostly teenage girls and unmarried women who announced their loyalty by wearing red garments. Although segregated from the male Boxers—Red Lanterns worshipped at their own altars and practiced martial arts at separate boxing grounds—they were important to the movement in counteracting the influence of Christian women. Indeed, one of the Boxers' greatest fears was that cunning Christian women would use their guile to weaken the Boxers' spirits. They claimed that the "purity" of the Red Lanterns could counter this threat. The Red Lanterns were supposedly capable of incredible feats: they could walk on water or fly through the air. Belief in their magical powers provided critical assistance for the uprising.

As the movement gained momentum, the Qing vacillated between viewing the Boxers as a threat to order and embracing them as a force to check foreign intrusion. Early in 1900, Qing troops clashed with the Boxers in an escalating cycle of violence. By spring, however, the Qing could no longer control the tens of thousands of Boxers roaming the vicinities of Beijing and Tianjin. Embracing the Boxers' cause, the empress dowager declared war against the foreign powers in June 1900.

Acting without any discernible plan or leadership, the Boxers attacked Christian and foreign symbols and persons. They harassed and sometimes killed Chinese Christians in parts of northern China, destroyed railroad tracks

Spheres of Influence

- British
- French
- British and French
- German
- Japanese
- Russian

Colonies

- British
- French
- Japanese
- ● Treaty port, 1842
- ● Treaty port, 1858–1889
- ● Treaty port, 1890–1907

Map 18.3 Foreign Spheres of Influence in China, 1842–1907

While technically independent, the Qing dynasty could not prevent foreign penetration and domination of its economy during the nineteenth century.

- Which five powers established spheres of influence in China?
- At what time was the greatest number of treaty ports established?
- According to your reading, what did the foreign powers hope to achieve within their spheres of influence? What kinds of local opposition did the foreign influence inspire?

The Boxer Uprising in China The Boxer Uprising was eventually suppressed by a foreign army made up of Japanese, European, and American troops that arrived in Beijing in August 1900. The picture here shows fighting between the foreign troops and the combined forces of Qing soldiers and the Boxers. After a period of indecision, the Qing court, against the advice of some of its officials, finally threw its support behind the struggle of the Boxers against the foreign presence, laying the ground for the military intervention of the imperialist powers.

and telegraph lines, and attacked owners of foreign objects such as lamps and clocks. In Beijing, the Boxers besieged foreign embassy compounds, where diplomats and their families cowered in fear. The Boxers also reduced the Southern Cathedral to ruins and then besieged the Northern Cathedral, where more than 3,000 Catholics and 40 French and Italian marines had sought refuge.

Foreign Involvement and Aftermath In August 1900, a foreign army of 20,000 troops crushed the Boxers. About half came from Japan; the rest came primarily from Russia, Britain, Germany, France, and the United States. Thereafter, the victors forced the Chinese to sign the punitive Boxer Protocol. It required the regime to pay an exorbitant compensation in gold (about twice the empire's annual income) for damages to foreign life and property. The protocol also authorized western powers to station troops in Beijing.

Even in defeat, the Boxers' anti-western uprising showed how much had changed in China since the Taiping Rebellion. Although the Boxers were primarily peasants, even they had felt the unsettledness generated by European inroads into China. Indeed, the Europeans' commercial and spiritual reach, once confined to elites and port cities, had extended across much of China. Whereas the Taiping Rebellion had mobilized millions against the Qing, the Boxers remained loyal to the dynasty and focused their wrath on foreigners and Chinese Christians. The Boxer Uprising, like the Maji Maji

Revolt in East Africa, revealed the widespread political opposition to westernization and the willingness of disaffected populations to resist western programs.

Worldwide Insecurities

While news of unrest in the distant colonies and in China generally did not lead Europeans to question their ways, conflicts closer to home tore at European confidence in this era. The rise of a European-centered world deepened rivalries within Europe. Numerous factors fostered conflict, including France's smoldering resentment at its defeat in the Franco-Prussian War (see Chapter 17), and led to a buildup of military forces, especially in Britain, Germany, and France. Tensions also increased as the European states competed for raw materials and colonial footholds. Not everyone, however, supported vast expenditures on the military. Many Europeans disapproved of spending on massive steam-powered warships. Others warned that the arms race would end in a devastating war. At the same time, the booms and busts of expanding industrial economies, challenges about the proper roles of women, and problems of uncontrolled urbanization shook the established order and had an impact across the globe. (See again Map 18.1.) These changes and insecurities transformed Europe and swept through the world.

Core Objectives

IDENTIFY and **DESCRIBE** political, economic, and social crises that swept through the world in this period, and **ANALYZE** the impact they had on different regions of the world.

FINANCIAL, INDUSTRIAL, AND TECHNOLOGICAL CHANGE

Economic developments helped make powers "great," but they could also unsettle societies. Indeed, pride about wealth and growth coincided with laments about changes in national and international economies. To begin with, Americans and Europeans recognized that the small-scale, laissez-faire capitalism championed by Adam Smith (see Chapter 14) was giving way to an economic order dominated by huge, heavily capitalized firms. Gone, it seemed, was Smith's vision of many small producers in vigorous competition with one another, all benefiting from efficient—but not exploitative—divisions of labor.

Instead of smooth progress, the economy of Europe and North America in the nineteenth century bounced between booms and busts: long-term business cycles of rapid growth followed by countercycles of stagnation. Late in the century, the pace of economic change accelerated. Large-scale steel production, railroad building, and textile manufacturing expanded at breakneck speed, while waves of bank closures, bankruptcies, and agricultural crises ruined many small property owners, including farmers. By the century's end, European and North American economies were dominated as never before by a few large-scale firms, such as John D. Rockefeller's Standard Oil and the large banking institutions in France, Britain, Germany, and the United States. The same was true in Japan, where *zaibatsu*—large companies with banking subsidiaries for finance and industrial wings dominating different sectors of the market—like Sumitomo, Mitsui, and Mitsubishi were the engine of Japan's extraordinary economic growth.

Financial Integration and Crises These were years of heady international financial integration. More and more countries joined the world system of borrowing and lending; more and more countries were linked financially through global loans and the fact that all of the major national currencies in the world, such as the American dollar, the British pound, and the French franc were exchanged at reliable rates. At the hub of this world system were the banks of London, which since the Napoleonic wars had been a major source of capital for international borrowers.

The rise of giant banks and huge industrial corporations caused alarm, for it seemed to signal an end to free markets and competitive capitalism. Rather than longing for the return of truly free markets, many critics sought reforms that would protect people from economic instability. The solution, many economists and politicians thought, was for the state to manage the national economies.

Banking especially seemed in need of closer government supervision. Many industrial societies already had central banks (banks that issued national currencies, fixed underlying interest rates, and in general controlled monetary policy); London's Bank of England had long since overseen local and international money markets. But governments did not have the resources to protect all—or even most—investments during times of crisis. Between 1890 and 1893, 550 American banks collapsed, and only the intervention of J. P. Morgan prevented the depletion of the nation's reserves of gold that stood behind the dollar.

The road to regulation of banking and finance, however, was hardly smooth. In 1907, a more serious crisis threatened. A panic on Wall Street led to a run on the banks. Once again, J. P. Morgan rescued the American economy from financial panic—by compelling financiers to commit unprecedented funds (eventually $35 million) to protect banks and trusts against depositors' panic. Morgan himself lost $21 million and emerged from the bank panic convinced that some sort of public oversight was needed. By 1913, the U.S. Congress ratified the Federal Reserve Act, creating boards to monitor the supply and demand of the nation's money. The crisis of 1907 also showed how national financial matters could quickly become international affairs as panicked American investors withdrew their funds from other countries, many of which relied on American capital.

Industrialization and the Modern Economy Backed by big banks, industrialists extended their enterprises to new places. For example, with loans from European investors, Russia built railways, telegraph lines, and factories. By 1900, Russia was producing half of the world's oil and a considerable amount of steel. Yet industrial development remained uneven: southern Europe and the American South continued to lag behind northern regions. The gap was even more pronounced in colonial territories, which contained few industrial enterprises aside from railroad building and mining.

By 1914, the factory and the railroad had become global symbols of the modern economy—and of its positive and negative effects. Everywhere, the coming of the railroad to one's town or village was a big event: for some, it represented an exhilarating leap into the modern world; for others, a terrifying abandonment of the past. Ocean liners, automobiles, and airplanes likewise could be both dazzling and disorienting.

For ordinary people, the new economy brought benefits and drawbacks. Factories produced cheaper goods, but they belched clouds of black smoke. Railways offered faster transport, but they ruined small towns unlucky enough to be left off the branch line. Machines (when operating properly) were more efficient than human and animal labor, but workers who used them felt reduced to machines themselves. Indeed, the American Frederick Winslow Taylor proposed a system of "scientific management" to make human bodies perform more like machines, maximizing the efficiency of workers' movements. But workers did not want to be managed or to cede control of the pace of production to employers. Labor's resistance to "Taylorization" led to numerous strikes. For strikers, as for those left out of the new economy, the course of progress had taken an unsettling turn.

THE "WOMAN QUESTION"

Complicating the situation was turmoil about the "woman question." In the west, female activists demanded that women be given more rights as citizens; more radical voices called for fundamental changes to the family and the larger society. At the same time, imperialists claimed that colonial rule was bringing great improvements to women in Asia and Africa. But the "woman question" was no more easily settled there than elsewhere.

Women's Issues in the West In western countries, for most of the nineteenth century, a belief in "separate spheres" had supposedly confined women to domestic matters, while leaving men in charge of public life and economic undertakings. (In practice, only women from middle- and upper-class families avoided working outside the home for wages.) However, as economic developments created new jobs for women and greater access to education, women increasingly found work as teachers, secretaries, typists, department store clerks, social workers, and telephone operators. These jobs offered greater economic and social independence. Some educated women spearheaded efforts to improve conditions for the urban poor and to expand the government's role in regulating economic affairs. Nonetheless, much of the population continued to think that higher education and public activism were not suitable for women.

In one important change, many women began to assert control over reproduction. Although in numerous countries the use of contraceptive devices was illegal, women still found a variety of ways to limit the number of children they bore. In addition to marrying late and sleeping apart, some used spermicidal herbs, which sometimes worked but sometimes killed the woman; others relied on a variety of sponges and other barriers, had their partners use condoms, or insisted on the practice of *coitus interruptus* (withdrawal). When contraception failed, many women turned to abortion, even though it was illegal. Successful contraception, by whatever means, depended on cooperation and communication and tended to be more effective as educational levels increased.

Early in the twentieth century, the birthrate in America was half of what it had been a century before. By having fewer children, families could devote more income to education, food, housing, and leisure activities. Declining birthrates, along with improved medicine, also meant that fewer women died in childbirth; more would see their children reach adulthood.

Still, changes in women's social status did not translate into full political rights at the national level, such as the vote. By the mid-nineteenth century, women's suffrage movements had appeared in several countries, but these campaigns bore little immediate fruit. In 1868, women received the right to vote in local elections in Britain. Within a few years, Finland, Sweden, and some American states allowed single, property-owning women the right to cast ballots—again, only in local elections. Women obtained the right to vote in national elections in New Zealand in 1893, in Australia in 1902, in Finland in 1906, and in Norway in 1913.

Despite these gains, male alarmists portrayed women's suffrage and women's rights as the beginning of civilization's end. Among women, views on feminism varied. Most middle-class women in Europe and the Americas were not seeking to make women equal to men. Indeed, many bourgeois women recoiled from the close relationships between socialism and feminism. In Latin America, for example, anarchists championed a version of feminism arguing that the abolition of private property would liberate women from their misery and that the traditional family was a bourgeois convention. Other women feared becoming too "mannish," and a few worried that equality would destroy female sensuality. Most, probably, looked to reform less in terms of voting rights and more in terms of better treatment within families and local communities.

Women's Status in Colonies In the colonial world, the woman question was also a contentious issue—but it was mainly argued among men. European authorities liked to boast that colonial rule improved women's status. Citing examples of traditional societies' treatment of women, they criticized the veiling of women in Islamic societies, the binding of women's feet in China, widow burning (*sati*) in India, and female genital mutilation in Africa. Europeans believed that prohibiting such acts was a justification for colonial intervention.

And yet, colonialism only added to women's burdens. As male workers headed into the export economy, formerly shared agricultural work fell exclusively on women's shoulders. In Africa, for example, the opening of vast gold and diamond mines drew thousands of men away to work in the mines, leaving women to tend to the farmstead and to do colonial tasks that men once did. Similarly, the rise of European-owned agricultural estates in Kenya and Southern Rhodesia depleted surrounding villages of male family members, who went to work on the estates. In these circumstances, women kept the local, food-producing economy afloat.

Nor did colonial "civilizing" rhetoric improve women's political or cultural circumstances. In fact, European missionaries preached a message of domesticity to Asian and African families, emphasizing that women's place was in the home raising children and that women's education should be different from men's. Thus, males overwhelmingly dominated the new schools that Europeans built. Moreover, the chiefs who collaborated with colonial officials consistently favored men. As a result, African women often lost landholding and other rights that they had enjoyed before the Europeans' arrival.

CLASS CONFLICT

As capitalism's volatility shook confidence in free market economies and sharpened conflicts between classes, the tone of political debate was transformed as new voices called for radical change. Although living conditions for European and North American workers improved over time, widening inequalities in income and the slow pace of reform bred frustration. Most workers remained committed to peaceful agitation, but some radicals favored violence against the state and its agents.

Strikes and Revolts In the Americas and in Europe, radicals adopted numerous tactics for asserting the interests of the working class. In Europe, the franchise was gradually expanded in hopes that the lower classes would prefer voting to revolution—and indeed, most of the new political parties that catered to workers had no desire to overthrow the state. But conservatives feared them anyway, especially as they gained electoral clout. The Labour Party, founded in Britain in 1900, quickly boasted a large share of the vote. By 1912, the German Social Democratic Party was the largest party in the Reichstag, though it lacked power since the Reichstag was only an advisory body. But it was not the legally sanctioned parties that sparked violent street protests and strikes in the century's last decades. A whole array of **syndicalists** (labor activists), **anarchists** (those who opposed government altogether), royalists, and socialists sprang up in this period, making work stoppages everyday affairs.

Although the United States had similar radical groups, they were few and small. Nonetheless, American workers were organizing. The labor movement's power burst forth dramatically in 1894. Spawned by wage cuts and firings following an economic downturn, the Pullman strike (directed against the maker of railway sleeping cars, George Pullman) involved approximately 3 million workers. The strike's conclusion, however, revealed the enduring power of the status quo. After hiring replacement workers to break the strike, Pullman requested federal troops to protect his operation. After its leaders were jailed, the strike collapsed. Although strikes and protests in the United States and Europe often failed to achieve their immediate goals, they worried those in power and ultimately led to important changes.

Revolution in Mexico Perhaps the most successful turn-of-the-century revolution occurred in Mexico. This peasant uprising thoroughly transformed the country. Fueled by the unequal distribution of land and by disgruntled workers, the **Mexican Revolution** erupted in 1910 when political elites split over the succession of General Porfirio Díaz after decades of his strong-arm rule. Dissidents balked when Díaz refused to step down, and peasants and workers rallied to the call to arms.

From the north (led by the charismatic Pancho Villa) to the south (under the legendary Emiliano Zapata), peasants, farmers, and other rural workers helped topple the Díaz regime. In the name of providing land for farmers and ending oligarchic rule, peasant armies defeated Díaz's troops and proceeded to destroy many large estates. The fighting lasted for ten brutal years, during which almost 10 percent of the country's population perished.

Thereafter, political leaders had to accept popular demands for democracy, respect for the sovereignty of peasant communities, and land reform. The revolution's most lasting legacy was perhaps the creation of rural communes for Mexico's peasantry. These communal village holdings, called *ejidos*, looked back to a precolonial heritage. The revolution spawned a set of new national myths based on the heroism of rural peoples, Mexican nationalism, and a celebration of the Aztec past.

Preserving Established Orders Although the Mexican Revolution succeeded in toppling the old elite, elsewhere in Latin America the ruling establishment remained united against assaults from below. Already, in 1897, the Brazilian army had mercilessly suppressed a peasant movement in the northeastern part of the country. Moreover, in Cuba, the Spanish and then the American armies crushed tenant farmers' efforts to reclaim land from sugar estates. In Guatemala, Maya Indians lost land to coffee barons.

In Europe and the United States, the preservation of established orders did not rest on repression alone. Here, elites also grudgingly agreed to gradual change. Indeed, by the century's end, left-wing agitators, muckraking reporters, and middle-class reformers began to win meaningful social improvements. Unable to suppress the socialist movement, Otto von Bismarck, the German chancellor, defused the appeal of socialism by enacting social welfare measures in 1883–1884, insuring workers against illness, accidents, and old age and establishing maximum working hours. In the United States, it took lurid journalistic accounts of unsanitary practices in Chicago slaughterhouses (including tales of workers falling into lard vats and being rendered into cooking fat) to spur the federal government into action. In 1906, President Theodore Roosevelt signed a Meat Inspection Act that provided for government supervision of meatpacking operations. In other cases (banking, steel production, railroads), the federal government's enhanced supervisory authority served corporate interests as well. These consumer and family protection measures reflected a broader reform movement, one dedicated to creating a more efficient society and correcting the undesirable consequences of urbanization and industrialization. At local and state levels, these **progressive reformers** attacked corrupt city governments that had allegedly fallen into the hands of immigrant-dominated "political machines." The progressives also attacked other vices, such as gambling, drinking, and prostitution—all associated with industrialized, urban settings. The creation of city parks preoccupied urban planners, who hoped parks' green spaces would serve as the city's "lungs" and offer healthier forms of entertainment than houses of prostitution, gambling dens, and bars. From Scandinavia to California, the proponents of old-age pensions and public ownership of utilities put pressure on lawmakers. Thousands of associations took shape against capitalism's harsher effects, and they occasionally succeeded in changing state policies. Indeed, the period leading up to World War I was one of rapid change, in which financial crises reverberated across the globe, European and American women pressed for their rights and also agitated for the rights of Asian and African women, and elites were forced to make reforms, though they tended to be limited, in the colonial and colonializers' worlds.

Cultural Modernism

As revolutionaries and reformers wrestled with the problems of progress, intellectuals, artists, and scientists struggled to make sense of change in their own societies and beyond. What we call **modernism**—the sense of having

progressive reformers
Members of the U.S. reform movement in the early twentieth century that aimed to eliminate political corruption, improve working conditions, and regulate the power of large industrial and financial enterprises.

modernism
In the arts, modernism refers to the effort to break with older conventions and seek new ways of seeing and describing the world.

Core Objectives

EXPLAIN how European modernism drew on Afro-Asian influences and represented uncertainty about ideas inherited from the Enlightenment.

broken with tradition—came to prominence in many fields, from physics to architecture, from painting to the social sciences.

Modernist movements were notably international. Egyptian social scientists read the works of European thinkers, while French and German painters flocked to museums to inspect artifacts from Egypt and artworks from other parts of Africa, Asia, and Oceania. As education spread and political reforms enfranchised more Americans and Europeans, changes in the meaning of culture occurred, causing it to be less elitist and more popular. Yet European elites did not give up their opera houses and paintings in favor of arts and entertainments that were appealing to urban workers or colonized peoples. Instead, the arts became more abstract: musicians abandoned the comfort of harmonic and diatonic sound (the eight-tone scale standard in classical western music at the time); writers and visual artists left realistic representation behind.

Above all, modernism in arts and sciences replaced the certainties of the Enlightenment with the unsettledness of the new age. Modernists challenged claims to provide complete, coherent explanations and representations of all kinds. With growing doubts about civilizing missions or urban and industrial "progress," artists and scientists struggled to understand a world in which human reason seemed inadequate.

POPULAR CULTURE COMES OF AGE

From the late eighteenth to the late nineteenth century, production and consumption of the arts, books, music, and sports changed dramatically. The change derived mainly from new urban settings, technological innovations, mass education, and increased leisure time. Middle-class art lovers eagerly purchased mass-produced engravings; millions attended dance halls and vaudeville shows (entertainment by singers, dancers, and comedians). For the first time, sports attracted mass followings. Soccer in Europe, baseball in the United States, and cricket in India had wildly devoted middle- and working-class fans. Thus did a truly **popular culture** emerge, delivering affordable and accessible forms of art and entertainment to "the masses."

By the nineteenth century's close, the press stood as a major form of popular entertainment and information. This was partly because publishers were offering different wares to different classes of readers and partly because many more people could read, especially in Europe and the Americas. By that time, the English *Daily Mail* and the French *Petit Parisien* boasted circulations of over 1 million. In the United States, urban dwellers, many of them immigrants, avidly read newspapers—some in English, others in their native languages. Banner headlines, sensational stories, and simple language drew in readers with little education or poor English skills.

popular culture
Affordable and accessible forms of art and entertainment available to people at all levels of society.

By now the kind of culture one consumed had become a reflection of one's real (or desired) status in society. For many Latin American workers, for example, reading one's own newspaper or comic strip was part of being a worker. Argentina's socialist newspaper, *La Vanguardia*, was one of Buenos Aires's most prominent periodicals, read and debated at work and in the cafés of working-class neighborhoods. Anyone seen reading the bourgeois paper, *La Prensa*, faced heckling and ridicule by fellow workers. As the community of cultural consumers broadened and as ideas from across the globe flooded in, writers, artists, and scholars struggled to adapt.

MODERNISM IN EUROPEAN CULTURE

In intellectual and artistic terms, Europe at the turn of the twentieth century experienced perhaps its richest age since the Renaissance. Artists' work reflected their doubts about the modern world, as represented by the railroad, the big city, and the factory. While the artists and writers of the mid-nineteenth century had largely celebrated progress, the painters and novelists of the century's end took a darker view. They turned away from reason, which the Enlightenment had championed, and descriptive prose as they searched for meanings that came from instinct and emotion. The primitive came to symbolize both Europe's lost innocence and the forces that reason could not control, such as sexual drives, religious fervor, or brute strength.

Europeans began to see the world in a fundamentally different way, aided by the experience of nonwestern visual arts. The painter who led the way in incorporating nonwestern themes into modern art was Pablo Picasso (1881–1973), who found in African art forms a radically new way of expressing

New Forms of Subjectivity Jean-Auguste-Dominique Ingres, one of the great realist artists of the nineteenth century, was one of Pablo Picasso's idols. The portrait of the newspaper baron Louis-François Bertin (*left*) embodies the artist's confidence in his own ability to represent an external reality just as it appears. Picasso refined his technique by copying Ingres's works at the Louvre. He clearly used Ingres as a model for his 1910 portrait of his own art dealer, Ambroise Vollard (*right*), which built on the work of the impressionists, in an effort to challenge the two-dimensional realism of his master.

human sentiments that was shocking to most European and American observers. Other artists were inspired by the sleekness and syncopation of machines or by the irrational content of dreams. And painting was not the only art form that displayed a modern style. Arnold Schönberg (1874–1951) composed the first piece of music that rejected traditional western tonality. World-famous dancers like Isadora Duncan (1877–1927) pioneered the expressive, free-form movements that laid the foundations for modern dance.

However, the arts alone did not undermine older views of the world. Even science, in which the Enlightenment had placed so much faith, challenged the idea that the world functioned according to easily understood natural laws. After 1900, pioneering physicists and mathematicians like Albert Einstein (1879–1955) challenged the idea that a single scientific theory, like Newton's, could explain everything. They took apart the Enlightenment's conviction that man could achieve full knowledge of, and control over, nature.

In a series of papers published between 1905 and 1915, Einstein worked out the special and general theories of relativity, which demonstrated that measurements of speed and gravitational pull were not purely objective but always conditioned by the relative position and conditions of the observer. Although most scientists continued to collect data, feeling certain that they could plumb nature's depths, some of their colleagues began to question the arrogance of this view.

From the time of the Enlightenment, Europeans had prided themselves on their "reason." To be rational was to be civilized and to master irrational urges; respectable, middle-class nineteenth-century men were thought to embody these virtues. But in the late nineteenth century, faith in rationality began to falter. Perhaps reason was *not* man's highest attainment, said some; perhaps reason was impossible for man to sustain, said others. Friedrich Nietzsche (1844–1900) claimed that conventional European attempts to assert The Truth—including science and Judeo-Christian moral codes—were nothing more than life-destroying quests for power. Sigmund Freud (1856–1939) began to excavate layers of the human subconscious, where irrational desires and fears lay buried. For Freud, human nature was not as simple as it had seemed to Enlightenment thinkers. Instead, he asserted, humans were driven by sexual longings and childhood traumas. Neither Nietzsche nor Freud was well loved among nineteenth-century liberal elites. But in the new century, Nietzsche would become the prophet for many antiliberal causes, from nudism to Nazism; and Freud's dark vision would become central to the twentieth century's understanding of the self.

CULTURAL MODERNISM IN CHINA

What it meant to be modern sparked debate beyond western Europe. Europeans provided one set of answers; thinkers elsewhere offered quite different answers. Chinese artists and scientists at the turn of the century selectively engaged western ideas and transformed them. Indeed, some scholars have described the late Qing period as a time of competing cultural *modernities*, in contrast to the post-Qing era, which pursued a single, western-oriented *modernity*. These forms of modernity involved critical reflection on Chinese traditions and mixed reactions to western culture.

As in the west, Chinese writers now had a wider readership. By the late nineteenth century, more than 170 presses in China were serving a potential readership of 2 to 4 million concentrated mostly in the urban areas. These cities were more economically and culturally vibrant than the hinterlands. Not only was there an expanding body of readers, but newly rich beneficiaries of the treaty-port economy now patronized the arts.

Painters from the lower Yangzi region, collectively known as the **Shanghai School**, adopted elements from both indigenous and foreign sources.

Shanghai School
Late nineteenth-century style of painting characterized by an emphasis on spontaneous brushwork, feeling, and the incorporation of western influences into classical Chinese pieces.

Although classically trained, they appropriated new western techniques into their art.

Similarly, fantasy novels drew on both western science and indigenous supernatural beliefs. Some experimental writers explicitly addressed Chinese–western relations. Depicting China at war with western powers, the novel *New Era* (1908) celebrated conventional military themes but also introduced western inventions such as electricity-repellent clothing and bulletproof satin.

Although steamships, telegraphs, and railroads captured public attention, there was little interest in changing fundamental Chinese beliefs. Indeed, even as Chinese intellectuals recognized new modes of knowledge, many of the elite insisted that Chinese learning remain the principal source of all knowledge. What kind of balance should exist between western thought and Chinese learning, or even whether the ancient classics should keep their fundamental role, was an issue that would haunt generations to come. In this respect, the Chinese dilemma reflected a worldwide challenge to accepting the impulses of modernism.

Modernism arose at a time when intellectuals began to question the values that had sustained Europe and North America throughout most of the nineteenth century. It reflected discontent with industrialization, income inequality, and colonial repression. Even though modernism had its origins and most profound impact in Europe, in many ways, especially in art, it drew upon nonwestern traditions and spread its influence throughout Asia and Africa among the educated classes.

Rethinking Race and Reimagining Nations

Core Objectives

EVALUATE the ways in which race, nation, and religion unified populations but also made societies more difficult to govern.

Ironically, at this time of huge population transfers and shared technological modernization, many European and American elites embraced the idea that the identities of peoples and nations were deeply rooted and unchangeable and were based on physical and cultural characteristics. By the century's close, racial roots had become a crucial part of identity. People wanted to know who they (and their neighbors) were—especially in terms of *biological* ancestry. Now the idea of inheritance took on new weight, in both cultural and biological forms. Nationalists spoke of the uniqueness of the Slavic soul, the German mind, Hindu spirituality, the Hispanic race.

Nationalist and racial ideas were different in different parts of the world. In Europe and America, debates about race and national purity reflected several concerns—above all, fear of being overrun by the brown, black, and yellow peoples beyond the borders of "civilization." By contrast, in India these ideas were part of the anticolonial debate, and they helped mobilize people politically. This was also the case in China, Latin America, and the Islamic world, where discussions of identity went hand in hand with opposition to western domination and corrupt indigenous elites.

As we will see, these new impulses produced a variety of national movements, from China's anti-Qing campaign to India's Swadeshi movement. At the same time, panethnic movements looked beyond the nation-state, envisioning communities based on ethnicity. Behind these movements was the notion that political communities should be built on racial purity.

NATION AND RACE IN NORTH AMERICA AND EUROPE

Americans and Europeans greeted the end of the century with a combination of pride and pessimism, and this mood influenced attitudes about national identity, race, and religion. In the early 1890s, for example, Americans flocked to extravagant commemorations of the four-hundredth anniversary of Christopher Columbus's discovery. Yet, at the same time, Americans—like many Europeans—feared for their future.

Regulating the Environment and Immigration Americans especially worried that the United States had exhausted its supposedly infinite supply of new land and resources—as evidenced by the disappearance of the buffalo, the erosion of soils, and the depletion of timber stands by aggressive logging companies. Conservationists' alarm grew more intense with the Census Bureau's 1890 announcement that the American frontier had "closed." When Theodore Roosevelt became president of the United States in 1901, he translated concerns about conserving natural resources into government policy. The market, insisted Roosevelt and like-minded conservationists, could not be trusted to protect "nature." Instead, federal regulation was necessary. This led in 1902 to the passage of the National Reclamation Act, which provided funding for large-scale dams and irrigation projects. Three years later, the Roosevelt administration orchestrated the establishment of the National Forest Service to manage the development of millions of acres of permanent public lands.

Another issue troubled the Americans: the need to maintain the dominance of persons of European descent. As a result, the government initiated new forms of racial discrimination where old forms (like slavery) had broken down. In the American West, animosity toward Chinese workers led to the 1882 Exclusion Act, which prohibited almost all immigration from China. In the American South, where most of the nation's 7 million African Americans resided, a system of "Jim Crow" laws—enacted after Reconstruction, especially in the 1890s and later, and in force until the 1960s—upheld racial segregation and inequality.

Theodore Roosevelt with John Muir President Theodore Roosevelt and Scottish-American conservationist John Muir (to the president's left) took a camping trip in Yosemite Valley, California, in 1903. The founder of the Sierra Club, Muir took this opportunity to urge Roosevelt to set aside additional land in Yosemite and other areas in the United States for national parks.

Americans from western Europe grew even more anxious as throngs of "swarthy" immigrants entered the United States from southern and eastern Europe. Even more threatening were darker peoples who were colonial subjects in the Philippines, Puerto Rico, and Cuba. Talk of the end of white America fueled support for more restrictive immigration policies.

Across the North Atlantic, European elites engaged in similar discussions about immigration and the environment. For them, the final divvying up of Africa was in many respects equivalent to the closing of the American frontier. The Germans and Italians, in particular, complained about the lack of new territories on which to plant their flags. The French and British, by contrast, worried about how to preserve their overseas empires in a period of intense international competition; both experienced widespread nativist campaigns on their respective mainlands, and England all but closed its borders with the Aliens Act of 1905.

New Social Issues in Europe Darwinist theory provoked new anxieties about inherited diseases, racial mixing, and the dying out of white "civilizers." Sexual relations between European colonizers and indigenous women—and their mixed offspring—had always been a part of European expansionism, but as racial identities hardened, many saw racial mixing as harmful to the supposedly superior white races. In addition, medical attention focused on homosexuality, regarding it as a disease and a threat to civilization.

Some people debated whether Jews—defined by religious practice or, increasingly, by ethnicity—could be fully assimilated into European society. Even though Jews had gained rights as citizens in most European countries by the late nineteenth century, powerful prejudices persisted. In the 1880s and 1890s, violent attacks known as pogroms, often involving police complicity, targeted the large Jewish populations in the Russian Empire's western territories and pushed the persecuted farther westward. These emigrants' presence, in turn, stirred up fear and resentment, especially in Austria, Germany, and France. Rumors circulated about Jewish bankers' conspiratorial powers, and anxieties over the "pollution" of the European races became widespread.

RACE-MIXING AND THE PROBLEM OF NATIONHOOD IN LATIN AMERICA

In Latin America, debates about identity chiefly addressed ethnic intermixing and the legacy of a system of government that, unlike in much of the North

Atlantic world, excluded rather than included most people. Social hierarchies reaching back to the sixteenth century ranked whites born in Spain and Portugal at the top, creole elites in the middle, and indigenous and African populations at the bottom. Thus, the higher on the social ladder, the more likely people were to be white.

Contested Mixtures and Invented Traditions "Mixing" did not lead to a shared heritage. Nor did it necessarily lead to homogeneity. In fact, the "racial" order did not stick, since some Iberians occupied the lower ranks, while a few people of color managed to ascend the social ladder. Moreover, starting in the 1880s, the racial hierarchy saw further disruption by the deluge of poor European immigrants; they flooded into prospering Latin American countrysides or into booming cities like Buenos Aires in Argentina and São Paulo in Brazil. Latin American societies, then, did not easily become homogeneous "nations."

Latin American leaders began to exalt bygone glories as a way to promote national identity and foster unity. Inventing successful myths could make a government seem more legitimate—as the heir to a rightful struggle of the past. In Mexico, many parades celebrated Aztec grandeur, thereby creating a mythic arc from the greatness of the Aztec past to the triumphal story of Mexican independence. As the government glorified the Aztecs with pageants, statues, and pavilions, however, it continued to ignore modern Aztec descendants, who lived in squalor. Thus, race in Latin America was a more fluid category than it was in North America and Europe.

SUN YAT-SEN AND THE MAKING OF A CHINESE NATION

Just as Latin Americans celebrated their past, Chinese writers emphasized the power and depth of Chinese culture—in contrast to the Qing Empire's failing political and social strength. Here, writers used race to emphasize the superiority of the Han Chinese. Here, too, the pace of change generated a desire to trace one's roots back to secure foundations. Moreover, traditions were reinvented in the hope of saving Chinese culture threatened by modernity.

Among those who thought most intensely about the future of China was **Sun Yat-sen** (1866–1925), whose life story symbolized the challenge of nation building. Sun was part of an emerging generation of critics of the old regime. Like his European counterparts, Sun dreamed of a political community reshaped along national lines. Born into a modest rural household in southern China, he studied medicine in the British colony of Hong Kong and then turned to politics during the Sino-Japanese War. When the Qing government rejected his offer of service to the Chinese cause, he became

Sun Yat-sen
(1866–1925) Chinese revolutionary and first provisional president of the Republic of China. Sun played an important role in the overthrow of the Qing dynasty and later founded the Guomindang, the Nationalist Party of China.

Adapting to the Environment: Russian Peasants Take on the Steppe

The Eurasian steppe extends for some 5,000 miles north of the Caucasus Mountains, from northern China and Mongolia to Hungary, and below the forest belt of the original Muscovy. When historians mention these grasslands at all, it is generally to treat them as a military highway for armies of nomads that formed their own short-lived empires and harassed others. In this telling, when steppe warriors stood in the way of imperial Russian state expansion, they were wiped out or bribed to enter into bargains with the state. In the case of the powerful freebooters of the Don River basin, known as Cossacks, the Russian Empire offered grants of land and respect for Cossack self-government in exchange for the Cossacks' help in defending the empire's southern frontier. But there is another, lesser known environmental history of the steppe—one that tells of wheat fields and locusts, of snowstorms and boundless skies, and of the ways in which peasant migrants from northern, watered forests learned to adapt their farming methods to the land.

Russians first became aware of the environmental peculiarities of this region soon after Catherine the Great annexed a large swathe of the southern steppe, dubbing it "New Russia." The tsarina had hoped to use this rich earth to feed Russians living on poorer northern lands. But already by the later eighteenth century, it was clear that increased farming was not yielding great increases in food production. Why not? Catherine sent officials to investigate, and at first they blamed the land, pointing to natural vegetation, recurring droughts, and other special qualities of the steppe environment. Over time, however, they realized that the problem lay in the farmers' practices, not in the land itself. The peasants were practicing farming as they had up north, grateful for the land but ignorant of it. Gradually, painfully, peasants as well as officials learned that because the steppe was different—hot and dry—it required

different methods. The old implements did not work either: a new type of plow was needed to break the heavier-rooted plant life, especially steppe fescue (feather grass).

A breakthrough occurred when a Mennonite farmer observed topsoil blowing off his field. He planted a line of trees to break the wind and, in winter, to help retain snow for moisture. Similarly, an agronomist noticed that ravines near the river were widening and advised peasants to leave a band of steppe grasses in place as they plowed, since the grasses would help hold down the soil. At first, many peasants resisted sowing less of the land. Eventually, however, they discovered that the advice enabled them to increase crop production because of reduced erosion. In other words, environmental awareness spread—and made a difference.

The geologist Vasily Dokuchaev (1846–1903) turned the environmental awareness of the settlers and peasants into the first form of soil science.

convinced that China's rulers were out of touch with the times. Subsequently he established an organization based in Hawaii to advocate the Qing downfall and the cause of republicanism. The cornerstone of his message was Chinese—specifically, Han—nationalism. Sun blasted the feeble rule by outsiders, the Manchus, and trumpeted a sovereign political community of "true" Chinese.

Replacing the Qing and Reconstituting a Nation Realizing that reforms were necessary, the Manchu court began overhauling the administrative system and the military in the aftermath of the Boxer Uprising. Yet these

Dokuchaev's breakthrough idea was this: the problem with steppe farming was not the steppe but the farmer. He made extensive studies across Russian regions, developed a theory of soil formation in relation to climate and human usage, and created the first soil classification system. He recommended crop rotations, longer fallow periods, and lighter plowing (to preserve topsoil). He wanted peasants to become stewards, not just exploiters, of the land.

By the latter part of the nineteenth century, agriculture in the steppe had taken off. Cossacks, too, had become successful farmers. New Russia, which was also called Ukraine, became a breadbasket (which it still is to a large extent). Imperial Russia became the world's leading agricultural exporter, feeding both Germany and Britain in the run-up to World War I.

Russia's environment was transformed. And yet, the agriculture of the steppe was not what we would call "sustainable." The minimal woods in the area were depleted (peasants continued to act as if they still lived in northern forests with endless supplies of timber), and the black-earth topsoil was significantly diminished. Later, this would spur the introduction of chemical fertilizers—which would increase crop yields but once again change the steppe ecosystem, adding pollutants to rivers. Like human history, the natural history of the steppe never stands still.

Harvest in the Ukraine **(1880)** This 1880 painting by Vladimir Orlovsky shows Ukrainian peasants bringing in the rich harvest of the steppe.

Questions for Analysis

- How did the steppe lands' usefulness to the Russian Empire change during the period described above?
- How did peasants, officials, and scientists learn to think differently about steppe lands?

Explore Further

Moon, David, *The Plough That Broke the Steppes: Agriculture and Environment on Russia's Grasslands, 1700–1914* (2013).

changes came too late. The old elites grumbled, and the new class of urban merchants, entrepreneurs, and professionals (who often benefited from business with westerners) regarded the government as outmoded. Peasants and laborers resented the high cost of the reforms, which seemed to help only the rulers.

A mutiny, sparked in part by the government's nationalization of railroads and its low compensation to native Chinese investors, broke out in the city of Wuchang in central China in 1911. As it spread to other parts of the country, Sun Yat-sen hurried home from traveling in the United States. Few people rallied to the emperor's cause, and the Qing dynasty collapsed and

Diego Rivera's *History of Mexico* This is one of the most famous works of Mexican art, a history of Mexico by the radical nationalist painter Diego Rivera. Completed in 1935, this work seeks to show a people fighting constantly against outside aggressors; it winds like a grand epic from their glorious preconquest days (lower center) to the conquest, the colonial exploitation, the revolution for independence, nineteenth-century invasions from France and the United States, and the popular 1910 revolution. It culminates in an image of Karl Marx, framed by a "scientific sun" (not shown here)—pointing to a future of progress and prosperity for all, as if restoring a modern Tenochtitlán of the Aztecs. This work captured many Mexicans' efforts to return to the indigenous roots of the nation and to fuse them with modern scientific ideas.

was replaced by the Republic of China, bringing an abrupt end to a dynastic tradition of more than 2,000 years.

China was soon reconstituted, and Sun's ideas, especially those regarding race, played a central role. The original flag of the republic, for example, consisted of five colors representing the citizenry's major racial groups: red for the Han, yellow for the Manchus, blue for the Mongols, white for the Tibetans, and black for the Muslims. But Sun had reservations about this multiracial flag, believing there should be only one Chinese race. The existence of different groups in China, he argued, was the result of incomplete assimilation—a problem that the modern nation now had to confront.

NATIONALISM AND INVENTED TRADITIONS IN INDIA

British imperial rule persisted in India, but the turn of the century saw cracks in its stranglehold. Four strands had woven the territory together: the consolidation of colonial administration, the establishment of railways and telegraphs, the growth of western education and ideas, and the development of colonial capitalism. Now it was possible to speak of India as a single unit. It was also possible for anticolonial thinkers to imagine seizing and ruling India by themselves. Thus a new form of resistance emerged, different from peasant rebellions of the past. Now, dissenters talked of Indians as "a people" who had both a national past and national traditions.

A Modernizing Elite Leaders of the nationalist opposition were western-educated intellectuals from colonial cities and towns. Although a tiny minority of the Indian population, they gained influence through their access to the official world and their familiarity with European knowledge and history. This elite group used their knowledge to develop modern cultural forms. For example, they turned colloquial languages (such as Hindi, Urdu, Bengali, Tamil, and Malayalam) into standardized, literary forms for writing novels and dramas. Now the publication of journals, magazines, newspapers, pamphlets, novels, and dramas surged, facilitating communication throughout British India.

Along with print culture came a growing public sphere where intellectuals debated social and political matters. By 1885, voluntary associations in big cities had united to establish a political party, the Indian National Congress. Lawyers, prominent merchants, and local notables dominated its early leadership. The congress demanded greater representation of Indians in administrative and legislative bodies, criticized the government's economic policies, and encouraged India's industrialization.

Underlying this political nationalism, embodied by the Indian National Congress, was cultural nationalism. The nationalists claimed that Indians might not be a single race but were at least a unified people, because of their unique culture and common colonial history.

Rewriting Traditions The recovery of traditions became a way to establish a modern Indian identity without acknowledging the recent subjugation by British colonizers. So Indian intellectuals (like those in Latin America) turned to the past and rewrote the histories of ancient empires and kingdoms. In this way, Indian intellectuals promoted the idea of India as a nation-state.

To portray Indians as a people with a unifying religious creed, intellectuals reconfigured Hinduism so that it resembled western religion. This was no easy task, for traditional Hinduism did not have a supreme textual authority, like the Bible or the Quran, a monotheistic God, an organized church, or an established creed. Nonetheless, nationalist Hindu intellectuals combined various philosophical texts, cultural beliefs, social practices, and Hindu traditions into a mix that they labeled the authentic Hindu religion. While fashioning hybrid forms, revivalists also narrowed the definition of Indian traditions.

As Hindu intellectuals looked back, they identified Hindu traditions and the pre-Islamic past as the only sources of India's culture. Other contributors to the region's mosaic past were forgotten; the Muslim past, in particular, had no prominent role.

Hindu Revivalism Hindu revivalism became a powerful political force in the late nineteenth century, when the nationalist challenge to the colonial regime took a militant turn. New leaders rejected constitutionalism and called for militant agitation. The British decision to partition Bengal in 1905 into two provinces—one predominantly Muslim, the other Hindu—drew militants into the streets to urge the boycott of British goods. Rabindranath Tagore, a famous Bengali poet and future Nobel laureate, composed stirring nationalist poetry. Activists formed voluntary organizations, called Swadeshi ("one's own country") Samitis ("societies"), that championed indigenous enterprises for manufacturing soap, cloth, medicine, iron, and paper, as well as schools for imparting nationalist education. Although few of these ventures succeeded, the efforts reflected the nationalist desire to assert Indians' autonomy as a people.

Unlike the insurgents of 1857, nationalist leaders in India at the turn of the twentieth century imagined a modern national community. Invoking religious and ethnic symbols, they formed modern political associations to operate in a national public arena. They did not seek a radical alternative to the colonial order; instead, they fought for the political rights of Indians as a secular, national community. In these new nationalists, British rulers discovered an enemy not so different from themselves.

THE PAN MOVEMENTS

India and China were not the only places where activists dreamed of founding new states. Across the globe, groups had begun to imagine new communities based on ethnicity or, in some cases, religion. **Pan movements** (from the Greek *pan*, "all") sought to link people across state boundaries. The grand aspiration of all these movements—which included pan-Asianism, pan-Islamism, pan-Africanism, pan-Slavism, pan-Turkism, pan-Arabism, pan-Germanism, and Zionism—was the rearrangement of borders in order to unite dispersed communities. But such remappings posed a threat to rulers of the Russian, Austrian, and Ottoman Empires, as well as to overseers of the British and the French colonial empires.

Pan-Islamism Within the Muslim world, intellectuals and political leaders begged their fellow Muslims to put aside their differences and unite under the banner of Islam in opposition to European incursions. The leading spokesman for pan-Islamism was the well-traveled Jamal al-Din al-Afghani

pan movements
Groups that sought to link people across state boundaries in new communities based on ethnicity or, in some cases, religion (e.g., pan-Germanism, pan-Islamism, pan-Slavism).

(1839–1897). Born in Iran and given a Shiite upbringing, he nonetheless called on Muslims worldwide to overcome their Sunni and Shiite differences so that they could work together against the west. Afghani called for unity and action, for an end to corruption and stagnation, and for acceptance of the true principles of Islam.

The pan-Islamic message only added to Muslims' confusion as they confronted the west. Indeed, Arab Muslims living as Ottoman subjects had many calls on their loyalties. Should they support the Ottoman Empire to resist European encroachments? Or should they embrace the Islamism of Afghani? Most decided to work within the fledgling nation-states of the Islamic world, looking to a Syrian or Lebanese identity, for example, as the way to deal with the west and gain autonomy. But Afghani and his disciples had struck a chord in Muslim culture, and their Islamic message has long retained a powerful appeal.

Sultan Abdul Hamid II Agrees to a Constitution In 1876, the new Ottoman sultan, Abdul Hamid II, agreed to reign as a constitutional monarch. Thanks in part to war with Russia, which commenced the next year, and in part to the sultan's own dictatorial instincts, the Ottoman Empire reverted to an absolute monarchy within two years, and the sultan began to promote himself as a Muslim leader.

Pan-Germanism and Pan-Slavism Pan-Germanism found followers across central Europe, where it often competed with a pan-Slavic movement that sought to unite all Slavs against their Austrian, German, and Ottoman overlords. This area had traditionally been ruled by German-speaking elites, who owned the land farmed by Slavic peasants. German elites began to feel increasingly uneasy as Slavic nationalisms (spurred by the midcentury revivals of traditional Czech, Polish, Serbian, and Ukrainian languages and cultures) became more popular. Even more threatening was the fact that the Slavic populations were growing faster than the German population. As pogroms in the Russian Empire's borderlands in the 1880s, as well as economic opportunities, drove crowds of eastern European Jews westward, German resentment toward these newcomers also increased.

The rhetoric of pan-Germanism inspired mass, grassroots political activism. It motivated central Europeans to think of themselves as members of a German *race*, their identities determined by blood rather than defined by state boundaries. This, too, was the lesson of pan-Slavism. Both movements led extremists to take actions that were dangerous to existing states. The organization of networks of radical southern Slavs, for example, unsettled Bosnia and Herzegovina (annexed by the Austrians in 1908). Indeed, it was a

Serbian proponent of plans to carve an independent Slav state out of Austrian territory in the Balkans who assassinated the heir to the Habsburg throne in June 1914. By August, the whole of Europe had descended into mass warfare, bringing much of the rest of the world directly or indirectly into the conflict as well. Eventually, the war would fulfill the pan-Slav, pan-German, and anti-Ottoman Muslim nationalist longing to tear down the Ottoman and Habsburg Empires. Intellectuals articulated the pan movements, but aspiring political leaders and secret societies took up their ideologies, leaving Europe and much of Asia at the end of the nineteenth century boiling with ideas of how to change the borders of states and the dominance of France and Britain.

Conclusion

Ever since the Enlightenment, Europeans had put their faith in "progress." Through the nineteenth century, educated, secular elites took pride in booming industries, bustling cities, and burgeoning colonial empires. Yet by the century's end, urbanization and industrialization seemed more disrupting than uplifting, more disorienting than reassuring. Moreover, colonized people's resistance to the "civilizing mission" fueled doubts about the course of progress.

The realization that "the people" were developing ways to unseat them terrified ruling elites. In colonial settings, nationalists learned how to mobilize large populations. In Europe, socialist and right-wing leaders likewise challenged liberals by appealing to the idea of popular sovereignty. A politics that relied on closed-door negotiations between "rational" gentlemen was unprepared to deal with modern ideas and identities.

Nor were elites able to control the scope of change, for the expansion of empires had drawn ever more people into an unbalanced global economy. Everywhere, disparities in wealth appeared. Moreover, the size and power of industrial operations threatened small firms and made individuals seem insignificant. Even some cities seemed too big and too dangerous. All these social and economic challenges stretched the capacities of gentlemanly politics.

They also stimulated creative energy. Western artists borrowed nonwestern images and vocabularies; nonwestern intellectuals looked to the west for inspiration, even as they formulated anti-western ideas. The upheavals of modern experience propelled scholars to study the past and to fabricate utopian visions of the future.

Even as these changes unsettled the European-centered world, they intensified rivalries among Europe's powers themselves. Although the world had become a smaller place and travel was easier and quicker, at least for those who had wealth and came from powerful societies, this increasing global integration had its limitations and contradictions. At its center—Europe—the global order was unstable. And in the massive conflict that destroyed this era's faith in progress, Europe would ravage itself. The Great War (described in Chapter 19) would yield an age of even more rapid change—with even more violent consequences.

Focus On
Sources of Global Anxieties and Expressions of Cultural Modernism

Global Trends

- Mass migrations and unprecedented urban expansion challenge national identities.

Africa and China: Anticolonialism

- The Anglo-Boer War and violent uprisings against colonial rule in Africa call Europe's imperializing mission into question.

- The Chinese rise up against European encroachments in the Boxer Uprising.

Europe and North America: Mounting Tensions

- Intense political rivalries, financial insecurities and crises, rapid industrialization, feminism, and class conflict roil Europe and spread to the rest of the world.

Mexico: Resentment toward Elites

- The most widespread revolution from below takes place in Mexico.

Cultural Modernism

- Increased earning power gives workers in wealthy nations the leisure to enjoy music, vaudeville shows, sports, and other forms of popular culture and to read mass-circulation newspapers.

- Elite culture explores new forms in painting, architecture, music, literature, and science in order to break with the past and differentiate itself more dramatically from popular culture.

- New ideas of race emerge, as does a renewed emphasis on the nation-state and nationalism.

Key Terms

anarchists p. 852

Boxer Uprising p. 844

Mexican Revolution p. 852

modernism p. 853

pan movements p. 866

popular culture p. 854

progressive reformers p. 853

Shanghai School p. 857

Sun Yat-sen p. 861

syndicalists p. 852

CHRONOLOGY	1870	1880	1890
Africa			
The Americas		Jim Crow laws in the United States 1890s–1960s	
Europe			
South Asia		Indian National Congress founded 1885 ●	
East Asia			

THINKING ABOUT GLOBAL CONNECTIONS

- **Thinking about Crossing Borders and an Unsettled World** How did mobility of different kinds unsettle established certainties in this period? Think in particular of the massive flight of farmers toward cities and the erosion of traditional social hierarchies; the prevalence of steamships and rail travel, which made long-distance journeys easier than ever before; and the emergence of the telephone and telegraph, which revolutionized communications.

- **Thinking about Changing Power Relationships and an Unsettled World** To what extent were challenges to western influence internal to the western tradition—the product of growing doubts and contradictions within the Enlightenment project—articulated by

Europeans like Nietzsche and Freud? To what degree were they external to that tradition—a reaction against the massive concentration of wealth and power centered in the west and the values that supported western dominance?

- **Thinking about Women and Gender in an Unsettled World** To what degree did the economic and technological breakthroughs of the nineteenth century improve women's lives? To what extent were women able to make claims on governments in different parts of the world? How did ordinary women take control of their bodies and their lives, and how did feminists challenge patriarchal cultures?

 Go to iNQUIZITIVE to see what you've learned—and learn what you've missed—with personalized feedback along the way.

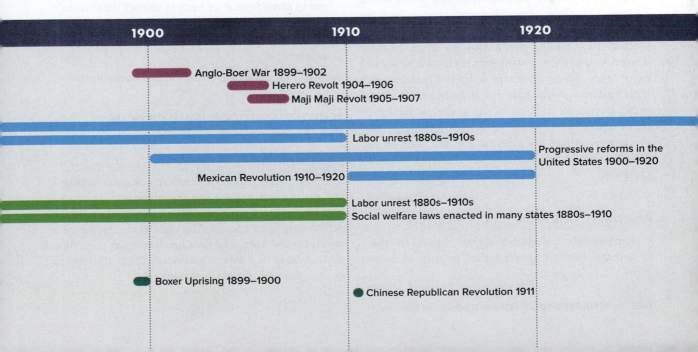

	1900	1910	1920

- Anglo-Boer War 1899–1902
- Herero Revolt 1904–1906
- Maji Maji Revolt 1905–1907
- Labor unrest 1880s–1910s
- Progressive reforms in the United States 1900–1920
- Mexican Revolution 1910–1920
- Labor unrest 1880s–1910s
- Social welfare laws enacted in many states 1880s–1910
- Boxer Uprising 1899–1900
- Chinese Republican Revolution 1911

Global Themes and Sources

Global Feminisms

The word *feminist* first entered common usage in French in the 1890s; shortly thereafter, it appeared in English and then in a wide array of languages. Demands for women's rights, however, emerged long before that, as we have seen, and they did so around the world.

Here we present a range of women's voices on women's rights. From the middle of the nineteenth century to the early twentieth, all four women spoke up on behalf of women and basic justice. All invoked religion in their writings. But they made their cases in very different ways: they differed in particular in their appreciation (or rejection) of women's difference from men and, in varying degrees, in their views of work, education, and the importance of motherhood. A former slave turned abolitionist orator and preacher, Sojourner Truth (c. 1787–1883) was unable to read or write. However, she left an indelible mark with her speeches. In the speech reprinted here, delivered at a women's rights convention in Akron, Ohio, in 1851, she rebukes the antifeminist statements of white male ministers. The next three documents were written by privileged women. Argentine writer María Eugenia Echenique centers her argument on equality of opportunity in an article published in a feminist journal. In a public speech Qiu Jin urges Chinese women to take their destiny into their own hands and encourages those who marry to be full partners with their husbands, while Bahithat al-Badiya concentrates in her lecture on equality in the workplace for Egyptian women.

Compare these documents. Pay attention to the different ways in which they all challenge women's exclusion.

Analyzing Global Feminisms Comparatively

- Explain what women's rights means to these authors. What supports rights, in their view, and what stands in the way of rights? Do the authors agree or disagree with one another?

- What social classes did these women represent? Explain the significance of class in each document.

- Compare the opinions of marriage and motherhood expressed in these documents.

- Compare the distinctions the texts draw between the private and public life.

"Ain't I a Woman?" (1851), Sojourner Truth

Born a slave in New York State, Sojourner Truth gained her freedom in 1827 and became well known as an abolitionist speaker and advocate of women's rights. This document is an extemporaneous speech to a women's convention in Akron, Ohio, in 1851, as remembered later by Frances D. Gage.

- Why did the other women at the meeting ask Gage not to allow Sojourner Truth to speak? What were they afraid of?

- What does Truth mean when she says, "Ain't I a woman?"

- What role does religion play in this document?

Reminiscences by Frances D. Gage.

Sojourner Truth.

The leaders of the movement trembled on seeing a tall, gaunt black woman in a gray dress and white turban, surmounted with an uncouth sun-bonnet, march deliberately into the church, walk with the air of a queen up the aisle, and take her seat upon the pulpit steps. A buzz of disapprobation was heard all over the house, and there fell on the listening ear, "An abolition affair!" "Woman's rights and niggers!" "I told you so!" "Go it, darkey!"

I chanced on that occasion to wear my first laurels in public life as president of the meeting. At my request order was restored, and the business of the Convention went on. Morning, afternoon, and evening exercises came and went. Through all these sessions old Sojourner, quiet and reticent as the "Lybian Statue," sat crouched against the wall on the corner of the pulpit stairs, her sun-bonnet shading her eyes, her elbows on her knees, her chin resting upon her broad, hard palms. At intermission she was busy selling the "Life of Sojourner Truth," a narrative of her own strange and adventurous life. Again and again, timorous and trembling ones came to me and said, with earnestness, "Don't let her speak, Mrs. Gage, it will ruin us. Every newspaper in the land will have our cause mixed up with abolition and niggers, and we shall be utterly denounced." My only answer was, "We shall see when the time comes."

The second day the work waxed warm. Methodist, Baptist, Episcopal, Presbyterian, and Universalist minister came in to hear and discuss the resolutions presented. One claimed superior rights and privileges for man, on the ground of "superior intellect"; another, because of the "manhood of Christ; if God had desired the equality of woman, He would have given some token of His will through the birth, life, and death of the Saviour." Another gave us a theological view of the "sin of our first mother."

There were very few women in those days who dared to "speak in meeting"; and the august teachers of the people were seemingly getting the better of us, while the boys in the galleries, and the sneerers among the pews, were hugely enjoying the discomfiture, as they supposed, of the "strong-minded." Some of the tender-skinned friends were on the point of losing dignity, and the atmosphere betokened a storm. When, slowly from her seat in the corner rose Sojourner Truth, who, till now, had scarcely lifted her head. "Don't let her speak!" gasped half a dozen in my ear. She moved slowly and solemnly to the front, laid her old bonnet at her feet, and turned her great speaking eyes to me. There was a hissing sound of disapprobation above and below. I rose and announced, "Sojourner Truth," and begged the audience to keep silence for a few moments.

The tumult subsided at once, and every eye was fixed on this almost Amazon form, which stood nearly six feet high, head erect, and eyes piercing the upper air like one in a dream. At her first word there was a profound hush. She spoke in deep tones, which, though not loud, reached every ear in the house, and away through the throng at the doors and windows.

"Wall, chilern, whar dar is so much racket dar must be somethin' out o' kilter. I tink dat 'twixt de niggers of de Souf and de womin at de Norf, all talkin' 'bout rights, de white men will be in a fix pretty soon. But what's all dis here talkin' 'bout?

"Dat man ober dar say dat womin needs to be helped into carriages, and lifted ober ditches, and to hab de best place everywhar. Nobody eber helps me into carriages, or ober mud-puddles, or gibs me any best place!" And raising herself to her full height, and her voice to a pitch like rolling thunder, she asked, "And a'n't I a woman? Look at me! Look at my arm! (and she bared her right arm to the shoulder, showing her tremendous muscular power). I have ploughed, and planted, and gathered into barns, and no man could head me! And a'n't I a woman? I could work as much and eat as much as a man—when I could get it—and bear de lash as well! And a'n't I a woman? I have borne thirteen chilern, and seen 'em mos' all sold off to slavery, and when I cried out with my mother's grief, none but Jesus heard me! And a'n't I a woman?

"Den dey talks 'bout dis ting in de head; what dis dey call it?" ("Intellect," whispered some one near.) "Dat's it, honey. What's dat got to do wid womin's rights or nigger's rights? If my cup won't hold but a pint, and yourn holds a quart, wouldn't ye be mean not to let me have my little half-measure full?" And she pointed her significant finger, and sent a keen glance at the minister who had made the argument. The cheering was long and loud.

"Den dat little man in black dar, he say women can't have as much rights as men, 'cause Christ wan't a woman! Whar did your Christ come from?" Rolling thunder couldn't have stilled that crowd, as did those deep, wonderful tones, as she stood there with outstretched arms and eyes of fire. Raising her voice still louder, she repeated, "Whar did your Christ come from? From God and a woman! Man had nothin' to do wid Him." Oh, what a rebuke that was to that little man.

Turning again to another objector, she took up the defense of Mother Eve. I can not follow her through it all. It was pointed, and witty, and solemn; eliciting at almost every sentence deafening applause; and she ended by asserting: "If de fust woman God ever made was strong enough to turn de world upside down all alone, dese women togedder (and she glanced her eye over the platform) ought to be able to turn it back, and get it right side up again! And now dey is asking to do it, de men better let 'em." Long-continued cheering greeted this. "'Bleeged to ye for hearin' on me, and now ole Sojourner han't got nothin' more to say."

Amid roars of applause, she returned to her corner, leaving more than one of us with streaming eyes, and hearts beating with gratitude. She had taken us up in her strong arms and carried us safely over the slough of difficulty turning the whole tide in our favor. I have never in my life seen anything like the magical influence that subdued the mobbish spirit of the day, and turned the sneers and jeers of an excited crowd into notes of respect and admiration. Hundreds rushed up to shake hands with her, and congratulate the glorious old mother, and bid her God-speed on her mission of "testifyin' agin concerning the wickedness of this 'ere people."

Source: Sojourner Truth, "Ain't I a Woman?" in *History of Woman Suffrage*, vol. 1, 2nd ed., edited by Elizabeth Cady Stanton, Susan B. Anthony, and Matilda Joslyn Gage (Rochester, NY: Charles Mann, 1889), 115–17.

PRIMARY SOURCE 18.2

"The Emancipation of Women" (1876), María Eugenia Echenique

In Argentina, the young writer María Eugenia Echenique (1851–1878) advocated scientific education for women. She presented her views in a leading women's newspaper, *La Ondina del Plata*, in July 1876, in reply to a critic who celebrated women's role as mothers who were responsible for the home and could only be corrupted by public life.

- **What, according to Echenique, is the principal obstacle standing in the way of women's rights?**
- **What is the relationship between motherhood and women's rights?**
- **Explain the significance of biological difference in this document.**

When emancipation was given to men, it was also given to women in recognition of the equality of rights, consistent with the principles of nature on which they are founded, that proclaim the identity of soul between men and women. Thus, Argentine women have been emancipated by law for a long time. The code of law that governs us authorizes a widow to defend her rights in court, just as an educated woman can in North America, and like her, we can manage the interests of our children, these rights being the basis for emancipation. What we lack is sufficient education and instruction to make use of them, instruction that North American women have; it is not just recently that we have proclaimed our freedom. To try to question or to oppose women's emancipation is to oppose something that is almost a fact, it is to attack our laws and destroy the Republic.

So let the debate be there, on the true point where it should be: whether or not it is proper for women to make use of those granted rights, asking as a consequence the authorization to go to the university so as to practice those rights or make them effective. And this constitutes another right and duty in woman: a duty to accept the role that our own laws bestow on her when extending the circle of her jurisdiction and which makes her responsible before the members of her family.

This, assuming that the woman is a mother. But, are all women going to marry? Are all going to be relegated to a life of inaction during their youth or while they remain single? Is it so easy for all women to look for a stranger to defend their offended dignity, their belittled honor, their stolen interests? Don't we see every day how the laws are trodden underfoot, and the victim, being a woman, is forced to bow her head because she does not know how to defend herself, exposed to lies and tricks because she does not know the way to clarify the truth?

Far from causing the breakdown of the social classes, the emancipation of women would establish morality and justice in them; men would have a brake that would halt the "imperious need" that they have made of the "lies and tricks" of litigations, and the science of jurisprudence, so sacred and magnificent in itself but degenerated today because of abuses, would return to its splendor and true objective once women take part in the forum. Generous and abnegated by nature, women would teach men humanitarian principles and would condemn the frenzy and insults that make a battlefield out of the courtroom.

"Women either resolve to drown the voice of their hearts, or they listen to that voice and renounce emancipation." If emancipation is opposed to the tender sentiments, to the voice of the heart, then men who are completely emancipated and study science are not capable of love. The beautiful and tender girl who gives her heart to a doctor or to a scientist, gives it, then, to a stony man, incapable of appreciating it or responding to her; women could not love emancipated men, because where women find love, men find it too; in both burns the same heart's flame. I have seen that those who do not practice science, who do not know their duties or the rights of women, who are ignorant, are the ones who abandon their wives, not the ones who, concentrated on their studies and duties, barely have time to give them a caress.

Men as much as women are victims of the indifference that ignorance, not science, produces. Men are more slaves of women who abuse the prestige of their weakness and become tyrants in their home, than of the schooled and scientific women who understand their duties and are capable of something. With the former the husband has to play the role of man and woman, because she ignores everything: she is not capable of consoling nor helping her husband, she is not capable of giving tenderness, because, preoccupied with herself, she becomes demanding, despotic, and vain, and she does not know how to make a happy home. For her there are no responsibilities to carry out, only whims to satisfy. This is typical, we see it happening every day.

The ignorant woman, the one who voluntarily closes her heart to the sublime principles that provoke sweet emotions in it and elevate the mind, revealing to men the deep secrets of the All-Powerful; the woman incapable of helping her husband in great enterprises for fear of losing the prestige of her weakness and ignorance; the woman who only aspires to get married and reproduce, and understands maternity as the only mission of women on earth—she can be the wife of a savage, because in him she can satisfy all her aspirations and hopes, following that law of nature that operates even on beasts and inanimate beings.

I would renounce and disown my sex if the mission of women were reduced only to procreation, yes, I would renounce it; but the mission of women in the world is much more grandiose and sublime, it is more than the beasts', it is the one of teaching humankind, and in order to teach it is necessary to know. A mother should know science in order to inspire in her children great deeds and noble sentiments, making them feel superior to the other objects in the universe, teaching them from the cradle to become familiar with great scenes of nature where they should go to look for God and love Him. And nothing more sublime and ideal than the scientific mother who, while her husband goes to cafes or to the political club to talk about state interests, she goes to spend some of the evening at the astronomical observatory, with her children by the hand to show them Jupiter, Venus, preparing in that way their tender hearts for the most legitimate and sublime aspirations that could occupy men's minds. This sacred mission in the scientific mother who understands emancipation—the fulfillment of which, far from causing the abandonment of the home, causes it to unite more closely—instead of causing displeasure to her husband, she will cause his happiness.

The abilities of men are not so miserable that the carrying out of one responsibility would make it impossible to carry out others. There is enough time and competence for cooking and mending, and a great soul such as that of women, equal to that of their mates, born to embrace all the beauty that exists in Creation of divine origin and end, should not be wasted all on seeing if the plates are clean and rocking the cradle.

Source: María Eugenia Echenique, "The Emancipation of Women," translated by Francisco Manzo Robledo, in *Reading about the World*, vol. 2, edited by Paul Brians et al. (Boston: Harcourt Brace College Publishing, 1999).

Injustices to Chinese Women (early twentieth century), Qiu Jin

Qiu Jin (1875–1907) was a Chinese revolutionary, feminist, and writer. She left her two children and an abusive marriage behind in 1903 to travel to Japan, where she wore men's clothing and learned to make bombs. She joined a range of overseas Chinese groups that strove to overthrow the Qing Empire and was later executed for her role in an abortive nationalist uprising. In the public address reprinted here, Qiu speaks out against arranged marriages and urges women to take charge of their own future.

- According to Qiu Jin, what is the principal obstacle standing in the way of women's rights?

- On what basis does Qiu criticize arranged marriages?

- What significance, if any, does motherhood have in this document? Does Qiu demand women's rights as mothers and educators of children or on some other basis?

An Address to Two Hundred Million Fellow Countrywomen

Alas! The greatest injustice in this world must be the injustice suffered by our female population of two hundred million. If a girl is lucky enough to have a good father, then her childhood is at least tolerable. But if by chance her father is an ill-tempered and unreasonable man, he may curse her birth: "What rotten luck: another useless thing." Some men go as far as killing baby girls while most hold the opinion that "girls are eventually someone else's property" and treat them with coldness and disdain. In a few years, without thinking about whether it is right or wrong, he forcibly binds his daughter's soft, white feet with white cloth so that even in her sleep she cannot find comfort and relief until the flesh becomes rotten and the bones broken. What is all this misery for? Is it just so that on the girl's wedding day friends and neighbors will compliment him, saying, "Your daughter's feet are really small"? Is that what the pain is for?

But that is not the worst of it. When the time for marriage comes, a girl's future life is placed in the hands of a couple of shameless matchmakers and a family seeking rich and powerful in-laws. A match can be made without anyone ever inquiring whether the prospective bridegroom is honest, kind, or educated. On the day of the marriage the girl is forced into a red and green bridal sedan chair, and all this time she is not allowed to breathe one word about her future. After her marriage, if the man doesn't do her any harm, she is told that she should thank Heaven for her good fortune. But if the man is bad or if he ill-treats her, she is told that her marriage is retribution for some sin committed in her previous existence. If she complains at all or tries to reason with her husband, he may get angry and beat her. When other people find out they will criticize, saying, "That woman is bad; she doesn't know how to behave like a wife." What can she do? When a man dies, his wife must mourn him for three years and never remarry. But if the woman dies, her husband only needs to tie his queue with a blue thread. Some men consider this to be ugly and don't even do it. In some cases, three days after his wife's death, a man will go out for some "entertainment." Sometimes, before seven weeks have passed, a new bride has already arrived at the door. When Heaven created people it never intended such injustice because if the world is without women, how can men be born? Why is there no justice for women? We constantly hear men say, "The human mind is just and we must treat people with fairness and equality." Then why do they greet women like black slaves from Africa? How did inequality and injustice reach this state?

Dear sisters, you must know that you'll get nothing if you rely upon others. You must go out and get things for yourselves. In ancient times when decadent scholars came out with such nonsense as "men are exalted, women are lowly," "a virtuous women is one without talent," and "the husband guides the wife," ambitious and spirited women should have organized and opposed them. When the second Chen ruler popularized footbinding, women should have challenged him if they had any sense of humiliation at all. . . . Men feared that if women were educated they would become superior to men, so they did not allow us to be educated. Couldn't the women have challenged the men and refused to submit? It seems clear now that it was we women who abandoned our responsibilities to ourselves and felt content to let men do everything for us. As long as we could live in comfort and leisure, we let men make all the decisions for us. When men said we were useless, we became useless; when they said we were incapable, we stopped questioning them even when our entire female sex had reached slave status. At the same time we were insecure in our good fortune and our physical comfort, so we did everything to please men. When we heard that men like small feet, we immediately bound them just to please them, just to keep our free meal tickets. As for their forbidding us to read and write, well, that was only too good to be true. We readily agreed. Think about it, sisters, can anyone enjoy such comfort and leisure without forfeiting dearly for it? It was only natural that men, with their knowledge, wisdom, and hard work, received the right to freedom while we became their slaves. And as slaves, how can we escape repression? Whom can we blame but ourselves since we have brought this on ourselves? I feel very sad talking about this, yet I feel that there is no need for me to elaborate since all of us are in the same situation.

I hope that we all shall put aside the past and work hard for the future. Let us all put aside our former selves and be resurrected as complete human beings. Those of you who are old, do not call yourselves old and useless. If your husbands want to open schools, don't stop them; if your good sons want to study abroad, don't hold them back. Those among us who are middle-aged, don't hold back your husbands lest they lose their ambition and spirit and fail in their work. After your sons are born, send them to schools. You must do the same for your daughters and, whatever you do, don't bind their feet. As for you young girls among us, go to school if you can. If not, read and study at home. Those of you who are rich, persuade your husbands to open schools, build factories, and contribute to charitable organizations. Those of you who are poor, work hard and help your husbands. Don't be lazy, don't eat idle rice. These are what I hope for you. You must know that when a country is near destruction, women cannot rely on the men any more because

they aren't even able to protect themselves. If we don't take heart now and shape up, it will be too late when China is destroyed.

Sisters, we must follow through on these ideas!

Source: Qiu Jin, "An Address to Two Hundred Million Fellow Countrywomen," in *Chinese Civilization: A Sourcebook*, 2nd ed., edited by Patricia Buckley Ebrey (New York: Free Press, 1993), pp. 342–44.

PRIMARY SOURCE 18.4

Industrialization and Women's Freedom in Egypt (1909), Bahithat al-Badiya

Malak Hifni Nasif (1886–1918) was born into a literary, middle-class Cairo family that encouraged her education. She was a member of the first graduating class of the Girls' Section of the 'Abbas Primary School in 1901 and continued her schooling in the Saniyyah Teacher Training College but had to quit when she married. She moved to the desert and began writing under the pseudonym Bahithat al-Badiya ("Seeker in the Desert").

- **How does the author's social background shape her views?**
- **Analyze the relationship between public and private in this text. What is the author's view of the idea of separate spheres for men and women?**
- **Explain al-Badiya's support for the veil.**

A Lecture in the Club of the Umma Party

Ladies, I greet you as a sister who feels what you feel, suffers what you suffer and rejoices in what you rejoice. . . .

Our meeting today is not simply for getting acquainted or for displaying our finery but it is a serious meeting. I wish to seek agreement on an approach we can take and to examine our shortcomings in order to correct them. . . . At the moment there is a semi-feud between us and men because of the low level of agreement between us. Men blame the discord on our poor upbringing and haphazard education while we claim it is due to men's arrogance and pride. This mutual blame which has deepened the antagonism between the sexes is something to be regretted and feared. God did not create man and woman to hate each other but to love each other and to live together so the world would be populated. If men live alone in one part of the world and women are isolated in another both will vanish in time.

Men say when we become educated we shall push them out of work and abandon the role for which God has created us. But, isn't it rather men who have pushed women out of work? Before, women used to spin and to weave cloth for clothes for themselves and their children, but men invented machines for spinning and weaving and put women out of work. In the past, women sewed clothes for themselves and their households but men invented the sewing machine. The iron for these machines is mined by men and the machines themselves are made by men. Then men took up the profession of tailoring and began to make clothes for our men and children. Before women winnowed the wheat and ground flour on grinding stones for the bread they used to make with their own hands, sifting flour and kneading dough. Then men established bakeries employing men. They gave us rest but at the same time pushed us out of work. . . .

I do not mean to denigrate these useful inventions which do a lot of our work. Nor do I mean to imply that they do not satisfy our needs. But, I simply wanted to show that men are the ones who started to push us out of work and that if we were to edge them out today we would only be doing what they have already done to us.

The question of monopolising the workplace comes down to individual freedom. One man wishes to become a doctor, another a merchant. Is it right to tell a doctor he must quit his profession and become a merchant or vice versa? No. Each has the freedom to do as he wishes. . . .

Specialised work for each sex is a matter of convention. It is not mandatory. We women are now unable to do hard work because we have not been accustomed to it. . . .

Nothing irritates me more than when men claim they do not wish us to work because they wish to spare us the burden. We do not want condescension,

we want respect. They should replace the first with the second. . . .

Men criticise the way we dress in the street. They have a point because we have exceeded the bounds of custom and propriety. We claim we are veiling but we are neither properly covered nor unveiled. I do not advocate a return to the veils of our grandmothers because it can rightly be called being buried alive, not *hijab*, correct covering. The woman used to spend her whole life within the walls of her house not going out into the street except when she was carried to her grave. I do not, on the other hand, advocate unveiling, like Europeans, and mixing with men, because they are harmful to us. . . .

If we had been raised from childhood to go unveiled and if our men were ready for it I would approve of unveiling for those who want it. But the nation is not ready for it now. . . .

Veiling should not prevent us from breathing fresh air or going out to buy what we need if no one can buy it for us. It must not prevent us from gaining an education nor cause our health to deteriorate. When we have finished our work and feel restless and if our house does not have a spacious garden why shouldn't we go to the outskirts of the city and take the fresh air that God has created for everyone and not just put in boxes exclusively for men. But, we should be prudent and not take promenades alone and we should avoid gossip. We should not saunter moving our heads right and left. . . .

The imprisonment in the home of the Egyptian woman of the past is detrimental while the current freedom of the Europeans is excessive. I cannot find a better model of today's Turkish woman. She falls between the two extremes and does not violate what Islam prescribes. She is a good example of decorum and modesty. . . .

If we pursue everything western we shall destroy our own civilisation and a nation that has lost its civilisation grows weak and vanishes.

Source: Bahithat al-Badiya, "A Public Lecture for Women Only in the Club of the Umma Party," from "Industrialization and Women's Freedom in Egypt," in *Opening the Gates: A Century of Arab Feminist Writing*, edited by Margot Badran and Miriam Cooke (Bloomington: Indiana University Press, 1990), pp. 228–34, 236.

Interpreting Visual Evidence

Global Modernism

Modernism was an international cultural movement that reacted against established traditions and sought to mark a break between the old and the new. In Europe, the movement's center, modernists challenged the Enlightenment belief in stable, universal truth. They criticized realism—the attempt to reproduce the natural world and human interactions faithfully, like a photograph—as naïve and superficial; they believed realists compressed a three-dimensional reality into two and left out the passions and often-irrational urges that motivate human behavior.

When the Franco-Spanish artist Pablo Picasso first showed his painting *Les Demoiselles d'Avignon* (The Courtesans of Avignon; 1907), his friends accused him of wasting his talents, and outraged critics likened the canvas to a broken pane of glass. Picasso broke all the rules of the art academies. He abandoned

Picasso, *Les Demoiselles d'Avignon.*

Ren Xiong, *Self-Portrait.*

perspective and proportion, distorted shapes, and borrowed from what at the time were considered primitive cultures in order to criticize the hypocrisies of bourgeois European culture. Rather than idealizing the human form of nymphs or classical goddesses, Picasso rendered it in jagged, jarring terms, presenting five common prostitutes in a brothel.

Influenced by Europe, modernists elsewhere challenged a different set of established traditions, but they too set out to redefine what it meant to be modern. For them, the problem was how to be Bengali, Chinese, or Egyptian, for example, and modern at the same time. In the self-portrait shown here (1850s), the Shanghai School artist Ren Xiong relied on old conventions in Chinese art, but the subject's pose, his facial expression, the physicality of his uncovered shoulder, and his engagement with the viewer all pointed in a new direction, as if to contrast the artist's experience with the established traditions of Chinese art.

The Indian artist Abanindranath Tagore painted a number of works that drew inspiration from Mughal art. His best known work, *Bharat Mata* (Mother India; 1905), presents a young woman with four arms, in the manner of Hindu gods, holding symbols of India's national aspirations—a book, sheaves of rice, Hindu prayer beads, and a white cloth—in an effort to create nationalist feeling in Indians across the subcontinent.

Tagore, *Bharat Mata*.

Questions for Analysis

1. Identify similarities in these works. Do you see connections in terms of the use of color or other artistic techniques? What characteristics, if any, do they share?

2. Who do you think made up the audiences for these works? With whom were the artists trying to communicate? To whom were they responding? How broad do you think they imagined their public was, compared to the audiences for the images reproduced in the Interpreting Visual Evidence section of Chapter 17?

3. What do you think each artist understood by the term *modern*, and how is this reflected in his work?

19

Of Masses and
Visions of the Modern

1910–1939

The last guns of the Great War (World War I) fell silent in a remote corner of East Africa. It took a full day for news of the armistice to reach that region, where African soldiers, under British and German officers, were battling for control of German East Africa. Here, 10,000 German-led African soldiers used guerrilla tactics to thwart the efforts of over 300,000 British-led African soldiers. Thousands of African troops died in these battles, beyond the spotlight of international opinion. Although most major battles occurred on European soil, campaigns bloodied the soil in sub-Saharan Africa, Egypt, Syria, and Turkey as well, and millions of African, Asian, and American soldiers were ferried across oceans to join the fight in Europe. The war's impact was thoroughly global.

Raging from August 1914 to November 1918, the Great War shook the foundations of the European-centered world. In addition to involving soldiers from Europe's colonies, it spread notions of freedom and self-determination and a growing disillusionment with European rule. Elsewhere, nations grappled with competing visions for building stable governments and strong economies.

This chapter deals with the Great War and its global impact. First, because the war was fought on a worldwide scale and to utter exhaustion in Europe, it required the resources of a large part of the world. It prompted production and consumption on a mass scale. Wartime leaders also used new media such as radio and film to promote

Chapter Outline

- The Quest for the Modern
- The Great War
- Mass Society: Culture, Production, and Consumption
- Mass Politics: Competing Visions for Building Modern States
- Conclusion

Core Objectives

- **IDENTIFY** the causes of World War I, and **ANALYZE** the effects of the war on regions both within and outside Europe.

- **EXPLAIN** how the development of modern, mass societies both caused and was affected by the Great Depression.

- **COMPARE** the ideologies of liberal democracy, authoritarianism, and anticolonialism, and **EVALUATE** the success of each in this period.

- **EXPLAIN** how access to consumer goods and other aspects of mass society influenced political conflict in Asia, Africa, and Latin America.

national loyalties and to discredit enemies—and thereby helped spread a mass culture. Second, the incomplete nature of the peace settlement contributed to the outbreak of the Great Depression. Third, political turmoil surrounding the war inflamed disputes over how to manage mass societies and build a better world. To this end, three distinct visions arose: liberal democracy, authoritarianism, and anticolonialism. These ideologies competed for preeminence in the decades leading up to World War II.

Global Storylines

- The Great War (World War I) engulfs the globe, exhausts Europe, and promotes production and consumption on a mass scale.

- The harsh terms of the peace settlement produce resentment in Germany and contribute to global economic problems.

- European countries' efforts to rebuild their economies after the Great War by cutting expenses and returning to the gold standard cause the Great Depression, which directly affects the entire global economy.

- Three strikingly different visions for building a better world arise: liberal democracy, authoritarianism, and anticolonialism.

The Quest for the Modern

When people spoke of "being modern" in the 1920s and 1930s, they disagreed about what it meant. For culture and the arts (see Chapter 18), the term *modernism* has a fairly precise meaning. It emerged in the late nineteenth century as a challenge to the supposedly conservative values of realism in Europe and to established artistic traditions elsewhere. In other fields, however, there was much less agreement. Reformers have always distinguished their ideas as modern or progressive while opposing accepted norms as backward or traditional. In the early twentieth century, most people agreed that in economic terms modernity involved mass production and mass consumption. In the west, for example, the automobile, the gramophone (record player), the cinema, and the radio reflected the benefits of economic progress and mass culture. In politics, being modern meant the involvement of the masses. Everywhere people favored strong leadership to reinvigorate their societies; some wanted more democracy to replace monarchical and colonial rule while others favored more authoritarian solutions.

The first political vision of being or becoming modern—the *liberal democratic* one—confronted economic failings that beset this period, such as the Great Depression, without sacrificing market economies or representative democracy. It widened participation in politics but also gave greater power to regulatory bureaucracies. After the Great Depression spread hard times and unemployment, this predominantly American and western European model linking capitalism and democracy no longer seemed so promising. Although many countries rejected the liberal perspective, the system survived in the United States, parts of western Europe, and several Latin American nations.

For many observers, liberal democracies failed to match the astonishing dynamism of a second perspective—*authoritarianism*. Authoritarian regimes rejected democracy, subordinated the individual to the state, managed and often owned most industries, used censorship and terror to enforce loyalty, and exalted an all-powerful leader. During this period, authoritarianism was evident in both right-wing dictatorships (including fascist Italy, Nazi Germany, dictatorial Spain and Portugal, and militaristic Japan) and a left-wing dictatorship (the Soviet Union).

The third vision—*anticolonialism*—also questioned the liberal democratic order, primarily because of its connection to colonialism. However, many anticolonialists did not reject representative democracy, private property, or free markets. Resentful of European rulers who preached democracy but practiced despotism, anticolonial leaders sought to oust their colonial rulers and then find their own path to modernity, their own vision of progress. They generally favored mixing western ideas with indigenous traditions.

Authoritarian and anticolonial visions of modernity both embraced technology and economic dynamism. They sought to take advantage of economic growth and mass support and redefine what freedom meant, while rejecting what they considered the hypocrisy and weakness of liberal democracy.

The Great War

Few events were more decisive in drawing men and women worldwide into national and international politics than the **Great War (World War I)**. For over four years, millions of soldiers from Europe, as well as from its dominions and colonies, killed one another. The war's carnage shook the hierarchies of prewar society around the world. Above all, the war made clear how much the power of the state now depended on the support of the people.

The war's causes were complex. At the heart of the European tensions, however, were nationalist rivalries, which pitted a rising Germany and a conflict-ridden Austria-Hungary against Britain, France, and Russia. Through most of the nineteenth century, Britain had been the preeminent power and Russia its principle rival (in Asia). By the century's end, however, the rise of Germany—Germany's industrial output surpassed Britain's—had driven Russia and France together. In 1907, Britain affiliated with them in the Triple Entente (later called the Allied Powers after Italy joined). Germany had allied with Austria-Hungary to form the Central Powers. The two rival blocs increasingly came into conflict in the Balkans, in territory formerly controlled by the Ottoman Empire

The assassination of Archduke Franz-Ferdinand of Austria in June 1914 set off a chain reaction. The assassin, a teenage Bosnian Serb named Gavrilo Princip, hoped to trigger an independence movement that would unite South Slav territories in the Austro-Hungarian Empire (see Chapter 18) with independent Serbia. The Austro-Hungarian emperor decided to take a firm stand, and the German kaiser backed him; the Russians declared support for the Serbs in an effort to uphold state prestige and stifle domestic political opposition. The British and French sought to prevent Germany and Austria from gaining any advantage. Throughout July, diplomats sought to negotiate a deal, but no one managed to prevent the outbreak of a war that would devastate all of Europe and drag its colonies into the warfare, too.

THE FIGHTING

Despite hopes for a swift resolution, the war became infamous for its duration and horrors. The initial German offensive stalled 30 miles outside Paris at the First Battle of the Marne, in September 1914. (See Map 19.1.) A stalemate

Great War (World War I) (August 1914–November 1918) A total war involving the armies of Britain, France, and Russia (the Allies) against those of Germany, Austria-Hungary, and the Ottoman Empire (the Central Powers). Italy joined the Allies in 1915, and the United States joined them in 1917, helping tip the balance in favor of the Allies, who also drew upon the populations and material of their colonial possessions.

Western Front

← Allied advance
← German advance
— The Western Front, November 1914
••• German offensive, spring 1918
–– The Western Front, March 1918
— Armistice Line, November 1918
✳ Major battle

Eastern Front

← Russian advance
← German advance
— Limit of Russian advance, 1914–1915
––– Limit of Austro-German advances, 1915–1916
— German penetration into Russia, June 1918
✳ Major battle

Map 19.1 World War I: The European and Middle Eastern Theaters

Most of the fighting in World War I, despite its designation as a world war, occurred in Europe. Although millions of soldiers fought on both sides, the territorial advances were relatively small. Look at the maps above, and identify all the countries where the Allies and Central Powers made advances.

• Which countries had to fight a two-front war?

• Did the armies of the Central Powers or the Allies gain the most territory during the war?

• According to your reading, how did those territorial gains affect the war's outcome?

Allies and colonies
Neutral nations that joined Allies
Central Powers
Neutral nations and empires that joined Central Powers and colonies
Neutral nations

← Allied advance
← Central Powers' advance
––– Maximum German Advance, 1918
— Armistice line, Nov. 11, 1918
— Armistice line, Treaty of Brest-Litovsk, 1918

Trenches in World War I The expectation of a short, decisive war turned out to be an illusion; instead, armies dug trenches and filled them with foot soldiers and machine guns. To advance entailed walking into a hail of machine-gun fire. Life in the trenches meant cold, dampness, rats, disease, and boredom.

ensued. Vast land armies dug trenches along the Western Front—from the English Channel through Belgium and France to the Alps—installing barbed wire and setting up machine-gun posts. Anything but glorious, life in the trenches mixed boredom, dampness, dirt, vermin, and disease, punctuated by the terror of being ordered to "go over the top" to attack the enemy's entrenched position. Doing so meant running across a "no man's land" in which machine guns mowed down almost all attackers. The war also witnessed new instruments of warfare, including poison gas; submarines; military aircraft, used primarily for reconnaissance; and, in the latter stages, tanks.

The death toll forced governments to call up more men than ever before. More than 70 million men worldwide fought in the war, including almost all of Europe's young adult males. From 1914 to 1918, 13 million served in the German army. In Russia more than 15 million men took up arms. In France around 8 million served, roughly 80 percent of men aged fifteen to forty-nine, a greater proportion than in any other major power. The British Empire mobilized nearly 9 million soldiers, and the 5.25 million troops of the United Kingdom (England, Scotland, Wales, and Ireland) constituted almost half the prewar population of men aged fifteen to forty-nine. Lord Kitchener—who had conquered Sudan in part by unleashing the machine gun on Sudanese warriors opposing conquest—had predicted to the British cabinet that the war in Europe "will not end until we have plumbed our manpower to the last military man." Over half of all the men mobilized for World War I were killed, injured, taken prisoner, or unaccounted for. Mass mobilization also undermined traditional gender boundaries. Tens of thousands of women served at or near the front as doctors, nurses, and technicians. Even more women mobilized on the "home front," taking on previously male occupations—especially in munitions plants. But women could also turn against the state. Particularly in central Europe and Russia, the war's demands for soldiers and supplies left farms untended and caused food shortages. Bread riots and peaceful protests by women, traumatized by loss and desperate to feed their children, put states on notice that their citizens expected compensation for their sacrifices. Indeed, civilian pressure forced many states to make promises they would have to fulfill after the war, in the form of welfare provisions, expanded suffrage, and pensions for widows and the wounded.

Empire and War The war's horrors reached around the globe. (See Map 19.2.) To increase their forces, the British and the French conscripted colonial subjects: India provided 1 million soldiers, who fought exclusively in the Middle Eastern theater; over 1 million Africans fought in Africa and Europe for their colonial masters, and another 3 million transported war supplies. Even the sparsely populated British dominions of Australia, New Zealand, and Canada dispatched over a million young men to fight for the empire.

The Ottoman decision to enter the war on the side of the Central Powers proved costly. In 1915–1916, as their fortunes declined, Ottoman forces massacred or deported 1.3 million Armenians, who were accused as a group of collaborating with the Russians. Many analysts regard these attacks as the world's first genocide, the intentional elimination of a whole people. The Ottoman alliance with the Central Powers made it inevitable that the British, French, and Russians, now enemies of the Ottomans, would draw up plans for dismembering the empire. Britain and France had long coveted Arab lands that remained under Ottoman control—what would later become Syria, Iraq, Lebanon, Jordan, and Palestine. No one foresaw the full consequences of the hastily drawn-up postwar borders in places such as Iraq and Syria: they would remain in existence until the twenty-first century, then be exploded by emancipated Shiites as well as by radical Sunni Islamists—notably al-Qaeda and the Islamic State of Iraq and Syria (ISIS), also known as the Islamic caliphate.

The Russian Revolution The war destroyed entire empires. The first to go was Romanov Russia. In February 1917, Tsar Nicholas II stepped down under pressure from his generals. They wanted to quash the mass unrest in the capital, St. Petersburg, which, they believed, threatened the war effort along the Eastern Front. Some members of the Russian parliament formed a provisional government; at the same time, grassroots councils (soviets) sprang up in factories, garrisons, and towns. The irony of Russia's February Revolution,

The Global View

GREENLAND

NORWAY
SWEDEN
FINLAND

CANADA

UNITED
KINGDOM
DENMARK
BALTIC SEA

GERMANY
POLAND

FRANCE
AUSTRIA-
HUNGARY

ROMANIA
ITALY
SERBIA
BLACK SEA
MONTENEGRO
BULGARIA
CAUCA

PORTUGAL
SPAIN
ALBANIA
GREECE
OTTOMAN
EMPIRE

UNITED
STATES
ATLANTIC
OCEAN
TUNISIA
IRAQ

MOROCCO
ALGERIA
LIBYA
EGYPT
ARAB

BRITISH
HONDURAS
BAHAMAS
RIO DE ORO

CUBA
JAMAICA
HONDURAS
NICARAGUA
WEST INDIES
GAMBIA
NIGERIA
ANGLO-
EGYPTIAN
SUDAN

BRITISH GUIANA
GUINEA
ETHIOPIA

COSTA
RICA
PANAMA
COLOMBIA
VENEZUELA
DUTCH GUIANA
FRENCH GUIANA
SIERRA LEONE
CAMEROON
UGANDA
KENYA

ECUADOR
GOLD COAST
TOGO

PERU
BRAZIL
GERMAN
EAST
AFRICA

BOLIVIA
NORTHERN
RHODESIA

PACIFIC
OCEAN
PARAGUAY
SOUTHERN
RHODESIA

CHILE
GERMAN
SOUTH
WEST
AFRICA
SOUTH
AFRICA

ARGENTINA
URUGUAY

Allied Powers, colonies, and allies
Central Powers and colonies
Neutral nations throughout the war
Troop movements

| 0 | | 1000 | | 2000 Miles |
| 0 | 1000 | | 2000 Kilometers | |

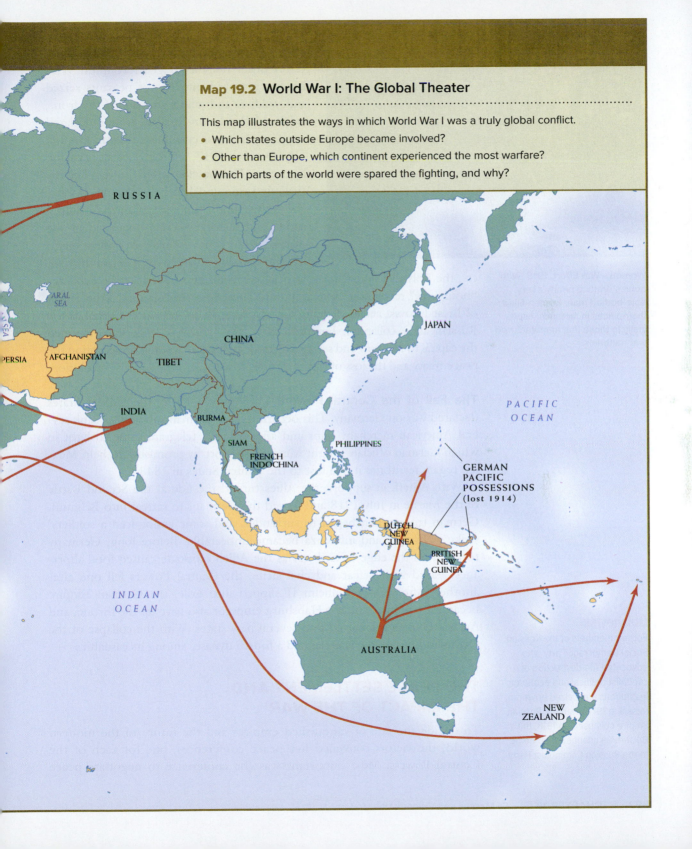

Map 19.2 World War I: The Global Theater

This map illustrates the ways in which World War I was a truly global conflict.

• Which states outside Europe became involved?

• Other than Europe, which continent experienced the most warfare?

• Which parts of the world were spared the fighting, and why?

RUSSIA

ARAL
SEA

PERSIA   AFGHANISTAN

CHINA

TIBET

JAPAN

INDIA

BURMA

SIAM

FRENCH
INDOCHINA

PHILIPPINES

PACIFIC
OCEAN

GERMAN
PACIFIC
POSSESSIONS
(lost 1914)

DUTCH
NEW
GUINEA

BRITISH
NEW
GUINEA

INDIAN
OCEAN

AUSTRALIA

NEW
ZEALAND

Women's War Effort, 1915 With armies drafting nearly every able-bodied man, women filled their places in factories, especially in those that manufactured war materials.

which brought an end to the monarchy, was that the military and civilian elites wanted to restore order, not encourage a revolution. With the tsar removed, millions of peasants seized land, soldiers and sailors abandoned the front, and borderland non-Russian groups declared autonomy from the crumbling Russian Empire.

In October 1917, left-wing socialists calling themselves **Bolsheviks** seized power. Led by Vladimir Lenin and Leon Trotsky, the Bolsheviks drew support among radicalized soldiers, sailors, and factory workers organized in the soviets. Arresting provisional government members and claiming power in the name of the soviets, the Bolsheviks proclaimed a socialist revolution to overtake the February "bourgeois" revolution. Several months later, Soviet Russia signed the Treaty of Brest-Litovsk, acknowledging German victory on the Eastern Front as the Russian army collapsed. For protection, the Bolshevik leadership relocated the capital to Moscow and set up a dictatorship. Lenin insisted on accepting the peace treaty and the loss of vast territories to safeguard the socialist revolution.

The Fall of the Central Powers On April 2, 1917, the United States declared war on Germany. This occurred after German submarines sank several American merchant ships and after a secret telegram came to light in which German officials sought Mexican support by promising to help Mexico regain territories it had lost to the United States in 1848.

With American support, the Allies turned the tide at the Second Battle of the Marne in July 1918 and forced the Germans to retreat into Belgium. German troops then began to surrender, and some announced a soldiers' strike as hunger and influenza became unbearable. Before long, Germany tottered on the edge of civil war as the Allied blockade caused food shortages. Faced with defeat and civil strife, the Central Powers fell one after another. After Kaiser Wilhelm II slipped into exile, the German Empire became a republic. The last Habsburg emperor also gave up the throne, and Austria-Hungary dissolved into several new states. With the collapse of the Ottoman Empire, the war claimed a fourth dynasty among its casualties.

THE PEACE SETTLEMENT AND THE IMPACT OF THE WAR

To decide the fate of vanquished empires and the future of the modern world, the victors convened five peace conferences, one for each of the Central Powers. Most important was the conference to negotiate peace

Bolsheviks Former members of the Russian Social Democratic Party who advocated the destruction of capitalist political and economic institutions and seized power in Russia in 1917 when the Russian Empire collapsed. In 1918, the Bolsheviks changed their name to the Russian Communist Party.

with Germany, held at Versailles, France, in January 1919. Delegates drew many of their ideas from American president Woodrow Wilson's "Fourteen Points," a blueprint he had devised for making peace in Europe. Wilson especially insisted that postwar borders be redrawn by following the principle of "self-determination of nations" and that an international League of Nations be set up to negotiate further quarrels. Such high-minded ideas were appealing, but once delegates got down to the business of carving up Europe and doling out Germany's colonies, negotiations became tense and difficult. Over the objections of the Americans and British, the French insisted on a punitive treaty that assigned Germany sole blame for the war and forced it to pay reparations.

BROKEN PROMISES AND POLITICAL TURMOIL

The war's hurricane of violence followed the invention of the Maxim gun and barbed wire (originally intended to hold livestock), pogroms in imperial Russian borderlands, British concentration camps in the Boer War, and Belgian horrors in the Congo, but still proved earth shattering in its scope. Violence became an enduring part of politics.

The American goal of making the world safe for democracy proved illusory. The idea of self-determination created intractable problems. Although President Wilson had intended self-determination to apply principally to the ethnic minorities within the Russian and Austro-Hungarian Empires and to European peoples still under Ottoman rule, other groups expected the term to apply to themselves as well. In Europe, making ethnic and political boundaries coincide proved impossible. Suddenly, 60 million people in central and eastern Europe emerged as inhabitants of new nation-states. (See Map 19.3.) Many were unhappy, as perhaps 25 million now lived in states in which they were ethnic minorities and vulnerable to persecution in the tumultuous years after the armistice. Furthermore, colonial subjects demanded states of their own. One of them, a photographer's assistant living in Paris named Nguyen Ai Quoc, the future Ho Chi Minh, famously challenged the American delegation at Versailles to take their own principles seriously and support his people's liberation from French rule, to no avail.

The Russian Revolution Vladimir Lenin died just six years and three months after the October 1917 revolution, but he lived on in his writings and in images, such as in this painting by Alexander Gerassimov called *Lenin on the Stand.* Artists and propagandists helped make Lenin an icon of the new Soviet order.

Map 19.3 Outcomes of World War I in Europe, North Africa, and Some of the Middle East

....

The political map of Europe and the Middle East changed greatly after the peace treaty of 1919.

- Comparing this map with Map 19.1, which shows the European and Middle Eastern theaters of war, identify the European countries that came into existence after the war.

- What happened to the Ottoman Empire, and what powers gained control over many territories of the Ottoman state?

- What states emerged from the Austro-Hungarian Empire?

Beyond Europe, the principle of self-determination galvanized anticolonial and nationalist sentiment, but these sentiments were almost entirely dashed by France and Britain's imperial ambitions. The British, after a long-drawn-out military campaign, suppressed a 1919 rebellion in Egypt, albeit only after promising Egyptian nationalists a limited form of autonomy. The Syrians, too, did not understand why they were less deserving of self-rule than the Czechoslovaks or Yugoslavs, but the French put down a Syrian nationalist revolt. In India, similarly inspired by Wilsonian ideals, a bloody confrontation between peaceful protesters, gathered in a garden in the city of Amritsar in the Punjab, resulted in the killing of 370 Indians and the wounding of 2,000 (although Indian eyewitnesses claimed that the dead totaled more than 1,000). In China, students, offended by the minor status accorded to their country at Versailles, launched a widespread protest in the name of Wilsonianism that solidified nationalist sentiment for this generation of students and later ones.

The bloodiest of all conflicts occurred in Iraq, where nearly 600,000 people—more than 20 percent of the population—rose up against British military efforts to force them into a colonial state. The rebellion's first stages were so successful that the Iraqis established an independent state in the middle Euphrates region, one that brought together Sunni and Shiite leaders and Arab officers and soldiers who had formerly served with the Ottoman army but desired an independent Iraqi state. Ultimately, British forces totaling 73,000, of whom 63,000 were Indian soldiers, were needed to crush the rebellion.

A final set of broken promises occurred in an Arab nationalist movement led by the emir of Mecca, Sharif Husayn. Believing that he had British military and political support to create an independent Arab state in Syria, parts of Palestine, Jordan, and Iraq, Sharif Husayn led a general Arab rebellion against the Ottoman Turks. He was disabused when the Bolsheviks published secret peace agreements that had been negotiated between the British and the French during the war. One of these was the Sykes-Picot Agreement (signed in 1916 by Mark Sykes on behalf of the British and François Georges-Picot for the French), which divided the Arab east between Britain and France. (See Map 19.4.) A second promise, for a homeland for the Jews in Palestine, also angered Arab nationalists: the Balfour Declaration of November 2, 1917, took the form of a letter sent by the British foreign secretary, Arthur James Balfour, to Baron Rothschild, leader of the British Jewish community, and fulfilled a Zionist aspiration for a national homeland for the Jewish people in Palestine. The declaration did acknowledge the rights of the local residents, stating that it was "clearly understood that nothing shall be done which may prejudice the civil and religious rights of existing non-Jewish communities in Palestine, or the rights and political status enjoyed by Jews in any other country." Nonetheless, the declaration failed to reconcile competing claims, and it ultimately led to the creation of the state of Israel and numerous Arab-Israeli wars.

Map 19.4 The Sykes-Picot Agreement

....

The Sykes-Picot Agreement was negotiated between British diplomat Mark Sykes and French diplomat François Georges-Picot in 1916. While the agreement reserved protectorates for the French in Syria and the British in Iraq, it also supported the creation of a politically independent Arab state or confederation of Arab states under an Arab chief.

- Why did the British and French governments want to divide up the Arab provinces of the Ottoman Empire?
- Compare the areas that were to be the Arab confederation (though dominated by the French and the British) with the areas in the map of ISIS that appears in the Epilogue (Map E.5). How similar are the territories in both maps?
- Why do you think that Arabs in particular and Muslims in general believed that this agreement was antithetical to their wishes and was an inadequate recompense for their contributions to the war effort? Why do you think that it continues to this day to fuel powerful grievances against the west?

Mass Society: Culture, Production, and Consumption

The war dramatically extended the making of mass societies. Even before 1914, democratic regimes had begun to extend the right to vote, in many cases making non–property holders and women eligible to cast ballots. Authoritarian regimes, meanwhile, had begun to mobilize the people via rallies and mass organizations. And new technologies, such as radio, were helping to create mass cultures that spanned geographic and class divides.

MASS CULTURE

New forms of communication and entertainment contributed to the new mass culture. In an effort to mobilize populations for total war, leaders had disseminated propaganda as never before—through public lectures, theatrical productions, musical compositions, and (censored) newspapers. Indeed, the war's impact had politicized cultural activities while broadening the audience for nationally oriented information and entertainment.

Postwar *mass culture* was distinctive. First, it differed from elite culture (opera, classical music, paintings, literature) because it reflected the tastes of the working and the middle classes, who now had more time and money to spend on entertainment. Second, mass culture relied on new technologies, especially film and radio, which could reach an entire nation's population and consolidate their sense of being a single state.

Radio Radio entered its golden age after World War I. Invented early in the twentieth century, it made little impact until the 1920s, when powerful transmitters permitted stations to reach much larger audiences—often with nationally syndicated programs. Radio "broadcasts" gave listeners a sense of intimacy with newscasters and stars, addressing consumers as personal friends and drawing them in to the lives of serial heroes.

Radio also was a way to mobilize the masses, especially in authoritarian regimes. The Italian dictator Benito Mussolini pioneered the radio address to the nation; later, Soviet and Nazi propagandists used it to great effect, as did the right-wing Japanese government. But even dictatorships could not exert total control over mass culture. For example, although the Nazis regarded jazz

Josephine Baker Reacting to the Great War's carnage, many Europeans looked longingly for supposedly pristine worlds that their own corrupting civilization had not destroyed. The African American entertainer Josephine Baker was a sensation on the stage in Paris after the war. Many of her shows exoticized or even caricatured her African descent.

Core Objectives

EXPLAIN how the development of modern, mass societies both caused and was affected by the Great Depression.

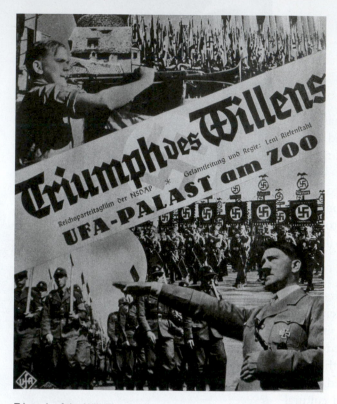

Triumph of the Will Though later denounced, Leni Riefenstahl's propaganda film of Adolf Hitler and the Nazi Party Congress won a Golden Lion at the 1935 Venice Biennale and an award at the 1937 World's Exhibition in Paris. Its poster featured the many mass rallies that projected an image of dynamism and collective will, which Hitler claimed to embody.

as racially inferior music and the Soviets regarded it as "bourgeois," neither could prevent young or old from tuning in to foreign radio broadcasts, smuggling gramophone records over the borders, or creating their own jazz bands.

Film and Advertising Film, too, had profound effects. For traditionalists, Hollywood by the 1920s signified vulgarity and decadence because the silver screen prominently displayed modern sexual habits. Like radio, film served political purposes. Here, again, antiliberal governments took the lead. German filmmaker Leni Riefenstahl's movie of the Nazi Nuremberg rally of 1934, *Triumph of the Will*, is a key example of propagandistic cinema. Nazi-era films were comedies, musicals, melodramas, detective films, and adventure epics—sometimes framed by racial stereotypes and political goals. Soviet film studios also produced Hollywood-style musicals alongside didactic pictures about socialist triumphs.

In market economies, radio and film grew into big businesses, and with expanded product advertising they promoted other enterprises as well. Especially in the United States, advertising became a major industry, with radio commercials shaping national consumer tastes. Increasingly, too, American-produced entertainment, radio programs, and cinematic epics reached an international audience. Thanks to new media, America and the world began to share mass-produced images and fantasies.

MASS PRODUCTION AND MASS CONSUMPTION

The same factors that promoted mass culture also enhanced production and consumption on a mass scale. In fact, World War I had relied on industrial might, for machine technologies produced war materials with abundant and devastating effect.

Never before had armies had so much firepower at their disposal. Whereas in 1809 Napoleon's artillery had discharged 90,000 shells over two days during the largest battle waged in Europe to that point, by 1916 German guns were firing 100,000 rounds of shells per hour for twelve hours at a time in the Battle of Verdun. To sustain military production, millions of men and women worked in factories at home and in the colonies. Producing huge quantities of identical guns, gas masks, bandage rolls, and boots, these factories reflected the modern world's demands for greater volume, faster speed, reduced cost, and standardized output—key characteristics of *mass production*.

The war reshuffled the world's economic balance of power, boosting the United States as an economic powerhouse. As the United States' share of world industrial production climbed above one-third in 1929 (roughly equal to that of Britain, Germany, and Russia combined), people around the globe regarded it as a "working vision of modernity" in which not only production but also consumption boomed.

The Automobile Assembly Line The most outstanding example of the relationship between mass production and consumption in the United States was the motor car. Before World War I, the automobile had been a rich man's toy. Then came Henry Ford, who founded the Ford Motor Company in 1903. Seeking to make more cars more quickly and cheaper, Ford used mechanized conveyors to send the auto frame along a track, or assembly line, where each worker performed one simplified task. By standardizing the manufacturing process and substituting machinery for manual labor, Ford's assembly line brought a new efficiency to the mass production of automobiles.

By the 1920s, a finished car rolled off Ford's assembly line every ten seconds. Although workers complained about becoming "cogs" in a depersonalized labor process, the system boosted output and reduced costs. Altogether, nearly 4 million jobs related directly or indirectly to the automobile—an impressive total in a labor force of 45 million workers.

After World War I, automobile ownership became more common among Americans. Ford further expanded the market for cars by paying his own workers $5 per day—approximately twice the average manufacturing wage in the United States. He understood that without *mass consumption*, increased purchasing power in the middle classes, and appetite for goods there could be no mass production. Whereas in 1920 Americans owned 8 million motor cars, a decade later they owned 23 million. The automobile's rapid spread seemed to demonstrate that mass production worked.

The Great Depression Not all was easy listening and smooth motoring in countries where mass societies were taking root. On October 24, 1929—Black Tuesday—the American stock market collapsed, plunging not only the American economy and its consumers, heavily in debt, but also international financial and trading systems into crisis. This event led the world into the **Great Depression**.

The causes of the Depression went back to the Great War. The efforts by European governments to slash spending and return to the prewar gold standard stifled growth and compromised their ability to pay their war debts. Political and economic instability in Germany, the linchpin of the European economy, made matters even more difficult. The financial terms of the Versailles

Great Depression
Worldwide depression following the U.S. stock market crash on October 29, 1929.

treaty required Germany to pay reparations to compensate for the costs of the war. The German government, however, was unable or unwilling to tax citizens at the rates that prevailed in victor countries, which would have enabled it to meet its treaty obligations. It opted instead to print more money. The resulting hyperinflation destroyed both the German economy and democracy.

To restore stability, Europeans borrowed heavily from the United States. Germany borrowed more from the United States than it paid in reparations, but that assistance was insufficient and short-lived. In 1928 and 1929, American banks pulled their support. Starting in central Europe, banks began to collapse. The panic then spread to the world's stock markets, which led to the Wall Street crash of 1929, which spurred more bank closures.

Financial turmoil produced a major reduction in world trade. Striving to protect workers and investors from the influx of cheap foreign goods, governments raised tariffs against imports. After the United States enacted protective tariffs, other governments abandoned free trade in favor of protectionism. Manufacturers cut back production, laid off millions of workers, and often went out of business. By 1935, world trade had shrunk to one-third of its 1929 level. The producers of raw materials, mainly found in the less developed economies, felt the harshest effects, for their international markets shut down almost completely. For example, world prices for Argentine beef, Chilean nitrates, and Indonesian sugar all dropped sharply.

The Great Depression forced people to rethink the core of laissez-faire liberalism (see Chapter 15), the idea that free markets regulate themselves and free trade leads to economic progress. By the late 1930s, the exuberant embrace of private mass production had ceded to a new conviction: state intervention to regulate the economy was critical to prevent disaster. In 1936, the British economist John Maynard Keynes published a landmark treatise, *The General Theory of Employment, Interest, and Money*. He argued that the market could not always adjust to its own failures and that sometimes the state had to stimulate it by increasing the money supply and creating jobs. Although the "Keynesian Revolution" took years to transform economic policy, many governments had doubts whether capitalism could be saved. The Great Depression did more than any other event to challenge the belief that liberal democracy and capitalism were the best way to achieve political stability and economic progress.

Core Objectives

COMPARE the ideologies of liberal democracy, authoritarianism, and anticolonialism, and EVALUATE the success of each in this period.

Mass Politics: Competing Visions for Building Modern States

In the aftermath of World War I, societies grappled with the question of how to build modern, prosperous states. The war upset class, gender, and colonial relations, which were already unsettled in the prewar period. On battlefronts and home fronts, countless workers, peasants, women, and colonial subjects had sacrificed and now expected to share in the fruits of peace. Many, even in victorious nations, lost confidence in traditional authorities who had failed to prevent the cataclysm and allowed it to go on so long. Amid widespread political turmoil, the states that retained some form of democracy revised the liberal vision, while authoritarianism gained in popularity and anticolonial movements gathered steam.

LIBERAL DEMOCRACY UNDER PRESSURE

The demands of fighting a total war had a profound effect on all the European states. All of them, including the democracies in Britain and France, seized the opportunity to experiment with illiberal policies. Indeed, the war brought both the suspension of many democratic rights and an effort by governments to manage industry and distribution. States on both sides of the conflict jailed many individuals who opposed the war. Governments regulated both production and, through rationing, consumption. Above all, the war and the economic crises that followed revolutionized the size and scope of the state.

British and French Responses to Economic Crises Britain and France retained their democracies, but even here, old-fashioned liberal democracy was on the run. Strife rippled across the British Empire, and in the home isles Britain gave independence to what became the Republic of Ireland in 1922. Britain's working-class Labour Party came to power twice between 1923 and 1931; but either alone or in coalition with Liberals and Conservatives, Labour could not lift the country out of its economic crisis.

Disorder was even more pronounced in France, which had lost 10 percent of its young men and seen the destruction of vast territory. In 1932–1933, six government coalitions came and went over the course of just nineteen months. Against the threat of a rightist coup, a coalition of the moderate and radical left, including the French Communist Party, formed the Popular Front government (1936–1938). It introduced the right of collective bargaining, a forty-hour workweek, two-week paid vacations, and minimum wages.

The American New Deal In the United States, too, markets and liberalism faced challenges. When the Great Depression shattered the nation's fortunes, pressure intensified to create a more secure political and economic system.

By the end of 1930, more than 4 million American workers had lost their jobs. As President Hoover insisted that citizens' thrift and self-reliance, not government handouts, would restore prosperity, the economic situation worsened. By 1933, industrial production had dropped by a staggering

50 percent since 1929. The hard times were even worse in the countryside, where farm income plummeted by two-thirds between 1929 and 1932.

In the 1932 presidential election, a Democrat, Franklin Delano Roosevelt, won in a landslide. He promptly launched what came to be called the New Deal, a set of programs and regulations that dramatically expanded the scope of the American national government and its role in the nation's economic life. In his first hundred days in office, Roosevelt obtained legislation to provide relief for the jobless and to rebuild the shattered economy. Among his administration's experiments were the Federal Deposit Insurance Corporation to guarantee bank deposits up to $5,000, the Securities and Exchange Commission to monitor the stock market, and the Federal Emergency Relief Administration to help states and local governments assist the needy. Subsequently, in 1935, the Works Progress Administration put nearly 3 million people to work building roads, bridges, airports, and post offices. In addition, the Social Security Act inaugurated old-age pensions supported by the federal government.

Never before had the U.S. federal government expended so much on social welfare programs or intervened so directly in the national economy. Yet the Depression lingered, and before long unemployment again climbed—from 7 million in 1937 to 11 million in 1938.

The New Deal did not substantially redistribute national income. Privately owned enterprises continued to dominate American society. Roosevelt's aim was not to destroy capitalism but to save it. In this regard the New Deal succeeded, for it staved off authoritarian solutions to modern problems.

Jim Crow The American New Deal left most African Americans behind. In the rural American South, "Jim Crow" laws mandated racial segregation, with African Americans forced to use separate, and usually unequal, facilities, including schools, hotels, and theaters, such as this one in Mississippi.

During the interwar years, liberal democratic regimes respected elections and defended private property against challenges from labor movements. But they intervened in markets and regulated people's lives in ways their prewar counterparts never would have contemplated.

AUTHORITARIANISM AND MASS MOBILIZATION

Like the liberal systems they challenged, authoritarian regimes came in various stripes. Right-wing dictatorships arose in Italy, Germany, and Japan. Although differing in important respects, they all disliked the left-wing dictatorship of the Soviet Union. The Soviets, in turn, hated the fascists.

The Soviet Union and Socialism The most dramatic blow against liberal capitalism occurred in Russia when the Bolshevik Party seized power and established a socialist regime. Fearing the spread of socialist revolutions, Britain, France, Japan, and the United States sent armies to Russia to contain Bolshevism. But after executing the tsar and his family, the Bolsheviks rallied support by defending the homeland against its invaders. They also mobilized people to fight (and win) a civil war (1918–1921) in the name of defending the revolution.

To revive the economy, which had been devastated by war, revolution, and civil war, the Bolsheviks grudgingly legalized private trade and private property. In 1924, with the country still recovering from civil war, the undisputed leader of the revolution, Lenin, died. Lenin had done more than anyone to shape the institutions of the revolutionary regime, including creating expectations for a single ruler. After eliminating his rivals, **Joseph Stalin** (1878–1953) emerged as the new leader of the Communist Party and the country, which soon became the Union of Soviet Socialist Republics (USSR), or Soviet Union.

Since socialism as a fully developed social and political order did not exist anywhere in the 1920s, no one was sure how it would actually work. Stalin resolved this dilemma by defining Soviet or revolutionary socialism in opposition to capitalism. Since capitalism had "bourgeois" parliaments serving the interests of the rich, socialism, as elaborated by Stalinist leaders, would have soviets (councils) of worker and peasant deputies. Since capitalism had unregulated markets, which led to inefficiency and unemployment, socialism would have economic planning and full employment. And since capitalism relied on the "exploitation" of private ownership, socialism would outlaw private trade and private property. In short, socialism would eradicate capitalism and then invent socialist forms in housing, culture, values, dress, and even modes of reasoning.

The efforts to build a noncapitalist society required class war, and these efforts began in the heavily populated countryside. As Stalin solidified his

Joseph Stalin
(1879–1953) Leader of the Communist Party and the Soviet Union; sought to create "socialism in one country."

УДАРНУЮ УБОРКУ—

БОЛЬШЕВИСТСКОМУ УРОЖАЮ

Collectivized Agriculture Soviet plans for the socialist village envisioned the formation of large collectives supplied with advanced machinery, thereby transforming peasant labor into an industrial process, and equality between men and women. Note the woman farmer who dominates the image, and the men and women working side by side. The realities behind the images of smiling farmers—such as in this poster, proclaiming "Let's Achieve a Victorious Harvest"—were low productivity, enormous waste, and often broken-down machinery.

control over the Soviet Union in the late 1920s, he sought to combine individual farms into larger units owned and worked collectively and run by regime loyalists. Tens of thousands of urban activists and Red Army soldiers led a drive to establish these collective farms and to compel farmers to sell all their grain and livestock at state-run collection points for whatever price the state was willing to pay (often very little).

In protest, many peasants burned their crops, killed their livestock, and destroyed their farm machinery. The government responded by deporting the protesters, along with many bystanders, to remote areas. Meanwhile, harvests again declined, and famine claimed millions more lives. Grudgingly, the regime allowed the collectivized peasants to have household plots. Here they could grow their own food and take some of their produce to approved markets. But few escaped the collectives, which depended on the state for seed, fertilizers, and machinery.

The year 1928 saw the beginning of a frenzied Five-Year Plan to "catch and overtake" the leading capitalist countries. As peasants were forced onto collective farms, millions of enthusiasts (as well as deported peasants) set about building a socialist urban utopia founded on advanced technology, almost all of it purchased from the Depression-mired capitalist countries. More than 10 million people helped build or rebuild hundreds of factories, hospitals, and schools. Huge hydroelectric dams, automobile and tractor factories, and heavy machine–building plants symbolized the promise of Soviet-style modernity, which eliminated unemployment during the capitalist Great Depression. Soviet authorities also started building socialism on the borderlands, and the USSR soon included several new republics (see Map 19.5), all of which acquired their own institutions—but under central rule from Moscow.

Mass Terror and Stalin's Dictatorship The Soviet political system became more ruthless as the state expanded. Police power grew the most, partly from forcing peasants into collectives and organizing mass deportations. As the party's ranks swelled, ongoing loyalty tests also led to the removal of party members, even when they professed absolute loyalty. From 1936 to 1938, trials of supposedly treasonous "enemies of the people" resulted

Map 19.5 The Soviet Union

The Union of Soviet Socialist Republics (USSR) came into being after World War I.

- How did its boundaries compare with those of the older Russian Empire, as shown in Map 17.5?
- Identify the Soviet republics other than Russia.
- What does the large number of Soviet republics suggest about the ethnic diversity within the Soviet Union?

in the execution of around 750,000 people and the arrest or deportation of several million more. They were sent to forced-labor camps, collectively known as the Gulag. Such purges decimated the loyal Soviet elite—party officials, state officials, intelligentsia, army officers, and even members of the police who had enforced the terror. Lenin and Stalin secured a communist regime based in Russia but did so through highly coercive and deeply resented methods. Nonetheless, Stalin's efforts at heavy industrialization were to pay off when Nazi Germany invaded the Soviet Union in World War II (see Chapter 20).

Italian Fascism Disillusionment with the costs of the Great War and fear of a communist takeover like that in Russia inspired violent political movements in many European countries, above all in Italy and Germany. In Italy, mass strikes, occupations of factories, and peasant land seizures swept the country in 1919 and 1920. Amid this disorder, authoritarian nationalists seized power. Their leader was **Benito Mussolini** (1883–1945), a former socialist journalist, who coined the term **fascism**. In the wake of the Russian Revolution of 1917, fascism represented a counterrevolution. It combined mass movements, which had emerged on the political left, with an aggressive, authoritarian nationalism and antisocialist and antiliberal values.

In 1919, Mussolini sought to organize alienated veterans into a mass political movement. In the early years, black-shirted vigilante squads received money from landowners and factory owners to beat up socialist leaders. Still, the fascists presented themselves as champions of the little guy, of peasants and (nonsocialist) workers, as well as of war veterans, students, and white-collar professionals.

In 1922, Mussolini announced a march on Rome. The march was a bluff, since Mussolini had no military support, yet it intimidated the king, who opposed fascist ruffians but feared bloodshed. So the king withheld use of the army against the lightly armed marchers. When the Italian government resigned in protest, the monarch invited Mussolini to become prime minister, despite the fact that fascists had won only a small minority of seats in the 1921 elections. Soon a series of decrees transformed Italy from a constitutional monarchy into a dictatorship. Within a few years, all parties except that of the fascists had been dissolved. The regime used parades, films, radio, and visions of recapturing Roman imperial grandeur to boost support during the troubled times of the Depression. Mussolini used his personal charisma to promote the idea that as *Il Duce* (the leader), he personified the power and unity of Italy.

Mussolini's dictatorship made deals with big business and the church. He left traditional elites in place and preserved their powerful institutions; thus, his regime fell short of a total social revolution. By the mid-1930s, Italian fascism had settled into a traditional form of conservatism. Nonetheless, as the first antiliberal, antisocialist alternative, the early phase of Italian fascism served as a model for other countries.

German Nazism In Germany, too, fear of Bolshevism and anger over the war's outcome propelled a violent, authoritarian party to power. Here, the dictator was **Adolf Hitler** (1889–1945), backed by the nationalist workers' movement, whose name he changed to the National Socialist German Workers' Party (*Nationalsozialistische Deutsche Arbeiterpartei*, or **Nazis**).

Unlike Mussolini, the young Hitler was never a socialist, but the Nazi's Twenty-Five Points (1920) combined nationalism with a heavy dose of anticapitalism. The party platform called for the renunciation of the Treaty of Versailles and for discrimination against Jews. It was an assertion of Germany's grievances against the world and of the small man's grievances against those whom the Nazis perceived as the rich. At first, Hitler and the Nazis were unsuccessful, and Hitler himself was arrested. He was sentenced to five years in prison for treason but served less than a year. While in prison he wrote an autobiographical and fanatically anti-Semitic treatise called *Mein Kampf* (My Struggle, 1925), which subsequently became wildly popular among Nazis.

As the Great Depression eroded popular support for the Weimar Republic (the democratic regime that came into existence after the Treaty of Versailles), conservative leaders sought to profit from Hitler's popularity. Germany's president appointed Hitler chancellor (prime minister) in 1933, even as the Nazi movement was declining as an electoral force. Like Mussolini, Hitler came to power legally, with the help of traditional elites. Yet neither leader won an electoral majority.

Hitler's first step as chancellor was to heighten fears of communist conspiracy. The burning of the Reichstag (parliament) building in Berlin gave the Nazis an opportunity to blame the fire on the communists. They immediately suspended civil liberties, including free speech and freedom of association, and attacked and imprisoned their opponents, especially communists. By July 1933, the Nazis were the only legal party and Hitler was dictator of Germany. Like Mussolini, Hitler relied on choreographed mass rallies and new media like film and radio, as well as his own personal charisma, to mobilize a mass following.

Hitler also unleashed a campaign of persecution against Jews. Like many other right-wing Germans, he believed that a Jewish-socialist conspiracy had stabbed the German army in the back, causing its surrender in World War I, and that intermarriage with Jews was destroying the supposed purity of the Aryan race (which included northern, white Europeans). Hitler and the Nazis did not believe that religious practice defined Jewishness; instead, they held, it was transmitted biologically from parents to children. Hitler encouraged the use of terror against Jews, destroying their businesses, homes, and marriages with non-Jews and ultimately eliminating all traces of Jewish life and culture in Nazi-dominated central Europe (see Chapter 20).

The Nazis won popular support for restoring order and reviving the economy, although the economic gains had more to do with timing than Nazi policy. In any case, Germany reemerged as a great power with expansionist aspirations. Just as Mussolini reached back to ancient Rome to connect fascism to the Italian past, Hitler, too, invoked history. He called his state the Third Reich—he considered the Holy Roman Empire (or Reich) the first and the Reich created by Bismarck in 1871 the second—to bolster its legitimacy.

Militarist Japan Unlike authoritarian regimes in Europe, the right-wing movement that emerged in Japan did not spring from wounded power and pride during World War I. In fact, because wartime disruptions reduced European and American competition, Japanese products found new markets in Asia. Although the government expanded the electorate and seemed headed toward liberal democracy in the early 1920s, Japan veered to the political right in 1926 when Emperor Hirohito came to power.

Adding Manchuria to its Korean and Taiwanese colonies in 1932 (see Map 19.6), Japan established the puppet state of Manchukuo. Meanwhile, at home, "patriots" carried out a campaign of terror against uncooperative businessmen and critics of the military. Unlike Italian fascism and German Nazism, Japanese authoritarianism had an explicitly religious dimension. The state in Japan took on a sacred aura through the promotion of an official religion, Shinto, and of Emperor Hirohito's divinity. By 1940, Hirohito and his closest advisers had merged all political parties into the Imperial Rule Assistance Association, ending even the semblance of democracy, and they advocated a radical form of racial purity. The Imperial Army divided the peoples of Asia into "master races," "friendly races," and "guest races," reserving a dominant position for the Japanese "Yamato Race."

Common Features of Authoritarian Regimes All the major authoritarian regimes of this period claimed that modern economies required state direction. In Japan, the government fostered huge business conglomerates (*zaibatsu*); in Italy, it encouraged big business to form cartels. The German state also regarded the private sector as the vehicle of economic growth, but it expected entrepreneurs to support the Nazis' racial, antidemocratic, and expansionist aims. The most thorough form of economic coordination occurred in the Soviet Union, which adopted American-style mass production while eliminating private enterprise. Instead, the Soviet state owned and managed all of the country's industry.

All these states relied heavily on mass organizations. Russia, Italy, and Germany had single mass parties; Japan had various rightist groups until the 1940 merger. All promoted dynamic youth movements, such as the Hitler Youth and the Union of German Girls, the Soviet Communist Youth League, and the Italian squads marching to the anthem "Giovinezza" (Youth).

Three of the four adopted extensive social welfare policies. The Nazis emphasized full employment, built public housing, and provided assistance to needy Aryan families. The Italian National Agency for Maternity and Infancy provided services for unwed mothers and infant care. Soviet programs addressed maternity, disability, sickness, and old age. Although Japan did not enact innovative social welfare legislation, its Home Affairs Ministry

Map 19.6 The Japanese Empire in Asia, 1933

Hoping to become a great imperial power like the European states, Japan established numerous colonies and spheres of influence early in the twentieth century.

- What were the main territorial components of the Japanese Empire?
- How far did the Japanese succeed in extending their political influence throughout East Asia?
- According to your reading, what problems did the desire to extend Japanese influence in China present to Japanese leaders?

Map legend:

- Japanese acquisitions as of 1895
- Japanese acquisitions, 1905–1910
- Japanese area of influence before 1914
- ← Japanese attack, 1914
- Extension of Japanese influence after 1918
- Occupied by Japan, 1920–1925
- Japan forms puppet state of Manchukuo, 1932
- Occupied by Japan, 1933

enlisted helpmates among civic groups, seeking to raise savings rates and improve child-rearing practices.

All these regimes, except the Soviet Union, were ambivalent about women in public roles. Even the Soviets, who claimed to support gender equality, eventually restricted abortion and rewarded mothers who had many children. Officials were eager to honor new mothers as a way to repair the loss of so many young men during the Great War. Yet many more women were also entering professional careers, and some were becoming their families' primary wage earners.

Finally, all the dictatorships used violence and terror as tools for remaking the sociopolitical order. The Italians and the Japanese were not shy about arresting political opponents, particularly in their colonies. However, it was the Nazis and especially the Soviets who filled concentration and labor camps with alleged enemies of the state, whether Jews or supposed counterrevolutionaries.

THE HYBRID REGIMES IN LATIN AMERICA

Core Objectives

EXPLAIN how access to consumer goods and other aspects of mass society influenced political conflict in Asia, Africa, and Latin America.

Latin American countries felt the same pressures that produced liberal democratic and authoritarian responses in Europe, Russia, and Japan. However, the Latin American leaders devised solutions that combined democratic and authoritarian elements.

Economic Turmoil Latin American states had stayed out of the fighting in World War I, but their export economies had suffered. As trade plummeted, popular confidence in oligarchic regimes fell, and radical agitation surged.

As in Europe, Latin American governments stepped in to manage volatile economic markets. More than in any other region, the Depression battered Latin America's trading and financial systems, as well as the standards of living of laborers, because all were so dependent on exports. Exporters of basic staples, from sugar to wheat, faced stiff competition from other exporters and evaporating demand for their commodities. The region in fact suffered doubly because it had borrowed so much money to invest in infrastructure and expansion. When the world's major banks failed, creditors called in their loans from Latin America. This move drove borrowers to default. In an effort to improve their economic prospects, Latin American governments—with enthusiastic backing from the middle classes, nationalist intellectuals, and urban workers—turned to their domestic rather than foreign markets as the main engine of growth. Here, too, the state took a much more interventionist role in market activity than in the ideal of classical liberalism.

After the war, Latin American elites confronted the mass age by establishing mass parties and encouraging interest groups to associate with them.

Collective bodies such as chambers of commerce, trade unions, peasant associations, and organizations for minorities like blacks and Indians all operated with state sponsorship. This form of modern politics, often labeled corporatist, used social groups to bridge the gap between ruling elites and the general population.

Corporatist Politics in Brazil Corporatist politics took hold especially in Brazil, where the old republic collapsed in 1930. In its place, a coalition led by the skilled politician Getúlio Vargas (1883–1954) cultivated a strong following by enacting socially popular reforms.

Dubbing himself the "father of the poor," Vargas encouraged workers to organize, erected monuments to national heroes, and supported the building of schools and the paving of roads. He made special efforts to appeal to Brazilian blacks, who had been excluded from public life since the abolition of slavery. Thus, he legalized many previously forbidden Afro-Brazilian practices, such as the ritual *candomblé* dance, whose African and martial overtones seemed threatening to white elites. Vargas also supported samba schools, organizations that not only taught popular dances but also raised funds for public works. Moreover, Vargas addressed maternity and housing policies and enfranchised women (although they had to be able to read, as did male voters). Although he condemned the old elites for betraying the country to serve the interests of foreign consumers and investors, he also arranged foreign funding and technical transfers to build steel mills and factories. However, he took this step to create domestic industry so that Brazil would not be so dependent on imports. In these and other ways, Brazil and other Latin American governments combined democratic and authoritarian institutions and methods as a response to the economic downturn of the depression.

Samba Dancers The dance started in the shantytowns of Rio de Janeiro and eventually became popular throughout the world, thanks to films, photographs, and long-playing records that featured samba music.

ANTICOLONIAL VISIONS OF MODERN LIFE

Debates over liberal-democratic versus authoritarian models engaged the world's colonial and semicolonial regions as well. But here there was a larger concern: What should be done about colonial authority? Throughout Asia, most educated people wanted to roll back the European and

Population Movements: Filling Up the Empty Spaces and Spreading Capitalism

As we have seen in Chapters 12 and 13, the European discovery of the Americas resulted in a vast movement of peoples across the Atlantic Ocean from Europe and Africa into the Western Hemisphere. These population movements, among the largest in world history up to that point, pale when measured against the long-distance migrations that occurred in the hundred years between 1840 and 1940. During these years, 150 million individuals of European and Asian descent filled up the less populated parts of the world, moving from Europe, South Asia, and China into the Americas, Southeast Asia, and northern Asia in unprecedented numbers and spreading a capitalist mode of production wherever they moved. A great many of the migrants went as laborers in the factories and on the plains of the Americas and on the rubber, sugar, tea, and coffee plantations springing up in the Dutch East Indies and East and southern Africa. They were as essential to the expansion of the capitalist system in these regions as the 12 million African captives transported to the Americas during the Atlantic slave trade were for the economic expansion of the Americas. Although the new watchword in economic relations was free labor, not all of the men and women who moved were in fact free workers. Indentured servitude—that is, agreeing to work for a certain number of years, usually between three and seven, in return for transportation to the region, food, housing, and clothing—was widely used with Chinese and Indian workers.

A good example of the movement and use of semi-coerced or indentured workers in less developed regions comes from East Africa. There, the British and Germans were engaged in a furious political rivalry to extend their control over territories, and British officials believed that constructing a railway from the coast of East Africa at the port of Mombasa to Kisumu at Lake Victoria would enhance their territorial ambitions in East Africa. They also concluded that they would be unable to recruit a sufficient supply of African workers to accomplish the task. Not surprisingly, they looked to the government of India to assist them in providing the necessary workforce.

The British government of India did more than help them. In all, it made available nearly 35,000 indentured South Asian workers on three-year contracts for the construction of what was known as the Uganda Railway, the track for which, covering a distance of 582 miles, was completed in a mere five years, from 1896 to 1901. The work was arduous and the living conditions in the work camps were horrific, yet the British official overseeing the construction concluded that had it not been for this workforce, it is doubtful that the project could have been completed in less than twenty years. The building of the Uganda Railway is one of many examples in which we see significant

American imperial presence. Some Asians even accepted Japanese imperialism as an antidote, under the slogan "Asia for the Asians." In Africa, however, where the European colonial presence was more recent, intellectuals still questioned the real meaning of colonial rule: Were the British and the French sincerely committed to African improvement, or were they obstacles to African peoples' well-being? (See Current Trends in World History: Population Movements: Filling Up the Empty Spaces and Spreading Capitalism.)

In Africa as well as Asia, then, the search for the modern encompassed demands for power sharing or full political independence. To overcome the contradictions of the democratic liberalism Europeans practiced at home and numbers of people moving to new places and regions, sometimes by their own choosing and sometimes not, to play an important role in the expansion of the capitalist system and the rivalries between colonial powers.

The Uganda Railway Indian workers cut rock for the Uganda Railway, built in 1896 to 1901, during the Scramble for Africa.

Questions for Analysis

- Why do you think that in some cases, like the building of the Uganda Railway, governments had to be involved in forcibly moving workers to where they were needed rather than letting market forces draw the workers to where work was available?
- What do you see as some of the similarities and differences between the treatment of the African slaves and the treatment of the forced or indentured servants during this period?

Explore Further

McKeown, Adam, *Melancholy Order: Asian Migration and the Globalization of Border* (2008).

the authoritarianism they exercised in colonial areas, educated Asians and Africans proposed various forms of nationalism.

Behind the Asian and African nationalist movements were profound disagreements about how best to govern nations once they gained independence and how to define citizenship. The democratic ethos of the imperial powers appealed to many intellectuals. Others liked the radical authoritarianism of fascism and communism, with their promises of rapid change. Whatever their political preferences, most literate colonial subjects also regarded their own religious and cultural traditions as sources for political mobilization. Thus Muslim, Hindu, Chinese, and African nationalist leaders used traditional values to gain the support of the rank and file. The colonial figures involved in political and intellectual movements insisted that the societies they sought to establish were going to be modern *and* at the same time retain their indigenous characteristics.

African Stirrings Africa contained the most recent territories to come under the Europeans' control, so anticolonial nationalist movements there were quite young. The region's fate remained very much in the hands of Europeans. After 1918, however, African peoples probed more deeply for the meaning of Europe's imperial presence.

There was some room (but not much) for voicing African interests under colonialism. The French had long held to a vision of assimilating their colonial peoples into French culture. In France's primary West African colony, Senegal, four coastal cities had traditionally elected one delegate (of mixed African and European ancestry) to the French National Assembly. This practice, limiting African representation to men of mixed ancestry, lasted until 1914, when Blaise Diagne (1872–1934), an African candidate, ran for office and won the seat in the French National Assembly, invoking his African origins and garnering the African vote. While the British allowed Africans to elect delegates to municipal bodies, they refused to permit colonial representatives to sit in Parliament.

Opposition was still not widespread in Africa, for protests ran up against not only colonial administrators but also western-educated African elites. Yet even this privileged group began to reconsider its relationship to colonial authorities. In Kenya, immediately after World War I, a small contingent of mission-educated Africans called on the British to provide more and better schools and to return lands they claimed European settlers had stolen. Although defeated in this instance, the young nationalists drew important lessons from their confrontation with the authorities. Their new spokesperson, Jomo Kenyatta (1898–1978), invoked their precolonial Kikuyu traditions as a basis for resisting colonialism. These early anticolonial movements prepared the foundations for more widespread resistance to colonial rule after World War II.

Imagining an Indian Nation As Africans explored the use of modern politics against Europeans, the war and its aftermath brought full-blown challenges to British rule in India. Indeed, the Indian nationalist challenge provided inspiration for other anticolonial movements.

For over a century, Indians had heard British authorities extol the virtues of liberal democracy, yet they were excluded from participation. In 1919, the British did slightly enlarge the franchise in India and allowed more local self-government, but these moves did not satisfy Indians' nationalist longings. During the 1920s and 1930s, the nationalists, led by

Mohandas Karamchand (Mahatma) Gandhi (1869–1948), laid the foundations for an alternative, anticolonial movement.

Gandhi and Nonviolent Resistance When Gandhi returned to India in 1915, after studying law in England and gaining a reputation for working on behalf of Indian immigrants in South Africa, he immediately became the focus of the Indian nationalist movement. He spelled out the moral and political philosophy of *satyagraha*, or **nonviolent resistance**, which he had developed while in South Africa. His message to Indians was simple: develop your own resources and inner strength and control the instincts and activities that encourage participation in colonial economy and government, and you shall achieve *swaraj* ("self-rule"). Faced with Indian self-reliance and self-control pursued nonviolently, Gandhi claimed, the British eventually would have to leave.

Indian nationalists urged people to oppose cooperation with government officials, to boycott goods made in Britain, to refuse to send their children to British schools, and to withhold taxes. Gandhi added his voice, calling for an all-India *satyagraha*. He also formed an alliance with Muslim leaders and began turning the Indian National Congress from an elite organization of lawyers and merchants into a mass organization open to anyone who paid dues, even the illiterate and poor.

Mohandas Karamchand (Mahatma) Gandhi
(1869–1948) Indian leader who led a nonviolent struggle for India's independence from Britain.

nonviolent resistance
Moral and political philosophy of resistance developed by Indian National Congress leader Mohandas Gandhi. Gandhi believed that if Indians pursued self-reliance and self-control in a nonviolent way, the British would eventually have to leave.

Gandhi and the Road to Independence (*Left*) Gandhi launched a civil disobedience movement in 1930 by violating the British government's tax on salt. Calling it "the most inhuman poll tax the ingenuity of man can devise," Gandhi, accompanied by his followers, set out on a monthlong march on foot covering 240 miles to Dandi on the Gujarat coast. The picture shows Gandhi arriving at the sea, where he and his followers broke the law by scooping up handfuls of salt. (*Right*) Gandhi believed that India had been colonized by becoming enslaved to modern industrial civilization. Indians would achieve independence, he argued, when they became self-reliant. Thus, he made the spinning wheel a symbol of *swaraj* and handspun cloth the virtual uniform of the nation.

When the Depression struck India in 1930, Gandhi singled out salt as a testing ground for his ideas on civil disobedience. Every Indian used salt, whose producer was a heavily taxed government monopoly. Thus, salt symbolized the Indians' subjugation to an alien government. To break the colonial government's monopoly, Gandhi began a 240-mile march from western India to the coast to gather sea salt for free. Accompanying him were seventy-one followers representing different regions and religions of India. News wire services and mass-circulation newspapers worldwide reported on the drama of the sixty-one-year-old Gandhi, wooden staff in hand, dressed in coarse homespun garments, leading the march. Thousands of people gathering en route were moved by the sight of the frail apostle of nonviolence encouraging them to embrace independence from colonial rule. By insisting that Indians follow their conscience (always through nonviolent protest), by exciting the masses through his defiance of colonial power, and by using symbols like homespun cloth to counter foreign, machine-spun textiles, Gandhi instilled in the people a sense of pride, resourcefulness, and Indian national awareness.

A Divided Anticolonial Movement in India Although Gandhi gained a mass following, his program met opposition from within, for many in the Indian National Congress Party did not share his vision of community as the source of public life. Cambridge-educated Jawaharlal Nehru (1889–1964), for example, believed that only by embracing science and technology could India develop as a modern nation.

Even less enamored were radical activists who wanted a revolution, not peaceful protest. In the countryside, these radicals sought to organize peasants to overthrow colonial domination. Other activists galvanized the growing industrial proletariat by organizing trade unions. Their stress on class conflict ran against Gandhi's ideals of national unity.

Religion, too, threatened to fracture Gandhi's hope for anticolonial unity. The Hindu-Muslim alliance crafted by nationalists in the early 1920s splintered over who represented them and how to ensure their political rights. The Muslim community found an impressive leader in Muhammad Ali Jinnah, who set about making the Muslim League the sole representative organization of the Muslim community. In 1940, the Muslim League passed a resolution demanding independent Muslim states in provinces where Muslims constituted a majority, on the grounds that Muslims were not a religious minority of the Indian nation but a nation themselves.

In 1937, the British belatedly granted India provincial assemblies, a national legislature with two chambers, and an executive. By then, however, India's people were deeply politicized. The Congress Party, which inspired the masses to overthrow British rule, struggled to contain the different ideologies and new political institutions, such as labor unions, peasant associations, religious parties, and communal organizations. Seeking a path to economic modernization, Gandhi, on one side, envisioned independent India as an updated collection of village republics organized around the benevolent authority of male-dominated households. Nehru, on another side, hoped for a socioeconomic transformation powered by science and state-sponsored economic planning. Both believed that India's traditions of collective welfare and humane religious and philosophical practices set it apart from the modern west. By the outbreak of World War II, India was well on its way toward political independence, but British policies and India's divisions foretold a violent end to imperial rule (see Chapter 20).

Chinese Nationalism Unlike India and Africa, China was never formally colonized. But foreign powers' "concession areas" on Chinese soil compromised its sovereignty. Indeed, foreign nationals living in China enjoyed many privileges, including immunity from Chinese law. Furthermore, unequal treaties imposed on the Qing government had robbed China of its customs and tariff autonomy. Thus, the Chinese nationalists' vision of a modern alternative echoed that of the Indian nationalists: ridding the nation of foreign domination was the initial condition of national fulfillment. For many, the 1911 Revolution (as the fall of the Qing dynasty came to be known; see Chapter 18) symbolized the first step toward transforming a crumbling agrarian empire into a modern nation.

Despite high hopes, the new republic could not establish legitimacy. For one thing, factional and regional conflicts made the government little more than a loose alliance of rural elites, merchants, and military leaders. Its intellectual inspiration came from the ideas of Sun Yat-sen, founder of the nationalist political party, the Guomindang. Under the banner of anti-imperialism, the party sponsored large-scale organizations of workers' unions, peasant leagues, and women's associations that looked to students and workers as well as the Russian Revolution for inspiration.

In 1926, amid a renewed tide of anti-foreign agitation, **Chiang Kai-shek** (1887–1975) seized control of the party following Sun's death. Chiang launched a partially successful military campaign to reunify the country and established a new national government in 1928 with its capital in Nanjing.

Peasant Populism in China: White Wolf For many Guomindang leaders, the peasant population represented a backward class. Thus, the leadership failed to tap in to the revolutionary potential of the countryside, which was alive with grassroots movements such as that of White Wolf.

From late 1913 to 1914, Chinese newspapers circulated reports about a roving band of armed men led by a mysterious figure known as White Wolf. This figure terrified members of the elite. It is unlikely that the band,

Chiang Kai-shek (1887–1975) Leader of the Guomindang following Sun Yat-sen's death who mobilized the Chinese masses through the New Life movement. In 1949, he lost the Chinese Revolution to the Communists and moved his regime to Taiwan.

Mustafa Kemal Ataturk
(1881–1938) Ottoman army officer and military hero who helped forge the modern Turkish nation-state. He and his followers deposed the sultan, declared Turkey a republic, and constructed a European-like secular state, eliminating Islam's hold over civil and political affairs.

rumored to have close to a million followers, had more than 20,000 members even at its height. But the mythology surrounding White Wolf was so widespread that the movement's impact reverberated well beyond its physical presence.

Popular myth depicted White Wolf as a Chinese Robin Hood with the mission to restore order. The band's objective was to rid the country of government injustices. Raiding major trade routes and market towns, White Wolf's followers gained a reputation for robbing the rich and aiding the poor. Stories of helping the poor won the White Wolf army many followers in rural China, where local peasants joined temporarily as fighters and then returned home when the band moved on. Although the White Wolf army lacked the power to restore order in the countryside, its presence reflected the changes that had to come in China.

A Postimperial Turkish Nation Of all the postwar anticolonial movements, none was more successful or more committed to European models than that of **Mustafa Kemal Ataturk** (1881–1938), who helped forge the modern Turkish nation-state. Until 1914, the Ottoman Empire was a colonial power in its own right. But having fought on the losing German side, it saw its realm shrink to a part of Anatolia under the Treaty of Sèvres, which ended the war between the Allies and the Ottoman Empire.

In 1920, an Ottoman army officer and military hero named Mustafa Kemal harnessed an outpouring of Turkish nationalism into opposition to Greek troops that had been sent to enforce the peace treaty. Rallying his own troops to defend the fledgling Turkish nation, Kemal reconquered most of Anatolia and the area around Istanbul and secured international recognition for the new state in 1923 in the Treaty of Lausanne. Thereafter, a vast, forcible exchange of populations occurred. Approximately 1.2 million Greek Christians left Turkey to settle in Greece, and 400,000 Muslims relocated from Greece to Turkey.

With the Ottoman Empire gone, Kemal and his followers moved to build a state based on Turkish national identity. First they deposed the sultan. Then they abolished the Ottoman caliphate and proclaimed Turkey a republic, whose supreme authority would be an elected House of Assembly. Later, after Kemal insisted that the people adopt European-style surnames, the assembly conferred on Kemal the mythic name Ataturk, "father of the Turks."

In forging a Turkish nation, Kemal looked to construct a European-style secular state and to eliminate Islam's hold over civil and political affairs. The Turkish elite replaced Muslim religious law with the Swiss civil code, instituted the western (Christian) calendar, and abolished the once-powerful dervish religious orders. They also sought to eliminate Arabic and Persian words from Turkish, substituted Roman script for Arabic letters, forbade polygamy, made wearing the fez (a brimless cap associated in Kemal's mind with old-fashioned ways) a crime, and instructed Turks to wear European-style hats. The veil, though not outlawed, was denounced as a relic. In 1934, the government enfranchised Turkish women, granted them property rights in marriage and inheritance, and allowed them to enter the professions. Schools were taken out of the hands of Muslim clerics, placed under state control, and, along with military service, became the chief instrument for making the masses conscious of belonging to a Turkish nation. Yet many villagers did not accept Ataturk's non-Islamic nationalism, remaining devoted to Islam and resentful of the prohibitions against dervish dancing.

In imitating Europe, Kemal also borrowed many of its antidemocratic models. Inspired by the Soviets, he inaugurated a five-year plan for the economy emphasizing centralized coordination by the government. During the 1930s, Turkish nationalists also drew on Nazi examples by advocating racial theories that celebrated central Asian Turks as the founders of all civilization. In another authoritarian move, Kemal occasionally rigged parliamentary elections, while using the police and judiciary to silence his critics. The Kemalist revolution in Turkey was the most far-reaching and enduring transformation that had occurred outside Europe and the Americas up to that point. It offered an important model for the founding of secular, authoritarian states in the Islamic world.

Nationalism and the Rise of the Muslim Brotherhood in Egypt Elsewhere in the Middle East, where France and Britain expanded their holdings at the Ottomans' expense, anticolonial movements borrowed from European models while putting their own stamp on nation-making and modernization campaigns. In Egypt, the British occupation predated the fall of the Ottoman Empire, but here, too, World War I energized the forces of anticolonial nationalism.

When the war ended, Sa'd Zaghlul (1857–1927), an educated Egyptian patriot, pressed for an Egyptian delegation to be invited to the peace conference at Versailles. He hoped to present Egypt's case for national independence. Instead, British officials arrested and exiled him and his most vocal supporters. When news of this action came out, Egypt burst into revolt. Rural rebels broke away from the central government, proclaiming local republics. Villagers tore up railway lines and telegraph wires, the symbols of British authority.

After defusing the conflict, British authorities tried to appease the Egyptian desire to control their own destiny. In 1922, Britain proclaimed Egypt independent, although it retained the right to station British troops on Egyptian soil. This provision was intended to protect traffic through the Suez Canal and foreign populations residing in Egypt, but it also enabled the British to continue to influence Egyptian politics. Two years later, elections placed Zaghlul's nationalist party, the Wafd, in office. But the British prevented the Wafd from exercising real power.

This subversion of independence and democracy provided an opening for antiliberal versions of anticolonialism in Egypt. During the Depression years, a fascist group, Young Egypt, garnered wide appeal. Much more influential and destined to have an enduring influence throughout the Arab world was an Islamic group founded in 1928, the Muslim Brotherhood, which attacked liberal democracy as a façade for middle-class, business, and landowning interests. The Muslim Brotherhood was anticolonial and anti-British, but its members considered mere political independence insufficient. Egyptians, they argued, must also renounce the lure of the west (whether liberal capitalism or godless communism) and return to a purified form of Islam. For the Muslim Brotherhood, Islam offered a complete way of life. A "return to Islam" through the nation-state created yet another model of modernity for colonial and semicolonial peoples.

Conclusion

The Great War and its aftermath accelerated the trend toward mass participation in a broad range of activities and the debate over how to define progress and organize the people. Because mass society meant production and consumption on a staggering scale, satisfying the populace became a pressing concern for rulers worldwide. Competing programs vied for influence in the new, broader, public domain.

Most programs fell into one of three categories: liberal democratic, authoritarian, or anticolonial. Liberal democracy defined the political and economic systems in most of western Europe and the Americas in the decade following World War I. Resting on faith in free enterprise and representative democracy (with a restricted franchise), liberal regimes had already been unsettled before the Great War. Turn-of-the-century reforms broadened electorates and brought government oversight and regulation into private economic activity. But during the Great Depression, dissatisfaction again deepened. Only far-reaching reforms, introducing greater regulation and more aggressive government intervention to provide for the citizenry's welfare, saved capitalist economies and democratic political systems in Britain, France, and North America from collapse.

Through the 1930s, liberal democracy was in retreat. Authoritarianism seemed better positioned to satisfy the masses while representing the dynamism of modernity. While authoritarians differed about the faults of capitalism, they joined in the condemnation of electoral democracy. Authoritarians mobilized the masses to put the interests of the nation above the individual. That mobilization often involved brutal repression, yet it seemed also to restore pride and purpose to a great number of people.

Meanwhile, the colonial and semicolonial world searched for ways to escape from European domination. In Asia and Africa, anticolonial leaders sought to eliminate foreign rule while turning colonies into nations and subjects into citizens. Some looked to the liberal democratic west for models of nation building, but others rejected liberalism because it was associated with colonial rule. Instead, socialism, communism, fascism, and a return to religious traditions offered more promising paths.

Focus On
World War I and Its Aftermath

The Great War

- The war destroys empires, starting with the Bolshevik Revolution against the tsarist regime in Russia, followed by the defeat and dissolution of the German, Austro-Hungarian, and Ottoman Empires.

- Mass mobilization sees more than 70 million men join the fighting, undermines traditional gender boundaries, and forces states to recognize their peoples' demands for compensation afterward.

- Popular culture spreads as leaders use the new media of radio and film to promote national loyalties and discredit enemies.

The Aftermath

- Liberal democracies in France, Britain, and the United States survive the Great Depression by enacting far-reaching changes in their political systems and free market economies.

- Authoritarian (communist and fascist) dictatorships with many political similarities emerge in the Soviet Union, Italy, Germany, Spain, and Portugal.

- Latin American leaders devise hybrid solutions that combine democratic and authoritarian elements.

- Peoples living under colonial rule in Asia and Africa mobilize traditional values to oppose imperial rulers.

- Key individuals emerge in the struggle to define newly independent nations: Kenyatta, Gandhi, Chiang Kai-shek, and Ataturk.

CHRONOLOGY

1900   **1910**   **1920**

The Americas
U.S. enters World War I 1917

Europe
World War I 1914–1918
Mussolini takes over Italy 1922

Soviet Union
Bolshevik Revolution 1917
Russian civil war 1918–1921

East Asia

Africa
Blaise Diagne (Senegal) elected to the French senate 1914
More than 1 million Africans fight in World War I 1914–1918
Jomo Kenyatta invokes Kikuyu tradition to oppose British colonialism in Kenya 1920s

South Asia

Middle East
Sykes-Picot Agreement 1916
Balfour Declaration 1917
Mustafa Kemal creates modern Turkish nation-state 1923

- **Thinking about Transformation & Conflict and Visions of the Modern** What was the relationship between war and progress in the early twentieth century? What new political, social, and cultural movements grew out of the Great War? Think in particular of the role of former soldiers in politics; the adaptation in peacetime of production practices developed for the war effort; and governments' willingness and ability to regulate the economy and people's everyday lives.

- **Thinking about Changing Power Relationships and Visions of the Modern** What, if anything, was left in this period of the tradition of classical liberalism, which trusted markets to regulate themselves and believed progress would result when individuals pursued their own self-interest? What role did government intervention—in the economy and society—play for the three major traditions discussed in this chapter: liberal democratic, authoritarian, and anticolonial? How central was state intervention to their respective views of progress and modernity?

- **Thinking about Gender and Visions of the Modern** What role did women play in the social transformations of the early twentieth century, both as participants and as symbols? Pay special attention to the role of women workers in war production and, increasingly, in professional careers thereafter; to women consumers in an era of mass production; and to governments' commitment to the ideal of gender equality and their (faltering) willingness to abide by that ideal.

Key Terms

Mustafa Kemal Ataturk p. 918

Bolsheviks p. 892

Chiang Kai-shek p. 917

fascism p. 906

Mohandas Karamchand (Mahatma) Gandhi p. 915

Great Depression p. 899

Great War (World War I) p. 886

Adolf Hitler p. 906

Benito Mussolini p. 906

Nazis p. 906

nonviolent resistance p. 915

Joseph Stalin p. 903

 Go to **INQUIZITIVE** to see what you've learned—and learn what you've missed—with personalized feedback along the way.

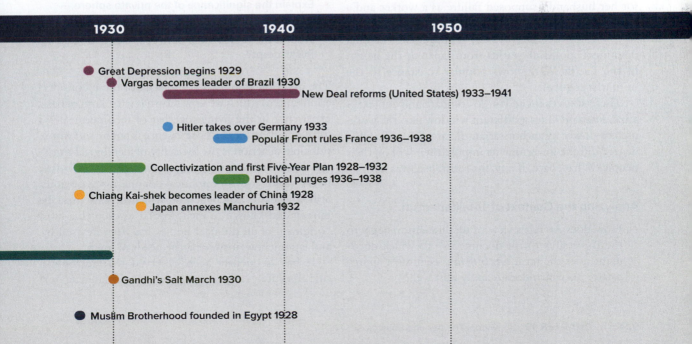

1930   1940   1950

- Great Depression begins 1929
- Vargas becomes leader of Brazil 1930
- New Deal reforms (United States) 1933–1941

- Hitler takes over Germany 1933
- Popular Front rules France 1936–1938

- Collectivization and first Five-Year Plan 1928–1932
- Political purges 1936–1938

- Chiang Kai-shek becomes leader of China 1928
- Japan annexes Manchuria 1932

- Gandhi's Salt March 1930

- Muslim Brotherhood founded in Egypt 1928

Global Themes and Sources

Comparing and Contextualizing Totalitarianism

The term *totalitarianism* emerged in the early twentieth century to refer to regimes that aspired to intervene more directly into people's everyday lives than previous dictatorships had done. While some writers gave the term a positive meaning, most used it critically, to condemn the erosion of basic freedoms. During the Cold War, anti-communist intellectuals in Europe and the United States linked Nazi Germany and the Soviet Union, and sometimes imperial Japan, and contrasted them with the "free world" of liberal democracies. Since the end of the Cold War, historians have largely abandoned the term, calling attention to the notable differences between Nazi Germany and the Soviet Union and to the role of ordinary people in policing one another in all the interwar dictatorships.

Hannah Arendt gave classic expression to the term *totalitarianism* in her 1951 *Origins of Totalitarianism*. The next two sources provide a more ambivalent view of state power: the letter to Marfa Gudzia shows one woman shaming another in Soviet Magnitogorsk for her husband's supposed failure as a worker and a man, while Victor Klemperer's diary shows ordinary Germans uninterested in Nazi propaganda. The final document, political graffiti from Japan at the height of the Pacific War, shows popular resistance to the militarist regime.

These sources invite you to compare and contextualize. Each provides a different window into the workings of power in authoritarian dictatorships. To what degree did the governments impose their will on their people? What space, if any, for resistance, was left?

Analyzing the Context of Totalitarianism

- How does Arendt's view of totalitarianism apply to the three subsequent documents? To which document does the term *totalitarian* seem most appropriate? To which does it apply least well?

- What role do ordinary people play in supporting or resisting the regime in the final three documents?

- Identify the nature and limits of state power in the final three documents.

PRIMARY SOURCE 19.1

The Origins of Totalitarianism (1951), Hannah Arendt

One of the most influential political philosophers of the twentieth century, Hannah Arendt (1906–1975), a Jew, fled Nazi Germany in 1933 and ultimately settled in the United States, where she received American citizenship in 1950. Her first major book, *The Origins of Totalitarianism*, linked Nazi Germany and the Soviet Union.

- **Arendt claims that totalitarianism marks a fundamentally new form of politics. On what grounds does she make this claim?**

- **Explain the significance of the private sphere — "[t]he whole sphere of private life"—in this passage.**

- **What is the relationship between ruler and ruled in this excerpt?**

The question we raised at the start of these considerations and to which we now return is what kind of basic experience in the living-together of men permeates a form of government whose essence is terror and whose principle of action is the logicality of ideological thinking. That such a combination was never used before in the varied forms of political domination is obvious. Still, the basic experience on which it rests must be human and known to men, insofar as even this most "original" of all political bodies has been devised by, and is somehow answering the needs of, men.

It has frequently been observed that terror can rule absolutely only over men who are isolated against each other and that, therefore, one of the primary concerns of all tyrannical government is to bring this isolation about. Isolation may be the beginning of terror; it certainly is its most fertile ground; it always is its result. This isolation is, as it were, pretotalitarian; its hallmark is impotence insofar as power always comes from men acting together, "acting in concert" ([Edmund] Burke); isolated men are powerless by definition.

Isolation and impotence, that is the fundamental inability to act at all, have always been characteristic of tyrannies. Political contacts between men are severed in tyrannical government and the human capacities for action and power are frustrated. But not all contacts between men are broken and not all human capacities destroyed. The whole sphere of private life with the capacities for experience, fabrication and thought are left intact. We know that the iron band of total terror leaves no space for such private life and that the self-coercion of totalitarian logic destroys man's capacity for experience and thought just as certainly as his capacity for action.

Source: Hannah Arendt, *The Origins of Totalitarianism* (1951; repr., San Diego: Harcourt Brace, 1973), p. 474.

Letter to Marfa Gudzia (1930s)

In this letter, a woman named Anna Kovaleva, wife of the best locomotive driver in the Soviet factory town of Magnitogorsk, writes to Marfa Gudzia, the wife of the worst, to criticize her for her husband's many shortcomings.

....

- Analyze the role of gender in this document. What is the source of Kovaleva's pride? How does she contribute to society?

- How does state power operate in this document?

- How did Kovaleva and her husband get their apartment?

....

Dear Marfa!

We are both wives of locomotive drivers of the rail transport of Magnitka. You probably know that the rail transport workers of the MMK [Magnitogorsk Metallurgical Complex] are not fulfilling the plan, that they are disrupting the supply of the blast furnaces, open hearths, and rolling shops. . . . All the workers of Magnitka accuse our husbands, saying that the rail workers hinder the fulfillment of the [overall] industrial plan. It is offensive, painful, and annoying to hear this. And moreover, it is doubly painful, because all of it is the plain truth. Every day there were stoppages and breakdowns in rail transport. Yet our internal factory transport has everything it needs in order to fulfill the plan. For that, it is necessary to work like the best workers of our country work. Among such shock workers is my husband, Aleksandr Panteleevich Kovalev. He always works like a shock worker, exceeding his norms, while economizing on fuel and lubricating oil. His engine is on profit and loss accounting. . . . My husband trains locomotive drivers' helpers out of unskilled laborers. He takes other locomotive drivers under his wing. . . . My husband receives prizes virtually every month. . . . And I too have won awards. . . .

My husband's locomotive is always clean and well taken care of. You, Marfa, are always complaining that it is difficult for your family to live. And why is that so? Because your husband, Iakov Stepanovich, does not fulfill the plan. He has frequent breakdowns on his locomotive, his locomotive is dirty, and he always overconsumes fuel. Indeed, all the locomotive drivers laugh at him. All the rail workers of Magnitka know him—for the wrong reasons, as the worst driver. By contrast, my husband is known as a shock worker. He is written up and praised in the newspapers. . . . He and I are honored everywhere as shock workers. At the store we get everything without having to wait in queues. We moved to the building for shock workers [*dom udarnika*]. We will get an apartment with rugs, a gramophone, a radio, and other comforts. Now we are being assigned to a new store for shock workers and will receive double rations. . . . Soon the Seventeenth Party Congress of our Bolshevik Party will take place. All rail workers are obliged to work so that Magnitka greets the Congress of Victors at full production capacity.

Therefore, I ask you, Marfa, to talk to your husband heart to heart, read him my letter. You, Marfa, explain to Iakov Stepanovich that he just can't go on working the way he has. Persuade him that he must work honorably, conscientiously, like a shock worker. Teach him to understand the words of comrade Stalin, that work is a matter of honor, glory, valor, and heroism.

You tell him that if he does not correct himself and continues to work poorly, he will be fired and lose his supplies. I will ask my Aleksandr Panteleevich to take your husband in tow, help him improve himself and become a shock worker, earn more. I want you, Marfa, and Iakov Stepanovich to be honored and respected, so that you live as well as we do.

I know that many women, yourself included, will say: "What business is it of a wife to interfere in her husband's work. You live well, so hold your tongue." But it is not like that. . . . We all must help our husbands to fight for the uninterrupted work of transport in the winter. OK enough. You catch my drift. This letter is already long. In conclusion, I'd like to say one thing. It's pretty good to be a wife of a shock worker. It's within our power. Let's get down to the task, amicably. I wait your answer.

Anna Kovaleva

Source: Stephen Kotkin, *Magnetic Mountain: Stalinism as a Civilization* (Berkeley: University of California Press, 1995), pp. 218–19.

Source: Stephen Kotkin, *Magnetic Mountain: Stalinism as a Civilization* (Berkeley: University of California Press, 1995), pp. 218–19.

PRIMARY SOURCE 19.3

Victor Klemperer's Diary (1938)

Victor Klemperer (1881–1960) was a scholar of the French Enlightenment whose diaries, published in Germany in 1995, shed light on everyday life in Nazi Germany.

- **According to Klemperer, how did the public respond to Goering's speech?**

- **Based on Klemperer's account, how would you characterize the relationship between rulers and ruled, between the Nazi state and ordinary Germans?**

- **Evaluate the influence of Nazi ideology in this document.**

September 11, Sunday

For the third time Georg has remitted 500M to me from the blocked account "of the deceased Frau Maria Kl." My joy is already no longer as great as the first two times. Because this time I was almost counting on the sum. Also it is only a very partial help; also I feel more humiliated than before, since he has not written me a single line since October and replied neither to my letter of condolence nor to my birthday greetings. Nevertheless the sum (which by the way I do not yet have in my hands, and no one knows what is going to happen tomorrow, everything is uncertain and every hour may bring new coercive measures and war), so nevertheless the money is a great relief to me at the moment. Eva was always preaching: Let the Öhlmanns come here during their holiday, then we can go for a trip with Grete. I had vacillated, the Öhlmanns' holiday came to an end, and Grete took the train to Kudowa. In view of the 500M we announced our visit to the Öhlmanns and drove to Leipzig yesterday. Luck with the weather and a very successful drive via Niederwartha, Meissen [. . .]. New rest house in Lonnewitz. Village just before Oschatz, "Long Distance Lorry Drivers' Restaurant." The huge vehicles outside, the huge portions inside. The Party Rally was coming over the loudspeaker. Announcement, the arrival of Field Marshal Goering. Introductory march, roars of triumph, then Goering's speech, about the tremendous rise, affluence, peace and workers' good fortune in Germany, about the absurd lies and hopes of its enemies, constantly interrupted by well-drilled roars of applause. But the most interesting thing about it all was the behavior of the customers, who all came and went, greeting and taking their leave with "Heil Hitler." But no one was listening. I could barely understand the broadcast because a couple of people were playing cards, striking the table with loud thumps, talking very loudly. It was quieter at other tables. One man was writing a postcard, one was writing in his order book, one was reading the newspaper. And landlady and waitress were talking to each other or to the cardplayers. Truly: Not one of a dozen people paid attention to the radio for even a single second, it could just as well have been transmitting silence or a foxtrot from Leipzig.

At the Öhlmanns' by two and then like the last time in early spring coffee and conversation in her little room until six. According to Trude Öhlmann's stories from the Deutsche Bücherei, where they get a great deal of official information, war is virtually certain. The air-raid precautions (we too have just had several practices, blackout, sirens), the preparations for mobilization all point to it. Mood of the public, of the workers in particular, is bad. If I talk to the butcher or the butter man here in Dresden, then there will certainly be peace, but if (as the day before yesterday) I listen to Wolf, the car man, then so many of his mates have been fetched straight from work to the army again: "Things are coming to a head now!" If I read the newspaper, see and hear the film reports, then we're doing soooo well, we love the Führer soo much and sooo unanimously—what is real, what is happening? That's how one experiences history. We know even less about today than about yesterday and no more than about tomorrow.

Source: Victor Klemperer, *I Will Bear Witness: The Diaries of Victor Klemperer*, translated by Martin Chalmers (London: Weidenfeld & Nicolson, 1998) pp. 267–68.

PRIMARY SOURCE 19.4

Political Graffiti in Imperial Japan (1941–1944)

These passages were collected by the imperial Japanese Thought Police from the walls of public and private places.

....

- Are these passages evidence of the strength or weakness of the Japanese state?
- What can you tell about people who wrote this graffiti? What values did they share?
- Does this source tell us more about the opinions of ordinary Japanese people or the anxieties of the government?

....

December 1941

Kill the emperor

Japan is losing in China

Why does our fatherland dare to commit aggression?
Ask the leaders why they're waging aggressive war against China.

Communism. Communism.
Workers of the world
Revolution now
. . . including the emperor

Look at the pitiful figures of the undernourished people.
Overthrow the government.
Shoot former Prime Minister Konoe, the traitor.

January 1942

Absolute opposition to the imperialist war.
Japan and Germany proclaim their domination throughout the world
But that won't make people happy.
True peace will come only when the Soviet Union obtains victory.
You laborers in military industry throughout the land—
Now is the time to become aware.

Soon we won't be able to eat.
Those who feel good being called soldiers of industry are big fools.
Win or lose, our lives won't change.
End the war (say the workers).
It's just puffing up the bourgeoisie
(says the proletariat).

March 1942

End the war.
In the end we'll lose and the people will suffer.

Her Majesty the Empress is a lecher

Sumitomo Metal is a cheating company that wrings the sweat and blood out of us workers for a pittance.
Kill those guys who decide on salaries.

June 1942

Soldiers carry weapons to kill.
What's become of things like personal character?
Ridiculous. All the more reason to commit suicide.

Capitalists are thieves, property is the fruit of
exploitation

—A Socialist

No rice. End the war.

End the war. Give us freedom.

July 1942

Capitalists ignited the war and are accumulating
wealth and hoarding it.
Give the people peace, liberty, and bread.

Destroy the aristocracy—those consuming parasites.

People's Revolution.
Japan Communist Party *banzai!*

What we believe in is nothing more than Idealism,
Liberalism, Individualism.
Become a youth of "originality."

August 1942

Overthrow the government
Raise wages

November 1942

Starvation and war dead.
The imperalist war intensified work.
Turn the war into insurrection.

Marxism *banzai*
Communist Party *banzai*

We demand repeal of the Peace Preservation Law.
We workers and farmers have been exploited as slaves
of the bourgeois landlords.
Let's throw off our submissive attitudes of the past.
Unite and overthrow Japanese imperialism and
overthrow the capitalists who have exploited and
repressed us.
Overthrow capitalism and imperialism.

No prospect of winning the war.
Kill Konoe Fumimaro.

Stop the war

December 1942

Kill the emperor
Bury the politicians, overthrow the capitalists

February 1943

Kill the dumb emperor

Don't make the farmers weep.
Kill the Minister of Agriculture
Kill Minister Ino.

Kill Tōjō

March 1943

Ridiculous to be a soldier—35 *sen* a day

May 1943

Communism *banzai*. Oppose the war.

Rid Japan of the war-mongering military.
The sword that kills one saves many.

End the war

June 1943

2,000 *yen* to whoever lops off the
emperor's head.

2,000 *yen* . . . for the empress.

Japan and the United States should cooperate for
world peace

The war is no good

July 1943

Kill the rich

Brave men! Carry out a Red revolution!
Soviet *banzai!* Japan Communist Party *banzai!*
Motherland Russia.

Attack the government's running-dog police.
You who have complaints against the government,
Join with comrades and gather under the red flag.
Anarchism. Anarchism.
Stand up, proletariat.

Destroy the bourgeoisie.

For what purpose have you all been fighting for seven years?

August 1943

Communist Party *banzai*.

Comrades of the country, band together under the flag of communism.

Do it. It's life.

Advance and overthrow the capitalists.

Concept of mutual help

Concept of joint responsibility

Concept of class struggle

. . . live with these.

September 1943

How long will the Great East Asian War last?

Three and a half years without food.

One after another, starvation. . . .

All the strong ones have perished. . . .

October 1943

Anglo-American victory, Japanese-German defeat

It's the military and bureaucrats who are profiting from the war under the beautiful name of "nation."

November 1943

To the Deity of Poverty, the Tōjō Cabinet, Liberty, and Equality:

Commoners die for the glory of a few.

For whom are we fighting this war that was started by the privileged class and the military group?

December 1943

What's wrong with liberalism and communism?

We have to reconsider this.

March 1944

Even in the Japanese empire,

Something that was bound to come has come.

What is it? Marxism.

Source: John W. Dower, *Japan in War and Peace: Selected Essays* (New York: New Press, 1993), pp. 124–28.

Interpreting Visual Evidence

Men, Machines, and Mass Production

Mass production of consumer goods reshaped economies and societies in the early twentieth century. Powered by coal and later electricity, the modern factory transformed work, first in Europe, the United States, and Japan and then, especially from 1950 onwards, around the world. The images gathered here provide several perspectives on mass production and its cult of efficiency—its efforts to streamline, to standardize productive activity, to maximize output and minimize cost—and its consequences for workers.

Large-scale manufacturing on assembly lines demands coordinated action. Engineers like Frederick Winslow Taylor (see Chapter 18) developed the field of "scientific management," the forerunner of ergonomics, to streamline the production process. Rather than shaping production to the needs and desires of skilled workers, Taylor tried to adapt machines and human bodies to one another. He and his followers broke down complex tasks into standardized, repeatable actions and then timed workers, imposing a predictable uniformity and minimizing accidents and

error. Gone were the days when farmers organized their days by the light of the sun.

The French inventor-scientist Étienne-Jules Marey (1830–1904) helped prepare the way for the scientific study of labor. He developed stop-action photography in 1882, with a photographic "gun" that took twelve frames per second, which helped pave the way for modern cinema. Here we look at a series of studies of human movement that would influence Taylor and facilitate the study of labor practices around the world.

Inspired by Pablo Picasso and Karl Marx, among others, the Mexican muralist Diego Rivera (1886–1957) was fascinated by labor. His Detroit mural (1923) of the Ford Motor Company depicted workers on an assembly line, celebrating the physical force of cosmopolitan groups of industrial workers. The final two images include a photograph of a Ford assembly line in Detroit and one from a Mitsubishi electric plant in Japan in the 1930s, representing iconic examples of modern factories, with standardized, streamlined production processes powered by electricity and massive machines.

Photographs by Étienne-Jules Marey.

Mural in Detroit by Diego Rivera.

Car assembly line at Ford plant.

Mitsubishi Electric Factory.

Questions for Analysis

1. Describe the relationship between workers and machines in these images, from the point of view of the workers.

2. Explain how engineers like Taylor, who were interested in maximizing production, could also use Marey's images to improve working conditions.

3. Explain the relationship between factory production and factory workers, as depicted in these images, and mass consumption and consumers, as presented in this chapter.

4. On balance, do the images of the human body and industrial work presented here promise alienation or liberation for workers?

20

The Three-World Order

1940–1975

In February 1945, the three leaders of the World War II Allies—President Franklin Delano Roosevelt of the United States, Prime Minister Winston Churchill of Great Britain, and Premier Joseph Stalin of the Soviet Union—met to prepare for the postwar world. By then, Germany, Italy, and Japan were losing the war. But the world's postwar reordering was a source of deep contention, for the three leaders had profoundly different visions for the future. Roosevelt envisioned independent nation-states protected by an international body and had no interest in restoring the old European empires. Churchill, however, resisted decolonization of the British Empire. Stalin sought above all to secure Soviet influence in eastern Europe and to weaken Germany so that it could never again menace the Soviet Union. When the fighting stopped, the European-centered order, shocked by World War I, had been shattered by World War II. Empires lay in ruins and faced dismantling by independence movements. The nation-state had emerged as the prevailing global political organization.

With the weakening of western Europe, a new three-world order emerged. Heading the "First World," the United States championed capitalism and democracy as the best way to bring unprecedented prosperity in the decades after 1945. The Soviet Union, despite having been the United States' crucial ally during World War II, became its chief adversary in the decades that followed. As leader of the communist "Second World,"

Chapter Outline

- World War II and Its Aftermath
- The Beginning of the Cold War
- Decolonization
- Three Worlds
- Tensions within the Three Worlds
- Conclusion

Core Objectives

- **EXPLAIN** the relationship between World War II and the three-world order.
- **ANALYZE** the extent to which World War II was a global war.
- **ANALYZE** the roles that the United States and the Soviet Union played in the Cold War.
- **IDENTIFY** the goals of Third World states in this period, and **EVALUATE** the degree to which these goals were achieved.
- **COMPARE** the civil rights issues in the First, Second, and Third Worlds, and **ASSESS** the ways each "world" addressed these and other basic rights.

the Soviet Union contested capitalist societies' claims and trumpeted socialism's accomplishments. As their spheres of influence expanded, the Americans and the Soviets (and their respective allies) engaged in a bitter ideological rivalry, known as the **Cold War** because no direct military conflict occurred between these two superpowers. Caught in between were formerly colonized and semicolonized peoples. Lumped together as the "Third World" by western intellectuals and by Asian, Latin American, and African leaders who embraced the idea of an alternative to the two dominant blocs, these nations emerged from the war eager to seek their own ways forward.

Global Storylines

- World War II shatters the European-centered global order, weakening Europe and Japan and unsettling empires.

- The United States and its liberal democratic allies (the First World) engage in a cold war with the Soviet Union and its communist allies (the Second World).

- Decolonized states in Asia, Africa, and Latin America (the Third World) struggle to find a "third way" but find themselves caught between the rival superpowers.

World War II and Its Aftermath

World War II was truly a global conflict, a devastatingly total one. It grew out of unresolved problems connected to the Great War. World War I had not been, as many had prophesied, "the war to end all wars." Especially influential were the resentments bred by the harsh provisions and controversial state boundaries set out in the treaties signed at the war's end. World War II also resulted from the aggressive ambitions and racial theories of Germany and Japan. By the late 1930s, German and Japanese ambitions to become colonial powers brought these dictatorships (which, along with Italy, constituted the Axis powers) into conflict with France, Britain, the Soviet Union, and eventually the United States (the Allied powers). Fighting occurred in Europe, Africa, Asia, and the Atlantic and Pacific Oceans as the warring nations mobilized millions of people and placed enormous demands on civilian populations.

THE BIG PICTURE

What was the relationship between World War II and the three-world order?

THE WAR IN EUROPE

World War II began in September 1939 with Germany's invasion of Poland and Britain's and France's decision to oppose it. Before it was all over in 1945, much of Europe, including Germany, had been leveled.

Blitzkrieg and Resistance Germany's early success was staggering. Nazi troops overran Poland, France, Norway, Denmark, Luxembourg, Belgium, and the Netherlands. Within less than two years, the Germans controlled virtually all of Europe from the English Channel to the Soviet border. (See Map 20.1.) Only Britain escaped Axis control, although Nazi bombers pulverized British cities. In 1939, Germany signed a nonaggression pact with the Soviets, but in 1941, the German army broke the pact and invaded the Soviet Union with 170 divisions, 3,000 tanks, and 3.2 million men—an invasion force of a size unmatched before or since. Here, as elsewhere, the Germans fought a *blitzkrieg* (lightning war) of tank-led assaults followed by motorized infantrymen and then foot soldiers. By October 1941, the Germans had reached the outskirts of Moscow. The Soviet Union seemed on the verge of a monumental defeat.

The Nazi war was not just a grab for land and raw materials; it was also a crusade for a new order based on race. Throughout Europe, Hitler established puppet governments that complied with deportation orders against Jews and dissidents. His new order made Europe a giant police state. It gave rise to collaborators, who worked with the Germans; resistance fighters, who opposed the German occupiers for varying reasons; and a wide range of options in between, as people struggled to make their way and take care of their families as best they could.

Axis powers, August 1939
Extent of Axis control, May 1941
Allies
Neutral nations
→ **Axis offenses**
→ **Allied offenses**
✳ **Major battles**

Battle of Britain
Aug. 1–Oct. 12, 1940

D-Day
June 6, 1944

Paris liberated
Aug. 25, 1944

VICHY FRANCE (occupied Nov. 1942)

Battle of the Bulge
Dec. 16, 1944–Jan. 31, 1945

Leningrad besieged
Sept. 1941–Jan. 1944

Germany invades Soviet Union
June 1941

Stalingrad
Aug. 21, 1942–Jan. 31, 1943

Rome liberated
June 4, 1944

El Alamein
June–Nov. 1942

Map 20.1 World War II: The European Theater

The Axis armies enjoyed great success during the early stages of World War II.

- Which parts of the European theater did the Allies control? The Axis? Which countries were neutral in 1941?
- Where did the major Allied and Axis campaigns take place?
- What was Germany's greatest geographic obstacle during World War II?

The Devastation of War In November 1942, Nazi troops entered Stalingrad, some 2,000 miles from Berlin. Hitler wanted to capture the city not only to exploit the surrounding wheat fields and the oil of the Caucasus, but also for its very name. With handheld flamethrowers and sometimes just their fists, Soviet troops drove out the Germans in February 1943.

In the east, the tide turned against the Germans and their collaborators after the ferocious battles of Stalingrad in 1942–1943 and Kursk in 1943. At the Battle of Stalingrad, the German army and its allies had 1.5 million men killed, wounded, or captured, compared with 750,000 Soviet troops suffering the same fates. Only six months later, at the Battle of Kursk, the largest tank conflict in world history, the Germans, boasting a tank force of more than 2,000, lost to a Soviet tank force twice its size. Once the Soviet army had blunted the initial German assault, it launched a massive counter-offensive. This move initiated the defeat of the German war effort on the Eastern Front, but full retreat took another two years as the Soviets drove Hitler's army slowly westward. The spectacular D-Day landing of western Allied forces in Normandy on June 6, 1944 (when the Germans had a mere 15 divisions in France, as compared with more than 300 on the Eastern Front), initiated Germany's defeat in the west. On April 30, 1945, as Soviet and Anglo-American forces converged on Berlin, Hitler committed suicide. Days later, Germany surrendered unconditionally.

The Bitter Costs of War The war in Europe had devastating human and material costs. This was particularly true in eastern Europe, where German forces leveled more than 70,000 Soviet villages, obliterated one-third of the Soviet Union's wealth, and inflicted 7 million Soviet military deaths (by contrast, the Germans lost 3.5 million soldiers) and at least 20 million civilian deaths. German bombing of British cities, such as London, took a heavy toll on civilians and buildings, as did Allied bombing of Axis war plants and cities like Dresden and Tokyo. Tens of millions were left homeless.

Europe's Jews paid an especially high price. Hitler had long talked of "freeing" Europe of all Jews. At the war's outset, the Nazis herded Jews into ghettos and labor camps, then seized their property. As the German army moved eastward, more and more Jews came under their control.

At first the Nazi bureaucrats considered deportation of Jews, but then ruled out transporting "subhumans" as too costly, and began instead to starve them and crowd them together in unsanitary ghettos. By summer 1941, special troops operating behind the army on the Eastern Front had begun mass shootings of communists and Jewish civilians, and by fall 1941, Hitler and the S.S.—the *Schutzstaffel*, or special security forces—were building a series of killing centers in the east. Cattle cars shipped Jews from all over Europe to these extermination sites, where Nazis used the latest technology, including the arsenic-based poison gas Zyklon B, to kill men, women, and children. The largest facility, Auschwitz, combined an extermination center and work camp in a single complex.

The deliberate extermination of the Jews, known as the **Holocaust**, claimed around 6 million lives. About half of this number died in the gas chambers of death camps; the others were shot, gassed in mobile vans, or succumbed to starvation or disease. The shift to a policy of extermination was both unimaginably brutal and rapid. At its core, the Holocaust was brief, intense mass murder. In mid-March 1942, roughly three-quarters of all victims of the Holocaust were still alive and one-quarter had been killed; within a year—by March 1943—the proportions were reversed, with three-quarters of the victims dead. The Nazis also turned their mass killing apparatus against Sinta and Roma (gypsies), homosexuals, communists, and Slavs, with deportations to the death camps continuing to the very end of the war.

These Nazi genocides—enormous in scale and reliant on modern, "enlightened" administrative practices—stood as a powerful challenge to European claims that science, technology, and an efficient bureaucracy would make life better for everyone. Lamenting connections between European culture and the Holocaust, German philosopher Theodor Adorno wrote that "to write poetry after Auschwitz is barbaric" (1949). Nazi crimes, he suggested, defied human understanding.

THE WAR IN THE PACIFIC

Like the war in Europe, the conflict in the Pacific transformed the military and political landscape. (See Map 20.2.) The war broke out when Japan's ambitions to dominate Asia targeted American interests and military might.

Japan's Efforts to Expand Japanese efforts to expand in Asia were already under way in the 1930s, but the outbreak of war in Europe opened opportunities for further expansion. Having fought with the Allies in World War I, Japan was granted control of the South Pacific Mandate (1919–1947) by the

SOVIET
UNION

ALASKA
(U.S.)

CANADA

MONGOLIA

MANCHUKUO

ALEUTIAN IS. (U.S.)

CHINA

KOREA JAPAN
• Tokyo

Hiroshima
Aug. 6, 1945

Midway
June 1942

TIBET

Nagasaki
Aug. 9, 1945

Iwo Jima
Feb. 1945

Pearl Harbor
Dec. 7, 1941

TAIWAN

BURMA
(Br.)

THAILAND

FRENCH
INDOCHINA

PHILIPPINES
(U.S.)

GUAM
(U.S.)

PACIFIC OCEAN

DUTCH EAST INDIES

JAPANESE
MANDATE

Guadalcanal
Aug. 1942–
Feb. 1943

INDIAN
OCEAN

AUSTRALIA

Coral Sea
May 1942

NEW
ZEALAND

0   1000   2000 Miles

0   1000   2000 Kilometers

Japanese Empire, 1936
Japanese control, Aug. 1942
Allies
Neutral nations
Allied offenses
Major battles
Atomic bomb targets

Map 20.2 World War II: The Pacific Theater

Like Germany and Italy, Japan experienced stunning military successes in the war's early years.

- In August, 1942, which areas in the Pacific theater were under the control of the Japanese, and which were under Allied control?

- What does tracing the route of the Allied offense tell you about their main strategy?

- What geographic factors influenced the American decision to drop atomic bombs on Hiroshima and Nagasaki to end the war, instead of invading Japan?

League of Nations. Japan's military forces invaded and occupied Manchuria in 1931—creating a puppet state called Manchukuo (1937–1945)—and then launched an offensive against the rest of China in 1937. Although the Japanese did not achieve China's complete submission, the invaders exacted a terrible toll on the population. Most infamous was the so-called rape of Nanjing, in which Japanese aggressors slaughtered at least 100,000 civilians and raped thousands of women in the Chinese city between December 1937 and February 1938.

Meanwhile, Germany's swift occupation of western Europe left the defeated nations' Asian colonies at the mercy of Japanese forces. After concluding a pact with Germany in 1940, the Japanese occupied French Indochina (Vietnam) in 1941 and made demands on the Dutch East Indies for oil and rubber. The chief remaining obstacle to their further expansion in the Pacific was the United States, which already had imperial interests in China and the Philippines as well as other Pacific islands. Hoping to strike the United States before it was prepared for war, the Japanese launched a surprise air attack on the American naval base at Pearl Harbor in Hawaii on December 7, 1941.

Now Japan's expansion shifted into high gear. With French Indochina already under their control, the Japanese turned against the American colony of the Philippines and against the Dutch East Indies, both of which fell in 1942. By coordinating their army, navy, and air force units and using tactical surprise, the Japanese seized a huge swath of territory that included British-ruled Hong Kong, Singapore, Malaya, and Burma while threatening the British Empire's hold on India as well.

Japan justified its aggression on the grounds that it was anticolonial and pan-Asian: Japan promised to drive out the European imperialists and to build a new order reflecting "Asia for Asians." In practice, however, the Japanese made oppressive demands on fellow Asians for resources, developed myths of Japanese racial purity and supremacy, and treated Chinese and Koreans with brutality.

Allied Advances and the Atomic Bomb Like the Germans in their war against the Soviet Union, the Japanese could not sustain their military successes against the United States. By mid-1943, U.S. forces had put the Japanese on the defensive. Fighting their way from island to island, American troops recaptured the Philippines, and a combined force of British, American, and Chinese troops returned Burma to Britain. The Allies then moved toward the Japanese mainland. By summer 1945, American bombers had all but devastated the major cities of Japan. Yet Japan did not surrender.

Anticipating that an invasion of Japan would cost hundreds of thousands of American lives, U.S. President Harry Truman unleashed the Americans' secret weapon. It was the work of a team of scientists who were predominantly

The Aftermath of the Atomic Bomb A view of Nagasaki less than half a mile from "ground zero" after the atomic bomb was dropped in August 1945. A few reinforced concrete buildings still stand.

European refugees. On August 6, 1945, an American plane dropped an atomic bomb on the city of Hiroshima, killing or maiming over 100,000 people and poisoning the air, soil, and groundwater for decades to come. Three days later, the Americans dropped a second atomic bomb on Nagasaki. Within days, Emperor Hirohito announced Japan's surrender, bringing the war to an official end. After the six years of World War II, much of East Asia and Europe lay in ruins; millions had died, and millions more were wounded, displaced, widowed, and orphaned. What the postwar world would look like, however, remained unclear.

The Beginning of the Cold War

The destruction of Europe and the defeat of Japan left a power vacuum, which the United States and the Soviet Union rushed to fill. Avoiding direct warfare, the Americans and Soviets vied for influence in postwar Europe and around the globe in a series of smaller, indirect conflicts.

Core Objectives

ANALYZE the roles that the United States and the Soviet Union played in the Cold War.

REBUILDING EUROPE

Communism and liberal democracy offered competing approaches to rebuilding states and societies in Europe after World War II. The task of

The Berlin Airlift In summer 1948, West Berlin seemed poised to become an outpost of the west inside the Soviet occupation zone. The Soviets responded by blocking western traffic into Berlin; the west countered with an airlift, forcing the Soviets to back down in May 1949 but hastening the division of Germany into two countries.

political rebuilding was daunting, for the old order had been discredited. Liberal democrats had to distance themselves from their prewar predecessors. Communism, by contrast, gained new appeal. Many eastern Europeans, reacting to the horrors of fascism and not knowing the extent of Stalin's crimes, looked to the Soviets for answers.

Europe's leftward tilt alarmed U.S. policymakers. They feared that the Soviets would use their ideological influence and the territory taken from the Nazis by the Red Army to spread communism. They also worried that Stalin might seize Europe's overseas possessions and create communist regimes outside Europe. But no one wished to fight another "hot" war. As President Truman began advocating a policy of containment to prevent the further advance of communism, an American journalist popularized the term *cold war* in 1946 to describe a new form of struggle in which both sides endeavored to avoid direct warfare.

Truman's containment policy was tested when the Soviets attempted to seize control of Berlin. Like the rest of Germany, Berlin had been partitioned into British, French, American, and Soviet zones of occupation, but the city itself was an island lying within the Soviet zone. In 1948, the Soviets attempted to cut the city off from western access by blocking routes between the western zones of Germany and the western zones of Berlin. The Allies responded with the Berlin Airlift, transporting supplies in planes to West Berlin in hope of keeping the population from capitulating to the Soviets. This crisis lasted for almost a year, until Stalin lifted the blockade in May 1949.

In that same year, occupied Germany was split into two hostile states: the democratic Federal Republic of Germany (West Germany) in the west, and the communist German Democratic Republic (East Germany) in the east. In 1961, leaders in the German Democratic Republic built a wall around West Berlin to insulate the east from capitalist propaganda and to halt a flood of émigrés fleeing communism. The Berlin Wall became the great symbol of a divided Europe and of the Cold War.

U.S. policymakers wanted to shore up democratic governments in Europe, so Truman promised American military and economic aid. Containing the spread of communism meant securing a capitalist future for Europe, a job that fell to Truman's secretary of state, General George C. Marshall. He launched the Marshall Plan, an ambitious program that provided over $13 billion in grants and credits to reconstruct Europe and facilitate an economic revival. U.S. policymakers hoped the aid would dim communism's appeal by fostering economic prosperity, muting class tensions, and integrating western European nations into an alliance of capitalist democracies.

Stalin saw the Marshall Plan as a threat to the Soviet Union and rejected the offer of support. He felt the same way about the formation in 1949 of the **North Atlantic Treaty Organization (NATO)**, a military alliance between countries in western Europe and North America. He believed that the Soviet Union, having sacrificed millions of people to the war against fascism, deserved to be dominant in eastern Europe. Soviet troops had occupied eastern European nations at the war's end, and in those nations, communists and leftist members of other parties formed Soviet-backed coalition governments. In 1955, the Soviets formally allied themselves with these communist nations in the **Warsaw Pact**, a military alliance of their own. (See Map 20.3.) The tense confrontations between NATO and the Warsaw Pact countries in Europe and in other parts of the world in the 1950s and 1960s brought the world to the brink of an atomic World War III.

WAR IN THE NUCLEAR AGE: THE KOREAN WAR

The dropping of the atomic bombs on Japan in 1945 changed military affairs forever. Spurred by the onset of the Cold War, the Soviets worked hard to

North Atlantic Treaty Organization (NATO)
International organization set up in 1949 to provide for the defense of western European countries and the United States from the perceived Soviet threat.

Warsaw Pact (1955–1991)
Military alliance between the Soviet Union and other communist states that was established in response to the creation of the North American Treaty Organization (NATO).

Map 20.3 NATO and Warsaw Pact Countries

....

The Cold War divided Europe into two competing blocs: those allied with the United States in the North Atlantic Treaty Organization (NATO) and those linked to the Soviet Union under the Warsaw Pact.

- Which nations had borders with nations belonging to the opposite bloc?

- Comparing this map with Map 20.1, explain how combat patterns in World War II shaped the dividing line between the two blocs.

- According to the map, where would you expect Cold War tensions to be the most intense?

Map labels: ICELAND; ATLANTIC OCEAN; U.S. and Canada are also part of NATO; NORWAY $236 million; FINLAND; SWEDEN $107 million; NORTH SEA; BALTIC SEA; SOVIET UNION; DENMARK $273 million; IRELAND $148 million; GREAT BRITAIN $3190 million; NETHERLANDS $1084 million; EAST GERMANY; POLAND; BELGIUM; Luxembourg and Belgium together receive $546 million; WEST GERMANY 1955 $1391 million; CZECHOSLOVAKIA; LUXEMBOURG; FRANCE $2714 million; SWITZ.; AUSTRIA $678 million; HUNGARY; ROMANIA; ITALY $1509 million; YUGOSLAVIA; BLACK SEA; PORTUGAL $51 million; SPAIN 1982; CORSICA; ADRIATIC SEA; BULGARIA; ALBANIA until 1968; BALEARIC ISLANDS; SARDINIA; GREECE 1952 $707 million; AEGEAN SEA; TURKEY 1952 $225 million; MEDITERRANEAN SEA; SICILY; CRETE; RHODES

Legend:
- NATO
- Warsaw Pact
- Neutral
- U.S. $ Marshall aid recipient

catch up to the Americans, and in 1949 tested their first nuclear bomb. Thereafter, each side rushed to stockpile nuclear weapons and update its military technologies. By 1960, the explosive power of these weapons had increased so greatly that nuclear war had the potential to destroy the world without a soldier firing a single shot. This sobering realization changed the rules of the game. Each side now possessed the power to inflict total destruction on the other, a circumstance that inhibited direct confrontations but sparked smaller conflicts in parts of Asia such as Korea, where Japan's defeat resulted in an uneasy standoff between the communist North, backed by the Soviet Union, and the South, backed by the U.S.

SOVIET
UNION

CHINA

Ch'ŏngjin

Hyesanjin

Chosan

3) Oct. 26, 1950

NORTH

Hŭngnam

KOREA

Pyongyang

Wonsan

SEA OF JAPAN

5) June 1951–July 1953

Kŭmhwa

38th parallel

Kaesong

4) Jan. 25, 1951

Seoul
Inch'ŏn

Sumchok

2) Sept. 30, 1950

SOUTH
KOREA

Taejŏn

YELLOW

Taegu

1) Sept. 15, 1950

SEA

JAPAN

- ← Advance by North Korean troops, June–Sept. 1950
- ← Advance by South Korean, U.N., and U.S. troops, Sept.–Oct. 1950
- ◄- - Advance by Chinese and North Korean troops, Nov. 1950–Jan. 1951
- ◄- - Advance by South Korean, U.N., and U.S. troops, Jan.–June 1951
- — Front line of North Korean troops
- — Front line of Chinese and North Korean troops
- — Front line of South Korean, U.N. and U.S. troops
- •••• Truce line, July 1953

Map 20.4 The Korean War

The Korean War was an early confrontation between the capitalist and communist blocs during the Cold War era.

- What were the dates of each side's farthest advance into the other side's territory?
- Why was this peninsula strategically important?
- According to your reading, how did the outcome of the war shape political affairs in East Asia for the next several decades?

In 1950, North Korean troops invaded South Korea, setting off the Korean War. (See Map 20.4.) President Truman ordered American troops to drive back the North Koreans. The Security Council of the United Nations— an international body established in 1945 to help prevent another world war—also sent troops from fifteen nations to restore peace. Within a year, the invaders had been routed and were near collapse. When U.N. troops

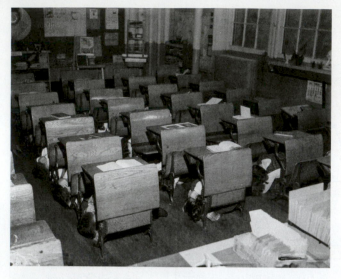

Atom Bomb Anxiety This photograph shows school-children taking shelter under their desks during an A-bomb drill in Brooklyn, New York, 1951. The Soviets had exploded their first test bomb in 1949. Underground bomb shelters were built in many American urban areas as places in which to survive a doomsday attack.

Core Objectives

IDENTIFY the goals of Third World states in this period, and EVALUATE the degree to which these goals were achieved.

decolonization
End of empire and emergence of new independent nation-states in Asia and Africa as a result of the defeat of Japan in World War II and weakened European influence after the war.

advanced north to the Chinese border, however, Stalin maneuvered his communist Chinese allies into rescuing the communist regime in North Korea and driving the South Korean and U.N. forces back to the old boundary in the middle of the Korean peninsula. The fighting continued until 1953, when an armistice divided the country at roughly the same spot as at the start of the war.

The Korean War energized America's anti-communist commitments and spurred a rapid increase in NATO forces. The United States now saw Japan as a bulwark against communism and resolved to rebuild Japanese economic power. Like West Germany, Japan went from being the enemy in World War II to being a valued U.S. ally as the Cold War rivalry between the United States and the Soviet Union spurred both sides to shore up alliances around the globe.

Decolonization

The unsettling of empires, including those established by Japan before and during World War II and the longer-standing colonies held by European states, inspired colonial peoples to reconsider their political futures. The resulting process of **decolonization** and nation building followed four general patterns: civil wars, negotiated independence, wars of independence, and incomplete decolonization.

THE CHINESE REVOLUTION

In China, the ousting of the Japanese occupiers intensified a civil war that eventually brought the Chinese Communist Party to power. The communist movement in China had its origins in post–World War I hostility toward the western powers. In that period, the communists had vowed to free China from colonialism, but had been outgunned by Chiang Kai-shek's nationalist regime and driven from China's cities; they retreated into the interior, where they founded base camps. In 1934, under attack by Chiang's forces, the communists, led by **Mao Zedong** (1893–1976), abandoned their bases and undertook an arduous 6,000-mile journey through the rugged terrain of northwestern China. (See Map 20.5.) In the course of this great escape, glorified in communist lore as the Long March, fewer than 10,000 of the approximately 80,000 people who started the journey reached their

Map 20.5 The Long March, 1934–1935

During the Long March, which took place during the struggle for power between the nationalist Guomindang and the communists within China, communist forces traveled over 6,000 miles to save their lives and their movement.

- What route did the communist forces take?
- Why did the communists take this particular route?
- How did this movement affect the outcome of this internal struggle in the long run?

Map legend:

/// Early Soviets (self-governing communist areas), 1927–1935
→ Route of the main Chinese communist forces from Ruijin after Guomindang assaults on Jiangxi Soviet area
→ Route of communist forces from other areas
⌐ Main communist base area, governed from Yan'an, 1935–1945
▪ "Liberated areas" dominated by local communist groups by 1945
HUNAN Province

destination. Fortunately for the communists, the Japanese invasion in 1937 diverted nationalist troops and offered Mao and the survivors a chance to regroup.

Mao's followers cultivated popular support by advocating the lowering of taxes, cooperative farming, and policies aimed at women's emancipation, such as the outlawing of arranged marriages and the legalization of divorce. Like many anticolonial reformers, Mao regarded women's emancipation as a key component in building a new nation, since he considered their oppression to be both unjust and an obstacle to progress.

Communist expansion in rural areas during World War II swelled the membership of the Communist Party from 40,000 in 1937 to over a million in 1945. After Japan's surrender, China's civil war between nationalists

Mao Zedong (1893–1976)

Chinese communist leader who rose to power during the Long March (1934). In 1949, he defeated the nationalists and established a communist regime in China.

and communists resumed. But the communist forces now had the numbers, the guns (mostly supplied by the Soviet Union), and the popular support to assault nationalist strongholds and seize power, establishing the People's Republic of China in 1949.

NEGOTIATED INDEPENDENCE IN INDIA AND AFRICA

In India and most of colonial Africa, gaining independence involved little bloodshed, although the aftermath was often extremely violent. The British, realizing that they could no longer rule India without coercion, bowed to the inevitable and withdrew. The same happened in many African colonies, where nationalists also succeeded in negotiating independence from European empires, although, as we shall see, there were notable exceptions.

India Unlike China, India achieved political independence without an insurrection. But it did veer dangerously close to civil war. The leadership of the Indian National Congress Party retained tight control over the mass movement that it had mobilized in the 1920s and 1930s (see Chapter 19). Even Gandhi hesitated to leave the initiative to the common people, believing that they had not yet assimilated the doctrine of nonviolence. Gandhi and the party leadership worked hard to convince the British that they, the middle-class leaders, spoke for the nation. At the same time, the threat of a mass peasant uprising with radical aims (like the communist revolution in China) encouraged the British to transfer power quickly.

As negotiations moved forward, Hindu-Muslim unity deteriorated. Whose culture would define the new nation? The Indian nationalism that had existed in the late nineteenth century reflected the culture of the Hindu majority. Yet this movement masked the multiplicity of regional, linguistic, caste, and class differences *within* the Hindu community, just as Muslim movements that arose in reaction to Hindu-dominated Indian nationalism overlooked divisions within their own ranks. Now the prospect of defining "India" created a grand contest between newly self-conscious communities. Riots broke out between Hindus and Muslims in 1946, which increased the mutual distrust between the Congress Party and Muslim League leaders. The specter of civil war haunted the proceedings as outgoing colonial rulers decided to divide the subcontinent into two states: India and Pakistan.

On August 14, 1947, Pakistan gained independence from Britain; a day later, India did the same. The euphoria of decolonization, however, was drowned in a frenzy of brutality. Shortly after independence, as many as 1 million Hindus and Muslims killed one another. Fearing further violence, 12 million Hindus and Muslims left their homes to relocate in the new countries where they would be in the majority. Although the British departed peacefully from India, the peoples inhabiting the subcontinent engaged in open warfare over differences that haunt the relationship between India and Pakistan to this day.

Africa for Africans Shortly after Indian independence, most African states also gained their sovereignty. Except in southern Africa, where minority white rule persisted, the old colonial states gave way to indigenous rulers.

The postwar years saw Africans move to cities in search of a better life. As expanding educational systems produced a wave of primary and secondary school graduates, these educated young people and other new urban dwellers became disgruntled when attractive employment opportunities were not forthcoming. Three groups—former servicemen, the urban unemployed or underemployed, and the educated—led the nationalist agitation that began in the late 1940s and early 1950s. (See Map 20.6.)

Faced with rising nationalist demands, and too much in debt to invest more in pacifying the discontented colonies, European powers agreed to decolonize. The Soviet Union and the United States also favored decolonization. Thus, decolonization in most of Africa was a rapid and relatively sedate affair. In 1957, the Gold Coast (renamed Ghana), under Prime Minister Kwame Nkrumah, became tropical Africa's first independent state. Other British colonial territories followed in rapid succession, so that by 1963, all of British-ruled Africa, except for Southern Rhodesia, was independent.

Decolonization in much of French-ruled Africa followed a similarly smooth path, although the French were initially resistant. Instead of negotiating independence, they tried first to accord fuller voting rights to their colonial subjects, even allowing Africans and Asians to send delegates to the French National Assembly. In the end, however, the French electorate had no desire to share the privileges of French citizenship with African and Asian populations. Thus, France dissolved its political ties with French West Africa and French Equatorial Africa in 1960, having given protectorates in Morocco and Tunisia their independence in 1956. Algeria, considered an integral part of France, was a different matter. France's desperate efforts to hold onto Algeria (see below) facilitated independence movements elsewhere in Africa.

The leaders of African independence movements believed that Africa's precolonial traditions would enable the region to move from colonialism right into a special African form of socialism, escaping the ravages of capitalism. Without rejecting western culture completely, they praised the so-called African personality, exemplified by the idea of "Negritude" developed by Senegal's first president, Léopold Sédar Senghor. Negritude, they claimed, was steeped in common African traditions and able to embrace social justice and equality while rejecting the unrestrained individualism that Africans felt lay at the core of European culture.

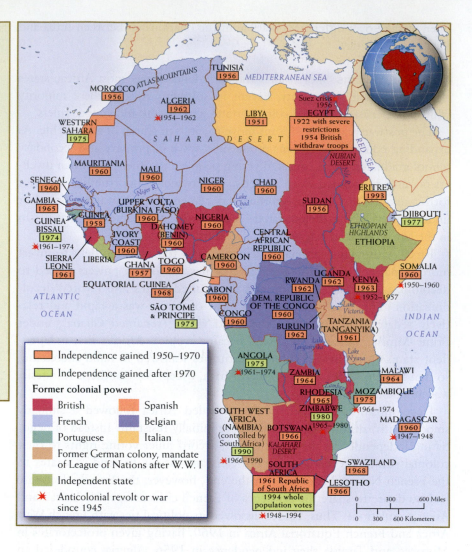

Map 20.6

Decolonization in Africa

....

African decolonization occurred after World War II, largely in the 1950s, 1960s, and 1970s.

- Find at least four areas that won independence in the 1950s and identify the former colonial power that ruled each area.

- What areas took longer to gain independence?

- According to your reading, what problems and tensions contributed to this uneven process of decolonization across Africa?

Map legend (within map):

- Independence gained 1950–1970
- Independence gained after 1970

Former colonial power
- British
- French
- Portuguese
- Spanish
- Belgian
- Italian
- Former German colony, mandate of League of Nations after W.W. I
- Independent state
- ✶ Anticolonial revolt or war since 1945

VIOLENT AND INCOMPLETE DECOLONIZATIONS

Although transfers of power in most of Africa and Asia ultimately occurred peacefully, there were notable exceptions. In Palestine, Algeria, Kenya, and southern Africa, the presence of European immigrant groups created violent conflicts that aborted any peaceful transfer of power—or left the process incomplete. In Vietnam, the process was also violent and delayed, partly because of France's desire to reimpose colonial control and partly because of the power politics of Cold War competition.

Palestine, Israel, and Egypt In Palestine, Arabs and Jews had been on a collision course since the end of World War I. Before that war, a group of

European Jews, known as Zionists, had argued that only a large-scale migration from existing states to their place of origin in Palestine could lead to Jewish self-determination. Zionism combined a yearning to return to the holy lands with a fear of anti-Semitism and anguish over increasing Jewish assimilation. Zionists wanted to create a Jewish state, and they won a crucial victory during World War I when the British government, under the Balfour Declaration, promised a homeland for the Jews in Palestine. But when the British took control of Palestine after 1918, they also guaranteed the rights of Palestinian Arabs.

As more Jews settled in Palestine, tensions arose between Zionists and Palestinian Arabs, and both grew dissatisfied with British rule. Arabs resented the presence of Jews, who displaced farmers who had lived on the land for generations and who openly sought their own independent state. Zionists became especially enraged when British authorities wavered in supporting their demands for more immigration. After World War II, the pressure to allow more immigration increased as hundreds of thousands of concentration camp survivors clamored for entry into Palestine, and Zionist militants began using force to attempt to gain control of the state.

In 1947, after the British announced that they would leave negotiations over the area's fate to the United Nations, that body voted to partition Palestine into Arab and Jewish territories. The Arab states rejected the partition, and the Jewish Agency, a nongovernmental organization that supported the immigration of Jews to Israel, only reluctantly accepted it. Although the Jews were delighted to have an independent state, they were unhappy about its small size, its indefensible borders, and the fact that it did not include all the lands that had belonged to ancient Israel. For their part, the Palestinians were shocked at the partition, and they looked to their better-armed Arab neighbors to regain the territories set aside for the new state of Israel.

The ensuing Arab-Israeli War of 1948–1949 shattered the legitimacy of Arab ruling elites. Arab states entered the war poorly prepared to take on the well-run and enthusiastically supported Israeli Defense Force. By the time the United Nations finally negotiated a truce, Israel had declared its independence (May 14, 1948) and extended its boundaries; more than 1 million Palestinians had become refugees in surrounding Arab countries.

Embittered by this defeat, a group of young army officers in Egypt plotted to overthrow the Egyptian regime, which they felt was corrupt and still under European influence. One of the officers, Gamal Abdel Nasser, became the head of a secret organization of junior military officers called the Free Officers movement. These men had ties with communists and other dissident groups, including the Muslim Brotherhood, which favored a return to Islamic rule. They launched a successful coup in 1952, forcing the king to abdicate and leave the country. The new regime dissolved the parliament, banned political parties (including the communists and the Muslim Brotherhood), and stripped the old elite of its wealth.

In 1956, Nasser moved to nationalize the Suez Canal Company (an Egyptian company, mainly run by French businessmen and experts), inciting the Israelis, the British, and the French to invade Egypt and seize territory along the Suez Canal. Opposition by the United States and the Soviet Union forced the invading countries to withdraw, providing Nasser with a spectacular diplomatic triumph. As Egyptian forces reclaimed the canal, Nasser's reputation as leader of the Arab world soared. He became the chief symbol of a pan-Arab nationalism that swept across the Middle East and North Africa and especially through the camps of Palestinian refugees.

The Algerian War of Independence The appeal of Arab nationalism was particularly strong in Algeria, where a population of 1 million European settlers (the *colons*) stood in the way of decolonization. Indeed, French leaders claimed that Algeria was an integral part of France. Although the *colons* were a minority in Algeria, they held the best land and generally lived in the major cities near the coast. They controlled Algeria's finances and all of its major public institutions.

Anticolonial nationalism in Algeria gathered force after World War II. The Front de Libération Nationale (FLN) emerged as the leading nationalist party in the 1950s, using violence to provoke its opponents and to make the local population choose between supporting the nationalist cause or the *colons*. The full-fledged revolt that erupted in 1954 pitted FLN troops and guerrillas against thousands of French troops. Atrocities and terrorist acts occurred on both sides.

The war dragged on for eight years, at a cost of perhaps 300,000 lives. On the French mainland, the war came as a terrible shock, for many, though not all, French citizens had accepted the idea that Algeria was not a colonial territory but part of France itself. The *colons* insisted that they had emigrated to Algeria in response to their government's promises and that yielding power to the nationalists would be a betrayal. After an insurrection led by *colons* and army officers brought down the French government in 1958, the new French president, Charles de Gaulle, negotiated a peace accord. Shortly after the handover of power to FLN leaders, 800,000 *colons* left Algeria. By late 1962, over nine-tenths of its European and indigenous Jewish population had departed.

Southern Africa The bloody conflict in Algeria highlights a harsh reality of African decolonization: the presence of European settlers often prevented the smooth transfer of power. South Africa, which held the continent's largest and wealthiest settler population (a mixture of Afrikaans- and English-speaking peoples of European descent), defied black majority rule longer than other African states. After winning the elections of 1948, the white Afrikaner–dominated National Party enacted an extreme form of racial segregation known as apartheid. Under apartheid, laws stripped Africans, Indians, and "colored" persons (those of mixed descent) of their few political rights. Racial mixing of any kind was forbidden, and schools were strictly segregated.

The ruling party tolerated no protest. Nelson Mandela, one of the leaders of the African National Congress (ANC), a group that campaigned for an end to discriminatory legislation, was repeatedly harassed, detained, and tried by the government, even though he had at first urged peaceful resistance. After the Sharpeville massacre in 1960, in which police killed demonstrators who were peacefully protesting the oppressive laws, Mandela and the ANC decided to oppose the apartheid regime with violence. A South African court sentenced Mandela to life imprisonment, and the government banned the ANC.

Women helped keep resistance flames burning. The most dynamic of these individuals was Winnie Mandela, wife of the imprisoned Nelson Mandela. Unlike many of the ANC leaders, who opposed the regime from exile, she remained in South Africa and openly and courageously spoke out against the apartheid government. Nonetheless, whites retained external support. Through the 1950s and 1960s, western powers (especially the United States) saw South Africa as a bulwark against the spread of communism in Africa.

Vietnam The same concern to contain communism also drew the United States into support for a conservative and pro-western regime in South Vietnam. Vietnam had come under French rule in the 1880s, and by the 1920s approximately 40,000 Europeans were living among and ruling over roughly 19 million Vietnamese. To promote an export economy of rice, mining, and rubber, the colonial rulers granted vast land concessions to French companies and local collaborators while leaving large numbers of peasants landless.

The colonial system also generated a new intelligentsia. Primarily schooled in French and Franco-Vietnamese schools, educated Vietnamese worked as clerks, shopkeepers, teachers, and petty officials. Yet they had few opportunities for advancement. Discontented, they turned from the traditional ideology of Confucianism to modern nationalism. Vietnamese intellectuals overseas, notably Ho Chi Minh, one of the original founders of the French Communist Party, took the lead in imagining a new Vietnamese nation-state.

When the French tried to restore their rule in Vietnam after Japan's defeat in 1945, Ho led the resistance. War with France followed (1946–1954). The Viet Minh (League for the Independence of Vietnam) used guerrilla tactics to undermine French positions. They were most successful in the north, but even in the south their campaign bled the French. Finally, in 1954, the anti-colonial forces won a decisive military victory. At a conference held in Geneva that year, Vietnam (like Korea) was divided into two zones. Ho controlled the north, while a government with French and American support took charge in the south.

During the early 1960s, U.S. involvement in Vietnam escalated as Ho's support for the Viet Cong (Vietnamese communist) guerrillas heightened American concerns about the spread of communism. In 1965, large numbers of American troops entered the country to fight on behalf of South Vietnam, while communist North Vietnam turned to the Soviet Union for supplies. Over the next several years, the United States sent some 500,000 soldiers to fight the Vietnam War, but peasant support enabled the Viet Cong to continue fierce guerrilla fighting. Even the bombing of villages and the deployment of counterinsurgency forces failed to prevent the spread of communism in Southeast Asia. In 1975, two years after the final withdrawal of American troops, the South Vietnamese government collapsed.

Thus, the process of decolonization varied across regions. Although most of the lands in Asia and Africa had gained independence by the mid-1960s, there were significant exceptions in Africa—South Africa, Southern Rhodesia, and the Portuguese colonies—and Asia—notably Vietnam. Although the British and French realized that they no longer had the resources to stem the nationalist tide that was spreading through the Third World, they tried to use military might to support areas of European settlement, above all in Algeria.

Three Worlds

World War II and postwar decolonization created a three-world order, in which the liberal democratic and capitalist First World and the communist Second World competed for global influence, notably among the newly decolonized Third World states. The war had made the Soviet Union and the United States into superpowers. Possessing nuclear weapons, superior armies, and industrial might, they vied for global influence. As decolonization spread, the two Cold War belligerents offered new leaders their models for modernization. The decolonized, however, had their own ideas. With the communist takeover in 1949, China had shrugged off semicolonial status, but Mao soon broke from Soviet direction. Other decolonized nations in Asia and Africa had underdeveloped economies and could not leap into either capitalist or communist industrial development. They drew some elements from communist and capitalist models, but politically tended to favor single-party states. Moreover, in some places colonial rule persisted, and civilians were not allowed even relative autonomy because the colonizers remained in place.

THE FIRST WORLD

As the Cold War spread in the early 1950s, western Europe and North America became known as the First World, or "the free world." Later on, Japan joined this group. First World states sought to organize the world on the basis of capitalism and democracy. Yet, in struggling against communism, the free world sometimes aligned with Third World dictators, thereby sacrificing its commitment to freedom and democracy for the sake of propping up pro-western regimes.

Western Europe The reconstruction of western Europe after World War II was a spectacular success. By the late 1950s, most nations' economies were thriving, thanks in part to massive American economic assistance. Improvements in agriculture were particularly impressive. As industrial production boomed and wages rose, goods that had been luxuries before the war—refrigerators, telephones, automobiles, indoor plumbing—became commonplace. Prosperity and the dismantling of national military establishments allowed governments to expand social welfare systems; by the late 1950s, education and health care were within the reach of virtually all citizens.

Western Europe's economic recovery blunted the appeal of socialism and communism. At the same time, the Cold War slowed down efforts to punish fascists, Nazis, and collaborators. Although war crimes trials brought the conviction of a number of prominent Nazis, the fear was that a complete purge of former Nazis would deprive Germany of political and economic leaders, leaving it susceptible to communist subversion.

The United States While Europe lay in ruins in 1945, the United States entered a period of economic expansion and a rising standard of living. Americans could afford more consumer goods than ever before—almost always U.S. manufactures. Home ownership became more common, especially in the burgeoning suburbs.

Yet anxieties about the future of the First World abounded. Following the Soviet Union's explosion of an atomic bomb, the communist revolution in China, and the outbreak of the Korean War, fear of the communist threat prompted increasingly harsh rhetoric. Anticommunist hysteria led a Republican senator from Wisconsin, Joseph McCarthy, to initiate a campaign to uncover closet communists in the State Department and in Hollywood in the 1950s. Televised congressional hearings broadcast his views to the entire

Civil Rights Movement The 1955 arrest of Rosa Parks, for refusing to give up her seat on a Montgomery, Alabama, bus to a white passenger, led to a boycott that brought Martin Luther King Jr. to prominence and galvanized the challenge to legal racial segregation in the American South.

nation, which pressured elected officials to support a strong anticommunist foreign policy and a large military budget.

Postwar American prosperity did not benefit all citizens equally. During the 1950s, nearly a quarter of the American population lived in poverty. But many African Americans, a group disproportionately trapped below the poverty line, participated in a powerful movement for equal rights and the end of racial segregation. The National Association for the Advancement of Colored People (NAACP) won court victories that mandated the desegregation of schools. Boycotts, too, became a weapon of the growing civil rights movement, as when Martin Luther King Jr. (1929–1968) led a successful strike against injustices in the bus system of Montgomery, Alabama. Here and in subsequent campaigns against white supremacy, King borrowed his most effective weapons—the commitment to nonviolent protest and the appeal to conscience—from Gandhi. As the civil rights movement spread, the federal government gradually supported programs promoting racial equality.

The Japanese "Miracle" Japan reemerged as an economic powerhouse in the postwar period. The war had ended with Japan's unconditional surrender in 1945, its dreams of dominating East Asia dashed and its homeland devastated. But after 1945, in an attempt to incorporate Japan into the First World, American military protection, investment, and transfers of technology helped to rebuild Japanese society. The Japanese government guided economic development through directed investment, partnerships with private firms, and protectionist trade policies. By the mid-1970s, Japan, formerly a dictatorship, became a politically stable civilian regime with a thriving economy, and the power of the emperor had been replaced with a parliamentary system.

THE SECOND WORLD

The Soviet Union, with its eastern and central European allies as well as Mongolia and North Korea, constituted the communist Second World. The scourge of World War II and the shadow of the Cold War fell heavily on the Soviets. Having suffered more deaths and more damage than any other industrialized nation, the Soviet Union was determined to insulate itself from future aggression from the west. That meant turning eastern Europe into a bloc of communist buffer states.

The Appeal of the Soviet Model The Soviet model's egalitarian ideology and success with rapid industrialization made it seem a worthy alternative to capitalism. Here, there was no private property and thus, in Marxist terms, no exploitation. Workers "owned" the factories and worked for themselves. The Soviet state promised full employment, boasting that a state-run economy would be immune from upturns and downturns in business cycles. Freedom from exploitation, combined with security, was contrasted with the capitalist model of owners hoarding profits and suddenly firing loyal workers when they were not needed.

The Soviet system touted protections for workers, inexpensive mass transit, paid maternity leave, free health care, and universally available education. Whereas under the Russian Empire less than one-third of the population had been literate, by the 1950s the literacy rate soared above 80 percent. True, Soviet policies did not provide material abundance of the sort that First World nations were enjoying. But if consumer goods were often scarce, they were always cheap. Likewise, while it sometimes took ten years to obtain a small apartment through waiting lists at work, when one's turn finally came the apartment carried low annual rent and could be passed on to one's children.

Few Soviet citizens knew how people lived in the capitalist world, so it was easy to believe in the advantages of the Soviet system. Government censors skewed news about the First World and suppressed unfavorable information about the Soviet Union and the communist bloc. Critics did not typically seek to overthrow the system and restore capitalism. Rather, they wanted the Soviet regime to introduce reforms that would create "socialism with a human face."

Repression of Dissent Few people outside the Soviet sphere knew just how inhuman Soviet communism was, and few within knew the extent of its brutality. Under Stalin, anyone suspected of opposing the regime risked imprisonment, forced labor, and often torture or execution. By the time of Stalin's death in 1953, its vast Gulag (labor camp complex) confined several million people, who dug for gold and uranium and survived on hunks of bread and gruel.

In 1956, the new party leader, Nikita Khrushchev, delivered a speech at a closed session of the Communist Party Congress in which he attempted to separate Stalin's crimes from true communism. The speech was never published in the Soviet Union, but party members distributed it to party organizations abroad. The crimes that Khrushchev revealed came as a terrible shock.

Soviet Ecocide

Before the twentieth century, the spread of peasant agriculture, as well as settlement in the steppe and forest zones and the hunting of fur-bearing forest animals, brought profound changes to the Russian environment, including soil degradation, deforestation, and depopulation of species. But the environmental impact of Soviet-era industrialization was staggering. No other industrial civilization poisoned its land, air, water, and people so systematically and over so long a time. Scholars have deemed the Soviet environmental catastrophe an "ecocide."

Soviet economic planners and propagandists celebrated the plumes of purple and orange smoke in their skies as evidence of the country's huge industrial production. Pollution-control devices remained unheard of well after their 1950s introduction in Europe and the United States; even when installed in Soviet factories, they were rarely turned on so as not to depress output. Sulfur dioxide, hydrogen sulfide, and solid phenols in the water, the food supply, and the air caused epidemic levels of respiratory and intestinal ailments, blood diseases, and birth defects. The giant steel plant at Magnitogorsk, once the pride of Stalin's industrial leap, became a zone of atmospheric and soil devastation 120 miles long and 40 miles wide; inside it, chronic bronchitis, asthma, and cancers attacked the population. In agriculture, the Soviet Union continued to use the insecticide DDT long after its 1972 banning in the United States.

In the 1970s, despite the socialist country's overall development, Soviet life expectancy began to decline and infant mortality to rise. By 1989, Soviet men lived an average of 63.9 years from birth, down from 66.1 in 1965. By the late 1980s, Infant mortality rose to 25.4 per 1,000, roughly the same as in Malaysia, a developing country, and Harlem. Alcoholism also contributed mightily to adverse health trends.

The April 1986 Chernobyl nuclear disaster exposed 20 million people in Ukraine and Belarus to excess radiation. Although there was no bomb concussion, the accident spewed more radioactive material into the atmosphere than had been released by the atomic bombs over Hiroshima and Nagasaki. The Chernobyl cleanup claimed around 7,000 lives.

Few symbols of Soviet ecocide surpass the Aral Sea—once a huge saline lake at the border between Kazakhstan and Uzbekistan. Because inflow into the lake was blocked by dams built for wasteful power plants and excess irrigation for cotton production, the lake shrank by two-thirds, giving way to huge white, lifeless salt flats. Soviet cosmonauts, looking down from space in 1975, were astonished to see immense storms of dust and salt over central Asia. Toxic salt rain wreaked enormous damage on human and animal lungs. Soviet Uzbekistan, with twice the population of Soviet Belarus, was served by only one-third the hospitals.

Lake Baikal, the world's largest body of fresh water, and once among the cleanest, suffered the construction from the 1950s of factories on its perimeter, especially a cellulose

Repercussions were far-reaching. Eastern European leaders interpreted Khrushchev's speech as an endorsement for political liberation and economic experimentation. Right away, Polish intellectuals began a drive to break free from the communist ideological straitjacket. Hungarian intellectuals and students held demonstrations demanding an uncensored press, free elections with genuine alternative parties, and the withdrawal of Soviet troops. But the seeming liberalization promised by Khrushchev's speech proved short-lived.

Rather than let eastern Europeans stray, the Soviet leadership crushed dissent. In Poland, the security police massacred strikers. In Hungary, tanks from the Soviet Union and other Warsaw Pact members invaded and cord plant (for tires on Soviet bombers) and pulp plant (for paper). The threat to Baikal, as well as the Aral Sea catastrophe, sparked grassroots environmental activism in an otherwise tightly controlled Soviet society. Scientists led the way in breaking censorship taboos, and people from all walks of life turned up at unsanctioned meetings and signed their names to petitions to stop the damage and protect the environment.

Aral Sea Catastrophe What was once one of the largest lakes in the world shrank to less than 10 percent of its original size due to the aggressive Soviet construction of irrigation canals in the sixties to bolster cotton production. Here, a shipping vessel is moored on the bed of the former Aral Sea, in present-day Kazakhstan.

Questions for Analysis

- Why do you think environmental degradation was so much more severe in the Soviet Union than in western countries?
- Why do you think environmental awareness developed much sooner in the United States than in the Soviet Union?

Explore Further

Feshbach, Murray and Friendly, Alfred Jr., *Ecocide in the USSR: Health and Nation under Siege* (1992).

Micklin, Philip, Aladin, N.V., and Plotnikov, Igor, eds., *The Aral Sea: The Devastation and Partial Rehabilitation of a Great Lake* (2014).

Wiener, Douglas R., *A Little Corner of Freedom: Russian Nature Protection from Stalin to Gorbachev* (2002).

installed a new government that aimed to smash all "counterrevolutionary" activities. The Second World remained very much the dominion of the Soviet Union.

Despite its repressive policies, the Soviet Union's status surged after the launching of Sputnik, the first satellite, into space in 1957. Students from Third World countries flocked to the Soviets' excellent educational system for training as engineers, scientists, army commanders, and revolutionaries. The updated 1961 Communist Party program predicted euphorically that within twenty years the Soviet Union would surpass the United States and eclipse the First World, but reckless industrialization left terrible scars both on the population and on the landscape.

THE THIRD WORLD

In the 1950s, the French demographer Alfred Sauvy coined the term **Third World** (*tiers monde*) to describe those countries that, like the "third estate" in the 1789 French Revolution, represented the majority of the world's population but were oppressed. By the early 1960s, the term characterized a large bloc of countries in Asia, Africa, and Latin America. All had experienced colonial domination and now aimed to create more just societies than those of the First and Second Worlds by finding a "third way" between capitalism and communism.

Limits to Autonomy Charting a third way proved difficult. Both the Soviets and the Americans saw the Third World as "underdeveloped." The western powers looked to two new instruments of global capitalism, the **World Bank** and the **International Monetary Fund (IMF)**, to help them develop their economies. Both institutions raised capital from all participating nations—but the most from the United States—and provided economic guidance in the Third World. The World Bank funded loans for projects intended to lift societies out of poverty (such as providing electricity in India and building roads in Indonesia), while the IMF supported the new governments' monetary systems when they experienced economic woes (as in Ghana, Nigeria, and Egypt). Yet both institutions also intruded on these states' autonomy.

Another force that threatened Third World economic autonomy was the multinational corporation. In the rush to acquire advanced technology, Africans, Asians, and Latin Americans struck deals with multinational corporations to import their know-how. Owned primarily by American, European, and Japanese entrepreneurs, firms such as United Fruit, Firestone, and Volkswagen expanded cash-cropping and plantation activities and established manufacturing branches worldwide. But such corporations impeded the growth of indigenous firms. Although the world's nations were more economically interdependent, the west still made the decisions—and reaped most of the profits.

Whether dealing with the west or with the Soviet Union, Third World leaders had limited options because they faced pressure to choose one Cold War side or the other. In hope of adding subservient client states to its bloc, the Soviet Union backed communist insurgencies around the globe, while the United States supported almost all leaders who declared their anticommunism. With the threat of nuclear war hanging over the two superpowers, they competed through proxy states that they armed to battle one another.

Nowhere was the militarization of Third World countries more threatening to economic development than in Africa. Whereas in the colonial era African states had spent little on military forces, this trend ended abruptly once the states became independent and were drawn into the Cold War. Civil wars, like the one that splintered Nigeria between 1967 and 1970, were opportunities for the superpowers to wield influence. When the west refused to sell weapons to the Nigerian government so it could suppress the breakaway eastern province of Biafra, the Soviets supplied MiG aircraft and other vital weapons, contributing to a destructive conflict and the ultimate triumph of the federal government of Nigeria.

Revolutionaries and Radicals As postcolonial states increasingly found themselves mired in debt and dependency, dissatisfaction grew. While some radicals seized power in the 1950s and 1960s, revolutionary transformation of society proved elusive.

Third World revolutionaries drew on the pioneering writings of Frantz Fanon (1925–1961). While serving as a psychiatrist in French Algeria, Fanon (who was born in a French Caribbean colony) became aware of the psychological damage of European racism. He subsequently joined the FLN and became a radical theorist of liberation. His 1961 book *The Wretched of the Earth* urged Third World peoples to achieve personal and national independence through violence against their European oppressors.

The Maoist Model While Fanon moved people with his writings, others did so by building political organizations and undertaking revolutionary social experiments. In 1958, Mao Zedong introduced the Great Leap Forward. Mao's program organized China into 24,000 social and economic units, called communes. Peasants took up industrial production in their own backyards. The campaign aimed to catapult China past the developed countries, but the communes failed to feed the people and the industrial goods were inferior. As many as 45 million people may have perished from famine and malnutrition, forcing the government to abandon the experiment in 1961.

The Cultural Revolution in China Young women were an important part of the Red Guards during the Cultural Revolution. Here, female Red Guards march in the front row of a parade in the capital city of Beijing under a sign that reads "Rise."

Fearing that China's revolution was losing spirit, Mao launched the Great Proletarian Cultural Revolution in 1966. This time Mao turned against his associates in the Communist Party and appealed to China's young people. They responded enthusiastically. Organized into "Red Guards," over 10 million of them journeyed to Beijing to participate in huge rallies, at which they pledged to cleanse the party of corrupt elements and remake Chinese society.

With help from the army, the Red Guards set out to rid society of the "four olds"—old customs, old habits, old culture, and old ideas. They ransacked homes, libraries, museums, and temples. They destroyed classical texts, artworks, and monuments. With its rhetoric of struggle against American imperialism and Soviet revisionism, the Cultural Revolution also targeted anything foreign. Knowledge of a foreign language was enough to compromise a person's revolutionary credentials. The Red Guards attacked government officials, party cadres, or just plain strangers in an escalating cycle of violence. Even family members and friends were pressured to denounce one another; all had to prove themselves faithful followers of Chairman Mao.

Given the costs of the Great Leap Forward and the Cultural Revolution, many of Mao's revolutionary policies were hard to celebrate. But radicals in much of the Third World were unaware of these costs and found the style of a rapid and massive—if deeply undemocratic—appeal to the masses attractive.

Latin American Revolution Most Third World radicals did not go as far as Mao, but they still dreamed of overturning the social order. In Latin America, such dreams excited those who wished to throw off the influence of U.S.-owned multinational corporations and local elites.

Reform programs in Latin America addressed numerous concerns. Economic nationalists urged greater protection for domestic industries and sought to curb the multinationals. Liberal reformers wanted to democratize political systems and redistribute land, lest discontent erupt into full-blown revolutions like China's. But when liberals and nationalists joined forces, as in Guatemala in the 1950s, their reforms met resistance from local conservatives and from the United States.

In Cuba, the failure of the government to address political, social, and economic concerns spurred a revolution. Since gaining its independence in the Spanish-American War of 1898, Cuba had been ruled by governments better known for their compliance with U.S. interests than with popular sentiment. In the 1930s, sugar planters, casino operators, and North American investors prospered, but middle- and working-class Cubans did not. In 1953, a group composed heavily of university students launched a botched assault on a military garrison. One of the leaders, a law student named **Fidel Castro** (1926–2016), gave a stirring speech at the rebels' trial, which made him a national hero. After his release from prison in 1955, he fled to Mexico. Several years later, he returned and started organizing guerrilla raids that brought him to power in 1959.

Castro then elbowed aside rivals and wrested control of the economy from the wealthy elite, who fled to exile. As his policies grew increasingly radical, American leaders began to plot his demise. It was over Cuba and its

Castro, Fidel (1926–2016)
Cuban communist leader who seized power in January 1959. Castro became increasingly radical as he consolidated power, announcing a massive redistribution of land and the nationalization of foreign oil refineries; he declared himself a socialist and aligned himself with the Soviet Union in the wake of the 1961 CIA-backed Bay of Pigs invasion.

radicalizing revolution that the world came closest to nuclear Armageddon in the Cuban Missile Crisis of 1962. To deter U.S. attacks, Castro appealed to the Soviet Union to install nuclear weapons in Cuba—a mere ninety miles off the coast of Florida. When U.S. intelligence detected the weapons, President John F. Kennedy ordered a blockade of Cuba, just as weapons-bearing Soviet ships were heading toward Havana. For several weeks, the world was paralyzed with anxiety as Kennedy, Khrushchev, and Castro matched threats. In the end, Kennedy succeeded in getting the Soviets to withdraw their nuclear missiles from Cuba.

By rejecting the power of capitalist industrial societies, Castro and his followers promoted revolution, not reform, as a way to achieve Third World liberation. The symbol of this new spirit was Castro's closest lieutenant, Ernesto "Che" Guevara (1928–1967). Shortly after receiving his medical degree in 1953, Guevara arrived in Guatemala in time to witness the CIA-backed overthrow of the progressive Jacobo Arbenz government. Thereafter, he became increasingly bitter about U.S. influences in Latin America. He joined Castro's forces and helped topple the pro-American regime in Cuba in 1958. After 1959, he held several posts in the Cuban government, but grew restive for more action. Latin America, he believed, should challenge the global power of the United States. Soon his casual military uniform, his patchy beard, his cigar, and his moral energy became legendary symbols of revolt.

To combat the germ of revolution, the Kennedy administration sent U.S. advisers throughout Latin America to dole out aid, explain how to reform local land systems, and demonstrate the benefits of liberal capitalism. Working with American advisers, Latin American militaries were trained to root out radicalism. Even Salvador Allende's democratically elected socialist government in Chile was not spared; the CIA and U.S. policymakers aided General Augusto Pinochet's military coup against the regime in 1973 and looked the other way while political opponents were butchered. By 1975, protesters had been liquidated in Argentina, Uruguay, Brazil, Mexico, Bolivia, and Venezuela.

Tensions within the Three Worlds

Each of the three "worlds" was beset by vulnerabilities and divisions. The United States experienced social unrest in this period on a scale not seen since the Great Depression, and other First World countries also experienced major protest movements. In the Second World, too, dissent challenged the Soviet Union's hold on world communism. In the Third World, the optimism generated at independence gave way quickly to discouragement and eventually despair. Finally, in the 1970s, the rising fortunes of oil-producing

Core Objectives

COMPARE the civil rights issues in the First, Second, and Third Worlds, and ASSESS the ways each "world" addressed these and other basic human rights.

Women Protest Sexism Insisting that "the personal is political," many women in the 1960s and 1970s argued that the problem of sexism went beyond equal rights and income equality: women's oppression began in the home, where they were treated merely as homemakers or as sex objects. At this 1971 rally in London, protesters suggested that women were being "crucified" by their association with these everyday objects: an apron, a net shopping bag, silk stockings, and an item of washing.

nations and of Japan introduced new problems in the relations within and among worlds.

TENSIONS WITHIN THE FIRST WORLD

Although the First World enjoyed great prosperity in the decades after World War II, lingering inequality created friction within these societies.

Women's Issues, Civil Rights, and Environmental Concerns In the First World, groups that believed that they had been left behind in the surge of economic growth expressed deep unhappiness. One issue was women's economic and political opportunities. Women in Italy, France, and Belgium did not obtain the right to vote until the end of World War II. Although women made gains in employment outside the home, they still awaited a decrease in domestic responsibilities.

A second source of concern, articulated most forcefully by students in Europe, was the deployment of nuclear weapons in their countries, as well as the rigid social and educational institutions that preserved power and high culture for the elite few. Protests reached their apex in Paris in 1968, when workers joined students in a general strike and clashed violently with police.

A rising crescendo of protests against racial discrimination in the United States propelled the U.S. federal government to enact civil rights legislation and to promote programs designed to end poverty. The Civil Rights Act of 1964 banned segregation in public facilities and outlawed racial discrimination in employment, and the Voting Rights Act of 1965 gave millions of previously disenfranchised African Americans an opportunity to exercise equal political rights. The Lyndon Baines Johnson administration also supported programs targeting social security, health, and education. Aided by impressive economic growth, these War on Poverty programs nearly halved the U.S. poverty rate.

But legacies of racism and inequality were not easy to overcome, and protest movements proliferated. In spite of Supreme Court decisions, most schools remained racially homogeneous not only in the South but across the United States, as "white flight" to the suburbs left inner-city neighborhoods and schools to minorities. Militant voices, like those of Malcolm X and the Black Panthers, became prominent. Instead of integration, these radicals advocated black separatism; instead of Americanism, they espoused embracing their African origins.

African American struggles inspired Native Americans, Mexican Americans, homosexuals, and women to initiate their own campaigns for equality and empowerment. Women now questioned a life built around taking care of home and family. In fact, the introduction of the birth control pill in 1960 and the publication of Betty Friedan's *The Feminine Mystique* in 1963 stand as watershed moments in American women's history. Because oral contraception allowed women to limit childbearing and to have sex with less fear of pregnancy, the resulting freedom helped unleash a sexual revolution. Moreover, Friedan blasted the myth of middle-class domestic contentment, describing the idealized 1950s suburban home as a "comfortable concentration camp" from which women must escape. Despite rising numbers of married women and college-educated women in the workforce, their compensation and opportunity for advancement lagged far behind those of men.

A year before Friedan authored her challenge to the subordination of women, Rachel Carson published *Silent Spring*, a book that was equally revolutionary in its attack against long-standing practices. In particular, Carson's book took on the use of synthetic pesticides such as dichlorodiphenyltrichloroethane (DDT), which she said caused cancer, devastated wildlife, and destroyed natural ecosystems. Although chemical manufacturers responded that pesticides had vastly multiplied agricultural yields, *Silent Spring* stirred opposition that ultimately led to the banning of DDT in the United States in 1972. More broadly, Carson's book spurred the development of an environmental movement that questioned many of the ideas about economic progress and material prosperity upon which the "American Dream" had rested.

The escalation of the Vietnam War prompted many white American college students to question the ideals of American society. As the United States increased troop levels there in the 1960s, it conscripted more and more men. After President Richard Nixon sent American troops into Cambodia in 1970 to root out North Vietnamese soldiers, students at over 500 campuses occupied buildings and closed down universities. At Kent State University in Ohio, National Guardsmen attempting to stop the protests killed four students. The United States withdrew from Vietnam in 1973, but not before the divisions created by the war had strained the country almost to the breaking point.

TENSIONS WITHIN WORLD COMMUNISM

The unity of the communist world also came under increasing pressure. As early as 1948, Yugoslavia had broken free of the Soviet yoke and embarked on its own road to building socialism. Other satellite states within the Soviet bloc had more trouble freeing themselves. In 1956, Poland and Hungary were forced back into line. Twelve years later, Czechoslovakia experienced the Prague Spring, in which communist authorities experimented with creating a democratic and pluralist socialist world. Workers and students rallied behind the reformist government of Alexander Dubček, calling for more freedom of expression, more autonomy for workers and consumers, and more debate within the ruling party. Once again, the Soviets crushed what they branded a "counterrevolutionary" movement. As their tanks rolled into Prague, the Czech capital, one desperate student doused himself with gasoline and lit a match—his public suicide a gesture of defiance against communist rule.

Thereafter, the Prague Spring served as a symbol for dissenters, who were divided between those who still wanted to reform socialism and those who wanted to overturn it. Underground reading groups proliferated throughout eastern Europe, and many Russians renewed their faith in Orthodox Christianity, their prerevolutionary religion. Many dissidents were exiled from the Soviet Union. Most famous by the early 1970s was the Russian novelist Alexander Solzhenitsyn. His masterwork, *The Gulag Archipelago*, rejected the notion that socialism could be reformed simply by a turn away from Stalin's policies. Yet very few people in the Soviet Union could obtain copies of Solzhenitsyn's exposé, which had been published abroad and was a best-seller in the west. In 1974, the author himself was expelled from the USSR.

Hungarian Revolt Khrushchev's secret 1956 speech denouncing Stalin's crimes unintentionally destabilized the communist bloc. Tanks of the Soviet-led Warsaw Pact forces crossed into Hungary to put down a revolt that year, restoring the Soviet-style system but damaging Soviet prestige. Some American officials and especially American-supported radio had encouraged the Hungarians to rise up but then did nothing to support them, damaging U.S. prestige. The upshot was a turn to "national communism" in the Soviet satellites as a way to promote stability and loyalty.

Still, there were important changes within the Second World. During the 1950s and 1960s, "national communism" became the rule throughout eastern Europe, even in countries that experienced Soviet invasions. National variations also arose within the Soviet Union, where Moscow conceded some autonomy to the Communist Party machines of its fifteen republics—in exchange for their fundamental loyalty. Dissidents were still persecuted, but by the 1970s, many fewer were murdered outright, and the population of the gulags declined.

Widespread dislike of the United States created a Sino-Soviet alliance in the years just after the Chinese Revolution of 1949. By the late 1950s, the Soviet Union had contributed massive military and economic aid to China. But the Chinese increasingly sought to define their own brand of Marxism and criticized Khrushchev's efforts to reduce tensions with the United States and the west. The divide raised China's profile throughout Asia and even in eastern Europe. Indeed, Romania achieved a measure of autonomy in foreign policy by playing off China and the Soviet Union. Albania declared its allegiance to China. African nations seeking Soviet aid increased their demands with subtle hints that they might consider deepening ties with China instead. Clearly, the Second World was no monolith.

TENSIONS WITHIN THE THIRD WORLD

In contrast to the First and Second Worlds, the Third World was never unified by economic, military, or political alliances. The Cold War pushed Third World states to choose between alignment with the First World or the Second. Nonetheless, radicalism nourished new hopes for unifying and empowering the Third World.

One effort at collaboration was the formation in 1960 of an alliance of oil exporters. The Organization of the Petroleum Exporting Countries (OPEC)—which included Algeria, Ecuador, Gabon, Indonesia, Iran, Iraq, Kuwait, Libya, Nigeria, Qatar, Saudi Arabia, the United Arab Emirates, and Venezuela—had little success in raising oil revenues through the 1960s, even though several members nationalized their oil fields. But after the fourth major Arab-Israeli war broke out in 1973, OPEC's Arab members decided to pressure Israel's First World allies by halting oil exports to them. Overnight, the embargo lifted oil prices more than threefold, a bonanza that enriched all oil producers and led to an oil crisis in the west. To many, the bulging treasuries of OPEC nations seemed like the Third World's revenge. Here were Saudi Arabian princes, Venezuelan magnates, and Indonesian ministers dictating world prices to industrial consumers.

But the realignment was not thorough. Third World producers of raw materials such as coffee and rubber tried unsuccessfully to duplicate OPEC's model, and OPEC itself had trouble controlling the world's oil market.

During the 1970s, oil discoveries in the North Sea, Mexico, and Canada reduced pressures on the large oil-consuming states to be more fuel efficient. With supply up, prices fell. To compensate for lost revenue, various OPEC states raised their own production, putting further downward pressure on prices.

Nor did oil revenues help overcome poverty and dependency in the Third World as a whole. To the contrary, most revenue surpluses from OPEC simply flowed back to First World banks or were invested in real-estate holdings in Europe and the United States. Some of these funds, in turn, were reloaned to the world's poorest countries in Africa, Asia, and Latin America, at high interest rates, to pay for more expensive imports—including oil! The biggest bonanza went to multinational petroleum firms, whose control over production, refining, and distribution yielded enormous profits.

For all the talk in the mid-1970s of changing the balance of international economic relations between the world's rich and poor countries, fundamental inequalities persisted. Those few Third World nations that appeared to break out of the cycle of poverty, like South Korea and Taiwan, did not achieve success through free trade and private-sector development. Rather, these nations regulated domestic markets, nurtured new industries, educated the populace, and required multinationals to work with local firms.

Conclusion

The three-world order arose on the ruins of European empires and their Japanese counterpart. First, the Soviet Union and the United States became superpowers. Second, World War II affirmed the nation-state rather than the empire as the primary form for organizing communities. Third, in spite of the rhetoric of individualism and the free market, the war and postwar reconstruction enhanced the reach and functions of the modern state. In the Third World, too, leaders of new nations saw the state as the primary instrument for promoting economic development.

The organization of the world into three blocs lasted into the mid-1970s. This arrangement fostered the economic recovery of western Europe and Japan from the wounds inflicted by war. These nations' recovery grew out of a Cold War alliance with the United States, where anticommunist hysteria accompanied an economic boom. The Cold War also cast a shadow over the citizens of the Soviet Union and eastern Europe. Gulags and political surveillance became widespread, while the Soviets and their satellite regimes mobilized resources for military purposes. The Third World, squeezed by its inability to reduce poverty on the one hand and by superpower rivalry on the other, struggled to pursue a "third way." While some states maintained democratic institutions and promoted economic development, many tumbled into dictatorships and authoritarian regimes, marked by high levels of corruption. In addition, they often suffered irreparable environmental damage.

In this context, Third World revolutionaries sought radical social and political transformation, seeking paths different from both western capitalism and Soviet communism. Though not successful, they energized considerable tensions in the three-world order. These tensions intensified in the late 1960s and early 1970s as Vietnamese communists defeated the United States, an oil crisis struck the west, and protests escalated in the First and Second Worlds. Thirty years after the end of World War II, the world order forged after 1945 was beginning to give way.

Focus On
World War II and a New Global Order

World War II

- World War II grows out of unresolved problems connected to World War I, especially the aggressive plans of Germany and Japan to expand their political and economic influence.

- The war brings huge human and material costs and ushers in an age of nuclear weapons.

- At war's end, the United States, fearing the spread of communism and Soviet influence, rebuilds war-torn Europe and Japan and creates military and political alliances to contain Soviet expansionist ambitions.

A New Global Order

- The Soviet Union and the United States become superpowers.

- Japan emerges as an economic powerhouse and a U.S. ally.

- A weakened Europe cannot resist demands for independence from Asian and African nationalists.

- Chinese communists engineer a revolution, while Indian nationalists and many African leaders achieve independence through negotiations.

- Elsewhere, especially in territories with large settler populations, decolonization is violent (Palestine, Algeria) or incomplete (southern Africa).

- Actions by Latin American reformers and revolutionaries spark counterinsurgency efforts by the United States and its regional allies.

- An insecure three-world order emerges after most Asian and African states achieve independence.

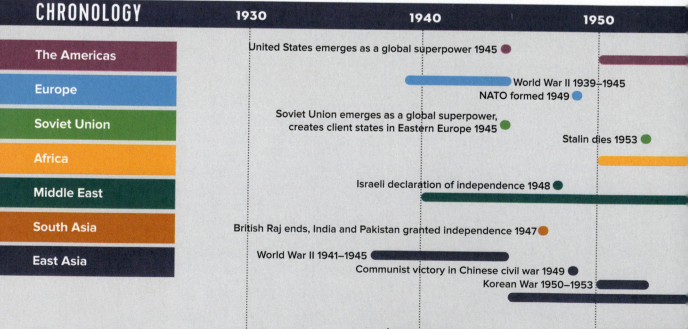

CHRONOLOGY

1930   1940   1950

The Americas
United States emerges as a global superpower 1945

Europe
World War II 1939–1945
NATO formed 1949

Soviet Union
Soviet Union emerges as a global superpower, creates client states in Eastern Europe 1945
Stalin dies 1953

Africa

Middle East
Israeli declaration of independence 1948

South Asia
British Raj ends, India and Pakistan granted independence 1947

East Asia
World War II 1941–1945
Communist victory in Chinese civil war 1949
Korean War 1950–1953
Japanese economic "miracle" 1950s–1970s

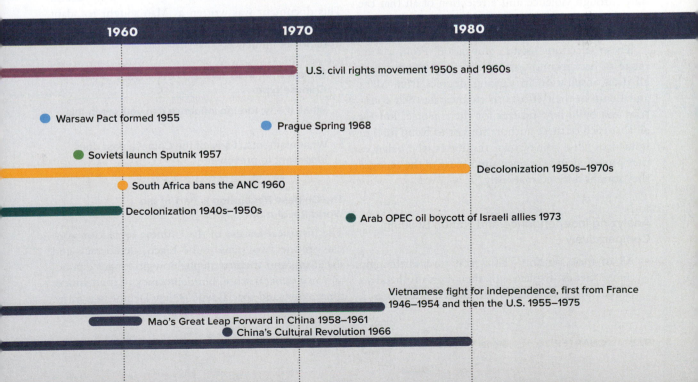

THINKING ABOUT GLOBAL CONNECTIONS

- **Thinking about Worlds Together, Worlds Apart and the Three-World Order** Explain how the collapse of a Europe-centered world changed how states interacted with one another. In what ways did the division of the globe into three rival worlds differ from the dominance of the European "great powers" that preceded it? Which world order do you think was more stable, the Europe-centered world or the three-world order that followed it? Do you think one system was more equitable than the other?

- **Thinking about Changing Power Relationships and the Three-World Order** Analyze Third World revolutionaries' ability to alter the dynamic of the Cold War. Where do you think power was located in this period?

To what degree did Washington and Moscow determine the course of world affairs, and to what degree were politicians in places like Cuba, Vietnam, and Algeria able to play the superpowers off against one another? How and to what degree were revolutionaries able to make claims on the First and Second Worlds in terms of economic, political, or military assistance?

- **Thinking about Environmental Impacts and the Three-World Order** In this period, for the first time, organized groups set out to defend the environment. What sparked their protests? Where were those organizations most fully developed? Where was ecological devastation most extreme? What force or forces opposed environmentalists?

Key Terms

Fidel Castro p. 962	Holocaust p. 938
Cold War p. 934	International Monetary Fund (IMF) p. 960
decolonization p. 946	

Mao Zedong p. 947	Third World p. 960
North Atlantic Treaty Organization (NATO) p. 943	Warsaw Pact p. 943
	World Bank p. 960

Go to **INQUIZITIVE** to see what you've learned—and learn what you've missed—with personalized feedback along the way.

1960 **1970** **1980**

U.S. civil rights movement 1950s and 1960s

Warsaw Pact formed 1955

Prague Spring 1968

Soviets launch Sputnik 1957

Decolonization 1950s–1970s

South Africa bans the ANC 1960

Decolonization 1940s–1950s

Arab OPEC oil boycott of Israeli allies 1973

Vietnamese fight for independence, first from France 1946–1954 and then the U.S. 1955–1975

Mao's Great Leap Forward in China 1958–1961

China's Cultural Revolution 1966

Global Themes and Sources

Comparing Independence and Nation Building

Intellectuals and political activists in the Third World sought to expel foreign colonizers and build new societies. As their nations struck out on their own, the overwhelming majority of these thinkers and leaders wanted to borrow at least some elements from their own established traditions, on the one hand, and from foreign influences, on the other.

In his "New Democracy" (1940), Mao Zedong set forth a new democratic culture—nationalistic, scientific, and mass-based—that he regarded as a transitional stage to the communist utopia of the future. Jawaharlal Nehru also celebrated science and technology in his "Note to the Members of the National Planning Committee" (1940), which sought a "third way" between capitalism and communism. In his speech on Negritude, Léopold Sédar Senghor presented a black culture different from, but not inferior to, European cultural forms. Frantz Fanon, inspired by Mao as well as Marx and Lenin, celebrated the power of violence to restore the self-respect of the colonized; only through violence and a rejection of all that the colonizers stood for, he thought, could the colonized ever truly free themselves.

These selections invite comparison. From a wide range of backgrounds, the authors represented here all drew inspiration in varying degrees from Marx and Lenin in their efforts to emancipate their countries and build new futures for their people. But for all that each of these authors sought to blend foreign influences with homegrown traditions, the balances they proposed and the pace and nature of the changes they sought differed markedly.

Analyzing Independence and Nation Building Comparatively

- All of these authors came from overwhelmingly rural societies. Explain why they drew on the ideas of Karl Marx, who famously likened peasants to a "sack of potatoes" and thought modern industry essential to end oppression of all kinds.

- Identify the balance between indigenous tradition and foreign influence in each selection. Which text draws most heavily on foreign sources and which rejects outside influences most completely?

- Analyze the relationship between the individual and the community described in each of these readings.

- Which of the readings do you consider most revolutionary and why? Do you think the idea of revolution was important to the authors?

PRIMARY SOURCE 20.1

"New Democracy" (1940), Mao Zedong

As chairman of China's Communist Party, Mao Zedong (1893–1976) ruled the People's Republic of China from its founding in 1949 until his death. This document was written as Mao sought to adapt communism to Chinese traditions and distance himself from Soviet influence.

- Explain what Mao means by democracy of the Chinese type.

- What, if any, foreign influence can you see in this text?

- What elements, if any, of the Chinese past does Mao want to preserve?

The Chinese Revolution Is Part of the World Revolution

The historical feature of the Chinese revolution consists in the two steps to be taken, democracy and socialism, and the first step is now no longer democracy in a general sense, but democracy of the Chinese type, a new and special type—New Democracy. How, then, is this historical feature formed? Has it been in existence for the past hundred years, or is it only of recent birth?

If we make only a brief study of the historical development of China and of the world, we shall understand that this historical feature did not emerge as a consequence of the Opium War but began to take shape only after the first imperialist world war and the Russian October Revolution.

After these events, the Chinese bourgeois-democratic revolution changes its character and belongs to the category of the new bourgeois-democratic revolution and, so far as the revolutionary front is concerned, forms part of the proletarian-socialist world revolution.

This "world revolution" refers no longer to the old world revolution—for the old bourgeois world revolution has long become a thing of the past—but to a new world revolution, the socialist world revolution. Similarly, to form "part" of the world revolution means to form no longer a part of the old bourgeois revolution but of the new socialist revolution. This is an exceedingly great change unparalleled in the history of China and of the world.

This correct thesis propounded by the Chinese Communists is based on Stalin's theory.

As early as 1918, Stalin wrote in an article commemorating the first anniversary of the October Revolution:

The great worldwide significance of the October Revolution chiefly consists in the fact that:

1. It has widened the scope of the national question and converted it from the particular question of combating national oppression in Europe into the general question of emancipating the oppressed peoples, colonies, and semi-colonies from imperialism.

2. It has opened up wide possibilities for their emancipation and the right path toward it, has thereby greatly facilitated the cause of the emancipation of the oppressed peoples of the West and the East, and has drawn them into the common current of the victorious struggle against imperialism.

3. It has thereby erected a bridge between the socialist West and the enslaved East, having created a new front of revolutions against world imperialism, extending from the proletarians of the West, through the Russian revolution to the oppressed peoples of the East.

Since writing this article, Stalin has again and again expounded the theoretical proposition that revolutions in colonies and semi-colonies have already departed from the old category and become part of the proletarian-socialist revolution.

The first step in, or the stage of, this revolution is certainly not, and cannot be, the establishment of a capitalist society under the dictatorship of the Chinese bourgeoisie; on the contrary, the first stage is to end with the establishment of a new-democratic society under the joint dictatorship of all Chinese revolutionary classes headed by the Chinese proletariat. Then the revolution will develop into the second stage so that a socialist society can be established in China.

New-Democratic Politics

As to the question of "political structure" [in the New Democracy], it is the question of the form of structure of political power, the form adopted by certain social classes in establishing their organs of political power to oppose their enemy and protect themselves. Without an adequate form of political power there would be nothing to represent the state. . . . But a system of really universal and equal suffrage, irrespective of sex, creed, property, or education, must be put into practice so that the organs of government elected can properly represent each revolutionary class according to its status in the state, express the people's will and direct revolutionary struggles, and embody the spirit of New Democracy. Such a system is democratic centralism. Only a government of democratic centralism can fully express the will of all the revolutionary people and most powerfully fight the enemies of the revolution.

The state system—joint dictatorship of all revolutionary classes. The political structure—democratic centralism. This is new-democratic government; this is a republic of New Democracy, the republic of the anti-Japanese united front, the republic of the new

Three People's Principles with the three cardinal policies, and the Republic of China true to its name.

New-Democratic Economy

We must establish in China a republic that is politically new-democratic as well as economically new-democratic.

Big banks and big industrial and commercial enterprises shall be owned by this republic.

Enterprises, whether Chinese-owned or foreign-owned, that are monopolistic in character or that are on too large a scale for private management, such as banks, railways, and airlines, shall be operated by the state so that private capital cannot dominate the livelihood of the people. This is the main principle of the control of capital.

This was also a solemn statement contained in the Manifesto of the First National Congress of the Nationalists during the period of the Nationalist-Communist cooperation; this is the correct objective for the economic structure of the new-democratic republic under the leadership of the proletariat. The state-operated industries are socialist in character and constitute the leading force in the national economy as a whole; but this republic does not take over other forms of capitalist private property or forbid the development of capitalist production that "cannot dominate the livelihood of the people," for China's economy is still very backward.

This republic will adopt certain necessary measures to confiscate the land of landlords and distribute it to those peasants having no land or only a little land, carry out Dr. Sun Yat-sen's slogan of "land to the tillers," abolish the feudal relations in the rural areas, and turn the land into the private property of the peasants. In the rural areas, rich peasant economic activities will be tolerated. This is the line of "equalization of land ownership." The correct slogan for this line is "land to the tillers." In this stage, socialist agriculture is in general not yet to be established, though the various types of cooperative enterprises developed on the basis of "land to the tillers" will contain elements of socialism.

New-Democratic Culture

A given culture is the ideological reflection of the politics and economy of a given society. There is in China an imperialist culture, which is a reflection of the control of imperialism over China politically and economically. This part of culture is advocated not only by the cultural organizations run directly by the imperialists in China but also by a number of shameless Chinese. All culture that contains a slave ideology belongs to this category. There is also in China a semi-feudal culture, which is a reflection of semi-feudal politics and economy and has as its representatives all those who, while opposing the new culture and new ideologies, advocate the worship of Confucius, the study of the Confucian canon, the old ethical code, and the old ideologies. Imperialist culture and semi-feudal culture are affectionate brothers, who have formed a reactionary cultural alliance to oppose China's new culture. This reactionary culture serves the imperialists and the feudal class and must be swept away.

Some Errors on the Question of the Nature of Culture

So far as national culture is concerned, the guiding role is fulfilled by Communist ideology, and efforts should be made to disseminate socialism and communism among the working class and to educate, properly and methodically, the peasantry and other sections of the masses in socialism.

A National, Scientific, and Mass Culture

New-democratic culture is national. It opposes imperialist oppression and upholds the dignity and independence of the Chinese nation. . . . China should absorb on a large scale the progressive cultures of foreign countries as an ingredient for her own culture; in the past we did not do enough work of this kind. We must absorb whatever we today find useful, not only from the present socialist or new-democratic cultures of other nations, but also from the older cultures of foreign countries, such as those of the various capitalist countries in the age of enlightenment. However, we must treat these foreign materials as we do our food, which should be chewed in the mouth, submitted to the working of the stomach and intestines, mixed with saliva, gastric juice, and intestinal secretions, and then separated into essence to be absorbed and waste matter to be discarded—only thus can food benefit our body; we should never swallow anything raw or absorb it uncritically. So-called wholesale Westernization is a mistaken viewpoint. China has suffered a great deal in the past from the formalist absorption of foreign things. Likewise, in applying Marxism to China, Chinese Communists must fully and properly unite the universal truth of Marxism with the specific practice of the Chinese revolution; that is to say, the truth of Marxism must be integrated with the characteristics of the nation and given a definite national form before it can be useful; it must not be applied subjectively as a mere formula. . . .

Communists may form an anti-imperialist and anti-feudal united front for political action with certain idealists and even with religious followers, but we can never approve of their idealism or religious doctrines. A splendid ancient culture was created during the long period of China's feudal society. To clarify the process of development of this ancient culture, to throw away its feudal dross, and to absorb its democratic essence is a necessary condition for the development of our new national culture and for the increase of our national self-confidence; but we should never absorb anything and everything uncritically.

The Twofold Task of the Chinese Revolution and the Chinese Communist Party

To complete China's bourgeois-democratic revolution (the new-democratic revolution) and to prepare to transform it into a socialist revolution when all the necessary conditions are present—that is the sum total of the great and glorious revolutionary task of the Communist Party of China. All members of the party should strive for its accomplishment and should never give up halfway. Some immature Communists think that we have only the task of the democratic revolution at the present stage but not that of the socialist revolution at the future stage; or that the present revolution or the agrarian revolution is in fact the socialist revolution. It must be emphatically pointed out that both views are erroneous. Every Communist must know that the whole Chinese revolutionary movement led by the Chinese Communist Party is a complete revolutionary movement embracing the two revolutionary stages, democratic and socialist, which are two revolutionary processes differing in character, and that the socialist stage can be reached only after the democratic stage is completed. The democratic revolution is the necessary preparation for the socialist revolution, and the socialist revolution is the inevitable trend of the democratic revolution. And the ultimate aim of all Communists is to strive for the final building of socialist society and communist society.

Source: Mao Zedong, *Selected Works*, in *Sources of Chinese Tradition*, 2nd ed., vol. 2, edited by Wm. Theodore de Bary and Richard Lufrano (New York: Columbia University Press, 2000), pp. 418–23.

PRIMARY SOURCE 20.2

"A Note to the Members of the National Planning Committee" (1940), Jawaharlal Nehru

Jawaharlal Nehru (1889–1964) was the first prime minister of India and a leading figure in Indian politics before and after independence. Here he combines a universalist, technocratic faith in planning with local traditions.

- Evaluate the balance of foreign influence and Indian tradition in this document.

- What does Nehru think planning can achieve? What risks does he want to avoid?

- What is Nehru's view of entrepreneurship and free markets?

Planning for the Future

To some it may appear that this is a most unsuitable time for planning, which is essentially a labour of peaceful co-operation. It may be argued that we should wait for better times and more stable conditions, for who knows what the outcome of the present conflict will be? On what foundation shall we build, when no man can foretell what that foundation will be? And yet though we are so uncertain of the future, this we know well that the future will be very different from the past or even from this changing present. Already we see vast political and economic changes taking shape in the womb of the future. Can we plan in India with all this doubt and uncertainty?

These considerations fill our minds, as they should, and we must give careful thought to them. And yet these very considerations lead us to a contrary conclusion. For it is this very time of change and uncertainty that demands mental activity and a vision of the future that we desire. If we are mere onlookers now, and passive and helpless agents of circumstances or the will of others, we barter away our claim to that future. Instead of preparing for it, we hand the reins to others. Every conflict ends sometime or other, every war is followed by a peace, temporary or more enduring, every work of destruction has to be followed by construction. That construction will be chaotic and wasteful unless previous thought has been given to it. A period of war and dynamic change therefore demands, even more than the static times of peace, the planned activity of the mind, so that, when time and opportunity come, this may be translated with all speed into the planned activity of the nation.

For, thinking and planning for the future is essential if that future is not to end in misdirected energy and chaos. It is foolish to imagine that when the present crisis at long last ends, a new or better arrangement of world affairs or our national affairs will automatically emerge out of it. It is equally unwise to allow matters to drift, protesting occasionally perhaps, but otherwise looking on helplessly, for fear that what we may do might involve a risk or be taken unfair advantage of by our opponents. The world is full of risks and dangers today. We cannot escape them. The greatest risk and danger is to drift and not give thought and energy to finding a way out. It is manifest that the old order has had its day and is dissolving, whether we like this or not. It has led to wars and upheavals and continuing conflicts which involve not only passion and hatred and an enormous waste of energy and resources, but also prevent us from achieving what is otherwise easily attainable. We have to understand the conflicts of forces that dominate the world today and seek to resolve these conflicts. It is certainly a possibility that the world may inevitably be led to social dissolution. We have to avoid that, if we can, but we cannot do so by shutting our eyes to the fact that the existing order is incapable of preventing this catastrophe. Something else, more in keeping with modern conditions, has to be evolved. Politics, in our country as elsewhere, dominates the scene and occupies men's minds. But the real changes that are shaping the world are deeper than politics. If we plan, we must consider them and have clear minds about them.

We shall thus have to consider, at this stage or later, the basic and fundamental policies that must govern our planning. Without a definite and clear-cut objective in view, and an understanding of the path we must pursue, we shall plan ineffectively or perhaps even in vain.

Already the NPC has given some thought to this matter and we have come to some general but fundamental decisions. It is well to recapitulate some of them. We are aiming at a free and democratic state, which has full political and economic freedom. In this state the fundamental rights of the individual and the group—political, economic, social and cultural—will be guaranteed, and the corresponding duties and obligations laid down. The state will be progressive and will utilize all scientific and other knowledge for the advancement of the people as a whole, and for the promotion of their happiness and material as well as cultural and spiritual well-being. The state will not permit the exploitation of the community by individuals or groups to the disadvantage of the former and to the injury of the nation as a whole. To realize the social objectives, the state has to plan through its representatives for the nation (whenever possible, in co-operation with other nations) and to co-ordinate the various activities of the nation so as to avoid waste and conflict and attain the maximum results. This planning will deal with production, distribution, consumption, investment, trade, income, social services, and the many other forms of national activity which act and react on each other. Briefly put, planning aims at the raising of the material and cultural standard of living of the people as a whole. In India our standards are so terribly low and poverty is so appalling that this question of raising standards is of the most vital importance. The NPC has suggested that national wealth should be increased between two and three times within the next ten years, and this should be so planned as to raise the general standard at least in a like measure.

Source: Jawaharlal Nehru, "A Note to the Members of the National Planning Committee," May 1, 1940, in *Jawaharlal Nehru: An Anthology*, edited by Sarvepalli Gopal (Delhi: Oxford University Press, 1980), pp. 304–6.

On Negritude (1959), Léopold Sédar Senghor

Léopold Sédar Senghor (1906–2001) was a Senegalese poet and politician. A leading figure in the Negritude movement, Senghor served as the first president of Senegal (1960–1980). This selection, drawn from a lecture at Oxford University and reprinted many times, presents a concise overview of the movement, which was established initially in poetry.

....

- Define Negritude.

- Explain the relationship between reason and emotion in this text.

- What does Senghor mean when he says that Negritude does not oppose European values but complements them?

....

PARADOXICALLY, it was the French who first forced us to seek its essence, and who then showed us where it lay. . . . when they enforced their policy of assimilation *and thus deepened our despair . . . Early on, we had become aware within ourselves that assimilation was a failure; we could assimilate mathematics or the French language, but we could never strip off our black skins nor root out our black souls. And so we set out on a fervent quest for the Holy Grail: our Collective Soul. And we came upon it.*

It was not revealed to us by the "official France" of the politicians who, out of self interest and political conviction defended the policy of assimilation. Its whereabouts was pointed out to us by that handful of freelance thinkers—writers, artists, ethnologists, and prehistorians—who bring about cultural revolutions in France. It was, to be quite precise, our teachers of Ethnology who introduced us to the considerable body of work already achieved in the understanding of Africa, by the University of Oxford.

What did we learn from all those writers, artists and teachers? That the early years of colonisation and especially, even before colonisation, the *slave trade* had ravaged black Africa like a bush fire, wiping out images and values in one vast carnage. That Negroid civilisation had flourished in the Upper Paleolithic

Age, and that the Neolithic Revolution could not be explained without them. That their roots retained their vigour, and would one day produce new grass and green branches . . .

Negritude is *the whole complex of civilised values— cultural, economic, social and political—which characterise the black peoples*, or, more precisely, the Negro-African world.

All these values are essentially informed by intuitive reason. Because this sentient reason, the reason which comes to grips, expresses itself emotionally, through that self-surrender, that coalescence of subject and object; through myths, by which I mean the archetypal images of the collective Soul, above all through primordial rhythms, synchronised with those of the Cosmos.

In other words, the sense of communion, the gift of myth-making, the gift of rhythm, such are the essential elements of Negritude, which you will find indelibly stamped on all the works and activities of the black man. . . .

In opposition to European racialism, of which the Nazis were the symbol, we set up an "anti-racial racialism". The very excesses of Naziism, and the catastrophes it engendered, were soon to bring us to our senses. Such hatred, such violence, above all, such weeping and such shedding of blood produced a feeling of revulsion—it was so foreign to our continent's genius: our *need to love.*

And then the anthropologists taught us that there is no such thing as a pure race: scientifically speaking, races do not exist. They went one better and forecast that, with a mere two hundred million people, we would in the end disappear as a "black race", through miscegenation.

At the same time they did offer us some consolation. "The focal points of human development", wrote Teilhard de Chardin, in 1939, "always seem to coincide with the points of contact and anastomosis of several nerve paths", that is, in the ordinary man's language, of several races.

If then we were justified in fostering the values of Negritude, and arousing the energy slumbering within us, it must be in order to pour them into the mainstream of cultural miscegenation (the biological process taking place spontaneously). They must flow towards the meeting point of all Humanity; they must be our contribution to the Civilisation of the Universal.

Biological miscegenation, then, takes place spontaneously, provoked by the very laws which govern Life, and in the face of all policies of Apartheid. It is a different matter in the realm of culture. Here, we remain wholly free to cooperate or not, to provoke or prevent the synthesis of cultures. This is an important point. For, as certain biologists point out, the psychological mutations brought about by education are incorporated in our genes, and are then transmitted by heredity. Hence the major role played by *Culture*.

Seen within this prospect of the Civilisation of the Universal, the colonial policies of Great Britain and France have proved successful complements to each other, and black Africa has benefited.

The policies of the former tended to reinforce the traditional native civilisation. As for France's policy, although we have often reviled it in the past, it too ended with a credit balance, through forcing us actively to assimilate European civilisation. This fertilised our sense of Negritude.

Today, our Negritude no longer expresses itself as opposition to European values, but as a *complement* to them. Henceforth, its militants will be concerned, as I have often said, *not to be assimilated, but to assimilate*. They will use European values to arouse the slumbering values of Negritude, which they will bring as their contribution to the Civilisation of the Universal.

Nevertheless, we still disagree with Europe: not with its values any longer (with the exception of Capitalism) but with its theory of the Civilisation of the Universal. . . .

In the eyes of the Europeans, the "exotic civilisations" are static in character, being content to live by means of archetypal images, which they repeat indefinitely. The most serious criticism is that they have no idea of the *pre-eminent dignity of the human person*.

My reply is this. Just as much as black Africa, taking this as an example, Europe and its North American offspring live by means of archetypal images. For what are Free Enterprise, Democracy, Communism, but *myths*, around which hundreds of millions of men and women organise their lives?

Negritude itself is a myth (I am not using the word in any pejorative sense), but a living, dynamic one, which evolves with its circumstances into a form of humanism.

Actually, our criticism of the [European] thesis is that it is monstrously anti-humanist. For if European civilisation were to be imposed, unmodified, on all Peoples and Continents, it could only be by force. That is its first disadvantage. A more serious one is that it would not be *humanistic*, for it would cut itself off from the complementary values of the greater part of humanity. As I have said elsewhere, it would be a universal civilisation; it would not be the Civilisation of the Universal.

Whereas our revised Negritude is humanistic. I repeat, it welcomes the complementary values of Europe and the white man, and indeed, of all other races and continents.

But it welcomes them in order to fertilise and re-invigorate its own values, which it then offers for the construction of a civilisation which shall embrace all Mankind.

The *Neo-Humanism* of the twentieth century stands at the point where the paths of all Nations, Races and Continents cross, where the Four Winds of the Spirit blow.

Source: Léopold Sédar Senghor, "What is Negritude?" *Negro Digest* (April 1962), 3–6.

PRIMARY SOURCE 20.4

On Decolonization (1961), Frantz Fanon

Frantz Fanon (1925–1961) was a psychiatrist and writer from the Caribbean island of Martinique. Fanon joined the Algerian Front de Libération Nationale and treated torture victims during the Algerian War of Independence (1954–1962). This selection, written at the very end of his life, drew on his wartime experience.

- Analyze the role of religion in this passage.
- Is this text Eurocentric?
- What role do traditional Muslim religious leaders ("the caids and the customary chiefs") play in this text?

In decolonization, there is therefore the need of a complete calling in question of the colonial situation. If we wish to describe it precisely, we might find it in the well-known words: "The last shall be first and the first last." Decolonization is the putting into practice of this sentence. That is why, if we try to describe it, all decolonization is successful.

The naked truth of decolonization evokes for us the searing bullets and bloodstained knives which emanate from it. For if the last shall be first, this will only come to pass after a murderous and decisive struggle between the two protagonists. That affirmed intention to place the last at the head of things, and to make them climb at a pace (too quickly, some say) the well-known steps which characterize an organized society, can only triumph if we use all means to turn the scale, including, of course, that of violence.

You do not turn any society, however primitive it may be, upside down with such a program if you have not decided from the very beginning, that is to say from the actual formulation of that program, to overcome all the obstacles that you will come across in so doing. The native who decides to put the program into practice, and to become its moving force, is ready for violence at all times. From birth it is clear to him that this narrow world, strewn with prohibitions, can only be called in question by absolute violence.

* * *

As soon as the native begins to pull on his moorings, and to cause anxiety to the settler, he is handed over to well-meaning souls who in cultural congresses point out to him the specificity and wealth of Western values. But every time Western values are mentioned they produce in the native a sort of stiffening or muscular lockjaw. During the period of decolonization, the native's reason is appealed to. He is offered definite values, he is told frequently that decolonization need not mean regression, and that he must put his trust in qualities which are well-tried, solid, and highly esteemed. But it so happens that when the native hears a speech about Western culture he pulls out his knife—or at least he makes sure it is within reach. The violence with which the supremacy of white values is affirmed and the aggressiveness which has permeated the victory of these values over the ways of life and of thought of the native mean that, in revenge, the native laughs in mockery when Western values are mentioned in front of him. In the colonial context the settler only ends his work of breaking in the native when the latter admits loudly and intelligibly the supremacy of the white man's values. In the period of decolonization, the colonized masses mock at these very values, insult them, and vomit them up.

* * *

But it so happens that for the colonized people this violence, because it constitutes their only work, invests their characters with positive and creative qualities. The practice of violence binds them together as a whole, since each individual forms a violent link in the great chain, a part of the great organism of violence which has surged upward in reaction to the settler's violence in the beginning. The groups recognize each other and the future nation is already indivisible. The armed struggle mobilizes the people; that is to say, it throws them in one way and in one direction.

The mobilization of the masses, when it arises out of the war of liberation, introduces into each man's consciousness the ideas of a common cause, of a national destiny, and of a collective history. In the same way the second phase, that of the building-up of the nation, is helped on by the existence of this cement which has been mixed with blood and anger. Thus we come to a fuller appreciation of the originality of the words used in these underdeveloped countries. During the colonial period the people are called upon to fight against oppression; after national liberation, they are called upon to fight against poverty, illiteracy, and underdevelopment. The struggle, they say, goes on. The people realize that life is an unending contest.

We have said that the native's violence unifies the people. By its very structure, colonialism is separatist and regionalist. Colonialism does not simply state the existence of tribes; it also reinforces it and separates them. The colonial system encourages chieftaincies and keeps alive the old Marabout confraternities. Violence is in action all-inclusive and national. It follows that it is closely involved in the liquidation of regionalism and of tribalism. Thus the national parties show no pity at all toward the caids and the customary chiefs. Their destruction is the preliminary to the unification of the people.

At the level of individuals, violence is a cleansing force. It frees the native from his inferiority complex and from his despair and inaction; it makes him fearless and restores his self-respect. Even if the armed struggle has been symbolic and the nation is demobilized through a rapid movement of decolonization, the people have the time to see that the liberation has been the business of each and all and that the leader has no special merit. From thence comes that type of aggressive reticence with regard to the machinery of protocol which young governments quickly show. When the people have taken violent part in the national liberation they will allow no one to set themselves up as "liberators." They show themselves to be jealous of the results of their action and take good care not to place their future, their destiny, or the fate of their country in the hands of a living god. Yesterday they were completely irresponsible; today they mean to understand everything and make all decisions. Illuminated by violence, the consciousness of the people rebels against any pacification. From now on the demagogues, the opportunists, and the magicians have a difficult task. The action which has thrown them into a hand-to-hand struggle confers upon the masses a voracious taste for the concrete. The attempt at mystification becomes, in the long run, practically impossible.

Source: Frantz Fanon, *The Wretched of the Earth*, trans. Constance Farrington (Grove Press, 1963), 37, 43, 93–95.

Interpreting Visual Evidence

War and Propaganda

Both the Allies and the Axis powers made major efforts to mobilize consent and win support, not only among soldiers but on the home front as well. Governments used propaganda—information and ideas that are spread in order to promote a certain political point of view—to shape public opinion during World War II. While Joseph Goebbels and the Nazi Ministry for Public Enlightenment and Propaganda were the most famous for their efforts to demonize the enemy and foster a sense of solidarity at home and among Germany's allies, they had analogs in Washington, London, Moscow, and Tokyo. Propaganda offices around the world enlisted journalists, cartoonists, and other visual artists, as well as radio and film, to spread their messages.

The first image, "Victory or Bolshevism," a poster by Hans Schweitzer, known as Mjölnir (the name of the Norse god Thor's hammer), contrasts a wholesome German community with the bleak prospect of a Soviet occupation after the German defeat at Stalingrad (1942–1943). The next two images show European propaganda that celebrates the loyalty of colonial subjects in their empires' war efforts. A recruitment poster for the British army shows seven uniformed soldiers from across the empire, prepared to fight for a common future. The photograph shows Free French

German poster, "Victory or Bolshevism."

British poster, "Together."

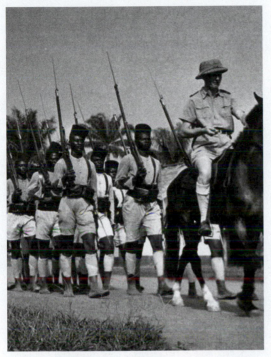

Free French troops train in Bouar.

眼で見る時局雑誌

漫画

二月號

大政翼贊會
宣傳部長室

30錢

Japanese poster portraying a villainous President Roosevelt.

troops—Resistance fighters who supported the Allies and opposed collaborationist Vichy France—marching in Bouar, French Equatorial Africa (today the Central African Republic). The final image shows a Japanese representation of the United States. It depicts a demonic Franklin Delano Roosevelt with grasping hands and an evil smile.

Questions for Analysis

1. Contrast the stereotypes presented to celebrate cooperation with those presented to demonize enemies. Do they differ in any meaningful ways?

2. Does the medium—poster, caricature, or photograph—shape the message these images convey? Is the photograph similar to or different from the posters and caricature? Do they appeal to audiences in the same way?

3. Analyze the role of gender in these images. How do the artists use masculine and feminine imagery, and to what effect?

21

Globalization

1970–2000

In the thirteenth century, few people could imagine moving beyond their local regions. The Venetian explorer Marco Polo, who traveled through China, and the Arab scholar Ibn Battuta, who traversed the Islamic world, were rare exceptions. In contrast, by the late twentieth century, people traversed in a matter of hours the distances that it took Marco Polo and Ibn Battuta years to cover. Many others staying at home could "travel" the world via the Internet, books, newspapers, and television.

But not all travelers moved about so comfortably. Many migrants—desperate to escape political chaos, persecution, or poverty—slipped across borders in the dark of night, traveled as human cargo inside shipping containers, or fled their homelands on foot. Billions of other people still had no access to the global age's technological wonders and economic opportunities. Thus, while the development of integrated worldwide cultural and economic structures—known as **globalization**—created new possibilities for some, it also caused deeper inequalities.

The forces driving global integration—and inequality—were no longer the political empires of old. By the mid-twentieth century, the European empires had lost their sway. The Cold War and decolonization movements that had produced the three-world order no longer influenced world affairs. Power structures in the First World, under stress in the 1970s, did not crack. But those in the Second World did. Thus, the Cold War ended with the implosion of the Soviet bloc. The Third World also splintered, with some areas becoming highly

Chapter Outline

- Removing Obstacles to Globalization
- Unleashing Globalization
- Characteristics of the New Global Order
- Citizenship in the Global World
- Conclusion

Core Objectives

- **DESCRIBE** the relationship between global migration, new technologies, and the spread of cultural influences during and after the Cold War.
- **EVALUATE** the degree to which globalization after the end of the Cold War changed societies, and **COMPARE** that globalization with earlier forms of globalization.
- **DESCRIBE** how globalization and population changes affected the environment, and vice versa.
- **IDENTIFY** the transnational forces that eroded the power of the nation-state in the last third of the twentieth century, and **EXPLAIN** how they did so.

advanced and others falling into deep poverty. To be sure, nation-states remained essential for establishing democratic institutions and protecting human rights, but supranational organizations—institutions that transcended nation-state borders, like the European Union and the International Monetary Fund (IMF)—often impinged on their autonomy. A new global order emerged with a unified marketplace and unhindered flows of capital, commerce, culture, and labor.

Global Storylines

- Following the collapse of the three-world order, new global markets and communications networks integrate the world but also create deep inequalities.

- New technologies and vast population movements make global culture more homogeneous.

- Globalization, supranational organizations (like the World Bank, the European Union, and the United Nations), and religious fundamentalism erode the power of the nation-state.

Removing Obstacles to Globalization

The collapse of the Soviet Union brought the Cold War to an end. At the same time, the capitalist First World gave up its last colonial possessions and the remnants of white settler supremacy disintegrated. But as this occurred, the formerly colonized Third World's dream of a "third way" also vanished. As empires withdrew, they revealed a world integrated by markets for capital and labor, culture, and technology, rather than forced loyalties to imperial masters or rival superpowers.

ENDING THE COLD WAR

A world divided between two hostile factions limited the prospects for a global exchange of peoples, ideas, and resources. There was widespread exchange within each of the rival blocs, but for other countries, the pressure from the Soviet Union and the United States to align with a superpower imposed limits to their interactions, even with neighboring states. Pushing against the Cold War superpower framework, however, were strong nationalist aspirations and religious movements, which the superpowers tried to control—or in some cases inflame—at great cost.

Mounting Costs Rivalry was enormously costly to the superpowers. The 1970s and 1980s saw the largest peacetime accumulation of arms in history. Despite myriad treaties and summits, the United States and the Soviet Union stockpiled nuclear and conventional weaponry. Furthermore, in 1983, U.S. president Ronald Reagan unveiled the Strategic Defense Initiative (nicknamed "Star Wars"), an elaborate and expensive plan to use satellites and space missiles to insulate the United States from incoming nuclear bombs. For both sides, these military spending sprees brought economic troubles.

Other pressures within and outside the United States and the Soviet Union also strained the Cold War order. The Soviet Union sent troops to prop up a puppet regime in Afghanistan, only to fall into a bloody war against insurgents financed and armed by the United States. The resulting stalemate undermined the image of the mighty Soviet armed forces, and mothers of Soviet soldiers protested their government's involvements abroad. In Europe and North America, the antinuclear movement rallied millions to the streets, while western industrialists worried about competition from Japan, which had been plowing money into rapid industrialization rather than arms. Political leaders also grappled with distressingly high unemployment rates. Thus, both sides shared a common crisis: fatigue from the Cold War, and an economic challenge from East Asia.

THE BIG PICTURE

What were the transnational forces that eroded the power of the nation-state in the last third of the twentieth century? How did they do so?

The Soviet Bloc Collapses In the end, the Soviet bloc collapsed. (See Map 21.1.) Even though planned economies employed the entire Soviet population, they failed to fill stores with sufficient consumer goods. Socialist health care and benefits lagged behind those provided in wealthy, capitalist countries. Authoritarian political structures in the Soviet bloc relied on deception and coercion rather than elections and civic activism. Although communists had promised to beat capitalism by building socialism on the way to achieving full communism, the communist paradise was nowhere on the horizon.

Lech Wałęsa A Polish electrician from the Lenin Shipyard in the Baltic port city of Gdańsk, Walesa spearheaded the formation of Solidarity, a mass independent trade union of workers who battled the communist regime that ruled in their name. He later was elected president of post-communist Poland.

Events in Poland were one catalyst in socialism's undoing. In 1978, the Catholic Church appointed a new pope, John Paul II, who came from Poland—the first non-Italian pope in over 450 years. The pope supported mass strikes at the Lenin Shipyard in Gdańsk, which led to the formation of the Soviet bloc's first independent trade union, Solidarity. As Communist Party members in Poland defected to its side, the union became a society-wide movement; it aimed not to reform socialism (as in Czechoslovakia in 1968; see Chapter 20) but to overcome it. A crackdown by the Polish military and police put most of Solidarity's leadership in prison and drove the movement underground, but Soviet intelligence officials secretly worried that Solidarity could not be easily eradicated.

The most consequential factor in the collapse of the Soviet superpower was the reform effort launched by Mikhail Gorbachev, who became general secretary of the Soviet Communist Party in 1985. Under this effort (known as *perestroika*, meaning "reconstruction"), Gorbachev permitted competitive elections for Communist Party posts, relaxed censorship, allowed civic associations, legalized small nonstate businesses, granted autonomy to state firms, and encouraged the Soviet republics to be responsible for their own affairs within the Soviet Union. These reforms were linked with dramatic arms-control initiatives to ease the superpower burden on the Soviet Union. Gorbachev then began withdrawing troops from Afghanistan and informed eastern European leaders that they could not count on Moscow's armed intervention to prop up their regimes.

Having set out to improve socialism, however, Gorbachev instead destabilized it. Civic groups called not for reform of the system, but for its liquidation. Eastern European states declared their intention to leave the Soviet orbit, and some of the Soviet republics began to push for independence. In response, disgruntled factions within the Communist Party and the Soviet

1989: Mass demonstrations, fall of the Berlin Wall
1990: Reunited with West Germany

1980 onward: Solidarity leads opposition
1981: Crackdown against Solidarity, driving it underground
1989: Solidarity wins 99 of the 100 seats in parliament that it is permitted to contest

1989: Mass demonstrations
1990: Multiparty elections
1993: Czechoslovakia splits into Czech Republic and Slovakia

1989: Removal of barbed wire on border with Austria allows East German tourists to cross westward
1990: Multiparty elections

1989: National uprising against Ceausescu
1992: First multiparty general election
1996: First non-Communist government

1990: Multiparty elections

1990: Multiparty elections
1991–1992: War between Croats and Serbs

1992: Fighting begins between Serbs and Bosnian Muslims
1995: Divided in two

1990: Multiparty elections
1991: Dissolved into warring states

1989: Loses autonomy from Serbia
1998–1999: Fighting between Serbs and ethnic Albanians
2000: First free elections

1989: Demonstrations
1990: Multiparty elections

1990: Multiparty elections
2001: Fighting erupts between Macedonians and ethnic Albanians

1990: Demonstrations, civil war
1991: Multiparty elections

Civil unrest

DENMARK
BALTIC SEA
NETHERLANDS
EAST GERMANY
Berlin
Leipzig
BELGIUM
LUX.
WEST GERMANY
FRANCE
SWITZERLAND
Gdańsk
POLAND
Warsaw
Prague
CZECHOSLOVAKIA
CZECH REPUBLIC
SLOVAKIA
Bratislava
AUSTRIA
Budapest
HUNGARY
SLOVENIA
CROATIA
BOSNIA-HERZOGOVINA
Belgrade
YUGOSLAVIA
SERBIA
MONTE-NEGRO
KOSOVO
ITALY
MACEDONIA
Tirana
ALBANIA
GREECE
ROMANIA
Timisoara
Bucharest
Danube R.
BULGARIA
Sofia
BLACK SEA
TURKEY
SOVIET UNION
MEDITERRANEAN SEA

0   100   200   300 Miles
0   100   200   300 Kilometers

Map 21.1 Collapse of the Communist Bloc in Europe

The Soviet Union's domination of eastern Europe ended precipitously in 1989. The political map of eastern and central Europe took on a different shape under European integration.

- What significant event in many communist countries signaled the collapse of communism?
- In what part of eastern and central Europe did the most political instability and conflict occur?
- According to your reading, why did the end of communist rule cause the reshuffling of political boundaries in the region?

military tried to preserve the destabilized old order by staging a coup attempt in 1991. However, the former Communist Party boss of Moscow and elected president of the Russian republic, Boris Yeltsin, rallied the opposition and faced down the hard-liners. Under Yeltsin, Russia, like Ukraine and the other Soviet republics, became a refuge for discontented Soviet elites. Thereafter, those elites abandoned the cause of the Soviet Union and divided up state property among themselves. Thus, the Soviet Union broke apart into independent states. (See Map 21.2.) The Cold War, which began as a tense stand-off between World War II allies, ended when the eastern bloc failed to keep up with the economic and technological development of its rivals.

AFRICA AND THE END OF WHITE RULE

Although the aftermath of World War II saw the dismantling of most of Europe's empires, remnants of colonial rule remained in southern Africa (see Map 20.6). Here, whites clung to centuries-old notions of their racial superiority over non-Europeans. Final decolonization meant that self-rule would return to all of Africa. The end of colonialism also set the stage for former colonies to find new trading and investment partners and to become more integrated with the wider world.

The Last Holdouts The last African territories under direct European control were the Portuguese colonies of southern and western Africa. However, by the mid-1970s, efforts to suppress African nationalist movements in those colonies had exhausted Portugal's resources. As African nationalist demands led to a hurried Portuguese withdrawal from Guinea-Bissau, Angola, and Mozambique, formal European colonialism in Africa came to an end.

But white rule still prevailed elsewhere in Africa. In Rhodesia, a white minority resisted international pressure to allow black rule. In the end, independent African states helped support a liberation guerrilla movement under Robert Mugabe. Surrounded, Rhodesian whites finally lost control in 1979. The new constitutional government renamed the country Zimbabwe, erasing from Africa's map the name of the long-deceased British expansionist Cecil Rhodes (see Chapter 17).

South Africa and Nelson Mandela The final outpost of white rule was South Africa, where the European minority was larger, richer, and more entrenched than elsewhere in the region. Yet in the countryside and cities, defiance of white rule was growing. Black South Africans lobbed rocks and crude bombs at tanks and organized mass strikes against the multinational-owned mines.

At the same time, pressures from abroad to end the racist apartheid system were mounting. The International Olympic Committee banned South

Map 21.2 The Breakup of the Soviet Union

The Soviet Union broke apart in 1991. Compare this map with Map 17.5, which illustrates Russian expansion in the nineteenth century.

- Which parts of the old Russian Empire remained under Russian rule, and which of its territories established their own states?
- In what areas did large migrations accompany the breakup, and for what reasons?
- According to your reading, how did the breakup of the Soviet Union change Russia's status in Europe and Asia?

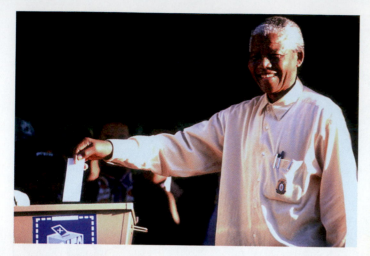

The End of Apartheid Nelson Mandela, running for president in 1994 as the candidate of the African National Congress, here casts a ballot in the first all-races election in South Africa. This election ended apartheid and saw the African National Congress take control of the Republic of South Africa.

African athletes starting in 1970. American students insisted that their universities divest themselves of companies with investments in South Africa. As international pressures grew, foreign governments—even that of the United States, once South Africa's staunchest ally—applied economic sanctions against South Africa. A swelling worldwide chorus demanded that **Nelson Mandela**, the imprisoned leader of the African National Congress (ANC), be freed. The white political elite eventually realized that it was better to negotiate new arrangements than to endure international condemnation and years of internal warfare against a majority population. Ensuing negotiations produced South Africa's first free, mass elections in 1994. These elections brought an overwhelming victory to the ANC and to Nelson Mandela, who was elected president.

Still, African leaders faced immense problems in building stable political communities. Although they set out to destroy the vestiges of colonial political structures and build African-based public institutions, those leaders struggled to find a third way between capitalism and communism. Ethnic and religious rivalries, held in check during the colonial period, now blazed forth. Civil wars erupted in many countries—most violently in Nigeria, Sudan, and Zaire (later called Democratic Republic of the Congo)—and military leaders were drawn into politics. By the 1990s, the continent was aflame with civil strife. Armed conflicts that started with the Cold War endured well after it ended, even though white rule had finally come to an end throughout the entire continent.

Unleashing Globalization

Core Objectives

DESCRIBE the relationship between global migration, new technologies, and the spread of cultural influences during and after the Cold War.

As obstacles to international integration began to dissolve, capital, commodities, people, and culture crossed borders with ever-greater freedom. Even though these movements had occurred throughout history, their scale changed dramatically in these years. Never had there been such unequal access to the fruits of exchange. Many Third World countries, as well as those of the former eastern communist bloc—which came to be collectively called the **developing world**—were largely left out. Several factors contributed to increasing integration and to new power arrangements: international banking, expanded international trade, population migrations, and technical breakthroughs in communications.

FINANCE AND TRADE

The increase in the international flow of goods and capital was well under way in the 1970s, but the end of the Cold War removed many impediments to globalization. During the 1990s, even the strongest nation-states felt the effects of economic globalization.

Global Finance and Deregulated Markets Major transformations in the world's financial system occurred in the 1970s. America's budget and trade deficits prompted president Richard Nixon to take the dollar off the gold standard, an action that enabled the yen, the lira, the pound, the franc, and other national currencies to cut their ties to the American dollar. Now international financiers enjoyed greater freedom from national regulators and found fresh business opportunities.

The primary agents of the heightened global financial activity were banks. Based mainly in London, New York, and Tokyo, big banks attracted large amounts of capital for lucrative ventures around the world. Revenues from oil producers provided a large infusion of cash into the global economy in the 1970s. At the same time, banks joined forces to issue mammoth loans to developing countries.

No international financial organization was more influential than the International Monetary Fund (IMF), which came into existence after World War II with a view to raising capital from all of the participating states so as to be able to lend funds to states in need. During the 1980s, it emerged as a central player, especially in response to debt crises in poor countries that emerged as the prospect of finding a third way between the superpower blocs began to fade. Throughout the 1970s, European, Japanese, and North American banks had loaned money on very easy terms to cash-strapped Third World and eastern-bloc borrowers. But what was once good business soon turned sour. In 1982, a wave of defaults, in which governments and other borrowers found themselves unable to repay their loans, threatened to overrun Latin America in particular. Throughout the 1980s, international banks and the IMF kept heavily indebted customers solvent. The IMF offered short-term loans to governments on condition that recipients produce balanced budgets, compel civilian populations to give up subsidies on essential products, and cease to import far more than they exported. Latin Americans led the way in reorganizing their finances and thus pioneered the process of expanding domestic production while at the same time engaging in robust international trade. All across the world, tariffs and other barriers to foreign trade crumbled, state enterprises became private firms, and foreign banks and multinational companies took a great interest in investing in these newly reformed economies.

Effects of Integrated Networks New technologies and institutions enabled many more financial investors and traders to participate in the integrated

Nelson Mandela (1918–2013)
Leader of the African National Congress (ANC) who was imprisoned for more than two decades by the apartheid regime in South Africa for his political activities, until worldwide protests led to his release in 1990. In 1994, Mandela won the presidency in South Africa's first free mass elections.

developing world
Term applied to poor countries of the Third World and the former eastern communist bloc seeking to develop viable nation-states and prosperous economies. The term has come under sustained criticism for suggesting that there is a single path of economic growth that countries everywhere follow. It has been replaced by equally problematic terms like "advanced economy" and "emerging markets."

networks of world finance. The Internet and online trading accelerated the movement of capital across borders. Rapid changes in financial and currency markets soon created problems, however. When the Mexican economy went into paralysis in 1994, the crisis was so extreme that not even the IMF could bail it out; the U.S. Treasury issued the largest international loan in history to pull Mexico out of its economic tailspin. Despite acting as the lender in that instance, the United States emerged in the new financial order as the world's largest borrower because it imported far more than it exported. Early in the new millennium, its net foreign debt soared past $2 trillion—a 700 percent increase since the early 1990s. Much of this debt was owed to China, which had a huge trade surplus with the United States.

Globalization increased commercial, as well as financial, interdependence. The total value of goods and services exchanged through world trade increased nearly tenfold between 1973 and 1998, and trade in Asia grew even faster. Whereas an American would once have worn American-made clothes (Levi's), driven an American car (a Ford), and watched an American television (made by Zenith), such was rarely the case by the century's end. Increasingly, American consumers bought foreign goods and services and sold a greater share of their own output abroad. This pattern had always been true of smaller regions like Central America and southern Africa. But in the 1980s, it intensified as countries with cheap and skilled labor, like China, India, and Brazil, were able to undersell their competitors in world markets.

International trade also shifted the international division of labor. After World War II, Europeans and North Americans dominated manufacturing, while Third World countries supplied raw materials. But by the 1990s this was no longer the case. Brazil became a major airplane maker, South Korea exported millions of automobiles, and China emerged as the world's largest source of textiles, footwear, and electronics.

The most remarkable global shift involved East Asian industry and commerce. Manufactured goods, including high-technology products, now came from the eastern fringe of Afro-Eurasia as often as from its western fringe. Japan blazed the Asian trail: between 1965 and 1990, its share of world trade doubled to almost 10 percent. China, too, flexed its economic muscle. When Deng Xiaoping took power in 1978, China was already a growing economy. Under Deng, China started to become an economic powerhouse. For the next two decades, China chalked up astounding 10 percent annual growth rates, swelling its share of world GDP (gross domestic product, the value of goods and services produced) from 5 percent to 12 percent.

For East Asia, the share of exports doubled in the same period. Smaller states whose governments subsidized economic development, like Singapore, Taiwan, South Korea, and Hong Kong, became mini-powerhouses. By the early 1990s, these countries and Japan were also major investors abroad.

As East Asia's share of world production quickly increased, the U.S. and European shares decreased.

Regional Trade Blocs and Growing Inequalities The industrialization of poor countries, combined with lower trade barriers, increased the pressures of world competition on national economies. Some areas responded by establishing regional trade blocs in an effort to create larger markets for themselves and stay competitive in an ever more integrated world economy.

The most complete regional integration occurred in Europe, where states slashed trade barriers and harmonized their commercial policies toward the rest of the world. In 1993, the Maastricht Treaty established the **European Union (EU)** under its current name, and what had been conceived as a trading and financial bloc began to evolve into a political union as well, a supranational organization that encroached on the sovereignty of its member states. In 2002, a number of the European Union states deepened their economic interdependence by adopting a single currency, the euro. A few of the EU states—most notably the United Kingdom—did not want to give up control of their own national currency. By 2012, the European Union had twenty-seven members, with seventeen members using the euro.

Although international trade increased during this period, it also became increasingly unequal. High-technology and high-value goods now occupied an ever-greater share of the manufacturing and exports of the world's richest countries. For rich countries as a whole, about half of total GDP reflected the production and distribution of goods such as computers, software, and pharmaceuticals and services such as insurance and banking, which, collectively, gave those countries a competitive advantage. Poor nations, by contrast, generally remained locked in the production of low-tech goods and the export of raw materials. Increasingly, technology and knowledge divided the world into affluent, technically sophisticated countries and poor, technically underdeveloped regions.

MIGRATION

Migration, a constant feature of world history, became more pronounced in the twentieth century. (See Map 21.3.) Although after 1970 fewer Europeans were on the move, many more Asians, Africans, and Latin Americans were, chasing jobs in the richer countries. By 2000, there were 120 million migrants scattered across 152 countries, up from 75 million in 1965.

Patterns of Migration Migratory flows often followed the contours of past colonial and political ties. Where North America and Europe had had colonies or dependencies, their political withdrawal left tracks for migrants to follow. Indians and Pakistanis moved to Britain; so did Jamaicans. Dominicans,

European Union (EU)
International body organized after World War II as an attempt at reconciliation between Germany and the rest of Europe. It initially aimed to forge closer industrial cooperation. Eventually, through various treaties, many European states relinquished some of their sovereignty, and the cooperation became a full-fledged union with a common parliament. Some EU members adopted a single currency, the euro.

The Global View

Map 21.3 World Migration, 1918–1998

The world's population continued to grow and move around in the twentieth century.

- Looking at this map, identify the countries that had the greatest increase in foreign-born people as a percentage of total population.

- Then compare the areas of most rapid population growth during the nineteenth century with those parts of the world that, according to this map, had the highest percentage of foreign-born people in the twentieth century. What are the similarities and differences?

- During the twentieth century, which parts of the world were the sending areas, and which were the receiving territories? See also Map 18.1.

East Europeans 1918–1919

East Europeans 1918–1919

Russian Jews to USA 1980s and 1990s

European Jews to USA 1930s

CANADA

UNITED STATES

MEXICO

1950–

1960–

GUATEMALA
NICARAGUA

BELIZE

CUBA

HAITI

Jamaicans, Haitians, and
Dominicans to USA 1990–

1960–1980

COLOMBIA

BRAZIL

West Indians to Britain

Spaniards to Mexico 1936

ATLANTIC
OCEAN

PACIFIC
OCEAN

GREAT
BRITAIN

SWITZ.
FRANCE

Algerian colons to
France 1962

SPAIN

1950–

MOROCCO

TUNISIA
ALGERIA

NIGER

1970–

IVORY
COAST

NIGERIA

1980

ARGENTINA

Foreign-born people as percentage of total population (latest available year)

- Less than 1.5%
- 1.5%–2.9%
- 3.0%–7.5%
- More than 7.5%
- Data not available
- ← Migration

0   1000   2000 Miles

0   1000   2000 Kilometers

ARCTIC OCEAN

Poles and Baltic peoples to Siberia 1939–1940

RUSSIA

GERMANY

POLAND

1918–1922

1930s and 1940s

UKRAINE

AUSTRIA

Russian Jews to Israel
1980s and 1990s

1945

GEORGIA

1922

1922

ITALY

TURKEY

2003

1950–1954

NORTH
KOREA

1945–

SYRIA

IRAQ

AFGHANISTAN

CHINA

SOUTH
KOREA

JAPAN

1950–

ISRAEL

1947–

1979

BANGLADESH

JORDAN

PAKISTAN

1947

EGYPT

1947–

LIBYA

1980–

1970–

INDIA

1947

HONG KONG

Chinese to Canada and USA 1980 –

1970–

SAUDI
ARABIA

1972

Falashas to
Israel 1991

THAILAND

VIETNAM

1975

Vietnamese to USA

SUDAN
mid
1980s

ETHIOPIA
1980s

MALAYSIA

Indians to USA 1990 –

PACIFIC
OCEAN

CONGO

RWANDA
1994

TANZANIA

Indians, Pakistanis,
and Bangladeshis
to Western Europe
and USA

Vietnamese
to France 1975

Southeast Asians to
Australia 1970s

INDONESIA

INDIAN
OCEAN

MOZAMBIQUE

BOTSWANA
1960–

1960–

AUSTRALIA

SOUTH
AFRICA

NEW
ZEALAND

Europeans to Australia/New Zealand 1918 –

Lagos, Nigeria During the twentieth century, Lagos was one of the fastest-growing and most crowded cities in Africa. Note the market and the mosque in the foreground, and the skyscrapers far in the distance.

Haitians, and Mexicans went to the United States. Algerians and Vietnamese moved to France. Where emerging rich societies cultivated close diplomatic ties, these relations opened migratory gates. This was true of Germany's relationship with Turkey, of Japan's with South Korea, and of Canada's with Hong Kong.

International migration was often an extension of regional and national migration from poorer rural areas to urban centers. In Nigeria, for example, rural-urban migration intensified after 1970. In 1900, Nigeria's capital at the time, Lagos, had a population of 41,847. At the century's end, Lagos had more than 10 million people, and this number was predicted to double by 2025. The key to Lagos's boom in the 1970s was the existence of large oil reserves in the country and the high prices that oil fetched in international markets. When OPEC sent oil prices soaring, money poured into Nigeria. The government kept most of that money in its largest city. That, in turn, spurred people to move to Lagos. This rural-urban migration increased Lagos's population by 14 percent per year in the 1970s and 1980s. No government—least of all a new, weakly supported one like Nigeria's—could cope with such a huge influx. Electricity supplies failed regularly in and around Lagos. There were never enough schools, teachers, or textbooks. But the city burst with the vitality of new arrivals, prompting one immigrant to exclaim, "It's a terrible place; I want to go there!"

One of the biggest changes in world migration patterns took place in the United States. Having all but closed its coastal borders on the Pacific in the late nineteenth century and on the Atlantic in the 1920s, the United States enacted a major immigration reform in 1965. By 2000, 27 million immigrants lived there, accounting for almost 10 percent of the population—double the share in 1970 and approaching levels not seen since the early twentieth century. The profile of migrants to the United States also changed. In 1970, there were more Canadians or Germans than Mexicans living in the United States. Over the next thirty years, the Mexican influx rose tenfold and by 2000 accounted for almost one-third of immigrants in the United States. The flow of legal and illegal immigrants from Mexico and Central America had an especially dramatic impact on the border states. The numbers migrating from Asia also surged, accounting for over 40 percent of all immigrants to the United States in the 1990s.

Temporary Migrants Some migrants moved for temporary sojourns—or at least that was their original intent. Into the 1950s and 1960s, southern Europeans moved northward; but when Spain, Portugal, Greece, and Italy also became wealthy societies, not only did the exodus decline, but these countries became magnets for Middle Eastern, North African, and later, eastern European migrants. The economic downturn in Europe in the 1970s and the resulting high unemployment rate, however, made their integration into European society difficult. Most migrants from Asia and Africa went initially to Europe in search of temporary jobs as "guest workers." With time, they and their families who followed them settled in their host countries, often living in dilapidated public housing projects, isolated from city centers and public services. The existence of welfare programs made them less likely to leave and return "home" than were earlier generations of labor migrants.

In Japan, too, immigrants were not easily incorporated. Tokyo's immigration policy in the 1970s resembled a guest-worker program. Discouraging permanent settlement and immigration, Japan encouraged itinerant workers to move to the country temporarily, yet its expanding economy required increasing numbers of these temporary migrants. Indeed, Japan's deep reluctance to recruit large numbers of foreign workers, for fear of their settling down, led to dire labor shortages. After Japan, the economic tigers of Hong Kong, Taiwan, and Malaysia all became hosts for temporary migrants. Millions of guest workers moved there, and ultimately those migrants sank deeper roots, especially once their children entered school.

Resident Noncitizens and Refugees Arguments in Los Angeles over schools and health care for resident noncitizens became part of a global debate over the rights and protections afforded to migrants. In Argentina, up to 500,000 undocumented Peruvians, Bolivians, and Paraguayans lived without rights as citizens. Even more staggering were the numbers of migrants— between 3 and 8 million—who moved from Mozambique, Zimbabwe, and Botswana to South Africa. In some Middle Eastern countries, like Saudi Arabia and Kuwait, foreign-born workers constituted over 70 percent of the workforce. In general, migrants were only partially accommodated by their host societies, while many were fully excluded. Thus, even though population movements flowed across political, kinship, and market networks, this demographic reshuffling heightened national concerns about the ethnic makeup of political communities.

Forced migrations remained a major problem. In contrast to earlier centuries' forced migration of slaves from Africa, this period's involuntary flows involved refugees fleeing civil war and torture. Many suffered for weeks, months, or years in refugee camps on the periphery of violence. The greatest concentration of refugees occurred in the world's poorest region—Africa. Many Africans were caught up in ethnic and religious conflicts that generated vast refugee camps, where their survival depended on the generosity of host governments and international contributions.

Whether migrants traveled in search of work or fled persecution, they posed a series of challenges for host countries. If migrants crossed borders easily, they often struggled to receive basic rights. Especially during economic downturns, discrimination often led to violent conflicts among recent immigrants, long-time residents (often themselves of immigrant origin), and the host country's security forces. Conflicts erupted over religion and culture, notably in French efforts to prevent women from wearing Muslim headscarves in public and the English-only movement in the United States. Governments in immigrant-receiving countries everywhere grappled with the challenge of extending citizenship to newcomers and then respecting their desires to dress, worship, and celebrate traditions as they did in their families' homelands.

GLOBAL CULTURE

Migrations and new technologies helped create a more global entertainment culture. In this domain, globalization is often equated with Americanization. Yet American entertainments themselves reflected artistic practices from across the globe as one mass culture met another. On the global scale, there was less cultural diversity in 2000 than in 1300; but in terms of individuals' everyday experience, the potential for experiencing cultural diversity, if one could afford the technology to do so, increased.

New Media Technology was key in spreading entertainment. In the 1970s, for example, cassette tapes became the dominant medium for popular music, sidelining the long-playing record and the short-lived eight-track tape. Television was another globalizing force, as American producers bundled old dramas and situation comedies for stations worldwide. Brazilian soap operas began to appear in Spanish-language TV markets throughout the Americas in the 1980s, often inducing Mexican viewers to rush home from work to catch the latest episode. Latin American television shows and music were distributed in the United States in areas with large Spanish-speaking populations. Bombay also produced its fair share of programs for viewers of British television and today produces roughly twice as many films per year as Hollywood. (See Current Trends in World History: Urbanization as a Global Phenomenon.) In terms of box-office revenues, Hollywood remains the leading producer of films in the world, helped in no small measure by its ability to send movies across borders and also by the actors from around the world who star in its films.

Television's globalizing effects were especially evident in sports. Soccer (known as football outside the United States) became an international passion, with devoted national followings for national teams. Indeed, by the 1980s, soccer was *the* world sport, with television ratings increasingly determining its schedule. Organizers of the 1986 World Cup in Mexico insisted that big soccer matches take place at midday so that the games could be televised live at prime time in Europe, even though teams had to play under the scorching sun. In many parts of the globe, major American sports also made particularly deep inroads as more people participated in them and as television broadcast American games in other countries. The National Basketball Association (along with the athletic footwear firm Nike) was particularly successful in international marketing; in the process, it made Michael Jordan the world's best-known athlete in the late twentieth century.

Cultural Exchanges Technology was not the only driving force of world cultures; migration and exchange were also important. For example, as people moved around, they brought their own musical tastes with them and borrowed others. Reggae, born in the 1960s among Jamaica's Rastafarians, became a sensation in London and Toronto, where large West Indian communities had migrated. Reggae's lyrics and realist imagery invoked a black countercultural spirit and a call for a return to African roots. Soon, Bob Marley and the Wailers, reggae's flagship band, played to audiences worldwide. In northeastern Brazil, where African culture was emerging from decades of disdain, Bob Marley became a folk hero. In Soweto, South Africa, populated by black workers, he was a symbol of resistance.

Reggae propelled a shift in black American music. In broadcasting reggae, DJs often merged sounds and chanted lyrics over a beat, a "talkover" form that soon characterized rap music as well. This was a disruptive concept in the late 1970s, but within ten years rap had become mainstream. Rap lyrics emulated reggae's realism by focusing on black problems, but they also opened a new domain of controversies by reflecting gang worldviews. On the world stage, Latino rappers stressed multicultural themes, often in "Spanglish." Asian rap stressed the genre as a vehicle for cross-cultural sharing and epitomized the ability of new cultural forms to bring peoples together.

Local Culture World cultures may have become more integrated and homogeneous, but they did not completely replace national and local cultures. Indeed, technology and migration often reinforced the appeal of "national" cultural icons as national celebrities gained popularity among emigrant groups abroad. Inexpensive new technology introduced these stars to more

Urbanization as a Global Phenomenon: Transforming Bombay into Mumbai

The city has played a pivotal role in world history since it first emerged thousands of years ago along the Tigris and Euphrates Rivers in Mesopotamia (modern-day Iraq). People have flocked to cities ever since for the social and economic advantages that these locations offer. By the end of the twentieth century, the proportion of people living in cities—usually defined as places having populations over 5,000 or 10,000—exceeded 50 percent in the wealthiest countries and was approaching that proportion in the less developed countries.

Of the burgeoning cities in the developing world, one of the most dynamic is Mumbai, in the state of Maharashtra, India. Acquired in the sixteenth century by the Portuguese, who then transferred its control to the English East India Company, Bombay (as it was named at the time) developed as a port city for colonial commerce. It profited from the cotton trade, developed a vibrant textile industry, attracted migrants from the countryside, and acquired a cosmopolitan image. India gained its independence from Britain in 1947, and in 1996 Bombay was renamed "Mumbai." It still epitomizes the modern face of the nation, and its increasingly heterogeneous population reflects the larger Indian melting pot.

Beginning in the 1980s, however, the nature of the city's relationship with the world economy started to change. The cotton textile industry, Bombay's economic backbone, went into a decline. Industrial employment fell sharply. The share of informal household enterprises, small shops, petty subcontractors, and casual labor rose, along with employment in banking and insurance. Economic liberalization removed hurdles for foreign businesses and brought the city directly into the global economy.

Today Mumbai occupies a strategic place in transnational geography. This is evident in the increasing presence of financial institutions, trading organizations, insurance companies, telecommunications corporations, and information technology enterprises with worldwide operations. Even the city's vibrant film industry addresses a global, not just a national, audience. Rather appropriately, Bombay cinema has been nicknamed "Bollywood." The city, however, still attracts a large number of poor migrants who live in slums or call the pavements their home. The gap between Mumbai's rich and poor has grown alarmingly. The millions who eke out a miserable living stand in stark contrast to a tiny elite enriched by the global economy.

Globalization has also affected Mumbai residents' identity. In the 1990s, the

and more people. In Egypt, the most popular singer of the Nasser years was Umm Kalthum, who became the favorite of Arab middle classes via radio. In 1975, she was given a state funeral, the likes of which had rarely been seen.

Nonetheless, as the market for world cultures grew increasingly competitive, performers increasingly employed a wider array of styles and also challenged biases and conventions. Among the breakthroughs that have occurred since the 1970s are the triumphs of black performers (Bob Marley, Dorothy Masuka), black athletes (Pelé, Michael Jordan), and black writers (Toni Morrison, Chinua Achebe). Competition also shattered some sexual biases. Women performers such as Madonna became popular icons. So did gay performers, starting with the Village People, whose campy multicultural anthem "YMCA" created a place for a new generation of gay, lesbian, and bisexual artists. Of course, beyond Europe and North America, challenging sexual conventions had its limits. In the Middle East, women video artists continued to wear veils—but

Bollywood Bombay cinema, or Bollywood, has an increasing global presence. This poster advertises *Devdas*, a three-hour romance that won awards in India and around the world.

political party then in power in Maharashtra was the Shiv Sena, a nativist regional party named after a seventeenth-century Maratha chieftain who opposed the Mughal Empire. As the industrial economy and trade unions gave way to the service sector and unorganized labor, the Shiv Sena utilized the social and political fluidity produced by globalization to win support for its nativist ideology. Mumbai's cosmopolitan image went up in smoke in 1992–1993, when the Shiv Sena led pogroms against the city's Muslim residents. In response, a Muslim underworld don, according to police investigations, engineered a series of bomb blasts in March 1993. Since then the city has experienced episodes of violence, none more gruesome than the terrorist attacks on two luxury hotels, a crowded railway station, and a Jewish center in November 2006. Ironically, the terrorists chose to attack Mumbai because of its economic importance and reputation as a cosmopolitan city.

Mumbai today illustrates the uneven effects of globalization. The society is sharply divided, economic disparities are great, and the city's politics is a cauldron of conflicting identities. These are the local forms in which this vast and influential city experiences globalization.

Questions for Analysis

- Contrast migration to Mumbai, as described here, with that to other parts of the world, notably western Europe and Japan, as described in the body of the chapter.
- How does Mumbai fit into the larger theme of "Worlds Together, Worlds Apart"?

Explore Further

Mehta, Suketu, *Maximum City: Bombay Lost and Found* (2005).
Prakash, Gyan, *Mumbai Fables* (2010).

now they swung their hips. Relatively homogeneous national cultures, often dominated by men representing the ethnic majority, gave way to a wider variety of entertainers and artists who broke loose from confining local cultures.

COMMUNICATIONS

Computer technology drove a revolution in global communications networks. In the late 1980s, while working in Switzerland, the British physicist Tim Berners-Lee devised a way to pool data stored on various computers. Whereas previous electronic links had existed only between major universities and research stations, Berners-Lee made data more accessible by creating the World Wide Web. With each use, each connection, and each datum entered, however, the Web grew unmanageably crowded and difficult to navigate. The early 1990s saw the first commercial browsers used in navigating the

Bob Marley In the 1970s, young Europeans and North Americans began to listen to music from the Third World. Among the most popular was Jamaican-based reggae, and its most renowned artist, Bob Marley. Marley's music combined rock and roll with African rhythms and lyrics about freedom and redemption for the downtrodden of the world.

Web. Suddenly people were communicating across global networks more easily than with neighbors and more inexpensively than with local phone calls.

These changes created a new generation of wealth. CEOs of top companies like General Motors, Royal Dutch Shell, and Merck now had less net worth than Michael Dell (computer hardware maker), Bill Gates (software maker), and Jeff Bezos (creator of online retailer Amazon.com). Shares of Internet firms, known as dot-coms, swept the world's stock markets. Money from these companies flowed globally as they established offices worldwide. Software and Internet technology firms developed enormous economies of scale, and thus those industries became prone to monopolization as they took over smaller companies.

While the Internet revolution provided new means to share and sell information, it also reinforced hierarchies between haves and have-nots. Great swaths of the world's population living outside big cities, especially in low-income countries, had no access to the Internet. The have-nots were poor not just from lack of capital, but from lack of access to knowledge and new media.

Characteristics of the New Global Order

Core Objectives

EVALUATE the degree to which globalization after the end of the Cold War changed societies and COMPARE that globalization with earlier forms of globalization.

While providing access to an unimaginable array of goods and services, globalization also deepened world inequalities. Family structures changed, and life spans increased. Education and good health determined one's status in society as never before. Populations expanded dramatically, requiring greater industrial and agricultural output from all parts of the world. While many parts of the world consumed more than ever before, others struggled with famine and the consequences of environmental change.

THE DEMOGRAPHY OF GLOBALIZATION

It took 160 years (1800–1960) for the world's population to increase from 1 billion to 3 billion; over the next 40 years (1960–2000), it jumped from 3 billion to over 6 billion. Behind this steepening curve were two important developments: a decline in mortality, especially among children, and a rise in life expectancy.

Population growth was hardly equal worldwide. (See Map 21.4.) In Europe, population growth peaked around 1900, and it moved upward only

Map 21.4 World Population Increases, 1950–1997

The world's population more than doubled between 1950 and 1997, rising from approximately 2.5 billion to nearly 6 billion.

- Which countries had the largest population increases over these five decades?
- Why do you suppose these countries experienced such high population increases?
- According to your reading, why did western Europe and Russia have the lowest population increases during this period?

World population increases, 1950–1997

- 0–49%
- 50%–99%
- 100%–149%
- 150%–199%
- 200%–249%
- 250%–300%
- Over 300%

gradually, from 400 million to 730 million, during the twentieth century, with little growth after the 1970s. North America's population quadrupled over the same period, mainly because of immigration. The other population booms in the twentieth century occurred in Asia (whose population grew by 400 percent), Africa (550 percent), and Latin America (700 percent). China and India each passed the billion-person mark. Population increases were greatest in cities. By the 1980s, the world's largest cities were Asian, African, and Latin American. Greater Tokyo-Yokohama had 30 million inhabitants, while Mexico City had 20 million, São Paulo 17 million, Cairo 16 million, Calcutta 15 million, and Jakarta 12 million.

Population growth slowed most dramatically in richer societies. For some, like Italy, the growth rate declined to zero, as the number of births no longer exceeded the number of deaths. More recently enriched societies like Korea, Taiwan, and Hong Kong also had fewer births. Societies that did not see their birthrates decline by the same rate (much of Africa, southern Asia, and impoverished parts of Latin America) had difficulty raising income levels. But even among poor nations, birthrates declined after the 1970s.

The most remarkable turnaround occurred in China, where the government instituted a "one-child family" policy in 1979 with rewards for compliance and penalties for transgression. The bias in favor of sons (long a feature of China's patrilineal system, which emphasized descent through the male line), together with the availability of ultrasound scanners, promoted the widespread—albeit illegal—practice of prenatal sex selection.

In general, however, declining family size resulted from choice. In rich countries, more women deferred having children as education, career prospects, and birth-control devices provided incentives and methods to postpone starting a family. In addition, love became a precondition to marriage and family formation in societies that had previously emphasized arranged marriages.

Families In many countries, the legal definition of families became more fluid in this period. Here again, the changes reflected women's choices and the relationship between love and marriage. First, couples chose to end their marriages at unprecedented rates. In Belgium and Britain late in the twentieth century, fewer than half of all marriages survived. China's divorce rate soared too. In Beijing, by century's end, it approached 25 percent—double the 1990 rate. As of 2000, women initiated more than 70 percent of divorces.

As marriages became shorter-lived, new forms of child-rearing proliferated. Europeans, including the supposedly more traditional Italians and Greeks, abandoned nuclear family conventions. In those European countries where divorce remained difficult, more couples lived together without getting married. In the United States, out-of-wedlock births constituted one-third of all births in the late 1990s, and only about half of American children were living in households with both parents (compared with nearly three-quarters of children in the early 1970s).

Aging Average life spans grew longer as more infants survived childhood and lived to be old. The populations of industrialized nations "grayed" considerably as their median ages increased and the percentages of populations over age sixty-five grew. In western Europe and Japan, this graying was especially pronounced. Japan's birthrate plummeted, and the citizenry aged at such a rate that the population began to decrease. From a population of 127 million in 2000, estimates forecast a decline to 105 million by 2050.

Aging populations presented new challenges for families. For centuries, being a parent meant providing for children until they could be self-sufficient.

Old age, the period of relatively unproductive labor, was brief. Communities and households absorbed the cost of caring for the elderly. Household savings became family bequests to future, not to older, generations. But as populations aged, retirees needed their own and society's savings to survive. So public and private pension funds swelled to accumulate pools of money to fund future care for the aged. In Germany, over 30 percent of the government's social policy spending went into the state pension fund.

In Africa, where publicly supported pension funds were rare, the aged faced bleaker futures. Whereas in earlier times the elderly were respected founts of wisdom, colonial rule and the postcolonial world elevated the status of the young—especially those with western educations and lifestyles. Then, in the 1970s, as birthrates soared, the demand on family resources for infant and child care rose at the very moment when societies' resource bases began to shrink. The elderly could no longer work, but neither could they rely on the household's support.

INEQUALITY AND ENVIRONMENTAL DEGRADATION

Health The spread of contagious diseases also reflected inequities in the globalized world. Although microbes have no respect for borders, the effects of public health regulations, antibiotics, and vaccination campaigns reduced the spread of contagions in some countries. By the late twentieth century, not only did nutrition and healthy habits determine social status (as they always had), but access to medicines did too.

What used to be universal afflictions in previous centuries now affected only certain peoples. Water treatment and proper sewerage, for example, had banished cholera from most urban centers by the mid-twentieth century. More recently, however, its deadly grip again reached across Asia and into the eastern Mediterranean, parts of Latin America and the Caribbean, and much of sub-Saharan Africa. Thus, diseases proliferated where urban squalor was most acute—in cities with the greatest post-1970s population growth.

In the 1970s, entirely new diseases began to devastate the world's population. Consider **HIV/AIDS**, an epidemic that, in its first two decades, killed 12 million people. Acquired immunodeficiency syndrome (AIDS) is caused by the human immunodeficiency virus (HIV), which spreads through blood and other body fluids. The virus may remain dormant in the bodies of infected people for some time, but eventually attacks the immune system, leaving them unable to fight off even the most common microbes. First detected in 1981, HIV/AIDS was initially stigmatized as a "gay cancer" (as it then appeared primarily in gay men) and received little attention. But as it spread to heterosexuals and public awareness about it increased, new campaigns urged the practice of safe sex, control of blood supplies, and restrictions on sharing hypodermic needles.

HIV/AIDS
An epidemic of acquired immunodeficiency syndrome (AIDS) caused by the human immunodeficiency virus (HIV), which compromises the ability of the infected person's immune system to ward off other diseases. First detected in 1981, AIDS killed 12 million people in the two decades that followed.

In Europe and North America, where the campaigns intensified and new drugs were eventually developed to keep the virus inactive, HIV/AIDS rates stabilized. The new drugs were very expensive, however, leaving the poor and disadvantaged still vulnerable to developing AIDS. By 2000, 33 million people had AIDS (the vast majority in poor countries) and even more were infected with HIV. (See Map 21.5.) At least two-thirds of those with AIDS lived in sub-Saharan Africa. In India, 7 million carried HIV; in China, the figure topped 1 million.

Education Access to education increasingly separated the haves from the have-nots. Moreover, because educational opportunities usually favored men, schooling shaped economic opportunities available to men and women. In sub-Saharan Africa and in India, for example, literacy rates as of 2000

Map 21.5 HIV Infection across the World, 1999

HIV, which leads to AIDS, spread across the whole world within two decades, providing further evidence of global interconnectedness. The outbreak began in Africa.

- Where in Africa have the highest rates of HIV infection occurred?
- Which countries *outside* the African continent have had the highest rates of infection, and why is this so?
- Which countries have the lowest rates of HIV infection, and why is this so?

were, respectively, 63 and 64 percent for men and only 39 and 40 percent for women. In the Arab world, the literacy gap between men and women had decreased somewhat by the end of the twentieth century. Yet low levels of literacy overall and the depressed levels for women continued to impede each region's efforts to combat poverty.

Gender bias also remained in rich societies. For decades, however, women and girls pressed for equal access to education, with some astounding results. In the United States, by the late 1980s, more than half of all college degrees went to women. Chinese women made even greater strides, although roadblocks persisted. Ironically, with China's market reforms (described later in this chapter), women's access to basic education regressed as families, particularly in rural areas, reverted to spending their limited resources on educating sons. Thus, in 2000, up to 70 percent of China's 140 million illiterate people were female.

African Women and Education
Though women's education lagged behind that of men in Africa, a number of women, like Stella Kenyi, pictured here, graduated from African high schools and attended universities at home or abroad. Kenyi taught business skills to men and women in Sudan after completing an undergraduate degree at Davidson College in North Carolina.

Women and Work Although more women held jobs outside the home, they lacked full equality at work. Limited by job discrimination and the burdens of child-rearing, women's participation in the workforce reached a fairly stable level by the 1980s. The percentage of women at the top of the corporate pyramid was considerably lower than their proportion in the labor force or their college graduation rates. Women worldwide had difficulties breaking through the "glass ceiling"—the seemingly invisible barrier that kept them from advancing to these high-level positions. Consequently, while the difference between men's and women's incomes narrowed, a significant gap persisted.

Working outside the home led to a problem inside the home: Who would take care of the children? Changing gender norms in rich countries sparked major migration streams. Jamaican and Filipino women, for example, migrated by the thousands in the 1970s and 1980s to Canada and Australia to work as nannies to raise money to send back home, where they had often left their own children. In South Africa and Brazil, local women worked as domestic servants and nannies. They were doing the jobs that once belonged to middle- and upper-class homemakers, women who now wanted the same rights as men: to parent *and* to work.

The deeply ingrained inequality between men and women prompted calls for change. Feminist movements arose mainly in Europe and North America in the 1960s, then became global in the 1970s. In 1975, the first truly international women's forum took place in Mexico City. But becoming global did not necessarily imply overturning local customs. What feminists called for was not the abolition of gender differences, but equal treatment—equal pay and equal opportunities for jobs and advancement.

Women took increasingly active stances against discrimination in government and in the workplace. Indeed, as economic integration intensified as a result of regional trade pacts (usually negotiated by men in the interest of male-owned and male-run firms), women struggled to ensure that globalization did not cut them out of new opportunities. For instance, after Argentina, Uruguay, Paraguay, and Brazil negotiated the Mercosur free trade pact, member governments built new highways and bridges, and traffic across South American borders soared. But as government efforts to foster approved trade grew, so did efforts to monitor illegal commerce. Women were responsible for one kind of illicit commerce: for generations, they had transported goods across the river separating Argentina and Paraguay. When customs officers tried to stop this practice in the mid-1990s, Argentine and Paraguayan women locked arms to occupy the new bridge that male truckers were using to ship Mercosur products, protesting the restrictions on their age-old enterprise.

The rising tide of global feminism culminated in the Fourth World Conference on Women, held in Beijing in 1995. Delegates from more than 180 governments attended the conference to produce "a platform for action" regarding women's rights in politics, business, education, and health. Alongside the official conference was the NGO Forum, a parallel conference for nearly 30,000 grassroots activists, who represented 2,000 nongovernmental organizations from every corner of the globe. Representatives planned strategies and coordinated programs for improving women's living and working conditions. What emerged from the conference were associations and groups that pledged to lobby for the rights of women and girls worldwide. One effect was to spotlight the ongoing shortage of opportunities for the advancement of women leaders.

Core Objectives

DESCRIBE how globalization and population changes affected the environment, and vice versa.

Agricultural Production The most immediate challenge facing many societies was how to feed their increasing populations. Yet changing agrarian practices resulted in a huge increase in food production. Starting in the 1950s, the "green revolution," which relied on chemical fertilizers, herbicides, and pesticides, produced dramatically larger harvests. Then, in the 1970s, biologists began developing genetically engineered crops, which multiplied yields at an even faster rate.

But these breakthroughs were not evenly distributed. American farmers, the biggest innovators, were also the greatest beneficiaries. For example, by century's end, they produced approximately one-ninth of the world's wheat and two-fifths of its corn. American exports accounted for about one-third of the world's international wheat trade and four-fifths of all corn exports. The most dramatic transformation of agriculture, however, occurred in China. Beginning in the late 1970s, the Chinese government broke up some of the old collective farms and restored the individual household as the basic economic unit in rural areas. Thereafter, agricultural output surged by roughly 9 percent per year and nearly doubled between 1978 and 1986.

While biology and chemistry allowed farmers in some countries to get more out of their land, others simply opened up new lands to cultivation. The most notorious frontier expansion occurred in the Amazon River basin. Migrants flocked to the Amazon frontier, largely from impoverished areas in northeastern Brazil. They cleared (by fire) cheap land, staked their claims, and, like nineteenth-century American homesteaders, tried to get ahead by cultivating crops and raising livestock. But the promise of bounty failed: the soils were poor and easily eroded, and land titles provided little security, especially once large speculators moved into the area. So the frontiersmen moved farther inland to repeat the cycle. By the 1980s, migrants to the Amazon River basin had burned away much of the rain forest, contaminated the environment, reduced the stock of diverse plant and animal life, and fostered social conflict in the Brazilian hinterland.

Not even "breadbasket" areas were always able to feed exploding populations. This was especially true in Africa from the 1970s onward, when domestic food production could not keep pace with population growth. (See Map 21.6.) Food shortages increased in frequency and duration, wiping out large numbers of people in sub-Saharan Africa. Children with protruding ribs became a clichéd image of the region.

What explained Africa's famines? As the Indian economist and Nobel laureate Amartya Sen observed, famines—and their increasing frequency—are not natural disasters; they are human-made. Food shortages in Africa stemmed largely from governments that ignored the rural sector and its politically unorganized farmers. Unable to persuade their governments to raise prices for their crops, the farmers lacked incentives to expand production. Food shortages were also by-products of global inequalities. At the urging of the IMF, African countries devoted hefty chunks of their economies to crops that could be exported to repay debts incurred in the 1970s. This focus left them without enough foodstuffs domestically, and thus they actually became food importers.

Natural Resources and the Environment The consumption of water, oil, and other natural resources became matters of international concern late in the twentieth century. So did pollution control and the disposal of waste products. Part of this internationalization reflected the recognition that individual nations could not solve environmental problems on their own. Air and water, after all, do not stop flowing at political boundaries.

Map 21.6 Food Consumption and Famine since the 1940s

There is perhaps no better indicator of the division of the world into rich and poor, haves and have-nots, than average food consumption and famine.

- Which parts of the world have had the most difficulty in feeding their populations?
- What have been some of the causes of famine and malnourishment in these regions?
- How much have famine and malnourishment been due to human actions, and how much to climate and other matters over which human beings have little control?

Americans consumed a disproportionate share of the world's natural resources. By 2000, they were using water at a per capita rate three times the world's average. Indeed, extensive irrigation was crucial to California's agricultural sector, the most productive and profitable in the world. And piping water to desert cities like Los Angeles allowed them to grow.

In the United States and Canada, attempts to curb energy consumption saw little success, and the United States grew more dependent on imported oil. In the late 1990s, North American demand for fuel-guzzling sport utility vehicles intensified the demand for oil imports. Dependence on foreign sources locked oil importers into recurring clashes with oil exporters.

As Canadians saw their northern lakes fill up with acid rain (precipitation laced with sulfur, mainly from coal-fired power plants), they urged their southern neighbor to curb emissions. Reciprocal agreements between Canada and the United States to cut sulfur emissions took shape in the 1980s. Europeans, also beset by acid rain, likewise negotiated regional environmental treaties. But some polluting industries simply moved overseas to poorer and less powerful nations. As the west cleaned up its environment, the rest of the world paid the price.

Other problems crossed national borders as well. These included **global warming:** increases in temperatures worldwide caused by the release of carbon into the atmosphere, mainly by the burning of fossil fuels. Global warming has the potential to change precipitation rates, sea level, and storm strength, and to shift the life cycles and migration patterns of flora and fauna—effects referred to collectively as **climate change**. International meetings in Rio de Janeiro and Kyoto in the 1990s urged restrictions on carbon emissions to avoid climate change, but a global accord proved impossible to achieve.

The response to these environmental crises has been uneven at best. Carbon emissions continued to grow with the rise in automobile traffic in cities like Tokyo, Mexico City, and Los Angeles. Where environmentalists acquired political power, they forced regulators to curb carbon emissions. But controls on emissions depended on power and wealth, for it was hard to impose restrictions in societies where high energy use seemed a necessity of economic life. Even the Japanese, pioneers of clean fuel as early as the 1960s, were polluters in other spheres long thereafter. For example, with increasing controls at home, Japanese industrialists went abroad to unload hazardous waste. U.S. industrialists did the same, sending hazardous waste to Mexico. Argentina and Canada sent their nuclear waste not abroad, but to poor provinces desperate for jobs.

At the end of the twentieth century, even though some states had enacted measures to protect the environment, global guidelines for regulating the impact of human activities on the environment had eluded the world's leaders. At the same time, inequalities between and within societies grew more pronounced. The most glaring were between the rich and poor countries, despite the well-to-do middle classes that emerged everywhere in the world and tended to congregate in the big cities.

Citizenship in the Global World

Since the nineteenth century, people had assumed that nation-states defined and protected the rights of citizens. But after the 1970s, people increasingly realized that international and supranational organizations often had more

Ecological Crisis in the Amazon Farmers and ranchers cut and burned the Amazon rain forest at a ferocious rate on frontier lands. In these remote regions, it was hard for local authorities to enforce conservation laws.

global warming
Upward temperature trends worldwide due to the release of carbon into the air, mainly by the burning of fossil fuels and other human activities.

climate change
A wide range of phenomena caused by global warming. These changes encompass not only rising temperatures, but also changes in precipitation patterns; ice mass loss on mountain glaciers around the world; shifts in the life cycles and migration patterns of flora and fauna; extreme weather events; and sea level rise.

supranational organizations

Organizations that transcend national boundaries, such as nongovernmental organizations (NGOs), the World Bank, and the International Monetary Fund (IMF).

influence over their lives than did their own national governments, especially in the developing world. However, these organizations failed to stop the violence that erupted in many regions during this period. Religion also undermined the influence of nation-states as religious groups came into conflict with one another and with secular principles.

SUPRANATIONAL ORGANIZATIONS

New organizations with goals and responsibilities that transcended national boundaries took shape after World War II for the purpose of facilitating global activities. These **supranational organizations**, which were intended to facilitate globalization and manage crisis situations, impinged on the autonomy of all but the most powerful states.

Among the most prominent supranational organizations were the World Bank and the International Monetary Fund, which provided vital economic assistance to poorer nations. The World Bank, originally named the International Bank for Reconstruction and Development, was designed primarily to provide financial assistance for big development projects. In contrast, the IMF provided funds and technical assistance to countries whose economies were in trouble. A good example of the World Bank's agenda was the financial support that it gave to the government of Ghana in the 1960s for the Volta River project, which was intended to create an electrical grid for that country. Nonetheless, both the World Bank and the IMF required that recipient governments implement far-reaching economic reforms, such as devaluation of the currency and the privatization of public-sector companies; these reforms were often deeply unpopular and led to charges that these international groups were agents of a new kind of imperialism.

Another set of supranational bodies, international nongovernmental organizations (NGOs), also stepped forward late in the twentieth century. Many championed human rights or highlighted environmental problems. Others, like the International Committee of the Red Cross, once dedicated to war relief, became more active in peacetime, sheltering survivors of natural disasters or providing food for famine victims. What united NGOs was not so much their goals, but the way they pursued them: autonomously, rather than through state power.

International NGOs reached a new level of influence in the 1970s because most nation-states at that time were still not democracies. Of the 121 countries in the world in 1980, only 37 were democracies, accounting for only 35 percent of the globe's population. People found it difficult to rely on authoritarians to uphold their rights as citizens. Indeed, despite adopting a Universal Declaration of Human Rights in 1948, the United Nations (another international organization created after World War II and intended to provide a forum for settling international problems) was a latecomer to enforcing human rights provisions, largely because its own members were the selfsame authoritarians.

NGOs, then, took the lead in trying to make the language of human rights stick. The brutality of military regimes in Latin America inspired the emerging network of international human rights organizations to take action. After the overthrow of Chile's Salvador Allende in 1973, political groups created by the Catholic Church protested the military junta's harsh repression. When the Argentine military began killing tens of thousands of innocent civilians in 1976 and news of their torture techniques leaked out, human rights organizations again took action. Prominent among them was Amnesty International. Formed in 1961 to defend prisoners of conscience (detained for their beliefs, color, sex, ethnic origin, language, or religion), Amnesty International catalogued human rights violations worldwide. By 2000, an extensive network of NGOs was informing the public, lobbying governments, and pressuring U.N. member nations to live up to commitments to respect the rights of citizens.

VIOLENCE

Supranational organizations and NGOs could play only a limited role in preserving peace and strengthening human rights. The end of the Cold War left entire regions in such turmoil that even the most effective humanitarian agencies could not prevent mass killings.

Consider the Balkans in the 1990s. In the territorial remains of Yugoslavia, groups of Serbs, Croats, Bosnians, ethnic Albanians, and others fought for control. Former neighbors, fueled by opportunistic leaders' rhetoric, no longer saw themselves as citizens of diverse political communities. Instead, demagogues trumpeted the superiority of ethnically defined states. Ethnic Serbians took up arms against their Croat neighbors, and vice versa. When international agencies moved in to try to bolster public authority, they failed, and Yugoslavia's ethnic mosaic imploded into civil war and ethnic cleansing.

Some of the most gruesome scenes of political violence occurred in Africa, where many nation-states struggled to uphold the rule of law for all citizens. Here, tension often erupted into conflict between ethnic groups. The failure of African agriculture to sustain growing populations, as well as unequal access to resources like education, made ethnic rivalries worse. Droughts, famine, and corruption fanned the rivalries into riots and killings—even into bitter civil wars and the breakdown of centralized authority.

Events in Rwanda reflected Africa's horrifying experience with political violence. Friction grew between the majority Hutus (agrarian people, often

Rwandan Refugees Perhaps as many as 800,000 Tutsis were killed in Rwanda in 1994 as the Hutu leadership turned against the country's Tutsi population.

very poor) and the minority Tutsis (herders, often with better education, wealthier, and chosen by the Belgians to rule over the Hutus) after the two peoples had intermarried and lived side by side for many generations. Some resentful Hutus blamed the Tutsis for all their woes. As tensions mounted, the United Nations dispatched peacekeeping troops. Moderate Hutus urged continued peaceful coexistence, only to be shouted down by government forces in command of radio stations and a mass propaganda machine. Although alerted to the impending problem, U.N. forces, fearing a clash and uncertain of their mandate, failed to prevent the violence.

The failure on the part of the international community, including the United States, which did not have troops on the ground and which had no clear policy toward Rwanda, gave the Hutu government a green light to wipe out its opponents. In 100 days of carnage in 1994, Hutu militias massacred 800,000 Tutsis and moderate Hutus. This was not, as many proclaimed, the militarization of ancient ethnic rivalries, for many Hutus were butchered as they tried to defend Tutsi friends, relatives, and neighbors. Meanwhile, the ensuing refugee crisis destabilized neighboring countries. The Rwanda genocide sent riptides across eastern and central Africa, creating a whole new generation of conflicts. This catastrophe is the starkest example of the failure of supranational organizations to deal with a crisis before it mushroomed into a genocide. Elsewhere, in famine areas and big development projects, supranational relief agencies enjoyed more success.

Some societies tried to put political violence behind them. In Argentina, El Salvador, Guatemala, and South Africa, the transition to democracy compelled elected rulers to establish commissions to inquire into past rulers' human rights abuses. These **truth commissions** were vital for creating a new aura of legitimacy for democracies and for promising to uphold the rights of individuals. In South Africa, many blacks backed the new president, Nelson Mandela, but also demanded a reckoning with the punitive experience of the apartheid past. To avoid a backlash against the former white rulers, the South African leadership opted to record the past events rather than avenge them. The long-term consequences of these efforts to address violent atrocities remain uncertain.

truth commissions
Commissions established to inquire into human rights abuses by previous regimes. In Argentina, El Salvador, Guatemala, and South Africa, these commissions were vital for creating a new aura of legitimacy for democracies and for promising to uphold the rights of individuals.

RELIGIOUS FOUNDATIONS OF POLITICS

Secular concerns for human rights and international peace were not the only foundations for politics after the Cold War. In many regions, people wanted religion to define the moral fabric of political communities. Very often, religion provided a way to reimagine the nation-state just as globalization was undermining national autonomy.

Hindu Nationalism In India, Hindu nationalism offered a communal identity for a country being rapidly transformed by globalization. In the 1980s, India freed market forces, privatized state firms, and withdrew from its role as welfare provider. Economic reforms under the ruling Congress Party sparked economic growth, thereby creating one of Asia's largest, best-educated, and most affluent middle classes. But because these changes also widened the gap between rich and poor, lower classes and castes formed political parties to challenge the traditional elites. With established hierarchies and loyalties eroding, Hindu nationalists argued that religion could now fill the role once occupied by a secular state. Claiming that the ideology of *Hindutva* (Hinduness) would bring the help that secular nationalism had failed to give, Hindu militants trumpeted the idea of India as a nation of Hindus (the majority), with minorities relegated to a lesser status. The chief beneficiary of the politics established by economic liberalization was a Hindu nationalist party, the Bharatiya Janata Party (BJP), or Indian People's Party. It was the political arm of an alliance of Hindu organizations devoted to establishing India as a Hindu state. In 1998 a BJP coalition came to power and sought to transform the nation-state into a moral community, but without challenging the economic forces of globalization.

Islamic Conservatism In some cases, religion provided a way to resist seemingly American-dominated globalization. One of the most spirited challenges arose in the Islamic Middle East, where many people believed that modernizing and westernizing programs were leading their societies toward rampant materialism and unchecked individualism. Critics included both traditional clerics and young western-educated elites whose job prospects seemed bleak and who felt that the promise of modernization had failed. Having criticized modernizing processes since the nineteenth century, Islamic conservatives flourished once more in the 1970s as global markets and social tensions undermined secular leadership.

The most revolutionary Islamic movement arose in Iran, where clerics forced the shah, the country's ruler, from power in 1979. The revolt pitted a group of religious officials possessing only pamphlets, tracts, and tapes against the military arsenal and the vast intelligence apparatus of the Iranian state. Shah Mohammad Reza Pahlavi had enjoyed U.S. technical and military support since the Americans helped place him on the throne in 1953. His bloated army and police force, as well as his brutally effective intelligence service, had crushed all challenges to his authority. The shah had also benefited from oil revenues, which soared after 1973. Yet the uneven distribution of income, the oppressive police state, and the royal family's ostentatious lifestyle fueled widespread discontent.

The most powerful critique came from the mullahs (Muslim scholars or religious teachers), who found in the Ayatollah Ruhollah Khomeini a courageous leader. Khomeini used his traditional Islamic education and his training in Muslim ethics to accuse the shah's government of gross violations of Islamic norms. He also identified the shah's ally, America, as the Great Satan. With opposition to his rule mounting, the shah fled the country in 1979. In his wake, Khomeini established a theocratic state ruled by a council of Islamic clerics. Although some Iranians grumbled about aspects of this return to Islam, they prided themselves on having inspired a revolution based on principles other than those drawn from the west.

Religious Conservatism in the United States The search for religious foundations for politics in the global age reached into western societies. Indeed, in the United States, religion became a potent force after the 1970s as the membership and activism of conservative, fundamentalist Protestant churches eclipsed that of mainstream denominations. Insisting on a literal interpretation of the Bible, Protestant fundamentalists argued against secularizing trends in American society. This traditionalist crusade took up a broad range of cultural and political issues. Religious conservatives (predominantly evangelical Protestants, but also some Catholics and Orthodox Jews) attacked many of the social changes that had emerged from the liberation movements of the 1960s. Shifting sexual and familial relations were sore points, but the religious conservatives especially targeted public leaders who, they felt, had abandoned the moral purpose of authority by legalizing abortion and supporting secular values.

Tiananmen Square
Largest public square in the world and site of the pro-democracy demonstrations in 1989 that ended with the killing of as many as a thousand protesters by the Chinese army.

ACCEPTANCE OF AND RESISTANCE TO DEMOCRACY

New sources of power and new social movements drastically changed politics in the global age. Increasingly, supranational organizations were decisive in defining the conditions of democratic citizenship. Perhaps most remarkable was how much democracy spread toward the end of the twentieth century. In South Africa, Russia, and Guatemala, elections now decided politicians' fates. In this sense, the world's societies embraced the idea that people had a right to choose their own representatives. Nevertheless, democracy did not triumph everywhere.

An important holdout was China. Mao Zedong died in 1976, and within a few years, his successor, Deng Xiaoping, opened the nation's economy to market forces. But Deng and other Chinese Communist Party leaders resisted multiparty competition. Instead of turning to capitalism and western-style democracy, they maintained that China should follow its own path to modernity. By the late 1980s, economic reforms had produced spectacular increases in production and rising standards of living for most of China's people. But the widening gap between rich and poor, together with increasing public awareness of corruption within the party and the government, triggered popular discontent. Worker strikes and slowdowns, peasant unrest, and student activism spread.

On April 22, 1989, some 100,000 people gathered in **Tiananmen Square** at the heart of Beijing in silent defiance of a government ban on assembling. The regime responded by declaring martial law. Two huge protest demonstrations followed, and residents erected barricades to defend the city against government troops. As the protest's momentum waned, a twenty-eight-foot icon, partly inspired by the Statue of Liberty, was unveiled at the square, capturing the imagination of the crowd and the attention of the cameras. But by then the government had assembled troops to crush the movement. In a night of terror that began at dusk on June 3, the People's Liberation Army turned its guns against the people. Estimates of the death toll range from hundreds into the thousands.

In Mexico, democracy finally triumphed, as the single party that had dominated the country for seventy-one years fell after the election of Vicente

Tiananmen Square This white plaster and Styrofoam statue, inspired in part by the Statue of Liberty and dubbed the Goddess of Democracy, was created by students in Beijing in the spring of 1989. It was brought to Tiananmen Square and unveiled at the end of May in an attempt to reinvigorate the democracy movement and the spirits of the protesters. For five days it captured worldwide attention, until it was toppled by a tank on June 4 and crushed as the Chinese People's Liberation Army cleared the square of its democracy advocates.

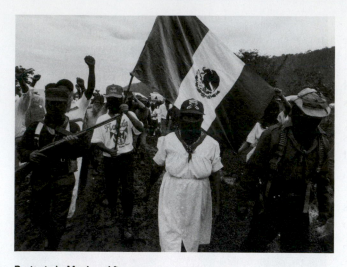

Protests in Mexico After generations of oppression and exclusion, peasants of Chiapas, in southern Mexico, called for democracy and respect for their right to land. When Mexican authorities refused to bend, peasants took up arms. While they knew that they posed no military threat to the Mexican army, the Zapatista rebels used the world media and international organizations to embarrass the national political establishment into allowing reforms.

Fox in 2000. Until that time, Mexican rulers had combined patronage and rigged elections to stay in office. By the 1980s, corruption and abuse permeated the system. The abuse of democratic rights fell hardest on poor communities, especially those with large numbers of indigenous people.

These events in Mexico, South Africa, and China showed that men and women in every corner of the earth yearned to choose their own leaders. In 1994, millions of previously disenfranchised South Africans lined up for hours to cast a vote for their new black African president, Nelson Mandela. That same year, Zapatista rebels drew worldwide attention to the plight of poor indigenous communities when militants occupied six towns in central and eastern Chiapas, Mexico, to protest the North American Free Trade Agreement. In China, the ruling Communist Party had to call in the army to prevent regime change and democratic reforms.

Conclusion

In the thirteenth century (and long before), a few travelers like Ibn Battuta and Marco Polo ventured over long distances to trade, to explore, and to convert souls; yet communications technology was rudimentary, making long-distance mobility and exchange expensive, rare, and perilous. The world was much more a series of communities set apart than a world bound together by culture, capital, and communications networks.

By the late twentieth century, that balance had changed. Food, entertainment, clothing, and even family life were becoming more similar worldwide. To be sure, some local differences remained. In 2000, local cultures lived on, and in some cases were revived, through challenges to the authority of nation-states. No longer did the nation-state or any single level of community life define collective identities. At the same time, worldwide purveyors of cultural and commercial resources offered all local communities the same kinds of products, from aspirin to Nike shoes. Exchanges across local and national boundaries became easier. For the first time, many of the world's peoples felt they belonged to a global culture.

New technologies, new methods of production and investment, and the greater importance of personal health and education created new possibilities—and greater inequalities. Indeed, the gaps between haves and have-nots in 2000 were astonishing. For as humanity harnessed new technologies to accelerate exchanges across and within cultures, an ever-larger gulf separated those who participated in global networks from those on the margins. This inequality produced a range of different political and cultural forms after the collapse of the three-world order. Thus, as the world became more integrated, it also grew apart along ever-deeper lines.

TRACING THE GLOBAL STORYLINES

Focus On
Globalization

Removing Obstacles to Globalization

- Communism's fall and the end of the Cold War improve prospects for global exchange of peoples, ideas, and resources.

- Final decolonization in Angola, Mozambique, and Guinea-Bissau and the end of apartheid in South Africa return self-rule throughout Africa.

Unleashing Globalization

- Financial deregulation and the end of the gold standard allow money to move freely across borders but lead to a Third World debt crisis.

- Widespread migrations occur as people in Africa, Asia, and Latin America move to Europe and America, following the tracks of their former colonizers.

- Revolutions in culture and communications make cultural diversity more possible for those who can afford it.

The New Global Order

- Globalization leads to dramatic population expansion, requiring greater agricultural and industrial output.

- Family structure changes, life spans increase, and more goods are available, yet inequalities deepen as education and good health determine social status as never before.

- As globalization erodes the power of the nation-state, greater violence occurs between and within states. Nongovernmental organizations (NGOs) and religion become resources for dealing with violence and inequality and for reimagining the nation-state.

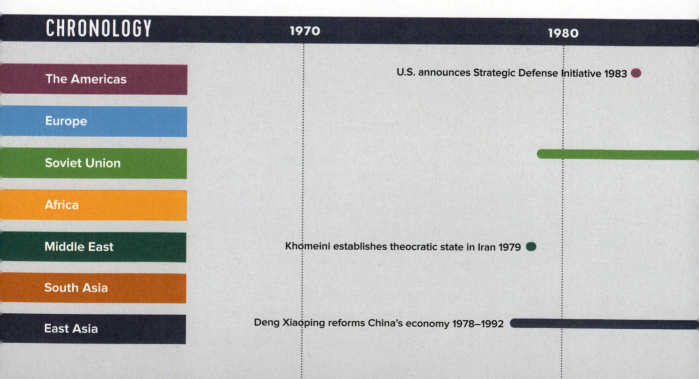

CHRONOLOGY

	1970	1980
The Americas		U.S. announces Strategic Defense Initiative 1983 ●
Europe		
Soviet Union		
Africa		
Middle East	Khomeini establishes theocratic state in Iran 1979 ●	
South Asia		
East Asia	Deng Xiaoping reforms China's economy 1978–1992	

- **Thinking about Worlds Together, Worlds Apart and Globalization** How did globalization shape patterns of inequality? After the Cold War, trade, migration, and communications reshaped the terms on which peoples interacted with one another around the world. Industry, agriculture, culture, and the arts all linked peoples and regions together in different ways. Consider differences in all these domains. What kinds of inequalities were most significant?

- **Thinking about Changing Power Relationships and Globalization** What kind of resistance movements did globalization generate, both within the world's wealthiest societies and elsewhere? How did the feminist, labor, and environmental reform movements resemble

and differ from their predecessors? How did Hindu nationalism and religious conservatism differ from each other and from earlier nationalist and religious or pan movements?

- **Thinking about Environmental Impacts and Globalization** Explain the relationship between globalization, climate change, and the environment. The consumption of water, oil, and other natural resources became major national and international issues in this period. How did the organization of agricultural and industrial production change, and what influence did those changes have on global warming, acid rain, and pollution? Identify efforts to limit damage to the environment and evaluate their success.

Key Terms

climate change p. 1013

developing world p. 993

European Union (EU) p. 995

globalization p. 986

global warming p. 1013

HIV/AIDS p. 1007

Nelson Mandela p. 993

supranational organizations p. 1014

Tiananmen Square p. 1018

truth commissions p. 1017

Go to **INQUIZITIVE** to see what you've learned—and learn what you've missed—with personalized feedback along the way.

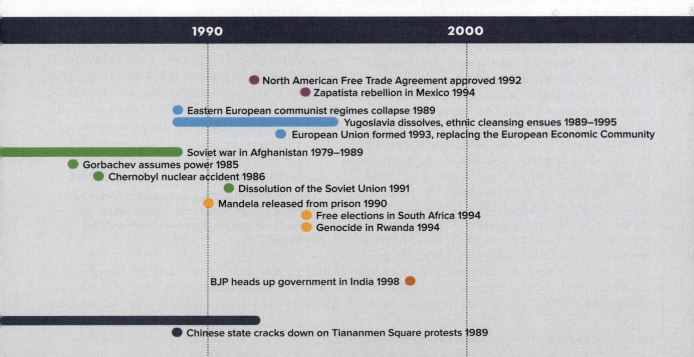

1990

2000

North American Free Trade Agreement approved 1992
Zapatista rebellion in Mexico 1994

Eastern European communist regimes collapse 1989
Yugoslavia dissolves, ethnic cleansing ensues 1989–1995
European Union formed 1993, replacing the European Economic Community

Soviet war in Afghanistan 1979–1989
Gorbachev assumes power 1985
Chernobyl nuclear accident 1986
Dissolution of the Soviet Union 1991
Mandela released from prison 1990
Free elections in South Africa 1994
Genocide in Rwanda 1994

BJP heads up government in India 1998

Chinese state cracks down on Tiananmen Square protests 1989

Global Themes and Sources

Comparing the Power of Grassroots Democracies

Despite the enormous economic and technological advances of the past 200 years, famine and dire poverty remain problems in many places. These problems have been particularly severe where unrepresentative, authoritarian leaders prevent foreign aid from reaching the needy and ordinary people from achieving self-sufficiency. Self-sufficiency has been further undermined by pervasive discrimination against women, which has limited their access to education and has therefore compromised economic growth for everyone, men and women alike.

Written by a dissident dramatist (and future politician) in 1978, the first document, excerpted from a long essay in political philosophy, explores the possibility for individuals to maintain their independence and dignity, and ultimately to undermine the communist dictatorships of eastern Europe. In the second document, from the General Council of the Zapatista Army for National Liberation (EZLN), a group of mostly Amerindians living in a jungle region in Chiapas, Mexico, seeks international support for its conflict with Mexican authorities. In the third, researchers for the World Bank report that better education, and especially better education for girls, improves economic development among the poor. The final selection, from economist and Nobel laureate Amartya Sen (1933–), argues that no major famine has occurred in a democratic country with a free press.

The selections presented here all call attention to the importance of grassroots democracy and equality in responding to political, economic, and ecological disasters and achieving at least a measure of autonomy. They raise big questions about the nature and location of power and the possibility of change. While there is an important comparative dimension to these selections—each understands the promise of grassroots democracy differently—they are all the product of a common context, a common reaction against monolithic, authoritarian forms of rule. Collectively, they call for both comparison and contextualization.

Analyzing the Power of Grassroots Democracies Comparatively and Contextually

- On what basis do the authors of these documents claim authority? In whose name do they speak? What goals do they seek to attain?

- What does justice mean from the perspectives of these four documents? Do the authors agree or disagree on what is just?

- What is the relationship between individual and collective rights in these documents? To what degree does each text consider individual liberties essential or harmful to the common good? Pay special attention to differences between the first document and the next three.

PRIMARY SOURCE 21.1

"The Power of the Powerless" (1978), Václav Havel

Václav Havel (1936–2011) was a Czech dramatist, founder of Charter 77, a civic initiative under communism (1976–1982) that defended human rights, and president of Czechoslovakia (1989–1992) and then the Czech Republic (1993–2003). His essay *The Power of the Powerless*, originally written in 1978, provided a model of what he called "living within the truth," a form of resistance against communism.

- What does Havel mean by "living within the truth"?
- Explain the significance of law in this document.
- Compare this selection with Friedrich Engels' and Karl Marx's *Bourgeoisie and Proletariat* (16.5). Is Havel's view of politics compatible with the manifesto?

A spectre is haunting eastern Europe: the spectre of what in the West is called "dissent." This spectre has not appeared out of thin air. It is a natural and inevitable consequence of the present historical phase of the system it is haunting. It was born at a time when this system, for a thousand reasons, can no longer base itself on the unadulterated, brutal, and arbitrary application of power, eliminating all expressions of nonconformity. What is more, the system has become so ossified politically that there is practically no way for such nonconformity to be implemented within its official structures.

***

And so the post-totalitarian system behaved in a characteristic way: it defended the integrity of the world of appearances in order to defend itself. For the crust presented by the life of lies is made of strange stuff. As long as it seals off hermetically the entire society, it appears to be made of stone. But the moment someone breaks through in one place, when one person cries out, "The emperor is naked!"—when a single person breaks the rules of the game, thus exposing it as a game—everything suddenly appears in another light and the whole crust seems then to be made of a tissue on the point of tearing and disintegrating uncontrollably.

When I speak of living within the truth, I naturally do not have in mind only products of conceptual thought, such as a protest or a letter written by a group of intellectuals. It can be any means by which a person or a group revolts against manipulation: anything from a letter by intellectuals to a workers' strike, from a rock concert to a student demonstration, from refusing to vote in the farcical elections, to making an open speech at some official congress, or even a hunger strike, for instance. If the suppression of the aims of life is a complex process, and if it is based on the multifaceted manipulation of all expressions of life, then, by the same token, every free expression of life indirectly threatens the post-totalitarian system politically, including forms of expression to which, in other social systems, no one would attribute any potential political significance, not to mention explosive power.

***

Like ideology, the legal code is an essential instrument of ritual communication outside the power structure. It is the legal code that gives the exercise of power a form, a framework, a set of rules. It is the legal code that enables all components of the system to communicate, to put themselves in a good light, to establish their own legitimacy. It provides their whole game with its "rules" and engineers with their technology. Can the exercise of post-totalitarian power be imagined at all without this universal ritual making it all possible, serving as a common language to bind the relevant sectors of the power structure together? The more important the position occupied by the repressive apparatus in the power structure, the more important that it functions according to some kind of formal code. . . .

If the exercise of power circulates through the whole power structure as blood flows through veins, then the legal code can be understood as something that reinforces the walls of those veins. Without it, the blood of power could not circulate in an organized way and the body of society would haemorrhage at random. Order would collapse.

A persistent and never-ending appeal to the laws—not just to the laws concerning human rights, but to all laws—does not mean at all that those who do so have succumbed to the illusion that in our system the law is anything other than what it is. They are well aware of the role it plays. But precisely because they know how desperately the system depends on it—on the "noble" version of the law, that is—they also know how enormously significant such appeals are. Because the system cannot do without the law, because it is hopelessly tied down by the necessity of pretending the laws are observed, it is compelled to react in some way to such appeals. Demanding that the laws be upheld is thus an act of living within the truth that threatens the whole mendacious structure at its point of maximum mendacity.

Over and over again, such appeals make the purely ritualistic nature of the law clear to society and to those who inhabit its power structures. They draw attention to its real material substance and thus, indirectly, compel all those who take refuge behind the law to affirm and make credible this agency of excuses, this means of communication, this reinforcement of the social arteries outside of which their will could not be made to circulate through society. They are compelled to do so for the sake of their own consciences, for the impression they make on outsiders, to maintain themselves in power (as part of the system's own mechanism of self-preservation and its principles of cohesion), or simply out of fear that they will be reproached for being "clumsy" in handling the ritual. They have no other choice: because they cannot discard the rules of their own game, they can only attend more carefully to those rules.

***

Hope for those who would liberate themselves, therefore, lies in a symbiosis of the moral and the social, of humanity and democracy, in the realization of a social order in which the formalized and functionalized structure of society will be regulated and controlled by this "newly discovered" spontaneous civic activity, which will be a permanent and essential source of social self-awareness, while the bureaucracies ruling society shrink to assume merely compliant executive roles.

Source: Václav Havel, "The Power of the Powerless," in *The Power of the Powerless: Citizens against the State in Central-Eastern Europe*, ed. John Keane (Armonk, NY: M. E. Sharpe, 1985), 23, 42–43, 74–77, 108–109.

PRIMARY SOURCE 21.2

Declaration of War against the Mexican Government (1993), EZLN

The Zapatista Army of National Liberation (EZLN) is a revolutionary political organization based in Chiapas, the southernmost state in Mexico. On January 1, 1994, it took up arms against the government, calling for a restoration of the principles of the Mexican Revolution and protesting the confiscation of poor people's land rights. This document, released in 1993, issues a call to arms.

- The document opens, "We are a product of 500 years of struggle." Who is "we"? Who does the document include as insiders, and whom—whether individuals or broad social forces—does it exclude?

- On what basis do the authors speak for the nation?

- What is the relationship between this declaration and the rule of law? Do the authors claim to uphold the law, or do they reject it and seek to overthrow it?

To the People of Mexico: Mexican Brothers and Sisters:

We are a product of 500 years of struggle: first against slavery, then during the War of Independence against Spain led by insurgents, then to avoid being absorbed by North American imperialism, then to promulgate our constitution and expel the French empire from our soil, and later the dictatorship of Porfirio Diaz denied us the just application of the Reform laws and the people rebelled and leaders like Villa and Zapata emerged, poor men just like us. We have been denied the most elemental preparation so they can use us as cannon fodder and pillage the wealth of our country. They don't care that we have nothing, absolutely nothing, not even a roof over our heads, no land, no work, no health care, no food nor education. Nor are we able to freely and democratically elect our political representatives, nor is there independence from foreigners, nor is there peace nor justice for ourselves and our children.

But today, we say ENOUGH IS ENOUGH.

We are the inheritors of the true builders of our nation. The dispossessed, we are millions and we thereby call upon our brothers and sisters to join this struggle as the only path, so that we will not die of hunger due to the insatiable ambition of a 70 year dictatorship led by a clique of traitors that represent the most conservative and sell-out groups. They are the same ones that opposed Hidalgo and Morelos, the same ones that betrayed Vicente Guerrero, the same ones that sold half our country to the foreign invader, the same ones that imported a European prince to rule our country, the same ones that formed the "scientific" Porfirista dictatorship, the same ones that opposed the Petroleum Expropriation, the same ones that massacred the railroad workers in 1958 and the students in 1968, the same ones [that] today take everything from us, absolutely everything.

To prevent the continuation of the above and as our last hope, after having tried to utilize all legal means based on our Constitution, we go to our Constitution, to apply Article 39 which says:

> "National Sovereignty essentially and originally resides in the people. All political power emanates

from the people and its purpose is to help the people. The people have, at all times, the inalienable right to alter or modify their form of government."

Therefore, according to our constitution, we declare the following to the Mexican federal army, the pillar of the Mexican dictatorship that we suffer from, monopolized by a one-party system and led by Carlos Salinas de Gortari, the maximum and illegitimate federal executive that today holds power.

According to this Declaration of War, we ask that other powers of the nation advocate to restore the legitimacy and the stability of the nation by overthrowing the dictator.

We also ask that international organizations and the International Red Cross watch over and regulate our battles, so that our efforts are carried out while still protecting our civilian population. We declare now and always that we are subject to the Geneva Accord, forming the EZLN as our fighting arm of our liberation struggle. We have the Mexican people on our side, we have the beloved tri-colored flag highly respected by our insurgent fighters. We use black and red in our uniform as our symbol of our working people on strike. Our flag carries the following letters, "EZLN," Zapatista National Liberation Army, and we always carry our flag into combat.

Beforehand, we refuse any effort to disgrace our just cause by accusing us of being drug traffickers, drug guerrillas, thieves, or other names that might be used by our enemies. Our struggle follows the constitution which is held high by its call for justice and equality.

Therefore, according to this declaration of war, we give our military forces, the EZLN, the following orders:

First: Advance to the capital of the country, overcoming the Mexican federal army, protecting in our advance the civilian population and permitting the people in the liberated area the right to freely and democratically elect their own administrative authorities.

Second: Respect the lives of our prisoners and turn over all wounded to the International Red Cross.

Third: Initiate summary judgments against all soldiers of the Mexican federal army and the political police that have received training or have been paid by foreigners, accused of being traitors to our country, and against all those that have repressed and treated badly the civil population and robbed or stolen from or attempted crimes against the good of the people.

Fourth: Form new troops with all those Mexicans that show their interest in joining our struggle, including those that, being enemy soldiers, turn themselves in without having fought against us, and promise to take orders from the General Command of the Zapatista National Liberation Army.

Fifth: We ask for the unconditional surrender of the enemy's headquarters before we begin any combat to avoid any loss of lives.

Sixth: Suspend the robbery of our natural resources in the areas controlled by the EZLN.

To the People of Mexico: We, the men and women, full and free, are conscious that the war that we have declared is our last resort, but also a just one. The dictators are applying an undeclared genocidal war against our people for many years. Therefore we ask for your participation, your decision to support this plan that struggles for work, land, housing, food, health care, education, independence, freedom, democracy, justice and peace. We declare that we will not stop fighting until the basic demands of our people have been met by forming a government of our country that is free and democratic.

Join the Insurgent Forces of the Zapatista National Liberation Army.

General Command of the EZLN
1993

Source: "First Declaration from the Lacandon Jungle," http://struggle.ws /mexico/ezln/ezlnwa.html (http://struggle.ws/mexico.html).

PRIMARY SOURCE 21.3

Why Gender Matters (2000), World Bank

The *World Development Report* is an annual report published since 1978 by the International Bank for Reconstruction and Development. The report for 2000–2001, which included this selection, was devoted to the topic "Attacking Poverty."

- Describe the effect of tuition on girls' school attendance.
- Evaluate the relative importance of barriers to girls' education posed by culture on the one hand and poverty on the other.
- What effect does expanding educational opportunity for girls have on boys?

Using Subsidies to Close Gender Gaps in Education

Evaluations of recent initiatives that subsidize the costs of schooling indicate that demand-side interventions can increase girls' enrollments and close gender gaps in education. A school stipend program established in Bangladesh in 1982 subsidizes various school expenses for girls who enroll in secondary school. In the first program evaluation girls' enrollment rate in the pilot areas rose from 27 percent, similar to the national average, to 44 percent over five years, more than twice the national average. After girls' tuition was eliminated nationwide in 1992 and the stipend program was expanded to all rural areas, girls' enrollment rate climbed to 48 percent at the national level. There have also been gains in the number of girls appearing for exams and in women's enrollments at intermediate colleges. While boys' enrollment rates also rose during this period, they did not rise as quickly as girls'.

Two recent programs in Balochistan, Pakistan, illustrate the potential benefits of reducing costs and improving physical access. Before the projects there were questions about whether girls' low enrollments were due to cultural barriers that cause parents to hold their daughters out of school or to inadequate supply of appropriate schools. Program evaluations suggest that improved physical access, subsidized costs, and culturally appropriate design can sharply increase girls' enrollments.

The first program, in Quetta, the capital of Balochistan, uses a subsidy tied to girls' enrollment to support the creation of schools in poor urban neighborhoods by local NGOs. The schools admit boys as long as they make up less than half of total enrollments. In rural Balochistan the second program has been expanding the supply of local, single-sex primary schools for girls by encouraging parental involvement in establishing the schools and by subsidizing the recruitment of female teachers from the local community. The results: girls' enrollments rose 33 percent in Quetta and 22 percent in rural areas. Interestingly, both programs appear to have also expanded boys' enrollments, suggesting that increasing girls' educational opportunities may have spillover benefits for boys.

Source: The World Bank, from "Using subsidies to close gender gaps in education," World Bank. 2001. *World Development Report 2000–2001: Attacking Poverty*, p. 122, Box 7.2. © World Bank. http://openknowledge.worldbank.org/handle/10986/11856 License: Creative Commons Attribution license (CC BY 3.0).

"Democracy as a Universal Value" (1999), Amartya Sen

This selection is drawn from Sen's work on the economics and politics of famines as well as political philosophy. In many famines, Sen has shown, food supplies remained adequate, while unemployment, rising prices, and unresponsive governments led to catastrophe. The current selection comes from a keynote address delivered in New Delhi, titled "Building a Worldwide Movement for Democracy."

- What does Sen mean by democracy?
- What, according to Sen, is the relationship between democracy and economic dynamism?
- Explain the significance of famines to Sen's argument.

In the summer of 1997, I was asked by a leading Japanese newspaper what I thought was the most important thing that had happened in the twentieth century. . . .

I did not, ultimately, have any difficulty in choosing one as the preeminent development of the period: the rise of democracy.

***

It is often claimed that nondemocratic systems are better at bringing about economic development. This belief sometimes goes by the name of "the Lee hypothesis," due to its advocacy by Lee Kuan Yew, the leader and former president of Singapore. He is certainly right that some disciplinarian states (such as South Korea, his own Singapore, and postreform China) have had faster rates of economic growth than many less authoritarian ones (including India, Jamaica, and Costa Rica). The "Lee hypothesis," however, is based on sporadic empiricism, drawing on very selective and limited information, rather than on any general statistical testing over the wide-ranging data that are available. A general relation of this kind cannot be established on the basis of very selective evidence. For example, we cannot really take the high economic growth of Singapore or China as "definitive proof" that authoritarianism does better in promoting economic growth, any more than we can draw the opposite conclusion from the fact that Botswana, the country with the best record of economic growth in Africa, indeed with one of the finest records of economic growth in the whole world, has been an oasis of democracy on that continent over the decades. We need more systematic empirical studies to sort out the claims and counterclaims.

There is, in fact, no convincing general evidence that authoritarian governance and the suppression of political and civil rights are really beneficial to economic development. Indeed, the general statistical picture does not permit any such induction. . . . The directional linkage seems to depend on many other circumstances, and while some statistical investigations note a weakly negative relation, others find a strongly positive one. If all the comparative studies are viewed together, the hypothesis that there is no clear relation between economic growth and democracy in *either* direction remains extremely plausible. Since democracy and political liberty have importance in themselves, the case for them therefore remains untarnished. . . .

We must go beyond the narrow confines of economic growth and scrutinize the broader demands of economic development, including the need for economic and social security. In that context, we have to look at the connection between political and civil rights, on the one hand, and the prevention of major economic disasters, on the other. Political and civil rights give people the opportunity to draw attention forcefully to general needs and to demand appropriate public action. The response of a government to the acute suffering of its people often depends on the pressure that is put on it. The exercise of political rights (such as voting, criticizing, protesting, and the like) can make a real difference to the political incentives that operate on a government.

I have discussed elsewhere the remarkable fact that, in the terrible history of famines in the world, no substantial famine has ever occurred in any independent and democratic country with a relatively free press. We cannot find exceptions to this rule, no matter where we look: the recent famines of Ethiopia, Somalia, or other dictatorial regimes; famines in the Soviet Union in the 1930s; China's 1958–61 famine with the failure of the Great Leap Forward; or earlier still, the famines in Ireland or India under alien rule. China, although it was in many ways doing much better economically than India, still managed (unlike India) to have a famine, indeed the largest recorded famine in world history: Nearly 30 million people died in the famine of 1958–61, while faulty governmental policies remained uncorrected for three full years. The policies went uncriticized because there were no opposition parties in parliament, no free press, and no multiparty elections. Indeed, it is precisely this lack of challenge that allowed the deeply defective policies to continue even though they were killing millions each year. The same can be said about the world's two contemporary famines, occurring right now in North Korea and Sudan.

Famines are often associated with what look like natural disasters, and commentators often settle for the simplicity of explaining famines by pointing to these events: the floods in China during the failed Great Leap Forward, the droughts in Ethiopia, or crop failures in North Korea. Nevertheless, many countries with similar natural problems, or even worse ones, manage perfectly well, because a responsive government intervenes to help alleviate hunger. Since the primary victims of a famine are the indigent, deaths can be prevented by recreating incomes (for example, through employment programs), which makes food accessible to potential famine victims. Even the poorest democratic countries that have faced terrible droughts or floods or other natural disasters (such as India in 1973, or Zimbabwe and Botswana in the early 1980s) have been able to feed their people without experiencing a famine.

Famines are easy to prevent if there is a serious effort to do so, and a democratic government, facing elections and criticisms from opposition parties and independent newspapers, cannot help but make such an effort. Not surprisingly, while India continued to have famines under British rule right up to independence (the last famine, which I witnessed as a child, was in 1943, four years before independence), they disappeared suddenly with the establishment of a multiparty democracy and a free press. . . .

The issue of famine is only one example of the reach of democracy, though it is, in many ways, the easiest case to analyze. The positive role of political and civil rights applies to the prevention of economic and social disasters in general. When things go fine and everything is routinely good, this instrumental role of democracy may not be particularly missed. It is when things get fouled up, for one reason or another, that the political incentives provided by democratic governance acquire great practical value.

Source: Amartya Sen, "Democracy as a Universal Value," *Journal of Democracy* 10, no. 3 (1999): 3–17, pp. 3, 6–9.

Interpreting Visual Evidence

Chimerica

The term "Chimerica" refers to the idea that the People's Republic of China and the United States of America make up a single, dominant economic entity. It was coined by the historian Niall Ferguson and the economist Moritz Schularick to describe the interdependent relationship that began in the last two decades of the twentieth century and has extended into the first decades of the twenty-first century. China began to open its economy in the early 1980s, and its exports of manufactured goods, especially to the United States—which rose from $51.5 billion in 1996 to $102 billion in 2001—eventually fueled the world economy. Combined, the two countries make up roughly 13 percent of the world's land surface, a quarter of its population, more than a third of its economic production, and, by some estimates, nearly half of all economic growth in the first decade of the new millennium. Chimerica is also a play on the word *chimera*: a fire-breathing female monster in Greek mythology, or an unrealizable dream, an illusion.

Modern Beijing.

Foxconn factory with suicide nets.

Retirement community near Phoenix, Arizona.

Walmart Supercenter.

Like Japan and Germany after World War II, China in this period concentrated on export-led industrial growth. But unlike those countries, China refused to let workers' wages rise as the economy grew, and its leaders refused to apply international standards to workplace safety, intellectual property, or environmental protections. In developed economies, where those protections applied and wages were higher, production costs were higher. As a result, competition from China cost millions of jobs in developed countries, including 2.9 million jobs in the United States alone from 2001 to 2012. Chinese leaders instead invested the surplus revenues abroad, mostly in the United States, where the influx of Chinese investment kept interest rates low. U.S. consumers used the resulting easy credit to purchase homes, cars, and goods like tablets and mobile phones, many of them manufactured in China.

The images presented here portray different aspects of what Ferguson and Schularick call Chimerica. The first shows modern Beijing, with massive new buildings, roadways, and smog; it shows both the robust growth of the Chinese economy—notice how new the buildings are—and its environmental costs. The second photograph shows protective nets around a factory run by Foxconn, one of Apple's leading suppliers in China, after a series of suicides in 2010 drew world attention to the company's labor practices. This image reflects some of the dire costs of producing consumer goods at low prices. The third image shows a massive retirement community near Phoenix, Arizona, filled with homes purchased at low interest rates, thanks to Chinese investment. The fourth image shows a Walmart superstore in Albany, New York, filled with inexpensive goods, many of them produced in China. Such "big-box" retail stores provide many jobs, but at much lower wages than the industrial jobs that

have disappeared. The final image shows an unofficial Apple store in Tehran, Iran; it shows the dominance of global brands for Chinese-made consumer items.

Unofficial Apple Store in Tehran.

Questions for Analysis

1. Explain the relationship between China and the United States presented by these images. How has each country benefited from this relationship, and what sacrifices has each made?

2. Looking at the first two images, identify the sacrifices ordinary Chinese people have made as a result of the policies that enabled their country to invest in the United States. What group or groups in China do you think benefited from these policies, and how?

3. With the second, third, and fourth images in mind, analyze the tradeoffs for ordinary Americans that have resulted from Chinese investment in the United States.

4. Examine the final image and consider the likely consequences of the growth of Chimerica for ordinary consumers and workers around the world.

Epilogue

2001–THE PRESENT

The new millennium closed the chapter on the bloody wars and ideological rivalries of the twentieth century. Although the Cold War was over, and global integration seemed greater than ever before in human history, the twentieth-first century brought new explosive hostilities and fresh economic and political challenges.

On September 11, 2001, nineteen hijackers commandeered four commercial airplanes. The hijackers slammed two of the planes into the World Trade Center in New York City and a third into the Pentagon, home of the U.S. Department of Defense, in Washington, D.C. The fourth plane was diverted from its intended target—the White House or the Capitol—and crashed in a field in southwestern Pennsylvania. A still rather unknown Muslim militant organization, al-Qaeda, headed by an equally little known Saudi, Osama bin Laden, claimed responsibility for the attacks, which took the lives of more than 3,000 Americans. What followed was a predictable and determined American military response: the invasions of Iraq, incorrectly blamed for engineering the attacks, and Afghanistan, where a fundamentalist Islamic government provided a haven for bin Laden and his al-Qaeda affiliates.

Economic turmoil added to the turbulence of terrorism and wars. The global economy and new technologies had brought the world together as never before, but the benefits of integration were unequally distributed. Consequently, when an economic crisis broke out in 2008, its effects were felt globally, but experienced unequally. An angry, populist politics of despair swept many parts of the world fighting back against the perceived negative effects of globalization. This wave of populism led to national election victories for conservative populist candidates, such as Donald Trump in the United States and Recep Tayyip Erdogan in Turkey. Populist political parties, including the right-wing Alternative für Deutschland (AfD) in Germany, gained substantial ground in national assemblies, and in Great Britain, a majority of voters opted for the so-called Brexit: leaving the European Union (EU).

Global Challenges

WAR ON TERROR

The terrorist attack of 9/11 repulsed people around the world. Anger focused on Osama bin Laden and al-Qaeda, the loosely organized militant network of Islamist groups that had organized the attack. The militants claimed that it was a response

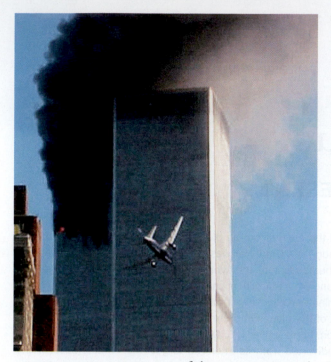

9/11 With the North Tower already aflame, this photograph captures a second hijacked jet an instant before it crashed into the South Tower of New York's World Trade Center on September 11, 2001.

to America's imperialist policies in the Middle East and retribution for American troops' presence in Saudi Arabia (during the first Iraq War). In the months and years that followed, countries grappled with a "war on terror," conflicts with militant Islamic groups, and a global economic crisis. George W. Bush, who had become president after a close and disputed election the year before the attack, gained broad public support for his tough talk about bringing terrorists to justice. Domestically, Bush pushed for security measures to curb future terrorist violence.

Internationally, President Bush declared a "global war on terror." With the backing of the majority of the American people, as well as strong support from many nations, Bush unsuccessfully sent American forces to Afghanistan to hunt down bin Laden, destroy al-Qaeda training camps, and topple the Taliban government that had provided a haven for the terrorists. Expanding the battlefront of the war on terror, the Bush administration ordered an invasion of Iraq in 2003, falsely charging its dictator, Saddam Hussein, with abetting the terrorist assault of 9/11 and producing weapons of mass destruction. As in Afghanistan, the initial offensive went well, but defeating the Iraqi army and finding Hussein proved easier than restoring order to the country or winning popular support.

In Afghanistan, U.S.-led coalition forces soon found themselves in a quagmire. Early successes collapsed as local warlords pursued their own goals and as the revitalized Taliban was able to regroup in neighboring Pakistan.

While the campaigns in Iraq and Afghanistan faltered, the United States accelerated its efforts to hunt down terrorist leaders. Under President Barack Obama, a daring operation in Pakistan ended with the death of Osama bin Laden in 2011. Even so, the American image suffered internationally as news of programs of extensive surveillance (including that of U.S. citizens), "rendition" of suspected militants to sites where they could be tortured to extract information, the inhumane treatment of Iraqi prisoners at the Abu Ghraib prison, and the harsh and indefinite detention of suspected terrorists at Guantanamo spread. The prospect that the new century would be one of peace and prosperity under an American order seemed increasingly remote.

CRISIS AND INEQUALITY IN THE GLOBAL ECONOMY

In 2008, the world economy fell into crisis. The problem began the previous year in the financial sector, the most globally interlinked sector of all. Seeking new sources of profits, investors from around the world had poured their money into riskier and riskier investments—many of which were so complex that not even the regulators in charge of monitoring the financial sector could understand them.

One of the most enticing of these risky bets was real estate in the United States, where a frenzy of investment in the early 2000s created a price "bubble." The bubble eventually burst, leading to a plunge in property values. By the summer of 2008, there was a worldwide panic, and the banking system nearly collapsed. As it became more difficult to borrow money and consumers stopped spending, factories shut down and stores went bankrupt.

The financial crisis brought signs of gathering discontent. In Europe, where, at last, economic and political integration within the European Union had seemed to promise an end to conflict between states, the crisis created new tensions. In Greece, radical new parties arose to protest austerity measures or to take out frustrations on immigrants, and many blamed the richer nations, especially the Germans, for having profited from the creation of the EU at the expense of the poorer nations. For the first time in decades, vehement nationalist slogans came into wide circulation, and politicians of the left and right hostile to the European project were elected. Some commentators predicted that the common currency (the euro)—and perhaps even the European Union in its current form—would not last, as exemplified by Great Britain's decision to leave the European Union. In the Americas, Mexico elected a trade skeptic, Andrés Manuel López Obrador. In the United States, the Trump administration pulled out of the Trans-Pacific Partnership (a trade agreement with twelve nations), sought to renegotiate the North American Free Trade Agreement with Mexico and Canada, and, in the name of national security, imposed restrictions on the importation of aluminum and steel.

Even as economies emerged from the crisis, economic inequality among individuals and regions led to new challenges. The very same ongoing integration of the world economy that globalized the economic crisis also produced fresh wealth across the world. Capital, technology, and media brought the world together ever more closely. The movement of ideas and images across national borders accelerated. Social media like Facebook provided new lines of communication and connections, particularly among the young. New aspirations for employment, prosperity, consumption, and political expression appeared.

These global economic and political stirrings were full of paradoxes and contradictions. The growth of prosperity and wealth around the world was highly unequal and accompanied by an unprecedented rise in the power and influence of corporations and financial institutions. Even as a global middle class came into being, inequality deepened. This sparked a range

Global Capitalism and the Great Contraction of 2008

According to the economic historian Charles Kindleberger, the twentieth century witnessed seven of the world's ten greatest global financial panics since the eighteenth century. To those crises now must be added the Great Contraction of 2008, a financial crisis almost as severe and long lasting as the Great Depression of 1929 (see Chapter 19). Although billions of people have been pulled out of poverty during the twentieth and twenty-first centuries, economic growth has come with a heavy price, namely, dramatic and alarming economic crises that have spread rapidly throughout the world, now tightly linked because of increased global integration. According to Kindleberger, "the years since the early 1970s are unprecedented in terms of volatility in the prices of commodities, currencies, real estate and stocks, and the frequency and severity of financial crises."

Many policymakers and economists believed that the lessons learned during the Great Depression rendered anything as severe as the losses of wealth and income, the high unemployment rates, and the sharp drop in consumer purchasing power in that period a thing of the past. Except for a few crying Cassandras, decision makers in the developed world were utterly unprepared for the financial crisis that was triggered by the bursting of a real-estate bubble in 2008, which in turn led to the implosion of some of the most powerful financial houses and manufacturers in the United States and throughout the world.

The signals of an approaching financial disaster were apparent to many, but were ignored, in part because Alan Greenspan, the guru of monetary policy at the Federal Reserve—America's central bank—and an ardent economic libertarian and free marketer, argued that the marketplace would bring about necessary corrections. In reality, risk and indebtedness were at record levels. Commercial and investment banks and insurance companies had tripled their indebtedness over the three decades leading up to 2008. Even when the Hongkong and Shanghai Banking Corporation (HSBC), based in London since 1991 and the seventh largest bank in the world in terms of assets, reported massive losses in its subprime housing loans, and Countrywide Business Credit filed for bankruptcy, the George W. Bush administration and Congress did not react. Only when Bear Stearns collapsed in March 2008 because of its heavy exposure to subprime mortgage loans did the U.S. Treasury intervene, providing a loan of nearly $30 billion to J. P. Morgan Chase to buy out Bear Stearns. But no support was forthcoming on September 18, 2008, when Lehman Brothers, a firm that had been in existence since 1850 and had survived the Civil War, World Wars I and II, and the Great Depression, filed for bankruptcy. Had the Treasury provided anywhere from $12 to $60 billion, the roiling financial crisis might have been averted. But it did not, and what had already been a dramatic economic and financial meltdown in the United States, the United Kingdom, Ireland, Spain, and Iceland now spread rapidly throughout Europe, Asia, Latin America, and parts of Africa. Millions lost their livelihoods and homes, corporations failed, trillions of dollars of wealth were destroyed, "and the once mighty US economy [was brought] to its knees, [leaving] all levels of government gasping for tax revenue."

The Great Contraction of 2008 did not last as long as the Great Depression of 1929. The unemployment rate

of protest movements outside conventional political and institutional forms like political parties and trade unions—none more powerful and dramatic than Occupy Wall Street (OWS), a movement that started in September 2011 in New York and was organized by a Canadian anarchist group called Adbusters, using social media to mobilize young people. It highlighted growing social and economic inequality and challenged the power of banks and corporations.

in the United States cratered out at 10 percent, not 25 percent, and hundreds of banks, not thousands, failed. The financial downturn of 2008 was not as sharp and did not persist as long as the 1929 depression largely because of the innovative policies championed by Ben Bernanke—Greenspan's successor at the Federal Reserve—and officials at the U.S. Treasury. It was perhaps fortuitous that Bernanke was at the Fed and Christina Romer was a high-ranking economic adviser in the Obama administration. Both had studied the Great Depression during their academic careers and were committed to monetary and financial policies that they believed would have pulled the United States out of the depression. Specifically, they thought it essential to protect the big banks, stimulate the economy, resist protectionism, and promote international cooperation. In keeping with these policies, the Treasury bailed out fourteen financial firms, including such heavy-hitters as Goldman Sachs, Morgan Stanley, Merrill Lynch, Bank of America, Citigroup, and J. P. Morgan Chase, as well as two automobile

manufacturers, General Motors and Chrysler. They did so by pressuring a rather unwilling Congress to set aside the stupendous sum of $700 billion in a program labeled TARP (Troubled Assets Relief Program). Although the majority of Americans thought the program was wrong-headed, rewarding the banks that had brought on the financial disaster, TARP was, according to Alan Blinder, an expert economist, "among the most successful—but least understood— economic policy innovations in our nation's history." In fact, the Treasury disbursed only $430 billion of the allocated $700 billion and eventually turned a profit of $25 billion as the businesses that received the funds repaid the equity injected into their companies.

Are financial crises likely to be with us in the future? Probably so, for it is the nature of humankind to become inordinately ebullient about financial gains to be made and to take on more debt than can be sustained. It would appear that financial bubbles, panics, manias, contractions, and even catastrophic depressions are an inevitable part of world capitalism.

Explore Further

Blinder, Alan S., *After the Music Stopped: The Financial Crisis, the Response, and the Work Ahead* (2013).

Eichengreen, Barry J., *Hall of Mirrors: The Great Depression and the Great Recession, and the Uses—and Misuses—of History* (2015).

Friedman, Milton and Schwartz, Anne Jacobson, *A Monetary History of the United States, 1867–1960* (1963).

Guillen, Mauro F., *The Architecture of Collapse: The Global System in the 21st Century* (2015).

Kindleberger, Charles P. and Aliber, Robert, *Manias, Panics, and Crashes: A History of Financial Crises*, 5th edition (2005).

Reinhart, Carmen M. and Rogoff, Kenneth S., *This Time Is Different: Eight Centuries of Financial Folly* (2009).

Sources: Charles P. Kindleberger and Robert Aliber, *Manias, Panics, and Crashes: A History of Financial Crises*, 5th edition (Hoboken, NJ: John Wiley & Sons, 2005), p. 1; Alan S. Blinder, *After the Music Stopped: The Financial Crisis, the Response, and the Work Ahead* (New York: Penguin, 2013), pp. 4, 178.

CLIMATE CHANGE

As the world population continues to grow and as more areas industrialize, the pressure on vital natural resources (especially oil and water) has inspired calls for greater conservation and more environmentally sustainable economic development. But the U.S. government's resistance to global regulations, as well as a rising demand for resources (especially by China and India), has made the future of the earth's environment uncertain.

Occupy Wall Street Inspired by other stirrings around the world, this largely national movement was fueled by methods as novel as social media and as traditional as sit-ins. Here, an Occupy Wall Street rally joins a labor union demonstration outside the New York County Courthouse in 2011.

Climate change has emerged as one of the most pressing issues for the new millennium. Despite difficulties in achieving a consensus on policy, scientists and environmental experts agree that the planet needs remedial action. Thus, when the Group of Eight (G8), a forum of leaders from Canada, France, Germany, Italy, Japan, Russia, the United Kingdom, and the United States, met in 2007, a key topic was climate change. It acknowledged that humankind is contributing to, if not causing, global warming through its emissions of greenhouse gases—especially by burning coal and oil for electricity, but also by clearing vegetation for farming, development, and timber. The result is climate change: rising temperatures, melting ice caps, drought in some regions, and more severe storms elsewhere. The effects on populations living close to sea level can be catastrophic. Hurricane Katrina in 2005, for example, left much of New Orleans and the Mississippi Gulf Coast in ruins. Hurricane Sandy had similar catastrophic effects on the shorelines of New Jersey and New York in 2013; and in 2018, Hurricane Maria devastated Puerto Rico. Elsewhere, prolonged drought has led to agrarian crises and food shortages; this situation crept up on Syria over many years and led to an outburst of opposition to the despotic government of Bashar al-Assad and a bloody civil war. The resulting refugee crisis has spilled over into Turkey and Europe.

A major breakthrough occurred in Paris in 2015 when, under the sponsorship of the United Nations Framework on Climate Change, most of the nations of the world gathered to hammer out an agreement that would limit the emission of greenhouse gases and hold down the increase in global temperature. The accord, scheduled to go into effect in 2020, aims to achieve a less than 1.5°C increase in global temperature. The two heaviest polluters, China and the United States, are crucial signatories. Yet the implementation of the agreement is left to the individual nations, each of which must file reports with the United Nations. Donald Trump, the American president elected in 2016, has repudiated American participation in the Paris accord and asserted that the entire science of climate change and global warming is a hoax.

The United States, the European Union, and Japan

Although the global challenges of the twenty-first century have touched virtually every corner of the world, local contexts continue to weigh heavily. Countries and regions have experienced globalizing forces in very different ways.

THE UNITED STATES

In the United States, the Obama administration sought to cope with the economic crisis while introducing health care reform. It encountered a conservative backlash in the shape of the Tea Party movement, which espoused the ideals of small government and market freedom and contributed to a stinging defeat of the Democrats in the 2010 congressional elections. From the opposite side of the ideological spectrum arose the Occupy Wall Street movement in 2011. Claiming to speak on behalf of 99 percent of Americans against the wealthiest 1 percent, the Occupy activists, consisting largely of young people, railed against the banks and financial institutions that the federal government had rescued from bankruptcy. Although the movement ran out of steam by the end of the year, it succeeded in inserting the nation's growing inequality into political discussions.

More stunning was the 2016 election, in which candidate Donald Trump, who had never held political office, inveighed against "inner-city" crime, immigrants, international trade, and long-standing American alliances and security arrangements. Although few pundits gave Trump much chance against a field of well-established and well-financed Republican Party opponents, his platform resonated with primary voters and gained him the party's nomination. Facing Hillary Clinton in the general election, Trump once more defied pollsters by winning a majority in the Electoral College (though losing the popular vote by nearly 3 million). Coming on the heels of Brexit, Trump's victory reflected the rising populist and nationalist tide against globalization.

A CHANGING WESTERN EUROPE

The American invasion of Iraq in 2003 created fractures in the alliance between the United States and western Europe. During the 1990s, the collapse of the Soviet Union and the development of the EU had caused some rumblings about the future of NATO, but disagreements remained muted at that time. In fact, in the immediate wake of 9/11, European allies rallied behind the United States. But as the American military entered Iraq, leaders in France and Germany sharply criticized U.S. foreign policy.

Far more serious divisions emerged over the fate of NATO and of the EU, whose membership peaked at twenty-eight countries, including ten that had formerly been part of the Soviet bloc. In a 2016 referendum on EU membership in Britain, in which voters could choose "Leave" or "Remain," "Leave" secured a majority. The trend toward EU expansion, whereby member states relinquished a significant degree of sovereignty as an answer to the legacies of war, ethnic cleansing, and genocide, was reversed over the issues of free integration within the union and the unlimited jurisdiction of the European Court of Justice.

Has *Homo sapiens* Entered a New Epoch—the Anthropocene?

The Earth came into being more than 4 billion years ago, and the first life forms appeared around 2 billion years ago. From the nineteenth century onward, geologists, earth scientists, evolutionary biologists, and others have been fine-tuning a time scale of Earth history, which they divide into eons, four of which have thus far existed and each of which spans hundreds and thousands of millions of years. The eons themselves are subdivided into eras, periods, epochs, and ages. Earth scientists base their geological divisions of the earth's history on the major changes that have taken place in the environment and climate of our planet and its life forms. Using these categories, they have created a geological time scale (GTS). Today, we live in the Cenozoic Era and the Holocene Epoch. The Cenozoic Era, which began roughly 65 million years ago with the extinction of the dinosaurs, has been called the Age of Mammals because the largest land animals of the era have been mammals. The Holocene Epoch, which began about 12,000 years ago, after the last major ice age, has had a stable climate and has been increasingly dominated by *Homo sapiens*. The term *Holocene* itself, meaning whole and recent, was first proposed by the British scientist Charles Lyall in 1833, and was adopted by the International Geological Congress in 1885 as the title for our epoch.

However, two scientists, Paul J. Crutzer and Eugene F. Stoemer, believe that we have entered a new geological epoch, dominated by the impact of humankind on the earth's environment, particularly its stratosphere. They first proposed the term "Anthropocene" to represent humankind's dominance in this new epoch. Their proposal appeared in an article published in May 2000 in the newsletter of the International Geosphere-Biosphere Programme (IGBP). Although their statement was only a short one, these authors dealt with virtually all of the factors that led them and their followers to assert that the environmental and geological impact of *Homo sapiens* has been so decisive that the world has indeed entered a new geological age. They stressed human population growth, the extinction of other species, the increase in atmospheric greenhouse gases, notably carbon dioxide and methane, and the destruction of rain forests. They concluded their essay by observing that "it seems to us more than appropriate to emphasize the central role of mankind in geology and ecology by proposing the term 'anthropocene' for the current geological epoch." Evidence from glacial ice cores showing a dramatic rise in greenhouse gas concentrations since the latter part of the eighteenth century caused them to argue that the Anthropocene began at the time of the industrial revolution.

Thus far, it has been mainly environmental historians who have taken up the challenge of studying the impact of humankind on the environment, though only a few have used the term "Anthropocene" proposed by Crutzer and Stoemer. They have, however, elaborated on the factors that Crutzer and Stoemer first laid out. Two environmental historians, J. R. McNeill and Peter Engelkes, in their essay "Into the Anthropocene: People and Their Planet," contend that "a new history of the earth has begun, that the Holocene is over, and something new has begun: the Anthropocene." They prefer the twentieth century rather than Crutzer's and Stoemer's claim for the later eighteenth century as the starting point of this epoch and conclude "that humankind emerged as the most powerful influence upon the global ecology." They cite the enormous expansion of the human population: a tenfold increase over three centuries, producing the present world population of 7.6 billion. The growth of the human population was exceedingly slow up to the beginning of the nineteenth century—only about 0.05 per year—but reached a full 2 percent per year in 1970. In their view, "no primate, perhaps no mammal, has ever engaged in such a frenzy of reproduction." As for the loading of the atmosphere with carbon dioxide, three-quarters of this loading took place during the most recent six and half decades (between 1945 and 2011). The number of vehicles increased from 40 million to 800 million during the same period. Moreover, the number of residents of cities expanded from about 200 million to 3.5 billion. Until it became possible to use fossil fuels such as coal, oil, and natural gas for energy, human beings relied on their own muscles to do most work. Fossil fuels have led to rapid economic progress throughout the world, but have also created problems of smog, general pollution, and the thinning of the ozone layer in the atmosphere that shields the earth from harmful radiation, as well as the critical problem of global warming.

Crutzer and Stoemer were optimistic in 2000 that world leaders would pay attention to the evidence, revealed by earth scientists, that human beings were upsetting the ecology and environment of the earth. Short of "an enormous volcanic eruption, an unexpected epidemic, a large scale nuclear war, an asteroid impact, a new ice age, or continued plundering of Earth's resources, [they expected] . . . mankind [to] remain a major geological force for many millennia, maybe millions of years to come." Yet, are earth scientists and well-informed political leaders and ruling elites nearly so sanguine these days?

Explore Further

Crutzer, Paul J. and Stoemer, Eugene F., "The Anthropocene," *IGBP Newsletter*, no. 41 (May 2000), pp. 17–18.

McNeill, J. R., *Something New under the Sun: An Environmental History of the Twentieth Century* (2000).

McNeill, J. R. and Engelkes, Peter, "Into the Anthropocene: People and Their Planet," in *Global Interdependence: The World after 1945*, ed. Akira Iriye (2014).

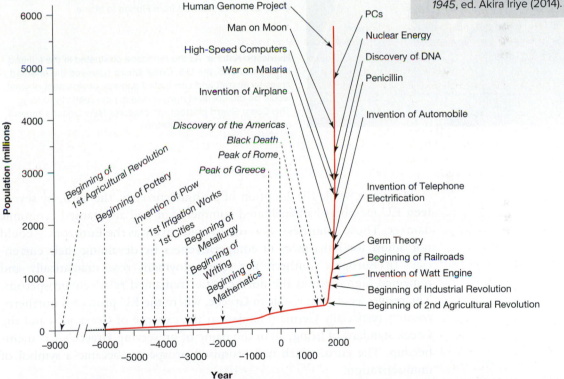

Population and Technology This graph tracks the world's increasing population over time alongside major technological developments. Where one skyrockets, so does the other, suggesting a starting point for the Anthropocene.

Source: J. R. McNeill and Peter Engelkes, "Into the Anthropocene: People and Their Planet," in *Global Interdependence: The World after 1945*, ed. Akira Iriye (Cambridge, MA: Belknap Press of Harvard University Press, 2014), 365–533.

Destruction by Hurricane Sandy on Ortley Beach, New Jersey Hurricane Sandy, moving ashore in New Jersey on October 29, 2012, was the second-costliest hurricane in U.S. history. Its high winds struck twenty-four states, including the entire eastern seaboard from Florida to Maine.

Hurricane Katrina As the hurricane dissipated in the tail end of August 2005, the U.S. Coast Guard surveyed the affected areas by aircraft and conducted damage assessment of what would be the costliest natural disaster in American history. This Coast Guard photograph captures New Orleans immediately after the passing of Katrina.

Moreover, while the adoption of a single currency, the euro, by seventeen EU members had facilitated commerce, it had also caused economic damage. Those countries—referred to collectively as the Eurozone—could not adjust for imbalances in competitiveness by devaluing their currencies. In Europe's southern tier, unemployment rose dramatically and remained high, even as the northern tier remained relatively prosperous. The results were most visible in Greece, where the EU protected northern-country (especially German) lenders at the expense of Greek jobs and the Greek standard of living, all in the name of preserving Greece's EU membership. The euro, which had promised prosperity, became a symbol of immiserization.

In addition, the EU's signature identity, democratic institutions, experienced significant erosion, beginning in Hungary and then Poland before spreading to much of the rest of Europe. Italy, which hosted the conference that led to the EU's founding Treaty of Rome (1958), elected a government in 2018 that was deeply critical of the Union. Europe's malaise put the long-term future of integration to the test.

DEMOGRAPHIC ISSUES

One threat to future peace and prosperity in Europe—and in the United States and Japan as well—comes from the interlocking issues of aging and immigration. Women in the European Union would have to bear two children on average to maintain its population of 500 million, but women in the EU now average only 1.5 children. Adding to the problem is the graying of the European population. With the percentage of elderly Europeans rising rapidly, sustaining the present ratio of workers to retirees and paying for the region's burgeoning number of pensioners will require the EU to attract around 15 million immigrants annually.

That number of immigrants has not been reached. European populations have been boosted by millions of immigrants, many of them Muslims, but sustainable economic growth has proved elusive. Islam has become the fastest-growing religion in Europe. The presence of Muslims in Europe's large cities threatens those who still equate Europe with Christendom and challenges those who believe that European integration requires complete cultural assimilation of all inhabitants.

Europe is not alone in confronting the problems of an aging population and the integration of immigrants. As its post–World War II baby boom generation ages, the United States faces a similar imbalance between retirees and workers that endangers its Social Security system. Likewise, the increase in immigration, particularly from Asia and Latin America, continues to shift the nation's ethnic composition. Donald Trump, who pledged to "build a wall" across the U.S.-Mexico border, made control of immigration central to his campaign for the presidency in 2016. (For a global look at population growth and life expectancies, see Maps E.1 and E.2.)

In many respects, the problem of an aging population presses hardest today on Japan. Like Europeans and North Americans, the Japanese are marrying later and having fewer children. Japan's female population now averages barely 1.37 children, compared with nearly 3.7 in 1950. At the same time, Japanese life expectancy has reached eighty-five, the highest in the world, which further tilts the nation's age pyramid. In 1970, the elderly (those over age sixty-five) represented around 7 percent of the population; in 2014, they made up more than 25 percent and are expected to hit 40 percent by 2050. Japan's population peaked at around 128 million and might decline to perhaps 120 million by 2050, with a substantial proportion over the working age. Such a downturn bodes ill for Japan's economy.

Like Europe and North America, Japan relies on immigrants to fill out its labor force. In the 1960s, the nation's booming economy led to labor shortages, but neither the government nor major corporations chose to invite in foreign laborers. By the 1980s, however, deepening labor shortages and the yen's rising value led to an expanded dependence on immigrant workers.

Percentage population increase, 2016

- Population loss
- 0.0%–0.9%
- 1.0%–1.9%
- 2.0%–2.9%
- 3.0% or more

0   1000   2000 Miles

0   1000   2000 Kilometers

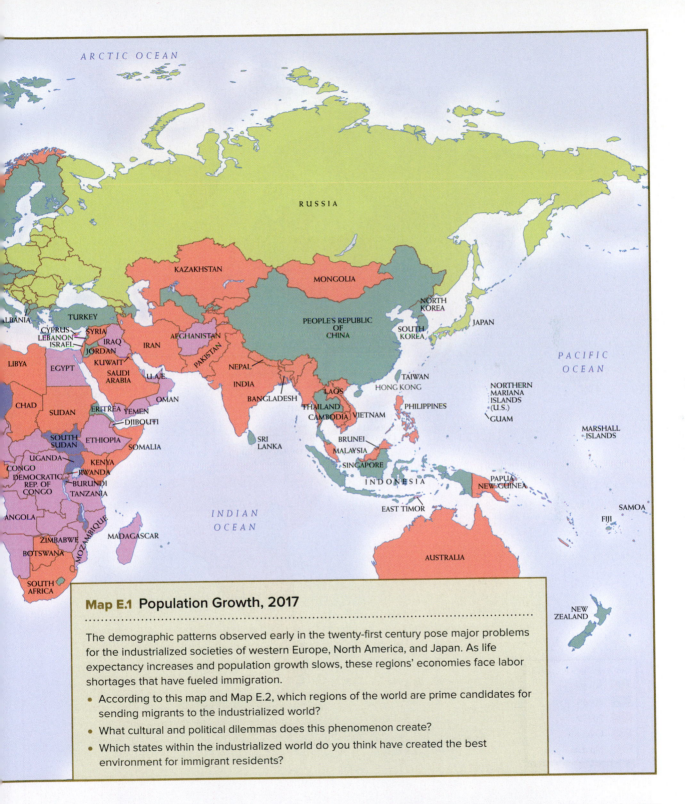

Map E.1 Population Growth, 2017

The demographic patterns observed early in the twenty-first century pose major problems for the industrialized societies of western Europe, North America, and Japan. As life expectancy increases and population growth slows, these regions' economies face labor shortages that have fueled immigration.

- According to this map and Map E.2, which regions of the world are prime candidates for sending migrants to the industrialized world?
- What cultural and political dilemmas does this phenomenon create?
- Which states within the industrialized world do you think have created the best environment for immigrant residents?

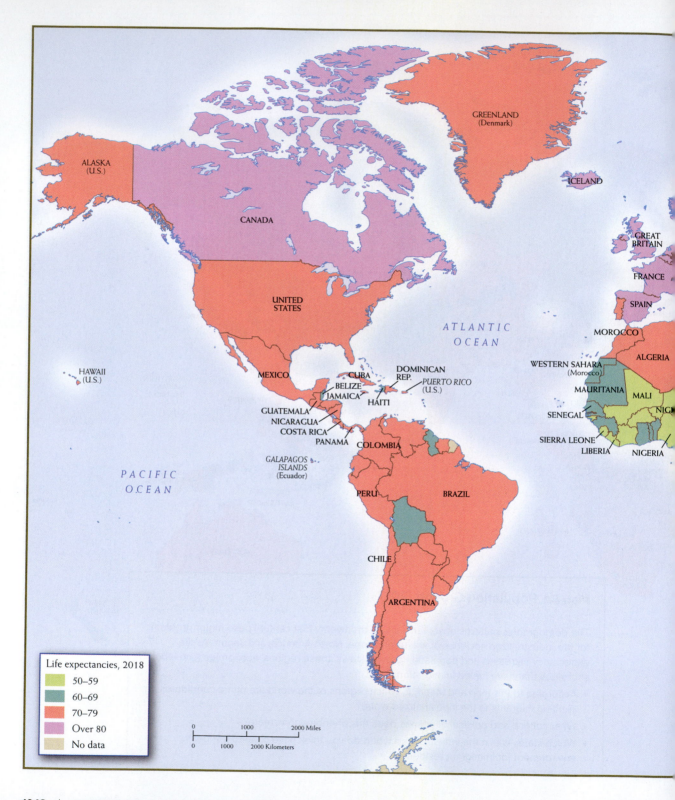

Life expectancies, 2018

- 50–59
- 60–69
- 70–79
- Over 80
- No data

Map E.2 Life Expectancies in Global Perspective, 2018

Increased attention to public health, medicine, nutrition, and education since the early nineteenth century has contributed to prolonging life expectancy around the world, as have the many scientific breakthroughs and technological advancements of the twentieth and twenty-first centuries.

- According to Map E.1 and this map, which regions experienced population increases but low life expectancies? Population decreases and high life expectancies? Explain.
- Which countries do not match the life expectancy trends of their geographic regions? Why?
- Do you note any correlations between a region's life expectancy and its physical environment? Why or why not?

Recent estimates put the number of foreign nationals in Japan at nearly 2 million, or around 1.5 percent of the total population. Most of them hail from the Korean Peninsula, the Philippines, Southeast Asia, Brazil, and Iran.

ANTI-IMMIGRANT SENTIMENTS

In Europe, where unemployment rates have remained higher than in Japan or North America, the political reaction against immigration has been sharpest. Far-right groups have demanded that immigration be halted or "foreigners" expelled, and that stance has now been adopted by politicians across the far-right spectrum. Support for these views varies among countries, but across Europe, the far right's electoral base appears to be around 15 percent; in some countries, it is above 25 percent. The Freedom Party in Austria regularly places cabinet representatives in coalition governments. Ultra-right forces such as France's National Front, Denmark's People's Party, and the League of Polish Families sometimes pressure governing coalitions to slow EU integration and immigration, especially from Muslim countries. The issue of accepting Muslim refugees from war-torn Syria has galvanized supporters and opponents in the EU's most powerful country, Germany, and it played a key role in the Northern League's election as part of a populist coalition government in Italy.

The pushback against immigration has become intertwined with the issues of terrorism and assimilation of Muslims into European societies. In Holland, the precipitating event was the grisly murder of filmmaker Theo van Gogh by Mohammed Bouyeri in 2004. Bouyeri claimed he was fulfilling his duty as a Muslim by assassinating van Gogh, who had made a film about the abuse of Muslim women. Following the assassination, many in Holland questioned the nation's traditional tolerance of diversity and expressed concern that Muslims were too alien in their values to ever fit into Dutch society. France confronted a similar debate after riots protesting police brutality and the country's failure to offer equal opportunity to all rocked a series of poor neighborhoods, notably in Paris, in 2005.

Although the Europeans stepped up their security procedures and intensified intelligence gathering, violence continued. The French satirical weekly *Charlie Hebdo* became the target of two terrorist attacks (in 2011 and 2015) after publishing deliberately irreverent depictions of the Prophet Muhammad. On November 13, 2015, terrorists claiming allegiance to the Islamic State in Iraq and Syria (ISIS) carried out a series of coordinated attacks: while one group struck outside a Paris stadium where France was playing Germany in a football (soccer) match, others attacked restaurants, cafes, and a concert hall. In all, 130 people were killed and many more injured. Just a few months later, a Tunisian, Anis Amri, also asserting allegiance to ISIS, struck in a market in Berlin, killing twelve.

The United States, too, was trying to cope with the threat of terrorism and the challenge of immigration. Since 9/11, the United States had not

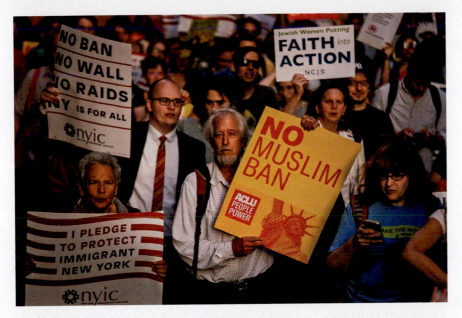

suffered another major attack, but smaller attacks raised the level of public alarm. While Americans often described themselves as a nation of immigrants, anti-immigrant sentiments also gathered popular support, fueled by candidate (and then President) Trump's nativist attacks on immigrants and refugees. Among its early, signature measures, the Trump administration imposed restrictions on immigration from Muslim countries (the so-called Muslim ban); separated children from parents who crossed the U.S.-Mexico border illegally; and sought to end the Deferred Action for Childhood Arrivals (DACA) policy of his predecessor, Barack Obama, which allowed some immigrants to remain and work in the United States.

In just a few years, the mood of the world's most advanced industrial societies has shifted decisively. The triumphant atmosphere that ushered in the new millennium has given way to a pessimistic outlook. In the year 2000, talk of the blessings of global integration dominated the political and economic scene; two decades later, prognosticators warn about the dangers emanating from disaffected members of their societies and from radicals, especially Islamic radicals, willing and able to unleash terror anywhere in the world.

Russia, China, and India

Fueling the anti-immigrant fires in Europe, Japan, and North America is the increasing number of jobs being "outsourced" to China, India, and other countries. In the past, businesses had turned to immigrants to fill low-wage positions (and to keep all wages down). But by the end of the twentieth century, it had become more economical to relocate manufacturing to places where cheap labor was already available.

ECONOMIC GLOBALIZATION AND POLITICAL EFFECTS

In the twenty-first century, business mobility has not been limited to low-skill and low-wage jobs. Technological advances—particularly in computers and communication—have enabled all sorts of enterprises to operate from almost any point on the globe. No longer do educated workers have to leave India or China for employment in Europe or North America, because it is increasingly cost-effective for corporations to shift certain operations to those countries. The globalized market economy has leveled the playing field in the competition for jobs, although countries with vast labor reserves, such as China, India, and Russia, still have a long way to go to achieve the per capita income levels enjoyed in the older capitalist societies. Nonetheless, Russia, China, and India have had healthy economic growth in the first years of the new century.

While Russia's economy was opening to the world, thanks to high oil prices, its political system seemed to be closing in on itself. President Vladimir Putin presided over a rebuilding of the central Russian state, which was widely welcomed in Russia. But the means used by Putin to reassert central state power led, once again, to personal rule. The president forcibly repossessed the two principal television stations from their billionaire owners and reassigned other valuable private properties, especially oil and gas companies, to the state, to be run by his former colleagues from the Soviet-era political police, the KGB. The Gorbachev-Yeltsin era's promise of a real legislature, an independent judiciary, and an end to arbitrary rule gave way, in the yearning for order and stability, to aggressive nationalism and an authoritarian executive.

As in Russia, leaders in China have encouraged market reforms while quashing political liberalization. Their economic strategies seem to be successful. Over the last three decades, China's economy has maintained an average growth rate of over 9 percent annually, although it has recently shown signs of slowing down. Consumer goods made in China dominate so many markets that it is virtually impossible, as several newspaper reporters have found, to supply an American family's needs with a "China-free" shopping list. Indeed,

Child Labor Girls in a Javanese village work in a factory transferring bundles of cotton yarn to bobbins to be used in hand-looms.

the Chinese economy has been the second largest in the world since late 2010, and some projections suggest that it will be the largest by midcentury, even though China's per capita income will still lag behind that of the United States.

In many ways, China's fortunes illustrate both the promises and the pitfalls of the economic reforms undertaken by many developing countries in the era of globalization. On the one hand, China's entry into the World Trade Organization (WTO) in 2001 signified its full integration into the global capitalist economy. On the other hand, the reforms have caused political, social, and environmental problems that defy easy solutions. A 2016 report from Peking University found that 1 percent of Chinese households controlled a third of the country's assets, while the poorest 25 percent of households owned just 1 percent of the country's wealth.

There are concerns, both at home and abroad, about the environmental impact of China's economic development. China's homes and factories, for instance, use 40 percent more coal than those in the United States, and Chinese city dwellers suffer from some of the world's worst smog and poorest air quality. But as its energy consumption and economy have soared, so has China's global standing.

China has embarked on an ambitious infrastructure program. Dubbed the "Belt and Road Initiative," the plan seeks to spread Chinese economic and political influence to some sixty countries, principally in Asia and Europe but also in Oceania and eastern Africa. By the early twenty-first century, China had become the number one trading partner with almost every country in Asia, displacing the United States. It has even become the top trading partner with Brazil, as well as with many countries in Africa. China has also replaced the United States as the number one customer for Saudi Arabian oil. Chinese-Indian economic relations have strengthened, too. Although China faces numerous challenges, it has regained the enormous global weight it held for centuries up until the eighteenth century.

India has also registered impressive economic growth in the new millennium. Since the 1990s, the Indian economy has become increasingly open. The nation's information technology sector boomed, and India became a favorite destination for global corporations, attracted by its sizable English-speaking population. Per capita income rose by 20 percent annually, and poverty declined by an average of over 2 percent annually, between 2004 and 2014.

Yet the benefits of economic liberalization were unequally experienced. High inflation hit the income of the salaried class hard. Inequality and poverty

Chinese Environmental Concerns Despite its prosperity, Hong Kong, like other major Chinese cities, suffers from severe air pollution, which threatens its future as a hub of international commerce. This picture shows part of the city's waterfront shrouded in smog.

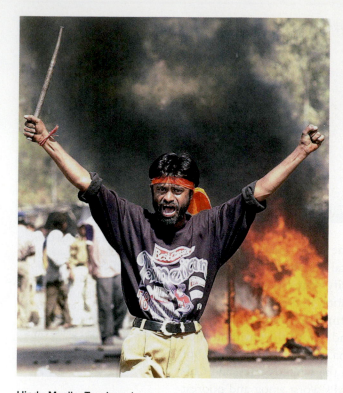

Hindu-Muslim Tensions In 2002, Gujarat was consumed by sectarian riots, set off by a train fire in which sixty Hindu pilgrims died. Although an Indian government investigation concluded that the fire was accidental, the incident sparked an orgy of violence by Hindu mobs against Muslims. Shown here is an angry right-wing Hindu Party activist.

remain acute problems. In an effort to boost the capitalist economy, the government declared an open season on land acquisition for real estate development, industrial parks, and mining, leading to the eviction of farmers and forest dwellers. The displaced people responded with armed insurgencies. In addition, the booming economy and new wealth created opportunities for corrupt practices. Riding on the widespread revulsion against corruption, the Bharatiya Janata Party (BJP), under Narendra Modi, swept the national elections and came to power in 2014.

Internal divisions and external rivalries have threatened to undo many benefits of economic globalization in India, China, and Russia. This is most clearly apparent in India, where the BJP, while advocating for the free market, has also aggressively championed *Hindutva* (Hinduness) as the bedrock of Indian identity.

Violence erupted in the state of Gujarat in February 2002 after sixty Hindu pilgrims perished in a fire that consumed a train compartment. Although the circumstances of the fire remain disputed, a rumor immediately spread that Muslims and a "foreign hand" were responsible. For the next few months, Hindu mobs went on a rampage, burning Muslim homes and hacking the residents to death. Over 2,000 Muslims lost their lives.

The ongoing tension with neighboring Pakistan poses further problems. Flexing its nationalist muscle, the Indian government exploded a nuclear device in 1998. Pakistan responded by exploding its own bombs, casting an ominous shadow over the two nations' unresolved conflict over Kashmir. In that contested province, terrorist violence repeatedly disturbed the peace and brought the nuclear-armed neighbors close to a potentially devastating war. The tension between the two countries escalated in 2008 when a small band of terrorists from Pakistan carried out raids in Mumbai, slaughtering many civilians and security personnel before being subdued.

The Middle East, Africa, and Latin America

In the Middle East, radical changes have been brought about by the Arab Spring and the growth of Islamic militancy, while more than a few countries in Africa have begun to achieve economic progress and gained political stability through democratic elections.

THE ARAB SPRING

The trigger for what became known as the Arab Spring was a seemingly futile act of protest. On December 17, 2010, Mohammed Bouazizi, a twenty-six-year-old Tunisian vegetable vendor and father of eight, set himself on fire outside a provincial office to protest the constant police harassment he had undergone. This singular act aroused the entire population of Tunisia against the ruling elite. Not only had the police confiscated Bouazizi's vegetable stand, and not for the first time, but a policewoman had slapped him in the face. In explaining his decision to take his life, his sister exclaimed, "In Sidi Bouzidi [where he resided] those with no connections and no money for bribes are humiliated and insulted and not allowed to live." As the story circulated through the country, crowds poured into the streets, demanding an end to the long-term dictatorship of Zine al-Abidine Ben Ali, who had taken over from Habib Bourguiba, Tunisia's president from independence in 1956 until 1978. The catchword of the protesters was "*dégage*" (get out). With the army refusing to suppress the dissenters and the security police overwhelmed, Ben Ali took the only way open to him: he departed for Saudi Arabia on January 14, 2011.

Young Egyptian radicals watched events in Tunisia with growing interest. If the Tunisians could get rid of their dictator, why not the Egyptians? On January 25, 2011—ironically, a holiday to honor Egypt's police

Arab Spring Day and night, Egyptians of all ages went to Cairo's Tahrir Square to protest the ongoing military rule after the ousting of Mubarak. Here, protestors burn the midnight oil to decry the dissolution of the parliament by Egypt's Supreme Constitutional Court, a move to consolidate power in the hands of military generals. Note the man documenting the heated demonstration with his video camera (bottom left), whose footage would probably have found its way to a wide array of social media sites for discussion and further dissemination.

forces—Egyptians of all backgrounds and ages assembled in Cairo's major plaza, Tahrir (Liberation) Square, to let Egypt's president, Hosni Mubarak, know that he was no longer wanted. On February 11, 2011, just three weeks after the first mass demonstration, Mubarak left office, turning the reins of power over to the Supreme Command of the Armed Forces.

The ouster of Ben Ali and Mubarak sent shock waves throughout the Arab world and sparked an outpouring of protest in all of its major cities. The protesters' demands were consistent: the end of repression, the establishment of democratic institutions, and the ousting of rulers who had stayed in power too long and who did not represent the will of the people. The results were astonishing. Monarchs in Jordan and Morocco promised new constitutions. Bahraini Shiites successfully demanded a new constitution from their Sunni king, and Ali Saleh, ruler of Yemen since 1978, fled the country. Even Muammar Qaddafi, the Libyan strongman, in power since ousting King Idris in 1969, felt the sting of protest, though his ouster and eventual execution on October 20, 2011, owed as much to NATO air power as it did to the rebel army that rose up to unseat him.

Where did the uprisings come from? In the first place, the Arab people, most of whom were young and had known only authoritarian rule, resented the fact that the wave of democratic reforms that had swept other regions had passed them by. They saw no reason why they, too, should not have leaders who represented their wishes, rather than rigged elections and fraudulent referendums that supported the wishes of the ruling elites. The young came to be known as the generation in waiting—waiting for jobs that never seemed to appear; waiting to have enough money to move out of their parents' homes; waiting to get married and start families. The fact that Hafez al-Assad of Syria had passed power to his son, Bashar al-Assad, and that Hosni Mubarak in Egypt was grooming his son, Gamal, to succeed him, heightened their rage. Although the uprisings often took names that suggested peaceful protest—such as the Jasmine Revolution in Tunisia and the White Revolution in Egypt—in reality these outbursts reflected deep-seated and long-standing fury at rulers who were repressive, corrupt, and unresponsive to their people.

Dictatorships and monarchies lost control over the media. The Qatari television station and newspaper *Al Jazeera*, founded in 1995, became an open forum for all kinds of opinions. One of its most dramatic and widely quoted programs featured an intense discussion about whether the Arab people had the right, like those in the west, to criticize their leaders. In addition, mobile phones, Facebook, Twitter, and other social media helped dissenters communicate with one another and enabled groups to organize large assemblies outside the purview of the state.

The early results led euphoric protesters to believe that they could create new and more open societies. Dictators were ousted, free elections were held, and new constitutions were promised. But the progress was hard to sustain. In Tunisia, which thus far had accomplished more than the other states, a moderate Muslim Brotherhood party, Al-Nahda, won control of the parliament. Egypt, too, held elections that were won by the Muslim Brotherhood party, Justice and Development, but nullified by the courts. It also elected a Muslim Brotherhood president, Muhammad Morsi. Yet President Morsi failed to establish an inclusive government and was ousted by Egypt's military leader, General Abdel-Fattah el-Sisi. On June 4, 2014, el-Sisi was elected president, promising to restore order to Egypt and imprisoning a large number of Muslim Brothers. Rebels in Sinai and the western desert, drawing inspiration from the rise of ISIS (discussed shortly), have challenged Sisi's government. The liberals and secularists who initiated the revolt against Mubarak have seen their aspirations dashed.

By far, the most lethal outcome of the Arab Spring has occurred in Syria. Beginning on March 15, 2011, protesters demanded the ouster of President Bashar al-Assad, formed a Free Syrian Army, gained international recognition for their movement from the United States and European states, and led protests that resulted in violent confrontation with Assad's forces, which resorted to the use of chemical weapons (sarin gas and chlorine bombs). In August 2012, U.S. President Obama declared that the use of chemical weapons would cross a "red line." A year later, on August 21, 2013, the Syrian military killed nearly 1,500 civilians in Damascus. Video footage showed people with bodies twitching, foaming at the mouth after exposure to sarin gas. Since 2013, thousands of Syrians have been injured and hundreds killed in chemical attacks. By the summer of 2014, when the United Nations stopped officially counting, more than 400,000 Syrians had lost their lives in the conflict and 12 million had been displaced, of whom 5 million sought refuge in Turkey, Lebanon, and Jordan. Another 1 million risked their lives on rickety boats bound for Europe. Even while the Americans and many others considered Assad's days to be numbered, the Syrian president defied the protesters and his western critics by gaining financial aid from Iran and crucial— indeed, regime-saving—military support from Hezbollah (a Shiite party established in Lebanon) and Russia.

Syrian Chemical Weapons Use A child receives treatment after an alleged gas attack on the Sakba and Hammuriye areas in Eastern Ghouta, Syria on March 7, 2018.

Although Bashar al-Assad remains in power, and a general rules Egypt, at this writing, the forces unleashed by the Arab Spring are still at work. The ideals enunciated by the protesters—open societies representative of the people, which promote economic progress—are still vibrant in the region.

ISLAMIC MILITANCY

Islamic militancy, dominated by al-Qaeda in the 1990s and the first decade of the twenty-first century, changed significantly with the emergence of ISIS in the early 2000s. As the Americans clipped the power of al-Qaeda, killing many of its important leaders, ISIS rose to take its place, becoming an even more formidable opponent.

Al-Qaeda's agenda was based on the belief that the west, and especially the United States, was the main force standing in the way of Islam's rise. Thus, the first order of business was to challenge American power: hence the attack on the World Trade Center and the Pentagon. The leaders of al-Qaeda (notably the Saudi Osama bin Laden and the Egyptian Ayman al-Zawahiri) came from elite families and were gradualists in their vision of liberating the Muslim world from western influence, believing that an Islamic state could emerge only after American power had been eroded. They were also uncomfortable with the kinds of violence that more radical Islamists, like the founders of ISIS, urged upon their followers. U.S. Navy Seals killed Osama bin Laden where he was hiding out, though really in plain sight, in Abbottabad, Pakistan, but the United States has yet to find Zawahiri in spite of offering $25 million for information concerning his whereabouts.

The founder of ISIS, Abu Musab al-Zarqawi, was an unlikely leader. A heavy drinker, a brawler, and a high school dropout, he found religion—in his case, militant Islam—which became his salvation and the purpose of his life. Al-Zarqawi made his way to Afghanistan in the 1990s to meet Osama bin Laden, whom he idolized. Those meetings did not generate much enthusiasm,

ISIS Fighters ISIS assembled a powerful group of soldiers, many from foreign countries (including the United States and Europe), and created a territorial state in western Syria and northern Iraq.

probably because al-Qaeda's leadership considered him too violent and hot-headed. Nonetheless, some high-ranking members of al-Qaeda accepted him into their ranks. When the Americans chased al-Zarqawi out of Afghanistan, he made his way to Iraq, anticipating that the Americans would invade and that he could put his form of radical and militant Islam into action there.

As the American occupation of Iraq faltered, al-Zarqawi's vision of a violent jihadi world rose to prominence. Here, because of his willingness to employ extreme violence, such as beheading prisoners and burning them alive, he earned the nickname "the Sheikh of the Slaughterers." As much as al-Zarqawi hated Americans, his rage against Iraqi Shiites was even more intense. In a country where Sunnis had exercised power for centuries in spite of being a minority, the dominance of Shiites in the new American-supported government enraged al-Zarqawi and his Sunni followers.

Although American troops killed al-Zarqawi in June 2006, the movement he led resurrected itself and became known as ISIS. Its unlikely new leader, Abu Bakr al-Baghdadi, had neither military nor bureaucratic experience when he assumed leadership of ISIS in May 2010. He was an Islamic scholar, trained in some of the minor Iraqi Muslim schools, eventually gaining his doctorate by writing an exegesis of the Quran. But he had something that the parent organization, al-Qaeda, lacked: a territorial state, based in northern and central Iraq, which became even more formidable following the departure of American forces from the country. After moving into war-torn Syria and conquering Mosul in northern Iraq in 2014, ISIS also took the name Islamic Caliphate, and Baghdadi announced to the world that he was the new state's first caliph.

At its height, after the conquest of Mosul in 2014, ISIS controlled territories in central Syria and northern Iraq equivalent in area to the United Kingdom. It also had a population of between 6 and 9 million; an army of 30,000; a capital city, Raqqa, in Syria; and large financial resources, amassed though oil revenues, looting, and taxes. (For a look at the territory held by the Islamic State and the population of Shiite Muslims in the Middle East, see Map E.3 and Table E.1.) By August 2016, ISIS was reported to operate in eighteen countries around the world, including Afghanistan and Pakistan.

The territories under its control rapidly diminished thereafter. In 2017, American military sources claimed that 98 percent of territory ISIS controlled had been recaptured. The Iraqi government declared its war against ISIS over, and Russia announced a partial withdrawal of Russian troops from Syria. Whether ISIS can regroup and realize its global ambitions seems doubtful. But radical, militant Islam is here to stay.

THE IRANIAN NUCLEAR DEAL

In mid-June 2015, Iran and the United States, Russia, China, Britain, France, Germany, and the European Union reached an agreement on an issue that

Islamic State

Iraqi government

Syrian government

Syrian rebel forces

Syrian and Iraqi Kurdish forces

Map E.3 Warring Factions in Iraq and Syria, March 27, 2017

This map shows the territories held by Kurdish fighters, ISIS, rebel Syrian fighters, and the Iraqi and Syrian governments.

- Compare the territories held by ISIS with the map of the boundaries set by the Sykes-Picot agreement (see Map 19.4). How similar are the territories that ISIS held in March 2017 to those that Sykes-Picot reserved for an Arab confederation?

- ISIS contends that the British-French agreements for the division of the Arab world after World War I need to be abolished. Why does ISIS hold these views?

- Why would the Turkish, Iraqi, and Syrian governments be dismayed that the Kurds have become the strongest militia fighting against ISIS?

Table E.1 Population of Shiite Muslims, 2009

	Estimated 2009 Shiite population	Approximate percentage of Muslim population that is Shiite
Iran	66–70 million	90–95
Iraq	19–22 million	65–70
Yemen	8–10 million	35–40
Azerbaijan	5–7 million	65–75
Syria	3–4 million	15–20
Lebanon	1–2 million	45–55
Kuwait	500,000–700,000	20–25
Bahrain	400,000–500,000	65–75
World total	154–200 million	10–13

Source: Mapping the Global Muslim Population (Washington, D.C.: Pew Research Center, October 7, 2009).

has troubled Iran's relations with the outside world for more than a decade and that resulted in the placing of severe economic sanctions on Iran. The agreement dealt with Iran's nuclear program, which the Iranians claimed was entirely for civil use; but the United States and many other countries believed that the Iranians were seeking to create nuclear weapon capability. The U.S. government, along with five other states, negotiated a nuclear agreement that was to run for ten years and would allow inspections of the Iranian nuclear facilities while permitting the Iranians to enrich uranium for civil, but not military, uses. The negotiating foreign powers agreed to lift the financial and economic sanctions, thus permitting Iran to engage in trade with the rest of the world and to gain access to its substantial financial resources, tied up in western banks.

Not everyone was pleased with the agreement. Benjamin Netanyahu, the Israeli prime minister, believed that the Iranians would subvert the treaty and build nuclear weapons. As a presidential candidate, Donald Trump called the agreement the worst ever signed; in 2018, as president, he pulled the U.S. out of the agreement. Trump further distanced the U.S. from its allies by agreeing to meet with North Korean dictator Kim Jong-un and accepting the latter's pledge to denuclearize without a timetable, an agreed-upon definition of what counts as denuclearization, or any measures of independent verification.

POVERTY, DISEASE, GENOCIDE

In much of the developing world, poverty, disease, and violence persist. The new millennium did not begin auspiciously for the peoples of Africa. The region remained the poorest in the world and suffered the uncontrolled and uncontrollable spread of HIV/AIDS. (For a global look at hunger and disparities in income, see Maps E.4 and E.5.)

Of the thirty-eight sub-Saharan African countries surveyed in the *World Bank Development Report* for 2009, all but seven were low-income countries. The poorest of the poor (Burundi, the Republic of the Congo, and Liberia) reported per capita incomes of U.S. $150 or less. Botswana, which enjoyed Africa's second-highest per capita income at $6,120 (behind only mineral-rich Gabon), was so devastated by HIV/AIDS that its average life expectancy, once the highest in Africa at close to seventy years, had tumbled to fifty-one years by 2007 and was one of the lowest in the world. (For a global look at HIV incidence, see Map E.6.) As Asian economies have prospered, Africa's share of global poverty has increased. In 2013, more than half of the people living in extreme poverty lived in Africa.

There have, however, been signs of progress. Ghana embraced parliamentary and presidential elections. Civil strife ended in Mozambique and Angola. South Africa convened a Truth and Reconciliation Commission to put the trauma of apartheid behind it and to stay on the course of parliamentary democracy while addressing the gross income inequality between whites and blacks that was a legacy of the twentieth century.

But these countries have been exceptions to the rule in a region where political instability has wrought misery and devastation. Many of Africa's countries (Liberia, Sierra Leone, Mali, the Ivory Coast, and the Central African Republic) were torn asunder by ethnic and personal rivalries, and the resulting conflicts required foreign interventions. Nigeria finally rid itself of its unwanted military dictatorship and moved to a civil, parliamentary system. But Nigeria's democratically elected presidents have barely been able to hold the country together. The people of the Niger Delta in the south of the country continue to rebel and to demand a larger share of the oil wealth their region produces, while in the impoverished northeast, a Muslim group calling itself Boko Haram (meaning no western learning) has carried out acts of shocking violence.

In 2011, just when Africa's longest-running civil war, pitting the animists and Christians of southern Sudan against the Muslim peoples of the north, had seemingly been resolved through the creation of a new state for the southerners, known as South Sudan, an ongoing dispute in western Sudan kept the Sudanese government in civil strife. In the region of Darfur, the state allowed local horse-riding nomads to carry out ethnic cleansing campaigns against settled agriculturalists. Thus, as in Rwanda in the 1990s (see Chapter 21), genocide has once more visited Africa. The conflict has also led to one of Africa's worst cases of displacement: as of 2018, over 4 million refugees have fled government terror and civil war to huddle in vast, miserable camps. But there is some reason for hope. In the West African country of Liberia, after years of pitiless civil war, the belligerents agreed to put down their guns in 2004. In 2005, remarkable elections swept Africa's first woman president, Ellen Johnson-Sirleaf, into office.

DEEPENING INEQUALITIES

Globalization has contributed to economic inequality in some of the poorest parts of the world. Compared with sub-Saharan Africa, Latin America's situation is not so bleak, but the divide between haves and have-nots has widened across the region, which has historically been the world's most unequal. The very rich in Buenos Aires live like the very rich in Boston; magnates of Mexico City drive the same cars, eat the same food, read the same books, and vacation in the same spots as their social cousins from New York. They send their children to private schools in the United States and the United Kingdom to join a cosmopolitan upper class. To Latin American elites, globalization has been a boon, as it has increased their wealth and has facilitated their integration into the international circulation of goods, ideas, and people. Many, in fact, identify less and less with a particular place in the world.

Some of the same features hold for the social bottom. Being disadvantaged and poor in southern Mexico looks a lot like being on the losing end in southern Africa: people cling to tiny parcels of land, migrate long distances for seasonal jobs, and fight against insensitive authorities for their basic needs. In many cases, the best solution to their problems is to leave—to move to cities or across borders in search of opportunities elsewhere.

Latin Americans have responded to these challenges in many ways. One sweeping trend is the election of left-wing governments. Most of these new leaders are not like the rebel firebrands of the 1960s. Instead, in Brazil, Chile, Argentina, and Uruguay, left-wing governments have offered policies designed to soften the blows of globalization and meet basic needs for land, schools, and decent housing. However, the same pressures of globalization that contribute to leftist electoral triumphs limit what these fledgling governments can do. Elsewhere, a more nationalist and populist brand of politics has emerged, one that rejects globalization altogether. Rather than softening the effects of globalization, its leaders promise to reverse them.

The appeal of anti-globalist politics is not limited to Latin America, or even to the developing nations. In the most advanced industrial societies, as well as in rapidly rising nations like China and India, programs to check globalization or buffer people from its destabilizing effects have found receptive

Prevalence of undernourishment (%), 2014–2016

- No data, significant concern
- <5.0%, very low
- 5.0%–9.9%, moderately low
- 10.0%–19.9%, moderately high
- 20.0%–29.9%, high
- >30.0%, very high
- No data

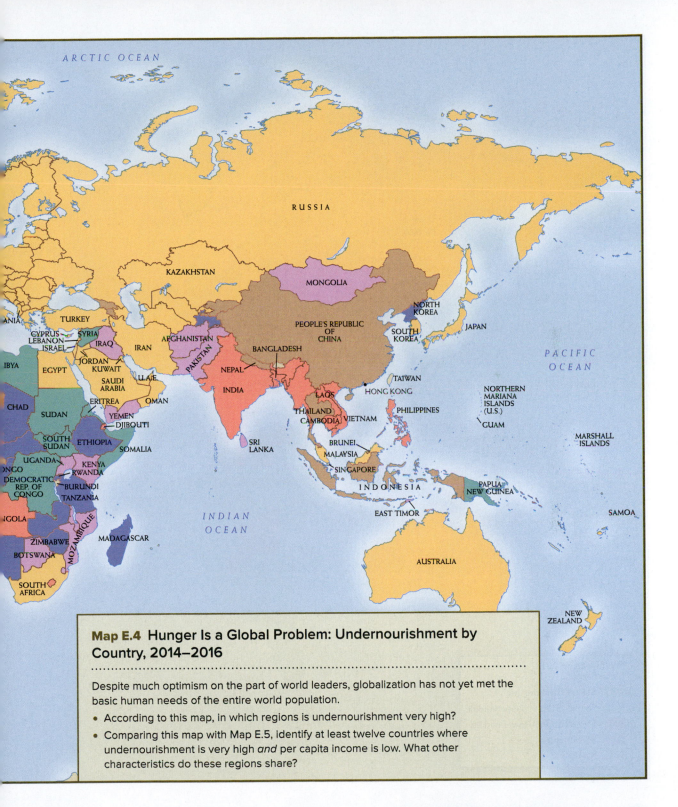

Map E.4 Hunger Is a Global Problem: Undernourishment by Country, 2014–2016

Despite much optimism on the part of world leaders, globalization has not yet met the basic human needs of the entire world population.

- According to this map, in which regions is undernourishment very high?
- Comparing this map with Map E.5, identify at least twelve countries where undernourishment is very high *and* per capita income is low. What other characteristics do these regions share?

World income, 2018
(Gross Domestic Product per capita)

- $18,000 or more, high
- $6,000–$17,999, upper middle
- $2,000–$5,999, lower middle
- $1,999 or less, low
- No data

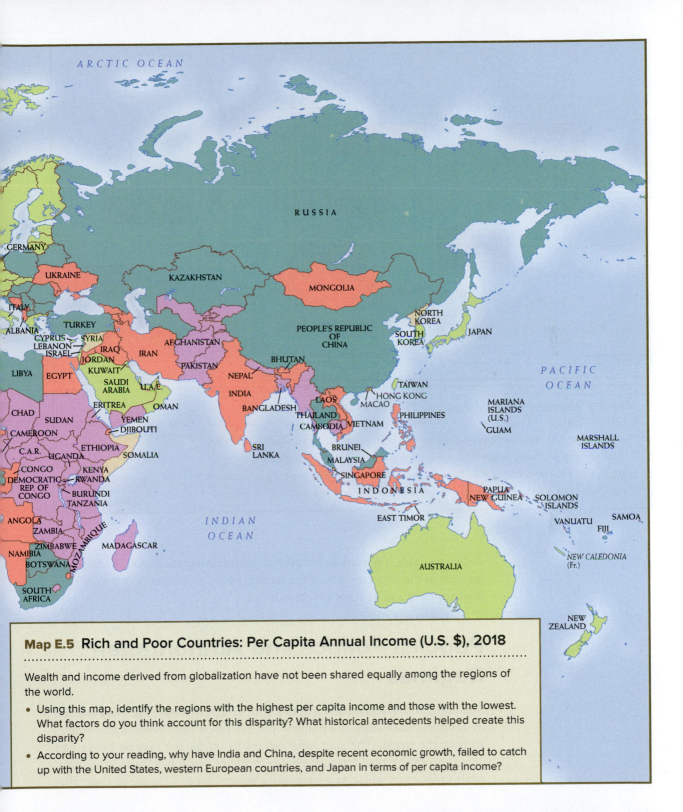

ARCTIC OCEAN

RUSSIA

GERMANY

UKRAINE

ITALY

ALBANIA

TURKEY

CYPRUS

LEBANON

ISRAEL

JORDAN

IRAQ

IRAN

KAZAKHSTAN

MONGOLIA

NORTH
KOREA

SOUTH
KOREA

JAPAN

PACIFIC
OCEAN

LIBYA

EGYPT

KUWAIT

SAUDI
ARABIA

U.A.E.

OMAN

AFGHANISTAN

PAKISTAN

NEPAL

BHUTAN

PEOPLE'S REPUBLIC
OF
CHINA

TAIWAN

HONG KONG

MACAO

INDIA

CHAD

SUDAN

ERITREA

YEMEN

DJIBOUTI

BANGLADESH

LAOS

THAILAND

CAMBODIA

VIETNAM

PHILIPPINES

MARIANA
ISLANDS
(U.S.)

GUAM

MARSHALL
ISLANDS

CAMEROON

C.A.R.

UGANDA

ETHIOPIA

SOMALIA

SRI
LANKA

BRUNEI

MALAYSIA

SINGAPORE

CONGO

DEMOCRATIC
REP. OF
CONGO

KENYA

RWANDA

BURUNDI

TANZANIA

INDONESIA

PAPUA
NEW GUINEA

SOLOMON
ISLANDS

SAMOA

VANUATU

FIJI

ANGOLA

ZAMBIA

ZIMBABWE

MOZAMBIQUE

MADAGASCAR

NAMIBIA

BOTSWANA

INDIAN
OCEAN

EAST TIMOR

NEW CALEDONIA
(Fr.)

AUSTRALIA

SOUTH
AFRICA

NEW
ZEALAND

Map E.5 Rich and Poor Countries: Per Capita Annual Income (U.S. $), 2018

Wealth and income derived from globalization have not been shared equally among the regions of the world.

- Using this map, identify the regions with the highest per capita income and those with the lowest. What factors do you think account for this disparity? What historical antecedents helped create this disparity?

- According to your reading, why have India and China, despite recent economic growth, failed to catch up with the United States, western European countries, and Japan in terms of per capita income?

Map E.6 Numbers of HIV-Positive People Worldwide, 2016

The spread of HIV threatens the development of human capital in the twenty-first century.

• According to this map, which region has the highest rate of HIV infection?

• Using Maps E.4 and E.5 for reference, what connections do you see between poverty and HIV prevalence?

• How does the spread of HIV compromise economic development in poorer regions of the world?

audiences. Still, opposition to deeper global integration continues to be greatest in the poorest parts of the world, where globalization's benefits are least apparent and its costs are often lethal.

Populist Politics and Authoritarian Regimes

Beginning with the financial crisis of 2008, groups that have felt marginalized by economic inequality and political powerlessness have asserted themselves all over the world. The successful efforts to rescue the biggest banks and investors of the global financial system, many of which had caused the crisis, while ordinary people largely became its victims, led to widespread anger that

Inequality in São Paulo, Brazil An aerial view of one of São Paulo's biggest slums, Favela Morumbi, which borders one of the city's richest neighborhoods, also called Morumbi.

was initially ignored—until political entrepreneurs perceived an opportunity. The last decade has experienced a resurgence of populist political sentiments that pit "the people" against their enemies. This politics of "us versus them" directs discontent and anger against illegitimate "others"—elites, immigrants, ethnic and religious minorities—that are portrayed as enemies of the nation. This kind of populism has taken many forms. In some countries, it has been highly autocratic. In democracies like those of Britain, Europe, and the United States, it has seen the rise of ethnic nationalists and the election or emergence of strong right-wing parties. In Britain, it also fueled the vote to leave the European Union.

In India, Prime Minister Narendra Modi rose to become that nation's strongman, claiming to embody the interests of the nation. With opposition parties dispirited and weak, he skillfully used social media to portray himself as a leader working tirelessly to advance India's interests against its foreign and domestic enemies. Taking a cue from their leader's aggressive nationalism, BJP politicians and Hindu vigilante groups targeted minorities, particularly Muslims.

In Turkey, similar religious and autocratic tendencies emerged under the presidency of Recep Tayyip Erdogan, who founded the Justice and Development Party (AKP) in 2001. Erdogan served as prime minister from 2003

Prime Minister Modi Meets with President Erdogan President Recep Tayyip Erdogan (*right*), of Turkey, met with the Indian Prime Minister, Narendra Modi, on November 16, 2015. Both men have used religion to enhance their popularity and the parties that they head, Erdogan fostering Islamism and Modi, Hinduism.

Families at the Border U.S. Border patrol agents stand at an open gate on the fence along the U.S.-Mexico border to allow Luis Eduardo Hernandez-Bautista to hug Ty'Jahnae Williams and his father, Eduardo Hernandez (not in view), as part of Universal Children's Day at the Border Field State Park, California, November 19, 2016.

until 2014 and thereafter as president, championing a party and movement that won an overwhelming majority in the parliamentary election in its first effort in 2001 and has been in control of Turkey's politics ever since. Although as mayor of Istanbul from 1994 to 1998, and then as prime minister, he promoted liberal and democratic policies, Erdogan embraced Islamist and authoritarian policies in the later years of his prime ministership (and especially after he became president). He intimidated journalists and intellectuals who opposed his efforts, and he curtailed freedom of speech, the press, and assembly. On July 15, 2016, a segment of the military attempted a coup d'état against the government, but their attempt failed, emboldening Erdogan to purge the country of people who favored liberal, secular policies. He obtained sweeping powers the following year in a referendum that shifted power decisively from the parliament to the executive, and in 2018 he was reelected president. Although Erdogan's Turkey is not an Islamic theocracy like Iran or a militant state like that of the Taliban in Afghanistan (and although it has joined the battle against ISIS), its shift toward Islamism and authoritarianism has been notable and has rendered its once-desired admission to the European Union impossible.

Nowhere did the rise of populism play out more dramatically than in the United States with the election of Donald Trump, an heir to a real estate fortune who became a celebrity thanks to television and new media such as Twitter. Even as he lost the popular vote, Trump won the U.S. presidency in 2016 by a majority of 77,000 combined votes in three hotly contested states, Pennsylvania, Michigan, and Wisconsin, which delivered his majority in the decisive Electoral College. Trump campaigned against immigration and free trade. Most fundamentally, he was supported by people who felt ignored in the national conversation and overlooked by the mainstream media and political establishment.

In many ways, Trump's campaign to "Make America Great Again" mirrored developments in Russia, even beyond the American president's profuse admiration for Russia's strongman leader. In Russia, too, a powerful sense of aggrieved nationalism, accusations of deception by the western media, contempt for any limits on executive power, and charges that the open, rules-based international order was rigged galvanized a wide following. The difference is that whereas Russia has always called into question the liberal world system, America created that system; U.S. withdrawal from that system therefore raises big questions about its future.

Conclusion: Globalization and Its Discontents

Globalization has had transforming effects, many of them decidedly good for large segments of the world's population, but some of them unsettling. Freer markets and international trade have created a global middle class, pulling nearly half a million Chinese out of poverty, as well as equally huge proportions of the poor in India, Southeast Asia, Egypt, Nigeria, South Africa, and many other communities around the world. Members of the new international middle class communicate with one another, read the same newspapers

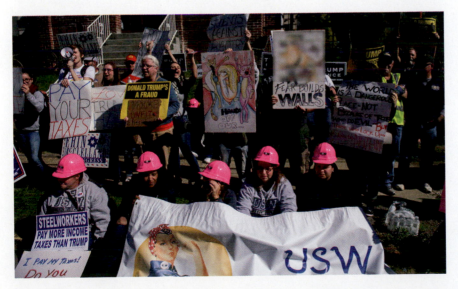

Steelworkers Protest
Protestors demonstrate outside a rally for Republican presidential candidate Donald J. Trump at Ambridge Area Senior High School on October 10, 2016, in Ambridge, Pennsylvania. Ambridge, named after the American Bridge Company, a steel fabricating plant that once employed 60,000 workers, is traditionally a Democratic stronghold, but it shifted Republican as a shrinking tax base and lost jobs devastated the former industrial community. Donald Trump would carry Beaver County, PA, with nearly 60 percent of the vote.

and journals, see the same films, wear the same clothes, and eat the same foods. Nor is everything made in America, as the Nobel Prize in Literature, the leading film actors of the world, and the major commentators on increasingly international television and radio networks demonstrate. The extremely high economic growth rates enjoyed by states once regarded as part of the developing world could not have been achieved without international trade networks and significant free trade agreements.

Nonetheless, the negative effects of globalization have been much in evidence, especially since the financial crisis of 2008. While major banks and large multinational corporations were bailed out, the less well off suffered grievously. In America, the hardest hit were white workers between the ages of forty-five and fifty-four who lacked a high school education. Their death rates became alarmingly high as the result of suicide, drug addiction and overdosing, and alcoholism, bringing about for the first time an overall decline in the average life span of white males. The marginalized no longer remained silent, however. They voted overwhelmingly for Brexit (Britain's departure from the European Union) and contributed to the rise of Islamic militancy, Hindu nationalism, Turkey's turn toward Islamism and authoritarianism, and the increasing popularity of right-wing, ethnic nationalist parties in Europe, many of which oppose immigrant communities and balk at allowing refugees into their countries. In the United States, they elected Donald Trump, thereby turning away from the economic and security agreements that were central to American leadership in the post–World War II period and the initial efforts to contain climate change. In short, globalization has drawn the world more closely together, enhancing the life prospects of many, but threatening those groups who, deprived of education and marketable skills, are ill equipped to take advantage of globalism's opportunities.

Further Readings

Chapter 1: Becoming Human

Arsuaga, Juan Luis, *The Neanderthal's Necklace: In Search of the First Thinkers*, trans. Anthony Klatt (2002). A stimulating overview of prehistory that focuses on the Neanderthals and compares them with *Homo sapiens*.

Barham, Lawrence, and Peter Mitchell, *The First Africans: African Archaeology from the Earliest Toolmakers to Most Recent Foragers* (2008). New findings on the evolution of hominids in Africa.

Barker, Graeme, *Agricultural Revolution in Prehistory: Why Did Foragers Become Farmers?* (2006). The most recent truly global and up-to-date study of this momentous event in world history.

Bellwood, Peter, *First Farmers: The Origins of Agricultural Societies* (2005). A state-of-the-art global history of the origins of agriculture including recent archaeological, linguistic, and microbiological data.

Bender, Michael L., *Paleoclimate* (2013). A definitive overview of the world's climate over the entire life of our universe, written by a renowned geoclimatologist.

Bogucki, Peter, *The Origins of Human Society* (1999). An authoritative overview of prehistory.

Brooke, John L., *Climate Change and the Course of Global History: A Rough Journey* (2014). An excellent overview of the impact of climate on history; particularly useful for the hominin period and the emergence of *Homo sapiens*.

Callaway, Ewen, "Oldest *Homo sapiens* Fossil Claim Rewrites Our Species' History," *Nature News*, June 7, 2017, doi:10.1038/nature.2017.22114. Describes and contextualizes Hublin's early *Homo sapiens* finds at Jebel Irhoud in Morocco.

Cauvin, Jacques, *The Birth of the Gods and the Origins of Agriculture*, translated by Trevor Watkins from the original 1994 French publication (2000). An important work on the agricultural revolution of Southwest Asia and the evolution of symbolic thinking at this time.

Cavalli-Sforza, Luigi Luca, *Genes, Peoples, and Languages*, translated by Mark Seielstad from the original 1996 French publication (2000). An expert's introduction to the use of gene research for revealing new information about the evolution of human beings in the distant past.

Childe, V. Gordon, *What Happened in History* (1964). A classic work by one of the pioneers in studying the early history and evolution of human beings. Though superseded in many respects, it is still an important place to start one's reading and a work of great power and emotion.

Christian, David, *Maps of Time: An Introduction to Big History* (2004). Offers an outline of Big History from the formation of the universe and planets, to the beginnings of life on earth, to humans, to the modern era; emphasizes the value of examining both collective learning and human extensification/intensification of the

earth's resources for making sense of human history at the grandest scale.

Clark, J. Desmond, and Steven A. Brandt (eds.), *From Hunters to Farmers: The Causes and Consequences of Food Production in Africa* (1984). Excellent essays on the agricultural revolution.

Coon, Carleton Stevens, *The Story of Man: From the First Human to Primitive Culture and Beyond*, 2nd ed. (1962). An important early work on the evolution of humans, emphasizing the distinctiveness of "races" around the world.

Cunliffe, Barry (ed.), *The Oxford Illustrated Prehistory of Europe* (1994). The definitive work on early European history.

Ehrenberg, Margaret, *Women in Prehistory* (1989). What was the role of women in hunting and gathering societies, and how greatly were women affected by the agricultural revolution? The author offers a number of stimulating generalizations.

Ehret, Christopher, *The Civilizations of Africa: A History to 1800* (2002). Although this is a general history of Africa, the author, a linguist and an expert on early African history, offers new information and new overviews of African peoples in very ancient times.

Fagan, Brian, *People of the Earth: An Introduction to World Prehistory* (1989). An authoritative overview of early history, widely used in classrooms.

Fage, J. D., and Roland Oliver (eds.), *The Cambridge History of Africa*, 8 vols. (1975–1984). A pioneering work of synthesis by two of the first and foremost scholars of the history of Africa. Volume 1 deals with African prehistory.

Frison, George C., *Survival by Hunting: Prehistoric Human Predators and Animal Prey* (2004). An archaeologist applies his knowledge of animal habitats, behavior, and hunting strategies to an examination of prehistoric hunting practices in the North American Great Plains and Rocky Mountains.

Gebauer, Anne Birgitte, and T. Douglas Price (eds.), *Transition to Agriculture in Prehistory* (1992). Excellent essays on the agricultural revolution, especially those written by the two editors.

Gibbons, Ann, "World's Oldest *Homo sapiens* Fossils Found in Morocco," *Science*, June 7, 2017, doi:10.1126/science.aan6934. An accessible discussion of Jebel Irhoud fossils that explains how they "fit" the picture of other hominid finds.

Harari, Yuval Noah, *Sapiens: A Brief History of Humankind* (2015). A largely successful overview of human history from the hominins to the present.

Hershkovitz, Israel, et al., "The Earliest Modern Humans Outside Africa," *Science* 359 (January 26, 2018): 456–59. Reviews the scientific evidence for the *Homo sapiens* fossils found at Mount Carmel, pushing back the date of *Homo sapiens* migration out of Africa closer to 180,000 years ago.

Hublin, Jean-Jacques, et al., "New Fossils from Jebel Irhoud, Morocco and the Pan-African Origin of *Homo sapiens*," Nature 546 (June 8, 2017): 289–92, doi:10.1038/nature22336. The report from Hublin's team that explains the significance of the Jebel Irhoud

site and of the identification of the fossils found there as *Homo sapiens*.

"Inter-Group Violence among the Early Holocene Hunter-Gatherers of West Turkana, Kenya," *Nature* 529 (January 21, 2016): 394–98. Describes a spectacular discovery of the remains of hunter-gatherers who engaged in warfare.

Johnson, Donald, Lenora Johnson, and Blake Edgar, *Ancestors: In Search of Human Origins* (1999). A good overview of human evolution, with insightful essays on *Homo erectus* and *Homo sapiens*.

Jones, Steve, Robert Martin, and David Pilbeam (eds.), *The Cambridge Encyclopedia of Human Evolution* (1992). A superb guide to a wide range of subjects, crammed with up-to-date information on the most controversial and obscure topics of human evolution and early history.

Ki-Zerbo, J. (ed.), *Methodology and African Prehistory*, vol. 1 of *General History of Africa* (1981). The first volume of UNESCO's general history of Africa, written for the most part by scholars of African heritage.

Klein, Richard G., and Blake Edger, *The Dawn of Human Culture* (2002). A fine and reliable guide to the tangled history of human evolution.

Leakey, Richard, *The Origin of Humankind* (1994). A readable and exciting account of human evolution, written by the son of the pioneering archaeologists Louis and Mary Leakey, a scholar of equal stature to his parents.

Lewin, Roger, *The Origin of Modern Humans* (1993). Yet another good overview of human evolution, with useful chapters on early art and the use of symbols.

Loewe, Michael, and Edward Shaughnessy (eds.), *The Cambridge*

History of Ancient China: From the Origins of Civilization to 221 B.C. (1999). A good review of the archaeology of ancient China.

Mathieson, Iain, et al., "Genome-Wide Patterns of Selection in 230 Ancient Eurasians," *Nature* 522 (November 23, 2015), published online. New DNA research on the skeletons of 230 West-Eurasians who lived between 6500 and 300 BCE shows the three waves of migrations into Europe in its distant past. These migrations came from Africa via Southwest Asia, Anatolia, and the Russian steppes.

Mellaart, James, *Çatal Höyük: A Neolithic Town in Anatolia* (1967). A detailed description of one of the first towns associated with the agricultural revolution in Southwest Asia.

Meredith, Martin, *Born in Africa: The Quest for Human Origins* (2011). A well-written and authoritative overview of the evolution of humankind from the earliest hominins to *Homo sapiens*.

Mithen, Steven, *The Prehistory of the Mind: The Cognitive Origins of Art and Science* (1996). A stimulating discussion of the impact of biological and cultural evolution on the cognitive structure of the human mind.

Olson, Steve, *Mapping Human History: Genes, Race, and Our Common Origins* (2003). Using the findings of genetics and attacking the racial thinking of an earlier generation of archaeologists, the author writes powerfully about the unity of all human beings.

Price, T. Douglas (ed.), *Europe's First Farmers* (2000). A discussion of the agricultural revolution in Europe.

Price, T. Douglas, and Anne Birgitte Gebauer (eds.), *Last Hunters—First Farmers: New Perspectives on* the *Prehistoric Transition to Agriculture* (1996). An exciting collection of essays by some of the leading scholars in the field studying the transition from hunting and gathering to settled agriculture.

Richter, Daniel, et al., "The Age of the Hominin Fossils from Jebel Irhoud, Morocco, and the Origins of the Middle Stone Age," *Nature* 546 (June 8, 2017): 293–96, doi:10.1038/nature22335. Reviews the methods used by scientists to determine the date of the *Homo sapiens* fossils at Jebel Irhoud.

Scarre, Chris (ed.), *The Human Past: World Prehistory and the Development of Human Societies* (2005). An encyclopedia and an overview rolled up into one mammoth volume, written by leading figures in the field of early human history.

Shaw, Thurstan, et al. (eds.), *The Archaeology of Africa: Food, Metals, and Towns* (1993). Up-to-date research on the earliest history of human beings in Africa.

Shreeve, James, "Mystery Man," *National Geographic* 228 (October 2015): 30–57. An authoritative and up-to-date account of the extraordinary discovery of fossil remains of a hominid species, now named *Homo naledi*.

Smith, Bruce D., *The Emergence of Agriculture* (1995). How early humans domesticated wild animals and plants.

Stringer, Christopher, and Robin McKie, *African Exodus: The Origins of Modern Humanity* (1996). Detailed data on why Africa was the source of human origins and why *Homo sapiens* is a recent wanderer out of Africa.

Tattersall, Ian, *The Fossil Trail: How We Know What We Think We Know about Human Evolution* (1995).

A passionately written book about early archaeological discoveries and the centrality of Africa in human evolution.

———, *Masters of the Planet: The Search for Our Human Origins* (2012). The most recent survey of human evolution.

———, *The World from Beginnings to 4000 BCE* (2008). A brief up-to-date overview of humanity's early history by a leading authority.

Van Oosterzee, Penny, *Dragon Bones: The Story of Peking Man* (2000). Describes how the late nineteenth-century unearthing of sites in China containing fossils of animals used for medicinal purposes led to the discovery of the fossils of Peking Man.

Weiss, Mark L., and Alan E. Mann, *Human Biology and Behavior: An Anthropological Perspective* (1996). The authors stress the contribution that biological research has made and continues to make to the unraveling of the mystery of human evolution.

Wrangham, Richard, *Catching Fire: How Cooking Made Us Human* (2009). The author shows how fire made it possible for humans to have a more varied and richer diet but also one that provided energy for the one organ—the brain—that consumes the most energy.

Chapter 2: Rivers, Cities, and First States, 3500–2000 BCE

Adams, Robert McCormick, *The Evolution of Urban Society* (1966). A classic study of the social, political, and economic processes that led to the development of the first urban civilizations.

Algaze, Guillermo, *Ancient Mesopotamia at the Dawn of Civilization* (2008). A compelling analysis of the complex environmental and social factors underlying the rise of the world's first urban culture in southern Mesopotamia.

———, *The Uruk World System: The Dynamics of Expansion of Early Mesopotamian Civilization* (1993). A compelling argument for the colonization of the Tigris-Euphrates basin by the proto-Sumerians at the end of the fourth millennium BCE.

Andrews, Carol, *Egyptian Mummies* (1998). An illustrated summary of Egyptian mummification and burial practices.

Bagley, Robert, *Ancient Sichuan: Treasures from a Lost Civilization* (2001). Describes the remarkable findings in southwestern China, particularly at Sanxingdui, that have challenged earlier accounts of the Shang dynasty's central role in the rise of early Chinese civilization.

Bar-Yosef, Ofar, and Anatoly Khazanov (eds.), *Pastoralism in the Levant: Archaeological Materials in Anthropological Perspectives* (1992). Classic study of the role of nomads in the development of societies in the Levant during the Neolithic period.

Bruhns, Karen Olsen, *Ancient South America* (1994). The best basic text on pre-Columbian South American cultures.

Butzer, Karl W., *Early Hydraulic Civilization in Egypt: A Study of Cultural Ecology* (1976). The best work on how the Egyptians dealt with the Nile floods and the influence that these arrangements had on the overall organization of society.

Cunliffe, Barry, *Europe between the Oceans, 9000 BC–AD 1000* (2008). A very up-to-date and spectacularly illustrated account of early Europe.

Feng, Li, *Early China: A Social and Cultural History* (2013). An important new study on the origins of Chinese culture.

Fukuyama, Francis, *The Origins of Political Order: From Prehistoric Times to the French Revolution* (2011). A superb overview of the powerful political elements that were behind the great river-basin societies in ancient times.

Habu, Junko, *Ancient Jomon of Japan* (2004). Study of prehistoric Jomon hunter-gatherers on the Japanese archipelago that incorporates several different aspects of anthropological studies, including hunter-gatherer archaeology, settlement archaeology, and pottery analysis.

Jacobsen, Thorkild, *The Treasures of Darkness: A History of Mesopotamian Religion* (1976). Best introduction to the religious and philosophical thought of ancient Mesopotamia.

Kemp, Barry J., *Ancient Egypt: Anatomy of a Civilization* (1989). A synthetic overview of the culture of the pharaohs.

Kramer, Samuel Noah, *The Sumerians: Their History, Culture and Character* (1963). Classic study of the Sumerians and their culture by a pioneer in Sumerian studies.

Pollock, Susan, *Ancient Mesopotamia: The Eden That Never Was* (1999). An analysis of the social and economic development of Mesopotamia from the beginnings of settlement until the reign of Hammurapi.

Possehl, Gregory L., *Indus Age: The Beginnings* (1999). The second of four volumes analyzing the history of the Indus Valley civilization.

Postgate, J. N., *Early Mesopotamia: Society and Economy at the Dawn of History* (1992). A study of the economic and political development of the Sumerian civilization.

Preziosi, Donald, and L. A. Hitchcock, *Aegean Art and Architecture* (1999). One of the best general guides to the figurative and decorative art produced both by the Minoans and Mycenaeans and by related early societies in the region of the Aegean.

Ratnagar, Shereen, *Trading Encounters: From the Euphrates to the Indus in the Bronze Age*, 2nd ed. (2004). A comprehensive presentation of the evidence for the relationship between the Indus Valley and its western neighbors.

———, *Understanding Harappa: Civilization in the Greater Indus Valley* (2001). Harappan site archaeological data of the last century organized into a historical narrative comprehensible to the general audience.

Rice, Michael, *Egypt's Legacy: The Archetypes of Western Civilization, 3000–300 BC* (1997). The author argues for the decisive influence of Egyptian culture on the whole of the Mediterranean and its later historical development.

Roaf, Michael, *Cultural Atlas of Mesopotamia and the Ancient Near East* (1990). A comprehensive compendium of the historical and cultural development of the Mesopotamian civilization from the Neolithic background through the Persian Empire.

Shaw, Ian (ed.), *The Oxford History of Ancient Egypt* (2000). The most up-to-date and comprehensive account of the history of Egypt down to the Greek invasion.

Thorp, Robert, *The Chinese Neolithic: Trajectories to Early States* (2005). Uses the latest archaeological evidence to describe the development of early Bronze Age cultures in northern and northwestern China from about 2000 BCE.

Tignor, Robert L., *Egypt: A Short History* (2011). An overview of the history of Egypt from the rise of the pharaohs to the present.

Wachsmann, Shelley, *Seagoing Ships and Seamanship in the Bronze Age Levant* (1998). Provides a compelling, in-depth, and well-documented review of the evidence for ships from several Bronze Age seafaring peoples (including Egyptians, Mycenaeans, and Sea Peoples) and also discusses activities such as shipbuilding, navigation, and piracy.

Wright, Rita P., *The Ancient Indus: Urbanism, Economy, and Society* (2010). A reconstruction of the Indus society with updated archaeological data.

Chapter 3: Nomads, Territorial States, and Microsocieties, 2000–1200 BCE

Allan, Sarah, *The Shape of the Turtle: Myth, Art, and Cosmos in Early China* (1991). Explains the roles of divination and sacrifice in artistic representations of the Shang cosmology.

Allen, James P., *Middle Egyptian: An Introduction to the Language and Culture of Hieroglyphs* (2000). An introduction to the system of writing and its use in Ancient Egypt.

Anthony, David W., *The Horse, the Wheel, and Language: How Bronze-Age Riders from the Eurasian Steppes Shaped the Modern World* (2007). A superb analysis of the origins and spread of the Indo-European peoples.

Arnold, Dieter, *Building in Ancient Egypt: Pharaonic Stone Masonry* (1996). Details the complex construction of monumental stone architecture in ancient Egypt.

Baines, John, and Jaromir Málek, *Atlas of Ancient Egypt* (1980). Useful compilation of information on ancient Egyptian society, religion, history, and geography.

Beal, Richard H., *The Organization of the Hittite Military* (1992). A detailed study based on textual sources of the world's first chariot-based army.

Behringer, Wolfgang, *A Cultural History of Climate* (2010). A general history of the impact of climate on many different societies.

Bogucki, Peter, and Pam J. Crabtree (eds.), *Ancient Europe 8000 BC–AD 1000: Encyclopedia of the Barbarian World*, 2 vols. (2004). An indispensable handbook on the economic, social, artistic, and religious life in Europe during this period.

Bruhns, Karen Olsen, *Ancient South America* (1994). The best basic text on pre-Columbian South American cultures.

Bryant, Edwin, *The Quest for the Origins of Vedic Culture: The Indo-Aryan Migration Debate* (2001). Insight into the highly charged debate on who the Indo-European speakers were, where they originated, and where they migrated to.

Castleden, Rodney, *The Mycenaeans* (2005). One of the best current surveys of all aspects of the Mycenaean Greeks.

Chadwick, John, *The Decipherment of Linear B*, 2nd ed. (1968). Not only a retelling of the story of the decipherment of the Linear B script, but also an introduction to the actual content and function of the tablets themselves.

Childs-Johnson, Elizabeth, "Fu Zi, the Shang Woman Warrior," in Lily Xiao Hong Lee, A. D. Stefanowska, and Sue Wiles (eds.), *Biographical Dictionary of Chinese Women, Antiquity through Sui, 1600 B.C.E.–618 C.E.* (2007), pp. 19–25. Offers a biography of Fu Hao (Fu Zi) that summarizes

much Chinese-language scholarship as well as a thorough discussion of the items found in her tomb.

Cline, E. H., *Sailing the Wine-Dark Sea: International Trade and the Late Bronze Age Aegean* (1994). An excellent account of the trade and contacts between the Aegean and other areas of the Mediterranean, Europe, and the Near East during the late Bronze Age.

Cunliffe, Barry, *Facing the Ocean: The Atlantic and Its Peoples, 8000 BC–AD 1500* (2001). An in-depth, highly useful treatment of western Europe during this period.

——— (ed.), *Prehistoric Europe: An Illustrated History* (1997). A state-of-the-art treatment of first farmers, agricultural developments, and material culture in prehistoric Europe.

Curry, Andrew, "Slaughter at the Bridge," *Science* 351 (March 25, 2016): 1384–89. New information on a battle among hunter-gatherer warriors in northern Europe in the thirteenth century BCE.

Davis, W. V., and L. Schofield, *Egypt, the Aegean and the Levant: Interconnections in the Second Millennium BC* (1995). A discussion of the complex interactions in the eastern Mediterranean during the "international age."

Doumas, Christos, *Thera: Pompeii of the Ancient Aegean* (1983). A study of the tremendous volcanic eruption and explosion that destroyed the Minoan settlement on the island of Thera.

Drews, Robert, *Coming of the Greeks: Indo-European Conquests in the Aegean and the Near East* (1988). A good survey of the evidence for the "invasions" or "movements of peoples" that reconfigured the world of the eastern Mediterranean and Near East.

Finley, M. I., *The World of Odysseus,* 2nd rev. ed. (1977; reprint, 2002). The classic work that describes what might be recovered about the social values and behaviors of men and women in the so-called Dark Ages of early Greek history.

Frankfort, Henri, *Ancient Egyptian Religion: An Interpretation* (1948; reprint, 2000). A classic study of Egyptian religion and culture during the pharaonic period.

Keightley, David N., *The Ancestral Landscape: Time, Space, and Community in Late Shang China, ca. 1200–1045 BC* (2000). Provides insights into the nature of royal kinship that undergirded the Shang court and its regional domains.

Kemp, Barry J., *Ancient Egypt: Anatomy of a Civilization* (2006). A definitive presentation of the history, culture, and religion of ancient Egypt.

Klein, Jacob, "The Marriage of Martu: The Urbanization of 'Barbaric' Nomads," in Meir Malul (ed.), *Mutual Influences of Peoples and Cultures in the Ancient Near East* (1996). A crucial text in the corpus of scholarship on Sumerian literature.

Kristiansen, Kristian, *Europe before History* (1998). The finest recent survey of all the major developmental phases of European prehistory.

McIntosh, Jane, *Handbook to Life in Prehistoric Europe* (2006). Highlights the archaeological evidence that enables us to re-create the day-to-day life of different prehistoric communities in Europe.

Pines, Yuri, *The Everlasting Empire: The Political Culture of Ancient China and Its Imperial Legacy* (2012). How imperial unity became the norm in ancient China.

Preziosi, Donald, and L. A. Hitchcock, *Aegean Art and Architecture*

(1999). One of the best general guides to the figurative and decorative art produced both by the Minoans and Mycenaeans and by related early societies in the region of the Aegean.

Quirke, Stephen, *Ancient Egyptian Religion* (1992). A highly readable presentation of ancient Egyptian religion that summarizes the roles and attributions of the many Egyptian gods.

The Rigveda, the Earliest Religious Poetry of India, trans. Stephanie W. Jamison and Joel P. Brereton (2014). A new translation of the earliest literature of South Asia, correcting errors made in earlier translations.

Robins, Gay, *The Art of Ancient Egypt* (1997). The most comprehensive survey to date of the art of pharaonic Egypt.

————, *Women in Ancient Egypt* (1993). An interesting survey of the place of women in ancient Egyptian society.

Romer, John, *Ancient Lives: Daily Life in Egypt of the Pharaohs* (1990). A discussion of the economic and social lives of everyday ancient Egyptians.

Sandars, N. K., *The Sea Peoples: Warriors of the Ancient Mediterranean* (1985). A readable discussion of a very complex period of Levantine history.

Simpson, William Kelly (ed.), *The Literature of Ancient Egypt: An Anthology of Stories, Instructions, and Poetry* (1972). A compilation of the most important works of literature from ancient Egypt.

Thapar, Romila, *The Past before Us: Historical Tradition of Early North India* (2013). A comprehensive evaluation of ancient Indian literature.

Thorp, Robert L., *China in the Early Bronze Age: Shang Civilization* (2005). Reviews the archaeological discoveries near Anyang, site of two capitals of the Shang kings.

Warren, Peter, *The Aegean Civilizations: From Ancient Crete to Mycenae*, 2nd ed. (1989). An excellent textual and pictorial guide to all the basic aspects of the Minoan and Mycenaean societies.

Wilson, John A., *The Culture of Ancient Egypt* (1951). A classic study of the history and culture of pharaonic Egypt.

Yadin, Yigael, *The Art of Warfare in Biblical Lands in the Light of Archaeological Discovery* (1963). A well-illustrated presentation of the machinery of war in the second and first millennia BCE.

Yoffee, Norman (ed.), *The Cambridge World History*, vol. 3, *Early Cities in Comparative Perspective* (2014). One of nine volumes that trace world history through individual articles written by experts.

Chapter 4: First Empires and Common Cultures in Afro-Eurasia, 1250–325 BCE

Ahlström, Gosta W., *The History of Ancient Palestine from the Paleolithic Period to Alexander's Conquests* (1993). An excellent survey of the history of the region by a renowned expert, with good attention to the recent archaeological evidence.

Aubet, Maria Eugenia, *The Phoenicians and the West*, 2nd ed. (2001). The basic survey of the Phoenician colonization of the western Mediterranean and Atlantic, with special attention to recent archaeological discoveries.

Behringer, Wolfgang, *A Cultural History of Climate*, trans. Patrick Camiller (2010). A summary view of the place of climate in historical change, written by an expert in historical climatology.

Benjamin, Craig (ed.), *The Cambridge World History*, vol. 4, *A World with States, Empires, and Networks, 1200 BCE–900 CE* (2015). An important overview of developments in the world, with individual chapters written by experts.

Briant, Pierre, *From Cyrus to Alexander: A History of the Persian Empire*, trans. Peter T. Daniels (2002). A complex and comprehensive history of the Persian Empire by its finest modern scholar.

Bright, John, *A History of Israel*, 4th ed. (2000). An updated version of a classic and still very useful overview of the whole history of the Israelite people down to the end of the period covered in this chapter.

Cook, J. M., *The Persian Empire* (1983). An older but still useful, and highly readable, standard history of the Persian Empire.

Fagan, Brian, *The Long Summer: How Climate Changed Civilization* (2004). An accessible overview of the role of climate in historical change, written by one of the leading historians of ancient history and an individual who has brought together considerable evidence about climate change and historical development.

Falkenhausen, Lothar von, *Chinese Society in the Age of Confucius (1000–250 BC): The Archaeological Evidence* (2006). A timely reassessment of early Chinese history that compares the literary texts on which it has traditionally been based with the new archaeological evidence.

Frye, Richard N., *The Heritage of Persia* (1963). This classic study of ancient Iran gives the political and literary history of the Persians and their successors.

Fukuyama, Francis, *The Origins of Political Order: From Prehuman*

Times to the French Revolution (2011). Argues that the first real kings in Chinese history and the first real states and dynasties did not appear until the Qin and Han.

Grayson, A. K., "Assyrian Civilization," in *Cambridge Ancient History*, vol. 3, pt. 2, pp. 194–228 (1992). The Assyrian and Babylonian empires and other states of the Near East, from the eighth to the sixth century BCE.

Hornung, Erik, *Akhenaten and the Religion of Light*, translated from the German by David Lorton (1999). An important, brief biography of Egypt's most controversial pharaoh.

———, *History of Ancient Egypt: An Introduction*, translated from the German by David Lorton (1999). An accessible overview of the history of ancient Egypt by a leading Egyptologist.

Isserlin, Benedikt J., *The Israelites* (1998). A very well-written and heavily illustrated history of all aspects of life in the regions of the Levant inhabited by the Israelites, equally good on the latest scholarship and the archaeological data.

Keay, John, *India: A History* (2010). A useful, readable overview of the sweep of Indian history.

Lancel, Serge, *Carthage: A History*, trans. Antonia Nevill (1997). By far the best single-volume history of the most important Phoenician colony in the Mediterranean (the first three chapters are especially relevant to materials covered in this chapter).

Lemche, Niels Peter, *Ancient Israel: A New History of Israelite Society* (1988). A quick, readable, and still up-to-date summary of the main phases and themes.

Lewis, Mark Edward, *Writing and Authority in Early China* (1999). A work that traces the changing uses of writing to command assent and obedience in early China.

Liu, Guozhong, *Introduction to the Tsinghua Bamboo-Strip Manuscripts*, trans. Christopher J. Foster and William N. French (2016). An important essay on the implications of these texts for our understanding of early Western Zhou history.

Liverani, Mario, *The Ancient Near East: History, Society and Economy* (2014). Parts 5 and 6 are especially relevant to the materials covered in this chapter.

Markoe, Glenn E., *Phoenicians* (2000). A thorough survey of the Phoenicians and their society as it first developed in the Levant and then expanded over the Mediterranean, with excellent illustrations of the diverse archaeological sites.

Matthews, Victor H., and Don C. Benjamin, *Social World of Ancient Israel, 1350–587 BCE* (1993). A thematic overview of the main occupational groups and social roles that characterized ancient Israelite society.

Oates, Joan, and David Oates, *Nimrud: An Assyrian Imperial City Revealed* (2001). A fine and highly readable summary of the state of our knowledge of the Assyrian Empire from the perspective of the early capital of Assurnasirpal II.

Oded, Bustenay, *Mass Deportations and Deportees in the Neo-Assyrian Empire* (1979). A detailed textual examination of the deportation strategy of the Assyrian kings. Good for in-depth research of the question.

Potts, D. T., *The Archaeology of Elam: Formation and Transformation of an Ancient Iranian State* (1999). The definitive study of the archaeology of western Iran from the Neolithic period through the Persian Empire.

Quinn, Josephine C., and Nicholas C. Vella (eds.), *The Punic Mediterranean* (2014). A valuable and readable collection of chapters on various aspects of how the Phoenician colonization of the Mediterranean led to the formation of new cultural identities.

Radner, Karen, *Ancient Assyria: A Very Short Introduction* (2015). A highly readable and up-to-date survey of all the important aspects of Assyrian government and society.

Shaughnessy, Edward L., *Sources of Western Zhou History: Inscribed Bronze Vessels* (1992). Detailed work on the historiography and interpretation of the thousands of ritual bronze vessels discovered by China's archaeologists.

Stein, Burton, *A History of India*, 2nd ed., edited by David Arnold (2010). One of the standard general histories of India, brought up to date by a leading historian of the subcontinent.

Tanner, Harold M., *China: A History* (2009). A readable and up-to-date overview of the sweep of Chinese history.

Thapar, Romila, *The Aryan: Recasting Constructs* (2011). On the rise of the theory of an Aryan race and the beginnings of Indian history.

———, *From Lineage to State* (1984). The only book on early India that uses religious literature historically and analyzes major lineages to reveal the transition from tribal society to state institutions.

Tignor, Robert L., *Egypt: A Short History* (2010). A succinct treatment of the entire history of Egypt from the pharaohs to the present, with three chapters on the ancient period.

Trautmann, Thomas, *India: Brief History of a Civilization* (2011). A highly readable survey of Indian history with emphasis on its early history.

Tubb, Jonathan N., *Canaanites* (1998). The best recent survey, well illustrated, of one of the main ethnic groups dominating the culture of the Levant.

Chapter 5: Worlds Turned Inside Out, 1000–350 BCE

Adams, William Y., *Nubia: Corridor to Africa* (1977). The authoritative historical overview of Nubia, the area of present-day Sudan just south of Egypt and a geographic connecting point between the Mediterranean and sub-Saharan Africa.

Allan, Sarah, *Buried Ideas: Legends of Abdication and Ideal Government in Early Chinese Bamboo-Slip Manuscripts* (2016). Four recently discovered Warring States texts challenge long-standing ideas about Chinese intellectual history.

Armstrong, Karen, *Buddha* (2001). A readable and impressive account of the life of the Buddha.

———, *The Great Transformation: The Beginning of Our Religious Traditions* (2006). A thorough investigation of a key moment in the evolution of religious thought, explaining the traditions that arose in the ninth century BCE in four regions of the civilized world as a response to the violence of the period.

Aubet, Maria Eugenia, *The Phoenicians and the West*, 2nd ed. (2001). The basic survey of the Phoenician colonization of the western Mediterranean and Atlantic, with special attention to recent archaeological discoveries.

Barker, Graeme, and Tom Rasmussen, *The Etruscans* (1998). The most up-to-date introduction to this important pre-Roman society in the Italian peninsula, with strong emphasis on broad social and material patterns of development as indicated by the archaeological evidence.

Bellah, Robert N., "What Is Axial about the Axial Age?" *European Journal of Sociology* 46, no. 1 (2005): 69–89. A useful categorical analysis of the four cases of axial "breakthrough"—ancient Israel, Greece, India, and China.

Benjamin, Craig (ed.), *The Cambridge World History*, vol. 4, *A World with States, Empires, and Networks, 1200 BCE–900 CE* (2015). Essays by experts on these centuries in world history. Especially important for thinking about the Axial Age is the chapter by Bjorn Wittrock, "The Axial Age in World History," pp. 101–19.

Bresson, Alain, *The Making of the Ancient Greek Economy: Institutions, Markets, and Growth in the City-States*, trans. Steven Rendall (2015). The most conceptually sophisticated and factually up-to-date account of the economic regimes of the Greek city-states.

Bruhns, Karen Olsen, *Ancient South America* (1994). A very useful overview of recent debates and conclusions about pre-Columbian archaeology in South America, including both the Andes and the lowland and coastal regions.

Burkert, Walter, *Greek Religion*, trans. John Raffan (1985). The best one-volume introduction to early Greek religion, placing the Greeks in their larger Mediterranean and Near Eastern contexts.

Cartledge, Paul (ed.), *The Cambridge Illustrated History of Ancient Greece* (2002). An excellent history of the Greek city-states down to the time of Alexander the Great.

Chakravarti, Uma, *The Social Dimensions of Early Buddhism* (1987). A description of the life of Buddha drawn from early Buddhist texts.

Cho-yun, Hsu, *Ancient China in Transition* (1965). An account of the political, economic, social, and intellectual changes that occurred during the Warring States period.

Coarelli, Filippo (ed.), *Etruscan Cities* (1975). A brilliantly and lavishly illustrated guide to the material remains of the Etruscans: their cities, their magnificent tombs, and their architecture, painting, sculpture, and other art.

Coe, Michael, et al. (eds.), *The Olmec World: Ritual and Rulership* (1996). A collection of field-synthesizing articles with important illustrations, based on one of the most comprehensive exhibitions of Olmec art in the world.

Confucius, *The Analects (Lun Yü)*, trans. D. C. Lau (1979). An outstanding translation of the words of Confucius as recorded by his major disciples. Includes valuable historical material needed to provide the context for Confucius's teachings.

Eisenstadt, S. N. (ed.), *The Origins and Diversity of the Axial Age* (1986). An important, original analysis of the great ancient civilizations and a systematic exploration of the conditions under which they developed.

Elman, Benjamin A., and Martin Kern (eds.), *Statecraft and Classical Learning: The Rituals of Zhou in East Asian History* (2010). Traces the long-term political rise of classical learning and state rituals in East Asia from the decline of the Eastern Zhou kingdom to the rise of later imperial dynasties in China, Japan, and Korea.

Falkenhausen, Lothar von, *Chinese Society in the Age of Confucius (100–250 BC)* (2006). The larger Chinese society under the influence of Confucian thought.

Finley, M. I., and H. W. Pleket, *The Olympic Games: The First Thousand Years* (2005). A fine description of the most famous of the Greek games; it explains how they exemplify the competitive spirit that marked many aspects of the Greek city-states.

Garlan, Yvon, *Slavery in Ancient Greece*, trans. Janet Lloyd (1988). A treatment of the emergence, development, and institutionalization of chattel slavery in the Greek city-states.

———, *War in the Ancient World: A Social History*, trans. Janet Lloyd (1976). A discussion of the emergence of the forms of warfare, including male citizens fighting in hoplite phalanxes and the development of siege warfare, that were typical of the Greek city-states.

Iliffe, John, *Africans: The History of a Continent*, 2nd ed. (2007). A first-rate scholarly survey of Africa from its beginnings, with a strong emphasis on demography.

Jaspers, Karl, *The Origin and Goal of History*, trans. Michael Bullock (1953). A book that reckons with the philosophy of the history of humankind and heightens our awareness of the present by locating it within the framework of the obscurity of prehistory.

Kagan, Donald, *The Peloponnesian War* (2004). A vivid description of the war that pitted the major Greek city-states, including Athens and Sparta, against one another over the latter half of the fifth century BCE.

Lancel, Serge, *Carthage: A History*, trans. Antonia Nevill (1997). By far the best single-volume history of the most important Phoenician colony in the Mediterranean.

Lewis, Mark Edward, *Sanctioned Violence in Early China* (1990). An analysis of the use of sanctioned violence as an element of statecraft from the Warring States period to the formation of the Qin and Han empires in the second half of the first millennium BCE.

———, *Writing and Authority in Early China* (1999). A revisionist account of the central role of writing and persuasion in models for the invention of a Chinese world empire.

Ling, Trevor, *The Buddha: Buddhist Civilization in India and Ceylon* (1972). An overview of Buddhism in India and Ceylon.

Lloyd, G. E. R., *Early Greek Science: Thales to Aristotle* (1970). An especially clear and concise introduction to the main developments and intellectuals that marked the emergence of critical secular thinking in the early Greek world.

Lloyd, G. E. R., and Nathan Sivin, *The Way and the Word: Science and Medicine in Early China and Greece* (2002). A comprehensive rethinking of the social and political settings in ancient China and city-state Greece that contributed to the different views of science and medicine that emerged in each place.

Mote, Frederick, *Intellectual Foundations of China* (1971). An early but still useful description of the seminal figures in China's early intellectual life.

Murray, Oswyn, *Early Greece*, 2nd ed. (1993). One of the best introductions to the emergence of the Greek city-states down to the end of the archaic age.

Ober, Josiah, *The Rise and Fall of Classical Greece* (2015). A compelling general interpretation of the rise of the Greek city-states in the sixth and fifth centuries BCE and their subsequent demise in the fourth century.

Osborne, Robin, *Archaic and Classical Greek Art* (1998). An outstanding book that clearly explains the main innovations in Greek art, setting them in their historical context.

———, *Greece in the Making, 1200–479 BC* (1999). The standard history of the whole early period of the Greek city-states, characterized by an especially fine and judicious mix of archaeological data and literary sources.

Pallottino, Massimo, *The Etruscans,* rev. ed., trans. J. Cremona (1975). A fairly traditional but still classic survey of all aspects of Etruscan history and political and social institutions.

Pines, Yuri, Paul R. Goldin, and Martin Kern (eds.), *Ideology of Power and Power of Ideology in Early China* (2015). A new assessment of state ideology and political legitimation under the Eastern Zhou dynasty during the Warring States era.

Provan, Iain, *Convenient Myths: The Axial Age, Dark Green Religion, and the World That Never Was* (2013). An illumination of two deeply rooted myths—the first being Karl Jasper's construct of world religions spontaneously emerging from a shared set of values, the second being David Suzuki's assertion that organized religion severed society's previous connection with nature—and their dangers.

Redford, Donald B., *From Slave to Pharaoh: The Black Experience of Ancient Egypt* (2004). A description of Egypt's twenty-fifth dynasty, which was made up of Sudanese conquerors.

Schaberg, David, *A Patterned Past: Form and Thought in Early Chinese Historiography* (2002). A comprehensive study of the intellectual content of historical anecdotes by the followers of Confucius collected around the fourth century BCE.

Schaps, David, *The Invention of Coinage and the Monetization of Ancient Greece* (2004). A new analysis that offers a broad overview of the emergence of coined money in the Near East and the eastern Mediterranean and its effects on the spread of money-based markets.

Sharma, J. P., *Republics in Ancient India, c. 1500 B.C.–500 B.C.* (1968). Relying on information from early Buddhist texts, this book first revealed that South Asia had not only monarchies but also alternative polities.

Shaw, Thurston, *Nigeria: Its Archaeology and Early History* (1978). An important introduction to the early history of Nigeria by one of that country's leading archaeologists.

Shinnie, P. L., *Ancient Nubia* (1996). An excellent account of the history of the ancient Nubians, who, we are discovering, had great influence on Egypt and on the rest of tropical Africa.

Snodgrass, Anthony, *Archaic Greece: The Age of Experiment* (1981). A good introduction to the archaeological evidence of archaic Greece.

Taylor, Christopher, Richard Hare, and Jonathan Barnes, *Greek Philosophers* (1999). A fine, succinct, one-volume introduction to the major aspects of the three big thinkers who dominated the high period of classical Greek philosophy: Socrates, Plato, and Aristotle.

Torok, Laszlo, *Meroe: Six Studies on the Cultural Identity of an Ancient African State* (1995). A good collection of essays on the most recent work on Meroe.

Welsby, Derek A., *The Kingdom of Kush: The Napatan and Meroitic Empires* (1996). A fine book on these two important Nubian kingdoms.

Chapter 6: Shrinking the Afro-Eurasian World, 350–250 BCE

Bradley, Keith, *Slavery and Rebellion in the Roman World, 140 B.C.–70 B.C.* (1989). A description of the rise of large-scale plantation slavery in Sicily and Italy, and a detailed account of the three great slave wars.

Bresson, Alain, *The Making of the Ancient Greek Economy: Markets and Growth in the City-States*, trans. Steven Rendall (2015). An up-to-date and theoretically well-informed analysis of the market economics of the Greek city-states in the Hellenistic era.

Browning, Iain, *Palmyra* (1979). A narrative of the history of the important desert city that linked eastern and western trade routes.

Casson, Lionel, *The Periplus Maris Erythraei* (1989). An introduction to a typical ancient sailing manual, this one of the Red Sea and Indian Ocean.

——, *Ships and Seamanship in the Ancient World* (1995). The classic account of the ships and sailors that powered commerce and war on the high seas.

Colledge, Malcolm, *The Art of Palmyra* (1976). A well-illustrated introduction to the unusual art of Palmyra with its mixture of eastern and western elements.

Fowler, Barbara H., *The Hellenistic Aesthetic* (1989). How the artists in this new age saw and portrayed their world in new and different ways.

Green, Peter, *Alexander to Actium: The Historical Evolution of the Hellenistic Age* (1990). The best general guide to the whole period in all of its various aspects, and well illustrated.

Habicht, Christian, *Athens from Alexander to Antony*, trans. Deborah L. Schneider (1997). The authoritative account of what happened to the great city-state of Athens in this period.

Hansen, Valerie, *The Silk Road: A New History* (2012). The most recent work on the Silk Road; authoritative on the eastern terminus of this vital trade route.

Herodotus, *The Histories*, 4 vols., trans. Tom Holland (2013). A basic work, which many scholars regard as the first world history. The translation given here was done by Brent Shaw and came from the original Greek.

Holt, Frank L., *Thundering Zeus: The Making of Hellenistic Bactria* (1999). A basic history of the most eastern of the kingdoms spawned by the conquests of Alexander the Great.

Hopkirk, Peter, *Foreign Devils on the Silk Road* (1984). A historiography of the explorations and researches on the central Asian Silk Road in the nineteenth and early twentieth centuries.

Juliano, Annette L., and Judith A. Lerner (eds.), *Nomads, Traders and Holy Men along China's Silk Road* (2003). A description of the travelers along the Silk Road in human terms, focusing on warfare, markets, and religion.

Kosmin, Paul J., *The Land of the Elephant Kings: Space, Territory, and Ideology in the Seleucid Empire* (2014). The best current analysis of the relationships of Seleucid kings, both with their own subjects and, especially, with the Mauryan kingdom of India and the nomadic peoples of central Asia.

Kuzima, E. E., *The Prehistory of the Silk Road* (2008). Valuable information on the early history of the Silk Road.

Lane Fox, Robin, *Alexander the Great* (1973). Still the most readable and in many ways the sanest biography of the world conqueror.

Lewis, Naphtali, *Greeks in Ptolemaic Egypt* (1986). An account of the relationships between Greeks and Egyptians as seen through the lives of individual Greek settlers and colonists.

Liu, Xinru, *Ancient India and Ancient China* (1988). The first work to connect political and economic developments in India and China with the evolution and spread of Buddhism in the first half of the first millennium.

——, *The Silk Road in World History* (2010). A study of the history of the great trade and communications route that connected the different regions of Afro-Eurasia between the third century BCE and the thirteenth century CE.

Long, Antony A., *Hellenistic Philosophy: Stoics, Epicureans, Sceptics*, 2nd ed. (1986). One of the clearest guides to the main new trends in Greek philosophical thinking in the period.

Martin, Luther H., *Hellenistic Religions: An Introduction* (1987). An introduction to the principal new Hellenistic religions and cults that emerged in this period.

Mendels, Doron, *The Rise and Fall of Jewish Nationalism* (1992). A sophisticated account of the various phases of Jewish resistance in Judah to foreign domination.

Miller, James Innes, *The Spice Trade of the Roman Empire, 29 B.C. to A.D. 641* (1969). A first-rate study of the spice trade in the Roman Empire.

Pomeroy, Sarah B., *Women in Hellenistic Egypt: From Alexander to Cleopatra* (1990). A highly readable investigation of women and family in the best-documented region of the Hellenistic world.

Ray, Himanshu P., *The Wind of Change: Buddhism and the Maritime Links of Early South Asia* (1994). Ray's study of Buddhism and maritime trade stretches from the Arabian Sea to the navigations between South Asia and Southeast Asia.

Rosenfield, John, *The Dynastic Art of the Kushans* (1967). Instead of focusing on the Gandharan Buddhist art itself, Rosenfield selects sculptures of Kushan royals and those representing nomadic populations in religious shrines to display the central Asian aspect of artworks of the period.

Rostovtzeff, Michael Ivanovich, *Caravan Cities*, trans. D. and T. Talbot Rice (1932). Though published more than seven decades ago, this small volume contains accurate descriptions of the ruins of many caravan cities in modern Jordan and Syria.

——, *The Social and Economic History of the Hellenistic World* (1941). A monumental achievement; one of the great works of history written in the twentieth century. An unsurpassed overview of all aspects of the politics and social and economic movements of the period. Despite its age, there is still nothing like it.

Schoff, Wilfred H. (ed. and trans.), *The Periplus of the Erythraean Sea* (1912). An invaluable tool for mapping names and places from the Red Sea to Indian coastal areas during this period.

Shipley, Graham, *The Greek World after Alexander, 323–30 BC* (2000). A more up-to-date survey than Peter Green's work (above), with more emphasis on the historical detail in each period.

Tarn, W. W., *Greeks in Bactria and India* (1984). The most comprehensive coverage of Greek sources on Hellenistic states in Afghanistan and northwest India.

Thapar, Romila, *Ashoka and the Decline of the Mauryas* (1973). Using all available primary sources, including the edicts of Aśoka and Greek authors' accounts, Thapar gives the most authoritative analysis of the first and the most important empire in Indian history.

Vainker, Shelagh, *Chinese Silk: A Cultural History* (2004). A work that traces the cultural history of silk in China from its early origins to the twentieth century and considers its relationship to the other decorative arts. The author draws on the most recent archaeological evidence to emphasize the role of silk in Chinese history, trade, religion, and literature.

Wood, Frances, *The Silk Road: Two Thousand Years in the Heart of Asia* (2004). Illustrated with drawings, manuscripts, paintings, and artifacts to trace the Silk Road to its origins as far back as Alexander the Great, with an emphasis on its importance to cultural and religious movements.

Young, Gary K., *Rome's Eastern Trade: International Commerce and Imperial Policy, 31 BC–AD 305* (2001). This study examines the taxation and profits of eastern trade from the perspective of the Roman government.

Chapter 7: Han Dynasty China and Imperial Rome, 300 BCE–300 CE

Barbieri-Low, Anthony J., and Robin D. S. Yates, *Law, State, and Society in Early Imperial China: A Study with Critical Edition and Translation of the Legal Texts from*

Zhangjiashan Tomb No. 247, 2 vols. (2015). A new account of changes in Western (Former) Han dynasty law in terms of its moralization via instituting Confucianism.

Bodde, Derk, *China's First Unifier: A Study of the Ch'in Dynasty as Seen in the Life of Li Ssu (280?–208 B.C.)* (1938). A classic account of the key Legalist adviser, Li Si, who formulated the Qin policy to enhance its autocratic power.

Bowman, Alan K., *Life and Letters on the Roman Frontier: Vindolanda and Its Peoples* (1994). An introduction to the exciting discovery of writing tablets at a Roman army base in northern Britain.

Bradley, Keith, *Slavery and Society at Rome* (1994). The best single overview of the major aspects of the slave system in the Roman Empire.

Chevallier, Raymond, *Roman Roads,* trans. N. H. Field (1976). A guide to the fundamentals of the construction, maintenance, administration, and mapping of Roman roads.

Coarelli, Fillipo (ed.), *Pompeii*, trans. Patricia Cockram (2006). A lavishly illustrated large volume that allows the reader to sense some of the wondrous wealth of the buried city of Pompeii.

Colledge, Malcolm A. R., *The Parthians* (1967). A bit dated but still a fundamental introduction to the Parthians, the major power on the eastern frontier of the Roman Empire.

Cornell, Tim, *The Beginnings of Rome: Italy and Rome from the Bronze Age to the Punic Wars, c. 2000 to 264 B.C.* (1995). The single best one-volume history of Rome through its early history to the first war with Carthage.

Cornell, Tim, and John Matthews, *Atlas of the Roman World* (1982). A history of the Roman world; much more than simply an atlas. It is provided not only with good maps and a gazetteer, but also with marvelous color illustrations and a text that guides the reader through the basics of Roman history.

Csikszentmihalyi, Mark, *Readings in Han Chinese Thought* (2006). A volume presenting a representative selection of primary sources to illustrate the growth of ideas in early imperial times; a useful introduction to the key strains of thought during this crucial period.

Dien, Albert E., "The Qin Army and Its Antecedents," in Liu Yang (ed.), *China's Terracotta Warriors: The First Emperor's Legacy* (2013). An account of the Qin army in light of its Warring States precedents.

Dixon, Suzanne, *The Roman Family* (1992). The best one-volume guide to the nature of the Roman family and family relations.

Garnsey, Peter, and Richard Saller, *The Roman Empire: Economy, Society, and Culture*, 2nd ed. (2014). A perceptive and critical introduction to three basic aspects of social life in the empire.

Giardina, Andrea (ed.), *The Romans*, trans. Lydia Cochrane (1993). Individual studies of important typical figures in Roman society, from the peasant and the bandit to the merchant and the soldier.

Goldsworthy, Adrian, *The Roman Army at War: 100 B.C.–A.D. 200* (1996). A summary history and analysis of the Roman army in action during the late Republic and early Empire.

Goodman, Martin, *The Roman World: 44 B.C.–A.D. 180* (1997). A newer basic history text covering the high Roman Empire.

Graf, David F., "The Silk Road between Syria and China," in Andrew Wilson and Alan Bowman (eds.), *Trade, Commerce, and the State in the Roman World* (2018), pp. 443–529. An exhaustive overview of relations between the Roman Empire and Han China, based on the most recent research of historians.

Hansen, Valerie, *The Silk Road: A New History* (2012). An important study of the Silk Road, based on much original research.

Harris, William, *Ancient Literacy* (1989). A basic survey of what is known about communication in the form of writing and books in the Roman Empire.

Hopkins, Keith, *Death and Renewal: Sociological Studies in Roman History*, vol. 2 (1983). Innovative studies in Roman history, including one of the best on gladiators and another on death and funerals.

———, *A World Full of Gods: Pagans, Jews and Christians in the Roman Empire* (1999). A somewhat unusual but interesting and provocative look at the world of religions in the Roman Empire.

Hughes, J. Donald, *Environmental Problems of the Greeks and Romans: Ecology in the Ancient Mediterranean*, 2nd ed. (2014). A much improved and expanded edition of a classic work on the environment in Greek and Roman antiquity and a state-of-the-art summary of our current knowledge.

Juliano, Annette L., and Judith A. Lerner (eds.), *Nomads, Traders and Holy Men along China's Silk Road* (2003). A description of the travelers along the Silk Road in human terms, focusing on warfare, markets, and religion.

Kern, Martin, and Michael Hunter (eds.), *The Analects: A Western Han Text?* (2013). Challenges the assumption that the Confucian

Analects was compiled before the Han Dynasty.

Knapp, Robert C., *Invisible Romans* (2011). A highly readable introduction to the lower orders of Roman imperial society: the poor, slaves, freedmen, prostitutes, gladiators, bandits, and pirates (among others).

Kraus, Theodore, and Leonard von Matt, *Pompeii and Herculaneum: The Living Cities of the Dead*, trans. Robert E. Wolf (1975). A huge, lavishly illustrated compendium of all aspects of life in the buried cities of Pompeii and Herculaneum as preserved in the archaeological record.

Liang, Cai, *Witchcraft and the Rise of the First Confucian Empire* (2014). A new account of the rise of the Confucians at the Former (Western) Han court during the famous witchcraft trials circa 91–87 BCE.

Liu, Xinru, *The Silk Road in World History* (2010). A short overview of the Silk Road, written by a scholar whose specialty is India, and of the manifold connections involving East Asia, South Asia, Southwest Asia, North Africa, and Europe.

Loewe, Michael, *The Government of the Qin and Han Empires: 221 BCE–220 CE* (2006). A useful overview of the government of the early empires of China. Topics include the structure of central government, provincial and local government, the armed forces, officials, government communications, the laws of the empire, and control of the people and the land.

Millar, Fergus, *The Crowd in the Late Republic* (1998). An innovative study of the democratic power of the citizens in the city of Rome itself.

———, *The Emperor in the Roman World, 31 B.C.–A.D. 337* (1992). Everything you might want to know about the Roman emperor, with special emphasis on his civil role as the administrator of an empire.

Potter, David S., *The Roman Empire at Bay: A.D. 180–395*, 2nd ed. (2014). A new basic text covering the later Roman Empire, including the critical transition to a Christian state.

Potter, David S., and David J. Mattingly (eds.), *Life, Death, and Entertainment in the Roman Empire* (1999). A good introduction to basic aspects of Roman life in the empire, including the family, feeding the cities, religion, and popular entertainment.

Qian, Sima, *Records of the Grand Historian: Qin Dynasty*, trans. Burton Watson, 3rd ed. (1995). The classic work of Chinese history in a readable translation. The Han dynasty's Grand Historian describes the slow rise and meteoric fall of the Qin dynasty from the point of view of the succeeding dynasty, which Sima Qian witnessed or heard of during his lifetime.

Southern, Pat, *The Roman Army: A Social and Institutional History* (2006). A fundamental guide to all aspects of the Roman army.

Todd, Malcolm, *The Early Germans*, rev. ed. (2004). A basic survey of the peoples in central and western Europe at the time of the Roman Empire.

Vainker, Shelagh, *Chinese Silk: A Cultural History* (2004). A work that traces the cultural history of silk in China from its early origins to the twentieth century and considers its relationship to the other decorative arts. The author draws on the most recent archaeological evidence to emphasize the role of silk in Chinese history, trade, religion, and literature.

Wells, Peter S., *The Barbarians Speak: How the Conquered Peoples Shaped Roman Europe* (1999). The cultures of the peoples of central and northern Europe at the time of the Roman Empire and their impact on Roman culture.

Wood, Frances, *The Silk Road: Two Thousand Years in the Heart of Asia* (2004). A work illustrated with drawings, manuscripts, paintings, and artifacts to trace the Silk Road to its origins as far back as Alexander the Great. The author stresses the importance of the Silk Road to cultural and religious movements.

Woolf, Greg (ed.), *The Cambridge Illustrated History of the Roman World* (2005). A good guide to various aspects of Roman history, culture, and provincial life.

———, *Rome: An Empire's Story* (2012). An up-to-date narrative of the Roman Empire told according to major themes that are particularly relevant to world history.

Chapter 8: The Rise of Universalizing Religions, 300–600 CE

Bowersock, Glen W., *Empires in Collision in Late Antiquity* (2013). Brilliant, short studies of the relations between Ethiopia, Arabia, and Byzantium as a background to the origins of Islam.

Bowersock, Glen W., Peter Brown, and Oleg Grabar (eds.), *Late Antiquity: A Guide to the Postclassical World* (1999). Essays and items for the entire period 150–750 CE. The volume covers the Roman, East Roman, Sasanian, and early Islamic worlds.

Brown, Peter, *The Rise of Western Christendom: Triumph and Diversity, A.D. 200–1000*, 2nd ed. (2003). The rise and spread of Christianity in Europe and Asia, with up-to-date bibliographies on all topics, maps, and time charts.

———, "The Silk Road in Late Antiquity," in V. H. Maier and J. Hickman (eds.), *Reconfiguring the Silk Road* (2014). Silk Road from the perspective of its western outlets and influences.

———, *Through the Eye of a Needle: Wealth, the Fall of Rome, and the Making of Christianity in the West, 350–550* (2012). Christianity and Roman society before and after the end of the empire.

———, *Treasure in Heaven: The Holy Poor in Early Christianity* (2016). On the social role of early Christian monasticism in Syria and Egypt.

———, *The World of Late Antiquity: From Marcus Aurelius to Muhammad, AD 150–750* (1989). A social, religious, and cultural history of the late Roman and Sasanian empires, with illustrations and a time chart.

Bühler, G. (trans.), *The Laws of Manu* (1886). The classic translation of one of India's most important historical, legal, and religious texts.

Canepa, Matthew P., *The Two Eyes of the Earth: Art and Ritual of Kingship between Rome and Sasanian Iran* (2009). An interesting look at how two great global powers, Rome and Iran, shared images of rulership.

Clynes, Tom, "Laser Scans Reveal Maya 'Megalopolis' below Guatemalan Jungle," *National Geographic News*, February 1, 2018, https://news.nationalgeographic.com/2018/02/maya-laser-lidar-guatemala-pacunam/. Highlights the use of LIDAR laser technology to uncover extensive Maya ruins, including additional pyramids, intercity road systems, defensive walls, irrigation systems, quarries, and other structures.

Coe, Michael D., *The Maya*, 6th ed. (1999). A work by the world's most famous Mayanologist, with recent evidence, analyses, and illustrations.

Cowgill, George L., "The Central Mexican Highlands and the Rise of Teotihuacan to the Decline of Tula," in Richard Adams and Murdo Macleod (eds.), *The Cambridge History of the Native Peoples of the Americas*, vol. 2, *Mesoamerica*, pt. 1 (2000). A thorough review of findings about urban states in central Mexico.

Fash, William L., *Scribes, Warriors and Kings: The City of Copan and the Ancient Maya* (2001). A fascinating and comprehensive study of one of the most elaborate of the Maya city-kingdoms.

Fisher, Greg (ed.), *Arabs and Empires before Islam* (2015). A collection of up-to-date studies on the relationships of various Arab groups with imperial powers, especially Rome and Persia.

———. *Between Empires: Arabs, Romans, and Sasanians in Late Antiquity* (2011). Arab, Roman, and Sasanian empires compared.

Fowden, Elizabeth Key, *The Barbarian Plain: Saint Sergius between Rome and Iran* (1999). The study of a major Christian shrine and its relations to Romans, Persians, and Arabs.

Fowden, Garth, *Empire to Commonwealth: The Consequences of Monotheism in Late Antiquity* (1993). A study of the relationship between empire and world religions in western Asia.

Gombrich, Richard F., and Sheldon Pollack (eds.), *Clay Sanskrit Library* (2005–2006). All major works from the Gupta and post-Gupta periods, in both Sanskrit and English versions. During the Gupta period, classical Sanskrit literature reached its apex, with abundant drama, poetry, and folk stories.

Gordon, Charles, *The Age of Attila* (1960). The last century of the Roman Empire in western Europe, vividly illustrated from contemporary sources.

Haldon, John, *The Empire That Would Not Die: The Paradox of Eastern Rome's Survival* (2010). Incorporates much new climatological evidence.

Hansen, Valerie, *The Silk Road: A New History* (2012). A detailed history of the Silk Road, based largely on Chinese sources.

Harper, Prudence, *The Royal Hunter: The Art of the Sasanian Empire* (1978). The ideology of the Sasanian Empire as shown through excavated hoards of precious silverware.

Heather, Peter, *The Fall of the Roman Empire: A New History of Rome and the Barbarians* (2006). A military and political narrative based on up-to-date archaeological material.

Herrmann, Georgina, *Iranian Revival* (1977). The structure and horizons of the Sasanian Empire as revealed in its monuments.

Hillgarth, Jocelyn (ed.), *Christianity and Paganism, 350–750: The Conversion of Western Europe*, rev. ed. (1986). A collection of contemporary sources.

Holcombe, Charles, *In the Shadow of the Han: Literati Thought and Society at the Beginning of the Southern Dynasties* (1994). A clear and concise account of the evolution of thought in China after the fall of the Han dynasty in 220 CE. The book presents the rise of Buddhism and Daoism as popular religions as well as elite interests in classical learning in a time of political division and barbarian conquest in North and South China.

La Vaissière, Étienne de, *Sogdian Traders: A History*, trans. James Ward (2005). A summary of historical facts about the most important trading community and its commercial networks on the Silk Road, from the early centuries CE to its demise in the ninth century CE.

Little, Lester (ed.), *Plague and the End of Antiquity: The Pandemic of 541–750* (2008). A series of debates over the nature and impact of the first great pandemic attested in global history.

Liu, Xinru, and Lynda Norene Shaffer, *Connections across Eurasia: Transportation, Communication, and Cultural Exchanges on the Silk Roads* (2007). A survey of trade and religious activities on the Silk Roads.

Lopez, Ariel G., *Shenoute of Atripe and the Uses of Poverty: Rural Patronage, Religious Conflict, and Monasticism in Late Antique Egypt* (2013). Places a leading Egyptian abbot in his full social context.

Maas, Michael, *The Age of Attila: The Cambridge Companion to the Age of Attila* (2013). Essays on this important age in the Late Antique period.

———, *Readings in Late Antiquity: A Source Book* (1999). Well-chosen extracts that illustrate the interrelation of Romans and non-Romans, and of Christians, Jews, and pagans.

——— (ed.), *The Cambridge Companion to the Age of Justinian* (2005). A survey of all aspects of the eastern Roman Empire in the sixth century CE.

Moffett, Samuel, *A History of Christianity in Asia*, vol. 1 (1993). Particularly valuable on Christians in China and India.

Munro-Hay, Stuart, *Aksum: An African Civilization of Late Antiquity* (1991). The origins of the Christian kingdom of Ethiopia.

Murdock, George P., *Africa: Its Peoples and Their History* (1959). A vital introduction to the peoples of Africa and their history.

Oliver, Roland, *The African Experience: From Olduvai Gorge to the Twenty-First Century* (1999). An important overview, written by one of the pioneering scholars of African history and one of the leading authorities on the Bantu migrations.

Payne, Richard. *A State of Mixture: Christians, Zoroastrians, and Iranian Political Culture in Late Antiquity* (2015). A new view of Christianity in Sasanian Iran.

Pines, Yuri, *Envisioning Eternal Empire: Chinese Political Thought of the Warring States Era* (2009). A critical comparative work that focuses on the Warring States period and discusses how the rise of an imperial ideology was formative in the Chinese commitment to imperial rule.

———, *The Everlasting Empire: The Political Culture of Ancient China and Its Imperial Legacy* (2012). Stresses the critical role that the Warring States period played in the formulation of an enduring imperial ideology.

Pourshariati, Parvaneh, *The Decline and Fall of the Sasanian Empire: The Sasanian-Parthian Confederacy and the Arab Conquest of Iran* (2008). An innovative perspective on the demise of the Sasanians and the relevance of their decline for the Arab conquest of Iran.

Pregadio, Fabrizio, *Great Clarity: Daoism and Alchemy in Early Medieval China* (2006). An examination of the religious aspects of Daoism. The book focuses on the relation of alchemy to the Daoist traditions of the third to sixth centuries CE and shows how alchemy was integrated into the elaborate body of doctrines and practices of Daoists at that time.

Rosenthal, Jean-Laurent, and R. Bin Wong, *Before and Beyond Divergence: The Politics of Economic Change in China and Europe* (2011). A spirited attempt to understand why Europe outperformed China in the period leading up to the twenty-first century.

Scheidel, Walter (ed.), *Rome and China: Comparative Perspectives on Ancient World Empires* (2009). The essays by Walter Scheidel and Nathan Rosenstein expertly compare the Roman and Han Empires.

Tempels, Placide, *Bantu Philosophy* (1959). A highly influential effort to argue for the underlying cultural unity of all the Bantu peoples.

Vansina, Jan, *Paths in the Rainforests: Toward a History of Political Tradition in Equatorial Africa* (1990). The best work on Bantu history.

Walker, Joel, *The Legend of Mar Kardagh: Narrative and Christian Heroism in Late Antique Iraq* (2006). Christians and Zoroastrians in northern Iraq and in Iran.

Yarshater, Ehsan, *Encyclopedia Iranica* (1982–). A guide to all aspects of the Sasanian Empire and to religion and culture in the regions between Mesopotamia and central Asia.

Zürcher, E., *The Buddhist Conquest of China: The Spread and Adaptation of Buddhism in Early Medieval China*, 3rd ed. (2007). A reissue of the classic account of the assimilation of Buddhism in China during the medieval period, with particular focus on the religious and philosophical success of Buddhism among Chinese elites in South China.

Chapter 9: New Empires and Common Cultures, 600–1000 CE

Ahmed, Leila, *Women and Gender in Islam* (1992). A superb overview of the relations between men and women throughout the history of Islam.

al-Azmeh, Aziz, *The Emergence of Islam in Late Antiquity: Allah and His People* (2014). A detailed and comprehensive treatment of the origins of Islam, written by a scholar aware of all historical sources of this period.

Aneirin, *Y Gododdin: Britain's Oldest Heroic Poem*, ed. and trans. A. O. H. Jarman (1988). A sixth-century Welsh text that describes the battle of the last Britons against the invading Anglo-Saxons.

Arberry, Arthur J., introduction to *The Koran Interpreted: A Translation*, trans. Arthur J. Arberry (1986). One of the most eloquent appreciations of this classical work of religion.

Augustine, *The City of God*, trans. H. Bettenson (1976). An excellent translation of Augustine's monumental work of history, philosophy, and religion.

Berkey, Jonathan P., *The Formation of Islam: Religion and Society in the Near East, 600–1800* (2005). A recent overview of the history of Islam before the modern era. It is particularly sensitive to the influence of external elements on the history of the Muslim peoples.

Bol, Peter, *This Culture of Ours: Intellectual Transitions in T'ang and Sung China* (1994). A study tracing the transformation of the shared culture of the Chinese learned elite from the seventh to the twelfth centuries.

Bowersock, G. W., *The Crucible of Islam* (2017). A classicist treatment of the origins of Islam.

———, *The Throne of Adulis: Red Sea Wars on the Eve of Islam* (2013). A vital study of the kingdom of Himyar, in present-day Yemen, a center of Judaism and Christianity before the rise of Islam in the Arabian Peninsula.

Brooke, John L., *Climate Change and the Course of Global History: A Rough Journey* (2014). An overview of a changing climate and its impact on historical developments.

Brown, Peter, *The Rise of Western Christendom: Triumph and Diversity, AD 200–1000*, 2nd ed. (2003). A description of the changes in Christianity in northern Europe and the emergence of the new cultures and political structures that coincided with this development.

Bulliet, Richard W., *Conversion to Islam in the Medieval Period: An Essay in Quantitative History* (1979). A study of the rate at which the populations overrun by Arab conquerors in the seventh century CE embraced the religion of their rulers.

———, *Cotton, Climate, and Camels in the Early Islamic State* (2009). A fascinating account of economic development on the Iranian plateau, with an emphasis on climate.

Cook, Michael, *The Koran: A Very Short Introduction* (2000). A useful overview of Islam's holy book.

———, *Muhammad* (1983). A brief but careful life of the Prophet that takes full account of the prolific and often controversial preexisting scholarship.

Creswell, K. A. C., *A Short Account of Early Muslim Architecture*, revised and supplemented by James W. Allan (1992). The definitive treatment of the subject, brought up to date.

Crone, Patricia, *The Nativist Prophets of Early Islam: Rural Revolt and Local Zoroastrianism* (2012). The rise of protest movements in Islam that led to the Abbasid takeover from the Umayyads.

Cross, S. H., and O. P. Sherbowitz-Wetzor (trans.), *The Russian Primary Chronicle* (1953). A vivid record of the Viking settlement of Kiev, of the conversion of Kiev, and of the princes of Kiev in the tenth and eleventh centuries.

Donner, Fred M., *The Early Islamic Conquests* (1981). The best account of the Arab conquests in the Persian and Byzantine empires in the seventh century.

———, *Muhammad and the Believers at the Origins of Islam* (2010). An Islamicist reexamines early historical sources on the origins of Islam and contends that the early Muslim believers did not separate from Christianity and Judaism until more than a half century had elapsed from Muhammad's first proclamations.

Duncan, John, *The Origins of the Chosŏn Dynasty* (2000). A historical account of the early Korean dynasties from 900 to 1400.

Elman, Benjamin, *Precocious China: Civil Examinations, 1400–1900* (2013). Summary of civil exams in China from medieval times.

Fage, J. D., *Ghana: A Historical Introduction* (1966). A brief but authoritative history of Ghana from earliest times to the twentieth century.

Fisher, Humphrey J., *Slavery in the History of Muslim Black Africa* (2001). A general history of the relations between North Africa and black Africa, focusing on one of the most important aspects of contact—the slave trade.

Fowden, Garth, *Before and after Muhammad: The First Millennium Refocused* (2014). The author sets Islam in its larger Greek and

Christian context; part of the work of the Late Antique scholarly community.

Grabar, Oleg, *The Shape of the Holy: Early Islamic Jerusalem* (1996). The best account of the architecture of early Islam, including the building and the purposes of the Dome of the Rock, one of Islam's early and iconic places of worship.

Graham-Campbell, James, *Cultural Atlas of the Viking World* (1994). A positioning of the Vikings against their wider background in both western and eastern Europe.

Haider, Najam, *The Origins of the Shi'a: Identity, Ritual, and Sacred Space in Eighth-Century Kufah* (2011). A definitive study on the origin of Shiism.

Hawting, G. R., *The First Dynasty of Islam: The Umayyad Caliphate, A.D. 661–750* (2000). The essential scholarly treatment of Islam's first dynasty.

Herrmann, Georgina, *Iranian Revival* (1977). The structure and horizons of the Sasanian Empire as revealed in its monuments.

Hillgarth, J. N. (ed.), *Christianity and Paganism, 350–750: The Conversion of Western Europe*, rev. ed. (1986). A collection of contemporary sources.

Hodges, Richard, and David Whitehouse, *Mohammed, Charlemagne, and the Origins of Europe* (1983). A spirited comparison of Islam and the rise of Europe.

Hodgson, Marshall G. S., *The Venture of Islam: Conscience and History in a World Civilization*, 3 vols. (1977). A magnificent history of the Islamic peoples. Its first volume, *The Classical Age of Islam*, is basic reading for anyone interested in the history of the Muslim world.

Holdsworth, May, *Women of the Tang Dynasty* (1999). An account of women's lives during the Tang dynasty.

Hourani, Albert, *History of the Arab Peoples* (2002). The best overview of Arab history.

Hoyland, Robert G., *In God's Path: The Arab Conquests and the Creation of an Islamic Empire* (2015). An overview of new findings about the origins of Islam.

Jones, Gwynn, *The Norse Atlantic Saga* (1986). The Viking discovery of America.

Kennedy, Hugh, *The Prophet and the Age of the Caliphate: The Islamic Near East from the Sixth to the Eleventh Century* (2004). A very good synthesis of the rise and spread of Islam.

Lee, Peter, et al. (eds.), *Sources of Korean Tradition*, vol. 1 (1996). A unique view of Korean history through the eyes and words of the participants or witnesses themselves, as provided in translations of official documents, letters, and policies.

Levtzion, Nehemia, *Ancient Ghana and Mali* (1980). The best introduction to the kingdoms of West Africa.

Levtzion, Nehemia, and Jay Spaulding, *Medieval West Africa: Views from Arab Scholars and Merchants* (2003). An indispensable source book on early West African history.

Levy-Rubin, Milka, *Non-Muslims in the Early Islamic Empire: From Surrender to Co-existence* (2011). The exploitation of non-Muslims in early Islam and their later conversion and rise to prominence.

Lewis, Bernard (trans.), *Islam from the Prophet Muhammad to the Capture of Constantinople*, vol. 2, *Religion and Society* (1974). A fine collection of original sources that portray various aspects of classical Islamic society.

———, *The Middle East: Two Thousand Years of History from the Rise of Christianity to the Present Day* (1995). A stimulating introduction to an area that has seen the emergence of three of the great world religions.

Lewis, David Levering, *God's Crucible: Islam and the Making of Europe, 570–1215* (2008). An exciting and well-written overview of the high period of Islamic power and cultural attainments.

Middleton, John, *The Swahili: The Social Landscape of a Mercantile Community* (2000). An exciting synthesis of the Swahili culture of East Africa.

Miyazaki, Ichisada, *China's Examination Hell* (1981). A study of China's examination system.

Nurse, Derek, and Thomas Spear, *The Swahili: Reconstructing the History and Language of an African Society, 800–1500* (1984). A work that explores the history of the Muslim peoples who lived along the coast of East Africa.

Peters, F. E., *Muhammad and the Origins of Islam* (1994). A work that explores the early history of Islam and highlights the critical role that Muhammad played in promoting a new religion and a powerful Arab identity.

Pourshariati, Parveneh, *Decline and Fall of the Sasanian Empire* (2008). Fundamental analysis of the end of the Sasanian Empire and the reasons for the success of the Arab/Muslim invasions.

Robinson, Chase F., *'Abd al-Malik* (2005). A short biography of the powerful Umayyad ruler who played a critical role in distinguishing Islam from the other monotheisms in the region, namely, Christianity, Judaism, and Zoroastrianism.

———, *The Formation of the Islamic World, Sixth to Eleventh Centuries*, vol. 1 of *The New Cambridge*

History of Islam (2010). The first volume of an authoritative and up-to-date six-volume overview of the history of Islam from the sixth century CE to the present.

Schirokauer, Conrad, David Lurie, and Suzanne Gay, *A Brief History of Japanese Civilization,* 2nd ed. (2005). A balanced account; chapters focus on developments in art, religion, literature, and thought as well as on Japan's economic, political, and social history in medieval times.

Shoemaker, Stephen J., *The Death of a Prophet: The End of Muhammad's Life and the Beginnings of Islam* (2012). A careful revision of the standard biographies of Muhammad, based on non-Muslim sources.

Smith, Julia, *Europe after Rome: A New Cultural History, 500–1000* (2005). A vivid analysis of society and culture in so-called Dark Age Europe.

Totman, Conrad, *History of Japan* (2004). A recent and readable summary of Japanese history from ancient to modern times.

Twitchett, Denis, *The Birth of the Chinese Meritocracy: Bureaucrats and Examinations in T'ang China* (1976). A description of the role of the written civil examinations that began during the Tang dynasty.

———, *Financial Administration under the T'ang Dynasty* (1970). A pioneering account—based on rare Dunhuang documents that survived from medieval times in Buddhist grottoes in central Asia—of the political and economic system undergirding the Chinese imperial state.

Whittow, Mark, *The Making of Byzantium, 600–1025* (1996). A study on the survival and revival of the eastern Roman Empire as a major power in eastern Europe and Southwest Asia.

Wood, Ian, *The Missionary Life: Saints and the Evangelization of Europe, 400–1050* (2001). The horizons of Christians on the frontiers of Europe.

Chapter 10: Becoming "The World," 1000–1300 CE

Allsen, Thomas, *Commodity and Exchange in the Mongol Empire: A Cultural History of Islamic Textiles* (1997). A study that uses golden brocade, the textile most treasured by Mongol rulers, as a lens through which to analyze the vast commercial networks facilitated by the Mongol conquests and control.

———, *Culture and Conquest in Mongol Eurasia* (2001). A work that emphasizes the cultural and scientific exchanges that took place across Afro-Eurasia as a result of the Mongol conquest.

Bagge, Svere, Michael Gelting, and Thomas Lundkvist (eds.), *Feudalism: New Landscapes of Debate* (2011). A collection of essays on interpretations of feudalism by experts on the topic.

Bartlett, Robert, *The Making of Europe: Conquest, Colonization and Cultural Change, 950–1350* (1993). The modes of cultural, political, and demographic expansion of feudal Europe along its frontiers, especially in eastern Europe.

Bay, Edna G., *Wives of the Leopards: Gender, Politics, and Culture in the Kingdom of Dahomey* (1998). A work that stresses the role of women in an important West African society and dips into the early history of this area.

Beach, D. N., *Shona and Zimbabwe, 900–1850: An Outline of Shona History* (1980). A good place to start for exploring the history of Great Zimbabwe.

Brooks, George E., *Landlords and Strangers: Ecology, Society, and Trade in Western Africa, 1000–1630* (1993). A survey assembled from primary sources of early West African history that stresses transregional connections.

Bulliet, Richard W., *Cotton, Climate, and Camels in Early Islamic Iran* (2009). An analysis of the upswing of the Iranian plateau economy after the Muslim conquest and its subsequent decline as a result of climate change.

Buzurg ibn Shahriyar of Ramhormuz, *The Book of the Wonders of India: Mainland, Sea and Islands,* ed. and trans. G. S. P. Freeman-Greenville (1981). A collection of stories told by sailors, both true and fantastic; they help us imagine the lives of sailors of the era.

Chappell, Sally A. Kitt, *Cahokia: Mirror of the Cosmos* (2002). A thorough and vivid account of the "mound people"; it explores not just what we know of Cahokia but how we know it.

Christian, David, *A Short History of Russia, Central Asia, and Mongolia,* vol. 1, *Inner Eurasia from Prehistory to the Mongol Empire* (1998). Essential reading for students interested in interconnections across the Afro-Eurasian landmass.

Curtin, Philip, *Cross-Cultural Trade in World History* (1984). A groundbreaking book on intercultural trade with a primary focus on Africa, especially the cross-Saharan trade and Swahili coastal trade.

Dawson, Christopher, *Mission to Asia* (1980). Accounts of China and the Mongol Empire brought back by Catholic missionaries and diplomats after 1240.

Di Cosmo, Nicola, Allen J. Frank, and Peter Golden (eds.), *The Cambridge History of Inner Asia: The Chinggisid Age* (2009). A definitive study of the Mongol period, written by the leading scholars of this period.

Ellenblum, Ronnie, *The Collapse of the Eastern Mediterranean: Climate Change and the Decline of the East, 950–1072* (2012). An analysis of the impact of freezing temperatures and drought on the societies of the eastern Mediterranean.

Foltz, Richard C., *Religions of the Silk Road: Overland Trade and Cultural Exchange from Antiquity to the Fifteenth Century* (1999). A study of the populations and the cities of the Silk Road as transmitters of culture across long distances.

Franklin, Simon, and Jonathan Shepherd, *The Emergence of Rus: 750–1200* (1996). The formation of medieval Russia between the Baltic and Black Seas.

Gibb, Hamilton A. R., *Saladin: Studies in Islamic History,* ed. Yusuf Ibish (1974). A sympathetic portrait of one of Islam's leading political and military figures.

Goitein, S. D., *Letters of Medieval Jewish Traders* (1973). The classic study of medieval Jewish trading communities based on the commercial papers deposited in the Cairo Geniza (a synagogue storeroom) during the tenth and eleventh centuries; it explores not only commercial activities but also the personal lives of the traders around the Indian Ocean basin.

———, *A Mediterranean Society: An Abridgment in One Volume,* rev. and ed. Jacob Lassner (1999). A portrait of the Jewish merchant community with ties across the Afro-Eurasian landmass, based largely on the documents from the Cairo Geniza (of which Goitein was the primary researcher and interpreter).

———, "New Light on the Beginnings of the Karim Merchant," *Journal of Social and Economic History of the Orient* 1 (1958). Goitein's description of Egyptian trade.

Goitein, S. D., and Mordechai A. Friedman, *India Traders of the Middle Ages: Documents from the Cairo Geniza* (2008). Collection of documents (translated into English) and authoritative essays that explore the eleventh- and twelfth-century trade conducted by several prominent Jewish families along the Mediterranean and Indian Ocean routes.

Harris, Joseph E., *The African Presence in Asia: Consequences of the East African Slave Trade* (1971). One of the few books that looks broadly at the impact of Africans and African slavery on the societies of Asia.

Hartwell, Robert, "Demographic, Political, and Social Transformations of China, 750–1550," *Harvard Journal of Asiatic Studies* 42 (1982): 365–442. A pioneering study of the demographic changes that overtook China during the Tang and Song dynasties, which are described in light of political reform movements and social changes in this crucial era.

Historical Relations across the Indian Ocean: Report and Papers of the Meeting of Experts Organized by UNESCO at Port Louis, Mauritius, from 15 to 19 July, 1974 (1980). Excellent essays on the connections of Africa with Asia across the Indian Ocean.

Hitti, Philip, *An Arab-Syrian Gentleman and Warrior in the Period of the Crusades: Memoirs of Usāmah ibn-Munqidh* (1929). The Crusaders seen through Muslim eyes.

Hodgson, Natasha, *Women, Crusading, and the Holy Land in Historical Narrative* (2007). A book dealing with the Crusades and focusing on the place of women in them.

Holt, P. M., *The Age of the Crusades: The Near East from the Eleventh Century to 1517* (1984). The Crusades period as seen from the eastern Mediterranean and through the lens of a leading British scholar of the area.

Huff, Toby E., *The Rise of Early Modern Science* (2009). A bold attempt to look at the rise of scientific work in the Islamic world, premodern China, and Europe, seeking to explain why the scientific revolution occurred in Europe rather than the Islamic world or China.

Hymes, Robert, and Conrad Schirokauer (eds.), *Ordering the World: Approaches to State and Society in Sung Dynasty China* (1993). A collection of essays that traces the intellectual, social, and political movements that shaped the Song state and its elites.

Ibn Battuta, *The Travels of Ibn Battuta,* trans. H. A. R. Gibb (2002). A readable translation of the classic book, originally published in 1929.

Ibn Fadlan, Ahmad, *Ibn Fadlan's Journey to Russia: A Tenth Century Traveler from Baghdad to the Volga River,* translated with commentary by Richard Frye (2005). A coherent summary of the observations of an envoy who traveled from Baghdad to Russia.

Irwin, Robert, *The Middle East in the Middle Ages: The Early Mamluk Sultanate, 1250–1582* (1986). Egypt under Mamluk rule.

Jeppie, Shamil, and Souleymane Bachir Diagne (eds.), *The Meanings of Timbuktu* (2008). New materials on the ancient Muslim city of Timbuktu by scholars who have been preserving its manuscripts and writing about its historical importance.

Khazanov, Anatoly M., *Nomads and the Outside World*, 2nd ed., trans. Julia Crookurden, with a foreword by Ernest Gellner (1994). A classic overview of nomadism, based on years of research, covering all of the nomadic communities of Afro-Eurasia.

Lancaster, Lewis, Kikun Suh, and Chai-shin Yu (eds.), *Buddhism in Koryo: A Royal Religion* (1996). A description of Buddhism at its height in the Koryo period, when the religion made significant contributions to the development of Korean culture.

Levtzion, Nehemia, and Randall L. Pouwels (eds.), *The History of Islam in Africa* (2000). A useful general survey of the place of Islam in African history.

Lewis, Bernard (trans.), *Islam: From the Prophet Muhammad to the Capture of Constantinople*, vol. 2, *Religion and Society* (1974). A fine collection of original sources that portray various aspects of classical Islamic society.

Lopez, Robert S., *The Commercial Revolution of the Middle Ages, 950–1350* (1976). An account focusing on the development around the Mediterranean of commercial practices such as the use of currency, accounting, and credit.

Lyons, Malcolm C., and D. E. P. Jackson, *Saladin: The Politics of the Holy War* (1984; reprint, 2001). The fundamental revisionist work on one of the more important historical figures of the time.

Maalouf, Amin, *The Crusades through Muslim Eyes*, trans. Jon Rothschild (1984). The European Crusaders as seen by the Muslim world.

Marcus, Harold G., *A History of Ethiopia* (2002). An authoritative overview of the history of this great culture.

Mass, Jeffrey, *Yoritomo and the Founding of the First Bakufu: The Origins of Dual Government in Japan* (1999). A revisionist account of how the Kamakura military leader Minamoto Yoritomo established the "dual polity" of court and warrior government in Japan.

McDermott, Joseph, *A Social History of the Chinese Book: Books and Literati Culture in Late Imperial China* (2006). The history of the book in China since the Song dynasty, with comparisons to the book's role in other civilizations, particularly the European.

McEvitt, Christopher, *The Crusaders and the Christian World of the East: Rough Tolerance* (2008). Excellent work on the relations of religious groups in the Crusader kingdoms.

McIntosh, Roderik, *The Peoples of the Middle Niger: The Island of Gold* (1988). A historical survey of an area often omitted from other textbooks.

Moore, Jerry D., *Cultural Landscapes in the Ancient Andes: Archaeologies of Place* (2005). The most recent and up-to-date analysis of findings based on recent archaeological evidence, emphasizing the importance of local cultures and diversity in the Andes.

Mote, Frederick W., *Imperial China, 900–1800* (1999). Still the best work on this period, written by an expert on the full scope of Chinese history. The chapter on the Mongols is superb.

Niane, D. T. (ed.), *Africa from the Twelfth to the Sixteenth Century*, vol. 4 of *General History of Africa* (1984). The fourth volume of

UNESCO's history of Africa covers four centuries of African history. This work features the scholarship of Africans.

Oliver, Roland (ed.), *From c. 1050 to c. 1600*, vol. 3 of *The Cambridge History of Africa*, ed. J. D. Fage and Roland Oliver (1977). Another general survey of African history. This volume draws heavily on the work of British scholars.

Peters, Edward, *The First Crusade* (1971). The Crusaders as seen through their own eyes.

Petry, Carl F. (ed.), *Islamic Egypt, 640–1517*, vol. 1 of *The Cambridge History of Egypt* (1998). A solid overview of the history of Islamic Egypt up to the Ottoman conquest.

Polo, Marco, *The Travels of Marco Polo*, ed. Manuel Komroff (1926). A solid translation of Marco Polo's famous account.

Popovic, Alexandre, *The Revolt of African Slaves in Iraq in the 3rd/9th Century*, trans. Leon King (1999). The account of a massive revolt against their slave masters by African slaves taken to labor in Iraq's mines and fields.

Rossabi, Morris, *A History of China* (2014). Part of the Blackwell History of the World series and an excellent overview of Chinese history.

Scott, Robert, *Gothic Enterprise: A Guide to Understanding the Medieval Cathedral* (2003). The meaning and social function of religious building in medieval cities in northern Europe.

Shaffer, Lynda Norene, *Maritime Southeast Asia to 1500* (1996). A history of the peoples of the southeast fringe of the Eastern Hemisphere, up to the time that they became connected to the global commercial networks of the world.

Shimada, Izumi, "Evolution of Andean Diversity: Regional Formations (500 BCE–CE 600)," in Frank Salomon and Stuart Schwartz (eds.), *South America*, vol. 3 of *The Cambridge History of the Native Peoples of the Americas* (1999), pt. 1, pp. 350–517. A splendid overview that contrasts the varieties of lowland and highland cultures.

Steinberg, David Joel, et al., *In Search of Southeast Asia: A Modern History, rev. ed.* (1987). An account of the emergence of the modern Southeast Asian polities of Cambodia, Burma, Thailand, and Indonesia.

Tanner, Harold M., *China: A History* (2009). Along with Rossabi, an excellent overview of the full history of China.

Tyerman, Christopher, *God's War: A New History of the Crusades* (2006). The balance of religious and nonreligious motivations in the Crusades.

Waley, Daniel, *The Italian City-Republics*, 3rd ed. (1988). The structures and culture of the new cities of medieval Italy.

Watson, Andrew, *Agricultural Innovation in the Early Islamic World: The Diffusion of Crops and Farming Techniques, 700–1100* (1983). An impressive study of the spread of new crops throughout the Muslim world.

West, Charles, *Reframing the Feudal Revolution: Political and Social Transformation between Marne and Moselle, c. 800–c. 1100* (2013). Big change seen through an intensely studied region.

Wickham, Chris, *Sleepwalking into a New World: The Emergence of Italian City Communes in the Twelfth Century* (2015). Origins of the city democracies of medieval Italy.

Chapter 11: Crises and Recovery in Afro-Eurasia, 1300–1500

Barkey, Karen, *Empire of Difference: The Ottomans in Comparative Perspective* (2008). A revisionist view of the rise and flourishing of the Ottoman Empire.

Bois, Guy, *The Crisis of Feudalism: Economy and Society in Eastern Normandy, c. 1300–1550* (1984). A good case study of a French region that illustrates the turmoil in fourteenth-century Europe.

Brook, Timothy, *Praying for Power: Buddhism and the Formation of Gentry Society in Late Ming China* (1994). An analysis of the role of a significant religious force in the political and social developments of the Ming.

Clunas, Craig, and Jessica Harrison-Hall (eds.), *Ming: 50 Years That Changed China* (2014). Developed to accompany an exhibition at the British Museum, this catalog includes richly illustrated scholarly essays that explore clothing, jewelry, courtly objects, and commerce during the Ming dynasty.

Dardess, John, *A Ming Society: T'ai-ho County, Kiangsi, Fourteenth to Seventeenth Centuries* (1996). A work that covers the different changes and developments of a single locality in China through the centuries.

Dols, Michael W., *The Black Death in the Middle East* (1977). One of the few scholarly works to examine the Black Death outside Europe.

Dreyer, Edward, *Early Ming China: A Political History, 1355–1435* (1982). A useful account of the early years of the Ming dynasty.

Faroqhi, Suraiya N., and Kate Fleet (eds.), *The Cambridge History of Turkey*, vol. 2, *The Ottoman Empire as a World Power, 1453–1603* (2013). An overview of this crucial period in Ottoman history, written by experts in the field.

Finkel, Caroline, *Osman's Dream: The Story of the Ottoman Empire, 1300–1923* (2005). The most authoritative overview of Ottoman history.

Hale, John, *The Civilization of Europe in the Renaissance* (1994). A beautifully crafted account of the politics, economics, and culture of the Renaissance period in western Europe.

He, Yuming, *Home and the World: Editing the "Glorious Ming" in Woodblock-Printed Books of the Sixteenth and Seventeenth Centuries* (2013). An insightful exploration of Ming society through a close look at its vibrant print culture and market for books.

Hodgson, Marshall, *The Venture of Islam: Conscience and History in a World Civilization*, vol. 3 (1974). A good volume on the workings of the Ottoman state.

Hoffman, Philip T., *Why Did Europe Conquer the World?* (2015). Makes an interesting case for the importance of Europe's use of gunpowder technologies.

Itzkowitz, Norman, *Ottoman Empire and Islamic Tradition* (1972). Another good book on the Ottoman state.

Jackson, Peter, *The Delhi Sultanate* (1999). A meticulous, highly specialized political and military history.

Jackson, Peter, and Lawrence Lockhart (eds.), *The Cambridge History of Iran*, vol. 6 (1986). A volume that deals with the Timurid and Safavid periods in Iran.

Jones, E. L., *The European Miracle* (1981). A provocative work on the economic and social recovery from the Black Death.

Kafadar, Cemal, *Between Two Worlds: The Construction of the Ottoman State* (1995). A thorough reconsideration of the origins of one of the world's great land empires.

Karamustafa, Ahmed, *God's Unruly Friends: Dervish Groups in the Islamic Later Middle Period, 1200–1550* (1994). A book that describes the unorthodox Islamic activities that were occurring in the Islamic world prior to and alongside the establishment of the Ottoman and Safavid empires.

Levathes, Louise, *When China Ruled the Seas: The Treasure Fleet of the Dragon Throne, 1405–33* (1994). A book that provides a lively account of the Zheng He expeditions.

Lowry, Heath W., *The Nature of the Early Ottoman State* (2003). New perspectives on the rise of the Ottomans to prominence.

McNeill, William, *Plagues and Peoples* (1976). A pathbreaking work with a highly useful chapter on the spread of the Black Death throughout the Afro-Eurasian landmass.

Morgan, David, *Medieval Persia, 1040–1797* (1988). Contains an informative discussion of the Safavid state.

Peirce, Leslie, *The Imperial Harem: Women and Sovereignty in the Ottoman Empire* (1993). A work that describes the powerful place that imperial women had in political affairs.

Pirenne, Henri, *Economic and Social History of Medieval Europe* (1937). A classic study of the economic and social recovery from the Black Death.

Reid, James J., *Tribalism and Society in Islamic Iran, 1500–1629* (1983). A useful account of how the Mongols and other nomadic steppe peoples influenced Iran in the era when the Safavids were establishing their authority.

Schäfer, Dagmar, *The Crafting of the 10,000 Things: Knowledge and Technology in Seventeenth-Century China* (2011). An innovative study of the philosophy of technology and crafts in the late Ming period with important implications for the global history of science.

Singman, Jeffrey L. (ed.), *Daily Life in Medieval Europe* (1999). An introductory description of the social and material world experienced by Europeans of different walks of life.

Tuchman, Barbara W., *A Distant Mirror: The Calamitous Fourteenth Century* (1978). A book that shows, in a vigorous way, how war, famine, and pestilence devastated Europeans in the fourteenth century.

Wittek, Paul, *The Rise of the Ottoman Empire* (1958). A work that contains vital insights on the emergence of the Ottoman state amid the political chaos in Anatolia.

Chapter 12: Contact, Commerce, and Colonization, 1450–1600

Axtell, James, *Beyond 1492: Encounters in Colonial North America* (1992). A wonderfully informed speculation about Indian reactions to Europeans.

Brady, Thomas A., Heiko A. Oberman, and James D. Tracy (eds.), *Handbook of European History 1400–1600: Late Middle Ages, Renaissance, and Reformation, vol. 1, Structures and Assertions* (1996). A good synthetic survey of recent literature and historiographical debates.

Brook, Timothy, *Vermeer's Hat: The Seventeenth Century and the Dawn of the Global World* (2008). An interesting look at the connections forged across the globe through the works of a well-known European artist.

Casale, Giancarlo, *The Ottoman Age of Exploration* (2010). The author places Ottoman exploration in a comparative context alongside European overseas expansion.

Cass, Victoria, *Dangerous Women: Warriors, Grannies, and Geishas of the Ming* (1999). An original study of Chinese female archetypes in memoirs, miscellanies, short stories, and novels.

Chaudhuri, K. N., *Trade and Civilisation in the Indian Ocean: An Economic History from the Rise of Islam to 1750* (1985). An excellent, comprehensive work that deals with the Indian Ocean economy and the appearance of European merchants there from the sixteenth century onward.

Clendinnen, Inga, *Aztecs: An Interpretation* (1991). Brilliantly reconstructs the culture of Tenochtitlán in the years before its conquest.

Crosby, Alfred W., *The Columbian Exchange: Biological and Cultural Consequences of 1492* (1972). A provocative discussion of the ecological consequences that followed the European "discovery" of the Americas.

———, *Ecological Imperialism: The Biological Expansion of Europe, 900–1900* (1986). Another important work on the ecological consequences of European expansion.

Curtin, Philip, *Cross-Cultural Trade in World History* (1984). A work stressing the role of trade and commerce in establishing cross-cultural contacts.

Faroqhi, Suraiya N. (ed.), *The Cambridge History of Turkey*, vol. 3, *The Later Ottoman Empire, 1603–1839* (2008). Definitive articles on this important period in Ottoman history.

Faroqhi, Suraiya N., and Kate Fleet (eds.), *The Cambridge History of Turkey*, vol. 2, *The Ottoman Empire as a World Power, 1453–1603* (2013). A collection of articles written by leading scholars of this crucial period in Ottoman history.

Febvre, Lucien, *The Problem of Unbelief in the Sixteenth Century: The Religion of Rabelais* (1982). A tour de force of intellectual history by the man who moved the study of the Reformation away from great men to the broader question of religious revival and mentalities.

Flynn, Dennis, and Arturo Giráldez (eds.), *Metals and Monies in an Emerging Global Economy* (1997). Contains several articles relating to silver and the Asian trade.

Frank, Andre Gunder, *ReOrient: Global Economy in the Asian Age* (1998). A reassessment of the role of Asia in the economic development of the world from around 1400 onward.

Glahn, Richard von, *The Economic History of China: From Antiquity to the Nineteenth Century* (2016). A masterful new survey of Chinese economic history.

———, *Fountain of Fortune: Money and Monetary Policy in China, 1000–1700* (1996). Includes an excellent analysis of the history of silver in Ming China.

Gruzinski, Serge, *The Conquest of Mexico* (1993). An important work on the conquest of Mexico.

Habib, Irfan, *The Agrarian System of Mughal India* (1963). One of the best studies on the subject.

Hall, Richard Seymour, *Empires of the Monsoon: A History of the Indian Ocean and Its Invaders* (1996). A very engaging journalistic account with fabulous details.

Hodgson, Marshall, *The Venture of Islam*, vols. 2 and 3 (1974). A magisterial work that includes the Indian subcontinent in its careful study of the political and cultural history of the whole Islamic world.

Hulme, Peter, *Colonial Encounters: Europe and the Native Caribbean, 1492–1797* (1986). Presents an interesting interpretation of the encounters of Europeans and Native Americans.

Lach, Donald F., *Asia in the Making of Europe*, 5 books in 3 vols. (1965–). Perhaps the single most comprehensive and innovative guide to the European voyages of discovery.

Lockhart, James, and Stuart Schwartz, *Early Latin America* (1983). One of the finest studies of European expansion in the late fifteenth century.

McCann, James, *Maize and Grace: Africa's Encounter with a New World Crop, 1500–2000* (2005).

Melville, Elinor G. K., *A Plague of Sheep: Environmental Consequences of the Conquest of Mexico* (1994). A history of the transformation of a valley in Mexico from the Aztec period to the era of Spanish rule.

Mignolo, Walter D., *The Darker Side of the Renaissance: Literacy, Territoriality, and Colonization* (1995). Uses literary theory and literary images to present provocative interpretations of the encounter of Europeans and Native Americans.

Ozbaran, Salih, *Ottoman Expansion toward the Indian Ocean in the 16th Century* (2009). An important treatment of the Ottoman entry into the Indian Ocean at a time when the Portuguese were also expanding there.

Pagden, Anthony, *European Encounters with the New World* (1993). A complex look at the deep and lasting imprint of the New World on its conquerors.

Parker, Geoffrey, *The Military Revolution: Military Innovation and the Rise of the West, 1500–1800* (1996). Traces the changes in technology and tactics in the early modern period and discusses the political significance of this "revolution."

Pelikan, Jaroslav, *Reformation of Church and Dogma (1300–1700)* (1988). An important overview of major religious controversies.

Phillips, William D., and Carla Rahn Phillips, *The World of Christopher Columbus* (1992). One of the finest studies of European expansion in the late fifteenth century.

Roper, Lyndal, *Martin Luther: Renegade and Prophet* (2016). A magisterial biography that demonstrates the ways in which Luther was a rebel but also a man of his time.

Russell-Wood, A. J. R., *The Portuguese Empire, 1415–1808* (1992). An important survey of early Portuguese exploration.

Chapter 13: Worlds Entangled, 1600–1750

Alam, Muzaffar, *The Crisis of Empire in Mughal North India* (1993). Represents the best of the new scholarly interpretations of the subject.

Bay, Edna, *Wives of the Leopard: Gender, Politics, and Culture in the Kingdom of Dahomey* (1998). A useful treatment of gender issues in Dahomey.

Blackburn, Robin, *The Making of New World Slavery: From the Baroque to the Modern, 1492–1800* (1997). A good place to begin when studying African slavery and the Atlantic slave trade, this book compares the early expansion of the plantation systems across the Atlantic and throughout the Americas.

Bushkovitch, Paul, *Peter the Great* (2016). An updated version of a standard work, offering a concise overview of one of Russia's most celebrated and energetic rulers.

Calloway, Colin G., *One Vast Winter Count: The Native American West before Lewis and Clark* (2003). A sweeping survey of North American Indian histories prior to the nineteenth century.

Crossley, Pamela, *A Translucent Mirror: History and Identity in Qing Imperial Ideology* (1999). The author deals with the formation of identities such as "Manchu" and "Chinese" during the Qing period.

Dale, Stephen F., *The Muslim Empires of the Ottomans, Safavids, and Mughals* (2010). A comparative overview of Islam's three most powerful empires of the sixteenth and seventeenth centuries.

Eltis, David, and David Richardson, *Atlas of the Transatlantic Slave Trade* (2010). This work contains the most up-to-date data on the Atlantic slave trade, including the numbers transported, where the captives came from, and where they landed.

Flynn, Dennis O., and Arturo Giráldez (eds.), *Metals and Money in an Emerging World Economy* (1997). A collection of articles about the place of silver in the world economy.

Forsyth, James, *A History of the Peoples of Siberia: Russia's North Asian Colony 1581–1990* (1992). A narrative overview of a violent history reminiscent of the western expansion of the United States.

Glahn, Richard von, *Fountains of Fortune: Money and Monetary Policy in China, 1000–1700* (1996). A discussion of the place of silver in the Chinese economy.

Halperin, Charles J., *Russia and the Golden Horde: The Mongol Impact on Medieval Russian History* (1985). A book on the rise of Muscovy, forebear of the Russian Empire, from within the Mongol realm.

Hämäläinen, Pekka, *The Comanche Empire* (2008). A book that inverts the conventional history of empires in North America by arguing that the Comanches were the most successful expansionist power in the middle of the continent during the eighteenth century.

Hartley, Janet, *Siberia: A History of the People* (2014). A vivid portrait of the diverse conquerors—fur traders, Cossack adventurers, political criminals—of a region larger than almost all continents.

Hattox, Ralph S., *Coffee and Coffeehouses: The Origins of a Social Beverage in the Medieval Near East* (1985). This work shows how widespread and popular coffee consumption and coffeehouses were around the world.

Herzog, Tamar, *Frontiers of Possession: Spain and Portugal in Europe and the Americas* (2015). An exploration of how Spanish and Portuguese rulers carved up the New World, less by military action and diplomatic treaties than by quarrels over land settlement and rights to trade and travel.

Huang, Ray, *1587, A Year of No Significance: The Ming Dynasty in Decline* (1981). An insightful analysis of the problems confronting the late Ming.

Lensen, George, *The Russian Push toward Japan: Russo-Japanese Relations 1697–1875* (1959). A discussion of why and how Japan established its first border with another state and how Russia pursued its ambitions in the Pacific.

Lockhart, James, *The Nahuas after the Conquest* (1992). A landmark study of the social reorganization of Mesoamerican societies under Spanish rule.

Lovejoy, Paul, *Transformations in Slavery: A History of Slavery in Africa* (1983). An excellent discussion of African slavery.

Mathee, Rudi, *Persia in Crisis, Safavid Decline, and the Fall of Isfahan* (2012). A study of the disintegration of the Safavid state.

Mikhail, Alan, *Nature and Empire in Ottoman Egypt: An Environmental History* (2011). An important study of the impact of the environment on Egypt in the eighteenth century.

Monahan, Erika, *The Merchants of Siberia: Trade in Early Modern Eurasia* (2016). A stirring account of entrepreneurs battling the harshest imaginable conditions to establish trading networks connecting the far-flung territories north of the ancient Silk Road.

Moon, David, *The Plough That Broke the Steppes: Agriculture and Environment in Russia's Grasslands, 1700–1913* (2013). A bold incorporation of environmental aspects to retell the epic story of Russia's most numerous social group.

Nakane, Chie, and Shinzaburo Oishi (eds.), *Tokugawa Japan: The Social and Economic Antecedents of Modern Japan* (1990). First-rate essays on Japanese village society, urban life, literacy, and culture.

Nwokeji, G. Uko, *The Slave Trade and Culture in the Bight of Biafra: An African Society in the Atlantic World* (2010). A study of the Aro peoples of southeastern Nigeria and their use of their commercial powers to promote a vigorous trade with European slavers on the coast.

Pamuk, Sevket, *A Monetary History of the Ottoman Empire* (2000). A discussion of the place of silver in the Ottoman Empire.

Parker, Geoffrey, Global Crisis: *War, Climate Change, and Catastrophe in the Seventeenth Century* (2013). A comprehensive and exhaustively researched study of the effects of the Little Ice Age on the governments and societies of the entire world in the seventeenth century.

——— (ed.), *The Thirty Years' War* (1997). The standard account of the conflict and its outcomes.

Perdue, Peter C., *China Marches West: The Qing Conquest of Central Asia* (2005). This volume chronicles the expansion of the Qing Empire to its northwest, drawing comparisons to other colonial empires and their legacies.

Platonov, S. F., *Ivan the Terrible* (1986). Covers the controversies over Russia's infamous tsar.

Rawski, Evelyn, *The Last Emperors: A Social History of Qing Imperial Institutions* (1998). This volume explores the mechanisms and processes through which the Qing court negotiated its Manchu identity.

Reid, Anthony, *Charting the Shape of Early Modern Southeast Asia* (1999). A collection of articles by a leading historian of Southeast Asia.

Spence, Jonathan, and John Wills (eds.), *From Ming to Ch'ing: Conquest, Region, and Continuity in Seventeenth-Century China* (1979). Covers the various aspects of a tumultuous period of dynastic transition.

Subramanyam, Sanjay, *From the Tigris to the Ganges: Explorations in Connected History* (2012). A study that demonstrates that Afro-Eurasia in the seventeenth and eighteenth centuries contained a porous network of empires, cultures, and economies.

Subramanyam, Sanjay, and Muzaffar Alam, *Indo-Persian Travels in the Age of Discoveries, 1400–1800* (2012). A lively portrait of cultural exchanges between Persia, central Asia, and India as seen in travel literature.

Taylor, Alan, *American Colonies: The Settling of North America* (2001). Brings together British, French, and Spanish colonial histories and shows how the fortunes of each were entangled with one another and with those of diverse Native American peoples.

Thornton, John K., *Africa and Africans in the Making of the Atlantic World, 1400–1800* (1998). A wonderful discussion of the large role African slaves played in the formation of the Atlantic world.

———, *The Kongolese Saint Anthony: Dona Beatriz Kimpa Vita and the Antonian Movement, 1684–1706* (1998). An excellent monograph on religious movements in the Kongo.

Toby, Ronald P., *State and Diplomacy in Early Modern Japan: Asia in the Development of the Tokugawa Bakufu* (1984). The author shows that the Japanese, far from being isolated from the outside world, engaged in vigorous and successful diplomacy.

Van Dusen, Nancy E., *Global Indios: The Indigenous Struggle for Justice in Sixteenth-Century Spain* (2015). A remarkable study of the ways that Spanish rulers enslaved Amerindians in the Americas and even exported them back to Europe.

Vilar, Pierre, *A History of Gold and Money* (1991). An excellent study of the development of the early silver and gold economies.

Chapter 14: Cultures of Splendor and Power, 1500–1780

Axtell, James, *The Invasion of America: The Contest of Cultures in Colonial North America* (1985). Discusses the strategies of Christian missionaries in converting the Indians, as well as the success of Indians in converting Europeans.

Babaie, Sussan, *Isfahan and Its Palaces: Statecraft, Shi'ism and the Architecture of Conviviality in Early Modern Iran* (2008). An overview of the city of Isfahan as the capital of the Safavid state.

Barmé, Geremie R., *The Forbidden City* (2008). A concise introduction to the history of one of the most important physical emblems of Chinese imperial power.

Berlin, Ira, *Many Thousands Gone: The First Two Centuries of Slavery in North America* (1998). Surveys the development of African-American culture in colonial North America.

Bleichmar, Daniela, *Visible Empire: Botanical Expeditions and Visual Culture in the Hispanic Enlightenment* (2012). A fascinating and beautifully illustrated history of creole botanical expeditions in the eighteenth century.

Brook, Timothy, *The Confusions of Pleasure: Commerce and Culture in Ming China* (1999). An insightful survey of Ming society.

Clunas, Craig, *Superfluous Things: Material Culture and Social Status in Early Modern China* (1991). A good account of the late Ming elite's growing passion for material things.

Collcutt, Martin, Marius Jansen, and Isao Kumakura, *A Cultural Atlas of Japan* (1988). A sweeping look at the many different forms of Japanese cultural expression over the centuries, including the flourishing urban culture of Edo.

Darnton, Robert, *The Business of the Enlightenment: A Publishing History of the Encyclopédie, 1775–1800* (1979). The classic study of

Europe's first great compendium of knowledge.

Dash, Mike, *Tulipomania: The Story of the World's Most Coveted Flower and the Extraordinary Passions It Aroused* (1999). A global perspective on and lively account of the spread of the tulip around the world as a flower signifying both beauty and status.

Doniger, Wendy, *The Hindus: An Alternative History* (2009). A deeply scholarly yet accessibly written history of Hinduism that takes into account both texts and popular practices and contains a lively account of dissenting traditions.

Elman, Benjamin A., *On Their Own Terms: Science in China, 1550–1900* (2005). A study of the development of "native" Chinese science and how the process interacted with the introduction of western science to China over the course of three and a half centuries.

Eze, Emmanuel Chukwudi (ed.), *Race and the Enlightenment: A Reader* (1997). Readings examining the idea of race in the context of the Enlightenment.

Fleischer, Cornell, *Bureaucrat and Intellectual in the Ottoman Empire: The Historian Mustafa Ali (1540–1600)* (1986). Offers good insight into the world of culture and intellectual vitality in the Ottoman Empire.

Grafton, Anthony, April Shelford, and Nancy Siraisi, *New Worlds, Ancient Texts: The Power of Tradition and the Shock of Discovery* (1995). A concise discussion of the impact of the New World on European thought.

Gutiérrez, Ramón, *When Jesus Came, the Corn Mothers Went Away: Marriage, Sexuality, and Power in New Mexico, 1500–1846* (1991). A provocative dissection of the spiritual dimensions of European colonialism in the Americas.

Harley, J. B., and David Woodward (eds.), *The History of Cartography*, vol. 2, book 2, *Cartography in the Traditional East and Southeast Asian Societies* (1994). An authoritative treatment of the subject.

Hart, Roger, *Imagined Civilizations: China, the West, and Their First Encounter* (2013). A treatment of the Jesuit mission to China as the first contact between Chinese and European cultures.

Horton, Robin, *Patterns of Thought in Africa and the West: Essays on Magic, Religion, and Science* (1993). Reflections on African patterns of thought and attitudes toward nature, which can help us understand African-American religious beliefs and resistance movements.

Huff, Toby, *Intellectual Curiosity and the Scientific Revolution: A Comparative Perspective* (2011). This book deals with Europe's scientific revolution comparatively, asking why it occurred Europe and not in China or the Islamic world.

Kai, Ho Yi (ed.), *Science in China, 1600–1900: Essays by Benjamin Elman* (2015). Elman, an expert on Chinese science, offers his latest word on China's scientific achievements in a context of Europe's transmission of science through the Jesuit mission.

Keene, Donald, *The Japanese Discovery of Europe: Honda Toshiaki and Other Discoverers, 1720–1798* (1952). A study of the ways Japan managed to incorporate knowledge from the outside world with the development of national traditions.

Ko, Dorothy, *Teachers of the Inner Chambers: Women and Culture in Seventeenth-Century China* (1994). Explores the lives of elite women in late Ming and early Qing China.

Lewis, Bernard, *Race and Color in Islam* (1979). Examines the Islamic attitude toward race and color.

Morgan, Philip D., *Slave Counterpoint: Black Culture in the Eighteenth-Century Chesapeake and Lowcountry* (1998). Describes the development of African-American culture in colonial North America.

Munck, Thomas, *The Enlightenment: A Comparative Social History, 1721–1794* (2000). A wonderful survey, with unusual examples from the periphery, especially from Scandinavia and the Habsburg Empire.

Necipoğlu, Gülru, *Architecture, Ceremonial, and Power: The Topkapi Palace in the Fifteenth and Sixteenth Centuries* (1991). A magnificently illustrated book that shows the enormous artistic talent that the Ottoman rulers poured into their imperial structure.

"Publishing and the Print Culture in Late Imperial China," special issue, *Late Imperial China* 17, no. 1 (June 1996). Contains a collection of important articles with a foreword by the French cultural historian Roger Chartier.

Qaisar, Ahsan Jan, *The Indian Response to European Technology, AD 1498–1707* (1998). A meticulous, scholarly work on this little-studied subject.

Rizvi, Athar Abbas, *The Wonder That Was India*, vol. 2, *A Survey of the History and Culture of the Indian Sub-continent from the Coming of the Muslims to the British Conquest, 1200–1700* (1987). A deeply learned work in intellectual history.

Safier, Neil, *Measuring the New World: Enlightenment Science and South America* (2008). Examines the ways in which European, and especially Parisian, surveyors set about gauging the curvature of the earth, starting in Quito, Ecuador. Along the way, they learned much more about local natural history, which flowed back to Paris to inform the Enlightenment.

Smith, Bernard, *European Vision and the South Pacific* (1985). An excellent cultural history of Cook's voyages.

Smith, Richard J., *Chinese Maps: Images of "All under Heaven"* (1996). Provides a good introduction to the history of cartography in China.

Sorkin, David, *The Religious Enlightenment: Protestants, Jews, and Catholics from London to Vienna* (2008). Discusses a wide range of thinkers who were able to reconcile Enlightenment thought with religious belief.

Welch, Anthony, *Shah Abbas and the Arts of Isfahan* (1973). Describes the astonishing architectural and artistic renaissance of the city of Isfahan under the Safavid ruler Shah Abbas.

Whitfield, Peter, *The Image of the World: Twenty Centuries of World Maps* (1994). A good introduction to the history of cartography in different parts of the world.

Wilks, Ivor, *Forests of Gold: Essays on the Akan and the Kingdom of Asante* (1993). A study that focuses on the Asante's drive for wealth.

Zilfi, Madeline C., *The Politics of Piety: The Ottoman Ulema in the Post-Classical Age (1600–1800)* (1988). Explores the cultural flourishing that took place within the Islamic world in this period.

Chapter 15: Reordering the World, 1750–1850

Allen, Robert C., *The British Industrial Revolution in Global Perspective* (2009). The most recent and authoritative study of the industrial revolution in Britain and its implications around the world.

Anderson, Fred, *Crucible of War: The Seven Years' War and the Fate of Empire in British North America, 1754–1766* (2000). The best synthesis of the "great war for empire" that set the stage for the American Revolution.

Bayly, C. A., *Indian Society and the Making of the British Empire* (1998). A useful work on the early history of the British conquest of India.

Blackburn, Robin, *The Overthrow of Colonial Slavery, 1776–1848* (1988). Places the abolition of the Atlantic slave trade and colonial slavery in a large historical context.

Cassel, Par Kristoffer, *Grounds of Judgement: Extraterritoriality and Imperial Powers in Nineteenth-Century China and Japan* (2012). A study of the idea and practice of extraterritoriality within the context of the triangular relationship between China, Japan, and the west.

Chaudhuri, K. N., *The Trading World of Asia and the East India Company, 1660–1760* (1978). An authoritative economic history of the East India Company's operations.

Crafts, N. F. R., *British Economic Growth during the Industrial Revolution* (1985). A pioneering study that emphasizes a long-term, more gradual process of adaptation to new institutional and social circumstances.

Daly, M. W. (ed.), *Cambridge History of Egypt, vol. 2, Modern Egypt, from 1517 to the End of the Twentieth Century* (1998). Contains authoritative essays on all aspects of modern Egyptian history, including the impact of the French invasion and the rule of Muhammad Ali.

de Vries, Jan, *Industrious Revolution: Consumer Behavior and the Household Economy, 1650 to the Present* (2008). A book on the lead-up to the industrial revolution, written by the leading economic historian who coined the term "industrious revolution."

Diamond, Jared, and James A. Robinson (eds.), *Natural Experiments of History* (2010). This book consists of eight comparative studies drawn from history, archaeology, economics, economic history, geography, and political science, covering a spectrum of approaches, ranging from a nonquantitative narrative style to quantitative statistical analyses.

Drescher, Seymour, *Abolition: A History of Slavery and Anti-Slavery* (2009). A recent and authoritative overview of slavery and its opponents.

Dubois, Laurent, *Avengers of the New World: The Story of the Haitian Revolution* (2004). The most up-to-date synthesis on the Haitian Revolution.

Elvin, Mark, *The Retreat of the Elephants: An Environmental History of China* (2004). A study of the different ways in which China's natural environment was shaped.

Findley, Carter, *Bureaucratic Reform in the Ottoman Empire: The Sublime Porte, 1789–1922* (1980). A useful guide to Ottoman reform efforts in the nineteenth century.

Geggus, David (ed.), *The Impact of the Haitian Revolution in the Atlantic World* (2001). A lively effort to disentangle the effects of the Haitian Revolution from those of the French Revolution.

Hevia, James, *Cherishing Men from Afar: Qing Guest Ritual and the Macartney Embassy of 1793* (1995).

Offers a definitive interpretation of the nature of Sino-British conflict in the Qing period.

Hobsbawm, Eric, *Nations and Nationalism since 1780* (1990). An important overview of the rise of the nation-state and nationalism around the world.

Howe, Daniel Walker, *What Hath God Wrought: The Transformation of America, 1815–1848* (2007). A Pulitzer Prize–winning interpretation of how new technologies and new ideas reshaped the economy, society, culture, and politics of the United States in the first half of the nineteenth century.

Hunt, Lynn, *Politics, Culture and Class in the French Revolution* (1984). Examines the influence of sociocultural shifts as causes and consequences of the French Revolution, emphasizing the symbols and practice of politics invented during the revolution.

Inikori, Joseph, *Africans and the Industrial Revolution in England* (2002). Demonstrates the important role that Africa and Africans played in facilitating the industrial revolution.

Isset, Christopher Mills, *State, Peasant, and Merchant in Qing Manchuria, 1644–1862* (2007). A study of the relationships between sociopolitical structures and peasant lives in a key region during the Qing.

James, C. L. R., *The Black Jacobins: Toussaint L'Ouverture and the San Domingo Revolution* (1938). A classic chronicle of the only successful slave revolt in history, it provides a critical portrait of their leader, Toussaint L'Ouverture.

Jones, E. L., *Growth Recurring* (1988). Discusses the controversy over why the industrial revolution took place in Europe, stressing the unique ecological setting that encouraged long-term investment.

Kinsbruner, Jay, *Independence in Spanish America* (1994). A fine study of the Latin American revolutions that argues that the struggle was as much a civil war as a fight for national independence.

Landers, Jane, *Atlantic Creoles in the Age of Revolutions* (2011). A collection of fascinating and unique portraits of Atlantic world creoles who managed to move freely and purposefully through French, Spanish, and English colonies, and through Indian territory, in the unstable century between 1750 and 1850.

Lieven, Dominic, *Russia Against Napoleon* (2010). Explains how outnumbered Russian forces were able to defeat the massive army that Napoleon assembled for his conquest of Russia.

Mokyr, Joel, *Enlightened Economy: An Economic History of Britain, 1700–1850* (2009). Perspectives on the evolution of the British economy in the era that produced the industrial revolution.

——, *The Lever of Riches* (1990). An important study of the causes of the industrial revolution that emphasizes the role of small technological and organizational breakthroughs.

Naquin, Susan, and Evelyn Rawski, *Chinese Society in the Eighteenth Century* (1987). A survey of mid-Qing society.

Neal, Larry, *The Rise of Financial Capitalism* (1990). An important study of the making of financial markets.

Nikitenko, Aleksandr, *Up from Serfdom: My Childhood and Youth in Russia, 1804–1824* (2001). One of the very few recorded life stories of a Russian serf.

Parthasarathi, Prasannan, *Why Europe Grew Rich and Asia Did Not: Global Economic Divergence, 1600–1800* (2011). A work that places the British industrial revolution in a global context, with much emphasis on India's textile industry before it was superseded by British manufacturers.

Pomeranz, Kenneth, *The Great Divergence: Europe, China, and the Making of the Modern World Economy* (2000). Offers explanations of why Europe and not some other place in the world, like parts of China or India, forged ahead economically in the nineteenth century.

Popkin, Jeremy D., *You Are All Free: The Haitian Revolution and the Abolition of Slavery* (2010). A revisionist account that calls attention to the role of local factors in the emancipation of Haiti's slaves.

Tackett, Timothy, *The Coming of the Terror in the French Revolution* (2017). An authoritative account of the most controversial phase of the French Revolution.

Taylor, Alan, *American Revolutions: A Continental History, 1750–1804* (2016). A sweeping interpretation of the founding of the United States that places the War of Independence in a North American perspective, bringing together the diverse revolutions that transformed societies and borders across the continent.

Wakeman, Frederic, Jr., "The Canton Trade and the Opium War," in John K. Fairbank (ed.), *The Cambridge History of China*, vol. 10 (1978), pp. 163–212. The standard account of the episode.

Wong, R. Bin, *China Transformed: Historical Change and the Limits of European Experience* (2000). Draws attention to the relative autonomy of merchant capitalists in relation to dynastic states in Europe as compared with China.

Wood, Gordon S., *Empire of Liberty: A History of the Early Republic, 1789–1815* (2009). An excellent synthesis of the history of the United States in the tumultuous years between the ratification of the Constitution and the War of 1812.

Wortman, Richard, *Scenarios of Power: Myth and Ceremony in Russian Monarchy*, 2 vols. (1995–2000). Examines how dynastic Russia confronted the challenges of the revolutionary epoch.

Chapter 16: Alternative Visions of the Nineteenth Century

Anderson, David M., *Revealing Prophets: Prophets in Eastern African History* (1995). Good discussion of the prophets in eastern Africa.

Beecher, Jonathan, *The Utopian Vision of Charles Fourier* (1983). A fine biography of this important thinker.

Boyd, Jean, *The Caliph's Sister: Nana Asma'u, 1793–1865, Teacher, Poet, and Islamic Leader* (1988). A study of the most powerful female Muslim leader in the Fulani religious revolt.

Brower, Benjamin Claude, *A Desert Named Peace: The Violence of France's Empire in the Algerian Sahara, 1844–1902* (2009). Examines colonial violence across a few fields of research and through multiple stories to reveal some unexpected causes—for instance, France's difficult revolutionary past and its sway on the military's institutional culture.

Clancy-Smith, Julia, *Rebel and Saint: Muslim Notables, Populist Protest, Colonial Encounter (Algeria and Tunisia, 1800–1904)* (1994).

Examines Islamic protest movements against western encroachments in North Africa.

Clogg, Richard, *A Concise History of Greece* (1997). A good introduction to the history of Greece in its European context.

Dalrymple, William, *The Last Mughal: The Fall of a Dynasty: Delhi, 1857* (2007). A deeply researched and riveting account of Delhi during the 1857 revolt.

Danziger, Raphael, *Abd al-Qadir: Resistance to the French and Internal Consolidation* (1977). Still the indispensable work on this important Algerian Muslim leader.

Dowd, Gregory E., *A Spirited Resistance: The North American Indian Struggle for Unity, 1745–1815* (1992). Emphasizes the importance of prophets like Tenskwatawa in the building of pan-Indian confederations in the era between the Seven Years' War and the War of 1812.

Guha, Ranajit, *Elementary Aspects of Peasant Insurgency in Colonial India* (1983). Not specifically on the Indian Rebellion of 1857, but includes it in its pioneering "subalternist" interpretation of South Asian history.

Hamilton, Carolyn (ed.), *The Mfecane Aftermath: Reconstructive Debates in Southern African History* (1995). Debates on Shaka's *Mfecane* movement and its impact on southern Africa.

Hiskett, Mervyn, *The Sword of Truth: The Life and Times of the Shehu Usman dan Fodio* (1994). An authoritative study of the Fulani revolt in northern Nigeria.

Johnson, Douglas H., *Nuer Prophets: A History of Prophecy from the Upper Nile in the Nineteenth and Twentieth Centuries* (1994). Deals with African prophetic and charismatic movements in eastern Africa.

Keddie, Nikki, *An Islamic Response to Imperialism: Political and Religious Writings of Sayyid Jamal ad-Din "al-Afghani"* (1968). Definitive information on the Afghani's life and influence, coupled with a translation of one of his most important essays.

Michael, Franz, and Chung-li Chang, *The Taiping Rebellion: History and Documents*, 3 vols. (1966–1971). The basic source for the history of the Taiping.

Mukherjee, Rudrangshu, *Awadh in Revolt 1857–58* (1984). A careful case study of the Indian Rebellion.

Omer-Cooper, J. D., *The Zulu Aftermath: A Nineteenth-Century Revolution in Bantu Africa* (1966). A good place to start in studying Shaka's *Mfecane* movement, which greatly rearranged the political and ethnic makeup of southern Africa.

Ostler, Jeffrey, *The Plains Sioux and U.S. Colonialism from Lewis and Clark to Wounded Knee* (2004). Uses the lens of colonial theory to track relations between the Sioux and the United States, offering fresh insights about the Ghost Dance movement.

Peires, J. B. (ed.), *Before and After Shaka* (1981). Discusses elements in the debate over Shaka's *Mfecane* movement.

Pilbeam, Pamela, *French Socialists before Marx: Workers, Women and the Social Question in France* (2001). Describes the development of a variety of socialist ideas in early nineteenth-century France.

Platt, Stephen R., *Autumn in the Heavenly Kingdom: China, the West, and the Epic Story of the Taiping Civil War* (2012). A study of the Taiping Rebellion from a global perspective.

Reed, Nelson, *The Caste War of Yucatan* (1964). A classic narrative of the Caste War of the Yucatán.

Restall, Matthew, *The Maya World* (1997). Describes in economic and social terms the origins of the Yucatán upheaval in southern Mexico.

Rugeley, Terry, *Rebellion Now and Forever: Mayans, Hispanics, and Caste War Violence in Yucatán, 1800–1880* (2009). Explains the combination of economic and cultural pressures that drove the Maya in the Yucatán to revolt in the Caste War.

Spence, Jonathan, *God's Chinese Son: The Taiping Heavenly Kingdom of Hong Xiuquan* (1996). A fascinating portrayal of the Taiping through the prism of its founder.

Sperber, Jonathan, *Karl Marx: A Nineteenth-Century Life* (2013). An engaging and authoritative biography of Marx that emphasizes his role as a radical journalist.

Stedman Jones, Gareth, *Karl Marx: Greatness and Illusion* (2016). Now the authoritative biography of the founder of communism, showing Marx's own ambivalence about what he had created.

Wagner, Rudolf, *Reenacting the Heavenly Vision: The Role of Religion in the Taiping Rebellion* (1982). A brief but insightful analysis of the religious elements in the Taiping's doctrines.

White, Richard, *The Middle Ground: Indians, Empires, and Republics in the Great Lakes Region, 1650–1815* (1991). A pathbreaking exploration of intercultural relations in North America that offers a provocative interpretation of the visions of Tenskwatawa and the efforts of Tecumseh to resist the expansion of the United States.

Chapter 17: Nations and Empires, 1850–1914

Berry, Sara, *Cocoa, Custom and Socio-Economic Change in Western Nigeria* (1975). Innovative study based on interviews with local farmers that suggests that farmer enterprise and microeconomic theory better explain the spectacular growth in cocoa production than grand economic theory.

Cain, P. A., and A. G. Hopkins, *British Imperialism: Innovation and Expansion, 1688–1914* (1993). An excellent discussion of British imperialism, especially British expansion into Africa.

Clark, Christopher, *Iron Kingdom: The Rise and Downfall of Prussia, 1600–1947* (2009). Includes an excellent discussion of the rise of German nationalism and Prussian power.

Cooper, Frederick, *Colonialism in Question: Theory, Knowledge, History* (2005). A collection of essays by one of the leading scholars of colonial studies.

Cronon, William, *Nature's Metropolis: Chicago and the Great West* (1991). Makes connections among territorial expansion, industrialization, and urban development.

Davis, John, *Conflict and Control: Law and Order in Nineteenth-Century Italy* (1988). A superb study of the north-south and other rifts after Italian political unification.

Frankel, S. Herbert, *Capital Investment in Africa: Its Course and Effects* (1938). A careful study based on a mass of detailed figures and statistics on the general economic development of states in sub-Saharan Africa.

Friesen, Gerald, *The Canadian Prairies* (1984). The most comprehensive account of Canadian westward expansion.

Gluck, Carol, *Japan's Modern Myths: Ideology in the Late Meiji Period* (1985). A study of how states fashion useful historical traditions to consolidate and legitimize their rule.

Headrick, Daniel R., *The Tools of Empire: Technology and European Imperialism in the Nineteenth Century* (1981). A useful general study of the relationship between imperialism and technology.

Herbst, Jeffrey, *States and Power in Africa: Comparative Lessons in Authority and Control* (2000). An overview of the impact of colonial rule on contemporary African states.

Hill, Polly, *The Gold Coast Cocoa Farmer: A Preliminary Survey* (1965). A socioeconomic report detailing three issues facing the cocoa farmer: labor; indebtedness and pledging; and income and expenditure.

Hine, Robert V., and John Mack Faragher, *The American West: A New Interpretive History* (2000). Presents an excellent synthesis of the conquests by which the United States expanded from the Atlantic to the Pacific.

Hobsbawm, Eric J., *Nations and Nationalism since 1780: Programme, Myth, Reality* (1993). An insightful survey of the origins and development of nationalist thought throughout Europe.

Hochschild, Adam, *King Leopold's Ghost* (1998). A full-scale, eminently readable study of Europe's most egregiously destructive colonial regime in Africa.

Judson, Peter, *The Habsburg Empire: A New History* (2016). An innovative history of the relationship between "the people" and the state in a multiethnic empire.

Lee, Leo Ou-fan, and Andrew Nathan, "The Beginnings of Mass Culture: Journalism and Fiction in the Late Ch'ing and Beyond," in David Johnson, Andrew Nathan, and Evelyn Rawski (eds.), *Popular Culture in Late Imperial China* (1985), pp. 360–95. An important article on the emergence of a mass-media market in late nineteenth- and early twentieth-century China.

Lieven, Dominic, *Empire: The Russian Empire and Its Rivals* (2000). A comparison of the British, Ottoman, Habsburg, and Russian empires.

Mackenzie, John M., *Propaganda and Empire* (1984). Contains a series of useful chapters showing the importance of the empire to Britain.

Mamdani, Mahmood, *Citizen and State: Contemporary Africa and the Legacy of Late Colonialism* (1996). A survey of the impact of European colonial powers on African political systems.

McClintock, Anne, *Imperial Leather: Race, Gender and Sexuality in the Colonial Contest* (1995). A study of the imperial relationship between Victorian Britain and South Africa from the point of view of cultural studies.

McNeil, William, *Europe's Steppe Frontier: 1500–1800* (1964). An excellent study of the definitive victory of Russia's agricultural empire over grazing nomads and independent frontier people.

Mitchell, B. R., *International Historical Statistics: Africa, Asia, and Oceania, 1750–2005* (2007). This comparative volume provides data from over two centuries for all principal areas of economic and social activity in both eastern and western Europe.

Montgomery, David, *The Fall of the House of Labor: The Workplace, the State, and American Labor Activism, 1865–1925* (1987). An excellent discussion of changes in work in the late nineteenth century.

Myers, Ramon, and Mark Peattie (eds.), *The Japanese Colonial Empire, 1895–1945* (1984). A collection of essays exploring different aspects of Japanese colonialism.

Needell, Jeffrey, *A Tropical Belle Epoque: Elite Culture and Society in Turn-of-the-Century Rio de Janeiro* (1987). Shows the strength of the Brazilian elites at the turn of the century.

Pan, Lynn (ed.), *The Encyclopedia of Chinese Overseas* (1999). A comprehensive coverage of the history of the Chinese diaspora.

Porter, Bernard, *The Absent-Minded Imperialists: What the British Really Thought about Empire* (2004). A careful dissection of the ways in which empire changed the British—and did not.

Prasad, Ritika, *Tracks of Change: Railways and Everyday Life in Colonial India* (2016). A detailed analysis of how railways transformed the everyday experience of Indians under colonial rule.

Stengers, Jean, *Combien le Congo a-t-il coûté à la Belgique* (1957). A detailed financial accounting of how much Leopold put into the Congo and how much he took out, underscoring just how ruthlessly he exploited this possession.

Topik, Steven, *The Political Economy of the Brazilian State, 1889–1930* (1987). An excellent discussion of the Brazilian state, and especially of its elites.

Walker, Mack, *German Home Towns: Community, State, and the General State, 1648–1871* (1971; reprint, 1998). A brilliant, street-level analysis of the Holy Roman Empire (the First Reich) and the run-up to the German unification of 1871 (the Second Reich).

Wasserman, Mark, *Everyday Life and Politics in Nineteenth-Century Mexico* (2000). Wonderfully captures the way in which people coped with social and economic dislocation in late nineteenth-century Mexico.

Weeks, Theodore R., *Nation and State in Late Imperial Russia: Nationalism and Russification on the Western Frontier, 1863–1914* (1996). A good discussion of the Russian Empire's responses to the concept of the nation-state.

White, Richard, *Railroaded: The Transcontinentals and the Making of Modern America* (2011). A searing exposé of the corruptions and a startling critique of the economic and environmental costs associated with the expansion of railroad lines across Canada, the United States, and Mexico.

Yung, Wing, *My Life in China and America* (1909). The autobiography of the first Chinese graduate of an American university.

Zarrow, Peter, *After Empire: The Conceptual Transformation of the Chinese State, 1885–1924* (2012). A history of the changing ideas regarding the Chinese state that eventually led to the abandonment of monarchical rule by the Chinese people.

Chapter 18: An Unsettled World, 1890–1914

Bayly, C. A., *The Birth of the Modern World, 1780–1914: Global Connections and Comparisons* (2004). A general study of the key political, economic, social, and cultural features of the modern era in world history.

Bergère, Marie-Claire, *Sun Yat-sen* (1998). Originally published in French in 1994, this is a judicious biography of the man generally known as the father of the modern Chinese nation.

Brinkley, Douglas, *Wilderness Warrior: Theodore Roosevelt and the Crusade to Save America* (2010).

An important account of Roosevelt's environmental policies, based on new research.

Chatterjee, Partha, *The Nation and Its Fragments* (1993). One of the most important works on Indian nationalism by a leading scholar of "subaltern studies."

Conrad, Joseph, *Heart of Darkness* (1899). First published in a magazine in 1899, this novella contained a searing critique of King Leopold's oppressive and exploitative policies in the Congo and was part of a growing concern for the effects that European empires were having around the world, especially in Africa.

Esherick, Joseph, "How the Qing Became China," in Joseph W. Esherick, Hasan Kayali, and Eric Van Young (eds.), *Empire to Nation: Historical Perspectives on the Making of the Modern World* (2006). A study of the processes through which the Qing Empire became the nation-state of China.

———, *The Origins of the Boxer Uprising* (1987). The definitive account of the episode.

Everdell, William R., *The First Moderns: Profiles in the Origins of Twentieth-Century Thought* (1997). A rich account of the many faces of modernism, focusing particularly on science and art.

Finnane, Antonia, *Changing Clothes in China: Fashion, History, Nation* (2008). An exploration of changing Chinese identities from the perspective of clothing.

Gay, Peter, *The Cultivation of Hatred* (1994). A provocative discussion of the violent passions of the immediate pre–Great War era.

Gilmartin, Christina, et al. (eds.), *Engendering China: Women, Culture, and the State* (1994). Analyzes politics and society in modern China from the perspective of gender.

Hochschild, Adam, *King Leopold's Ghost: A Story of Greed, Terror, and Heroism in Colonial Africa* (1998). A well-written account of the violent colonial history of the Belgian Congo under King Leopold in the late nineteenth century.

Judge, Joan, *The Precious Raft of History: The Past, the West, and the Woman Question in China* (2008). An insightful exploration of the "woman question" in China at the turn of the twentieth century.

Katz, Friedrich, *The Life and Times of Pancho Villa* (1998). An exploration of the Mexican Revolution that shows how Villa's armies destroyed the forces of Díaz and his followers.

Keddie, Nikki, *An Islamic Response to Imperialism: Political and Religious Writings of Sayyid Jamal ad-Din "al-Afghani"* (1968). Definitive information on the Afghani's life and influence, coupled with a translation of one of his most important essays.

Kern, Stephen, *The Culture of Time and Space 1880–1918* (1986). A useful study of the enormous changes in the experience of time and space in the age of late industrialism in Europe and America.

Kuhn, Philip, *Chinese among Others: Emigration in Modern Times* (2008). An overview of the history of Chinese migration.

McKeown, Adam, *Melancholy Order: Asian Migration and the Globalization of Borders* (2008). An examination of global migration patterns since the mid-nineteenth century and how regulations designed to restrict Asian migration to other parts of the world led to the modern regime of migration control.

Meade, Teresa, *"Civilizing" Rio: Reform and Resistance in a Brazilian City, 1889–1930* (1997). A wonderful study of cultural and class conflict in Brazil.

Moon, David, *The Plough That Broke the Steppes: Agriculture and Environment on Russia's Grasslands, 1700–1914* (2013). A pathbreaking study of Russian environmental history before the twentieth century.

Morris, Edmund, *Theodore Rex* (2002). A thorough biography of Theodore Roosevelt.

Pick, Daniel, *Faces of Degeneration: A European Disorder, c. 1848–c. 1918* (1993). A study of Europe's fear of social and biological decline, particularly focusing on France and Italy.

Pretorius, Fransjohn (ed.), *Scorched Earth* (2001). A study of the Anglo-Boer War in terms of its environmental impacts.

Saler, Michael (ed.), *The Fin de Siècle World* (2014). A comprehensive anthology of essays on turn-of-the-century politics and culture across the world.

Sarkar, Sumit, *The Swadeshi Movement in Bengal* (1973). A comprehensive study of an early militant movement against British rule.

Schorske, Carl E., *Fin-de-Siècle Vienna: Politics and Culture* (1980). The classic treatment of the birth of modern ideas and political movements in turn-of-the-century Austria.

Trachtenberg, Alan, *The Incorporation of America: Culture and Society in the Gilded Age* (1982). A provocative synthesis of changes in the American economy, society, and culture in the last decades of the nineteenth century.

Wang, David Der-wei, *Fin-de-Siècle Splendor: Repressed Modernities of Late Qing Fiction, 1849–1911* (1997). A fine work that attempts to locate the "modern" within the writings of the late Qing period.

Warren, Louis, *Buffalo Bill's America: William Cody and the Wild West Show* (2005). A superb portrait of William F. Cody, the person; of Buffalo Bill, the persona Cody (and others) created; and of the popular culture his Wild West shows brought to audiences in Europe and North America.

Warwick, Peter, *Black People and the South African War, 1899–1902* (1983). An important study that reminds readers of the crucial involvement of black South Africans in this bloody conflict.

Womack, John, Jr., *Zapata and the Mexican Revolution* (1968). A major work on the Mexican Revolution that discusses peasant struggles in the state of Morelos in great detail.

Chapter 19: Of Masses and Visions of the Modern, 1910–1939

Akcam, Taner, *The Young Turks' Crime against Humanity: The Armenian Genocide and Ethnic Cleansing in the Ottoman Empire* (2012). An exhaustive examination of the factors that impelled the Turkish authorities to carry out ethnic cleansing against the Armenians during World War I.

Aksakal, Mustafa, *The Ottoman Road to War in 1914: The Ottoman Empire and the First World War* (2008). An important study of the personalities and factors that led the Ottomans to join with Germany and Austria-Hungary during World War I, a fateful decision that ultimately spelled the end of the Ottoman Empire.

Anderson, Scott, *Lawrence in Arabia: War, Deceit, Imperial Folly, and the Making of the Middle East* (2013). A new and authoritative biography of T. E. Lawrence, with significant new material on British policies in the Middle East as seen through the eyes of a strong pro-Arab figure.

Bloxham, Donald, *The Great Game of Genocide: Imperialism, Nationalism, and the Destruction of the Ottoman Armenians* (2005). The definitive work on the Armenian genocide, set in a wide historical context.

Brown, Judith, *Gandhi: Prisoner of Hope* (1990). A biography of Gandhi as a political activist.

Clark, Christopher, *Sleepwalkers: How Europe Went to War* (2012). A reexamination of the crucial role of Austria-Hungary in triggering the world war.

De Grazia, Victoria, and Ellen Furlough (eds.), *The Sex of Things: Gender and Consumption in Historical Perspective* (1996). Path-breaking essays on how gender affects consumption.

Dumenil, Lynn, *The Modern Temper: America in the 1920s* (1995). A general discussion of American culture in the decade after World War I.

Fainsod, Merle, *Smolensk under Soviet Rule* (1989). The most accessible and sophisticated interpretation of the Stalin revolution in the village.

Friedman, Edward, *Backward toward Revolution: The Chinese Revolutionary Party* (1974). An insightful look at the failure of liberalism in early republican China through the prism of the short-lived Chinese Revolutionary Party.

Gelvin, James, *Divided Loyalties: Nationalism and Mass Politics in Syria at the Close of Empire* (1998). Offers important insights into the development of nationalism in the Arab world.

Horne, John (ed.), *A Companion to World War I* (2010). A collection of articles written by leading scholars of World War I; the most comprehensive and up-to-date work on this war.

———, *State, Society, and Mobilization during the First World War* (1997). Essays on what it took to wage total war among all the belligerents.

Johnson, G. Wesley, *The Emergence of Black Politics in Senegal* (1971). A useful examination of the stirrings of African nationalism in Senegal.

Kennedy, David M., *Freedom from Fear: The American People in Depression and War, 1929–1945* (1999). A wonderful narrative of turbulent years.

Kershaw, Ian, *Hitler*, 2 vols. (1998–2000). A masterpiece combining biography and context.

Kimble, David, *A Political History of Ghana* (1963). An excellent discussion of the beginnings of African nationalism in Ghana.

Kotkin, Stephen, *Magnetic Mountain: Stalinism as a Civilization* (1995). Recaptures the atmosphere of a time when everything seemed possible, even creating a new world.

———, *Stalin*, vol. 1, *Paradoxes of Power* (2014). A sweeping history of the tsarist regime, world war, Russian Revolution, civil war, and rise of Stalin.

Lambert, Nicholas A., *Planning Armageddon: British Economic Warfare and the First World War* (2012). Mines new archives to show that the British had an aggressive plan before the war to destroy Germany financially, which the British government approved and began to enact until the United States forced them to back off.

LeMahieu, D. L., *A Culture for Democracy: Mass Communication and the Cultivated Mind in Britain between the Wars* (1988). One of the great works on mass culture.

Lyttelton, Adrian, *The Seizure of Power: Fascism in Italy, 1919–1929* (1961). Still the classic account.

Marchand, Roland, *Advertising the American Dream: Making Way for Modernity, 1920–1945* (1985). An excellent discussion of the force of mass production and mass consumption.

Mazower, Mark, *Dark Continent: Europe's Twentieth Century* (1999). A wide-ranging overview of Europe's tempestuous twentieth century.

McGirr, Lisa, *The War on Alcohol: Prohibition and the Rise of the American State* (2016). Emphasizes the power of cultural reaction against modernity that brought about Prohibition and the irony that its enforcement helped to expand the power of the modern state.

McKeown, Adam, *Melancholy Order: Asian Migration and the Globalization of Border* (2008). A major study of the vast movement of peoples around the globe between the middle of the nineteenth and the twentieth centuries.

Morrow, John H., Jr., *The Great War: An Imperial History* (2004). Places World War I in the context of European imperialism.

Musgrove, Charles D., *China's Contested Capital: Architecture, Ritual, and Response in Nanjing* (2013). An exploration of how the Chinese Nationalist capital of Nanjing served as a focal point for the making of a nation and a new form of mass politics.

Nottingham, John, and Carl Rosberg, *The Myth of "Mau Mau": Nationalism in Kenya* (1966). Dispels the myths in describing the roots of nationalism in Kenya.

Pedersen, Susan, *The Guardians: the League of Nations and the Crisis of Empire* (2015). Skillfully reexamines the neglected effort to regulate the colonial world under a so-called mandate system.

Rosenberg, Clifford, *Policing Paris: The Origins of Modern Immigration Control between the Wars* (2006). Explores the first systematic efforts to enforce distinctions of nationality and citizenship status in a major urban setting.

Rutledge, Ian, *Enemy on the Euphrates: The British Occupation of Iraq and the Great Arab Revolt, 1914–1921* (2014). An impassioned investigation of Britain's effort to take control of the oil-rich territory of Iraq and the determined resistance of the Iraqi peoples.

Strand, David, *An Unfinished Republic: Leading by Word and Deed in Modern China* (2011). A study of how the need for popular support led to a new political culture characterized by public speaking and performance in early twentieth-century China.

Suny, Ronald Gregor, *"They Can Live in the Desert but Nowhere Else": A History of the Armenian Genocide* (2015). A careful, document-based analysis of the Armenian genocide.

Taylor, Jay, *The Generalissimo: Chiang Kai-shek and the Struggle for Modern China* (2009). The first serious biographical study of Chiang Kai-shek in English, although its reliance on Chiang's own diary as a source does raise some questions of historical interpretation.

Thorp, Rosemary (ed.), *Latin America in the 1930s* (1984). An important collection of essays on Latin America's response to the shakeup of the interwar years.

Tsin, Michael, *Nation, Governance, and Modernity in China: Canton, 1900–1927* (1999). An analysis of the vision and social dynamics behind the Guomindang-led revolution of the 1920s.

Vianna, Hermano, *The Mystery of Samba* (1999). Discusses the history of samba, emphasizing its African heritage as well as its persistent popular content.

Wakeman, Frederic, Jr., *Policing Shanghai, 1927–1937* (1995). An excellent account of Guomindang rule in China's largest city during the Nanjing decade.

Winter, J. M., *The Experience of World War* (1988). A comprehensive presentation of the many sides of the twentieth century.

Young, Louise, *Japan's Total Empire: Manchuria and the Culture of Wartime Imperialism* (1998). An innovative case study of Japanese imperialism and mass culture with broad implications.

Chapter 20: The Three-World Order, 1940–1975

Aburish, Said K., *Nasser: The Last Arab* (2004). An impressive look at Egypt's most powerful political leader in the 1950s and 1960s.

Anderson, Jon Lee, *Che Guevara: A Revolutionary Life* (1997). A sweeping study of the radicalization of Latin American nationalism.

Bayly, Christopher, and Tim Harper, *Forgotten Armies: Britain's Asian Empire and the War with Japan* (2004). A brilliant social and military history of the Second World War as fought and lived in South and Southeast Asia.

Chatterjee, Partha, *Nationalist Thought and the Colonial World: A Derivative Discourse?* (1986). An influential interpretation of the ideological and political nature of Indian nationalism and the struggle for a postcolonial nation-state.

Cook, Alexander C. (ed.), *Mao's Little Red Book: A Global History* (2014). A look at the global impact of the Chinese Cultural Revolution through the lens of the iconic "little red book" of quotations from Mao.

Crampton, R. J., *Eastern Europe in the Twentieth Century and After,* 2nd ed. (1997). Comprehensive overview covering all Soviet-bloc countries.

Dikötter, Frank, *Mao's Great Famine: The History of China's Most Devastating Catastrophe, 1958–1962* (2010). A recent detailed account of one of the greatest man-made disasters in twentieth-century history.

Dower, John W., *Embracing Defeat: Japan in the Wake of World War II* (1999). A prize-winning study of the transformation of one of the war's vanquished.

Elkins, Caroline, *Imperial Reckoning: The Untold Story of Britain's Gulag in Kenya* (2005). Pulitzer Prize–winning study of the brutal war to suppress the nationalist uprising in Kenya in the 1950s that ultimately led to independence for that country.

Evans, Martin, *Algeria: France's Undeclared War* (2011). Gives the history of the Algerian nationalist movements and provides an overview of the Algerian war for independence.

Feshbach, Murray, and Alfred Friendly, Jr., *Ecocide in the USSR: Health and Nation under Siege* (1992). A crucial study of ecological disasters in the Soviet Union.

Gao, Yuan, *Born Red: A Chronicle of the Cultural Revolution* (1987). A gripping personal account of the Cultural Revolution by a former Red Guard.

Gordon, Andrew (ed.), *Postwar Japan as History* (1993). Essays covering a wide range of topics on postwar Japan.

Hargreaves, John D., *Decolonization in Africa* (1996). A good place to start when exploring the history of African decolonization.

Hasan, Mushirul (ed.), *India's Partition: Process, Strategy and Mobilization* (1993). A useful anthology of scholarly articles, short stories, and primary documents on the partition of India.

Iriye, Akira, *Power and Culture: The Japanese-American War, 1941–1945* (1981). A discussion that goes beyond the military confrontation in Asia.

Jackson, Kenneth T., *Crabgrass Frontier: The Suburbanization of the United States* (1985). An insightful and influential consideration of the movement of the American population from cities to suburbs.

Jalal, Ayesha, *The Sole Spokesman: Jinnah, the Muslim League and the Demand for Pakistan* (1985). A study of the high politics leading to the violent partition of British India.

Keep, John L. H., *Last of the Empires: A History of the Soviet Union 1945–1991* (1995). A detailed overview of the core of the "Second World."

Morris, Benny, *Righteous Victims: A History of the Zionist-Arab Conflict, 1881–1999* (2000). On the Arab-Israeli War of 1948.

Pantsov, Alexander V., *Mao: The Real Story,* trans. Steven I. Levine (2012). A well-researched biography of Mao Zedong.

Patterson, James T., *Grand Expectations: The United States, 1945–1974* (1996). Synthesizes the American experience in the postwar decades.

Patterson, Thomas, *Contesting Castro* (1994). The best study of the tension between the United States and Cuba. Culminating in the Cuban Revolution, it explores the deep American misunderstanding of Cuban national aspirations.

Roberts, Geoffrey, *Stalin's Wars: From World War to Cold War, 1939–1953* (2007). A reassessment of Stalin's wartime leadership that conveys the vast scale of what took place.

Saich, Tony, and Hans van de Ven (eds.), *New Perspectives on the Chinese Communist Revolution* (1995). A collection of essays reexamining different aspects of the Chinese communist movement.

Schram, Stuart, *The Thought of Mao Tse-tung* (1989). Standard work on the subject.

Tignor, Robert L., *W. Arthur Lewis and the Birth of Development Economics* (2006). An intellectual biography of the Nobel Prize–winning, West Indian–born economist, who proposed formulas to promote the economic development of less developed societies and then sought to implement them in Africa and the West Indies.

Wiener, Douglas R., *A Little Corner of Freedom: Russian Nature Protection from Stalin to Gorbachev* (2002). A groundbreaking book about Russian environmentalism.

Zubkova, Elena, *Russia after the War: Hopes, Illusions, and Disappointments, 1945–1957* (1998). Uses formerly secret archives to catalogue the devastation and difficult reconstruction of one of the war's victors.

Chapter 21: Globalization, 1970–2000

Collier, Paul, *The Bottom Billion: Why the Poorest Countries Fail and What Can Be Done about It* (2007). Shows that despite the world's advancing prosperity, more than a billion people have been left behind in abject poverty.

Davis, Deborah (ed.), *The Consumer Revolution in Urban China* (2000). A look at the different aspects of the recent, profound social transformation of urban China.

Davis, Mike, *City of Quartz: Excavating the Future in Los Angeles* (1990). Offers provocative reflections on the recent history, current condition, and possible future of Los Angeles.

Dutton, Michael, *Streetlife China* (1999). A fascinating portrayal of the survival tactics of those inhabiting the margins of society in modern China.

Eichengreen, Barry, *Globalizing Capital: A History of the International Monetary System* (1996). An insightful analysis of how international capital markets changed in the period from 1945 to 1980.

Ferguson, Niall, and Moritz Schularick, "'Chimerica' and the Global Asset Market Boom," *International Finance* 10, no. 3 (Winter 2007): 215–39. Coined the term "Chimerica" to designate a single, intertwined economic entity made up of a productive partner, China, and a consuming partner, the United States.

Gourevitch, Philip, *We Wish to Inform You That Tomorrow We Will Be Killed with Our Families: Stories from Rwanda* (1999). A volume that reveals the hatreds that culminated in the Rwanda genocide.

Guillermoprieto, Alma, *Looking for History: Dispatches from Latin America* (2001). A collection of articles by the most important journalist reporting on Latin American affairs.

Han Minzhu (ed.), *Cries for Democracy: Writings and Speeches from the 1989 Chinese Democracy Movement* (1990). A collection of documents from the events leading up to the incident in Tiananmen Square on June 4, 1989.

Herbst, Jeffrey, *States and Power in Africa: Comparative Lessons in Authority and Control* (2000). Explores the political dilemmas facing modern African polities.

Honig, Emily, and Gail Hershatter, *Personal Voices: Chinese Women in the 1980's* (1988). A record of Chinese women during a period of rapid social change.

Huang, Yasheng, *Capitalism with Chinese Characteristics: Entrepreneurship and the State* (2008). A sharp, unsentimental inside look at China's market economy and its future prospects.

Kavoori, Anandam P., and Aswin Punathambekar (eds.), *Global Bollywood* (2008). A collection of essays by leading scholars of Indian cinema on different aspects of the processes by which the Hindi film industry became Bollywood.

Klitgaard, Robert, *Tropical Gangsters* (1990). On the intimate connections between corrupt native elites and international aid agencies.

Kotkin, Stephen, *Armageddon Averted: The Soviet Collapse, 1970–2000* (2001). Places the surprise fall of the Soviet Union in the context of the great shifts in the post–World War II order.

Macekura, Stephen, *Of Limits and Growth: The Rise of Global Sustainable Development in the Twentieth Century* (2016). Explores the rise of global environmental politics in the 1970s and 1980s and the debate about resources and climate change.

Mamdani, Mahmood, *When Victims Become Killers: Colonialism, Nativism, and the Genocide in Rwanda* (2001). Discusses the genocide in Rwanda in light of the legacy of colonialism.

Mehta, Suketu, *Maximum City: Bombay Lost and Found* (2005). Examines one of the great, and contradictory, cities in the era of globalization.

Miller, Chris, *The Struggle to Save the Soviet Economy: Mikhail Gorbachev and the Collapse of the USSR* (2016). An insightful analysis of internal debates in Moscow over rival directions for the Soviet economy and the response to Chinese reforms after 1978.

Mottahedeh, Roy, *The Mantle of the Prophet: Religion and Politics in Iran,* 2nd ed. (2008). Perhaps the best book on the 1979 Iranian Revolution and its aftermath.

Nathan, Andrew, and Perry Link, *The Tiananmen Papers* (2002). An inside look at the divisions within the Chinese elite in connection with the 1989 crackdown.

Portes, Alejandro, and Rubén G. Rumbaut, *Immigrant America,* 2nd ed. (1996). A good comparative study of how immigration has transformed the United States.

Prakash, Gyan, *Mumbai Fables* (2010). A spirited account of the rise of India's most modern city, a center of intellectual, commercial, and political vitality.

Prunier, Gerald, *Africa's World War: Congo, the Rwandan Genocide, and the Making of a Continental Catastrophe* (2009). A chilling discussion of the spillover effects of the Rwandan genocide on central, eastern, and southern Africa.

Punathambekar, Aswin, *From Bombay to Bollywood: The Making of a Global Media Industry* (2013). A study of the transformation of the Indian film industry that globalizes its content and reach.

Reinhart, Carmen, and Kenneth Rogoff, *This Time Is Different: Eight Centuries of Financial Folly* (2009). Explains the latest financial crash using historical perspective.

Ruggie, John Gerard, *Just Business: Multinational Corporations and Human Rights* (2013). Shows how even big businesses became involved in human rights advocacy.

Sen, Amartya, *Poverty and Famines: An Essay on Entitlement and*

Deprivation (1982). A major study that reoriented the study of famines from a narrow concentration on food supply to broader questions of ownership, exchange, and democracy.

Sikkink, Kathryn, *The Justice Cascade: How Human Rights Prosecutions Are Changing World Politics* (2011). Shows how new forms of global organizing and new social norms are changing the political rules across borders.

Stein, Judith, *Pivotal Decade: How the United States Traded Factories for Finance in the Seventies* (2010). A comprehensive study of the rise of American banking and the decline of heartland industries.

Ther, Philipp, *Europe since 1989: A History* (2016). A concise account of European integration and neoliberalism since the fall of the Berlin Wall.

Van Der Wee, Hermann, *Prosperity and Upheaval: The World Economy, 1945–1980* (1986). Describes very well the transformation and problems of the world economy, particularly from the 1960s onward.

Westad, Odd Arne, *The Global Cold War: Third World Interventions and the Making of Our Times* (2007). A genuinely global perspective on the Cold War and its consequences.

Winn, Peter, *Americas: The Changing Face of Latin America and the Caribbean* (1992). A useful portrayal of Latin America since the 1970s.

Epilogue: 2001–The Present

Achcar, Gilbert, *Morbid Symptoms: Relapse in the Arab Uprising* (2016). An up-to-date overview of the difficulties that the proponents of the Arab Spring encountered, with long and detailed treatments of Syria and Egypt.

Blinder, Alan S., *After the Music Stopped: The Financial Crisis, the Response, and the Work Ahead* (2013). A definitive and detailed treatment of the Great Contraction.

Christensen, Thomas J., *The China Challenges: Shaping the Choices of a Rising Power* (2015). A survey of "China's Rise" and the challenges and choices the country faces in the contemporary world.

Cleveland, William L., and Martin Bunton, *A History of the Modern Middle East*, 6th ed. (2016). The sixth edition of an important textbook that covers the whole of the Middle East from 1800 to the present.

Cooper, Frederick, *Africa in the World: Capitalism, Empire, Nation-State* (2014). An overview of Africa's place in global history, based on the most recent scholarship.

Crutzer, Paul J., and Eugene F. Stoemer, "The Anthropocene," IGBP Newsletter, no. 41 (May 2000): 17–18. The first coining of the term Anthropocene and the argument for a new geologic epoch.

Darwall, Rupert, *The Age of Global Warming: A History* (2013). An accessible narrative describing how scientists became increasingly aware of the threat of climate change and the multinational effort to reduce carbon emissions.

Deaton, Angus, *The Great Escape: Health, Wealth, and the Origins of Inequality* (2013). An examination of rising inequality by a Nobel Prize–winning authority who emphasizes that contemporary well-to-do individuals have largely failed to help those not so fortunate to achieve their potential.

Eichengreen, Barry J., *Hall of Mirrors: The Great Depression and the Great Recession, and the Uses—and Misuses—of History* (2015). The expert on the Great Depression now writes about the Great Contraction.

Esposito, John L., Tamara Sonn, and John O. Voll, *Islam and Democracy after the Arab Spring* (2016). An analysis of the prospects of democracy in Muslim countries, with case studies of Tunisia, Egypt, and Turkey, among others.

Ferguson, James, *Give a Man a Fish: Reflections on the New Politics of Distribution* (2015). An analysis of social welfare programs in southern Africa, which involve cash payments to the poorest members of societies, and their implications for neoliberal capitalism.

Franco, Jean, *Cruel Modernity* (2013). An examination of the cultural dimensions of Latin America's experience with recent neoliberal policies and the tensions and violence of relatively stateless societies.

Friedman, Milton, and Anne Jacobson Schwartz, *A Monetary History of the United States, 1867–1960* (1963). A classic account of monetary policy. Still essential reading even though it leaves off in 1960.

Gerges, Fawaz A., *ISIS: A History* (2016). One of a series of books that explores the rise of ISIS and stresses the place of violence in building a new Islamic state.

Guillen, Mauro F., *The Architecture of Collapse: The Global System in the 21st Century* (2015). A work that stresses the interconnectedness and complexity of the global capitalist system and argues that global financial systems have an "intrinsic propensity to instability, disruption, and crisis."

Jaffrelot, Christophe, *Saffron Modernity in India: Narendra Modi and His Experiment with Gujarat* (2014). A political history of how Narendra Modi emerged dominant in Gujarat using anti-Muslim nationalist ideology, captured the leadership of the BJP, and built a personality cult that catapulted him to national leadership.

Judis, John, *The Populist Explosion: How the Great Recession Transformed American and European Politics* (2016). A book by a journalist and political analyst that argues that the contemporary populist upsurges on both the right and the left are responses to neoliberal globalization.

Kindleberger, Charles P., and Robert Aliber, *Manias, Panics, and Crashes: A History of Financial Crises*, 5th edition (2005). A brilliant overview of the financial crises that have beset the global economy prior to the Great Contraction of 2008.

Lepore, Jill, *The Whites of Their Eyes: The Tea Party's Revolution and the Battle over American History* (2011). A history of the American far right and the Tea Party and their imagination of a nostalgic American past.

Lynch, Marc, *The New Arab Wars: Uprisings and Anarchy in the Middle East* (2016). Brings the narrative of the Arab Spring and the ambitions of its diverse proponents up to the present.

McCants, William, *The ISIS Apocalypse: The History, Strategy, and Doomsday Vision of the Islamic State* (2015). An important study of ISIS based on a wide reading of its own publications.

McNeill, J. R., *Something New under the Sun: An Environmental History of the Twentieth Century* (2000). An important overview of the environmental history of the twentieth century, with considerable statistical data that underscore the impact of humans on the environment and the atmosphere.

McNeill, J. R., and Peter Engelkes, "Into the Anthropocene: People and Their Planet," in Akira Iriye (ed.), *Global Interdependence: The World after 1945* (2014). Two environmental historians embrace the concept of the Anthropocene Epoch.

Milankovic, Brian, *Global Inequality: A New Approach for the Age of Globalization* (2016). Using the most up-to-date data on worldwide incomes, the author shows how the last quarter century has yielded a convergence in global income distribution across societies and the widening of a gap within societies.

Moubayed, Sami, *Under the Black Flag: At the Frontier of the New Jihad* (2015). A study of the rise of jihadism within the Arab world, with a concentration on Syria.

Muller, Jan-Werner, *What Is Populism?* (2016). The sharpest analysis yet of the nature and prospects of populism, especially its relations to political establishments, which it condemns but on which it depends.

Owen, Roger, *The Rise and Fall of Arab Presidents for Life, with a New Afterword* (2014). A study that examines the emergence of Arab leaders who endeavored to hold on to power for as long as they lived, with insights into the actions of those who brought many of those leaders down during the Arab Spring.

Pietz, David A., *The Yellow River: The Problem of Water in Modern China* (2015). A critical look at health and environmental issues in China today, from a historical perspective through the lens of one of its major rivers.

Radelet, Steven, *Emerging Africa: How Seventeen Countries Are Leading the Way* (2010). An Afro-optimist sees many African countries enjoying economic growth and political stability, proving that Africa can join much of the rest of the world in achieving economic and political progress.

————, *The Great Surge: The Ascent of the Developing World* (2015). An overview of the extraordinary progress that many of the countries in what once was called the Third World have achieved in the economic and political realms.

Reid, Michael, *Forgotten Continent: The Battle for Latin America's Soul* (2009). A journalistic account of how Latin America grappled with market openings, new democratic forces, and the search for policies to close the gap between the haves and have-nots.

Shambaugh, David, *China Goes Global: The Partial Power* (2013). An analysis of China's role in the global arena and its impact, from economics to culture.

Trenin, Dmitri, *Should We Fear Russia?* (2016). A clear-eyed view of what contemporary Russia is and is not.

Warwick, John, *Black Flags Flying: The Rise of ISIS* (2015). A detailed account of the leadership groups within ISIS and its relationship to al-Qaeda.

Weiss, Michael, and Hassan Hassan, *ISIS: Inside the Army of Terror* (2015). An account based on interviews and wide reading of western and Arabic sources on the rise of ISIS.

Wright, Lawrence, *The Looming Tower: Al-Qaeda and the Road to 9/11* (2006). A Pulitzer Prize–winning study of the origins and evolution of al-Qaeda.

————, *The Terror Years: From al-Qaeda to ISIS* (2016). Primarily a study of the decline of the power of al-Qaeda, which created an opening for the more territorially based ISIS.

Glossary

Abd al-Rahman III Islamic ruler in Spain who held a countercaliphate and reigned from 912 to 961 CE.

aborigines Original, native inhabitants of a region, as opposed to invaders, colonizers, or later peoples of mixed ancestry.

absolute monarchy Form of government in which one body, usually the monarch, controls the right to tax, judge, make war, and coin money. The term *enlightened absolutist* was often used to refer to state monarchies in seventeenth- and eighteenth-century Europe.

acid rain Precipitation containing large amounts of sulfur, which comes mainly from coal-fired power plants.

adaptation Ability to alter behavior and to innovate, finding new ways of doing things.

African National Congress (ANC) Multiracial organization founded in 1912 in an effort to end racial discrimination in South Africa.

Afrikaners Descendants of the original Dutch settlers of South Africa; formerly referred to as Boers.

Agones Athletic contests in ancient Greece.

Ahmosis Egyptian ruler in the southern part of the country who ruled from 1550 to 1525 BCE; Ahmosis used Hyksos weaponry—chariots in particular—to defeat the Hyksos themselves.

Ahura Mazda Supreme God of the Persians, believed to have created the world and all that is good and to have appointed earthly kings.

AIDS See HIV/AIDS.

Akbarnamah Mughal intellectual Abulfazl's *Book of Akbar*, which attempted to reconcile the traditional Sufi interest in the inner life within the worldly context of a great empire.

Alaric II Visigothic king who issued a simplified code of innovative imperial law.

Alexander the Great (356–323 BCE) Leader who used novel tactics and new kinds of armed forces to conquer the Persian Empire, which extended from Egypt and the Mediterranean Sea to the interior of what is now Afghanistan and as far as the Indus River valley. Alexander's conquests broke down barriers between the Mediterranean world and Southwest Asia and transferred massive amounts of wealth and power to the Mediterranean, transforming it into a more unified world of economic and cultural exchange.

Alexandria Port city in Egypt named after Alexander the Great. Alexandria was a model city in the Hellenistic world. It was built up by a multiethnic population from around the Mediterranean world.

Al-Khwarizmi Scientist and mathematician who lived from 780 to 850 CE and is known for having modified Indian digits into Arabic numerals.

Allied Powers Name given to the alliance between Britain, France, Russia, and Italy, all of which fought against Germany and Austria-Hungary (the Central Powers) in World War I. In World War II, the name was used for the alliance between Britain, France, and the United States, all of which fought against the Axis powers (Germany, Italy, and Japan).

allomothering System in which mothers relied on other women, including their own mothers, daughters, sisters, and friends, to help in the nurturing and protecting of their children.

alluvium Area of land created by river deposits.

alphabet A mid-second-millennium BCE Phoenician system of writing based on relatively few letters (twenty-two) that combined to make sounds and words. Adaptable to many languages, the alphabet was simpler and more flexible than writing based on symbols for syllables and ideas.

American Railway Union Workers' union that initiated the Pullman strike of 1894, which led to violence and ended in the leaders' arrest.

Amnesty International Nongovernmental organization formed to defend "prisoners of conscience"—those detained for their beliefs, race, sex, ethnic origin, language, or religion.

Amorites Name, which means "westerners," used by Mesopotamian urbanites to describe the transhumant herders who began to migrate into their cities in the late third millennium BCE.

Amun Once-insignificant Egyptian god elevated to higher status by Amenemhet (1991–1962 BCE).

Amun means "hidden" in Ancient Egyptian; the name was meant to convey the god's omnipresence.

Analects Texts that included the teachings and cultural ideals of Confucius.

anarchists Advocates of anarchism, the belief that society should be a free association of its members, not subject to government, laws, or police.

Anatolia The area now mainly known as modern Turkey. In the sixth millennium BCE, people from Anatolia, Greece, and the Levant took to boats and populated the Aegean. Their small villages endured almost unchanged for two millennia.

Angkor Wat Magnificent temple complex that crowned the royal palace of the Khmer Empire in Angkor, adorned with statues representing the Hindu pantheon of gods.

Anglo-Boer War (1899–1902) Anticolonial struggle in South Africa between the British and the Afrikaners over the gold-rich Transvaal. In response to the Afrikaners' guerrilla tactics and in order to contain the local population, the British instituted the first concentration camps. Ultimately, Britain won the conflict.

animal domestication Gradual process that occurred simultaneously with or just before the domestication of plants, depending on the region.

annals Historical records. Notable annals are the cuneiform inscriptions that record successful Assyrian military campaigns.

Anti-Federalists Critics of the U.S. Constitution who sought to defend the people against the power of the federal government and insisted on a Bill of Rights to protect individual liberties from government intrusion.

apartheid Racial segregation policy of the Afrikaner-dominated South African government. Legislated in 1948 by the Afrikaner National Party, it had existed in South Africa for many years.

Arab-Israeli War of 1948–1949 Conflict between Israeli and Arab armies that arose in the wake of a U.N. vote to partition Palestine into Arab and Jewish territories. The war shattered the legitimacy of Arab ruling elites.

Aramaic Dialect of a Semitic language spoken in Southwest Asia; it became the lingua franca of the Persian Empire.

Aristotle (384–322 BCE) Philosopher who studied under Plato but came to different conclusions about nature and politics. Aristotle believed in collecting observations about nature and discerning patterns to ascertain how things worked.

Aryans Nomadic charioteers who spoke Indo-European languages and entered South Asia in 1500 BCE. The early Aryan settlers were herders.

Asante state State located in present-day Ghana, founded by the Asantes at the end of the seventeenth century. It grew in power in the next century because of its access to gold and its involvement in the slave trade.

ascetic One who rejects material possessions and physical pleasures.

Asiatic Society Cultural organization founded by British Orientalists who supported native culture but still believed in colonial rule.

Aśoka Emperor of the Mauryan dynasty from 268 to 231 BCE; he was a great conqueror and unifier of India. He is said to have embraced Buddhism toward the end of his life.

Assur One of two cities on the upper reaches of the Tigris River that were the heart of Assyria proper (the other was Nineveh).

Aśvaghosa First known Sanskrit writer. He may have lived from 80 to 150 CE and may have composed a biography of the Buddha.

Ataturk, Mustafa Kemal (1881–1938) Ottoman army officer and military hero who helped forge the modern Turkish nation-state. He and his followers deposed the sultan, declared Turkey a republic, and constructed a European-like secular state, eliminating Islam's hold over civil and political affairs.

Atlantic system New system of trade and expansion that linked Europe, Africa, and the Americas. It emerged in the wake of European voyages across the Atlantic Ocean.

Atma Vedic term signifying the eternal self, represented by the trinity of deities.

Atman In the Upanishads, an eternal being who exists everywhere. The atman never perishes, but is reborn or transmigrates into another life.

Attila Sole ruler of all Hunnish tribes from 433 to 453 CE. Harsh and much feared, he formed the first empire to oppose Rome in northern Europe.

Augustus Latin term meaning "the Revered One"; title granted by the Senate to the Roman ruler Octavian in 27 BCE to signify his unique political position. Along with his adopted family name, *Caesar*, the military honorific *imperator*, and the senatorial term *princeps*, *Augustus* became a generic term for a leader of the Roman Empire.

australopithecines Hominid species, including *anamensis*, *afarensis* (Lucy), and *africanus*, that appeared in Africa beginning around 4 million years ago and, unlike other animals, sometimes walked on two legs. Their brain capacity was a little less than one-third of a modern human's. Although not humans, they carried the genetic and biological material out of which modern humans would later emerge.

Austro-Hungarian Empire Dual monarchy established by the Habsburg family in 1867; it collapsed at the end of World War I.

authoritarianism Centralized and dictatorial form of government, proclaimed by its adherents to be superior to parliamentary democracy and especially effective at mobilizing the masses. This idea was widely accepted in parts of the world during the 1930s.

Avesta Compilation of Zoroastrian holy works transmitted orally by priests for millennia and eventually recorded in the sixth century BCE.

Awadh Kingdom in northern India; one of the first successor states to have gained a measure of independence from the Mughal ruler in Delhi, and the most prized object for annexation by the East India Company.

Axial Age Pivotal period in the mid-first millennium BCE when radical thinkers, such as Zoroaster in Persia, Confucius and Master Lao in East Asia, Siddhartha Gautama (the Buddha) in South Asia, and Socrates in the Mediterranean, offered dramatically new ideas that challenged their times.

Axis powers The three aggressor states in World War II: Germany, Japan, and Italy.

Aztec Empire Mesoamerican empire that originated with a league of three Mexica cities in 1430 and gradually expanded through the Central Valley of Mexico, uniting numerous small, independent states under a single monarch who ruled with the help of counselors, military leaders, and priests. By the late fifteenth century, the Aztec realm may have embraced 25 million people. In 1521, the Aztecs were defeated by the conquistador Hernán Cortés.

baby boom Post–World War II upswing in U.S. birth rates, which reversed a century of decline.

Bactria (c. 200–50 BCE) Hellenistic kingdom in Gandhara region (modern Pakistan), with a major city at Aï Khanoum. Its people and culture are sometimes called "Indo-Greek" because of the blending of Indian and Greek populations and ideas.

Bactrian camel Two-humped animal domesticated in central Asia around 2500 BCE. The Bactrian camel was heartier than the one-humped dromedary and became the animal of choice for the harsh and varied climates typical of Silk Road trade.

Baghdad Capital of the Islamic empire under the Abbasid dynasty, founded in 762 CE (located in modern-day Iraq). In the medieval period, it was a center of administration, scholarship, and cultural growth for what came to be known as the Golden Age of Islamic science.

Baghdad Pact (1955) Middle Eastern military alliance between countries friendly with America that were also willing to align themselves with the western countries against the Soviet Union.

Balam Na Stone temple and place of pilgrimage for the Maya people of Mexico's Yucatán Peninsula.

Balfour Declaration Letter (November 2, 1917) written by Lord Arthur J. Balfour, British foreign secretary, that promised a homeland for the Jews in Palestine.

Bamboo Annals Shang stories and foundation myths that were written on bamboo strips and later collected.

Bantu Language first spoken by people who lived in the southeastern region of modern Nigeria around 1000 CE.

Bantu migrations Waves of population movement from West Africa into eastern and southern Africa during the first millennium CE, bringing new agricultural practices to these regions and absorbing much of the hunting and gathering population.

barbarian Derogatory term used to describe pastoral nomads, painting them as enemies of civilization; the term *barbarian* used to have a more neutral meaning than it does today.

barbarian invasions Violent migration of people in the late fourth and fifth centuries from the frontiers of the Roman Empire into its western provinces. These migrants had long been used as non-Roman soldiers.

basilicas Early Christian churches modeled on Roman law-court buildings that could accommodate over a thousand worshippers.

Battle of Adwa (1896) Battle in which the Ethiopians defeated Italian colonial forces; it inspired many of Africa's later national leaders.

Battle of Wounded Knee (1890) Bloody massacre of Sioux Ghost Dancers by U.S. armed forces.

Bay of Pigs (1961) Unsuccessful invasion of Cuba by Cuban exiles supported by the U.S. government. The invaders intended to incite an insurrection in Cuba and overthrow the communist regime of Fidel Castro.

Bedouins Nomadic pastoralists in the deserts of Southwest Asia.

Beer Hall Putsch (1923) Nazi intrusion into a meeting of Bavarian leaders in a Munich beer hall in an attempt to force support for their cause; Adolf Hitler was imprisoned for a year after the incident.

Beghards (1500s) Eccentric European group whose members claimed to be in a state of grace that allowed them to do what they pleased—ranging from adultery, free love, and nudity to murder; also called Brethren of Free Speech.

bell beaker Ancient drinking vessel, an artifact from Europe, so named because its shape resembles an inverted bell.

Berenice of Egypt Egyptian queen who helped rule over the kingdom of the Nile from 320 to 280 BCE.

Beringia Prehistoric thousand-mile-long land bridge that linked Siberia and North America (which had not been populated by hominids). About 18,000 years ago, *Homo sapiens* edged into this landmass.

Berlin Airlift (1948) Supply of vital necessities to West Berlin by air transport, primarily under U.S. auspices, initiated in response to a land and water blockade of the city instituted by the Soviet Union in the hope that the Allies would be forced to abandon West Berlin.

Berlin Wall Wall dividing the city of Berlin, built in 1961 by communist East Germany to prevent its citizens from fleeing to West Germany; torn down in 1989.

Bhakti Religious practice that grew out of Hinduism and emphasizes personal devotion to gods.

big men Leaders of the extended household communities that formed village settlements in African rain forests.

big whites French plantation owners in Saint-Domingue (present-day Haiti) who created one of the wealthiest slave societies.

Bilad al-Sudan Arabic for "the land of the blacks"; it consisted of the land lying south of the Sahara.

bilharzia Debilitating waterborne illness that was widespread in Egypt, where it infected peasants who worked in the irrigation canals.

Bill of Rights First ten amendments to the U.S. Constitution; ratified in 1791.

bipedalism Walking on two legs, thereby freeing hands and arms to carry objects such as weapons and tools; one of several traits that distinguished hominids.

Black Death Great epidemic of the bubonic plague that ravaged Europe, East Asia, and North Africa in the fourteenth century, killing large numbers of people, including perhaps as much as one-third of the European population.

Black Jacobins Nickname for the rebels in Saint-Domingue, including Toussaint L'Ouverture, a former slave who led the slaves of this French colony in the world's largest and most successful slave insurrection.

Black Panthers Radical African American group in the 1960s and 1970s that advocated black separatism and pan-Africanism.

black shirts Fascist troops of Mussolini's regime; these squads received money from Italian landowners to attack socialist leaders.

Black Tuesday (October 29, 1929) Historic day when the U.S. stock market crashed, plunging the United States and international trading systems into crisis and leading the world into the Great Depression.

blitzkrieg "Lightning war"; type of warfare waged by the Germans during World War II, using coordinated aerial bombing campaigns along with tanks and infantry in motorized vehicles.

bodhisattvas In Mahayana Buddhism, enlightened beings who have earned nirvana but remain in this world to help others reach it.

Bolívar, Simón (1783–1830) Venezuelan leader who urged his followers to overcome their local identities and become "American." He wanted the liberated South American countries to form a Latin American confederation, urging Peru and Bolivia to join Venezuela, Ecuador, and Colombia in the "Gran Colombia."

Bolsheviks Former members of the Russian Social Democratic Party who advocated the destruction of capitalist political and economic institutions and seized power in Russia in 1917 when the Russian Empire collapsed. In 1918, the Bolsheviks changed their name to the Russian Communist Party.

Book of the Dead Ancient Egyptian funerary text that contains drawings and paintings as well as spells describing how to prepare the jewelry and amulets that were buried with a person in preparation for the afterlife.

bourgeoisie A French term originally designating non-noble city dwellers (*Bürger* in German). They sought to be recognized not by birth or aristocratic title but by property and ability. In the nineteenth century, *bourgeois* came to refer to non-noble property owners, especially those who controlled modern industry. A bourgeois was an individual. We can refer to "bourgeois values." *Bourgeoisie* refers to the entire class, as in the French bourgeoisie as a whole.

Boxer Protocol Written agreement between the victors of the Boxer Uprising and the Qing Empire in 1901 that placed western troops in Beijing and required the regime to pay exorbitant damages for foreign life and property.

Boxer Uprising (1899–1900) Chinese peasant movement that opposed foreign influence, especially that of Christian missionaries; it was put down after the Boxers were defeated by an army composed mostly of Japanese, Russians, British, French, and Americans.

Brahma One of three major deities that form a trinity in Vedic religion. Brahma signifies birth. *See also* Vishnu *and* Siva.

Brahmans Vedic priests who performed rituals and communicated with the gods. Brahmans provided guidance on how to live in balance with the forces of nature as represented by the various deities. Brahmanism was reborn as Hinduism sometime during the first half of the first millennium CE.

British Commonwealth of Nations Union formed in 1926 that conferred "dominion status" on Britain's white settler colonies in Canada, Australia, and New Zealand.

British East India Company *See* East India Company.

bronze Alloy of copper and tin brought into Europe from Anatolia; used to make hard-edged weapons.

brown shirts Troops of German men who advanced the Nazi cause by holding street marches, mass rallies, and confrontations and by beating Jews and anyone who opposed the Nazis.

Buddha "Enlightened One." The term was applied to Kshatriya-born Siddhartha Gautama (c. 563–483 BCE), whose ideas—about the relationship between desire and suffering and how to eliminate both through wisdom, ethical behavior, and mental discipline in order to achieve contentment (*nirvana*)—offered a radical challenge to Brahmanism.

Buddhism Major South Asian religion that aims to end human

suffering through the renunciation of desire. Buddhists believe that removing the illusion of a separate identity would lead to a state of contentment (*nirvana*). These beliefs challenged the traditional Brahmanic teachings of the time and provided the peoples of South Asia with an alternative to established traditions.

bullion Uncoined gold or silver.

Byzantium Modern term for the Eastern Roman Empire (which would last until 1453), centered at its "New Rome," Constantinople, which was founded in 324 CE by Constantine on the site of the Greek city Byzantium.

Cahokia Commercial city on the Mississippi for regional and long-distance trade of commodities such as salt, shells, and skins and of manufactured goods such as pottery, textiles, and jewelry; marked by massive artificial hills, akin to earthen pyramids, used to honor spiritual forces.

calaveras Allegorical skeleton drawings by the Mexican printmaker and artist José Guadalupe Posada. The works drew on popular themes of betrayal, death, and festivity.

caliphate Islamic state, headed by a caliph—chosen either by election from the community (Sunni) or from the lineage of Muhammad (Shia)—with political authority over the Muslim community.

Calvin, Jean (1509–1564) A French theologian during the Protestant Reformation. Calvin developed a Christianity that emphasized moral regeneration through church teachings and laid out a doctrine of predestination.

candomblé Yoruba-based religion in northern Brazil; it interwove African practices and beliefs with Christianity.

Canton system System officially established by imperial decree in

1759 that required European traders to have Chinese guild merchants act as guarantors for their good behavior and payment of fees.

caravan cities Cities (like Petra and Palmyra) that were located along land routes of the Silk Roads and served as hubs of commerce and cultural exchange between travelers and merchants participating in long-distance trade.

caravans Companies of men who transported and traded goods along overland routes in North Africa and central Asia; large caravans consisted of 600–1,000 camels and as many as 400 men.

caravanserais Inns along major trade routes that accommodated large numbers of traders, their animals, and their wares.

caravel Sailing vessel suited for nosing in and out of estuaries and navigating in waters with unpredictable currents and winds.

carrack Ship used on open bodies of water, such as the Mediterranean.

Carthage City in what is modern-day Tunisia; emblematic of the trading aspirations and activities of merchants in the Mediterranean. Pottery and other archaeological remains demonstrate that trading contacts with Carthage were as far-flung as Italy, Greece, France, Iberia, and West Africa.

cartography Mapmaking.

caste system Hierarchical system of organizing people and distributing labor.

Caste War of the Yucatán (1847–1901) Conflict between Maya Indians and the Mexican state over Indian autonomy and legal equality, which resulted in the Mexican takeover of the Yucatán Peninsula.

Castro, Fidel (1926–2016) Cuban communist leader who seized power in January 1959. Castro became increasingly radical as he consolidated power, announcing a massive redistribution of land and the nationalization of foreign oil refineries; he declared himself a socialist and aligned himself with the Soviet Union in the wake of the 1961 CIA-backed Bay of Pigs invasion.

Çatal Hüyük Site in Anatolia discovered in 1958. It was a dense honeycomb of settlements filled with rooms whose walls were covered with paintings of wild bulls, hunters, and pregnant women. Çatal Hüyük symbolizes an early transition to urban dwelling and dates to the eighth millennium BCE.

cathedra Bishop's seat, or throne, in a church.

Catholic Church *See* Roman Catholic Church.

Cato the Elder (234–149 BCE) Roman statesman, often seen as emblematic of the transition from a Greek to a Roman world. He wrote a manual for the new economy of slave plantation agriculture, invested in shipping and trading, learned Greek rhetoric, and added the genre of history to Latin literature.

caudillos South American local military chieftains.

cave drawings Images on cave walls. The subjects are most often large game, although a few are images of humans. Other elements are impressions made by hands dipped in paint and pressed on a wall as well as abstract symbols and shapes.

Celali revolts (1595–1610) Peasant and artisan uprisings against the Ottoman state.

Central Powers Alliance of Germany and Austria-Hungary in World War I.

Chan Chan City founded between 850 and 900 CE by the Moche people in what is now modern-day Peru. It became the largest city of the Chimú Empire with a core population of 30,000 inhabitants.

Chan Santa Cruz Separate Maya community formed as part of a crusade for spiritual salvation and the complete cultural separation of the Maya Indians; means "little holy cross."

Chandra Gupta II King who reigned in South Asia from 320 to 335 CE. He shared his name with Chandragupta, the founder of the Mauryan Empire.

Chandravamsha One of two main lineages (the lunar one) of Vedic society, each with its own creation myth, ancestors, language, and rituals. Each lineage included many clans. *See also* Suryavamsha.

chapatis Flat, unleavened Indian bread.

chariot Horse-drawn vehicle with two spoked and metal-rimmed wheels that revolutionized warfare in the second millennium BCE and was made possible through the interaction of pastoralists and settled communities.

charismatic Person who uses personal strengths or virtues, often laced with a divine aura, to command followers.

Charlemagne Emperor of the west and heir to Rome from 764 to 814 CE.

chartered companies Firms that were awarded monopoly trading rights over vast areas by European monarchs (for example, the Virginia Company and the Dutch East India Company).

Chartism (1834–1848) Mass democratic movement to pass the Peoples' Charter in Britain, granting male suffrage, secret ballot, equal electoral districts, and annual parliaments and absolving the requirement of property ownership for members of the parliament.

chattel slavery Form of slavery that sold people as property, the rise of which coincided with the expansion of city-states. Chattel slavery was eschewed by the Spartans, who also rejected the innovation of coin money.

Chavín Agrarian people living from 1400 to 200 BCE in complex societies in what is now Peru. They manufactured goods (ceramics, textiles, and precious metals), conducted limited long-distance trade, and shared an artistic and religious tradition, most notably at Chavín de Huántar.

Chernobyl (1986) Site in the Soviet Union (in present-day Ukraine) of the meltdown of a nuclear reactor.

Chiang Kai-shek (1887–1975) Leader of the Guomindang following Sun Yat-sen's death who mobilized the Chinese masses through the New Life movement. In 1949, he lost the Chinese Revolution to the Communists and moved his regime to Taiwan.

Chimú Empire South America's first empire, centered at Chan Chan, in the Moche Valley on the Pacific coast from 1000 through 1470 CE, whose development was fueled by agriculture and commercial exchange.

chinampas Floating gardens used by Aztecs in the 1300s and 1400s to grow crops.

China's Sorrow Name for the Yellow River, which, when it changed course or flooded, could cause mass death and waves of migration.

chinoiserie Chinese silks, teas, tableware, jewelry, and paper; popular among Europeans in the seventeenth and eighteenth centuries.

Christendom Entire portion of the world in which Christianity prevailed.

Christianity New religious movement originating in the Eastern Roman Empire in the first century CE, with roots in Judaism and resonance with various Greco-Roman religious traditions. The central figure, Jesus, was tried and executed by Roman authorities, and his followers believed he rose from the dead. The tradition was spread across the Mediterranean by his followers, and Christians were initially persecuted—to varying degrees—by Roman authorities. The religion was eventually legalized in 312 CE, and by the late fourth century CE it became the official state religion of the Roman Empire.

Church of England Established form of Christianity in England dating from the sixteenth century.

city Highly populated concentration of economic, religious, and political power. The first cities appeared in river basins, which could produce a surplus of agriculture. The abundance of food freed most city inhabitants from the need to produce their own food, which allowed them to work in specialized professions.

city-state Political organization based on the authority of a single, large city that controls outlying territories.

Civil Rights Act (1964) U.S. legislation that banned racial segregation in public facilities, outlawed racial discrimination in employment, and marked an important step in correcting legal inequality.

civil rights movement Powerful movement for equal rights and the end of racial segregation in the United States that began in the 1950s with court victories against school segregation and nonviolent boycotts.

civil service examinations Set of challenging exams instituted by the Tang to help assess potential bureaucrats' literary skill and knowledge of the Confucian classics.

Civil War, American (1861–1865) Conflict between the northern and southern states of America that led to the abolition of slavery in the United States.

clan A social group comprising many households, claiming descent from a common ancestor.

clandestine presses Small printing operations that published banned texts in the early modern era, especially in Switzerland and the Netherlands.

climate change A wide range of phenomena caused by global warming. These changes encompass not only rising temperatures, but also changes in precipitation patterns; ice mass loss on mountain glaciers around the world; shifts in the life cycles and migration patterns of flora and fauna; extreme weather events; and sea level rise.

Clovis people Early humans in America who used basic chipped blades and pointed spears in pursuing prey. They extended the hunting traditions they had learned in Afro-Eurasia, such as establishing campsites and moving with the herds. They were known as "Clovis people" because the type of arrowhead point that they used was first found by archaeologists at a site near Clovis, New Mexico.

Code of Manu Brahmanic code of law that took shape in the third to fifth centuries CE and expressed ideas going back to Vedic times. Framed as a conversation between Manu (the first human and an ancient lawgiver) and a group of wise men, it articulated the rules of the hierarchical *varna* system.

codex Early form of book, with separate pages bound together; it replaced the scroll as the main medium for written texts. The codex emerged around 300 CE.

cognitive skills Skills such as thought, memory, problem solving, and—ultimately—language. Hominids were able to use these skills and their hands to create new adaptations, like tools, which helped them obtain food and avoid predators.

Cohong Chinese merchant guild that traded with Europeans under the Qing dynasty.

coins Form of money that replaced goods, which previously had been bartered for services and other products. Originally used mainly to hire mercenary soldiers, coins became the commonplace method of payment linking buyers and producers throughout the Mediterranean.

Cold War (1945–1990) Ideological rivalry in which the Soviet Union and eastern Europe opposed the United States and western Europe, but no direct military conflict occurred between the two rival blocs.

colonies Regions under the political control of another country.

colons French settlers in Algeria.

colosseum Huge amphitheater in Rome completed by Titus and dedicated in 80 CE. Originally begun by Flavian, the structure is named after a colossal statue of Nero that formerly stood beside it.

Columbian exchange Movements between Afro-Eurasia and the Americas of previously unknown plants, animals, people, diseases, and products that followed in the wake of Columbus's voyages.

commanderies The thirty-six provinces (*jun*) into which Shi Huangdi divided territories. Each commandery had a civil governor, a military governor, and an imperial inspector.

Communist Manifesto Pamphlet published by Karl Marx and Friedrich Engels in 1848 at a time when political revolutions were sweeping Europe. It called on the workers of all nations to unite in overthrowing capitalism.

Compromise of 1867 Agreement between the Habsburg state and the peoples living in Hungarian parts of the empire that the state would be officially known as the Austro-Hungarian Empire.

concession areas Territories, usually ports, where Chinese emperors allowed European merchants to trade and European people to settle.

Confucian ideals The ideals of honoring tradition, emphasizing the responsibility of the emperor, and respect for the lessons of history, promoted by Confucius, which the Han dynasty made the official doctrine of the empire by 50 BCE.

Confucianism Ethics, beliefs, and practices stipulated by the Chinese philosopher Kong Qiu, or Confucius, which served as a guide for Chinese society up to modern times.

Confucius (551–479 BCE) Radical thinker whose ideas—especially about how ethical living that was centered on *ren* (benevolence), *li* (proper ritual), and *xiao* (filial piety toward ancestors living and dead) shaped the politically engaged superior gentleman—transformed society and government in East Asia.

cong tube Ritual object crafted by the Liangzhu, made of jade and used in divination practices.

Congo Free State Large colonial state in Africa created by Leopold II, king of Belgium, during the 1880s and ruled by him alone. After rumors of mass slaughter and enslavement, the Belgian parliament took possession of the colony.

Congress of Vienna (1814–1815) International conference to reorganize Europe after the downfall of Napoleon. European monarchies agreed to respect one another's borders and to cooperate in guarding against future revolutions and war.

conquistadors Spanish military leaders who led the conquest of the New World in the sixteenth century.

Constantine Roman emperor who converted to Christianity in 312 CE. In 313, he issued a proclamation that gave Christians new freedoms in the empire. He also founded Constantinople (at first called "New Rome").

Constantinople Capital city of Byzantium, which was founded as the New Rome by the emperor Constantine.

Constitutional Convention (1787) Meeting to formulate the Constitution of the United States of America.

Contra rebels Opponents of the Sandinistas in Nicaragua; they were armed and financed by the United States and other anticommunist countries (1980).

conversos Jewish and Muslim converts to Christianity in the Iberian Peninsula and the New World.

Coptic Form of Christianity practiced in Egypt. It was doctrinally different from Christianity elsewhere, and Coptic Christians had their own views of the nature of Christ.

Corn Laws Laws that imposed tariffs on grain imported to Great Britain, intended to protect British farming interests. The Corn Laws were abolished in 1846 as part of a British movement in favor of free trade.

cosmology Branch of metaphysics devoted to understanding the order of the universe.

cosmopolitans Meaning "citizens of the world," as opposed to a city-state, this term refers particularly to inhabitants of the large, multiethnic cities that were nodes of exchange in the Hellenistic world.

Council of Nicaea Church council convened in 325 CE by Constantine and presided over by him as well. At this council, a Christian creed was articulated and made into a formula that expressed the philosophical and technical elements of Christian belief.

Counter-Reformation Movement to counter the spread of the Reformation; initiated by the Catholic Church at the Council of Trent in 1545. The Catholic Church enacted reforms to attack clerical corruption and placed a greater emphasis on individual spirituality. During this time, the Jesuits were founded to help revive the Catholic Church.

coup d'état Overthrow of an established state by a group of conspirators, usually from the military.

creation narratives Narratives constructed by different cultures that draw on their belief systems and available evidence to explain the origins of the world and humanity.

creed From the Latin *credo* meaning "I believe," an authoritative statement of belief. The Nicene Creed, formulated by Christian bishops at the Council of Nicaea in 325 CE, is an example of one such formal belief statement.

creoles Persons of full-blooded European descent who were born in the Spanish American colonies.

Crimean War (1853–1856) War waged by Russia against Great

Britain and France. Spurred by Russia's encroachment on Ottoman territories, the conflict revealed Russia's military weakness when Russian forces fell to British and French troops.

crossbow Innovative weapon used at the end of China's Warring States period that allowed archers to shoot their enemies with accuracy, even from a distance.

Crusades Wave of attacks launched in the late eleventh century by western European Christians against Muslims. The First Crusade began in 1095, when Pope Urban II appealed to the warrior nobility of France to free Jerusalem from Muslim rule. Four subsequent Crusades were fought over the next two centuries.

Cuban Missile Crisis (1962) Diplomatic standoff between the United States and the Soviet Union that was provoked by the Soviet Union's attempt to base nuclear missiles in Cuba; it brought the world close to a nuclear war.

cult Religious movement, often based on the worship of a particular god or goddess.

cultigen Organism that has diverged from its ancestors through domestication or cultivation.

cuneiform Wedge-shaped form of writing. As people combined rebus symbols with other visual marks that contained meaning, they became able to record and transmit messages over long distances by using abstract symbols or signs to denote concepts; such signs later came to represent syllables, which could be joined into words. By impressing these signs into wet clay with the cut end of a reed, scribes engaged in cuneiform.

Cyrus the Great Founder of the Persian Empire. This sixth-century ruler (559–529 BCE) conquered the Medes and unified the Iranian kingdoms.

czar *See* tsar.

Daimyo Ruling lords who commanded private armies in pre-Meiji Japan.

dan Fodio, Usman (1754–1817) Fulani Muslim cleric whose visions led him to challenge the Hausa ruling classes, whom he believed were insufficiently faithful to Islamic beliefs and practices. His ideas gained support among those who had suffered under the Hausa landlords. In 1804, his supporters and allies overthrew the Hausa in what is today northern Nigeria.

Daoism East Asian philosophy of the Axial Age introduced by Master Lao and expanded by his student Zhuangzi. It was remarkable for its emphasis on following the *dao* (the natural way of the cosmos) and that the best way to do that was through *wuwei* (doing nothing).

dar al-Islam Arabic for "the House of Islam"; describes a sense of common identity.

Darius I (521–486 BCE) Leader who put the emerging unified Persian Empire onto solid footing after Cyrus the Great's death.

Darwin, Charles (1809–1882) British scientist who became convinced that the species of organic life had evolved under the uniform pressure of natural laws, not by means of a special, one-time creation as described in the Bible.

D-Day (June 6, 1944) Day of the Allied invasion of Normandy under General Dwight Eisenhower to liberate western Europe from German occupation.

Dear Boy Nickname of an early human skull discovered in 1931 by a team of archaeologists named the Leakeys. Other objects discovered with Dear Boy demonstrated that by his time, early humans had begun to fashion tools and to use them for butchering animals and possibly for hunting and killing smaller animals.

Decembrists Russian army officers who were influenced by events in revolutionary France and formed secret societies that espoused liberal governance. They launched a revolt that was put down by Nicholas I in December 1825.

Declaration of Independence U.S. document stating the theory of government on which America was founded.

Declaration of the Rights of Man and Citizen (1789) French charter of liberties formulated by the National Assembly that marked the end of dynastic and aristocratic rule. The seventeen articles later became the preamble to the new constitution, which the assembly finished in 1791.

decolonization End of empire and emergence of new independent nation-states in Asia and Africa as a result of the defeat of Japan in World War II and weakened European influence after the war.

Delhi Sultanate (1206–1526) A Turkish Muslim regime in northern India that, through its tolerance for cultural diversity, brought political integration without enforcing cultural homogeneity.

democracy The idea that people, through membership in a nation, should choose their own representatives and be governed by them.

Democritus Thinker in ancient Greece who lived from 470 to 360 BCE; he deduced the existence of the atom and postulated that there was such a thing as an indivisible particle.

demotic writing The second of two basic forms of ancient Egyptian writing. Demotic was a cursive script written with ink on papyrus, on pottery, or on other absorbent objects. It was the most common and practical form of writing in Egypt and was used for administrative record keeping and in private or pseudo-private forms like letters and works of literature. *See also* hieroglyphs.

developing world Term applied to poor countries of the Third World and the former eastern communist bloc seeking to develop viable nation-states and prosperous economies. The term has come under sustained criticism for suggesting that there is a single path of economic growth that countries everywhere follow. It has been replaced by equally problematic terms like "advanced economy" and "emerging markets."

devshirme The Ottoman system of taking non-Muslim children in place of taxes in order to educate them in Muslim ways and prepare them for service in the sultan's bureaucracy.

dhamma Moral code espoused by Aśoka in the Kalinga edict, which was meant to apply to all—Buddhists, Brahmans, and Greeks alike.

dhimma system Ottoman law that permitted followers of religions other than Islam, such as Armenian Christians, Greek Orthodox Christians, and Jews, to choose their own religious leaders and to settle internal disputes within their religious communities as long as they accepted Islam's political dominion.

dhows Ships used by Arab seafarers whose large sails were rigged to maximize the capture of wind.

Dien Bien Phu (1954) Site of a defining battle in the war between French colonialists and the Viet Minh that secured North Vietnam for Ho Chi Minh and his army and left the south to form its own

government with French and American support.

Din-I-Ilahi "House of worship" in which the Mughal emperor Akbar engaged in religious debate with Hindu, Muslim, Jain, Parsi, and Christian theologians.

Diogenes Greek philosopher who lived from 412 to 323 BCE and who espoused a doctrine of self-sufficiency and freedom from social laws and customs. He rejected cultural norms as out of tune with nature and therefore false.

Directory Temporary military committee in France that took over affairs of the state from the radicals in 1795 and held control until the coup of Napoleon Bonaparte.

divination Rituals used to communicate with gods or royal ancestors and to foretell future events. Divination was used to legitimize royal authority and demand tribute.

Djoser Ancient Egyptian king who reigned from 2630 to 2611 BCE. He was the second king of the Third Dynasty and celebrated the Sed festival in his tomb complex at Saqqara.

domestication Bringing a wild animal or plant under human control.

Dominion in the British Commonwealth Canadian promise to keep up the country's fealty to the British crown, even after its independence in 1867. Later applied to Australia and New Zealand.

Dong Zhongshu Emperor Wu's chief minister, who advocated a more powerful view of Confucius by promoting texts that focused on Confucius as a man who possessed aspects of divinity.

double-outrigger canoes Vessels used by early Austronesians to cross the Taiwan Straits and colonize islands in the Pacific. These sturdy canoes could cover over 120 miles per day.

Duma Russian parliament.

Dutch learning Broad term for European teachings that were strictly regulated by the shoguns inside Japan.

dynastic cycle Political narrative in which influential families vied for supremacy. Upon gaining power, they legitimated their authority by claiming to be the heirs of previous grand dynasts and by preserving or revitalizing the ancestors' virtuous governing ways. This continuity conferred divine support.

Earth Summit (1992) Meeting in Rio de Janeiro between many of the world's governments in an effort to address international environmental problems.

East India Company (1600–1858) British charter company created to outperform Portuguese and Spanish traders in the Far East; in the eighteenth century the company became, in effect, the ruler of a large part of India.

Eastern Front Battlefront between Berlin and Moscow during World War I and World War II.

Edict of Nantes (1598) Edict issued by Henry IV to end the French Wars of Religion. The edict declared France a Catholic country but tolerated some Protestant worship.

Eiffel Tower Steel monument completed in 1889 for the Paris Exposition. It was twice the height of any other building at the time.

eight-legged essay Highly structured essay form with eight parts, required on Chinese civil service examinations.

Ekklesia Church or early gathering committed to leaders chosen by God and fellow believers.

Ekpe Powerful slave trade institution that organized the supply and purchase of slaves inland from the Gulf of Guinea in West Africa.

Elamites A people with their capital in the upland valley of modern Fars who became a cohesive polity that incorporated transhumant people of the Zagros Mountains. A group of Elamites who migrated south and west into Mesopotamia helped conquer the Third Dynasty of Ur in 2400 BCE.

empire Group of states or ethnic groups governed, through a range of methods and with varying degrees of centralization, by a single sovereign power.

Enabling Act (1933) Emergency act passed by the Reichstag (German parliament) that helped transform Hitler from Germany's chancellor, or prime minister, into a dictator following the suspicious burning of the Reichstag building and a suspension of civil liberties.

enclosure A movement in which landowners took control of lands that traditionally had been common property serving local needs.

encomenderos Commanders of the labor services of the colonized peoples in Spanish America.

encomiendas Grants from European Spanish governors to control the labor services of colonized peoples.

Endeavor Ship of Captain James Cook, whose celebrated voyages to the South Pacific in the late eighteenth century supplied Europe with information about the plants, birds, landscapes, and people of this uncharted territory.

Engels, Friedrich (1820–1895) German social and political philosopher who collaborated with Karl Marx on many publications, including the *Communist Manifesto*.

English Navigation Act of 1651 Act stipulating that only English ships could carry goods between the mother country and its colonies.

English Peasants' Revolt (1381) Uprising of serfs and free farm workers that began as a protest against a tax levied to raise money for a war on France. The revolt was suppressed, but led to the gradual emergence of a free peasantry as labor shortages made it impossible to keep peasants bound to the soil.

enlightened absolutists Seventeenth- and eighteenth-century monarchs who claimed to rule rationally and in the best interests of their subjects and who hired loyal bureaucrats to implement the knowledge of the new age.

Enlightenment Intellectual movement in eighteenth-century Europe, which extended the methods of the natural sciences, especially physics, to society, stressing natural laws and reason as the basis of authority.

entrepôts Multiethnic trading stations, often supported and protected by regional leaders, where traders exchanged commodities and replenished supplies in order to facilitate long-distance trade.

Epicurus Greek philosopher who espoused emphasis on the self. He lived from 341 to 279 BCE and founded a school in Athens called The Garden. He stressed the importance of sensation, teaching that pleasurable sensations were good and painful sensations bad. Members of his school sought to find peace and relaxation by avoiding unpleasantness or suffering.

Estates-General French quasi-parliamentary body called in 1789 to deal with the financial problems that afflicted France. It had not met since 1614.

Etruscans A dominant people on the Italian Peninsula until the fourth century BCE. The Etruscan states were part of the foundation of the Roman Empire.

eunuchs Surgically castrated men who rose to high levels of military, political, and personal power in several empires (for instance, the Tang and the Ming Empires in China; the Abbasid and Ottoman Empires; and the Byzantine Empire).

Eurasia The combined area of Europe and Asia.

European Union (EU) International body organized after World War II as an attempt at reconciliation between Germany and the rest of Europe. It initially aimed to forge closer industrial cooperation. Eventually, through various treaties, many European states relinquished some of their sovereignty, and the cooperation became a full-fledged union with a common parliament. Some EU members adopted a single currency, the euro.

evolution Process by which species of plants and animals change over time, through the favoring, through reproduction, of certain traits that are useful in that species' environment.

Exclusion Act of 1882 U.S. congressional act prohibiting nearly all immigration from China to the United States; fueled by animosity toward Chinese workers in the American West.

Ezo Present-day Hokkaido, Japan's fourth main island.

fascism Form of hypernationalism that emerged in Europe after World War I, in which a charismatic leader was followed by a mass party and supported by established elites and churches and existing government institutions. Fascist movements were widespread but came to power only in Italy and Germany.

Fatehpur Sikri Mughal emperor Akbar's temporary capital near Agra.

Fatimids Shiite dynasty that ruled parts of the Islamic empire beginning in the tenth century CE. They were based in Egypt and founded the city of Cairo.

February Revolution (1917) The first of two uprisings of the Russian Revolution, which led to the end of the Romanov dynasty.

Federal Deposit Insurance Corporation (FDIC) Organization created in 1933 to guarantee all bank deposits up to $5,000 as part of the New Deal in the United States.

Federal Republic of Germany (1949–1990) Country formed from the areas of Germany occupied by the Allies after World War II. Also known as West Germany, this country experienced rapid demilitarization, democratization, and integration into the world economy.

Federal Reserve Act (1913) U.S. legislation that created a series of boards to monitor the supply and demand of the nation's money.

Federalists Supporters of the ratification of the U.S. Constitution, which was written to replace the Articles of Confederation.

feminist movements Movements that call for equal treatment for men and women—equal pay and equal opportunities for obtaining jobs and advancement. Feminism arose mainly in Europe and in North America in the 1960s and then became global in the 1970s.

Ferangi Arabic word meaning "Frank," which was used to describe Crusaders.

Fertile Crescent An area in Southwest Asia, bounded by the Mediterranean Sea in the west and the Zagros Mountains in the east; site of the world's first agricultural revolution.

feudalism System instituted in medieval Europe after the collapse of the Carolingian Empire (814 CE) whereby each peasant was under the authority of a lord.

fiefdoms Medieval economic and political units.

First World Term invented during the Cold War to refer to western Europe and North America (also known as the "free world" or the west); Japan later joined this group. Following the principles of liberal modernism, First World states sought to organize the world on the basis of capitalism and democracy.

five pillars of Islam Five practices that unite all Muslims: (1) proclaiming that "there is no God but God and Muhammad is His Prophet"; (2) praying five times a day; (3) fasting during the daylight hours of the holy month of Ramadan; (4) traveling on pilgrimage to Mecca; and (5) paying alms to support the poor.

Five-Year Plan Soviet effort launched under Stalin in 1928 to replace the market with a state-owned and state-managed economy in order to promote rapid economic development over a five-year period and thereby "catch and overtake" the leading capitalist countries. The First Five-Year Plan was followed by the Second Five-Year Plan (1933–1937), and so on, until the collapse of the Soviet Union in 1991.

Flagellants European social group that came into existence during the Black Death in the fourteenth century; they believed that the plague was the wrath of God.

floating population Poor migrant workers in China who supplied labor under Emperor Wu.

Fluitschips Dutch shipping vessels that could carry heavy, bulky cargo with relatively small crews.

flying cash Letters of exchange—early predecessors of paper money—first developed by guilds in the northern Song province Shanxi that eclipsed coins by the thirteenth century.

fondûqs Complexes in caravan cities that included hostels, storage houses, offices, and temples.

Forbidden City of Beijing Palace city of the Ming and Qing dynasties.

Force Publique Colonial army used to maintain order in the Belgian Congo; during the early stages of King Leopold's rule, it was responsible for bullying local communities.

Fourierism Form of utopian socialism based on the ideas of Charles Fourier (1772–1837), who envisioned communes where work was made enjoyable and systems of production and distribution were run without merchants. His ideas appealed to the middle class, especially women, as a higher form of Christian communalism.

free labor Wage-paying rather than slave labor.

free markets Unregulated markets.

Free Officers Movement Secret organization of Egyptian junior military officers who came to power in a coup d'état in 1952, forced King Faruq to abdicate, and consolidated their own control through dissolving the parliament, banning opposing parties, and rewriting the constitution.

free trade (laissez-faire) Domestic and international trade unencumbered by tariff barriers, quotas, and fees.

Front de Libération Nationale (FLN) Algerian anticolonial, nationalist party that waged an eight-year war against French troops, beginning in 1954, that forced nearly all of the 1 million European colonists to leave.

Fulani Muslim group in West Africa that carried out religious revolts at the end of the eighteenth and the beginning of the nineteenth centuries in an effort to return to the pure Islam of the past.

fur trade Trading of animal pelts (especially beaver skins) by Indians for European goods in North America.

Gandharan style Style of artwork, especially statuary, originating in the Gandharan region of modern Pakistan, that blends Hellenistic artistic influences with Buddhist stylistic features and subjects.

Gandhi, Mohandas Karamchand (Mahatma) (1869–1948) Indian leader who led a nonviolent struggle for India's independence from Britain.

garrison towns Stations for soldiers originally established in strategic locations to protect territorial acquisitions. Eventually, they became towns. Alexander the Great's garrison towns evolved into cities that served as centers from which Hellenistic culture was spread to his easternmost territories.

garrisons Military bases inside cities; often used for political purposes, such as protecting rulers, putting down domestic revolts, or enforcing colonial rule.

gauchos Argentine, Brazilian, and Uruguayan cowboys who wanted a decentralized federation, with autonomy for their provinces and respect for their way of life.

Gdansk shipyard Site of mass strikes in Poland that led in 1980 to the formation of the first

independent trade union, Solidarity, in the Soviet bloc.

gender relations A relatively recent development that implies roles emerged only with the appearance of modern humans and perhaps Neanderthals. When humans began to think imaginatively and in complex symbolic ways and give voice to their insights, perhaps around 150,000 years ago, gender categories began to crystallize.

genealogy History of the descent of a person or family from a distant ancestor.

Geneva Peace Conference (1954) International conference to restore peace in Korea and Indochina. The chief participants were the United States, the Soviet Union, Great Britain, France, the People's Republic of China, North Korea, South Korea, Vietnam, the Viet Minh party, Laos, and Cambodia. The conference resulted in the division of North and South Vietnam.

Genoa One of two Italian cities (the other was Venice) that linked Europe, Africa, and Asia as nodes of commerce in 1300. Genoese ships linked the Mediterranean to the coast of Flanders through consistent routes along the Atlantic coasts of Spain, Portugal, and France.

German Democratic Republic (1949–1990) Country formed from the areas of Germany occupied by the Soviet Union after World War II. Also known as East Germany.

German Social Democratic Party Founded in 1875, the most powerful socialist party in Europe before 1917.

Ghana The most celebrated medieval political kingdom in West Africa.

Ghost Dance American Indian ritual performed in the nineteenth

century in the hope of restoring the world to precolonial conditions.

Gilgamesh Heroic narrative written in the Babylonian dialect of Semitic Akkadian. This story and others like it were meant to circulate and unify the kingdom.

Girondins Liberal revolutionary group that supported the creation of a constitutional monarchy during the early stages of the French Revolution.

global warming Upward temperature trends worldwide due to the release of carbon into the air, mainly by the burning of fossil fuels and other human activities.

globalization Development of integrated worldwide cultural and economic structures.

globalizing empires Empires that cover immense territory, exert significant influence beyond their borders, include large, diverse populations, and work to integrate conquered peoples.

Gold Coast Name that European mariners and merchants gave to that part of West Africa from which gold was exported. This area was conquered by the British in the nineteenth century and became a British colony; upon independence, it became Ghana.

Goths One of the groups of "barbarian" migrants into Roman territory in the fourth century CE.

government schools Schools founded by the Han dynasty to provide an adequate number of officials to fill positions in the administrative bureaucracy. The Imperial University had 30,000 members by the second century BCE.

Gracchus brothers Two tribunes, the brothers Tiberius and Gaius Gracchus, who in 133 and 123–121 BCE attempted to institute land reforms that would guarantee all of Rome's poor citizens a basic amount of land that would qualify them for army service. Both men were assassinated.

Grand Canal A thousand-mile-long connector between the Yellow and Yangzi Rivers created in 486 BCE to link the north and south of China.

grand unity Guiding political idea embraced by Qin rulers and ministers with an eye toward joining the states of the Central Plains into one empire and centralizing administration.

"greased cartridge" controversy Controversy spawned by the rumor that cow and pig fat had been used to grease the shotguns of the sepoys in the British army in India. Believing that this was a British attempt to defile their religions and speed their conversion to Christianity, the sepoys mutinied against the British officers.

Great Depression Worldwide depression following the U.S. stock market crash on October 29, 1929.

great divide The division between economically developed nations and less developed nations.

Great East Asia Co-Prosperity Sphere Term used by the Japanese during the 1930s and 1940s to refer to Hong Kong, Singapore, Malaya, Burma, and other states that they seized during their attempt to dominate Asia.

Great Flood One of many traditional Mesopotamian stories that were transmitted orally from one generation to another before being recorded. The Sumerian King List refers to this crucial event in Sumerian memory and identity. The Great Flood narrative assigned responsibility for Uruk's demise to the gods.

Great Game Competition over areas such as Turkistan, Persia (present-day Iran), and Afghanistan. The British (in India) and the Russians believed that controlling these areas was crucial to preventing their enemies' expansion.

Great League of Peace and Power Iroquois Indian alliance that united previously warring communities.

Great Leap Forward (1958–1961) Plan devised by Mao Zedong to achieve rapid agricultural and industrial growth in China. The plan, which failed miserably, may have led to the deaths of as many as 45 million people from famine and malnutrition.

great plaza at Isfahan The center of Safavid power in the seventeenth century created by Shah Abbas (r. 1587–1629) to represent the unification of trade, government, and religion under one supreme political authority.

Great Proletarian Cultural Revolution (1966–1976) Mass mobilization of urban Chinese youth inaugurated by Mao Zedong in an attempt to reinvigorate the Chinese Revolution and to prevent the development of a bureaucratized Soviet style of communism; with this movement, Mao turned against his longtime associates in the Communist Party.

Great Trek Afrikaner migration to the interior of Africa after the British Empire abolished slavery in 1833.

Great War (World War I) (August 1914–November 1918) A total war involving the armies of Britain, France, and Russia (the Allies) against those of Germany, Austria-Hungary, and the Ottoman Empire (the Central Powers). Italy joined the Allies in 1915, and the United States joined them in 1917, helping tip the balance in favor of the Allies, who also drew upon the populations and material of their colonial possessions.

Greek Orthodoxy Branch of eastern Christianity, originally centered in Constantinople, that emphasizes the role of Jesus in helping humans achieve union with God.

Greek philosophers "Wisdom lovers" of the ancient Greek city-states, including Socrates, Plato, Aristotle, and others, who pondered such issues as self-knowledge, political engagement and withdrawal, and evidence-based inquiry to understand the order of the cosmos.

Greenbacks An American political party of the late nineteenth century that worked to advance the interests of farmers by promoting cheap money.

griots Counselors and other officials serving the royal family in African kingships. They were also responsible for the preservation and transmission of oral histories and repositories of knowledge.

Group Areas Act (1950) Act that divided South Africa into separate racial and tribal areas and required Africans to live in their own separate communities, including the "homelands."

guerrillas Portuguese and Spanish peasant bands who resisted the revolutionary and expansionist efforts of Napoleon; after the French word *guerre*.

guest workers Migrants seeking temporary employment abroad.

Gulag Administrative name for the vast system of forced labor camps under the Soviet regime; it originated in a small monastery near the Arctic Circle and spread throughout the Soviet Union and to other Soviet-style socialist countries. Penal labor was required of both ordinary criminals (rapists, murderers, thieves) and those accused of political crimes (counterrevolution, anti-Soviet agitation).

Gulf War (1991) Armed conflict between Iraq and a coalition of thirty-two nations, including the United States, Britain, Egypt, France, and Saudi Arabia. It was started by Iraq's invasion of Kuwait, which it had long claimed, on August 2, 1990.

gunpowder Explosive powder. By 1040, the first gunpowder recipes were being written down. Over the next 200 years, Song entrepreneurs invented several incendiary devices and techniques for controlling explosions.

gunpowder empires Muslim empires of the Ottomans, Safavids, and Mughals that used cannonry and gunpowder to advance their military causes.

Guomindang Nationalist Party of China, founded just before World War I by Sun Yat-sen and later led by Chiang Kai-shek.

Habsburg Empire Ruling house of Austria, which once ruled both Spain and central Europe but came to settle in lands along the Danube River; it played a prominent role in European affairs for many centuries. In 1867, the Habsburg Empire was reorganized into the Austro-Hungarian Empire, and in 1918 it collapsed.

hadith Sayings, attributed to the Prophet Muhammad and his early converts, used to guide the behavior of Muslim peoples.

Hagia Sophia Enormous and impressive church sponsored by Justinian and built starting in 532 CE. At the time, it was the largest church in the world.

hajj Pilgrimage to Mecca; an obligation for Muslims.

Hammurapi's Code Legal code created by Hammurapi (r. 1792–1750 BCE). The code divided society into three classes—free, dependent, and slave—each with distinct rights and responsibilities.

Han agrarian ideal Guiding principle for the free peasantry that made up the base of Han society. In this system, peasants were honored for their labors, while merchants were subjected to a range of controls, including regulations on luxury consumption, and were belittled for not engaging in physical labor.

Han Chinese Inhabitants of China proper who considered others to be outsiders and felt that they were the only authentic Chinese.

Han Fei Chinese state minister who lived from 280 to 223 BCE; a proponent and follower of Xunzi.

Han military Like its Roman counterpart, a ruthless military machine that expanded the Han Empire and created stable conditions that permitted the safe transit of goods by caravans. Emperor Wu heavily influenced the transformation of the military forces and reinstituted a policy that made military service compulsory.

Hangzhou City and former provincial seaport that became the political center of the Chinese people in their ongoing struggles with northern steppe nomads. It was also one of China's gateways to the rest of the world by way of the South China Sea.

Hannibal Great general from Carthage whose campaigns in the third century BCE swept from Spain toward the Italian peninsula. He crossed the Pyrenees and the Alps with war elephants. He was unable, however, to defeat the Romans in 217 BCE.

Harappa One of the two largest of the cities that, by 2500 BCE, began to take the place of villages throughout the Indus River valley (the other was Mohenjo Daro). Each covered an area of about 250 acres and probably housed 35,000 residents.

harem Secluded women's quarters in a Muslim household.

Harlem Renaissance Cultural movement in the 1920s that was based in Harlem, a part of New York City with a large African American population. The movement gave voice to black novelists, poets, painters, and musicians, many of whom used their art to protest racism; also referred to as the "New Negro movement."

harnesses Tools made from wood, bone, bronze, and iron for steering and controlling chariot horses. Harnesses discovered by archaeologists reveal the evolution of headgear from simple mouth bits to full bridles with headpiece, mouthpiece, and reins.

Hatshepsut Leader known as ancient Egypt's most powerful woman ruler. Hatshepsut served as regent for her young son, Thutmosis III, whose reign began in 1479 BCE. She remained co-regent until her death.

Haussmannization Redevelopment and beautification of urban centers; named after the city planner who "modernized" mid-nineteenth century Paris.

Heian period Period from 794 to 1185 CE during which the pattern of regents ruling Japan in the name of the sacred emperor began.

Hellenism Process by which the individuality of the cultures of the earlier Greek city-states gave way to a uniform culture that stressed the common identity of all who embraced

Greek ways. This culture emphasized the common denominators of language, style, and politics to which anyone, anywhere in the Afro-Eurasian world, could have access.

hieroglyphs One of two basic forms of Egyptian writing that were used in conjunction throughout antiquity. Hieroglyphs are pictorial symbols; the term derives from a Greek word meaning "sacred carving." They were employed exclusively in temple, royal, and divine contexts. *See also* demotic writing.

hijra Tradition of Islam whereby one withdraws from one's community to create another, holier, one. The practice is based on the Prophet Muhammad's withdrawal from the city of Mecca to Medina in 622 CE.

Hinayana Buddhism (termed "Lesser Vehicle" Buddhism by the Mahayana/"Greater Vehicle" school; also called Theraveda Buddhism) A more traditional, conservative branch of Buddhism that accepted the divinity of the Buddha but not of bodhisattvas.

Hindu revivalism Movement to reconfigure traditional Hinduism to be less diverse and more amenable to producing a narrowed version of Indian tradition.

Hinduism Ancient Brahmanic Vedic religion that emerged as the dominant faith in India in the third century CE. It reflected rural and agrarian values and focused on the trinity of Brahma (birth), Vishnu (existence), and Shiva (destruction).

Hiroshima Japanese port devastated by an atomic bomb on August 6, 1945.

Hitler, Adolf (1889–1945) German dictator and leader of the Nazi Party who seized power in Germany after its economic collapse in the Great Depression. Hitler and his Nazi regime started World War II in Europe and systematically murdered Jews and other non-Aryan groups in the name of racial purity.

Hittites An Anatolian chariot warrior group that spread east to northern Syria, though they eventually faced weaknesses in their own homeland. Rooted in their capital at Hattusa, they interacted with contemporary states both violently (as at the Battle of Qadesh against Egypt) and peacefully (as in the correspondence of the Amarna letters).

HIV/AIDS An epidemic of acquired immunodeficiency syndrome (AIDS) caused by the human immunodeficiency virus (HIV), which compromises the ability of the infected person's immune system to ward off other diseases. First detected in 1981, AIDS killed 12 million people in the two decades that followed.

Holocaust Deliberate racial extermination by the Nazis of Jews, along with some other groups the Nazis considered "inferior" (including Sinta and Roma [gypsies], Jehovah's Witnesses, homosexuals, and people with mental illness) that claimed the lives of around 6 million European Jews.

Holy Roman Empire Enormous realm that encompassed much of Europe and aspired to be the Christian successor state to the Roman Empire. In the time of the Habsburg dynasts, the empire was a loose confederation of principalities that obeyed an emperor elected by elite lower-level sovereigns. Despite its size, the empire never effectively centralized power; it was split into Austrian and Spanish factions when Charles V abdicated to his sons in 1556.

Holy Russia Name applied to Muscovy and then to the Russian Empire by Slavic Eastern Orthodox clerics who were appalled by the Muslim conquest in 1453 of Constantinople (the capital of Byzantium and of eastern Christianity) and who were hopeful that Russia would become the new protector of the faith.

home charges Fees India was forced to pay to Britain as its colonial master; these fees included interest on railroad loans, salaries to colonial officers, and the maintenance of imperial troops outside India.

hominids The family, in scientific classification, that includes gorillas, chimpanzees, and humans (that is, *Homo sapiens*, in addition to our now-extinct hominid ancestors such as the various australopithecines as well as *Homo habilis*, *Homo erectus*, and *Homo neanderthalis*).

Homo The genus, in scientific classification, that contains only "true human" species.

Homo caudatus "Tailed man," believed by some European Enlightenment thinkers to be an early human species.

Homo erectus Species that emerged about 1.8 million years ago, had a large brain, walked truly upright, migrated out of Africa, and likely mastered fire. *Homo erectus* means "standing man."

Homo habilis Species, confined to Africa, that emerged about 2.5 million years ago and whose toolmaking ability truly made *it* the forerunner, though a very distant one, of modern humans. *Homo habilis* means "skillful man."

Homo sapiens The first humans; emerged in Africa as early as 300,000 years ago and migrated out of Africa beginning about 180,000 years ago. They had bigger brains and greater dexterity than previous hominid species, whom they eventually eclipsed.

homogeneity Uniformity of the languages, customs, and religion of a particular people or place. It can also be demonstrated by a consistent calendar, set of laws, administrative practices, and rituals.

horses Animals used by full-scale nomadic communities to dominate the steppe lands in western Afro-Eurasia by the second millennium BCE. Horse-riding nomads moved their large herds across immense tracts of land within zones defined by rivers, mountains, and other natural geographic features. In the arid zones of central Eurasia, the nomadic economies made horses a crucial component of survival.

Huguenots French Protestants who endured severe persecution in the sixteenth and seventeenth centuries.

humanism The Renaissance aspiration to develop a greater understanding of the human experience than the Christian scriptures offered by reaching back into ancient Greek and Roman texts.

Hundred Days' Reform (1898) Abortive modernizing reform program of the Qing government of China.

hunting and gathering Lifestyle in which food is acquired through hunting animals, fishing, and foraging for wild berries, nuts, fruit, and grains, rather than planting crops, vines, or trees. As late as 1500 CE, as much as 15 percent of the world's population still lived by this method.

Hyksos Chariot-driving, axe- and composite-bow-wielding, Semitic-speaking people (their name means "rulers of foreign lands") who invaded Egypt, overthrew the Thirteenth Dynasty, set up their own rule over Egypt, and were expelled by Ahmosis to begin the period known as New Kingdom Egypt.

Ibn Sina Philosopher and physician who lived from 980 to 1037 CE. He was also schooled in the Quran, geometry, literature, and Indian and Euclidian mathematics.

ideology Dominant set of ideas of a widespread culture or movement.

Il Duce (leader) Name used by the fascist Italian leader Benito Mussolini.

Iliad Epic Greek poem about the Trojan War, composed several centuries after the events it describes. It was based on oral tales passed down for generations.

Il-Khanate Mongol-founded dynasty in thirteenth-century Persia.

imam Muslim religious leader and politico-religious descendant of Ali; believed by some to have a special relationship with Allah.

Imperial University Founded in 136 BCE by Emperor Wu (Han Wudi) not only to train future bureaucrats in the Confucian classics but also to foster scientific advances in other fields.

imperialism Acquisition of new territories by a state and the incorporation of these territories into a political system as subordinate colonies.

Imperium Latin word used to express Romans' power and command over their subjects. It is the basis of the English words *empire* and *imperialism.*

Inca Empire Empire of Quechua-speaking rulers in the Andean valley of Cuzco that encompassed a population of 4 to 6 million. The Incas lacked a clear inheritance system, causing an internal split that Pizarro's forces exploited in 1533.

Indian Institutes of Technology (IIT) Institutions originally designed as engineering schools to expand knowledge and to modernize India, which produced a generation of pioneering computer engineers, many of whom moved to the United States.

Indian National Congress Formed in 1885, a political party deeply committed to constitutional methods, industrialization, and cultural nationalism.

Indian National Muslim League Founded in 1906, an organization dedicated to advancing the political interests of Muslims in India.

Indo-European migrations The migrations, tracked linguistically and culturally, of the peoples of a distinct language group (including Sanskrit, Persian, Greek, Latin, and German) from central Eurasian steppe lands into Europe, Southwest Asia, and South Asia.

Indo-Greek Of or relating to the fusion of Indian and Greek culture in the area under the control of the Bactrians, in the northwestern region of India, around 200 BCE.

Indu Name used for what we would today call India by Xuanzang, a Chinese Buddhist pilgrim who visited the area in the 630s and 640s CE.

indulgences Church-sponsored fund-raising mechanism that gave certification that one's sins had been forgiven in return for money.

industrial revolution Gradual accumulation and diffusion of old and new technical knowledge that led to major economic changes in Britain, northwestern Europe, and North America. It resulted in large-scale industry and the harnessing of fossil fuels, which allowed economic growth to outpace the rate of population increase.

industrious revolution Dramatic economic change in which households that had traditionally produced for themselves decided to work harder and longer hours in order to produce more for the market, which enabled them to increase their income and standard of living. Areas that underwent the industrious revolution shifted from peasant farming to specialized production for the market.

innovation Creation of new methods that allowed humans to make better adaptations to their environment, such as the making of new tools.

Inquisition General term for a tribunal of the Roman Catholic Church that enforced religious orthodoxy. Several inquisitions took place over centuries, seeking to punish heretics, witches, Jews, and those whose conversion to Christianity was called into doubt.

internal and external alchemy In Daoist ritual, use of trance and meditation or chemicals and drugs, respectively, to cause transformations in the self.

International Monetary Fund (IMF) Agency founded in 1944 to help restore financial order in Europe and the rest of the world, to revive international trade, and to offer financial support to Third World governments.

invisible hand As described in Adam Smith's *The Wealth of Nations*, the idea that the operations of a free market produce economic efficiency and economic benefits for all.

iron Malleable metal found in combined forms almost everywhere in the world; it became the most important and widely used metal in world history after the Bronze Age.

Iron Curtain Term popularized by Winston Churchill after World War II to refer to a rift that divided western Europe, under American influence, from eastern Europe, under the domination of the Soviet Union.

irrigation Technological advance whereby water delivery systems and water sluices in floodplains or riverine areas were channeled or redirected and used to nourish soil.

Islam A religion that dates to 610 CE, when the Prophet Muhammad believed God came to him in a vision. Islam (which means submission—in this case, to the will of God) requires its followers to act righteously, to submit themselves to the one and only true God, and to care for the less fortunate. Muhammad's most insistent message was the oneness of God, a belief that has remained central to the Islamic faith ever since.

Jacobins Radical French political group that came into existence during the French Revolution; executed the French king and sought to remake French culture.

Jacquerie (1358) French peasant revolt in defiance of feudal restrictions.

jade The most important precious substance in East Asia; associated with goodness, purity, luck, and virtue. Jade was carved into such items as ceremonial knives, blade handles, religious objects, and elaborate jewelry.

Jagat Seths Enormous trading and banking empire in eastern India during the first half of the eighteenth century.

Jainism System of thought, originating in the seventh century BCE, that challenged Brahmanism. Spread by Vardhamana Mahavira, Jainism encouraged purifying the soul through self-denial and nonviolence.

Jaja (1821–1891) A merchant prince who founded the Opobo city-state, in what is known in modern times as the Rivers state of Nigeria.

janissaries Corps of infantry soldiers conscripted as children under the *devshirme* system of the Ottoman Empire and brought up with intense loyalty to the Ottoman state and its sultan. The sultan used these forces to clip local autonomy and to serve as his personal bodyguards.

jatis Social groups as defined by Hinduism's caste system.

Jesuits Religious order founded by Ignatius Loyola to counter the inroads of the Protestant Reformation; the Jesuits, or the Society of Jesus, were active in politics, education, and missionary work.

jihad Literally, "striving" or "struggle." This word also connotes military efforts, or "striving in the way of God." In addition, it came to mean spiritual struggles against temptation or inner demons, especially in Sufi, or mystical, usage.

Jih-pen Chinese for "Japan."

Jim Crow laws Laws that codified racial segregation and inequality in the southern part of the United States after the Civil War.

jizya Special tax that non-Muslims were forced to pay to their Islamic rulers in return for which they were given security and property and granted cultural autonomy.

jong Large oceangoing vessels built by Southeast Asians that plied the regional trade routes from the fifteenth century to the early sixteenth century.

Judah The southern kingdom of David, which had been an Assyrian vassal until 612 BCE, when it became a vassal of Assyria's successor, Babylon, against whom the people of Judah rebelled, resulting in the destruction of Jerusalem in the sixth century BCE.

Julius Caesar Formidable Roman general who lived from 100 to 44 BCE. He was also a man of letters, a great orator, and a ruthless military man who boasted that his campaigns had led to the deaths of over a million people.

junks Large seafaring vessels used in the South China seas after 1000 CE, which helped make shipping by sea less dangerous.

Justinian Roman or Byzantine emperor who ascended to the throne in 527 CE. In addition to his many building projects and military expeditions, he issued a new law code.

Kabuki Theater performance that combined song, dance, and skillful staging to dramatize conflicts between duty and passion in Tokogawa, Japan.

kamikaze Japanese for "divine winds," or typhoons; such a storm saved Japan from a Mongol attack.

kanun Highly detailed system of Ottoman administrative law that jurists developed to deal with matters not treated in the religious law of Islam.

Karim Loose confederation of shippers banding together to protect convoys.

karma Literally, "fate" or "action"; in Confucian thought, a universal principle of cause and effect.

Kassites Nomads who entered Mesopotamia from the eastern Zagros Mountains and the Iranian plateau as early as 2000 BCE. They gradually integrated into Babylonian society by officiating at temples. By 1745 BCE, they had asserted order over the region, and they controlled southern Mesopotamia for the next 350 years, creating one of the territorial states.

Keynesian Revolution Post-Depression economic ideas developed by the British economist John Maynard Keynes, wherein the state took a greater role in managing the economy, stimulating it by increasing the money supply and creating jobs.

KGB Soviet political police and spy agency, formed as the Cheka not long after the Bolshevik coup in October 1917. Grew to more than 750,000 operatives with military rank by the 1980s.

Khan Mongol ruler acclaimed at an assembly of elites, who was supposedly descended from Chinggis Khan on the male line; those not descended from Chinggis continually faced challenges to their legitimacy.

Khanate Major political unit of the vast Mongol Empire. There were four Khanates, including the Yuan Empire in China, forged by Chinggis Khan's grandson Kublai.

Kharijites Radical sect from the early days of Islam. The Kharijites seceded from the "party of Ali" (who themselves came to be known as the Shiites) because of disagreements over succession to the role of the caliph. They were known for their strict militant piety.

Khmer A people who created the most powerful empire in Southwest Asia between the tenth and thirteenth centuries in what is modern-day Cambodia.

Khomeini, Ayatollah Ruhollah (1902–1989) Iranian religious leader who used his traditional Islamic education and his training in Muslim ethics to accuse Shah Reza Pahlavi's government of gross violations of Islamic norms. He also identified the shah's ally, America, as the great Satan. The shah fled the country in 1979; in his wake, Khomeini established a theocratic state ruled by a council of Islamic clerics.

Khufu A pyramid, among those put up in the Fourth Dynasty in ancient Egypt (2575–2465 BCE), which is the largest stone structure in the world. It is in an area called Giza, just outside modern-day Cairo.

Khusro I Anoshirwan Sasanian emperor who reigned from 530 to 579 CE. He was a model ruler and was seen as the personification of justice.

Kiev City that became one of the greatest cities of Europe after the eleventh century. It was built to be a small-scale Constantinople on the Dnieper.

Kikuyu Kenya's largest ethnic group; organizers of a revolt against the British in the 1950s.

King, Martin Luther, Jr. (1929–1968) Civil rights leader who borrowed his most effective weapon—the commitment to nonviolent protest and the appeal to conscience—from Gandhi.

Kingdom of Jerusalem What Crusaders set out to liberate from Muslim rule when they launched their attacks.

Kizilbash Mystical, Turkish-speaking tribesmen who facilitated the Safavid rise to power.

Knossos Area in Crete where, during the second millennium BCE, a primary palace town existed.

Koine Greek Simpler than regional versions of Greek such as Attic or Ionic, this "common Greek" dialect became an international language across the regions influenced by Hellenism and facilitated trade of goods and ideas.

Koprulu reforms Reforms named after two grand viziers who revitalized the Ottoman Empire in the seventeenth century through administrative and budget trimming as well as by rebuilding the military.

Korean War (1950–1953) Cold War conflict between Soviet-backed North Korea and U.S.- and U.N.-backed South Korea. The two sides seesawed back and forth over the same boundaries until 1953, when an armistice divided the country at roughly the same spot as at the start of the war. Casualties included 33,000 Americans, at least 250,000 Chinese, and up to 3 million Koreans.

Koryo dynasty Leading dynasty of the northern-based Koryo kingdom in Korea. It is from this dynasty that the name "Korea" derives.

Kremlin Moscow's walled city center, whose name was once synonymous with the Soviet government.

Kshatriyas Originally the warrior caste in Vedic society, the dominant clan members and ruling caste who controlled the land.

Ku Klux Klan Racist organization that first emerged in the U.S. South after the Civil War and then gained national strength as a radically traditionalist movement during the 1920s.

Kublai Khan (1215–1294) Mongol leader who seized southern China after 1260 and founded the Yuan dynasty.

kulak Originally a pejorative word used to designate better-off peasants, a term used in the late 1920s and early 1930s to refer to any peasant, rich or poor, perceived as an opponent of the Soviet regime. Russian for "fist."

Kumarajiva Renowned Buddhist scholar and missionary who lived from 344 to 413 CE. He was brought to China by Chinese regional forces from Kucha, modern-day Xinjiang.

Kushans Northern nomadic group that migrated into South Asia in 50 CE. They unified the tribes of the region and set up the Kushan Empire, which embraced a large and diverse territory and played a critical role in the formation of the Silk Roads.

Labour Party Political party founded in Britain in 1900 that represented workers and was based on socialist principles.

laissez-faire The concept that the economy works best when it is left alone—that is, when the state does not regulate or interfere with the workings of the market.

"Land under the Yoke of Ashur" Lands not in Neo-Assyria proper, but under its authority, which had to pay the Neo-Assyrian Empire exorbitant amounts of tribute.

language System of communication reflecting cognitive abilities. Natural language is generally defined as words arranged in particular sequences to convey meaning and is unique to modern humans.

language families Related tongues with a common ancestral origin; language families contain languages that diverged from one another but share grammatical features and root vocabularies. More than a hundred language families exist.

Laozi Also known as Master Lao; perhaps a contemporary of Confucius, and the person after whom Daoism is named. His thought was elaborated upon by generations of thinkers.

latifundia Broad estates that produced goods for big urban markets, including wheat, grapes, olives, cattle, and sheep.

League of Nations Organization founded after World War I to solve international disputes through arbitration; it was dissolved in 1946 and its assets were transferred to the United Nations.

Legalism Also called Statism, a system of thought about how to live an ordered life. Developed by Master Xun, or Xunzi (310–237 BCE), it is based on the principle that people, being inherently inclined toward evil, require authoritarian control to regulate their behavior.

Lenin, Nikolai (1870–1924) Leader of the Bolshevik Revolution in Russia and the first leader of the Soviet Union.

Liangzhu Culture spanning centuries from the fourth to the third millennium BCE that represented the last new Stone Age culture in the Yangzi River delta. One of the Ten Thousand States, it was highly stratified and is known for its jade objects.

liberalism Political and social theory that advocates representative government, free trade, and freedom of speech and religion.

limited-liability joint-stock company Company that mobilized capital from a large number of investors, called shareholders, who were not to be held personally liable for financial losses incurred by the company.

Linear A and B Two linear scripts first discovered on Crete in 1900. On the island of Crete and on the mainland areas of Greece, documents of the palace-centered societies were written on clay tablets in these two scripts. Linear A script, apparently written in Minoan, has not yet been deciphered. Linear B was first deciphered in the early 1950s.

"Little Europes" Urban landscapes between 1100 and 1200 composed of castles, churches, and towns in what are today Poland, the Czech Republic, Hungary, and the Baltic States.

Little Ice Age A period of global cooling—not a true ice age—that extended roughly from the sixteenth to the nineteenth century. The dates, especially for the start of the period, remain the subject of scientific controversy.

Liu Bang Chinese emperor from 206 to 195 BCE; after declaring himself the prince of his home area of Han, in 202 BCE, Liu declared himself the first Han emperor.

llamas Animals domesticated in the Americas that are similar in utility and function to camels in Afro-Eurasia. Llamas can carry heavy loads for long distances.

Long March (1934–1935) Trek of over 10,000 kilometers by Mao Zedong and his communist followers to establish a new base of operations in northwestern China.

Longshan peoples Peoples who lived in small agricultural and riverine villages in East Asia at the end of the third millennium BCE. They set the stage for the Shang dynasty in terms of a centralized state, urban life, and a cohesive culture.

lord Privileged landowner who exercised authority over the people who lived on his land.

lost generation The 17 million former members of the Red Guard and other Chinese youth who were denied education from the late 1960s to the mid-1970s as part of the Chinese government's attempt to prevent political disruptions.

Louisiana Purchase (1803) American purchase of French territory from Napoleon that included much of the present-day United States between the Mississippi River and the Rocky Mountains.

Lucy Relatively intact skeleton of a young adult female australopithecine unearthed in the valley of the Awash River in 1974 by an archaeological team working at a site in present-day Hadar, Ethiopia. The researchers nicknamed the skeleton Lucy. She stood just over 3 feet tall and walked upright at least some of the time. Her skull contained a brain within the ape size range, but her jaw and teeth were humanlike. Lucy's skeleton was relatively complete and at the time was the oldest hominid skeleton ever discovered.

Luftwaffe German air force.

Luther, Martin (1483–1546) A German monk and theologian who sought to reform the Catholic Church; he believed in salvation through faith alone, the importance of reading scripture, and the priesthood of all believers. His Ninety-Five Theses, which enumerated the abuses by the Catholic Church as well as his reforms, started the Protestant Reformation.

Maastricht Treaty (1991) Treaty that formed the European Union, a fully integrated trading and financial bloc with its own bureaucracy and elected representatives.

Ma'at Term used in ancient Egypt to refer to stability or order, the achievement of which was the primary task of Egypt's ruling kings, the pharaohs.

Maccabees Leaders of a riot in Jerusalem in 166 BCE that was a response to a Roman edict outlawing the practice of Judaism.

madrassas Higher schools of Muslim education that taught law, the Quran, religious sciences, and the regular sciences.

magnetic needle compass A navigational instrument invented by the Chinese that helped guide sailors on the high seas after 1000 CE.

Mahayana Buddhism "Great Vehicle" Buddhism; an accessible form of Buddhism that spread along the Silk Roads and included in its theology a divine Buddha as well as bodhisattvas.

Mahdi The "chosen one" in Islam whose appearance was believed to foretell the end of the world and the final day of reckoning for all people.

maize Grains, the crops that the settled agrarian communities across the Americas cultivated, along with legumes (beans) and tubers (potatoes).

Maji-Maji Revolt (early 1900s) Swahili insurrection against German colonialists; inspired by the belief that those who were anointed with specially blessed water (*maji*) would be immune to bullets. It resulted in 200,000–300,000 African deaths.

Mali Empire West African empire, founded by the legendary king Sundiata in the early thirteenth century. It facilitated thriving commerce along routes linking the Atlantic Ocean, the Sahara, and beyond.

Mamluks (Arabic for "owned" or "possessed") Military men who ruled Egypt as an independent regime from 1250 until the Ottoman conquest in 1517.

Manaus Opera House Opera house built in the interior of Brazil in a lucrative rubber-growing area at the turn of the twentieth century.

Manchukuo Japanese puppet state in Manchuria in the 1930s.

Manchus Descendants of the Jurchens who helped the Ming army recapture Beijing in 1644 after its seizure by the outlaw Li Zicheng. The Manchus numbered around 1 million but controlled a domain that included perhaps 250 million people. Their rule lasted more than 250 years and became known as the Qing dynasty.

mandate of heaven Religious ideology established by Zhou leaders to communicate legitimate transfer and retention of royal power as the will of their supreme god. The mandate later became Chinese political doctrine.

Mande A people who lived in the area between the bend in the Senegal River to the west and the bend in the Niger River to the east and between the Senegal River to the north and the Bandama River to the south. Also known as the Mandinka. Their civilization emerged around 1100.

Mandela, Nelson (1918–2013) Leader of the African National Congress (ANC) who was imprisoned for more than two decades by the apartheid regime in South Africa for his political activities, until worldwide protests led to his release in 1990. In 1994, Mandela won the presidency in South Africa's first free mass elections.

Manifest Destiny Belief that it was God's will for the American people to expand their territory and political processes across the North American continent.

manorialism System in which the manor (a lord's home, its associated industry, and surrounding fields) served as the basic unit of economic power; an alternative to the concept of feudalism (the hierarchical relationships of king, lords, and peasantry) for thinking about the nature of power in western Europe from 1000 to 1300 CE.

Mao Zedong (1893–1976) Chinese communist leader who rose to power during the Long March (1934). In 1949, he defeated the nationalists and established a communist regime in China.

maroon community Sanctuary for runaway slaves in the Americas.

Marshall Plan Economic aid package given by the United States to Europe after World War II in hopes of a rapid period of reconstruction and economic gain that would secure the countries that received the aid from a communist takeover.

martyr Literally meaning "witness," a person executed by Roman authorities for maintaining his or her Christian beliefs rather than worshipping the emperor.

Marx, Karl (1818–1883) German philosopher and economist who created Marxism and believed that a revolution of the working classes would overthrow the capitalist order and create a classless society.

Marxism A current of socialism created by Karl Marx and Friedrich Engels. It stressed the primacy of economics and technology—and, above all, class conflict—in shaping human history. Economic production provided the foundation, the "base" for society, which shaped politics, values, art, and culture (the superstructure). In the modern, industrial era, they believed class conflict boiled down to a two-way struggle between the bourgeoisie (who controlled the means of industrial production) and the proletariat (workers who had only their labor power to sell).

mass consumption Increased purchasing power and appetite for goods in the prosperous and mainly middle-class societies of the early twentieth-century, stemming from mass production.

mass culture Distinctive form of popular culture that arose in the wake of World War I. It reflected the tastes of the working and middle classes, who now had more time and money to spend on entertainment, and relied on new technologies, especially film and radio, that could

reach an entire nation's population and consolidate their sense of being a single state.

mass production System in which factories were set up to produce huge quantities of identical products, reflecting the early twentieth-century world's demands for greater volume, faster speed, reduced cost, and standardized output.

Mastaba Word meaning "bench" in Arabic; it refers to a huge flat structure identical to earlier royal tombs of ancient Egypt.

Mau-Mau Revolt (1952–1957) Uprising orchestrated by a Kenyan guerrilla movement; this conflict forced the British to grant independence to the black majority in Kenya.

Mauryan Empire (321–184 BCE) The first large-scale empire in South Asia, stretching from the Indus in the west to the mouth of the Ganges in the east and nearly to the southern tip of the Indian subcontinent; begun by Chandragupta Maurya, in the aftermath of Alexander's time in India, and expanded to its greatest extent by his grandson Aśoka.

Mawali Non-Arab "clients" to Arab tribes in the early Islamic empire. Because tribal patronage was so much a part of the Arabian cultural system, non-Arabs who converted to Islam affiliated themselves with a tribe and became clients of that tribe.

Maxim gun European weapon that was capable of firing many bullets per second; it was used against Africans in the conquest of the continent.

Mayas Civilization that ruled over large stretches of Mesoamerica; it was composed of a series of kingdoms, each built around ritual centers rather than cities. The Mayas engaged neighboring peoples in warfare and trade and expanded borders through tributary relationships. They were not defined by a great ruler or one capital city, but by their shared religious beliefs.

McCarthyism Campaign by U.S. Republican senator Joseph McCarthy in the late 1940s and early 1950s to uncover closet communists, particularly in the State Department and in Hollywood.

Meat Inspection Act (1906) Legislation that provided for government supervision of meatpacking operations; it was part of a broader progressive reform movement dedicated to correcting the negative consequences of urbanization and industrialization in the United States.

Mecca Arabian city in which the Prophet Muhammad was born. Mecca was a trading center and pilgrimage destination in the pre-Islamic and Islamic periods. Exiled in 622 CE because of resistance to his message, Muhammad returned to Mecca in 630 CE and claimed the city for Islam.

Medes Rivals of the Assyrians and the Persians. The Medes inhabited the area from the Zagros Mountains to the modern city of Tehran; known as expert horsemen and archers, they were eventually defeated by the Persians.

megalith Literally, "great stone"; the word *megalith* is used when describing structures such as Stonehenge. These massive structures are the result of cooperative planning and work.

megarons Large buildings found in Troy (level II) that are the predecessors of the classic Greek temple.

Meiji Empire Empire created under the leadership of Mutsuhito, emperor of Japan from 1868 until 1912. During the Meiji period Japan

became a world industrial and naval power.

Meiji Restoration (1868–1912) Reign of the Meiji Emperor, which was characterized by a new nationalist identity, economic advances, and political transformation.

Mencius Disciple of Confucius who lived from 372 to 289 BCE.

mercantilism Economic theory that drove European empire builders. In this economic system, the world had a fixed amount of wealth, which meant one country's wealth came at the expense of another's. Mercantilism assumed that colonies existed for the sole purpose of enriching the country that controlled the colony.

Mercosur Free-trade pact between the governments of Argentina, Brazil, Paraguay, and Uruguay.

meritocracy Rule by persons of talent.

Meroitic kingdom Thriving kingdom from the fourth century BCE to 300 CE. A successor to Kush, it was influenced by both Egyptian and Sudanic cultures.

mestizos Mixed-blood offspring of Spanish settlers and Amerindians.

métis Mixed-blood offspring of French settlers and Amerindians.

Mexican Revolution (1910–1920) Conflict fueled by the unequal distribution of land and by disgruntled workers; it erupted when political elites split over the succession of General Porfirio Díaz after decades of his rule. The fight lasted over ten years and cost 1 million lives, but it resulted in widespread reform and a new constitution.

Mfecane movement African political revolts in the first half of the nineteenth century that were caused by the expansionist methods of King Shaka of the Zulu people.

microsocieties Small-scale, fragmented communities that had little interaction with others. These communities were the norm for peoples living in the Americas and islanders in the Pacific and Aegean from 2000 to 1200 BCE.

Middle Kingdom Period of Egyptian history lasting from about 2040 to 1640 BCE, characterized by a consolidation of power and building activity in Upper Egypt.

migration Long-distance travel for the purpose of resettlement. In the case of early humans, the need to move was usually a response to an environmental shift, such as climate change during the Ice Age.

millenarian Believer in the imminent coming of a just and ideal society.

millenarian movement Believer (usually religious) in the cataclysmic destruction of a corrupt, fallen society and its replacement by an ideal, utopian future.

Millets Minority religious communities of the Ottoman Empire.

minaret Slender tower within a mosque from which Muslims are called to prayer.

minbar Pulpit inside a mosque from which Muslim religious speakers broadcast their message to the faithful.

Ming dynasty Successor to the Mongol Yuan dynasty that reinstituted and reinforced Han Chinese ceremonies and ideals, including rule by an ethnically Han bureaucracy.

Minoans A people who built a large number of elaborate, independent palace centers on Crete, at Knossos, and elsewhere around 2000 BCE. Named after the legendary King Minos, said to have ruled Crete at the time, they sailed throughout the Mediterranean and by 1600 BCE had planted colonies on many Aegean islands, which in turn became trading and mining centers.

mission civilisatrice Term French colonizers used to refer to France's form of "rationalized" colonial rule, which attempted to bring "civilization" to the "uncivilized."

mitochondrial DNA Form of DNA found in mitochondria, structures located outside the nuclei of cells. Examining mitochondrial DNA enables researchers to measure the genetic variation among living organisms, including human beings. Only females pass mitochondrial DNA to their offspring.

Moche A people who extended their power and increased their wealth at the height of the Chimú Empire over several valleys in what is now Peru.

Model T Automobile manufactured by the Ford Motor Company, which was the first to be priced reasonably enough to be sold to the masses.

modernism In the arts, modernism refers to the effort to break with older conventions and seek new ways of seeing and describing the world.

Mohism School of thought in ancient China, named after Mo Di, or Mozi, who lived from 479 to 438 BCE. It emphasized one's obligation to society as a whole, not just to one's immediate family or social circle.

monarchy Political system in which one individual holds supreme power and passes that power on to his or her next of kin.

monasticism From the Greek word *monos* (meaning "alone"), the practice of living without the ties of marriage or family, forsaking earthly luxuries for a life of prayer and study. While Christian monasticism originated in Egypt, a variant of ascetic life had long been practiced in Buddhism.

monetization An economic shift from a barter-based economy to one dependent on currency.

Mongols Combination of nomadic forest and steppe peoples who lived by hunting and livestock herding and were expert horsemen. Beginning in 1206, the Mongols launched a series of conquests that brought far-flung parts of the world together under their rule. By incorporating conquered peoples and adapting some of their customs, the Mongols created a unified empire that stretched from the Pacific Ocean to the shores of the eastern Mediterranean and the southern steppes of Eurasia.

monotheism The belief in only one god; to be distinguished from polytheism (the belief in many gods) and henotheism (the belief that there may be many gods but one is superior to the others).

Moors Term employed by Europeans in the medieval period to refer to Muslim occupants of North Africa, the western Sahara, and the Iberian Peninsula.

mosque Place of worship for the people of Islam.

mound people Name for the people of Cahokia, since its landscape was dominated by earthen monuments in the shapes of mounds. The mounds were carefully maintained and were the loci from which Cahokians paid respect to spiritual forces. *See also* Cahokia.

Mu Chinese ruler (956–918 BCE) who put forth a formal bureaucratic system of governance, appointing officials, supervisors, and military captains to whom he was not related. He also instituted a formal legal code.

muckrakers Journalists who aimed to expose political and commercial corruption in late nineteenth- and early twentieth-century America.

Muftis Experts on Muslim religious law.

Mughal Empire One of Islam's greatest regimes. Established in 1526, it was a vigorous, centralized state whose political authority encompassed most of modern-day India. During the sixteenth century, it had a population of between 100 and 150 million.

Muhammad (570–632 CE) Prophet and founder of the Islamic faith. Born in Mecca in Saudi Arabia and orphaned when young, Muhammad lived under the protection of his uncle. His career as a prophet began around 610 CE, with his first experience of spiritual revelation.

Muhammad Ali (r. 1805–1848) Ruler of Egypt who initiated a set of modernizing reforms that sought to make it competitive with the great powers.

mullahs Religious leaders in Iran who in the 1970s led a movement opposing Shah Reza Pahlavi and denounced American materialism and secularism.

multinational corporations Corporations based in many different countries that have global investment, trading, and distribution goals.

Muscovy The principality of Moscow. Originally a mixture of Slavs, Finnish tribes, Turkic speakers, and many others, Muscovy used territorial expansion and commercial networks to consolidate a powerful state and expanded to become the Russian Empire, a huge realm that spanned parts of Europe, much of northern Asia, numerous North Pacific islands, and even—for a time—a corner of North America (Alaska).

Muslim Brotherhood Egyptian organization founded in 1938 by Hassan al-Banna. It attacked liberal democracy as a cover for middle-class, business, and landowning interests and fought for a return to a purified Islam.

Muslim League National Muslim party of India.

Mussolini, Benito (1883–1945) Italian dictator and founder of the fascist movement in Italy. During World War II, he allied Italy with Germany and Japan.

Muwahhidin Literally, "unitarians"; followers of the Wahhabi movement that emerged in the Arabian Peninsula in the eighteenth century.

Mycenaeans Mainland competitors of the Minoans who took over Crete around 1400 BCE. Migrating to Greece from central Europe, they brought their Indo-European language, chariots, and metalworking skills, which they used to dominate until 1200 BCE.

Nagasaki Second Japanese city to be hit by an atomic bomb near the end of World War II.

Napoleon Bonaparte (1769–1821) General who rose to power in a postrevolutionary coup d'état, eventually proclaiming himself emperor of France. He placed security and order ahead of social reform and created a civil legal code. Napoleon expanded his empire through military action, but after his disastrous Russian campaign, the united European powers defeated Napoleon and forced him into exile. He escaped and reassumed command of his army but was later defeated at the Battle of Waterloo.

Napoleonic Code Legal code drafted by Napoleon in 1804; it distilled different legal traditions to create one uniform law. The code confirmed the abolition of feudal privileges of all kinds and set the conditions for exercising property rights.

National Assembly of France Governing body of France that succeeded the Estates-General in 1789 during the French Revolution. It was composed of, and defined by, the delegates of the Third Estate.

National Association for the Advancement of Colored People (NAACP) A U.S. civil rights organization, founded in 1910, dedicated to ending inequality and segregation for black Americans.

National Recovery Administration (NRA) U.S. New Deal agency created in 1933 to prepare codes of fair administration and to plan for public works. It was later declared unconstitutional.

nationalism The idea that members of a shared community called a nation should have sovereignty within the borders of their state.

nation-state Form of political organization that derived legitimacy from its inhabitants, often referred to as citizens, who in theory, if not always in practice, shared a common language, common culture, and common history.

native learning Japanese movement to promote nativist intellectual traditions and the celebration of Japanese texts.

native paramountcy British form of "rationalized" colonial rule, which attempted to bring "civilization" to the "uncivilized" by proclaiming that when the interests of European settlers in Africa clashed with those of the African population, the latter should take precedence.

natural rights Belief that emerged in eighteenth-century western Europe and North America that rights fundamental to human nature were discernible to reason and should be affirmed in human-made law.

natural selection Charles Darwin's theory that populations grew faster than the food supply, creating a "struggle for existence" among species. In later work he showed how the passing on of individual traits was also determined by what he called sexual selection—according to which the "best" mates are chosen for their strength, beauty, or talents. The outcome: the "fittest" survived to reproduce, while the less adaptable did not.

Nazis (National Socialist German Workers' Party) German organization dedicated to winning workers over from socialism to nationalism; the first Nazi Party platform combined nationalism with anticapitalism and anti-Semitism.

Neanderthals Members of an early wave of hominids from Africa who settled in western Afro-Eurasia, in an area reaching from present-day Uzbekistan and Iraq to Spain, approximately 150,000 years ago.

negritos Hunter-gatherer inhabitants of the East Asian coastal islands who migrated there around 28,000 BCE but by 2000 BCE had been replaced by new migrants.

Negritude The idea of a black identity and culture different from, but not inferior to, European cultural forms; shaped by African and African American intellectuals like Senegal's first president, Léopold Sédar Senghor.

Nehemiah Jewish eunuch of the Persian court who was given permission to rebuild the fortification walls around the city of Jerusalem from 440 to 437 BCE.

Neo-Assyrian Empire Afro-Eurasian empire that dominated around

950 BCE. The Neo-Assyrians extended their control over resources and people beyond their own borders, and their empire lasted for three centuries.

Nestorian Christians Denomination of Christians whose beliefs about Christ differed from those of the official Byzantine church. Named after Nestorius, former bishop of Constantinople, they emphasized the human aspects of Jesus.

New Deal President Franklin Delano Roosevelt's package of government reforms that were enacted during the 1930s to provide jobs for the unemployed, social welfare programs for the poor, and security to the financial markets.

New Economic Policy Enacted decrees of the Bolsheviks between 1921 and 1927 that grudgingly sanctioned private trade and private property.

New Negro movement *See* Harlem Renaissance.

New World Term applied to the Americas that reflected the Europeans' view that anything previously unknown to them was "new," even if it had existed and supported societies long before European explorers arrived on its shores.

nirvana Literally, "nonexistence"; *nirvana* is the state of complete liberation from the concerns of worldly life, as in Buddhist thought.

Nō drama Masked theater favored by Japanese bureaucrats and regional lords during the Tokugawa period.

Noble Eightfold Path Buddhist concept of a way of life by which people may rid themselves of individual desire to achieve *nirvana*. The path consists of wisdom, ethical behavior, and mental discipline.

Nok culture Spectacular culture that arose in present-day Nigeria in the sixth century BCE. Iron smelting occurred there around 600 BCE. Thus the Nok people made the transition from stone to iron materials.

nomads People who move across vast distances without settling permanently in a particular place. Often pastoralists, nomads and transhumant herders introduced new forms of chariot-based warfare that transformed the Afro-Eurasian world.

nongovernmental organizations (NGOs) Term used to refer to private organizations like the Red Cross that play a large role in international affairs. See *supranational organizations*.

nonviolent resistance Moral and political philosophy of resistance developed by Indian National Congress leader Mohandas Gandhi. Gandhi believed that if Indians pursued self-reliance and self-control in a nonviolent way, the British would eventually have to leave.

North American Free Trade Agreement (NAFTA) Treaty negotiated in the early 1990s to promote free trade between Canada, the United States, and Mexico.

North Atlantic Treaty Organization (NATO) International organization set up in 1949 to provide for the defense of western European countries and the United States from the perceived Soviet threat.

Northern Wei dynasty Regime founded in 386 CE by the Tuoba, a people originally from Inner Mongolia, that lasted one and a half centuries. The rulers of this dynasty adopted many practices of the earlier Chinese Han regime. At the same time, they struggled to consolidate authority over their own nomadic people. Ultimately, several decades of intense internal conflict led to the dynasty's downfall.

Northwest Passage Long-sought marine passageway between the Atlantic and Pacific Oceans along the northern coast of North America.

Oceania Collective name for the lands of Australia and New Zealand and the islands of the southwest Pacific Ocean.

Odyssey An epic tale, composed in the eighth century BCE, of the journey of Odysseus, who traveled the Mediterranean back to his home in Ithaca after the siege of Troy.

oikos The word for "small family unit" in ancient Greece, similar to the *familia* in Rome. Its structure, with men as heads of household over women and children, embodied the fundamental power structure in Greek city-states.

oligarchy Clique of privileged rulers.

Olmecs Mesoamerican people, emerging around 1500 BCE, whose name means "inhabitants of the land of rubber," one of their major trade goods. Living in decentralized agrarian villages, this complex, stratified society shared language and religious ideas that were practiced at sacred ritual centers.

open door policy Policy proposed by U.S. Secretary of State John Hay that would give all foreign nations equal access to trade with China. As European imperial powers carved out spheres of influence in late nineteenth-century China, American leaders worried that the United States would be excluded from trade with China.

Opium Wars (1839–1842, 1856–1860) Wars fought between the British and Qing China over British trade in opium; the result was that China granted to the British the right to trade in five different ports and ceded Hong Kong to the British.

oracle bones Animal bones inscribed, heated, and interpreted by Shang ritual specialists to determine the will of the ancestors.

Organization of Petroleum Exporting Countries (OPEC) International association established in 1960 to coordinate price and supply policies of oil-producing states.

orientalism Genre of literature and painting that portrayed the non-western peoples of North Africa and Asia as exotic, sensuous, and economically backward with respect to Europeans.

orientalists Western scholars who specialized in the study of the East.

Orrorin tugenensis Predecessor to hominids that first appeared 6 million years ago.

Ottoman Empire A Turkish warrior band that transformed itself into a vast, multicultural, bureaucratic empire that lasted from the early fourteenth century through the early twentieth century and encompassed Anatolia, the Arab world, and large swaths of southern and eastern Europe.

Pacific War (1879–1883) War between Chile and the alliance of Bolivia and Peru.

pagani Pejorative word used by Christians to designate pagans.

palace Official residence of the ruler, his family, and his entourage. The palace was both a social institution and a set of buildings. It first appeared around 2500 BCE, about a millennium later than the Mesopotamian temple, and quickly joined the temple as a defining landmark of city life. Eventually, it became a source of power rivaling the temple, and palace and temple life often blurred, as did the boundary between the sacred and the secular.

Palace of Versailles The palace complex, 11 miles away from the French capital of Paris, built by Louis XIV in the 1670s and 1680s to house and entertain his leading clergymen and nobles, with the hopes of diverting them from plotting against him.

Palmyra Roman trading depot in located modern-day Syria; part of a network of trading cities that connected various regions of Afro-Eurasia.

pan movements Groups that sought to link people across state boundaries in new communities based on ethnicity or, in some cases, religion (e.g., pan-Germanism, pan-Islamism, pan-Slavism).

Pansophia Ideal republic of inquisitive Christians united in the search for knowledge of nature as a means of loving God.

papacy The institution of the pope, the Catholic spiritual leader in Rome.

papal Of, relating to, or issued by a pope.

Parthians Horse-riding people who pushed southward around the middle of the second century BCE and wiped out the Greek kingdoms in Iran. They then extended their power all the way to the Mediterranean, where they ran up against the Roman Empire in Anatolia and Mesopotamia.

pastoral nomads Peoples who move with their herds in perpetual motion across large areas, like the steppe lands of Inner Eurasia, and facilitate long-distance trade.

pastoralism A way of life in which humans herd domesticated animals and exploit their products (hides/fur, meat, and milk). Pastoralists include nomadic groups that range across vast distances, as well as transhumant herders who migrate seasonally in a more limited range.

paterfamilias Latin for "father of the family," the foundation of the Roman social order.

patria Latin, meaning "fatherland."

patrons In the Roman system of patronage, men and women of wealth and high social status who protected dependents or "clients" of a lower class.

Pax Mongolica The political and especially the commercial stability that the vast Mongol Empire provided for the travelers and merchants of Eurasia during the thirteenth and fourteenth centuries.

Pax Romana Latin term for "Roman Peace," referring to The period from 25 BCE to 235 CE, when conditions in the Roman Empire were relatively settled and peaceful, allowing trade and the economy to thrive.

Pax Sinica Modern term (paralleling the term Pax Romana) for the "Chinese Peace" that lasted from 149 to 87 BCE, a period when agriculture and commerce flourished, fueling the expansion of cities and the growth of the population of Han China.

Peace Preservation Act (1925) Act instituted in Japan that specified up to ten years' hard labor for any member of an organization advocating a basic change in the political system or the abolition of private property.

Pearl Harbor American naval base in Hawaii on which the Japanese launched a surprise attack on December 7, 1941, bringing the United States into World War II.

Peloponnesian War War fought between 431 and 404 BCE between two of Greece's most powerful city-states, Athens and Sparta.

Peninsular War (1808–1814) Conflict in which the Portuguese and

Spanish populations, supported by the British, resisted an invasion of the Iberian Peninsula by the French under Napoleon.

peninsulares Spaniards who, although born in Spain, resided in the Spanish colonial territories. They regarded themselves as superior to Spaniards born in the colonies (creoles).

Peoples' Charter Document calling for universal suffrage for adult males, the secret ballot, electoral districts, and annual parliamentary elections. It was signed by over 3 million British between 1839 and 1842.

periplus "Sailing around" manual that preserved firsthand knowledge of navigation strategies and trading advice.

Persepolis Darius I's capital city in the highlands of Fars; a ceremonial center and expression of imperial identity as well as an important administrative hub of the Persian Empire.

Peterloo Massacre (1819) The killing of 11 and wounding of 460 following a peaceful demonstration for political reform by workers in Manchester, England.

Petra Literally, "rock"; city in modern-day Jordan that was the Nabataean capital. It profited greatly by supplying provisions and water to travelers and traders. Many of its houses and shrines were cut into the rocky mountains.

phalanx Military formation used by Philip II of Macedonia, whereby heavily armored infantry were closely arrayed in battle.

Philip II of Macedonia Father of Alexander the Great, under whose rule Macedonia developed into a large ethnic and territorial state. After unifying Macedonia, Philip went on to conquer neighboring states.

philosophes Enlightenment thinkers who applied scientific reasoning to human interaction and society as opposed to nature.

philosophia Literally, "love of wisdom"; a system of thought that originally included speculation on the nature of the cosmos, the environment, and human existence. It eventually came to include thought about the nature of humans and life in society.

Phoenicians An ethnic group in the Levant known for their ships, trading, and alphabet, and referred to in Hebrew scripture as the Canaanites. The term *Phoenician* (Greek for "Purple People") derives from the major trade good they manufactured, a rare and expensive purple dye.

phonemes Primary and distinctive sounds that are characteristic of human language.

piety Strong sense of religious duty and devoutness, often inspiring extraordinary actions.

plant domestication The practice of growing plants, harvesting their seeds, and saving some of the seeds for planting in subsequent growing cycles, resulting in a steady food supply. Plant domestication was practiced as far back as 5000 BCE in the southern Levant and spread from there into the rest of Southwest Asia.

plantation slavery System whereby labor was used for the cultivation of crops wholly for the sake of producing surplus that was then used for profit; slave plantations were a crucial part of the growth of the Mediterranean economy.

Plato (427–347 BCE) Disciple of the great philosopher Socrates; his works are the only record we have of Socrates's teaching. He was also the author of formative philosophical works on ethics and politics.

plebs The "common people" of Rome, whose interests were protected by officials called tribunes.

Pochteca Archaic term for merchants of the Mexicos.

polities Politically organized communities or states.

polyglot communities Societies composed of diverse linguistic and ethnic groups.

popular culture Affordable and accessible forms of art and entertainment available to people at all levels of society.

popular sovereignty The idea that the power of the state resides in the people.

populists Members of a political movement that supported U.S. farmers in late nineteenth-century America. The term is often used generically to refer to political groups who appeal to the majority of the population.

potassium-argon dating Major dating technique based on the decay of potassium into argon over time. This method makes possible the dating of objects up to a million years old.

potato famine (1840s) Severe famine in Ireland that led to the rise of radical political movements and the migration of large numbers of Irish to the United States.

potter's wheel Fast wheel that enabled people to mass-produce vessels in many different shapes. This advance, invented at the city of Uruk, enabled potters to make significant technical breakthroughs.

pottery Vessels made of mud and, later, clay used for storing and transporting food.

Prague Spring (1968) Program of liberalization by which communist authorities in Czechoslovakia strove to create a democratic and pluralist socialism; crushed by the Soviets, who branded it a "counterrevolutionary" movement.

predestination Belief of many sixteenth- and seventeenth-century Protestant groups that God had foreordained the lives of individuals, including their bad and good deeds.

primitivism Western art movement of the late nineteenth and early twentieth centuries that drew upon the so-called primitive art forms of Africa, Oceania, and pre-Columbian America.

progressive reformers Members of the U.S. reform movement in the early twentieth century that aimed to eliminate political corruption, improve working conditions, and regulate the power of large industrial and financial enterprises.

proletarians Industrial wage workers.

prophets Charismatic freelance religious men of power who found themselves in opposition to the formal power of kings, bureaucrats, and priests.

Prophet's Town Indian village in present-day Indiana that was burned down by American forces in the early nineteenth century.

Protestant Reformation Religious movement initiated by sixteenth-century monk Martin Luther, who openly criticized the corruption in the Catholic Church and voiced his belief that Christians could speak directly to God. His doctrines gained wide support, and those who followed this new view of Christianity rejected the authority of the papacy and the Catholic clergy, broke away from the Catholic Church, and called themselves "Protestants."

Protestantism Division of Christianity that emerged in western Europe from the Protestant Reformation.

Proto-Indo-European The parent of all the languages in the Indo-European family, which includes, among many others, English, German, Norwegian, Portuguese, French, Russian, Persian, Hindi, and Bengali.

Pullman Strike (1894) American Railway Union strike in response to wage cuts and firings.

Punic Wars Series of three wars fought between Rome and Carthage from 264 to 146 BCE that resulted in the end of Carthaginian hegemony in the western Mediterranean, the growth of Roman military might (army and navy), and the beginning of Rome's aggressive foreign imperialism.

puppet states Governments with little power in the international arena that follow the dictates of their more powerful neighbors or patrons.

Puritans Seventeenth-century reform group of the Church of England; also known as dissenters or nonconformists.

Qadiriyya Sufi order that facilitated the spread of Islam into West Africa.

Qadis Judges in the Ottoman Empire.

qanats Underground water channels, vital for irrigation, that were used in Persia. Little evaporation occurred when water was being moved through qanats.

Qing dynasty (1644–1911) Minority Manchu rule over China that incorporated new territories, experienced substantial population growth, and sustained significant economic growth.

Questions of King Milinda (Milindapunha) Name of a second-century BCE text espousing the teachings of Buddhism as set forth by Menander, a Yavana king. It featured a discussion between the king and a sophisticated Buddhist sage named Nagasena.

Quetzalcoatl Ancient deity and legendary ruler of Native American peoples living in Mexico.

Quran The scripture of the Islamic faith. Originally a verbal recitation, the Quran was eventually compiled into a book with its verses in the order in which we have them today. According to traditional Islamic interpretation, the Quran was revealed to Muhammad by the angel Gabriel over a period of twenty-three years.

radicals Widely used term in nineteenth-century Europe that referred to those individuals and political organizations that favored the total reconfiguration of Europe's old state system.

radiocarbon dating Dating technique using the isotope C^{14}, contained by all living organisms, which plants acquire directly from the atmosphere and animals acquire indirectly when they consume plants or other animals. When organisms die, the C^{14} they contain begins to decay into a stable nonradioactive isotope, C^{12}. The rate of decay is regular and measurable, making it possible to ascertain the ages of fossils that leave organic remains up to 40,000 years.

raj British crown's administration of India following the end of the East India Company's rule after the Rebellion of 1857.

raja "King" in the Kshatriya period in South Asia; could also refer to the head of a family, but indicated the person who had control of land and resources in South Asian city-states.

Ramadan Ninth month of the Muslim year, during which all Muslims must fast during daylight hours.

rape of Nanjing Attack against the Chinese in which the Japanese slaughtered at least 100,000 civilians and raped thousands of women between December 1937 and February 1938.

Rashtriya Swayamsevak Sangh (RSS) (1925) Campaign to organize Hindus as a militant, modern community in India; translated in English as "National Volunteer Organization."

Rebellion of 1857 Indian uprising against the East India Company whose aims were religious purification, an egalitarian society, and local and communal solidarity without the interference of British rule.

rebus Probably originating in Uruk, a representation that transfers meaning from the name of a thing to the sound of that name. For example, a picture of a bee can represent the sound "b." Such pictures opened the door to writing: a technology of symbols that uses marks to represent specific discrete sounds.

Reconquista Spanish reconquest of territories lost to the Islamic empire, beginning with Toledo in 1061.

Red Guards Chinese students who were the shock troopers in the early phases of Mao Zedong's Great Proletarian Cultural Revolution in 1966–1968.

Red Lanterns Female supporters of the Chinese Boxers who dressed in red garments. Most were teenage girls and unmarried women.

Red Turban movement Diverse religious movement in China during the fourteenth century that spread the belief that the world was drawing to an end as Mongol rule was collapsing.

Reds Bolsheviks.

Reich German empire composed of Denmark, Austria, and parts of western France (1933–1945).

Reichstag The German parliament.

Reign of Terror Campaign at the height of the French Revolution in the early 1790s that used violence, including systematic execution of opponents of the revolution, to purge France of its enemies and to extend the revolution beyond its borders; radicals executed as many as 40,000 persons who were judged enemies of the state.

Renaissance Term meaning "rebirth" used by historians to characterize the cultural flourishing of European nations between 1430 and 1550, which emphasized a break from the church-centered medieval world and a new concept of humankind as the center of the world.

republican government Government in which power and rulership rest with representatives of the people, not with a king.

res publica Term (meaning "the public thing") used by Romans to describe their Republic, which was advised by a Senate and was governed by popular assemblies of free adult males, who were arranged into voting units, based on wealth and social status, to elect officers and legislate.

Restoration (1815–1848) European movement after the defeat of Napoleon to restore Europe to its pre-French-revolutionary status and to quash radical movements.

Rift Valley Area of northeastern Africa where some of the most important early human archaeological discoveries of fossils were made, especially one of an intact skull that is 1.8 million years old.

river basin Area drained by a river, including all its tributaries. River basins were rich in fertile soil, water for irrigation, and plant and animal life, which made them attractive for human habitation. Cultivators were able to produce surplus agriculture to support the first cities.

riverine Of or relating to an area whose inhabitants depend on irrigation for their well-being and whose populations are settled near great rivers. Egypt was, in a sense, the most riverine of all these cultures, in that it had no hinterland of plains, as did Mesopotamia and the Indus Valley. Away from the banks of the Nile, there is only largely uninhabitable desert.

Roman army Military force of the Roman Empire. The Romans devised a military draft that could draw from a huge population. In their encounter with Hannibal, they lost up to 80,000 men in three separate encounters and still won the war.

Roman Catholic Church Western European Christianity, centered on the papacy at Rome, that emphasizes the atoning power of Jesus's death and aims to expand as far as possible.

Roman law The legal system of Rome, under which disputes were brought to public courts and decisions were made by judges and sometimes by large juries. Rome's legal system featured written law and institutions for settling legal disputes.

roving bandits Large bands of dispossessed and marginalized peasants who vented their anger at tax collectors in the waning years of the Ming dynasty.

Royal Road A 1,600-mile road from Sardis in Anatolia to Susa in Iran; used by messengers, traders, the army, and those taking tribute to the king in the fifth century BCE.

Russification Programs to assimilate people of over 146 dialects into the Russian Empire.

Sack of Constantinople Rampage in 1204 by the Frankish armies on the capital city of Constantinople.

sacred kingships Institutions that marked the centralized politics of West Africa. The inhabitants of these kingships believed that their kings were descendants of the gods.

Sahel The area of sub-Saharan Africa spanning the continent just south of the Sahara Desert.

St. Bartholomew's Day Massacre (1572) Roman Catholic massacre of French Protestants in Paris.

St. Patrick Former slave brought to Ireland from Britain who later became a missionary, also called the "Apostle of Ireland." He died in 470 CE.

Salt March (1930) A 240-mile trek to the sea in India, led by Mohandas Gandhi, to gather salt for free, thus breaking the British colonial monopoly on salt.

Samurai Japanese warriors who made up the private armies of Japanese daimyos.

Sandinista coalition Left-leaning Nicaraguan coalition of the 1970s and 1980s.

Sanskrit cosmopolis Cultural synthesis based on Hindu spiritual beliefs expressed in the Sanskrit language that unified South Asia in place of a centralized empire.

Santería African-based religion, blended with Christian influences, that was first practiced by slaves in Cuba.

Sargon the Great King of Akkad, a city-state located near present-day Baghdad. Reigning from 2334 to 2279 BCE, Sargon helped bring the competitive era of city-states to an end and sponsored monumental works of architecture, art, and literature.

Sasanian Empire Empire that succeeded the Parthians in the mid-220s CE in Inner Eurasia. The Sasanian Empire controlled the trade crossroads of Afro-Eurasia and possessed a strong armored cavalry, which made it a powerful rival to Rome. The Sasanians were also tolerant of Judaism and Christianity, which allowed Christians to flourish.

sati Hindu practice whereby a widow was burned to death on the pyre of her dead husband.

satrap Governor of a province in the Persian Empire. Each satrap was a relative or intimate associate of the king.

satrapy Province in the Persian empire, ruled over by a governor, called a satrap, who was usually a relative or associate of the king.

satyagraha *See* nonviolent resistance.

scientific method Method of inquiry based on experimentation in nature. Many of its principles were first laid out by the philosopher Sir Francis Bacon (1561–1626), who claimed that real science entailed the formulation of hypotheses that could be tested in carefully controlled experiments.

Scramble for Africa European rush to colonize parts of Africa at the end of the nineteenth century.

scribes Those who wield writing tools; from the very beginning they were at the top of the social ladder, under the major power brokers.

Scythian ethos Warrior ethos that embodied the extremes of aggressive horse-mounted culture. In part, the Scythian ethos was the result of the constant struggle between settlers, hunter-gatherers, and nomads on the northern frontier of Europe around 1000 BCE.

Sea Peoples Migrants from north of the Mediterranean who invaded cities of Egypt, Asia Minor, and the Levant in the second millennium BCE.

SEATO (Southeast Asia Treaty Organization) Military alliance of pro-American, anticommunist states in Southeast Asia from 1954 to 1977.

Second World Term invented during the Cold War to refer to the communist countries, as opposed to the west (or First World) and the former colonies (or Third World).

second-generation societies First-millennium BCE societies that innovated on their older political, religious, and cultural ideas by incorporating new aspects of cultures they encountered to reshape their way of life.

Seleucus Nikator Successor of Alexander the Great who lived from 358 to 281 BCE. He controlled Mesopotamia, Syria, Persia, and parts of the Punjab.

Self-Strengthening movement A movement of reformist Chinese bureaucrats in the latter half of the nineteenth century that attempted to adopt western elements of learning and technological skill while retaining their core Chinese culture.

Semu Term meaning "outsiders," or non-Chinese people—Mongols, Tanguts, Khitan, Jurchen, Muslims, Tibetans, Persians, Turks, Nestorians, Jews, and Armenians—who became a new ruling elite over a Han majority population in the late thirteenth century.

sepoys Hindu and Muslim recruits of the East India Company's military force.

serfs Peasants who farmed the land and paid fees to be protected and governed by lords under a system of rule called feudalism.

settled agriculture Humans' use of tools, animals, and their own labor to work the same plot of land for more than one growing cycle.

It involves switching from a hunting and gathering lifestyle to one based on farming.

Seven Years' War (1756–1763) Worldwide war that ended when Prussia defeated Austria, establishing itself as a European power, and when Britain gained control of India and many of France's colonies through the Treaty of Paris.

sexual revolution Increased freedom in sexual behavior, resulting in part from advances in contraception, notably the introduction of oral contraception in 1960, that allowed men and women to limit childbearing and to have sex with less fear of pregnancy.

shah Traditional title of Persian rulers.

shamans Certain humans whose powers supposedly enabled them to commune with the supernatural and to transform themselves wholly or partly into beasts.

shamisen Three-stringed instrument, often played by Japanese geisha.

Shandingdong Man A *Homo sapiens* whose fossil remains and relics can be dated to about 18,000 years ago. His physical characteristics were close to those of modern humans, and he had a similar brain size.

Shang state Dynasty in northeastern China that ruled from 1600 to 1045 BCE. Though not as well defined by borders as the territorial states in the southwest of Asia, it did have a ruling lineage. Four fundamental elements of the Shang state were a metal industry based on copper, pottery making, standardized architectural forms and walled towns, and divination using animal bones.

Shanghai School Late nineteenth-century style of painting characterized by an emphasis on spontaneous brushwork, feeling, and the incorporation of western influences into classical Chinese pieces.

sharecropping System of farming in which tenant farmers rented land and gave over a share of their crops to the land's owners. Sometimes seen as a cheap way for the state to conduct agricultural affairs, sharecropping often resulted in the impoverishment and marginalization of the underclass.

sharia Body of Islamic law that has developed over centuries, based on the Quran, the sayings of Muhammad (*hadith*), and the legal opinions of Muslim scholars (*ulama*).

Sharpeville Massacre (1960) Massacre of sixty-nine black Africans when police fired upon a rally against the recently passed laws requiring nonwhite South Africans to carry identity papers.

Shawnees Native American tribe that inhabited the Ohio Valley during the eighteenth century.

Shays's Rebellion (1786) Uprising of armed farmers that broke out when the Massachusetts state government refused to offer them economic relief.

Shi Huangdi Title taken by King Zheng in 221 BCE when he claimed the mandate of heaven and consolidated the Qin dynasty. He is known for his tight centralization of power, including standardizing weights, measures, and writing; constructing roads, canals, and the beginnings of the Great Wall; and preparing a massive tomb for himself filled with an army of terra-cotta warriors.

Shiism One of the two main branches of Islam, practiced in the Safavid Empire. Although always a minority sect in the Islamic world, Shiism contains several subsects, each of which has slightly different interpretations of theology and politics.

Shiites Minority tradition within modern Islam that traces political succession through the lineage of Muhammad and breaks with Sunni understandings of succession at the death of Ali (cousin and son-in-law of Muhammad and fourth caliph) in 661 CE.

Shinto Literally, "the way of the gods"; Japan's official religion, which promoted the state and the emperor's divinity.

shoguns Japanese military commanders. From 1192 to 1333, the Kamakura shoguns served as military "protectors" of the ruler in the city of Heian.

Shotoku Prince in the early Japanese Yamoto state (574–622 CE) who is credited with having introduced Buddhism to Japan.

shudras Literally, "small ones"; workers and slaves from outside the Vedic lineage.

Siddhartha Gautama *See* Buddha.

Sikhism Islamic-inspired religion that calls on its followers to renounce the caste system and to treat all believers as equal before God.

Silicon Valley Valley between the California cities of San Francisco and San Jose, known for its innovative computer and high-technology industries.

silk Luxury textile that became a vastly popular export from China (via the Silk Roads) to the cities of the Roman world.

Silk Roads More than 5,000 miles of trade routes linking China, central Asia, and the Mediterranean. They were named for the silk famously traded along their land and sea routes, although ideas, people, and many other high-value commodities also moved along their lengths.

Silla One of three independent Korean states that may have emerged as early as the third century BCE. These states lasted until 668 CE, when Silla took control over the entire peninsula.

Silver Islands Term used by European merchants in the sixteenth century to refer to Japan because of its substantial trade in silver with China.

Sino-Japanese War (1894–1895) Conflict over the control of Korea in which China was forced to cede the province of Taiwan to Japan.

Sipahi Urdu for "soldier."

Siva The third of three Vedic deities, signifying destruction. *See also* Brahma *and* Vishnu.

small seal script Unified script that was used to the exclusion of other scripts under the Qin with the aim of centralizing administration; its use led to a less complicated style of clerical writing than had been in use under the Han.

social contract The idea, drawn from the writings of British philosopher John Locke, that the law should bind both ruler and people.

Social Darwinism Belief that Charles Darwin's theory of evolution was applicable to humans and justified the right of the ruling classes or countries to dominate the weak.

social hierarchies Distinctions between the privileged and the less privileged.

Social Security Act (1935) New Deal act that instituted old-age pensions and insurance for the unemployed.

socialism Political ideology that calls for a classless society with collective ownership of all property.

Socrates (469–399 BCE) Philosopher of Athens who encouraged people to reflect on ethics and morality. He stressed the importance of honor and integrity as opposed to wealth and power. Plato was his student.

Sogdians A people who lived in central Asia's commercial centers and maintained the stability and accessibility of the Silk Roads. They were crucial to the interconnectedness of the Afro-Eurasian landmass.

Solidarity The Soviet bloc's first independent trade union, established in Poland at the Gdansk shipyard.

Song dynasty Chinese dynasty that took over the mandate of heaven for three centuries starting in 976 CE. It ruled in an era of many economic and political successes, but it eventually lost northern China to nomadic tribes.

Song porcelain Type of porcelain perfected during the Song dynasty that was light, durable, and quite beautiful.

South African War (1899–1902) *See* Anglo-Boer War.

Soviet bloc International alliance that included the eastern European countries of the Warsaw Pact as well as the Soviet Union, but also came to include Cuba.

Spanish-American War (1898) War between the United States and Spain in Cuba, Puerto Rico, and the Philippines. It ended with a treaty in which the United States took over the Philippines, Guam, and Puerto Rico; Cuba won partial independence.

speciation The formation of species.

specie Money in coin.

species A group of animals or plants sharing one or more distinctive characteristics.

spiritual ferment Process that occurred after 300 CE in which religion touched more areas of society and culture than before and in different, more demanding ways.

Spring and Autumn period Period between the eighth and fifth centuries BCE during which China was ruled by the feudal system. In this anarchic and turbulent time, there were 148 different tributary states.

S.S. (*Schutzstaffel*) Hitler's security police force.

Stalin, Joseph (1879–1953) Leader of the Communist Party and the Soviet Union; sought to create "socialism in one country."

steel A metal more malleable and stronger than iron that became essential for industries like shipbuilding and railways.

stoicism Widespread philosophical movement initiated by Zeno (334–262 BCE). Zeno and his followers sought to understand the role of people in relation to the cosmos. For the Stoics, everything was grounded in nature. Being in love with nature and living a good life required being in control of one's passions and thus indifferent to pleasure or pain.

Strait of Malacca Seagoing gateway to Southeast and East Asia.

Strategic Defense Initiative Master plan, championed by U.S. president Ronald Reagan in the 1980s, that envisioned the deployment of satellites and space missiles to protect the United States from incoming nuclear bombs; nicknamed "Star Wars."

stupa Dome monument marking the burial site of relics of the Buddha.

Suez Canal Channel built in 1869 across the Isthmus of Suez to connect the Mediterranean Sea with the

Red Sea in order to lower the costs of international trade.

Sufi brotherhoods Sufi religious orders that were responsible for the expansion of Islam into many regions of the world.

Sufism Emotional and mystical form of Islam that appealed to the common people.

sultan Islamic political leader. In the Ottoman Empire, the sultan combined a warrior ethos with an unwavering devotion to Islam.

Sumerian King List Text that recounts the making of political dynasties. Recorded around 2000 BCE, it organizes the reigns of kings by dynasty, one city at a time.

Sumerian pantheon The Sumerian gods, each of whom had a home in a particular floodplain city. In the Sumerian belief system, both gods and the natural forces they controlled had to be revered.

Sumerian temples Homes of the gods and symbols of Sumerian imperial identity. Sumerian temples also represented the gods' ability to hoard wealth at sites where people exchanged goods and services. In addition, temples distinguished the urban from the rural world.

Sun Yat-sen (1866–1925) Chinese revolutionary and first provisional president of the Republic of China. Sun played an important role in the overthrow of the Qing dynasty and later founded the Guomindang, the Nationalist Party of China.

Sunnis Majority sect within modern Islam that follows a line of political succession from Muhammad, through the first four caliphs (Abu Bakr, Umar, Uthman, and Ali), to the Umayyads and beyond, with caliphs chosen by election from the *umma* (not from Muhammad's direct lineage).

superior man In the Confucian view, a person of perfected moral character, fit to be a leader.

superpowers Label applied to the United States and the Soviet Union after World War II because of their size, their possession of the atomic bomb, and the fact that each embodied a model of civilization (capitalism and communism, respectively) applicable to the whole world.

supranational organizations Organizations that transcend national boundaries, such as nongovernmental organizations (NGOs), the World Bank, and the International Monetary Fund (IMF).

survival of the fittest Charles Darwin's belief that as animal populations grew and resources became scarce, a struggle for existence arose, the outcome of which was that only the "fittest" survived to reproduce.

Suryavamsha The second lineage of two (the solar) in Vedic society. *See also* Chandravamsha.

Swadeshi movement Voluntary organizations in India that championed the creation of indigenous manufacturing enterprises and schools of nationalist thought in order to gain autonomy from Britain.

syndicalists Advocates of syndicalism, a movement of workplace associations that included unskilled labor and sought a replacement for capitalism led by workers.

tabula rasa Term used by John Locke to describe the human mind before it begins to acquire ideas from experience; Latin for "clean slate."

Taiping Heavenly Kingdom (Heavenly Kingdom of Great Peace) Religious sect established by the Chinese prophet Hong Xiuquan

in the mid-nineteenth century. Hong Xiuquan believed that he was Jesus's younger brother. The group struggled to rid the world of evil and "restore" the heavenly kingdom, imagined as a just and egalitarian order.

Taiping Rebellion (1850–1864) Rebellion by followers of Hong Xiuquan and the Taiping Heavenly Kingdom against the Qing government over the economic and social turmoil caused by the Opium War. Despite raising an army of 100,000 rebels, the rebellion was crushed.

Taj Mahal Royal palace of the Mughal Empire, built by Shah Jahan in the seventeenth century in homage to his wife, Mumtaz.

Tale of Genji Japanese work written in the early eleventh century by Lady Murasaki that gives vivid accounts of Heian court life; Japan's first novel.

talking cure Psychological practice developed by Sigmund Freud whereby the symptoms of neurotic and traumatized patients would decrease after regular periods of thoughtful discussion.

Talmud Huge volumes of oral commentary on Jewish law eventually compiled in two versions, the Palestinian and the Babylonian, in the fifth and sixth centuries BCE.

Talmud of Jerusalem Codified written volumes of the traditions of Judaism; produced by the rabbis of Galilee around 400 CE.

Tang dynasty (608–907 CE) Regime that promoted a cosmopolitan culture, turning China into the hub of East Asian cultural integration, while expanding the borders of its empire. In order to govern such a diverse empire, the Tang established a political culture and civil service based on Confucian teachings. Candidates for the civil service were required to take examinations, the first of their kind in the world.

Tanzimat Reorganization period of the Ottoman Empire in the mid-nineteenth century; its modernizing reforms affected the military, trade, foreign relations, and civilian life.

tappers Rubber harvesters in Brazil, most of whom were either Indian or mixed-blood people.

Tarascans Mesoamerican society of the 1400s; rivals to and sometimes subjects of the Aztecs.

Tatish Ruler of Chan Santa Cruz during the Caste War of the Yucatán. The name means "father."

Tecumseh (1768–1813) Shawnee who circulated Tenskwatawa's message of Indian renaissance among Indian villages from the Great Lakes to the Gulf Coast. He preached the need for Indian unity, insisting that Indians resist any American attempts to get them to sell more land. In response, thousands of followers renounced their ties to colonial ways and prepared to combat the expansion of the United States.

Tekkes Schools that taught the devotional strategies and religious knowledge needed for students to enter Sufi orders and become masters of the brotherhood.

temple Building where believers worshipped their gods and goddesses and where some peoples believed the deities had their earthly residence.

Tenskwatawa (1775–1836) Shawnee prophet who urged disciples to abstain from alcohol and return to traditional customs, reducing dependence on European trade goods and severing connections to Christian missionaries. His message spread to other tribes, raising the specter of a pan-Indian confederacy.

Teotihuacán City-state in a large, mountainous valley in present-day Mexico; the first major community to emerge after the Olmecs.

territorial state A kingdom made up of city-states and hinterlands joined together by a shared identity, controlled through the centralized rule of a charismatic leader, and supported by a large bureaucracy, legal codes, and military expansion.

Third Estate The French people minus the clergy and the aristocracy; this term was popularized in the late eighteenth century and used to exalt the power of the bourgeoisie during the French Revolution.

Third Reich The German state from 1933 to 1945 under Adolf Hitler.

Third World A collective term used for nations of the world, mostly in Asia, Latin America, and Africa, that were not highly industrialized like First World nations or tied to the Soviet bloc (the Second World). It implies a revolutionary challenge to the existing (liberal, capitalist) order.

Thirty Years' War (1618–1648) Conflict begun between Protestants and Catholics in Germany that escalated into a general European war fought against the unity and power of the Holy Roman Empire.

Tiananmen Square Largest public square in the world and site of the pro-democracy demonstrations in 1989 that ended with the killing of as many as a thousand protesters by the Chinese army.

Tiers monde Term meaning "Third World," coined by French intellectuals to describe countries seeking a "third way" between Soviet communism and western capitalism.

Tiglath Pileser III Assyrian ruler from 745 to 728 BCE who instituted reforms that changed the administrative and social structure of the empire to make it more efficient, and who introduced a standing army.

Tiwanaku Another name for Tihuanaco, the first great Andean polity, on the shores of Lake Titicaca.

Tlaxcalans Mesoamerican society of the 1400s; these people were enemies of the powerful Aztec Empire.

Tokugawa shogunate Hereditary military administration founded in 1603 that ruled Japan while keeping the emperor as a figurehead; it was toppled in 1868 by reformers who felt that Japan should adopt, not reject, western influences.

Toltecs Mesoamerican peoples who filled the political vacuum left by Teotihuacán's decline; established a temple-filled capital and commercial hub at Tula.

Tomb Culture Warlike group from Northeast Asia who arrived by sea in the middle of the third century CE and imposed their military and social power on southern Japan. These conquerors are known today as the tomb culture because of their elevated necropolises near present-day Osaka.

Topkapi Palace Palace complex located in Istanbul that served as both the residence of the sultan, along with his harem and larger household, and the political headquarters of the Ottoman Empire.

total war All-out war involving civilian populations as well as military forces, often used in reference to World War II.

transhumant herders Pastoral peoples who move seasonally from lowlands to highlands in proximity to city-states, with which they trade the products of their flocks (milk, fur, hides) for urban products (manufactured goods, such as metals).

Trans-Siberian Railroad Railroad built over very difficult terrain between 1891 and 1903 and subsequently expanded; it created an overland bridge for troops, peasant settlers, and commodities to move between Europe and the Pacific.

Treaty of Brest-Litovsk (1918) Separate peace between imperial Germany and the new Bolshevik regime in Russia. The treaty acknowledged the German victory on the Eastern Front and withdrew Russia from the war.

Treaty of Nanjing (1842) Treaty between China and Britain following the Opium War; it called for indemnities, the opening of new ports, and the cession of Hong Kong to the British.

Treaty of Tordesillas (1494) Treaty in which the pope decreed that the non-European world would be divided into spheres of trade and missionary responsibility between Spain and Portugal.

trickle trade Method by which a good is passed from one village to another, as in the case of obsidian among farming villages; the practice began around 7000 BCE. Also called "down-the-line trade."

Tripartite Pact (1940) Pact that stated that Germany, Italy, and Japan would act together in all future military ventures.

Triple Entente Alliance developed before World War I that included Britain, France, and Russia.

Troy City founded around 3000 BCE in the far west of Anatolia. Troy is legendary as the site of the war that was launched by the Greeks (the Achaeans) and that was recounted by Homer in the *Iliad*.

Truman Doctrine (1947) Declaration promising U.S. economic and military intervention, whenever and wherever needed, for the sake of preventing communist expansion.

Truth and Reconciliation Commission Quasi-judicial body established after the overthrow of the apartheid system in South Africa and the election of Nelson Mandela as the country's first black president in 1994. The commission was to gather evidence about crimes committed during the apartheid years. Those who showed remorse for their actions could appeal for clemency. The South African leaders believed that an airing of the grievances from this period would promote racial harmony and reconciliation.

truth commissions Commissions established to inquire into human rights abuses by previous regimes. In Argentina, El Salvador, Guatemala, and South Africa, these commissions were vital for creating a new aura of legitimacy for democracies and for promising to uphold the rights of individuals.

tsar Russian word derived from the Latin *Caesar* to refer to the Russian ruler of Kiev, and eventually to all rulers in Russia. Also given as czar.

Tula Toltec capital city; a commercial hub and political and ceremonial center.

Uitlanders Literally, "outsiders"; British populations living in Afrikaner republics, who were denied voting rights and subjected to other forms of discrimination in the late nineteenth century.

ulama Arabic word that means "learned ones" or "scholars"; used for those who devoted themselves to knowledge of Islamic sciences.

Umayyads Family who founded the first dynasty in Islam. They established family rule and dynastic succession to the role of caliph. The first Umayyad caliph established Damascus as his capital and was named Mu'awiya ibn Abi Sufyan.

umma Arabic word for "community"; used to refer to the Islamic polity or Islamic community.

Universal Declaration of Human Rights (1948) U.N. declaration that laid out the rights to which all human beings are entitled.

universalizing religions Religions that appeal to diverse populations; are adaptable to new cultures and places; promote universal rules and principles; proselytize new believers, often through missionaries; foster community; and, in some cases, do all of this through the support of an empire.

universitas Term used from the end of the twelfth century to denote scholars who came together, first in Paris. The term is borrowed from the merchant communities, where it denoted the equivalent of the modern union.

untouchables Caste in the Indian system whose jobs, usually in the more unsanitary aspects of urban life, rendered them "ritually and spiritually" impure.

Upanishads First-millennium BCE Vedic wisdom literature, in the form of a dialogue between students and teacher; together with the Vedas, they brought a cultural and spiritual unity to much of South Asia.

urban-rural divide Division between those living in cities and those living in rural areas. One of history's most durable worldwide distinctions, the urban-rural divide eventually encompassed the globe. Where cities arose, communities adopted lifestyles based on the mass production of goods and on specialized labor. Those living in the countryside remained close to nature, cultivating the land or tending livestock. They diversified their labor and exchanged their grains and animal products for necessities available in urban centers.

utopian socialism The most visionary of all Restoration-era movements. Utopian socialists like Charles Fourier dreamed of transforming states, workplaces, and human relations and proposed plans to do so.

Vaishyas Householders or lesser clan members in Vedic society who worked the land and tended livestock.

Vardhamana Mahavira Advocate of Jainism who lived from 540 to 468 BCE; he emphasized interpretation of the Upanishads to govern and guide daily life.

varna Sanskrit for "color"; refers to the four ranked social groups within early Vedic society (priests, warriors, commoners, and laborers). The term *caste*, which derives from the term *casta* ("race/breed" in Spanish and Portuguese) is a later, anachronistic term often used for these divisions.

vassal states Subordinate states that had to pay tribute in luxury goods, raw materials, and manpower as part of a broad confederation of polities under a king's protection.

Vedas Rhymes, hymns, and explanatory texts composed and orally transmitted in Sanskrit by Brahman priests. They shaped the society and religious rituals of Vedic peoples and became central texts in Hinduism.

Vedic people People who came from the steppes of Inner Asia around 1500 BCE and entered the fertile lowlands of the Indus River basin, gradually moving as far south as the Deccan plateau. They called themselves Aryan, which means

"respected ones," and spoke Sanskrit, an Indo-European language.

veiling Practice of modest dress required of respectable women in the Assyrian Empire, introduced by Assyrian authorities in the thirteenth century BCE.

Venus figures Representations of the goddess of fertility drawn on the Chauvet Cave in southeastern France. Discovered in 1994, they are probably about 35,000 years old.

Versailles Conference (1919) Peace conference among the victors of World War I; resulted in the Treaty of Versailles, which forced Germany to pay reparations and to give up its colonies to the victors.

Viet Cong Vietnamese communist group committed to overthrowing the government of South Vietnam and reunifying North and South Vietnam.

Viet Minh (League for the Independence of Vietnam) Group founded in 1941 by Ho Chi Minh to oppose the Japanese occupation of Indochina; it later fought the French colonial forces for independence.

Vietnam War (1965–1975) Conflict that resulted from U.S. concern over the spread of communism in Southeast Asia. The United States intervened on the side of South Vietnam in its struggle against peasant-supported Viet Cong guerrilla forces, who wanted to reunite Vietnam under a communist regime. Faced with antiwar opposition at home and ferocious resistance from the Vietnamese, American troops withdrew in 1973; the puppet South Vietnamese government collapsed two years later.

Vikings Warrior group from Scandinavia that used its fighting skills and sophisticated ships to raid and trade deep into eastern Europe, southward

into the Mediterranean, and westward to Iceland, Greenland, and North America.

Vishnu The second of three Vedic deities, signifying existence. *See also* Brahma *and* Siva.

viziers Bureaucrats of the Ottoman Empire.

vodun Mixed religion of African and Christian customs practiced by slaves and free blacks in the colony of Saint-Domingue.

Voting Rights Act (1965) Law that granted universal suffrage in the United States.

Wafd Nationalist party that came into existence during a rebellion in Egypt in 1919 and held power sporadically after Egypt was granted limited independence from Britain in 1922.

Wahhabism Early eighteenth-century reform movement organized by Muhammad Ibn Abd al-Wahhab, who preached the absolute oneness of Allah and a return to the pure Islam of Muhammad.

Wang Mang Han minister who usurped the throne in 9 CE because he believed that the Han had lost the mandate of heaven. He ruled until 23 CE.

war ethos Strong social commitment to a continuous state of war. The Roman army constantly drafted men and engaged in annual spring military campaigns. Soldiers were taught to embrace a sense of honor that did not allow them to accept defeat, and those who repeatedly threw themselves into battle were commended.

War of 1812 Conflict between Britain and the United States arising from U.S. grievances over oppressive British maritime practices in the Napoleonic Wars.

War on Poverty U.S. president Lyndon Johnson's push for an increased range of social programs and increased spending on social security, health, education, and assistance for the disabled.

Warring States period Period extending from the fifth century to 221 BCE, when China's regional warring states were unified by the Qin dynasty.

Warsaw Pact (1955–1991) Military alliance between the Soviet Union and other communist states that was established in response to the creation of the North American Treaty Organization (NATO).

Weimar Republic (1919–1933) Constitutional republic of Germany that was subverted by Hitler soon after he became chancellor.

Western Front Battlefront that stretched from the English Channel through Belgium and France to the Alps during World War I.

White and Blue Niles The two main branches of the Nile, rising out of central Africa and Ethiopia, respectively. They come together at the present-day capital city of Sudan, Khartoum.

White Lotus Rebellion Series of uprisings in northern China (1790–1800s) inspired by mystical beliefs in folk Buddhism and, at times, the idea of restoring the Ming dynasty.

White Wolf Mysterious militia leader, depicted in popular myth as a Chinese Robin Hood whose mission was to rid the country of the injustices of Yuan Shikai's government in the early years of the Chinese Republic (1910s).

Whites "Counterrevolutionaries" of the Bolshevik Revolution (1918–1921) who fought the Bolsheviks (the Reds); included former supporters of the tsar, Social Democrats, and large independent peasant armies.

witnessing Dying for one's faith, or becoming a martyr.

Wokou Supposedly Japanese pirates, many of whom were actually Chinese subjects of the Ming dynasty.

Works Progress Administration (WPA) New Deal program instituted in 1935 that put nearly 3 million people to work building roads, bridges, airports, and post offices.

World Bank International agency established in 1944 to provide economic assistance to war-torn and poor countries. Its formal title is the International Bank for Reconstruction and Development.

World War I *See* Great War.

World War II (1939–1945) Worldwide war that began in September 1939 in Europe, and even earlier in Asia, and pitted Britain, the United States, and the Soviet Union (the Allies) against Nazi Germany, Japan, and Italy (the Axis).

Wu (r. 140–87 BCE) Also known as Han Wudi, or the "Martial Emperor"; the ruler of the Han dynasty for more than fifty years, during which he expanded the empire through his extensive military campaigns.

Wu Zhao Chinese empress who lived from 626 to 706 CE. She began as a concubine in the court of Li Shimin and became the mother of his son's child. She eventually gained power equal to that of the emperor, and she named herself regent when she finagled a place for one of her own sons after their father's death.

Xiongnu The most powerful and intrusive of the nomadic peoples of Inner Asia; originally pastoralists from the eastern part of the Asian steppe in what is modern-day Mongolia. They appeared along the frontier with China in the late Zhou dynasty and by the third century BCE had become the most powerful of all the pastoral communities in that area.

Xunzi (310–237 BCE) Confucian moralist whose ideas were influential to Qin rulers. He believed that rational statecraft was more reliable than fickle human nature and that strict laws and severe punishments could create stability in society.

Yalta Accords Results of a meeting between President Roosevelt, Prime Minister Churchill, and Premier Stalin held in the Crimea in 1945 to plan for the post–World War II order.

Yavana kings Sanskrit name for Greek rulers, derived from the Greek name for the area of western Asia Minor called Ionia, a term that was then extended to anyone who spoke Greek or came from the Mediterranean.

yellow press Newspapers that sought mass circulation by featuring sensationalist reporting.

Yellow Turbans One of several local Chinese religious movements that emerged across the empire, especially under Wang Mang's officials, who considered him a usurper. The Yellow Turbans, so called because of the yellow scarves they wore around their heads, were Daoist millenarians.

Yin City that became the capital of the Shang dynasty in 1350 BCE, ushering in a golden age.

Young Egypt Antiliberal, fascist group that gained a large following in Egypt during the 1930s.

Young Italy Nationalist organization founded in 1832, made up of young students and intellectuals devoted to the unification and renewal of the Italian state.

Yuan dynasty Dynasty established by the Mongols after the defeat of the Song. The Yuan dynasty was strong from 1280 to 1368; its capital was at Dadu, or modern-day Beijing.

Yuan Mongols Mongol rulers of China who were overthrown by the Ming dynasty in 1368.

Yuezhi A Turkic nomadic people who roamed pastoral lands to the west of the Xiongnu territory of central Mongolia. They had friendly relationships with the farming societies in China, but detested the Xiongnu and had frequent armed clashes with them.

Zaibatsu Large-scale, family-owned corporations in Japan, consisting of factories, import-export businesses, and banks, that dominated the Japanese economy until 1945.

Zamindars Archaic tax system of the Mughal Empire in which decentralized lords collected tribute for the emperor.

Zapatistas Group of indigenous rebels that rose up against the Mexican government in 1994 and drew inspiration from an earlier Mexican rebel, Emiliano Zapata.

Zheng *See* Shi Huangdi.

Zheng He Ming naval commander who, from 1405 to 1433, led seven massive naval expeditions to impress other peoples with Ming might and to establish tributary relations with Southeast Asia, Indian Ocean ports, the Persian Gulf, and the east coast of Africa.

Zhong Shang Administrative central complex of the Shang.

Zhongguo Term originating in the ancient period and subsequently used to emphasize the central cultural and geographic location of China in the world; means "Middle Kingdom."

ziggurat Stepped platform that served as the base of a Sumerian temple, which had evolved from the earlier elevated platform base by the end of the third millennium BCE.

Zionism Political movement advocating the reestablishment of a Jewish homeland in Palestine.

Zoroaster Sometimes known as Zarathustra, thought to have been a teacher around 1000 BCE in eastern Iran and credited with having solidified the region's religious beliefs into a unified system that moved away from animistic nomadic beliefs. The main source for his teachings is a compilation called the Avesta.

Zoroastrianism Dualistic Persian religion, based on the teaching of Zoroaster, in which forces of light and truth battle with those of darkness and falsehood.

Zulus African tribe that, under Shaka, created a ruthless warrior state in southern Africa in the early 1800s.

Credits

Front Matter

Photos p. ii: HIP/Art Resource, NY; p. vii: Erich Lessing/Art Resource; p. viii: The Trustees of the British Museum/Bridgeman Images; p. ix: Scala/Art Resource; p. x: Dagli Orti/Louvre/Bridgeman Images; p. xi (left): Lou-Foto/Alamy Stock Photo; p. xiii (middle): agefotostock Art Collection/age footstock; p. xiii (right): Erich Lessing/Art Resource, NY; p. xii (top): Cleveland Museum of Art, OH, USA/ Dudley; p. Allen Fund/Bridgeman Images; p. xii (bottom): Erich Lessing/Art Resource, NY; p. xiii (right): Dean Conger/ Getty Images; p. xiii (left): Getty Images; p. xiv: Patrick Ward/Getty Images; p. xv: HIP/Art Resource, NY; p. xvii: Snark/Art Resource; p. xvii (top): Fine Art Images/ Heritage Images/Getty Images; p. xvii (bottom): Reunion de Musees Nationaux/ Art Resource; p. xviii: Scala/Art Resource, NY; p. xix: Christophel Fine Art/UIG via Getty Images; p. xx: Pictures from History/ Bridgeman Images; p. xxi: Granger Collection; p. xxii: SuperStock; p. xxiii (top): The Illustrated London News Picture Library/ The Bridgeman Images; p. xxiii (bottom): © Hulton-Deutsch Collection/CORBIS/ Corbis via Getty Images; p. xxiv: AP Photo/Anat Givon; p. xxv: Jeff Swensen/ Getty Images.

Chapter 1

Photos Pages 2–3: Erich Lessing/Art Resource; p. 12: Robert Preston/Alamy; p. 15: John Reader/Science Source; p. 17: Pascal Goetgheluck/Science Source; p. 18: Lionel Bret/Science Source; p. 25: Alamy Stock Photo; p. 27: Erich Lessing/Art Resource; p. 33: Kimbell Art Museum, Fort Worth, Texas/Art Resource, NY; p. 41: De Agostini Picture Library/Getty Images; p. 52 (left): Fine Art Images/Heritage Images/Getty Images; p. 52 (right): Patrick Aventurier/Getty Images; p. 53 (right): Subhendu Sarkar/LightRocket via Getty Images; p. 53 (left): Ronald Wittek/EPA/ REX/Shutterstock; p. 53 (middle): CM Dixon/Print Collector/Getty Images.

Text Primary Source 1.1: "From Rg-Veda 10.90," in *Sources of Indian Tradition 2nd Ed., Vol. 1, From the Beginning to 1800*, edited and revised by Ainslie T. Embree. pp. 18–19. Copyright © 1988 Columbia University Press. Reprinted with permission of the publisher. Primary Source 1.2: Genesis 1:1–31. Scripture quotations are from the New Revised Standard Version Bible, copyright © 1989 National Council of the Churches of Christ in the United States of America. Used by permission. All rights reserved. Primary Source 1.3: "The Creation of the Universe" from the *Huainanzi* in *Sources of Chinese Tradition, 2nd Ed. Vol. 1: From Earliest Times to 1600*, compiled by Wm. Theodore de Bary and Irene Bloom, pp. 346–347. Copyright © 1999 Columbia University Press. Reprinted with permission of the publisher. Primary Source 1.4: Excerpts from *Popol Vuh: The Sacred Book of the Ancient Quiché Maya*, pp. 165–168. English version by Delia Goetz & Sylvanus G. Morley, from the Spanish translation by Adrián Recinos. Copyright © 1950 The University of Oklahoma Press. Reproduced with permission. All rights reserved. Primary Source 1.5: "Yoruba Creation Narrative" as translated by P.J. Criss. Reprinted by permission of the Estate of P.J. Criss.

Chapter 2

Photos Pages 54–55: The Trustees of the British Museum/Bridgeman Images; p. 62: Granger Collection; p. 64: Peter Bull Art Studio; p. 66: Courtesy of Penn Museum, image B16693; p. 68 (top left): Alamy Stock Photo; p. 68 (top right): Erich Lessing/Art Resource, NY; p. 68 (bottom left): Ancient Art and Architecture/Alamy Stock Photo; p. 68 (bottom right): © The Trustees of the British Museum/Art Resource, NY; p. 77 (left): World History Archive/Alamy Stock Photo; p. 77 (right): Heritage Image Partnership Ltd/Alamy Stock Photo; p. 79:

Dinodia Photos/Alamy Stock Photo; p. 82: Richard Ashworth/Robert Harding/Getty Images; p. 86: © Asian Art & Archaeology, Inc./CORBIS/Corbis via Getty Images; p. 87: HIP/Art Resource; p. 91: Image Hans Elbers/Getty Images; p. 98 (top): Forman/Universal Images Group/Getty Images; p. 98 (bottom all): Borromeo/Art Resource, NY; p. 99 (top): Zens photo/ Getty Images; p. 100: DEA/ G. DAGLI ORTI/Getty Images; p. 102 (left): Egyptian National Museum, Cairo, Egypt/ Bridgeman Images; p. 102 (right): HIP/Art Resource; p. 103 (top): Alamy Stock Photo; p. 103 (bottom): Réunion des Musées Nationaux/Art Resource.

Text Primary Source 2.1: Inscription translation for Item #18390 (Tablet from 3rd Dynasty of Ur) from British Museum, Collection Online. Copyright © The Trustees of the British Museum, 2018. Reprinted by permission of the British Museum. Primary Source 2.2: Excerpts from "The Offering Ritual," from *Writings of the Ancient World: The Ancient Egyptian Pyramid Texts* 2nd Ed., translated by James P. Allen. Copyright © 2015 by SBL Press. Reprinted with permission. Primary Source 2.5: Doc. 116 from *Documents in Mycenaean Greek*, 2nd ed. by M. Ventris and J. Chadwick (Cambridge: Cambridge University Press, 1973), p. 245. Reprinted by permission of Cambridge University Press.

Chapter 3

Photos Pages: 104–105: Scala/Art Resource; p. 110 (left): Art Resource, NY; p. 110 (top right): Scala/Art Resource; p. 110 (bottom right): JTB Photo Communications/Alamy; p. 113: John Beasley/Alamy Stock Photo; p. 118 (left): Peter Horree/ Alamy Stock Photo; p. 118 (right): DEA/S. VANNINI/De Agostini/Getty Images; p. 120 (top right): Eric Lessing/Art Resource; p. 122 (left): bpk, Berlin/orderasiatisches Museum, Staatliche Museen, Berlin, Germany/Olaf M. Tessmer/Art Resource, NY;

p. 122 (right): De Agostini Picture Library/ Bridgeman Images; p. 126: ephotocorp/ Alamy Stock Photo; p. 129: Hobart and Edward Small Moore Memorial Collection, Gift of Mrs. William H. Moore. Yale University Art Gallery; p. 133: Lyndon Giffard Images/Alamy Stock Photo; p. 137: Bill Curtsinger/National Geographic/Getty Images; p. 138: Erich Lessing/Art Resource; p. 152 (left): The Granger Collection; p. 153 (left): The Granger Collection; p. 153 (right): © Vanni Archive/ Art Resource, NY.

Text Primary Source 3.3: Exodus 20:1–17 and Leviticus 26:14–26. Scripture quotations are from the New Revised Standard Version Bible, copyright © 1989 National Council of the Churches of Christ in the United States of America. Used by permission. All rights reserved. Primary Source 3.5: Zuo zhuan translated by Earnest Caldwell in "Social Change and Written law in Early Chinese Legal Thought," *Law and History Review* 32(1), p. 15. Reprinted by permission of Cambridge University Press.

Chapter 4

Photos Pages: 154–155: Dagli Orti/Louvre/Bridgeman Images; p. 160 (left): © A. Paul Jenkin/Animals Animals; p. 160 (right): Alexander Frolov/Alamy Stock Photo; p. 162: World History Archive/ Alamy Stock Photo; p. 166: © The Trustees of the British Museum/Art Resource, NY; p. 167: British Museum/Bridgeman Images; p. 171: Lloyd Cluff/Getty Images; p. 172 (top): Erich Lessing/Art Resource, NY; p. 174: Scala/Art Resource, NY; p. 177 (left): © Dagli Orti/Shutterstock; p. 177 (right): © North Wind Picture Archives/ The Image Works; p. 181: Dinodia Photos/ Alamy Stock Photo; p. 182 © The Trustees of the British Museum/Art Resource, NY; p. 185 Giraudon/Art Resource; p. 187: Freer Gallery of Art, Smithsonian Institution, USA/Bridgeman Images; p. 200 (left): Granger Collection; p. 200 (right): Bridgeman Images; p. 201: Image copyright © The Metropolitan Museum of Art. Image source: Art Resource, NY.

Text Primary Source 4.1: "Featured Object Number 8, May 1990, Human-Headed Winged Bull from Khorsabad (OIM A7369)," translated by John A. Brinkman, Oriental Institute Museum, 1990, pp. 3–4, https://oi.uchicago.edu/sites/

oi.uchicago.edu/files/uploads/Lamassu_ A7369_1990_factsheet.pdf. Courtesy of the Oriental Institute of the University of Chicago. Primary Source 4.2: Behistun Inscription, translated by Roland G. Kent in *Old Persian: Grammar, Texts, Lexicon,* 2nd Revised Ed. pp. 131–32. Copyright © 1953 American Oriental Society. Reprinted with permission. Primary Source 4.3: "Zhou Succession Story," from *Early Chinese Literature,* edited by Burton Watson, pp. 35–36. Copyright © 1962 Columbia University Press. Reprinted with permission of the publisher.

Chapter 5

Photos Pages 202–203 (left): Lou-Foto/ Alamy Stock Photo; (middle): agefotostock Art Collection/age footstock; (right): Erich Lessing/Art Resource, NY; p. 211: Pictures from History/Bridgeman Images; p. 213: Erich Lessing/Art Resource, NY; p. 216 (left): Paul Almasy/Corbis/VCG via Getty Images; p. 216 (right): © Corbis/VCG/ Getty; p. 219: Borromeo/Art Resource, NY; p. 222 (top): Robert Harding/Alamy Stock Photo; p. 223 (left): Erich Lessing/ Art Resource, NY; p. 223(right): HIP/Art Resource, NY; p. 225: Scala/Art Resource, NY; p. 229 (left): Peter Langer/Getty Images; p. 229 (right): Jess Kraft/Shutterstock; p. 235: Eric Lafforgue/agefootstock; p. 248 (left): Erich Lessing/Art Resource, NY; p. 248 (right): Musee du Quai Branly et des Arts Premiers, Paris, France/De Agostini Picture Library/G. Dagli Orti/Bridgeman Images; p. 249 (top): Museo Nacional de Antropologia, Mexico City, Mexico/ Photo © Boltin Picture Library/Bridgeman Images; p. 249 (bottom): Bridgeman Images.

Text Primary Source 5.1: Ahunuvaiti Gatha, Yasna 33:1–14 from *The Gathas: The Hymns of Zarathushtra* (1999), translated by D.J. Irani, edited by K.D. Irani. Reprinted by permission of the Estate of K.D. Irani. Primary Source 5.2: Confucius, from *The Analects (Norton Critical Editions),* edited by Michael Nylan, translated by Simon Leys. Copyright © 2014 by W.W. Norton & Company, Inc. *The Analects of Confucius* translation copyright © 1997 by Pierre Ryckmans. Used by permission of W. W. Norton & Company, Inc. Primary Source 5.4: Plato, excerpts from *The Apology of Socrates.* Translated by Cathal Woods and Ryan Pack. Reprinted with permission.

Chapter 6

Photos Pages 250–251: Cleveland Museum of Art, OH, USA/Dudley P. Allen Fund/ Bridgeman Images; p. 256 (top): Erich Lessing/Art Resource, NY; p. 257 (bottom): Lauros/Giraudon/Bridgeman Images; p. 258: Vanni/Art Resource, NY; p. 267: Dea Picture Library/Getty Images; p. 268 (left): Brian A. Vikander/Getty Images; p. 268 (right): Bridgeman Images; p. 270 (bottom): © The Cleveland Museum of Art; p. 272 (left): Image copyright ©The Metropolitan Museum of Art. Image source: Art Resource, NY; p. 272(right): Image copyright © The Metropolitan Museum of Art/Art Resource, NY; p. 276 (top): Heritage Image Partnership Ltd/Alamy Stock Photo; p. 276 (middle): Pjr Studio/Alamy Stock Photo; p. 276 (bottom): Paul Fearn/Alamy Stock Photo; p. 278: DEA/G. Dagli Orti/Getty Images; p. 280: NASA/JPL; p. 294 (top left): Birmingham Museums and Art Gallery/Bridgeman Images; p. 294 (top center left): Birmingham Museums and Art Gallery/Bridgeman Images; p. 294 (middle left): Dilip Rajgor/ Dinodia Photo; p. 294 (bottom right): Lou-Foto/Alamy Stock Photo; p. 295 (bottom left): HIP/Art Resource, NY.

Text Primary Source 6.1: Arrian, from *The Campaigns of Alexander,* translated by Aubrey de Sélincourt, revised with an introduction and notes by J. R. Hamilton (Penguin Classics 1958, Revised edition 1971). Copyright © the Estate of Aubrey de Sélincourt, 1958. Introduction and Notes copyright © J. R. Hamilton, 1971. Reproduced by permission of Penguin Books Ltd. Primary Source 6.2: Aśoka, "The Kalinga Edict," from *Inscriptions of Aśoka,* translated by D.C. Sircar. Reprinted by permission of the Publications Division of the Ministry of Information and Broadcasting of India, 1967. Primary Source 6.4: Excerpts from *The Perfection of Wisdom in Eight Thousand Lines & Its Verse Summary* translated by Edward Conze. Copyright © 1973 by Edward Conze. Reprinted with the permission of The Permissions Company, Inc., on behalf of City Lights Books, www. citylights.com.

Chapter 7

Photos Pages 296–297: Erich Lessing/Art Resource, NY; p. 303: Snark/Art Resource, NY; p. 304 (top): Louis Mazzatenta/

National Geographic Image Collection; p. 304 (bottom): Bridgeman Images; p. 305: British Museum/Art Resource, NY; p. 306: DeAgostini/Getty Images; p. 308 (left): Artokoloro Quint Lox Limited/Alamy Stock Photo; p. 308 (middle): Asian Art & Archaeology, Inc./Getty Images; p. 308 (right): Asian Art & Archaeology, Inc./Getty Images; p. 317: Vanni/Art Resource, NY; p. 319: Atlantide Phototravel/Getty Images; p. 320 (left): Cultura RM/Alamy Stock Photo; p. 320 (right): Scala/Art Resource, NY; p. 321: HIP/Art Resource, NY; p. 329: Erich Lessing/Art Resource, NY; p. 340 (bottom left): Krzysztof Dydynski/Getty Images; p. 340 (top right): Alamy Stock Photo; p. 340 (bottom right): Alamy Stock Photo; p. 341 (left): robertharding/Alamy Stock Photo; p. 341 (right): Getty Images.

Text Primary Source 7.1: Dong Zhongshu, "Responsibilities of Han Rulership" in *Sources of Chinese Tradition, 2nd Ed. Vol. 1: From Earliest Times to 1600*, compiled by Wm. Theodore de Bary and Irene Bloom, pp. 298–300. Copyright © 1999 Columbia University Press. Reprinted with permission of the publisher. Primary Source 7.3: Pan Chao, excerpts from "Lessons for Women," *Pan Chao: Foremost Woman Scholar of China*. Translated by Nancy Lee Swann. Reprinted by permission of the East Asian Library and Gest Collection at Princeton University. Primary Source 7.4: Musonius Rufus, in Mary R. Lefkowitz & Maureen B. Fant, eds. *Women's Life in Greece and Rome: A Source Book in Translation*. Second Edition. pp. 50–54. © 1982, 1992 Mary F. Lefkowitz and Maureen B. Fant. Reprinted with permission of Johns Hopkins University Press.

Chapter 8

Photos Pages 342–343 (bottom right): Dean Conger/Getty Images; p. 342 (left): Getty Images; p. 349: Granger Collection; p. 351: Scala/Art Resource, NY; p. 355: Getty Images; p. 360 (left): Art Resource; p. 360 (right): Getty Images; p. 362: akg-images/Werner Forman; p. 368: Zhang Peng/LightRocket via Getty Images; p. 369: Réunion des Musées Nationaux/Art Resource, NY; p. 373: EDU Vision/Alamy Stock Photo; p. 376: Angelo Hornak/Getty Images; p. 377: Werner Forman/Art Resource, NY; p. 390 (left): Getty Images; p. 390 (right): Art Resource, NY; p. 391 (top): Art Resource, NY; p. 391 (bottom): Art Resource NY.

Text Primary Source 8.2: Excerpts from *Egeria: Diary of a Pilgrimage*, translated and annotated by George E. Gingras, Copyright © 1970 by Rev. Johannes Quasten and Rev. Walter J. Burghardt, S.J. and Thomas Comerford Lawler. Paulist Press, Inc., New York/Mahwah, NJ. Reprinted by permission of Paulist Press, Inc. www.paulistpress.com. Primary Source 8.5: From *Srimad Bhagavatam: Third Canto*, translated by A.C. Bhaktivedanta Swami Prabhupāda (Bhaktivedanta Book Trust, 1974), p. 16. Quoted text courtesy of The Bhaktivedanta Book Trust International, Inc. www.Krishna.com.

Chapter 9

Photos Pages 392–393: Patrick Ward/Getty Images; p. 396: Abid Katib/Getty Images; p. 407 (left): Ian Murray/age footstock; p. 407 (right): Patrick Ward/Getty Images; p. 411 (left): Michel Piccaya/Shutterstock; p. 411 (right): B.O'Kane/Alamy Stock Photo; p. 416 (left): Werner Forman/Art Resource, NY; p. 416 (right): Kurt Scholz/SuperStock; p. 418: Julia Waterlow/Eye Ubiquitous/Getty Images; p. 422 (left): CulturalEyes-AusGS/Alamy; p. 422 (right): Paul Fearn/Alamy Stock Photo; p. 425: Giraudon/Bridgeman Images; p. 427 (left): Alamy Stock Photo; p. 427 (right): Alamy Stock Photo; p. 429: Werner Forman/Art Resource; p. 430: Alamy Stock Photo; p. 440 (left): Leemage/Corbis via Getty Images; p. 440 (right): © The British Library Board, Cotton Nero D IV f259; p. 441 (from top down): © The British Library Board, OR.8210/P.2; p. 441: Bridgeman-Giraudon/Art Resource, NY; p. 441 (center): V&A Images, London/Art Resource, NY; p. 441 (bottom left): San Diego Museum of Art, USA/Edwin Binney 3rd Collection/Bridgeman Image; p. 441 (top right): Getty Images Editorial.

Text Primary Source 9.1: "Sura 4" translated by Marmaduke Pickthall in *Qur'an: A Norton Critical Edition*, edited by Jane Dammen McAuliffe. Copyright © 2014 by W.W. Norton & Company, Inc. Used by permission of W.W. Norton & Company, Inc. Primary Source 9.3: "The Book of Analects for Women: Consort Song," translated by Heying Jenny Zhan and Robert Bradshaw in *Journal of Historical Sociology* 9(3), pp. 261–269. Copyright © 1996 Blackwell Publishers Ltd. Reprinted by permission of John Wiley & Sons, Inc.

Chapter 10

Photos Pages 442–443: HIP/Art Resource, NY; p. 446: Granger Collection; p. 447: Nik Wheeler/Getty Images; p. 449: Alamy Stock Photo; p. 455: De Agostini Picture Library/Getty Images; p. 460: Granger Collection, NY; p. 461 (bottom): Hemis/Alamy Stock Photo; p. 466: British Library, London, UK/© British Library Board. All Rights Reserved/Bridgeman Images; p. 470: HIP/Art Resource, NY; p. 473 (top): Thomas Cockrem/Alamy Stock Photo; p. 475 (bottom): INTERFOTO/Alamy Stock Photo; p. 482: akg-images; p. 494: Giraudo/Art Resource, NY; p. 495 (bottom): Pictorial Press Ltd/Alamy Stock Photo; p. 495 (top): Art Resource, NY.

Text Primary Source 10.1: Rabban Bar Sāwmā, from *The Monks of Kublai Khan, Emperor of China: Medieval Travels from China through Central Asia to Persia and Beyond*, translated by Sir E.A. Wallis Budge. Originally published by Harrison & Sons, Ltd. in 1928 for the Religious Tract Society. Reprinted by permission of Lutterworth Press. Primary Source 10.3: From *Ibn Battuta: Travels in Asia & Africa, 1325–1354* translated by H. A. R. Gibb, pp. 55–57. Copyright © 1929 George Routledge & Sons. Reprinted by permission of Taylor & Francis Books (UK). Primary Source 10.4: Al-'Umarī, from *Corpus of Early Arabic Sources for West African History*, translated by J.F.P. Hopkins, edited and annotated by N. Levtzion and J.F.P. Hopkins (Cambridge: Cambridge University Press, 1981). © University of Ghana, International Academic Union, Cambridge University Press 1991. Reprinted with the permission of Cambridge University Press.

Chapter 11

Photos Photos 496–497: Snark/Art Resource; p. 500: The Granger Collection, New York; p. 504: Emo Bardazzi/Electa/Mondadori Portfolio via Getty Images; p. 508: Album/Art Resource; p. 509: Muhammed Enes Yldrm/Anadolu Agency/Getty Images; p. 510: Stapleton

Collection, UK/Bridgeman Art Library; p. 517: The Granger Collection; p. 519 (left): Scala/Art Resource; p. 519 (right): Scala/Art Resource; p. 522: Réunion des Musées Nationaux/Art Resource, NY; p. 523 (China): Detail from the painting 'Beauties in History', attributed to the Ming Dynasty artist Qiu Ying (c. 1492–1552)/Pictures from History/Bridgeman Images; p. 524: The Granger Collection, New York; p. 525: © RMN-Grand Palais/Art Resource, NY; p. 528 (left): The Picture Art Collection/Alamy Stock Photo; p. 528 (right): A. HARLIN/National Geographic Creative; p. 542 (right): Opkapi Palace Museum, Istanbul, Turkey/Bridgeman Images; p. 542 (left): Bridgeman Images; p. 543: The Granger Collection, New York.

Text Primary Source 11.1: Michael Dols, "Ibn al-Wardi's Risalah al-Naba' 'an al-Waba', a Translation of a Major Source for the History of the Black Death in the Middle East" in *Near Eastern Numismatics, Iconography, Epigraphy and History: Studies in Honor of George C. Miles*, ed. Dickran K. Kouymjian (Beirut: American University of Beirut, 1974), 447–454. Reprinted by permission of the American University of Beirut Press. Primary Source 11.2: Marchione di Coppo Stefani, Cronaca Fiorentina, edited by Niccolo Rodolico, Vol. 30 of Rerum Italicarum Scriptores (Citta di Castello: S. Lapi, 1903–1913), as translated by Duane Osheim at http://www2.iath.virginia.edu/osheim/marchione.html. Reprinted by permission of Duane Osheim. Primary Source 11.3: Ibn Khaldûn, excerpts from *The Muqaddimah: An Introduction to History Vol. 1*, translated by Franz Rosenthal (New York: Pantheon Books, 1958). © 1958 by Bollingen Foundation, Inc. Reprinted by permission of Princeton University Press. Primary Source 11.4: al-Maqrizi, "The Guide to the Knowledge of Dynasties and Kings," translated by Hamid Irbouh and excerpted in *The Middle East and Islamic World Reader*, copyright © 2003, Revised edition copyright © 2012 by Marvin Gettleman and Stuart Schaar. Used by permission of Grove/Atlantic, Inc. Any third party use of this material, outside of this publication, is prohibited.

Chapter 12

Photos Pages 544–545: Fine Art Images/Heritage Images/Getty Images; p. 548:
Reunion des Musees; Nationaux/Art Resource, NY; p. 549: akg-images/Cameraphoto; p. 554: Christophel Fine Art/UIG via Getty Images; p. 555: Bildarchiv Preussischer Kulturbesitz/Art Resource, NY; p. 558 (left): The Granger Collection, New York; p. 559: The Granger Collection, New York; p. 559 (right): HIP/Art Resource, NY; p. 565 (top): Francois Guenet/Art Resource; p. 567 (bottom): The Granger Collection; p. 578: Bridgeman Images; p. 588 (left): Scala/Art Resource, NY; p. 588 (right): The Granger Collection; p. 589: Reunion des Musees Nationaux/ Art Resource.

Text Primary Source 12.1: Book Twelve of the Florentine Codex, translated by James Lockhart in *We People Here: Nahuatl accounts of the conquest of Mexico* (Berkeley: University of California Press, 1993), pp. 56–86. Reprinted by permission of the University of California Press. Primary Source 12.4: T'ien-Tsê Chang, from *Sino-Portuguese Trade From 1514 to 1644: A Synthesis of Portuguese and Chinese Sources* (Leyden: E.J. Brill, 1934), pp. 51–52. Reprinted by permission of Brill Academic Publishers.

Chapter 13

Photos Pages 590–591: Reunion de Musees Nationaux/Art Resource; p. 595 right: British Museum, London/E.T. Archives, London/SuperStock; p. 595 left: Chester Beatty Library and Gallery of Oriental Art, Dublin/Bridgeman Images; p. 598: Rijksmuseum, Amsterdam, The Netherlands/Bridgeman Images; p. 602: MPI/Getty Images; p. 605: MPI/Getty Images; p. 608 (left): North Wind Picture Archives; p. 608 (right): Private Collection/Bridgeman Images; p. 609: Sarin Images / GRANGER , All rights reserved; p. 613: DEA/G. DAGLI ORTI/Getty Images; p. 622: Gianni Dagli Orti/Shutterstock; p. 627: Musee Bargoin, Clermont-Ferrand, France/Bridgeman Images; p. 630: Chateau de Versailles, France/Bridgeman Images; p. 642 (left): Image copyright © The Metropolitan Museum of Art. Image source: Art Resource, NY; p. 642 (right): Bridgeman Images; p. 643 (top): Museum of Fine Arts, Boston, Massachusetts, USA/William Sturgis Bigelow Collection/Bridgeman Images; p. 643 (bottom): Image Copyright © Metropolitan Museum of Art Image source: Art Resource, NY.

Text Primary Source 13.1: Olaudah Equiano, from *Interesting Narrative of the Life of Olaudiah Equiano, or Gustavus Vassa, The African, Written by Himself: A Norton Critical Edition*, edited by Werner Sollors. Copyright © 2001 by W. W. Norton & Company, Inc. Used by permission of W. W. Norton & Company, Inc. Primary Source 13.4: Katherine Holt, "Population by Racial Classification, Santiago de Iguape 1835," "Free and Freed Population by Racial Classification, Iguape 1835," and "Enslaved Population by Place of Birth, Santiago do Iguape, 1835." From The Bahian History Project, www.mappingbahia.org. Reproduced with permission from Katherine Holt.

Chapter 14

Photos Pages 644–645: Scala/Art Resource, NY; p. 649 (left): ART Collection/Alamy Stock Photo; p. 649 (right): Victoria & Albert Museum, London/Art Resource, NY; p. 651: Dea Picture Library/Getty Images; p. 655 (left): George Rinhart/Corbis via Getty Images; p. 655 (right): Underwood & Underwood/Library of Congress/Corbis/VCG via Getty Images; p. 656: Werner Forman/Art Resource, NY; p. 658: British Library, London, UK © British Library Board. All Rights Reserved/Bridgeman Images; p. 661: Image copyright © The Metropolitan Museum of Art/Art Resource, NY; p. 667 (top): Private Collection/Bridgeman Images; p. 667 (bottom): Private Collection/Bridgeman Images; p. 670: Alamy Stock Photo; p. 673 (left): Album/Art Resource, NY; p. 673 (right): Museo de America, Madrid/The Bridgeman Images; p. 677 (left): HIP/Art Resource, NY; p. 677 (right): The Granger Collection, New York; p. 690 (bottom left): Art Collection 3/Alamy Stock Photo; p. 690 (top right): Fine Art Images/Heritage Images/Getty Images; p. 690 (top left): Library of Congress, Geography and Map Division; p. 690 (bottom right): Private Collection/Photo © Christie's Images/Bridgeman Images; p. 691 (bottom right): Library of Congress, Geography and Map Division; p. 691 (bottom left): Art Collection 4/Alamy Stock Photo; p. 691 (top): Private Collection/Bridgeman Images.

Text Primary Source 14.1: Excerpts from *Montesquieu: The Spirit of the Laws*, Cambridge Texts in the History of Political Thought, translated and edited by Anne

M. Cohler, Basia Carolyn Miller and Harold Samuel Stone (Cambridge: Cambridge University Press, 1989), pp. 338–339. Reprinted by permission of Cambridge University Press. Primary Source 14.3: Jean-Jacques Rousseau, from *Rousseau's Political Writings: A Norton Critical Edition*, edited by Alan Ritter and Julia Conaway Bondanella, translated by Julia Conaway Bondanella. Copyright © 1988 by W.W. Norton & Company, Inc. Used by permission of W.W. Norton & Company, Inc. Primary Source 14.4: "The Testament of Shimai Soshitsu," from *Sources of Japanese Tradition, 2nd. Ed. Vol. 2: 1600 to 2000*, compiled by Wm. Theodore de Bary, Carol Gluck, and Arthur E. Tiedemann, pp. 310–313. Copyright © 2005 Columbia University Press. Reprinted with permission of the publisher. Primary Source 14.5: Excerpts from "Two Edicts from the Ch'ien-Lung Emperor to King George III of England," in J. Mason Gentzler (ed.), *Changing China: readings in the history of China from the Opium War to the present*. Copyright © 1977 Praeger Publishers. Reprinted by permission of Cengage Learning.

Chapter 15

Photos Pages 692–693: Christophel Fine Art/UIG via Getty Images; p. 699: Library of Congress; p. 702: Hulton Archive/Getty Images; p. 706: The Granger Collection, New York; p. 709: The Granger Collection, New York; p. 713: The Granger Collection, New York; p. 715: The Granger Collection, New York; p. 723: National Army Museum, London/Bridgeman Images; p. 725 (left): British Library, London, UK © British Library Board. All Rights Reserved/Bridgeman Images; p. 725 (right): De Agostini/Biblioteca Ambrosiana/Getty Images; p. 736 (left): Louvre, Paris, France/Giraudon/Bridgeman Images; p. 736 (right): Fine Art Images/Heritage Images/Getty Images; p. 737 (left): Musee Girodet, Montargis, France/Peter Willi/Bridgeman Images; p. 737 (right): © The Metropolitan Museum of Art/Art Resource, NY.

Text Primary Source 15.2: Abd al-Rahman al-Jabarti, *Al-Jabarti's Chronicle of the first seven months of the French occupation of Egypt*, translated by S. Moreh (Leiden, E.J. Brill, 1975), 39–40, 42–43, 46–47 © 1975 E.J. Brill, Leiden, Netherlands. Reprinted by permission of the publisher.

Chapter 16

Photos Pages 738–739: Pictures from History/Bridgeman Images; p. 745: Paul Fearn/Alamy Stock; Photo; p. 748 (left): British Library Board. All Rights Reserved/Bridgeman Images; p. 748 (right): Universal History Archive/UIG/Bridgeman Images; p. 751: The Granger Collection, New York; p. 757: The Granger Collection, New York; p. 763 (left): The Granger Collection, New York; p. 763 (right): Granger Collection; p. 766: Witold Skrypczak/Alamy Stock Photo; p. 769: Felice Beato/Universal History Archive/UIG via Getty Images; p. 785 (left): World History Archive/Alamy Stock Photo; p. 785 (right): Courtesy of Heidelberg Centre for Transcultural Studies, University Heidelberg; p. 785 (bottom): Art Collection 2/Alamy Stock Photo.

Text Primary Source 16.2: Nana Asma'u, "Gikku Bello" from Beverly Mack & Jean Boyd (eds.), *One Woman's Jihad: Nana Asma'u, Scholar and Scribe*. Copyright © 2000 by Beverly B. Mack and Jean Boyd. Reprinted with permission of Indiana University Press. Primary Source 16.4: From "The Principles of the Heavenly Nature," in *Sources of Chinese Tradition, 2nd Ed., Vol. 2: From 1600 through the Twentieth Century*, compiled by Wm. Theodore de Bary and Richard Lufrano, pp. 226–30. Copyright © 2000 Columbia University Press. Reprinted with permission of the publisher. Primary Source 16.5: Karl Marx and Friedrich Engels, from "Bourgeoisie and Proletariat," in *The Marx-Engels Reader*, 2nd ed. (New York: W.W. Norton & Company, 1972), pp. 335–345. Edited by Robert C. Tucker.

Chapter 17

Photos Pages 786–787: Granger Collection; p. 795: Time & Life Pictures/Getty Images; p. 800: Bridgeman Images; p. 804 (left): Illustrated London News/ Mary Evans Picture Library; p. 804 (right): Military History Collection/Alamy Stock Photo; p. 808 (left): Hulton Archive/Getty Images; p. 808 (right): Private Collection/Bridgeman Images; p. 810: Roger-Viollet, Paris/The Bridgeman Art Library; p. 812: Shutterstock; p. 813: Erich Lessing/Art Resource, NY; p. 814: Shutterstock; p. 832 (left): Kawanabe Kyosai, 'School for Spooks' (Bake-bake gakko), no.3 from the series 'Drawings for Pleasure by Kyosai' (Kyosai rakuga), Kawanabe Kyosai Memorial Museum; p. 832 (right): Granger Collection, All rights reserved; p. 833 (right): Library of Congress.

Chapter 18

Photos Pages 834–835: SuperStock; p. 840 (left): Hulton Archive/Getty Images; p. 843: ullstein bild/Granger Collection; p. 846: SuperStock; p. 855 (left): © National Gallery, London/Art Resource, NY; p. 856 (left): Erich Lessing/Art Resource, NY; p. 856 (right): Scala/Art Resource, NY; p. 860: PhotoQuest/Getty Images; p. 863: Private Collection/Photo © Christie's Images/Bridgeman Images; p. 864: Schalkwijk/Art Resource, NY. © 2018 Banco de Mexico Diego Rivera Frida Kahlo Museums Trust, Mexico, D.F./Artists Rights Society (ARS), New York p. 867: Gianni Dagli Orti/Shutterstock; p. 880 (left): © Estate of Pablo Picasso/Artists Rights Society (ARS), New York. Digital Image © The Museum of Modern Art/Licensed by Scala/Art Resource, NY; p. 880 (right): Paul Fearn/Alamy Stock Photo; p. 881: Art Collection 2/Alamy Stock Photo.

Text Primary Source 18.2: Maria Eugenia Echenique: "The Emancipation of Women." Translated by Francisco Manzo Robledo in Paul Brians, et. al. *Reading About the World, Vol. 2*. (1999). Reprinted by permission of Francisco Manzo Robledo. Primary Source 18.3: Qui Jin, "An Address to Two Hundred Million Fellow Countrywomen." Reprinted with the permission of Simon & Schuster Publishing Group, a division of Simon & Schuster, Inc. from the Free Press edition of *Chinese Civilization: A Sourcebook*, 2nd Edition by Patricia Buckley Ebrey. Copyright © 1993 by Patricia Buckley Ebrey. Copyright © 1981 by The Free Press. All rights reserved. Primary Source 18.4: Bahithat al-Badiya "A Lecture in the Club of the Umma Party (1909)" from Margot Badran and Miriam Cooke (eds.), *Opening the Gates: An Anthology of Arab Feminist Writing*, 2nd edition. Copyright © 2004 by Margot Badran and Miriam Cooke. Reprinted with permission of Indiana University Press.

Chapter 19

Photos Pages 882–883: The Illustrated London News Picture Library/The Bridgeman Images; p. 887: adoc-photos/Corbis via Getty Images; p. 892: Hulton Archive/

Getty Images; p. 893 (left): Alamy Stock Photo; p. 897: © SF Palm/Stageimage/The Image Works; p. 898: The Granger Collection, New York/The Granger Collection; p. 902: Marion Post Wolcott/Library of Congress; p. 904: The Granger Collection, New York/The Granger Collection; p. 911: Genevieve Naylor/Getty Images; p. 913: The Granger Collection, New York/The Granger Collection; p. 915 (left): The Illustrated London News Picture Library/Mary Evans Picture Library; p. 915 (right): Private Collection/Bridgeman Images; p. 930: Getty Images; p. 931 (top): Detroit Institute of Arts, USA/Gift of Edsel B. Ford/Bridgeman Images. © 2018 Banco de Mexico Diego Rivera Frida Kahlo Museums Trust, Mexico, D.F. / Artists Rights Society (ARS), New York; p. 931 (bottom left): Granger Collection; p. 931 (bottom right): © Everett Collection Inc./Alamy.

Text Primary Source 19.1: Hannah Arendt, excerpt from *The Origins of Totalitarianism*. Copyright © 1973, 1968, 1966, 1958, 1951, 1948 by Hannah Arendt and renewed 2001, 1996, 1994, 1986 by Lotte Kohler, Copyright renewed 1979 by Mary McCarthy West, Copyright renewed 1976 by Hannah Arendt. Reprinted by permission of Houghton Mifflin Harcourt Publishing Company. All rights reserved. And by permission of Penguin Books Ltd. Primary Source 19.2: Letter from Anna Kovaleva to Marfa Gudzia in Stephen Kotkin, *Magnetic Mountain: Stalinism as a Civilization* (Berkeley: University of California Press, 1995), pp. 218–219. Reprinted by permission of the University of California Press. Primary Source 19.3: Victor Klemperer. "1938" from *I Will Bear Witness, Volume 1: A Diary of the Nazi Years: 1933–1941*, translated by Martin Chalmers, translation copyright © 1998 by Martin Chalmers. Used by permission of Random House, an imprint and division of Penguin Random House LLC. All rights reserved. And by permission of The Orion Publishing Group. Primary Source 19.4: Excerpt from *Japan in War and Peace* - Copyright © 1993 by John W. Dower. Reprinted by permission of The New Press. www.thenewpress.com and by permission of Georges Borchardt Inc. for the author.

Chapter 20

Photos Pages 932–933: © Hulton-Deutsch Collection/CORBIS/Corbis via Getty Images; p. 937 (right): Laski Diffusion/ Getty Images; p. 941 (left): Photo Researchers/Getty Images; p. 942: Walter Sanders/The LIFE Picture Collection/ Getty Images; p. 946: Bettmann/Getty Images p. 956 (left): AP Photo; p. 958: STRINGER/AFP/Getty Images; p. 961 (left): Roger-Viollet/The Image Works; p. 963: Rolls Press/Popperfoto/Getty Images; p. 966: Hulton-Deutsch Collection/CORBIS/Corbis via Getty Images; p. 982 (left): Art Resource Image Reference; p. 982 (top right): DEA/G. COSTA/Getty Images; p. 982 (top left): George Rodger/ Magnum Photos; p. 983: Pictures from History/Granger, NYC.

Text Primary Source 20.1: Mao Zedong, *Selected Works*, in *in Sources of Chinese Tradition, 2nd Ed., Vol. 2: From 1600 through the Twentieth Century*, compiled by Wm. Theodore de Bary and Richard Lufrano, pp. 418–23. Copyright © 2000 Columbia University Press. Reprinted with permission of the publisher. Primary Source 20.2: Jawaharlal Nehru, "A Note to the Members of the National Planning Committee," May 1, 1940, in *Jawaharlal Nehru: An Anthology*, edited by Sarvepalli Gopal (Delhi: Oxford University Press, 1980), pp. 306–7. Reprinted by permission of the Jawaharlal Nehru Memorial Fund. Primary Source 20.3: Léopold Sédar Senghor, "What is Negritude?" *Negro Digest* (April 1962), 3–6. Primary Source 20.4: Frantz Fanon, "On Violence." From *The Wretched of the Earth*. English translation copyright © 1963 by Présence Africaine. Used by permission of Grove/Atlantic, Inc. Any third party use of this material, outside of this publication, is prohibited.

Chapter 21

Photos Pages 984–985: AP Photo/Anat Givon; p. 988: Hulton Archive/Getty Images; p. 992 (left): Peter Magubane/Time Life Pictures/Getty Images; p. 998: Frédéric Soltan/Corbis via Getty Images; p. 1003: Mary Evans/Eros International/Ronald Grant/Everett Collection; p. 1004: Mike Prior/Redferns/Getty Images; p. 1009: Vanessa Vick/Redux; p. 1013: Morley Read/ Alamy Stock Photo; p. 1016: Peter Turnley/ Getty Images; p. 1019: Jeff Widener/AP/ Wide World Photos; p. 1020 (left): Clive Shirley/Panos Pictures; p. 1032 (top left): Getty Images; p. 1032 (top right): REUTERS/Bobby Yip; p. 1032 (bottom right): Jim Thompson/Albuquerque Journal/ ZUMA Wire/Alamy Live News; p. 1032 (bottom left): Getty Images; p. 1033: Farshid M. Bina/picture-alliance/dpa/AP Images.

Text Primary Source 21.1: Václev Havel, "The Power of the Powerless, in *The Power of the Powerless: Citizens Against the State in Central-eastern Europe* (M.E. Sharpe, 1985), edited by John Keane. © 1985 Taylor & Francis. Reprinted by permission of Taylor and Francis Books UK. Primary Source 21.3: The World Bank, From "Using subsidies to close gender gaps in education," World Bank. 2001. *World Development Report 2000–2001: Attacking Poverty*, p. 122, Box 7.2. © World Bank. https://openknowledge.worldbank.org/handle/10986/11856 License: Creative Commons Attribution license (CC BY 3.0). Primary Source 21.4: Amartya Kumar Sen, "Democracy as a Universal Value." *Journal of Democracy* 10:3 (1999), 6–9. © 1999 National Endowment for Democracy and the Johns Hopkins University Press. Reprinted with permission of Johns Hopkins University Press.

Epilogue

Photos Pages 1034–1035: Jeff Swensen/ Getty Images; p. 1035 (right): AP Photo/ Carmen Taylor; p. 1040: AP Photo/Jason DeCrow; p. 1044 (left): Kyle Niemi/U.S. Coast Guard via Getty Images; p. 1044 (right): AP Photo/Rich Schultz; p. 1051: AP Photo/Andres Kudacki; p. 1052: Dean Conger/Getty Images; p. 1053: Timothy O'Rourke/Bloomberg via Getty Images; p. 1054: Sebastian D'Souza/AFP/Getty Images; p. 1055: AP Photo/Pete Muller; p. 1057: Khaled Akasha/Anadolu Agency/ Getty Images; p. 1058: Handout/Alamy Stock Photo; p. 1069 (top: top): AP/ Wide World Photos; p. 1069 (bottom): Kayhan Ozer/Anadolu Agency/Getty Images; p. 1070: Mike Blake/Reuters; p. 1071: Jeff Swensen/Getty Images.

Line Art p. 1043: Figure 1 from "Catching up with the Economy," *American Economic Review* 89(1): 1–12. Copyright American Economic Association; reproduced with permission of the American Economic Review.

Back Matter

Photos Map of the world: National Geographic.

Index

Italic page references indicate maps, illustrations, or chronology entries.

Atlantic world (*continued*)
    and economy, 628, 714
    and mercantilism, 631
    and new colonies in Americas, 605
    revolutions of national independence in, *696–97*
    and slave trade, 608, 637–41, 711
    transformations in, 693–94, 695–98
atma (eternal self), 361, *362*
atman (universal being), 183
atoma (atoms), 225
atomic warfare, 940–41, *941*, 943–46, *946*, 955, 960
Attila, 353
Augustine of Hippo, 425–26
Augustus ("the Revered One"), 318
Augustus, emperor of Rome, 318–19, *331, 340*, 340–41, *341*
Aurangzeb (Mughal ruler), 573, *634*
Auschwitz-Birkenau concentration camp, 938
Australia, 675, *677*, 677–78, 850, 889, 1009
australopithecines, 7–15, *13*
Australopithecus afarensis, 7, *10, 11*, 12, 14, *18*
Australopithecus africanus, 7, *11*, 12, *17, 44*
Australopithecus anamensis, 10, 11
Austria
    between 1750–1850, 702, 704
    between 1850–1914, 799, 860, 866, 868
    and alternative visions of nineteenth century, 754, 758
    anti-immigrant sentiments, 1050
    and consolidation of nation-states in Europe, 799
    and culture between 1600–1780, 666
    and Napoleonic Empire, 704
    and pan movements, 866, 868
    and race, 860
    and religious wars, 627
    see also Austro-Hungarian Empire
Austro-Hungarian Empire, 799, 892, *894*
Austronesia, settlement of, 132–33
Austronesians, as colonizers, *133*
Austronesians, migration of, 132–34, *133, 134*

authorianism, 1068–71
authoritarianism, 885, 896, 898, 900, 903–10, 969, 1024
    see also dictatorships
authority
    between 1600–1750, 614–15, 617, 620
    between 1750–1850, 723–24
    between 1850–1914, 811, 837, 841, 843
    between 1910–1939, 900
    in Aztec society, 557–58
    and culture in Americas between 1600–1780, 671
    and Enlightenment, 664, 665
    and Europe, 623
    in Han vs. Roman empires, 340–41
    and imperialism, 811, 841
    see also specific nations and empires
automobiles, 885, 899
Avebury, 89
Avercamp, Hendrick, *598*
Averroës (Ibn Rushd), 452
Avicenna, 406–7
Awadh kingdom (India), 767
Axial Age, 204–5, 220, 226–27, 248–49
    Greek city-states of, 366
    modern critiques of, 226–27
    philosphers of, 366
    scholarly perspectives on, 226–27
    updated definition of, 226–27
Axis Powers, 935, 937, 982
Azamgarh Proclamation, 774, 777–79
Azores, 515
Aztecs, 373, 557–58, 563, *566, 567, 580*, 588, *588*, 690, 762, 852, 861, *864*
    agriculture of, 557
    religious beliefs of, 558
    see also Mexica society

Babur ("Tiger") (Mughal ruler), 573
baby boomer generation, 1045
Babylon, Babylonia, 119–20, *141*, 261
    Hittite sacking of, 123
    ideas borrowed from, 168
Babylonian Talmud, 357
Bacon, Sir Francis, 663
Bactria, Bactrians, 269–70, 326
Bactrian camel, 160–61

Baghdad, Iraq, 443, 449–50, 452, 501, 506
    as Abbasid capital, 393, 400, 405–6, *406*, 411, 425
    as crossroads of civilizations, 393
    libraries and learning centers in, 405–6
    Mongol sacking of, 479, *485*, 506
Bahamas, 555
Bake-Bake Gakkō (Kyosai), 832, *832*
Baker, Josephine, *897*
balance of power
    between 1600–1750, 593
    between 1750–1850, 695, 724
    between 1850–1914, *798*, 847
    between 1910–1939, 899
    and consolidation of nation-states in Europe, *798*
    and globalization, 1013
    and production and consumption, 899
    and Qing dynasty, 724
    and three-world order, 935
    and worldwide insecurities, 847
Balfour, Arthur James, 895
Balfour Declaration (1917), 951
Bali, 273, 460
Balkans
    between 1850–1914, 868
    and globalization, 1015
    and Islamic revivalist movements, 744
    and Ottoman Empire, 508
    and pan movements, 868
    violence in, 1015
Balkh (Bactra), 405
ball courts, Mayan, 377
ballplayers, Olmec, 231
Baltic Sea, 548, 623, 626
Baluchistan Mountains, 79
"Bamboo Annals," 127
Bamiyan, 358, *360*
bananas, in sub-Saharan Africa, 372
Banda Islands, 611
banking, 647–49, 802, 815, 900, 993
    see also money, monetary system
Bank of America, 1039
Bank of England, 848
ban liang, 294, *295*
Bantu people, 236, 344, 370–73, *371*, 379, *380–81*, 407, 747
baptism, Egyptian-Greek, 260
Barbados, 636, 637–38

of Ottoman Empire, 508–9, 510–11, 512, 523–24, 543
of Persian Empire, 168–69, 170
in Russia, 624
in Soviet Union, 819, 903
in territorial states, 112, 118
see also administration; *specific nations and empires*
burials, ancient, 102, *102–3,* 152
Burma (Myanmar), 620, 803, 840, 940
Burundi, 1062
Bush, George W.
and economic crisis, 1038
and war on terror, 1036
Buyid family, 449–50
Byblos, 116
Byzantine Empire, Byzantium, 354–55, 357, 378, *380–81,* 423, 450, 465, 479, 482, 530
and Arabia, *432*
and Islam, 397, 401, *402–3,* 405
and Ottoman Empire, 508–10
Turks and, 450

Cabral, Pedro Alvares, 556
Caffa, 497
Cahokia, 473–75, *474,* 484
Cairo, Egypt, *411, 448,* 449, 452, 840, 1005, *1055,* 1056
as maritime commercial center, 445–46
as Umayyad capitol, 411
Calcutta, India, 578, 1005
calendars
Chinese, 187
lunar, 129
Mayan, 377
Olmec, 231
Calicut (Malabar coast), 551
California, 1012–13
caliphs, caliphates, 397, 400–401, 404–5, 405–6, *406, 407,* 409–11, 450
Umayyad, 397
Uthman, 398
Calvin, Jean, 570
Cambodia, 460, 965
camels, *160,* 160–61, 162, 201, 278, 281, 358, 452
Cameroon, 843
Canada
between 1750–1850, 698
between 1850–1914, 793, *822*
between 1910–1939, 889

and American Revolution, 698
and culture between 1600–1780, 673
and expansion and nation-building, *791,* 793
and French claims in Americas, 601
and globalization, 995–98, 1009, 1012–13
and oil, 967–68
World War I and, 889
canals
in China, 185–86, 201, 304, 416–17
Persian, 171
rice cultivation and, 417
Canary Islands, 555
Canon of Medicine, 407
Canton, China, 527, 620, *622,* 725, 749
Cape of Good Hope, 551
Cape Verde Islands, 516, 564
capital
between 1850–1914, 789, 792, 802, 815
and expansion and nation-building, 789, 792
and industry, science, and technology, 802
and Japanese transformation and expansion, 815
capitalism, 1038–39
between 1850–1914, 647–49, 802, 815, 837, 851–53, 865
between 1910–1939, 885, 898–900, 903, 904, 911
and alternative visions of nineteenth century, 740, 756, 758, 774–83
and decolonization, 949, 972
and Great Depression, 901–3
and industry, science, and technology, 802
laissez-faire, 740, 847
liberal, 901–3
and mass politics, 901–3, 911
and population movements, 912–13
and stock market crash, 899, 900
and Third World, 960
and three-world order, 933, 935, 955
and worldwide insecurities, 647–49, 851–53

see also cold war; *specific nations and empires*
Caracas, Venezuela, 707
caravan cities, 276, 277–78, 283
caravans, 548, *549*
caravansarais, *549*
caravan trading, 273, *274–75,* 277–78, 281
carbohydrates, from corn, 564
Caribbean
between 1600–1750, 602–3, 631
between 1750–1850, 698, 704, 712–13
between 1850–1914, 802, 812
and alternative visions of nineteenth century, 764
and commerce and colonization between 1450–1600, 555–56, 568
and deforestation, 708
and economy, 608, 712–13
and imperialism, 812
map about, *604*
and mercantilism, 631
and new colonies in Americas, 602–3, 608
plantation complex in, 602–3
revolutions in, 704
see also specific nations and islands
Caribs, 556–57
Carson, Rachel, 965
Carthage, 175, 220, 222, *223, 254–55, 285,* 427
Christian persecution in, 343, 349, 350
Hellenism of, 261, 262–63, 283
Roman wars with, 262, *285,* 316
slaves in, 316
cartography, 445, *494,* 494–95, *495,* 654–57, *690,* 690–91, *691*
cassava, 564
caste. *See* social class, caste
caste *(varna),* 454
Caste War of the Yucatán, 765, *766*
Castile, 515–16, *533*
Castro, Fidel, 962–63, *971*
Catalan Atlas, 494, 495, 551, *554*
Çatal Höyük, Anatolia, 41, *41*
catapult, 163
Catherine the Great, 862
Catherine the Great, empress of Russia, 626

and globalization, 987, 1014–15,
1016–17, 1019–20
invention of, 220
and Latin American corporatism,
911–14
and mass politics, 901–3, 911–14
and Mexican Revolution, 852,
1024
and political structure, 973–74
power of grassroots, 1014
and three-world order, 954–55
and transformation in Atlantic
world, 695
and worldwide insecurities, 852
"Democracy as a Universal Value" (Sen),
1024, 1028–30
Democratic Republic of the Congo, 992
Democritus, 225
demographic changes, 1045–50
and age, 1045
and gender, 1045
and immigration, 1045
and religion, 1045
demography, of globalization, 1004–7
Demoiselles d'Avignon, Les (Picasso),
880, 880–81
demokratia (democracy), 220
de Montesquieu, Baron, 682–83
demotic writing, 76
Deng Xiaoping, 994, 1019, *1022*
Denmark, 427, 666, 711, 935, 1050
deportation. *see* forced migration
deregulation, 993
dervishes, 450
Descartes, René, 649
de Secondat, Charles, 682–83
Detroit News, 983, *983*
developing world, 992, 993
devshirme, 511, *542,* 543
Dhamapada, 219
dhamma (morals), 265–67
dharma (religious teachings), 265–67,
361
Dharmarajika monastery, *216*
Dhaskalio (Agean island), 88
dhows, 282, 445, 446, *447,* 452, 494
Diagne, Blaise, 914
diamonds, 851
"Diamond Sutra," 440, *441*
Díaz, Porfirio, 766, 852
dichlorodiphenyltrichloroethane
(DDT), 958, 965
dictator, Roman, 317

dictatorships, 898, 903–10, 969
see also authoritarianism; *specific*
people and dictatorships
Diderot, Denis, 664, *667*
Digest (of Roman laws), 354
Din, Rashid al-, *482*
Diogenes, 259
Dionysus, *225,* 260, 261, 269
diplomacy
Amarna letters and, 123–24
in China, 279
Chinese-Roman, 326–27
disrupted by peripheral societies,
160
early empires and, 160
languages of, 123
marriage as, 123–24, 179, 181, 188
peace treaties and, 123
of Romans, 326–27
territorial states and, 118,
123–24, *257,* 264
disease
between 1600–1750, 602–3,
608, *608*
between 1910–1939, 892
in Africa, 1062–63
and Afro-Eurasia population in
14th century, 501, 504
and commerce and colonization
between 1450–1600, 554–55,
557, 560, 562
and imperialism in Oceania, 678
and new colonies in Americas,
602–3, *608*
and slave trade, 605, 608
and Soviet ecocide, 958
and World War I, 889
see also Black Death; malaria
diversity
between 1850–1914, 789, 795,
796, 797, 815, 817
and consolidation of nation-states
in Europe, 796, 797
and expansion and nation-building,
789
and Russian transformation and
expansion, 819
divination
Bantu, 373
by oracle bones, *128, 130*–31
"divine right," 629
divorce, 1006
Djoser, king of Egypt, 73–74

DNA analysis, 3, 8–9, 22
dogs
domestication of, 27
ritual sacrifice of, 130
Dokuchaev, Vasily, 862–63
domestication of animals and plants, 4,
26–40, *28,* 84, 133–34
domesticity, 813, 850, 851
Dominican religious order, 543, 672
Dominican Republic, 556, 995–97
Doña Marina, 559
Dostoevsky, Fyodor, 757
dot-coms, 1004
Douglass, Frederick, 734–35
Doux Commerce, 682–83
draft. *see* conscription
Dresden Codex, 441, *441*
dress. *see* clothes, clothing
drinking vessels, 91
dromedaries, *160,* 160–61
drought
in 11th and 12th century CE
Egypt, 449
in Afro-Eurasia in 1200 BCE, 157
in Afro-Eurasia in 2000 BCE, 107,
111–12, 112–13, 119, 139
in Afro-Eurasia in 2200–2150
BCE, 105–6
bubonic plague (Black Death)
and, 499
drugs, Chavín priests and, 228
Dubcek, Alexander, 966
Duncan, Isadora, 856
Dunhuang, *368,* 440
Dutch
between 1600–1750, 611, 623,
628, 631
and Asia in seventeenth and eighteenth centuries, 611
and colonization between
1450–1600, 572, 576
and commerce and trade, 572,
576
and culture, 658, 659–60
and economy, 628
and Japan, 623, 658, 659–60
and landscape, *598*
and Little Ice Age, *598*
and mercantilism, 631, *634*
and Mughal Empire, 575
and political fluctuations in
Europe, 628
and religious wars, 572

labor (*continued*)

    and Russia, 624–26, 904

    and strikes, 718

    and wages, 718, 1032–33

    and World War II, 938

    and worldwide insecurities, 849, 851–53

    see also assembly lines; slaves, slavery; *specific types of labor*

labor disputes, late nineteenth-century, *870–71*

Labour Party (Great Britain), 851, 901

Lacandon jungle, *376*

"Lady" (Aegean deity), 137

Lagos, Nigeria, 995–98, *998*

Lahore, 548

Lake Baikal (Russia), 958–59

Lake Nyanza (Africa), 372

Lake Texcoco (Mexico), 557

Lamb, Charles, 594

Lancashire, England, *715*

land

    between 1600–1750, 628–29

    between 1750–1850, 698, 699–700

    and alternative visions of nineteenth century, 763–64, 767

    and American Revolution, 699–700

    and economic and political fluctuations in Europe, 628–29

    and Indian Rebellion of 1857, 767

    and insurgencies against colonizing and centralizing states, 763–64, 767

    see also agriculture; farmers; peasants; planters, plantations

land bridge, Bering Straits, 19, 22

"Land of Ashur," 164, *165,* 166

"Land under the Yoke of Ashur," 164, *165*

language

    between 1750–1850, 721

    between 1850–1914, 796, 797, 865

    in China, 962

    common, 157, 168, 252, 257–58, 277–78, 329

    common origins of, 107

    and consolidation of nation-states in Europe, 796, 797

    diplomatic, 124

families, *24,* 107

    of *Homo sapiens,* 3–4, 7, 18, 23–24, *24,* 43

    in India, 721, 865

    official, 268

    and transformation in Atlantic world, 695

    see also writers, writing; *specific language families and languages*

L'Anse aux Meadows, 429

Laozi (Master Lao), 210, 312

Last Supper (Leonardo da Vinci), *519*

Lat Dior (Muslim warlord), 808

Late Antique period, 398–99

"Late Antiquity," 423

Later Han dynasty, 311–12, 329

Latin America, 1063

    between 1850–1914, 794–95, 811, 835, 850, 853, 855, 859, 860–61

    between 1910–1939, 910–11

    and anti-colonialism, 934

    corporatism in, 910–11

    and culture, 671–74, 855

    elites in, 1063

    European migrants in, 860

    and expansion and nation-building, *710,* 794–95

    and globalization, 993, 995–97, 1000, 1001, 1007

    health care in, 1007

    and imperialism, 811

    and politics, 910–11

    population of, 1005

    and race, 636, *640–41,* 859, 860–61

    and three-world order, 934, 960, 962–63

    and worldwide insecurities, 850, 853

Latin American confederation, 707–11

Latin language, 107, 262, 299, 329, 426, 513

La Venta, 231–32

Lawgiver, 591

laws

    Indian, 363–64

    Qin, 302, 304

    Roman, 321, 354

    see also legal codes; penal codes

Laws of Manu, 217, 363, 379

leadership, 619–20, 742, 907, 949

League for the Independence of Vietnam, 953–54

League of Nations, 893, 938–40

League of Polish Families, 1050

Leakey, Louis S. B., 14–15, *15*

Leakey, Mary Nicol, 14–15, *15*

Lebanon, *894,* 1057

legal codes, formalization of, 112, 188, 299

    see also laws; penal codes

legalism, in China, 210–11, 213, 302

legal system, 714

    see also sharia

Lenin, Vladimir, 892, *893,* 903, 905, 972

Leo Africanus's Travels in Africa (1550), 585–86

Leo III, Pope, 427

Leonardo da Vinci, *519*

Leonidus, 174

Leopold II, king of Belgium, 806, *808,* 810–11, *811,* 843

Leo X, Pope, 569

Lesotho, 999

Levant

    Aegean and, 88

    agriculture in, *30–31*

    borderland of 1000–400 BCE, 174–75, *176,* 177–78, 219–20

    city-states in, 219–20, *221*

    Egyptian expansion into, 118–19

Leviathan (Hobbes), 599

Lewis, Samuel, 712

Lewis, William, 712

li (proper ritual), 208

Liang Qichao, 820

Liangzhu culture, 87

liberalism

    between 1750–1850, 722–23, 736

    between 1850–1914, 797, 857

    between 1910–1939, 885, 901–3, 906, 908, 911, 914

    and alternative visions of nineteenth century, 754, 765

    and capitalism, 901–3

    and consolidation of nation-states in Europe, 797

    and cultural modernism, 857

    and Great Depression, 901

    in India, 722–23

    and insurgencies against colonizing and centralizing states, 765

    and Italian fascism, 906

oil, 803, 848, 940, 963–64, 967–68, *971*, 998, 1011–13
Okinawa, 815, 817
Old Akkadian period, conflict during, 162
Old Babylonian era, 119–20, *122*
Old Kingdom, of Egypt, *72*, 73–77, *77*, 112, 162
Olduvai Gorge, 15
oligarchies
    in Greece, 220
    in South Asia, 213, 215, 219
Olmecs, 205, *206–7*, 229–32, *230*, 237, *238*, 248, *249*, 557
    cities of, 231–32
    decline of, 232, 373
    human sacrifice of, 231, 237
    priestly class of, 230, 231–32
Olympic Games, 221, 990–91
OPEC (Organization of Petroleum Exporting Countries), 967–68, *971*, 998
"open door" policy, 843
Opera House (Manaus, Brazil), 795, *795*
Opis (Upî), 251
opium, 724–27, *725*, 749
Opium War (1839–1842), *723*, 724–27, *725*, *726*, *729*, 749, 751–52
Opobo, 712
oracle bones, *128*, 130–31
oral tradition
    in South Asia, 182, 217, 218
    in sub-Saharan Africa, 370
Orange Free State, 806, 841
Orhan (Ottoman chief), 507
orientalism, 812
"Orientalist" scholarship, 721
Origin of Species (Darwin), 802–3, *822*
Orissa, India, 721
Orléans, France, 515
Orlovsky, Valdimir, *863*
Orrorin tugenenis, *11*
Orrorin tugenensis, *11*, 12, 14, *18*
Oseberg ship, *429*
Osiris, 75, 259–60
Osman, chief of Ottomans, 506–7, *507*, *532*
Ostend, Belgian Congo, 810–11
Ottoman Empire, *507*, 516, 519, 521, 530, *532–33*, 543, 545–46, 550–51, 717, 737
    between 1600–1750, 591–92, 610, 612–14, 620, 623, 624, 633

    between 1750–1850, 693, 719–21, 727
    between 1850–1914, 805, 817, 819, 866–67
    between 1910–1939, 889, 892, *894*, 918–19
    agriculture in, 506
    and alternative visions of nineteenth century, 741, 755
    and anti-colonialism, 918–19
    and Asia in seventeenth and eighteenth centuries, 610, 612–14
    bureaucracy of, 508–9, 510–11, 512, 523–24, 543, 612, 721
    and climate change, 612, 614, 632
    and coffeehouses, 594
    collapse of, 892, 917
    and colonization between 1450–1600, 548, 550–51, 579
    and commerce and trade, 547, 548, 550–51, 579
    Constantinople conquered by, *508*, 508–9, 516, *533*
    and culture, 648–51, *649*, 650–51, *651–52*
    diversity in, 510–12
    and drought, 615
    economy in, 591–92, 612–14, 720, 721
    education in, 720
    and Egypt, 550
    end of, 593
    and Enlightenment, 670
    expansion of, 508–10, 547, 548, 549–50, 612–14
    and famine, 615
    gender in, 510
    and Greek independence, *696–97*, 755, *772*
    and imperialism, 805
    and Islamic revivalist movements, 744
    Jamal al-Din al-Afghani and, 866–67
    and Little Ice Age, 599, 614
    and mass politics, 918–19
    and Mughal Empire, 614–15
    and Muslims, 550
    and pan movements, 866–67
    and persistence and change in Eurasia, 719–21
    and Portugal, 547

    reform of, 719–21
    religious tolerance in, 506–8
    rise of, 452, 506–12
    and Russia, 624, 817, 819
    and Safavid Empire, 550, 612–14
    as Sunni, 506–7, 517, 530–31
    and Syria, 550
    Tanzimat of, 720
    Topkapi Palace, 656
    transformation of, 612–14
    and Turkey, 918–19
    Turkish-speaking peoples in, 498, 505–6
    vulnerability of, 720
    warrior ethos of, 506–7
    in West Asia, 548
    and World War I, 889, 892, *894*
"Out of Africa" thesis, 3–4, 6
overland commerce, 547–48
Ovid (Roman poet), 326
Oyo Empire, 564–65, 660–62, *680*

Pachacuti (Yupanqui), 561
Pacific coast, Chavín exploration of, 228
Pacific islands, microsocieties on, 132–34, *133*
Pacific Ocean, 624, *939*, 940
pagodas, 369
Paine, Thomas, 699
paintings, 542–43, *542–43*, 543, 588, *588*, *589*, 658, *659*, 784, *785*, 853, 854, *880*, 880–81, *881*, *1020*
Pakistan, 948–49, *970*, 995–97, 1054
Palace of Versailles, 656
palaces, 269, *376*, *377*, 510–11
    Aegean, 88, 135–37
    Assyrian, *166*, 166–67
    Han, 306
    Mesopotamian, 65
    Olmec, 231
    Persian, *200*, 201, 253
    Shang, *129*
Palenque, 375, *376*
Paleolithic bone carving, 26
Palestine, 450, *894*, 950–51, *970*
    ancient Egyptian presence in, 119
    as home of Jesus, 324
palm oil, 712
Palmyra, 277–78, *278*, 280
Pancantantra stories, 357
Panjikent, 355, 357, 358
pan movements, 762–63, *763*, 859, 866–68, 940, 952, 957

papacy, 569

    see also Catholics

paper

    invention of, 279, 404

    silk used as, 279, *280*

papyrus, oldest, 74

Paraguay, 999, 1010

Paris, France, 465–66, *630*

    between 1750–1850, 701, 703

    between 1850–1914, 799

    between 1910–1939, 893

    Bar Sāwmā's visit to, 443

    and consolidation of nation-states in Europe, 799

    and religious wars, 572

Paris, Treaty of (1783), 700

Paris accord, 1040

Parks, Rosa, *956*

Parliament, British, 513

    between 1600–1750, 630–31

    between 1750–1850, 699, 711–12

    between 1850–1914, 793, 813

    and alternative visions of nineteenth century, 756

    and American Revolution, 699

    and dynastic monarchies, 630–31

    and expansion and nation-building, 793

    and imperialism, 813

    and slave trade, 711–12

parliaments

    between 1750–1850, 699

    between 1910–1939, 889

Parsi theology, 575

Parthians, 276, 325, 341

Parvati, 390, *391*

Pasargadae, 172

pastoralism, 27, 28–29, 35, 60, 78–79, 168, 325

    see also nomads

pastorialism, 28–29, 449

Pat, Jacinto, 765

paterfamilias, 321

patriarchy, 42, 66, 93, 130, 167, 187–88, 208, 210, 306–7, 401, 404, 619

    see also gender

patrilineage, 66, 130–31, 187–88

patronage system, Roman, 321

Paul of Tarsus, 322, 324

Pax Romana, 318, *323*

Pax Sinica, 309, *310*

Peace of Lausanne (1923), 919

Peace of Paris, *600*

Pearl Harbor, 940

peasant revolts, 353, 512

    see also slaves, slavery, rebellions of; workers' mutinies

peasants

    between 1600–1750, 598, 619–20, 624–26, 628–29

    between 1750–1850, 701, 703, 708, 717–18, 719, 723–24, 725

    between 1850–1914, 794, 815, 817, 847, 851–53, 862–64

    between 1910–1939, 900, 903–4, 917–18

    and alternative visions of nineteenth century, 740, 746, 749, 767, 769–70

    and China, 619

    in China, 616–17, 619–20, 724, 725, 749, 847, 862–64, 917–18, 961

    Chinese empires' dependence on, 303, 307, 328–29

    and decolonization, 948, 953–54

    and democracy, 1020

    displacement by slavery, 260, 317–18

    and dynastic monarchies, 629–30

    and expansion and nation-building, 794

    and French Revolution, 701, 703

    and globalization, 1020

    in India, 723, 767, 769–70

    and insurgencies against colonizing and centralizing states, 769–70

    in Islamic world, 746

    and Italian fascism, 904

    in Japan, 815

    and Little Ice Age, 598

    in Mexico, 852

    in Mughal Empire, 575, 615

    and politics, 900, 903–4

    and populism, 917–18

    and revolutions in Caribbean and Iberian America, 708

    runaway, 626

    in Russia, 624–26, 719, 817, 892, 903, 904

    in Soviet Union, 903–4

    and three-world order, 961

    uprisings by, 794, 851–53, 917–18

    in Vietnam, 953–54

    and worldwide insecurities, 851–53

Peking Man, 17–18

Peking Man *(Homo erectus), 10–11*

Peking Man *(Homo erectus),* 17–18, 19

Pelé, 1002

Peleset, 173

Peloponnesian War, 222

penal codes

    Han, 304

    Qin, 302

    see also laws; legal codes

peninsulares, 707

Peninsular War (1808–1813), 704

Pentagon, 1035

People's Party (Denmark), 1050

People's Party (India), 1017

People's Republic of China, 948

pepper trade, 548, 578, 611

periplus, 282

Periplus Maris Erythraei, 327, 328

Periplus Maris Erythraei (Periplus of the Red Sea), 282

Perpetua, Vibia, 349, 390, *390*

Perry, Matthew, 814, *814*

Persepolis

    capital city of, 168, *171, 172*

    palace at, *200,* 201, 253

Persia, Persians

    between 1600–1750, 615

    between 1850–1914, 817, 819

    Christians in, 344

    and climate change, 632

    and culture between 1600–1780, 650

    emigration to Iranian plateau from, 167–68

    and Islam, 401

    learning in, 405–6

    Mongol rule in, 482

    and Russia, 817, 819

    Sasanian Empire of, 355, 356–57

    see also Iran; Safavid Empire

Persian Empire, 167–73, 188, 189, 191, *191,* 206–7, 223, 253, 261–62, 478

    Alexander's defeat of, 253, 261–62

    bureaucracy of, 168–69, 170

    fringes of, 173–78, *176, 216*

    imperial identity of, 168–70, 172–73

    infrastructure of, 168–70, 170–71

radical Islam, 1058–59
radicalism, 754–59
    between 1750–1850, 699, 703
    between 1850–1914, 841, 850,
      851–53
    between 1910–1939, 901, 911,
      916
    and alternative visions of nine-
      teenth century, 752–59
    and French Revolution, 703
    and imperialism, 841
    and Latin American corporatism,
      910–11
    and mass politics, 901, 911, 916
    and three-world order, 961–63
    and "woman question," 850
    and worldwide insecurities, 850,
      851–53
radio, 883, 885, 893, 897–98, 906
railroads
    between 1850–1914, 790, *791,*
      792, 802, 805, 810, 819–921,
      846, 849, 865
    in Canada, *791*
    in China, 819–921, 844, 863
    in Europe, 846
    in India, 768, 805, 865
    in Russia, 819, *823,* 849
    and spread of capitalism through
      migration, 912–13
    in United States, 790, *791,* 792,
      846, 851–52
    and worldwide insecurities, 849
    see also specific railroads
"Raj, the," 805, *823, 970*
rajas (Vedic chiefs), 453–54
Ramayana, 181, *181,* 361
Ramses II, king of Egypt, 235
Ramses III, king of Egypt, *235*
Rani of Jhansi, 784, *785*
rap music, 1001
Ravenna, Archbishop's Chapel from,
    390
Ravi River, 78–79
Re (Egyptian god), 113
Reagan, Ronald, 987
realism, *736, 736–37, 737,* 880
rebellions, 307, 311–12, 329, *331,* 525,
    612–13
    see also peasant revolts; slaves,
      slavery, rebellions of; workers'
      mutinies
Reconquista, *484–85*

Reconstruction, 790, 859
Red Army, 942
Red Eyebrows uprising, 311
Red Guards, 961–62
redistribution of land, by Wang Mang,
    311
redistribution of wealth, by Alexander,
    253
"Red Lanterns," 844
Red Sea, 395, 446, 548, 605
    commerce on, 281–82
    Nile linked to, 171
    and *Periplus Maris Erythraei,* 282
Red Turban Movement, 500, 520
Reformation, 518–19
refugee crisis, 1040, 1050, 1057, 1062
Regency of Algiers, 744
reggae, 1001
registration, of subjects, 302
regulation, 848, 853, 900
Reich, German, 799
Reichstag, German, 799, 851–52, 907
Reign of Terror, 703
Reims Cathedral, 515
reincarnation, 183, 271
Reis, Piri, 549
religion
    between 1600–1750, 592,
      611–12, 614, 622–23, 624,
      627–28, 631
    between 1750–1850, 702, 719,
      721
    between 1850–1914, 796,
      864–66, 867
    between 1910–1939, 908
    Aegean, 137
    in Africa, 992
    and alternative visions of nine-
      teenth century, 741–46, 749,
      751–52, 774
    in Americas, 671–72
    art and, *390, 390–91, 391*
    and Aztecs, 558
    in China, 654, 749
    and coffeehouses, 594
    and commerce and colonization
      between 1450–1600, 546,
      557–58, 569–73
    and consolidation of nation-states
      in Europe, 796
    and culture, 646, 647–52, 654,
      662, 665–66, 671–72
    and demographic changes, 1045

    and direct revelation, 260
    and dynastic monarchies, 631
    in early cities, 57, 60
    and economic and political fluc-
      tuations in Europe, 627–28
    in Egypt, 73–75, 720
    and Enlightenment, 662,
      665–66, 666–68
    in Europe, 569–73, *571*
    and family, 774, 1018
    and French Revolution, 702
    and gender, 259, 349
    and globalization, 992, 1017–18
    in Great Britain, 665–66
    in Han China, 308
    Hellenistic, 259–60
    of *Homo sapiens,* 40–41
    in India, 865–66
    and Islamic world, 647–52,
      741–46
    and Little Ice Age, 598
    Mesopotamian, 63–65
    and Mughal Empire, 573
    and Ottoman Empire, 721
    and pan movements, 866–68
    of Persian Empire, 170
    and politics, 627–28, 908,
      1017–18
    representations of holiness in,
      390, 390–91, 391
    and revival of trade, 546
    in Russia, 624, 719
    and Safavid Empire, 611–12
    Sumerian pantheon, 65
    and tensions in world commu-
      nism, 966
    and transformation of Europe, 624
    universalizing, 156–57, 343–44,
      348, 358–61, 361–63, 363–
      64, 368–69, 378–79, 390,
      393–94, 411, 421, 425–26,
      430–31
    and war between 1600–1750,
      627–28
    wars over, 570
    and writing, 217, 345, 349, 350,
      351, 364–65, 368–69, *440,*
      440–41, *441*
    see also clergy; Protestant Refor-
      mation; *specific religions*
religious synthesis, of Mahayana Bud-
    dhism, 270–73
ren (humaneness), 208

Renaissance, 498–99, 515, 517–20, 579, 855
    art and architecture of, 517–18
    religious themes in, 517–18
    secular learning in, 518–19
Ren Xiong, *880*, 881
reproductive rights, 850, 965
Republic, The (Plato), 225
Res publica, 317–18
Restoration period (1815–1848), 752, *773*
revivalist movements, Islamic, 745
revolts. *see* peasant revolts; rebellions; slaves, slavery, rebellions of; workers' mutinies
revolutions
    of 1848, 758–59
    global themes and sources, 730–35
    map about, *696–97*
    rhetoric of, 698
    in Third World, 961–63
    see also specific revolutions
Reza Shah Pahlavi, Mohammad, shah of Iran, 1018
rhetoric, Greek, 262
Rhine river, as Roman frontier, 325–27
Rhodes, Cecil, 806, *808*, 990
Rhodesia, 806, 851, 949, 954, 990
    see also Zimbabwe
Ricci, Matteo, 655
rice, 45, 548, 593, 619
    as East Asian staple crop, 33–35, 84
    "Green Revolution" and, 417
    as South Asian staple crop, 179, 213, 215, 264
    wet-field cultivation of, 417
Richelieu, Cardinal, 629
Riefenstahl, Leni, 898, *898*
Rift Valley, 11
Rig-Veda, 124, 182
Rio de Janeiro, Brazil, 707, 794
riots, rioting
    in Byzantium, 354–55
    supression of, 354–55
ritual centers, of Mayans, 375
Rivera, Diego, *864*, 930, *931*
River-basin societies (3500–2000 BCE), *114*, 114–15
riverine cities (3500–2000 BCE), *58–59*, 92–93
    in East Asia, 84–87, *85*
    in Egypt, 70–77, *72*

in Indus Valley, 78–83, *80*
in Mesopotamia, 62–70, *69*
rulers and gods in, 57, 63–64
specialization of labor in, 55–56, 57, 60, 63–64, 65–66, 81
trade in, 57, 60, *61, 72, 80,* 83, 91, 92–93
writing invented in, 56, 57, 66–67, 75–76
roads, 266–67
    Qin, 302–3
    Roman, 322
Robespierre, Maximilien, 703
Rockefeller, John D., 848
rock temple at Bamiyan, 358
rodents, as disease carriers, 499–500
Rodrigues, Manoel Lopes, 784
Roger II, King of Sicily, 494
Roman-Carthage war, 285, 316
Roman Catholic Church, 569
Roman Empire, 272–73, 277, 298–300, *323, 352,* 364, *380–81*
    administration of, 317–19, 321–22, 325–27, 354–55
    alphabet of, *177,* 262
    armies of, 313, 316–17, 317–18, 318–19, 351, 353
    beginnings of, 262, 312–17
    Carthage at war with, 262, *285,* 316
    Christianity as state faith of, 343, 345–50, *348,* 357, 364
    Christians persecuted in, 324, 343–44, 345, 349
    civil wars in, 366–67
    civil wars of, 317–18, 349, 353
    comparisons with other large empires, 340–41
    comparison with Han Empire, 366–67
    conquests of, *285,* 313–17, *314–15,* 322
    decline and fall of, 366–67, 423
    of the East, 354–55, 378 (*See also* Byzantine Empire, Byzantium)
    economy of, 261, 321–22, *323,* 326–28
    entertainment in, *320,* 320–21
    farmers and soldiers of, *317*
    frontiers of, *323,* 324, 325–26, 356–57
    Han China and, *328*

Hellenism of, 261–62
images of power in, *340,* 340–41, *341*
imperial system of, 298–300, 318–19, 349–50
infrastructure of, 319–21, *320,* 321–22, *323*
laws of, 321, 354–55, *380*
learning in, 354–55, 404, 517–18
overextension of, 351, 353, 412, 427
Pax Romana of, 318, *323*
roads in, 266–67, *267*
and Silk Road, 326–27, *328*
slaves in, 316, 317–18, 319, 321–22, 326–28
social relations in, 317–18, 321
symbols of, 349–50
towns and cities of, *319,* 319–21, *320, 323*
warfare and, 366–67
of the West, 351, 353
"Roman" identity, 299–300, 345, 350
Romanovs, 624, 629, *634,* 889
Rome
    Bar Sāwmā's visit to, 443
    city-state of, 220, 313
    imperial metropolis of, 320
    Justinian's reclamation of, 354–55
    Mussolini's march on, 906
    papacy in, 353, *433*
    see also Roman Empire
Romer, Christina, 1039
Romulus Augustulus, emperor of Rome, 353
Roosevelt, Franklin Delano, 901–3, 933
Roosevelt, Theodore, 853, 859, *860*
Rothschild, Baron, 895
Rouen, France, 515
Rousseau, Jean-Jacques, 684–85
Royal Academy of Sciences (France), 663
Royal Road (Zagros Mountains), 171
Royal Society, British, 663, 675–77
Royal Tombs of Ur, 102, *102*
rubber, 229, 232, 795, 802, 803, 809, 810–11, 940
Ruggieri, Michele, 670
rulership, and personality, 120, 259
Rumi, Jalal al-Din, 450

spies, as tool of empire, 169
spiritualism, spirituality, 573
Spring and Autumn period, of China, 205, 211–13, *239*
Sputnik, 959, *971*
Sri Lanka (Ceylon), 805
Stalin, Joseph, 903–4, 933, 942, 943, 957, 958, 966, *970*
Stalingrad, 937
standardization
 Persian, 170
 Qin, 302, 303
 Roman, 322
Standard Oil, 792, 801, 847
Stanley, Henry Morton, 806, *808*, 810
statecraft, 210–11, 327, 364–65
 see also diplomacy
states, 793
steam engines, 714–15, *728*
steamships, 802
steel, 801
 Sasanian use of, 357
 and Soviet ecocide, 958
steppe peoples, as barbarians, 480
stimulants, 594–95
Stoa Poikile, 259
stock exchanges, 628
stock market, crash of American, 899, 900
Stoemer, Eugene F., 1042–43
Stoicism, 259–60
stone beehive huts, *427*
Stonehenge, 89, *91*
Strategic Defense Initiative ("Star Wars"), 987, *1022*
Street of the Dead, *373*, 375
strikes, 718, 850, 851–52
Study for Portrait of an Indian (Girodet–Trioson), 737, *737*
stupas, *216, 268, 270, 271, 272*
sub-Saharan Africa, 1063
 between 1100–1400, *484–85*
 between 1600–1750, 593
 between 1850–1914, 822
 between 1910–1939, 883
 agriculture in, 234, 370–72
 and alternative visions of nineteenth century, 749
 Bantu peoples of, 343–44, 370–73, *371, 379, 380–81*
 c. 500 BCE, 232–36, *233, 236*, 248, *248*
 dense village life in, 92–93

education in, 1008, *1009*
and globalization, 1007, 1008, 1011
health care in, 1007
Hellenism in, 261
and HIV/AIDS, 1008
and increasing economic linkages, 593
Islam in, *408*
oral tradition in, 370
population of, 749
trade in, *408*
see also specific people, and regions
subsistence farming, decline of, 56, 81, 321–22
suburbanization, 955
succession
 between 1600–1750, 615–16, 619–20, 626, 629–31
 and dynastic monarchies, 629–31
 and Japan, 620
 and Mughal Empire, 615–16
 and Russia between 1600–1750, 626
"successor kingdoms," Hellenistic, 256–58, 269–70, *285*
Sudan, 235, 809, 992, 1062
Sudanic savanna region, 234, 235–36
Suez Canal, 802, 920, 952
Suez Canal Company, 952
Sufis, Sufism, 449, 450–52, *485*, 648
sugar
 between 1600–1750, 593, 594, 595, 601–2, 602–3
 between 1750–1850, 636, *640–41*, 704–6, 708, *709*, 713, 714
 between 1850–1914, 794, 853
 between 1910–1939, 900
 and Americas, 601–2, 602–3
 and colonization between 1450–1600, 564–68, *566*
 and commerce and trade, 564–68, *566*
 and economy, 593, 594, 595, 713, 714
 and environmental degradation, 708
 and expansion and nation-building, 794
 and Great Depression, 900
 and insurgencies against colonizing and centralizing states, 764–65

refining of, 714
and revolutions in Caribbean and Iberian America, 708–9
and slave trade, *606–7*
and three-world order, 962
and worldwide insecurities, 853
suicide, in Roman Empire, 318
Sui dynasty, 412, 416–17
Suleiman, Ottoman emperor, 510, 650
Suleiman the Magnificent, 545, 549, 591
Suleymaniye Mosque, *509*, 511
sultans, 454, 508–9, 510–11, 612, *649*, 649–50
 see also Ottoman Empire; *specific people*
Sumatra, 133, 460
Sumerian pantheon, 65
Sumerians, Sumer, 63–70, 121, 393
 conflict among city-states, 162
 writing and texts of, *68*
Summa contra Gentiles (Thomas Aquinas), 466
Sundiata, 468
Sunnis, 866
 in Ottoman Empire, 506–7, 517, 530–31
 Shiite schism with, *406*, 409–11, 449–50
 see also Ottoman Empire
Sun Yat-sen, 861–64, 917
supranational organizations, 987, 1014–15
Supreme Court, U.S., 964
Susa, 172
Swadeshi Movement, 859, 866
Swahili, Swahilis, 407, 470
Swahili coast, 605
swaraj, 915
Sweden, 626
Switzerland, 570
Sykes, Mark, 895, *896*
Sykes-Picot Agreement, 895, *896*
syndicalism, 852
Syracuse, city-state of, 258
Syria, 393, 397, 450, 466, 479, 883, *894*, 1040, 1056, 1057, *1057, 1060*
 and 1200 BCE drought, 157
 Black Death in, 501
 and chemical weapons, 1057
 civil war in, 1057
 Hellenism in, 256, 257, 261
 Islamic conquest of, 397

urban-rural divide, 60, 78–79, 92–93, 106, 226
Urkesh, 68
Uruguay, 963, 1010, 1063
Uruk, 63, 67
    Gilgamesh, king of, 65, 68, 121–22, *122*
    as oldest city, 55–56
    writing and, 67, 121
Uruk, Mesopotamia, 64
USSR. *See* Soviet Union
U.S. Steel, 792, 801
Uthman caliphate, 398
Utnapishtim, 121
utopians, 752–59
Uzbekistan, 958
    see also Samarkand

Vaishyas, 181–82
Valens, 351–53
Valley of the Kings, *110*
values
    of Greeks, 259–60
    of Romans, 318–19
    see also ethics; morals
van Gogh, Theo, 1050
Vargas, Getúlio, 911, *923*
varna (caste), 454
varna (castes), 181–82, 213, 215–16, 217, 361–62, 363
Varna, ancient burial at, 102, *103*
Vatican. *see* papacy
Vedas, 182–83
Vedic people, 124–26, 140, *141*, 188, 189, *190–91*, 213
    between 1500–400 BCE, 178–83, *180*
    armies of, 162
    caste system of, 213, 215–16, 217
    Hymns of, 178–79, 181, 182
    religion of, 124, *126*
    Sanskrit of, 124
    Sixteen State period of, 213–15, 225, 237
    splintered states of, 178–79
    varna system of, 181–82
    worship rituals of, 124, *126*
Vedic religion, 360–62, 455–56, 460–61
    see also Brahmanism
vegetarianism, Hindu, 456
veiling, in Assyria, 167

Venezuela, 706, 709, 963, 967
Venice, 515
"Venus" figures, 26, 52–53, *53*, 341
Veracruz, 559
Verdun, Battle of (1916), 899
Versailles, 629, *630*
Versailles, Palace of, 656
Versailles, Treaty of (1919), 893, 900, 907, 919
Via Appia, 266
Victoria, queen of England, 770
"Victory or Bolshevism" (German poster), 982, *982*
Vienna, *613*, 614, 789
Viet Cong, 954
Viet Minh, 953–54
Vietnam, 412, 620, 950–51, 953–54, *970–71*, 996–98
    Champa rice from, 417
    in Chinese empires, 303, 309, 412, 417
    and World War I, 940
Vietnam War, 965, 969, *970–71*
Vigarny, Felipe, *517*
Vikings, 423, 427–29, *433*
    in Constantinople, 429, *433*
    slave trade of, *428*, 428–29
Villa, Pancho, 853
Vimalaprava (Jain monk), 441
Virgil (Roman poet), 326
Virginia, 599, *605*, 674
Virginia Company, 594
Vishnu, 361–62, *362*, 456
visual evidence, interpreting of
    in Axial Age, 248–49, *248–49*
    bronze-working, 152–53, *152–53*, *153*
    burials and long-distance trade, 102–3, *102–3*
    "Chimerica," *1032*, 1032–33, *1032–33*
    coinage, 294–95, *294–95*
    conflict and consent, *588*, 588–89, *589*
    framing the subject, *736*, 736–37, *737*
    gender of nations, 784, *785*
    global modernism, *880*, 880–81, *881*
    images of power, *340*, 340–41, *341*
    making boundaries, inspiring loyalty, *542*, 542–43, *543*

men, machines, and mass production, *930*, 930–31, *931*
    prehistoric art, 52–53, *52–53*, *53*
    representations of holiness, *390*, 390–91, *391*
    transmission of religious knowledge, *440*, 440–41, *441*
    tribute, 200–201, *200–201*, *201*
    war and propaganda, *982*, 982–83, *983*
    world maps, *494*, 494–95, *495*, *690*, 690–91, *691*
    world of goods, *642*, 642–43, *643*
Vladivostok, Russia, 819
VOC. *see* Dutch East India Company
volcanic eruptions
    Mount Vesuvius and, *319*
    in second millennium BCE, 137
Voltaire, 664–65, 668
Volta River Project (Ghana), 1014
voting
    between 1750–1850, 695, 699
    between 1850–1914, 790, 794, 796, 797, 850
    between 1910–1939, 893, 904, 907
    and American Revolution, 699
    and decolonization, 949
    and expansion and nation-building, 790, 794, 796, 797, 799–801
    and German Nazism, 907
    and mass politics, 907
    and transformation in Atlantic world, 695
    and women, 850, 893, 964
    and worldwide insecurities, 850
    see also elections
Voting Rights Act (U.S., 1964), 964

Wafd party (Egypt), 920
Wahhabi Movement, 742, 744, 771, *772*
Wajid Ali Shah, Nawab, 767
Waldseemuller map, 536
Waldseemüller map, 691, *691*
Walesa, Lech, *988*
walls. *see* defensive walls
Wall Street, 1038, *1040*
Walmart, 1033, *1033*
wanax (ruler), 137–38
Wang, empress of China, 415
Wang Mang, 311–12, *331*

NORTH POLAR REGION

GLOBAL SATELLITE MOSAIC

The beauty and complexity of Earth's landscape comes alive in this Global Satellite Mosaic. The mosaic was created for the National Geographic Society by NASA's Jet Propulsion Laboratory from more than 500 satellite images from the National Oceanic and Atmospheric Administration. The cloud-free images show Earth in its natural colors as it would be seen from space. One can easily identify the world's major glaciers, deserts, mountain ranges, and rain forests. For example, follow the green ribbon of lush vegetation from the Poles into the stark, dry Sahara. The mountain ranges seem to rise off the map thanks to digital elevation databases from the Department of Defense. The deepest areas of the ocean realm are colored dark blue in contrast to the light blue areas highlighting continental shelves, submarine ridges, and underwater mountains.

BIOSPHERE

Thousands of satellite images combined to show a picture of biological productivity. In the oceans, red, yellow, and green indicate waters rich in phytoplankton. On land, green areas show high potential plant productivity, tan areas suffer from productivity limitations due to aridity and temperature.

THE W
SATELL

SOUTH POLAR
REGION

ANTARCTICA

THE NEED FOR SATELLITES

ORLD
E MAP

SURFACE
TEMPERATURE